THE OXFORD HANDBOOK OF

ENERGY POLITICS

THE OXFORD HANDBOOK OF

ENERGY

POLITICS

Edited by

KATHLEEN J. HANCOCK

and

JULIANN EMMONS ALLISON

OXFORD

UNIVERSITY PRESS

OXFORD
UNIVERSITY PRESS

Oxford University Press is a department of the University of Oxford. It furthers
the University's objective of excellence in research, scholarship, and education
by publishing worldwide. Oxford is a registered trade mark of Oxford University
Press in the UK and certain other countries.

Published in the United States of America by Oxford University Press
198 Madison Avenue, New York, NY 10016, United States of America.

Library of Congress Cataloging-in-Publication Data
Names: Hancock, Kathleen J., editor. | Allison, Juliann Emmons, 1965–editor.
Title: The Oxford handbook of energy politics /
Edited by Kathleen J. Hancock and Juliann Emmons Allison.
Description: New York : Oxford University Press, [2021] |
Identifiers: LCCN 2020018523 (print) | ISBN 9780190861360 (hardback) |
LCCN 2020018524 (ebook) | ISBN 9780190861391 (epub) | ISBN 9780190861377
Subjects: LCSH: Energy policy. | Power resources—Political aspects.
Classification: LCC HD9502.A2 O987 2020 (print) | LCC HD9502.A2 (ebook) | DDC 333.79—dc23
LC record available at https://lccn.loc.gov/2020018523
LC ebook record available at https://lccn.loc.gov/2020018524

1 3 5 7 9 8 6 4 2

Printed by Sheridan Books, Inc., United States of America

To those academics, engineers, policymakers, and activists who are working to bring cheaper, cleaner, and more sustainable energy to peoples around the world. Special mention, in memoriam, to our collaborator and contributor Prof. Azra Tutuncu, Harry D. Campbell Chair, Department of Petroleum Engineering, and Director, Unconventional Natural Gas and Oil Institute at the Colorado School of Mines.

Contents

PART III   MAJOR ENERGY PLAYERS AND REGIONS

PART IV CONCLUSION

About the Editors

KATHLEEN J. HANCOCK is associate professor of political science at the Colorado School of Mines. Her recently published work focuses on the intersection of regionalism and energy issues, particularly renewable energy in Africa. Previous publications include her book *Regional Integration: Choosing Plutocracy*; a coedited 2015 special issue of *Energy Research and Social Science* and numerous articles in journals such as *International Studies Perspective, International Studies Review, Foreign Policy Analysis, Asian Perspective*, and *China and Eurasia Forum*; and a variety of book chapters. In 2015 and 2016 she was a senior scholar at the Free University-Berlin. Her work has been funded by the German foundation Fritz Thyssen Stiftung, the International Studies Association, the Institute on Global Conflict and Cooperation/MacArthur Fellowship, the Institute for International Education, and the Institute for Security and Development Policy.

JULIANN EMMONS ALLISON is associate professor of gender and sexuality studies at the University of California, Riverside. Her teaching and research emphasize feminist global political economy, critical environmental justice in the context of air quality and energy politics and policy, and community-based social change. Allison's current research examines the sustainability of Southern California's warehousing industry, gender and transitions to renewable energy sources, and ecological grief. Her research has been funded by the National Science Foundation, the American Alpine Club, the California Energy Commission, the California Department of Transportation, the Energy Foundation, and the Haynes Foundation. Her recent work appears in *Energy Research and Social Science*, the *Journal of Labor and Society*, and the *Journal of Poverty*.

Contributors

Saleem H. Ali, University of Delaware

Juliann Emmons Allison, University of California, Riverside

Kyle Bahr, Tohoku University

Lucy Baker, University of Sussex

Margarita Balmaceda, Harvard University

Erika Boeing, Rensselaer Polytechnic Institute

Elina Brutschin, Webster Vienna Private University

Jesse Burton, University of Cape Town

Timothy C. Coburn, University of Tulsa

Jeff D. Colgan, Brown University

Katrine Danielsen, KIT Royal Tropical Institute

Laurence L. Delina, Boston University

Savannah Fitzwater, National Nuclear Security Administration, US Department of Energy

Sara Fuller, Macquarie University

Sylvia Gaylord, Codex Consulting

Kathleen J. Hancock, Colorado School of Mines

Andreas Heinrich, University of Bremen

Lior Herman, Hebrew University of Jerusalem

Christina E. Hoicka, York University

Mirza Sadaqat Huda, The OSCE Academy in Bishkek

Llewelyn Hughes, Australian National University

Trevor Incerti, Yale University

Jessica Jewell, International Institute for Applied Systems Analysis; University of Bergen

Phillip Y. Lipscy, University of Toronto

Julie MacArthur, University of Auckland

Eliza Massi, Trade and Investment Section, Embassy of Brazil in London

Matto Mildenberger, University of California, Santa Barbara

Jonas Nahm, School of Advanced International Studies, Johns Hopkins University

Jewellord Nem Singh, Leiden University

Stefano Palestini, Pontificia Universidad Católica de Chile

Srinivas Parinandi, University of Colorado, Boulder

Lydia Powell, Energy and Climate Change, ORF Centre for Resources Management, Observer Research Foundation, India

Antulio Rosales, University of Oslo

Miriam Sánchez, City University of Hong Kong

Karina Standal, Centre for International Climate and Environmental Research

Jessica Steinberg, Indiana University

Jan B. Stockbruegger, Brown University

Leah C. Stokes, University of California, Santa Barbara

Nora Szarka, Deutsches Biomasseforschungszentrum (DBFZ) gGmbH

Kacper Szulecki, University of Oslo

Hilton Trollip, University of Cape Town

Azra N. Tutuncu, (formerly) Colorado School of Mines

Kirsten Westphal, Stiftung Wissenschaft und Politik

Jeffrey D. Wilson, Murdoch University

Tanja Winther, University of Oslo

Eckart Woertz, GIGA Institute for Middle East Studies; University of Hamburg

Wojtek Wolfe, Rutgers University, Camden

Acknowledgments

The idea for this *Handbook* emerged from several workshops organized by one or both editors and sponsored by the International Studies Association. These events convinced us that the narrative that only a handful of political scientists were working on issues of energy politics was no longer accurate. In fact, a community of talented international relations scholars, comparative political scientists, and other international studies scholars, many of them still working toward their PhDs or recently graduated, is working on in this important area of research. This *Handbook* brings together more than forty scholars from around the world, who cite over a thousand others, demonstrating there is indeed an energy politics literature.

We thank all the *Handbook* contributors, the more than sixty anonymous reviewers, and the scholars cited in the *Handbook*. Each of the *Handbook*'s chapters is a window into a world of technological and institutional innovations that we could not have covered on our own. We thank the physical scientists and engineers who produced comprehensive chapters on energy resources and technologies that are technically accurate and accessible to social science scholars and energy policy makers. Our social science contributors provided extensive literature reviews, and thoughtful, forward-looking research agendas represent both critical additions to the broader literature on energy politics and gracious service to political science and related disciplines. The anonymous reviewers contributed significant time and expertise, sometimes providing second reviews, to ensure that chapters are comprehensive without sacrificing necessary detail and designed to support innovative future scholarship and practice.

Despite this wellspring of collaborative scholarship, *The Oxford Handbook of Energy Politics* could not have been produced without the vision, commitment, and patience of Oxford University Press senior editor Molly Balikov, who, from our first meeting, was a strong advocate for the project. We also thank development editor Alyssa Callan, whose prompt replies and organizational skills were instrumental in helping us complete the project. Prompt copyediting by Kulothungan ArulMozhi and his team of editors was much appreciated by the authors and editors. Finally, we thank the Oxford delegates who reviewed and approved our proposal and then the final product. Knowing we had to meet their high standards, we required double-blind peer reviews for all chapters, which further improved already excellent drafts.

We thank the Lama Foundation, which provided workspace in New Mexico's Sangre de Cristo Mountains and nourishment—social support as well as room and board—for Juliann during summer 2018. We thank the International Studies Association, our primary professional organization, for funding several workshops related to energy politics. Without this support, our community might not have come together to create the *Handbook*. In addition, we thank Tanja Börsel and Thomas Risse for modeling how to edit a great *Oxford Handbook*.

An important final step was finding the cover artwork, *Advent of Hope*. We are grateful to artist Jennifer Boes for allowing us to use her painting. We see the rising sun bringing the city out of darkness as representing hope for the energy future.

Of course the time and attention we devoted to this *Handbook* were not only ours. We thank our families, who tolerated delays and working "vacations," provided space for us to vent as much as to celebrate, and loved us regardless of our progress on "the Oxford handbook." Kathleen thanks John, Jamie, and Willa. Juliann thanks Raymond (Ted), Quentin, Reiley, Parker, and Olivia Allison.

—Kathleen J. Hancock and Juliann Emmons Allison

PART I

OVERVIEW

CHAPTER 1

....

THE POLITICS OF ENERGY IN A CHANGING CLIMATE

An Introduction

....

JULIANN EMMONS ALLISON AND
KATHLEEN J. HANCOCK

THE EMERGENCE OF CONTEMPORARY ENERGY POLITICS

....

THE origin story of contemporary energy politics begins with the 1970s oil crisis (Araújo 2014; Van de Graaf et al. 2016). In October 1973, members of the Organization of Arab Petroleum Exporting Companies (OAPEC) responded to the United States' sending a $2.2-billion emergency aid package to Israel in the Yom Kippur War with an oil embargo. The embargo ended US, Canadian, UK, Dutch, and Japanese oil imports from OAPEC states and initiated a series of production reductions that pushed the price of oil from $2.90/barrel to $11.65/barrel four months later. Oil importers were unprepared for the embargo, not to mention for the Organization of the Petroleum Exporting Countries' (OPEC's) decision to continue raising prices for oil, their primary source of revenue. At the time, coordination among oil-consuming states, as members of the Organisation for Economic Co-operation and Development (OECD), in response to the emergent sellers' market had not advanced beyond recommendations for emergency planning, including oil reserves and sharing schemes (Lantzke 1975). Consequently, their initial responses amounted to "zero-sum competitive stockpiling and hoarding of their reserves" (Florini 2011). A nearly year-long negotiation among oil consumers convened by the United States yielded an international energy program consisting of oil reserves, demand restraints, and sharing. The OECD Council created the International Energy Agency (IEA) to administer the program.

While the oil price shock appeared to be a victory for oil-exporting nations, which gained wealth and international influence at the expense of importers, Ross (2013) argues that high oil prices stimulated investments in energy efficiency and alternative energy resources and prompted energy and environmental policy changes by oil-consuming states that "fortuitously" yielded reductions in greenhouse gas (GHG) emissions. In North America, for example, the United States established stringent fuel efficiency standards and expanded efforts to develop unconventional fuels and renewable energy resources (see Emmons Allison and Parinandi in this volume), while Canada, a net oil exporter, created Petro-Canada to wrest control of oil (and gas) production and revenue streams from US and other foreign companies (Muller 2008). Elsewhere, including in the embargo's European targets and Japan, policy makers re-emphasized public transportation, and both renewable and nuclear energy options rose in prominence (Char and Csik 1987; Pisarski and Terra 1975; Sinha 1974; see chapters by Massi and Singh and Incerti and Lipscy in this volume). Publication of the First Assessment Report by the International Panel on Climate Change (IPCC) in 1990, followed by the negotiation of the United Nations Framework Convention on Climate Change two years later, reignited these efforts with the intent to reduce carbon dioxide emissions. Global per capita energy consumption has increased "consistently" since recovering from the abrupt decline associated with the 1973 oil embargo, with most of this growth occurring in middle- and low-income[1] nations, especially Brazil, China, India, and other major emerging economies. As expected, trends in energy consumption are associated with rising per capita emissions of carbon dioxide (and other GHGs). Yet these rising emissions are arguably lower than they would have been in the absence of gains in energy efficiencies and technological developments due to states' policy responses to the embargo (Ross 2013; see Malewitz 2016; Stecker 2016).

The relationship between the IEA, the closest we come to a "world energy organization" (Van de Graaf 2013a), and climate change is less clear. In addition to its core responsibilities for oil crisis management and gathering and disseminating data and other information about energy resources, the IEA's role has expanded to include energy security, economic development, and environmental protection—in particular, climate change mitigation (now adaptation). Yet Van de Graaf (2013b) argues that the IEA has not yet adapted to the "new global energy landscape," which requires engagement with non-OECD consumer states and OPEC members, leadership in the world's transition to sustainable energy, and integration of energy and climate change regime complexes— each of which exists as "an array of partially overlapping and non-hierarchical institutions that includes more than one international agreement or authority" (Alter and Raustiala 2018). This conceptualization of the potential for the IEA's contribution to international energy governance is an improvement over the siloing of energy apart from its externalities—for example, climate change, accidents, toxics, and waste (Florini and Sovacool 2011; see also Lesage and Van de Graaf 2016).

Muttitt's (2018) unforgiving investigation suggests otherwise. He argues that the IEA continues to encourage members to enact energy policies and direct investments that are likely to increase fossil fuel use and accelerate climate change. Indeed, Van de Graaf's (2013a; see also Colgan, Keohane, and Van de Graaf 2012) explanation for the establishment of the International Renewable Energy Agency (IRENA) in 2009 rests, in part, on the IEA's failure to include states outside of the OECD and to fund its renewable energy initiatives—for example, data analysis and collaboration with government and industry experts through its Renewable Energy Working Party (REWP) and Renewable Industry Advisory Board (RIAB). These practical concerns fueled national (especially German, Danish, and Spanish) and activist views of the IEA "as a fossil fuels and nuclear lobby that underestimates the potential of renewable sources of energy" (Van de Graaf 2013a, 26). Van de Graaf argues that the belief in the IEA's capture by retrograde interests, in comparison to these nations' and activists' own moral and financial commitments to renewables, motivated IRENA's creation to facilitate international cooperation in the adoption of renewable energy. The desire to have a voice within the new institution and green posturing arguably explain IRENA's phenomenal growth, from 75 founding members in 2009 to 160 in January 2019 (Van de Graaf 2013a).

The upshot of this substantive and institutional history is an energy landscape that raises critical issues political scientists are just beginning to tackle, including new energy sources, production technologies, and consumption patterns; governmental and nongovernmental stakeholders; and an array of often overlapping security, socioeconomic, and environmental crises. *The Oxford Handbook of Energy Politics* supports research initiatives by international relations (IR) scholars, comparative political scientists, and others concerning energy politics by summarizing and critiquing a diverse literature to provide insights into and a foundation for teaching and research on critical energy issues. This introductory chapter provides a brief conceptual and technical overview of the world's primary energy resources—fossil fuels, renewable energy, and nuclear power—and related infrastructures. This overview is followed by an introduction to the theory and substance of contemporary energy politics covered in the *Handbook*, including energy interdependence and regional governance of energy resources and electrical power; energy security, foreign policy, and conflict over energy resources; energy markets and finance and corporate social responsibility (CSR); energy justice and the gender dimensions of energy politics; and the global and national politics of climate change adaptation. The conceptual and technical overview and the introduction to international and comparative energy politics provide a foundation for understanding the energy politics of major "players," the states and regions that dominate energy institutions and markets—historically, Europe, the Middle East and North Africa, and the United States—or represent central challenges to them. The increasing presence of emerging market nations such as China and Brazil and the rising demand for energy resources and power by the world's poorest nations, including those in sub-Saharan Africa,[2] threaten to both destabilize regional and global energy equilibria and undermine global initiatives to manage climate change.

Energy Resources: A Conceptual and Technical Overview

The world's energy resources include all the various fuels used for heating and cooling, electricity generation, and other energy conversion processes. These resources are generally categorized as fossil fuels (coal, oil, and natural gas from decayed plant and animals); renewable resources, including geothermal, hydro-, solar, tidal, wave, and wind power in addition to some forms of biomass; and energy released during nuclear fission or fusion. The technologies required to extract, harvest, or create these resources are increasingly complex, and the institutions and facilities that govern and enable their use continue to change. Technical innovations during the Industrial Revolution emphasized harnessing the energy in fossil fuels to power steam engines and factories, heat homes and cook food, and generate electricity. The success of nuclear fission manifest in the US bombing of Hiroshima and Nagasaki not only hastened the end of World War II in the Pacific but also catalyzed the use of nuclear power for electricity generation as well as military weapons throughout the Cold War and into the current era. Most recently, the combined effects of peak oil warnings (Hubbert 1979) and evidence of warming attributable to GHG emissions (King 2015) have placed a premium on renewables. Consequently, the following overview is best understood as a "snapshot" of critical energy resources and associated infrastructures during the late twentieth and early twenty-first centuries. In that context, this *Handbook*'s technical chapters collectively serve as an accessible, stand-alone reference, as well as a strong foundation for the volume's social science chapters.

Fossil Fuels, Renewable Energy, and the Nuclear Option

Despite the waning of easily accessible oil and the climate crisis, the vast majority of the world's energy is derived from fossil fuels; coal, oil, and natural gas continue to be central to energy industries and politics. Azra N. Tutuncu's *Handbook* chapter on the future of fossil fuels explains that recent and successful efforts—initially by the United States, and later by Canada, China, and Argentina—to extract hard-to-reach, unconventional oil and gas reserves has unleashed scrutiny by fossil fuels experts, governments, and environmental and social activists. Hydraulic fracturing, or "fracking," is currently the most controversial fossil fuel issue, particularly in the United States, where it is the primary method for extracting shale oil and gas. Fracturing is a process of injecting fluid—mostly water, but also including sand or other proppants suspended with the aid of thickening agents—at high pressure into subsurface formations to fracture the shale and release oil and/or gas. Critics are concerned that fracturing often contaminates water, pollutes the air, increases earthquake risks, and is likely to accelerate climate change (Miller 2017; see also Clarke et al. 2014; O'Hara et al. 2012; Whitmarsh et al. 2015). Tutuncu's review suggests that research by, and collaboration among, representatives of fossil fuel industries, universities, and other scientific research institutions; federal and state government agencies in the United States and abroad; and environmental organizations is more likely than not to develop innovative technologies and practices that will improve existing extraction techniques and reduce the environmental risks and other negative impacts associated with extracting oil and gas from "tight" reservoirs, or those with low porosity and low permeability (Davis Graham and Stuggs et al. 2019).

Kyle Bahr, Nora Szarka, and Erika Boeing's *Handbook* chapter on the renewable energy transition responds differently to the pollution and other environmental and social externalities associated with the combustion of fossil fuels. Bahr and co-authors review posits renewable energy as a better bet than cleaner fossil fuel technologies for reducing water and air pollution and the risks of earthquakes and climate-related disasters because it is abundant and self-replenishing (Ellabban, Abu-Rub, and Blaabjerg 2014). Thus, renewable energy also has the potential to eliminate energy resource scarcities and ensure energy security over the long term, once technological developments ensure the sustainability of the entire production chain necessary to produce it (Dahren 2016). In contrast to the case of shale and other tight reservoirs, which feature polluting energy resources (oil and natural gas) and extraction technologies (fracturing), renewable energy resources—that is, solar irradiance and wind—are often sustainable, while the technologies that enable their use, such as fabricating solar panels (Nuñez 2014) or constructing the plastic composite blades for modern wind turbines (De Decker 2019), may not be. Recognizing the challenges as well as the benefits associated with the prospect of transitioning our reliance on fossil fuels to renewable energy—specifically, solar, wind, bioenergy, geothermal, and hydropower—Bahr and co-authors suggest that while there is much room for expansion of current renewable energy use globally, scientists and policy makers must proceed with an awareness of the technical characteristics of these resources and technologies, so that the future global use of renewable energy will be both ambitious and realistic.

Concerns about the environmental and social costs of producing energy from fossil fuels and even renewable energy resources in the current context of simultaneously increasing demands for energy and climate change adaptation (in the absence of viable mitigation) strategies underscore the re-emergence of nuclear power as a viable energy resource. Once a nuclear power plant is constructed, electricity generation is inexpensive relative to competing fossil fuel and renewable energy resources, as well as clean and efficient, making it perfect as a source of baseload energy for power sources, such as solar and wind, that are not consistently available (Sovacool 2011). Unfortunately, nuclear energy's production generates a prodigious amount of radioactive waste, and while nuclear accidents are statistically rare, they can be catastrophic. The Chernobyl, Ukraine (1986), and Fukushima, Japan (2011), nuclear accidents, for example, have been identified as the cause of four thousand (World Health Organization 2016) and two thousand (World Health Organization 2013) deaths, respectively, in addition to widespread ecological contamination. These disasters understandably temper enthusiasm for nuclear power, evidenced by the halving of new commercial nuclear reactors worldwide—from 406 to 194—over the thirty years following Chernobyl (Beale 2016) and the expectation that the Fukushima accident will likewise impact the expansion of nuclear reactors to generate electricity (Hayashi and Hughes 2013; Joskow and Parsons 2012). These findings support Sovacool's (2011) argument that the costs associated with nuclear power production are sufficiently large and unavoidable that most nations cannot realistically invest in them. Savannah Fitzwater's *Handbook* chapter provides an overview of the fundamentals of nuclear technology and assessment of the costs and benefits of using nuclear energy for electricity production today. Fitzwater, Fitzwater's review includes future areas of nuclear power development, including small modular reactors, advanced Generation IV reactor designs, and the expansion of non-electric applications of nuclear power, in light of the current state of nuclear power.

Infrastructure: The Core of Fossil Fuel Energy and Electricity Generation

Both of this *Handook's* chapters on infrastructure—for fossil fuels, by Timothy C. Coburn, and electricity generation, by Christina E. Hoicka and Julie MacArthur— identify these technical systems' role in organizing economies and supporting social lives. Coburn refers to the pipelines, drilling platforms, refineries, ports, terminals, processing plants, and storage facilities that constitute the oil and gas infrastructure as an industrial "lifeline" (see Huber 2015). Hoicka and MacArthur argue that electricity infrastructure manifest in a network of wires, towers, dams, and turbines is the "substrate" of modern life. Like Coburn and Hoicka and MacArthur, social scientists, policy analysts, and other energy experts increasingly recognize the significance of energy infrastructures beyond their primary capacities as technologies for producing, transporting, converting, and storing energy and electrical power. Energy infrastructures interact reflexively with environmental justice, political power and mobilization, political economy, and institutional design (Hoicka and MacArthur in this volume). Yet many scholars whose expertise lies in energy security, the political economy of energy, energy governance, and other aspects of the international and comparative politics of energy do not adequately consider these concerns (Kuzemko 2016; Geels 2014). Coburn responds to this knowledge deficit with an overview of pipelines, refineries, storage tank farms and batteries, railroads, LNG plants and terminals, and offshore drilling and production platforms. In addition, he also introduces a set of important current topics, including digitization of infrastructure, cybersecurity and infrastructure, and infrastructure and the environment. Hoika and MacArthur follow suit with a technical overview of the key elements of an electricity system—demand, generation, transmission, and distribution—and a discussion of trends capable of refiguring current electricity infrastructures: increased demand for electricity due to urbanization; increased reliance on renewable energy; and increased grid flexibility, including distributed generation.

Energy Politics: Key Theories, Concepts, and Issues

Energy use is widely understood to be "personal." That is, individuals' decisions about travel, diet and nutrition, heating and cooling, education and training, and work life "depend in some way on energy and the price of energy" (Institute for Energy Research 2010). Scholars and practitioners additionally regard energy to be "the most significant international resource system" (Zimmer 2011). Energy resources and power generation technologies are critical to nations' security, as well as to national, international, and global political economies. Hence, changes in the availability of energy resources or electricity supplies—due to natural disasters, technological issues, and/or political dissension—tend to precipitate social unrest, economic volatility, policy conflicts, political violence, and increasingly, ecological crises. Because these issues are common to many nations and in many cases—for example, declining fossil fuel resources, climate change, and energy injustice— and cannot be contained within any one of them, social science theories, concepts, and issues are apt sources for political analysis and policy guidance.

Authors of this *Handbook's* theoretical and conceptual chapters are predominantly scholars of IR and/or comparative politics (see Russett 2003). International relations examines interactions between and among sovereign nation-states,[3] such as national security, political economy, governance, environmental protection, cultural preservation, terrorism, social movements, and other sources of common problems and (potential) collective action. In contrast, comparative politics analyzes the similarities and differences among selected nations, subnational units, and societies or other groups of individuals. Specifically, these chapters provide an international and comparative review of the literatures on energy interdependence and regional governance of energy resources and electrical power; energy security, conflict over energy resources, and energy employed as a global political tool; issues relevant to the international and comparative political economies (IPE and CPE) of energy (markets and finance, CSR, energy justice, and the gender dimensions of energy politics); and the global politics of climate change adaptation. Each chapter illuminates areas of strength and weakness around a particular aspect of energy politics and provides corresponding suggestions for further research.

Energy Interdependence and Regionalism

Both Jeffrey D. Wilson's chapter on energy interdependence and Kathleen J. Hancock, Stefano Palestini, and Kacper Szulecki's chapter on energy regionalism recognize the significance of institutions for collaborative decision-making and policy implementation among national and/or regional energy authorities for effective energy politics. Wilson's conceptual approach to energy interdependence underscores the relationship between the political economy of energy (linking energy producers and consumers through trade and financial institutions) and energy security for nations and their citizens. He argues that the resulting "coordination game" embodies tensions between a geopolitical, zero-sum behavioral logic that favors nationalist policy approaches and a more cooperative, global governance logic representative of the contemporary liberal international political economy.

The outcome of these tensions for the formation and operation of regional energy organizations—ASEAN, EU, SADC, ECOWAS, Eurasian Union, NAFTA, and UNASUR—constitutes the substance of Hancock and co-authors' systematic review of the literatures on regional governance. They argue that the institutions governing the extraction of coal, petroleum, and uranium; the generation, transmission, and distribution of renewable and nuclear energy resources; and infrastructures associated with these complex processes are well documented—however, the literature in comparative politics on regionalism generally has not yet focused adequately on energy. Consequently, they join

Wilson in suggesting that future research should address theoretical lapses in the existing research. Both Wilson and Hancock and co-authors call for theories that address the politics of national, and regional, energy policy choices; in addition, Hancock and colleagues urge renewed attention to institutional design as a means of ensuring that regional organizations yield more efficient and effective energy policies.

Energy Security, Conflict, and Global Politics

The inter- and intranational relationships discussed in Wilson's and Hancock and co-authors' chapters may serve to forestall conflicts related to threats to energy security, understood as the continuous availability of sufficient supplies of energy at affordable prices. Klare (2014) argues that securing energy resources has been a "conspicuous factor" in many recent conflicts, including the Islamic State of Iraq and Syria's (ISIS's) quest for statehood and China's claims on oil in the South China Sea as well as the more obvious Gulf Wars. Jessica Jewell and Elina Brutschin's *Handbook* chapter interrogates the concept of energy security, which finds different expressions in the literature depending on context and the interests of scholars and practitioners. They examine five approaches to understanding energy security, which can be characterized as realist, analyses of risks to energy and power supplies, definitional, associated with securitization, and critical. Given these multiple approaches, they conceptualize energy security as "low vulnerability of vital energy systems" to provide bases for productive theoretical and empirical research around the material and intersubjective aspects of "vulnerability" and "vitality" of energy systems. Jewell and Brutschin suggest that greater clarity around the meaning of energy security will facilitate much-needed explanations for the gap between energy securitization and action, as well as greater understanding of the relationships among energy security and other energy policy goals.

Handbook chapters by Jeff D. Colgan and Jan B. Stockbruegger and by Lior Herman, on energy and international conflict and global politics, respectively, emphasize the role of conventional, material definitions of energy as oil and gas resources. Colgan's historical and analytical review covers World War I, the first war in which oil played a crucial role; the 1973 oil crisis; wars caused by revolutionary petro-states such as Iraq and Iran; the rise of terrorist groups such as al-Qaeda and the Islamic State; and the role of energy in Russia's assertive behavior in Europe and Syria. His review identifies eight mechanisms linking oil to international conflict and outlines a research agenda emphasizing the continued military presence of the United States in the Persian Gulf and strategic competition between the United States and China over China's maritime oil supply routes in the South China Sea. In contrast to Colgan's bird's-eye view of energy conflicts, Herman reviews the literatures on energy as both a "carrot" (incentive) and a "stick" (threat) for influencing international politics and political economies. He argues that this body of work reflects a key theoretical division between realist and liberal scholars favoring, respectively, "energy diplomacy"—that is, managing energy's geopolitical consequences—and "energy governance"—that is, institutions to ensure energy reliability, mitigate associated risks, and provide emergency assistance. Colgan's critique of this literature highlights theoretical lacunae specific to national and international energy issues, including renewable energy resources and technologies, transit states, energy firms, sovereign wealth funds, and civil society.

Critical Issues of International and Comparative Political Economy of Energy

Kuzemko, Lawrence, and Watson's (2019) appraisal of research in IPE on energy reports that scholars have focused on fossil fuels, especially oil, national and transnational corporate actors, and national interests. These foci are understandable. As recently as 2018, the world's energy consumption continued to be fueled by oil (32 percent), with coal (26 percent) and natural gas (23 percent) bringing our dependence on fossil fuels to over 80 percent (Enerdata 2019). The top ten oil-producing nations—the United States, Saudi Arabia, Russia, Canada, China, Iraq, Iran, the UAE, Brazil, and Kuwait—are responsible for 70 percent of the world's oil production (US Energy Information Agency [EIA] 2018); all of the top ten oil companies in terms of production are either state owned—Saudi Aramco, Kuwait Petroleum Company (KPC), National Iranian Oil Company (NIOC), China National Petroleum Company (CNPC), Abu Dhabi National Oil Company (ADNOC), and PEMEX—or transnational—Rosneft (Russia), ExxonMobil (U.S.), Petrobras (Brazil), and Chevron (US) (Ali 2019). And oil remains endemic to the national interest, whether conceived theoretically "in terms of power," objectively as a "tangible" policy goal, or procedurally in the context of democratic decision-making, in most cases (Krasner 1989; Nye 2002; Nye and Frazier 1991; Nincic 1999). Wojtek Wolfe's *Handbook* chapter responds to the prevailing primacy of oil by offering geographically sensitive analysis of the political economy of oil markets that includes studies of the US shale revolution and China's emergence as a major oil importer. Wolfe's review and analysis of these recent shocks anticipate future research on issues related to managing oil market volatility.

Research on the IPE and CPE of energy has broadened with the expansion of energy resources available and deepened as scholars and policy makers increasingly consider the social dimensions of resource extraction and power generation, transmission, and distribution. Their insights have informed theoretical and substantive debates concerning relationships between energy and development, environmental justice, and gender equity that have become pitched in the context of climate change threats. Jessica Steinberg's *Handbook* chapter on the CSR of energy resources responds to one of the theoretical strains concerning increased demand for energy and power—especially in lower middle- and low-income nations—given globalized markets that are heavily influenced by corporations rather than nation-states (Babic, Garcia-Bernardo, and Heemskerk 2019; Grosser and Moon 2005). Steinberg relates CSR, or firms' voluntary provision of social and economic benefits to communities affected by their operations, to the growth of CSR in energy sectors, with trends toward privatization and the deregulation of energy infrastructure. This transition shifted the onus for incentivizing communities to welcome hazardous conventional or novel, alternative energy operations from governments to businesses (Babic, Garcia-Bernardo, and Heemskerk 2019; Grosser and Moon 2005). Steinberg's review of the literature on CSR conceptualizations, empirical regularities, and policy efforts related to energy suggests that the distinguishing characteristics of energy companies—costly start-ups, long time horizons, large environmental impacts, and insulation from consumers—might explain their willingness to conform to international norms favoring CSR rather than risk reputational costs associated with violating them. Steinberg argues that climate change ups the ante for energy companies seeking to succeed in middle- and low-income nations committed to reducing GHG emissions.

Handbook chapters on energy justice and gender equity around energy, by Sara Fuller and Karina Standal, Tanja Winther, and Katrine Danielsen, respectively, consider key ethical issues associated with energy. Energy justice extends justice theory to energy policy, production, systems, consumption, activism, and security as well as climate change (Jenkins et al. 2016). Fuller's review of the energy justice literature is situated in the more extensive literature on distributive, procedural, and recognition justice that has been applied to natural and built environments. Yet it focuses on two key strands of research: (1) energy access and affordability and (2) the politics of energy production. With respect to energy access and affordability, the literature includes fuel poverty (individual or household access to affordable energy, usually manifest in higher income nations) and energy poverty (energy access and security, largely in poorer nations). This distinction captures significant gendered spatial inequalities. Specifically, in many areas lacking access to modern energy services, fuel collection and use is "women's work" (see Clancy et al. 2007; Kowasari and Zerriffi 2011).

Standal and co-authors take up this thread in their chapter, which interrogates the relationship between gender discrimination and women's access to both energy resources and decision-making power. Their review suggests that much of the literature on this relationship presents women in middle- and low- income nations as victims of energy poverty, which has successfully channeled much-needed resources to them; however, this narrative renders these women responsible for sustainable economic growth via their choice of cleaner forms of energy (Standal and Winther 2016). An alternative narrative identified by Standal and co-authors recognizes women's right to basic services, including energy, which is codified by the United Nations Sustainable Development Goal 7[4] and implicit in the Convention on the Elimination of All Forms of Discrimination Against Women (CEDAW). This approach provides a basis for critiquing the "deep" structures of inequality underlying observed distributions of energy access and security. It also develops Fuller's review of the literature on the politics of energy production, which tends to distinguish between "good" (e.g., renewable, and/or distributed) energy technologies and "bad" (e.g., unconventional fossil fuel and nuclear) sources of energy and power. Inequitable social and geographic access to these resources, especially in the context of ongoing transitions to lower-carbon energy regimes, has important political and justice implications (Bickerstaff, Walker, and Bulkeley 2013), addressed by both Standal and colleagues' and Fuller's proposed research agendas.

Energy Politics in an Era of Climate Change

Handbook chapters on the IPE and CPE of energy politics anticipate Llewelyn Hughes's chapter, which examines the implications of climate change for both our continued reliance on fossil fuel resources and the ongoing transition to alternatives that generate fewer GHG emissions. While political scientists, along with economists, have played important roles in integrating energy and climate policy-making (see Barbier and Pearce 1990), with few exceptions—notably Young (1989)—their theoretical contributions arrived late in the game (see Bernauer 2013; Javeline 2014; Keohane 2015). Rai and Victor's (2009) framework for evaluating India's options for responding to climate-related threats without reducing reliance on fossil fuels so much that economic development is jeopardized is among the first efforts by IR and comparative politics scholars to integrate energy and climate change politics. Over the ensuing decade, these scholars persisted in this effort to integrate research on securing access to energy and power and ensuring adaptation to a changing climate (see Victor and Yueh 2010; Toke and Vezirgiannidou 2013). Hughes synthesizes and critiques this research with an emphasis on studies that yield more general findings concerning the transformation of technological, institutional, and social systems support for a lower-carbon future, though particularly significant results pertaining to specific economic sectors (Schmidt and Sewerin 2017) and/or nations (Ansolabehere and Konisky 2014) are also included. His review concludes with a call for future research on the political economy of developing and deploying low-carbon and negative emissions strategies rapidly and on a global scale.

Major Energy Players: Resources, Regions, and Redistribution

The world's historically major energy "players"—Europe, Russia, the Middle East, and the United States—remain critically important to understanding contemporary energy politics. Yet *Handbook* chapters covering the world's major regions and some of the nations that are, or may become, central to the energy politics of a more environmentally constrained and technologically innovative future suggest that rising demands for energy, electrical power, and political influence are poised to transform regional and global energy markets. The *Handbook's* approach to major energy players reflects the continued primacy of nations, while recognizing that nation-level approaches to the politics of securing access to energy at home and empowering themselves by contributing to the same abroad are also regional. *Handbook* chapters focusing on nations and regions reflect and often directly incorporate insights developed in the technical and more theoretical chapters. The *Handbook's* technical chapters provide insights into the geographical distribution of fossil fuel resources—which continue to dominate energy infrastructures and interactions—and opportunities and constraints associated with developing the technological and institutional alternatives offer a starting point for considering national and international energy politics. The theoretical chapters demonstrate that in addition to geography, climate, and associated prevailing winds and hydropower resources, energy politics is influenced by political-economic histories, relationships, and institutions.

A Geography of Energy Resources

Table 1.1 summarizes *Handbook* chapters on regions and nations in terms of their role among the world's top oil producers, consumers, net oil exporters, nuclear power producers, and capacities for solar and wind generation. In addition to reflecting the *Handbook's* breadth of coverage in terms of global energy use, Table 1.1 reveals three trends relevant to the worldwide transition from reliance on fossil fuels to renewable energy resources and technologies. First, all of the world's top consumers of oil *except* Saudi Arabia have invested in alternative sources of energy and electrical power. *Handbook* chapters covering the politics of energy in the United States (Juliann Emmons Allison and Srinivas Parinandi), North America (Matto Mildenberger and Leah C. Stokes), the European Union (Kirsten Westphal), China (Jonas Nahm), India (Lydia Powell), Japan (Trevor Incerti and Phillip Y. Lipscy), Asia (Mirza Sadaqat Huda and Saleem H. Ali), and Brazil (Eliza Massi and Jewellord Nem Singh) identify literatures that recognize the relationship between nations' fossil fuel consumption and their fiscal responsibilities and/or international obligations to increase reliance on alternative, lower-carbon sources of energy and electrical power. In contrast, Margarita Balmaceda and Andreas Heinrich's chapter covering Russia as well as Eckart Woertz's on the Middle East and North Africa, reflect resistance to transition from fossil fuels to renewables in the absence of clear economic benefits.

Table 1.1 World's Top Ten Oil Producers, Consumers, and Net Exporters; Nuclear Power Producers; and Investors in Solar and Wind Energy

Nation/Region	Oil Producer	Oil Consumer	Net Oil Exporter	Nuclear	Solar Installed	Wind Installed
United States	X	X		X	X	X
North America	X *Canada*	X *Canada*				X *Canada*
European Union		X *Germany*		X *France*	X *Germany Italy, UK, France*	X *Germany Spain, Italy, UK, France*
Russia/Eurasia	X *Russia*	X *Russia*	X *Russia*	X		
China	X	X		X	X	X
India		X			X	X
Japan		X			X	
Asia Pacific		X *ROK*		X *ROK*	X *ROK, Australia*	
Brazil	X	X				X
Venezuela			X			
Middle East & North Africa	X *Saudi Arabia, Iraq, Iran, UAE, Kuwait*	X *Saudi Arabia*	X *Saudi Arabia, Kuwait, UAE, Iran*			
Sub-Saharan Africa			X *Nigeria, Angola*			

Sources: International Renewable Energy Agency (2018); US Energy Information Administration (2018, 2019).

Second, among the nations that are top ten oil producers *and* consumers, the United States, Canada, and China are also recognized for their commitments to renewable energy. China is the world's biggest investor in *both* solar and wind power. In addition to having the world's largest installed capacity for solar and wind power, by 2017 China owned five of the world's largest solar-module manufacturing companies and the world's largest wind-turbine manufacturer (Slezak 2017). The US installed solar capacity is third (behind Japan), and its installed wind energy capacity is second only to China's (International Renewable Energy Agency 2018). While Canada's installed wind power capacity is commendable, its renewable energy star power comes from hydropower (International Renewable Energy Agency 2018). With the exception of Russia's investment in tidal energy, neither that nation nor Saudi Arabia ranks among the world's top investors in or users of renewable resources (Bernstein 1995; International Renewable Energy Agency 2018). Finally, none of the world's top ten net oil exporters have *yet* (the United States is poised to join this group, according to Emmons Allison and Parinandi) made major investments in renewable energy, which may contribute to our understanding of Russia's and Saudi Arabia's divergence from other high- and upper middle-income nations[5] included in the *Handbook* with respect to energy politics.

Renewables have become the cheapest energy source in much of the world, according to IRENA (2019); however, historically, coal's relatively low cost and abundance have made it a key source of energy for middle- and low-income nations. Still, Table 1.2 suggests that trends among the nations and regions covered in the *Handbook* are similar for oil and coal, despite changes in major players. That is, all of the world's top consumers of coal *except* South Africa have invested in alternative sources of energy and electrical

Table 1.2 World's Top Ten Coal Producers and Consumers; Nuclear Power Producers; and Investors in Solar and Wind Energy

Nation/Region	Coal Producer	Coal Consumer	Nuclear	Solar Installed	Wind Installed
United States	X	X	X	X	X
North America					X Canada
European Union	X Germany, Poland	X Germany Poland Turkey	X France	X Germany Italy, UK, France	X Germany Spain, Italy, UK, France
Russia/Eurasia	X Russia, Kazakhstan	X Russia	X		
China	X		X	X	X
India	X	X		X	X
Japan		X		X	
Asia Pacific	X Australia Indonesia	X Australia ROK	X ROK	X ROK Australia	
Brazil					X
South Africa	X	X			

Sources: Enerdata (2019); US Energy Information Administration (2019); International Renewable Energy Agency (2018).

power. South Africa's sun exposure and abundant coastlines are prime opportunities for renewable energy technologies, and the nation's 2019 Integrated Resource Plan embraces solar and wind energy; however, renewable energy integration faces stiff opposition from Eskom (state-owned public utility), and organized labor fearing job losses, and coal interests, according to Lucy Baker, Jesse Burton and Hilton Trollip's *Handbook* chapter (see also Winkler 2019). And except for Russia and South Africa, the nations that are top ten coal producers *and* consumers are also among the world's biggest investors in solar and/or wind power. The US and Chinese commitments to renewable energy were previously elaborated. While Germany has less installed solar and wind capacity than either of these nations, renewables surpassed fossil fuels with respect to electricity generation in 2019 (Eckert 2019). Australia is outranked by Germany in terms of installed solar capacity, but its renewable energy sector—including wind and solar—was growing faster than Germany's by fall 2019 (Stocks, Blakers, and Baldwin 2019).

Theoretical Insights for Regions, Nations, and Societies

Together, Wilson's chapter on energy interdependence, Hancock, Palestini, and Szulecki's chapter on energy regionalism, and Herman's chapter on energy foreign policy provide foundational contexts for understanding how geographical locations and regional energy institutions and organizations are interrelated. Contributions by Jewell and Brutschin and Colgan and Stockbruegger on energy security and conflict, respectively, illuminate energy's historical role as a theoretical and material source of political power. Wolfe's review of the IPE literature on energy reaffirms the centrality of oil markets as a means for evaluating the energy politics of nations and regions. These international, strategic contexts suggest, for instance, that developing and implementing mutually beneficial energy strategies or collective energy policies may be more effective in the presence of a common threat. For example, Westphal's review of the literatures on EU energy politics supports the expectation that energy cooperation may have been more successful in Europe than elsewhere because of a lack of fossil fuel resources and enmity toward the better-resourced Soviet Union. Woertz's review of the literatures on energy politics of the Middle East and North Africa (MENA) similarly suggests that a common demand for resource sovereignty in opposition to transnational oil companies contributed to the Middle East nations' formation of OPEC. Colgan's and Wolfe's historical contextualizations provide another source of insight. Both Balmaceda and Heinrich's coverage of the literatures on the energy politics of Russia and Eurasia and Huda and Ali's corresponding work on Asia capture the force of historical ties on contemporary energy relationships and policies. Balmaceda and Heinrich, for instance, underscore the relatively low infrastructural costs and smoother politics associated with Eurasian nations' opting to "turn East" by increasing trade with China and Asia along with Russia rather than opposing the region's de facto leader (see also Hart 2016). Huda and Ali's review similarly illuminates Asia's challenging military-strategic history, which has dominated the region's approach to energy; the latter has recently broadened to include environmental and social considerations.

In contrast to these strategic and historical insights, theoretical chapters covering energy justice and gender, by Fuller and Standal and colleagues, respectively, especially under conditions of climate change, underscore domestic political and broader societal implications of the global energy system. With respect to politics, for example, Mildenberger and Stokes and Emmons Allison and Parinandi both suggest that federal policymaking institutions and long-standing power asymmetries among the United States, Canada, and Mexico have made regional cooperation difficult but supported the establishment of extensive subnational energy and climate policy regimes. Sylvia Gaylord's chapter on Latin America,[6] considered together with Massi and Singh's and Antulio Rosales and Miriam Sánchez's reviews of the literatures on Brazil and Venezuela, respectively, reflect on challenges associated with cooperative energy and climate politics— here due to contested subnational politics in the context of energy deregulation and transition to lower-carbon fuels and renewable energy technologies. Powell's and Baker and colleagues' approaches to the energy politics of India and South Africa, respectively, illustrate the societal challenges faced by MICs and low-income nations seeking to ensure (energy) justice while transitioning from dependence on abundant and low-cost coal. Powell's review suggests that neoliberal economic commitments and deeply rooted class, caste, and gender cleavages have so far doomed energy redistribution programs in India. Baker and co-authors' review adds corruption and structural racism to the social challenges faced by South Africa, which is a major player in the world's "coal game" (see Table 1.2); the nation relies heavily on coal domestically and is the world's fifth largest coal exporter (US Energy Information Agency 2019; see also Delina in this volume). While the coal industry is part of the institutionalized and racialized socioeconomic inequality and environmental injustice experienced by many poor South Africans, organized resistance is weak (Carruthers 2019; Peek and Taylor 2014).

Conclusion

This introductory chapter has mirrored the organization of the *Handbook* as a whole, which opens with chapters intended to provide conceptual and technical overviews of the world's primary energy resources—fossil fuels, renewable energy, and nuclear power—and related infrastructures. The overview is followed by a collection of chapters devoted to the literatures in IR and comparative politics on energy concepts and key issues: energy interdependence and regional governance of energy resources and electrical power; energy security, foreign policy, and conflict over energy resources; energy markets and finance and CSR; energy justice and the gender dimensions of energy politics; and the global and national dimensions of climate change adaptation. The *Handbook's* final substantive section introduces the world's major energy players and reviews literatures on the history and politics of the following nations and regions: the United States, North America, the European Union, Russia and Eurasia, China, India, Japan, the Asia Pacific region, Brazil, Venezuela, Latin America, MENA, South Africa, and sub-Saharan Africa. It concludes with a summary of the *Handbook's* major contributions, with an emphasis on critical areas for future research, and identifies the technologies, concepts, issues, and geographies that have been overlooked either because there is insufficient literature available to review them or because the appropriate scholar or expert has not yet emerged to cover extant work. The research reviewed in the *Handbook* will contribute to broadening and deepening the community of scholars and practitioners interested in energy politics and provide a strong basis for future research on energy politics and related issues, as well as more effective policy-making efforts.

NOTES

1. This chapter adopts World Bank categorizations of countries as "high-income" (gross national income [GNI] per capita over $12,376), "middle-income" (MICs, GNI per capita between $1,026 and $12,375; the dividing line between lower/upper MICs is $3,995), and "low-income" (GNI per capita $1,025 or lower).
2. Sub-Saharan Africa is a contested term in the context of postcolonial theorizing (see Aspinall 2011); however, the scholarship on the energy politics of this African subregion continues to employ the concept.
3. The use of "nation-state" here signals a theoretical convention in the study of IR. The more broadly understood "nation" is used otherwise.
4. UN Sustainable Development Goal 7: Ensure access to affordable, reliable, sustainable and modern energy.
5. Russia was reclassified from "high-income" country to upper MIC in 2015.
6. The *Handbook* treats Mexico as a part of North America rather than Latin America.

REFERENCES

Ali, Umar. 2019. "Top ten companies by oil production." *Offshore Technology*, 14 May. https://www.offshore-technology.com/features/companies-by-oil-production/

Alter, Karen, and Kal Raustiala. 2018. "The Rise of International Regime Complexity." *Annual Review of Law and Social Science* 14: 329–349.

Ansolabehere, Stephen, and David M. Konisky. *Cheap and Clean: How Americans think about Energy in the age of Global Warming.* Cambridge, MA: MIT Press, 2014.

Araújo, K. 2014. "The Emerging Field of Energy Transitions: Progress, Challenges, and Opportunities." *Energy Research & Social Science* 1: 112–121.

Aspinall, Peter J. 2011. "Who Is 'Black African' in Britain? Challenges to official categorisation of the sub-Saharan African origin population." *African Identities* 9, no. 01: 33–48.

Babic, Milan, Javier Garcia-Bernardo, and Eelke M. Heemskerk. 2019. "The Rise of Transnational State Capital: State-Led Foreign Investment in the 21st Century." *Review of International Political Economy*: 1–43.

Barbier, Edward B., and David W. Pearce. 1990. "Thinking Economically about Climate Change." *Energy Policy* 18, no. 1: 11–18.

Beale, Charlotte. 2016. "Has the Chernobyl Disaster Affected the Number of Nuclear Plants Built?" *The Guardian*, April 30. https://www.theguardian.com/environment/2016/apr/30/has-chernobyl-disaster-affected-number-of-nuclear-plants-built.

Bernauer, Thomas. 2013. "Climate Change Politics." *Annual Review of Political Science* 16: 421–448.

Bernstein, Lev B. 1995. "Tidal Power Development—a Realistic, Justifiable and Topical Problem of Today." *IEEE Transactions on Energy Conversion* 10, no. 3: 591–599.

Bickerstaff, Karen, Gordon Walker, and Harriet Bulkeley, eds. 2013. *Energy Justice in a Changing Climate: Social Equity and Low-Carbon Energy*. London: Zed Books.

Carruthers, Jane. 2019. "Energy, Environment, and Equity in South Africa." *Environmental Justice* 12, no. 3: 112–117.

Char, N. L., and B. J. Csik. 1987. "Nuclear Power Development: History and Outlook." *IAEA Bulletin* (March). https://www.iaea.org/sites/default/files/publications/magazines/bulletin/bull29-3/29304781925.pdf.

Clancy, Joy, Fareeha Ummar, Indira Shakya, and Govind Kelkar. 2007. "Appropriate Gender-Analysis Tools for Unpacking the Gender-Energy-Poverty Nexus." *Gender & Development* 15, no. 2: 241–257.

Clarke, Huw, Leo Eisner, Peter Styles, and Peter Turner. 2014. "Felt Seismicity Associated with Shale Gas Hydraulic Fracturing: The First Documented Example in Europe." *Geophysical Research Letters* 41, no. 23: 8308–8314.

Colgan, Jeff D., Robert O. Keohane, and Thijs Van de Graaf. 2012. "Punctuated Equilibrium in the Energy Regime Complex." *The Review of International Organizations* 7, no. 2: 117–143.

Dahrén, Börje. 2016. "Renewable Energy—Not Always Sustainable." Phys.org, October 31. https://phys.org/news/2016-10-renewable-energy-sustainable.html.

De Decker, Kris. 2019. "How to Make Wind Power Sustainable Again." *Resilience*, June 27. https://www.resilience.org/stories/2019-06-27/how-to-make-wind-power-sustainable-again/.

Eckert, Vera. 2019. "Renewables Overtake Coal as Germany's Main Energy Source." Reuters, January 3. https://www.reuters.com/article/us-germany-power-renewables/renewables-overtake-coal-as-germanys-main-energy-source-idUSKCN1OX0U2.

Ellabban, Omar, Haitham Abu-Rub, and Frede Blaabjerg. 2014. "Renewable Energy Resources: Current Status, Future Prospects and Their Enabling Technology." *Renewable and Sustainable Energy Reviews* 39: 748–764.

Enerdata. 2019. *Global Statistical Yearbook*. https://yearbook.enerdata.net/

Florini, Ann. 2011. "The International Energy Agency in Global Energy Governance." *Global Policy* 2: 40–50.

Florini, Ann, and Benjamin K. Sovacool. 2011. "Bridging the Gaps in Global Energy Governance." *Global Governance* 17: 57–74.

Geels, Frank W. 2014. "Regime Resistance against Low-Carbon Transitions: Introducing Politics and Power into the Multi-Level Perspective." *Theory, Culture & Society* 31, no. 5: 21–40.

Graham Davis & Stubbs, LLP, Gray Reed & McGraw, LLP, Vorys, Sater, Seymour and Pease LLP. 2019. "Hydraulic Fracturing Law and Practice." LexixNexis.

Grosser, Kate, and Jeremy Moon. 2005. "The Role of Corporate Social Responsibility in Gender Mainstreaming." *International Feminist Journal of Politics* 7, no. 4: 532–554.

Hart, Michael. 2016. "Central Asia's Oil and Gas Now Flows to the East." *The Diplomat*, August 18. https://thediplomat.com/2016/08/central-asias-oil-and-gas-now-flows-to-the-east/.

Hayashi, Masatsugu, and Larry Hughes. 2013. "The Fukushima Nuclear Accident and Its Effect on Global Energy Security." *Energy Policy* 59: 102–111.

Hubbert, M. King. 1979. "Hubbert Estimates from 1956 to 1974 of US Oil and Gas." In *Methods and Models for Assessing Energy Resources*, 370–383. London: Pergamon.

Huber, Matthew. "Theorizing energy geographies." *Geography Compass* 9, no. 6 (2015): 327–338.

Institute for Energy Research. 2010. "A Primer on Energy and the Economy: Energy's Large Share of the Economy Requires Caution in Determining Policies that Affect It." https://www.instituteforenergyresearch.org/uncategorized/a-primer-on-energy-and-the-economy-energys-large-share-of-the-economy-requires-caution-in-determining-policies-that-affect-it/.

International Renewable Energy Agency (IRENA). 2018. "Country Rankings." https://www.irena.org/Statistics/View-Data-by-Topic/Capacity-and-Generation/Country-Rankings.

International Renewable Energy Agency (IRENA). 2019. "Renewable Power Generation Costs 2018." https://www.irena.org/-/media/Files/IRENA/Agency/Publication/2019/May/IRENA_Renewable-Power-Generations-Costs-in-2018.pdf.

Javeline, Debra. 2014. "The Most Important Topic Political Scientists Are Not Studying: Adapting to Climate Change." *Perspectives on Politics* 12, no. 2: 420–434.

Jenkins, Kirsten, Darren McCauley, Raphael Heffron, Hannes Stephan, and Robert Rehner. 2016. "Energy Justice: A Conceptual Review." *Energy Research & Social Science* 11: 174–182.

Joskow, Paul L., and John E. Parsons. 2012. "The Future of Nuclear Power after Fukushima." *Economics of Energy & Environmental Policy* 1, no. 2: 99–114.

Keohane, Robert O. 2015. "The Global Politics of Climate Change: Challenge for Political Science." *PS: Political Science & Politics* 48, no. 1: 19–26.

King, Andrew. 2015. "Where and When Did the First Evidence of Climate Change Emerge?" World Economic Forum, October 2. https://www.weforum.org/agenda/2015/10/where-and-when-did-the-first-evidence-of-climate-change-emerge/.

Klare, Michael. 2014. "Twenty-First Century Energy Wars: How Oil and Gas Are Fueling Global Conflicts." Energy Post, July 15. https://energypost.eu/twenty-first-century-energy-wars-oil-gas-fuelling-global-conflicts/.

Kowsari, Reza, and Hisham Zerriffi. 2011. "Three Dimensional Energy Profile: A Conceptual Framework for Assessing Household Energy Use." *Energy Policy* 39: 7505–7517.

Krasner, Stephen D. 1989. *Defending the National Interest: Raw Materials Investments and US Foreign Policy*. Princeton, NJ: Princeton University Press.

Kuzemko, Caroline. 2016. "Energy Depoliticisation in the UK: Destroying Political Capacity." *The British Journal of Politics and International Relations* 18, no. 1: 107–124.

Kuzemko, Caroline, Andrew Lawrence, and Matthew Watson. 2019. "New Directions in the International Political Economy of Energy." *Review of International Political Economy* 26, no. 1: 1–24.

Lantzke, Ulf. 1975. "The Oil Crisis: In Perspective." *Daedalus* 104, no. 4: 217–227.

Lesage, Dries, and Thijs Van de Graaf. 2016. *Global Energy Governance in a Multipolar World*. New York, NY: Routledge.

Malewitz, Jim. 2016. "Energy Crisis,2 Futures: How Denmark and Texas Answered a Challenge." *The Texas Tribune*, November 21. https://www.texastribune.org/2016/11/21/denmark-texas-climate/.

Miller, Aimee. 2017. "Research Shows U.S. and UK Share Similar Fracking Concerns." *UCSB Daily Nexus*, April 30. http://dailynexus.com/2017-04-30/research-shows-u-s-and-uk-share-similar-fracking-concerns/.

Muller, Ian. 2008. "Evolving Priorities: Canadian Oil Policy and the United States in the Years Leading up to the Oil Crisis for 1973." University of Waterloo. https://uwspace.uwaterloo.ca/bitstream/handle/10012/3705/Ian_Muller_Thesis.pdf?sequence=1&isAllowed=y.

Muttitt, Greg. 2018. "Off Track: How the International Energy Agency Guides Energy Decisions Toward Fossil Fuel Dependence and Climate Change." Oil Change International, in collaboration with the Institute for Energy Economics and Financial Analysis. http://priceofoil.org/content/uploads/2018/04/OFF-TRACK-the-IEA-Climate-Change.pdf.

Nincic, Miroslav. 1999. "The National Interest and Its Interpretation." *The Review of Politics* 61, no. 1: 29–55.

Nuñez, Christina. 2014. "How Green Are Those Solar Panels, Really?" *National Geographic*, November 11. https://www.nationalgeographic.com/news/energy/2014/11/141111-solar-panel-manufacturing-sustainability-ranking/.

Nye, J. S., Jr., and C. Frazier. 1991. "Why the Gulf War Served the National Interest." *Atlantic Monthly* 268, no. 1: 54–60.

Nye, Joseph S., Jr. 2002. "Limits of American Power." *Political Science Quarterly* 117, no. 4: 545–559.

O'Hara, S., M. Humphrey, R. Jaspal, B. Nerlich, and M. Poberezhskaya. 2012. " Shale Gas in the UK: What the People Think?" June 29. https://core.ac.uk/download/pdf/30629777.pdf.

Peek, Bobby, and Tristen Taylor. 2014. "Eskom Cannot Continue to Ignore Reality." *Business Day*, December 10. http://www.bdlive.co.za/opinion/2014/12/10/eskom-cannot-continue-to-ignore-reality.

Pisarski, Alan E., and Neils de la Terra. 1975. "American and European Transportation Responses to the 1973–74 Oil Embargo." *Transportation* 4, no. 3: 291–312.

Rai, Varun, and David G. Victor. 2009. "Climate Change and the Energy Challenge: A Pragmatic Approach for India." *Economic and Political Weekly* 44, no. 1: 78–85.

Ross, Michael. 2013. "How the 1973 Oil Embargo Saved the World." *Foreign Affairs*, October 15. https://www.foreignaffairs.com/articles/north-america/2013-10-15/how-1973-oil-embargo-saved-planet.

Russett, Bruce. 2003. "Integrating the Subdisciplines of International and Comparative Politics." *International Studies Review* 5, no. 4: 9–12.

Schmidt, Tobias S., and Sebastian Sewerin. 2017. "Technology as a Driver of Climate and Energy Politics." *Nature Energy* 2, no. 6: 1–3.

Sinha, R. P. 1974. "Japan and the Oil Crisis." *The World Today* 30, no. 8: 335–344.

Slezak, Mikey. 2017. "China Cementing Global Dominance of Renewable Energy and Technology." *The Guardian*, January 6. https://www.theguardian.com/environment/2017/jan/06/china-cementing-global-dominance-of-renewable-energy-and-technology.

Sovacool, Benjamin K. 2011. "An International Comparison of Four Polycentric Approaches to Climate and Energy Governance." *Energy Policy* 39, no. 6: 3832–3844.

Standal, Karina, and Tanja Winther. 2016. "Empowerment through Energy? Impact of Electricity on Care Work Practices and Gender Relations." *Forum for Development Studies* 43, no. 1: 27–45.

Stecker, Tiffany. 2016. "How the Oil Embargo Sparked Energy Independence in Brazil." *Climate Wire* (blog), *Scientific American*, October 17. https://www.scientificamerican.com/article/how-the-oil-embargo-sparked-energy-independence-in-brazil/.

Stocks, Mathew, Andrew Blakers, and Ken Baldwin. 2019. "Australia Is the Runaway Global Leader in Building New Renewable Energy." The Conversation, September 4. https://theconversation.com/australia-is-the-runaway-global-leader-in-building-new-renewable-energy-123694.

Toke, David, and Sevasti-Eleni Vezirgiannidou. 2013. "The Relationship between Climate Change and Energy Security: Key Issues and Conclusions." *Environmental Politics* 22, no. 4: 537–552.

US Energy Information Administration (EIA). 2018. "Frequently Asked Questions: What Countries Are the Top Producers and Consumers of Oil?" https://www.eia.gov/tools/faqs/faq.php?id=709&t=6.

US Energy Information Administration (EIA). 2019. "Nuclear Energy Explained: Nuclear Power Plants." https://www.eia.gov/energyexplained/nuclear/nuclear-power-plants.php.

Van de Graaf, T. 2013a. "Fragmentation in Global Energy Governance: Explaining the Creation of IRENA." *Global Environmental Politics* 13, no. 3: 14–33.

Van de Graaf, T. 2013b. *The Politics and Institutions of Global Energy Governance*. New York, NY: Springer.

Van de Graaf, T., B. K. Sovacool, A. Ghosh, F. Kern, and M. T. Klare. 2016. "States, Markets, and Institutions: Integrating International Political Economy and Global Energy Politics." In *The Palgrave Handbook of the International Political Economy of Energy*, edited by Thijs Van de Graaf, Benjamin K. Sovacool, Arunabha Ghosh, Florian Kern, and Michael T. Klare, 3–44. London: Palgrave Macmillan.

Victor, David G., and Linda Yueh. 2010. "The New Energy Order: Managing Insecurities in the Twenty-First Century." *Foreign Affairs* 89, no. 1: 61–73.

Whitmarsh, Lorraine, Nick Nash, Paul Upham, Alyson Lloyd, James P. Verdon, and J-Michael Kendall. 2015. "UK Public Perceptions of Shale Gas Hydraulic Fracturing: The Role of Audience, Message and Contextual Factors on Risk Perceptions and Policy Support." *Applied Energy* 160: 419–430.

Winkler, Hartmut. 2019. "Is South Africa on the Cusp of a Major Shift in Energy Policy?" The Conversation, February 4. https://theconversation.com/is-south-africa-on-the-cusp-of-a-major-shift-in-energy-policy-109903.

World Health Organization. 2013. "Health Risk Assessment from the Nuclear Accident after the 2011 Great East Japan Earthquake and Tsunami." https://apps.who.int/iris/bitstream/handle/10665/78218/9789241505130_eng.pdf;jsessionid=78D631884276438E90C9A8FF04E1EDFA?sequence=1.

World Health Organization. 2016. "Chernobyl's Legacy: Health, Environmental and Socio-Economic Impacts." https://www.who.int/mediacentre/news/releases/2005/pr38/en/.

Young, Oran R. 1989. *International Cooperation: Building Regimes for Natural Resources and the Environment*. Ithaca, NY: Cornell University Press.

Zimmer, Karl S. 2011. "New Geographies of Energy: Introduction to the Special Issue." *Annals of the Association of American Geographers* 101, no. 4: 705–711.

CHAPTER 2

....

FOSSIL FUELS

A Technical Overview

....

AZRA N. TUTUNCU

FOSSIL *fuel* is defined as organic matter from the remains of plants and other hydrocarbon-containing materials of biological origin deposited in anoxic (oxygen deficient) environments and subjected to high pressure and temperatures over millions of years (US Energy Department.)[1] Coal, oil, and natural gas are the three types of fossil fuel that have been at the center of the energy industry for centuries. Although mounting evidence of climate change as a consequence of fossil fuel combustion has spawned increased investment in, and adoption of, renewable energy for electricity production and transportation fuels (biofuels), coal and natural gas remain the dominant source for electricity; oil, in the form of gasoline, plays that role for transportation. As depicted in Figure 2.1, 81 percent of the world's energy was derived from fossil fuels in 2018. Perhaps surprisingly, wood remains the world's largest source of renewable energy.

In the context of the ongoing climate crisis, fossil fuels have been further scrutinized due to increased efforts, initially by the United States and later Canada, China, and Argentina, to extract unconventional oil and gas reserves. Extracting these resources presents unique challenges that require regulation to ensure economic efficiency, environmental protection, and political support. In 2017, 90 percent of the gas wells in the United States required hydraulic fracturing, which yielded more than half of the nation's oil and gas (Powell 2017). Hydraulic fracturing is currently the most controversial fossil fuel issue, particularly in the United States, where it is the primary method for extracting shale oil and gas. Fracturing is a process of injecting fluid—mostly water, but also including sand or other proppants suspended with the aid of thickening agents—at high pressure into subsurface formations to fracture the shale and release oil and/or gas. The sand (and proppants) sustain the fractures, allowing oil and/or gas to seep into the wellbore (Tutuncu 2017). Contrary to public perceptions, fracturing is not drilling; rather, a well is drilled to enable the injection of fluids required to fracture, or create cracks in, rock formations to release oil, natural gas, and brine.

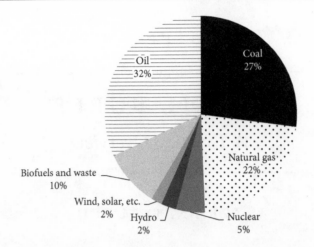

FIGURE 2.1 Global energy supply.

Source: Data from International Energy Agency (2019b). Figure created by Handbook editors.

These perceptions are important to the future of fossil fuel use because public opinion can be the central barrier to developing new energy sources and technologies. Although the investment needed to construct the most efficient gas-fired plant is $1,100 per kilowatt, compared with $3,700 for the most efficient coal-fired plant (IEA 2017), neither the public in the United States, the world's largest producer of fracked gas for export, nor that in the United Kingdom, which is accelerating fracturing developments, "is enthusiastic about the new fracturing technology that utilizes shale development" due to fear of water contamination, air pollution, the risk of accelerating climate change, and earthquakes (Miller 2017; see Allison and Parinandi in this volume; Clarke et al. 2014; O'Hara et al. 2012; Whitmarsh et al. 2015). The water that is used, produced, and wasted; air and water that are contaminated; noise pollution; seismic activity due to fluid injection; and social impacts of fracturing are among the most critical issues associated with these resources (Jackson et al. 2014).

In response to public concern and evidence of air and water pollution and earthquake risk, the fossil fuel industry, academia, federal and state government agencies in the United States and abroad, and environmental organizations have been closely collaborating to develop innovative technologies and practices and improve the existing techniques to reduce the environmental risks and impacts associated with extracting gas from "tight" reservoirs, or those with low porosity and low permeability. Research and development (R&D) will continue to play a major role in fundamentally understanding these complex reservoirs and bringing technology enhancements to optimize the production from these unconventional reserves safely and sustainably (Tutuncu, 2017). Public outreach and education about fossil fuels are expected to contribute further to finding and advancing those solutions to ensure the use of fracturing technologies in an economically viable way that does not jeopardize the natural environment or the public interest.

Types of Fossil Fuels

There are three primary varieties of fossil fuel: coal, oil, and natural gas. In addition to providing energy to heat and cool our homes, cook and store our food, and fuel modern methods of transportation, they are found in numerous commonly used items, including plastics, computers, personal care products, and pharmaceuticals. In addition, fossil fuel industries employ millions of people and generate revenue from taxes and royalties. While the public costs of fossil fuel extraction and combustion, from contaminated water and earthquakes to air pollution and climate change, portend continued phenomenal growth in renewable energy—6.3 percent in 2017 (Richard 2018)—fossil fuels are expected to provide most of the world's energy for some time (Rissman 2013). The remainder of this section provides an overview of fossil fuel types, brief histories of their uses as energy, and production and consumption trends, and suggests employing controversies that exist as bases for developing thoughts on the future of fossil fuels.

Coal

Coal is mined in solid state: chunks of black rock composed of carbon, nitrogen, hydrogen, and sulfur. High-energy anthracite coal is abundant, found in nearly every nation, though it may not always be extracted easily or economically. Lignite, which is high in oxygen and hydrogen relative to carbon, and soft bituminous coal are less energy rich. All three kinds of coal are fossilized mud from Carboniferous-period swamps. The carbon energy stored in coal was captured, along with a number of contaminants, through plant photosynthesis. Burning coal reverses this sequestration process, yielding soot and air pollutants, including mercury, lead, sulfur dioxide, nitrogen oxides, particulates, and other heavy metals. Efforts to reduce this pollution consist of technologies to improve coal fire efficiency—for example, flue gas desulfurization (wet scrubbing) and coal washing to remove sulfur, ash, and other impurities—and carbon capture and storage (CCS) techniques for separating carbon dioxide from the gases produced by generating electricity and other industrial processes. The success of these approaches is manifest in contemporary power plants, which emit 90 percent fewer pollutants—sulfur dioxide and nitrogen oxides, in particular—than the 1970s-era plants that they replaced (Institute for Energy Research 2017).

Coal has been used as a fuel source since the Roman Empire (100–200 BCE), but large-scale coal use did not begin until the Industrial Revolution, when it was first burned to generate steam to power engines. By the end of the nineteenth century, steam had been deployed to generate electricity, and coke, a derivative of coal that has been baked to isolate carbon, had replaced charcoal in the production of steel. The world's dependence on coal for energy peaked before the start of World War I; although coal extraction and combustion have declined since then, coal remains a significant source of energy in some regions. As shown in Figures 2.2 and 2.3, China/Asia Pacific possesses, and depends on, some of the world's largest coal reserves; this equivalence of coal reserves and use obtains for other regions as well (Ritchie and Roser 2015). Still, according

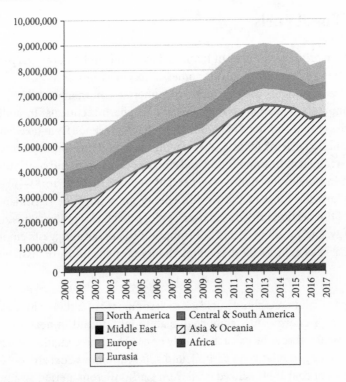

FIGURE 2.2 Coal production by world region*.

Source: Data from USEIA (2019b). Figure created by Handbook editors.

* In million short tons (Mst); 1 short ton = 2,000 lbs.

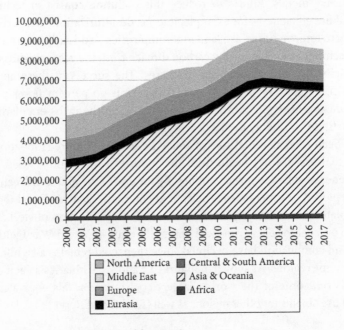

FIGURE 2.3 Coal consumption by world region*.

Source: Data from USEIA (2019b). Figure created by Handbook editors.

* In million short tons (Mst); 1 short ton = 2,000 lbs.

to the World Coal Association (n.d.), international coal trade reached 1,169 million tons in 2018, accounting for about 21 percent of total coal consumed. Global coal trade has increase by 148 percent since 2000.

Oil

Crude oil, or simply "oil," is a liquid mix of hydrocarbons that may be processed in combination with other liquids to create gasoline and other petroleum products. It is important to note that "petroleum" is used interchangeably with oil and categorically to include crude oil, natural gas, and products of petroleum refineries and from the extraction of hydrocarbons at natural gas processing plants (US Energy Information Administration 2018). The latter usage is arguably most appropriate when (light) crude oil and natural gas occur together, which has sometimes been the case in more than half of US wells (US Energy Information Administration 2013).

Oil and natural gas originated millions of years ago in source rocks that formed from sediments deposited in very quiet water, usually in swamps on land or in deep marine settings, composed of fine-grained minerals that trapped the remains of organic materials, like algae, small wood fragments, and plants. When these sediments were buried by overlying sediments, the increasing pressure and temperature compacted the sediments into rocks. Increasing temperatures initiated pyrolyzation (cooking) of organic-rich sediments (> 120° C [250° F]), expelling oil and natural gas. The higher the burial temperature, the more organic matter matured, and fluid pressure increased via this "cooking process." When sediments have very low porosity and high permeability, or almost no connection between the small pore spaces, the increased fluid pressure introduces small cracks and natural fractures in the formation. Oil and gas expelled from these cracks typically migrate upward to higher porosity, fine-grained sedimentary formations until "trapped" by some less permeable cap rock such as shale or sandstone. The porosity and fluid characteristics of conventional reservoirs permit oil or gas to flow easily into wellbores, the holes drilled to extract oil, gas, and other subsurface resources.

If the trap rises into an oxidizing zone, where oil and water mix, bacterial degradation and evaporation may convert the oil to high-density and -viscosity heavy oil (Head et al. 2003), which requires costly extraction methods, such as surface mining, cold production, and thermal recovery, as well as upgrading—processing beyond the norm—prior to transport and refining. Like heavy oil, tight oil and gas, shale oil and gas, oil shale, coalbed methane, and gas-hydrate deposits constitute unconventional reservoirs, which means it is difficult or impossible for oil or gas to flow through pores into a standard well. These reservoirs require alternative extraction techniques, including hydraulic fracturing for tight oil and gas and shale oil and gas, and steam-assisted gravity drainage for oil, or "tar," sands where bitumen—a thick, sticky, black oil—is found. Table 2.1 lists the world's top twenty heavy oil reservoirs. Extracting these resources may require enhanced oil recovery (EOR)—that is, gas, thermal, or chemical injection—in situ heating methods to release and recover hydrocarbons, and/or fracturing.

The protracted economic viability of unconventional sources of oil and gas may be attributed to American businessman George Mitchell's innovative combination of

Table 2.1 Regional Distribution of Heavy Oil and Bitumen around the Globe

Company Name	Country	Market Value (Billion USD)	Gas Production (MMCF/D)	Oil Production (Million BBL/D)
ExxonMobil	US	344.1	2,936	4.10
Royal Dutch Shell	The Netherlands	306.5	785	2.95
Chevron	US	248.1	970	2.62
Petro China	China	220.2	9,370	4.07
BP	UK	152.6	1,659	3.24
Sinopec	China	138.6	444	1.32
Total	France	121.9	527	2.35
Petrobras	Brazil	92.6	504	2.55
Statoil	Norway	90.2	819	1.81
ConocoPhillips	US	81.3	905	1.59

Source: Meyers et al. (2007).

hydraulic fracturing with horizontal drilling in the 1990s; the astronomically increasing price of crude oil (223 percent) over nearly two decades prior to crashing in 2014 (Macrotrends n.d.); and the availability of low interest rates for investment in energy production following the 2008 economic crisis (McClean 2018). While the fracturing process is more expensive than drilling, it is cost effective in comparison to low-volume "stripper" wells up to a "break-even" or benchmark per barrel price, used to predict producer responses to market prices. The estimated break-even price for fracked oil was as high as $70 per barrel (World Bank 2016) when world oil prices dropped precipitously, from nearly $120 to $36 per barrel between late 2014 and the end of 2016 (Macrotrends n.d.). By the end of 2018, the break-even fracked oil price ranged between $40 and $60 per barrel (Cunningham 2019) throughout the US shale "plays," the term for the fine-grained sedimentary rock that might contain hydrocarbons. The word price for oil then was $51, according to West Texas Intermediate (WTI or NYMEX) data (Macrotrends n.d.).

The use of crude oil for fuel originated in China during the fourth century BCE, but the distillation of fuel from oil fields in what is now Azerbaijan was not recorded until the ninth century AD. Drilling and distillation technologies developed further and spread rapidly over the following three centuries, and oil was used widely in the form of a kerosene-like fuel for heating and lighting in the Middle East, Central Asia, and Europe by the twelfth century. Scottish chemist James Young and Canadian geologist Abraham Pineo Gesner, respectively, distilled paraffin (from coal) and kerosene (from coal, bitumen, and oil shale) to fuel lamps in the mid-1800s. Kerosene proved to be a game changer. The fuel burned cleaner than competing products, such as whale oil, and was cheaper to produce. Gesner founded the Kerosene Gaslight Company in Halifax, Nova Scotia, in 1850, followed by the North American Kerosene Gas Light Company four years later. Meanwhile, a Polish inventor, Ignacy Lukasiewicz, developed a technique for refining kerosene from "rock oil" seeps in 1852; the first rock oil mine was constructed near Krosno, Poland, two years later, in part to satisfy demand for this new fuel. The first modern, commercial oil well was drilled in 1859 by Edwin Drake, a Seneca Oil Company contractor hired to identify oil deposits in Titusville, Pennsylvania, now that there was a lucrative gas light market.

Oil became the energy source following widespread use of electricity (the light bulb was invented in 1879) and increased automobile ownership (the first gasoline-fueled car was built in 1888). Gasoline sales surpassed those of kerosene by 1919. One hundred years later, 98 percent of the energy used for transportation—including gasoline, diesel, jet fuel, propane, and residuals—is derived from crude oil (Maritime Executive 2019). As indicated in Figure 2.4, the United States had out produced Saudi Arabia by 2014; this achievement is attributable to the "shale boom" (Egan 2019).

Figures 2.5 and 2.6 show that Africa and the Middle East produce much more oil than they consume, and states in the Asia/Pacific region consume far more oil than they produce.

Natural Gas

Natural gas is the lightest of the hydrocarbons produced via the process explained in the previous section: a mix of decomposed organic material, mud, silt, and sand sealed into an oxygen-free space and exposed to heat and pressure over a long period of time.

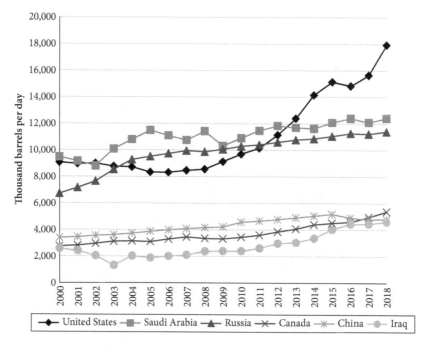

FIGURE 2.4 Top oil-producing countries, 2000–2018.

Source: Data from USEIA (2019b). Figure created by Handbook editors.

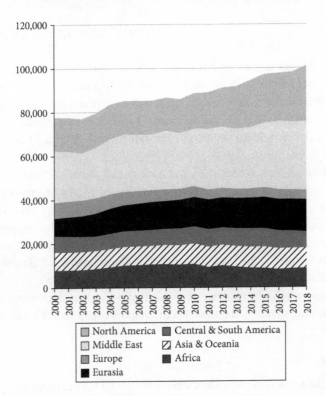

FIGURE 2.5 Petroleum and other liquids production, by world region, 2000–2018.*

Source: Data from USEIA (2019b). Figure created by Handbook editors.

* Millions of barrels/day.

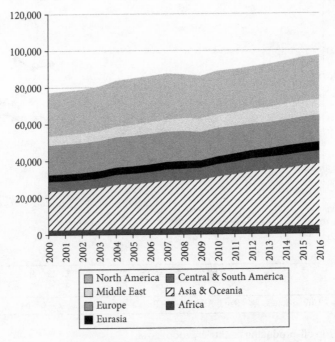

FIGURE 2.6 Petroleum and other liquids consumption, by world region, 2000–2016.*

Source: Data from USEIA (2019b). Figure created by Handbook editors

* Millions of barrels/day.

Natural gas is composed mostly of methane—an odorless, colorless gas—though it may also contain other alkanes (compounds of hydrogen and carbon, such as ethane and propane) as well as carbon dioxide, nitrogen, hydrogen sulfide, and/or helium. Because natural gas produces less carbon dioxide per unit of energy released than oil or coal, natural gas is widely considered to be cleaner than either coal or oil.

Once created, natural gas is lower density than the rock that contains it, so it rises to the surface and, in the presence of enough heat or a spark, may catch fire. These mysterious fires were the source of ancient myths, including the Greek's story of the Oracle of Delphi, whose prophesies were said to be inspired by the flame and accompanying smoke. The Chinese (ca. 500 BCE) were the first to use natural gas for fuel; they crafted "pipelines" from bamboo to transport gas for boiling water. Natural gas, distilled from bituminous coal, was not used commercially—as fuel for lamps in England—until the late eighteenth century. Cleaner natural gas extracted from the ground largely replaced this manufactured variation in the United States by the mid-nineteenth century. Although Drake's oil well also produced natural gas, William Hart is credited with digging the first well, in Fredonia, New York, specifically intended to recover gas, which was ultimately marketed by the Fredonia Gas Light Company. The zenith of natural gas lighting was short lived. (Kerosene) oil replaced gas for lighting within decades following Thomas Edison's invention of the electric light bulb; the first oil-fired plant opened for business in 1895.

The nascent natural gas industry was "saved" by Robert Bunsen's invention in 1891 of an adjustable gas "burner," which anticipated the use of natural gas for heating/cooling and fueling appliances. Contemporary uses of natural gas extend from heating and cooling and electricity generation—directly and as "backup" power for renewable energy applications, such as solar and wind (IEA 2017)—to the production of fertilizer, antifreeze, plastics, pharmaceuticals, fabrics, and many chemicals, and, in the form of compressed natural gas (CNG), for use as vehicle fuel. In addition, natural gas is transformed into cleaner-burning variants of fuels, such as gasoline and diesel, in gas-to-liquids (GTL) plants. Reaching this level of penetration into the energy economy depended on the development of efficient means of natural gas transport. The first natural gas pipeline was built about the same time as the Bunsen burner was invented, and the United States invested in the construction of pipeline infrastructure following World War I; however, the welding, pipe-rolling, and metallurgical technologies necessary to build efficient pipelines were not developed until the mid-twentieth century. By 2019 there were more than 300,000 miles of transmission pipeline systems (connecting processing facilities to distribution hubs) and 2.1 million distribution pipelines in the United States alone (American Petroleum Institute 2019; see also Coburn in this volume).

Considered in the context of relatively reduced reliance on coal, trends in the production and consumption of natural gas, shown in Figures 2.7 and 2.8, suggest a transition from coal- to gas-fired power plants. In addition to being cleaner, a gas-fired power station takes much less time to start and stop than a coal-fired plant. This unique flexibility

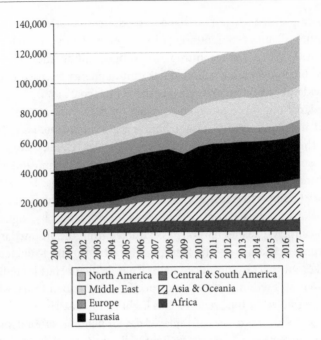

FIGURE 2.7 Dry natural gas production, by world region.

Source: Data from USEIA (2019b). Figure created by Handbook editors.

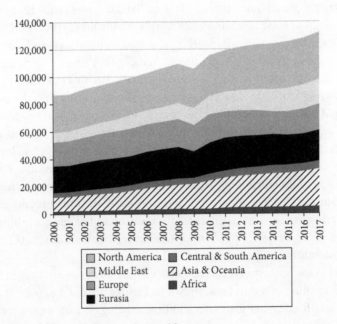

FIGURE 2.8 Natural gas consumption, by world region.

Source: Data from USEIA (2019b). Figure created by Handbook editors.

of gas power makes natural gas the perfect partner for wind, solar, and other renewable energy technologies, eliminating their limitations, such as cloudy or windless days. Demand for natural gas is expected to increase significantly due to its role as a cleaner (than other fossil fuel) energy source and its abundance. The quantity of recoverable natural gas resources has grown with the discovery of new reserves and advances in horizontal drilling and multistage hydraulic fracturing technologies.

The Unconventional Hydrocarbon Revolution

"Unconventional" oil or natural gas is not a fixed point; rather, it is gas or oil regarded as too difficult or expensive to extract. For example, "deep" natural gas produced far below (fifteen thousand feet or more) "conventional" drilling depths (less than about three thousand feet below the surface) was not tapped until the 1970s, when deep drilling, exploration, and extraction technologies were developed sufficiently to make this resource economical. Deep natural gas is arguably conventional by twenty-first-century standards, though still more costly to extricate than reserves located closer to the earth's surface (Inkpen and Moffett 2011). Keeping this caveat in mind, unconventional (oil and) gas resources also include tight oil and gas, shale oil and gas, geo-pressurized zones, coalbed methane, and Arctic and seabed hydrates.

Tight and Shale Oil and Gas

Tight oil or gas is "trapped" in unusually hard, impermeable, nonporous rock—usually sandstone or limestone. Shale oil or gas is crude oil or natural gas trapped in shale, a soft, fine-grained sedimentary rock composed of mud or clay that breaks easily into thin, parallel layers. Oil and natural gas tend to become stuck between thicker shale deposits that "sandwich" a thinner area of shale containing hydrocarbons. Extracting these resources usually requires the use of horizontal wells in combination with hydraulic fracturing. Horizontal drilling improves the productivity of fracked reservoirs by increasing the number of fractures and therefore also the flow of oil and gas (Inkpen and Moffett 2011; University of Calgary 2017).

Oil Shale

Oil shale is a sedimentary rock with deposits of kerogen, consisting of organic compounds that have not experienced sufficient geologic pressure, heat, and time to become conventional oil. Kerogen may be converted to crude oil by heating it to very high temperatures—up to 950°F in an oxygen-free environment—a process called "retorting." Retorting may occur above ground or in situ, by burying heaters in gaps in the shale for years until the rock reaches temperatures of at least 650°F and releases the oil (Center for Sustainable Systems 2018). The complexity and costs of these complex and lengthy processes continue to anticipate a lengthy timeline to commercial production of oil shale under most conditions (Glatz 2013).

Geopressurized Zones

Geopressurized zones within a rock formation are characterized by unusually high pressure for their depth. These areas formed ten to twenty-five thousand feet below the surface when impermeable sediments, such as clay, were deposited and compacted very quickly on top of more porous, absorbent sediments—for example, sand or silt—making it impossible for any liquids or gases to escape. Extracting oil and gas from geopressurized zones is particularly complicated and expensive (Inkpen and Moffett 2011).

Coalbed Methane

Many coal seams also contain natural gas, which usually remains trapped underground until mining activities release it. Historically, coalbed methane was regarded as a nuisance in the mining industry. Any methane that accumulated in a mine was diluted by ventilation—airway tunnels, drill holes, and shafts—and drainage boreholes to protect miners (Flores 1998; Inkpen and Moffett 2011); since the 1970s, it has increasingly been recovered for commercial use. Like deep gas, coalbed methane might arguably be categorized as a conventional fossil fuel by the late 1990s (Flores 1998).

Arctic and Seabed Hydrates

Methane hydrate—also called methane clathrate, hydromethane, methane ice, fire ice, natural gas hydrate, and gas hydrate—is a solid "ice" that consists of a methane molecule surrounded by a lattice or "cage" of water molecules at temperatures above freezing and pressures over one atmosphere (Inkwell and Moffett 2011). These conditions obtain in four environments: (1) in sedimentary rock formations below the Arctic permafrost; (2) in sediments deposited along continental margins; (3) in deepwater sediments, like those found in inland lakes and seas; and (4) under the Antarctic ice (King 2019). Cold seeps are formed when hydrate "beds" leak gases into the water (Levin et al. 2016).

Production of oil and gas from unconventional formations is indicative of the most recent revolution in the fossil fuels sector. The United States initiated this revolution, providing government incentives for developing domestic fossil fuel resources in the interest of energy independence. Net oil imports to the United States fell precipitously in the wake of the OPEC oil embargo—a consequence of higher world oil prices and increased domestic conservation—and then rose through the early 2000s before declining again (US Energy Information Administration 2019a). The catalyst for this transition was the discovery of large oil fields in the Gulf of Mexico and elsewhere (beginning in the 1980s) and tight and shale oil and gas formations throughout the lower forty-eight states (from the mid-2000s). The discovery of shale oil and gas, in particular, provided the context in which small, independent Mitchell Energy combined hydraulic fracturing with horizontal drilling in 1997 (McClean 2018). Mitchell's success in Texas's Barnett shale has been transferred to other US shale basins by numerous independent companies, including Chesapeake Energy and Continental Resources, both of which pioneered entirely shale-based assets with success in Oklahoma, Wyoming, North Dakota, Texas, and Pennsylvania. As Figure 2.6 indicates, shale reserves exist on every continent.

The United States has been tapping its share of these resources so aggressively that the US Energy Information Administration (USEIA 2018) expects shale gas to account for 90 percent of the nation's natural gas production by 2050.

THE FUTURE OF FOSSIL FUELS

Crude oil and natural gas provide energy for manufacturing, transportation, and electricity generation, in addition to their use as feedstock to make other chemicals for household goods, medicine, and agriculture. Demand for fossil fuel energy and petroleum products is likely to escalate as the world's population and GDP per capita rise. Thus, despite evidence of the environmental consequences of reliance on fossil fuels and continuing support for renewable energy, fossil fuels, especially natural gas, will remain central to societies' energy mixes for some time. This section considers current fossil fuel opportunities and challenges given the rising demand for energy in the context of greater expert and popular awareness of the impacts of coal, oil, and natural gas on ecologies and climate.

Fossil Fuel Opportunities

Evidence of large, untapped fossil fuel reserves represents the greatest opportunity inherent in the unconventional hydrocarbon revolution. The sheer volume of resources justified investments in research and development necessary to identify and enhance technologies and processes for recovering unconventional fuels in an economically and ecologically sustainable manner. Consequent increases in oil and gas production, especially in the United States and Canada, have reverberated throughout the world energy economy to create employment, spur growth in remote sensing and other information technologies (IT), and provide opportunities for applied research.

Economic Opportunities

The discovery, extraction, and use of unconventional fossil fuel resources has transformed the United States from an oil-importing nation to one that is on track to become a net exporter of energy, defined as crude oil and refined petroleum products, or crude oil and natural gas, subject to the construction of the necessary LNG infrastructure (U.S. Energy Information Administration 2019a; see Coburn in this volume). A much-cited IHS Energy report (2012) concluded that activity in the US unconventional oil and natural gas industry had already contributed $237 billion to the nation's GDP by 2012 and was projected to nearly double that amount by 2035. The fossil fuel sector has also created a significant number of jobs, not only in the coal mines and oil and gas "fields," but also in the local economies where these operations are ongoing. IHS Energy (2012) reported that 1.7 million workers were employed directly by the unconventional oil and gas industry in 2012, and this number was projected to reach 3 million by 2020. More recently, the Department of Energy (2017) reported that fuel production and electricity generation employed 1.9 million workers in 2016, with over half (1.1 million) working in the fossil fuel sector; an additional 2.3 million workers were employed in energy transmission, distribution, and storage jobs.

Energy, Environment, and Information Technology

Advances in IT have enhanced all aspects of energy projects, from document management, data analysis, and telecommunications to monitoring drilling, well stimulation, and production in the field. Remote sensing in oil and natural gas fields is widely used to collect information; however, efficient use of the data is occurring slowly, especially with respect to real-time processing. Still, GPU-accelerated analytics that accelerate production models to improve decision-making help well operators visualize, analyze, and respond to immense volumes of sensor and production data, including pump pressures, flow rates, and temperatures. Similar computational capabilities are enabling companies to accelerate exploration and other upstream activities by providing faster and more advanced interpretation of "big" seismic and geoscience data.

Applied Research and Technology

Regulation to protect environments and the public requires increased understanding of the impacts of fossil fuel exploration, extraction, distribution, transmission, and use, as well as the development of technologies for managing them. The advent of unconventional oil and natural gas operations has generated extensive cooperation among federal and state governments and regulatory agencies, oil companies, affected communities, public interest groups, and major research universities and organizations. In particular, academic programs in petroleum engineering, geoscience, and related areas, and other research enterprises generally, continue to improve technological and other capacities to evaluate unconventional fossil fuel resources with respect to climate and other environmental and public health challenges.

Fossil Fuel Challenges

The growth and development of the fossil fuel sector has required overcoming numerous intellectual and technical challenges. In addition, there have been and continue to be individual and social challenges associated with "hidden" costs of fossil fuel production and use. These costs, or externalities, are left out of the market price of fossil fuels, despite their environmental impacts or (public) health consequences. Fossil fuel externalities include climate change, in addition to air pollution and respiratory illness; land degradation, which can destroy livelihoods and wildlife habitats; contaminated water and, in the case of major spills, irredeemable ecological loss (see Allison and Parinandi and Mildenberger and Stokes in this volume); and unusual seismic activity, including earthquakes. Due to contemporary economic and political emphasis on unconventional fossil fuels, this section emphasizes the role these resources play in climate change, the availability and quality of water, and earthquake risk.

Greenhouse Gas Emissions

One of the key challenges for the use of fossil fuels is that they release carbon dioxide (CO_2) when they burn. Research studies associate CO_2 emissions directly with climate change. Natural gas is twice as clean as coal or oil in terms of its contribution to CO_2 concentrations in the atmosphere (International Energy Agency 2017), making transitions from coal to gas for electrical power generation promising. The catch is that natural gas is a major source of another greenhouse gas, methane, which is roughly thirty times more potent as a greenhouse gas than CO_2. Moreover, methane linkage throughout the natural gas supply chain—estimated at 1.4 percent (US Environmental Protection Agency 2018)—adds to the methane released when gas burns. Others have disputed this number: Alvarez et al. (2018) found that in 2015, supply chain emissions were about 60 percent higher than the EPA's estimate.

Research on methods for reducing both CO_2 and methane is promising. CO_2 sequestration, and caprock sealing to capture and trap CO_2 underground during the production process, is one possibility (Espinoza and Santamarina 2017). Perhaps more promising is the use of methane fuel cells to produce electricity from natural gas with low emissions of pollutants—not only CO_2 and methane, but also nitrogen oxides, sulfur oxides, volatile organic compounds, and particulates. A fuel cell is an electrochemical device that converts the energy from methane in natural gas directly into electricity through a chemical reaction with oxygen fuel (International Energy Agency 2017; Santhanam et al. 2016).

Water Use and Contamination

Water used to extract shale gas, in particular, is among the chief concerns raised by the public as well as regulatory organizations. The implementation of hydraulic fracturing requires large quantities of fresh water (any impurities may reduce the efficiency of additives)—as much as two to eight million gallons per well (US Environmental Protection Agency 2016)—and produces a substantial flowback of fracturing fluid and briny formation water. While the amount of water required for fracturing appears substantial, it is small compared to the quantities devoted to agriculture, manufacturing, and power plant cooling (Magill 2015). Yet even a relatively small volume of water diverted to natural gas production may be problematic in arid regions. In addition, drilling too close to aquifers and/or improper disposal of wastewater can lead to contamination. Tainted water has become less likely as drilling practices have improved; however, failure to contain or clean (and reuse) waste that has been mixed with chemicals during the fracturing process continues to be an issue (Harrabin 2016). Shale oil and gas operators and water regulators continue to collaborate in the development of management practices designed to minimize water use and pollution as well as costs (Craig 2012).

Injection-Induced Seismicity

If there is a fault near fracturing operations, then the injection of liquids underground associated with hydraulic fracturing can induce seismicity that is much greater than any normal microseismic tremors—five to six orders of magnitude below the smallest quakes humans can feel—associated with the process (Tutuncu and Bui 2016). This induced seismicity was first noticed in the Rocky Mountain Arsenal during the injection of waste fluids into a high-porosity formation close to a theretofore unknown fault. The result was a significant number of earthquakes up to magnitude 5.3 in a previously aseismic area. Research points to a correlation between the fluid injection and the earthquakes' occurrence (Evans 1966; Tutuncu and Bui 2016).

In order to assure that no seismicity is induced during these operations, most hydraulic fracturing treatments are monitored using devices called geophones, which convert ground movement into voltage, which is then recorded at the surface and distributed to the connected seismology stations. The deviation of this measured voltage from the base line is called the seismic response and is analyzed for the structure of the earth.

FINAL CONSIDERATIONS

As energy technologies change, so will our choice of fossil fuels. Changes in societies' primary energy fuel from wood to coal to oil and natural gas have yielded significant reductions in air pollution and concomitant efforts to limit water usage and contamination. Indeed, the fossil fuel sector has long been a source of innovation, producing technological breakthroughs that have improved the lives of millions. Increased reliance on solar and wind power and on hybrid and electrical auto use reflects this trend, yet the fossil fuels and byproducts long embedded in our daily lives will persist as foundation sources of energy. Energy investments easily reflect this expectation. Investment in solar, wind, and other green energy *is* at historically high levels—$333.5 billion in 2017, according to Bloomberg New Energy Finance (Deign 2019). But, according to the International Energy Agency (2019a), it is not enough, especially when investments in fossil fuel exploration and production remain insufficient, barring discovery of a "game-changing" alternative. "Whichever way you look, we are storing up risks for the future" (Hill 2019).

ACKNOWLEDGMENTS

From Kathleen J. Hancock, coeditor, The Oxford Handbook of Energy Politics:

As the Harry D. Campbell Chair and director of the Unconventional Natural Gas and Oil Association at the Colorado School of Mines, Dr. Tutuncu was a star in her field, both technically and as a communicator. Demonstrating her commitment to working with scholars from all disciplines, she quickly and enthusiastically agreed to write this chapter for the Handbook.

Sadly, Dr. Tutuncu passed away shortly before her chapter went to press. She will be sorely missed by me and her many friends and colleagues at Mines and beyond.

From Dr. Erdal Ozkan, professor of petroleum engineering, Colorado School of Mines:

Dr. Tutuncu was a personal friend for over forty years and a colleague at Colorado School of Mines for the past nine years. I am deeply saddened to write these words in her memoriam, but I am conciliated by the belief that she used every moment of her life to do what she cherished the most: serving humanity through science and engineering. It is a great loss, but she has left a legacy to be carried forth by her students and colleagues.

NOTE

1. Editorial note: In our last communication with Dr. Tutuncu, she indicated the chapter was nearly ready to go but that she wanted to do a final review before submitting it. Given her sudden death, we sent the chapter to two anonymous reviewers, both with PhDs in petroleum engineering, to ensure that no edits were needed from a technical perspective. Both agreed the chapter was ready for publication.—Kathleen Hancock and Juliann Allison

REFERENCES

Alvarez, Ramón A., Daniel Zavala-Araiza,David R. Lyon, David T. Allen, Zachary R. Barkley, Adam R. Brandt, Kenneth J. Davis, Scott C. Herndon, Daniel J. Jacob, Anna Karion, Eric A. Kort, Brian K. Lamb, Thomas Lauvaux, Joannes D. Maasakkers, Anthony J. Marchese, Mark Omara, Stephen W. Pacala, Jeff Peischl, Allen L. Robinson, Paul B. Shepson, Colm Sweeney, Amy Townsend-Small, Steven C. Wofsy, and Steven P. Hamburg. 2018. "Assessment of methane emissions from the U.S. oil and gas supply chain." *Science* 361, no. 6398: 186–188.

American Petroleum Institute. 2019. "Pipeline 101: Natural Gas Pipelines." https://pipeline101. com/Why-Do-We-Need-Pipelines/Natural-Gas-Pipelines.

BLM (Bureau of Land Management). 2018. "About the BLM Oil and Gas Program." US Department of the Interior. https://www.blm.gov/programs/energy-and-minerals/oil-and-gas/about.

Clarke, Huw, Leo Eisner, Peter Styles, and Peter Turner. 2014. "Felt Seismicity Associated with Shale Gas Hydraulic Fracturing: The First Documented Example in Europe." *Geophysical Research Letters* 41. doi:10.1002/2014GL062047.

Craig, Robin Kundis. 2012. "Hydraulic Fracturing (Fracking), Federalism, and the Water-Energy Nexus." *Idaho Law Review* 49: 241.

Cunningham, Nick. 2019. "The Myth of Cheap Shale Oil." OilPrice.com, May 22. https://oilprice. com/Energy/Crude-Oil/The-Myth-Of-Cheap-Shale-Oil.html.

Deign, Jason. 2019. "Global Renewable Energy Investment on the Rise." Greentech Media, January 1. https://www.greentechmedia.com/articles/read/global-renewable-energy-investment#gs.yw3xhd.

Egan, Matt. 2019. "America Is Set to Surpass Saudi Arabia in 'Remarkable' Milestone." CNN, March 21. https://www.cnn.com/2019/03/08/business/us-oil-exports-saudi-arabia/index.html.

Espinoza, D. Nicolas, and Juan Carlos Santamarina. 2017. "CO_2 Breakthrough—Caprock Sealing Efficiency and Integrity for Carbon Geological Storage." *International Journal of Greenhouse Gas Control* 66: 218–229.

Evans David M. 1966. "The Denver Area Earthquakes and the Rocky Mountain Arsenal Disposal Well." *The Mountain Geologist* 3: 23–36.

Flores, Romeo M. 1998. "Coalbed Methane: From Hazard to Resource." *International Journal of Coal Geology* 35, nos. 1–4: 3–26.

Glatz, Guenther. 2013. "Oil Shale Pyrolysis." http://large.stanford.edu/courses/2013/ph240/glatz2/.

Harrabin, Roger. 2016. "Does Fracking Affect the Water Supply?" *BBC News*, October 6. https://www.bbc.com/news/uk-37578189.

Head Ian M., Darren M. Jones, Steve R. Larter. 2003. "Biological activity in the deep subsurface and the origin of heavy oil." *Nature* 426: 344–352.

Hill, Joshua S. 2019. "Fossil Fuel Investment Increased in 2018, as Renewables Stalled: IEA." https://reneweconomy.com.au/fossil-fuel-investment-increased-in-2018-as-renewables-stalled-iea-27425/.

Inkpen, Andrew and Michael H. Moffett. 2011. *The Global Oil and Gas Industry: Management, Strategy, and Finance*. Tulsa, OK: PenWell Corporation.

Institute for Energy Research. 2017. "Cleaned-Up Coal and Clean Air: Facts about Air Quality and Coal-Fired Plants. https://www.instituteforenergyresearch.org/uncategorized/cleaned-coal-clean-air-facts-air-quality-coal-fired-power-plants/

International Energy Agency (IEA). 2017. "World Energy Outlook 2017: A World in Transformation." https://www.iea.org/weo2017/.

International Energy Agency (IEA). 2019a. "World Energy Investment." https://reneweconomy.com.au/fossil-fuel-investment-increased-in-2018-as-renewables-stalled-iea-27425/.

International Energy Agency (IEA). 2019b. "World Energy Balances." https://webstore.iea.org/world-energy-balances-2019.

Jackson, Robert B., Avener Vengosh, J. William Carey, Richard J. Davies, Thomas H. Darrah, Francis O'Sullivan, and Gabrielle Pétron. 2014. "The Environmental Costs and Benefits of Fracking." *Annual Review of Environment and Resources* 39: 327–362.

King, Hobart M. 2019. "Methane Hydrate: The World's Largest Resource Is Trapped Beneath Permafrost and Ocean Sediment." https://geology.com/articles/methane-hydrates/.

Levin, Lisa A., Amy R. Baco, David A. Bowden, Ana Colaco, Erik E. Cordes, Marina R. Cunha, Amanda W. J. Demopoulos, et al. 2016. "Hydrothermal Vents and Methane Seeps: Rethinking the Sphere of Influence." *Frontiers in Marine Science* 3: 72.

Macrotrends. N.d. https://www.macrotrends.net/1369/crude-oil-price-history-chart

Magill, Bobby. 2015. "Water Use Rises as Fracking Expands." *Scientific American* July 1.

Maritime Executive, The. 2019. "Transport Uses 25 Percent of World Energy." https://www.maritime-executive.com/article/transport-uses-25-percent-of-world-energy.

McClean, Bethany. 2018. "How America's 'Most Reckless Billionaire' Created the Fracking Boom." *The Guardian*, August 30. https://www.theguardian.com/news/2018/aug/30/how-the-us-fracking-boom-almost-fell-apart.

Meyer, Richard F., Emil D. Attanasi, and Philip A. Freeman. 2007. "Heavy Oil and Natural Bitumen Resources in Geological Basins of the World." USGS Report 2007–1084.

Miller, Aimee. 2017. "Research Shows U.S. and UK Share Similar Fracking Concerns." *UCSB Daily Nexus*, April 30. http://dailynexus.com/2017-04-30/research-shows-u-s-and-uk-share-similar-fracking-concerns/.

O'Hara, Sarah, Mat Humphrey, Rusi Jaspal, Brigitte Nerlich, and Marianna Poberezhskaya. 2012. "Shale Gas in the UK: What the People Think." http://www.nottingham.ac.uk/news/pressreleases/2012/july/fracking.aspx.

Powell, Tarika. 2017. "Is your Natural Gas Actually Fracked?" Sightline Institute, October 30. https://www.sightline.org/2017/10/30/is-your-natural-gas-actually-fracked/.

Richard, Craig. 2018. "Renewables Fasted Growing Energy Source in 2017." *Wind Power Monthly*, April 22. https://www.windpowermonthly.com/article/1460160/renewables-fastest-growing-energy-source-2017.

Rissman, Jeffrey. 2013. "We Will Not Run Out of Fossil Fuel." *LiveScience* 14 (June). https://www.livescience.com/37469-fuel-endures.html.

Ritchie, Hannah, and Max Roser. 2015. "Fossil Fuels." Our World in Data. https://ourworldindata.org/fossil-fuels.

Santhanam, K.S.V., Gerald A. Takacs, J. Miri Massoud, Alla V. Bailey, Thomas D. Allston, and Roman J. Press. 2016. *Clean Energy: Hydrogen/Fuel Cells Laboratory Manual*. Singapore: World Scientific Publishing Company.

Tutuncu, Azra N. 2017. "Chapter 2: Hydraulic Fracturing Fundamentals." In *Hydraulic Fracturing Law and Practice*, edited by Davis Graham and Stubbs LLP, and LexisNexis Matthew Bender.

Tutuncu, Azra N., and T. Bui Binh. 2016. "A Coupled Geomechanics and Fluid Flow Model for Induced Seismicity Prediction in Oil and Gas Operations and Geothermal Applications." *Journal of Natural Gas Science and Engineering* 29: 110–124.

University of Calgary. 2017. "Energy Education: Horizontal Well." https://energyeducation.ca/encyclopedia/Horizontal_well.

US Energy Department. 2020. "Energy Sources: Fossil." https://www.energy.gov/science-innovation/energy-sources/fossil

U.S. Energy Information Administration (EIA). 2013. Drilling often results in both oil and gas production. Today in Energy, 29 October. https://www.eia.gov/todayinenergy/detail.php?id=13571.

US Energy Information Administration (USEIA). 2018. "Annual Energy Outlook 2018 with Projections to 2050." Report #AEO2018, February 6. www.eia.gov/aeo.

U.S. Energy Information Administration. 2019a. "US is Expected to Export more Energy than it Imports by 2020." https://www.eia.gov/todayinenergy/detail.php?id=38152.

US Energy Information Administration (USEIA). 2019b. "International." https://www.eia.gov/beta/international/index.php.

US Environmental Protection Agency. 2016. *Hydraulic Fracturing for Oil and Gas: Impacts from the Hydraulic Fracturing Water Cycle on Drinking Water in the United States*. EPA-600-R-16-236Fa. https://epa.gov/hfstudy

US Environmental Protection Agency. 2018. *Inventory of U.S. Greenhouse Gas Emissions and Sinks, 1990–2016*. https://www.epa.gov/ghgemissions/inventory-us-greenhouse-gas-emissions-and-sinks-1990-2016

Whitmarsh, Lorraine, Nick Nash, Paul Upham, Alyson Lloyd, James P. Verdon, and Michael Kendall. 2015. "UK Public Perceptions of Shale Gas Hydraulic Fracturing: The Role of Audience, Message and Contextual Factors on Risk Perceptions and Policy Support." *Applied Energy* 160: 419–430.

World Bank. 2016. "Commodity Markets Outlook." http://pubdocs.worldbank.org/en/743431507927822505/CMO-October-2017-Full-Report.pdf.

World Coal Association. N.d. "Coal Market and Pricing." https://www.worldcoal.org/coal/coal-market-pricing.

CHAPTER 3

NUCLEAR POWER

A Technical Overview

SAVANNAH FITZWATER

It is not too much to expect that our children will enjoy in their homes electrical energy too cheap to meter…will know of great periodic regional famines in the world only as matters of history…will travel effortlessly over the seas and under them and through the air with only a minimum of danger and at great speeds…and will experience a lifespan far longer than ours, as disease yields and man comes to understand what causes him to age.

This is the forecast for an age of peace.

—Lewis Strauss, Chairman, United States
Atomic Energy Commission (1954)

WHILE the hopes and idealism of the new atomic age were tempered by the reality of and experiences gained in constructing and operating nuclear power plants, many believe that nuclear power still has the potential to change the world for the better. Supporters of nuclear power argue that nuclear power plants will play a key role in providing clean energy to a world population that continues to grow. However, the future of nuclear power will inevitably continue to be influenced by a complicated history and technically challenging environment.

GLOBAL OVERVIEW

In 2016 approximately two-thirds of the world's gross electricity production was generated from fossil fuels. As shown in Figure 3.1, nuclear power comprised slightly more than 10 percent of the world's gross electricity production, considerably less than fossil fuels (International Energy Agency 2018).

At the end of 2018 there were 451 operational reactors in thirty countries and Taiwan, across five continents. Over half were in just four countries; the United States, France, China, and Russia collectively have 238. While Japan had thirty-nine operable reactors,

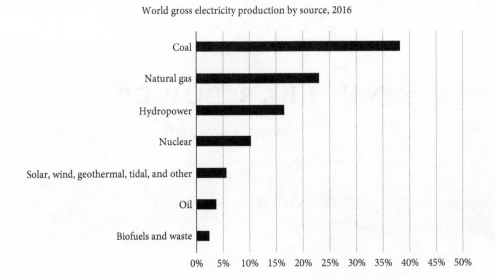

World gross electricity production by source, 2016

FIGURE 3.1 World gross electricity production by source, 2016.

Source: Data from International Energy Agency (2018).

the vast majority have not resumed operations following the post-Fukushima shut-downs. As shown in Table 3.1, the majority of countries and Taiwan each have fewer than ten nuclear reactors (International Atomic Energy Agency 2019b).

The portion of energy from nuclear power in each country varies substantially, from single digit percentages in Argentina, Brazil, China, India, Japan, Iran, Mexico, the Netherlands, Pakistan, and South Africa to more than 50 percent in France, Hungary, Slovakia, and Ukraine (see Figure 3.2). Although accounting for small percentages of national production, China and Japan each have a large number of reactors (see Table 3.1) (International Atomic Energy Agency 2019b).

In addition to existing reactors, a large number are under construction (see Table 3.2). Most of these reactors are being built at existing power plants, which would expand the number of reactor units already operating at these sites. Obvious exceptions to this are found in countries that do not already have nuclear power, including Bangladesh, Belarus, Turkey, and the United Arab Emirates. A small number of nuclear reactors are being constructed in countries that do not fall into either of these categories (International Atomic Energy Agency 2019b).

ORIGINS OF NUCLEAR POWER
AND THE MILITARY

Nuclear science advanced considerably during World War II as a result of the United States' "unprecedented collaboration of military, scientific, and corporate resources" in the development of the first nuclear weapon (Stacy 2000). In 1942, as part of the Manhattan Project, scientists at the University of Chicago demonstrated the first

Table 3.1 Operating Nuclear Reactors Worldwide, 2018

	Number of Operational Reactors	Net Capacity (MWe)	Nuclear Electricity Supplied (TWe-h)
Argentina	3	1,633	6.5
Armenia	1	375	1.9
Belgium	7	5,918	27.3
Brazil	2	1,884	14.8
Bulgaria	2	1,966	15.4
Canada	19	13,554	94.4
China	46	42,858	277.1
Czech Republic	6	3,932	28.3
Finland	4	2,784	21.9
France	58	63,130	395.9
Germany	7	9,515	71.9
Hungary	4	1,902	14.9
India	22	6,255	35.4
Iran, Islamic Republic of	1	915	6.3
Japan	39	36,974	49.3
Korea, Republic of	24	22,444	127.1
Mexico	2	1,552	13.2
Netherlands	1	482	3.3
Pakistan	5	1,318	9.3
Romania	2	1,300	10.5
Russia	36	27,252	191.3
Slovakia	4	1,814	13.8
Slovenia	1	688	5.5
South Africa	2	1,860	10.6
Spain	7	7,121	53.4
Sweden	8	8,613	65.9
Switzerland	5	3,333	24.5
Taiwan, China	5	4,448	26.7
Ukraine	15	13,107	79.5
United Kingdom	15	8,923	59.1
United States of America	98	99,061	808.0
Total	**451**	**396,911**	**2,562.8**

Source: Data from International Atomic Energy Agency (2019b).

controlled nuclear fission reaction. This experiment, referred to as the Chicago Pile no. 1, or CP-1, was a landmark event in nuclear history (Montgomery and Graham 2017; Stacy 2000). The first reactors were built as part of the Manhattan Project, not to produce electricity but in support of the US weapons programs (Marcus 2010; Montgomery and Graham 2017). By 1954, just a few short years later, the first nuclear reactor to supply electricity to the grid, the AM-1, started operation in Obninsk, Soviet Union (now Russia), using a design similar to the later developed Reaktor Bolshoy Moshchnosti Kanalyniy (RBMK; high-power channel reactor) design. The pilot size and ongoing debate over whether the original purpose was for plutonium production limits the applicability of the

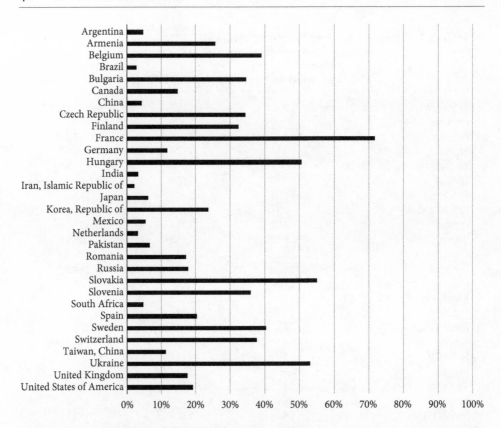

FIGURE 3.2 Nuclear share of electricity generation, 2018.

Source: Data from International Atomic Energy Agency (2019b).

AM-1 for commercial-scale electricity production. Another commonly cited nuclear "first" is the Calder Hall 1 reactor in Sellafield, United Kingdom. Calder Hall produced commercial quantities of electricity beginning in 1956 but was designed and built as a dual-purpose facility to produce plutonium and electricity (Marcus 2010).

The Shippingport Atomic Power Station in the United States began operating in 1957 and was the first commercial-scale reactor with the sole purpose of electricity production for civilian applications. Like many other nuclear developments, the development of this was not entirely separated from military nuclear applications due to the significant involvement of Admiral Hyman Rickover and the initial use of a highly enriched uranium (HEU) reactor core from a canceled aircraft carrier (Marcus 2010; Montgomery and Graham 2017; Smil 2003; Weinberg 1994).

It was not until the 1960s that countries without nuclear weapons programs began to use nuclear power for commercial purposes. In 1962 Belgium's BR-3 in Mol became the first reactor to connect to the grid in a country not involved in nuclear weapons development. While the BR-3 was a smaller-scale, low-power reactor, Italy quickly followed suit in 1963 with the reactor at Latina, a large-scale, commercial-sized reactor connected to the grid (Marcus 2010). These two reactors marked a major milestone, demonstrating that nuclear energy could exist separately from nuclear weapons.

Table 3.2 Reactors Under Construction, 2018

	Number of Reactors	Net Capacity (MWe)
Argentina	1	25
Bangladesh	2	2,160
Belarus	2	2,220
Brazil	1	1,340
China	11	10,982
Finland	1	1,600
France	1	1,630
India	7	4,824
Japan	2	2,653
Korea, Republic of	5	6,700
Pakistan	2	2,028
Russia	6	4,573
Slovakia	2	880
Taiwan, China	2	2,600
Turkey	1	1,114
Ukraine	2	2,070
United Arab Emirates	4	5,380
United Kingdom	1	1,640
United States of America	2	2,234
Total	55	56,643

Source: Data from International Atomic Energy Agency (2019b).

In just over a half century, the nuclear field saw great advancements, largely, although not exclusively, driven by the US military complex during and following World War II. As early as 1944, Enrico Fermi warned his fellow nuclear pioneers that the public might not accept a source of energy that had some relation to weapons (Weinberg 1994). The original intersection of civilian and defense applications was undeniable and would have a lasting impact on the perception and use of peaceful nuclear science and technologies for decades to come (Montgomery and Graham 2017). Today, however, they are largely separated. Many countries have nuclear power plants, but only five are recognized as nuclear weapons states under the Nuclear Non-proliferation Treaty (NPT). Since the NPT opened for signature in 1968 and entered into force in 1970, it has had unparalleled impact on the international landscape (Montgomery and Graham 2017; United Nations, n.d.).

Nuclear Reactor Fundamentals

Although development of nuclear reactors kicked off during the 1940s, a variety of reactor concepts have been designed, built, and tested in this relatively short period. Understanding the various components and designs of nuclear reactors sheds light on the history, politics, and policies surrounding nuclear power and why nuclear reactors have specific costs and benefits relative to other electricity sources.

Reactor Components

In many ways, nuclear power plants are complex, technological systems. However, all reactors have the same basic components: reactor core, coolant, control elements, moderator, reactor vessel, and steam generator (Lamarsh and Baratta 2001).

The reactor core contains the fuel, generally low enriched uranium (LEU) in the form of uranium dioxide pellets. These pellets are placed end-to-end inside metal tubes, to form long fuel rods. These long fuel rods are gathered together in bundles, which are the groupings used to move fuel into, around, and out of a reactor core. Reactors that use heavy water, such as the Canadian deuterium uranium (CANDU) reactors, use natural uranium instead of LEU as a fuel (Cochran and Tsoulfanidis 1990; Lamarsh and Baratta 2001).

Coolant flows through the reactor core and is used to carry heat away from the fuel. Most reactors, pressurized water reactors (PWRs) and boiling water reactors (BWRs), use light water, or H_2O. Other reactors, such as the CANDU reactors, use heavy water, ^2H_2O or D_2O, as a coolant (Lamarsh and Baratta 2001). In addition to light water and heavy water, nuclear reactors can also be cooled using helium or carbon dioxide gas. Fast reactors use liquid metal, such as sodium or lead, or gas to remove heat from the reactor core while minimizing moderation of neutrons (Cochran and Tsoulfanidis 1990; International Atomic Energy Agency 2012).

Control elements help control the operations of the reactor. Control elements come in many shapes and forms, most commonly rods, but also drums or fins. Despite the differences in shape, all control elements are made of a neutron-absorbing material. When control rods or fins are inserted into a reactor core, or in the case of drums, rotated to be exposed to the core, the reactivity of the reactor core decreases. Control elements effectively act as a throttle to control the power of a reactor. Control elements are most commonly made of a boron compound but can also be made with cadmium or other neutron-absorbing materials (Lamarsh and Baratta 2001).

Thermal reactors use a moderator to slow down neutrons from the fuel. In PWRs and BWRs, light water serves a dual purpose as both a coolant and a moderator, as does heavy water in pressurized heavy water reactors (PHWRs) (Lamarsh and Baratta 2001). In other types of reactors, such as the RBMK, a type of light water graphite reactor, and in gas-cooled reactors (GCR), graphite is used as a moderator. Fast reactors do not use a moderator (Lamarsh and Baratta 2001; Shultis and Faw 2002). (Note: CP-1, mentioned previously as the first example of controlled nuclear fission, also used graphite as a moderator; Marcus 2010; Sovacool, Brown, and Valentine 2016).

Finally, the reactor vessel varies based on the type of reactor. For PWRs and BWRs, which operate under pressure, the reactor vessel is also a pressure vessel and is made from steel. The thickness of the pressure vessel varies, with PWRs requiring a thicker vessel than BWRs. In the case of CANDUs, the reactor vessel is actually a pressure tube design, turned horizontally, as opposed to the vertical design of the PWRs and BWRs. While most pressure vessels are made of steel, high temperature gas reactors have used prestressed concrete as a pressure vessel (Cochran and Tsoulfanidis 1990; Lamarsh and Baratta 2001; Montgomery and Graham 2017).

Types of Nuclear Reactors

A nuclear reactor fundamentally produces two things: neutrons and heat (Stacy 2000). Another way to describe a commercial nuclear reactor is as a complex, commercial-sized tea kettle (Herbst and Hopley 2007), working to heat water to sufficiently high temperatures to rotate industrial turbines and generate electricity. Currently operating reactors have a number of different designs, including the PWR, BWR, PHWR, GCR, light water graphite reactor (LWGR), and fast reactors (International Atomic Energy Agency 2019a), each of which is described in the following paragraphs.

Pressurized water reactors: PWRs are the most common type of reactor. In PWRs, LEU is used as a fuel and light water as both a moderator and coolant. PWRs have a vertical reactor pressure vessel. The control rods are inserted into the reactor core from the top. As the name implies, PWRs operate under pressure. Heat is transferred from the primary loop to the secondary loop and turned into steam via the steam generator; this steam is used to rotate the turbine and generate electricity (see Figure 3.3). The Soviet, now Russian, Vodo-Vodyanoi Energetichesky Reactor (VVER) reactors are similar to PWRs but have some unique design characteristics, such as hexagonal fuel bundles. The International Atomic Energy Agency (IAEA) Power Reactor Information System (PRIS) database includes VVERs as a type of PWR despite the differences between VVERs and Western PWRs (Cochran and Tsoulfanidis 1990; International Atomic Energy Agency 2018c; Goldberg and Rosner 2011; Lamarsh and Baratta 2001).

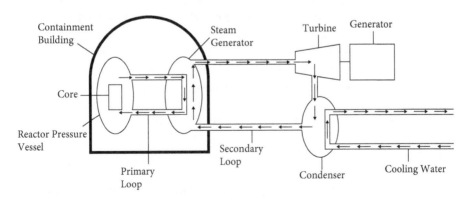

FIGURE 3.3 Pressurized water reactor diagram.

Source: Shultis and Faw (2002); Lamarsh and Baratta (2001).

Boiling water reactors: BWRs also use LEU as a fuel, light water as a moderator and coolant, and a vertical reactor vessel. Unlike in a PWR, a BWR's control rods are inserted from the bottom of the reactor core. In a BWR, a single coolant loop is used, in which water that has flowed through the reactor core becomes steam and is used to rotate the turbine to produce electricity. BWRs are the second most common type of commercial nuclear power plant in operation today (Cochran and Tsoulfanidis 1990; International Atomic Energy Agency 2019b; Lamarsh and Baratta 2001).

Pressurized heavy water reactors: PHWRs use heavy water, ^2H_2O or D_2O, as a coolant and moderator. The most common version of a PHWR is the CANDU reactor design, which can use natural uranium as a fuel. A CANDU reactor uses a horizontal vessel design with pressurized tubes that contain the fuel and coolant. The CANDU reactors can support online refueling during operations, providing high reactor availability (Cochran and Tsoulfanidis 1990; International Atomic Energy Agency 2018d; Lamarsh and Baratta 2001).

Gas cooled reactors: The first GCRs used natural uranium as a fuel, carbon dioxide gas as a coolant, and graphite as a moderator, and were generally focused on plutonium production for weapons first and electricity production second. Over the years, the United Kingdom transitioned to advanced gas reactors (AGRs), which use LEU as fuel but maintain carbon dioxide gas and graphite as the coolant and moderator. Most research now is on the next phase of GCR development, the high temperature gas reactor (HTGR). The HTGRs use helium as a coolant instead of carbon dioxide and potentially use two steam generators (Cochran and Tsoulfanidis 1990; Lamarsh and Baratta 2001; Montgomery and Graham 2017; Shultis and Faw 2002).

Light water graphite reactors: LWGRs, such as the RBMK, use LEU as fuel, light water as a coolant, and graphite as a moderator. The RBMK uses a concrete reactor vessel with a removable steel cap to support refueling during operations and plutonium production. Similar to the CANDU reactors, the multiple channels that hold the reactor fuel assemblies are pressurized (Lamarsh and Baratta 2001; Montgomery and Graham 2017).

Fast reactors: Fast reactor designs come in a variety of forms but represent the smallest number of operable reactors at this point. According to the IAEA PRIS database, two fast reactors are operating in Russia, and one fast reactor is operable but not currently producing electricity in China (International Atomic Energy Agency 2019g, 2019c, 2019d, 2019e). Different types of fast reactors can be fueled with uranium, thorium, and plutonium, while also burning up other actinides—making them a flexible design choice. Fast reactors do not use a moderator, but depending on the design, use liquid metal, gas, or molten salt as a coolant (Lamarsh and Baratta 2001; Montgomery and Graham 2017).

Impacts

Despite the seemingly diverse spectrum of reactor designs, the PWR is by far the most common reactor design, representing 66 percent of all commercial reactors (International Atomic Energy Agency 2019b). This is due in large part to the selection of PWRs as the choice of reactor type for the US Navy in the 1950s. Because reactor operators were most familiar with PWRs, in terms of both design and operational experience, utilities were influenced in their selection of reactor types in the United States and around the world (Montgomery and Graham 2017; Smil 2003; Stacy 2000; Weinberg 1994). Furthermore, since many utilities have multi-reactor unit sites (Ferguson 2009), the number of PWRs around the world is even higher. What is particularly notable is that a variety of other designs have been developed, and many have reached commercialization—Canada and the CANDUs, the United Kingdom and GCRs, and the then Soviet Union and RBMKs and PWRs (Weinberg 1994).

As early as the 1940s, there were concerns about the then believed lack of availability of uranium deposits to provide sufficient material for weapons, and later, for reactors, although this was later discovered to be untrue (Montgomery and Graham 2017; Stacy 2000; Weinberg 1994). Before that discovery, fast reactors were developed as a solution, with the potential to create more fuel than consumed, but also with the potential to create plutonium (Shultis and Faw 2002; Weinberg 1994). Unsurprisingly, proliferation concerns about the potential production of plutonium are a deterrent for many people when evaluating reactor options (Montgomery and Graham 2017).

Positive Aspects of Nuclear Energy

Scholarship on and supporters of nuclear power identify several benefits associated with this technology as an energy source. The benefits vary based on the perspectives of an individual or organization but generally include greenhouse gas emission-free electricity generation, baseload and load following operations, and low costs over time (Herbst and Hopley 2007). As with any complex technological issue, there are nuances that should be explored further.

Greenhouse Gas Emissions

An advantage often discussed is nuclear power's greenhouse gas emission-free energy generation. This idea is not new (Weinberg 1994), but has been more vocally embraced by the nuclear industry in recent years (Sovacool, Brown, and Valentine 2016). From 1970 to 2015 the production of approximately 68 gigatonnes of CO_2 was avoided through the use of nuclear power. This has the potential to make nuclear power plants a key contributor to reducing emissions and battling climate change (International Atomic Energy Agency 2018e; Lovering, Yip, and Nordhaus 2016).

Others have argued that although fuel is not burned, per se, during a nuclear power plant's operations, just as in a fossil fuel plant, the full life cycle of nuclear power generation does release greenhouse gases (Smil 2010; Sovacool, Brown, and Valentine 2016). This is technically accurate; greenhouse gas producing fossil fuel power plants are often used not only in the construction of nuclear plants, but also to power parts of the fuel cycle. However, nuclear power is comparable to hydropower and wind power in terms of greenhouse gas per kilowatt-hour over the full life cycle (International Atomic Energy Agency 2018e; Sovacool, Brown, and Valentine 2016).

Baseload and Load Following Operations

Nuclear power plants are often considered to only be a source of baseload power. Once a reactor is brought up to full operations, it will generally remain at that same power level for an extended period of time. Any major changes in the operations, whether a decrease or full outage, happen as a result of scheduled refueling and maintenance or due to unscheduled events. This stability provides advantages in terms of the design and license of the reactors, operations, maintenance, fuel management, and costs (Herbst and Hopley 2007; International Atomic Energy Agency 2018b).

Nuclear power plants in France, Germany, Slovakia, and the Czech Republic have operated in a load following, or flexible, mode for years (FORATOM 2018). As seen in Figure 3.2, in 2018 more than 70 percent of France's electricity was generated by nuclear power (International Atomic Energy Agency 2019b). Since the majority of France's power comes from nuclear reactors, and demand on the grid inevitability varies, some of these reactors—up to two-thirds of the reactors in France—must be operated in a load following mode to be sufficiently responsive (Lokhov 2011; FORATOM 2018). Based on work with its member states, the IAEA states that variation in demand from the grid can be generally categorized based on the time of day, day of the week, time of the year, and weather conditions (International Atomic Energy Agency 2018b). Nuclear power's ability to be a strong supplier of baseload power, and provide responsive, load following operations across a wide variety of conditions, makes it a key part of a diverse energy portfolio.

Costs over Time

Nuclear power plants can operate for an extraordinarily long period of time before retirement, second only to hydropower. In the United States, LWRs were initially licensed to operate for forty years, but many have already applied and been approved for an extension to operate for sixty years, and a smaller number have already applied for an extension to eighty years (Montgomery and Graham 2017; Nuclear Regulatory Commission 2018). The first license extension from 60 to 80 years was granted to Turkey Point in December 2019 (World Nuclear News 2019). Globally, LWRs "produce electricity...between 2.5 and 7 cents/kWh" (Sovacool, Brown, and Valentine 2016), but production costs have averaged even lower in the United States, reaching 1.89 c/kWh in 2000 and 1.66 c/kWh in 2006 (Herbst and Hopley 2007; Goldberg and Rosner 2011). A long lifespan, which allows for capital costs to be recovered earlier in the operating life cycle, along with the historically lower operating costs, shortened outage and refueling cycles, and regulatorily approved power uprates, can make nuclear power very appealing (Ferguson 2009; Sovacool, Brown, and Valentine 2016; Goldberg and Rosner 2011).

NEGATIVE ASPECTS OF NUCLEAR ENERGY

Criticisms of nuclear power have also emerged over the years. Some scholars believe that the obstacles to nuclear energy fall into two key issue areas—the high upfront costs associated with building large-scale, commercial power plants, and the public perception and anxiety, not only about nuclear energy, but also about "radiation, the threat of nuclear war, deceitful government, and indifferent corporate power" (Montgomery and Graham 2017). Other scholars have proposed that this list of key issues includes cost, safety, waste, and risk of proliferation (Deutch et al. 2003) or the view of "nuclear power as a categorical evil" and concerns about operations and waste (Smil 2003). Holistically, the negative aspects of nuclear energy include concerns about what to do with spent nuclear fuel or waste; the complexities and costs associated with the design, construction, and licensing of nuclear power plants; and fears about safety and of accidents.

Spent Nuclear Fuel

Critics of nuclear power often cite worries about spent nuclear fuel, or nuclear waste. In a once through, or open, fuel cycle, the front end of the fuel cycle includes mining and milling, conversion, enrichment, and fuel fabrication. These activities can be seen on the right side of the outer ring in Figure 3.4. The back end of the fuel cycle includes the storage and disposition of spent nuclear fuel, seen on the left side of the outer ring in Figure 3.4.

The first underground repository for nuclear waste was located in Asse, Germany, in a converted salt mine and opened in 1967. While the Asse repository is no longer accepting nuclear waste and has faced some challenges with the preexisting mine (versus a dedicated facility), it has provided invaluable experience and data on underground waste storage (Marcus 2010). In the United States, Yucca Mountain is the long-planned geological repository for commercial spent nuclear fuel, but it has faced decades of political contention, ultimately resulting in delays. The US Department of Energy also has a geological repository at the Waste Isolation Pilot Plant (WIPP), located in Carlsbad, New Mexico, for radioactive waste produced as a result of defense activities. The waste stored at WIPP is transuranic (TRU) waste, that is, materials contaminated with radioactive elements heavier than uranium on the periodic table. The TRU waste disposed of at WIPP includes "tools, rags, protective clothing, sludges, soil and other materials contaminated with radioactive elements, mostly plutonium" (Department of Energy—Waste Isolation Pilot Plant n.d.-a). After fifteen years of successful operations, the government

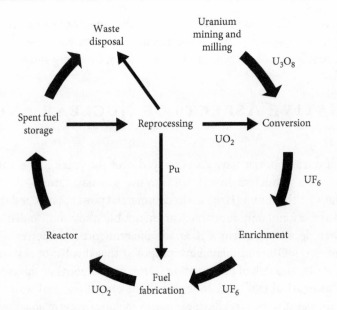

FIGURE 3.4 Nuclear fuel cycle.

Source: Cochran and Tsoulfanidis (1990); Deutch et al. (2003); Lamarsh and Baratta (2001).

shut down active operations at WIPP in February 2014 due to a vehicular fire and an unrelated waste drum breach, which released a very small amount of radioactive material into the air at the surface of WIPP ("WIPP Recovery—Accident Description" n.d.):

> The 13 employees present during the radioactive release event on February 14 were tested for internal radioactive contamination after the event. Initial fecal samples measured some radioactivity above normal background levels, with follow-up urine samples showing no detectable amounts of radioactivity. All had negative chest counts, which indicated they have no detectable radioactive contamination deep in their lungs. The 140 employees at the site the following day were also offered testing, with 118 showing no detectable levels of contamination. The remaining 22 were notified that their exposure was below the 10 millirem level, which is about the same exposure a person would get from a chest x-ray.
>
> ("WIPP Recovery—Accident Description" n.d.)

Subsequent radiological modeling indicated that any potential exposure was below the regulatory requirement (Department of Energy—Waste Isolation Pilot Plant n.d.-b). In April 2017 TRU waste shipments to WIPP resumed (Department of Energy—Waste Isolation Pilot Plant n.d.-a, n.d.-c, n.d.-d; NRC n.d.). Other parts of the world have also pursued geological repositories for their spent nuclear fuel. The most successful examples of progress made toward establishing deep geological repositories have been in Sweden, Finland, and South Korea. A noticeable aspect of the success of these efforts is the local communities' support for the repositories (Montgomery and Graham 2017).

An alternative to the open fuel cycle is the closed fuel cycle, in which the spent nuclear fuel is reprocessed. These activities are seen in the center of Figure 3.4. France has been the notable success story in reprocessing; other countries, including the United States, have long-standing policies prohibiting civilian reprocessing. Other countries with active reprocessing activities include China, India, Japan, Russia, and the United Kingdom (Montgomery and Graham 2017).

Design, Construction, and Licensing Delays

Nuclear power plants represent a significant investment in terms of time and perhaps more significantly, of costs. As of 2018, seventeen countries and Taiwan were pushing forward with new nuclear construction. The countries with the most new nuclear construction include China, India, Russia, South Korea, and the United Arab Emirates, as seen in Table 3.2 (International Atomic Energy Agency 2019b). Some critics argue that a negative of nuclear power plants is the very expensive and lengthy design, licensing, and construction process. The pursuit of nuclear power has seen three historical periods of construction. The mid-1950s to mid-1970s showed a steady average construction of reactors for the first half of the period, then a drastic increase in the second half. The second period, from the mid-1970s to mid-2000s, showed a decrease in construction of reactors, due in part to the effects of Three Mile Island and Chernobyl on public perception and regulatory requirements, but also due to increasing construction costs and decreasing oil prices. Most recently, the "Nuclear Renaissance" began in the mid-2000s and was marked by a large increase in nuclear construction efforts worldwide (World Energy Council 2011).

More important than recognizing that nuclear construction is a dauntingly expensive and time-consuming endeavor is trying to understand *why* it has gotten to this point. This wasn't always the case. While many studies on nuclear power plant construction focused on the United States and France in the post–Three Mile Island period and the associated skyrocketing costs, new research shows that these costs increases weren't as severe as originally thought. Since the United States and France were forerunners in designing and building commercial nuclear power fleets, both countries also incurred additional costs from the associated challenges of a new technology. When looking at Asian countries and taking into account the entire time period of nuclear reactor construction in the United States and France, the construction costs and timelines are significantly reduced. As a latecomer to the commercial nuclear power industry, South Korea has actually seen *decreases* in the costs to build nuclear power plants (Lovering, Yip, and Nordhaus 2016; Hayashi and Hughes 2012; Escobar Rangel and Leveque 2013). One reactor achieved criticality in Japan after just four years and one day from the time construction started (Goldberg and Rosner 2011). Nuclear energy is not alone in this phenomenon, but the high-visibility construction of nuclear power plants (e.g., countless news headlines about Vogtle Units 3&4, the last of the new nuclear construction in the United States, from mid-2018 to early 2019) and frequently cited high historical costs (see Smil 2003 and Sovacool, Brown, and Valentine 2016 as examples) are a difficult narrative to overcome.

Major Accidents at Commercial Nuclear Power Plants

The biggest negative mostly commonly associated with nuclear energy is the fear of an accident with serious health impacts. Despite many years of safe operations, Alvin Weinberg's statement that "a nuclear accident anywhere is a nuclear accident everywhere" (Weinberg 1986) reflects that the potential for an accident at a nuclear power plant is often at the forefront of discussions on nuclear energy. To date there have been three major accidents at commercial nuclear power plants: Three Mile Island, Chernobyl, and Fukushima. Each happened for different reasons and under differing scenarios, but collectively they have had a significant impact on the nuclear industry as a whole.

Three Mile Island: The first major event at a commercial nuclear power plant happened in 1979 at the Three Mile Island (TMI) Unit 2 in the United States. During normal, full-power operations, feedwater flow to the reactor was lost during maintenance activities. This situation, in and of itself, was not abnormal. As planned, when the heat and pressure began to rise, the control rods were inserted into the reactor core to bring down the pressure, and a pressure relief valve automatically opened. However, when the relief valve failed to close, reactor coolant drained away, exposing the reactor core. The high temperature of the reactor core, without proper cooling, ultimately melted part of the reactor core within the reactor pressure vessel. While the failure of the automatic valve closure was a mechanical problem, the bigger problem was the failure of the reactor operators to correctly interpret the control signals that there was an issue in the reactor (Lamarsh and Baratta 2001; Montgomery and Graham 2017; Herbst and Hopley 2007; Marcus 2010).

Testing and monitoring of TMI and the surrounding areas showed that very low levels of radiation were released. Despite these low levels, nuclear scholars often agree that the chaotic rumors and media reporting of the events unfolding at TMI, combined with the public's increasing concern about public health, safety, and the environment, resulted in a severe backlash against the nuclear industry. Estimates vary, but between 120,000 and 200,000 individuals, or half the local population, were so afraid of the potential radiation that they temporarily moved away from the area immediately surrounding TMI. No formal evacuation was ordered, although pregnant women and children were advised to leave. Multiple studies on cancer rates and life expectancy, including infant mortality rates, were conducted over the years. These studies, including a twenty-year follow-up study, all showed that the accident did not increase cancer rates or lower life expectancy. However, the psychological impact was clearly seen in health evaluations conducted afterward, with some individuals showing signs of anxiety and stress. After the accident, 100,000 protesters marched against nuclear power in Washington, D.C. Individuals who evacuated, along with businesses and the local and state governments, were compensated for the financial impacts of the accident. The other reactor unit at TMI, TMI 1, operated until September 2019, while TMI 2 undergoes decommissioning (Lamarsh and Baratta 2001; Marcus 2010; Ropeik 2012; Montgomery and Graham 2017; Weart 2012; Herbst and Hopley 2007; Nuclear Energy Institute 2009; World Nuclear Association 2019).

Chernobyl: In 1986 a steam explosion and fire occurred at the Chernobyl reactor in Ukraine (then part of the Soviet Union), near the Ukraine-Belarus border. As part of a test, operators shut off the automatic shutdown system, a key safety feature that included the coolant pump, to determine how long the reactor could continue producing power via the turbines after the primary electrical system in the plant was lost. Tragically, this decision, combined with the unique characteristics of the RBMK design, resulted in a runaway reaction. The reactor core quickly heated, ultimately resulting in a steam explosion, which blew the steel cap off the reactor vessel. (The RBMK reactor uses a very different reactor vessel design than a PWR or BWR, as discussed previously, in which the cap is designed to be removed during operations for refueling and plutonium production.) The subsequent second explosion and fire caused radioactive materials to be spread across widely populated areas. A ten-kilometer evacuation zone was finally ordered several days after the accident, impacting approximately forty-five thousand residents. Radioactivity was detected in Russia, Belarus, Ukraine, and other parts of Europe, including Scandinavia, but the highest radiation levels were measured in an approximately fifty-thousand-square-kilometer area (Montgomery and Graham 2017; Herbst and Hopley 2007; Lamarsh and Baratta 2001).

The events at Chernobyl caused the deaths of thirty-one individuals in 1986: two workers were killed by the explosion, twenty-eight workers and emergency responders died from acute radiation syndrome, and one person died from an unrelated heart condition (The Chernobyl Forum 2005). Of the approximately five million people who lived in the fifty-thousand-square-kilometer zone of the highest radiation, most received doses lower than background radiation levels (The Chernobyl Forum 2005; Montgomery and Graham 2017). Those who were directly impacted became known as the Chernobyl victims, and they reported psychological effects including depression and anxiety at higher rates than normal. Thyroid cancer is a key focus of studies, with more than eleven thousand cases diagnosed by 2016, most of whom have cancer in remission. It is important to note that while a large portion of these thyroid cancer cases were likely caused by Chernobyl, some may have occurred without the accident (World Health Organization 2016; The Chernobyl Forum 2005; Montgomery and Graham 2017). Studies on the potential impacts on various aspects of reproductive health were carried out for years afterward. Given the low levels of radiation that most of the impacted people were exposed to, the conclusion of international organizations was that

> there is no evidence or any likelihood of observing decreased fertility among males or females in the general population as a direct result of radiation exposure. These doses are also unlikely to have any major effect on the number of stillbirths, adverse pregnancy outcomes or delivery complications or the overall health of children.
>
> (The Chernobyl Forum 2005)

Long-term health studies of the individuals impacted by Chernobyl are ongoing (World Health Organization 2016).

Fukushima: On March 11, 2011, a massive 9.0 earthquake struck off the coast of Japan, creating a tsunami that devastated the coastline. One of the areas heavily impacted was the Fukushima prefecture, where the Fukushima-Daichi nuclear power plants are located. The tsunami was greater than the flood wall protecting the power plant was designed to protect against and ultimately caused both on-site and off-site power to be lost. Without power, reactor operators were unable to cool the three operating reactors or the spent fuel pools at the site effectively. Without active cooling measures, the reactors eventually overheated, melting the fuel in the reactor cores and creating hydrogen explosions from the compromised reactor pressure vessels (International Atomic Energy Agency 2015).

Unsurprisingly, this accident swiftly yielded global impacts. A Worldwide Independent Network/Gallup International Association poll of forty-seven countries taken shortly after the accident showed 91 percent of respondents were aware of the earthquake and tsunami, and 81 percent of respondents were aware of the damaged reactors (Worldwide Independent Network/Gallup International Association 2011). In Japan, all of the operating reactors were shut down soon after the tsunami, and Japan increased its import of natural gas, coal, and petroleum and reduced energy demand to compensate (Hayashi and Hughes 2012). While operations of some plants in Japan have resumed, most have not (International Atomic Energy Agency 2019b). Germany announced it would shut down all seventeen of its operating nuclear power plants by 2022, which had previously provided 23 percent of Germany's electricity (Evans 2011; Hayashi and Hughes 2012). The response in Germany was not entirely unexpected, as Germany has a history of antinuclear sentiment (Montgomery and Graham 2017; Weart 2012). In Italy, efforts to pursue nuclear plants again were voted down, and a permanent ban was approved. Switzerland voted to phase out its five operating nuclear power plants by 2034. However, most countries continued operating existing reactors or pursuing the construction of new reactors (Hayashi and Hughes 2012).

While Fukushima was a major accident like Chernobyl, there were notable differences. The mandatory evacuation area increased incrementally on March 11 and 12, until it reached a twenty-kilometer area. By March 25, those within twenty to thirty kilometers who had been sheltering in place were advised to evacuate. Restrictions on food originating from the impacted area were also announced (International Atomic Energy Agency 2015). Despite radiation being released from the plant, no radiation-related deaths or health impacts have been identified, although studies will continue for many more years. There have been reports of psychological impacts, though, including depression, anxiety, and post-traumatic stress disorder (International Atomic Energy Agency 2015). Because Japan faced so much hardship from the earthquake and tsunami, it can be difficult to determine whether the psychological impacts were solely attributable to fears about the Fukushima plant, but based on the impacts of TMI and Chernobyl, there is a likely connection (International Atomic Energy Agency 2015). One way to explore this issue more thoroughly is to look at the psychological impacts of those not only from the area surrounding Fukushima, but from other areas impacted by the earthquake and tsunami as well. The findings of Hasegawa and colleagues show that while post-traumatic stress disorder was seen across all of the impacted areas, chronic anxiety and guilt, an ambiguous loss experience, separated families/communities, and self-stigma were unique to Fukushima (Hasegawa et al. 2016). The evacuated zone is being slowly remediated, with some residents able to return. Decommissioning efforts at the Fukushima reactors are ongoing, with continued international collaboration (International Atomic Energy Agency 2015).

Impacts: After each of these accidents, there was a decrease in public support for nuclear power. The initial imagery of the TMI cooling towers, the remains of the Chernobyl reactor, and later the explosion at Fukushima had a strong effect on the public (Weart 2012). The media coverage of Fukushima was particularly problematic, with around the clock news focused on it. Unfortunately, this news was often incorrect or exaggerated, which was further amplified by the lack of information from the utility (Montgomery and Graham 2017). Less often discussed are the positive outcomes from these accidents. After each one, lessons learned were identified and major improvements were made across the nuclear industry. Based on the lessons from Chernobyl, evacuations, food restrictions, and remediation requirements at Fukushima were based on very conservative, very low levels of radiation. While this was difficult for residents, it likely resulted in a better scenario. After each accident, the worldwide nuclear industry focused on new, improved training programs, along with additional safety reviews and retrofits of reactors, for ongoing improvements (Montgomery and Graham 2017; World Energy Council 2011; Nuclear Energy Institute 2009; Herbst and Hopley 2007).

Public Perceptions

Beyond the facts about greenhouse gases; baseload and load following operations; economics; spent nuclear fuel; design, licensing, and construction delays; and accidents, the public perceptions have shaped the politics behind nuclear energy. Nuclear technology is depicted in countless books, movies, and television shows. Some notable, historic examples include General Electric's comic book *Adventures Inside the Atom* (1948) and cartoon *A Is for Atom* (1952), King Feature's *Dagwood Splits the Atom* (1949), and Walt Disney's book (1956) and television show (1957) *Our Friend the Atom*. Other positive depictions that have remained in the pop culture arena for much longer include *Spiderman*, the *Teenage Mutant Ninja Turtles*, *The Incredible Hulk*, and *The Fantastic Four*, in which ordinary individuals become superheroes as a result of exposure to radioactive materials (Szasz 2004; Weart 2012). These fictional depictions show the potential peaceful uses and outcomes of nuclear, or atomic, energy in a format that is palatable to the public. In the mid-1950s, surveys showed that a majority of the public felt optimistic regarding civilian nuclear power (Weart 2012).

But the media have also portrayed nuclear energy in a negative light. Common depictions in movies include monsters created by exposure to radioactive materials, such as *Godzilla* (1954), *Them* (1954), and *Night of the Living Dead* (1968), and accidents at a nuclear power plant or facility, such as *The China Syndrome* (1979) and *Silkwood* (1983) (Ulaby 2011). *The China Syndrome* was a particularly high-impact antinuclear movie due to the timing of its release, less than two weeks before the TMI accident (Ropeik 2012). Following six weeks of front-page headlines about TMI, protestors marched in Washington, D.C. (Morris 2000). It is impossible to say if the public's response to TMI would have been as severe without the release of *The China Syndrome*, but the timing was certainly damaging to the nuclear industry.

In books, the themes trend toward nuclear, or nuclear-related, apocalyptic and post-apocalyptic scenarios, beginning with Huxley's *Ape and Essence* (1948) and continuing with Percy's *The Dead Lands* (2016). These books tend to be published after the Bulletin of the Atomic Scientists' Doomsday Clock moves toward midnight, indicating the seriousness of the public's concerns (*The Economist* 2017). Furthermore, some of the same comic strip storylines, which showed a positive spin on nuclear technologies, also showed villains who had powers from nuclear technologies—as early as 1941 in a *Batman* comic (Weart 2012).

In more recent years, new documentaries such as *Pandora's Promise* (2013), *NOVA: The Nuclear Option* (2017), and *The New Fire* (2018) have become widely available to the public, through both hard copies and Internet streaming. In theory, the goal of these documentaries is to educate and perhaps convince those who are on the fence about nuclear to have a more favorable outlook. However, previous research showed that public support for or against nuclear power was not tied to knowledge about the technology. Instead, those who were in the middle of the spectrum on support for or against for nuclear power tended to follow the position of authority figures (Weart 2012). In the United States, the Nuclear Energy Institute also launched the "Voices for Nuclear Energy" campaign in 2016, with several high-profile individuals stating their support for nuclear energy. This group includes representation from industry, think tanks, and both sides of the US political spectrum—even household names such as Bill Gates and Robert Downey Jr ("Voices for Nuclear Energy" n.d.). (For a more in-depth exploration of the public's perception and fear of nuclear issues, see Weart 2012.)

THE FUTURE OF NUCLEAR ENERGY

Scientists and engineers are continually trying to improve the field of nuclear energy, particularly through reactor designs. All of the Generation I, early prototype reactors have been shut down. The currently operating reactors are primarily Generation II designs and include PWRs, BWRs, CANDUs, RBMKs, and AGRs. A smaller, but growing, number of operating reactors and reactors under construction are Generation III and

III+ designs, which include CANDU-6, System 80, Westinghouse advanced pressurized 600 (AP600), advanced boiling water reactor (ABWR), VVER-1200, advanced CANDU reactor (ACR-1000), European pressurized reactor (EPR), economic simplified boiling water reactor, advanced pressurized water reactor (APWR) APR-14000, European ABWR (EU-ABWR), advanced pressurized reactor (APWR), ATMEA 1, and the advanced pressurized 1000 (AP1000). These designs are considered to be advancements of Generation II reactors. In 2018 the first four AP1000 reactor units were connected to the grid in China. The next phase of nuclear energy lies in designs that are still being developed, including small modular reactors (SMRs) and Generation IV reactors (Goldberg and Rosner 2011; Sovacool, Brown, and Valentine 2016; International Atomic Energy Agency 2018a, 2019f; Generation IV International Forum 2014; World Nuclear News 2018).

Small Modular Reactors

Unlike large-scale, traditional commercial nuclear reactors, SMRs have the potential for considerably more flexible construction and siting requirements. Existing commercial reactors are designed to provide large amounts of electricity, usually on the order of 1,000 MWe, but in some cases more than 1,600 MWe. SMRs are generally defined as producing 300 MWe or less, and many produce less than 50 MWe (World Nuclear Association 2018; Goldberg and Rosner 2011; Holgate and Saha 2018). The current fleet of reactors is best suited for electricity for larger population areas, even though the reactors may be situated in more rural areas outside of cities. The developers of SMRs and nuclear experts argue that SMRs provide the potential for nuclear power generation in smaller markets and more remote locations, which have smaller electrical grids that would be unable to support a larger source of electricity (International Atomic Energy Agency 2018a; Goldberg and Rosner 2011; Holgate and Saha 2018). The physical size for many SMRs is much smaller than the current fleet of reactors, and some designs may be small enough to be transported by railroad, trucks, or barges. This varies based on design selection and whether or not multiple units will be co-located or operate as stand-alone power sources (International Atomic Energy Agency 2018a; Holgate and Saha 2018). (For more information on electrical infrastructure, see Hoicka and MacArthur in this volume.)

Another potential advantage of SMRs may be reduced construction costs compared to commercial scale nuclear power plants. As previously discussed, the price tag of a nuclear power plant skyrocketed in the United States following the TMI accident (Montgomery and Graham 2017), which had ripple effects in other countries as well. Because SMRs are designed to be substantially smaller, less complex, and able to be manufactured in a modular fashion, construction costs may be cheaper than the current fleet of LWRs. However, once SMRs are constructed and operating, the cost for electricity generation may be higher than large LWRs (International Atomic Energy Agency 2018a; Holgate and Saha 2018).

Generation IV Reactors

Generation IV reactor designs are the innovative advancement of current nuclear designs. The Generation IV International Forum (GIF) selected the following six designs to focus international cooperative research on: the gas-cooled fast reactor (GFR), lead-cooled fast reactor (LFR), molten salt reactor (MSR), sodium-cooled fast reactor (SFR), supercritical-water-cooled reactor (SCWR), and very-high-temperature reactor (VHTR). The GIF focuses on four goals in the pursuit of Generation IV designs: sustainability, safety and reliability, economic competitiveness, and proliferation resistance and physical protection. These six types of reactors represent a suite of options for the future of nuclear power. Each reactor is at a different stage of maturity; MSRs and SFRs were demonstrated in a noncommercial setting more than fifty years ago, but SFRs and VHTRs have been focused on by some GIF member countries. Admirably, GIF is developing an entire fuel cycle as part of the system that integrates with the new reactor designs. This foresight may help alleviate some of the concerns about waste discussed previously. GIF is also considering lessons from Fukushima, including an expanded focus on heat removal for novel coolants operating at higher temperatures (Montgomery and Graham 2017; Generation IV International Forum 2014).

Non-electrical Applications

Another area that will continue to see ongoing exploration and development is the use of heat from a nuclear power plant for non-electrical applications. Potential uses for this heat could include "seawater desalination, district heating, hydrogen production, oil extraction and other petrochemical applications, and propelling large tankers and container ships" (International Atomic Energy Agency 2018e). The first reactor used primarily for district heating started operations in Sweden in 1964 (Marcus 2010). The application of excess heat from nuclear power plants to hydrogen production and desalination was proposed several decades ago, with the first nuclear-powered desalination taking place in Antarctica from 1966 to 1972 and the first commercial-scale desalination starting in 1973 in what is now Kazakhstan; however, most desalination plants are still powered by fossil fuels (International Atomic Energy Agency 2018e; Marcus 2010; Rhodes 2018).

In 2017 more than seventy reactors in twelve countries were usable for district heat, process heat, or desalination, as seen in Table 3.3 (International Atomic Energy Agency 2017). In addition to the countries listed in Table 3.3, China, Finland, France, and Sweden have also used nuclear power for district heating, and Canada, Germany, and Norway have also used nuclear power for process heating (International Atomic Energy Agency 2017, 2007; Ferguson 2009). Some of the Generation IV designs could also play a key role in direct hydrogen production, including GFRs, LFRs, MSRs, and VHTRs, due to their high operating temperatures (Goldberg and Rosner 2011).

Table 3.3 Non-electric Applications of Nuclear Power in 2017

District Heating	Process Heating	Desalination
Bulgaria	India	India
Czech Republic	Russia	Japan
Hungary	Slovakia	Pakistan
Romania	Switzerland	
Russia		
Slovakia		
Switzerland		
Ukraine		

Source: Data from International Atomic Energy Agency (2017).

CONCLUSION

Nuclear energy produced more than 17 percent of the world's electricity generation at its peak in 1996 (IEA Statistics 2013) and produced more than 10 percent in 2018 (International Energy Agency 2018), from 451 operational nuclear reactors in thirty countries and Taiwan (International Atomic Energy Agency 2019b). The majority of these countries do not have nuclear weapons, but in some minds, nuclear power is inextricably linked to nuclear weapons. Despite the disconnect between the two, the decades-old perception leads some to question whether it is wise to continue to operate and construct new nuclear power plants. However, the only way to truly evaluate the potential benefits and drawbacks of nuclear power as an energy solution is to view it from the same perspective as other sources of energy, not through the lens of nuclear weapons.

As the world continues to face the growing evidence of climate change, the sources of energy we pursue will become more important than ever. For many people, nuclear energy represents part of the solution, providing baseload and load following power, free of greenhouse gases, that can help sustain growing populations (Smil 2010). New reactor designs have the potential to overcome many of the economic, political, and technical challenges that have arisen during the development and operations of this complex technology. Despite the closing of nuclear power plants in Germany, there are seventeen countries and Taiwan with fifty-five reactors under construction—with the largest numbers being built in China, Russia, and India (International Atomic Energy Agency 2019b). The current fleet of nuclear power plants, along with the new reactors being built and designed, will undoubtedly play a unique role in a balanced solution to the energy challenges we face. Perhaps one day the peaceful benefits envisioned during the atomic age will finally be realized, and electricity truly will be too cheap to meter.

Author Note

The views expressed in this chapter are solely those of the author and are not the views of the US Department of Energy.

The National Nuclear Security Administration, or the US Government.

References

The Chernobyl Forum. 2005. "Chernobyl's Legacy: Health, Environmental and Socio-Economic Impacts and Recommendations to the Governments of Belarus, the Russian Federation and Ukraine." www.iaea.org/sites/default/files/chernobyl.pdf.

Cochran, Robert G., and Nicholas Tsoulfanidis. 1990. *The Nuclear Fuel Cycle: Analysis and Management*. 2nd ed. La Grange Park, IL: American Nuclear Society.

Department of Energy—Waste Isolation Pilot Plant. n.d.-a "History/Timeline." http://wipp.energy.gov/historytimeline.asp.

Department of Energy—Waste Isolation Pilot Plant. n.d.-b "Radiological Modeling Results." Waste Isolation Pilot Plant. https://wipp.energy.gov/Special/Modeling%20Summary.pdf.

Department of Energy—Waste Isolation Pilot Plant. n.d.-c "Transuranic (TRU) Waste." Waste Isolation Pilot Plant. http://wipp.energy.gov/tru-waste.asp.

Department of Energy—Waste Isolation Pilot Plant. n.d.-d "WIPP Recovery/Restart." Waste Isolation Pilot Plant. http://wipp.energy.gov/recoveryrestart.asp.

Deutch, John, Ernest Moniz, Eric Beckjord, Michael Driscoll, Stephen Ansolabehere, John Holdren, Paul Joskow, et al. 2003. *The Future of Nuclear Power: An Interdisciplinary MIT Study*. Cambridge, MA: Massachusetts Institute of Technology. http://web.mit.edu/nuclearpower/pdf/nuclearpower-full.pdf.

The Economist. 2017. "Charting Trends in Apocalyptic and Post-Apocalyptic Fiction," April 12. https://www.economist.com/blogs/prospero/2017/04/writing-end-world.

Escobar Rangel, Lina, and Francois Leveque. 2013. "Revisiting the Nuclear Power Construction Costs Escalation Curse." *IAEE Energy Forum*, Third Quarter.

Evans, Stephen. 2011. "German Nuclear Plants To Be Shut." *BBC News*, May 30, Europe section. https://www.bbc.com/news/world-europe-13592208.

Ferguson, Charles. 2009. "A Nuclear Renaissance?" In *Energy Security Challenges for the 21st Century*, edited by Gal Luft and Anne Korin, 295–307. Santa Barbara, CA: Praeger Security International.

FORATOM. 2018. "Flexible Operations of Nuclear Power Plants." Brussels, Belgium: FORATOM. http://www.foratom.org/downloads/flexible-operation-of-nuclear-power-plants/.

Generation IV International Forum. 2014. "Technology Roadmap Update for Generation IV Nuclear Energy Systems." Paris: Organisation for Economic Cooperation and Development – Nuclear Energy Agency.

Goldberg, Stephen, and Robert Rosner. 2011. *Nuclear Reactors: Generation to Generation*. Cambridge, MA: American Academy of Arts and Sciences.

Hasegawa, A., T. Ohira, M. Maeda, S. Yasumura, and K. Tanigawa. 2016. "Emergency Responses and Health Consequences after the Fukushima Accident; Evacuation and Relocation." *Clinical Oncology* 28, no. 4: 237–244. doi:10.1016/j.clon.2016.01.002.

Hayashi, Masatsugu, and Larry Hughes. 2012. "The Fukushima Nuclear Accident and Its Effect on Global Energy Security." *Energy Policy* 59: 102–111.

Herbst, Alan M., and George W. Hopley. 2007. *Nuclear Energy Now: Why the Time Has Come for the World's Most Misunderstood Energy Source.* Hoboken, NJ: John Wiley & Sons.

Holgate, Laura S. H., and Sagatom Saha. 2018. "America Must Lead on Nuclear Energy to Maintain National Security." *The Washington Quarterly* 41, no. 2: 7–25.

IEA Statistics. 2013. "Electricity Production from Nuclear Sources (% of Total)." The World Bank/Data. https://data.worldbank.org/indicator/EG.ELC.NUCL.ZS?end=2015&start=1960&view=chart.

International Atomic Energy Agency. 2007. "Advanced Application of Water Cooled Nuclear Power Plants." TECDOC 1584. Vienna: International Atomic Energy Agency.

International Atomic Energy Agency. 2012. "Liquid Metal Coolants for Fast Reactors Cooled By Sodium, Lead, and Lead-Bismuth Eutectic." No. NP-T-1.6. IAEA Nuclear Energy Series. Vienna: International Atomic Energy Agency.

International Atomic Energy Agency, ed. 2015. "The Fukushima Daiichi Accident: Report by the Director General." Vienna: International Atomic Energy Agency.

International Atomic Energy Agency. 2017. "Nuclear Power Reactors in the World." IAEA-RDS-2/37. Reference Data Series no. 2. Vienna: International Atomic Energy Agency.

International Atomic Energy Agency. 2018a. "Advances in Small Modular Reactor Technology Developments: A Supplement to IAEA Advanced Reactors Information System (ARIS)." Vienna: International Atomic Energy Agency.

International Atomic Energy Agency. 2018b. "Non-Baseload Operation in Nuclear Power Plants: Load Following and Frequency Control Modes of Flexible Operations." NP-T-3.23. IAEA Nuclear Energy Series. Vienna: International Atomic Energy Agency.

International Atomic Energy Agency. 2018c. "Operational & Long-Term Shutdown Reactors." Power Reactor Information System (PRIS), February 11. https://www.iaea.org/PRIS/WorldStatistics/OperationalReactorsByCountry.aspx.

International Atomic Energy Agency. 2018d. "The Database on Nuclear Power Reactors." Power Reactor Information System (PRIS), February 11. https://www.iaea.org/pris/.

International Atomic Energy Agency. 2018e. "Climate Change and Nuclear Power 2018." Vienna: International Atomic Energy Agency.

International Atomic Energy Agency. 2019a. "Glossary of Terms in PRIS Reports." PRIS—Glossary. https://pris.iaea.org/PRIS/Glossary.aspx.

International Atomic Energy Agency. 2019b. "Nuclear Power Reactors in the World." Reference Data Series no. 2. Vienna: International Atomic Energy Agency. https://www.iaea.org/publications/13552/nuclear-power-reactors-in-the-world.

International Atomic Energy Agency. 2019c. "BELOYARSK-3." PRIS—Reactor Details, June 13. https://pris.iaea.org/PRIS/CountryStatistics/ReactorDetails.aspx?current=484.

International Atomic Energy Agency. 2019d. "BELOYARSK-4." PRIS—Reactor Details, June 13. https://pris.iaea.org/PRIS/CountryStatistics/ReactorDetails.aspx?current=451.

International Atomic Energy Agency. 2019e. "CEFR (China Experimental Fast Reactor)." PRIS—Reactor Details, June 13. https://pris.iaea.org/PRIS/CountryStatistics/ReactorDetails.aspx?current=1047.

International Atomic Energy Agency. 2019f. "China, People's Republic Of." PRIS—Country Details, June 13. https://pris.iaea.org/PRIS/CountryStatistics/CountryDetails.aspx?current=CN.

International Atomic Energy Agency. 2019g. "PRIS—Reactor Status Reports—Operational & Long-Term Shutdown—By Type." PRIS, June 13. https://pris.iaea.org/PRIS/WorldStatistics/OperationalReactorsByType.aspx.

International Energy Agency. 2018. "Electricity Information: Overview." https://webstore.iea.
    org/electricity-information-2018-overview.

Lamarsh, John R., and Anthony J Baratta. 2001. *Introduction to Nuclear Engineering.* 3rd ed.
    Upper Saddle River, NJ: Prentice Hall.

Lokhov, Alexey. 2011. "Load-Following with Nuclear Power Plants." *NEA News* 29, no. 2: 18–20.

Lovering, Jessica R., Arthur Yip, and Ted Nordhaus. 2016. "Historical Construction Costs of
    Global Nuclear Power Reactors." *Energy Policy* 91 (April): 371–382. doi:10.1016/j.enpol.2016.01.011.

Marcus, Gail H. 2010. *Nuclear Firsts: Milestones on the Road to Nuclear Power Development.* La
    Grange Park, IL: American Nuclear Society.

Montgomery, Scott L., and Thomas Graham Jr. 2017. *Seeing the Light: The Case for Nuclear
    Power in the 21st Century.* New York: Cambridge University Press.

Morris, Robert C. 2000. *The Environmental Case for Nuclear Power: Economic, Medical, and
    Political Considerations.* St. Paul, MN: Paragon House.

NRC "Glossary—Transuranic Waste." n.d. https://www.nrc.gov/reading-rm/basic-ref/glossary/
    transuranic-waste.html.

Nuclear Energy Institute. 2009. "The TMI 2 Accident: Its Impacts, Its Lessons." Fact Sheet.
    Washington, DC: Nuclear Energy Institute.

Nuclear Regulatory Commission. 2018. "NRC: Status of Subsequent License Renewal
    Applications." Nuclear Regulatory Commission, July 13. https://www.nrc.gov/reactors/
    operating/licensing/renewal/subsequent-license-renewal.html.

Rhodes, Richard. 2018. *Energy: A Human History.* New York: Simon & Schuster.

Ropeik, David. 2012. "The Rise of Nuclear Fear-How We Learned to Fear the Radiation."
    Scientific American Blog Network, June 15. https://blogs.scientificamerican.com/guest-blog/
    the-rise-of-nuclear-fear-how-we-learned-to-fear-the-bomb/.

Shultis, J. Kenneth, and Richard E. Faw. 2002. *Fundamentals of Nuclear Science and Engineering.*
    New York: Marcel Dekker, Inc.

Smil, Vaclav. 2003. *Energy at the Crossroads: Global Perspectives and Uncertainties.* Cambridge,
    MA: The MIT Press.

Smil, Vaclav. 2010. *Energy Myths and Realities: Bringing Science to the Energy Policy Debate.*
    Washington, DC: American Enterprise Institute.

Sovacool, Benjamin, Marilyn Brown, and Scott Valentine. 2016. *Fact and Fiction in Global
    Energy Policy: 15 Contentious Questions.* Baltimore, MD: Johns Hopkins University Press.

Stacy, Susan M. 2000. "Proving the Principle: The History of The Idaho National Engineering and
    Environmental Laboratory 1949–1999." DOE/ID-10799. Washington, DC: U.S. Department
    of Energy, Idaho Operations Office.

Strauss, Lewis. 1954. "Remarks Prepared by Lewis L. Strauss, Chairman, United States Atomic
    Energy Commission, For Delivery At The Founder's Day Dinner, National Association Of
    Science Writers, On Thursday, September 16, 1954, New York, New York." *Speech presented
    at the National Association of Science Writers Founder's Day Dinner,* New York, NY. https://
    www.nrc.gov/docs/ML1613/ML16131A120.pdf.

Szasz, Ferenc M. 2004. "Atomic Comics." In *Atomic Culture: How We Learned to Stop Worrying
    and Love the Bomb,* edited by Scott C. Zeman and Michael A. Amundson, 12–13. Boulder:
    University of Press of Colorado.

Ulaby, Neda. 2011. "Movie Mutants Give a Face to Our Nuclear Fears." NPR, March 30. https://
    www.npr.org/2011/03/30/134950737/movie-mutants-give-a-face-to-our-nuclear-fears.

United Nations. n.d. "Treaty on the Non-Proliferation of Nuclear Weapons (NPT)." https://
    www.un.org/disarmament/wmd/nuclear/npt/.

"Voices for Nuclear Energy." n.d. Nuclear Energy Institute. https://www.nei.org/voices-for-nuclear-energy.

Weart, Spencer. 2012. *The Rise of Nuclear Fear*. Cambridge, MA: Harvard University Press.

Weinberg, Alvin. 1986. "A Nuclear Power Advocate Reflects on Chernobyl." *The Bulletin of the Atomic Scientists* 42, no. 7: 57–60.

Weinberg, Alvin. 1994. *The First Nuclear Era: The Life and Times of a Technological Fixer*. Woodbury, NY: American Institute of Physics.

"WIPP Recovery—Accident Description." n.d. http://wipp.energy.gov/wipprecovery-accident-desc.asp.

World Energy Council. 2011. "World Energy Perspective: Nuclear Energy One Year After Fukushima." London: World Energy Council.

World Health Organization. 2016. "1986–2016: Chernobyl at 30." World Health Organization. https://www.who.int/ionizing_radiation/chernobyl/Chernobyl-update.pdf

World Nuclear Association. 2018. "Small Nuclear Power Reactors." March. http://www.world-nuclear.org/information-library/nuclear-fuel-cycle/nuclear-power-reactors/small-nuclear-power-reactors.aspx.

World Nuclear Association. 2019. "Three Mile Island 1." September. http://www.world-nuclear.org/reactor/default.aspx/THREE%20MILE%20ISLAND-1

World Nuclear News. 2018. "Fourth Chinese AP1000 Connected to Grid." World Nuclear News, December 27. http://www.world-nuclear-news.org/Articles/Fourth-Chinese-AP1000-connected-to-grid.

World Nuclear News. 2019. "Turkey Point Licensed for 80 Years of Operation." World Nuclear News, December 6. https://world-nuclear-news.org/Articles/Turkey-Point-licensed-for-80-years-of-operation.

Worldwide Independent Network/Gallup International Association. 2011. "Japan Earthquake and Its Impact on Views about Nuclear Energy." Zurich: Worldwide Independent Network/Gallup International Association.

CHAPTER 4

....

THE INFRASTRUCTURE
FOR ELECTRICITY
A Technical Overview

....

CHRISTINA E. HOICKA AND JULIE MACARTHUR

ELECTRICITY infrastructure provides a substrate for modern life through the network of wires, towers, dams, and turbines that literally powers our economic and social practices. Despite its importance, electricity infrastructure is often depoliticized, left to the technical experts and relegated to a solely technical matter of "keeping the lights on" (Geels 2014; Kuzemko 2016). However, neglect of either the technical or sociopolitical aspects of the electricity sector comes with the very real risk of stalling progress toward much-needed low-carbon transitions (Diesendorf and Elliston 2018; Wolsink 2012). Furthermore, the socioeconomic impacts associated with adapting to climate change are global. The Paris Agreement requires a full set of mitigation options (Creutzig et al. 2016), and current forecasts show that renewable electricity would need to make up at least 40 percent, but up to 63 percent, of new electricity supply by 2040 in order to meet the targets set out by the agreement (IEA 2017). Other experts go further, arguing that 100 percent renewable energy is a desirable and achievable goal (Diesendorf and Elliston 2018). Any large, politically sustainable increase in renewable energy will require a fundamental shift in the varied elements of electricity infrastructure covered in this chapter.

Infrastructures are often both literally and discursively hidden from view, which is problematic as the sector is undergoing a revolution unlike any seen for more than a century (Burke and Stephens 2018; Mcfarlane and Rutherford 2008). In analyses of electricity infrastructures, the word "power" comes with a double meaning: political and economic power, and the electrons that power our lives. So while electricity infrastructures are certainly a highly technical field operationally, they are political in their distributive consequences, governance, spatial arrangements, and policy designs. For many people, access to electricity remains a luxury they have yet to enjoy, despite its importance to modern transport, communication, and industry. Nearly 14 percent of the world's population—1.1 billion people, mostly dwelling in rural sub-Saharan Africa and developing Asia—lack access to electricity (IEA 2017). Thus it is no surprise that the electricity sector is expected to continue to grow, particularly in developing economies. Yet for those living in wealthy nations, this growth and its implications are easily overlooked.

Evolutionary trends in electricity infrastructure are technology dependent but also policy driven and mediated by social acceptance and participation. These distinct elements are each better understood when the technical aspects are demystified and distinguished. Written with social scientists in mind, this chapter provides an overview of the technical aspects of over a century of electricity infrastructure developments, as well as the new technological trends that are essential to understanding the structure and evolution of the sector in distinct contexts. We start with an explanation of the main elements of the electricity infrastructure: electricity basics, demand, generation, transmission and distribution, and how the characteristics of these elements affect the management of electricity infrastructure. This section is followed by an explanation of the important characteristics of electricity generation and demand: size, sensitivity to geography, and power density. Building on these concepts and characteristics, we then focus on three broad global trends as having important influence: growth and the increase in electricity demand in urban centers, the increase in renewable power generation, and the need for increased flexibility of electricity grids and distributed infrastructures to maintain reliability in renewable power. These developments carry with them sociotechnical change; we preface debates that will be dealt with in more detail later in the volume—energy policy, energy justice, community energy, gendered infrastructure, and social movements—by weaving in a discussion of the sociotechnical issues raised by contemporary trends after each section.

Electricity Basics: Demand, Generation, and Transmission and Distribution

Electricity systems and markets are highly technical, dynamic, and complex, and they vary around the world (Martinot 2016). These variations depend on a range of factors: the geography of resources (e.g., Pasqualetti 2012); political organization (Victor and Heller 2007); and the shape, design, and size of human settlements that make up demand centers (Owens 1992, 1986). The main benefit of electricity is that it is an intermediary form of energy that can travel long distances. Electricity generation converts primary forms of energy into heat, light, or motion (Boyle 2012). Electricity infrastructure, illustrated in Figure 4.1, is made up of power generation that travels long distances over transmission and distribution to demand centers, such as cities, buildings, and industries, for electrical use. The infrastructure that moves generated power along these points is collectively known as "the grid." Recently, technologies for electricity system flexibility, such as "smart" grids, which use real-time information, battery

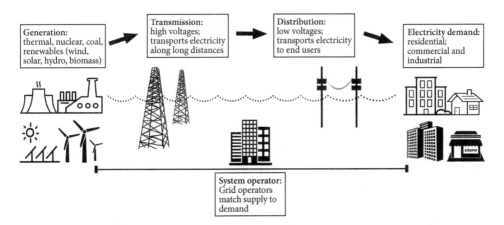

FIGURE 4.1 Electricity infrastructure.

storage technology, and super (high-voltage) grids, have allowed for increased shares of renewable electricity generation.

Electrical energy (see Box 4.1 for this and other technological definitions) is the energy released due to the movement or rearrangement of electrons in atoms. This energy can be the result of electric currents in metals or of the rearrangement of bonds between atoms in molecules (chemical energy). Generators convert kinetic energy into electrical energy with the use of magnets and coil wires that spin and release electrons to create a current (Boyle 2012). The earliest sources of generation were coal, natural gas, and hydroelectricity, which needed to be transported over long distances from the point of generation to the point of use (Smil 2006). The inventions that enabled electricity systems are steam turbines, transformers, the conversion of direct current (DC) to alternating current (AC) electricity, and high-voltage transmission (Smil 2006). The amount of energy produced or used (demand) depends on the amount of power (W) over time (hours) used or produced, measured as the product of the power used over time, in watt-hours (Wh).

Electricity Demand

On a global scale, the largest sources of electricity demand include industrial motors, appliances (e.g., washing machines, refrigerators, dishwashers), cooking, space heating and cooling, information and communication technology (ICT), and lighting (IEA 2017); these sources power the services responsible for industrialization; economic growth; and social outcomes related to health, education, and gender equality. The demand curve, illustrated in Figure 4.2, depicts the total amount of electricity demand (in MW, or 10^6W) in an energy system at any given time of day. The shape and peak of the demand curve, which gives the total amount of demand from end uses on a particular energy system at each time of day, will depend on factors such as climate, weather,

Box 4.1 Electricity Concepts and Terminology

Voltage and power. Voltage (measured in volts) is the potential between points on a wire. **Power**, measured in watts (W), is the rate at which energy is being converted from one form to another. The amount of power (P) carried by a wire from a generator to a device is a product of the voltage (V, potential between points on a wire) and current of electrons (I). To transmit large amounts of power over long distances, transmission lines operate at high voltages. Due to resistance in power lines, power losses are a key concern for transporting electricity long distances, as well as losses in conversions that occur between generation source and demand load.

Energy. Energy is measured in joules (J) or watt-hours (Wh) and is the capacity to do work. It comes from various processes, such as thermal (heat), chemical, kinetic (movement), gravitational, and electrical. Electrical energy is the energy released due to the movement or rearrangement of electrons in atoms. This can be due to electric currents in metals or due to the rearrangement of bonds between atoms in molecules (chemical energy) (Boyle 2012, 5–6). Electrical energy is measured in watt-hours (Wh), or the amount of time that power has been used or converted.

Electricity use. Electrical loads are rated by the power used (watts). The amount of energy used is measured in Wh and depends on the amount of time a device is used. A range of electrical loads in households and business is outlined in Table 4.2. When large amounts of energy are used or produced, the terminology used is kilowatt (i.e., kW or 10^3W), megawatt (i.e., MW or 10^6 W), gigawatt (i.e., GW or 10^9 W), and terawatt (i.e., TW or 10^{12} W).

Current. This is the rate at which electrons pass through a wire, measured in amps (A).

Direct current. Electrons flow from positive to negative terminals.

Alternating current. Electrons change direction from positive to negative. The frequency, measured in hertz (Hz), is how often they change direction per second.

Capacity factor. The actual output over a given period of time divided by the maximum possible output. For example, if a 1 MW (10^6 W) wind turbine produces 3,000 MWh per year, the maximum output is 8,760 MWh per year, and the capacity factor is 34.2 percent.

Thermodynamics. The **first law of thermodynamics** states that energy is conserved, even when transformed from one form to another. However, due to the **second law of thermodynamics**, in the case of conversions to and from electricity, typically the "useful" energy (output) is less than the energy input. The difference in energy between output and input is typically diffused as heat. For example, in a light bulb, where the main output is light (lumens), heat is lost due to inefficiency. Newer, more efficient light bulbs are not as warm to touch.

Energy efficiency. The ratio of useful energy output/energy input, usually defined as a percentage. The more efficient a device is, the less energy is lost, which allows less energy to be used to produce an energy service (e.g., lighting, heating, cooling, mechanical work).

Transporting electricity. Electricity (generation) is generated at voltages between 12.5 and 25 kV. Given that a combination of low current and high voltage is preferable for long-distance transmission, the generated low current is first transformed (stepped-up) to between 100 and 800 kV before being sent to long-distance markets, transformed again (stepped down) to safer, lower, voltages for distribution within cities (usually 12 kV), and then stepped down again to lower voltages (110–250V depending on the country) for household/organization use. Transformers can reduce or increase the voltage with almost no loss of energy, very reliably, and quietly.

Power density. The amount of land (space, measured in area, or m²) over which power is used or produced (Smil 2016).

Source: Boyle (2012); Everett et al. (2012); Smil (2006, 2016).

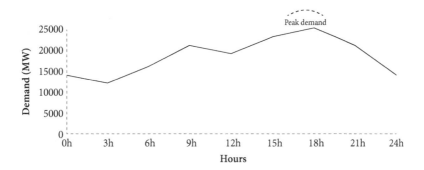

FIGURE 4.2 Electricity demand curve.

levels of industrialization, technology, the built environment, and culture. The area under the curve is the amount of electricity used in MWh. The electricity requirements of various household, commercial, and industrial equipment are presented later in the chapter in Table 4.2. The current global energy system size is 21,000 TWh (i.e., 10^{12} Wh) per year (IEA 2017). When an end use is more energy efficient (defined in Box 4.1), less energy is required to provide the same level of service that electricity use provides.

Electricity Generation

Electricity systems have existed for over a century, and the mix of generation fuels has undergone many transformations. Electricity systems have evolved from being predominantly based on fossil fuels and hydroelectricity generation to including nuclear power generation in the 1950s, and in recent years electricity generation from renewable sources (wind, hydro, solar PV) has increased substantially. Since 1990 the power sector has been the largest sectoral contribution to growth of greenhouse gas emissions (IEA 2017). The electricity sector currently provides 21,000 TWh per year globally and is responsible for nearly 40 percent of energy-related greenhouse gas emissions. The sector is also responsible for nearly 60 percent of the world's coal use and 36 percent of natural gas use (IEA 2017).

There are many forms of primary fuels for electricity generation, each with varying environmental impacts. Thermal power, which is historically and currently the dominant form of electricity generation, produces high-temperature steam that drives turbines and generators to produce electricity (see, e.g., Everett et al. 2012; Smil 2006). Thermal electricity generation is produced by the heat that results from the combustion of fossil fuels, coal, natural gas, or oil, or from the heat provided by nuclear fission splitting uranium atoms (see, e.g., Everett et al. 2012; Smil 2006). Thermal electricity generation requires substantial amounts of water to produce steam and for cooling (Sovacool, Axsen, and Kempton 2017). Hydroelectricity produces electricity by converting both gravitational and kinetic energy. Wind power converts kinetic energy into electricity using turbines and a generator. Solar power is produced from electromagnetic energy by using the sun's energy to release electrons. Each of these sources produces distinct climate emissions impacts based on the technology, placement, and materials used (see Table 4.1; Schlomer et al. 2014).[1] Despite these differences, in practice, the trend of fossil fuel generation (either with carbon capture and storage or without) entails significantly larger emissions impacts than do renewable sources of power. This distinction is most striking in the comparison of coal and natural gas to wind and solar power.

Several characteristics differentiate how the various forms of power generation contribute to an electricity system and are managed: the size (usually measured in MW), capacity factor, and dispatchability of the resource (Sims et al. 2011). In 2017 the global installed capacity of electricity generation was over 2,000 GW of coal; close to 1,700 GW of natural gas; close to 1,200 GW of hydroelectric; 500 GW of wind power; just under 500 GW each of oil, nuclear, and solar photovoltaic; and close to 200 GW of other renewables (IEA 2017).

Some of the largest electricity generation stations in the world are hydroelectric dams. For example, three dams in the world—China's Three Gorges, Brazil's Itaipu, and the US Grand Coulee—are rated at 6 GW (i.e., 10^9 W) in size (Smil 2016). Nuclear power plants in the United States range in size from 500 to 4,000 MW (i.e., 10^6 W) (US EIA 2017). (For a technical discussion of nuclear power, see Fitzwater in this volume.) Fossil fuel power

Table 4.1 Life-Cycle Assessment of GHG Emissions (gCO_2 eq./kWh) Including Albedo Effect

Type of Energy	Minimum	Maximum
Coal	740	910
Coal + carbon capture & storage (CCS)	100	250
Coal—cofiring with biomass	620	890
Gas (combined cycle)	410	650
Gas (cc) + CCS	94	340
Biomass—dedicated	130	420
Geothermal	6	79
Hydropower	1	2,200
Nuclear	3.7	110
Concentrated solar power (CSP)	8.8	63
Solar PV—rooftop	26	60
Solar PV—utility	18	180
Wind—onshore	7	56
Wind—offshore	2	81

Source: Data in this table are drawn from Schlomer et al. (2014, 1335)

plants can range in size from a few megawatts (MW) to several thousand megawatts (MW) (US EIA 2018). (For a technical discussion of fossil fuels, see Tutuncu this volume.) Solar photovoltaic installations can be as small as 1 kW (i.e., 10^3 W) in size, and those connected to households and rooftops, which may not be grid connected, range in size from 1 to 10 kW (IEA 2017). A wind turbine can be as large as 4 MW in size (Smil 2016). By comparison, peak household electricity use varies depending on energy end uses and behaviors of the household, but are generally on the order of 1 to 2 kW (De Almeida et al. 2011; Pollution Probe and Center for Urban Energy 2015).

The capacity factor (see Box 4.1 for definition) and dispatchability (see Box 4.2 for definition) of power generation are interrelated concepts that are important to grid

---

Box 4.2 Electricity Grid Concepts and Terminology

Grid operator. "Keeps the lights on, operates transmission, and may run the electricity market; usually called independent system operator or transmission system operator" (226).

Electricity market. "The buying and selling of wholesale electricity on the grid by generators, retailers, and wholesale consumers, in advance or in real time, through a stock-market-like exchange" (225).

Balancing area. Geographic and technical scope of a power grid in which supply and demand must be continuously balanced; typically controlled by one balancing authority.

Transmission and distribution. Transmission networks interconnect large power plants with centers of power demand; distribution networks serve power to local areas and neighborhoods (225).

Generation fleet. "All of the dispatchable power plants connected to a grid" (230).

Baseload plants. "Power plants that generally run continuously at constant output year-round or those with the lowest marginal operating costs and, as such, always dispatched first" (231).

Intermediate plants. "Plants designed to run part time, often cycled multiple times per day" (231).

Peaking plants. "Plants designed to run only a few hours per day, at peak hours" (232).

Dispatchable resources. "Resources that the grid operator can directly control; dispatched according to market scheduling or as ancillary services markets" (234).

Ancillary service. "An operational process, usually market-based, in which generators respond to grid operator signals to keep the grid operating within required technical parameters of power, voltage, and frequency; also referred to as grid service or ancillary market" (226).

Variable renewables. "Renewables such as wind and solar whose output is autonomously determined by the strength of wind and sun; usually not controllable by power grid" (226).

Capacity value. "Effective fraction of renewable capacity that can be counted in determining reserve capacity needs; also referred to as effective load carrying capacity" (229).

Combined heat and power plants (CHPs). "Power plants that produce both heat and power simultaneously, providing heat as hot water or steam to nearby buildings or industries" (226).

Pumped hydro as storage. "Hydropower with a lower and upper reservoir that acts as a battery when water is pumped uphill to the upper reservoir" (229).

Source: Martinot (2016).

operators who are trying to balance supply and demand within the voltage and other technical constraints on a power grid. The capacity factor is the actual output over a given period of time divided by the maximum possible output. The capacity factor of nuclear power tends to be 90 percent (Bruckner et al. 2014) and 60–85 percent for coal-fired-generation (Smil 2016). The capacity factor of wind power ranges from 20 to 45 percent (depending on whether offshore or onshore), solar ranges from 12 to 27 percent, and hydropower from 20 to 95 percent (run of river) or 30 to 60 percent (reservoir) (Sims et al. 2011). Dispatchable resources are power generation that a grid operator can directly control in order to balance generation and demand on the electricity grid and maintain reliability. "Demand response" refers to electricity loads that are coordinated to be reduced at the grid operator's signal. For example, in the case of a surge of demand, to balance the grid, grid operators would both increase dispatchable generation while dispatching demand response resources. Because wind and solar power generation are variable (Hoicka and Rowlands 2011; Sims et al. 2011), they can be predicted but are considered less dispatchable. However, some forms of generation that are predictable are also less dispatchable as their output is less variable. For example, nuclear power that has a 90 percent capacity factor is usually considered a base load resource that operates continuously and is dispatched first, whereas intermediate and peaking resources are more controllable and can be ramped up in response to the electricity demand on the system (see Box 4.2 for definitions).

Transmission and Distribution

Electricity transmission and distribution infrastructure elements both move electricity between generation facilities (supply) and end users (demand). The difference between the two is that transmission infrastructure carries large amounts of power at high voltages from a power generation plant to a substation, where the voltage is "stepped down" (reduced) to smaller wires to carry the power to end users along distribution lines. Both transmission and distribution cables can be run over ground via towers or "undergrounded" or buried, which is increasingly the case (Smil 2016). For example, a large high-voltage transmission cable runs between the south and north islands of New Zealand underwater, connecting the hydropower-generation-rich south with urban demand centers in the north. Higher voltages allow thinner wires to carry the same amount of power (Everett et al. 2012). Electricity is generated at low voltages that range between 12.5 and 25 kV and needs to be converted to much higher voltages to transport large amounts of power over long distances. Given that a combination of low current and high voltage is preferable for long-distance transmission, the generated low current is first transformed (stepped up) to the voltages of the transmission wires that range between 100 and 800 kV, before being sent to long-distance markets or load centers; transformed again (stepped down) to safer, lower voltages for distribution within cities (usually 12 kV); and then stepped down again to lower voltages (110–250V depending on the country) for household and organization use (Smil 2016). In the past, due to materials of components, landscape, and design, alternating current (AC) could more easily convert power between high and low voltages than direct current (DC) to transmit power over long distances (Smil 2006). Transformers can reduce or increase the voltage with almost no loss of energy, very reliably, and quietly (Smil 2006).

Managing the Electricity Grid

Electricity use (loads) will vary throughout the day, moment by moment, and by location, and the electricity grid is typically designed and managed to serve electricity at peak times (see Figure 4.2). Due to the first and second laws of thermodynamics (defined in Box 4.1), useful energy is lost at each transformation across the grid, from generation to transmission to distribution to end use. If the load (demand) on the grid rises, the voltage tends to drop, which is a signal to increase generation (Everett et al. 2012). (See Boxes 4.1, 4.2, and 4.3 for information on electricity grids and markets.) In order to maintain reliable electricity for demand centers, grid operators must maintain the voltage and frequency of grid components within tightly specified limits by continuously matching supply to demand while also optimizing generation (supply) resources. Depending on where generation and demand centers are located, this can potentially happen over long distances. Dispatchable resources are used for the purpose of allowing grid operators to keep resources in excess of predicted demand (Bruckner et al. 2014; Martinot 2016). This need to balance grid resources at all times often results in the underutilization of generation and transmission resources; in the United States, 8 to 12 percent of peak electricity demand occurs during 80 to 100 hours per year, and the generation, transmission, and distribution resources designed and built to serve this peak remain underutilized for the other 90 percent of the year (Sovacool, Axsen, and Kempton 2017).

The implications of management errors, generation shortfalls, and critical demand peaks can be serious, including brownouts, when voltage across the system drops due to insufficient power generation, and blackouts, in which power becomes unavailable due to system failure. According to World Bank data tracking the number of power outages per month globally, regions hardest hit are in south Asia, sub-Saharan Africa, and the Middle East and North Africa (MENA). Niger, for example, experienced twenty-two power outages a month in 2017, while Argentina had only 0.8 (World Bank 2019). These outages are unpredictable and undermine industrial, commercial, and residential activities in affected locations. These crises have economic implications; for example, the specific costs of interruption can include lost production or sales, damage to equipment or materials, extra overhead, and additional labor and overtime costs (Sullivan et al. 2015). For instance, in India the largest blackout in history left nearly 8 percent of the world's population (620 million people) without power for one to two days in July 2012. The blackout shut down commuter trains in Delhi, left people unable to draw water due to the failure of electric pumps, and shut down office buildings because elevators could not run without electricity (Yardley and Harris 2012). These power system failures can be the result of technical glitches, simple human error, or natural disasters. They can also, however, be the result of manipulation by profit-seeking actors manipulating supply in order to capture rents—the most famous example of this being Enron's role in California's energy crisis in 2000 (Beder 2003; Spitz 2005).

We now turn to three of the important trends that will shape the future of energy infrastructures: (1) urbanization and the growth of electricity demand centers, including the electrification of transportation; (2) the projected increase in amount and share of renewable electricity; and (3) increased flexibility of the electricity grid and distributed infrastructure.

Trend 1: The Growth of Electricity Demand Centers

Energy demand is projected to grow due to population growth and economic growth, and most of this growth is projected to occur in urban centers. The world's population growth, from under 1 billion in 1800 to 7.2 billion in 2012, has coincided with a twenty-fold increase in energy use (Araújo 2014). Nearly 1.1 billion people, mostly dwelling in rural sub-Saharan Africa and developing Asia, currently lack access to electricity (IEA 2017), and the world's population is projected to reach 9.5 billion by 2050, with most growth occurring in these same regions (Araújo 2014). Urban centers have grown significantly, from 2 percent of the worlds' population in 1800, to 43 percent in 1990, to 54 percent in 2016, and are expected to absorb nearly all future population growth (UN Habitat 2016). The current energy system uses 21,000 TWh per year (IEA 2017), and the IEA projects it will grow to somewhere between 32,000 and 37,000 TWh by 2040 (IEA 2017). The majority of this growth is projected to occur in developing economies, with the largest increase from industrial motor systems, space cooling, large appliances and cooking, information and communication technology (ICT), and small appliances (IEA 2017). In 2015 the United Nations General Assembly adopted the Sustainable Development Goals (SDGs), which include improving the accessibility and quality of modern energy services (SDG-7), promoting economic development and industrialization (SDG-9), and supporting consumption (SDG-12) (Seto et al. 2016).

Spatial organization, land uses, and planning have an important impact on levels of energy use and greenhouse gas emissions. The development and spatial distribution of existing energy systems has had a strong influence on the organization and governance of human settlements and current levels of energy use (Owens 1992, 1986). For example, energy use and emissions will depend on the relative location, shape, and built density of industrial, commercial, and residential centers (Jaccard, Failing, and Berry 1997; Owens 1986, 1992). More specifically, whether these areas are mixed use or made up of high-rises or low-density housing impacts technology choice and transportation, electricity use, and behaviors (Jaccard, Failing, and Berry 1997; Owens 1992, 1986). The industrial, commercial, and residential sectors are characterized respectively by the intensive use of motors and lighting (industrial); cooling, lighting, and other equipment (commercial); and heating, cooling, lighting, and appliances (residential) (IEA 2017). The concentration of energy demand in urban centers minimizes the land-use impacts of buildings and electricity line losses from long-distance delivery (Araújo 2014). However, energy system designs are considered to be in carbon lock-in, which means that existing infrastructures and technologies, institutions, and behavioral norms act together to constrain the rate and magnitude of reductions to carbon emissions and changes in energy systems (Seto et al. 2016).

Power density (W/m^2) is a useful concept to measure the impact of these trends on energy demand. The measure of power density describes the amount of land (space, measured in area, or m^2) over which power is used or produced (Smil 2016). Table 4.2

Table 4.2 Size and Power Density Characteristics of Electricity Installations and Uses

Installation Type	Range of Sizes	Power Density (W/m^2)
Fossil-fueled electricity plant	1–3,500 MW (order of magnitude)[d]	300–3,000[c]
Nuclear electricity plant	500 to 4,000 MW[a]	500[c]
Hydroelectricity plant	0.1–1,500 (MW) (run of river)[b] 1 MW to 20 GW (reservoir)[b]	3[c]
Solar electricity plant	< 1kW to 100 MW[b]	5[c]
Wind power plant	5–300[b] MW 2–4[e] MW (turbine)	1 (turbine), 50 (footprint)[c]
Electricity transmission	100–800 kV[c]	30[c]
Modern economy (use)	–	3[c]
Urban area	–	10–30[c]
City downtown	–	100[c]
House	–	10–50[c]
High-rise building, city downtown, factory, supermarket	–	300–1000[c]
Motor	~5–400 kW[f]	
Refrigerator	120 W[g]	
Laptop	30 W[g]	
Central air conditioning	2–5 kW[h]	
Room air –conditioning	1 kW[h]	
Light bulb (incandescent)	40–150W[i]	
Light bulb (compact fluorescent)	23 W[h]	
Light bulb (LED)	8–25 W[i]	
Clothes dryer	1.8–5 kW[h]	
Dishwasher	1.2–2.4 kW[h]	
Portable heater	750–1100 kW[h]	

Source: Data in this table are drawn from
[a] US EIA (2017);
[b] Sims et al. (2011);
[c] Smil (2016);
[d] US EIA (2018);
[e] Greenblatt et al. (2017)
[f] U.S. Department of Energy (2011);
[g] Menezes et al. (2014);
[h] Attari et al. (2010);
[i] Bradford (2017)

presents the range of sizes and power densities of loads and of various electricity installations and uses. This increased power density of energy demand, particularly if high-rise buildings or industry increase in a particular location, can also improve the economics of district energy for heating or cooling (explained in Box 4.3) (Owens 1986; Rezaie and Rosen 2012). Smil (2016) estimates that the mean global energy use by urban centers is 55 percent: "The weighted global mean is thus about 75 percent of energy used in urban or industrial regions, and that total (12.5 TW in 2012), prorated over 580,000 km^2, results in a power density of about 22 W/m^2." In Singapore, a high-density city, the twenty-four-hour maximum has reached 113 W/m^2 in the commercial district (Smil 2016). However, if growth of electricity demand in a dense downtown core outpaces the size of the transmission lines, it can also lead to local bottlenecks in delivering supply, local congestion, and constraints on matching supply to demand (Toronto Hydro et al. 2014). In order to meet local electricity needs, increased flexibility and localized management techniques, such as conservation, storage, and distributed generation, would be required; these factors are discussed in the section on grid flexibility and distributed infrastructure.

Box 4.3 Additional Electricity Grid Concepts and Terminology

Peak shaving. A technique to reduce electricity demand (load management) during times of high load and thus reduce costs of expensive infrastructure, only for short periods.

Distributed energy. "The production of heat or electrical power near the point of use on the distribution network, and other practices that can balance loads at a similarly local scale" (Kuzemko et al. 2017).

District energy. "District energy involves multi-building heating and cooling, in which heat and/or cold is distributed by circulating either hot water or low-pressure steam through underground piping. District networks incorporate an underground system of piping from one or more central sources to industrial, commercial and residential users. The heat delivered to buildings can also be used for air conditioning by adding a heat pump or absorption chiller" (Rezaie and Rosen 2012, 3).

Smart grid. Digitally enabled electricity infrastructure (Palensky and Kupzog 2013).

Microgrid. Autonomous systems can be as small as individual homes or groups of homes working on the low voltage distribution grid (Sims et al. 2011). A small grid with generation, consumption, and sometimes storage that can operate in a grid-connected and "isolated" mode (Palensky and Kupzog 2013).

Stand-alone systems. Off-grid systems for individual households or groups of consumers (IEA 2017).

Prosumers. Energy end users who become participants in the electricity market, buying and selling energy (Yeager 2004).

Brownout. Lack of generation supply requires a drop in voltage across the grid that necessitates reduced electricity demand.

Blackout. Interruption of electricity to the grid that can lead to economic losses and social disruption.

Another large expected increase in electricity demand, including in urban centers, is the electrification of vehicles. The transportation sector is the second largest source of CO_2 emissions (IEA 2017) and is responsible for 14 percent of global greenhouse gas emissions (IPCC Working Group III 2014). Transportation is strongly dependent on oil, and the IEA (2017) predicts that emissions from transportation will continue to grow past the peak of emissions from coal. Due to their potential for reduced greenhouse gas emissions, electric vehicles are considered an important option to decarbonize the transportation sector, just as they play an important role in increasing electricity demand. The main potential benefit of vehicle-to-grid integration (VGI) of electric vehicles is that it could contribute to decarbonizing both the transportation and electricity sectors simultaneously. Recent estimates suggest that plug-in electric vehicles (PEVs) must make up at least 40 percent of new vehicle sales globally by 2040 to contribute to stabilizing emissions at 450 ppm (Sovacool, Axsen, and Kempton 2017). Electric vehicles also contribute to better local air quality and less noise. Electric vehicles currently make up 0.2 percent of the global fleet of vehicles (IEA 2017), and the current stock of electric vehicles is 3 million, mainly in the United States, European Union, and China (IEA 2018). China also has 99 percent of the market of electric buses and two-wheelers (IEA 2018). In the last two years a number of countries have announced policies to ban the sale of new cars with combustion engines using gasoline or diesel, including Norway by 2025, India and Ireland by 2030, and France and the United Kingdom by 2040. However, when charging, electric vehicles will contribute a large load to the demand curve (see Figure 4.2). For example, in Canada, peak electricity demand of a house is about 2kW, while that of an electric vehicle is 8kW, which would increase that local household peak demand five times (Pollution Probe and Center for Urban Energy 2015). These moves will drive demand for new electricity generation at the same time that they will provide for distributed grid storage in the form of the family car (Sovacool, Axsen, and Kempton 2017; Wolsink 2012).

Demand Growth: Implications for Social Scientists

Studying the politics of infrastructures renders visible the ways in which our physical systems are shaped by diverse actors and institutions and are geographically embedded in distinct cultures and practices (Sovacool 2014). It is an all-too-common mistake of natural scientists to neglect the reflexive relationship between technical or biophysical developments and sociopolitical ones. While land uses and settlement patterns, building structure, and the efficiency of end-use technologies all have a strong influence on energy demand (Creutzig et al. 2016; Jaccard, Failing, and Berry 1997; Owens 1992, 1986; Smil 2016), energy demand is also strongly influenced by culture, behaviors, and practices that are embedded in complex social, technological, and institutional systems (Creutzig et al. 2016; Seto et al. 2016).

Social scientists interested in electricity infrastructures will be attuned to the fact that this trend toward increased demand from growing urban populations, increased electricity access, and vehicle electrification will not affect all equally. Seizing the benefits of energy access and use will be contingent upon political mobilization to address fuel poverty (lack of access) and economic inequality (Day, Walker, and Simcock 2016; Middlemiss and Gillard 2015). For those individuals and communities who are able to connect, the benefits are significant, which is why international agencies from the World Bank to the UNDP have focused on energy access as a key pillar to sustainable development. Chapters in this volume on energy justice (Fuller), citizen action (Cauchon), and gender (Standal et al.) illustrate how access to energy services is a prerequisite for the eradication of poverty, economic development, improvements in health, gender equality, and education (Goldemberg, Johansson, and Anderson 2004). As households ascend the "energy ladder," or switch from biomass and locally polluting fuels to modern fuels that are cleaner at the point of use, such as electricity, their members may engage in more formal economic activity, enjoy improved health, and possibly also reduce their environmental impacts. Women and children, who are typically most responsible for household labor in economically challenged situations, arguably benefit most from these changes (Kroon, Brouwer, and Beukering 2013).

Social researchers need to ask questions, then, not only about the geographies of this new demand, but also about who has the power (used in a dual sense) to demand, consume, and control electricity access within them. They will also have much to add on the historical and ideological drivers of electricity infrastructures and how these have shaped who can, and does, gain access to the benefits of electricity. For example, histories of the sector uncover how the first power networks were private and available to wealthy urban citizens. Electricity access expanded in many jurisdictions through programs of nationalization through the early twentieth century, to aid in industrialization projects and to extend services beyond the elite (Hausman, Hertner, and Wilkins 2008). However, since the postwar era, when natural monopoly characteristics were used to justify mass public ownership, system governance has transformed radically again due to both technological developments and ideological ones.

Beginning with Chile and the United Kingdom, electricity restructuring trends have accelerated since the 1990s; many national electricity systems have been restructured, with key elements (generation, distribution, or retailing) being privatized partially or outright, while others remain centralized monopolies (Beder 2003). At an ideological level, neoliberalism has provided a strong catalyst for privatization. These restructuring processes have not been uniform globally, nor are they uncontested, particularly where neoliberal restructuring and public infrastructure sales come as a form of conditionality for international loans or development aid (Anderson 2009; Agyeman, Bullard, and Evans 2003). In these restructured systems, private market actors, rather than public utilities, make key resource allocation decisions, with implications for pricing (and access), siting, resource use, international trade, and overall sectoral coordination (Cohen 2006; MacArthur 2016). These processes have opened up fertile ground for social scientists to examine whether and how comparative political economies shape trends such as energy use and access.

TREND 2: INCREASE IN RENEWABLE ENERGY

With the recent rise of new renewables developments, together with their increasing cost competitiveness, new technological, socioeconomic, and political challenges and opportunities have emerged. Again, technological innovations to meet the Paris Agreement goals to decrease carbon emissions come with a forecast increase in renewable power as 40 percent of new additions of power generation by 2040, to 15,688 TWh of power generation (IEA 2017). In a more ambitious scenario that aims to reduce poverty by achieving universal access to electricity and has more stringent reduction of energy-related pollutants, 63 percent of total power generation is to be generated by renewable power, to 22,664 TWh (IEA 2017). However, there are many social, economic, and environmental benefits associated with renewable power, and 100 percent renewable powered systems have been modeled as both technologically and economically feasible (Diesendorf and Elliston 2018). One root of the debate over whether 40 percent or 100 percent of renewable energy power should be the goal is that renewable power, particularly solar and wind, is more variable than the incumbent thermal power or hydroelectricity, and this requires different grid design, geography, and management techniques than have been used historically.

Since 2007 renewable sources of electricity generation have more than doubled, from close to 1,000 GW (10^6 W) installed capacity in 2007 to over 2,000 GW installed capacity in 2017 (IRENA 2017b). This growth has been driven by targeted public policies encouraging the development of new renewables; these, together with market and technological developments, have led to sharp declines in the cost of new solar and wind installations, making them cost-competitive in many instances with fossil fuels (IRENA 2017a). In the case of solar photovoltaic, costs have declined 69 percent since 2010 (IRENA 2017a, 2). Most of this new capacity has been from renewable hydropower, onshore wind, solar photovoltaic, and solid biomass electricity generation (IRENA 2017b). The IEA estimates 500 GW wind power, just under 500 GW solar photovoltaic, and close to 200 GW other renewables were reached in 2017 (IEA 2017). However, power generation from nonrenewable sources (coal and natural gas) have also continued to grow alongside renewable growth, as total demand increases.

A key challenge is how to integrate renewables into end-use sectors (heating, cooling, transport, etc.) (IRENA 2017a, 3). The characteristics of geography and power density help us to better understand the major trends that are affecting the evolution and transition of electricity infrastructures and how these are interacting spatially with human settlements. The geography (see, e.g., Bridge et al. 2013; Pasqualetti 2012) and power density (W/m²) (Smil 2016) characteristics of supply and demand in electricity infrastructures provide a more nuanced conception of the spatial reorganization of electricity infrastructure that could occur in a transition to a low-carbon electricity system. This view enables a better understanding of the important trends in electricity infrastructure, setting the playing field of challenges and opportunities for citizens and policy makers.

Smil (2016) points out that in matching supply (generation) to demand (load) over a grid, one of the historic advantages of thermal power plants (with power densities ranging from 300 to 3,000 W/m²) is that they operate at power densities that are one or two orders of magnitude higher than the power densities of households (10–50 W/m²) and two to four times the power densities required by large urban areas (10–30 W/m²). Consequently, in the case of thermal generation, a smaller spatial area is required to produce electricity that is delivered to a larger spatial area for demand. However, based on the information provided in Table 4.2, if a thermal generation plant, which might be 1,000 MW, were to be replaced by wind power, the number of turbines required to replace one thermal power plant (several hundred) would result in a large increase in the land use required to produce the same amount of electricity. Because wind power has a power density that is several orders of magnitude lower than that of thermal generation, an equivalent amount of power generation requires more land.

The geographical relationship between fuel types and electricity generation varies between renewable and nonrenewable resources and affects the location of transmission and distribution lines that connect electricity generation to energy demand centers. Fuel sources of coal, natural gas, oil, and uranium all must be extracted from the land. The deposits of these fuels are location dependent, but uranium and extracted fossil fuels are generally transported to a secondary location for electricity generation. Renewable power from hydro, wind, and solar installations is produced on location, usually selected for the strength of the renewable resource to be converted to electricity. Wind power can be produced both on land and offshore. Solar power tends to be ubiquitous across regions with similar profiles for solar electricity generation. Solar panels and tiles can be embedded into the infrastructure of demand centers, with the possibility to be installed on rooftops and other structures. This distinction explains, in part, why renewable power therefore may in some ways be considered more sensitive to location than centralized forms of generation, such as fossil fuels and nuclear energy (Pasqualetti 2012). Therefore, the share of low-carbon electricity sources, such as nuclear power and renewable energy, will affect the reorganization of the electricity grid.

Increased Renewables: Implications for Social Scientists

The shift to new sources of power and new actors with them opens up a host of challenges and opportunities for social science researchers. One fruitful line of work is the important role that public policies have played in driving new technological developments and reshaping the cost curves for technology. It is commonplace for renewable energy research to underplay, or disregard completely, the crucial role of government policy actions in underpinning the development and increased penetration (leading to lower costs) of these new power sources. Markets for these new technologies are not natural; they are constructed and maintained by social and political decisions of the past and present. Feed-in tariff structures; mandates and targets for new renewable procurement; and incentives for particular actors, particularly in countries such as Germany and Denmark, have each driven the nationally distinct profiles that exist today. National policies have also driven the broader global trend to higher shares of new renewables (Gan and Smith 2011; OECD 2015; Tobin et al. 2018). The rise of renewables industries in particular countries, such as solar manufacturing in China and wind in Germany, is also providing scope for a shifting geopolitics of the energy sector more broadly, as renewables become cost competitive with fossil fuels and climate commitments put pressure on fossil fuel industries and uses (Scholten and Bosman 2016; Stratfor 2018).

Public policies that underpin the expansion of renewables will need to contend with mobilization and lobbying by powerful incumbent interests from fossil fuel and utility sectors (Hess 2014; Oreskes and Conway 2010). Diesendorf and Elliston (2018) argue, for example, that "vested interests are having a similar effect to the former campaign by the tobacco industry to sow doubts about the serious adverse health impacts of their product and hence delay action. Vested interests are arguably the main barrier to a RE future" (326) Political scientists are well versed in the notion that not all interactions are win-win and that any particular change is likely to generate both winners and losers.

A further implication of the rise of renewables, and particularly new renewables, is that this transition may enable a shift toward a form of "energy democracy" or "community power," organized by and for local community development needs (Schumacher 1973; Sheer 2007). This kind of democratization is possible because the new renewable power needed to fulfill the energy demand and its corresponding density outlined in trend 1 requires a new political geography. Renewable power is associated with larger land use requirements across a wider geographic area (e.g., Schroth et al. 2012) than power generated from thermal generation; thus an increase in renewables may also involve an increase in the number of communities and local actors involved in or affected by power generation. This is politically significant, as it can entail a shift in actors, goals, and with them, sector governance.

Prosumers are participants in the electricity market, sometimes through intermediaries, in buying and selling electricity (Yeager 2004). Prosumer activity from more distributed power generation *may* lead to a range of behavioral changes, from increased citizen learning about energy infrastructures (due to local visibility) to a potential for citizen engagement, but the degree, shape, and practice will vary significantly by the institutional design of distributed energy: regulatory setting, ownership structures, and governance (Chilvers and Longhurst 2016; Hoicka and MacArthur 2018; van Veelen and van der Horst 2018). In fact, the more "local" and visible our energy infrastructures become, the more urban centers are going to need to address the challenges of NIMBY (not in my backyard) opposition to developments perceived as visibly intrusive or disruptive (Devine-Wright 2011). Historically some localities have been less impacted by the footprint of electricity infrastructure in the form of large transmission towers or generation plants, shifting the impacts to rural and poorer communities (Agyeman, Bullard, and Evans 2003).

One manifestation of these changes falls under the umbrella of "energy democracy." While the term is relatively new and notoriously slippery, with first mentions appearing online in 2010 (Burke and Stephens 2018; van Veelen and van der Horst 2018), the concept is not. It centers on a desire to harness the energy transition to restructure the political economy of the energy sector around new institutional configurations, allowing for enhanced citizen participation, learning, and local economic development (Devine-Wright 2011; Szulecki 2018; MacArthur 2016; Walker and Devine-Wright 2008). Community-based localism seeks to redistribute both decision-making and material benefits (jobs, economic rents, or savings) to those most affected by the nearby infrastructure, thus enhancing the political acceptability and radical potential of infrastructural change. There are particular groups, such as indigenous peoples, who have particularly strong claims for local ownership and development, given the dispossession of the lands energy infrastructures are built on through processes of colonial occupation (Bargh 2012; Castree 2004; MacArthur and Matthewman 2018). Local generation on apartments, schools, churches, and universities brings institutional and local actors into the infrastructural decision-making network in a way they were excluded from previously, at least in theory. Much depends on the broader policy settings around buying and selling power, as well as those involved in building design and investment.

Much has also yet to be learned about the actual practice of democracy (deliberative versus representative) at these local levels, as well as the range and scale of potential benefits from this democratization of electricity generation. Furthermore, it is by no means guaranteed that localization is a panacea for resolving thorny conflicts over "who owns the energy transition," project siting, or the distribution of resources (Mey and Diesendorf 2017; Sovacool 2014; Walker 2011). Instead of planning being captured by centralized or remote technocrats, it may prove that powerful local actors foreclose genuine learning or debate (Van Veelen 2018). It is also likely that large-scale plants and powerful incumbent actors will coexist and continue to dominate energy infrastructures, with local generation and distribution networks playing a relatively minor or niche role. Or it may prove the case that local energy systems are more suited to specific developmental, cultural, or resource contexts, and "scale up" only in particular settings. As a result, the rise of distributed renewable generation has opened up, technically at least, space for localized forms of energy ownership not seen since the birth of the sector more than a century ago.

TREND 3: INCREASE IN GRID FLEXIBILITY AND DISTRIBUTED INFRASTRUCTURES

Any large increase in renewable energy combined with growth of electricity demand and its density requires a fundamental shift in the geography and elements of electricity infrastructure. The combination of increased density of electricity demand (described in trend 1), with the growth of renewable power generation (described in trend 2) that has the characteristics of lower power density combined with intermittency, will lead to a shift in the geography of all elements of energy infrastructure. Existing electricity grid technologies can accommodate somewhere between 20 and 40 percent of electricity from renewable electricity (Bruckner et al. 2014; Martinot 2016). In recent years grids have become "smarter" (now called "smart grids"), as grid-related information and new grid management technologies and materials have increased and are allowing for better coordination among the elements of generation, demand, and distribution. However, in order to reach a higher share of renewable electricity, new designs that provide for more balancing and flexible options are required by the electricity grid (Bruckner et al. 2014; Martinot 2016). Matching supply to demand under these circumstances leads to three major shifts in electricity infrastructure: (1) the possibility of super grids that can transport large volumes of power over long distances to demand centers; (2) an increase in grid flexibility to match intermittent renewable power generation to demand that varies with time; and (3) an increase in distributed infrastructures. These elements are depicted in Figure 4.3 as the super grid, the smart grid, the microgrid, and distributed generation.

Super Grids

Renewable power generation is more geographically sensitive than many forms of thermal power generation. With an increase in renewable power to somewhere between 40 and 100 percent of generation, the power density of the generation fleet is forecast to decrease, meaning that more land coverage will be required for power generation (Schroth et al. 2012), which will need to be transported from various regions to dense urban centers (Palensky and Kupzog 2013). Some of this renewable power may be abundant but located far from demand centers. Furthermore, renewable power, particularly solar and wind, can be variable based on the available resource at any time of day, seasonally, or among locations. Super grids can transport large amounts of power over

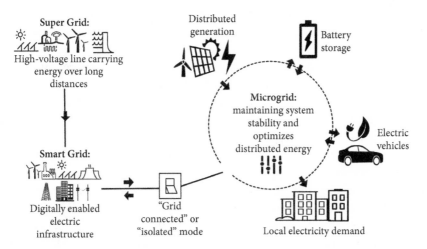

FIGURE 4.3 Increase in renewable power, smart grids, super grids, flexible grids, and distributed generation.

long distances, including over continents. These grids allow for an averaging effect across volatile and geographically dispersed loads, which make it easier to integrate this generation into the system (Palensky and Kupzog 2013). Using super grids to transport various forms of renewable energy from a range of locations can average out variability (Palensky and Kupzog 2013). For example, "Although China plans to extend 1,000-kV AC and 800-kV DC transmission lines to cover rising energy demand, the United States is considering the super grid approach for outage prevention, and the European Union is considering it for wind integration. In Europe, the so-called Club of Rome has proposed a super grid connecting northern Africa and Europe, potentially allowing the European Union to be supplied with renewable energy collected in African deserts" (Palensky and Kupzog 2013, 209).

Flexibility to Manage Variability

Some renewable power sources (mainly solar and wind) are not as dispatchable as thermal power generation. Instead, they are considered intermittent and variable with a low capacity factor. Hydroelectricity has a range of capacity factors and options for dispatchability that are context dependent. When a generation shortfall occurs, the voltage drops across the system, which is an indicator to system managers to increase generation. In order to manage the electricity grid with an increasing amount of intermittent renewable power supply with rising demand, these elements are becoming increasingly sensitive to location and time and require more sensitive coordination in real time across the electricity grid (Palensky and Kupzog 2013). Electricity grids have already begun the transformation toward smarter or "smart" grids through digitally enabled elements that affect all aspects of electricity infrastructure to enhance control, management, and resilience (Palensky and Kupzog, 2013). In order to maintain reliability under these new circumstances and avoid brownouts and blackouts, distribution systems are under pressure for major transformation to build in flexibility (Martinot 2016). Examples of these flexibility options are described in Boxes 4.2 and 4.3, and include prosumers, aggregators, virtual power plants, microgrids, peer-to-peer, storage, and increasing the time sensitivity of loads (Martinot 2016). Furthermore, in order to manage the variability of renewable power generation, electricity can also be stored and deployed as dispatchable generation during periods of high demand in an electrical grid. There are five main types of electrical storage systems: mechanical, such as pumped hydroelectricity, compressed air, and flywheel; electrochemical, such as batteries; chemical, such as hydrogen and compressed natural gas; electrical storage systems, such as double-layer capacitors and superconducting magnetic energy storage; and thermal storage (International Electrotechnical Commission 2011). For example, when solar power is combined with thermal storage, the capacity factor can reach 42 percent and the dispatchability and predictability also improve (Sims et al. 2011). Electric vehicles also have the potential to contribute local energy storage and flexible management activities on the electricity grid that would contribute to increasing renewable power.

Depending on how they are deployed, widespread electric vehicle adoption could help increase the penetration of renewable electricity generation into the grid (Sovacool, Axsen, and Kempton 2017).

Distributed Infrastructures

The combined growth of electricity demand and urbanization means that the power density of settlements is increasing. The profiles of energy generation and energy usage are shifting as the power densities of renewables are lower than thermal generation; an increasing number of demand centers may have power densities that are equal to or an order of magnitude larger than the power densities of supply. The result, in the case of the demand centers, may be increased congestion and constraints in delivering electricity from outside regions to an area with a higher power density of demand (Toronto Hydro et al. 2014) and the need for more distributed generation. Furthermore, a larger land area is required for renewable power generation than for thermal power generation (e.g., Schroth et al. 2012). If energy demand grows rapidly, some of this will result in congestion, as transmission and distribution power lines can only carry so much electricity. The solutions to address the challenge of supplying electricity to demand centers involve three main types of innovations: distributed energy, demand reduction, and demand response (Kuzemko et al. 2017). Distributed energy is the production of heat or electrical power near the point of use on the distribution network, as well as other practices that can balance loads at a similarly local scale (Kuzemko et al. 2017). Demand reduction, particularly at peak times, brings down system costs, as less electricity generation and other infrastructure is required to meet demand and less electricity is used overall (or slows growth of the electricity system) (Kuzemko et al. 2017). Demand reduction involves a reduction of energy used, either by reducing the use of an energy service or by improving the energy efficiency of the service. Demand response is a mechanism in which end-user loads are reduced, sometimes on short notice, sometimes by intermediary aggregators of many small loads that grid operators can deploy to balance supply and demand, sometimes for intermittent renewable power. All of these possibilities are enhanced and enabled by the flexibility options, which include prosumers, aggregators, virtual power plants, microgrids, peer-to-peer, storage, and increasing the time sensitivity of loads (Martinot 2016). Embedding these innovations into the electricity grid depends on the complex relationships between infrastructures and technology, institutions, and behaviors.

Electric Vehicles

Vehicle electrification is both a driver and a complement to these trends toward end-user participation, flexibility, and storage. The International Renewable Energy Agency predicts that electricity storage capacity will need to grow by 150 percent by 2030 to deal with growing demand, supply of variable power, and the rise of electric-vehicle-dominated fleets (IRENA 2017a, 4). This expectation is based on the fact that electric vehicles (EVs) are powered by energy stored in batteries, which could act as storage and balancing resources for renewable power that is produced in excess of demand requirements on the grid. Other potential benefits that are useful for grid operators include the improved utilization of existing generation capacity and distribution infrastructure, backup power (on reserve for reliability resources), load balancing (of renewable power), reduced peak loads, reduced forecast uncertainty, and using (storing) intermittent renewable energy (Sovacool, Axsen, and Kempton 2017). The benefits depend on whether EVs are restricted to charging mainly at off-peak times (i.e., overnight); this increases the utilization of grid resources outside of the 80 to 100 peak hours of the year that the system tends to be sized for and avoids increasing peak electricity demand, which contributes to congestion and constraints in supplying electricity. The deployment of EVs depends on the availability of charging options (IEA 2018). The charging infrastructure, in turn, depends on the vehicle range (distance that can be traveled between battery charge); the location of charging stations (e.g., whether at home, at work, in public parking lots, or along a highway); and the rate of power charging of the battery (rate of charge measured in watts; the time needed can range from minutes to hours) (Sovacool, Axsen, and Kempton 2017). It has been estimated that 87 percent of vehicle-days in the United States can be met by charging EVs once a day (Sovacool, Axsen, and Kempton 2017). However, the potential benefits of EVs hinge on how they and VGI relate to other elements of energy infrastructures: distribution grids, storage, generation, social acceptance, and policy support. For example, pollution from total particulate and SOx emissions could increase if EVs are powered by coal-fired power plants (Sovacool, Axsen, and Kempton 2017; IEA 2018). If electricity consumption is increased from thermal power generation, such as coal, natural gas, oil, or nuclear power, in addition to increasing greenhouse gas emissions, this could increase water use for cooling and steam production of these power plants, potentially reducing water availability (Sovacool, Axsen, and Kempton 2017).

These technologies are required to achieve goals of increasing renewable power while also increasing reliability and the efficiency of managing a range of resources.

Grid Flexibility: Implications for Social Scientists

In a review of studies and critiques of a 100 percent renewable energy future, Diesendorf and Elliston (2018) conclude that the key barriers are political, institutional, and cultural, rather than technical or economic. The smart grid elements discussed in trend 3 also raise a number of puzzles for social scientists over the effects on diverse populations and the role of resistance and opposition to these changes. Technocrats and physical scientists often underestimate the implementation challenges entailed in rapidly shifting human behavior on such a mass scale. The deployment of distributed infrastructure and flexible grid technology depends on whether or not actors are willing to engage with them. Wolsink (2012), along with other social scientists studying the challenges of demand infrastructures, argues that "smart" infrastructures can be used to monitor and control households by utilities, rather than reflexively engage them in managing their energy use in ways that suit their norms, practices, and needs. Hargreaves, Nye, and Burgess (2010, 6118) have also pointed out important social aspects of demand response technologies: "If the wind fails to blow, would households be willing to go to bed in the dark? Forego cooked breakfast and coffee? Not watch Eastenders?" Technology thus provides a means for decision-making transformation but in no way guarantees that practices will adjust to meet targets set centrally, particularly if the end users are not integrated into the design, delivery, and planning of the technological developments early on. One particularly fruitful line of research on the social aspects of household energy use is the degree to which gender is often a neglected part of decision makers' planning, despite the fact that women in many countries tend to play key roles in house-hold energy decision-making, through daytime use patterns in particular (see also Standal et al., this volume; Baruah 2017; Clancy and Roehr 2003; Fraune 2015; Räty and Carlsson-Kanyama 2010).

Social norms, acceptability, and culturally and demographically rooted practices play key roles in how and where densified and "smart" demand technologies will shape actual practices (Verbong, Beemsterboer, and Sengers 2013). Just as new generation infrastruc-ture is too often developed solely from technical and economic perspectives, new smart, flexible grids and EV infrastructure also lack deep social analysis. However, the institu-tional designs come with significant distributional impacts and potential barriers to effectiveness. On this front, Wolsink (2012) argues that a successful rollout requires sociopolitical acceptance (stakeholders, public, policy makers), community acceptance (place, residents, local authorities), and market acceptance (consumers, firms, inves-tors) (827). Furthermore, institutional "lock-ins" for an effective radical infrastructural shift may come from lack of storage capacity, price distortions, or discriminatory system access. Consider, for example, the decisions that are likely to emerge from the develop-ment of the necessary charging networks. A sociotechnical perspective points us not only to the financial and technical aspects of this infrastructure but also to issues of political power, culture, and psychology. Sovacool, Axsen, and Kempton put the chal-lenge of widespread EV uptake as follows: "It must confront an array of obstacles cutting across technical dimensions such as batteries and communication systems, financial ones such as purchase price and first-cost, negative environmental externalities, and behavioral challenges including notions of inconvenience, trust, confusion, and range anxiety" (2017, 399). "Range anxiety" is a psychological phenomenon wherein consum-ers are reluctant to purchase or use EVs because they are worried about running out of power and being stranded. This may push some to stay with hybrid or combustion engine (fossil fuel powered) vehicles, despite initiatives to encourage (financially or oth-erwise) EV uptake. Infrastructures matter, as do the culturally and demographically specific meanings given to those infrastructures.

Among the additional sociopolitical considerations raised by EV and related infrastructures are the distributive challenges related to affordability, access, and ownership. In a context within which many states are bringing in carbon pricing at the same time that EVs are still expensive compared to conventional vehicles, there is a risk of deepening fuel poverty for disadvantaged members of the population. Incentives for EV ownership, such as priority parking, ability to drive in high-occupancy vehicle lanes, and cheap fuel (in the form of electricity), then accrue to society's privileged. Wolsink (2012, 829) also raises interesting questions about who owns and designs the charging infrastructure. For example, will it be designed and run by centralized energy businesses and distributed mainly along roadways, as gas stations are currently, or will it be structured near or in residential areas and owned by local and community resident associations? The answer to this question has implications again for issues of local acceptance, financial cost and benefit distribution, and energy democracy.

CONCLUSION

Electricity grids are machines, infrastructures, cultural artifacts, and sets of both business and social practices (Bakke 2017). This chapter has outlined how the technical aspects of modern electricity infrastructures are constituted, with significant differences among the interconnected areas of power generation, transmission and distribution, storage, and load management. Each of these elements is currently in the process of significant change, but how these changes manifest between distinct social and national contexts is largely dependent on political values, actors, and institutions. Social science researchers represent a growing but still minority voice in the sector more broadly, often dominated by engineers and planners. However, many important questions remain and deserve attention, particularly those that seek to understand the distributive and social justice implications of new grid designs, those that probe the effectiveness of policy mixes for spurring low-carbon transitions, and those that investigate the distinct practices of energy politics and policy in developing and non-Western nations. While we may see the seeds of a radically distributed new grid network, with strong roles for prosumers, local renewable generation, and EVs, these shifts will also entail significant stranded assets for incumbent electricity companies and states that have invested billions in the existing infrastructure. The debates in this area are just beginning in many jurisdictions, and scholars of comparative political economy and public policy will have much to keep them busy.

ACKNOWLEDGMENTS

The authors thank research associate Susan Wyse for bringing the content of Figures 4.1, 4.2, and 4.3 to life.

NOTE

1. A significant debate exists about the life cycle analysis (LCA) impact of various technologies, which vary significantly over time, geography, materials used, project boundary, and other assumptions made by researchers. For a discussion of these issues see Turconi (2013) on the importance of integrating three distinct life-cycle phases (fuel, plant operation, and infrastructure); Heath and Mann (2012) on the importance of large-scale reviews of LCA analyses; Hertwich et al. (2015)for a systemwide, as opposed to facility-based, LCA approach; and Pehl et al. (2017) for a large-scale comparative LCA that incorporates energy, economy, and land-use modeling to 2050.

REFERENCES

Agyeman, Julian, Robert Bullard, and Bob Evans. 2003. *Just Sustainabilities: Development in an Unequal World*. Cambridge, MA: MIT Press.

Almeida, Aníbal De, Paula Fonseca, Barbara Schlomann, and Nicolai Feilberg. 2011. "Characterization of the Household Electricity Consumption in the EU, Potential Energy Savings and Specific Policy Recommendations." *Energy and Buildings* 43, no. 8: 1884–1894. doi:10.1016/j.enbuild.2011.03.027.

Anderson, John A. 2009. "Electricity Restructuring: A Review of Efforts around the World." *The Electricity Journal* 33, no. 3: 70–86.

Araújo, Kathleen. 2014. "The Emerging Field of Energy Transitions: Progress, Challenges, and Opportunities." *Energy Research & Social Science* 1: 112–121. doi:10.1016/j.erss.2014.03.002.

Attari, Shahzeen Z, Michael L. Dekay, Cliff I. Davidson, Wändi Bruine, and De Bruin. 2010. "Supporting information: Public Perceptions of Energy Consumption and Savings." *Proceedings of the National Academy of Sciences of the United States of America* 5. https://www.pnas.org/content/107/37/16054

Bakke, Gretchen. 2017. *The Grid: The Fraying Wires Between Americans and Our Energy Future*. New York: Bloomsbury Academic.

Bargh, Maria. 2012. "Rethinking and Re-shaping Indigenous Economies: Māori Geothermal Energy Enterprises." *Journal of Enterprising Communities: People and Places in the Global Economy* 6, no. 3: 271–283. doi:10.1108/17506201211258423.

Baruah, Bipasha. 2017. "Renewable Inequity? Women's Employment in Clean Energy in Industrialized, Emerging and Developing Countries." In *Climate Change and Gender in Rich Countries: Work, Public Policy and Action*, edited by Marjorie Griffin Cohen, 70–86. New York: Routledge.

Beder, Sharon. 2003. *Power Play: The Fight to Control the World's Electricity*. New York: The New Press.

Boyle, Godfrey, ed. 2012. *Renewable Energy: Power for A Sustainable Future*. 3rd ed. Oxford: Oxford University Press.

Bradford, Alina. 2017. "Watts vs. Lumens: How to Choose the Right LED Light Bulb." CNET. https://www.cnet.com/how-to/watts-vs-lumens-how-to-choose-the-right-led-light-bulb/.

Bridge, Gavin, Stefan Bouzarovski, Michael Bradshaw, and Nick Eyre. 2013. "Geographies of Energy Transition: Space, Place and the Low-Carbon Economy." *Energy Policy* 53: 331–340. doi:10.1016/j.enpol.2012.10.066.

Bruckner, T., I. A. Bashmakov, Y. Mulugetta, H. Chum, A. de la Vega Navarro, J. Edmonds, A. Faaij, et al. 2014. "Energy Systems." In *IPCC Fifth Assessment Report*, edited by O. Edenhofer,

R. Pichs-Madruga, Y. Sokona, E. Farahani, S. Kadner, K. Seyboth, A. Adler, et al., 527–532. Cambridge, UK, and New York: Cambridge University Press. doi:10.1017/CBO9781107415416.

Burke, Matthew J., and Jennie C. Stephens. 2018. "Political Power and Renewable Energy Futures: A Critical Review." *Energy Research & Social Science* 35 (January): 78–93. doi:10.1016/J.ERSS.2017.10.018.

Castree, Noel. 2004. "Differential Geographies: Place, Indigenous Rights and 'Local' Resources." *Political Geography* 23, no. 2: 133–167. doi:10.1016/J.POLGEO.2003.09.010.

Chilvers, Jason, and Noel Longhurst. 2016. "Participation in Transition(s): Reconceiving Public Engagements in Energy Transitions as Co-Produced, Emergent and Diverse." *Journal of Environmental Policy & Planning* 18, no. 5: 585–607. doi:10.1080/1523908X.2015.1110483.

Clancy, Joy, and Ulrike Roehr. 2003. "Gender and Energy: Is There a Northern Perspective?" *Energy for Sustainable Development* 7, no. 3: 44–49. doi:10.1016/S0973-0826(08)60364-6.

Cohen, Marjorie Griffin. 2006. "Electricity Restructuring's Dirty Secret." In *Nature's Revenge: Reclaiming Sustainability in an Age of Corporate Globalization*, edited by Josée Johnston, Michael Gismondi, and James Goodman. Canada, Peterborough: Broadview Press, 73–95.

Creutzig, Felix, Blanca Fernandez, Helmut Haberl, Radhika Khosla, Yacob Mulugetta, and Karen C. Seto. 2016. "Beyond Technology: Demand-Side Solutions for Climate Change Mitigation." *Annual Review of Environment and Resources* 41, no. 1: 173–198. doi:10.1146/annurev-environ-110615-085428.

Day, Rosie, Gordon Walker, and Neil Simcock. 2016. "Conceptualising Energy Use and Energy Poverty Using a Capabilities Framework." *Energy Policy* 93 (June): 255–264. doi:10.1016/J.ENPOL.2016.03.019.

Devine-Wright, Patrick. 2011. *Renewable Energy and the Public: From NIMBY to Participation*. London: Earthscan.

Diesendorf, Mark, and Ben Elliston. 2018. "The Feasibility of 100% Renewable Electricity Systems: A Response to Critics." *Renewable and Sustainable Energy Reviews* 93 (October): 318–330. doi:10.1016/J.RSER.2018.05.042.

Everett, Bob, Godfrey Boyle, Stephen Peake, and Janet Ramage, eds. 2012. *Energy Systems and Sustainability: Power for a Sustainable Future*. 2nd ed. Oxford: Oxford University Press.

Fraune, C. 2015. Gender matters: Women, renewable energy and citizen participation in Germany. Energy Research and Social Science 7: 55–65.

Gan, Jianbang, and C. T. Smith. 2011. "Drivers for Renewable Energy: A Comparison Among OECD Countries." *Biomass and Bioenergy* 35, no. 11: 4497–4503.

Geels, Frank W. 2014. "Regime Resistance against Low-Carbon Transitions: Introducing Politics and Power into the Multi-Level Perspective." *Theory, Culture & Society* 31, no. 5: 21–40. doi:10.1177/0263276414531627.

Goldemberg, J., T. B. Johansson, and D. Anderson. 2004. *World Energy Assessment: Overview 2004 Update*. New York: United Nations Development Programme, United Nations Department of Economic and Social Affairs, World Energy Council. https://www.undp.org/content/undp/en/home/librarypage/environment-energy/sustainable_energy/world_energy_assessmentoverview2004update.html.

Greenblatt, J. B., Brown, N. R., Slaybaugh, R., Wilks, T., & Mccoy, S. T. (2017). The Future of Low-Carbon Electricity. *Annual Review of Environment and Resources*, 42, 289–316. doi:10.1146/annurev-environ

Hargreaves, Tom, Michael Nye, and Jacquelin Burgess. 2010. "Making Energy Visible: A Qualitative Field Study of How Householders Interact with Feedback from Smart Energy Monitors." *Energy Policy* 38, no. 10: 6111–6119. doi:10.1016/J.ENPOL.2010.05.068.

Hausman, William J., Peter Hertner, and Mira Wilkins. 2008. *Global Electrification: Multinational Enterprise and International Finance in the History of Light and Power 1878–2007*. Cambridge MA: Cambridge University Press.

Heath, Garvin A., and Margaret K. Mann. 2012. "Background and Reflections on the Life Cycle Assessment Harmonization Project." *Journal of Industrial Ecology* 16 (April): S8–S11. doi:10.1111/j.1530-9290.2012.00478.x.

Hertwich, Edgar G., Thomas Gibon, Evert A. Bouman, Anders Arvesen, Sangwon Suh, Garvin A. Heath, Joseph D. Bergesen, Andrea Ramirez, Mabel I. Vega, and Lei Shi. 2015. "Integrated Life-Cycle Assessment of Electricity-Supply Scenarios Confirms Global Environmental Benefit of Low-Carbon Technologies." *Proceedings of the National Academy of Sciences of the United States of America* 112, no. 20: 6277–6282. doi:10.1073/pnas.1312753111.

Hess, David J. 2014. "Sustainability Transitions: A Political Coalition Perspective." *Research Policy* 43, no. 2: 278–283. doi:10.1016/J.RESPOL.2013.10.008.

Hoicka, Christina E., and Julie L. MacArthur. 2018. "From Tip to Toes: Mapping Community Energy Models in Canada and New Zealand." *Energy Policy* 121 (October): 162–174.

Hoicka, Christina E., and Ian H. Rowlands. 2011. "Solar and Wind Resource Complementarity: Advancing Options for Renewable Electricity Integration in Ontario, Canada." *Renewable Energy* 36, no. 1: 97–107. doi:10.1016/j.renene.2010.06.004.

International Electrotechnical Commission. 2011. "Electrical Energy Storage—White Paper." doi:10.1002/bse.3280020501.

International Energy Agency (IEA). 2017. "World Energy Outlook 2017." Paris. 1–15. doi:10.1016/0301-4215(73)90024-4.

International Energy Agency (IEA). 2018. "Global EV Outlook 2018." Paris. https://www.iea.org/gevo2018/

IPCC Working Group III. 2014. "Summary for Policymakers." Presented at Climate Change 2014: Mitigation of Climate Change; Contribution of Working Group III to the Fifth Assessment Report of the Intergovernmental Panel on Climate Change, 1–33. doi:10.1017/CBO9781107415324.

International Renewable Energy Agency (IRENA). 2017a. "Renewable Power: Sharply Falling Generation Costs." https://www.irena.org/-/media/Files/IRENA/Agency/Publication/2017/Nov/IRENA_Sharply_falling_costs_2017.pdf.

International Renewable Energy Agency (IRENA). 2017b. "Statistics Time Series Trends in Renewable Energy." International Renewable Energy Agency. 2017. http://resourceirena.irena.org/gateway/dashboard/?topic=4&subTopic=16.

Jaccard, M., L. Failing, and T. Berry. 1997. "From Equipment to Infrastructure: Community Energy Management and Greenhouse Gas Emission Reduction." *Energy Policy* 25: 1065–1074.

Kroon, Bianca Van Der, Roy Brouwer, and Pieter J. H. Van Beukering. 2013. "The Energy Ladder: Theoretical Myth or Empirical Truth? Results from a Meta-Analysis." *Renewable and Sustainable Energy Reviews* 20: 504–513. doi:10.1016/j.rser.2012.11.045.

Kuzemko, Caroline. 2016. "Energy Depoliticisation in the UK: Destroying Political Capacity." *The British Journal of Politics and International Relations* 18, no. 1: 107–124. doi:10.1111/1467-856X.12068.

Kuzemko, Caroline, Catherine Mitchell, Matthew Lockwood, and Richard Hoggett. 2017. "Policies, Politics and Demand Side Innovations: The Untold Story of Germany's Energy Transition." *Energy Research & Social Science* 28 (June): 58–67. doi:10.1016/J.ERSS.2017.03.013.

MacArthur, Julie L. 2016. *Empowering Electricity: Co-Operatives, Sustainability, and Power Sector Reform in Canada*. Vancouver: University of British Columbia Press.

MacArthur, Julie L., and Steve Matthewman. 2018. "Populist Resistance and Alternative Transitions: Indigenous Ownership of Energy Infrastructure in Aotearoa New Zealand." *Energy Research & Social Science* 43. doi:10.1016/j.erss.2018.05.009

Martinot, Eric. 2016. "Grid Integration of Renewable Energy: Flexibility, Innovation, and Experience." *Annual Review of Environment and Resources* 41, no. 1: 223–251. doi:10.1146/annurev-environ-110615-085725.

Mcfarlane, Colin, and Jonathan Rutherford. 2008. "Political Infrastructures: Governing and Experiencing the Fabric of the City." *International Journal of Urban and Regional Research* 32, no. 2: 363–374. doi:10.1111/j.1468-2427.2008.00792.x.

Menezes, A. C., A. Cripps, R. A. Buswell, J. Wright, and D. Bouchlaghem. 2014. "Estimating the Energy Consumption and Power Demand of Small Power Equipment in Office Buildings." *Energy and Buildings* 75: 199–209. doi:10.1016/j.enbuild.2014.02.011.

Mey, Franziska, and Mark Diesendorf. 2017. "Who Owns an Energy Transition? Strategic Action Fields and Community Wind Energy in Denmark." *Energy Research & Social Science* (October). doi:10.1016/J.ERSS.2017.10.044.

Middlemiss, Lucie, and Ross Gillard. 2015. "Fuel Poverty from the Bottom-up: Characterising Household Energy Vulnerability through the Lived Experience of the Fuel Poor." *Energy Research & Social Science* 6 (March): 146–154. doi:10.1016/J.ERSS.2015.02.001.

Oreskes, Naomi, and Erik Conway. 2010. *Merchants of Doubt*. New York: Bloomsbury Academic.

Organisation for Economic Co-operation and Development (OECD). 2015. "Climate Change Mitigation—Policies and Progress—En." Paris. 2015. doi:10.1787/9789264238787-en.

Owens, Susan. 1986. *Energy, Planning and Urban Form*. London, UK: Pion Limited.

Owens, Susan. 1992. "Land-Use Planning for Energy Efficiency." *Applied Energy* 43: 81–114.

Palensky, Peter, and Friederich Kupzog. 2013. "Smart Grids." *Annual Review of Environment and Resources* 38: 201–226. doi:10.1146/annurev-environ-031312-102947.

Pasqualetti, Martin J. 2012. "Reading the Changing Energy Landscape." In *Sustainable Energy Landscapes. Designing, Planning and Development*, edited by Sven Stremke and Andy van den Dobbelsteen, 11–44. New York: CRC Press, Taylor & Francis Group. http://ebookcentral.proquest.com/lib/york/reader.action?docID=1019592&ppg=31.

Pehl, Michaja, Anders Arvesen, Florian Humpenöder, Alexander Popp, Edgar G. Hertwich, and Gunnar Luderer. 2017. "Understanding Future Emissions from Low-Carbon Power Systems by Integration of Life-Cycle Assessment and Integrated Energy Modelling." *Nature Energy* 2, no. 12: 939–945. doi:10.1038/s41560-017-0032-9.

Pollution Probe and Center for Urban Energy. 2015. "Electric Mobility Adoption and Prediction (EMAP) Informing the Development of an Electric Vehicle Deployment Strategy for the City of Toronto." Pollution Probe. https://www.pollutionprobe.org/publications/electric-mobility-adoption-and-prediction-emap-toronto/

Räty, R., and A. Carlsson-Kanyama. 2010. "Energy Consumption by Gender in Some European Countries." *Energy Policy* 38, no. 1: 646–649. doi:10.1016/J.ENPOL.2009.08.010.

Rezaie, Behnaz, and Marc A. Rosen. 2012. "District Heating and Cooling: Review of Technology and Potential Enhancements." *Applied Energy* 93: 2–10. doi:10.1016/j.apenergy.2011.04.020.

Schlomer, Steffen, Thomas Brukner, Lew Fulton, Edgar Hertwich, Alan McKinnon, Daniel Perczyk, Joyashreee Roy, et al. 2014. "Technology-Specific Cost and Performance Parameters." In *Climate Change 2014: Mitigation of Climate Change. Contribution of Working Group III to the Fifth Assessment Report of the Intergovernmental Panel on Climate Change*, edited by O. Edenhofer, R. Pichs-Madruga, Y. Sokona, E. Farahani, S. Kadner, K. Seyboth, A. Adler, et al. Cambridge, UK: Cambridge University Press. https://www.ipcc.ch/site/assets/uploads/2018/02/ipcc_wg3_ar5_annex-iii.pdf

Scholten, Daniel, and Rick Bosman. 2016. "The Geopolitics of Renewables; Exploring the Political Implications of Renewable Energy Systems." *Technological Forecasting and Social Change* 103 (February): 273–283. doi:10.1016/J.TECHFORE.2015.10.014.

Schroth, Olaf, Ellen Pond, Rory Tooke, David Flanders, and Stephen Sheppard. 2012. "Spatial Modeling for Community Renewable Energy Planning: Case Studies in British Columbia, Canada." In *Sustainable Energy Landscapes: Designing, Planning and Development*, edited by Sven Stremke and Andy van den Dobbelsteen, 311–312. New York: CRC Press, Taylor & Francis Group.

Schumacher, E. F. 1973. *Small Is Beautiful?: A Study of Economics as If People Mattered*. London: Blond and Briggs.

Seto, Karen C., Steven J. Davis, Ronald B. Mitchell, Eleanor C. Stokes, Gregory Unruh, and Diana Ürge-Vorsatz. 2016. "Carbon Lock-In: Types, Causes, and Policy Implications." *Annual Review of Environment and Resources* 41, no. 1: 425–452. doi:10.1146/annurev-environ-110615-085934.

Sheer, Herman. 2007. *Energy Autonomy*. London: Earthscan.

Sims, R., P. Mercado, W. Krewitt, G. Bhuyan, D. Flynn, H. Holttinen, G. Jannuzzi, S. Khennas, Y. Liu, M. O'Malley, et al., 2011. "Integration of Renewable Energy into Present and Future Energy Systems". In *IPCC Special Report on Renewable Energy Sources and Climate Change Mitigation*, edited by O. Edenhofer, R. Pichs-Madruga, Y. Sokona, K. Seyboth, P. Matschoss, S. Kadner, T. Zwickel, P. Eickemeier, G. Hansen, S. Schlömer, and C. von Stechow. Cambridge, UK and New York: Cambridge University Press. https://www.ipcc.ch/site/assets/uploads/2018/03/Chapter-8-Integration-of-Renewable-Energy-into-Present-and-Future-Energy-Systems-1.pdf

Smil, Vaclav. 2006. *Energy: Beginner's Guide*. Oxford: Oneworld Publications.

Smil, Vaclav. 2016. *Power Density: A Key to Understanding Energy Sources and Uses*. Paperback. Cambridge, MA: MIT Press.

Sovacool, Benjamin K. 2014. "What Are We Doing Here? Analyzing Fifteen Years of Energy Scholarship and Proposing a Social Science Research Agenda." *Energy Research & Social Science* 1 (March): 1–29. doi:10.1016/J.ERSS.2014.02.003.

Sovacool, Benjamin K., Jonn Axsen, and Willett Kempton. 2017. "The Future Promise of Vehicle-to-Grid (V2G) Integration: A Sociotechnical Review and Research Agenda." *Annual Review of Environment and Resources* 42: 377–406.

Spitz, Laura. 2005. "The Gift of Enron: An Opportunity to Talk about Capitalism, Equality, Globalization, and the Promise of a North-American Charter of Fundamental Rights." *Ohio State Law Journal* 66: 315–396.

Stratfor. 2018. "Forecasting the Geopolitics of Renewable Energy." https://worldview.stratfor.com/article/how-renewable-energy-will-change-geopolitics.

Sullivan, Michael J., Matthew Mercurio, Josh Schellenberg, and Sullivan & Co. Freeman. 2015. "Estimated Value of Service Reliability for Electric Utility Customers in the United States." *Lawrence Berkeley National Laboratory* 1–51. https://emp.lbl.gov/publications/estimated-value-service-reliability.

Szulecki, Kacper. 2018. "Conceptualizing Energy Democracy." *Environmental Politics* 27, no. 1: 21–41. doi:10.1080/09644016.2017.1387294.

Tobin, Paul, Nicole M. Schmidt, Jale Tosun, and Charlotte Burns. 2018. "Mapping States' Paris Climate Pledges: Analysing Targets and Groups at COP 21." *Global Environmental Change* 48 (January): 11–21. doi:10.1016/J.GLOENVCHA.2017.11.002.

Toronto Hydro, Hydro One, IESO, and Ontario Power Authority. 2014. "Central Toronto Integrated Regional Resource Plan (IRRP) Introduction to the Engagement and IRRP Overview."

Turconi, Roberto, Alessio Boldrin, and Thomas Astrup. 2013. "Life Cycle Assessment (LCA) of Electricity Generation Technologies: Overview, Comparability and Limitations." *Renewable and Sustainable Energy Reviews* 28 (December): 555–565. doi:10.1016/J.RSER.2013.08.013.

UN Habitat. 2016. "World Cities Report 2016—Urbanization and Development: Emerging Futures." doi:10.1016/S0264-2751(03)00010-6. Retrieved from http://wcr.unhabitat.org/main-report/

US Department of Energy. 2011. "Buying an Energy-Efficient Electric Motor." Motor Challenge Program. https://energy.gov/sites/prod/files/2014/04/f15/mc-0382.pdf.

US Energy Information Administratrion (US EIA). 2017. "How Much Electricity Does a Nuclear Power Plant Generate?" https://www.eia.gov/tools/faqs/faq.php?id=104&t=3.

US Energy Information Administratrion (US EIA). 2018. "U.S. Energy Mapping System." https://www.eia.gov/state/maps.php?v=Coal.

Veelen, Bregje van. 2018. "Negotiating Energy Democracy in Practice: Governance Processes in Community Energy Projects." *Environmental Politics* 27, no. 4: 644–665. doi:10.1080/096 44016.2018.1427824.

Veelen, Bregje van, and Dan van der Horst. 2018. "What Is Energy Democracy? Connecting Social Science Energy Research and Political Theory." *Energy Research & Social Science* 46 (December): 19–28. doi:10.1016/j.erss.2018.06.010.

Verbong, Geert P. J., Sjouke Beemsterboer, and Frans Sengers. 2013. "Smart Grids or Smart Users? Involving Users in Developing a Low Carbon Electricity Economy." *Energy Policy* 52 (January): 117–125. doi:10.1016/J.ENPOL.2012.05.003.

Victor, David, and Thomas C. Heller. 2007. *The Political Economy of Power Sector Reform.* Cambridge, UK: Cambridge University Press.

Walker, Gordon. 2011. "The Role for 'Community' in Carbon Governance." *Wiley Interdisciplinary Reviews: Climate Change* 2, no. 5: 777–782. doi:10.1002/wcc.137.

Walker, Gordon, and Patrick Devine-Wright. 2008. "Community Renewable Energy: What Should It Mean?" *Energy Policy* 36, no. 2: 497–500.

Wolsink, Maarten. 2012. "The Research Agenda on Social Acceptance of Distributed Generation in Smart Grids: Renewable as Common Pool Resources." *Renewable and Sustainable Energy Reviews* 2, no. 16: 822–835.

World Bank. 2019. "Enterprise Surveys Dataset. Power Outages in Firms in a Typical Month (Number)." https://data.worldbank.org/indicator/IC.ELC.OUTG.

Yardley, Jim, and Gardiner Harris. 2012. "2nd Day of Power Failures Cripples Wide Swath of India." *New York Times*, July 31https://www.nytimes.com/2012/08/01/world/asia/power-outages-hit-600-million-in-india.html?_r=2.

Yeager, Kurt E. 2004. "Electricity for the 21st Century?: Digital Electricity for a Digital Economy." *Technology in Society* 26: 209–221. doi:10.1016/j.techsoc.2004.01.031.

CHAPTER 5

....

OIL AND GAS INFRASTRUCTURE

A Technical Overview

....

TIMOTHY C. COBURN

INFRASTRUCTURE is the life blood of the energy industry. It enables the movement and transport of energy products to markets and customers. The fluidity and volatility of energy products and the special requirements for storing, managing, and handling them prompt additional concerns and considerations related to health, safety, and the environment (HSE) that directly impact the way infrastructure is conceived, valued, constructed, and regulated. The energy value chain begins below the surface in parts of the earth that cannot be fully visualized, even with today's sophisticated measurement technology, and it intersects with almost every surface geography, including cities, rural farmland, nature preserves, oceans and waterways, and all points in between.

Infrastructure drives the economic engine of the energy industry. Both the upstream sector, which encompasses oil and gas exploration and production, and the downstream sector, which is engaged in refining and transforming produced hydrocarbons into consumer products and delivering them to the point of sale, require significant infrastructure. The midstream sector, which provides the physical link between the points of production and delivery, is completely dependent on the availability of infrastructure.

Energy markets cannot expand or transform without meaningful infrastructure growth and enhancement. Absent sufficient infrastructure, increased demand at point A cannot be satisfied by supply that exists at point B. The solution is not as simple as rerouting delivery trucks or changing flight schedules. Similarly, if new or additional supply becomes available at point C, but there is insufficient infrastructure to move it to points where demand exists, then the promise of markets cannot be realized.

With global economic and population growth comes increased demand for energy. Despite rapid advances in renewable resources, oil, gas, and other fossil fuels are likely to be part of the overall mix for years to come (see chapters by Tutuncu and Hoicka and MacArthur, in this volume; Davidson and Gross 2018), continuing to boost infrastructure requirements. In the United States alone, oil and gas infrastructure commerce is projected to exceed $80 billion by 2024 (Gupta and Bais 2018), and total investment is expected to balloon to as high as $1.34 trillion by 2035 (Petak et al. 2017).

Oil and gas infrastructure is expensive and time-consuming to develop. Including engineering, procurement, construction, and commissioning, infrastructure can consist of mega projects in size and scope that take years to complete at a cost of hundreds of millions to billions of dollars each. In the United States, most energy companies are privately owned, and the cost of developing new infrastructure is generally borne by the owners. Outside the United States, government entities often own energy companies and directly or indirectly shoulder the cost of infrastructure development and enhancement. Nongovernmental organizations and investors from around the world also help fund infrastructure development (Ernst & Young 2015).

Energy infrastructure is pervasive across the landscape of developed countries. In developing economies such as India, Mexico, and Venezuela, construction of new energy infrastructure is frequently at the forefront of social, political, and economic discourse. The centrality of energy infrastructure is the result of increasing demand brought on by increasing population, improving economic status, greater awareness driven by the proliferation of social media and communications technology, and a rising movement to eliminate energy inequity around the globe. Oil and gas facilities tend to permeate the landscape of many political jurisdictions and often loom large as the most visible icons on the horizon. This situation tells only part of the story, though, because many of the assets exist below ground or along the seafloor.

OVERVIEW

Oil and gas infrastructure is defined here as assets and facilities used to produce, process, refine, store, distribute, and transport energy and its associated resources, fuels, and products around the world (Fullmer 2009; IHS Global 2013; Petak, Manik, and Griffith 2018). Oil and gas infrastructure is perhaps more prevalent in onshore settings, but there are significant offshore elements as well. Some of the most complex and expensive examples are located in marine settings. Further, all infrastructure requires an adequate operating power supply, which may involve the co-location of dedicated or specialized electrical connections or power-generating facilities.

This chapter discusses five specific asset categories: pipelines, refineries, storage tank farms and batteries, liquefied natural gas (LNG) plants and terminals, and offshore drilling and production platforms. A section on rail cars is also included because of the critical role that railroads play in the transportation and distribution of products in North America, Russia, India, and other countries. The chapter also contains brief sections on the digitization of infrastructure, cybersecurity and infrastructure, and infrastructure and the environment. Not addressed here are specialized assets used to develop unconventional hydrocarbon resources, various types of oceangoing vessels, and over-the-road tanker trucks and related motorized carriers.

Because of its dominance in most infrastructure categories, the focus is on the United States, which has the world's longest network of oil and gas pipelines (Dhiraj 2018), the largest refining capacity (Garside 2019b), and the largest number of oil ports (Garside 2018). While other countries such as China and Nigeria are investing heavily in infrastructure (Reportlinker/GlobalData 2019), the United States is expected to remain at the forefront for the foreseeable future.

PIPELINES

Pipelines are the centerpiece of the oil and gas infrastructure complex. Pipelines connect all other facets, serving as the most essential link in the movement of crude oil and natural gas between the points of production and consumption. There are two major classes of pipeline systems: those that transport liquids and those that transport gas. Beyond the point of initial production, gas and oil are not transported through the same type of pipe due to compositional differences. Pipelines are further characterized as gathering systems (networks of flow lines that transport oil and gas from the wellhead to storage and/or processing facilities), transmission systems (cross-country "trunk" lines), or distribution systems (used to deliver gas to end users). In the United States, pipelines can serve intrastate or interstate markets. There are other important distinctions and characterizations as well, such as differences in onshore and offshore pipelines in the United Kingdom and classifications associated with international or transcontinental border crossings.

Liquids pipelines are used to transport crude oil and refined products, such as natural gas liquids (NGLs). They serve as the connectors in the liquids transportation chain, moving crude oil from the wellhead to a gas and crude oil separator, then to a storage tank, and on to a pumping station to maintain flow to reach tankers at oil export ports, rail cars at oil terminals, refineries, or large storage facilities. Refined products leave refineries via different pipelines on their way to similar destinations (e.g., ships/ports, trucks/terminals, storage tanks), from which they are delivered to end users and consumers.

In contrast to liquids pipelines, gas pipeline systems deliver product directly to end users. However, raw gas must first be purified of corrosive constituents and inert gases. In addition, heavier hydrocarbons, such as propane and butane, are removed and handled as separately marketable byproducts. After initial gathering at the wellhead, gas is sent to a processing plant. Processing plants are smaller and more numerous than refineries and are located relatively close to production. These plants may be owned by entities other than the gas producers or pipeline owners and may receive gas from multiple production sites.

In the United States, gathering systems and lines are found primarily in major oil-producing regions, including offshore areas and urban settings. This infrastructure is ubiquitous in other countries as well, although in the Middle East, for example, producing areas are sometimes more distant from urban centers. Generally, gathering lines are comparatively short in length; have small diameters (no more than eighteen inches and generally much less); operate under low pressure (e.g., 700 psi); and often exist as inter-connected networks supporting flow from multiple wells to central collection/storage sites, treatment plants, or processing facilities. Pipelines supporting offshore develop-ment also generally fall into this category. Small-diameter (twelve inches or smaller) "flowlines" operating under low pressure (roughly 250 psi) transport raw production that may contain a mixture of constituents from individual wells to gathering lines (API 2016; Hillier 2017).

Transmission, or "trunk," lines are designed to transport crude oil from producing regions to refineries or points of export located in the same or a different country. Transmission lines also move refined products cross-country or intercontinentally from refineries to major markets and/or points of export. Transmission lines are much longer than gathering lines, have greater pipe diameters (generally eight to twenty-four inches, but sometimes larger), and operate at higher pressures (generally 200–1,200 psi) to maintain flow. Compressors, pressure gauges, valves, regulators, and/or pump stations exist along the route to ensure constant pressure and flow (API 2016; Hillier 2017).

Distribution systems encompass mainlines and service lines used by utility compa-nies to deliver gas to homes and businesses. Service lines are the small-diameter (usually two inches or smaller) connections between meters and customers. Mainlines are intermediate-diameter (two to twenty-four inches) pipes operating at low pressure (generally under 200 psi) that connect trunk lines and service lines (API 2016; Hillier 2017). The points at which mainlines connect to trunk lines are called city gate stations. The key function of these stations is to reduce the incoming gas pressure to satisfy safety regulations as the gas flows into smaller diameter mainline pipes.

Depending on the setting, feeder lines may be regarded as components of gathering systems or of distribution systems. Feeder lines are composed of small-diameter (e.g., six to twelve inches) pipes and tubing that transport products between production sites, terminals, storage tanks, processing facilities, and larger pipeline systems. Feeder lines also sometimes distribute gas to homes and businesses (API 2016; Hillier 2017).

Pipelines are constructed by piecing together sections of pipe or tubing of the same diameter. Most pipelines are assembled by welding together segments of steel pipe in trenches along a preplanned route. If the route intercepts a byway, important topographical feature, or other substantive obstacle, it may be necessary to significantly deepen, divert, or reroute the trench path. Some portions of the assembled pipeline may have different diameters, which affects flow characteristics. Storage facilities can be added at these transitional points to buffer the change in flow, creating a series of intermediate entry and exit points. Such storage facilities may also provide a terminus for redirecting flow into another connecting pipeline. Pumping (oil) and compressor (gas) stations are used to propel the fluids along the pipeline route to maintain flow and pressure.

Except at entry and exit points, onshore pipelines are generally buried in the ground for safety and aesthetic reasons. Offshore pipelines generally traverse along the seafloor. Pipe burial is a regulatory requirement in many countries, with burial depths ranging from three to six feet in most circumstances. The most recognizable above-ground example in the United States is a segment of the Trans-Alaska Pipeline that is constructed on supports to protect the permafrost and other environmentally sensitive parts of the landscape (see Figure 5.1). In developing countries, pipelines may be left above ground or buried at shallow depths due to cost, technology limitations, or other constraints. Unprotected pipelines can lead to environmental and societal complications, including weather impacts, theft, vandalism, and sabotage.

Pipelines operate around the clock. In most countries, the systems are highly automated, with centrally controlled operations for starting and stopping pumps, opening and closing valves, and filling and emptying tanks as required. Supervisory control and data acquisition (SCADA) systems in control rooms continuously monitor pump pressures, flow rates, storage tank levels, and the locations of specific batches of product along the entire route.

Pipeline companies in the United States and Canada are guaranteed revenue so long as products are moving, regardless of commodity price (because once production begins, oil and gas must be transported away from the wellhead by some mechanism, regardless of the cost, or wells must be shut in). Pipelines operate under a fee-based structure based on the volume of product moving along the system. In this sense, they are common carriers, available for hire to transport in exchange for a fee. Pipeline companies are legally bound to transport products as long as there is sufficient space or capacity, the fee is paid, and there are no reasonable grounds for refusal.

FIGURE 5.1 A section of the trans-Alaska pipeline.

Source: US Library of Congress, Carol M. Highsmith Collection.

Another important characteristic is that product flow/shipment is unidirectional. It is possible for lines to be "turned around" in order to reverse the flow, but it is not an automatic or inexpensive process. Other factors—political, economic, or environmental— also impact these initiatives. Kirkwood (2015) discusses various case studies and best practices in pipeline reversal.

In many countries, the pipeline system is owned by the government or government-controlled companies/entities. However, in the United States and Canada, pipelines are constructed, owned, and operated by private or publicly traded companies, most of which operate in the midstream sector. Some vertically integrated oil and gas companies, as well as electric utilities and other organizations, may own and operate pipeline systems to serve their own internal interests.

Eminent domain is often at the forefront of pipeline construction projects. A question of eminent domain arises when operators route pipelines across the private property of individuals who will not voluntarily sell/convey rights-of-way for access and construction purposes. A declaration of eminent domain effectively allows a pipeline owner/operator to seize the property in question for public use at fair market value over the protests of the owner. The principle of eminent domain is exercised to one degree or another in a number of countries under various names, such as expropriation and compulsory acquisition.

In the United States, the authority to invoke eminent domain with regard to oil pipelines rests entirely with state governments (the situation is different for gas pipelines), but for over a century most of them have conveyed this authority to pipeline companies, electric and gas utilities, and other entities that provide energy and transportation services by defining pipelines and related infrastructure as a "public use" under state law. In most cases, pipeline companies are able to obtain the necessary easements through voluntary transactions with landowners.

The extent, size, and total composition of pipeline infrastructure is difficult to gauge due to continuous growth and expansion, as well as inconsistency in the ways that pipelines are categorized (see https://www.cia.gov/library/publications/the-world-factbook/fields/383.html#US). However, the United States, Russia, Canada, and China are generally considered the top four in terms of total length; the United States dominates with nearly ten times more than Russia. In the United States, there are 300,654 miles of gas transmission lines, 18,152 miles of gas gathering lines, and 2,223,089 miles of distribution lines (USPHMSA 2017). While natural gas is the predominant commodity, these figures also include hydrogen, landfill, propane, synthetics, and other gases. In addition, the United States has 3,333 miles of crude oil gathering lines, 79,081 miles of crude oil transmission lines, and 62,349 miles of refined products transmission lines (USPHMSA 2017). Gathering and distribution systems are not associated with the production of refined products.

Regulatory Concerns

Many experts consider pipelines the safest and most efficient way to transport oil and gas. Given the extent of the pipeline networks around the world, the frequency of safety-related incidents is comparatively low. However, because of the volatile and flammable nature of oil, gas, and refined products, there is always the potential for leaks, spills, and explosions to occur. Indeed, there have been a number of such incidents in recent years resulting from pipe ruptures due to corrosion and degradation, excessive pressure buildups, physical encounters with heavy equipment and vehicles, improper/unsupervised/unauthorized excavation, soil erosion, climate/weather impacts, spillover impacts from other accidents or fires, and the like.

In the United States, various federal and state agencies regulate pipelines to ensure safe operations and fair and competitive markets. At the federal level, the Pipeline and Hazardous Materials Safety Administration (PHMSA) in the US Department of Transportation regulates pipeline safety and tracks and reports pipeline-related safety incidents. The PHMSA reported a total of 301 significant pipeline incidents of all types during 2017, resulting in seven fatalities and thirty-three other injuries, at a total cost of about $261.5 million (USPHMSA 2018). The total number reported by PHMSA has been relatively stable over the last twenty years. (See Simmons [2015] for a comprehensive discussion of pipeline safety issues.)

The Federal Energy Regulatory Commission (FERC) and PHMSA regulate interstate pipelines. FERC is responsible for regulating the interstate transmission and sale of natural gas, interstate transportation of oil via pipelines, siting and abandonment of interstate natural gas pipelines and storage facilities, and gas pipeline facilities at import and export locations. FERC's authority extends to eminent domain decisions for interstate gas pipelines. Its jurisdiction is limited to regulation of rates and terms and conditions of service offered by the pipeline companies and the guarantee of equal service conditions to provide shippers with equal access to pipeline transportation. It has no oversight authority for oil pipeline construction or abandonment of service related to oil facilities.

The PHMSA is responsible for regulating, monitoring, and enforcing safety postcommissioning of pipeline projects. Safety compliance inspections are conducted by individual states, whose own requirements must mirror or exceed those of the federal government. (See Pless [2011] for more discussion and a state-by-state listing of regulatory responsibilities.)

Regulation of offshore transmission and gathering lines in federal waters on the Outer Continental Shelf (OCS) falls to the PHMSA/Office of Pipeline Safety or the Bureau of Safety and Environmental Enforcement (BSEE) within the US Department of the Interior. FERC has no responsibility for pipeline transportation or safety in the OCS region.

A variety of other regulatory regimes exist beyond the United States. The European Union, for example, maintains regulatory authority over pipelines crossing international boundaries among its member countries, but each country retains governance of pipelines that exist solely within its own boundaries. In Canada, the division of authority is similar to that of the United States, whereas in Australia, the Australian Energy Regulator maintains regulatory authority in all jurisdictions except Western Australia, where the Economic Regulation Authority retains responsibility. In Mexico, pipeline regulation remains in flux as the country continues to grapple with oil and gas industry reforms, although most authority still rests with the federal government.

Countries sometimes make agreements among themselves regarding the construction, handling, and operation of pipelines that cross borders. There is no single international regulatory agency that governs financial transactions, safety considerations, and related issues (Siddiky 2012). Cross-border pipelines can be economically advantageous to all parties (Cardinale 2019), but they can also spawn political unrest and conflict (Stevens 2009). Stevens (2003) provides an extensive exposé of the challenges, problems, prospects, and case studies associated with cross-border pipelines around the world, though there are some standout cases. Disagreement between the United States and Russia regarding construction of the Nordstream 2 Pipeline into Germany via the Baltic Sea bypassing Ukraine is a current source of international conflict. The Keystone XL Pipeline spanning Canada and the United States created domestic conflict on both sides of the border in the mid-2000s. The Trans-Arabian Pipeline (Tapline) from Dhahran, Saudi Arabia, to Zahrani, Lebanon, was similarly fraught with difficulties throughout its existence (1950–1982) due to the Arab-Israeli conflict (Kaufman 2014).

REFINERIES

Oil refineries are expensive, huge, and somewhat monolithic industrial complexes at which crude oil is transformed into one or more consumer or commercial products, such as gasoline, diesel, heating oil, and jet fuel. Refineries may also produce a variety of petrochemicals used to create other kinds of consumer products, such as plastics. There are 650–700 refineries of various types scattered throughout the world. The largest one is Jamnagar Refinery in Gujarat, India, with a processing capacity of over 1.2 million barrels per day. Five of the ten largest facilities in terms of processing capacity are located in the Texas-Louisiana corridor of the US Gulf Coast (see Figure 5.2). (See https://en.wikipedia.org/wiki/List_of_oil_refineries for a worldwide list of refineries and their capacities.)

In the United States, refineries are owned and operated by private or publicly traded companies, most of which function in the midstream or downstream sectors. Some vertically integrated oil and gas companies, as well as other entities, may own and operate refineries to serve their own internal interests. Delta Airlines made news in 2012 when it purchased the Trainer Refinery in Delaware County, Pennsylvania, through its Monroe Energy subsidiary to provide a reliable source of jet fuel (Mouawad 2012). In many other countries, refineries are owned by the government or government-controlled companies/entities.

With 135 operable refineries, the United States has the largest refining capacity in the world, followed by China, Russia, and India (USEIA 2018; BP 2019). Nonetheless, the total number of US refineries has steadily declined from about 300 in the early 1980s due to a number of economic, technological, and regulatory factors, including high volatility in commodity prices; a change from net exporter to net importer status (followed by a more recent return to net exporter status), requiring changes in the processes and

FIGURE 5.2 An oil refinery in Groves, Texas, near Port Arthur.

Source: US Library of Congress, Carol M. Highsmith Collection.

equipment necessary to accommodate different feedstocks (e.g., light sweet crude to heavy sour crude); the imposition of more stringent emissions and related environmental controls; advancing automation; improvements in automotive fuel economy; and general industry consolidation. Capable of processing approximately 636,000 barrels per day and employing approximately fifteen hundred people, the Port Arthur, Texas, refinery is the largest such facility in North America and among the top ten largest in the world (Motiva 2017). Saudi ownership of the facility ensures an ongoing market for imported Middle East crudes and those of similar quality that are more difficult to refine.

Storage Tank Farms and Batteries

A tank farm/battery is an industrial facility comprising a number of massive cylindrical holding vessels, usually situated entirely above ground, plus auxiliary equipment, such as pumps, meters, and valves, that receives, collects, and stores crude or refined products from pipelines, trucks, rail cars, or marine carriers. Generally, the products are held on a temporary basis until they can be sold, blended, and/or returned to the transportation system for ultimate delivery. Usually constructed of steel, oil tanks come in a variety of types and sizes, with the largest ones holding as much as sixteen million gallons, or 381,000 barrels. (See www.alloiltank.com or https://petrowiki.org/Oil_storage for more details.) Sometimes referred to as depots, terminals, or storage fields, tank farms can be used to temporarily remove products from the transportation system when there is insufficient capacity (i.e., oversupply or excess inventory). Some of the most iconic and recognizable infrastructure assets, tank farms are found in various urban, rural, and remote settings of the political jurisdictions in which oil and gas are produced and are almost always located in close proximity to pipelines, refineries, or ports (see Figure 5.3).

There are about forty-nine hundred tank farms/terminals of all types located across 161 countries (https://www.tankterminals.com, 2019), with nearly half located in North America (MapSearch 2019). As with refineries, some of the largest are located along the Texas and Louisiana Gulf Coast. The most extensive is in Cushing, Oklahoma, which serves as the primary point of convergence for most oil pipelines in the United States. The approximately three hundred storage tanks located at Cushing are owned by several different companies and can collectively hold eighty to eighty-five million barrels of product. The storage capacity at Cushing is almost as large as the total storage capacity of Canada (Oil Sands Magazine 2019), and more tanks are being added every year (Money 2018). The Louisiana Offshore Oil Port (LOOP), the second largest storage entity in the United States, serves as the primary point of entry for offloading oil imported via maritime carriers, as well as oil produced in the Gulf of Mexico. Another significant tank farm is the thirty-million-barrel facility at St. James, Louisiana, which serves as part of the US Department of Energy's Strategic Petroleum Reserve.

FIGURE 5.3 An aerial view of Savannah, Georgia, showing oil storage tanks along the Savannah River.

Source: US Library of Congress, Carol M. Highsmith Collection.

Natural gas is typically stored underground in depleted reservoirs, aquifers, or salt formations/caverns (USEIA 2015). Such facilities are connected by pipelines plus associated surface equipment such as valves, compressors, and other control mechanisms. Although less common, gas can also be stored above ground in tanks, gasometers (or gasholders, which are more commonly found in Europe), and pipelines. Gas storage tanks are considerably different in size, shape, scope, and construction than their oil tank cousins because of the compositional differences in the two fluids. Tanks are most commonly used to store gas in its liquefied state.

LNG Plants and Terminals

The purpose for liquefying natural gas is to enhance its storability and transportability. When liquefied, the volume of natural gas is reduced, and it can be transported to markets around the world by special tankers and marine vessels. LNG can also be transported over land by trucks and rail cars.

Excess natural gas supply, particularly in the Middle East, and resources stemming from the "shale gas revolution" in the United States have increased the potential for markets in other parts of the world, but only to the extent that the gas can be transported to those locations. This situation has spurred significant growth in global infrastructure to support exports and imports of natural gas commodities. Specifically, because extensive transoceanic pipeline systems are not feasible, intercontinental transportation of gas between nonadjoining countries via conventional technology is not an economically viable proposition. Hence, alternative means must be developed to move the supply to the most important points of demand. Recently, significant investment has been directed to developing LNG infrastructure around the globe.

LNG infrastructure comprises import/export terminals; storage facilities; specially equipped tankers; berthing and mooring facilities for tankers; and associated offloading/onloading mechanisms, connecting lines, meters, valves, and control equipment. On the export end, natural gas is received from the point of production via pipeline and is liquefied or condensed in a liquefaction plant/terminal by significantly lowering its temperature. LNG is then loaded onto tankers and shipped to commercial ports. On the import end, LNG is received and offloaded from tankers, regasified at a regasification plant/terminal by raising its temperature, and then sent via pipeline to end-use customers (e.g., power plants). Sufficient storage (e.g., refrigerated/cryogenic LNG containment tanks) must be available at both the export and import locations.

The liquefaction and regasification processes are complex, involving a number of phases, special equipment/technology, and significant handling and safety precautions. Liquefaction involves four main steps: pretreatment, acid gas removal and dehydration, removal of heavy hydrocarbons via fractionation, and separation and liquefaction (Cameron LNG 2017). An LNG liquefaction and purification facility is typically referred to as an "LNG train." The term "train" pertains to the turbines, compressors, and related equipment employed sequentially during the conversion process. Regasification is accomplished by passing LNG through a heat exchanger using sea water. Regasification plants can be situated onshore or can be mounted on floating barges that can be towed to various sites. Barge-mounted facilities are referred to as floating regasification units (FRUs) and floating storage and regasification units (FSRUs) if storage is involved. (See GIIGNL [n.d.] and Adesina et al. [2017] for more about the LNG process chain.)

There are 152 active LNG plants operating in the United States, along with 228 LNG tanks (USPHMSA 2017). Most of these plants help optimize natural gas distribution throughout the country. Today, there are only two commercial liquefaction terminals fully operational in the United States: Cheniere Energy Partners' Sabine Pass facility in Cameron Pass, Louisiana, and Dominion Energy's Cove Point facility on Chesapeake Bay in Lusby, Maryland. These two facilities supply all LNG exports in the lower forty-eight states. A number of other facilities have been approved and are in various construction and engineering stages (Stern 2018), with most being located in the Texas-Louisiana Gulf Coast region. Due to the cost, size, and complexity of LNG liquefaction facilities, expansion and greenfield development can take years to complete and are constrained by the economics of commodity prices, shipping costs, and other market forces.

LNG is a more robust business venture outside of the United States, with commensurately more focus on infrastructure. There are approximately forty liquefaction terminals located in just under twenty countries in Asia, the Middle East, South America, Europe, and Australia. The top ten LNG exporters in terms of volume are Qatar, Australia, Malaysia, Nigeria, Indonesia, Algeria, Russia, Trinidad, Oman, and Papua New Guinea (Frangoul 2017; Hall 2017). Further, there are more than one hundred regasification terminals, the largest concentration of which are in Japan and China. Many more facilities are in the planning and approval stages, but none of these are likely to materialize without favorable project economics tied to commodity and transportation pricing.

In addition to these land-based facilities, the worldwide LNG tanker fleet consists of 478 ships and vessels, including conventional craft acting as FSRUs (IGU 2018). The first floating liquefaction (FLNG) project became operational during 2017 in Malaysia (IGU 2018). (See IGU [2018] for more about LNG markets and infrastructure.)

LNG bunkering involves outfitting watergoing vessels with the capability to transport and deliver LNG as fuel to other marine vessels for their own purposes, a process similar to that of midair refueling of aircraft. The delivery vessels require special equipment to upload LNG at docks and ports along waterways, hold/store the fuel until the destination vessels are encountered, and then offload the LNG to the receiving craft. The practice can encompass ship-to-ship, terminal-to-ship, and truck-to-ship operations, allowing both oceangoing ships and river-navigating boats to be refueled mid-voyage. As such, it promises to expand the use of LNG as a marine fuel. Bunkering is most commonly practiced in northern Europe (Pitpoint 2019) but is beginning to filter its way into maritime operations in Southeast Asia and the United States.

RAIL CARS

Rail transportation provides a significant alternative to pipelines for moving oil and refined products, particularly when pipelines are inaccessible or capacity is unavailable. Rail cars may also serve as temporary oil storage facilities but are not yet viable for transporting natural gas, either in compressed or liquefied form.

While rail transportation of oil is notably a North American phenomenon, other countries such as Russia and India also include rail as part of their petroleum transportation portfolios and have done so for years. In the late 1990s, for example, approximately 40 percent of refined products and crude oil was shipped by rail in India (Malhotra 1997). As the "shale revolution" evolved in the United States and Canada, the railroads in those countries became major players in the transportation of crude oil out of the Williston Basin region of North Dakota and Montana because a viable pipeline network did not exist. With additional pipelines, dependence on rail transportation is diminishing in the United States. Rail shipment remains one of the most operationally efficient means to transport oil out of Canada, but the economics of doing so are highly dependent on commodity prices (Yourex-West 2019).

In the United States, rail cars, also known as tanker cars, typically carry about thirty thousand gallons (about 715 barrels) of crude oil each. Only certain types of rail cars are allowed to transport crude oil. Previously two types of cars, known as DOT-111s (or TC-111s in Canada) and CPC-1232s, were used to transport oil, ethanol, natural gas liquids, and other volatile commodities, but after a series of accidents in the mid-2000s, these were ultimately banned. The type of rail car now in use is labeled DOT-117 (or TC-117 in Canada), and such units must adhere to rigid safety standards set by the US and Canadian governments.

Rails and railway rights-of-way are part of a multipurpose asset class called "shared infrastructure" (USDOE 2015), assets that in the United States and Canada belong to publicly traded companies. In many cases the cars, or rolling stock, are owned by the railroads, and oil producers pay them a shipping fee in much the same way that an individual might pay Federal Express to ship a Christmas package. However, some energy companies purchase their own cars and pay the railroads a toll for access to rails (similar to airlines paying landing fees to airports). Alternatively, energy companies may lease cars or participate in a variety of other transportation arrangements. In addition, onboarding and offloading terminals are situated at specific locations along the route of the track, complete with storage facilities (see Figure 5.4). There are approximately 130 such terminals in the United States providing rail-to-rail, rail-to-pipe, or transloading capabilities, most of which are privately owned and/or publicly traded by entities other than the railroads (OpenDataSoft 2014) and may simultaneously serve other purposes.

Rail transportation offers a number of advantages, particularly in the United States, where railroads provide direct access to every refinery. Rail transportation

FIGURE 5.4 Offshore oil platform, floating storage unit, and shuttle vessels.

Source: © Kanok Sulaiman/123RF

affords the flexibility to shift delivery of products on relatively short notice to accommodate market opportunities and customer demand. In addition, track can be laid and/or rerouted much more quickly than pipelines if the need arises, leading to a relatively fast response to infrastructure investment requirements. Rail transportation also satisfies the demands of some producers to deliver "pure barrels," that is, volumes that have not been mixed with those from other sources in a pipeline. Although slower, rail transportation may be cost effective relative to some other modes of transportation.

In recent years the safety of transporting oil by rail has been an important concern. Long trains of rail cars fully loaded with volatile products passing through urban centers to terminals or ports can pose problems. High-profile accidents in North America involving tanker cars continue to dampen the public's appetite for this kind of industrial activity, despite significant new safety regulations. Indeed, rail transportation is now one of the most highly regulated business ventures across the continent. The Federal Railroad Administration (FRA), the PHMSA, and the Transportation Security Administration (TSA) (all agencies within the US Department of Transportation) share in the regulation of railroads, including the physical assets themselves and the movement of hazardous materials (HAZMAT). Transport Canada performs similar tasks in Canada. (See Simmons [2015] for more about safety issues surrounding the transportation of oil by rail.)

Offshore Drilling and Production Platforms

Offshore oil platforms are massive industrial structures that are connected to the seafloor in a way that facilitates exploring for, producing, storing, and processing oil and natural gas found in rock formations beneath the seabed. They may comprise singular structures or incorporate multiple pods or modules connected by bridges and other infrastructure. For example, the main platform or another module may contain residential facilities for the on-site workforce, with separate modules to accommodate drilling, processing, and power supply. The "topsides" facilities (main upper-level deck outside the splash zone) generally house a wide array of machinery, equipment, and amenities such as pumps, compressors, valves, a control room, a gas flare stack, revolving cranes, risers, survival craft, power generating equipment, docking units for marine shuttle craft, and a helicopter pad, in addition to specialized tools, instruments, and apparatus used in drilling and production.

Other kinds of equipment, machinery, fixtures, and tools associated with drilling, producing, and maintaining wells are found in the well bay, a work area below the topsides deck immediately under the drilling apparatus. These items typically include "Christmas trees": mechanical assemblages of valves, fittings, meters, and sensors used to control well flow, monitor various well performance characteristics, and conduct necessary interventions (e.g., blowout preventers, risers, production manifolds and separators, motors, pumps, piping outlets, flowlines). The drilling floor itself features the drilling apparatus, stacks of drill pipe, a collection of drill bits, drill collars, various fluid diverter and separator lines, storage tanks for mud and water, kill and choke lines to prevent blowouts, and so forth. A platform may have a single well bay that accommodates one or more wellheads, or there may be an additional well bay if a second drilling apparatus is present.

A wide variety of offshore assemblages can be collectively referred to as "platforms." Some are fixed in place using concrete or steel pilings anchored into the seabed and are essentially immobile and intended to remain at their locations for a very long time. Some can float but be linked with tie lines or flow lines to the seafloor (e.g., floating production, storage, and offloading systems [FPSOs], or floating storage and offloading systems [FSOs]). Floating units, which may have a ship-like appearance, are maneuvered to a location and moored there for an extended period of time but are not necessarily used for drilling purposes. Other assemblages include compliant towers, semisubmersibles, jack-up drilling rigs, drill ships, tension-leg units, spars, and gravity-based structures. (See Roach [2014] and Singh [2016] for more details.) Selection of the type of platform depends on a number of factors, including overall environmental conditions, water depth, wave height, prevailing winds, ocean currents, susceptibility to extreme climate events, condition of the seafloor, length of use, and intended purpose.

Produced fluids are generally transported through pipeline systems or shuttle tankers. If shuttle tankers are used, the platform must be equipped with onloading facilities, and the receiving port, terminal, or other transshipment facility must have offloading and storage capabilities as well.

Offshore platforms are sometimes referred to as "cities on the sea" because they encompass everything needed to maintain life and work activities. They are effectively self-sufficient, generating power using diesel and/or waste gas, supplying water via desalination, and receiving supplies and provisions from the mainland via various platform supply vessels. Workers generally remain on platforms for extended periods of time, and the working conditions can be harsh despite operator efforts to provide the comforts of home.

Some platforms may operate unstaffed. Such platforms are comparatively small structures, sometimes referred to as "toadstools," whose features may be limited to a single well bay, a helipad to support remote transportation and delivery of supplies and personnel, plus an emergency shelter and various safety equipment. Most unstaffed platforms are operated remotely and are only periodically visited for maintenance. Some installations serve only as conductor support systems or satellite platforms, connected to a parent platform by flow lines.

Offshore platforms may be constructed and assembled in stages at various locations, possibly far from their designated operating sites. Depending on the location of the final assembly site and the size of the structure, a platform may be towed into position by tugboats or transported by heavy-lift marine vessels. Additional assembly of various components may occur once the main structure is in position.

Clearly offshore platforms are highly complex structures that, in and of themselves, constitute complete industrial complexes. As such, they take years to plan and construct, at a cost of hundreds of millions of dollars. The financial burden associated with constructing a platform is often leveraged through joint ventures and partnerships among operators and associated companies and organizations. It is not unusual for multiple parties to share the financial risk in return for potential production rewards.

In January 2018 there were 1,238 active drilling and production rigs of all types, with the greatest concentrations being in the North Sea (184), the Gulf of Mexico (175), the Persian Gulf (159), Far East Asia (155), and Southeast Asia (152). Counting those in the Gulf of Mexico, there were 203 in US waters (Garside 2019a). The total number of offshore structures is, however, much larger.

Offshore oil and gas operations, platforms, and related structures in US federal waters fall under the jurisdiction of the Bureau of Safety and Environmental Enforcement (BSEE). The Bureau of Ocean Energy Management (BOEM) is responsible for managing the OCS leasing program, conducting resource assessments, and licensing seismic surveys. In addition, individual states regulate all such activity within their respective state waters.

Decommissioning of offshore platforms is one of the most significant infrastructure issues the oil and gas industry must face in coming years. This is particularly true in the Gulf of Mexico, where new development is steadily declining (Parker 2018). Due to increasing requirements of the BSEE, it is estimated that more than two thousand structures will have to be removed from the Gulf of Mexico (Parker 2018). Dismantling of deepwater platforms will involve especially massive projects requiring significant investments of time, money, personnel, and technology.

A Note on Oil and Gas Infrastructure as Relationship-Specific Assets (RSAs)

The physical assets that comprise oil and gas infrastructure can be variously described as relationship-specific; that is, it may not be possible to repurpose, reconfigure, or redeploy them for some other use without impacting their economic value. For example, a refinery really cannot be repositioned for use in some other industry—for example as a smelter, water purification plant, or manufacturing facility—but it *can* be upgraded or enhanced to handle different kinds of crudes or produce different products, thereby potentially increasing its value. Similarly, offshore drilling platforms might be difficult to repurpose at the same value (Scafidi and Gilfillian 2019; Buit et al. 2011), while oil tankers can be successfully converted to FPSOs having potentially more value (Mierendorff 2011). Employing sound risk mitigation principles and practices, petroleum pipelines can also be repurposed to transport different fluids (oil to gas, gas to oil, refined products to NGLs, etc.) (Fielden 2018; Hurdle 2018), but using them to move other gases such as carbon dioxide (CO_2) would, in many cases, be physically inappropriate (Buit et al. 2011). Because the spectrum of oil and gas infrastructure is so broad, the extent to which assets can be repurposed and recouped or enhanced value can be estimated is not fully known. (See IGI Global [n.d.] for a general description of the various forms of asset specificity originally described by Williamson [1991].)

The Digitization of Infrastructure

Like many other industries, oil and gas is experiencing a digital revolution, with profound impacts on the infrastructure that drives the industry's economic success. Digital strategies and technologies are increasingly being embraced to manage, optimize, and maintain the industry's physical assets, fed by rapidly expanding data collection and analytics capabilities. Spelman et al. (2017) paint a particularly promising picture of an industry empowered by digital technologies, Big Data, analytics, and the Industrial Internet of Things (IIOT) as a means to improve operating margins and more fully address critical issues such as water consumption, emissions reduction, safety, and human capital.

Today, information technology is practically indistinguishable from the operational fabric of refineries, terminals, pipelines, and drilling platforms, the digital oil field

(DOF) being but one example of the kind of enterprise that is being envisioned and embraced throughout the industry (Holland 2012; Carvajal, Maucec, and Cullick 2018). End-to-end, IIOT-leveraged connections across an oil and gas company's entire infrastructure footprint "ensure that all systems, equipment, sensors, and data are communicating and learning" from decisions made and actions taken throughout the company (Spelman et al. 2017). Moving forward, reliance on autonomous operations, plus the use of robots and drones to monitor and inspect assets such as wellheads, tanks, pipelines, and flare stacks, seems likely to become the norm rather than the exception, particularly in remote and/or inhospitable locations.

INFRASTRUCTURE CYBERSECURITY

Cybersecurity of infrastructure is a major priority for the oil and gas industry across the entire value chain. Because today's infrastructure operations are increasingly automated, more and more digital, and highly interconnected from an information technology perspective, the potential for intrusion, disruption, or even destruction is very real. The reliance on sensors and other data streaming devices, remote communications, industrial control systems (ICSs) (e.g., SCADA systems), and process control networks (PCNs) presents countless opportunities for bad actors to compromise the operational integrity of pipelines, refineries, production platforms, and the like. Further, as the natural gas supply becomes more closely integrated with electric utilities, there is additional potential for substantial disruption of the power grid via the pipeline gateway. Dancy and Dancy (2017) discuss pipeline vulnerability and potential liability in the face of realized disruptions. Despite these concerns, natural gas systems are quite resilient because "production, gathering, processing, transmission, distribution and storage of natural gas is geographically diverse, highly flexible and elastic, characterized by multiple fail-safes, redundancies and backups" (NGC/ONGSCC 2018).

Leaders and managers of oil and gas companies around the world recognize the seriousness of the problem and are instigating layered defense systems to prevent attacks and mitigate their effects. In the United States, many companies adhere to the Cybersecurity Framework (CSF) of the National Institute of Standards and Technology (NIST), which provides "common language organizations can use to assess and manage cybersecurity risk" (NGC/ONGSCC 2018). Other important resources include the American Petroleum Institute (API) Standard 1164, which specifically addresses pipelines; the US Department of Energy's cybersecurity capability maturity model; and the International Society of Automation (ISA)/International Electrotechnical Commission (IEC) 62443 Series of Standards on Industrial Automation and Control Systems Security. API regularly encourages communication, collaboration, and information sharing among its members on infrastructure security issues as a critical component of the industry's cyber defense strategy (API 2019.)

INFRASTRUCTURE AND THE ENVIRONMENT

Any discussion of oil and gas infrastructure would be incomplete without an acknowledgment of its relationship to environmental quality. Because so much has already been written on this subject (e.g., E&P Forum/UNEP 1997; Wilson 2012; Cordes et al. 2016), one cannot do justice to the many varying perspectives in a single chapter. Whether pro or con, the topic rarely fails to engender a vigorous response, be it political, economic, scientific, or emotional. The oil and gas industry has a substantial infrastructure footprint across the globe, and the potential for accidents, spills, releases, and contamination is significant. Still, coming at the situation from more of a "half full" position, the frequency of occurrence is relatively low when expressed in terms of the totality of infrastructure that exists. Mindful that even one accident on the scale of the 2010 Deepwater Horizon explosion is too many, oil and gas industry players strive to maintain the safest and cleanest operating environment possible.

Lately, much of the controversy pertaining to oil and gas infrastructure has centered on drilling activities, both onshore and offshore, and on the construction/expansion of pipelines and their associated endpoint terminals (e.g., Keystone XL and Dakota Access in the United States). Heretofore, such assets were regularly planned and constructed, and such tasks were executed, with relatively little fanfare. Recent events, however, have more keenly focused the public's eye on such issues as encroachment on private property, particularly in urbanized areas; disturbance of lands deemed sacred by indigenous peoples; and water use and pollution. Further, in some parts of the world, infrastructure projects such as transcontinental pipelines arouse concerns not only about the environment but of sovereignty and national security.

The potential contribution of greenhouse gas emissions from the world's collective oil and gas infrastructure, along with the energy-water nexus, is front and center in the contemporary discourse about climate change. These issues are particularly thorny and do not have forthright or cost-effective solutions. The extent to which oil and gas infrastructure may or may not contribute to climate change continues to be debated, yet the world's seemingly unquenchable thirst for energy—and hence more infrastructure—has a definite blunting effect on the argument. Ironically, due to geographic concentration close to oceans and waterways, many of the world's oil and gas infrastructure assets are themselves among the most vulnerable to the negative impacts of climate change (Cruz and Krausmann 2013).

SUMMARY REMARKS

Oil and gas infrastructure plays a vital role in the global economy. Its physical assets are vast and diverse, and they are found in nearly every country. People around the globe depend on these assets to produce and deliver the fuel they need to generate electricity, heat/cool their homes, and power transportation to get them to and from the market-place. They also rely on the associated industrial processes to produce consumer goods and raise living standards. Yet costs associated with new projects continue to spiral, while access to land and water resources is diminishing. There are political and social challenges as well. As companies race to incorporate the most advanced contemporary digital technology to improve the efficiency of these facilities, they face relentless assaults from cyber intruders. Finally, increasing worldwide concern over climate change and environmental preservation brings added pressure to an already stressed system striving to satisfy the world's growing thirst for energy.

Despite these concerns and trade-offs, infrastructure will undoubtedly continue to be the lifeblood of the oil and gas industry. Under virtually all economic scenarios today, oil and gas infrastructure remains a primary catalyst for expansion and development around the world.

References

Adesina, Ezekiel, Ben Asante, Natalia Cambia, Fisoye Delano, Richard Donohoe, Nicholas J. Fulford, Paulino Gregorio, et al. 2017. *Global LNG Fundamentals*. U.S. Department of Energy, United States Energy Association, and the U.S. Agency for International Development. https://www.energy.gov/sites/prod/files/2017/10/f37/Global%20LNG%20 Fundamentals_0.pdf.

American Petroleum Institute (API). 2016. "Pipeline 101: How Do Pipelines Work?" https://pipeline101.org/How-Do-Pipelines-Work.

American Petroleum Institute (API). 2019. "Cybersecurity." https://www.api.org/news-policy-and-issues/cybersecurity.

British Petroleum (BP). 2019. "BP Statistical Review of World Energy, 68th Edition." https://www.bp.com/content/dam/bp/business-sites/en/global/corporate/pdfs/energy-economics/statistical-review/bp-stats-review-2019-full-report.pdf.

Buit, Luuk, Albert van den Noort, Dennis Triezenberg, Machiel Mastenbroek, and Fred Hage. 2011. "Existing Infrastructure for the Transport of CO2." Gasunie Engineering BV, Report WP2.1/D2.1.1 for Project CO2Europipe: Towards a Transport Infrastructure for Large-Scale CCS in Europe, on Behalf of the European Commission, Seventh Framework Programme. http://www.co2europipe.eu/Publications/D2.1.1%20-%20Existing%20infrastructure%20 for%20the%20transport%20of%20CO2.pdf.

Cameron LNG. 2017. "Natural Gas and the Liquefaction Process." https://cameronlng.com/wp-content/uploads/2018/10/Natural-Gas-and-the-Liquefaction-Process-CLNG.pdf.

Carvajal, Gustavo, Marko Maucec, and Stan Cullick. 2018. *Intelligent Digital Oil and Gas Fields: Concepts, Collaboration, and Right-Time Decisions*. Cambridge, MA: Gulf Professional Publishing.

Cardinale, Roberto. 2019. "The Profitability of Transnational Energy Infrastructure: A Comparative Analysis of the Greenstream and Galsi Gas Pipelines." *Energy Policy* 131: 347–357.

Cordes, Erik E., Daniel O. B. Jones, Thomas A. Schlacher, Diva J. Amon, Angelo F. Bernardino, Sandra Brooke, Robert Carney, et al. 2016. "Environmental Impacts of the Deep-Water Oil and Gas Industry: A Review to Guide Management Strategies." *Frontiers of Environmental Science* 16: 1–26. doi:10.3389/fenvs.2016.00058.

Cruz, Ana, and Elisabeth Krausmann. 2013. "Vulnerability of the Oil and Gas Sector to Climate Change and Extreme Weather Events." *Climate Change* 121, no. 1: 41–53.

Dancy, Joseph R., and Victoria A. Dancy. 2017. "Terrorism and Oil & Gas Pipeline Infrastructure Vulnerability and Potential Liability for Cybersecurity Attacks." *Oil and Gas, Natural Resources, and Energy Journal* 2, no. 6: 579–619.

Davidson, Debra J., and Matthias Gross, eds. 2018. *The Oxford Handbook of Energy and Society*. New York: Oxford University Press.

Dhiraj, Amarendra B. 2018. "Countries with the Longest Network of Oil and Gas Pipelines in the World." *CEO Magazine*, December 3. https://ceoworld.biz/2018/12/03/countries-with-the-longest-network-of-oil-and-gas-pipelines-in-the-world.

E&P Forum/UNEP (Oil Industry International Exploration and Production Forum and United Nations Environment Programme). 1997. "Environmental Management in Oil and Gas Exploration and Production." Joint E&P Forum/UNEP Technical Publication, UNEP IE/PAC Technical Report 37, E&P Forum Report 2.72/254. https://wedocs.unep.org/bitstream/handle/20.500.11822/8275/-Environmental%20Management%20in%20Oil%20%26%20Gas%20Exploration%20%26%20Production-19972123.pdf?sequence=2&isAllowed=y.

Ernst & Young. 2015. "Infrastructure Investments." EYGM Ltd. https://www.ey.com/Publication/vwLUAssets/EY-infrastructure-investments-for-insurers/$FILE/EY-infrastructure-investments-for-insurers.pdf.

Fielden, Sandy. 2018. "One Way or Another—Gas to Crude Pipeline Conversions." *RBN Energy*, April 18. https://rbnenergy.com/one-way-or-another-gas-to-crude-pipeline-conversions.

Frangoul, Anmar. 2017. "10 Titans of Liquefied Natural Gas." *CNBC: Sustainable Energy*, May 2. https://www.cnbc.com/2017/05/02/10-titans-of-liquefied-natural-gas.html.

Fullmer, Jeffrey E. 2009. "What in the World Is Infrastructure?" *Infrastructure Investor*, July/August, 30–32. https://30kwe1si3or29z2yo2obgbet-wpengine.netdna-ssl.com/wp-content/uploads/2018/03/what-in-the-world-is-infrastructure.pdf.

Garside, Melissa. 2018. "Number of Oil Ports Worldwide as of 2018, by Country." Statista, the Statistics Portal, November 2. https://www.statista.com/statistics/938693/global-oil-ports-number-by-country.

Garside, Melissa. 2019a. "Number of Offshore Rigs Worldwide as of January 2018 by Region." Statista, the Statistics Portal, April 11. https://www.statista.com/statistics/279100/number-of-offshore-rigs-worldwide-by-region.

Garside, Melissa. 2019b. "Countries with the Largest Refinery Capacity Worldwide from 2010 to 2018." Statista, the Statistics Portal, June 28. https://www.statista.com/statistics/273579/countries-with-the-largest-oil-refinery-capacity.

Group International des Importateurs de Gaz Naturel Liquefie (GIIGNL). n.d. "The LNG Process Chain." The International Group of Liquefied Natural Gas Importers, LNG Information Paper 2. https://giignl.org/sites/default/files/PUBLIC_AREA/About_LNG/4_LNG_Basics/lng_2_-_lng_supply_chain_7.3.09-aacomments-aug09.pdf.

Gupta, Ankit, and Aditya Singh Bais. 2018. "Oil and Gas Infrastructure Market in U.S. to Exceed $80 bn by 2024." *Global Market Insights*, November. https://www.gminsights.com/industry-analysis/us-oil-and-gas-infrastructure-market.

Hall, Jason. 2017. "The World's 8 Largest Liquefied Natural Gas Exporters." *The Motley Fool*, August 23. https://www.fool.com/investing/2017/08/23/the-worlds-8-largest-liquefied-natural-exporte.aspx.

Hillier, Alan. 2017. "Types of Pipeline Every Oil and Gas Engineer Should Know About." Mirage Portable Performance, November 14. https://blog.miragemachines.com/types-of-pipeline-every-oil-and-gas-engineer-should-know-about.

Holland, Dutch. 2012. *Exploiting the Digital Oilfield: 15 Requirements for Business Value.* Bloomington, IN: Xlibris.

Hurdle, John. 2018. "Sunoco Wants to Use Older Pipeline to Pump NGLs Over Unfinished Sections of ME2." *State Impact Pennsylvania*, July 3. https://stateimpact.npr.org/pennsylvania/2018/07/03/sunoco-wants-to-use-older-pipeline-to-pump-ngls-over-unfinished-sections-of-me2.

IGI Global. n.d. "What Is Asset Specificity." https://www.igi-global.com/dictionary/asset-specificity/1593.

IHS Global. 2013. "Oil & Natural Gas Transportation & Storage Infrastructure: Status, Trends, & Economic Benefits." Prepared on Behalf of the American Petroleum Institute (API). https://www.api.org/~/media/Files/Policy/SOAE-2014/API-Infrastructure-Investment-Study.pdf.

International Gas Union (IGU). 2018. "2018 World LNG Report, 27th World Gas Conference Edition." https://www.igu.org/sites/default/files/node-document-field_file/IGU_LNG_2018_0.pdf.

Kaufman, Asher. 2014. "Between Permeable and Sealed Borders: The Trans-Arabian Pipeline and the Arab-Israeli Conflict." *International Journal of Middle East Studies* 46: 95–116.

Kirkwood, Mike. 2015. "Pipeline Reversals and Conversions: Case Studies and Best Practices." *Pipeline & Gas Journal*, September 2015. https://info.tdwilliamson.com/hubfs/Article/PAPER-Article-INTEG-MDS-PipelineReversalsandConversions.pdf.

Malhotra, M. 1997. "Incentives Needed to Expand India's Oil Transportation Infrastructure." *Oil and Gas Journal* 95, no. 43: 27–29.

MapSearch. 2019. "GIS Asset Data for the Energy Industry." Pennwell Corporation. https://www.mapsearch.com/products/tank-farms-storage-terminals-maps-and-gis-data.html.

Mierendorff, Ross. 2011. "Critical Success Factors for Efficient Conversion of Oil Tankers to Floating Production Storage Offloading Facilities (FPSOs)." DBA thesis, Southern Cross University.

Money, Jack. 2018. "Canadian Firm Is Building Storage at the Cushing Terminal, It Announced This Week." *The Daily Oklahoman*, May 17. https://newsok.com/article/5594861/canadian-firm-is-building-storage-at-the-cushing-terminal-it-announced-this-week.

Motiva Enterprises (Motiva). 2017. "North America's Largest Refinery." https://www.motiva.com/About/What-We-Do/Our-Production.

Mouawad, Jad. 2012. "Delta Buys Refinery to Get Control of Fuel Costs." *New York Times*, April 30. https://www.nytimes.com/2012/05/01/business/delta-air-lines-to-buy-refinery.html.

Natural Gas Council and Oil and Natural Gas Subsector Coordinating Council (NGC/ONGSCC). 2018. "Defense-in-Depth: Cybersecurity in the Natural Gas & Oil Industry." http://naturalgascouncil.org/wp-content/uploads/2018/10/Defense-in-Depth-Cybersecurity-in-the-Natural-Gas-and-Oil-Industry.pdf.

Oil Sands Magazine. 2019. "747 Million Barrels and Counting: A Look at Latest Estimates of US Crude Oil Storage Capacity." June 12. https://www.oilsandsmagazine.com/news/2017/6/7/747-million-barrels-and-counting-a-look-at-the-latest-estimates-of-us-crude-storage-capacity.

OpenDataSoft. 2014. "Crude Oil Rail Terminals." https://public.opendatasoft.com/explore/dataset/crude-oil-rail-terminals/information/?location=4,38.32142,-97.06299&basemap=jawg.streets, updated December 14.

Parker, Selwyn. 2018. "Gulf of Mexico: Decommissioning Adds to the Offshore Boom." *Offshore Support Journal*, November 20. https://www.osjonline.com/news/view,gulf-of-mexico-decommissioning-adds-to-the-offshore-boom_55949.htm.

Petak, Kevin, Julio Manik, and Andrew Griffith. 2018. "North America Midstream Infrastructure through 2035: Significant Development Continues." ICF International, on Behalf of the Interstate Natural Gas Association of America (INGAA). https://www.ingaa.org/File.aspx?id=27961&v=db4fb0ca.

Petak, Kevin, Harry Vidas, Julio Manik, Srirama Palagummi, Anthony Ciatto, and Andrew Griffith. 2017. "U.S. Oil and Gas Investment through 2035." ICF International, on Behalf of the American Petroleum Institute (API). https://www.api.org/~/media/Files/Policy/Infrastructure/API-Infrastructure-Study-2017.pdf.

Pitpoint Clean Fuels (Pitpoint). 2019. "Green Light for Construction of Europe's First LNG Bunkering Station." https://www.pitpoint.nl/en/lng-bunkering-station.

Pless, Jacquelyn. 2011. "Making State Gas Pipelines Safe and Reliable: An Assessment of State Policy." National Conference of State Legislatures, March. http://www.ncsl.org/research/energy/state-gas-pipelines-federal-and-state-responsibili.aspx.

Reportlinker/GlobalData. 2019. "Global Planned Refining Industry Outlook to 2023—Capacity and Capital Expenditure Forecasts with Details of All Planned Refineries." *CISION PR Newswire*, March 11. https://www.prnewswire.com/news-releases/global-planned-refining-industry-outlook-to-2023---capacity-and-capital-expenditure-forecasts-with-details-of-all-planned-refineries-300810095.html.

Roach, Eric. 2014. "Oil and Gas Offshore Rigs: A Primer on Offshore Drilling." *DrillingInfo*, May 8. https://info.drillinginfo.com/offshore-rigs-primer-offshore-drilling.

Scafidi, Jonathan, and Stuart M. V. Gilfillian. 2019. "Offsetting Carbon Capture and Storage Costs with Methane and Geothermal Energy Production through Reuse of a Depleted Hydrocarbon Field Coupled with a Saline Aquifer." *International Journal of Greenhouse Gas Control* 90. doi:10.1016/j.ijggc.2019.102788.

Siddiky, Chowdhury I. A. 2012. *Cross-Border Pipeline Arrangements: What Would a Single Regulatory Framework Look Like?* Alphen aan den Rijn, The Netherlands: Wolters Kluwer.

Simmons, Elton. 2015. *Oil and Gas Transportation: Pipeline and Rail Infrastructure Issues.* New York: Nova Publishers.

Singh, Bikram. 2016. "Different Types of Offshore Oil and Gas Production Structures." Marine Insight. https://www.marineinsight.com/offshore/different-types-of-offshore-oil-and-gas-production-structures.

Spelman, Mark, Bruce Weinelt, Pedro Gomez, Renée van Heusden, Reema Siyam, Muqsit Ashraf, Vivek Chidambaram, et al. 2017. "Digital Transformation: Oil and Gas Industry." World Economic Forum (WEF), in Collaboration with Accenture. http://reports.weforum.org/digital-transformation/wp-content/blogs.dir/94/mp/files/pages/files/dti-oil-and-gas-industry-white-paper.pdf.

Stern, Gary M. 2018. "America's LNG Export Boom Hinges on Infrastructure." Icons of Infrastructure, Informa USA, Inc. https://iconsofinfrastructure.com/americas-lng-export-hinges-on-infrastructure.

Stevens, Paul. 2003. "Cross-Border Oil and Gas Pipelines: Problems and Prospects." Center for Energy, Petroleum, and Mineral Law and Policy, University of Dundee, on Behalf of the Joint UNDP/World Bank Energy Sector Management Assistance Programme (ESMAP).

Stevens, Paul. 2009. "Transit Troubles: Pipelines as a Source of Conflict." Chatham House/Royal Institute of International Affairs. https://www.chathamhouse.org/sites/default/files/public/Research/Energy%2C%20Environment%20and%20Development/r0309_pipelines.pdf.

US Department of Energy (USDOE). 2015. "Quadrennial Energy Review (First Installment): Energy Transmission, Storage, and Distribution Infrastructure." Office of Policy, Presidential

Quadrennial Energy Review Task Force. https://www.energy.gov/policy/downloads/quadrennial-energy-review-first-installment.

US Energy Information Administration (USEIA). 2015. "Natural Gas: The Basics of Underground Natural Gas Storage." https://www.eia.gov/naturalgas/storage/basics.

US Energy Information Administration (USEIA). 2018. "Frequently Asked Questions: When Was the Last Refinery Built in the United States?" https://www.eia.gov/tools/faqs/faq.php?id=29&t=6.

US Pipeline and Hazardous Materials Safety Administration (USPHMSA). 2017. "Data and Statistics: Pipeline Mileage and Facilities." https://www.phmsa.dot.gov/data-and-statistics/pipeline/pipeline-mileage-and-facilities.

US Pipeline and Hazardous Materials Safety Administration (USPHMSA). 2018. "Data and Statistics: Pipeline Incident 20 Year Trends." https://www.phmsa.dot.gov/data-and-statistics/pipeline/pipeline-incident-20-year-trends.

Williamson, Oliver E. 1991. "Comparative Economic Organization: The Analysis of Discrete Structured Alternatives." *Administrative Science Quarterly* 36: 269–296.

Wilson, Tim. 2012. "Pipelines: Environmental Considerations (In Brief)." Canadian Library of Parliament, Publication No. 2012-37-E. https://bdp.parl.ca/staticfiles/PublicWebsite/Home/ResearchPublications/InBriefs/PDF/2012-37-e.pdf.

Yourex-West, Heather. 2019. "Oil by Rail Shipments Collapse Amid Alberta Government Production Cuts." *Global News*, February 15. https://globalnews.ca/news/4966966/alberta-oil-rail-shipments-collapse.

FURTHER READING

Banbulyak, Alexei, Bjorn Frantzen, and Rune Rautio. "Oil Transport from the Russian Part of the Barents Region—2015 Status Report." The Norwegian Barents Secretariat and Akvaplan-niva, Norway. http://deb.akvaplan.com/downloads/Oil_Transport_2015_internet.pdf.

Beath, John, Nyx Black, Marjorie Boone, Guy Roberts, Brandy Rutledge, Amgad Elgowainy, Michael Wang, et al. 2014. "Contribution of Infrastructure to Oil and Gas Production and Processing Carbon Footprint." *Environmental Science and Technology* 47, no. 20: 11739–11746. https://greet.es.anl.gov/publication-oil-gas-prod-infra.

Dismukes, David. E 2014. "Onshore Oil and Gas Infrastructure to Support Development in the Mid-Atlantic OCS Region." Acadian Consulting Group, on Behalf of US Department of the Interior, Bureau of Ocean Energy Management, Gulf of Mexico OCS Region. OCS Study BOEM 2014-657, Contract M09C00007. https://www.boem.gov/ESPIS/5/5402.pdf.

Energy Union Choices. 2016. "A Perspective on Infrastructure and Energy Security in the Transition." Report Prepared on Behalf of the European Climate Foundation, Third Generation Environmentalism (E3G), Cambridge Institute for Sustainable Leadership, Regulatory Assistance Project (RAP), Agora Energiewende, and World Wildlife Fund (WWF). https://www.e3g.org/docs/Energy_Union_Choices.pdf.

Ernst & Young. 2017. "Digitization and Cyber Disruption in Oil and Gas." EYGM Ltd. https://www.google.com/url?sa=t&rct=j&q=&esrc=s&source=web&cd=1&ved=2ahUKEwjq9c6zwYDlAhUEUaoKHUivCBkQFjAAegQIAhAC&url=https%3A%2F%2Fwww.ey.com%2FPublication%2FvwLUAssets%2Fey-wpc-digitization-and-cyber%2F%24FILE%2Fey-wpc-digitization-and-cyber.pdf&usg=AOvVaw19jBsasVQ9H2uAluX-BC6G.

Hillmer-Pegram, Kevin. 2014. "A Synthesis of Existing, Planned, and Proposed Infrastructure and Operations Supporting Oil and Gas Activities and Commercial Transportation in Arctic Alaska." University of Alaska-Fairbanks, North by 2020, North Slope Science Initiative. http://catalog.northslopescience.org/catalog/entries/3811-a-synthesis-of-existing-planned-and-proposed.

ICF Resources. 2016. "The Fuel and Petrochemical Supply Chains: Moving Fuels and Products That Power Progress." Report Prepared on Behalf of the American Fuel & Petrochemical Manufacturers (AFPM). https://www.afpm.org/system/files?file=attachments/Supply-Chain-Report-2018.pdf.

Kiss, Andás, Adrienn Selei, and Borbála T. Tóth. 2016. "A Top-Down Approach to Evaluating Cross-Border Natural Gas Infrastructure Projects in Europe." *The Energy Journal* 37: 61–79.

Klaus, Alexandra B., and Danielle Meinhardt. 2015. "Transporting Oil and Gas: Infrastructure Challenges." *Iowa Law Review* 100, no. 3: 947–1053. https://ilr.law.uiowa.edu/print/volume-100-issue-3/transporting-oil-and-gas-u-s-infrastructure-challenges.

Makholm, Jeff D. 2006. "The Theory of Relationship-Specific Investments, Long-Term Contracts and Gas Pipeline Development in the United States." Draft White Paper, National Economic Research Associates, Inc., Prepared for the Workshop on Energy Economics and Technology, Dresden University of Technology, Dresden, Germany, April 21. https://tu-dresden.de/bu/wirtschaft/ee2/ressourcen/dateien/lehrstuhlseiten/ordner_veranstaltungen_alt/ordner_enerday/ordner_enerday_2006/ordner_download_enerday_06/Makholm_paper.pdf.

Miranova, Irina. 2010. "Russian Gas in China: Complex Issues in Cross-Border Pipeline Negotiations." Energy Charter Secretariat. https://energycharter.org/what-we-do/trade-and-transit/trade-and-transit-thematic-reports/russian-gas-in-china-complex-issues-in-cross-border-pipeline-negotiations-2010.

Mittal, Anshu, Andrew Slaughter, and Paul Zonneveld. 2017. "Protecting the Connected Barrels: Cybersecurity for Upstream Oil and Gas." Deloitte & Touche LLP. https://www2.deloitte.com/insights/us/en/industry/oil-and-gas/cybersecurity-in-oil-and-gas-upstream-sector.html.

Murrill, Brandon J. 2016. "Pipeline Transportation of Natural Gas and Crude Oil: Federal and State Regulatory Authority." Congressional Research Service, Report 7-5700/R44432. https://fas.org/sgp/crs/misc/R44432.pdf.

Oh, Miyeon. 2015. "Cross-Border Oil and Gas Pipelines: The Intersection of Politics, Geography, and Energy Markets." PhD dissertation, Johns Hopkins University.

Omonbude, Ekpen J. 2013. "*Cross-Border Oil and Gas Pipelines and the Role of the Transit Country: Economics, Challenges, and Solutions.* London: Palgrave Pivot.

Randolph, Kevin. 2018. "NETL Releases Database of Global Oil, Natural Gas Infrastructure Information." *Daily Energy Insider*, November 30. https://dailyenergyinsider.com/news/12137-netl-releases-database-global-oil-natural-gas-infrastructure-information.

Rodrigue, Jean-Paul. 2017. "International Oil Transportation." In *The Geography of Transport Systems*, 4th ed., edited by Jean-Paul Rodrigue, Claude Comtois, and Brian Slack, . New York: Routledge. https://transportgeography.org/?page_id=6757.

Slaughter, Andres, Anshu Mittal, and Vivek Bansal. 2018. "The New Frontier: Bringing the Digital Revolution to Midstream Oil and Gas." Deloitte Insights. https://www2.deloitte.com/us/en/insights/industry/oil-and-gas/digital-transformation-midstream-oil-and-gas.html?id=us%3A2sm%3A3tw%3A4di4729%3A%3A6er%3A20181101171000%3A&utm_source=tw&utm_campaign=di4729&utm_content=er&utm_medium=social&linkId=59024455.

Verrastro, Frank, Michelle Melton, Sarah O. Ladislaw, Lisa Hyland, and Kevin Book. 2015. *Delivering the Goods: Making the Most of North America's Evolving Oil Infrastructure.* Washington, DC: Center for Strategic & International Studies, Energy and National Security Program. https://www.csis.org/analysis/delivering-goods.

Vinogradov, Sergei, and Gokce Mete. 2013. "Cross-Border Oil and Gas Pipelines in International Law." *German Yearbook of International Law* 56: 1–42.

Walton, Brett. 2014. "Fossil Fuel Boom Rewiring North America's Energy Infrastructure." *NewSecurityBeat,* December 15. https://www.newsecuritybeat.org/2014/12/fossil-fuel-boom-rewiring-north-americas-energy-infrastructure.

Yafimava, Katja. 2018. "Building New Gas Transportation Infrastructure in the EU—What Are the Rules of the Game?" The Oxford Institute for Energy Studies, OIES Paper NG 134. Oxford, England.

Zhiltsov, Sergey. S. 2016. "Russia's Policy Toward the Pipeline Transport in the Caspian Region: Results and Prospects." In *Oil and Gas Pipelines in the Black-Caspian Seas Region,* The Handbook of Environmental Chemistry 51, edited by Sergey S. Zhiltsov, Igor S. Zonn, and Andrey G. Kostianoy, 85–94. Cham, Switzerland: Springer International Publishing.

Zonneveld, Paul, and Andrew Slaughter. 2017. "An Integrated Approach to Combat Cyber Risk: Securing Industrial Operations in Oil and Gas." Deloitte Touche Tohmatsu Ltd. https://www2.deloitte.com/content/dam/Deloitte/global/Documents/Energy-and-Resources/intergrated-approach-combat-cyber-risk-oil-gas.pdf.

CHAPTER 6

RENEWABLE ENERGY

A Technical Overview

KYLE BAHR, NORA SZARKA, AND ERIKA BOEING

GROWING concerns over sustainability, resource scarcity, energy security, greenhouse gas emissions, and other social and environmental issues related to the use of fossil fuels have led to a search for clean, economical, and sustainable alternatives to fossil fuels (Helbling et al. 2011; Ölz, Sims, and Kirchner 2007; US Energy Information Administration [EIA] 2017a). Among these alternatives, renewable energy resources have come to hold a significant place in public discourse and in energy markets because of their abundance, ability to replenish themselves, and potential to be produced economically, as well as the relative lack of emissions involved in their use (Ellabban, Abu-Rub, and Blaabjerg 2014). When talking about renewable energy, it is important to make a distinction between renewable energy *resources* (solar irradiance, wind, geothermal heat, etc.) and the renewable energy *technologies* that allow those resources to be put to some useful purpose (photovoltaics, wind turbines, geothermal power plants, etc.). (For technical overviews on nuclear energy and fossil fuels, see Fitzwater and Tutuncu, respectively, in this volume; for technical overviews on infrastructure, see Coburn [oil and gas] and Hoicka and MacArthur [electricity] in this volume.)

There are many definitions of renewable energy resources, but they all include some description of the self-replenishing or continuous nature of the resource (Ellabban, Abu-Rub, and Blaabjerg 2014; US Energy Information Administration EIA 2017a). In this chapter, *renewable energy resources* are defined as a renewable form of primary energy, meaning that they exist naturally in the universe without human intervention. *Renewable energy technologies*, on the other hand, are technologies that use renewable energy resources to produce mechanical work, heat, or electricity. These processes represent the conversion from primary to secondary energy, which may more easily be stored, transported, or used in residential and industrial applications.

To understand the relationships between renewable resources and technologies, it is necessary to have a basic understanding of the units that these resources are measured in. Energy itself (e.g., heat, light, etc.) has International System (SI) units of Joules (J), but many applications (e.g., electricity generation) refer to power, which is the rate at which energy is consumed or produced and has the units of J/s, or watts (W). Because watts are such a small unit of power, it is more common to use kilowatts (kW) or megawatts (MW) when speaking about power on the residential or industrial scale. One common mistake is to confuse or conflate kilowatts with kilowatt-hours. The difference is that whereas the kWh is a measure of energy, the kW is a measure of *power* (energy per unit time). If an electronic appliance or device is rated to 100W, that means that it consumes 100 Joules of energy every second. If that 100W appliance were to be powered for one hour, it would consume 100Wh of energy. It is important to understand this crucial concept because the prices associated with energy production technologies are quite different depending on whether they are based on power (kW) or energy (kWh). Consumers typically pay for their energy usage (kWh), but capital equipment for energy generation is often purchased based on its maximum power rating (kW).

The useful application of renewable energy sources often involves the conversion of energy from one form to another with a renewable energy technology. Energy can take several forms, including radiation, heat, motion, electricity, and others. How we use renewable energy resources depends on (1) the natural form that the resource takes (primary energy), (2) the potential usefulness of energy in that natural form, and (3) the ability to convert that natural form into another form that can be used for other applications. For example, solar energy is the radiant energy emitted by the sun. That radiant energy takes the form of heat and light, which can be used directly to see by, grow plants, dry clothes, and so on, or it can be converted to electricity using the methods described later in this chapter.

"Renewable energy" as a topic encompasses a wide range of resources and technologies that fall within the purview of distinct fields and disciplines. Each of these academic and industrial areas focuses on different concerns and questions regarding the unique physical nature of its renewable resource of interest and the technologies associated with harnessing that resource. Because each resource and technology is so different from the others, it is sometimes difficult to make direct comparisons regarding environmental impacts, resource availability, secondary resource usage (the resources required to produce the associated technologies), emission of carbon and other pollutants, and optimum methods of energy distribution (Campos-Guzmán et al. 2019).

Like fossil fuels, renewable energy resources are distributed unevenly across the globe. The velocity and consistency of wind, for example, vary from place to place. Unlike fossil fuels, however, which can easily be transported from their deposits to their end-use locations, renewable energy resources must generally be used in place, with the exception of biomass fuels. It would be impractical, for example, to transport geothermally heated water over long distances to supply a demand in a place where that heat does not naturally occur. Thus, conversion of renewable energy resources to electricity is a popular application; electricity can be transported and converted to more useful forms of energy relatively easily. It can also be stored to some degree, although large-scale storage is not yet practical, and the energy being produced and consumed on a given grid must be carefully balanced at any given time. In addition to electricity generation, heat and transport fuels can also be generated from renewable resources, and a combination of conversion to electricity (or heat or gas) for grid distribution and in situ, direct-use applications should be considered (International Energy Agency [IEA] 2018). Indeed, there is a growing body of literature discussing the desirability of local production and consumption of renewable resources, as opposed to the long-distance utilization of those resources via a central distribution network (United Nations 2019; see Hoicka and MacArthur in this volume for a discussion of such distributed resources).

This chapter highlights five specific areas of renewable energy research: solar, wind, bioenergy, geothermal, and hydropower. It focuses on global trends in research, utilization, and challenges but uses local examples to illustrate features. The goal of this chapter is to provide an overview of a very broad field as a primer for social scientists and policy makers to understand the basic terminology and processes associated with the various resources and technologies, as well as to serve as a starting point for further investigation. We start with a simple technical overview of the technologies and resources, then move on to a discussion of the benefits and challenges of each renewable energy source and technology. The chapter concludes with a description of the state of the industry for each renewable energy sector, including worldwide potential and usage, key players, and industry challenges faced by each.

Overview of Renewable Energy Resources and Technologies

This section provides an overview of a selection of renewable energy resources (solar, wind, bioenergy, geothermal, and hydropower) and discusses the direct utilization of and electricity generation from these resources. In all cases, we provide simple technical descriptions that help demonstrate how the technical mechanisms and constraints of these resources and technologies have real-world policy implications.

Because several of the energy conversion processes described in this chapter make use of turbines and generators, it is necessary to understand the basic mechanisms these systems use to convert mechanical energy into electrical energy and other forms of work. Turbines consist of some configuration of fins or blades attached to a shaft, which rotates as the fins are pushed by a fluid (Sadiku 2018). In the case of wind energy, the blades are pushed by air molecules in the wind. In hydropower, they are pushed by flowing water (Figure 6.1); in thermodynamic cycle systems, they are pushed by an expanding gas (such as steam) that results from a phase change[1] (Figure 6.2). In direct-use cases, the rotational energy of the turbine is used to directly produce some form of mechanical work (grinding, pumping, milling, etc.). In electricity generation applications, the turbine shaft is connected to a generator shaft, either directly or through a series of gears. The generator then uses the rotational energy provided by the turbine to produce electricity based on Faraday's law of induction, which states that a current will be created in

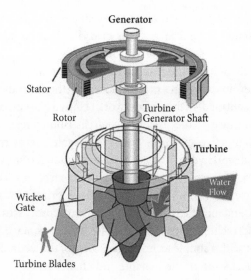

FIGURE 6.1 Hydro-turbine schematic.

Source: US Army Corps of Engineers (2012).

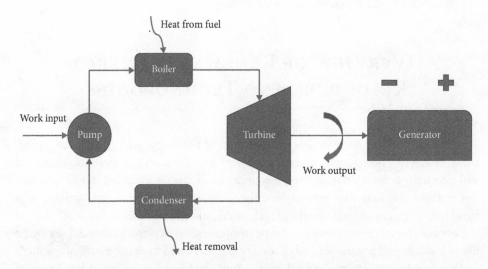

FIGURE 6.2 The Carnot cycle, typical in steam power generation systems.

a conducting wire as it moves through an electric field (Meier 2006; Sadiku 2018). One common way this is done is by attaching coils of wire to the generator shaft, which rotates within a housing that contains powerful magnets; this rotation generates an electric current. The magnitude of the current is proportional to the rate of travel of the wire through the magnetic field, and thus the amount of electricity that can be produced is proportional to the rotational velocity of the shaft (Meier 2006; Sadiku 2018).

Another important concept is the efficiency of the energy usage application. Different equations are used to calculate efficiency for different circumstances, but efficiency is roughly defined as the useful output of a conversion process compared to its input. Efficiency is generally expressed as a percentage (US Energy Information Administration

[EIA] 2018). This ratio of output to input can be used to determine the efficiency of electrical, thermal, fuel, and mechanical conversion. Efficiency represents an important measure of improvement potential for energy conversion technologies, as there are theoretical maximum limits to the efficiency that can be achieved by different technologies. For example, the Carnot limit (theoretical maximum efficiency) of a gas-fired steam turbine generator is around 51 percent, depending on the operating and ambient temperatures of the plant (Cullen and Allwood 2010). Because maximum theoretical limits express the idealized conversion of energy, actual operating efficiencies are usually much lower than their theoretical limits, as in the case of the Betz limit described in the wind section of this chapter. It is important to understand that although these technical limits constrain our overall ability to harness renewable energy resources, there is still much room for efficiency improvement in many sectors.

SOLAR

Solar energy is electromagnetic radiation emitted from the sun in the form of light and heat. It includes radiation in the ultraviolet (UV), visible, and infrared (IR) portions of the electromagnetic (EM) spectrum (Russell 2007). To put these areas of the EM spectrum into familiar terms, UV radiation is what causes sunburns when it interacts with skin tissue, visible light allows us to see, and IR radiation is the heat that can be felt on a sunny day. These phenomena demonstrate that there are more options available for utilizing this resource than just harnessing visible light.

Direct utilization of solar radiation is fundamental to life on earth. It is the source of energy that fuels photosynthesis, keeps the environment within a temperature range at which biochemical processes are possible, and drives the water cycle that produces fresh clean water in the form of precipitation. In terms of human activities, the drying of clothes, food, and building materials have relied on the sun since the beginning of history (Gopal et al. 2008). Solar energy has also been used to cook, heat homes, and disinfect and heat water for domestic use. All of these direct-use activities take advantage of the usefulness of the primary energy that solar radiation provides. One obvious limitation, however, is that just like visible light, UV and IR radiation can only be used directly when the sun is shining directly on the earth's surface. On cloudy days, only a portion of that radiation reaches the surface, and at nighttime there is none at all. Additionally, because the seasons are caused by the tilting of the earth toward or away from the sun, the amount of time that the sun shines on the surface varies according to the time of year. The ability to store this energy and use it at times when its source is not directly available is one of the major advantages of converting solar radiation into electricity, which can be stored, transferred, and accessed according to demand.

Electricity from solar radiation is produced in one of two ways: photovoltaics (PV) and concentrated solar power (CSP). A PV solar panel is composed of multiple photoelectric cells, which are flat pieces of semiconducting material (typically silicon) that are made in such a way that one side is positively charged (has a relative lack of electrons) and the other is negatively charged (has a relative excess of electrons) (Chapin, Fuller, and Peaarson 1954; Kazmerski 2006; Tyagi et al. 2013). When solar radiation strikes the surface of the cell, it causes electrons to flow from the positive side to the negative side. Metal contacts running along the surface of the material create a pathway for the electrons to flow, causing an electric current. One important thing for social scientists and policy makers to understand is that the amount of power produced by a PV array is proportional to the surface area of the cells in that array, which directly impacts the land required to build a PV plant of a desired power output.

CSP systems, less familiar to most people than PV, work in a fundamentally different way. CSP generates electricity through a thermodynamic power cycle similar to other thermal-based electricity generation technologies like gas turbines or even nuclear reactors. Heat is used to produce steam, which is run through a turbine, producing electricity (Crow and Shippen 2002). In CSP applications, heat comes from concentrating solar radiation on a point or line that contains a working fluid that produces the steam used to run a turbine. The heat is directed to the working fluid by using mirrors to refocus solar radiation onto a point (in the case of circular arrays) or a line (in the case of trough arrays) that contains the working fluid (Kalogirou 2004). Water/steam is a relatively common working fluid, but molten salt is also often used due to its high heat capacity, or ability to resist changes in temperature (Gawlik and Hassani 1997; Tomarov, Shipkov, and Sorokina 2016; Zeyghami and Nouraliee 2015). This high heat capacity allows the working fluid to retain heat and produce electricity when radiant energy from the sun is unavailable (e.g., at night or on cloudy days). The amount of heat that can be transferred to the working fluid is dependent on the amount of sunlight that can be focused on it, which means that the land use requirements for CSP are also typically quite large.

Wind

The energy in wind comes from the kinetic energy of air molecules as they move from areas of high pressure to those of low pressure (Rivkin, Randall, and Silk 2014). These pressure differentials are caused by differences in the absorption of solar radiation between the equator and the poles, and also by the Coriolis force, which is the result of friction between the air and the rotating planet.

Wind energy has been directly utilized in many ways throughout history, including ship sails and windmills. Windmills consist of large sails or blades that cause a shaft to rotate as they are struck by the wind, thereby converting the kinetic energy in the air molecules to mechanical energy that can be used to grind grain, pump water, or saw lumber (Muendel and Hills 1996). Windmills, in their most basic form, have been around since about 700 BC, when they were used in the Afghan highlands to grind grain (Ackermann 2004). They became widespread in Europe, particularly in the Netherlands, around 1100 AD, when they were used for the same purposes. Electric wind turbines work on a similar principle (albeit with many technological advances over time), but in this case the rotating shaft is used to turn a generator shaft and generate electricity, as previously described (Rivkin, Randall, and Silk 2014). The power output of a wind turbine is given by equation 1:

$$P = 0.5\rho A C_p v^3 \tag{1}$$

where P is power, ρ is the density of the air, A is the surface area that the wind turbine blades can cover (also referred to as the swept area), v is the velocity of the wind, and C_p is the power coefficient. The power coefficient describes what percentage of the energy in the wind a wind turbine is able to extract. The maximum theoretical limit for this value is the previously mentioned Betz limit, which has a value of 0.593, but values are more typically around 0.35–0.45 (Betz 1966).

To understand the design criteria and limitations of wind power generation, social scientists and policy makers should understand a few important features of this equation. The first is that A (swept area) and v (wind velocity) have a large impact on overall power output. The swept area may be increased by increasing the length of the blades. The velocity term in equation can be increased by (1) situating turbines in areas with high winds (such as offshore); and (2) increasing the height of the turbine, because greater wind speeds are found higher in the atmosphere (Rivkin, Randall, and Silk 2014). Wind velocity is the most influential factor on total output of a wind turbine, as the power output (P) scales with the cube of the wind velocity (v), meaning that a small difference in the wind velocity can have a very strong impact on the amount of power that can be produced. Wind turbines in the 1980s stood only 17 meters tall; in 2000, they were 70 meters tall; and today, some are over 100 meters tall (US Department of Energy 2015). Expected future trends include material and logistics advances that will allow for even larger towers and longer blade length (Wiser et al. 2012).

Bioenergy

Bioenergy may be defined as "energy generated from the conversion of solid, liquid and gaseous products derived from biomass," where biomass is the organic matter, or biological material, available on a renewable basis (International Energy Agency [IEA] 2019). Using the terminology of the other resources and technologies covered so far, biomass is a renewable resource that may be utilized directly or indirectly to produce energy in some form. A direct-use example is the burning of wood for heating buildings or for cooking, while a more complex use example is converting vegetable oils to biodiesel, which may then be used in transportation or to run a generator. More than 80 percent of the total primary energy supply of biomass is in the form of solid biomass—wood chips, wood pellets, fuel wood, and so on—typically in rural areas and in lower income countries. More efficient and complex uses of bioenergy are increasing (World Bioenergy Association 2018), and bioenergy in many countries is playing an important role in developing sustainable, economical, and secure energy systems (Thrän 2015).

In contrast to the other topics covered in this chapter—which are sources of renewable energy in the form of mechanical, radiant, or heat energy—biomass contains stored solar energy in the form of chemical potential energy, which can be converted to other forms of energy (power, heat, or transport fuel) on an as-needed basis. As Figure 6.3 shows, biomass can be converted through different chemical processes, or pathways, into solid (e.g., fuelwood, charcoal, pellets, etc.), liquid (e.g., bioethanol, biodiesel), and gaseous (e.g., biogas) biofuels. The type of pathway that is used depends on the raw materials—or feedstocks—used and the desired product (Thrän et al. 2018).

The three main pathways shown in Figure 6.3 are (1) thermal-chemical conversion, in which biomass is heated to facilitate a chemical change (e.g., creating charcoal from wood through pyrolysis); (2) physical-chemical conversion, in which the feedstock is subjected to some kind of physical process to separate or chemically change components (e.g., compression and (trans-)esterification of canola seeds to produce biodiesel); and (3) biochemical, in which biological processes are used for the conversion of biomass (e.g., anaerobic digestion of feedstock into bioethanol) (Thrän et al. 2018). It is important to note that the chemical structure and properties of products such as biodiesel and bioethanol are identical to diesel and ethanol manufactured synthetically from petrochemical raw materials, and that the "bio" prefix denotes the fact that they were produced

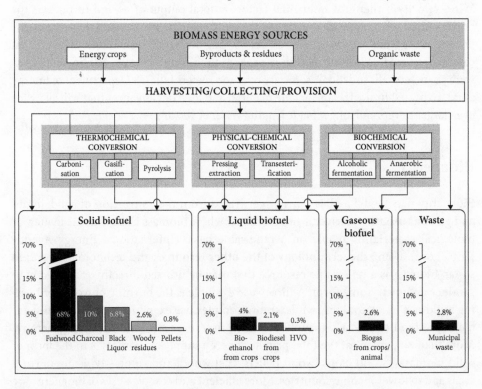

FIGURE 6.3 Conversion pathways of biomass into energy.

Source: Reproduced from Daniela Thrän et al., "Bioenergy Carriers—From Smoothly Treated Biomass towards Solid and Gaseous Biofuels," *Chemie Ingenieur Technik*, Volume 90, Issue 1–2, pages 68–84. © 2018 WILEY-VCH Verlag GmbH & Co. KGaA, Weinheim.

from renewable biological feedstock. The implications of this are discussed in the "Benefits and Challenges" section of this chapter.

Figure 6.3 also shows three classifications of feedstock: energy crops, byproducts and residues, and organic waste. Energy crops, also called dedicated plants, are woody or herbaceous plants grown and harvested for the specific purpose of producing energy from them. Willow or poplar trees are common examples of woody energy crops, and Miscanthus and elephant grass are widely utilized herbaceous grasses. As the name implies, byproducts and residues are residual matter that originate from various sectors. For example, they may come from the agricultural sector in the form of crop harvest residues; from the forestry sector in the form of forest residues; or from various food, wood, and other processing industries. Organic waste is the biological or organic portion of municipal waste that can be captured and separated during municipal waste processing.

The fuels produced from biomass can be used to generate electricity, provide heat for buildings and high-temperature industrial applications, and serve as fuel in the transportation sector. The type of production and use of a specific biofuel depends on the properties of the raw material from which it was made. Woody biomass, for example, is well suited for combustion and thus for providing heat and power (International Renewable Energy Agency [IRENA] 2019b). Biogas can be produced by anaerobic fermentation (fermentation in the absence of oxygen) from various biomass sources (e.g., animal manure, municipal and agricultural waste, sewage or food waste). Because biogases such as biomethane are chemically identical to their natural gas counterparts, they can be used with existing natural gas infrastructure such as natural gas power plants and vehicles. Sugar and starchy biomass (such as sugar beets or cereals) can be fermented to alcohol, which can then be used as a fuel in the transport sector. The variety of options and flexibility of use are some of the main benefits of using bioenergy from biomass. The issue of land-use competition that is inherent in growing crops for energy (as opposed to food) is discussed in the "Benefits and Challenges" section of this chapter.

Geothermal

Geothermal energy is heat that migrates from the core and mantle to the surface of the earth. Technologies used to harness this energy can include electricity generation on a large or small scale, as well as direct usage of hot water in applications ranging from bathing and cooking to industrial drying and district heating (Taylor 2005). Usage of geothermal energy is dependent on access to a heat source, such as a magma chamber, that is close enough to the surface that high-temperature water may be obtained through natural surface manifestations (e.g., hot springs) or by drilling, although lower-temperature technologies (such as geothermal heat pumps) can be powered by the natural geothermal gradient that is present everywhere in the world. Figure 6.4 shows a simplified schematic with some of the features of a typical geothermal system. Note that not every feature is found in every geothermal system (e.g., not every exploited reservoir has an injection well).

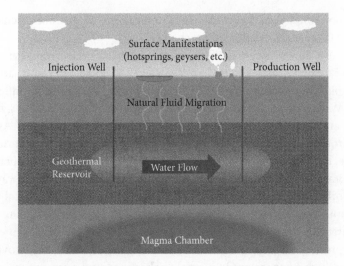

FIGURE 6.4 Geothermal reservoir system.

Direct use of geothermal dates to the beginning of human history; the main historical use has been bathing, but it has also been used for several other activities, including cooking and space heating (Kubota 2015; Shortall and Kharrazi 2017). In addition to these traditional direct-usage schemes, many modern applications have developed with the improvement of materials, drilling techniques, and other industrial technologies. Examples of modern direct uses for geothermal energy include space heating (district heating, heat pumps, snow melting, etc.), industrial food drying, heated greenhouses, and several others (Bratley 2018; Fridleifsson 1998). The appropriate use for a given geothermal resource depends on several factors, including the geothermal gradient, the depth of a potential reservoir, water temperature, and the flow rate of geothermally heated water at the surface (Dickson and Fanelli 2004).

Electricity from geothermally heated water was first generated at Lardarello, Italy, in 1904 (Bratley 2018). Typical modern geothermal power plants use the turbine-generator technologies described previously, with steam, hot water, or a mix of both coming from a geothermal well and the steam being expanded through a turbine after being separated from any liquid water. The fraction of the fluid that is steam compared to liquid is known as its *quality*, and the quality determines what kind of process it will go through to produce electricity.

There are three types of geothermal power generation systems, based on the temperature and quality of the geothermal fluid: dry steam systems, flash systems, and binary systems. In the rare cases when it exists naturally, superheated (dry) steam can be piped from a producing wellhead directly to a turbine (Moses 1961; Zarrouk and Moon 2014). Single or double flash plants—which represent the majority of geothermal power generation—first separate the vapor (steam) from the liquid phase through a process known as "flashing" before sending the steam to the turbine (Zarrouk and Moon 2014). Binary power plants use geothermal fluid to heat a separate working fluid in a heat exchanger, which is then sent to a turbine while the geothermal fluid is reinjected into the ground, often without ever being exposed to the atmosphere. If the boiling point of the working fluid is lower than that of water (isobutane or propane, for example), then electricity production is possible at much lower temperatures than with steam (as low as 74°C) (Bertani 2015; Gawlik and Hassani 1997; Tomarov, Shipkov, and Sorokina 2016; Zeyghami and Nouraliee 2015).

In addition to the treatment of steam at the surface, geothermal electricity production systems may also be enhanced through the management and design of the reservoir itself. Used geothermal fluid or other water may be reinjected into the reservoir to maintain the flow rate, pressure, and other parameters at the production well. Additionally, one of the main factors that influences the production rate of geothermal fluids is the permeability of the rock in which the geothermal fluid is found. Permeability represents the ease with which fluid may travel through a given medium. In rock types with insufficient permeability, the reservoir may be stimulated—or hydraulically fractured—in order to increase the amount of geothermal fluid available to the turbine (Tester et al. 2006; Williamson et al. 2001). Engineered (or enhanced) geothermal systems (EGS) are artificial geothermal reservoirs that are created by hydraulically fracturing hot, dry rock, usually at a significant depth (Tester et al. 2006, 1–9; see also Tutuncu in this volume). The fractures can be created in such a way that a continuous pathway is created between an injection well and a production well. There are still many elements of EGS that have yet to be understood, and only a few experimental EGS currently exist (Guo et al. 2015; Majer et al. 2007).

Hydropower

Most people are fairly familiar with the water cycle, in which water in the oceans is heated by the sun until it evaporates and forms clouds. As these clouds move to higher elevations, they cool and produce precipitation, which falls on the earth and collects in rivers and streams. These rivers continue to move to lower elevations until they deposit their water into lakes and eventually back into the oceans. As the water flows toward lower elevations, its gravitational potential energy is converted to kinetic energy, which can then be used to produce work.

The primary energy source in hydropower is the gravitational potential energy stored in water that is located at a height above the surface of the earth. The mass of the earth exerts a force on objects at its surface, which compels them to move from higher to lower elevations. The amount of potential stored in an object can be calculated by equation 2:

$$PE_{grav} = m \times g \times h \qquad (2)$$

where m is the mass of the object, g is the acceleration due to gravity ($9.8m/s^2$), and h is the height of the object (Harbick, Suh, and Bains 2019). Thus, the potential energy of an object can be increased by increasing either its mass or height. Because water is a fluid, the density of the fluid (the amount of mass in a given volume) can be substituted for mass in equation 2 to calculate the hydrostatic pressure, or force per area exerted due to the weight of the fluid, yielding equation 3:

$$P = \rho \times g \times h \tag{3}$$

where P is the hydrostatic pressure and ρ is the density of the water.

Because the density of water is constant, the way to increase the hydrostatic pressure—and by extension, the potential energy—in a hydrosystem is to increase the height of the water, which may be accomplished by transporting the water from higher upstream to produce work at a point lower downstream or by damming a river or stream to increase the height of the water level at the point where work is produced.

Like wind applications, direct-use hydropower has been used for a very long time to produce mechanical work, such as grinding grain and milling lumber (US Department of Energy 2019). There are many variations in hydro direct-use configurations throughout the world, but in general water from upstream (sometimes stored in a millpond to control the flow) flows over or under a waterwheel, which is attached to a shaft. As the waterwheel rotates, the shaft is used to produce mechanical work of some kind.

Hydroelectricity generation is the largest renewable electricity generation method in use today, and it works on principles already discussed in this chapter. A dam is used to build up the height of a river and control the flow of water through a turbine located at the base of the dam. Because the flow of water (and therefore electricity generation) is steady and controllable, hydro has been one of the most widely used renewable methods of meeting electricity demands (Ellabban, Abu-Rub, and Blaabjerg 2014). This flexibility also allows for excess energy to be used to pump water from downstream back up into the reservoir during times when the demand is low, in order to keep the height and hydrostatic pressure consistent and available for periods of high demand. Such systems are called pumped storage hydroelectric (PSH) or pumped hydroelectric energy storage (PHES) systems (Energy Storage Association 2019). It is important to note that more energy is consumed in pumping water back into the reservoir than is produced by the same amount of water powering a turbine, but the benefit is in the flexibility of balancing the supply with the demand, which is one of the major challenges of electricity production, particularly for renewable energy technologies such as solar and wind (Energy Storage Association 2019).

Benefits and Challenges

Each of the resources and technologies discussed in this chapter has potential benefits, as well as challenges that must be overcome in order to increase its total usage worldwide. In this section we discuss the pros and cons of both the renewable energy resources themselves and the technologies that allow us to use those resources to perform useful work. Table 6.1 lists some key advantages and disadvantages that are either inherent in each of the renewable energy resources or are a consequence of their conversion to secondary energy and work. Sources for the various pros and cons in Table 6.1 are provided in the following discussion.

The most obvious benefit of solar is its virtually infinite renewability, which will continue independent of any human activity on earth (Ellabban, Abu-Rub, and Blaabjerg 2014). Additionally, every place in the world receives direct sunlight and thus has at least some solar energy potential, although the amount and stability of solar irradiation varies widely from place to place, making it less feasible in some locations and difficult to forecast in others. The energy resource itself is clean, and the generation of electricity from solar produces no direct emissions of carbon or other impactful substances—though it

Table 6.1 Advantages and Disadvantages of Renewable Energy Resources

Renewable Energy Resource	Benefits	Challenges
Solar	Source is globally available Electricity production is clean Increasing efficiency gains have led to decreasing price (electricity) Wide range of direct uses	Cyclical (day/night, summer/winter) Variability of supply (cloud cover, dust, etc.) Uneven global distribution Large footprint/land use competition
Wind	Source is globally available Electricity production is clean Increasing efficiency gains have led to decreasing price (electricity)	Cyclical (daily and seasonally) Variability of supply Uneven global distribution Wildlife impacts (birds and bats)
Biomass	Broad range of feedstock types; waste as feedstock Flexible, demand-oriented supply of power, heat, and transport Time frame of renewability (growing season) Compatibility with existing infrastructure, potential for negative emissions	Possible competition of land and biomass use Requires responsible and sustainable management of the land and resource Costs are dependent on the supply chain
Geothermal	Stable/constant energy supply Abundance of energy at depth Clean	Scarcity/uneven distribution of heat near the surface Cost of drilling Induced seismicity Water use Uneven global distribution
Hydropower	Stability of energy supply Renewability	Infrastructure required for use GHG emissions from reservoirs Ecological/sociological impact of dams Uneven global distribution

is important to understand that the full environmental impact of any sector must be understood through a full cradle-to-grave lifecycle assessment (Aung 2013; Haapala and Prempreeda 2014).

As mentioned in the overview of solar, solar energy conversion potential is directly proportional to irradiated surface area, which means that often a large amount of land is needed to produce the energy required by a market (Hernandez et al. 2014). This land area may be all in one location, as is the case for solar farms used to supply electricity to a central grid, or located over a much wider area (e.g., on rooftops) in a distributed generation system (Hakimi and Moghaddas-Tafreshi 2009; Meier 2006; Rivkin, Randall, and Silk 2014). Land use competition may not be as important a factor in distributed systems, since the installation of solar panels on rooftops doesn't preclude the purpose for which the structure was built, but solar farms located in agricultural areas may limit agricultural production in those areas. While it is possible to use unproductive land, or land that does not require direct sunlight (parking lots, rooftops, etc.), Hernandez et al. (2015) found that nearly 30 percent of solar installations in California—the largest solar-producing state in the United States—are located on cropland. Due to land constraints, in recent years some companies have been considering the use of floating solar farms on both freshwater bodies and the ocean. Over 1GW of early floating solar projects have been built, primarily in East Asia (World Bank Group, ESMAP, and SERIS 2019).

Because wind energy actually comes from temperature differences on the earth's surface (as discussed in the technology overview section), wind has many of the same advantages and disadvantages as solar; the wind itself is clean, abundant, and available most places on earth. In both solar and wind electricity generation, increases in electricity conversion efficiencies have substantially decreased the price per kW over recent decades (International Energy Agency [IEA] 2018). Additionally, advances in materials science disciplines have led to the development of thinner, lighter, and stronger materials, which translates to greater heights and blade lengths for wind turbines.

The spatial variability in both wind and solar potential across the surface of the earth is not trivial, however, as it greatly affects the amount and kind of work that can be done with these resources (Jerez et al. 2013). An even bigger challenge is the variability of wind velocity and solar irradiation over time. As an example, Figure 6.5 shows the electricity generated from renewable sources in California over the course of a day (CAISO 2019). The dotted line in Figure 6.5 shows California's electricity demand during that same day, plotted on the secondary (right-side) axis. Note that the demand varies between around 16GW and 30GW, while the supply varies between 0 and 2.2GW—an order of magnitude difference between average supply and demand that relates to the 10 percent contribution of renewables to California's electricity supply on that day. This graph shows the variability of electricity produced by each renewable resource compared to the trend in demand. The electricity supply shown in this graph is a direct reflection of the availability of the resources themselves and the installed capacity of their respective electricity generation plants.

Note in Figure 6.5 that the demand peaks around 6:00 p.m., when there is a relative decrease in the electricity available through solar and wind. Currently, renewable energy

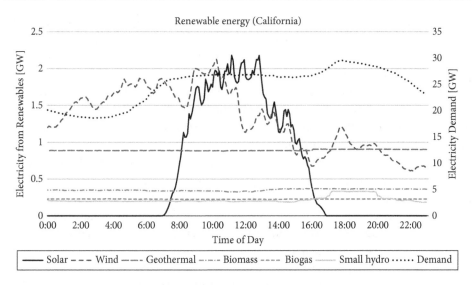

FIGURE 6.5 California electricity supply from renewable sources (left axis) and California electricity demand (right axis) over the course of a day (January 14, 2019).

Source: Data from CAISO (2019).

supply offsets the supply from fossil fuels, and variations in the renewable electricity supply are sometimes compensated for using batteries, which store excess electricity during off-peak hours and discharge that electricity to the grid when it is needed (McPherson and Tahseen 2018). The fluctuation of solar and wind availability is also cyclical over the course of a year, with more sunlight being available in the summertime and less in the wintertime and wind varying geographically according to seasonal trends (Jerez et al. 2013).

Biomass has the advantage of flexibility in its conversion to energy, use and convertibility to different final energy types, and ability for its feedstocks to be produced relatively quickly. Like fossil fuels, it is flexible in terms of its electricity and heat generation, which can be produced on demand. Consequently, bioenergy is often framed as a key transition component, especially in countries where there is an increasing share of fluctuating renewable energy sources. Biomass is also a flexible type of energy resource in terms of convertibility; it can be transformed into solid, liquid, or gaseous fuels for not only the power sector but also transportation and heating/cooling applications (Thrän et al. 2018). Additionally, because biofuels are chemically identical to those produced by processing fossil fuels, they may be used in existing infrastructure. Biogas (e.g., biomethane), for example, can be injected into the natural gas grid after appropriate upgrading (International Energy Agency [IEA] 2016).

Within the biospheric carbon cycle, bioenergy can be considered "carbon neutral" because the carbon that is released during its conversion was previously sequestered from the atmosphere as plants that are used for bioenergy are subsequently regrown. However, other steps during the whole bioenergy supply chain might be associated with emissions, such as the harvesting, transport, and processing or use of bioenergy (International Energy Agency [IEA] 2016), and the impacts of direct and indirect land use change. Biomass, geothermal, and hydro all have the advantage of providing a constant source of energy, whether for electricity or direct use (note that the lines representing those technologies in Figure 6.5 are fairly constant throughout the twenty-four-hour period). Additionally, geothermal and biomass can be used directly in heating applications (such as space and water heating or cooking) and in high-temperature industrial heating processes, which represent a significant proportion of overall thermal energy use (see the annual US thermal energy usage in Figure 6.6, which breaks down the demand for various heating and cooling applications).

The primary cost of geothermal energy production is in drilling, which increases exponentially with depth (DiPippo 2015; Tester et al. 2006, chap. 6). As a result, access to geothermal energy is limited to geothermal heat sources that are located close enough to the surface to be economically exploitable. These shallow resources are generally located near tectonic boundaries and other areas where the crust is thinner than usual, generating excessive geothermal potential around the "ring of fire," or the area surrounding the Pacific Ocean (Japan, Indonesia, New Zealand, and western North and South America), and other areas such as Iceland on the Mid-Atlantic rift zone and Kenya's Great Rift Valley (Acharya 1984). The concentration of geothermal resources around tectonic boundaries means that the feasibility of shallow geothermal energy production worldwide

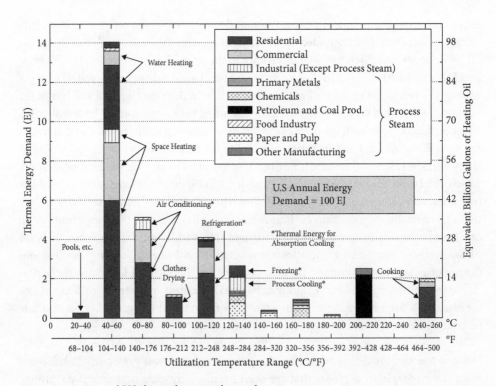

FIGURE 6.6 Annual US thermal energy demand.

Source: Adapted with permission of Royal Society of Chemistry from Don B. Fox, Daniel Sutter, and Jefferson W. Tester, "The Thermal Spectrum of Low-Temperature Energy Use in the United States," *Energy & Environmental Science*, Issue 10, © 2011; permission conveyed through Copyright Clearance Center, Inc.

is somewhat limited. At greater depths, however, the temperature in the crust is constant—meaning that as drilling technologies and techniques advance, geothermal energy can be available on a huge scale worldwide (Tester et al. 2006).

One other challenge associated with geothermal energy is that the injection of fluid used to stimulate and maintain geothermal reservoirs has been found to trigger seismic events (earthquakes), which can cause damage on the surface (Majer et al. 2007; Majer and Peterson 2007; Meier, Rodríguez, and Bethmann 2015). Much research is being conducted on the causes and mechanisms of induced seismicity in order to mitigate the impact of these events in the future.

As mentioned in Table 6.1, hydropower can deliver a stable and constant supply of energy, either for electricity production or direct use. Pumped hydro storage systems can also be used to maintain the necessary hydrostatic pressure by pumping water back up to the reservoir during periods of low demand, which contributes to the stability and renewability of the resource. The main challenges of hydro are related to the huge land areas that are lost when dams are built and valleys are flooded. This loss of land area may include delicate ecosystems; areas of natural beauty; and residential, agricultural, and industrial areas, the citizens of which must be relocated. Additionally, there is an increasing awareness of the massive quantities of greenhouse gasses emitted (particularly methane) by hydroelectric systems (Deemer et al. 2016). This is a significant issue that must be addressed if hydropower is to be an effective tool for mitigating climate change.

State of the Industries

Each of the energy sectors discussed in this chapter is represented by an industry. Due to the varied nature of uses and the limited space afforded for explanation, this section focuses primarily on the electricity generation applications of the renewable energy resources described in this chapter. Though it is sometimes difficult to directly compare these industries, there are several factors to look at when making comparisons. This section discusses three: the worldwide installed capacity, the rate of increase of installed capacity, and the price of the energy product (US dollars [USD] per kWh for electricity generation applications). The prices discussed in this section are based on the levelized cost of energy (LCOE), which is a measure of the average total cost of construction and operation of a generation system divided by the expected total energy output over its lifetime. This measure allows prices for energy produced by different methods to be consistently compared.

The worldwide installed capacity is the power (GW) that could be generated at a given time based on the infrastructure that is already in operation. The projected growth of a given sector depends on many characteristics that are unique to that sector. For example, geothermal potential depends on drilling technology/costs and the availability of geothermal heat within the currently viable drilling range, whereas solar electricity generation depends on the costs of materials, the efficiency of current technologies, cyclical patterns of solar availability, and current storage technologies. Table 6.2 lists the 2017 installed capacity of electricity generation, as well as the added capacity in 2017 and the LCOE (USD per kWh) for each technology. The following capacity and usage values and information come from a forecasting report done by the International Energy Agency (IEA 2018). What follows is a discussion of the state of each industry and key industrial indicators in each sector.

While hydropower had the greatest share of renewable capacity worldwide in 2017, solar and wind energy both outstripped it in terms of added capacity, with 55 percent of all new renewable power capacity coming from solar PV development, 28 percent from wind development, and 12.5 percent from hydropower. The growth in PV development was largely facilitated by the decrease in price for silicone PV modules, which fell by 26–32 percent in 2018. China dominated the growth, with an increase of 44GW, followed by India (9GW), the United States (8GW), and Japan (6GW). Concentrated solar power (CSP) was only 5.5GW in 2018, but that represents an increase of 430 percent since 2010. The small overall capacity for CSP is reflective of the relatively high price (USD 0.185/ kWh LCOE).

For wind, improvements to the capacity factor and increases in the range of operating conditions led to an increase in installed capacity worldwide of 45.4GW. As in solar, this growth was dominated by China, with an increased installed capacity of 18.5GW, in spite of having lower capacity factors than the United States, which had an increased installed capacity of 6.8GW in onshore wind. Increases in capacity in China and the United States were followed by Germany (2.7GW), India (2.4GW), Brazil (2.1GW), and France (1.6GW). The average LCOE of onshore wind electricity declined by 13 percent from 2017, to USD 0.056/kWh. Offshore wind electricity saw the biggest increases in China (1.8GW), the United Kingdom (1.3GW), and Germany (1GW) (International Energy Agency [IEA] 2018; International Renewable Energy Agency [IRENA] 2019a). Offshore wind was facilitated by increases in capacity factors and swept areas of larger turbines but inhibited by the high cost of building offshore at increasing distances from ports.

Table 6.2 Installed Capacity and Added Capacity by Technology, 2017

Technology	Installed Capacity (2017)	Added Capacity (2017)	Global Weighted-Average Cost of Electricity (USD/kWh, 2018)
Solar (electric)	397GW	94GW	0.085 (PV) 0.185 (CSP)
Wind (electric)	514GW	47GW	0.056 (Onshore) 0.127 (Offshore)
Biomass (total)	109GW	5GW	0.062
Geothermal (electric)	13.2GW	1GW	0.072
Hydro (electric)	1,152GW	21GW	0.047

Sources: International Energy Administration (IEA) (2018); and International Renewable Energy Agency (IRENA) (2019a).

Biomass accounted for 73 percent of primary energy from renewable sources in 2014, and renewable sources accounted for 12.7 percent of total global primary energy (Bharadwaj et al. 2017). China, India, Nigeria, the United States, and Brazil were the top five nations worldwide regarding the primary energy supply of biomass in 2014, though the way that biomass is used to generate energy in each of these nations varies greatly (different levels of complexity in uses, e.g., heating, cooking, biofuels). A significant share (87 percent) of the feedstock came from the forestry industry, 10 percent was animal and agricultural byproducts and energy crops, and 3 percent was from the waste sector (municipal solid waste and landfill gas). The Nordic countries, the Baltic countries, and Germany are the leading countries for primary energy biomass in Europe (Eurostat 2018). As previously mentioned, a broad range of bioenergy conversion pathways exists, and bioenergy is often generated at the local or regional scale, which has led to a sizable number of large and small companies in the various sectors and regions.

Geothermal electricity production remains a relatively small-growth industry, with only 500MW added in 2018. The limitations to increasing geothermal capacity are the high cost of drilling (particularly in high-temperature, high-pressure conditions) and the site-specific challenges at each potential development, which are highly dependent on the geology and hydrology characteristics of that specific area. The LCOE of geothermal increased from USD 0.05/kWh to 0.08/kWh between 2010 and 2012, after which it decreased and has remained fairly steady between USD 0.06/kWh and 0.07/kWh. The fact that costs have not seen significant improvement has led to a lack of rapid growth and expansion in geothermal, contrary to what is seen in some other renewable energy technologies today.

Hydropower projects are also very site specific, and each river basin presents unique challenges, which may increase or reduce the average cost significantly. Between 2010 and 2018 the LCOE increased slightly, due in large part to the number of hydro projects in southeast Asia, which have experienced a higher cost due to the logistical difficulties of building in more remote locations that are farther from existing grids and other infrastructural needs. The worldwide installed capacity of hydroelectric plants increased by 21GW in 2017, which is greater than increases in capacity for geothermal or biomass but less than half that of increases from wind and solar in the same year.

Summary

Global concerns surrounding energy security, resource reserves, and climate change have led to a renewed and reinvigorated interest in renewable sources of energy to meet society's demand in recent decades. This supply comes in the form of energy converted to electricity, but also in the form of other kinds of thermal and mechanical work that can be achieved by these renewable energy resources. This chapter has discussed several of the main renewable energy resources, including solar, wind, biomass, geothermal, and hydro. Each of these resources is fundamentally different from the others, and thus the technology used to harness each resource operates on different physical, chemical, and biological principles. Each energy source and its associated conversion technologies has many benefits and challenges that must be carefully considered when making decisions about what technologies ought to be pursued (and to what degree) by policy makers around the world. These policy decisions must be informed, constrained, and fostered by the technical limitations and opportunities of the resources and technologies, as well as the availability of those resources in any given geographic region. On a global scale, there is much room for expansion of current renewable energy utilization to meet the needs of society with clean and renewable technologies. The authors of this chapter encourage current and future policy makers and policy scientists to understand the technical characteristics of these resources and technologies, so that the future global use of renewable energy will be both ambitious and realistic.

Note

1. A phase change occurs when a substance transitions from one to another of the three states of matter: solid, liquid, or gas. In the case of steam, the phase changes from liquid water to gas, creating usable energy as the gas expands and drives mechanical components such as a piston or turbine.

References

Acharya, Hemendra. 1984. "Influence of Plate Tectonics on Locations of Geothermal Fields." *Pure and Applied Geophysics* 121: 853–867.

Ackermann, Thomas, ed. 2004. *Wind Power in Power Systems*. 2nd ed. Chichester, UK: John Wiley & Sons.

Aung, Kendrick T. 2013. "Economic and Life Cycle Analysis of Renewable Energy Systems." ASEE Annual Conference and Exposition, Conference Proceedings. https://peer.asee.org/economic-and-life-cycle-analysis-of-renewable-energy-systems.

Bertani, Ruggero. 2015. "Geothermal Power Generation in the World 2010–2014 Update Report." *Proceedings World Geothermal Congress* (April): 1–19. doi:10.1016/j.geothermics .2011.10.001.

Betz, Albert. 1966. *Introduction to the Theory of Flow Machines*. Edited and translated by D. G. Randall. Oxford: Pergamon Press. doi:10.1016/c2013-0-05426-6.

Bharadwaj, Kummamuru, Andrew Lang, Cristina Calderon, Douglas Bradley, Gilles Gauthier, Hazir Farouk, Heinz Kopetz, et al. 2017. "WBA Global Bioenergy Statistics 2017." Stockholm. https://worldbioenergy.org/uploads/WBA GBS 2017_hq.pdf.

Bratley, James. 2018. "History of Geothermal Energy." Clean Energy Ideas. http://www.clean-energy-ideas.com/articles/history_of_geothermal_energy.html.

CAISO. 2019. "Supply and Renewables." 2019. http://www.caiso.com/TodaysOutlook/Pages/supply.aspx.

Campos-Guzmán, Verónica, M. Socorro García-Cáscales, Nieves Espinosa, and Antonio Urbina. 2019. "Life Cycle Analysis with Multi-Criteria Decision Making: A Review of Approaches for the Sustainability Evaluation of Renewable Energy Technologies." *Renewable and Sustainable Energy Reviews* 104. doi:10.1016/j.rser.2019.01.031.

Chapin, D. M., C. S. Fuller, and G. L. Pearson. 1954. "A New Silicon P-n Junction Photocell for Converting Solar Radiation into Electrical Power [3]." *Journal of Applied Physics* 25, no. 5: 676–677. doi:10.1063/1.1721711.

Crow, I. G., and K. Shippen. 2002. "Electricity Generation." In *Plant Engineer's Reference Book*, 22-1, 22-3–22-33: Oxford, UK: Elsevier. doi:10.1016/B978-075064452-5/50077-8.

Cullen, Jonathan M., and Julian M. Allwood. 2010. "Theoretical Efficiency Limits for Energy Conversion Devices." *Energy* 35, no. 5: 2059–2069. doi:10.1016/j.energy.2010.01.024.

Deemer, Bridget R., John A. Harrison, Siyue Li, Jake J. Beaulieu, Tonya Delsontro, Nathan Barros, José F. Bezerra-Neto, et al. 2016. "Greenhouse Gas Emissions from Reservoir Water Surfaces: A New Global Synthesis." *BioScience* 66, no. 11: 949–964. doi:10.1093/biosci/biw117.

Dickson, Mary H., and Mario Fanelli. 2004. "What Is Geothermal Energy?" International Geothermal Association. 2004. https://www.geothermal-energy.org/explore/what-is-geothermal/.

DiPippo, Ronald. 2015. "Geothermal Power Plants: Evolution and Performance Assessments." *Geothermics* 53: 291–307. doi:10.1016/j.geothermics.2014.07.005.

Ellabban, Omar, Haitham Abu-Rub, and Frede Blaabjerg. 2014. "Renewable Energy Resources: Current Status, Future Prospects and Their Enabling Technology." *Renewable and Sustainable Energy Reviews* 39: 748–764. doi:10.1016/j.rser.2014.07.113.

Energy Storage Association. 2019. "Pumped Hydroelectric Storage." http://energystorage.org/energy-storage/technologies/pumped-hydroelectric-storage.

Eurostat. 2018. "Renewable Energy Statistics—Statistics Explained." http://ec.europa.eu/eurostat/statistics-explained/index.php?title=Renewable_energy_statistics.

Fridleifsson, Ingvar B. 1998. "Direct Use of Geothermal Energy around the World." *GHC Bulletin* (December): 4–9.

Gawlik, K., and V. Hassani. 1997. "Advanced Binary Cycles: Optimum Working Fluids." *IECEC-97 Proceedings of the Thirty-Second Intersociety Energy Conversion Engineering Conference* (Cat. No. 97CH6203) 3 (November): 1809–1814. doi:10.1109/IECEC.1997.656697.

Gopal, Sarvepalli, Sergai Tikhvinsky, I. A. Abu-Lughad, G Weinberg, I. D. Thiam, and W. Tao, eds. 2008. *History of Humanity—The Twentieth Century: Scientific and Cultural Development*. Vol. 7, *History of Humanity: Scientific and Cultural Development*. Paris: UNESCO.

Guo, Bin, Pengcheng Fu, Yue Hao, and Charles R Carrigan. 2015. "Thermal Drawdown-Induced Flow Channeling in A Single Heterogeneous Fracture in Geothermal Reservoir." *Proceedings of the 40th Workshop on Geothermal Reservoir Engineering* 61: SGP-TR-204. doi:10.1016/j.geothermics.2016.01.004.

Haapala, Karl R., and Preedanood Prempreeda. 2014. "Comparative Life Cycle Assessment of 2.0 MW Wind Turbines." *International Journal of Sustainable Manufacturing* 3, no. 2: 170–185. http://www.ourenergypolicy.org/wp-content/uploads/2014/06/turbines.pdf.

Hakimi, S. M., and S. M. Moghaddas-Tafreshi. 2009. "Optimal Sizing of a Stand-Alone Hybrid Power System via Particle Swarm Optimization for Kahnouj Area in South-East of Iran." *Renewable Energy* 34, no. 7: 1855–1862. doi:10.1016/j.renene.2008.11.022.

Harbick, Brittanie, Laura Suh, and Amrit Paul Bains. 2019. "Potential Energy." Chemistry LibreTexts. https://chem.libretexts.org/Bookshelves/Physical_and_Theoretical_Chemistry_Textbook_Maps/Supplemental_Modules_(Physical_and_Theoretical_Chemistry)/Thermodynamics/Energies_and_Potentials/Potential_Energy.

Helbling, Thomas, Joong Shik Kang, Michael Kumhof, Dirk Muir, Andrea Pescatori, and Shaun Roache. 2011. "Oil Scarcity, Growth and Global Imbalances." In *World Economic*

Outlook: Tensions from the Two-Speed Recovery, 89–124. Washington, DC: International Monetary Fund. http://www.imf.org/external/pubs/ft/weo/2011/01/pdf/c3.pdf.

Hernandez, R. R., S. B. Easter, M. L. Murphy-Mariscal, F. T. Maestre, M. Tavassoli, E. B. Allen, C. W. Barrows, et al. 2014. "Environmental Impacts of Utility-Scale Solar Energy." *Renewable and Sustainable Energy Reviews* 29: 766–779. doi:10.1016/j.rser.2013.08.041.

Hernandez, Rebecca R., Madison K. Hoffacker, Michelle L. Murphy-Mariscal, Grace C. Wu, and Michael F. Allen. 2015. "Solar Energy Development Impacts on Land Cover Change and Protected Areas." *Proceedings of the National Academy of Sciences* 112, no. 44: 13579–13584. doi:10.1073/pnas.1602975113.

International Energy Agency (IEA). 2016. "Task 38: Climate Change Effects of Biomass and Bioenergy Systems." http://task38.ieabioenergy.com/wp-content/uploads/2013/09/task38_description_2013.pdf.

International Energy Agency (IEA). 2018. "Renewables 2018—Market Analysis and Forecast from 2018 to 2023." https://www.iea.org/renewables2018/transport/.

International Energy Agency (IEA). 2019. "Bioenergy and Biofuels." https://www.iea.org/topics/renewables/bioenergy/.

International Renewable Energy Agency (IRENA). 2019a. "Renewable Power Generation Costs in 2018." Abu Dhabi, UAE. ISBN: 9789292601263, https://www.irena.org/publications/2019/May/Renewable-power-generation-costs-in-2018.

International Renewable Energy Agency (IRENA). 2019b. "Solid Biomass Supply for Heat and Power: Technology Brief." Abu Dhabi, UAE. ISBN: ISBN 978-92-9260-107-2, https://www.irena.org/publications/2019/Jan/Solid-Biomass-Supply-for-Heat-and-Power

Jerez, S., R. M. Trigo, A. Sarsa, R. Lorente-Plazas, D. Pozo-Vázquez, and J. P. Montávez. 2013. "Spatio-Temporal Complementarity between Solar and Wind Power in the Iberian Peninsula." In "European Geosciences Union General Assembly," special issue, *Energy Procedia* 40: 48–57. doi:10.1016/j.egypro.2013.08.007.

Kalogirou, Soteris A. 2004. "Solar Thermal Collectors and Applications." *Progress in Energy and Combustion Science* 30, no. 3: 231–295. doi:10.1016/J.PECS.2004.02.001.

Kazmerski, Lawrence L. 2006. "Solar Photovoltaics R&D at the Tipping Point: A 2005 Technology Overview." *Journal of Electron Spectroscopy and Related Phenomena* 150, no. 2: 105–135. doi:10.1016/j.elspec.2005.09.004.

Kubota, Hiromi. 2015. "Social Acceptance of Geothermal Power Generation in Japan." *World Geothermal Congress 2015* (April): 19–25.

Majer, E., R. Baria, M. Stark, S. Oates, J. Bommer, B. Smith, and H. Asanuma. 2007. "Induced Seismicity Associated with Enhanced Geothermal Systems." *Geothermics* 36, no. 3: 185–222. doi:10.1016/j.geothermics.2007.03.003.

Majer, E., and J. Peterson. 2007. "The Impact of Injection on Seismicity at The Geysers, California Geothermal Field." *International Journal of Rock Mechanics and Mining Sciences* 44, no. 8: 1079–1090. doi:10.1016/j.ijrmms.2007.07.023.

McPherson, Madeleine, and Samiha Tahseen. 2018. "Deploying Storage Assets to Facilitate Variable Renewable Energy Integration: The Impacts of Grid Flexibility, Renewable Penetration, and Market Structure." *Energy* 145 (February): 856–870. doi:10.1016/J.ENERGY.2018.01.002.

Meier, Alexandra Von. 2006. "Electric Power Systems: A Conceptual Introduction." doi:10.1002/0470036427.

Meier, Peter M., Andrés Alcolea Rodríguez, and Falko Bethmann. 2015. "Lessons Learned from Basel: New EGS Projects in Switzerland Using Multistage Stimulation and a Probabilistic

Traffic Light System for the Reduction of Seismic Risk." *World Geothermal Congress* (April): 19–25.

Moses, P. 1961. "Geothermal Gradients." in *Drilling and Production Practice*. Dallas, TX: American Petroleum Institute, 57–63.

Muendel, John, and Richard L. Hills. 1996. "Review of Power from Wind: A History of Windmill Technology." *Technology and Culture* 36, no. 3: 692–694. doi:10.2307/3107262.

Ölz, Samantha, Ralph Sims, and Nicolai Kirchner. 2007. "Contribution of Renewables to Energy Security." IEA Information Paper.

Rivkin, D. A., M. Randall, and L. Silk. 2014. *Wind Power Generation and Distribution*. The Art and Science of Wind Power. Burlington, MA: Jones & Bartlett Learning. https://books .google.co.jp/books?id=lRu21EhpAawC.

Russell, Randy. 2007. "The Multispectral Sun—Windows to the Universe." https://www .windows2universe.org/?page=/sun/spectrum/multispectral_sun_overview.html.

Sadiku, Matthew N. O. 2018. *Elements of Electromagnetics*. 7th ed. New York, USA: Oxford University Press. doi:10.1007/978-1-4471-0597-8.

Shortall, Ruth, and Ali Kharrazi. 2017. "Cultural Factors of Sustainable Energy Development: A Case Study of Geothermal Energy in Iceland and Japan." *Renewable and Sustainable Energy Reviews* 79 (May): 101–109. doi:0.1016/j.rser.2017.05.029.

Taylor, Robin. 2005. "Identifying New Opportunities for Direct-Use Geothermal Development." San Diego, CA. https://ww2.energy.ca.gov/2005publications/CEC-500-2005-108/CEC-500-2005-108.PDF

Tester, Jefferson W., Brian J. Anderson, Anthony S. Batchelor, David D. Blackwell, Ronald DiPippo, E. M. Drake, J. Garnish, et al. 2006. "The Future of Geothermal Energy: Impact of Enhanced Geothermal Systems on the United States in the 21st Century." Boston, MIT. www1.eere.energy.gov/geothermal/pdfs/future_geo_energy.pdf.

Thrän, Daniela. 2015. *Smart Bioenergy: Technologies and Concepts for a More Flexible Bioenergy Provision in Future Energy Systems*. Cham, Switzerland: Springer International Publishing.

Thrän, Daniela, Eric Billig, André Brosowski, Marco Klemm, Stefanie B. Seitz, and Janet Witt. 2018. "Bioenergy Carriers—From Smoothly Treated Biomass towards Solid and Gaseous Biofuels." *Chemie Ingenieur Technik* 90, nos. 1–2: 68–84. doi:10.1002/cite.201700083.

Tomarov, G. V., A. A. Shipkov, and E. V. Sorokina. 2016. "Choice of Optimal Working Fluid for Binary Power Plants at Extremely Low Temperature Brine." *Thermal Engineering* 63, no. 12: 887–895. doi:10.1134/S0040601516120065.

Tyagi, V. V., Nurul A. A. Rahim, N. A. Rahim, and Jeyraj A. L. Selvaraj. 2013. "Progress in Solar PV Technology: Research and Achievement." *Renewable and Sustainable Energy Reviews* 20 (April): 443–461. doi:10.1016/J.RSER.2012.09.028.

United Nations. 2019. "Energy Sector Transformation: Decentralized Renewable Energy for Universal Energy Access." New York. https://sustainabledevelopment.un.org/content/ documents/17589PB24.pdf.

US Army Corps of Engineers. 2012. "A Turbine Connected to a Generator Produces Power inside a Dam." https://www.usgs.gov/media/images/a-turbine-connected-a-generator-produces-power-inside-a-dam.

US Department of Energy. 2015. "Wind Vision: A New Era for Wind Power in the United States." http://www.osti.gov/scitech.

US Department of Energy. 2019. "History of Hydropower." https://www.energy.gov/eere/ water/history-hydropower.

US Energy Information Administration (EIA). 2017a. "Renewable Energy." *U.S. Energy Information Administration Glossary*. https://www.eia.gov/tools/glossary/index.php.

US Energy Information Administration (EIA). 2017b. "Renewable Energy Resources." *U.S. Energy Information Administration Glossary*. https://www.eia.gov/tools/glossary/index.php?id=R.

US Energy Information Administration (EIA). 2018. "Energy Efficiency." U.S. Energy Information Administration Glossary. 2018. https://www.eia.gov/tools/glossary/index.php?id=E.

Williamson, Kenneth H., Richard P. Gunderson, Gerald M. Hamblin, Darrell L. Gallup, and Kevin Kitz. 2001. "Geothermal Power: Technology Brief." *Proceedings of the IEEE 89* (December): 111–113.

Wiser, R., Z. Yang, M. Hand, O. Hohmeyer, D. Infield, P. H. Jensen, V. Nikolaev, et al. 2012. "Wind Energy." In *Renewable Energy Sources and Climate Change Mitigation: Special Report of the Intergovernmental Panel on Climate Change*, edited by Ottmar Edenhofer, Ramón Pichs Madruga, Youba Sokona, Kristin Seyboth, Patrick Matschoss, Susanne Kadner, Timm Zwickel, et al., 49:535–608. New York: Cambridge University Press. doi:10.1017/CBO9781139151153.

World Bank Group, ESMAP, and SERIS. 2019. "Where Sun Meets Water: Floating Solar Market Report." Washington, DC. http://documents.worldbank.org/curated/en/579941540407455831/Floating-Solar-Market-Report-Executive-Summary.

World Bioenergy Association. 2018. "WBA Global Bioenergy Statistics 2018." https://world-bioenergy.org/uploads/181017%20WBA%20GBS%202018_Summary_hq.pdf

Zarrouk, Sadiq J., and Hyungsul Moon. 2014. "Efficiency of Geothermal Power Plants: A Worldwide Review." *Geothermics* 51: 142–153. doi:10.1016/j.geothermics.2013.11.001.

Zeyghami, Mehdi, and Javad Nouraliee. 2015. "Effect of Different Binary Working Fluids on Performance of Combined Flash Binary Cycle." *Proceedings of World Geothermal Congress* (April): 19–25.

PART II

ENERGY CONCEPTS AND ISSUES

CHAPTER 7

....

ENERGY
INTERDEPENDENCE

....

JEFFREY D. WILSON

ENERGY interdependence plays a major role in international politics. Energy is both an essential input for modern economies and a major source of wealth for hydrocarbon-rich countries, whose economies depend on energy exploitation. But owing to the arbitrary geographic distribution of energy resources, few countries can independently achieve energy security. Energy-rich producers need to gain access to important markets for capital and exports, while energy-poor consumers need to access affordable energy inputs from abroad. These imperatives mean global energy systems are characterized by deep patterns of interdependence, in which trade and investment ties connect consumers who need to buy with producers who need to sell. This interdependence is facilitated by a "regime complex" of interlocking international institutions, which allow governments to negotiate principles, rules, and coordination schemes to cooperatively manage world energy markets. By benefiting both producers and consumers, international markets and institutions function as a "global public good" that can improve the energy security of all parties.

However, negotiating international arrangements for energy interdependence is highly charged. Despite the potential for cooperation to create mutual gains, producing and consuming economies have conflicting interests. Producers favor high prices that maximize returns, consumers prefer low prices that improve energy security, and both sides seek to set international rules that vest them with control over these important markets. Energy interdependence is therefore a coordination game, in which the benefits of intergovernmental cooperation are overlaid by distributional tensions over how to share joint gains.

As a consequence, governmental approaches to interdependence are characterized by two distinct behavioral logics. One is a competitive geopolitical approach, in which states assert national control over their energy sectors and become enmeshed in conflicts over energy trade and investment. The other is a cooperative global energy governance approach, in which states adopt market-based energy frameworks and seek to augment the operation of international markets through negotiated policy coordination. Depending on their distinct political and economic features, some governments adopt geopolitical energy policies, and others adopt global energy governance policies. Cycles in global energy markets have also historically driven a back and forth between these two logics, with competitive behavior dominant during boom phases and cooperative behavior emerging during busts.

This chapter explores how these competing imperatives structure the politics of energy interdependence. It begins by conceptualizing energy interdependence as an international coordination game, then reviews scholarly theories of competitive and cooperative behavioral logics. It goes on to connect these logics to states' energy policy choices, identifying nationalist and liberal frameworks and their effects on domestic and international energy markets. It then explores how the tension between these competing logics conditions attempts to build governance regimes for energy interdependence, with cooperative/liberal behavior driving the construction of multilateral institutions while competitive/nationalist policies simultaneously limit their achievements. The chapter concludes by mapping an agenda for future research into energy interdependence, which should focus attention on the political factors that determine the balance between these two behavioral logics.

ENERGY INTERDEPENDENCE AS A COORDINATION GAME

Interdependence is a key feature of global energy systems. All modern economies rely on reliable supplies of energy—traditionally from hydrocarbons, but increasingly from renewable sources such as wind, solar, hydro, and geothermal—to power their electricity, transportation, and industrial systems. Energy is also a major source of economic rents for resource-rich countries, particularly those in the developing world that rely on the exports, investment, and tax revenues generated by energy exploitation. Moreover, these natural resources are arbitrarily spread around the globe, so geographic patterns of consumption and production do not match. Energy demand comes primarily from countries that have large and/or industrialized economies, particularly developed Western states, and the rapidly industrializing economies of Asia. The Organisation for Economic Co-operation and Development (OECD) and China alone currently consume two-thirds of the world's primary energy supply (BP 2017). The largest and most economically viable energy resources are concentrated in a small number of states. The world's top 10 energy producers account for 84 percent of global output and 80 percent of exports (see Table 7.1). As very few countries possess the natural resources to achieve self-sufficiency using contemporary technologies, most rely on imports from energy-rich suppliers to meet their needs.

Table 7.1 Top 10 Energy Producers and Policy Regimes, 2015

	Primary Energy Production (Quad BTU)	Share World Production	Share World Exports	Energy Policy Regimes		
				State Ownership	Trade Restrictions	Subsidization Rate
OPEC	107.0	19.8%	34.6%	SOE dominance	Yes	^
China	103.1	19.1%	1.5%	SOE monopoly	Yes	4%
United States	83.5	15.4%	5.5%	None	No	None
Russia	56.0	10.5%	11.5%	SOE dominance	Yes	22%
EU-27	29.9	5.5%	15.0%	Mixed	No	None
Canada	20.5	3.8%	4.1%	None	No	None
Iran	14.4	2.7%	2.0%	SOE dominance	Yes	65%
Australia	14.4	2.7%	2.5%	None	No	None
India	14.3	2.6%	1.7%	SOE dominance	No	6%
Indonesia	13.1	2.4%	1.8%	SOE monopoly	Yes	27%
Top 10 subtotal	456.2	84.6%	80.2%			
World	**540.7**					

Source: Author's calculations, from USEIA (2016), UNCTAD (2017a), and IEA (2015).
^ OPEC subsidization rates range from 17% in Angola to 91% in Venezuela.

The result is deep patterns of economic interdependence between energy-rich and energy-poor countries, which take two principal forms. The first is international trade in energy commodities, which was valued at $1.5 trillion in 2016 and accounts for a tenth of all world trade (UNCTAD 2017a). A significant portion of global hydrocarbons is traded, with half of oil, 30 percent of gas, and 20 percent of coal output being exported (see Figure 7.1). The second is foreign investment, in which multinational resource corporations provide capital, infrastructure, and technical skills to help energy-rich economies—often in the developing world—build their energy production and export sectors. Over the last decade, cross-border investment in the mining and petroleum sectors has averaged $126 billion per year (UNCTAD 2017b). These trade and investment ties mean national energy systems are fundamentally interdependent, with energy-rich producers accessing foreign capital and export markets, while energy-poor consumers secure supplies that are otherwise unavailable within their own economies.

From an economic perspective, energy interdependence is a mutually beneficial, shared interest. Connecting consumers that need to buy with producers that wish to sell offers benefits for parties on both sides of the arrangement. But from a political perspective, there is also a perennial tension between their interests. Producers wish to maximize the economic rents their energy industries domestically generate, through high prices and buoyant investment inflows. Consumers prioritize energy security—the *continuous availability* of *appropriate* energy inputs at *affordable* prices (UNDP 2000)—for their industries and households and thus favor lower prices and investment levels. In this way,

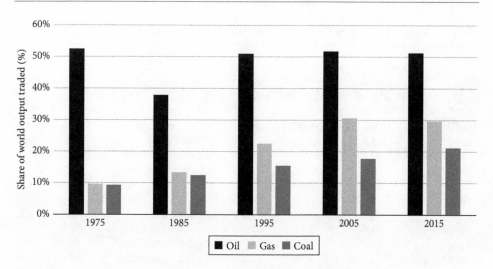

FIGURE 7.1 International trade intensity for hydrocarbons, 1975–2015.

Source: Author's calculations, from IEA (2017a).

energy interdependence should be conceived as a coordination game,[1] wherein cooperation creates gains for all parties, but these are overlaid by distributional tensions over how the joint gains are to be shared. Indeed, this coordination game is somewhat mandatory for states with few or no energy resources of their own. The politics of energy interdependence is concerned with whether and how states can coordinate policy for shared energy security goals and how such coordination schemes distribute their benefits.

The politics of this coordination game is also influenced by the volatile character of global energy markets (Colgan et al. 2012; Vivoda 2009; Wilson 1987). The often five- to ten-year lead times facing the construction of energy projects create lags among demand, investment, and the emergence of new supply. As a result, global energy markets have historically exhibited very pronounced cycles, in which "boom" phases of high prices alternate with "busts," in which markets collapse. As Figure 7.2 shows, two major boom/bust cycles have occurred in the post–World War II period. The first was during the energy crises of the 1970s, when growing global demand and cartel activity by the Organization of the Petroleum Exporting Countries (OPEC) resulted in oil prices increasing more than tenfold between 1973 and 1981. This boom was followed by a bust in the mid-1980s and then a decade of relative price stability. A second global resource boom occurred in the 2000s, driven by soaring natural resource demand from rapidly industrializing developing economies. This boom saw prices increase sixfold in the decade to 2012, before yet another collapse after 2014 returned them to more normal levels. These market cycles have asymmetrical distributional effects, with booms favoring producers at the expense of consumers' energy security, while busts make energy more affordable for consumers but harm the interests of producing economies. During the heightened volatility that occurs during the transition between these two phases, distributional conflicts between producer and consumer states can become highly charged.

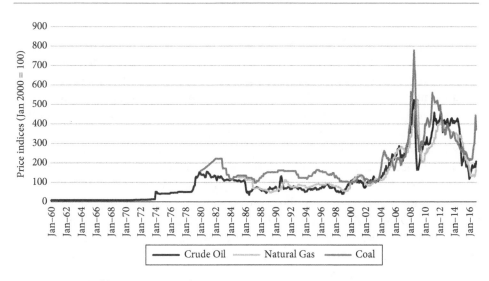

FIGURE 7.2 World energy price indices, 1960–2016.

Source: Author's calculations, from IMF (2017) and UNCTAD (2017a).

THEORIZING ENERGY INTERDEPENDENCE: COMPETITIVE AND COOPERATIVE BEHAVIORAL LOGICS

Two theoretical accounts are prominent among scholars of international energy politics, which respectively identify distinct behavioral logics as shaping patterns of interdependence. The first, which is often called the *geopolitical approach*, derives from realist international relations (IR) theory[2] and views energy interdependence as a source of interstate conflict. It begins by conceptualizing energy as scarce assets of strategic value. As reliable access is essential for both the smooth functioning of economies and the effective use of military capabilities, states place a high priority on securing their energy supplies (Klare 2008). But because natural endowments are unevenly distributed around the globe, most states are subject to a degree of "external dependency," wherein they rely on imports from foreign suppliers to meet their energy needs (Russett 1984). Additionally, energy wealth is often monopolized by a small group of countries, such as the OPEC member states, which hold 71 percent of world oil reserves (BP 2017, 12). This energy and economic inequality subjects consumer states to heightened energy security risks, as supply can be easily interrupted by civil disturbances, acts of terrorism, or the political decisions of producing governments (Peters and Westphal 2013). Energy is a leading example of what Haglund (1986) has labeled "strategic minerals": commodities that are essential for military and economic security but are primarily obtained via imports, and whose supply is therefore a matter of geopolitics and national security.

For some theorists, these features mean energy interdependence is an inherently conflictual political domain. Global energy reserves are argued to be a fixed and declining pie, over which states engage in zero-sum competition for access and control (Jain 2014; Klare 2008). Several factors are identified as potential drivers of energy competition. Some point to energy market cycles. As prices rise during boom phases, growing consumer anxieties over energy insecurity see governments "politicize" energy issues and become prone to conflictual behavior (Vivoda 2009; Wilson 1987). Others draw attention to the behavior of "miscreant" suppliers, who for political reasons have on occasion threatened to withhold access. During the 1970s blame was placed on the OPEC members who fomented the 1973 and 1979 oil crises (Vernon 1983), while in recent years attention has focused on Russian threats to withhold energy supply to eastern European consumers (Aalto 2012). Others point to increasingly conflictual great power relationships—caused by declining US hegemony (Wesley 2007), emerging patterns of multipolarity (Lesage et al. 2010), and the rise of China (Tunsjo 2013)—as creating a geopolitical environment in which energy conflicts become more likely.

Several types of interstate energy conflict are prevalent. One is the use of the "energy weapon," a form of economic sanction in which an energy producer withholds (or threatens to withhold) exports to coerce a change of behavior in the consumer (O'Sullivan 2013). The OPEC oil embargoes of the 1970s (Licklider 1988) and Russian gas threats against Ukraine during the mid-2000s (Pirani et al. 2009) are both significant examples. Another type of conflict is competitive "races" for energy, in which consumer states use mercantilistic tools (such as state-backed investments and energy diplomacy) to secure preferential access to key energy suppliers. During the mid-2000s the governments of China, Japan, and South Korea engaged in such a race to lock up new energy supplies from Africa, Latin America, and Central Asia in competition with each other (Wilson 2017). In extreme cases, these tensions can also manifest as "resource wars": armed conflicts that are at least in part fought over possession of natural resource wealth (Le Billon 2004). Westing (1986) has identified twelve such wars during the twentieth century, including both world wars, the Six-Day War of 1967, the Congo Civil War in 1960–1964 and Nigerian Civil War in 1967–1970, and the Falklands War in 1982, among others. More recently, Colgan and Stockbruegger (in this volume) argue that up to half of all interstate wars since 1973 have been connected to oil conflicts in some way.

A contrasting theoretical account, labeled *global energy governance*, draws on liberal international relations theory to conceptualize energy interdependence as a cooperative domain. This behavior is informed by the fact that very few governments, with the exception of a small number of oil-rich states, possess the full range of energy resources their economies require (Verrastro and Ladislaw 2007). As a result, cooperative behavior that provides governance regimes for energy interdependence is a shared interest that can benefit all parties. For consumers, the development of open and transparent energy markets helps facilitate the cross-border investment and trade flows needed to provide reliable access to energy supplies. For producers, cooperating to manage market volatility makes it easier for governments to plan investment in important but costly energy projects. For both sides, growing concerns about energy scarcity and climate change also create incentives to cooperatively manage the ongoing and complex energy transition from traditional (oil and coal) to newer energy sources such as natural gas and renewables. These factors mean that energy interdependence is not intrinsically a zero-sum domain of interstate conflict, but can potentially be a positive-sum game in which cooperation augments the energy security of both producers and consumers (Goldthau and Witte 2010; Lesage et al. 2010). Two types of governance institutions are identified as critical in producing such positive-sum interactions.

First, international energy markets play a key role in mediating interdependence. In competitive, transparent, and open markets, energy insecurity is addressed by the price mechanism. As energy becomes scarce, upward price movements call forth additional production from marginal reserves, ensuring a long-run balance between demand and supply. Well-managed markets are also more economically efficient, providing a stable environment for energy investments and ensuring capital is allocated to the most productive projects (Harris and Naughton 2007). They can also depoliticize energy relationships by facilitating trade between any parties wishing to sell or buy, and if not monopolized by a small group they make the coercive use of the energy weapon less likely (Goldthau and Witte 2009). For these reasons, analysts have labeled energy markets a *global public good* (Dubash and Florini 2011; Goldthau 2011), as they serve the energy security interests of both producers and consumers.

Second, intergovernmental institutions facilitate energy cooperation. As well-functioning energy markets require shared rules and governance practices, there are strong incentives for governments to take collective action to support such markets. These actions can include information sharing to reduce transaction costs, the management of price volatility and its deleterious effects, and the setting of rules for national energy policies that increase confidence in market transparency (Florini and Sovacool 2009; Victor and Yueh 2010). These shared interests have led to the progressive creation of an "energy regime complex": an interrelated set of global institutions to cooperatively manage interdependent world markets (Colgan et al. 2012). Table 7.2 outlines nine of the major multilateral energy institutions in operation today, highlighting the diversity of their contributions to global energy governance. Some are treaty-based bodies, which set rules for members' energy policy; some facilitate dialogue between producers and consumers; and others promote non-binding coordination toward the realization of mutually agreed energy policy principles. As Goldthau and Witte (2009) have argued, this combination of markets and institutions functions as a set of "rules of the game" for energy interdependence, which ameliorate conflict tendencies and enable positive-sum cooperation to occur.

The behavioral logics identified by geopolitical and global energy governance theories should not be conceptualized as an exclusive binary. Rather, they function as ideal types that bound a spectrum of possible behaviors that are variably expressed in different national and historical contexts. At certain times competitive geopolitical behaviors have been dominant, for example during the energy crises of the 1970s that pitted oil producer (OPEC) and consumer (International Energy Agency, IEA) cartels against each other for control of world energy pricing (Licklider 1988). At other times cooperative

Table 7.2 Major Multilateral Organizations Active in Energy Issues

Name	Year Established	Key Objectives	Institutional Design	Share World Energy Trade 2016 (Exports/Imports)
International Energy Agency (IEA)	1974	Consumer-side oil market stabilization, market integration	Treaty for oil, non-binding coordination elsewhere	33.5%/55.0%
Organization of Petroleum Exporting States (OPEC)	1960	Producer-side oil market stabilization	Treaty	35.5%/2.9%
Energy Charter Treaty (ECT)	1991	Market integration	Treaty	34.6%/37.7%
International Energy Forum (IEF)	1991	Information sharing	Dialogue body	88.9%/81.4%
Gas Exporting Countries Forum (GECF)	2001	Information sharing	Dialogue body	29.0%/2.0%
Group of Seven (G7)	1975	Market integration, energy transition	Non-binding coordination	15.7%/32.5%
Group of Twenty (G20)	2008	Market integration, energy transition, subsidy reform	Non-binding coordination	46.5%/61.7%
Asia-Pacific Economic Cooperation (APEC)	1991	Market integration, energy transition, subsidy reform	Non-binding coordination	36.5%/51.2%
International Renewable Energy Agency (IRENA)	2009	Energy transition	Non-binding coordination	88.3%/89.0%

Source: Adapted from Sovacool and Florini (2012) and Wilson (2015a).

global governance behavior has dominated instead, such as during the 1990s, when a collapse in world prices led to more cordial relations among states and the adoption of market-based governance practices (Stevens 2013). And within certain historical contexts, governments have adopted different strategies to manage their energy relationships. In recent years the European Union (EU) has been a staunch advocate for cooperative and market-based energy governance regimes (Westphal in this volume; Goldthau and Sitter 2015), while Russia has adopted a more competitive and state-controlled approach through the nationalization of its oil sector and the threatened use of the energy weapon (Aalto 2012). There are also distinct patterns on a geographic level, with major differences between energy governance regimes in different regions of the global economy (Hancock et al. in this volume).

A prominent critique of the geopolitical and global energy governance approaches concerns their ability to adequately explain the conditions giving rise to their identified behavioral logics. Both conceptualize energy interdependence as an "international game" played between states, with the debate being over whether this game is conflictual or cooperative. This discourse reflects a systemic mode of theorizing, inherited from realist and liberal IR theory (Stoddard 2013). However, it also means that the domestic politics of energy is largely excluded from the theoretical analysis. This omission is significant and problematic because a range of domestic political dynamics shapes governments' energy policy decisions. These dynamics can include state-firm bargaining, competition between bureaucratic groups, and interest group politics regarding how the benefits (and risks) of energy exploitation are shared among stakeholders (Hancock and Vivoda 2014; Hughes and Lipscy 2013). Without devoting attention to the domestic politics of energy policy, it is impossible to account for the full array of political factors that shape how governments approach the international game of energy interdependence (Wilson 2017). As several recent contributions have argued,[3] the research agenda for studies of energy interdependence lies in identifying both the *domestic* and *international* conditions that give rise to different expressions of these behavioral logics in various national, regional, and temporal contexts.

State Strategies: Energy Nationalism and Liberalism

These behavioral logics reveal that while energy interdependence is a somewhat mandatory coordination game, governments face a choice over whether to adopt competitive or cooperative approaches to their energy relationships. On the one hand, the necessity of international trade and investment to develop energy industries requires a degree of openness to and participation in international markets. On the other, the desire to maximize the gains from interdependence—whether in the form of capturing rents for producers or securing energy supplies for consumers—means pressures exist for states to intervene in the operation of these markets. This choice is manifested in state policy through two distinct strategies, known respectively as energy nationalism and energy liberalism, which are differentiated by the use of state- or market-based mechanisms for managing energy interdependence.

Energy nationalism is a strategy whereby governments use interventionist policies to assert control over their energy sectors. These policies are underpinned by the view that the laissez-faire approach will expose economies to the vicissitudes of international energy markets and that governments should instead manage these markets through a range of policy interventions (Wilson 2015b). One such policy intervention involves state ownership requirements, in which governments restrict foreign and private investment and require their energy sectors to be wholly or majority controlled by state-owned enterprises (SOEs). Another intervention is state controls on trade flows, including export taxes, licensing regimes, and quantitative restrictions. These allow governments, rather than private corporations, to determine with whom energy will be traded. A third policy intervention is energy subsidy regimes, under which price controls and producer subsidies are used to lower domestic energy prices relative to international levels. Subsidies act as a form of protection for energy-consuming industries, and energy prices are set not by market processes but by governmental decisions. The defining political-economic characteristic of energy nationalism is that states assert control of trade and investment to manage these flows in a way that maximizes the capture of energy rents.

Energy nationalism is very common. The archetypical nationalists are the Gulf States, which tightly control their energy sectors through state ownership rules and export controls associated with participation in the OPEC oil cartel (Marcel 2006). Russia also exercises control of its oil sector through state ownership of both production and export pipeline facilities (Aalto 2012). Many governments in the developing world—including Brazil, China, India, and Indonesia—have investment regimes mandating a degree of local or state ownership, to ensure these important sectors contribute to national development goals (Wilson 2015b). Most energy-rich governments maintain extensive subsidy regimes, which were collectively worth $321 billion in 2015 (IEA 2015). Indeed, energy nationalism is found in most major energy producers today. As Table 7.1 shows, six of the world's top 10 energy producers intervene in markets via a mix of state ownership, trade control, and energy subsidy policies. With these six players producing 57 percent of world output, global energy markets are subject to significant levels of state intervention.

Energy liberalism is an alternative strategy, in which governments instead deploy market-based energy policy regimes. Drawing on economic ideas regarding the efficacy of free markets, this strategy is rationalized by the belief that well-functioning international markets provide the best guarantee of energy security (McGowan 2008). At the domestic level, energy liberalism eschews the interventionist policies seen in more nationalistic jurisdictions, favoring investment rules that attract foreign capital, open trade regimes that allow private firms to determine patterns of supply, and energy pricing based on international market movements (Haselip and Hilson 2005). At the international level, this approach calls for the promotion of strategies to integrate national energy markets, through mutually negotiated trade and investment liberalization, the construction of cross-border energy infrastructure, and the cooperative management of market volatility. While energy liberalism means governments must forego opportunities to capture rents through intervention, its advocates argue that the efficiency and transparency offered by market mechanisms offer better outcomes than the nationalistic alternative.

Globally, there are four major energy players that use liberal policy frameworks: Australia, Canada, the EU, and the United States. All have open energy investment regimes, do not impose trade controls or subsidize domestic energy prices, and with the exception of the EU[4] do not have rules mandating state ownership or a major presence of SOEs in their energy sectors (Goldthau and Sitter 2015; Wilson 2015b). They have also been active supporters of international efforts to liberalize world energy markets. All are members of the IEA, which in recent years has become an important forum for advancing energy market liberalization efforts (van de Graaf 2012). The EU was the driving force behind the 2001 Energy Charter Treaty, a post–Cold War attempt to bring together eastern and western Europe through energy market integration (McGowan 2008). Australia has taken a leadership role in promoting gas market liberalization and subsidy reform, working with these partners through both the Asia-Pacific Economic Cooperation (APEC) (2017) and G20 Summit processes (Wilson 2016). While accounting for only a quarter of world energy production, these developed Western economies function as a powerful bloc advocating liberal approaches to energy interdependence.

There has also been a cyclical pattern of alternation between energy nationalism and liberalism over the past half-century. States' policy choices are closely correlated to cycles in world energy markets, with boom periods empowering countries to engage in nationalistic interventions, while during busts liberal policies are adopted (Vivoda 2009). In the immediate postwar period liberal policies were dominant, as producer states sought investment from Western energy firms. This gave way to a period of nationalism during the boom years of the 1960s and 1970s, when many developing economies sought to assert their independence from Western powers by nationalizing their energy sectors. An energy bust in the 1980s saw market-based approaches return to favor, as declining prices caused governments to liberalize their investment and trade regimes to secure their positions in increasingly competitive world markets. The resource boom of the early 2000s has again seen the pendulum swing back toward nationalism, with renationalization and trade controls reimposed in countries as diverse as Russia, Brazil, Indonesia, Venezuela, and Kazakhstan (Joffe et al. 2009; Stevens 2013). Wilson (1987) has described this back and forth as a "petro-political cycle," under which *economic cycles* (in world energy prices) drive a *political cycle* of alternation between nationalist and liberal policy strategies.

Importantly, the choice governments make between these two strategies structures patterns of international energy politics. Energy nationalism is a major cause of competitive behavior predicted by geopolitical analyses. The presence of SOEs, trade restrictions, and price-distorting subsidy regimes undermines the transparency and openness of international markets. This weakens their ability to function as a global public good, making governments wary about relying on market-based approaches to interdependence (Hughes 2011). By framing energy security as a *national* problem, they also reduce the likelihood of institutional cooperation between producers and consumers. Conversely, liberalism contributes to an environment in which global energy governance cooperation can flourish. By treating energy as "just another commodity," market-based policies act to depoliticize interdependence (McGowan 2008), and if adopted by many states they can function as a shared agenda underpinning multilateral cooperation (Andrews-Speed et al. 2002). In this way, the nature of the coordination game for energy interdependence is inherently neither zero- nor positive-sum. Rather, variations in the strategies states employ determine which behavioral logic is dominant. During periods when nationalism is widespread, competitive behavior is common, while liberal policies encourage cooperative behavior.

GOVERNANCE CHALLENGES: STATE BEHAVIOR AND INTERNATIONAL COORDINATION

The tension between competitive/nationalist and cooperative/liberal behaviors is a critical determinant of patterns of global energy governance. The international governance regimes for energy differ qualitatively from those in other domains of the global economy. Many other areas of economic cooperation are based on a central, formalized, and treaty-based body, such as the World Trade Organization (WTO) for trade and the International Telecommunications Union (ITU) for communication networks. In contrast, energy governance is characterized by a regime complex (Colgan et al. 2012) comprised of a set of overlapping institutions that range from formal treaties to informal dialogue bodies and non-binding coordination schemes (see Table 7.2). A defining feature of this regime complex is the dominance of "soft-law" approaches, in which governments favor dialogue-based mechanisms to negotiate informal and voluntary energy policy reforms (Wilson 2015a). This approach to institution building means international energy cooperation is a more open-ended process. Rather than a one-off negotiation of agreed rules within a single framework (e.g., a trade agreement), energy cooperation is an iterative process of negotiating non-binding standards across a diverse set of institutions. In this context, the balance between competitive and cooperative energy policy behavior becomes important in determining institutional processes and outcomes. Attempts to expand the landscape of multilateral energy institutions to better reflect contemporary market realities and efforts to reform energy subsidy and pricing regimes are two recent initiatives in global energy governance that illustrate this dilemma.

Since the 1970s, two major energy organizations—the IEA and OPEC—have dominated global energy governance. Respectively functioning as consumer and producer cartels, their initially antagonistic relationship has more recently transformed into one of "collaborative management," in which the bodies work together to manage oil market volatility (Goldthau and Witte 2011). However, the evolving nature of the world energy market has undermined their status. As industrialization has proceeded in a range of developing economies, these organizations' share of world energy markets has steadily fallen. The transition toward unconventional and renewable sources has also reduced the importance of oil as an energy source (see Tutuncu in this volume for a discussion of unconventional sources). OPEC now accounts for only 23 percent of world energy production, and the IEA for only 41 percent of consumption (USEIA 2016). As a result, several attempts have been launched to develop new institutions that better reflect today's energy markets.

The first of these institutional innovations was the formation of the International Energy Forum (IEF), a biennial summit of seventy-two producer and consumer countries first held in 1991 and formalized in 2003 (IEF 2017). In 2001 it was matched by the creation of the Gas Exporting Countries Forum (GECF), a twelve-member body whose members hold two-thirds of proven world gas reserves (GECF 2017). Both the IEF and

GECF are dialogue bodies, which convene ministerial summits and host technical working groups to facilitate information sharing. Unlike older treaty-based institutions, these energy forums focus solely on providing a space for dialogue and do not impose any formal rules or policy commitments on member states. The IEA and OPEC have also attempted to update their memberships via partnerships with new energy players. OPEC extended a membership invitation to Brazil and Russia in 2008 and in 2011 made a landmark agreement to "coordinate" with Russia on oil production decisions (Goldthau and Witte 2011). The IEA has made similar moves, opening "outreach programs" with Brazil, China, Mexico, Russia, and South Africa and in 2015 creating an "associate member" status, which has since been taken up by China, Indonesia, India, Thailand, Singapore, and Morocco (IEA 2017b). Driven by the cooperative behavioral logic, the result of these actions has been a much-needed modernization of the membership of multilateral energy institutions.

However, the utility of these institution-building efforts has been limited by the presence of energy nationalists. With domestic policy regimes emphasizing state control, these governments have only been willing to participate in efforts that do not constrain their energy policy autonomy. The IEA's outreach partners and associate members are only partially integrated with the organization, participating in dialogue and information-sharing activities but not joining the more important Coordinated Emergency Response Measures system for oil sharing during a supply crisis. OPEC's overtures to Brazil and Russia have been rebuffed, as membership in the OPEC quota system would require giving up autonomy over their oil production decisions (Goldthau and Witte 2011). While many governments have proven willing to join the new dialogue bodies, it is precisely because these bodies impose negligible policy constraints. Neither the IEF nor the GECF has articulated an agreed set of policy principles, nor do they have any rules for members' energy trade or investment policy. Indeed, the IEF Charter (IEF 2011) explicitly states that it will not "create any legally binding rights or obligations" for its members. As energy "talkshops," these organizations' dialogue-only approach makes it easy for autonomy-conscious states to participate, but at the cost of preventing any formal rule making from occurring (Wilson 2015a). The presence of energy nationalists means that cooperative imperatives have been channeled toward lower-cost, and lower-impact, dialogue-only activities.

Energy subsidy and pricing regimes are central to a second example of how the balance between competitive and/or cooperative energy policy behavior drives institutional processes and outcomes. These subsidies are widely considered to be a major cause of energy insecurity. By artificially lowering energy prices, they distort price signals, encourage wasteful consumption, and if funded by energy SOEs weaken these firms' ability to invest in new productive assets. They also divert scarce governmental resources away from more effective energy security measures (such as support for renewables or energy infrastructure). However, reform of energy subsidies is politically a very difficult process. A wide range of interest groups, including households, industrial firms, and the transportation sector, benefit from artificially low energy prices. This means subsidies are a populist policy that is easy to enact but difficult to reduce or reform (Victor 2009). Given the interdependent nature of energy markets—in which price movements in one economy spill over to others—there is also an international dimension to subsidy reform, which is most effective where governments agree to jointly reduce subsidies in a coordinated manner. International agreements may also help by applying "external" pressure that makes it easier to manage domestic vetoes of subsidy reform efforts.

Several efforts to coordinate energy subsidy reform have been launched in recent years (see Box 7.1). The first and most significant was made at the G20's Pittsburgh Summit in September 2009, at which members made a non-binding agreement to phase out "inefficient" fossil fuel subsidies over the medium term (G20 2009). This commitment was extended to the Asia-Pacific region, the global epicenter of energy consumption growth, when APEC adopted an almost identical commitment at its Singapore Summit in November of the same year (APEC 2009). Both added peer-review mechanisms to monitor implementation in 2013. In June 2010, eight major non-G20 countries established the "Friends of Fossil-Fuel Subsidy Reform," designed to build broader international consensus behind the need for subsidy reforms. In 2015 the Friends issued a "Fossil Fuel Subsidy Reform Communiqué," articulating a three-step strategy for implementing such reforms, which has subsequently been endorsed by thirty-five governments (FFFSR 2015). The connection among subsidy reform, environmental sustainability, and development was also recognized in 2015 when the reduction of inefficient subsidies was included as an explicit target in the UN Sustainable Development Goals (UN 2015, 12C). A broad consensus has now formed behind cooperative energy subsidy reform efforts.

However, the soft-law design of these agreements has left space for energy nationalists to shirk commitments to reform. All four instruments (including the peer-review mechanisms) are explicitly non-binding; while governments are encouraged to reform subsidies, the choice to do so is entirely voluntary. Moreover, all four instruments left the issue of what constituted an "inefficient" subsidy undefined, allowing governments to individually determine whether their subsidy regimes were affected or not. These

Box 7.1 Recent International Efforts to Promote Energy Subsidy Reform

G20: Commitment to "phase out and rationalize over the medium term inefficient fossil fuel subsidies" (Group of Twenty 2009); addition of voluntary peer-review mechanism (2013).

Asia-Pacific Economic Cooperation: Commitment to "rationalise and phase out over the medium-term fossil fuel subsidies that encourage wasteful consumption" (APEC 2009); addition of voluntary peer-review mechanism (2017).

Friends of Fossil Fuel Reform Subsidy Reform: Established 2010; issued "Fossil Fuel Subsidy Reform Communiqué" encouraging transparent, ambitious, and safeguard-supported strategies for subsidy reform (FFFSR 2015).

UN Sustainable Development Goals: Includes goal of "rationalizing inefficient fossil-fuel subsidies that encourage wasteful consumption" (UN 2015).

loopholes have enabled energy nationalists to declaratively support the instruments while making few if any policy changes. In APEC, only five small economies[5] have completed peer reviews, with none of the major energy players (particularly Russia, China, and the United States) willing to submit its subsidy reform efforts to scrutiny. In reporting to the G20, eight governments claimed that their subsidy regimes were not inefficient and thus not bound by the reform commitment (G20 Information Centre 2012).

Many governments are reluctant to report because they have made only minimal reforms to their subsidy regimes. Research by the Overseas Development Institute (ODI) has found that while some small economies have made progress, several major G20 and/or APEC members—including Russia, China, Indonesia, Saudi Arabia, and the United States—continue to heavily subsidize fossil fuels. The value of these subsidies is massive, with G20 governments collectively offering $70 billion in direct subsidies and $374 in indirect support through SOEs and government-owned financial institutions in 2013–2014 (ODI 2015). To be sure, the global value of energy subsidies has declined in recent years, falling from a peak of $493 billion in 2013 to $321 billion in 2015 (IEA 2015). But as recent IEA (2017c) analysis shows, the bulk of this decline is attributable to falling energy prices, not the effects of systematic subsidy reforms. As energy subsidies are a key component of these governments' nationalistic energy policy regimes, they have exploited the voluntarist nature of international instruments to largely ignore agreed reforms. Despite almost a decade of cooperative effort, energy nationalism continues to subject global energy markets to significant and distorting state interventions.

A FUTURE RESEARCH AGENDA: THE POLITICAL DRIVERS OF ENERGY BEHAVIORAL LOGICS

Interdependence is a defining feature of the global energy system. But in a coordination game—in which joint gains through cooperation are overlaid by distributional conflicts—states respond in different ways. A geopolitical behavior logic expects states to view interdependence as a zero-sum game, adopting nationalistic policies at home and abstaining from international agreements that constrain their energy autonomy. A global energy governance logic conversely offers a positive-sum approach, wherein liberal energy policy regimes are complemented by efforts to develop international institutions to augment and support markets. The balance between these two logics structures the tenor of international energy politics, with the former driving intergovernmental conflicts while the latter facilitates cooperative institution building. Often the two coexist, as exemplified by recent efforts to modernize the membership of multilateral institutions and foster consensus around subsidy reform. In such contexts, the tension between the two logics produces energy governance institutions that fall short of their desired goals, due to the need to compromise between the liberal and nationalistic preferences of different players. In this way, the relative strength of conflictual and cooperative behavior determines how the coordination game of energy interdependence plays out.

The agenda for future research therefore lies in identifying the political and economic conditions that give rise to these contrasting energy policy behaviors. Existing scholarship has already identified a leading *economic* factor—energy market cycles—as a key driver. Since the postwar period, there has been a close temporal correlation between world energy markets and states' policy choices, with boom periods leading to the spread of competitive energy nationalism and busts replacing it with cooperative liberal approaches (Stevens 2013; Vivoda 2009). This alternation has again occurred during the most recent market cycle, with nationalistic policies rising during the global boom of 2005–2012, then subsiding as prices have fallen since 2014 (Wilson 2017). As this pattern has consistently been observed for several decades, it is likely that economic cycles will continue to shape the balance between competitive and cooperative behavior in years to come.

However, further work to explain the political drivers of these behavior logics is needed. The utility of this avenue for research is indicated by the fact that different governments express different behaviors even within the same global market cycle. The most recent boom period provides an instructive example. Many governments in the developing world—including Brazil, Indonesia, India, and Russia—moved toward energy nationalism during this period, while others (such as the Gulf States) maintained preexisting nationalist policies (Stevens 2013). Yet this pattern was not universal. Several developed economies—including Australia, Canada, the United States, and the EU—maintained a liberal policy framework at home and advocated for cooperation in international fora. Such behavior reflects these states' unique political attributes: liberal market economies that favor cooperative and market-based approaches to economic governance (Goldthau and Sitter 2015; Wilson 2017). This diversity of responses indicates that *economic* market cycles are only part of the picture, and an analysis of the *political* factors driving energy policy behavior is also needed to explain the diversity of responses seen among the major players in the global energy system. Future scholarship should focus on how the unique political attributes of key producers and consumers structure their approach to energy interdependence.

As a corollary, greater attention should also be paid to the domestic politics underlying energy policy choices. By conceptualizing energy interdependence as a coordination game, existing theories have usefully identified two potential behavioral logics for how states interact over energy. But there is demonstrable variation—both between countries and over time—in whether governments choose cooperative/liberal strategies or competitive/nationalistic ones. The character of the international coordination game therefore does not fully determine the strategic choices governments make, which requires attention to ways in which energy is intertwined in a variety of domestic-level political and economic processes. As van de Graaf has succinctly argued: "State preferences in global energy are shaped to a large extent by the domestic political economy. The way in which a country's energy sector is structured matters significantly for the preferences it will develop towards global energy governance. Factors such as the dependence on foreign suppliers, the strength of national energy companies, the degree of liberalisation of energy markets, and the presence of influential environmental or industry lobby groups all contribute to explaining national positions in global energy discussions" (2013, 156).

It is only by combining analysis of the international politics of energy coordination with the domestic politics of energy policy decisions that a complete account of energy interdependence can be developed. The agenda for future research lies in building on existing theories of the international dimension through the addition of systematic analyses of domestic drivers. This will allow for a more comprehensive explanation of the variable patterns of energy cooperation and conflict observed in recent years and help identify the factors and conditions that enable robust and mutually beneficial global energy governance systems.

NOTES

1. In game theory, a coordination game featuring two agents is popularly known as the "battle of the sexes" game. For a discussion in the international relations context, see Snidal (1985).
2. For a discussion of energy politics and realist IR theory, see Stoddard (2013).
3. For a critique of the absence of domestic political analysis in theories of international energy politics, see Hancock and Vivoda (2014), Keating et al. (2012), Van de Graaf (2013), and Wilson (2017).
4. While many EU governments have privately owned energy sectors, some eastern European members maintain SOE monopolies in their electricity and gas sectors. Overall, SOEs account for 40 percent of turnover in the EU energy sector (European Commission 2016, 8).
5. Peru, New Zealand, Philippines, Taiwan, and Vietnam. Author's compilation, from APEC EWG (2017).

REFERENCES

Aalto, Pami, ed. 2012. *Russia's Energy Policies: National, Interregional and Global Levels.* Cheltenham, UK: Edward Elgar.

Andrews-Speed, Philip, Xuanli Liao, and Roland Dannreuther. 2002. "The Strategic Implications of China's Energy Needs." Adelphi Papers no. 346. London: International Institute for Strategic Studies.

APEC Energy Working Group (APEC EWG). 2017. "EWG Meetings Document Database," https://www.ewg.apec.org/meetings.html

Asia-Pacific Economic Cooperation (APEC). 2009. "The Singapore Declaration: Sustaining Growth, Connecting the Region, 14 November 2009," https://www.apec.org/Press/Features/2009/0201_APEC_Singapore_2009_Sustaining_Growth_Connecting_the_Region

BP. 2017. *BP Statistical Review of World Energy 2017.* London: BP PLC.

Colgan, Jeff D., Robert O. Keohane, and Thijs van de Graaf. 2012. "Punctuated Equilibrium in the Energy Regime Complex." *Review of International Organisations* 7, no. 2: 117–143.

Dubash, Navroz K., and Ann Florini. 2011. "Mapping Global Energy Governance." *Global Policy* 2, no. S1: 6–18.

European Commission. 2016. *State-Owned Enterprises in the EU: Lessons Learnt and Ways Forward in a Post-Crisis Context*. Brussels: European Commission.

Florini, Ann, and Benjamin K. Sovacool. 2009. "Who Governs Energy? The Challenges Facing Global Energy Governance." *Energy Policy* 37: 5239–5248.

Friends of Fossil Fuel Subsidy Reform (FFFSR). 2015. "Fossil-Fuel Subsidy Reform Communiqué," http://fffsr.org/communique/

Gas Exporting Countries Forum (GECF). 2017. "About the GECF," http://www.gecf.org/aboutus/about-gecf

Goldthau, Andreas. 2011. "The Public Policy Dimension of Energy Security." In *The Routledge Handbook of Energy Security*, edited by Benjamin K. Sovacool, 129–145. Abingdon, UK: Routledge.

Goldthau, Andreas, and Jan Martin Witte. 2009. "Back to the Future or Forward to the Past? Strengthening Markets and Rules for Effective Global Energy Governance." *International Affairs* 85, no. 2: 373–390.

Goldthau, Andreas, and Jan Martin Witte, eds. 2010. *Global Energy Governance: The New Rules of the Game*. Washington, DC: Brookings Institution Press.

Goldthau, Andreas, and Jan Martin Witte. 2011. "Assessing OPEC's Performance in Global Energy." *Global Policy* 2, no. S1: 31–39.

Goldthau, Andreas, and Nick Sitter. 2015. *A Liberal Actor in a Realist World: The European Union Regulatory State and the Global Political Economy of Energy*. Oxford: Oxford University Press.

Graaf, Thijs van de. 2012. "Obsolete or Resurgent? The International Energy Agency in a Changing Global Landscape." *Energy Policy* 48: 233–241.

Group of Twenty. 2009. "Leaders' Statement: The Pittsburgh Summit," https://www.oecd.org/g20/summits/pittsburgh/G20-Pittsburgh-Leaders-Declaration.pdf

Group of Twenty. 2013. "G20 Leaders' Declaration St Petersburg," http://www.g20.utoronto.ca/2013/2013-0906-declaration.html

G20 Information Centre. 2012. *2011 Cannes G20 Summit Final Compliance Report*. Toronto: University of Toronto Press.

Haglund, David G. 1986. "The New Geopolitics of Minerals: An Inquiry into the Changing International Significance of Strategic Minerals." *Political Geography Quarterly* 5, no. 3: 221–240.

Hancock, Kathleen J., and Vlado Vivoda. 2014. "International Political Economy: A Field Born of the OPEC Crisis Returns to Its Energy Roots." *Energy Research & Social Science* 1: 206–216.

Harris, Stuart, and Barry Naughton. 2007. "Economic Dimensions of Energy Security in the Asia-Pacific." In *Energy Security in Asia*, edited by Michael Wesley, 174–194. London: Routledge.

Haselip, James, and Gavin Hilson. 2005. "Winners and Losers from Industry Reforms in the Developing World: Experiences from the Electricity and Mining Sectors." *Resources Policy* 30, no. 2: 87–100.

Hughes, Llewelyn. 2011. "Resource Nationalism in the Asia-Pacific: Why Does It Matter?" In *Asia's Rising Energy and Resource Nationalism: Implications for the United States, China, and the Asia-Pacific Region*, 7–14. Seattle, WA: National Bureau of Asian Research.

Hughes, Llewelyn, and Phillip Y. Lipscy. 2013. "The Politics of Energy." *Annual Review of Political Science* 16, no. 1: 449–469.

International Energy Agency (IEA). 2015. "Energy Subsidies Database," http://www.worlden-ergyoutlook.org/resources/energysubsidies/.

International Energy Agency (IEA). 2017a. "Energy Balance Flows Database," https://www.iea.org/Sankey/

International Energy Agency (IEA). 2017b. "Non-Member Countries," https://www.iea.org/countries/non-membercountries/

International Energy Agency (IEA). 2017c. *Tracking Fossil Fuel Subsidies in APEC Economies: Toward a Sustained Subsidy Reform*. Paris: International Energy Agency.

International Energy Forum (IEF). 2011. *International Energy Forum Charter*. Riyadh, Saudi Arabia: International Energy Forum.

International Energy Forum (IEF). 2017. "IEF Overview," https://www.ief.org/about-ief/ief-overview.aspx

International Monetary Fund (IMF). 2017. "IMF Primary Commodity Prices Database," http://www.imf.org/external/np/res/commod/index.aspx

Jain, Purnendra. 2014. "Energy Security in Asia." In *Oxford Handbook of the International Relations of Asia*, edited by Rosemary Foot, John Ravenhill, and Saadia Pekkanen, 547–568. Oxford: Oxford University Press.

Joffe, George, Paul Stevens, Tony George, Jonathan Lux, and Carol Searle. 2009. "Expropriation of Oil and Gas Investments: Historical, Legal and Economic Perspectives in a New Age of Resource Nationalism." *Journal of World Energy Law & Business* 2, no. 1: 3–23.

Keating, Michael F., Caroline Kuzemko, Andrei V. Belyi, and Andreas Goldthau. 2012. "Introduction: Bringing Energy into International Political Economy." In *Dynamics of Energy Governance in Europe and Russia*, edited by Caroline Kuzemko, Andrei V. Belyi, Andreas Goldthau, and Michael F. Keating, 1–19. Basingstoke, UK: Palgrave Macmillan.

Klare, Michael. 2008. *Rising Powers, Shrinking Planet: The New Geopolitics of Energy*. New York: Henry Holt.

Le Billon, Philippe. 2004. "The Geopolitical Economy of 'Resource Wars.'" *Geopolitics* 9, no. 1: 1–28.

Lesage, Dries, Thijs van de Graaf, and Kirsten Westphal. 2010. *Global Energy Governance in a Multipolar World*. Farnham, UK: Ashgate Publishing.

Licklider, Roy. 1988. "The Power of Oil: The Arab Oil Weapon and the Netherlands, the United Kingdom, Canada, Japan, and the United States." *International Studies Quarterly* 32, no. 2: 205–226.

Marcel, Valerie. 2006. *Oil Titans: National Oil Companies in the Middle East*. London: Chatham House.

McGowan, Francis. 2008. "Can the European Union's Market Liberalism Ensure Energy Security in a Time of 'Economic Nationalism'?" *Journal of Contemporary European Research* 4, no. 2: 90–106.

O'Sullivan, Meghan. 2013. "The Entanglement of Energy, Grand Strategy and International Security." In *Handbook of Global Energy Policy*, edited by Andreas Goldthau, 30–47. Chichester, UK: Wiley-Blackwell.

Overseas Development Institute (ODI). 2015. *Empty Promises: G20 Subsidies to Oil, Gas and Coal Production*. London: Overseas Development Institute.

Peters, Susanne, and Kirsten Westphal. 2013. "Global Energy Supply: Scale, Perception and the Return to Geopolitics." In *International Handbook of Energy Security*, edited by Hugh Dyer and Maria Julia Trombetta, 92–113. Cheltenham, UK: Edward Elgar.

Pirani, Simon, Jonathan Stern, and Katja Yafimava. 2009. *The Russo-Ukrainian Gas Dispute of January 2009: A Comprehensive Assessment*. Oxford: Oxford Institute for Energy Studies.

Russett, Bruce. 1984. "Dimensions of Resource Dependence: Some Elements of Rigor in Concept and Policy Analysis." *International Organization* 38, no. 3: 481–499.

Snidal, Duncan. 1985. "Coordination versus Prisoners' Dilemma: Implications for International Cooperation and Regimes." *American Political Science Review* 79, no. 4: 923–942.

Sovacool, Benjamin K., and Ann Florini. 2012. "Examining the Complications of Global Energy Governance." *Journal of World Energy & Natural Resources Law* 30, no. 3: 235–263.

Stevens, Paul. 2013. "History of the International Oil Industry." In *Global Resources: Conflict and Cooperation*, edited by Roland Dannreuther and Wojciech Ostrowski, 13–32. Basingstoke, UK: Palgrave Macmillan.

Stoddard, Edward. 2013. "Reconsidering the Ontological Foundations of International Energy Affairs: Realist Geopolitics, Market Liberalism and a Politico-Economic Alternative." *European Security* 22, no. 4: 437–463.

Tunsjo, Oystein. 2013. *Security and Profit in China's Energy Policy: Hedging against Risk*. New York: Columbia University Press.

United Nations (UN). 2015. "Sustainable Development Goals," https://sustainabledevelopment.un.org/sdgs

United Nations Conference on Trade and Development (UNCTAD). 2017a. "UNCTADStat Database," http://unctadstat.unctad.org/

United Nations Conference on Trade and Development (UNCTAD). 2017b. *World Investment Report 2017*. New York: United Nations.

United Nations Development Program (UNDP). 2000. *World Energy Assessment: Energy and the Challenge of Sustainability*. New York: United Nations.

United States Energy Information Administration (USEIA). 2016. "International Energy Statistics Database," http://www.eia.doe.gov/cfapps/ipdbproject/IEDIndex3.cfm?tid=1&pid=1&aid=2

Van de Graaf, Thijs. 2013. *The Politics and Institutions of Global Energy Governance*. London: Palgrave Macmillan.

Vernon, Raymond. 1983. *Two Hungry Giants: The United States and Japan in the Quest for Oil and Gas*. Cambridge, MA: Harvard University Press.

Verrastro, Frank, and Sarah Ladislaw. 2007. "Providing Energy Security in an Interdependent World." *Washington Quarterly* 30, no. 4: 95–104.

Victor, David G. 2009. *The Politics of Fossil-Fuel Subsidies*. Manitoba, Winnipeg: International Institute for Sustainable Development.

Victor, David G., and Linda Yueh. 2010. "The New Energy Order." *Foreign Affairs* 89, no. 1: 61–73.

Vivoda, Vlado. 2009. "Resource Nationalism, Bargaining and International Oil Companies: Challenges and Changes in the New Millennium." *New Political Economy* 14, no. 4: 517–534.

Wesley, Michael. 2007. "The Geopolitics of Energy Security in Asia." In *Energy Security in Asia*, edited by Michael Wesley, 1–12. London: Routledge.

Westing, Arthur H. 1986. "Wars and Skirmishes Involving Natural Resources: A Selection from the Twentieth Century." In *Global Resources and International Conflicts: Environmental Factors in Strategic Policy and Action*, edited by Arthur H. Westing, 204–210. Oxford: Oxford University Press.

Wilson, Ernest J., III. 1987. "World Politics and International Energy Markets." *International Organization* 41, no. 1: 125–149.

Wilson, Jeffrey D. 2015a. "Multilateral Organisations and the Limits to International Energy Cooperation." *New Political Economy* 20, no. 1: 85–106.

Wilson, Jeffrey D. 2015b. "Understanding Resource Nationalism: Economic Dynamics and Political Institutions." *Contemporary Politics* 21, no. 4: 399–416.

Wilson, Jeffrey D. 2016. "The Challenge of Australia's Resource Power Moment." In *Australia in World Affairs 2011–2015: Navigating the New International Disorder*, edited by Mark Beeson and Shahar Hameiri, ch. 10. Melbourne: Oxford University Press.

Wilson, Jeffrey D. 2017. *International Resource Politics in the Asia-Pacific: The Political Economy of Conflict and Cooperation*. Cheltenham, UK: Edward Elgar.

CHAPTER 8

THE POLITICS OF ENERGY REGIONALISM

KATHLEEN J. HANCOCK, STEFANO PALESTINI, AND KACPER SZULECKI

THROUGHOUT the world, energy increasingly operates at a regional level. In Central America, southern Africa, western Africa, and northern Europe, states have linked themselves together via regional electricity grids (Del Barrio-Alvarez, Komatsuzaki, and Horii 2014; Oseni and Pollitt 2016). Members of the Association of Southeast Asian Nations (ASEAN) are joined through a regional gas pipeline (Sovacool 2010). The Arctic region faces a unique set of energy-related challenges best addressed in a regional context (Sidortsov 2016). Gas and oil pipelines give Russia leverage over regional neighbors (Ziegler 2013). The European Union (EU) recently formed its Energy Union, calling for a "resilient, reliable, secure and growingly renewable and sustainable" energy system (Jean-Claude Juncker, quoted in Westphal this volume). The North American Free Trade Agreement (NAFTA) includes several energy provisions (Stern 2007). In federal systems, subnational units have long created their own energy systems. In sum, energy regionalisms are a reality around the world.

A small but growing group of scholars has been asking important empirical and theoretical questions about energy regionalism. What regional arrangements aim at governing energy flows, markets, and politics? How do they emerge, and what drives regional integration in the energy sector? What effects does energy regionalism have on energy security and on the economic and social development of the regions and their populations? Research has been ongoing and increasing steadily, highlighting empirical cases in world regions. However, the research lacks an overt agenda that would provide real leverage over these questions.

This chapter first analyzes the results of a systematic search through political science, international relations, and energy journals to determine the type and extent of publications that link regions and energy. We then categorize the different units of analysis these studies use, look at the way they define and perceive regions, assess the theoretical approaches, and identify the main weaknesses in the literature. Finally, we propose a future research agenda on energy regionalism centered around three sets of questions about drivers, institutional design, and effects.

WHY REGIONALISM?

Energy has arguably become a regional issue. This development is due to a concurrence of different processes and the impact of source-specific energy materialities (Balmaceda 2018). First, the expansion of renewable energy sources and of electricity transmission infrastructure is often at odds with a state-centric logic (Lagendijk 2008). Power systems can be more efficient if they are designed and governed from a regional perspective, and regional grids allow states to diversify energy sources (Puka and Szulecki 2014). For example, South Africa can draw on hydroelectric sources via the Southern African Power Pool, offsetting its coal-heavy production, and Zambia can incorporate coal generation into its otherwise 100 percent hydroelectric production (Hancock 2018). Second, since the late 1960s, natural gas transmission pipelines have been built in various parts of the world, providing largely inflexible infrastructural backbones for new regions. These functional regions emerged from necessity to find governance solutions even in such politically hostile areas as divided Europe during the Cold War. Third, understanding how regionalisms—concepts, institutions, and organizations—intersect with energy politics can affect the success of development programs. For example, regional energy infrastructures meant to improve standards of living in lower income states sometimes flourish and at other times fail disastrously, benefiting only elites and fueling corruption. Development goals may thus go unreached and aid may be wasted due to a poor understanding of regional dynamics. Finally, energy externalities, such as air and water pollution, often have regional implications. As such, individual states have too narrow a scope, and global or even pan-continental forums, such as the African Union, might have too broad a scope. Regional solutions may provide the best governance structures.

At the scholarly level, our focus on energy regionalisms stems from three rarely linked trends. First, academics recognize the importance and specific characteristics of regions and have shown increased interest in rigorously comparing formal and informal institutions and issues between regions (e.g., Acharya 2012; Balsiger and VanDeveer 2012; Börzel and Risse 2016; Hameiri 2013; Lombaerde et al. 2010). Second, a wide variety of energy issues, driven by climate change, new energy players in the developing world, tensions between Russia and the European Union, and the rise of China, among other factors, are the focus of a growing group of international studies scholars. *The Oxford Handbook of Energy Politics* is but one example of the growing scholarship on a wide range of issues now covered under the larger umbrella of politics and energy. Third, whereas energy has long been viewed as a security issue, scholars increasingly analyze energy in a wider range of contexts. The interest in these new linkages is demonstrated by six recent journal special issues that focus on regions and energy: one dedicated to Africa (Hancock 2015a), another to the Arctic (Sidortsov 2016), three to the EU (Szulecki 2016; Szulecki and Claes 2019; Herranz-Surrallés, Solorio and Fairbrass 2020), and a sixth to energy regionalisms more broadly and covering several regions (Balmaceda and Westphal forthcoming; Goldthau, Richert, and Stetter forthcoming; Hancock forthcoming; Hermann and Ariel forthcoming; Johnson and VanDeveer forthcoming; Palestini forthcoming).

Energy and Regions: The State of the Art

We first discuss the results of a systematic search for journal articles that include energy and regions, some of which place regions front and center and some in which the region is more background. Drawing on our own areas of expertise, we have also analyzed the larger literature, including books, chapters, and works in progress.

Some scholars have observed that energy issues are not adequately covered in mainstream journals for political science and international relations scholars (Hancock and Vivoda 2014; Sovacool 2014). To see how well energy regionalism is covered, we searched eighty-six major peer-reviewed journals in international relations, political science, public policy, and energy studies (see Appendix), covering publications from 2000 to 2017. Through this systematic search, we identified fifty-two articles that deal with the combination of energy (using a variety of keywords in addition to energy, such as electricity, pipelines, coal, petroleum, oil, natural gas, nuclear, renewables, hydropower, and biofuels) and regions (in addition to the word "region," we searched for major regional organizations [European Union, ASEAN, etc.] and world regional groups [Africa, Asia, Southeast Asia, etc.]).

We found that these articles cover a wide range of regions, with the European Union dominating, both as a single focus area and in comparative articles (see Figure 8.1). This finding is consistent with the larger body of literature on regions. The Middle East and North Africa (MENA) has a higher percentage of coverage than it would in the larger literature. One might think this is due to oil and gas playing such a prominent role in the region, but interestingly, two of the three articles are on nuclear energy and one is on renewable energy. North America is more studied in our energy sample than is generally the case in the broader regionalism literature. This might be due to a particularly active group of scholars or because energy is the key factor in the region.

The topics covered in energy regionalism show an increasing concern with climate change, renewable energy of all varieties, and even energy efficiency (see Figure 8.2). As in the world of energy consumption, however, the bulk of articles are about oil, natural gas, and the pipelines used to carry those products. About a third of the articles focus on major formal regional organizations, mostly the EU plus some on ASEAN.

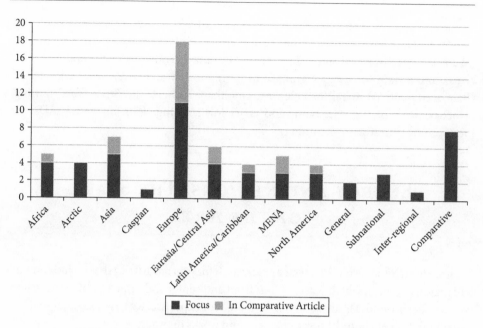

FIGURE 8.1 Articles by world region.

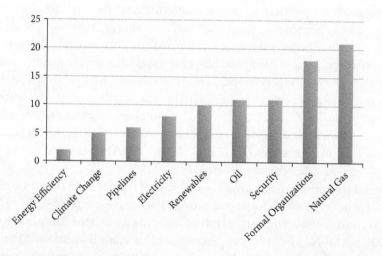

FIGURE 8.2 Articles by major topics.

As in the larger body of regionalism literature, there is a growing interest in evaluating energy issues on a regional scale (see Figure 8.3). Special issues partially account for this increase, as well as new publication outlets, notably *Energy Research & Social Science*, which was founded in 2014.

Energy scholars have sometimes complained about the challenges of getting published in general international relations and other politics journals. Our findings support the conclusion that general political journals publish much less on energy regionalism than do the two main energy-focused journals for social sciences: *Energy Policy* and the

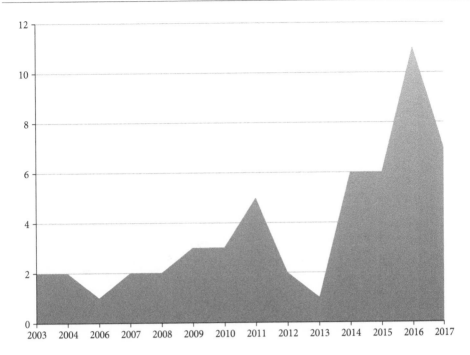

FIGURE 8.3 Articles by year.

previously noted *Energy Research & Social Science*. Of the general journals, only six published two or more articles on energy regionalism, with many not publishing any. Figure 8.4 shows all those journals that published two or more articles on energy regionalism during the 2000–2017 time period we analyzed. We do not claim there is a bias against publishing energy regionalism research, only that scholars looking for energy regionalism articles will be most likely to find them outside the broader based journals. Of the broader journals, *Review of Policy Research, International Affairs, Journal of International Relations and Development, Foreign Policy Analysis, International Studies Perspectives*, and *Journal of European Integration* have each published at least two articles over the seventeen-year period examined here.

Combining the journal articles found through our systematic search with published and unpublished work known from our own research, we find that more work needs to be done in three areas: first, the conceptualization of core concepts such as region and regionalism; second, more systematic research on the different energy contexts and how they affect types of regionalism; and third, a more systematic engagement with theories in order to explain the emergence of and the variation in energy regionalism.

Defining Energy Regions

Our journal search shows that the literature lacks a unified conceptualization of key concepts such as region and regionalism. While many articles take these concepts for

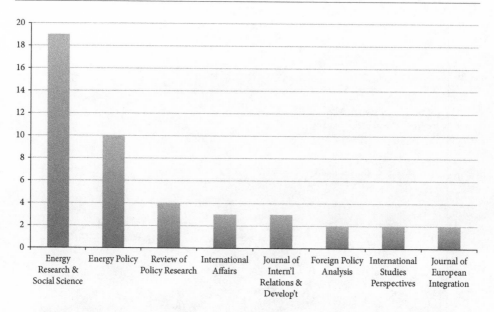

FIGURE 8.4 Major journals.

granted, others provide ad hoc definitions. For instance, scholars focusing on formal organizations assume their regions of reference from those who belong to the organization (Aalto 2014a; Baccini, Lenzi and Thurner 2013; Jinnah and Lindsay 2015; Stern 2007; Van den Hoven and Froschauer 2004). Thus, "European Union" functions as a shorthand for Europe, "ASEAN" for Southeast Asia, and "Eurasia" for the post-Soviet space (compare Balmaceda and Heinrich this volume). Other authors reference the Southern Cone region to discuss to the energy integration efforts within MERCOSUR (Hira and Amaya 2003). Still others label the region of reference as South America whether the focus is on Argentina, Bolivia, and Chile (Mares and Martin 2012) or Bolivia, Brazil, and Venezuela (Guimarães and Maitino 2019). In addition, Mares and Martin (2012) use the energy bilateral experience between Chile and other countries to draw generalizable lessons for broader South American energy integration, while Fritzsche, Zeijli and Tänzler (2011) look at Morocco to describe the relevance of global energy governance for Arab countries and MENA.

For some scholars, energy is what gives the region significance. Oil, argues Woertz (this volume), has shaped the very idea of the Middle East (and North Africa), providing a cornerstone for what we now perceive as the "naturalized" MENA region. For Brutschin and Schubert (2016), the Arctic is interesting and important for its undiscovered oil and gas reserves, as well as the melting ice opening up new trade routes and growing tensions along international borders. The Caspian states are linked by their petroleum-based economies and the fact that these are state-led industries (Alieva 2012). Prontera (2015) deals with the region that is constructed by the trans-Adriatic pipeline. Stroup, Kujawa, and Ayres (2015) study the Vermont-Canadian border region, which is constructed by decades of energy cooperation between Vermont and Québec.

The imagined regional space between Canada's hinterland and heartland region underlies Netherton's (2007) study on hydroelectric regimes. Meierding (2017) considers the South China Sea as a region precisely because of the oil and gas the littoral states want to explore.

We also find that the vast majority of the literature conceives of regions as made up of states, the common practice among international relations scholars, whereas subnational concepts (provinces, territories, states within federal states, etc.) are rarely used in the political science and policy literature on energy regionalism, even though national energy governance is explained by subnational factors. An exception is Selin and VanDeveer (2011). Focusing on environmental regions rather than energy per se, these authors provide a multiscalar definition of region that is not fixed to countries and that allows for different levels of jurisdiction. For these authors, therefore, there is no fundamental distinction between supranational and subnational regionalism. They define North American climate change regionalism as "a dynamic, political, multilevel context in which local, state, provincial, and federal actors formulate economic, environmental, and energy policies within their own jurisdictions. Furthermore, the exact number and definition of the particular levels of jurisdiction is neither always clear, nor static. As such, 'local' politics might include small towns, counties, large cities, or multi-jurisdictional metropolitan areas. Similarly, states and provinces make policy individually, but they also work in groups both within and across national boundaries" (Selin and VanDeveer 2011, 296).

While the bulk of political scientists focus on energy regions from an international perspective, a few study energy with a subnational understanding of region (Carroll, Stephenson, and Shaw 2011; Carter and Eaton 2016; Netherton 2007; Olson-Hazboun et al. 2016; Pratt 1985). Even fewer evaluate how subnational units from different states might form their own type of region. Stroup, Kujawa, and Ayres (2015), for instance, explore the subnational energy regionalism between two neighboring subnational jurisdictions: Vermont and the province of Québec. Energy relations between these two jurisdictions "reveal a complex interplay between energy flows and the environmental and policy discourses that surround them" (Stroup, Kujawa, and Ayres 2015, 301). Similarly, Pratt (1985) focuses on the tension between nationalism (Canadian identity) and regionalism, understood as the local identity of Canadian provinces. Smith (2007) looks at English regions in the context of devolution and EU membership in a multilevel governance framework, identifying a tension between formal administrative arrangements and the networked governance of renewables. Notably, none of the publications we reviewed evaluated subnational regionalism in non-Western states.

A handful of studies consider energy interregionalism. Chacha (2012) compares continental and subregional agreements, arguing that the regional integration agreements are the best way to reap the gains of cooperation. Interregionalism can also describe conscious efforts of one region to implement its legal regimes, order, or values in another, usually with the EU as the self-proclaimed model (Western Balkans in Fagan 2010; MENA in Charokopos 2015). The motives for these efforts are then the object of explanation. Antkiewicz and Momani (2009), for example, conclude that the European

Commission and its bureaucratic interests best explain the negotiations with the Gulf Cooperation Council. The most extensively researched case of energy interregionalism is the relationship between the EU and Eurasia via Russian oil and gas pipelines and exports (see Balmaceda and Heinrich this volume; Aalto et al. 2014). That said, scholars generally do not frame their contributions as interregional. Most studies present as international relations studies that happen to discuss the relationship of a regional organization (the EU) with a state from another region (Russia and Eurasia), or they are conducted from a European perspective in which Eurasia is not seen as a region comparable to Europe.

Some authors explicitly link energy regionalism to security. Alieva (2012) argues that security concerns of the elite are the driving force behind cooperation in the Caspian region. In her exploration of whether intergovernmental joint development agreements between rivals can lead to cooperation, Meierding (2017) finds that rarely are rivals able to co-develop hydrocarbons. Some authors argue that these energy sources have led to regional cooperation rather than conflict (Alieva 2012; Hancock 2009). Andreosso-O'Callaghan and Hwang (2009) argues that Northeast Asia could gain greater security through energy cooperation in the same way Europe did through the European Coal and Steel Commission.

Energy Content

As depicted in Figure 8.2, most energy regionalism scholarship evaluates fossil fuels, primarily oil and gas (e.g., Guimarães and Maitino 2019; Mares and Martin 2012; Prontera 2015; Valdivia 2015), electricity (e.g., Barrio-Álvarez et al. 2014; Hancock 2018, Netherton 2007; Oseni and Pollitt 2016; Van den Hoven and Froschauer 2004), or both (Hira and Amaya 2003; Palestini and Agostinis 2018). Wind energy has received the least coverage, with only Mukasa et al. 2015 specifically dedicated to wind energy, and even then the study, which focuses on how Africa could better use the wind to generate electricity, does not focus on regionalism per se. Similarly, with the exception of Shapiro (2014), biofuels are not explicitly covered in the regional literature we reviewed. A handful of articles analyze nuclear energy (Chacha 2012; Jackson 2009; Jewell 2011; Van Den Hoven and Froschauer 2004).

Many publications are indifferent regarding the characteristics of the energy resource and instead focus on political science concepts: identity politics (Pratt 1985), governance (Palestini and Agostinis 2018), diffusion (Charokopos 2015), policy coherence (Strambo, Nilsson, and Månberger 2015), conflict (Valdivia 2015), multilateralism (Belyi 2012), and power politics and regional leadership (Guimarães and Maitino 2019). Exceptions are those pieces focusing on power pools that make explicit the physical and, consequently, institutional differences between hydrocarbon and electricity sectors (Oseni and Pollitt 2016; Cayo 2011). Historical research has shown the integrative qualities of electric infrastructures, which emerged in the early twentieth century around resources and river basins and displayed transnational and *regional* rather than national dynamics

(Lagendijk 2008, 2016). As these qualities visibly vary between sectors, Balmaceda (2018) argues persuasively that scholars must take into account the way materialities of different energy sources impact governance frameworks.

Energy infrastructure plays a key role in a number of studies. Founded around existing regional trade organizations, the African power pools, which consist of electricity grids and energy markets, can be seen as deepening regional integration (Chacha 2012), a point others make about energy pipelines for Russia and some of its neighbors (Hancock 2006). For others, security and ethnic conflicts override potential regional cooperation that could be realized through existing or planned energy infrastructure, such as electricity grids in Central Asia (Bohr 2004) and pipelines in the Caspian region (Bahgat 2002).

Explaining Energy Regionalism

To explain energy regionalism, some scholars explicitly draw on international relations (IR) theories (Baccini et al. 2013; Emerson 2015; Guimaraes and Martino 2019; Jinnah and Lindsay 2015; Palestini and Agostinis 2018). This approach is most visible in research on energy regionalism in Europe, which benefits from the robust literature on European integration (see Westphal this volume). Beyond that, Prontera (2015) takes Susan Strange's work in international political economy as a broad framework for his analysis of Italian energy policy, whereas Stroup, Kujawa, and Ayres (2015) refer to the "New Regionalism Approach" without elaborating much on it. Unsurprisingly, some articles by economists draw on economic theories. Stern (2007) and Oseni and Pollitt (2016) base their analyses on international trade theory. In her analysis of energy integration strategies in Latin America, geographer Gabriela Valdivia (2015) uses critical oil geopolitics (Mitchell 2011; Tsing 2005 as her primary theoretical framework. Stroup, Kujawa, and Ayres (2015), Hancock (2015b), and Bruszt and Palestini (2016) reference the comparative regionalism theories. Skalamera (2016) explains Russian reluctance to join the Energy Charter Treaty, thus addressing obstacles to regionalism. Ziegler (2013) examines the EU and Russia, finding that trust is a key factor in the success or failure of energy cooperation. Oseni and Pollitt (2016) and Palestini and Agostinis (2018) explain the emergence of energy cooperation between states. Both Palestini and Agostinis (2018) and Hancock (2009) focus on the role of regional powers such as Brazil, Venezuela, and Russia. Alieva (2012) puts the attention on nonstate actors such as firms and transnational corporations, as well as social media.

With some exceptions, the vast majority of articles focus on empirics over theory. To some extent this is a natural beginning. We must first understand what is out there before we can get some theoretical leverage. However, this has left unanswered a variety of important questions. What drives this kind of cooperation? Why is energy increasingly governed regionally, if that is indeed the case? How can lessons from the most advanced regional integration projects, like the European Union, be drawn and used in other geographic contexts? The current literature does not address these questions in an organized way.

Future Research Agenda

The previous section has shown that there is a considerable literature dealing with the link between regions and energy politics. However, the scholars seldom engage in dialogue with each other, lack common theoretical frameworks, and frequently do not address similar research questions. In short, there does not appear to be an organized research agenda. As we have seen, there is no single definition in the literature of what exactly energy regionalism is. Although theoretical eclecticism can be a virtue in certain cases, lack of agreement on the definition of the object of study constitutes a hindrance. We propose that energy regionalism is politically led cooperation and integration initiatives between state and nonstate actors and across territorial units that seek to govern energy relationships and deliver energy-related collective goods (see Johnson and VanDeveer 2019).

In this section we outline what a research agenda on energy regionalism would look like were it to be a coherent scholarly project. Following discussion of key works in comparative regionalism (Börzel and Risse 2016; Solingen 2008), we anchor this agenda around three factors: the *drivers*, the *institutional design*, and the *effects* of energy regionalism. We also draw on the work of scholars working on the broader literature of energy politics. In addition, we tackle two issues that need to be taken seriously by future students of energy regionalism: *theory* and *comparison and generalization*.

The Drivers of Energy Regionalism

A first set of research questions should identify the factors that drive states and nonstate actors to engage in energy cooperation and integration. Some of these factors may be common to regionalism in other issue areas. For instance, a certain level of economic and security interdependence or the presence of a regional hegemon is arguably a necessary condition for energy cooperation to unfold. However, in the case of energy, two other levels of explanation must be brought into the analysis. The first is the spatial (geographic) characteristics and the material (also infrastructural) conditions of the specific region. Energy infrastructure creates very inflexible relations between actors and brings in path dependencies, which are difficult to break out of in energy cooperation (Hayter 2004). The second level has to do with the physical properties (materialities) of the energy resource. Natural gas, oil, and electricity vary a great deal in terms of their transportability, processing, distribution, and storage, with a direct impact on the regional governance of the resources (Balmaceda 2018).

When dealing with drivers, students of energy regionalism need to cope with the relationship between interdependence and regionalism. Liberal scholars have largely assumed that this relation is positive: increasing (economic) interdependence leads to more regionalism (see Mattli 1999; Moravcsik 1993). However, evidence from the energy field indicates that energy interdependencies within a shared geographical region can lead either to regional cooperation or to conflict. For instance, hydrocarbon producers in Central Asia strive to establish independent export routes and shake loose from asymmetrical interdependencies with Russia (Balmaceda and Heinrich this volume). In North America, high energy interdependencies between the three federal states (Canada, the United States, and Mexico) have not translated into regional energy institutions. On the contrary, Mexico and Canada remain locked in a highly asymmetrical relationship with the United States under NAFTA and now USMCA (see Mildenberger and Stokes this volume). We need to understand the conditions that lead to cooperative or conflictive patterns of energy interdependencies. Are certain types of energy resources and their physical properties more prone to lead to more conflictive forms of interdependence?

Another important question that emerges is whether regional paymasters and strong regional institutions are potentially able to transform negative interdependencies into positive ones and lead toward energy integration. This seems particularly important in hydrocarbon-dependent regions, as highlighted by Woertz (this volume) in the case of MENA. While the literature on comparative regionalism has established the importance of regional hegemons or paymasters for the emergence and institutionalization of regionalism (e.g., Mattli 1999; Pedersen 2002), the evidence from the energy field is less reassuring. The agenda on energy regionalism will benefit from future studies that unpack the role of regional hegemons in energy cooperation. One possible way forward is to distinguish between regional powers that perceive energy regionalism predominantly as a foreign policy or diplomatic tool (Russia, Venezuela) and those that see it as an economic or developmental tool (Brazil, China, South Africa). Another possible, and perhaps more productive, approach is to analyze regional power in terms of members' economic and political regime type (Belyi and Talus 2015). For instance, regional powers whose economies and national energy sectors are organized as liberal market economies will probably have completely different attitudes toward regional energy integration than those whose economies are organized as state-capitalist economies (Loe 2019; Ostrowski 2015). Similarly, illiberal regimes will have a different approach to energy regionalism than liberal-democratic regimes, which tend to favor market integration and privatization. These different categorizations can provide useful hypotheses to test in ongoing cases of hegemonic regional integration projects such as the Belt and Road Initiative or the Eurasian Economic Union (for the former see Huda and Ali this volume, and for the latter see Balmaceda and Heinrich this volume).

Students of energy regionalism can also shed light on the role of political and institutional actors normally overlooked by the larger literature on comparative regionalism. Jinnah and Lindsay (2015) have highlighted the role of general secretariats in managing institutional overlap and brokering information. The case of the power pools highlights the role played by regional development banks (RDBs), such as the Interamerican Development Bank and the African Development Bank, in brokering agreements among a variety of state and nonstate actors in order to interconnect electric infrastructure and design regional market rules (Oseni and Pollitt 2016; Palestini Forthcoming).

The case of the RDBs is particularly interesting, as they have been a rather neglected object of study for comparative regionalism. The drive for regionalism can also come from unexpected sources. Hancock (2018) has highlighted the role of mining companies as main drivers of energy regionalism in Africa. What other nonstate actors play key roles in energy regionalism, and when do they matter most?

Further work should also look at identity. When do regional identities fragment larger regional spaces by excluding those who do not share the claimed identity, and how can regional identities be mobilized to turn interdependencies into cooperation? For example, in recent years Poland has strived to create an alternative energy community, now institutionalized in the Three Seas Initiative, going partly against EU regionalist tendencies (Zbińkowski 2019). Similarly processes of region building can be observed in the Black Sea region, the Caspian Sea region, the Western Balkans, and the Mediterranean. A comparative regionalism perspective, possibly combined with conceptual frameworks developed by critical geopolitics (Ó Tuathail 1996), can help to unpack how identities matter.

The Institutional Design of Regional Energy Governance

A second set of questions concerns the regional arrangements that govern energy flows, markets, and energy politics. In other words, how does the institutional design of regional arrangements vary, and which factors explain that variation? Energy regionalisms vary significantly, from regions in which energy cooperation is governed through treaties, agreements, and other types of *legalized* rules (Abbott et al. 2000; Closa and Casini 2016), to regions in which cooperation is almost exclusively led by power politics, diplomacy, or shared values. Some regions, like Southeast Asia and Oceania, have to deal with very high internal diversity, which means that despite the existence of formal regional institutions (e.g., ASEAN), energy regionalism encounters significant obstacles (Fünfgeld 2019).

Attempts to explain this variation risk falling into circular argumentation: identity-based regions emerge from well-developed market economies (such as in the context of the Nordic countries and Western Europe), where in turn market making is facilitated by preexistent regional identities (Aalto 2014b; Belyi and Makarychev 2015). More fine-grained empirical research, including historical and process-tracing analyses, is needed to unpack this two-way causal relationship between informal institutions (shared values and identity discourses) and formal regional energy institutions (agreements, treaties, organizations) (Aalto, 2016). Historians of energy infrastructures (e.g., Schot and Lagendijk 2008) have laid the groundwork for such research, exploring the ways in which shared values emerged within the energy engineers' epistemic community, which enabled increasing regionalism in Western Europe after World War II. Transmission system operators (TSOs), governing translocal grids, are in a good position to initiate depoliticized regional integration schemes (Puka and Szulecki 2014), which can with time be scaled up and spill over to other areas, such as in the Nordic region.

Scholars should also look beyond the black and white of supranational versus intergovernmental governance to identify the wider array of grays on the spectrum. Whereas the EU can be perceived as the foremost case of supranationality in certain policy areas (Westphal this volume), outside of Europe states delegate a variety of energy regulation and executive competences to regional institutions (Aalto 2015). As noted previously, RDBs have traditionally been ignored in the literature. They resemble innovative governance modes, tools, and frameworks, such as multi-stakeholder part-nerships (Szulecki, Pattberg, and Biermann 2011) or nodes in a "polycentric governance" framework (Jordan et al. 2018). More research is needed to establish under which condi-tions orchestration is prone to emerge and under which conditions a transition from orchestrated initiatives to supranationalism is expected (Palestini Forthcoming).

Another crucial aspect of the institutional design of regionalism, and of energy region-alism in particular, is the issue of institutional and organizational overlap (Sovacool and Cooper 2013). Research is needed to establish the causes of overlap and its consequences. In the case of Latin America, overlapping regionalism and regime complexity have been driven by parallel and sometimes competitive political projects of regional integration (Nolte 2014). While some of them have been based on open regionalism and trade liberalization, other projects have put emphasis on political and non-economic policy cooperation. This also seems to be the case for energy regionalism. Whereas projects such as MERCOSUR electric and gas integration and SIEPAC have been mostly oriented by market-making objectives, the petro-programs established by Venezuela were oriented by foreign policy objectives (Palestini Forthcoming). But it is not clear whether overlapping regionalism always leads to rivalry and incoherence. Scholarship needs to explore what determines success and failure; this leads us to the next set of questions.

The Effects of Energy Regionalism

One of the general conclusions of *The Oxford Handbook of Comparative Regionalism* (Börzel and Risse 2016) was that there is sparse literature on the effects and results of regionalism across policy and governance fields. Energy regionalism is not an excep-tion. Actors engage in regionalism with different goals in mind. Thus, which of these goals one should focus on when trying to account for effects and results is not obvious. In addition, scholars and disciplines vary in their approaches to regionalism and energy; consequently, the literatures are interested in different effects. Underlying the resulting range of approaches are fundamental distinctions among those who regard energy as a commodity, as a national/strategic resource, as a public good, or as an ecological entity (for a similar discussion in the case of the Asia-Pacific region, see Huda and Ali this volume; for the case of South America see Sabbatella and Santos forthcoming).

How do we account for the many and varied effects of energy regionalism? Following the framework proposed by Sovacool (2011), a possible way forward is to identify the impact of regionalism on four components of *energy security*: availability, affordability, efficiency, and sustainability. This conception, though not unproblematic (Cherp and Jewell 2014; Szulecki 2017), has the merit of encompassing traditional national security concerns with economic and developmental issues. The task of students of energy regionalism will be to single out the specific effects of regional arrangements on these elements.

While traditional theories about regional integration focused almost exclusively on the positive effects of regionalism (e.g., delivery of public goods, economic development, international peace), the agenda on energy regionalism should also pay equal attention to possible negative effects and conflict outcomes. For instance, large energy integration projects such as cross-national pipelines, mega dams, and electric grids have become sources of social conflict, as they have been perceived as part of an extra-activist economic model that especially affects local communities (for a discussion on energy projects and extra-activism in Latin America, see Gaylord this volume).

Furthermore, scholars should systematically explore how regional agreements created for other purposes, notably trade, can be harnessed for energy integration as well; where there are already overlapping agreements, they should assess which are successful in enhancing energy security as defined by the United Nations Development Programme: "the availability of energy at all times in various forms, in sufficient quantities and at affordable prices without unacceptable or irreversible impact on the environment" (UNDP 2004, 42).

Theory Building, Comparison, and Generalization

Finally, to get more leverage on their research, energy regionalism scholars need to focus on theory building, comparisons, and generalizations. These issues cut across the three sets of questions presented in this chapter.

First, we need to focus on theory and theory building. The current lack of common theoretical frameworks or paradigms can be explained in part by the multidisciplinary character of energy regionalism. International relations scholars rely on IR theories, geographers on political geography theory, economists on international economics theory, and so on, hindering the emergence of a common set of theoretical frameworks. In addition, many publications lack theory altogether. The issue of theory and theory building is debated in the broader field of comparative regionalism. Some authors have proposed the use of an encompassing framework such as "diffusion theory" to account for regionalism and its development (Börzel and Risse 2016; Risse 2016). Others have advocated for the production of more ad hoc theories of regionalism (Solingen and Malnight 2016) or for drawing on the canon of (mostly European) integration theories (Laursen 2003, 2010). Closa (2015) has forcefully made the case for mainstreaming comparative regionalism, using standard theories in political science and IR to account for the emergence, design, and effects of regionalism. A crucial aspect in this discussion is that researchers of energy regionalism will benefit from theories that break with traditional state-centric assumptions and instead adopt frameworks that are open to different classes of political actors, levels of governance, and material as well as environmental factors (for the case of the Asia-Pacific region, see the discussion in Huda and Ali this volume; for the use of IPE approaches in the study of energy regionalism, see Sabbatella and Santos forthcoming). There are important lessons to be learned from European integration research (see Westphal in this volume); however, the specificity of the European Union has already been identified as a limit to generalizability.

Belyi and Makarychev (2015) have proposed a framework to study energy regionalism (in their case, specifically hydrocarbons). Drawing on Buzan (2004), they propose classifying energy regions in regional systems, regional societies, and regional communities. Systems are based on interdependencies but are void of normative contents. Societies are based on formal institutions, namely rules and procedures, whereas communities are organized around informal institutions and mainly shared values and regional identities. In this approach, communities, based on identities, are the ideal scenario in which "participants are capable of systematically resolving their disputes in a peaceful way based on engagement and inclusion" (Buzan 2004, 64). This framework could well prove fruitful for energy regionalism scholars and would provide a much-needed coherent approach.

Second, scholars need to more systematically compare and generalize across regions and between different sources of energy. Some regions, particularly sub-Saharan Africa, remain understudied *as regions* not merely sets of individual countries (see Delina this volume, as well as our review). For instance, the study of power pools could be developed in cross-regional terms, as there are well-developed cases of regional power pools in Africa, Europe, and the Americas. The study of drivers of energy regionalism could also benefit from a cross-regional perspective, examining, for instance, the role of energy companies, RDBs, and general secretariats in different regional settings. A second alternative is to proceed through cross-sectoral comparisons. We could advance the knowledge in the field by looking at how actors within a region deal with electric versus hydrocarbon regionalism, or how the institutional design of regionalism varies across different types of renewables. Cross-regional and cross-sectoral approaches are not exclusive and can be productively combined to bring about a truly comparative energy regionalism agenda.

Political scientists are devoting more attention to energy than they have in a long time, just as they are more systematically expanding research on regionalism. Bringing together these two lines of scholarship will continue to bear considerable fruit from academic and policy perspectives. With the rise of renewable energy in response to climate change; changes in the power and identity of major state and nonstate regional, subnational, and transnational actors; the continued power of oil and natural gas in geopolitics; and the continued development of regional relationships and organizations, the scholarly community has a great deal of important work ahead.

References

Aalto, Pami. 2014a. "Energy Market Integration and Regional Institutions in East Asia." *Energy Policy* 74: 91–100. doi:10.1016/j.enpol.2014.08.021

Aalto, Pami. 2014b. "Institutions in European and Asian Energy Markets: A Methodological Overview." *Energy Policy* 74: 4–15. doi:10.1016/j.enpol.2014.08.022

Aalto, Pami. 2015. "States and Markets in Energy Policy." In *States and Markets in Hydrocarbon Sectors*, edited by Andrei Belyi and Kim Talus, 40–60. Hampshire, UK: Palgrave Macmillan.

Aalto, Pami. 2016. "The New International Energy Charter: Instrumental or Incremental Progress in Governance?" *Energy Research & Social Science* 11: 92–96.

Aalto, Pami, David Dusseault, Michael D. Kennedy, and Markku Kivinen. 2014. "Russia's Energy Relations in Europe and the Far East: Towards a Social Structurationist Approach to Energy Policy Formation." *Journal of International Relations and Development* 17, no. 1: 1–29. doi:10.1057/jird.2012.29

Abbott, Kenneth W., et al. 2000. "The Concept of Legalization." *International Organization* 54, no. 3: 401–419.

Acharya, Amitav. 2012. "Comparative Regionalism: A Field Whose Time Has Come?" *The International Spectator: Italian Journal of International Affairs* 47, no. 1: 3–15.

Alieva, Leila. 2012. "Globalization, Regionalization and Society in the Caspian Sea Basin: Overcoming Geography Restrictions and Calamities of Oil Dependent Economies." *Southeast European and Black Sea Studies* 12, no. 3: 443–453.

Andreosso-O'Callaghan, Bernadette and Hae-Du Hwang. 2009. "Energy Cooperation and Emerging Regionalism in North-East Asia Relative Impact on APEC and ASEM in Terms of Inter-Regionalism." *Journal of Korea Trade* 13, no. 1: 65–88.

Antkiewicz, Agata, and Bessma Momani. 2009. "Pursuing Geopolitical Stability through Interregional Trade: the EU's Motives for Negotiating with the Gulf Cooperation Council." *Journal of European Integration* 31, no. 2: 217–235.

Baccini, Leonardo, Veronica Lenzi & Paul W. Thurner. 2013. "Global Energy Governance: Trade, Infrastructure, and the Diffusion of International Organizations." *International Interactions* 39, no. 2: 192–216.

Bahgat, Gawdat. 2002. "Pipeline Diplomacy: The Geopolitics of the Caspian Sea Region." *International Studies Perspectives* 3, no 3: 310–327.

Balmaceda, Margarita M. 2018. "Differentiation, Materiality, and Power: Towards a Political Economy of Fossil Fuels." *Energy Research & Social Science* 39: 130–140.

Balmaceda, Margarita M., and Kirsten Westphal. Forthcoming. "Cross-regional Production Chains, Competitive Regionalism and the Deepening of Regulatory Fault Lines in Euro-Asia." In "Energy Regionalisms," special issue, *Review of Policy Research*.

Barrio-Alvarez, Daniel del, Shunsaku Komatsuzaki, and Hideyuki Horii. 2014. "Regional Power Sector Integration: Critical Success Factors in the Central American Electrictiy Market." *OIDA International Journal of Sustainable Development* 17, no. 12: 119–136.

Balsiger, Jörg, and Stacy D. VanDeveer. 2012. "Navigating Regional Environmental Governance." *Global Environmental Politics* 12, no. 3: 1–17.

Belyi, Andrei. 2012. "The EU's Missed Role in International Transit Governance." *Journal of European Integration* 34, no. 3: 261–276.

Belyi, Andrei, and Andrey Makarychev. 2015. "Regional Institutions and Energy Markets: Systems, Societies, Communities." In *States and Markets in Hydrocarbon Sectors*, edited by Andrei Belyi and Kim Talus, 61–80. Hampshire, UK: Palgrave Macmillan.

Belyi Andrei and Kim Talus (eds). 2015. States and Markets in Hydrocarbon Sectors, Palgrave Macmillan, Basingstoke.

Bohr, Annette. 2004. "Regionalism in Central Asia: New Geopolitics, Old Regional Order." *International Affairs* 80, no. 3: 485–502.

Börzel, Tanja A., and Thomas Risse, eds. 2016. *The Oxford Handbook of Comparative Regionalism*. Oxford: Oxford University Press.

Brutschin, Elina, and Samuel R. Schubert. 2016. "Icy Waters, Hot Tempers, and High Stakes: Geopolitics and Geoeconomics of the Arctic." *Energy Research & Social Science* 16: 147–159.

Bruszt, Laszlo, and Stefano Palestini. 2016. "Regional Development Governance." In *The Oxford Handbook of Comparative Regionalism*, edited by Tanja Börzel and Thomas Risse, 374–404. Oxford: Oxford University Press.

Buzan, Barry. 2004. *From International to World Society? English School Theory and the Social Structure of Globalisation*. Cambridge: Cambridge University Press.

Carroll, Myles, Eleanor Stephenson, and Karena Shaw. 2011. "BC Political Economy and the Challenge of Shale Gas: Negotiating a Post-staples Trajectory." *Canadian Political Science Review* 5, no. 2: 165–176.

Carter, Angela V., and Emily M. Eaton. 2016. "Subnational Responses to Fracking in Canada: Explaining Saskatchewan's 'Wild West' Regulatory Approach." *Review of Policy Research* 33, no. 4: 393–419.

Cayo, Juan Miguel. 2011. "Power Integration in Central America: From Hope to Mirage?". In *Getting the Most Out of Free Trade Agreements in Central America*, edited by Humerto López and Rashmi Shankar, 123–150. Washington DC: World Bank.

Chacha, Mwita. 2012. "Regional Integration and Nuclear Energy in Africa." *African Security Review* 21, no. 4: 38–50.

Charokopos, Michael. 2015. "EU External Action and the Reproduction of the 'Rationality Myth': The EU Energy and Aviation Policies vis à vis its Neighbours in the Western Balkans and the Southern Mediterranean." *Journal of European Integration* 37, no. 5: 517–534. doi:10. 1080/07036337.2015.1019878

Cherp, Aleh and Jessica Jewell. 2014. "The Concept of Energy Security: Beyond the Four As." *Energy Policy* 75: 415–421.

Closa, Carlos. 2015. "Mainstreaming Regionalism." EUI Working Papers, RSCAS 2015/12. Florence, Italy.

Closa, Carlos, and Lorenze Casini. 2016. *Comparative Regional Integration. Governance and Legal Models*. Cambridge, UK: Cambridge University Press.

Del Barrio-Alvarez, Daniel, Shunsaku Komatsuzaki, and Hideyuki Horii. 2014. "Regional Power Sector Integration: Critical Success Factors in the Central American Electricity Market." *OIDA International Journal of Sustainable Development* 7, no. 12: 119–136.

Emerson, Guy. 2015. "Strong Presidentialism and the Limits of Foreign Policy Success: Explaining Cooperation between Brazil and Venezuela." *International Studies Perspectives* 16, no. 4: 484–499.

Fagan, Adam. 2010. "The New Kids on the Block – Building Environmental Governance in the Western Balkans." *Acta Politica* 45: 203–228.

Fritzsche, Kerstin, Driss Zejli, Dennis Tänzler. 2011. "The Relevance of Global Energy Governance for Arab Countries: The Case of Morocco." *Energy Policy* 39, no. 8: 4497–4506.

Fünfgeld, Anna. 2019. "ASEAN Energy Connectivity: Energy, Infrastructure and Regional Cooperation in Southeast Asia." *Indonesian Quarterly* 46, no. 4: 315–343.

Goldhthau, Andreas, Joern Richert, and Stephan Stetter. Forthcoming. "Leviathan Awakens: Gas Finds, Energy Governance and the Emergence of the Eastern Mediterranean as a Geopolitical Region." In "Energy Regionalisms," special issue, *Review of Policy Research*.

Guimarães, Feliciano de Sá, and Martin Egon Maitino. 2019. "Socializing Brazil into Regional Leadership: The 2006 Bolivian Gas Crisis and the Role of Small Powers in Promoting Master Roles Transitions." *Foreign Policy Analysis* 15, no. 1: 1–20.

Hameiri, Shahar. 2013. "Theorising Regions Through Changes in Statehood: Rethinking the Theory and Method of Comparative Regionalism." *Review of International Studies* 39, no. 2: 313–335.

Hancock, Kathleen J. 2006. "The Semi-Sovereign State: Belarus and the Russian Neo-Empire." *Foreign Policy Analysis* 2, no. 2: 117–136.

Hancock, Kathleen J. 2009. *Regional Integration: Choosing Plutocracy.* New York: Palgrave.

Hancock, Kathleen J. 2015a. "Renewable Energy in Sub-Saharan Africa: Contributions from the Social Sciences (Special Issue)". *Energy Research & Social Science* 5: 1–8.

Hancock, Kathleen J. 2015b. "Energy Regionalism and Diffusion in Africa: How Political Actors Created the ECOWAS Center for Renewable Energy and Energy Efficiency." *Energy Research & Social Science* 5: 105–115.

Hancock, Kathleen J. 2018. "Electric Regionalism: African states, Development Banks, and Mining Companies." Presented at the International Studies Association Annual Convention. San Francisco, April 4–7.

Hancock, Kathleen J. Forthcoming. "Electric Regionalism: Regional Organizations and the African Power Pools." In "Energy Regionalisms," special issue, *Review of Policy Research.*

Hancock, Kathleen J., and Vlado Vivoda. 2014. "International Political Economy: A Field Born of the OPEC Crisis Returns to Its Energy Roots." *Energy Research and Social Science* 1, no. 1: 206–217.

Hayter, R. 2004. "Economic Geography as Dissenting Institutionalism: The Embeddedness, Evolution and Differentiation of Regions." *Human Geography* 86, no. 2: 95–115.

Herman, Lior, and Jonathan Ariel. Forthcoming. "Comparative Energy Regionalism: NAFTA and the EU." In "Energy Regionalism," special issue, *Review of Policy Research.*

Herranz-Surrallés, Anna, Israel Solorio, and Jenny Fairbrass. 2020. "Renegotiating authority in the Energy Union: A Framework for Analysis." *Journal of European Integration* 42, no. 1: 1–17.

Hira, Anil, and Libardo Amaya. 2003. "Does Energy Integrate?" *Energy Policy* 31, no. 2: 185–199.

Jackson, Ian. 2009. "Nuclear Energy and Proliferation Risks: Myths and Realities in the Persian Gulf." *International Affairs* 85, no. 6: 1157–1172.

Jewell, Jessica. 2011. "A Nuclear-Powered North Africa: Just a Desert Mirage or Is There Something on the Horizon?" *Energy Policy* 39, no. 8: 4445–4457.

Jinnah, Sikina, and Abby Lindsay. 2015. "Secretariat Influence on Overlap Management Politics in North America: NAFTA and the Commission for Environmental Cooperation." *Review of Policy Research* 32, no. 1: 124–145.

Johnson, Corey, and Stacy D. VanDeveer. Forthcoming. "Regionalisms in Theory and Practice." In "Energy Regionalisms," special issue, *Review of Policy Research.*

Jordan, Andrew, Huitema, Dave, Van Asselt, Harro and Johanna Forster. 2018. *Governing Climate Change. Polycentricity in Action?* Cambridge: Cambridge University Press.

Lagendijk, Vincent. 2008. *Electrifying Europe: The Power of Europe in the Construction of Electricity Networks.* Amsterdam: Amsterdam University Press.

Lagendijk, Vincent. 2016. "Europe's Rhine Power: Connections, Borders, and Flows." *Water History* 8, no. 2: 23–39.

Laursen, Finn. 2003. *Comparative Regional Integration: Theoretical Perspectives.* Aldershot, UK: Ashgate, 53–73.

Laursen, Finn. 2010. *Comparative Regional Integration: Europe and Beyond.* Surrey, UK: Ashgate.

Loe, Julia S. P. 2019. "Clash of Realities: Gazprom's Reasoning on the EU Gas Trade." *Europe-Asia Studies* 71, no. 7: 1122–1139.

Lombaerde, Philippe De, Fredrik Söderbaum, Luk Van Langenhove, and Francis Baert. 2010. "The Problem of Comparison in Comparative Regionalism." *Review of International Studies* 36 (June): 731–753.

Mares, Davis R., and Jermey M Martin. 2012. "Regional Energy Integration in Latin America: Lessons from Chile's Experience with Natural Gas." *Third World Quarterly* 33, no. 1: 53–69. http://www.jstor.org/stable/41341211.

Mattli, Walter. 1999. "Explaining Regional Integration Outcomes." *Journal of European Public Policy* 6, no. 1: 1–27.

Meierding, Emily. 2017. "Joint Development in the South China Sea: Exploring the Prospects of Oil and Gas Cooperation between Rivals." *Energy Research & Social Science* 24: 65–70.

Mitchell, Timothy. 2011. *Carbon Democracy: Political Power in the Age of Oil.* London: Verso.

Moravcsik, Andrew. 1993. "Preferences and Power in the European Community: A Liberal Intergovernmentalist Approach." *JCMS: Journal of Common Market Studies* 31, no. 4: 473–524. doi:10.1111/j.1468-5965.1993.tb00477.x.

Mukasa, Alli D., Emelly Mutambatsere, Yannis Arvanitis, and Thouraya Triki. 2015. "Wind Energy in Sub-Saharan Africa: Financial and Political Causes for the Sector's Under-Development." *Energy Research & Social Science* 5: 90–104.

Netherton, Alexander. 2007. "The Political Economy of Canadian Hydro-Electricity: Between Old 'Provincial Hydros' and Neoliberal Regional Energy Regimes." *Canadian Political Science Review* 1, no. 1: 107–124.

Nolte, Detlef. 2014. "Latin America's New Regional Architecture: A Cooperative or Segmented Regional Governance Complex?" EUI Working Papers. RSCAS 2014/89 Florence.

Olson-Hazboun, Shawn K., Richard S. Krannich, and Peter G. Robertson. 2016. "Public Views on Renewable Energy in the Rocky Mountain Region of the United States: Distinct Attitudes, Exposure, and Other Key Predictors of Wind Energy." *Energy Research & Social Science* 21 (November): 167–179.

Oseni, Musiliu O., and Michael G. Pollitt. 2016. "The Promotion of Regional Integration of Electricity Markets: Lessons for Developing Countries." *Energy Policy* 88: 628–638. http://www.sciencedirect.com/science/article/pii/S030142151530094X.

Ostrowski, Wojciech. 2015. "State Capitalism and the Politics of Resources." In *States and Markets in Hydrocarbon Sectors*, edited by Andrei Belyi and Kim Talus, 83–102. Hampshire, UK: Palgrave Macmillan.

Ó Tuathail, Gearóid. 1996. *Critical Geopolitics. The Politics of Writing Global Space.* Minneapolis: University of Minnesota Press.

Palestini, Stefano. Forthcoming. "Turning the Lights On: The Interamerican Development Bank and the Orchestration of the Central American Electric System." In "Energy Regionalisms," special issue, *Review of Policy Research.*

Palestini, Stefano, and Giovanni Agostinis. 2018. "Constructing Regionalism in South America: The Cases of Transport Infrastructure and Energy within UNASUR." *Journal of International Relations and Development* 21, no. 1: 46–74.

Pedersen, Thomas. 2002. "Cooperative Hegemony Power, Ideas and Institutions in Regional Integration." *Review of International Studies* 28, no. 4: 677–696. http://journals.cambridge.org/production/action/cjoGetFulltext?fulltextid=129108.

Pratt, Larry. 1985. "Energy, Regionalism and Canadian Nationalism." *Newfoundland and Labrador Studies* 1, no. 2: 175–199.

Prontera, Andrea. 2015. "Italian Energy Security, the Southern Gas Corridor and the New Pipeline Politics in Western Europe: From the Partner State to the Catalytic State." *Journal of International Relations and Development* 21: 464–494.

Puka, Lidia, and Kacper Szulecki. 2014. "The Politics and Economics of Cross-Border Electricity Infrastructure: A Framework for Analysis." *Energy Research & Social Science* 4: 124–134.

Risse, Thomas. 2016. "The Diffusion of Regionalism." In *The Oxford Handbook of Comparative Regionalism*, edited by Tanja Börzel and Thomas Risse, 87–108. Oxford: Oxford University Press.

Sabbatella, Alejandro and Thauan Santos. Forthcoming. "The IPE of Regional Energy Integration in South America." In *The Routledge Handbook to Global Political Economy. Conversations and Inquiries*, edited by Ernesto Vivares. London and New York: Routledge.

Schot, Johan, and Vincent Lagendijk. 2008. "Technocratic Internationalism in the Interwar Years: Building Europe on Motorways and Electricity Networks." *Journal of Modern European History* 6, no. 2: 196–217.

Selin, Henrik, and Stacy D. VanDeveer. 2011. "Climate Change Regionalism in North America." *Review of Policy Research* 28, no. 3: 295–304.

Shapiro, Matthew A. 2014. "Establishing 'Green Regionalism' Environmental Technology Generation across East Asia and Beyond." *Journal of Contemporary Eastern Asia* 13, no. 2: 41–56.

Sidortsov, Roman. 2016. "A Perfect Moment during Imperfect Times: Arctic Energy Research in a Low-Carbon Era." *Energy Research & Social Science* 16 (June): 1–7.

Skalamera, Morena. 2016. Invisible but not indivisible: Russia, the European Union, and the importance of "Hidden Governance." *Energy Research & Social Science* 12: 27–49.

Smith, Adrian. 2007. "Emerging in Between: The Multi-Level Governance of Renewable Energy in the English Regions." *Energy Policy* 35, no. 12: 6266–6280.

Solingen, Etel. 2008. "The Genesis, Design and Effects of Regional Institutions: Lessons from East Asia and the Middle East." *International Studies Quarterly* 52, no. 2: 261–294. http://doi.wiley.com/10.1111/j.1468-2478.2008.00501.x.

Solingen, Etel, and Joshua Malnight. 2016. "Globalization, Domestic Politics and Regionalism." In *The Oxford Handbook of Comparative Regionalism*, edited by Tanja Börzel and Thomas Risse, 64–86. Oxford: Oxford University Press.

Sovacool, Benjamin K. 2010. "The political economy of oil and gas in Southeast Asia: heading towards the natural resource curse?" *The Pacific Review* 23 (2):225–259.

Sovacool, B. K., and C. J. Cooper. 2013. *The Governance of Energy Megaprojects: Politics, Hubris and Energy Security*. Cheltenham, UK: Edward Elgar.

Sovacool, Benjamin. 2009. "Energy Policy and Cooperation in Southeast Asia: The History, Challenges, and Implications of the Trans-ASEAN Gas Pipeline (TAGP) Network." *Energy Policy* 37, no. 6: 2356–2367.

Sovacool, Benjamin K. 2011. "Introduction: Defining, Measuring, and Exploring Energy Security." In *The Routledge Handbook of Energy Security*, edited by B. Sovacool, 1–42. London: Routledge.

Sovacool, Benjamin K. 2014. "What Are We Doing Here? Analyzing Fifteen Years of Energy Scholarship and Proposing a Social Science Research Agenda." *Energy Research & Social Science* 1, no. 1: 1–29.

Stern, David I. 2007. "The Effect of NAFTA on Energy and Environmental Efficiency in Mexico." *Policy Studies Journal* 35, no. 2: 291–322.

Strambo, Claudia, Måns Nilsson, André Månberger. 2015. "Coherent or Inconsistent? Assessing Energy Security and Climate Policy Interaction within the European Union." *Energy Research & Social Science* 8 (June): 1–12.

Stroup, Laura, Richard Kujawa, and Jeffrey Ayres. 2015. "Envisioning a Green Energy Future in Canada and the United States: Constructing a Sustainable Future in the Context of New Regionalisms?" *American Review of Canadian Studies* 45, no. 3: 299–314.

Szulecki, Kacper. 2016. "European Energy Governance and Decarbonization Policy: Learning from the 2020 Strategy." *Climate Policy* 8, no. 5: 543–547.

Szulecki, Kacper. 2017. "The Multiple Faces of Energy Security: An Introduction." In *Energy Security in Europe: Divergent Perceptions and Policy*, edited by Kacper Szulecki, 1–29. London: Palgrave Macmillan.

Szulecki, Kacper and Dag Harald Claes. 2019. "Towards Decarbonization: Understanding EU Energy Governance, Politics and Governance." *Politics and Governance* 7, no. 1: 1–5.

Szulecki, Kacper, Philipp Pattberg, and Frank Biermann. 2011. "Explaining Variation in the Effectiveness of Transnational Energy Partnerships." *Governance* 24, no. 4: 713–736.

Tsing, Anna. 2005. *Friction: An Ethnography of Global Connection*. Princeton, NJ: Princeton University Press.

UNDP. 2004. World Energy Assessment: Overview 2004 Update. New York: United Nations.

Valdivia, Gabriela. 2015. "Oil Frictions and the Subterranean Geopolitics of Energy Regionalisms." *Environment and Planning* 47, no. 7: 1422–1439.

Van Den Hoven, Drian, and Karl Froschauer. 2004. "Limiting Regional Electricity Sector Integration and Market Reform: The Cases of France in the EU and Canada in the NAFTA Region." *Comparative Political Studies* 37, no. 9: 1079–1103.

VanDeveer, S. 2011. "Networked Baltic Environmental Cooperation." *Journal of Baltic Studies* 42, no. 1: 37–55.

Zbińkowski, Grzegorz. 2019. "The Three Seas Initiative and Its Economic and Geopolitical Effect on the European Union and Central and Eastern Europe." *Comparative Economic Research. Central and Eastern Europe* 22, no. 2: 105–119.

Ziegler, Charles E. 2013. "Energy Pipeline Networks and Trust: The European Union and Russia in Comparative Perspective". *International Relations* 27, no. 1: 3–29.

Appendix: List of Journals Reviewed

Acta Politica
American Journal of Political Science
American Political Science Review
Annual Review of Political Science
Brazilian Political Science Review
British Journal of Political Science
Canadian Foreign Policy
Canadian Political Science Review
Chinese Political Science Review
Comparative Political Studies
Conflict Management and Peace Science

Current History
Energy Policy
Energy Research & Social Sciences
Ethnopolitics
European Journal of International Relations
European Political Science Review
European Union Politics
Foreign Affairs
Foreign Policy
Foreign Policy Analysis
Global Environmental Politics
Graduate Journal of Asia-Pacific Studies
Greek Political Science Review
Human Rights Quarterly
Indian Journal of Political Science
International Affairs Forum
International Interactions
International Organization
International Political Science Review
International Politics
International Security
International Studies Perspectives
International Studies Quarterly
International Studies Review
Interventions: International Journal of Postcolonial Studies
Japanese Journal of Political Science
Josef Korbel Journal of Advanced International Studies
Journal of Conflict Resolution
Journal of European Integration
Journal of Human Rights
Journal of International and Area Studies
Journal of International Relations and Development
Journal of Peace Research
Journal of Policy Analysis and Management
Journal of Political Economy
Journal of Political Science(South Carolina)
Journal of Politics
Journal of Public Administration Research
Journal of Religion, Conflict and Peace
Latin American Perspectives
National Political Science Review
New England Journal of Political Science
New Global Studies
Party Politics
Policy & Politics
Policy and Society
Policy Studies Journal

Politica y Gobierno
Political Analysis
Political Behavior
Political Geography
Political Research Quarterly (WPSA)
Political Science Quarterly
Political Studies
Politics & Gender
Politics & Policy
Polity (NEPSA)
Public Opinion Quarterly
Questions in Politics (Georgia Political Science Association)
Res Publica
Resource & Energy Economics
Review of Environmental Economics and Policy
Review of International Organizations
Review of International Studies
Review of Policy Research
Revista de Ciencia Politica
Security Studies
Social Science Quarterly
Swiss Political Science Review
The Illinois Political Science Review (Illinois)
The Nonproliferation Review
The Washington Quarterly
Third World Quarterly
World Affairs

....

CHAPTER 9

ENERGY POLITICS
AND GENDER

....

KARINA STANDAL, TANJA WINTHER, AND
KATRINE DANIELSEN

HISTORICALLY, and across geographies, there has been a gendered division of labor in which women's lives have generally been linked to unpaid activities within the home, while men have had formal, paid work in public spaces (Moore 1988; Raju 2011). This division has resulted in a process of social differentiation, in which activities tied to the masculine are assigned a higher value than feminine ones (e.g., domestic work, informal and unskilled labor) and women have been disadvantaged in terms of income, education, and job opportunities. The devaluation of women's work can be clearly viewed through the prism of energy; historically, and in many current contexts, women have been delegated the energy-related tasks of cooking and provision of household fuels (Standal and Winther 2016). Within the energy sector, women occupy significantly fewer positions than men as professionals, researchers, or decision makers (Clancy and Roehr 2003; Kaminara 2015; Winther, Ulsrud, and Saini 2018).

Regardless of this underrepresentation of women in the energy sector and related decision-making, national energy policies have predominantly been understood as belonging to the domains of technology and economy and, more recently, connected to climate change issues, ignoring the existence of gender-based differences in people's social positions, experiences, perceptions, needs, and values. The primary exception to this generalization has been the recent focus on women and energy in international development policy (Cecelski 2005; Standal forthcoming). For women's and feminist struggles, the energy-development-gender nexus has in some aspects become a dynamic space in which to seek recognition of women's right to have ownership and control of resources and representation (see Agarwal 2010; Kelkar 2017). However, the focus on energy and gender in development policy has primarily been framed around gender equality as instrumental to ideological currents of increasing productivity and economic growth in the global South, enabled through development interventions to secure women's access to modern energy (e.g., World Bank 2018, 52). Incorporation of gender in energy politics has thus by and large been presented as an issue in "developing countries," while energy issues in the global North have generally been projected as gender neutral, in line with a perception of Western societies as already gender equal, but in reality gender differences have been dismissed altogether (Clancy and Roehr 2003; Kaminara 2015).

Scholars (especially those who study international development) have recently started developing a body of literature on gender and energy politics. However, the field has been dominated by engineers and economists (Listo 2018, 9) and by "grey literature" authored by nongovernmental organizations (NGOs) and policy makers. This literature tends to focus on the immediate effects of energy access, such as increased productivity, income opportunities, or positive health benefits, disregarding issues of household inequality in distribution and control of resources and gender discriminatory practices in society (Haves 2012, 2).[1] Further, a recent article (Winther et al. 2017) observed that quantitative studies have looked at single indicators (e.g., women's time use) to measure the impact of electrification, while qualitative case studies have adopted a more holistic approach to energy and gender, encompassing underlying mechanisms and power relations at play. However, only a few published studies have looked into energy in relation to gender roles and power relations (e.g., Standal and Winther 2016; Winther et al. 2017) or made a critical analysis of the gendered politics of energy (e.g., Crewe 1997; Listo 2018; Marshall, Ockwell, and Byrne 2017).

In this chapter we address gender dimensions of energy politics by exploring discourses on micro and macro levels that produce and reproduce gender roles, framing how energy influences women and men differently and affects their access to and benefits from energy. Also recognized in development practices and the grey literature (e.g., Reeves and Baden 2000), gender denotes the socially constructed rights, identities, roles, and responsibilities of women and men; hence gender concerns the relations of power between women and men in a given context. Energy politics is here understood as positions of governance involved in distributing power and energy resources among members of society. We conceptualize positions of governance in broad terms, encompassing policies, strategies, legislation, and institutions, as well as micro politics on the local level and within households. Our underlying ambition is to show that knowledge production in the field of energy and gender is highly politicized, though often in subtle ways. We point to some epistemological consequences of this in our analysis. As the topic of energy is immensely broad, we primarily, but not exclusively, focus on resources of modern energy such as electricity and clean cookstoves. Electricity and cookstoves represent key debates and narratives within energy policy concerning the energy-gender nexus (e.g., World Bank 2018) and links to other important energy-related issues, such as the environment, forest conservation, and the neoliberal growth agenda.

We structure the analysis according to four overarching contemporary policy and research discourses framing women's and men's positions in benefiting from and participating in decision-making on energy issues: (1) energy as gender neutral; (2) the drudgery approach: women as victims of energy poverty; (3) the empowerment approach: women as game changers through access to modern energy; and (4) the gender and rights-based approach: women as rights holders. Each of these overarching discourses defines a salient governance position that is considered to produce social processes that influence gendered outcomes of energy-related distribution of power and resources. The examination of these discourses draws on a critical review of relevant literatures (e.g., Danielsen 2012; Standal and Winther 2016; Winther et al. 2017). We conclude with suggestions for future research with a general call to incorporate gender, as well as other intersecting identities such as class and ethnicity, into the analysis of energy politics at all levels, especially in the context of contemporary challenges of climate change and growing inequality.[2]

POLITICS OF NEUTRALITY: MARGINALIZING GENDER DIFFERENCES IN ENERGY

Energy politics has mainly been perceived as an economic and technical issue, coupled with policies of industrialization and national security, in which gender has been assumed to have little relevance. As stated by Kaminara (2015, 1), "When policy makers make decisions with respect to energy issues, they often do so considering that those decisions affect women and men in the same way." However, several studies conducted in both the global North and South show that gender "matters" in energy both for the promotion of renewable sources (Henning 2005) and because lack of adequate energy disempowers women (e.g., Clancy et al. 2011; Standal and Winther 2016; Winther et al. 2017). These studies show that gender is a key issue for understanding the politics of energy and the important relationships between micro and macro levels.

As Henning (2005) and Kaminara (2015) note, the widespread perception that the global North and especially Scandinavia is gender equal has led policy makers to assume that energy policy decisions affect women and men in the same way. In her ethnography on the adoption of domestic renewable energy technologies in Swedish households, Henning (2005) shows that government strategies (such as subsidies), as well as the engineers designing such technologies (in this case pellet stoves and household solar photovoltaic [PV] systems), tend to emphasize technological development over the users' preferences and social practices.[3] When Swedish policy makers assumed that subsidies for rooftop solar systems and switching from oil heating to pellet stoves would lead to a transition toward decarbonization, they did not take into account that aesthetics and gender roles posed a significant barrier to a green transition, by which we mean increased renewable energy replacing fossil fuels. Henning (2005) demonstrated that Swedish women tended to "control" the kitchen and living room spaces and resisted implementing new technologies that broke with their ideas of an attractive home even when subsidies and reduced cost made such a switch profitable. Similarly, a study of households that adopted solar systems for producing electricity in Italy, Norway,

Serbia, the United Kingdom, and Ukraine found women to be much less engaged in implementing and use of the solar PV systems than men (Standal, Westskog, and van Kraalingen forthcoming). Most of the women interviewed felt they had inadequate knowledge and skills concerning solar technology compared to their male partners. The same study also observed a bias in media presentations and solar companies' advertisements. When addressing consumers, they tended to speak to what Strenger (2014) calls the "Resource Man": the well-educated, techno-savvy male who is interested in energy technology and makes the household decisions. The study showed that the reproduction of men as the "natural" and skillful consumers of new energy technology makes women less inclined to invest in new renewable energy systems unless they are persuaded by their male partners. Further, when policies are assumed to be gender neutral, they discount differing needs of women and men, as well as overlooking societal groups who might lack necessary skills or comfort in adopting new technology. Without explicitly addressing women, policies may fail to help states transition to a renewable energy economy in time to tackle pressing global climate change problems.

The assumption of gender neutrality has impacts beyond households. Women are underrepresented in energy and climate policymaking and as professionals in the energy industry and businesses and thus have limited decision-making power for ensuring that the low-carbon energy transition is carried out in a socially equitable way (Diekman, Weisgram, and Belanger 2015; Kaminara 2015). On the one hand, energy companies with a large number of women on their boards of directors engaged in more investment in renewable energy and greater consideration of environmental risks in their financial decision-making (IRENA 2017). On the other hand, as Ross (2012, 118) points out, the underrepresentation of women in energy sector employment and policymaking has another distributional effect: when a country's exports are heavily biased toward the extractive industries, such as oil or mining, other job opportunities tend to diminish because products exported from such countries are expensive and thus less competitive on the global market, a complex process called the Dutch disease. The diminished work opportunities are often found in sectors of high female employment such as manufacturing, thus negatively affecting women (Hancock and Sovacool 2018; Ross 2012, 118).

Several countries face challenges similar to those just described and the complexities of energy poverty, or lack of access to adequate, affordable, reliable, and safe if not also ecologically sustainable energy. Despite an unsustainable increase in energy consumption in the world, especially in the Gulf nations and global North, energy poverty persists in poorer and isolated areas in the global South and eastern Europe. About 1.1 billion people lack access to electricity, and 2.8 billion used traditional fuels for cooking in 2017 (IEA 2017). The effects of energy poverty are well known; traditional fuels globally take about 4.3 million lives annually through indoor air pollution (WHO 2018). Further, lack of electricity has negative effects on education and income-generating opportunities (Clancy et al. 2011; Winther et al. 2017). Energy poverty is correlated with the feminization of poverty, meaning gender discrimination that results in women having lower income and other human capital (e.g., education) than men. This poverty is enforced by poor access to energy and insufficient opportunities to invest in greater access, as well as limited energy-related job opportunities (Clancy et al. 2011; Munien and Ahmed 2012). It is therefore not surprising that energy policies that incorporate gendered aspects are concerned with energy access (mostly in terms of electricity and clean cooking technologies).

In the global arena, there is considerable emphasis on providing universal access to modern forms of energy, such as Sustainable Development Goal (SDG) 7 (ensure access to affordable, reliable, sustainable, and modern energy for all) and the initiative Sustainable Energy for All (SE4ALL) (World Bank 2018). Although it is acknowledged that SDG 7 is a key conditional factor for other goals, such as gender (SDG 5), SDG 7 (and the targets for its measurement) does not include gender dimensions, but rather follows the trend of gender-blind energy policies.[4] Similarly, a recent review of national policies in Nepal, Kenya, and India as well as global initiatives found that these policies tend to be gender neutral (ENERGIA 2016). As an example, despite a persistently high rate of energy poverty and the fact that the associated conditions foster distinctly gendered experiences of it, Indian policy makers envision the energy future as centralized energy provision for national economic growth (Mohan and Topp 2018). According to a gender audit of renewable energy programs (Parikh et al. 2009, x), India was expected to invest more than $100 billion in the energy sector, including renewables, during its eleventh five-year plan (2007–2012), but less than 2 percent of this would go toward alleviating the energy poverty suffered by women and children. (For more on Indian energy politics, see Powell in this volume). Further, gender as a dimension of energy development policy competes with other agendas such as recentering growth in national policies and private-sector-led development (see McEwan et al. 2017; Standal forthcoming).

One problem is that the household is used as a gender-neutral unit, camouflaging the gender-differentiated nature of obtaining access and appliances and deciding on, and benefiting from, electricity's uses. Another problem is the lack of attention to how women's inclusion in policy formulation and the supply chain could help balance existing, and possibly growing, gender inequality. This tendency relates to general trends of devaluation of women's work (i.e., women's energy-related care work within the family) in the contemporary economic context of globalization (neoliberalization and the capitalist market economy) (Peterson 2005). The presumed neutrality of energy (as well as the economy) stems from how technology and current economic context is dominated from positions of power in which men (with the right socioeconomic and ethnic/racial status) have a privileged position (Peterson 2005).

POLITICS OF VICTIMIZATION: REPRESENTATIONS OF WOMEN IN THE DRUDGERY AGENDA

It is a well-documented phenomenon that women in the global South carry a disproportionately heavy burden of drudgery, as they fetch water, procure and collect fuel, and perform various domestic chores (Khandker, Ali, and Barnes 2014; van de Walle et al. 2015).

Research on India, Afghanistan, Kenya, and Zanzibar, in particular, confirms this picture (Standal and Winther 2016; Winther 2008; Winther et al. 2017). The continued uses of traditional biomass and cooking technologies is often perceived to be a main reason for these enduring practices, but the lack of other infrastructures (water, health, and transport) also has important and negative impacts on many women's lives (Clancy et al. 2011; Winther et al. 2017). Women have been projected as facing the brunt of the burden in energy poverty and thus have been actively used to raise awareness and action among policy makers and donors (Abdelnour 2015; Listo 2018). To combat this situation, access to modern energy is considered important, and one of the most visible, current representations of women and their drudgery is voiced by promotors of clean cookstoves (e.g., the Global Alliance for Clean Cookstoves [GACC] and the ENERGIA network on gender and sustainable energy).

Taking a closer look at how the problem of drudgery has been framed in the realm of cooking and clean cookstoves provides an illustration of "gender myths" that have been constructed in energy policy to achieve a range of other policy agendas (Abdelnour 2015; Crewe 1997; Listo 2018). According to Crewe (1997), the emphasis on cookstoves first appeared on the international agenda in the 1970s out of a concern for deforestation. Households were conceived to be the cause of the problem, and clean cookstoves were promoted for its mitigation. Researchers have found that it was industry and businesses that primarily caused deforestation, and the stoves (developed in laboratories by male experts) were not widely adopted because the emphasis on simple technical and decontextualized solutions did not fit the needs of (female) cooks. The effort to implement clean cookstoves proved especially difficult in South and Southeast Asia (Urmee and Gyamfi 2014). The problem of sexual violence in conflict zones has also been used to galvanize attention and action for clean cookstoves from the late 1990s, which reinforces the image that simple technological solutions offer salvation to complex issues of gender relations and violent conflicts (Abdelnour 2015). From the 2000s, women's drudgery was perceived as a health problem, both for the physically heavy burden involved in fuel collection and for indoor air pollution. This matches the present rhetoric of organizations such as GACC, which observe that lack of modern energy constitutes the fifth highest risk factor for disease in developing countries due to the use of traditional fuels (Ezzati and Kammen 2002), many times higher than malaria or HIV-related diseases. Women also suffer healthwise from carrying heavy loads of wood for heating and cooking (Kelkar et al. 2017; Matinga et al. 2010), and their responsibility for biomass wood collection contributes to spinal injuries, pregnancy complications, and premature births (Matinga 2010; Pope et al. 2010). Thus, clean cookstoves were again considered to be the solution, but to a different problem (women's health rather than deforestation). More recently, climate change caused by biomass energy use and pollution has become a main concern on the international development agenda (e.g., World Bank, GACC), to which the solution again would be improved cookstoves (Grieshop, Marshall, and Kandlikar 2011).

The shifting argumentation and politicization regarding introducing clean cookstoves is striking, and only in the second and third phases (sexual violence and health) were women and their needs put at the center of the discussion. However, this position is also difficult, partly because it tends to reduce women's domain to that of health and the reproductive sphere. This follows how women's health has been approached in development. Yamin and Boulanger (2013) have argued that the former Millennium Development Goals 4 (reduce child mortality) and 5 (improve women's maternal health) triggered a shift in development discourses away from the progressive agenda developed in international initiatives such as the UN Conference on Women in Beijing (1995), which had emphasized women's rights and gender inequality as barriers to women's health and well-being, toward priorities centered on women's roles as child bearers and caretakers. Another problem with the discourse focusing on cookstoves is that it tends to reduce cooking and eating, which are complex, gendered cultural practices (Matinga 2010; Winther 2008), to a question of technological "quick fixes." The long history of failed cookstove programs (Urmee and Gyamfi 2014) testifies to the naiveté of such an approach. The potential use of such cookstoves depends on women's opportunities for paid work, which augment the socially perceived value of their time and their negotiating power in the household (Nathan et al. 2018). In summary, the problem of the drudgery discourse is that it tends to victimize women by focusing solely on their health, confining their position to the reproductive sphere, and suggesting simplified solutions through new end-user technology without considering existing socio-material aspects, gender norms, and women's position within the household and beyond. Critiques of victimizing women in development (e.g., Cornwall, Harrison, and Whitehead 2007) have also influenced a shift of focus from victims to "game changers," wherein women have an instrumental role in changing the economic conditions from poverty to progress through energy access (Listo 2018; Standal forthcoming).

Politics of Empowerment: Representations of Women as Game Changers

More recently, and particularly with the issuing of the World Bank's (2012) *World Development Report 2012: Gender Equality and Development*, women have come to be regarded as game changers for moving to sustainable energy practices and achieving economic growth (Chant and Sweetman 2012). The focus on women as victims of energy poverty has been used in conjunction with presenting women as the solution to wider developmental challenges. For example, organizations such as the GACC have worked for the integration of women in economic productivity related to production, advertisement, and sale of clean cookstoves. The same strategy has been adopted by promoting poor women as energy entrepreneurs in attempts to increase access to modern energy, such as through the gender and energy network ENERGIA and the publication *Boiling Point*, a practitioner's journal for those working with household energy and cookstoves. Studies that have looked at women-targeted electrification initiatives observe that not only does the inclusion of women balance the general trend to only recruit men in the management and operation of electricity provision, but such inclusion may also result in changed local perceptions of women's capabilities and hence a modification of local gender norms (Sovacool et al. 2013; Standal and Winther 2016; Winther, Ulsrud, and Saini 2018).

The argument for involving women as energy agents is that many women in the South are already involved in small and microenterprises, and their lack of access to modern energy impinges on their productive potential. Further, women's roles as household energy managers and their networks (with other women) put them in a distinctive position to increase awareness of and deliver energy products and services: "This role goes beyond women just being the users of energy services, but as *change agents* in the energy sector: in selling, maintaining and financing energy products and services" (emphasis added).[5]

This focus is similar to ideas that were forwarded in the 1970s paradigm of Women in Development (WiD), in which women were perceived as the "missing link" in development (e.g., Boserup 1970), and it communicates an instrumental way of understanding gender equality (and development). Feminist critique of WiD's idea of women as homogenous and economic actors isolated from social structures and gender relations led to the paradigm of gender and development (GAD) in the 1990s. However, GAD also continued to promote instrumental approaches through its major emphasis on micro-credit as a means to achieve poverty alleviation through women's economic integration (Kumar 2013). Within the energy policy field it has been assumed that combining women's access to credit with their role as agents in energy systems would lead to transitions toward new energy technologies (Biswas, Bryce, and Diesendorf 2001; Cecelski 2000). This scenario assumes a win-win game in which general development goals and women's increased involvement in the energy chain are achieved at the same time. Implicitly, energy came to be regarded as a path to women's empowerment. However, a recent review of studies on women's empowerment through access to modern energy reveals a need to clarify what is meant by empowerment: "An epistemological problem in such reviews is that the examined studies use different definitions of empowerment and various methodologies" (Winther et al. 2017, 389). In cases where empowerment is specified, it is often taken to mean women's increased short-term economic opportunities or simply reduced drudgery, not long-term control over resources. These mechanisms, and how they relate to the concept of women's empowerment and gender equality, continue to be under-researched (Winther et al. 2017, 389).

In the same way that Cornwall, Harrison, and Whitehead (2007, 6) illustrated how particular images of women's relationship to the environment turn into potent fairy tales of "women as conservers of resources and guardians of nature," so have women become presented as potent game changers who turn modern energy access into economic productivity. These representations have transformed the image of "the poor woman" living in the global South to an enabling social actor increasing well-being for her family and community. This discourse conveys the moral message of women being a deserving and efficient tool within the ideologies of neoliberal economic integration in development to achieve energy development. However, such a framing risks overestimating the capacity of women and limits the focus to the realm of energy, as if expecting that this sector can and is attuned to the broader social transformation necessary, and the concept of empowerment itself carries grand promises without being clear about what it entails.

POLITICS OF JUSTICE: WOMEN AS RIGHTS HOLDERS

The gender- and rights-based approach to energy (see Danielsen 2012 for an elaborated discussion) is a radically different and less obvious politicization of energy access than the three discourses already presented. Here, the fundamental element is the acknowledgment of access to energy as a prerequisite for realizing economic and social rights such as gender equality, food, and health (Danielsen 2012). This narrative implies that women are positioned as rights holders who have a legitimate claim to access energy. The state is the primary duty bearer and should realize women's energy rights. In this discourse, access to energy is perceived as a universal entitlement, and energy poverty is analyzed and challenged from a social justice perspective. For example, Dugard (2009) uses a rights framework to analyze South Africa's legislation and argues that access to electricity, while not considered a right in and of itself, can be implied by other rights obligations in the constitution, such as the right to adequate housing.

The positioning of access to energy as a right resonates with the recent formulation of SDG 7. The rationale is that energy is crucial for achieving almost every SDG, from the eradication of poverty, through advancements in health, to combating climate change. At the level of international human rights law, however, access to energy has not been established explicitly as a human right, though article 14 of the Convention on the Elimination of All Forms of Discrimination Against Women (CEDAW) obligates state parties to the convention to "ensure to such women the right...to enjoy adequate living conditions, particularly in relation to...electricity" (quoted in Tully 2006, 536). Similarly, turning to the level of national law,[6] South African legislation refers to the elimination of women's discrimination in access to electricity (Dugard 2009).

Another example can be found in the recent policy for gender mainstreaming in energy access of the Economic Community of West African States (ECOWAS 2015). Building on gender equality commitments within the Human Rights and Committee on *Elimination of Discrimination against Women*, the policy endorsed by the member states in the ECOWAS, aims to align the member states energy interventions to ensure equal access to resources and energy-related decision-making for men and women on the policy level and in the energy-related workforce, research, businesses, and households. This policy initiative combines a rights-based approach with instrumental agendas, as the policy is set in place to ensure a rapid and just expansion of energy access in the ECOWAS region to meet the targets of SE4ALL and SDG7.[7]

The international community also has obligations to contribute to the realization of energy rights through recognition of and assistance to the primary duty bearer in making energy rights real. Several countries, such as the ECOWAS member states, are signatories to or have ratified CEDAW; in addition, some countries have incorporated other frameworks that integrate women's rights and gender equality in energy issues.

However, despite legal and policy commitments at various levels, energy poverty persists. And as access to energy is curtailed by unequal gender relations, women are disproportionately affected (Cecelski 2005; Kohlin et al 2011). To explain why women's right to energy is not realized, there is a need for an analysis of injustices that women experience through energy politics and its governance positions. Fraser's (2009) theory of social justice provides a useful framework for such analysis, as it distinguishes three interrelated "rights failures" leading to such injustices: recognition failures, redistribution failures, and representation failures. Different rights failures, in turn, lead to different struggles and rights claims.

To start with, recognition failures include the following. First, women's right to energy fails because recognition is lacking of the (economic) value of their work, such as firewood collection, as pointed out previously in this article. Similarly, insufficient investment in improved cooking technology at the household and national levels signifies a lack of recognition of the value of women's reproductive roles, while at the same time there is limited recognition of women's roles as farmers, entrepreneurs, and business owners, with related energy needs (Batliwalaa and Reddy 2003). Moreover, it is well documented that women's rights are often suppressed because women are perceived as occupying a lower social position than men and as having rights only through their relationships with men (such as land and property rights) (Agarwal 2010). Realizing these rights is often a key precondition for the shaping of access to energy and other services (Winther et al. 2017). Finally, as Kohlin and colleagues point out (2011), women often internalize social norms that place a low value on their worth and contribution, negatively affecting their access to energy services.

Recognition failures lead to recognition claims. In this discourse, such claims include advocacy for the explicit consideration of gender equality in energy policy, goals, and targets (e.g., Cecelski 2000; ENERGIA/UNDP 2006) based on the premise that energy legislation and regulation can provide the basis for shifts in social expectations about the roles and responsibilities of men and women and the rights and entitlements they should enjoy (Danielsen 2012).

Turning to redistribution failures, unequal access to resources affects the realization of women's energy rights. Women who lack access to land and property are limited in their ability to benefit from energy facilities that require land, notably solar systems, wind turbines, and biofuel plants. Limited income is a barrier to women's investing in technology that could improve the productivity of their labor, and limited access to credit reduces their ability to pay the upfront costs of improved energy technology or connection fees to the electric grid (Parikh et al. 2009). Despite these rights failures, state development institutions increasingly consider gender aspects less relevant than including the private sector in energy development cooperation in India (Standal forthcoming; see also McEwan et al. 2017). This is in line with the observation of Tully (2006) and Dugard (2009) that commercial interests often have driven national level electricity distribution, as opposed to concerns to create sustainable basic services for poor people.

Redistribution failures can lead to redistribution claims, such as demands for women's land rights, lobbying and collective action for the provision of credit facilities accessible to women, and demands for access to basic services such as energy access. Women rights holders, communities, and civil society organizations demand to be heard and try to influence energy politics. In India, for example, a group of indigenous women used the corporate social responsibility (CSR) policy for international wind-power cooperation as a basis to claim electricity and drinking water for households close to wind farms (AGECC 2010), and a local women's group used singing and folklore in a final attempt to awaken local politicians to their plight regarding village electricity in relation to state commitments (Sinha 2003).

The third rights failure of representation concerns the discourse of neutrality and women's under- or misrepresentation in energy governance, which brings about unequal control between women and men over the process of providing access to energy services. Both on the provision and user sides, energy governance institutions that have key decision-making power concerning the gendered access to energy services tend to be dominated by men (Winther et al. 2017; Winther, Ulsrud, and Saini 2018). Moreover, meaningful use of electricity always requires access to appliances, which are commonly controlled by men, who tend to have more negotiating power to decide which appliances to purchase and use (Standal forthcoming; Winther et al. forthcoming).

Representation failures result in claims for measures to increase women's decision-making positions in institutions dealing with natural resources and energy (see Agarwal 2010). From an energy justice perspective, equal representation of women in energy governance is both a right in itself and a contribution to ensuring accountability of duty bearers to social justice and gender equality in the energy sector (Goldthau and Sovacool 2012). Furthermore, the thinking is that the inclusion of more women and members of marginalized groups in formal energy institutions, who may act as role models for others, can result in a positive change of attitudes on gender in the sector (Danielsen 2012).

The analysis of various rights failures sheds light on the complex interactions and power relations between actors in energy system governance, including those in formal positions as well as ordinary citizens. It shows that the delivery of energy rights fails in practice because they are "overruled" by social institutions and norms that shape the roles and relationships between men and women (Danielsen 2012). These norms permeate energy governance structures and institutions, including legal and regulatory frameworks, policies, and programs, and thus mediate the realization of women's energy rights. The analysis also shows that rights realization is negatively influenced by "principles of cost reflectivity" (Dugard 2009: 282) as opposed to rights concerns.

INVESTIGATING ENERGY POLITICS AS IF WOMEN (AND GENDER INEQUALITY) REALLY MATTERED

A main conclusion of this article is that gender and energy are always politicized, whether or not this is acknowledged by stakeholders.[8] By referring to empirical research in the global North and global South, we show that energy is indeed gendered, from the political and policy levels in the ways energy systems are set up and managed to how energy is used in gendered local contexts. Investigating energy from a gender perspective has relevance beyond women's and men's positions for benefiting from energy; it asks questions of social justice in general, needed to ensure energy management on all levels. Thirty years have passed since Waring (1988) posed her feminist critique of political economy, *If Women Counted: A New Feminist Economics*, but her arguments about women's invisibility in the capitalist economy are still valid. In the same vein, energy politics has either assumed gender relations to be irrelevant or conflated them to a rhetorical/strategic focus on women to engage action or as enablers of producing economic growth. Gender in the politics of energy has thus largely produced narratives that provide limited imaginaries of women's agency in and relevance to the (everyday) politics of energy in their lives.

As an example; in the victimization policy discourse, women's burden and the problem of drudgery appear on the agenda but have limited impact in practice due to the fragmentation of policy into sector-oriented (e.g., electrification, stove programs) approaches rather than comprehensive development strategies aiming to induce structural changes. Correspondingly, in the literature on drudgery (e.g., impact of electrification), contributions from research have mainly sought to quantify outcomes (time use on activities) rather than looking at why and how changes occur and the structural factors that restrain women's empowerment. Similarly, in the empowerment discourse, individual women's agency is considered in a vacuum, while the structures in which women operate (as do policies and interventions) are neglected. Thus the underlying epistemological stance within these discourses is a simplified theory of change in which one single input (e.g., introduce cookstoves, involve women in supply chains) is expected to create changes in gender relations. Further, this politicization of gender and energy lends itself to the ideologies of the growth paradigm, which have been responsible for removing important social services (e.g., health services, education, rights to maternity leave) that are essential for women's equal participation in the economy.[9]

To borrow Moser's (1989) conceptualization of catering to women's practical versus strategic interests, the politicization of the gender dimensions of energy seldom enters into the politics of power between men and women. Rather, framing and discourses related to women and energy stay within providing women with practical resources and services to improve their lives or are instrumental to other political discourses and policies like deforestation, decarbonization, and smart economics. From the empowerment discourse, we nonetheless take home the lesson that women's involvement in interventions and energy systems may produce positive effects not only for themselves but also for wider groups of women in the given context. The focus on women has also led to an atmosphere of reconceptualization of women's legitimate (though in limited terms) right to have ownership and control of resources through representation in decision-making, such as forest governance in India and Nepal (Agarwal 2010).

The rights-based discourse is promising in its holistic approach, and this perspective provides a tool for examining the deeper unequal structures as well as holding stakeholders in supply accountable for reproducing gender equality (or not). Still, there is a risk that progressive laws and regulations will not necessarily, at least in the short term, materialize into social change on the ground.

A FUTURE RESEARCH AGENDA

To better understand the politics of energy in all its forms, more research is required into how different hierarchies of privilege (including gender, race, and class) create social differentiation. This need has become imminent due to the global challenges of climate change and growing economic inequality (Terry 2009). First, in general terms there is a necessity to broaden the research horizon geographically and study energy politics through the prism of gender in the global North also. Second, the argument of this article is that we need research on energy that has gender as a governing analytical focus to be relevant. Adding gender or women to an analysis of energy, which is the mainstay of current research in the field (especially quantitative research), will surely provide knowledge on the gendered experiences and outcomes of energy, as has been the case with the focus on women in relation to clean cookstoves. However, simply adding women or gender to the analysis would camouflage the ways conceptual frameworks and structures are produced, and reproduced, in a mode that favors some identities (e.g., the masculine expert) over others. We argue that if gender were applied analytically, rather than as an aspect added on, the discourses on victimization, empowerment, and rights would provide solutions (policy), results (social change), and valid knowledge (research). Ultimately, such analysis would also expose how we come to value and privilege different gendered identities in the first place, which would produce knowledge on what the problematic positions of power are and how their consequences might be mitigated and resolved (Peterson 2005). Such an analysis would also provide knowledge on how other groups in society become "feminized" and therefore marginalized in the politics of energy (e.g., migrants, the disabled, and ethnic groups). A shift of analytical focus would require a shift in epistemological foundation, hence in what is regarded as knowledge. It would require a more constructivist approach (as opposed to positivist/rationalist) that considers gender as an analytical lens and not only empirical categories distinguishing between women and men. This would also allow for a broader understanding of energy in relation to linkages across sectors, levels, and boundaries.

There is a small but emerging research group working from such an approach, and the idea of politics of access has also been broadened within academia to conceptualizations of energy justice.[10] However, as discussed in the last section, there is a need for more research on injustices that women experience through energy politics and its governance to understand energy injustice better from women's perspectives. In particular, what formal and informal accountability mechanisms exist? What methods are used to make energy rights claims? And what actions work to achieve energy rights outcomes and energy justice for women? Energy justice is also coupled with another issue that urgently warrants research: how we can best move toward a low-carbon energy transition. The perils of climate change require researchers to provide knowledge that can help the birth of a future energy system, in terms of energy for households, livelihoods, and transportation. Concepts related to our future energy systems, such as low carbon and energy transition, are portrayed in a similar manner to the existing energy system: a gender-neutral issue belonging to the domains of economy and technology. Research that addresses issues of social equity, in which gender is one of the most pervasive factors, will be of key importance to provide the contextual knowledge needed to move toward a future in which "no one is left behind" and which builds on climate and energy policies that are acceptable to the general public.

NOTES

1. In the Listo (2018, 11) literature review of articles concerning energy poverty and development in the journal Energy for Sustainable Development from 2001 to 2016, only thirty-six out of more than four hundred mentioned gender. Even fewer explored gender or women as their core focus.
2. This chapter deals with gender in energy politics. For more information on the impact of energy access on gender relations, see Winther et al. (2017), Clancy et al. (2011), and Nye (1991).
3. Theories of social practice have been the focus of a growing body of scholarship seeking to understand energy-related consumer behavior and choices; see, e.g., Wilhite (2008) and Shove (2003). Social practice theory rejects simplified economic theories of rational choice (e.g., *homo economicus*) as inadequate to understand consumption.
4. Similarly, in the Global Tracking Framework, set up to monitor the development of access through the SE4ALL initiative, there are no indicators for measuring the gender dimension of access to modern energy (Winther et al. forthcoming).
5. Editorial, "Boiling Point Issue 66: Women, Energy and Economic Empowerment," http://www.energia.org/boiling-point-women-energy-and-economic-empowerment/.

6. In some countries electricity has been given the status of a fundamental right, and in others this remains a controversy addressed in the judicial system.

7. For a discussion on energy policy in the ECOWAS countries, see Hancock (2015). For a discussion on the development-gender-energy nexus in the ECOWAS region, see Aglina, Agbejule, and Nyamuame (2016).

8. The title of this section was inspired by Cynthia Enloe's (2013) book *Seriously! Investigating Crashes and Crises as If Women Really Mattered.*

9. The most prominent feature of this has been the structural adjustment programs implemented in the global South, but in the global North the integration into the capitalist economy has limited the possibilities for women to claim social services (see Enloe 2013; Waring 1988).

10. Energy justice is an emerging academic field, as well as becoming an important issue in energy policies in Europe to ensure just energy transition in the processes of decarbonization. For more information see Sovacool and Dworkin (2015).

REFERENCES

Abdelnour, Samer. 2015. "The Cookstove–Rape Prevention Myth and the Limits of Techno-saviorism." In *Sustainable Access to Energy in the Global South*, edited by S. Hostettler, A. Gadgil, and E. Hazboun, 205–215. London: Springer.

Agarwal, Bina. 2010. *Gender and Green Governance: The Political Economy of Women's Presence within and beyond Community Forestry.* Oxford: Oxford University Press.

AGECC. 2010. *Energy for a Sustainable Future: Summary Report and Recommendations.* New York: The Secretary-General's Advisory Group on Energy and Climate Change.

Aglina, Moses K., Adebayo Agbejule, and Godwin Y. Nyamuame. 2016. "Policy Framework on Energy Access and Key Development Indicators: ECOWAS Interventions and the case of Ghana." *Energy Policy* 97: 332–342.

Batliwalaa, Srilatha and Amulya K. N. Reddy. 2003. "Energy for Women and Women for Energy (Engendering Energy and Empowering Women)". *Energy for Sustainable Development* 7, no. 3: 33–43.

Biswas, Wahidul K., Paul Bryce, and Mark Diesendorf. 2001. "Model for Empowering Rural Poor through Renewable Energy Technologies in Bangladesh." *Environmental Science & Policy* 4, no. 6: 333–344.

Boserup, Ester. 1970. *Women's Role in Economic Development.* New York: St. Martin's Press.

Cecelski, Elizabeth. 2000. "Enabling Equitable Access to Rural Electrification: Current Thinking on and Major Activities in Energy, Poverty and Gender." Briefing Paper, Asia Alternative Energy Unit.

Cecelski, Elizabeth. 2005. "Energy, Development and Gender: Global Correlations and Causality." Department for International Development (DFID), https://assets.publishing.service.gov.uk/media/57a08c97ed915d622c001441/R8346-2005_cecelski.pdf.

Chant, Sylvia, and Caroline Sweetman. 2012. "Fixing Women or Fixing the World? 'Smart Economics', Efficiency Approaches, and Gender Equality in Development." *Gender & Development* 20, no. 3: 517–529.

Clancy, Joy S., and Ulrike Roehr. 2003. "Gender and Energy: Is There a Northern Perspective?" *Energy for Sustainable Development* 7, no. 3: 44–50.

Clancy, Joy, Tanja Winther, Margaret Matinga, and Sheila Oparaocha. 2011. "Gender Equity in Access to and Benefits from Modern Energy and Improved Energy Technologies." Background Paper for *World Bank World Development Report 2012*.

Cornwall, Andrea, Elizabeth Harrison, and Ann Whitehead. 2007. "Gender Myths and Feminist Fables: The Struggle for Interpretive Power in Gender and Development." *Development and Change* 38, no. 1: 1–20.

Crewe, Emma. 1997. "The Silent Traditions of Developing Cooks." In *Discourses of Development: Anthropological Perspectives*, edited by R. D. Grillo and R. L. Stirrat, 59–80. Oxford and New York: Berg.

Danielsen, Katrine. 2012. "Gender Equality, Women's Rights and Access to Energy Services: An Inspiration Paper in the Run-up to Rio+20." Ministry of Foreign Affairs Denmark.

Diekman, Amanda, Erica Weisgram, and Aimee Belanger. 2015. "New Routes to Recruiting and Retaining Women in STEM: Policy Implications of a Communal Goal Congruity Perspective." *Social Issues and Policy Review* 9, no. 1: 52–88.

Dugard, Jackie. 2009. "Power to the People? A Rights-based Analysis of South Africa's Electricity Services." In *Electric Capitalism: Recolonising Africa on the Power Grid*, edited by David A. McDonald, 249–263. Cape Town: HSRC Press.

ECOWAS. 2015. "ECOWAS Policy for Gender Mainstreaming in Energy Access," https://www.afdb.org/fileadmin/uploads/afdb/Documents/Generic-Documents/ECOWAS_Policy_for_Gender_Mainstreaming_in_Energy_Access.pdf

ENERGIA. 2016. "Exploring Factors That Enhance and Restrict Women's Empowerment through Electrification (EFEWEE): Scoping Study Report for the Gender and Energy Research Programme: ENERGIA," http://www.energia.org/cm2/wp-content/uploads/2016/07/RA1-Scoping-Report.pdf

ENERGIA/UNDP. 2006. "Incorporating Women's Concerns into Energy Policies." Fact Sheet.

Enloe, Cynthia. 2013. *Seriously! Investigating Crashes and Crises as if Women Really Mattered*. Berkeley: University of California Press.

Ezzati, Majid, and Danile M. Kammen. 2002. "The Health Impacts of Exposure to Indoor Air Pollution from Solid Fuels in Developing Countries: Knowledge, Gaps, and Data Needs." *Environmental Health Perspectives* 110, no. 11: 1057–1068.

Fraser, N. 2009. *Scales of Justice: Reimagining Political Space in a Globalizing World*. New York: Columbia University Press.

Goldthau, Andreas, and Benjamin Sovacool. 2012. "The Uniqueness of the Energy Security, Justice, and Governance Problem." *Energy Policy* 41: 232–240.

Grieshop, Andrew P., Julian D. Marshall, and Milind Kandlikar. 2011. "Health and Climate Benefits of Cookstove Replacement Options." *Energy Policy* 39, no. 12: 7530–7542.

Hancock, Kathleen. 2015. "Energy Regionalism and Diffusion in Africa: How Political Actors Created the ECOWAS Center for Renewable Energy and Energy Efficiency." *Energy Research & Social Science* 5: 105–115.

Hancock, Kathleen, and Benjamin Sovacool. 2018. "International Political Economy and Renewable Energy: Hydroelectric Power and the Resource Curse." *International Studies Review*, no. 0: 1–18.

Haves, Emily. 2012. *Does energy access help women?* Ashden Report, https://www.ashden.org/files/pdfs/reports/Ashden_Gender_Report.pdf.

Henning, Anette. 2005. "Equal Couples in Equal Houses: Cultural Perspectives on Swedish Solar and Bio-pellet Heating Design." In *Sustainable Architectures: Cultures and Natures in Europe and North America*, edited by S. Guy, and S. A. Moore, 89–104. New York: Spoon Press.

IEA. 2017. "Energy Access Outlook. From Poverty to Prosperity." World Energy Outlook Special Report.

IRENA. 2017. "Renewable Energy and Jobs: Annual Review 2017," http://www.irena.org/-/media/Files/IRENA/Agency/Publication/2017/May/IRENA_RE_Jobs_Annual_Review_2017.pdf

Kaminara, Androulla. 2015. "The Gender Dimensions of Energy Policy." Opinion Piece, University of Oxford.

Kelkar, Govind, et al. 2017. "Energy, Gender and Social Norms in Indigenous Rural Societies." *Economic & Political Weekly* 52, no. 1: 67–74.

Khandker, S. R., H. A. Samad, R. Ali, and D. F. Barnes. 2014. "Who Benefits Most from Rural Electrification? Evidence in India." *Energy Journal* 35, no. 2: 75–96.

Kohlin, Gunnar, Erin O. Sills, S. K. Pattanayak, and Christoffer Wilfrong. 2011. "Energy, Gender and Development: What Are the Linkages? Where Is the Evidence?" Background Paper for *World Bank World Development Report 2012*.

Kumar, Lakshmi. 2013. "Illusion of Women Empowerment in Micro-credit: A Case Study." *Economic & Political Weekly* 48, no. 15: 70–76.

Listo, Romy. 2018. "Gender Myths in Energy Poverty Literature: A Critical Discourse Analysis." *Energy Research and Social Science*, no. 38: 9–18.

Marshall, Mipsie, David Ockwell, and Rob Byrne. 2017. "Sustainable Energy for All or Sustainable Energy for Men? Gender and the Construction of Identity within Climate Technology Entrepreneurship in Kenya." *Progress in Development Studies* 17, no. 2: 148–172.

Matinga, Margaret. N. 2010. "We Grow Up with It: An Ethnographic Study of the Experiences, Perceptions and Responses to the Health Impacts of Energy Acquisition and Use in Rural South Africa." PhD thesis, University of Twente, The Netherlands.

McEwan, Cheryl, Emma Mawdsley, Glenn Banks, and Regina Scheyvens. 2017. "Enrolling the Private Sector in Community Development: Magic Bullet or Sleight of Hand?" *Development and Change* 48, no. 1: 28–52.

Mohan, Aniruddh, and Kilian Topp. 2018. "India's Energy Future: Contested Narratives of Change." *Energy Research and Social Science*, no. 44: 75–82.

Moore, Henrietta L.1988. *Feminism and Anthropology*. Cambridge, UK: Polity Press.

Moser, Caroline O. N. 1989. "Gender Planning in the Third World: Meeting Practical and Strategic Gender Needs." *World Development* 17, no. 11: 1799–1825.

Munien, Suveshnee, and Fathima Ahmed. 2012. "A Gendered Perspective on Energy Poverty and Livelihoods: Advancing the Millennium Development Goals in Developing Countries." *Agenda: Empowering Women for Gender Equity* 26, no. 1: 112–123.

Nathan, Dev, Indira Shakya, R. Rengalakshmi, Manjula M. S. GaIkwad, and Govind Kelkar. 2018. "The Value of Rural Women's Labor in Production and Wood Fuel Use: A Framework for Analysis." *Economic & Political Weekly* 53, nos. 26–27: 56–63.

Nye, David. 1991. *Electrifying America. Social Meanings of a New Technology, 1880-1940*. Cambridge: MIT Press.

Parikh, Jyoti, Konsam Sangeeta, Chandrashekhar Singh, and Aysecan Oztop. 2009. "Gender Analysis of Renewable Energy in India: Present Status, Issues, Approaches and New Initiatives." Energia, Integrated Research and Action for Development (IRADe).

Peterson, V. Spike. 2005. "How (the Meaning of) Gender Matters in Political Economy." *New Political Economy* 10, no. 4: 499–521.

Pope, Daniel P., Vinod Mishra, Lisa Thompson, Amna R. Siddiqui, Eva A. Rehfuess, Martin Weber, et al. 2010. "Risk of Low Birth Weight and Stillbirth Associated with Indoor Air

Pollution from Solid Fuel Use in Developing Countries." *Epidemiologic Reviews* 32, no.1: 70–81.

Raju, Saraswati. 2011. "Conceptualizing Gender, Space and Race." In *Gendered Geographies: Space and Place in South Asia*, edited by Saraswati Raju, 1–28. New Delhi: Oxford University Press.

Reeves, Hazel, and Sally Baden. 2000. "Gender and Development: Concepts and Definitions." Prepared for the Department for International Development (DFID). Bridge Development-Gender, Report no. 55.

Ross, Michael. 2012. *The Oil Curse: How Petroleum Wealth Shapes the Development of Nations.* Princeton, NJ: Princeton University Press.

Shove, Elizabeth. 2003. "Users, technologies and expectations of comfort, cleanliness and convenience." *Innovation: The European Journal of Social Science Research.* 16, no. 2: 193–207.

Sinha, Shrish. 2003. "Tare Tare Kiss: The Story of a Tribal Women's Self-help Group's Struggle to Get Electricity in Their Village." *Energy for Sustainable Development* 7, no. 3: 30–32.

Sovacool Benjamin K., and Michael H. Dworkin. 2015. "Energy Justice: Conceptual Insights and Practical Applications." *Applied Energy* 142: 435–444.

Sovacool, Benjamin K., S. Clarke, K. Johnson, M. Crafton, J. Eidsness, and D. Zoppo. 2013. "The Energy-Enterprise-Gender Nexus: Lessons from the Multifunctional Platform (MFP) in Mali." *Renewable Energy* 50: 115–125.

Standal, Karina. Forthcoming. "Challenges of Gender, Power and Change in Solar Energy Interventions in Rural India: Imagined Beneficiaries and the Makings of Women's Empowerment in the Village Electrification Project." PhD diss., University of Oslo.

Standal, Karina, and Tanja Winther. 2016. "Empowerment through Energy? Impact of Electricity on Care Work Practices and Gender Relations." *Forum for Development Studies* 43, no. 1: 27–45.

Standal, Karina, Hege Westskog, and Imre van Kraalingen. Forthcoming. "Case-study: 'From Consumer to Prosumer.'" Synthesis report ENABLE.EU.

Strenger, Yolande. 2014. "Smart Energy in Everyday Life: Are You Designing for Resource Man?" *Interactions* 21, no. 4: 24–31.

Terry, Geraldine. 2009. "No Climate Justice without Gender Justice: An Overview of the Issues." *Gender and Development* 17, no. 1: 5–19.

Tully, Steven R. 2006. "The Contribution of Human Rights to Universal Energy Access." *Northwestern Journal of International Human Rights* 4: 518–548.

Urmee, Tania, and Samuel Gyamfi. 2014. "A Review of Improved Cookstove Technologies and Programs." *Renewable and Sustainable Energy Reviews* 33: 625–635.

Van de Walle, D., M. Ravallion, V. Mendiratta, and G. Koolwal. 2015. "Long-Term Gains from Electrification in Rural India." *World Bank Economic Review* (October): 1–36.

Waring, Marilyn. 1988. *If Women Counted: A New Feminist Economics.* San Francisco: Harper and Row.

WHO. 2018. "Household Air Pollution and Health." World Health Organization Fact Sheet, http://www.who.int/en/news-room/fact-sheets/detail/household-air-pollution-and-health.

Wilhite, Harold. 2008. *Consumption and the Transfomation of Everday Life: A View from South India.* New York, Palgrave Macmillan.

Winther, Tanja. 2008. *The Impact of Electricity. Development, Desires and Dilemmas.* Oxford: Berghahn Books.

Winther, Tanja, Kirsten Ulsrud, and Anjali Saini. 2018. "Solar Powered Electricity Access: Implications for Women's Empowerment in Rural Kenya." *Energy Research and Social Science*, no. 44: 61–74.

Winther, Tanja, Margaret Matinga, Kirsten Ulsrud, and Karina Standal. 2017. "Women's Empowerment through Electricity Access: Scoping Study and Proposal for a Framework of Analysis." *Journal of Development Effectiveness* 9, no. 3: 389–417.

Winther, Tanja, Anjali Saini, Deborshi Brahmachari, Debajit Palit, Rashmi Murali. Forthcoming. "In the Light of What We Cannot See: Exploring the Interconnections between Gender and Electricity Access." *Gender, Technology and Development.*

World Bank. 2012. "World Development Report 2012: Gender Equality and Development." Washington, DC, https://openknowledge.worldbank.org/handle/10986/4391.

World Bank. 2018. "Tracking SDG7: The Energy Progress Report 2018." Washington, DC, https://trackingsdg7.esmap.org/data/files/download-documents/tracking_sdg7-the_energy_progress_report_full_report.pdf.

Yamin, Elicia Ely, and Vanessa Boulanger. 2013. "From Transforming Power to Counting Numbers: The Evolution of Sexual and Reproductive Health and Rights in Development, and Where We Want to Go from Here." Harvard University: Working Paper Series.

CHAPTER 10

THE POLITICS OF ENERGY JUSTICE

SARA FULLER

ISSUES of justice permeate everyday energy consumption in multiple ways. As an example, a resident in northeast England reported changing her household energy practices in response to high energy prices: "I've stopped baking so that I don't have to use the oven.... [T]hat's how I control my spending on my electric is how much I use my oven which is stupid, it's heat or eat." While low income is an important explanatory factor, it is only part of the account, which also includes feelings of exploitation and powerlessness in the face of consistently rising energy bills, limited potential to implement energy efficiency measures, and a lack of accessible information regarding energy costs. This situation, replicated across many parts of the world, illustrates not only how energy vulnerability is multilayered but more significantly how energy is interconnected with ideas of justice.

While energy justice as a distinct field of enquiry is still relatively new, normative concerns about justice within energy systems draw on a long history of environmental justice scholarship. In its broadest form, the concept of energy justice captures "a global energy system that fairly disseminates both the benefits and costs of energy services, and one that has representative and impartial energy decision-making" (Sovacool and Dworkin, 2015, 436). Thus, moving toward a more "just" approach to energy policy and practice needs to not only consider issues of distribution—who gets what, where, and why—but also give proper recognition to the diversity of needs and capabilities of individuals who experience energy injustice and create more equitable procedures for involving them in decisions about their energy futures.

This chapter reviews the scholarly literature on energy justice. It first considers the emergence of the concept of energy justice, primarily within the environmental justice literature, particularly focusing on the ideas of distributive, procedural, and recognition justice. Next, it explores the two key strands of literature that have emerged: one concerning the dynamics of energy consumption in terms of access and affordability and the second involving the politics of energy production, largely in relation to infrastructure.

Finally, it sets out an agenda for future energy justice research in terms of three broad themes: connection and multiplicity, framing and discourses, and transitions and responsibility.

Conceptualizing Energy Justice

Energy justice has garnered significant attention within the social sciences literature over the last decade (Jenkins et al. 2016; McCauley 2018; Sovacool et al. 2016). Sovacool and Dworkin (2015, 436) define the concept as "a global energy system that fairly disseminates both the benefits and costs of energy services, and one that has representative and impartial energy decision-making." The concept of energy justice is rooted in the environmental justice literature, which draws on social justice theory to advance claims of (in)justice. It has primarily sought to identify normative and analytical principles that utilize established ideas of distribution, procedure, and recognition.

Energy concerns have been central to environmental justice claims since the emergence of the environmental justice movement in the United States in the 1970s. The environmental justice movement can be traced to grassroots struggles against the distribution of toxic waste and hazardous and polluting industries (Agyeman et al. 2002), drawing attention to particular groups facing disproportionate impacts of environmental "bads" (Bullard 1999). Environmental justice research, in its first wave, focused on distributive outcomes in terms of quantitative evaluations of the spatial distributions of environmental hazards and assessing whether burdens are inequitably borne by one or more minority groups (Taylor 2000). Such distributional approaches, drawing on the work of social justice theorists (e.g., Rawls 1971), primarily seek to ensure the fair distribution of goods and services.

Recent literature reflects the shifting boundaries of environmental justice scholarship, activism, and praxis (Agyeman et al. 2016; Schlosberg 2013; Sze and London 2008). This literature identifies that the "organising frame" of environmental justice has moved beyond its initial focus on polluting facilities to encompass a much wider range of issues, including green space, transportation, water, food, and energy (Schlosberg 2013), alongside increasing concern for global-local relationships (Sikor and Newell 2014; Sze and London 2008). In part this reflects the globalizing of environmental justice frames, through a "horizontal" emergence of environmental justice discourse in new settings around the world and a "vertical" extension of environmental justice frames across national borders (Walker 2009). In this context, energy systems have become an important domain of environmental justice research; as Sze and London (2008, 1339) argue, "energy has become a new front-line in environmental justice research and activism."

Alongside this expansion of boundaries, environmental justice analyses have moved beyond a purely distributive realm to include procedural justice and justice as recognition, as well as the interrelations among these dimensions (Schlosberg 2007, 2004). Procedural justice concerns the fairness of decision-making in terms of access to information about environmental risks (Agyeman et al. 2002) or the "institutional conditions which inhibit or prevent people from participating in determining their actions or conditions of their actions" (Young 1990, 94). Justice as recognition extends the concept further by including awareness of the cultural, social, and economic bases of inequalities (Fraser 1997). This principle of recognition, relevant to both distributive and procedural justice, suggests not only that marginalized and vulnerable groups must be taken into consideration, but also that wider issues of social injustice, including forms of exclusion and discrimination, should be considered. Both issues of procedure and recognition are significant for understanding energy justice.

Reflecting these multiple strands, Schlosberg (2004) develops a trivalent conception of environmental justice, requiring simultaneous attention to distribution, procedure, and recognition: "equity in the distribution of environmental risk, recognition of the diversity of the participants and experiences in affected communities, and participation in the political processes which create and manage environmental policy" (517). These dimensions of distributive, procedural, and recognition justice have been widely accepted in the energy justice literature and influential both in terms of guiding exploration of the theoretical connections between energy and justice and shaping a research agenda that has produced a significant body of empirical evidence.

A specific focus of this more recent energy justice work has been to use these principles of distribution, procedure, and recognition to identify injustices and articulate "just" policy responses in the arena of energy (Jenkins et al. 2016; Sovacool and Dworkin 2015; Sovacool et al. 2017; Walker and Day 2012). Other scholarship seeks to position energy justice as an issue distinct from environmental and climate justice, which "provides a way of bounding and separating out energy concerns from the wider range of topics addressed within both environmental and climate justice analysis campaigning" (Bickerstaff et al. 2013, 2).

Overall, the concept of energy justice is fundamentally intertwined with that of environmental justice. Well-established conceptualizations of distribution, procedure, and recognition have remained at the forefront, alongside the recent emergence of frameworks that seek to position energy justice as an independent concept. Nonetheless, these new approaches and frameworks demonstrate that the concept of energy justice is dynamic and that the relationship among justice, equity, and energy is being reframed and reconstituted in multiple ways. As such, energy justice is relevant not only in terms of pushing theoretical boundaries but also in terms of its application in practice and has garnered significant attention in the academic literature.

EXPLORING THE JUSTICE DIMENSIONS OF ENERGY CONSUMPTION AND PRODUCTION

In its broadest form, the existing energy justice literature sets out to interrogate the costs and benefits of energy systems. Two strands of literature have emerged, involving the dynamics of energy consumption in terms of access and affordability and the politics of energy production, largely in relation to infrastructure.

Energy Consumption: Access and Affordability

There are two well-established concepts that consider issues of justice in relation to energy deprivation: fuel poverty and energy poverty. In the Global North fuel poverty is the most frequent justice framing relating to individual or household access to affordable energy. In contrast, the concept of energy poverty has largely been adopted in the Global South to capture issues regarding access to energy and energy security.

The concept of fuel poverty emerged in the United Kingdom in relation to conditions whereby households are unable to sufficiently heat their homes due to low incomes or energy inefficient housing that also correspond with infrastructural legacies, housing structures, or changes in the affordability of utility services (Boardman 1991, 2010; Bouzarovski and Petrova 2015). A burgeoning body of research over the last decade has sought to map the prevalence of fuel poverty in many parts of the world. This literature has been particularly strong in Europe, with scholarship highlighting regional European inequalities (Bouzarovski 2014; Bouzarovski and Tirado Herrero 2017a; Thomson and Snell 2013) alongside empirical studies from Northern Europe (Brunner et al. 2012; Dubois 2012), Southern Europe (Papada and Kaliampakos 2016; Tirado Herrero and Jiménez 2016), and Central and Eastern Europe (Bouzarovski and Tirado Herrero 2017b; Petrova et al. 2013). While research is less evident in other parts of the Global North, studies from the United States (Harrison and Popke 2011; Hilbert and Werner 2016; Reames 2016) and Australia/New Zealand (Chester and Morris 2016; Howden-Chapman et al. 2012; Lawson et al. 2015) provide important contributions to this growing body of evidence.

From the outset, these understandings of fuel poverty have been regarded as a matter of injustice, whereby the fact that people suffer discomfort leading to ill health and mortality is morally wrong and requires collective action to redistribute resources. These studies have often focused on uneven distributive outcomes, including, for example, across social groups such as disabled people (Snell et al. 2015), young people (Petrova 2018), and older people (Chard and Walker 2016). Overall, this literature has made important contributions to understanding the multiple ways that fuel poverty is an uneven socio-spatial phenomenon.

Going beyond a purely distributive focus, Walker and Day (2012, 70) argue that fuel poverty also needs to be regarded in terms of procedural justice and the cultural and political recognition of vulnerable and marginalized social groups whereby "procedure and recognition can each be seen as both a component and a condition of justice; separate forms and experiences of injustice in themselves, but deeply tied to distributional inequalities." This dimension of recognition has resonance with a capabilities approach, which judges justice in terms of people's capabilities to achieve well-being in relation to specific energy services (Day et al. 2016). This explicit framing not only draws attention to the multiple injustices arising from circumstances of fuel poverty but also deepens understandings of the ways in which responses to fuel poverty can be shaped (Gillard et al. 2017; Snell et al. 2015).

Energy poverty debates in the Global South , in contrast, have largely been framed in the context of development, with a specific focus on access to energy and energy security. Statistics suggest that more than one-third of the world's population has limited access to modern energy services, while approximately one-quarter of the population, mostly in rural areas, has no direct access to electricity (Kowsari and Zerriffi 2011). This lack of energy services is seen to constrain socioeconomic development and is thus positioned as both a cause and an effect of rural poverty (Ahlborg and Hammar 2014).

Applications of energy justice are more nascent in Global South–focused scholarship. Nonetheless it is apparent that how and why justice comes to matter in these debates is highly related to socio-spatial inequalities, particularly in relation to gender (Bouzarovski and Petrova 2015). Energy in the Global South is "women's business, both in terms of collecting fuel, and in using that fuel for domestic chores and productive activities" (Clancy et al. 2007, 241). These gendered dimensions of energy are embedded both in the division of labor and in uneven distributions of power over energy services (Clancy et al. 2007). Gender is significant in terms of energy justice not only through the lenses of distribution, procedure, and recognition, but also because, as Pachauri and Rao (2013) argue, failure to address the gender dimensions of energy poverty will limit any transition to improved energy services.

The connection between energy access and justice is thus fundamentally intertwined with questions of energy supply and transitions to "modern" energy systems. This connection is commonly exemplified through the concept of an "energy ladder." "Households switch from traditional energy systems to modern energy systems… at the speed and extent allowed by factors such as household income, fuel and equipment costs, availability and accessibility of fuels, reliability of modern fuel distribution, and, to a lesser extent, relative fuel prices" (Kowsari and Zerriffi 2011, 7508). Well-established critiques of this approach, however, highlight the importance of specific historic and cultural contexts rather than a single linear transition (Masera et al. 2000). In practice, justice questions therefore emerge not only in terms of household energy practices, but also more significantly as a means to question modernist development paradigms and discourses of energy transitions (Munro et al. 2017).

Overall, a key strength of energy justice and consumption literature is its conceptual depth, which reflects a significant broadening of the research agenda in recent years. Conceptually, a narrow focus on fuel poverty and income in the Global North now incorporates a wider vocabulary, including concepts such as energy poverty, energy vulnerability, and energy precarity (Bouzarovski et al. 2017; Middlemiss and Gillard 2015; Petrova 2018). Furthermore, understandings of justice have broadened beyond distributive analyses to capture, for example, connections between energy justice and ethical consumption (Hall 2013) and interrelationships between energy use and poverty from a capabilities perspective (Day et al. 2016).

This literature thus provides significant insights into patterns of energy poverty in various regions around the world. However, not only is there still unevenness in terms of the empirical research conducted in different parts of the world, but there are also relatively few studies that attempt to capture a holistic understanding of global energy deprivation (Bouzarovski and Petrova 2015; Day et al. 2016; Li et al. 2014). Consequently, while there is a great deal of knowledge about energy poverty in relation to some energy services and practices (particularly space heating), there is much less understanding in relation to other types of energy consumption. While some important studies are emerging in this space (Petrova 2018; Simcock et al. 2016), there is still a need for further research that explicitly considers a wider range of energy practices and services in both the Global North and South.

Energy Production and the Politics of Energy Infrastructure

Beyond individual or household experiences of energy justice, research has also considered the ways in which principles of justice play out in the politics of energy infrastructures, most notably in relation to energy production. Reflecting its historical legacy in environmental justice scholarship, this literature is explicitly framed around the dimensions of distributive, procedural, and recognition justice.

Much of the empirical evidence associated with distributive outcomes has emerged from research in the United States. For example, studies have drawn attention to the uneven distribution of energy production facilities, such as the proximity of nuclear energy plants to Native American territories or petrochemical plants in low income and ethnic minority communities (Carruthers 2007; Endres 2009; Sze and London 2008). This work particularly draws connections with the activist origins of the environmental justice movement (Sze 2005). There is also literature that considers the energy justice implications of "new" systems of energy provision in terms of, for example, the environmental justice implications of hydraulic fracturing (fracking; see Tutuncu, this Handbook, for more on this technology) (Clough and Bell 2016). Drawing on a distributive environmental justice paradigm, this research has created a large body of evidence about the social and spatial impacts of energy systems infrastructure.

Such analyses of energy production are often bound up in normative assumptions of "good" and "bad" energy technologies. Energy production facilities, such as nuclear energy or fracking, tend to be framed in terms of negative impacts and lend themselves more easily to energy justice analyses. However, it is also important to look at the justice implications of renewable energy technologies. Going beyond framings that highlight the benefits of a low carbon transition, there is a rapidly growing body of work that explores the justice implications of renewable and community energy schemes (Bailey and Darkal 2018; Forman 2017; Fuller and Bulkeley 2013). These studies have not only identified distributive concerns in terms of siting decisions and the provision of financial and material benefits that might arise from such schemes (Cowell et al. 2011), but have also highlighted procedural and recognition considerations, in terms of how and by whom such projects are developed (Walker and Devine-Wright 2008).

The academic literature exploring justice in relation to energy production in the Global South highlights conflicts between energy security and neoliberal economic development. Well-established work on resource conflicts, such as oil in Nigeria (Watts, 2004) and biofuels in India (Baka, 2013), has been complemented recently by studies that explicitly apply an energy justice frame. This work includes analyses of unconventional gas extraction in Mexico (Silva Ontiveros et al. 2018) and studies of energy transitions in Mozambique (Castán Broto et al. 2018). One important study considers energy justice in the context of solar energy megaprojects in India (Yenneti et al. 2016). Drawing on a framework of spatial justice and accumulation by dispossession, the research highlights the justice consequences of megaprojects in terms of unequal distributions of benefits and burdens associated with exploitative land-grabbing practices. Future studies of this nature will be significant given that much energy production in countries of the Global South is directed toward export, highlighting the importance of a global perspective on energy justice issues and given the likely uptake of large-scale renewable energy projects in the Global South in the future.

Overall, while the literature on energy production and justice is less comprehensive than that on access and affordability to energy, it has provided significant insights into empirical cases and specific parts of the energy system. In so doing, it draws explicitly on environmental justice discourses and has systematically analyzed distributive, procedural, and recognition perspectives on energy infrastructure and technology.

Despite ongoing calls for "whole systems" analyses, there is still much less work that examines energy systems as a whole, although connections between energy consumption and production are much more visible in the Global South. There are some notable exceptions here. For example, Mulvaney (2013, 231) explores solar energy commodity chains and suggests that the inherent tension between innovation and environmental justice makes it necessary to examine "various sites connected by solar energy commodity chains and how different kinds of innovations reshape relations between production systems, workers, communities, and ecosystems." Similarly Adams et al. (2013) undertake a whole systems analysis of microgeneration technologies, while Healy et al. (2019) introduce the concept of "embodied energy injustices" to "explicitly consider hidden and distant injustices (upstream or downstream) arising from the extraction, processing, transportation and disposal of energy resources" (220). Overall, however, current research still tends to focus on specific parts of the energy system, which is a limitation in terms of identifying a comprehensive picture of energy justice issues.

A Future Research Agenda

The existing literature has made significant contributions—theoretical, empirical, and methodological—to understandings of how questions of justice relate to energy. This final section proposes a research agenda through three key themes:

connection and multiplicity, framing and discourses, and transitions and responsibility.

Connection and Multiplicity

A key theme to guide future research is that of connection and multiplicity. This should not only support integration and whole systems approaches to justice within energy systems at a macro level but also incorporate wider understandings of vulnerability and intersectionality at a micro level.

As a starting point, there are significant opportunities to offer a synthesis across the multiple bodies of energy justice literature. While some energy consumption literature has started to address this task (Bouzarovski and Petrova 2015; Day et al. 2016), there are still relatively few studies that attempt to capture a holistic understanding of energy poverty or provide approaches that can be applied across the Global North and South. In the realm of energy production, future research should examine how injustices are constructed and experienced across energy systems (Adams et al. 2013; Mulvaney 2013). In particular, it should consider how the spatial distribution of energy resources and supply chains may create energy vulnerabilities in terms of demand (Bouzarovski and Simcock 2017) and also explicitly draw out the connections and tensions between global and local in terms of formulations of justice (Batel and Devine-Wright 2017; Holifield et al. 2009).

At the same time, there is a need for research on the micropolitics of energy systems. While energy justice scholarship in the realms of both production and consumption has produced significant insights into patterns and processes of vulnerability, there is scope to explicitly draw on ideas of relationality and social context to enable in-depth interrogation of social connectedness and situatedness within power structures. In this context, energy justice research would benefit from engagement with the literature on intersectionality and vulnerability. Intersectionality as a feminist approach focuses on mutually constitutive forms of social oppression rather than on single axes of difference and explicitly draws out intersecting forms of social difference such as gender, race, ethnicity, class, disability, or age (Crenshaw 1991; Hopkins 2019). (For a detailed analysis of gender and energy politics, see Standal, Danielson, and Winther, this volume.) Another avenue would be closer engagement with the literature on "the vulnerable subject" to explore the interplay between human agency and structural constraints (Brown 2017). This research would not only extend current interpretations of identity and vulnerability in the context of energy systems but also provide the basis for a critique and potential repositioning of existing power and institutional structures.

These approaches would be supported by methodological advances that would enable the tracing of interconnections across micro and macro scales. There is a significant body of energy poverty scholarship that is quantitative in its approach. New quantitative frameworks attempt to capture the multidimensional nature of energy poverty (Okushima 2017; Thomson et al. 2017; Tirado Herrero 2017). There is a clear need to keep pushing this research trajectory to improve the detection of energy poverty across a more diverse array of vulnerable groups to inform more robust and evidence-based policy and practice.

Qualitative methodologies in energy justice research have started to provide significant insights into the lived experience of energy poverty (e.g., Chard and Walker 2016; Middlemiss and Gillard 2015; Waitt et al. 2016). There is still a need for more research in this arena to provide alternative perspectives on matters of energy (in)justice and help actors articulate what is important to them (Groves et al. 2017). While much of this work is interview centered, ethnography is emerging as an important means to bridge micro and macro level perspectives and bring all elements of everyday lives into view (Smith and High 2017). Overall, qualitative, experience-centered methodologies would reveal further insights into the mechanisms that shape everyday energy practices, not only how lives and practices intersect in the context of energy systems change, but also how energy systems can be shaped and resisted by mundane practices that might promote justice.

Framing and Discourses

The second key arena for further research relates to unpacking the frames and discourses of energy justice. New research in this vein should support theoretical enquiry that seeks to disrupt binaries of production and consumption alongside conceptual and empirical development that interrogates how and by whom the discourse of energy justice is being shaped and negotiated.

One branch of energy justice scholarship that has recently emerged focuses on identifying normative and evaluative principles to inform energy justice in practice (Jenkins et al. 2016; Sovacool et al. 2017). While this work has guided empirical case studies and provided insights into the nature of energy justice across energy systems, these understandings offer only partial accounts of energy justice and are themselves "social constructions that emerge from particular historical and cultural contexts" (Smith and High 2017, 1). Future research should thus promote more critical and situated explorations of multiplicity and complexity in energy justice and could question whether a universal understanding of energy justice is possible or desirable (LaBelle 2017).

An entry point for this research is the assumption that experiences and articulations of justice in practice depend on a process of co-construction of meaning (Rasch and Köhne 2017; Schlosberg 2013). An important priority for research that seeks to support future policy development is to draw out locally constructed and grounded approaches to energy justice (Forman 2017; Groves et al. 2017; Rasch and Köhne 2017). Further research should explore the construction of frames and discourses of energy justice "from below" to promote a stronger understanding of complexity; develop a more nuanced understanding of the politics, contestations, and tensions associated with energy justice; and engage with the specificities of experiences of energy (in)justice. This work should also open up a wider reading of energy justice through the lens of energy ethics and morality (Hall et al. 2013). This would not only facilitate the emergence of everyday accounts of energy justice based on people making their own judgments about the "rightness and wrongness of energy" (Smith and High 2017), but would also support a wider reading of "what matters" when considering the ethical and political aspects of energy transitions (Groves et al. 2017).

This work would benefit from a multidisciplinary perspective and greater integration of research from across disciplines (such as geography, development studies, and economics) to provide greater understandings of the complex interconnections. Such multidisciplinary work would be greatly supported by the integration of alternative understandings and interpretations from non-Western perspectives (particularly experiences from the Global South) to extend the vocabulary and frameworks of energy justice (Malakar et al. 2019; Munro et al. 2017). It would also challenge the existing geographic bias in the literature; further research in different parts of the world and a wider range of empirical case studies would support more diverse and nuanced framing(s) and challenge the potential application of universal approaches.

There is also scope for more critical engagement with the literature on framing and contentious politics. The notion of framing has emerged from a well-established body of political sociology or "contentious politics" literature (Benford and Snow 2000), wherein frames are "cognitive schemata" used to make sense of situations, attribute blame, identify solutions, and motivate participation. Existing research suggests the lack of an explicit energy justice frame and that activist movements have drawn, more implicitly, on discourses of environmental justice (Fuller and McCauley 2016). This raises important questions for future research about if and how the discourse of energy justice matters for politics and creating change. In this context, there is still little work evaluating how energy justice frames shift as they move into new political and cultural contexts (Sze and London 2008; Walker 2009), which suggests a need for further research to explore how energy justice is being mobilized, problematized, and resisted.

Transitions and Responsibility

A final arena for further research relates to energy justice in the context of low carbon energy transitions and climate change. Further research should consider how future energy vulnerability might be structured through changing thermal conditions and patterns of future energy demand, in terms of not only technology adoption but also adaptive practices. For example, increased use of air conditioning may in the future trigger new energy vulnerabilities in dwellings that have poor cooling characteristics or that cannot afford cooling systems (Moore et al. 2017; Nicholls and Strengers 2018). In such cases, the problem of fuel poverty under conditions of climate change may shift from one of principally inadequate heating in winter to also feature inadequate cooling in summer. Future research should explicitly consider cooling practices in the context of energy poverty and explore a wider range of adaptive practices in the context of changing climatic conditions to enable more just responses to climate change.

The issue of climate change raises questions not only about the direct impacts of climate change on energy justice but also in terms of how social and policy responses to climate change may have implications for how to consider and understand energy justice. For example, questions have been raised about the extent to which efforts to reduce energy consumption and support the deployment of energy technologies through the use of subsidies and related costs levied across the population may have important justice elements (Passey et al. 2018; Stockton and Campbell 2011). Framing questions of energy in relation to climate change thus brings new spatial and temporal dimensions to the forefront, which in turn raise questions about the adequacy of under-standings about what being "just" in energy terms may entail (Bickerstaff et al. 2013; Byrne and Portanger 2014). To date however, there has been limited research about the implications of applying a climate change frame to such analyses. In this context, further research is needed to more carefully explore attempts to decarbonize energy systems through new models of energy provision, new configurations of responsibility, and new patterns of energy use.

Such changes in energy systems may also trigger a redistribution of responsibilities. Shifting governance arrangements and discourses of ecological modernization mean that responsibilities for addressing energy transitions have increasingly been placed on individuals, communities, civil society, and corporate actors, rather than being positioned as an issue for government (Fuller 2017; Newell et al. 2015; Paterson and Stripple 2010). These shifts are significant because individual mechanisms not only have limited capacity to challenge development models that are sustained by high consumption, but also raise questions about the justice of asking all individuals to reduce their energy consumption. Further research should explicitly seek to identify and address the underlying structural mechanisms that underpin existing inequalities in energy consumption, with a focus on both "overconsumption" as well as "underconsumption," both of which are important in light of the complex role that energy services play in enabling well-being (Day et al. 2016).

In addition, there is a need for a more critical justice perspective on technocentric approaches that seek to reconfigure energy demand and practices. For example, smart home technologies for households to manage their energy use may further entrench existing inequalities by sustaining energy-intensive ways of life for some households or increasing domestic energy vulnerabilities where the benefits of such technologies are not evenly distributed (Tirado Herrero et al. 2018). Understanding the implications of such technocentric approaches is a significant area for future research to inform a more careful consideration of the emerging justice implications.

Overall, there is a need for research that explores how justice principles should be part of responses to climate change from multiple perspectives. Ideally, this research would include temporal dimensions, in terms of changes in energy systems over time, and the associated spatial, political, and economic transitions required to facilitate a low carbon energy system. Consequent knowledge gains would provide important insights into how existing understandings of energy justice might be challenged in relation to climate change and the policy imperatives of responding to justice issues through the notion of low carbon transitions.

REFERENCES

Adams, Charlotte, Sandra Bell, Philip Taylor, Varvara Alimisi, Guy Hutchinson, Ankit Kumar, and Britta Turner. 2013. "Equity across Borders: A Whole Systems Approach to Micro-Generation." In *Energy Justice in a Changing Climate*, edited by Karen Bickerstaff, Gordon Walker, and Harriet Bulkeley, 116–138. London: Zed Books.

Agyeman, Julian, Robert D. Bullard, and Bob Evans. 2002. "Exploring the Nexus: Bringing Together Sustainability, Environmental Justice and Equity." *Space and Polity* 6: 77–90.

Agyeman, Julian, David Schlosberg, Luke Craven, and Caitlin Matthews. 2016. "Trends and Directions in Environmental Justice: From Inequity to Everyday Life, Community, and Just Sustainabilities." *Annual Review of Environment and Resources* 41: 321–340.

Ahlborg, Helene, and Linus Hammar. 2014. "Drivers and Barriers to Rural Electrification in Tanzania and Mozambique—Grid-Extension, Off-Grid, and Renewable Energy Technologies." *Renewable Energy* 61: 117–124.

Bailey, Ian, and Hoayda Darkal. 2018. "(Not) Talking about Justice: Justice Self-Recognition and the Integration of Energy and Environmental-Social Justice into Renewable Energy Siting." *Local Environment* 23: 335–351.

Baka, Jennifer. 2013. "The Political Construction of Wasteland: Governmentality, Land Acquisition and Social Inequality in South India." *Development and Change* 44: 409–428.

Batel, Susana, and Patrick Devine-Wright. 2017. "Energy Colonialism and the Role of the Global in Local Responses to New Energy Infrastructures in the UK: A Critical and Exploratory Empirical Analysis." *Antipode* 49: 3–22.

Benford, Robert D., and David A. Snow. 2000. "Framing Processes and Social Movements: An Overview and Assessment." *Annual Review of Sociology* 26: 611–639.

Bickerstaff, Karen, Gordon Walker, and Harriet Bulkeley. 2013. "Introduction: Making Sense of Energy Justice." In *Energy Justice in a Changing Climate*, edited by Karen Bickerstaff, Gordon Walker, and Harriet Bulkeley, 1–13. London: Zed Books.

Boardman, Brenda. 1991. *From Cold Homes to Affordable Warmth*. London: Belhaven Press.

Boardman, Brenda. 2010. *Fixing Fuel Poverty: Challenges and Solutions*. London: Earthscan.

Bouzarovski, Stefan. 2014. "Energy Poverty in the European Union: Landscapes of Vulnerability." *Wiley Interdisciplinary Reviews: Energy and Environment* 3: 276–289.

Bouzarovski, Stefan, and Saska Petrova. 2015. "A Global Perspective on Domestic Energy Deprivation: Overcoming the Energy Poverty–Fuel Poverty Binary." *Energy Research & Social Science* 10: 31–40.

Bouzarovski, Stefan, and Neil Simcock. 2017. "Spatializing Energy Justice." *Energy Policy* 107: 640–648.

Bouzarovski, Stefan, and Sergio Tirado Herrero. 2017a. "The Energy Divide: Integrating Energy Transitions, Regional Inequalities and Poverty Trends in the European Union." *European Urban and Regional Studies* 24: 69–86.

Bouzarovski, Stefan, and Sergio Tirado Herrero. 2017b. "Geographies of Injustice: The Socio-Spatial Determinants of Energy Poverty in Poland, the Czech Republic and Hungary." *Post-Communist Economies* 29: 27–50.

Bouzarovski, Stefan, Sergio Tirado Herrero, Saska Petrova, Jan Frankowski, Roman Matoušek, and Thomas Maltby. 2017. "Multiple Transformations: Theorizing Energy Vulnerability as a Socio-Spatial Phenomenon." *Geografiska Annaler: Series B, Human Geography* 99: 20–41.

Brown, Kate. 2017. "Introduction: Vulnerability and Social Justice." *Social Policy and Society* 16: 423–427.

Brunner, Karl-Michael, Markus Spitzer, and Anja Christanell. 2012. "Experiencing Fuel Poverty: Coping Strategies of Low-Income Households in Vienna/Austria." *Energy Policy* 49: 53–59.

Bullard, Robert D. 1999. "Dismantling Environmental Racism in the USA." *Local Environment* 4: 5–19.

Byrne, Jason, and Chloe Portanger. 2014. "Climate Change, Energy Policy and Justice: A Systematic Review." *Analyse & Kritik* 2: 315–343.

Carruthers, David V. 2007. "Environmental Justice and the Politics of Energy on the US-Mexico Border." *Environmental Politics* 16: 394–413.

Castán Broto, Vanesa, Idalina Baptista, Joshua Kirshner, Shaun Smith, and Susana Neves Alves. 2018. "Energy Justice and Sustainability Transitions in Mozambique." *Applied Energy* 228: 645–655.

Chard, Rose, and Gordon Walker. 2016. "Living with Fuel Poverty in Older Age: Coping Strategies and Their Problematic Implications." *Energy Research & Social Science* 18: 62–70.

Chester, Lynne, and Alan Morris. 2016. "A New Form of Energy Poverty Is the Hallmark of Liberalised Electricity Sectors." *Australian Journal of Social Issues* 46: 435–459.

Clancy, Joy, Fareeha Ummar, Indira Shakya, and Govind Kelkar. 2007. "Appropriate Gender-Analysis Tools for Unpacking the Gender-Energy-Poverty Nexus." *Gender & Development* 15: 241–257.

Clough, Emily, and Derek Bell. 2016. "Just Fracking: A Distributive Environmental Justice Analysis of Unconventional Gas Development in Pennsylvania, USA." *Environmental Research Letters* 11: 25001. https://iopscience.iop.org/article/10.1088/1748-9326/11/2/025001.

Cowell, Richard, Gill Bristow, and Max Munday. 2011. "Acceptance, Acceptability and Environmental Justice: The Role of Community Benefits in Wind Energy Development." *Journal of Environmental Planning and Management* 54: 539–557.

Crenshaw, Kimberle. 1991. "Mapping the Margins: Intersectionality, Identity Politics, and Violence against Women of Color." *Stanford Law Review* 43: 1241–1299.

Day, Rosie, Gordon Walker, and Neil Simcock. 2016. "Conceptualising Energy Use and Energy Poverty Using a Capabilities Framework." *Energy Policy* 93: 255–264.

Dubois, Ute. 2012. "From Targeting to Implementation: The Role of Identification of Fuel Poor Households." *Energy Policy* 49: 107–115.

Endres, Danielle. 2009. "From Wasteland to Waste Site: The Role of Discourse in Nuclear Power's Environmental Injustices." *Local Environment* 14: 917–937.

Forman, Alister. 2017. "Energy Justice at the End of the Wire: Enacting Community Energy and Equity in Wales." *Energy Policy* 107: 649–657.

Fraser, Nancy. 1997. *Justice Interruptus: Critical Reflections on the "Postsocialist" Condition.* New York: Routledge.

Fuller, Sara. 2017. "Configuring Climate Responsibility in the City: Carbon Footprints and Climate Justice in Hong Kong." *Area* 49: 519–525.

Fuller, Sara, and Harriet Bulkeley. 2013. "Energy Justice and the Low Carbon Transition: Assessing Low Carbon Community Programmes in the UK." In *Energy Justice in a Changing Climate*, edited by Karen Bickerstaff, Gordon Walker, and Harriet Bulkeley, 61–78. London: Zed Books.

Fuller, Sara, and Darren McCauley. 2016. "Framing Energy Justice: Perspectives from Activism and Advocacy." *Energy Research & Social Science* 11: 1–8.

Gillard, Ross, Carolyn Snell, and Mark Bevan. 2017. "Advancing an Energy Justice Perspective of Fuel Poverty: Household Vulnerability and Domestic Retrofit Policy in the United Kingdom." *Energy Research & Social Science* 29: 53–61.

Groves, Christopher, Karen Henwood, Fiona Shirani, Gareth Thomas, and Nick Pidgeon. 2017. "Why Mundane Energy Use Matters: Energy Biographies, Attachment and Identity." *Energy Research & Social Science* 30: 71–81.

Hall, Sarah Marie. 2013. "Energy Justice and Ethical Consumption: Comparison, Synthesis and Lesson Drawing." *Local Environment* 18: 422–437.

Hall, Sarah Marie, Sarah Hards, and Harriet Bulkeley. 2013. "New Approaches to Energy: Equity, Justice and Vulnerability." Introduction to the special issue, *Local Environment* 18: 413–421.

Harrison, Conor, and Jeff Popke. 2011. " 'Because You Got to Have Heat': The Networked Assemblage of Energy Poverty in Eastern North Carolina." *Annals of the Association of American Geographers* 101: 949–961.

Healy, Noel, Jennie C. Stephens, and Stephanie A. Malin. 2019. "Embodied Energy Injustices: Unveiling and Politicizing the Transboundary Harms of Fossil Fuel Extractivism and Fossil Fuel Supply Chains." *Energy Research & Social Science* 48: 219–234.

Hilbert, Anthony, and Marion Werner. 2016. "Turn Up the Heat! Contesting Energy Poverty in Buffalo, NY." *Geoforum* 74: 222–232.

Holifield, Ryan, Michael Porter, and Gordon Walker. 2009. "Spaces of Environmental Justice: Frameworks for Critical Engagement." *Antipode* 41: 591–612.

Hopkins, Peter. 2019. "Social Geography I: Intersectionality." *Progress in Human Geography* 43: 937–947.

Howden-Chapman, Philippa, Helen Viggers, Ralph Chapman, Kimberley O'Sullivan, Lucy Telfar Barnard, and Bob Lloyd. 2012. "Tackling Cold Housing and Fuel Poverty in New Zealand: A Review of Policies, Research, and Health Impacts." *Energy Policy* 49: 134–142.

Jenkins, Kirsten, Darren McCauley, Raphael Heffron, Hannes Stephan, and Robert Rehner. 2016. "Energy Justice: A Conceptual Review." *Energy Research & Social Science* 11: 174–182.

Kowsari, Reza, and Hisham Zerriffi. 2011. "Three Dimensional Energy Profile: A Conceptual Framework for Assessing Household Energy Use." *Energy Policy* 39: 7505–7517.

Labelle, Michael Carnegie. 2017. "In Pursuit of Energy Justice." *Energy Policy* 107: 615–620.

Lawson, Rob, John Williams, and Ben Wooliscroft. 2015. "Contrasting Approaches to Fuel Poverty in New Zealand." *Energy Policy* 81: 38–42.

Li, Kang, Bob Lloyd, Xiao-Jie Liang, and Yi-Ming Wei. 2014. "Energy Poor or Fuel Poor: What Are the Differences?" *Energy Policy* 68: 476–481.

Malakar, Yuwan, Matthew Herington, and Vigya Sharma. 2019. "The Temporalities of Energy Justice: Examining India's Energy Policy Paradox Using Non-Western Philosophy." *Energy Research & Social Science* 49: 16–25.

Masera, Omar R., Barbara D. Saatkamp, and Daniel M. Kammen. 2000. "From Linear Fuel Switching to Multiple Cooking Strategies: A Critique and Alternative to the Energy Ladder Model." *World Development* 28: 2083–2103.

McCauley, Darren. 2018. *Energy Justice*. Basingstoke: Palgrave Macmillan.

Middlemiss, Lucie, and Ross Gillard. 2015. "Fuel Poverty from the Bottom-Up: Characterising Household Energy Vulnerability through the Lived Experience of the Fuel Poor." *Energy Research & Social Science* 6: 146–154.

Moore, Trivess, Ian Ridley, Yolande Strengers, Cecily Maller, and Ralph Horne. 2017. "Dwelling Performance and Adaptive Summer Comfort in Low-Income Australian Households." *Building Research & Information* 45: 443–456.

Mulvaney, Dustin. 2013. "Opening the Black Box of Solar Energy Technologies: Exploring Tensions Between Innovation and Environmental Justice." *Science as Culture* 22: 230–237.

Munro, Paul, Greg Van der Horst, and Stephen Healy. 2017. "Energy Justice for All? Rethinking Sustainable Development Goal 7 through Struggles over Traditional Energy Practices in Sierra Leone." *Energy Policy* 105: 635–641.

Newell, Peter, Harriet Bulkeley, Karen Turner, Christopher Shaw, Simon Caney, Elizabeth Shove, and Nicholas Pidgeon. 2015. "Governance Traps in Climate Change Politics: Re-framing the Debate in Terms of Responsibilities and Rights." *Wiley Interdisciplinary Reviews: Climate Change* 6: 535–540.

Nicholls, Larissa, and Yolande Strengers. 2018. "Heatwaves, Cooling and Young Children at Home: Integrating Energy and Health Objectives." *Energy Research & Social Science* 39: 1–9.

Okushima, Shinichiro. 2017. "Gauging Energy Poverty: A Multidimensional Approach." *Energy* 137: 1159–1166.

Pachauri, Shonali, and Narasimha D. Rao. 2013. "Gender Impacts and Determinants of Energy Poverty: Are We Asking the Right Questions?" *Current Opinion in Environmental Sustainability* 5: 205–215.

Papada, Lefkothea, and Dimitris Kaliampakos. 2016. "Measuring Energy Poverty in Greece." *Energy Policy* 94: 157–165.

Passey, Robert, Muriel Watt, Anna Bruce, and Iain MacGill. 2018. "Who Pays, Who Benefits? The Financial Impacts of Solar Photovoltaic Systems and Air-Conditioners on Australian Households." *Energy Research & Social Science* 39: 198–215.

Paterson, Matthew, and Johannes Stripple. 2010. "My Space: Governing Individuals' Carbon Emissions." *Environment and Planning D: Society and Space* 28: 341–362.

Petrova, Saska. 2018. "Illuminating Austerity: Lighting Poverty as an Agent and Signifier of the Greek Crisis." *European Urban and Regional Studies* 25: 360–372.

Petrova, Sask, Michael Gentile, Iilka Henrik Mäkinen, and Stefan Bouzarovski. 2013. "Perceptions of Thermal Comfort and Housing Quality: Exploring the Microgeographies of Energy Poverty in Stakhanov, Ukraine." *Environment and Planning A* 45: 1240–1257.

Rasch, Elisabet Dueholm, and Michiel Köhne. 2017. "Practices and Imaginations of Energy Justice in Transition: A Case Study of the Noordoostpolder, the Netherlands." *Energy Policy* 107: 607–614.

Rawls, John. 1971. *A Theory of Justice*. Cambridge, MA: Belknap Press.

Reames, Tony Gerard. 2016. "Targeting Energy Justice: Exploring Spatial, Racial/Ethnic and Socioeconomic Disparities in Urban Residential Heating Energy Efficiency." *Energy Policy* 97: 549–558.

Schlosberg, David. 2004. "Reconceiving Environmental Justice: Global Movements and Political Theories." *Environmental Politics* 13: 517–540.

Schlosberg, David. 2007. *Defining Environmental Justice: Theories, Movements and Nature*. Oxford: Oxford University Press.

Schlosberg, David. 2013. "Theorising Environmental Justice: The Expanding Sphere of a Discourse." *Environmental Politics* 22: 37–55.

Sikor, Thomas, and Peter Newell. 2014. "Globalizing Environmental Justice?" *Geoforum* 54: 151–157.

Silva Ontiveros, Letizia, Paul G. Munro, and Maria de Lourdes Melo Zurita. 2018. "Proyectos de Muerte: Energy Justice Conflicts on Mexico's Unconventional Gas Frontier." *The Extractive Industries and Society* 5: 481–489.

Simcock, Neil, Gordon Walker, and Rosie Day. 2016. "Fuel Poverty in the UK: Beyond Heating?" *People, Place and Policy* 10: 25–41.

Smith, Jessica, and Mette M. High. 2017. "Exploring the Anthropology of Energy: Ethnography, Energy and Ethics." *Energy Research & Social Science* 30: 1–6.

Snell, Carolyn, Mark Bevan, and Harriet Thomson. 2015. "Justice, Fuel Poverty and Disabled People in England." *Energy Research & Social Science* 10: 123–132.

Sovacool, Benjamin K., Matthew Burke, Lucy Baker, Chaitanta Kumar Kotikalapudi, and Holle Wlokas. 2017. "New Frontiers and Conceptual Frameworks for Energy Justice." *Energy Policy* 105: 677–691.

Sovacool, Benjamin K., and Michael H. Dworkin. 2015. "Energy Justice: Conceptual Insights and Practical Applications." *Applied Energy* 142: 435–444.

Sovacool, Benjamin K., Raphael J. Heffron, Darren McCauley, and Andreas Goldthau. 2016. "Energy Decisions Reframed as Justice and Ethical Concerns." *Nature Energy* 1: 16024.

Stockton, Helen, and Ron Campbell. 2011. *Time to Reconsider UK Energy and Fuel Poverty Policies?* York: Joseph Rowntree Foundation Viewpoint.

Sze, Julie. 2005. "Race and Power: An Introduction to Environmental Justice Energy Activism." In *Power, Justice and the Environment: A Critical Appraisal of the Environmental Justice Movement*, edited by David Naguib Pellow and Robert J. Brulle, 101–115. Cambridge, MA: MIT Press.

Sze, Julie, and Jonathan K. London. 2008. "Environmental Justice at the Crossroads." *Sociology Compass* 2: 1331–1354.

Taylor, Dorceta E. 2000. "The Rise of the Environmental Justice Paradigm." *American Behavioral Scientist* 43: 508–580.

Thomson, Harriet, Stefan Bouzarovski, and Carolyn Snell. 2017. "Rethinking the Measurement of Energy Poverty in Europe: A Critical Analysis of Indicators and Data." *Indoor and Built Environment* 26: 879–901.

Thomson, Harriet, and Carolyn Snell. 2013. "Quantifying the Prevalence of Fuel Poverty across the European Union." *Energy Policy* 52: 563–572.

Tirado Herrero, Sergio. 2017. "Energy Poverty Indicators: A Critical Review of Methods." *Indoor and Built Environment* 26: 1018–1031.

Tirado Herrero, Sergio, and Luis Jiménez. 2016. "Energy Poverty, Crisis and Austerity in Spain." *People, Place and Policy* 10: 42–56.

Tirado Herrero, Sergio, Larissa Nicholls, and Yolande Strengers. 2018. "Smart Home Technologies in Everyday Life: Do They Address Key Energy Challenges in Households?" *Current Opinion in Environmental Sustainability* 31: 65–70.

Waitt, Gordon, Kate Roggeveen, Ross Gordon, Katherine Butler, and Paul Cooper. 2016. "Tyrannies of Thrift: Governmentality and Older, Low-Income People's Energy Efficiency Narratives in the Illawarra, Australia." *Energy Policy* 90: 37–45.

Walker, Gordon. 2009. "Globalizing Environmental Justice: The Geography and Politics of Frame Contextualization and Evolution." *Global Social Policy* 9: 355–382.

Walker, Gordon, and Rosie Day. 2012. "Fuel Poverty as Injustice: Integrating Distribution, Recognition and Procedure in the Struggle for Affordable Warmth." *Energy Policy* 49: 69–75.

Walker, Gordon, and Patrick Devine-Wright. 2008. "Community Renewable Energy: What Should It Mean?" *Energy Policy* 36: 497–500.

Watts, Michael. 2004. "Resource Curse? Governmentality, Oil and Power in the Niger Delta, Nigeria." *Geopolitics* 9: 50–80.

Yenneti, Komali, Rosie Day, and Oleg Golubchikov. 2016. "Spatial Justice and the Land Politics of Renewables: Dispossessing Vulnerable Communities through Solar Energy Mega-Projects." *Geoforum* 76: 90–99.

Young, Iris Marion. 1990. *Justice and the Politics of Difference*. Princeton, NJ: Princeton Press.

CHAPTER 11

....

THE ENERGY POLITICS
OF CORPORATE SOCIAL
RESPONSIBILITY

....

JESSICA STEINBERG

In the province of Tete, Mozambique, coal company Rio Tinto provided livestock management training and houses to communities in and around its coal concession. In Kazakhstan, where oil extraction is a primary economic activity, the national oil and gas company provides financial aid to war veterans and supports the construction of infrastructure for regional administrative centers (Smirnova 2012). In Laos, revenues from a hydropower project support educational initiatives for youth living around the dam (Sparkes 2014). In each of these widely differing contexts, firms are extracting resources that they will turn into an energy source, while engaging in the provision of social or economic goods where they operate. The kinds of activities vary across firms, national and local contexts, and levels of development. However, all of these voluntary activities fall under the category of corporate social responsibility, or CSR.

This chapter seeks first to provide some background on the concept of CSR and in particular in the energy sector, providing a brief overview of its interdisciplinary conceptual development. Next, I explain what is specific to CSR in the energy sector, elaborating on the characteristics that shape its nature and extent in that (primarily non-renewable) sector. I then provide some exploration of the empirical regularities found in the literature and highlight measurement issues inherent in empirical studies of CSR. Because these empirical studies of CSR are not often broken out by sector, much of the academic literature covered here is not specifically focused on the energy sector, though I attempt, wherever possible, to highlight those items that are. I then discuss the policy implications, exploring the role of international governmental and market schemes to improve CSR practices and effectiveness. Finally, I explore areas for further research, suggesting that the changing climate and permeability of global capital create new challenges for understanding, studying, and incentivizing CSR in the energy sector.

The concept of CSR gained prominence as a subject of scholarship across a broad array of disciplines in the 1990s and early 2000s. This popularity coincided with the Exxon Valdez oil spill in the United States, as well as the move toward privatization of energy (and other) sectors in developing countries.[1] However, some disciplines have sought to understand CSR since much earlier than this, reflecting a broader, less context-dependent concept of CSR. In the 1930s the business and ethics literature sought to understand the societal responsibility of the private firm. Since then theories, conceptualizations, and frameworks for thinking about CSR have proliferated. In a well-cited article (Carroll 1991), Carroll develops what he calls a "pyramid of CSR," in which the author breaks down the concept of CSR into component parts that correspond to a firm's priorities across its economic, legal, ethical, and social responsibilities. With the goal of convincing business leaders to adopt such policies, this work is explicitly normative in much of its discussion, a characteristic of CSR that should be disentangled from those works seeking to understand the analytic purchase of the concept and the empirical regularities characterizing its practice.

More recently, the business and management scholarship has explored CSR as both a form and result of "stakeholder engagement" in the behavior of private entities; the relevant stakeholders usually include consumers, shareholders, government, and local communities. This procedural notion of CSR emphasizes the sufficient participation and engagement of a scripted set of actors labeled "stakeholders." This focus on the relationships among stakeholders explicitly considers the importance of stakeholders' expectations about firm behavior and performance. For example, Aguinis and Glavas (2012) define CSR as "context specific organizational actions and policies that take into account stakeholders' expectations and the triple bottom line of economic, social and environmental performance." Thus the need to consider whether firm behavior meets some predefined set of expectations in order to be considered CSR. Campbell (2007) suggests a more minimal definition of CSR: corporations must not knowingly do anything to harm their stakeholders (which includes investors, employees, customers, suppliers, and local community members), but if harm is done, the company must take steps to address the situation immediately.

Moving away from the business and management language of "stakeholders," anthropological considerations of CSR focus on the processes, meanings, and power structures produced and reproduced by a firm's engagement at the site of its operations (Gilberthorpe and Banks 2012). In comparison, in economics scholars speak of private firm regulation and "beyond compliance," evaluating firm incentives to voluntarily invest in social and environmental goods where they operate. The focus is on the optimal level of CSR and whether or when it corresponds to improved financial performance (McWilliams and Siegel 2001). CSR is not widely studied in political science, but where it is, it is explored in the context of nonstate goods provision (Steinberg 2016) and bargaining over the supply of local goods (Amengual 2018).

There is much at stake in defining CSR (Campbell 2007) beyond resolution of disciplinary-based conceptualizations. First, differences in the definitional scope of CSR shape what stakeholders believe they are entitled to and what firms might expect to provide. (Should activities extend beyond employees? Should CSR include both environmental and social goods?) Second, failing to consider the difference between local expectations of firm behavior and international standards of firm behavior may lead to the development of CSR standards and policies that do not in any way match the local and national contexts in which firms are embedded. And third, which actors constitute legitimate stakeholders has significant on-the-ground implications. For example, there are often trade-offs in protecting the interests of each of the different actors, and it is not obvious whether or under what conditions CSR should benefit one over the other. Firm investment brings with it the potential for national (and local) revenue accumulation, but it may adversely affect local communities, and CSR efforts need to successfully recognize both constituencies as relevant stakeholders. Thus, variations in the meaning and conceptualization of CSR may have significant implications. Though it is helpful to have a working definition, it is important to consider that the forms, practices, and incentives for CSR might differ across sectors, a consideration that few studies have acknowledged.

Across this multitude of approaches, CSR is at once a set of principles and norms and a collection of policies and regulatory frameworks, while still others view it as a disparate and context-specific set of practices on the ground. Because CSR is multidisciplinary, with conceptual definitions, drivers, and empirical trends proliferating in the business and management literature, political science, economics, anthropology, and sociology, there is significant variation in the conceptualizations of CSR. All told, Dahlsrud (2008) identifies at least thirty-seven definitions of CSR, suggesting that these varied disciplinary approaches in fact correspond to as many definitions of CSR. Though each of these approaches applies the traditions and signatures of its disciplinary canon to the topic of CSR, emphasizing different characteristics and relationships, there are shared tendencies. For the purposes of this chapter, I consider CSR to be a (a) voluntary or quasi-voluntary (b) discretionary set of (c) behaviors, policies, or practices relating to social, environmental, and cultural goods (d) by a private firm or corporate entity. These four defining characteristics are largely shared across disciplinary conceptualizations, though some approaches emphasize the less tangible or material dimensions of CSR.

The kinds of voluntary investments that firms make as part of a CSR portfolio vary, but they might include infrastructure investments, electrical grid extension, health services and clinics, recreational facilities, livelihood or vocational training, environmental services, or the provision or protection of cultural goods. In developing countries and in regions where service provision is limited, firms may step in to provide such services. For example, in Zambia copper companies provide medical clinics to local communities. In wealthier countries, firms might provide cultural goods, research and development investment, or educational scholarships. Oil companies in Alaska provide educational scholarships to Alaskan natives. Firm investment may also yield local benefits such as local employment, or knock-on industries, which can benefit both the firm and other stakeholders. However, these additional effects are not usually considered part of a definition of CSR, though firms often include these benefits in reports of their CSR efforts.

CSR in the Energy Sector

Given the multitude of disciplinary approaches to CSR in general, this chapter focuses primarily on conceptualizations, empirical regularities, and policy efforts related to CSR in the energy sector. While there is some literature focusing specifically on the energy sector, it is limited relative to that which focuses on CSR more broadly or on other industries. Thus, it is imperative to ask the question: How is CSR in the energy sector unique? What is particular about the energy sector that is likely to affect the way CSR by energy firms is conceived, implemented, and studied?

First, firms operating in the energy sector have fewer exit options than those operating in other sectors.[2] The location of natural resources such as coal and oil is determined by nature. While social, economic, political, and historical factors shape whether, when, and how the resource is extracted, the location of the firm's extractive operations is constrained by nature. As a result, energy and mining companies have limited choices when it comes to selecting a site for operations, and this means that companies often find themselves operating in regions with existing populations or regions that are particularly environmentally vulnerable.

Second, the energy sector often has high sunk costs relative to other sectors. Depending on the resource, the extraction of natural resources such as coal can require large swaths of land for the construction of a mine and for the storage of overburden and tailings. For oil and natural gas, this extensive space might include drilling wells or constructing offshore platforms and rigs. Because these sunk costs are site specific (at the site of extraction), firms are often disinclined to relocate their operations once the infrastructure has been constructed. The energy industry, perhaps more than any other industry, is threatened by Vernon's obsolescing bargain hypothesis (Vernon 1971). In this theory, firms hold most of the bargaining power vis-à-vis potential host governments in deciding where to invest, leading host governments to provide concessions to firms to make investment more attractive. However, once firms have begun constructing the infrastructure to support that investment and paid fixed start-up costs, bargaining power shifts from the firm to the host government, since the firm's costs are difficult to recuperate. This shift is particularly likely in the energy sector, where investment is especially capital intensive. Abandoning existing operations and beginning new ones is particularly costly, making energy firms subject to the whims of host governments and more likely to do what they can to ensure continued access to raw materials.

Third, the extractive sector has a long time horizon relative to other industries. In order to reap the benefits of the high sunk costs, firms are often allocated twenty- or thirty-year contracts over an energy concession (and occasionally these contracts are extended). This extended time frame ensures firms have a particularly strong interest in maintaining the capacity to operate in the chosen location. In order to do so, firms may need to consider the best way to maintain relationships with local residents, and this may involve different forms of CSR.

Fourth, the energy sector has a greater environmental footprint than other industries. As aa result, it can create greater costs for local communities than the non-extractive sector. Water can be easily contaminated with runoff from mine tailings. Large swaths of land where residents live may be required for overburden, and dust and noise pollution can result from the transport of raw materials. This higher environmental footprint can create a greater range of social and environmental responsibilities for the firm, as well as significant local demand for compensation.

Finally, in other sectors the consumer is a primary stakeholder who may drive the firm's behavior through making decisions about consumption based on firm behavior. Some arguments about why firms (of all types) engage in CSR rely on this relationship as a driver of firm behavior. However, because of the geographical distance, processing requirements, and industrial use of energy sector end products, the link between individual consumer choices and firm behavior is attenuated in the energy sector. Furthermore, this sector is particularly costly to boycott—there are limited low cost substitutions, making consumer pressure less likely to reach a level that could affect energy companies. Collective action on the part of the consumer that could put pressure on firms to behave in a socially and environmentally responsible manner is therefore less likely. As a consequence, it is more likely that the focus of energy sector CSR investments will be on those in the immediate geographic area of extraction, since they are the more proximal stakeholders. To be sure, consumers can and do switch energy sources, particularly wealthier consumers who can afford the cost of doing so (given the less developed infrastructure for alternative energy sources such as solar, as discussed in the chapter by Cauchon). However, absent a significant awareness campaign and mobilization effort around a particular firm's social and environmental impact, it is unlikely that the availability of alternative energy sources will improve an energy firm's behavior with respect to CSR.

These characteristics are largely shared between the nonrenewable energy sector (oil, gas, coal) and the mining industry—and thus the extractives more generally are likely to exhibit similar CSR tendencies and to be grouped together in the academic literature. Renewable energy sources, in contrast, are usually more spatially diffuse, may have lower sunk costs, and are slightly less site specific (though to be sure, there are optimal regions for solar, wind, and water power). Furthermore, they are likely to have a lower environmental footprint, limiting the demand for ongoing CSR efforts in the area of environmental mitigation. Additionally, renewable energy is a relatively new sector, and as a consequence there has been little theoretical or empirical work on CSR in the renewable energy sector (with the exception of the timber sector). As a result, this chapter addresses CSR drivers and empirical regularities in the nonrenewable energy sector, focusing on oil, gas, and mining.

In addition to this focus on nonrenewable resources, this chapter explores CSR efforts by foreign firms. While it is certainly the case that domestic firms invest in energy resources in their home countries (and consequently make domestic CSR investments), this chapter takes seriously the focus of this handbook on the *international* political economy of energy and therefore primarily considers CSR as it relates to foreign direct investment (FDI) in the nonrenewable energy sector. One consequence of focusing on CSR in this energy sector is that much of the study of this empirical phenomenon is devoted to countries with significant energy sectors, many of which remain low income in spite of their natural resource endowments. CSR has come to be viewed by some as a strategy of economic development delivery, ensuring that many of these studies focus on CSR practices in the energy industry in emerging markets where there are vulnerable local or indigenous populations (Latin America, Africa, and central Eurasia). As a consequence, studies of CSR often intersect with studies of governance, state capacity, economic development, and local politics.

DRIVERS OF CSR IN THE ENERGY SECTOR

If CSR is voluntary and discretionary, what motivates energy firms to invest in it or explains variation in degrees and type of investment? There is a multitude of arguments about what drives CSR, including actor-specific explanations (firm and state characteristics), transnational norms, and explicitly strategic motivations. While few of these theorized drivers of CSR have been ruled out, some of these explanations go further in explaining CSR investments and practices in the energy sectors than others. Perhaps the dominant explanation for firm investment in CSR is that characteristics of the firm drive such investment. For example, firm culture may be shaped by firm origin, in particular the labor and environmental practices in the firm's home country (Hart 1995; Waldman, Siegel, and Javidan 2006) Alternatively, firms may have long histories that shape their managerial practices, affecting the extent to which they engage in CSR. In addition, some argue that firm size matters. Firms may be more likely to engage in CSR, suggesting that it is a question of firm capacity as well as impact: larger firms have both a larger social impact and a larger profit margin and therefore have a greater capacity to invest in CSR. Others argue for a more U-shaped relationship between firm size and CSR (Udayasankar 2008). Finally, and relatedly, firms that are publicly held (which tend to be larger in terms of capitalization) may invest in CSR, since they are more vulnerable to reputation effects of failing to behave in a socially responsible manner (of course this presumes that such behavior or the consequences of its failure are observable to an international audience). Specifically, reputation arguments rely on the role of the consumer in exerting pressure on firms that fail to live up to consumer demands for environmentally and socially sustainable production. International reputation costs are borne out in firm share price, and it is for this reason that firms invest in CSR.

Arguments that focus on firm-centric drivers of CSR suggest that energy operations managed or held by the same firm should exhibit similar strategies of CSR investment. However, it is important to keep in mind that firm behavior with respect to CSR varies across projects owned or managed by the same firm, suggesting that firm characteristics may not be the only driver of CSR. Additionally, many energy projects are not managed by the same firm for the duration of the extractive contract, and as Hilson (2011) points out, there may be limited incentive for companies that inherit projects and associated CSR policies to follow through or maintain the same level and type of investment.

A state-centric approach to understanding the drivers of CSR suggests that government regulations, and the government's capacity to enforce them, shape CSR activities. Hilson (2011), building on Ostlund (1977), suggests that the 1970s marked a turning point in firm perceptions of firms' social responsibilities. Legislation that emerged out of the "conservation decade" compelled firms to mitigate social and environmental impacts to comply with new regulations. Specifically, pre-extraction assessments in the form of environmental and social impact assessments (EIAs), reporting requirements, and local investment requirements have compelled firms to invest more in ensuring socially and environmentally responsible practices. States require EIAs, in which firms detail the ways in which operations will impact both the environment and the social well-being of local populations, which have certainly proliferated. Notably, these do not constitute voluntary and discretionary practices, but instead legally binding ones. However, in practice firms may develop CSR practices that build directly on or derive from regulatory requirements (and locally, it is often difficult for residents to know the difference between legally required and voluntary practices by the firm). Furthermore, monitoring and enforcement varies with political will and with state capacity, making it all the more surprising that firms might invest in social and environmental goods at all.

Beyond firm- or state-specific characteristics, it is indisputable that a shift in norms took place in the 1990s. The transnational spread of norms regarding multinational firm conduct in host countries might be expected to affect the way firms behave, yielding a collective movement toward social spending in regions of foreign investment in the energy sector (Jones-Luong 2014). Such norms have led to the emergence of standardized and accepted practices, which yield reputation costs for firms that are found to have violated them. This argument suggests that increases in CSR since the 1990s might be attributed to a norms cascade. This is supported by the fact that most mining companies have established CSR or community relations departments to handle CSR-related issues, institutionalizing the appearance of investment in environmental and social stewardship. Similar arguments have focused on international legitimacy. Du and Vieira (2012) argue that oil companies, which are often embroiled in controversy as a result of their significant environmental and social footprints, rely on CSR to build international legitimacy. However, there is diversity even within the energy sector regarding company CSR policies; the degree of compliance with these norms varies, and the implementation of CSR policies varies with local contexts (Frynas 2005). Empirical evidence on the effectiveness of norms as drivers of CSR is mixed, despite well-publicized efforts to signal the emergence, proliferation, and acceptance of these norms (Dashwood 2007). While norms can explain a general trend toward CSR investment in the energy sector (or at the very least, rhetoric about its importance), an argument that norms motivate firms to invest in CSR does not provide a theoretical explanation of why CSR levels and types continue to vary.

Recently scholars have considered a more context-specific, explicitly strategic explanation of CSR. They have argued that CSR is aimed at preventing local conflict that could be costly to firm operations. This argument takes seriously the characteristics of the energy sector previously discussed (limited exit costs, sunk costs, significant environmental costs). Scholars such as Amengual (2018) and Steinberg (2016) argue that the local context matters in driving and shaping voluntary firm transfers. Because firms have limited exit options and significant sunk costs, as well as long time horizons, they have an interest in providing CSR or other social investments in order to secure a social license to operate that minimizes the likelihood of local resistance to firm operations. Since resistance can involve rioting, blockading roads, destruction of equipment, and even threats to the safety of personnel, firms seek to strategically mitigate the likelihood of resistance through CSR engagement.

MEASUREMENT AND EMPIRICAL REGULARITIES

Given the range of drivers of CSR, practices are likely to vary across firm ownership, firm size, type of resource, form of resource extraction, and location of extraction. How might scholars and practitioners measure CSR, especially when it varies so much? Is there a systematic, empirically observable indicator of how much energy firms invest in CSR? If CSR is context specific, especially for the energy industry, then obtaining or developing a standardized reporting requirement presents a significant challenge. Furthermore, the variety of conceptualizations of CSR make measuring and observing it difficult. As a consequence of the measurement and standardization challenges, most empirical studies of CSR in the energy sector have been single or comparative case studies, including South Africa (Dawkins and Ngunjiri 2008; Fig 2005; Hamann 2004), Nigeria (Frynas 2001; Watts 2004), Angola (Wiig and Kolstad 2010), Azerbaijan (Gulbrandsen and Moe 2007), Peru (Bebbington et al. 2008), and Bolivia (Amengual 2018). These studies detail how CSR is negotiated, distributed, and interpreted in the regions in and around extraction.

While existing efforts to develop and collect standardized data on CSR across energy companies have come to fruition, there are some sources that are worth mentioning specifically. Many studies of CSR rely on company website reporting, yearly sustainability reports, and annual financial reports (Kolk and Lenfant 2010). In fact, the energy industry was one of the earliest to adopt sustainability reporting, which usually includes reports on CSR strategies (Patten 1991). However, these sources are drafted by the company, a fact that introduces a significant bias in our understanding of the amount and nature of CSR efforts. Firms have an incentive to overstate their investment in CSR in a public forum to promote their reputations and build legitimacy. This is exacerbated by the fact that monitoring such a geographically disparate set of activities is costly. Even when monitoring is attempted, the limited independence of assessors has been criticized (Fonseca 2010). As an alternative to some of these sources, some scholars rely on the Dow Jones Sustainability Index (DJSI), which is based on a standardized combination of self-reporting and media reports, or the privately held CSR Hub. Notably, both of these measures are at the company level and thus cannot be applied to specific operational contexts.

Whether and how energy companies report their CSR investments and activities is an empirical question in and of itself. On average, firms based in wealthier countries are more likely to report on CSR activities (KPMG 2011), though Baskin (2006) argues that reported CSR in emerging markets is more developed than previously thought, finding that two-thirds of firms based in non–Organisation for Economic Co-operation and Development (OECD) countries had either a sustainability report or portion of their websites devoted to CSR. Du and Vieira (2012) provide a qualitative analysis of website content of six oil companies to evaluate the way companies use CSR to gain legitimacy, particularly given the controversial nature of oil and gas companies. They find that initiatives about the environment and local communities received the most attention, relative to issues targeting customers and employees, with five out of six producing stand-alone corporate social responsibility reports. In another study of sixty-five energy companies operating in the three central African countries Angola, Democratic Republic of the Congo, and Congo, two-thirds of the companies report on CSR, and smaller, less visible companies were less likely to report on CSR (Kolk and Lenfant 2010). However, reports were relatively generic and did not correspond to the context in which companies were operating. There is even less empirical understanding of the predictors of the *kinds* of CSR activities in which firms are likely to engage.

Whether the reporting of CSR investments translates into actual sustainable social and environmental investment is not clear, and some skepticism remains (Frynas 2005). However, reporting on CSR in and of itself may be beneficial to the firm for other reasons. Hughey and Sulkowski (2012) find that increased data availability about CSR activities for international oil companies improves companies' CSR reputations. (Ekatah et al. 2012; Pätäri et al. 2011) find some evidence of a positive relationship between CSR and sustainability reporting (as measured by inclusion in the DJSI) and corporate financial performance in the energy sector. It remains difficult to separate the reporting of CSR from the actual performance of CSR activities, which has led many to draw conclusions about the relationship between CSR and corporate financial performance based on CSR reported. Pätäri et al. (2014) provide an overview of empirical studies evaluating the relationship between CSR and corporate financial performance in the energy sector. The vast majority of these studies are individual and comparative case studies (with the exception of Hughey and Sulkowski [2012] and Pätäri et al. [2012]). Overall, these studies demonstrate a generally positive relationship between social sustainability and financial performance, consistent with empirical work of the relationship between reported CSR and financial performance that extends beyond the energy sector (Margolis and Walsh 2003; Orlitzky, Schmidt, and Rynes 2003).

Recently several scholars have turned their attention to the operational risk associated with failed CSR policies, focusing on evaluating the cost of what they call "company- community" conflict. Studies of the mining sector in Latin America (Amengual 2018; Arce 2014; Bebbington et al. 2008) and to a lesser extent in Africa (Arce and Miller 2016; Steinberg 2019) have detailed the prevalence of protest and resistance around mining and resource extraction, and a few of these studies explicitly link protest and instability to firm- community relationships and CSR failures (Amengual 2018; Franks et al. 2014; Steinberg 2016). In a study of fifty company-community conflicts in the mining industry, Franks et al. (2014) and Davis and Franks (2014) find that companies can lose up to US$20 million per week in net present value; in the initial exploration phase, each day of delay cost firms approximately US$10,000, and during advance exploration, US$50,000 per day. Firms may use CSR in hopes of mitigating these potential costs by preventing mobilization and resistance around firm operations. However, firms are not always successful. Idemudia (2010) finds that in spite of a change in mentality toward CSR by oil companies operating in the Niger delta, corporate community conflict persists, and few perceptions of the oil company on the ground have changed. In these empirical studies, CSR is seen as a strategic conflict mitigation strategy.

Policy Implications and Avenues for Further Research

While more research on CSR in the energy sector is required to understand the particular contours of CSR practices by extractive firms, it is important to pause and take stock of existing policies in place aimed at mitigating the effects of energy and resource extraction. The cascade of transnational norms regarding firm behavior, whether effective in driving successful CSR investment or not, have yielded governance schemes at the international level, as well as a smattering of national regulations relating to CSR. A number of initiatives and codes of conduct have emerged to incentivize transparency in the energy and mining sector and to coordinate and standardize the behavior of firms in and around their operations in host countries. The World Bank and the International Monetary Fund Voluntary Principles specify guidelines for firm behavior and treatment of local populations and the environment. Initiatives such as Publish What You Pay, Revenue Watch, and Extractive Industry Transparency Initiative (EITI) are aimed at ensuring transparency in energy and mineral revenue payments between governments and firms. Only recently, however, has EITI begun to record firms' social investments. The United Nations Global Compact (a commitment by a network of business, labor, and nongovernmental organizations to support a set of CSR principles drawn from existing international declarations, formed in 1999 by Kofi Annan), the Global Reporting Initiative, and business's International Council on Mining and Metals (ICMM) Sustainable Development Charter (a code of conduct outlining management principles to be followed by the mining and metals industry that emerged out of the Global Mining Initiative in 1998) are some of the most prominent initiatives in this transnational norms cascade.

While these global governance initiatives are aimed at providing shared standards and creating reputation costs for firms that fail to consider the social and environmental consequences of their activities, a broad push toward local, participatory development has led to a more local focus. Free prior and informed consent (FPIC) is a policy first developed by the UN for indigenous communities, in which firms are required to get the consent of local residents before beginning operations. FPIC, in conjunction with the informal consultation process that most firms engage in to communicate CSR activities and secure buy-in from local communities, has demonstrated the turn toward local, if informal, standards of firm behavior. Acknowledging that mere participation has been insufficient to ensure communities benefit from extraction through CSR practices, formal community development agreements (CDAs) have become increasingly common since the mid-2000s. While an agreed upon definition remains elusive, CDAs tend to be agreements between the community and the extractive firms specifying the local distribution of costs and benefits associated with extraction.[3] These agreements often include royalty or profit sharing, the establishment of community foundations, and government revenue earmarking. According to Sarkar et al. (2010), CDAs should help to "avert or mitigate negative project impacts, improve stakeholder relationships, and promote mutually beneficial sustainable benefits from the mining industry, including equitable and pro-poor benefits for local communities." However, it is not yet clear when CDAs are likely to be effective, especially if the host country is one in which there is limited state capacity for enforcement.

The preceding exploration suggests there are debates yet to be resolved and much room for further research in the area of CSR and energy. First, while it may not be necessary to settle on a single definition and scope of CSR in the energy sector (as long as practitioners and scholars are clear by what they mean by CSR), we may wish to take pause to consider the durability of such a concept, even one that is vague. More broadly, as the social sciences press further on the notion of CSR as the private delivery of development, to what extent will the idea of CSR be subsumed by broader considerations of the role of private corporations and entities in governance, especially as the Westphalian paradigm of statehood is continuously challenged?

Second, theoretical and empirical approaches to studying CSR should disaggregate across multiple dimensions, including south-south versus north-south FDI, sector type, and renewable versus nonrenewable energy. Regarding FDI, more FDI is occurring between low- and middle-income countries (in the energy sector and beyond), as opposed to primarily from wealthy to developing countries. To what extent do our theories about the drivers of CSR hold as this change in global capital advances? Many have sounded alarms about a race to the bottom in which firms invest in the regions that have the lowest standards of environmental and social protections. Owing to the "right to development" in low-income countries, states may competitively lower standards to attract FDI. There is little evidence that this has occurred so far, but the new trend in FDI among developing countries might cause us to renew evaluation of the potential for a race to the bottom, particularly if firms from developing countries are more capital constrained.

Research on CSR should also disaggregate across sectors. The energy sector has particular characteristics that shape the nature of CSR, as I laid out earlier in this chapter. However, few studies have disaggregated energy-related CSR from other types, making it difficult to interpret the empirical regularities associated with energy-related CSR as opposed to other types. The different characteristics of the sectors suggest that we ought to see differences, but current research does not allow us to identify these differences. Disaggregating across sectors will help to unpack the ways in which CSR is practiced and understood in the energy sector.

In addition to disaggregating across sectors, studies of CSR should also consider how CSR practices are likely to vary between nonrenewable and renewable energy, and whether this is a relevant distinction. While we might expect renewable energy to have a smaller environmental and social footprint, this does not undermine the need to understand the costs and drivers of mitigation of even those limited externalities. Much of the world is charting a path toward greater reliance on renewable energy in the face of climate change. As a result, we might expect to see increased private (and public) investment in renewable energy sites. Scholars should develop a strong conceptual framework differentiating between renewable and nonrenewable energy as it relates to CSR activities. In addition, they should begin to evaluate the empirical regularities associated with CSR in the renewable energy sector.

Finally, as energy exploration expands to new frontiers, what does this imply for CSR? Rising temperatures in the Arctic have created a scramble over the potential reserves of oil and natural gas in the region. The region is currently home to no preexisting human populations, other than climate change research teams and those vying to establish sovereignty. However, the region is likely to be particularly susceptible to environmental externalities from extraction. As the region becomes more habitable, what might CSR look like in the Arctic? Is it a relevant concept? In the changing landscape of energy extraction and use, owing to climate change and increased reliance on renewable energy sources, changing patterns of FDI, and greater transparency, the study of CSR remains important, as there may be an important role for it to play in preventing backlash against new sources and sites of energy extraction.

Notes

1. This was a result of the Washington Consensus and the accompanying structural adjustment programs.
2. This is primarily true of the nonrenewable, extractive energy sector, which is the focus of this chapter, as opposed to the renewable energy industry.

3. Varieties of CDAs include voluntary agreements, indigenous land use agreements, community contracts, landowner agreements, shared responsibilities agreements, empowerment agreements, and community joint venture agreements.

References

Aguinis, Herman, and Ante Glavas. 2012. "What We Know and Don't Know about Corporate Social Responsibility: A Review and Research Agenda." *Journal of Management* 38, no. 4: 932–968.

Amengual, Matthew. 2018. "Buying Stability: The Distributive Outcomes of Private Politics in the Bolivian Mining Industry." *World Development* 104: 31–45.

Arce, Moises. 2014. *Resource Extraction and Protest in Peru*. Pittsburgh: University of Pittsburgh Press.

Arce, Moises, and Rebecca E. Miller. 2016. "Mineral Wealth and Protest in Sub-Saharan Africa." *African Studies Review* 59: 83–105.

Baskin, Jeremy. 2006. "Corporate Responsibility in Emerging Markets." *Journal of Corporate Citizenship* 24, no. 1: 29–47.

Bebbington, Anthony, Denise Humphreys, Jeffrey Bury, Jeannet Lingan, Juan Pablo Muñoz, and Martin Scurrah. 2008. "Mining and Social Movements: Struggles Over Livelihood and Rural Territorial Development in the Andes." *World Development* 36, no. 12: 2888–2905.

Campbell, John L. 2007. "Why Would Corporations Behave in Socially Responsible Ways? An Institutional Theory of Corporate Social Responsibility." *Academy of Management Review* 32, no. 3: 946–967. http://amr.aom.org/content/32/3/946.short.

Carroll, Archie B. 1991. "The Pyramid of Corporate Social Responsibility: Toward the Moral Management of Organizational Stakeholders." *Business Horizons* 34, no. 4: 39–48.

Dahlsrud, Alexander. 2008. "How Corporate Social Responsibility Is Defined: An Analysis of 37 Definitions." *Corporate Social Responsibility and Environmental Management* 15, no. 1: 1–13.

Dashwood, Hevina S. 2007. "Canadian Mining Companies and Corporate Social Responsibility: Weighing the Impact of Global Norms." *Canadian Journal of Political Science/Revue canadienne de science politique* 40, no. 1: 129–156.

Davis, Rachel, and Daniel M. Franks. 2014. "Costs of Company-Community Conflict in the Extractive Sector." Corporate Social Responsibility Initiative Report. Cambridge, MA: Harvard Kennedy School.

Dawkins, Cedric, and Faith Wambura Ngunjiri. 2008. "Corporate Social Responsibility Reporting in South Africa: A Descriptive and Comparative Analysis." *Journal of Business Communication* 45, no. 3: 286–307.

Du, Shuili, and Edward T. Vieira. 2012. "Striving for Legitimacy Through Corporate Social Responsibility: Insights from Oil Companies." *Journal of Business Ethics* 110, 4: 413–427.

Ekatah, Innocent, Martin Samy, Roberta Bampton, and Abdel Halabi. 2011. "The Relationship Between Corporate Social Responsibility and Profitability: The Case of Royal Dutch Shell PLC." *Corporate Reputation Review* 14, no. 4: 249–261.

Fig, David. 2005. "Manufacturing Amnesia: Corporate Social Responsibility in South Africa." *International Affairs* 81, no. 3: 599–617.

Fonseca, Alberto. 2010. "How Credible Are Mining Corporations' Sustainability Reports? A Critical Analysis of External Assurance under the Requirements of the International Council on Mining and Metals." *Corporate Social Responsibility and Environmental Management* 17, no. 6: 355–370.

Franks, D. M., R. Davis, A. J. Bebbington, S. H. Ali, D. Kemp, and M. Scurrah. 2014. "Conflict Translates Environmental and Social Risk into Business Costs." *Proceedings of the National Academy of Sciences* 111, no. 21: 7576–7581.

Frynas, Jdrzej George. 2001. "Corporate and State Responses to Anti-Oil Protests in the Niger Delta." *African Affairs* 100, no. 398: 27–54.

Frynas, Jedrzej George. 2005. "The False Developmental Promise of Corporate Social Responsibility: Evidence from Multinational Oil Companies." *International Affairs* 81, no. 3: 581–598.

Gilberthorpe, Emma, and Glenn Banks. 2012. "Development on Whose Terms? CSR Discourse and Social Realities in Papua New Guinea's Extractive Industries Sector." *Resources Policy* 37, no. 2: 185–193.

Gulbrandsen, Lars H., and Arild Moe. 2007. "BP in Azerbaijan: A Test Case of the Potential and Limits of the CSR Agenda?" *Third World Quarterly* 28, no. 4: 813–830.

Hamann, Ralph. 2004. "Corporate Social Responsibility, Partnerships, and Institutional Change: The Case of Mining Companies in South Africa." In *Natural Resources Forum: A United Nations Sustainable Development Journal* 28: 278–290. Wiley Online Library. https://onlinelibrary-wiley-com.proxyiub.uits.iu.edu/doi/abs/10.1111/j.1477-8947.2004.00101.x

Hart, Stuart L. 1995. "A Natural-Resource-Based View of the Firm." *Academy of Management Review* 20, no. 4: 986–1014.

Hilson, Gavin. 2011. "Inherited Commitments: Do Changes in Ownership Affect Corporate Social Responsibility (CSR) at African Gold Mines?" *African Journal of Business Management* 5, no. 27: 10921–10939.

Hughey, Christopher J., and Adam J. Sulkowski. 2012. "More Disclosure = Better CSR Reputation? An Examination of CSR Reputation Leaders and Laggards in the Global Oil & Gas Industry." *Journal of Academy of Business and Economics* 12, no. 2: 24–34.

Idemudia, Uwafiokun. 2010. "Rethinking the Role of Corporate Social Responsibility in the Nigerian Oil Conflict: The Limits of CSR." *Journal of International Development* 22, no. 7: 833–845.

Jones-Luong, Pauline. 2014. "Empowering Local Communities and Enervating the State? Foreign Oil Companies as Public Goods Providers in Azerbaijan and Kazakhstan." In *The Politics of Non-State Social Welfare* ed. By Melani Cammett and Lauren MacLean, 57–76. Ithaca, NY: Cornell University Press.

Kolk, Ans, and François Lenfant. 2010. "MNC Reporting on CSR and Conflict in Central Africa." *Journal of Business Ethics* 93: 241–255.

KPMG. 2011. "KPMG International Survey of Corporate Responsibility Reporting 2011." Technical report. https://www.kpmg.de/docs/survey-corporate-responsibility-reporting-2011.pdf

Margolis, Joshua D., and James P Walsh. 2003. "Misery Loves Companies: Rethinking Social Initiatives by Business." *Administrative Science Quarterly* 48, no. 2: 268–305.

McWilliams, Abagail, and Donald Siegel. 2001. "Corporate Social Responsibility: A Theory of the Firm Perspective." *Academy of Management Review* 26, no. 1: 117–127.

Orlitzky, Marc, Frank L. Schmidt, and Sara L. Rynes. 2003. "Corporate Social and Financial Performance: A Meta-analysis." *Organization Studies* 24, no. 3: 403–441.

Ostlund, Lyman E. 1977. "Attitudes of Managers toward Corporate Social Responsibility." *California Management Review* 19, no. 4: 35–49.

Pätäri, Satu, Heli Arminen, Anni Tuppura, and Ari Jantunen. 2014. "Competitive and Responsible? The Relationship between Corporate Social and Financial Performance in the Energy Sector." *Renewable and Sustainable Energy Reviews* 37: 142–154.

Pätäri, Satu, Ari Jantunen, Kalevi Kyläaheiko, and Jaana Sandströom. 2012. "Does Sustainable Development Foster Value Creation? Empirical Evidence from the Global Energy Industry: Does Sustainable Development Foster Energy Firms' Value Creation?" *Corporate Social Responsibility and Environmental Management* 19, no. 6: 317–326.

Patten, Dennis M. 1991. "Exposure, Legitimacy, and Social Disclosure." *Journal of Accounting and Public Policy* 10, no. 4: 297–308.

Sarkar, Sunrita, Alastair Gow-Smith, Tunde Morakinyo, Roberto Frau, and Matthew Kuniholm. 2010. "Mining Community Development Agreements—Practical Experiences and Field Studies." Technical report, Environmental Resources Management. http://siteresources. worldbank.org/INTEXTINDWOM/Resources/CDA_Report_FINAL.pdf

Smirnova, Yelena. 2012. "Perceptions of Corporate Social Responsibility in Kazakhstan." *Social Responsibility Journal* 8, no. 3: 404–417.

Sparkes, Stephen. 2014. "Corporate Social Responsibility: Benefits for Youth in Hydropower Development in Laos." *International Review of Education* 60, no. 2: 261–277.

Steinberg, Jessica. 2016. "Strategic Sovereignty: A Model of Non-state Goods Provision and Resistance in Regions of Natural Resource Extraction." *Journal of Conflict Resolution* 60, no. 8: 1503–1528.

Steinberg, Jessica. 2019. *Mines, Communities, and States: The Local Politics of Natural Resource Extraction in Africa.* Cambridge, UK: Cambridge University Press.

Udayasankar, Krishna. 2008. "Corporate Social Responsibility and Firm Size." *Journal of Business Ethics* 83, no. 2: 167–175.

Vernon, Raymond. 1971. "Sovereignty at Bay: The Multinational Spread of US Enterprises." *Thunderbird International Business Review* 13, no. 4: 1–3.

Waldman, David A., Donald S. Siegel, and Mansour Javidan. 2006. "Components of CEO Transformational Leadership and Corporate Social Responsibility." *Journal of Management Studies* 43, no. 8: 1703–1725.

Watts, Michael. 2004. "Resource Curse? Governmentality, Oil and Power in the Niger Delta, Nigeria." *Geopolitics* 9: 50–80.

Wiig, Arne, and Ivar Kolstad. 2010. "Multinational Corporations and Host Country Institutions: A Case Study of CSR Activities in Angola." *International Business Review* 19, no. 2: 178–190.

CHAPTER 12

··

THE POLITICS OF
ENERGY SECURITY

··

JESSICA JEWELL AND ELINA BRUTSCHIN

WHEN asked about the main concerns of energy ministers, the then director of the International Energy Agency (IEA), Maria van der Hoeven, replied, "It's always about energy security. Always....For exporting countries it's about security of demand, for importing countries about security of supply" (quoted in Beckman 2012, para. 14). This quote highlights both energy security's importance in shaping policy decisions and the fact that it means different things for different states: for exporting states the importance of buyers to sell oil to and for importing states the importance of reliable suppliers from whom to buy oil. This major division in market power resulted in the formation of two international organizations that focus on energy security: the Organization of the Petroleum Exporting Countries (OPEC), representing the exporters, and the IEA, representing the importers.[1]

But the world is made up of more than just oil producers and suppliers, and oil is no longer the only energy security concern. Energy security now includes everything from ensuring connections for gas pipelines to the reliability of electricity systems. Debates about energy security extend beyond these technical issues to what is a threat, and for whom. Various scientific disciplines have engaged in this policy debate for decades. One challenge that they have encountered is that energy security means different things in different contexts and has also changed over time (Ciută 2010). This conceptual ambiguity is often deliberately used by policy makers and scholars to promote certain national and international policies. In this chapter we focus on national energy security and how it influences both international and domestic energy politics since self-preservation, that is, maintaining security, is the core imperative of the nation-state (Clinton, Thompson, and Morgenthau 2005; Morgenthau 1948).

In this chapter we show how today's energy security literature exhibits five different approaches to defining energy security and we systematically analyze their strengths and weaknesses. More importantly, we argue that defining energy security as "low vulnerability of vital energy systems" bridges both the material and intersubjective nature of energy security. We then unpack the key concepts of vulnerability and vital energy systems with connections to historical policy problems and seminal scholarly contributions. Finally, we conclude by showing how the complexity of the policy problem and the interdisciplinary nature of the research field shape its future research agenda.

THE LANDSCAPE OF TODAY'S ENERGY SECURITY LITERATURE

Since the 1970s, the field of energy security has expanded from the study of imported oil in industrialized countries to addressing a wider range of risks and energy systems. This expansion has led to a dizzying array of approaches to defining and measuring energy security. This situation arises not only from the increasing complexity of energy systems and potential threats but also from the fact that energy security contains both material and perceptual elements. Scholars have struggled with conceptualizing energy security by either searching for a universal definition or rejecting any universality in favor of energy security as a purely contingent and subjective notion. These tensions are partly a result of historical developments. Since scholarship on energy security has mirrored the policy problems and strategies states have pursued, this has led to different epistemological approaches. Until the 1980s, energy security mainly meant stable oil supply and purchases; importing states relied on oil for military use and later electricity, transport, and heating, while exporting states relied on oil for stable government revenues. During this time, both major oil producers and oil consumers set up international organizations (OPEC and the IEA) to try to gain control over the oil market. In addition, importing states tried to increase oil supply security by curbing domestic oil use through phasing it out of electricity and cutting down on oil-intensive industries (Ikenberry 1986) and by increasing production under state control through increasing domestic production and acquiring overseas assets (Katzenstein 1977).

Following these efforts and the general oversupply of oil in the 1980s, concerns over oil decreased. The establishment of the IEA and the rising belief in the usefulness of markets for securing energy supplies reflected a new paradigm of security through effective markets rather than through government intervention. However, as the strategies to diversify away from oil bore fruit, energy security began to mean not just secure oil supplies but also reliable gas supplies (Aalto 2016; Brutschin 2017; Prontera 2017), resilient electricity systems (Lovins and Lovins 1982), and stability of critical infrastructure (Farrell, Zerriffi, and Dowlatabadi 2004). Amid this growing complexity—of both technologies and issues—policy makers and scholars have struggled to find conceptual and definitional clarity. In many ways the search to redefine energy security has mirrored the "cottage industry" of "redefining security" in the national security and international relations communities that took place at the end of the Cold War

(Baldwin 1997, 5). Just as there was no clearly dominant conventional security threat at the end of the Cold War, since the turn of the century there has been no clearly dominant energy security threat. We are no longer living in the 1970s, when oil scarcity concerns and the realist perspective dominated, or in the 1980s and 1990s, when the oil glut and growing international interdependence led to liberalism dominating the research agenda. There have been five main approaches to sorting through the confusion and complexity (see Table 12.1), which we discuss in the following sections along with their central questions, approaches, and typical sectoral analysis.

The Geopolitical Approach

The first and oldest approach, firmly rooted in realism, proceeds from the premise that the main energy security concerns are and will be associated with national security needs and will be very similar in nature: a continuous struggle between exporters and importers for power and influence. For scholars within this line of thought, the twin concepts of "supply security" and "demand security" are central (Yergin 1988). Reflecting the importance of oil and later gas, scholars within this approach analyze how energy

Table 12.1 Five Dominant Approaches in the Energy Security Literature

Approach	Central Question(s)	Material or Intersubjective[a]	Typical Sectoral Focus
Geopolitical	How does control over energy resources affect state power and national security?	material	oil and increasingly gas
Indicator and Assessment Frameworks	How does energy security vary between states, over time, and between different scenarios or policies? How can we measure and evaluate these differences?	material	different energy sectors and services
Polysemic Energy Security	How do different social groups perceive energy security?	subjective	diverse energy policy issues (climate, energy poverty, and other energy policy issues)
Securitization	How does an (energy) issue become an energy security issue, and how is it used to achieve different goals?	intersubjective	diverse energy policy issues (in practice primarily oil and gas)
Deductive	What are the conceptual foundations of energy security, and how do material factors interact with intersubjective perceptions of energy security?	material and intersubjective	various configurations of energy systems (fuels, carriers, and users)

[a]"Intersubjective" refers to the perceived meaning that exists between actors.

security concerns might motivate internal and external conflicts and shape foreign policies (Moran and Russell 2009). (For more discussion on the interaction between energy and conflict, see Colgan and Stockbruegger in this volume.) Energy supply disruptions are often metaphorically referred to as an "energy weapon," first during the 1970s oil crisis with the "Arab oil weapon" (Paust and Blaustein 1974) and more recently with the "Russian energy weapon" following the 2006 disruption of Russian gas supplies to Europe (Smith Stegen 2011). There has been no shortage of studies of the geopolitics of pipelines, liquefied natural gas (LNG) terminals, and storage facilities in Eurasia (Correljé and van der Linde 2006; Orttung and Overland 2011), most often coined in classic realist terms, as well as parallel studies of struggles for influence over Asian energy markets (Lesbirel 2004; Calder 2008), particularly in light of rising Asian energy demand (Kumar Singh 2013; Li and Leung 2011).

The Global Energy Assessment (GEA), a landmark study that analyzes energy security in over 150 countries shows that most people in the world live in countries exposed to signficiant oil supply risks due to its relative scarcity, its geographic concentration, and the lack of easy substitutes in the transport sector (Cherp et al. 2012). The GEA also shows that natural gas is even more problematic than oil in specific regions, for example northern Eurasia. This means that by focusing on the geopolitics of oil and gas supply and demand, studies in the first strand address some important aspects of the contemporary energy security landscape. Still, they fail to acknowledge the increasing complexity and dynamism of this landscape, in which technological innovation, economic development, and new political imperatives may play more important roles than the traditional exporter-importer geopolitics.

Indicator and Assessment Frameworks

While the second approach also does not engage in fundamental rethinking of the concept of energy security, it does acknowledge that today's challenges are more complex than those of the 1970s and therefore require more advanced analysis. Such analyses often came in the form of sophisticated tools and frameworks for measuring the risks to energy systems, sometimes between primary and secondary fuels (such as crude oil, oil products, natural gas, coal, biofuels, nuclear power, and hydropower) (IEA 2011; Jewell 2011), but also extended to electricity (Bazilian et al. 2006; Stirling 1994, 1998) and even to energy services (such as transport and industrial demand) more generally (Jansen 2009; Jansen and Seebregts 2010). One prominent debate within this literature has been whether it is more useful to provide universal indices that bake all risks into a single number, such as the "Supply/Demand" Index (Scheepers et al. 2007), or to design frameworks that enable policy comparison of the risks among different policy options (Cherp and Jewell 2010). In the former, all risks are boiled down into a single number; in the latter, the analysis highlights which risks might increase or decrease under different policy and technology options. For example, limiting nuclear power may increase national electricity diversity but also decrease the independence of fuels supplying the electricity sector.

An earlier critique of indicators comes from Cherp and Jewell (2010), who argue that scholars should not strive to quantify risks in "universal indicators" but rather develop "contextualized frameworks" to analyze risks in different systems, jurisdictions, and time periods and under different scenarios. Cherp and Jewell (2013) further developed this approach and codified it into a systematic energy security assessment framework based on the concepts of risks, resilience and vital energy systems. Practically, this framework was applied in the GEA to analyze the political and techno-economic risks and resilience capacities of over 150 countries (Cherp et al. 2012), at the International Energy Agency's Model for Short-term Energy Security (IEA 2011; Jewell 2011),and for analyzing long-term energy scenarios (Guivarch et al. 2015; Guivarch and Monjon 2017; Jewell, Cherp, and Riahi 2014; Jewell et al. 2016). In these assessments, special attention is given to indicator interpretation and how different parts of the energy system interact. With the advance of computer modeling some of these studies sought to evaluate potential development of energy security in the future (Cherp et al. 2016; Grubb, Butler, and Twomey 2006; Jewell, Cherp, and Riahi 2014; Kruyt et al. 2009). While providing more advanced assessments, this strand does not engage with conceptual debate on the role of perceptions and interests of various actors in shaping the intersubjective nature of energy security.

The remaining three approaches seek to directly engage with the intersubjective nature of energy security and specifically the perceived diversity of its meanings. All of them start from the observation that there is no universal agreement on the meaning of energy security. However, these remaining strands diverge in how they deal with this fact.

Energy Security as a Polysemic Concept

The third major strand of energy security literature wrestles with conceptual questions by starting from the idea that energy security has many meanings (polysemic) that fluctuate with time and context (slippery) (Chester 2010) and then proceeds to compile a long list of dimensions and indicators for how it can be measured. This starting point has been interpreted to mean that there is no need for conceptual clarity; this then becomes a self-fulfilling prophecy as the concept of energy security indeed becomes polysemic and slippery. Some scholars now cast as wide a net as possible to encompass what energy security includes and then categorize definitions into "dimensions." This strand of literature has identified over a dozen different dimensions and hundreds of indicators of energy security from interviews (Sovacool 2011), literature reviews (Ang, Choong, and Ng 2015; Sovacool and Brown 2010), or surveys (Demski et al. 2018). Many of these scholars (e.g. Hughes 2012; Kruyt et al. 2009) start from the "four A's" (availability, accessibility, affordability, and acceptability), which first appeared in a report by the Asia Pacific Energy Research Center (APERC 2007). Cherp and Jewell (2014) suggest that the language was likely borrowed from the field of healthcare access (Penchansky and Thomas 1981).

This strand has been criticized for a number of conceptual and methodological flaws. To begin with, it falls into the trap that Baldwin identified as "cloaking normative and empirical debate[s] in conceptual rhetoric" (1997, 5). For example, some scholars and activists call climate change an energy security issue in order to move it higher on the energy agenda. However, while climate change is a pressing societal issue, whether or not it is an energy security issue is a conceptual and not a normative question. Methodologically, these studies generally fail to ask interviewees to prioritize among different dimensions, which can lead to a laundry list of energy issues that may or may not be security issues (Cherp 2012). The literature reviews also have no method of identifying which dimensions are security issues and which are merely energy issues. As a result, dimensions and indicators can range from national oil import dependence to "energy literacy of users" (Sovacool 2011) without reflecting on which issues are the most important.

The Securitization Approach

If the third strand accepts that virtually anything can be viewed as an energy security concern, under the fourth strand, with its disciplinary roots in critical political studies, particularly the Copenhagen school of security studies (Buzan 1983), energy security issues are associated with an existential threat. This strand focuses on analyzing the process of "securitization," in which social actors lift an issue out of the political realm and frame it as an existential threat (Buzan, Wæver, and Wilde 1998). While the original Copenhagen school emphasized that a speech act from a powerful person is enough to successfully securitize a "referent object" (often a state), later contributions have argued that in order to be successful, securitization must also be audience centered, context dependent, and power laden (Balzacq 2005).

When applied to energy, contributions range from simply documenting the use of "energy security" to promote certain technological or policy options (Littlefield 2013; Watson and Scott 2009) to analyzing how and why energy securitization has been successful for a given referent object, such as oil in China (Leung et al. 2014) and natural gas in Israel (Fischhendler and Nathan 2014; Fischhendler 2018). In addition, there is a new stream of literature that documents unsuccessful securitization moves, such as discussions about the Nord Stream gas pipeline in Poland (Heinrich 2018), a concept known as "security jargon" (Heinrich and Szulecki 2018). These contrasting observations highlight an important weakness of this genre that stems from their lack of detailed analysis of material realities of energy systems and their inability to predict when a securitization move will be successful and therefore to explain why different political concepts of energy security emerge in different circumstances.

The Deductive Approach

The final strand is distinct in its premise that different views on energy security reflect not different concepts of energy security, but rather different expressions of the same universal concept in different circumstances. This builds on a tradition in classic security studies that analyzes different instances of security (e.g., military, environmental, food) as expressions of a universal security concept rather than different types of security (Baldwin 1997; Wolfers 1952).[2] Scholars following this approach have searched for a concept of energy security that would be sufficiently generic to be applicable under diverse configurations of energy systems (e.g., not only exporting and importing, developing, and industrialized countries today, but also energy systems that may emerge in the future as a result of low-carbon transitions [Jewell, Cherp, and Riahi 2014]) and yet sufficiently concrete to accurately reflect today's concerns.

In "The Concept of Energy Security: Beyond the 4 As" (2014), Cherp and Jewell propose a definition of energy security as "low vulnerability of vital energy systems," closely aligned with a classic definition of security as low probability of damage to acquired values (Baldwin 1997), and argue that this definition would facilitate comparison of energy security issues across different contexts. Cherp and Jewell (2014) also propose a method of identifying the meaning of energy security in a particular context by clarifying the meaning of "vulnerability" and "vital energy systems" that is in line with the eight questions (see Box 12.1) that Baldwin (1997) proposed should be asked to clarify any instance of security.

This approach recognizes that energy security is both material and subjective and thus enables policy comparison and cross-disciplinary dialogue (Table 12.1). An energy system can be vulnerable due to material qualities that expose it to disruptions; at the same time, such qualities may or may not be perceived as acceptable within a given policy context. Similarly, a system may be defined as vital because of material qualities (such as fuels for the military) or simply because important actors have the power to

---

Box 12.1 Baldwin's (1997) Key Questions of Security

Security of what?[a]
Security for whom?
Security for which values?
Security at what level?
Security at what costs?
Security at what time frame?
From what threats?
By what means?

---

[a] This question was added by Cherp and Jewell (2014).

cast them as vital in a given policy context. Accordingly, this approach answers an often-neglected call in Chester (2010) to have a robust debate on the meaning of energy security based on articulating and comparing the underlying assumptions. However, in contrast to Chester (2010), Cherp and Jewell (2011, 2014) argue that different views of energy security result from different perspectives on the same issue, rather than on fundamentally different issues. As we elaborate in the next section, any contribution to this debate must be explicit about the answers to Baldwin's key security questions as well as the meaning of low vulnerability and vital energy systems.

Key Concepts in Energy Security

Energy security can be defined as low vulnerability of vital energy systems (Cherp and Jewell 2014), a definition that parallels the classic one of security as low probability of damage to acquired values (Baldwin 1997). In the following subsections we explain how vulnerability reflects the idea of low probability of damage and how vital energy systems relate to the idea of acquired values. We frequently refer to the questions of security outlined in Box 12.1. We relate these questions to the concepts framing the overarching definition (see Figure 12.1). In each case, we both trace the intellectual history and provide specific illustrations to guide readers in applying the same concepts and questions to analyzing any energy security situation they may encounter in their own research or practice.

Vulnerability

Low vulnerability (see Figure 12.1) corresponds to Baldwin's (1997) low probability of damage. Wolfers (1952) defined security as "the absence of threats," but Baldwin recognized that security includes not only the exposure to threats but also how a state is able to respond to those threats. In the field of energy security, vulnerabilities of energy systems have been described as the combination of their exposure to risks and their resilience (Cherp and Jewell 2014; IEA 2011; Jewell 2011). For example, if a state is highly dependent on natural gas from an unreliable supplier (high risk), its vulnerability will be lower if the state either switches to other energy sources (minimizes exposure to the risk of disruption) or establishes natural gas storage and mechanisms to rapidly switch the demand to other fuels (maximizes the resilience or the ability to respond to disruptions) (Jewell, 2011). This dual concept of risk/resilience is similar to the idea of "sensitivity" reflecting the exposure to risks and "vulnerability" defined as capacity to respond to disruptions from this exposure[3] (Keohane and Nye 1977, 2001).

Much of the scholarship on energy security has focused on the source of risk and has evolved over the last several decades to address different policy challenges, rooted in distinct disciplinary communities. Each perspective answers the questions, "What to protect?," "For what values?," and to some extent "By what means?" slightly differently.

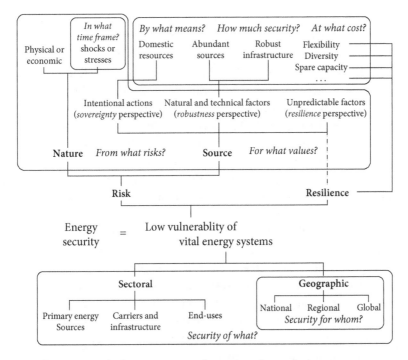

FIGURE 12.1 Energy security key concepts and questions for analysis.

Source: Reprinted from Aleh Cherp and Jessica Jewell, "The Concept of Energy Security: Beyond the Four As,"
Energy Policy 75: 415–421. Copyright © 2014, with permission from Elsevier.

The oldest, sovereignty, perspective has its roots in international relations and political science; it arose during World Wars I and II, when access to fuels for military use became crucial (see Colgan and Stockbruegger in this volume), and was consolidated during the oil crises (Deese 1979; Nye, Deese, and Alm 1981).

The sovereignty perspective views intentional actions from foreign actors as the main risk and the main response mechanisms as increasing domestic supplies (Katzenstein 1977) and decreasing the use of imported fuels (Ikenberry 1986). While this strategy has been quite successful in electricity, where IEA members have mostly phased-out oil, it is more difficult to implement in the transport sector.[4] One of the rare successful cases is Brazil, whose ethanol program and use of flexible-fuel cars helped reduce reliance on oil imports (Goldemberg 2007). The second, robustness, perspective has its roots in engineering and systems analysis and arose from concerns over resource scarcity and infrastructural rigidity (Lovins and Lovins 1982; Meadows et al. 1972). The robustness perspective views natural and technical factors as the main risks and thus aims to switch to abundant sources and invest in infrastructure. Part of this perspective is the "peak oil" theory: the belief that the rate of oil production is bell shaped, and US (and other producers') production will eventually peak, making oil a strategic resource (Chapman 2014). While some political scientists take peak oil as a given (Friedrichs 2010; Klare 2008), an increasing number of analysts believe that oil can be supplied far into the future in sufficient quantities given the current pace of technological advances and right market conditions (Bentley et al. 2004). Finally, the resilience perspective has its roots in economics and complexity science. It became dominant during market liberalization in the 1990s with the growing realization that energy systems will always face largely unpredictable risks, and the focus should therefore be on their resilience, that is, the ability to recover from disruptions (Awerbuch 1995; Bar-Lev and Katz 1976).

Risks can also be differentiated by their time horizon (shocks versus stresses), their nature (physical versus economic), and their source (Cherp and Jewell 2014; Winzer 2012). Contemporary energy security literature generally distinguishes between shocks and stresses[5] (Stirling 2011; Winzer 2012). Shocks or transitory risks are those that are fleeting and episodic. An example is a transit country dispute or an electricity outage due to a technical problem. On the other hand, stresses are enduring pressures such as domestic resource depletion, increasing demand leading to growing energy imports, and an aging power sector creating a dangerous capacity gap. Sometimes measures to increase energy security at one time horizon may negatively affect security at another time horizon. For example, Nye, Deese, and Alm (1981) document how the United States imposed import quotas during the 1960s, when Middle Eastern supplies were cheap and secure. This resulted in active exploitation and eventual depletion of US oil reserves, leading to a supply shortage. In the 1970s the United States dropped import quotas when exposure to Middle Eastern supplies had become expensive and risky. Thus, clarifying the time horizon answers the question "Security in what time frame?" (Baldwin 1997).

Another dominant distinction in the nature of energy security depicted in Figure 12.1 is between physical and economic risks (Gupta 2008; Kendell 1998). For example, the IEA definition of energy security refers not only to uninterrupted availability of energy sources but also to their "affordable price" (IEA 2018). The 1970s oil embargoes are a clear example of physical disruptions leading to a rise in the price of oil and economic price shocks. Deese (1979) emphasized that prices can disrupt normal economic activity if they are not affordable, and Yergin refers to "reasonable prices" in his definition of energy security (1988, 111). This has led many scholars to include affordability as an attribute (or dimension) of energy security, though the literature has been inconsistent on whom energy should be affordable for and in which sense (ranging from the prices being low enough for consumers [Kruyt et al. 2009] to the same prices being high enough for investors [APERC 2007] – see Cherp and Jewell [2014]).

Other scholars have problematized the issue of affordability, arguing that it is impossible to distinguish when an energy price rise becomes an energy security risk and when it is simply a market signal of a supply shortage or rising demand (Keppler 2007). Cherp and Jewell (2014) instead proposed the concept of economic risk to highlight the fact that energy costs and prices may become a relevant consideration in energy security when they can destabilize energy systems. For example, in California following deregulation, wholesale electricity prices rose 500 percent over a year (1999–2000), and two of the largest utilities were forced to declare bankruptcy (Joskow 2003). High prices for energy services can also lead to political instability (e.g., in Kyrgyzstan in 2010 [Harding 2010] and Bulgaria in 2013 [BBC 2013]), and price controls can result in underinvestment and shortages (e.g., in China in the power sector in 2004–2005 [Leung et al. 2014]).

From the beginning, energy security scholars have recognized that all risks cannot be controlled and that a state's vulnerability arises not just from its exposure to risks but also from its capacity to respond to those risks (Keohane and Nye 1977, 2001). In contemporary energy security studies this concept is generally referred to as energy system "resilience" (see Figure 12.1). This concept can be traced back to Winston Churchill, who on the eve of World War I, when asked about the issue of energy security and the British navy's dependence on Persian oil, said, "Safety and certainty in oil lie in variety and variety alone" (Yergin 2006, 69). What is crucial in this idea is that if a particular energy source, supply route, or technology is disrupted, the same energy service can be delivered by another source, route, or technology. In Churchill's case, this could be oil from another country but could not be, say, coal or firewood, as these would not power Britain's navy. In more flexible energy systems, switching to diverse sources is also possible. For example, in Finland over 40 percent of natural gas users are able to switch to another energy source in case of disruption (IEA 2012).

Following the 1970s oil embargo, resilience became a major policy goal for oil importers through the establishment of an integrated worldwide oil market, backed up by IEA member countries' strategic oil reserves. Competitive markets with their variety of actors are inherently resilient systems since both supply and demand can respond to shortages and disruptions. Throughout the 1980s and 1990s, proponents of energy market deregulation continued to argue that market liberalization would improve the resilience of energy systems, although critics questioned whether it was possible to maintain balance among different electricity supply options and ensure long-term capacity to meet demand in a fully liberalized electricity market (Helm 2002).

Stirling (1994) operationalized the diversity of the electricity supply by borrowing a diversity index from ecology (and further elaborated its different components in Stirling 2010), while Jansen, Van Arkel, and Boots (2004) expanded diversity indicators to integrate the political stability of exporters. Skea (2010) proposed policy options to value diversity by placing a tax on the level of market share a given energy technology takes up in an electricity system. While diversity indices have been widely used and are particularly useful in comparative (IEA 2011; Jewell 2011) and long-term assessments (Grubb, Butler, and Twomey 2006; Jewell, Cherp, and Riahi 2014; Kruyt et al. 2009), they have been criticized for being too abstract (Gracceva and Zeniewski 2014).

An alternative approach, which may be more relevant for contexts in which the risks are clear, is to model the impact of policy or technology shocks. This can be done through quantifying "unmet demand" through a series of stochastic model runs under different policy and technology shocks (Martišauskas, Augutis, and Krikštolaitis 2018). Another approach is is from Lilliestam and Ellenbeck (2011) who modeled the relative cost for Europe and for exporting countries of a hypothetical cut in renewable energy supply from North Africa. Another example comes from the European Union (EU), which simulated two scenarios: complete disruption of gas supplies from Russia and disruption of gas supplies through Ukraine (European Commission 2014). The tests highlighted the weaknesses of Eastern European countries stemming from poor inter-connections. The IEA also uses shock-based scenarios with its member countries, though its exercises are generally not model based but rather thought experiments with member country representatives.

Resilience also includes other policies that increase a state's capacity to respond. The IEA distinguishes between external and domestic resilience (IEA 2011; Jewell 2011). External resilience can relate to alternative trade routes and suppliers and mitigates risks from foreign supply. Domestic resilience includes, for example, spare production capac-ities, stockpiling, and emergency plans (Yergin 2006). These measures mitigate risks arising from both foreign and domestic sources. A recent trend in strengthening resil-ience, particularly evident in the EU, is building interconnections and LNG terminals, which account for all the EU's Key Energy Security Infrastructure Projects (European Commission 2017).

Ultimately, energy security responses and resilience strategies relate to three of Baldwin's key questions on vulnerability: "Security by what means?," "How much security?," and "Security at what cost?" The first question primarily relates to energy security measures. Over time a variety of strategies of increasing energy security have been tried, including military interventions, acquiring overseas energy assets, diversifying suppliers and consumers, nationalizing resources and infrastructure, liberalizing markets, subsidizing domestic energy, and creating infrastructural redundancies and strategic storage. In designing these measures, policy makers also have to answer the question "How much security?," because in the real world vulnerability of vital energy systems cannot be reduced to zero. This question is closely connected to another security question, "At what cost?" These two questions relate to one of Wolfers's reflections, that theoreti-cally, when states design their energy security strategies, "the sky is the limit" (1952, 494). Practically, states are constrained not only by their budgets but also in their technologi-cal, political, and institutional capacity to implement various energy security measures. Sometimes it is a difference in these capacities rather than in concepts of energy security that leads to different energy security priorities. As we discuss in the research agenda section, identifying these constraints is a promising avenue for future research.

Vital Energy Systems

The concept of "vital energy systems" is as important for understanding contemporary energy security challenges as is the concept of vulnerability. Discussions of energy secu-rity implicitly use the notion of energy systems. For example, most experts and policy makers understand that disruptions of oil supply cannot be alleviated by nuclear, solar, or wind power (except with electric vehicles). Analysts therefore assess vulnerabilities of oil supplies separately from those of electricity or heat provision; they are two different energy systems. In another example, a small country may be concerned with getting all its energy supplies from one unfriendly exporter, but these concerns are dramatically lower if the same country is connected to an international electricity or gas network that makes it part of a larger and hence more secure system.

Formally speaking, an energy system consists of energy resources, technologies, and uses linked together by energy, material, knowledge, and economic flows stronger than linkages outside of the system. Energy systems can be delineated along geographical or sectoral boundaries (Cherp and Jewell 2013). For example, one can speak of the global oil market security, energy security of China, or security of electricity supply in California. Churchill was concerned about oil supply for the British navy, which formed a specific, well-defined sector in the national economy and required specific sources of energy. The bulk of the energy security literature deals with energy security of nation-states, which is natural given that the state's raison d'être is to protect security (Clinton, Thompson, and Morgenthau 2005; Morgenthau 1948). However, some scholars use the term "household energy security" (Jain 2010). By linking energy security to specific energy systems, it is possible to answer two of Baldwin's security questions: "Security of what?" and "Security for whom?"

Up until the mid-1990s, most of the energy security literature focused on oil security (Deese 1979; Keohane and Nye 2001; Nye, Deese, and Alm 1981). While oil supply is still the energy system that affects the most people in the most countries, there are also concerns about the importance of energy export revenues for oil- and gas-exporting countries, natural gas in Eurasia, aging infrastructure in industrialized countries, and the need to scale up energy systems to meet growing demand in rapidly growing, under-developed economies (Cherp et al. 2012). In their assessment of future energy security, Jewell et al. (2014) and Cherp et al. (2016) evaluated security of new energy systems such as worldwide markets for hydrogen and biomass, which may become important (or "vital"; see later discussion) in the twenty-first century.

The boundaries of energy systems can be drawn not only along physical flows of fuel and electricity, but also along supply chains and technological know-how. This analysis will probably become more important as energy systems become increasingly based on solar, wind, and possibly nuclear energy. Some early analyses show that in particular, nuclear energy creates new and underappreciated patterns of technological dependency between countries (Brutschin and Jewell 2018; Jewell and Ates 2015), which may with time become energy security concerns.

What gets defined as an energy system is also subjective. For example, sometimes imports from friendly countries are defined as domestic sources and thus part of the same system (Scheepers et al. 2007). This is how Western European countries have often treated oil and gas imports from Norway, Denmark, and the Netherlands. How people draw energy system boundaries depends in part on their values and worldviews.

The adjective "vital" emphasizes that in order to be associated with energy security concerns, an energy system should support critical social functions (Cherp et al. 2012). This reflects the idea that energy security is linked to the protection of "national values and objectives" (Yergin 1988), what Baldwin (1997) calls "acquired values" (as opposed to aspirational values). Though such values and objectives vary from one society to the other (which partially explains the national variation in energy security priorities), almost all states are concerned about political independence and stability, human well-being (e.g., adequate nutrition, safety, access to medical care), and economic competitiveness. Insofar as a particular energy system supports these values, they are justifiably viewed as vital. For example, disruptions of oil supplies to North Korea and Cuba following the collapse of the Soviet Union in the early 1990s led to widespread hunger, famine, and many premature deaths as food production and other social functions were disrupted (Ayers 2017).

The concept of vital energy systems also helps to explain "demand security" (Yergin 1988), that is, concerns of oil- and gas-exporting countries about stability of oil and gas markets and prices. In many such societies, energy export revenues support truly vital social functions such as healthcare, education, maintenance and construction of infrastructure, and defense, as well as domestic fuel prices. Disruption of export revenues, whether due to political disputes, disruption of transit routes, sudden drops in market prices, or depletion of reserves available for exports, is therefore perceived as a threat to national security. Some have argued that the collapse of the Soviet Union in 1991 was linked to low oil prices (Strayer 1998) and the shortage of basic necessities, and political instability in Venezuela in the 2010s has been linked to low oil prices. The concept of vital energy systems facilitates analysis of oil and gas export revenues in much the same terms as we analyze other types of systems: clearly and specifically delineating their geographic and sectoral boundaries; identifying the nature (physical or economic), time horizons (shocks or stresses), and source (political or techno-economic) of risks; and assessing resilience (e.g., diversity, shock buffers, etc.).

The distinction between acquired values and aspirational values inherent in the definition of vital energy systems is an important one and helps to distinguish energy security from other energy policy goals and objectives. For example, providing universal access to modern energy for people who do not currently have it is an aspirational value and thus should be differentiated from energy security (Pachauri and Cherp 2011), while safeguarding existing services is linked to protecting acquired values and thus is an energy security concern. A similar argument can be applied to reducing greenhouse gas emissions, which is also an aspirational value that should be considered in parallel and not mixed with energy security concerns. (Not all scholars agree with this perspective; see Hippel et al. 2011; Sovacool and Brown 2010; Sovacool and Mukherjee 2011; Vivoda 2010).

Central to these lines of thinking is that not all energy priorities are the same, and only the ones that endanger critical social functions and/or national values and objectives are energy security priorities. Of course, what is a vital energy system varies from one country to another, both for objective reasons (as countries have different configurations of energy sources, infrastructures, and services) and because various societies (and groups within societies) differ in their values and in what they view as vital. Ultimately, how vital energy systems are defined in political debates makes them intersubjective constructs (Heinrich and Szulecki 2018, 33). As we discuss in the next subsection, identifying how energy security is used as a tool to influence domestic politics is also a promising research direction.

Summary of Key Concepts

Our approach to analyzing energy security can explain and reconcile divergent views of different countries and constituencies on energy security. Moreover, it can enable a meaningful discussion between materialist and critical schools of energy security by systematically exploring what is considered vital and vulnerable and why. Specifically, the concept of vulnerability encapsulates the ideas of risk and resilience prominent in the energy security literature. Risks can differ in their nature (physical versus economic, shocks versus stresses) and their source (actions of humans versus natural and technical processes). The nature and source of risks relate to key security questions: Security over what time frame?, Security from what risks?, and Security for what values? Strategies to reduce risks to energy security strongly overlap with strategies to increase resilience of energy systems and their ability to respond to disruptions and address another key security question: Security by what means? Although theoretically states will try to achieve the highest level of (energy) security, there are cost and practical limitations on which security measures a state can pursue. Teasing out that level addresses these questions: How much security (i.e., at what level)? and Security at what costs? Finally, the concept of vital energy systems highlights the need to be explicit about which energy system is evaluated or framed as the target of an energy security policy in a given context. This answers the key questions: Security of what? and Security for whom?

FUTURE RESEARCH AGENDA

Many current tensions in energy security scholarship arise from the fact that energy security reflects both material aspects of energy systems and their subjective perception. Thus it can be approached from a materialist or a critical perspective. At first glance, these two fundamentally different approaches have little in common. However, as Baldwin writes, a clear social science concept has the potential to show that scholars from seemingly different schools "have more in common than generally acknowledged" (1997, 6). Defining energy security as the low vulnerability of vital energy systems provides room for both the material and the constructivist interpretations of energy security while enabling their dialogue.

The key questions for future energy security research are: What makes an energy system vital and vulnerable? Answering this question requires advancing both material and critical studies on energy security. First, we need to understand what material characteristics link an energy system to critical social system, expose it to risks, and define its capacities to respond to disruptions. Second, we need to understand how the concepts of vitality and vulnerability are shaped by various social actors. It is critically important that these two knowledge domains continue to build bridges between each other. The concepts and key energy security questions "Security of what?," "Security for whom?," and "Security from what threats" (as well as the other five questions discussed throughout the chapter) can enable this dialogue and help clarify how this universal concept of energy security is expressed under different circumstances. Ultimately, this approach will enable policy learning and comparison and a deeper understanding of why different states view similar energy security risks differently and pursue different strategies.

How Do Material Factors Shape What Is Defined as Vulnerable and Vital?

Materialist analysis can investigate the role disruptions in the energy system play in shaping energy policy responses. For example, Cheon and Urpelainen (2015) have shown that energy research and development (R&D) expenditures rise with increasing shares of global oil supply from the Middle East and thus show the importance of the global oil market in national policymaking. Material studies should be explicit about vital energy systems and sensitive to which energy measures address which risks. A good example of this is Brutschin and Fleig (2018), who show how dependence on unstable oil suppliers leads to increased R&D expenditures on biofuels, the primary substitute for oil in transportation. The conceptual clarity of vital energy systems also enables systematic comparative analysis over time and across scenarios (e.g., Guivarch et al. 2015). But materialist analysis does not need to be only quantitative. For example, Leung et al. (2014) use process tracing to explain why oil, not coal or electricity, is viewed as the most important vital energy system in China even though over the past twenty years the country has regularly suffered from coal and electricity disruptions but has not had any oil shortages. Their answer is the memory of the discontinuation of oil supplies from the Soviet Union in the 1960s and US-led oil trade blockades in the 1960s and 1970s, combined with powerful national oil companies who have the power to persuade policymakers that oil continues to represent a threat. Thus, qualitative analysis can show how historical events can continue to shape the definition of what is vulnerable and vital. Finally, there needs to be much more empirical work on historical energy disruptions. Skea et al. (2012) are a rare example; they showed that in spite of all the discussion in the United Kingdom over geopolitical risks to gas security, most of the historical gas disruptions there were technical. Teasing out why this is the case connects to the next major promising area of research.

How Do Power, Values, and Trust Influence How Energy Security Is Defined?

While material factors can shape perceptions of vulnerability and vitality of energy systems, we also need more research on how ideas of power, values, and trust interact with material factors. This may help address several puzzles in the energy security literature.

For example, in spite of the EU's focus on European gas imports, several scholars have argued that Russia would face more losses than Europe in the case of a gas cutoff (Goldthau 2008; Smith Stegen 2011). What role do power and imagination play in how energy security vulnerabilities are perceived even when a material analysis shows that a disruption is unlikely? The Chinese example shows how a material vulnerability can lead to the creation of a powerful national actor that continues to securitize a given system even when a particular threat is no longer omnipresent (Leung et al. 2014). This example shows how important it is to integrate historical material analysis into analyses of power and vulnerability.

Finally, a promising avenue of research is to analyze how vital energy systems come to be defined differently. For example, Heinrich (2018) investigates why Germany and Poland hold different views on the Nord Stream gas pipeline that extends under the Baltic Sea, directly connecting Russia to EU markets. Germany views the pipeline as a natural improvement to EU energy security because it clearly diversifies gas supply routes. In contrast, Poland believes that Nord Stream threatens its national security by reducing its power to negotiate with Russia over energy supplies (the power that many Polish politicians associate with their control over transit pipelines going through their territory). In other words, while for Germany the common European gas (and electricity) market is a vital energy system whose security is enhanced by Nord Stream, for Poland (another member of the same market) it threatens energy security by taking Polish sovereignty away from transit energy routes, seen as an energy system more vital than the overall gas supply to the EU.

What Explains the Gap between Rhetoric and Action?

In projecting energy security discourses onto energy policies, there is often a gap between rhetoric and action. A concept useful for advancing this agenda is Heinrich and Szulecki's (2018) idea of energy security jargon (2018), which refers to when a politician or policy maker talks about energy security but does not do (nor even intend to do) anything about it. When and why is there a gap between rhetoric and action? Is it because jargon reflects true motivations, but some states or actors do not have adequate capacity to translate these motivations into action? Or is it because jargon does not have much to do with motivation in the first place and is simply used to serve political purposes not related to energy security (or even energy at all)?

If it is a matter of a state having strong motivations but insufficient capacity, we can build on earlier efforts to evaluate and measure state capacity. For example, Deese (1981) and Gaylord and Hancock (2013) argue that developing countries have less capacity to implement policies to respond to oil disruptions, and Ikenberry (1986) showed that even among industrialized countries the state capacity to respond to the oil crisis varied in the level of market intervention and available policy instruments. More recent literature has shown the importance of state capacity in introducing new energy technologies. For example, Jewell (2011) shows that nuclear power could only be introduced in sufficiently large, rich economies with rapidly expanding electricity demand or in states that were concurrently pursuing nuclear weapons; that is, where the technology was linked to a core imperative of the state. That capacity is often beyond a state's control should also be considered. For example, Katzenstein (1977) demonstrated the role domestic resources played in national strategies to respond to the oil crisis – with oil-rich countries ramping up production and oil-poor countries looking for other strategies to respond. More recent literature shows that this lesson also applies to newer technologies. Cherp et al. (2017) show that unfavorable wind technology conditions explain why it was the resource-rich Germany and not the resource-poor Japan that led to the earlier (and still higher) penetration of wind power.

On the other hand, perhaps the gap between energy security jargon and energy security action is a result of energy security being used as a tool to advance different agendas (perhaps energy, perhaps not). Fischhendler and Nathan (2014) show how different actors in the same government use "energy security" to advance different goals (some of which are not even related to energy security, such as advancing free market ideology by the private sector). Kester (2018) shows how earthquakes from natural gas production in the Netherlands were used by a local population to challenge the importance of natural gas production for security of supply at the national level. However, there is far too little research which documents how actors use energy security to advance their own agendas at the national level. In teasing out how actors cloak their own interests in energy security jargon in different contexts, it is useful to revisit the key questions: "Energy security for whom?," "Energy security for what values?," "Energy security of what?," and "Energy security by what means?" (Box 12.1; Cherp and Jewell, 2014). Answering these questions can help clarify how different actors use the concept of energy security to advance different energy and policy agendas.

How Does the Energy Security Agenda Interact with Other Energy Policy Agendas?

Energy security has long been central to states' energy policies. The increasing conceptual clarity about energy security provides the foundation for better understanding and informing these energy policies in the future. It also enables the rigorous analysis of how energy security will enhance or constrain energy policies to meet other energy policy objectives, such as mitigating climate change and increasing industrial competitiveness. For example, we need to establish the role energy security plays in shaping climate and technology policies which impact the energy system. Kuzemko (2014) has documented how the rise of the fear of imported Russian gas in the UK led to an increase in attention to not only energy security but also climate change and other energy problems. Another approach is to study the "consistency" or "coherence" between different policy objectives of defined measures in a given context (Strambo, Nilsson, and Månsson 2015). However, we also need to clarify the role of energy security as a "co-benefit" of climate policies. For example, Jewell et al. (2016) show that while climate policies benefit energy security, ambitious energy independence policies can lead to an increase in both coal and renewables.

Further exploring these questions in concrete policy contexts means that energy policies (including climate-friendly ones such as renewable policies) need to be analyzed as energy policies (rather than as environmental policies), which requires bridging knowledge from different disciplines. One promising approach uses political science, energy economics, and the sociology of technology to analyze national energy transitions (Cherp et al. 2018). Accomplishing this will be necessary to understand whether and under what conditions we can meet our climate goals.

NOTES

1. This division is also often reflected in academic debates in which energy security is depicted as a struggle for oil resulting in a zero-sum game between consumers and suppliers; see Wilson in this volume.
2. Note that both Wolfers (1952) and Baldwin (1997) discuss security in general and not specifically energy security.
3. During the 1970s oil crisis, Japan had a much higher sensitivity than the United States because it had a higher share of imported oil. However, under their framework, two countries importing the same share of oil might have different alternatives to coping with shocks. For example, one country might have strategic oil stocks while the other does not.
4. Though that may be changing in the twenty-first century as states and cities pursue strategies to switch certain parts of the vehicular fleet to electric (Mersky et al. 2016) or compressed natural gas (Misra 2007).
5. This echoes early distinctions between short-term (two years), intermediate (two to ten years), and long-term (ten years or more) oil security problems made by Nye (1981).

REFERENCES

Aalto, Pami. 2016. *The EU-Russian Energy Dialogue: Europe's Future Energy Security*. Abingdon and New York: Routledge.

Ang, B. W., W. L. Choong, and T. S. Ng. 2015. "Energy Security: Definitions, Dimensions and Indexes." *Renewable and Sustainable Energy Reviews* 42 (February): 1077–1093. doi:10.1016/j.rser.2014.10.064.

APERC. 2007. "A Quest for Energy Security in the 21st Century: Resources and Constraints." Institute of Energy Economics, Japan.

Awerbuch, Shimon. 1995. "Market-Based IRP: It's Easy!!!" *The Electricity Journal* 8, no. 3: 50–67. doi:10.1016/1040-6190(95)90201-5.

Ayers, John C. 2017. *Sustainability: An Environmental Science Perspective*. Boca Raton: CRC Press.

Baldwin, David A. 1997. "The Concept of Security." *Review of International Studies* 23, no. 1: 5–26.

Balzacq, Thierry. 2005. "The Three Faces of Securitization: Political Agency, Audience and Context." *European Journal of International Relations* 11, no. 2: 171–201. doi:10.1177/1354066105052960.

Bar-Lev, Dan, and Steven Katz. 1976. "A Portfolio Approach to Fossil Fuel Procurement in the Electric Utility Industry." *The Journal of Finance* 31, no. 3: 933–947. doi:10.2307/2326437.

Bazilian, Morgan, Fergal O'Leary, Brian O Gallachoir, and Martin Howley. 2006. "Security of Supply in Ireland 2006." Energy Policy Statistical Support Unit. http://inis.iaea.org/Search/search.aspx?orig_q=RN:38108706.

BBC. 2013. "Bulgaria PM to Resign over Protests." *BBC News*, February 20, sec. Europe. https://www.bbc.com/news/world-europe-21516658.

Beckman, Karel. 2012. "We Must Find Mechanisms to Strengthen Cooperation with the Emerging Economies." *European Energy Review*, March. https://www.elektormagazine.com/news/-We-must-find-mechanisms-to-strengthen-cooperation-with-the-emerging-economies-.

Bentley, R. W. and M. R. Smith, 2004. "World Oil Production Peak – A Supply- Side Perspective." *International Association for Energy Economics Newsletters*, 13 (Third Quarter): 25–28.

Brutschin, Elina. 2017. *EU Gas Security Architecture—The Role of the Commission's Entrepreneurship*. London: Palgrave Macmillan.

Brutschin, Elina, and Andreas Fleig. 2018. "Geopolitically Induced Investments in Biofuels." *Energy Economics* 74 (August): 721–732. doi:10.1016/j.eneco.2018.06.013.

Brutschin, Elina, and Jessica Jewell. 2018. "International Political Economy of Nuclear Energy." In *Handbook of the International Political Economy of Energy and Natural Resources*, edited by Andreas Goldthau, Michael F. Keating, and Caroline Kuzemko, 322–341. Cheltenham: Edward Elgar Publishing.

Buzan, Barry. 1983. *People, States, and Fear: The National Security Problem in International Relations*. Chapel Hill: University of North Carolina Press.

Buzan, Barry, Ole Wæver, and Jaap de Wilde. 1998. *Security: A New Framework for Analysis*. Boulder, CO: Lynne Rienner Publishers.

Calder, Kent E. 2008. "Japan's Energy Angst: Asia's Changing Energy Prospects and the View from Tokyo." *Strategic Analysis* 32, no. 1: 123–129. doi:10.1080/09700160701559359.

Chapman, Ian. 2014. "The End of Peak Oil? Why This Topic Is Still Relevant Despite Recent Denials." *Energy Policy* 64 (January): 93–101. doi:10.1016/j.enpol.2013.05.010.

Cheon, A., and J. Urpelainen. 2015. "Escaping Oil's Stranglehold: When Do States Invest in Energy Security?" *Journal of Conflict Resolution* 59, no. 6: 953–983. doi:10.1177/0022002713520529.

Cherp, Aleh. 2012. "Defining Energy Security Takes More Than Asking Around." In "Frontiers of Sustainability," special section, *Energy Policy* 48 (September): 841–842. doi:10.1016/j.enpol.2012.02.016.

Cherp, Aleh, Adeola Adenikinju, Andreas Goldthau, Francisco Hernandez, Larry Hughes, Jaap Jansen, Jessica Jewell, et al. 2012. "Energy and Security." In *Global Energy Assessment—Toward a Sustainable Future*, 325–384. Cambridge, UK, and New York: Cambridge University Press; Laxenburg, Austria: International Institute for Applied Systems Analysis.

Cherp, Aleh, Vadim Vinichenko, Jessica Jewell, Masahiro Suzuki, and Miklós Antal. 2017. "Comparing Electricity Transitions: A Historical Analysis of Nuclear, Wind and Solar Power in Germany and Japan." *Energy Policy* 101: 612–628. doi:10.1016/j.enpol.2016.10.044.

Cherp, Aleh, and Jessica Jewell. 2010. "Measuring Energy Security: From Universal Indicators to Contextualized Framework." In *The Routledge Handbook of Energy Security*, edited by Benjamin K. Sovacool, 330–355. Abingdon and New York: Routledge.

Cherp, Aleh, and Jessica Jewell. 2011. "The Three Perspectives on Energy Security: Intellectual History, Disciplinary Roots and the Potential for Integration." *Current Opinion in Environmental Sustainability* 3, no. 4: 202–212. doi:10.1016/j.cosust.2011.07.001.

Cherp, Aleh, and Jessica Jewell. 2013. "Energy Security Assessment Framework and Three Case-Studies." In *International Handbook of Energy Security*, edited by Hugh Dyer and Maria Julia Trombetta, 146–173. Cheltenham, UK, and Northampton, MA: Edward Elgar Publishing.

Cherp, Aleh, and Jessica Jewell. 2014. "The Concept of Energy Security: Beyond the Four As." *Energy Policy* 75: 415–421. doi:10.1016/j.enpol.2014.09.005.

Cherp, Aleh, Jessica Jewell, Vadim Vinichenko, Nico Bauer, and Enrica De Cian. 2016. "Global Energy Security under Different Climate Policies, GDP Growth Rates and Fossil Resource Availabilities." *Climatic Change* 136, no. 1: 83–94. doi:10.1007/s10584-013-0950-x.

Cherp, Aleh, Vadim Vinichenko, Jessica Jewell, Elina Brutschin, and Benjamin Sovacool. 2018. "Integrating Techno-Economic, Socio-Technical and Political Perspectives on National Energy Transitions: A Meta-Theoretical Framework." *Energy Research & Social Science* 37 (March): 175–190. doi:10.1016/j.erss.2017.09.015.

Chester, Lynne. 2010. "Conceptualising Energy Security and Making Explicit Its Polysemic Nature." *Energy Policy* 38, no. 2: 887–895. doi:10.1016/j.enpol.2009.10.039.

Ciută, Felix. 2010. "Conceptual Notes on Energy Security: Total or Banal Security?" *Security Dialogue* 41, no. 2: 123–144. doi:10.1177/0967010610361596.

Clinton, David, Kenneth Thompson, and Hans Morgenthau. 2005. *Politics Among Nations*. Boston: McGraw-Hill Education.

Correljé, Aad, and Coby van der Linde. 2006. "Energy Supply Security and Geopolitics: A European Perspective." *Energy Policy* 34, no. 5: 532–543. doi:10.1016/j.enpol.2005.11.008.

Deese, David A. 1979. "Energy: Economics, Politics, and Security." *International Security* 4, no. 3: 140–153. doi:10.2307/2626698.

Deese, David A. 1981. "The Oil-importing Developing Countries." In *Energy and Security*, edited by David A. Deese and Joseph S. Nye, 229–261. Cambridge: Ballinger Publishing Company.

Demski, Christina, Wouter Poortinga, Lorraine Whitmarsh, Gisela Böhm, Stephen Fisher, Linda Steg, Resul Umit, Pekka Jokinen, and Pasi Pohjolainen. 2018. "National Context Is a Key Determinant of Energy Security Concerns across Europe." *Nature Energy* 3, no. 10: 882–888. doi:10.1038/s41560-018-0235-8.

European Commission. 2014. "Communication from the Commission to the European Parliament and the Council on the Short Term Resilience of the European Gas System." COM(2014) 654. https://ec.europa.eu/energy/sites/ener/files/documents/2014_stresstests_com_en_0.pdf.

European Commission. 2017. "EU Invests €444 Million in Key Energy Infrastructure." http://europa.eu/rapid/press-release_IP-17-280_en.htm.

Farrell, Alexander E., Hisham Zerriffi, and Hadi Dowlatabadi. 2004. "Energy Infrastructure and Security." *Annual Review of Environment and Resources* 29, no. 1: 421–469. doi:10.1146/annurev.energy.29.062403.102238.

Fischhendler, Itay. 2018. "The Use of Intangible Benefits for Promoting Contested Policies: The Case of Geopolitical Benefits and the Israeli Gas Policy." *Geopolitics* 23, no. 4: 929–953. doi: 10.1080/14650045.2017.1350842.

Fischhendler, Itay, and Daniel Nathan. 2014. "In the Name of Energy Security: The Struggle over the Exportation of Israeli Natural Gas." *Energy Policy* 70 (July): 152–162. doi:10.1016/j.enpol.2014.03.020.

Friedrichs, Jörg. 2010. "Global Energy Crunch: How Different Parts of the World Would React to a Peak Oil Scenario." *Energy Policy* 38, no. 8: 4562–4569. doi:10.1016/j.enpol.2010.04.011.

Gaylord, Sylvia, and Kathleen J. Hancock. 2013. "Developing World: National Energy Strategies." In *International Handbook of Energy Security*, edited by Hugh Dyer and Maria Julia Trombetta, 206–239. Cheltenham: Edward Elgar.

Goldemberg, J. 2007. "Ethanol for a Sustainable Energy Future." *Science* 315, no. 5813: 808–810. doi:10.1126/science.1137013.

Goldthau, Andreas. 2008. "Rhetoric versus Reality: Russian Threats to European Energy Supply." *Energy Policy* 36, no. 2: 686–692. doi:10.1016/j.enpol.2007.10.012.

Gorelick, Steven M. 2009. *Oil Panic and the Global Crisis: Predictions and Myths*. Chichester: Wiley-Blackwell.

Gracceva, Francesco, and Peter Zeniewski. 2014. "A Systemic Approach to Assessing Energy Security in a Low-Carbon EU Energy System." *Applied Energy* 123 (June): 335–348. doi:10.1016/j.apenergy.2013.12.018.

Grubb, Michael, Lucy Butler, and Paul Twomey. 2006. "Diversity and Security in UK Electricity Generation: The Influence of Low-Carbon Objectives." *Energy Policy* 34, no. 18: 4050–4062. doi:10.1016/j.enpol.2005.09.004.

Guivarch, Céline, and Stéphanie Monjon. 2017. "Identifying the Main Uncertainty Drivers of Energy Security in a Low-Carbon World: The Case of Europe." *Energy Economics* 64 (May): 530–541. doi:10.1016/j.eneco.2016.04.007.

Guivarch, Céline, Stéphanie Monjon, Julie Rozenberg, and Adrien Vogt-Schilb. 2015. "Would Climate Policy Improve the European Energy Security?" *Climate Change Economics* 06, no. 02: 1550008. doi:10.1142/S2010007815500086.

Gupta, Eshita. 2008. "Oil Vulnerability Index of Oil-Importing Countries." *Energy Policy* 36, no. 3: 1195–1211. doi:10.1016/j.enpol.2007.11.011.

Harding, Luke. 2010. "Kyrgyzstan Capital Bloodied, Looted and Chaotic after Overthrow of Bakiyev." *The Guardian*, April 8, sec. World News. https://www.theguardian.com/world/2010/apr/08/kyrgyzstan-revolt-over-kurmanbek-bakiyev.

Heinrich, Andreas. 2018. "Securitisation in the Gas Sector: Energy Security Debates Concerning the Example of the Nord Stream Pipeline." In *Energy Security in Europe*, edited by Kacper Szulecki. London: Palgrave Macmillan. doi:10.1007/978-3-319-64964-1_3.

Heinrich, Andreas, and Kacper Szulecki. 2018. "Energy Securitisation: Applying the Copenhagen School's Framework to Energy." In *Energy Security in Europe*, edited by Kacper Szulecki. London: Palgrave Macmillan. doi:10.1007/978-3-319-64964-1_2.

Helm, Dieter. 2002. "Energy Policy: Security of Supply, Sustainability and Competition." *Energy Policy* 30, no. 3: 173–184. doi:10.1016/S0301-4215(01)00141-0.

Hippel, D. V., Suzuki, T., Williams, J. H., Savage, T., & Hayes, P. 2011. "Energy security and sustainability in Northeast Asia." *Energy Policy* 39, no. 11, 6719–6730. doi:10.1016/j.enpol.2009.07.001

Hughes, L. 2012. "A generic framework for the description and analysis of energy security in an energy system." *Energy Policy* 42, 221–231. doi:10.1016/j.enpol.2011.11.079.

IEA. 2011. "Measuring Short-Term Energy Security." https://www.iea.org/publications/freepublications/publication/Moses.pdf.

IEA. 2012. "Oil and Gas Security: Country Chapter Finland." https://www.iea.org/publications/freepublications/publication/CountryChapterFinland.pdf.

IEA. 2018. "Energy Security." https://www.iea.org/topics/energysecurity/.

Ikenberry, G. John. 1986. "The Irony of State Strength: Comparative Responses to the Oil Shocks in the 1970s." *International Organization* 40, no. 01: 105–137.

Jain, Garima. 2010. "Energy Security Issues at Household Level in India." In "The Role of Trust in Managing Uncertainties in the Transition to a Sustainable Energy Economy," special section, *Energy Policy* 38, no. 6: 2835–2845. doi:10.1016/j.enpol.2010.01.016.

Jansen, J. C. 2009. "Energy Services Security: Concepts and Metrics." Energy Research Centre of the Netherlands. https://www.ecn.nl/docs/library/report/2009/e09080.pdf.

Jansen, J. C., and Ad J. Seebregts. 2010. "Long-Term Energy Services Security: What Is It and How Can It Be Measured and Valued?" In "Energy Security—Concepts and Indicators," special section, *Energy Policy* 38, no. 4: 1654–1664. doi:10.1016/j.enpol.2009.02.047.

Jansen, J. C., W. G. Van Arkel, and M. G. Boots. 2004. "Designing Indicators of Long-Term Energy Supply Security." Petten, Netherlands: ECN. https://www.ecn.nl/publicaties/PdfFetch.aspx?nr=ECN-C-04-007.

Jewell, Jessica. 2011. "The IEA Model of Short-Term Energy Security (MOSES)." Paris: OECD/IEA. https://www.iea.org/media/freepublications/oneoff/moses_paper.pdf.

Jewell, Jessica, and Seyithan Ahmet Ates. 2015. "Introducing Nuclear Power in Turkey: A Historic State Strategy and Future Prospects." *Energy Research & Social Science* 10 (November): 273–282. doi:10.1016/j.erss.2015.07.011.

Jewell, Jessica, Aleh Cherp, and Keywan Riahi. 2014. "Energy Security under De-Carbonization Scenarios: An Assessment Framework and Evaluation under Different Technology and Policy Choices." *Energy Policy* 65 (February): 743–760. doi:10.1016/j.enpol.2013.10.051.

Jewell, Jessica, Vadim Vinichenko, David McCollum, Nico Bauer, Keywan Riahi, Tino Aboumahboub, Oliver Fricko, et al. 2016. "Comparison and Interactions between the Long-Term Pursuit of Energy Independence and Climate Policies." *Nature Energy* 1, no. 6: 16073. doi:10.1038/nenergy.2016.73.

Joskow, Paul L. 2003. "California's Electricity Crisis." SSRN Scholarly Paper ID 443484. Rochester, NY: Social Science Research Network. https://papers.ssrn.com/abstract=443484.

Katzenstein, Peter J. 1977. "Conclusion: Domestic Structures and Strategies of Foreign Economic Policy." *International Organization* 31, no. 4: 879–920.

Kendell, J. M. 1998. *Measures of Oil Import Dependence.* Washington, DC: US Energy Information Agency.

Keohane, Robert Owen, and Joseph S. Nye. 1977. *Power and Interdependence: World Politics in Transition.* Boston: Little, Brown.

Keohane, Robert Owen, and Joseph S. Nye. 2001. *Power and Interdependence.* New York: Longman.

Keppler, Jan Horst. 2007. "International Relations and Security of Energy Supply: Risks to Continuity and Geopolitical Risks." Brussels: Directorate General External Policies of the Union. European Parliament. http://www.europarl.europa.eu/meetdocs/2004_2009/documents/dv/studykeppl/studykeppler.pdf.

Kester, Johannes. 2018. *The Politics of Energy Security: Critical Security Studies, New Materialism and Governmentality.* Abingdon and New York: Routledge.

Klare, Michael. 2008. *Rising Powers, Shrinking Planet: The New Geopolitics of Energy.* New York: Henry Holt and Company.

Kruyt, Bert, D. P. van Vuuren, H. J. M. de Vries, and H. Groenenberg. 2009. "Indicators for Energy Security." In "China Energy Efficiency," special issue, *Energy Policy* 37, no 6: 2166–2181. doi:10.1016/j.enpol.2009.02.006.

Kumar Singh, Bhupendra. 2013. "South Asia Energy Security: Challenges and Opportunities." *Energy Policy* 63 (December): 458–468. doi:10.1016/j.enpol.2013.07.128.

Kuzemko, Caroline. 2014. "Politicising UK Energy: What 'Speaking Energy Security' Can Do." *Policy & Politics* 42, no. 2: 259–274. doi:10.1332/030557312X655990.

Lesbirel, S. Hayden. 2004. "Diversification and Energy Security Risks: The Japanese Case." *Japanese Journal of Political Science* 5, no. 1: 1–22. doi:10.1017/S146810990400129X.

Leung, Guy C. K., Aleh Cherp, Jessica Jewell, and Yi-Ming Wei. 2014. "Securitization of Energy Supply Chains in China." *Applied Energy* 123 (June): 316–326. doi:10.1016/j.apenergy.2013. 12.016.

Li, Raymond, and Guy C. K. Leung. 2011. "The Integration of China into the World Crude Oil Market since 1998." *Energy Policy* 39, no. 9: 5159–5166. doi:10.1016/j.enpol.2011.05.048.

Lilliestam, Johan, and Saskia Ellenbeck. 2011. "Energy Security and Renewable Electricity Trade—Will Desertec Make Europe Vulnerable to the 'Energy Weapon'?" *Energy Policy* 39, no. 6: 3380–3391. doi:10.1016/j.enpol.2011.03.035.

Littlefield, Scott R. 2013. "Security, Independence, and Sustainability: Imprecise Language and the Manipulation of Energy Policy in the United States." *Energy Policy* 52 (January): 779–788. doi:10.1016/j.enpol.2012.10.040.

Lovins, Amory B., and L. Hunter Lovins. 1982. *Brittle Power: Energy Strategy for National Security*. Andover, MA: Brick House Publishing Company.

Martišauskas, Linas, Juozas Augutis, and Ričardas Krikštolaitis. 2018. "Methodology for Energy Security Assessment Considering Energy System Resilience to Disruptions." *Energy Strategy Reviews* 22 (November): 106–118. doi:10.1016/j.esr.2018.08.007.

Meadows, D. H., D. L. Meadows, J. Randers, and W. W. Behrens. 1972. *The Limits to Growth*. New York: Universe Books.

Mersky, Avi Chaim, Frances Sprei, Constantine Samaras, and Zhen (Sean) Qian. 2016. "Effectiveness of Incentives on Electric Vehicle Adoption in Norway." *Transportation Research Part D: Transport and Environment* 46 (July): 56–68. doi:10.1016/j.trd.2016.03.011.

Misra, Ashutosh. 2007. "Contours of India's Energy Security: Harmonising Domestic and External Options." In *Energy Security in Asia*, edited by Michael Wesley, 68–87. London and New York: Routledge.

Moran, Daniel, and James A. Russell. 2009. *Energy Security and Global Politics: The Militarization of Resource Management*. Routledge. https://www.routledge.com/Energy-Security-and-Global-Politics-The-Militarization-of-Resource-Management/Moran-Russell/p/book/9780415776387.

Morgenthau, Hans Joachim. 1948. *Politics Among Nations: The Struggle for Power and Peace*. New York: A. A. Knopf.

Nye, Joseph S. 1981. "Energy and Security." In *Energy and Security*, edited by David A. Deese and Joseph S. Nye, 391–427. Cambridge: Ballinger Publishing Company.

Nye, Joseph S., David A. Deese, and Alvin L. Alm. 1981. "Conclusion: A U.S. Strategy for Energy Security." In *Energy and Security*, edited by David A. Deese and Joseph S. Nye, 391–427. Cambridge: Ballinger Publishing Company.

Orttung, Robert W., and Indra Overland. 2011. "A Limited Toolbox: Explaining the Constraints on Russia's Foreign Energy Policy." *Journal of Eurasian Studies* 2, no. 1: 74–85. doi:10.1016/j. euras.2010.10.006.

Pachauri, Shonali, and Aleh Cherp. 2011. "Energy Security and Energy Access: Distinct and Interconnected Challenges." In "Energy Systems," special issue, *Current Opinion in Environmental Sustainability* 3, no. 4: 199–201. doi:10.1016/j.cosust.2011.07.006.

Paust, Jordan J., and Albert P. Blaustein. 1974. "The Arab Oil Weapon—A Threat to International Peace." *The American Journal of International Law* 68, no. 3: 410–439. doi:10.2307/2200513.

Penchansky, Roy, and J. William Thomas. 1981. "The Concept of Access: Definition and Relationship to Consumer Satisfaction." *Medical Care* 19, no. 2: 127–140.

Prontera, Andrea. 2017. *The New Politics of Energy Security in the European Union and Beyond: States, Markets, Institutions.* London and New York: Taylor & Francis.

Scheepers, Martin, Ad J. Seebregts, Jacques de Jong, and Hans Maters. 2007. "EU Standards for Energy Security of Supply." Energy Research Centre of the Netherlands. https://www.ecn.nl/docs/library/report/2007/e07004.pdf.

Skea, Jim. 2010. "Valuing Diversity in Energy Supply." In "Large-Scale Wind Power in Electricity Markets," special issue, *Energy Policy* 38, no. 7: 3608–3621. doi:10.1016/j.enpol.2010.02.038.

Skea, Jim, Modassar Chaudry, and Xinxin Wang. 2012. "The Role of Gas Infrastructure in Promoting UK Energy Security." *Energy Policy* 43 (April): 202–213. doi:10.1016/j.enpol.2011.12.057.

Smith Stegen, Karen. 2011. "Deconstructing the 'Energy Weapon': Russia's Threat to Europe as Case Study." *Energy Policy* 39, no. 10: 6505–6513. doi:10.1016/j.enpol.2011.07.051.

Sovacool, Benjamin K. 2011. "Evaluating Energy Security in the Asia Pacific: Towards a More Comprehensive Approach." In "Asian Energy Security," special issue, *Energy Policy* 39, no. 11: 7472–7479. doi:10.1016/j.enpol.2010.10.008.

Sovacool, Benjamin K., and Marilyn A. Brown. 2010. "Competing Dimensions of Energy Security: An International Perspective." *Annual Review of Environment and Resources* 35, no. 1: 77–108. doi:10.1146/annurev-environ-042509-143035.

Sovacool, Benjamin K., and Ishani Mukherjee. 2011. "Conceptualizing and Measuring Energy Security: A Synthesized Approach." *Energy* 36, no. 8: 5343–5355. doi:10.1016/j.energy.2011.06.043.

Stirling, Andrew. 1994. "Diversity and Ignorance in Electricity Supply Investment: Addressing the Solution Rather Than the Problem." *Energy Policy* 22, no. 3: 195–216. doi:10.1016/0301-4215(94)90159-7.

Stirling, Andrew. 1998. "On the Economics and Analysis of Diversity." Science Policy Research Unit (SPRU), Electronic Working Papers Series 28, 1–156.

Stirling, Andrew. 2010. "Multicriteria Diversity Analysis: A Novel Heuristic Framework for Appraising Energy Portfolios." In "Energy Security—Concepts and Indicators," special issue, *Energy Policy* 38, no. 4: 1622–1634. doi:10.1016/j.enpol.2009.02.023.

Stirling, Andrew. 2011. "From Sustainability, through Diversity to Transformation: Towards More Reflexive Governance of Technological Vulnerability." In *Vulnerability in Technological Cultures: New Directions in Research and Governance,* edited by Anique Hommels, Jessica Mesman, and Wiebe E. Bijker, 305–332. Cambridge, MA: MIT Press.

Strambo, Claudia, Måns Nilsson, and André Månsson. 2015. "Coherent or Inconsistent? Assessing Energy Security and Climate Policy Interaction within the European Union." *Energy Research & Social Science* 8 (July): 1–12. doi:10.1016/j.erss.2015.04.004.

Strayer, Robert W. 1998. *Why Did the Soviet Union Collapse? Understanding Historical Change.* Armonk, NY: M. E. Sharpe.

Vivoda, V. 2010. "Evaluating energy security in the Asia-Pacific region: A novel methodological approach." *Energy Policy,* 38(9), 5258–5263. doi:10.1016/j.enpol.2010.05.028.

Watson, Jim, and Alister Scott. 2009. "New Nuclear Power in the UK: A Strategy for Energy Security?" *Energy Policy* 37, no. 12: 5094–5104. doi:10.1016/j.enpol.2009.07.019.

Winzer, Christian. 2012. "Conceptualizing Energy Security." *Energy Policy* 46 (supp. C): 36–48. doi:10.1016/j.enpol.2012.02.067.

Wolfers, Arnold. 1952. " 'National Security' as an Ambiguous Symbol." *Political Science Quarterly* 67, no. 4: 481–502. doi:10.2307/2145138.

Yergin, Daniel. 1988. "Energy Security in the 1990s." *Foreign Affairs* (Fall). https://www.foreignaffairs.com/articles/united-states/1988-09-01/energy-security-1990s.

Yergin, Daniel. 2006. "Ensuring Energy Security." *Foreign Affairs* (March/April). https://www.foreignaffairs.com/articles/2006-03-01/ensuring-energy-security.

....

CHAPTER 13

ENERGY AND
INTERNATIONAL
CONFLICT

....

JEFF D. COLGAN AND JAN B. STOCKBRUEGGER

FROM World War II to the invasion of Iraq in 2003, journalists, analysts, and others often point to oil and energy as root causes of war and international conflict. Yet the rhetoric around such wars often lacks serious rigor, and scholars debate the actual significance of oil and energy as a causal force. How and to what extent do they matter for international conflict?

This chapter begins with the issue of oil and conflict, then moves on to the broader role of energy. We focus on oil because of its key strategic role in the modern age, especially in transportation and the military. In the transportation sector, there is no real substitute for oil, at least at present. Other sources of energy, such as coal and gas, are generally used for electricity generation, where they can be more easily replaced. Furthermore, oil is the only energy commodity that is traded on truly global markets, which means that generally oil supplies can be shifted from one region to another relatively easily and at a very similar price. The effects of oil on international conflict are larger than the effects of any other source of energy. One study finds that since the beginning of the modern oil age in 1973, oil has contributed to between one-quarter and one-half of interstate wars (Colgan 2013a, 149).

We argue that oil and energy have mattered for international security in the last century in ways that are *conditional* and depend on *interactions* with other political and economic variables. Consequently, we differ with policy makers and scholars who tend to boil down energy's impact to a single, monolithic effect, such as that oil politics does (Klare 2004) or does not (Meierding 2016) lead to war. The literature shows that the reality is more complex and is conditional on other factors. Identifying those factors and showing their systematic effects is an area in which many fertile research questions presently lie. There is a large body of research on the domestic effects of the oil industry and the relationship between oil and civil war (e.g., Bellin 2004; Colgan 2015; Collier and Hoeffler 2004; Le Billon 2012; Lujala 2010; Paine 2016; Ross 2013, 2015), but we focus here on international relations. We consider the domestic impacts of the energy and oil industry only insofar as as they affect international security. And we bracket the role of energy in international political economy (e.g., Graaff 2012; Hancock and Vivoda 2014; Shaffer 2009).

Drawing on the extant literature, we first review eight mechanisms linking oil to international conflict. We then draw on these mechanisms to show how oil has contributed to international wars, always in combination with other factors, and how it has shaped the strategies of states during these wars. We start with World War I, the first war in which oil played a crucial role, and end with twenty-first-century conflicts. Finally, we briefly analyze the literature on conflict and natural gas, coal, and nuclear energy. We conclude by proposing a research agenda.

FROM OIL TO WAR: EIGHT MECHANISMS

We review the literature in the context of Colgan's (2013a) eight mechanisms connecting oil to international conflict, which he groups into three broad pathways. The first pathway is associated with the relationship between oil consumers and producers, while the second and third pathways deal with the interests of producers and consumers, respectively. These pathways do not include indirect effects of oil on conflict, such as conflicts induced by climate change, and they also exclude the ways in which oil shapes military tactics during war, such as the German U-boat campaign aimed at disrupting Britain's oil supplies. Instead, the pathways described here focus on the political effects of the oil industry that lead to international conflict.

The first pathway, ownership and market structure, includes mechanisms through which various actors on either the supply side (producers) or the demand side (consumers) have incentives to change the structure of the oil industry to their own advantage. This pathway includes three specific mechanisms: resource wars, wars over market control, and conflict fueled by grievances associated with the oil industry.

Mechanism 1 is resource wars. Oil is a high-value natural resource that is crucial to domestic economies. It is relatively easy to loot, refine, and sell on international markets. Armies also need access to oil in times of international conflict to operate and fight (Kelanic 2016; Markowitz 2013). Both survival and profits thus motivate states to conquer territory that holds large oil reserves. This leads to resource wars, which include Iraq's 1990 invasion of Kuwait and Japan's 1941 conquest of Southeast Asia. We discuss both wars in more detail later in this chapter. Despite their large hold on the popular discourse of oil and war, however, classic resource wars are actually quite rare (Koubi et al. 2014; Meierding 2016; Victor 2007).

Meierding (2016) argues that oil wars are actually a myth, but her claim goes too far. She defines oil wars as "intense militarized conflicts in which states attempt to gain direct, sustained control over known or prospective oil resources" (261). Japan's attack in 1941 and Iraq's in 1990 clearly qualify, but she dismisses them because "Japanese and Iraqi officials believed that foreign petroleum access was a requirement for regime survival. Security needs, not oil greed, were the fundamental cause of their attacks" (260). This argument is flawed; the fact that policy makers saw oil as essential for their security is evidence *for*, not against, the existence of oil wars.

Mechanism 2 is the risk of market domination. In this mechanism, states fight over potential control over oil markets. A state that conquers or threatens to conquer territory holding important oil reserves might undermine the global oil market through its dominance. Other states thus have incentives to intervene and to ensure that no single producer can control the supply and price of oil in international markets. This mechanism explains why, for instance, the United States went to war with Iraq in 1991. As we discuss later in the chapter, the United States did not aim to seize oil reserves in Kuwait or Iraq, but rather to protect and to secure the continued functioning of the international market for oil.

Mechanism 3 is oil industry grievances. In this mechanism, the economic inequalities created by the oil industry, and the perceived exploitation associated with them, lead to grievances among domestic social actors. These grievances trigger conflict and contribute to the radicalization of parts of the population. Grievances are also fueled by the presence of multinational oil companies and foreign workers in a petro-state (Vitalis 2006). (In this article we use the term *petro-state* to mean any state that is a net exporter of oil). Some jihadi terrorist groups, such as al-Qaeda, have used these grievances to legitimize their activities and to recruit followers (Moran and Avery 2009, 82). The 1980 Iran hostage crisis, in which fifty-two Americans were held for over a year, can be partially explained by this mechanism.

The second broad pathway captures three mechanisms that describe how violent conflict is caused by changing incentives in petro-states associated with income from the oil industry. These are petro-aggression, petro-insurgency, and the externalization of civil wars in petro-states.

Mechanism 4 is petro-aggression, a form of resource-backed conflict. States do not fight over oil, as in oil wars, but they use income from oil to finance wars, and oil income can also distort domestic politics, which affects foreign policy. Colgan (2010, 2013b) shows that petro-states engage in militarized international disputes at a higher rate than do non-petro-states (see also Hendrix 2017; Kim and Woods 2016). This result is driven by petro-states being led by revolutionary leaders. Revolutionary leaders are more aggressive and risk accepting than non-revolutionary leaders. Revenues from oil amplify this propensity by allowing leaders to finance aggressive and sometimes revisionist foreign policies. Oil thus makes it more likely that the leader will decide to launch an international conflict, as happened in Libya under Muammar al-Gaddafi or in Iraq under Saddam Hussein.

Mechanism 5 is petro-insurgency. Revenues generated by oil can support foreign insurgencies and terrorist organizations. Petro-states are not the only states to support foreign insurgencies, of course, but they seem to engage in such practices at a higher rate

(Colgan 2013b). Oil revenues allowed Libya to bankroll several terrorist and insurgent organizations in the 1980s (St. John 1987), and Iran has provided funding for Hezbollah in Lebanon as well as for the Palestinian Hamas and other nonstate military actors (Giraldo and Trinkunas 2007).

Mechanism 6 is externalization of civil wars in petro-states. Oil is associated with corruption, weak and fragile state institutions, and grievances driven by economic inequality. Oil also provides funding for domestic insurgents. Thus most scholars find petro-states are more likely to experience internal conflict and civil war than are other states (though some scholars disagree; see Basedau and Lay 2009; Smith 2004). Civil wars, in turn, can create spillover effects that affect neighboring countries or lead to international interventions (Gleditsch et al. 2008; Salehyan 2009; Schultz 2010). Sudan, for instance, attacked Chad in 2009 for its support of rebel groups operating in Dafur, and an international coalition led by the North Atlantic Treaty Organization (NATO) intervened in 2011 in Libya, leading to the downfall of the Gaddafi regime.

The last broad pathway concerns consumer politics and how states address their economic and military reliance on oil imports. It includes two mechanisms, conflicts over transit routes and oil as an obstacle to multilateralism.

Mechanism 7 is transit routes. International politics of pipelines and shipping lanes can generate conflict. The flow of oil could be disrupted in times of war and instability. Oil-importing states thus have an incentive to take action and to secure shipping lanes (Kelanic 2016; Lind and Press 2018; O'Sullivan 2013). This dynamic could lead to a security dilemma that escalates or amplifies international conflict. Tensions between China and the United States related to maritime shipping in the South China Sea and the Strait of Malacca illustrate this mechanism (Glaser 2013).

It is important to point out that this mechanism could also affect oil-exporting states. The United States intervened in the "Tanker War" to secure the flow of oil from the Persian Gulf to global markets in 1987. Also, maritime piracy and multinational naval efforts to protect merchant shipping are related to the transit route mechanism (Nevers 2015). Oil embargoes are a similar but different mechanism. Oil embargoes are rare and can usually be mitigated by the market (Gholz and Press 2010).

Mechanism 8 is oil as an obstacle to multilateralism. Oil can be an obstacle to multilateral cooperation efforts to prevent conflict and enhance international security. Ross and Voeten (2016), for instance, have shown that petro-states are less likely to join intergovernmental organizations, and they often do not accept compulsory international jurisdiction and arbitration. Furthermore, a petro-state can provide privileged access to oil in return for support in international disputes. Such relationships often undermine multilateral cooperation and prevent joint initiatives to address issues such as nuclear proliferation, humanitarian crises, and the escalation of an international conflict. Historically, this mechanism by itself is not associated with international conflict. Nevertheless, issues such as Iran's nuclear program, which China and Russia have shielded from international pressure, intensify security competition and tensions between rival states.

Brief History of Oil and Wars, from World War I to the Present

We briefly review here the history of oil and war, drawing on the eight mechanisms outlined in the preceding section. We include both direct and contextual effects of oil. Direct effects are situations in which the presence of oil or income from oil has a significant impact on how key actors make decisions related to war and when war breaks out. Contextual effects capture the ways in which oil has shaped the political environments in the past or when it has had a small influence on how actors make decisions that are relevant to war onset and duration. Our overview starts with World War I, when oil emerged as a key strategic resource in international affairs.

World War I and World War II

World War I (also known as the Great War) was the first motorized war in history. Winston Churchill, the First Lord of the Admiralty of the British Royal Navy, made key decisions in 1912 and 1913 to convert the British fleet from coal to oil (Yergin 1991, 156). This shift enhanced the operational capabilities of the navy, but it also made the navy more dependent on oil imports from America and the Middle East. The United States supplied nearly 90 percent of Britain's oil requirements during World War I, and Germany threatened those supplies through submarine warfare. Emergency oil shipments from the United States and the establishment of an effective convoy system enabled the Allies to continue their war efforts (Kelanic 2016, 200; Winegard 2016, 104).

A British naval blockade of Germany also imposed oil shortages on that country. In response, German forces seized oil fields in Romania, which were among the largest in Europe. It also tried to occupy the oil fields of Baku (Winegard 2016, 93–99, 180).

Control over oil became a strategic imperative for Britain even after the end of the Great War. The Slade memo of July 1918 envisioned an anticipatory British strategy aimed at securing access to oil reserves in Mesopotamia. Britain controlled only 5 percent of the world's oil production before the war; after the war, and as a direct result of its expansion into the Middle East, Britain, and British companies had direct access to nearly 50 percent of known global oil reserves (Kelanic 2016, 200; Winegard 2016, 107).

Oil scarcity (mechanism 1) had become a driving force in the Allied and German war strategies, though it was not a cause of the war's onset. This trend continued during World War II. Oil considerations did not cause Adolf Hitler's decision to attack Poland in 1939. However, overcoming oil scarcity played an important role in his strategic thinking, and it shaped Germany's military campaigns. Hitler's "Four-Year Plan" of 1936 aimed at making Germany self-sufficient in terms of raw materials, especially oil (Hayward 1995, 97). Yet Germany had not achieved its objective of oil self-sufficiency when the Allies imposed a naval blockade on Germany in response to Hitler's invasion of Poland.

Hitler's decision to attack the Soviet Union in June 1941 was at least partly motivated by his desire to overcome Germany's reliance on Soviet food and raw materials, including oil (Tooze 2007, 422–424). Yet Germany's oil problems increased when the Wehrmacht was unable to achieve a quick Blitzkrieg victory over the Soviet forces and to conquer the oil-rich Caucasus region (Hayward 1995). The German navy's submarine campaign failed to disrupt Allied oil shipments, which allowed Allied forces to expand the war effort on the western front. The oil factor thus favored the Allies, and it reduced Germany's ability to wage a "total war" on two fronts simultaneously (Kelanic 2016).

Oil scarcity triggered Japan's entry into World War II (mechanism 1). Japan was poor in natural resources and depended on oil imports from the United States, especially for its military (Yergin 1991, 307). In July 1941 the United States imposed an oil embargo on Japan in response to Japan's continued war in China and East Asia. Negotiations to resolve the dispute failed, and in December 1941 Japan attacked the US Pacific Fleet in Pearl Harbor and launched a military campaign to conquer Southeast Asia. Japan's main strategic objective was the oil fields in the Dutch East Indies, which it occupied in January 1942 (Lehmann 2009, 142–144; Meierding 2016, Paine 2017, 143–178).

Japan had conquered vital oil reserves, but it was unable to protect its seaborne oil transit routes against US submarine attacks. By 1944 the US Navy was destroying more tankers than Japan could build. Oil shortages crippled Japan's military capabilities and industrial capacities, which contributed to its eventual defeat (Blair 2001). The struggle over oil and oil supply lines thus contributed to the onset (in the Pacific), dynamics, and outcome of World War II.

Oil and Conflict since 1945

Oil considerations have also caused many wars and interventions since the end of World War II. One such case was the 1953 military coup d'état in Iran, orchestrated by the US Central Intelligence Agency (CIA). The Iranian crisis began in 1951 when the new prime minister, Mohammad Mosaddegh, drawing on domestic grievances, nationalized Iran's British-controlled oil industry and expelled foreign oil officials from the country (mechanism 3). Britain retaliated by declaring an oil boycott against Iran. When Mosaddegh began to tilt toward the Soviet Union, US president Dwight D. Eisenhower approved a CIA mission to help Mosaddegh's domestic rivals overthrow the government (mechanism 6). The shah of Iran re-established his authority, and a new consortium of mainly British and US companies regained control over Iran's oil industry. Over time, the United States became the dominant player in Middle East oil (Painter 1986; Yergin 1991).

The next crisis in which oil played a major role was the 1956 Suez Canal crisis (Marcel 2006, 24). Two-thirds of Europe's oil passed through this strategic waterway, which was controlled by the British-owned Suez Canal Company. In July 1956 Egyptian president Gamal Abdel Nasser nationalized the Suez Canal to take over its revenues.

Concerned about the security of oil supplies and trade (mechanism 7), among other issues, Britain, France, and Israel conspired to restore Western control over the canal by force. But the operation failed, and the Soviet Union and the United States forced the three invading countries to stop their military operations. Egypt kept control over the Suez Canal, and Britain, France, and Israel eventually withdrew their troops from the country.

The oil shock linked to the 1973 Yom Kippur War between Israeli and Arab forces marked a major transition in energy politics. Oil was not a direct cause of the war, but it influenced the conduct of the war in two ways. First, Saudi Arabia used its oil income to subsidize Egypt's military buildup and armament program (Bronson 2006). Libya, another petro-state, provided troops that fought alongside Egyptian forces (mechanism 4). Second, Saudi Arabia and other Arab countries imposed an oil embargo on Israel's supporters (mechanism 7). The embargo had no effect on the outcome of the war, but it spurred a massive change in the international oil order (Colgan 2013a).

The Arab oil embargo had only a limited tangible impact on the global oil market (Stern 2016), but it raised the profile of OPEC (Colgan 2014) and contributed to the "oil scarcity ideology" (Stern 2016) and fear of the "oil weapon" (Venn 1986). Access to Middle Eastern oil became a national security priority for the United States (Crane et al. 2009; Deutch et al. 2006; Duffield 2007; Gause 2009; Yetiv 2004). The oil crisis also raised the price of oil and the revenues of petro-states. This allowed the latter to play a more active role in international affairs. Hence, the period after 1973 also saw a number of cases of petro-aggression (mechanism 4).

The most prominent cases of petro-aggression involve Libya, Iraq, and Iran, which have been analyzed in detail by Colgan (2013b). In Libya, the revolutionary government of Muammar al-Gaddafi depended almost entirely on oil revenues. Oil enhanced his domestic power, reduced his accountability, and allowed him to pursue an aggressive foreign policy. Gaddafi fought a protracted border war with Chad, and Libyan troops supported Uganda in its war against Tanzania (1978–1979); he also financed and supported several insurgencies and terrorist organizations in Africa and the Middle East.

Another example of petro-aggression is Iraq. The revolutionary Baath Party under Saddam Hussein used oil revenues to consolidate its domestic authority and to increase the size of the armed forces, spending as much as 18 percent of Iraq's gross domestic product on the military. In 1980 Hussein attacked Iran to conquer the Shatt al Arab waterway and the oil region of Khuzestan. The war shattered Iraq's non-oil economy, but income from oil kept Hussein in power and allowed him to keep fighting until 1988. In 1990 Iraq invaded Kuwait to take control of its oil fields and to eliminate its war debt to the Kuwaiti government (mechanisms 1 and 4). An American-led military coalition intervened in 1991 to free Kuwait and to prevent Iraq from achieving a dominant position in the international oil market (mechanism 2).

Oil revenues also facilitated Iran's aggressive behavior, especially following the Islamic Revolution in 1979. The revolutionary regime led by Ayatollah Ruhollah Khomeini was not responsible for starting the Iran-Iraq War, as discussed previously. However, oil revenues allowed the regime to continue the war and to reject Iraqi offers to start peace negotiations. The Islamic Revolution was caused, at least in part, by economic inequalities and foreign exploitation in the US-dominated oil industry and its association with the corrupt and repressive regime of the shah (mechanism 3). Iran currently provides military and financial support to the regime of Bashar al-Assad in Syria, as well as to Shia militias in Iraq, the Houthi rebels in Yemen, and Hezbollah in Lebanon (mechanism 5). Furthermore, Iran has long worked on developing nuclear capabilities. Efforts to create a stronger and more effective United Nations (UN) sanction regime were undermined by Russia and China, which had concluded preferential commercial deals with Iran (mechanism 8).

The post-1973 period saw several cases of civil wars in petro-states that triggered international interventions (mechanism 6). This includes the civil wars in Angola, Iraq, and Libya. The oil industry in Angola created grievances leading to the outbreak of civil war in 1975, which led to military interventions by Cuba and South Africa that were supported by the United States and the Soviet Union (Ross 2013). The Libyan civil war broke out in 2011 and triggered a NATO-led and UN-sanctioned military intervention that ended with the execution of Gaddafi in October 2011 by Libyan insurgents (Kuperman 2013). Yet the civil war has continued, and it is fueled, at least in part, by struggles over Libya's oil industry. The United States and its allies have bombed Islamic State in Iraq and Syria (ISIS) positions in the country and elsewhere.

The connection between oil and terrorism, which remains controversial in the literature, grew in salience after 1973 (Lee 2018; Yetiv 2011). For example, the perceived US dominance over the oil industry in the Middle East fueled grievances that facilitated the rise of terrorist organizations such as al-Qaeda. Osama Bin Laden, moreover, funded al-Qaeda with money that his family had made in Saudi Arabia's booming oil economy (Colgan 2013a). Oil also facilitated the rise of ISIS, which captured oil fields and funded its operations with oil revenues. In Iraq, ISIS also benefited from economic and political inequalities associated with the oil industry (mechanism 3). Several external actors, including the United States, Russia, and Iran, are involved in the wars in Syria and Iraq, where they fight alongside domestic actors against ISIS and other threats (Byman 2016).

Conflicts over oil transit routes (mechanism 7) played a part in World Wars I and II and have continued to be important since then. The "Tanker War" was part of the Iran-Iraq War, as both sides attacked tankers that carried shipments of the other side's oil. The US Navy eventually intervened in the conflict in 1987 after Kuwait threatened to request Soviet assistance to protect oil shipments in the Persian Gulf (Hughes and Long 2015). Maritime piracy also affects transit routes, though it has been a relatively minor threat because of deterrence by governments and the shipping industry. In 2009, for instance, a multinational naval fleet was deployed to contain the rise of piracy in the Gulf of Aden; since 2011, ship owners have started to deploy private armed guards on-board their vessels (Nevers 2015).

Finally, oil also played an important role in America's military interventions in Iraq in 1991 and 2003. These interventions, and the larger US military presence in the Middle East, are poorly explained in terms of resource wars or US efforts to exploit Iraq's oil resources (mechanism 1). While the United States did not try to take over ownership of

Iraq's oil fields (Cramer and Thrall 2012), oil did matter. In 1991 the United States and other governments were interested in, among other things, preventing Iraq from dominating the global oil market (mechanism 2). Fear of oil market domination also underpinned the 1980 Carter doctrine and the creation of the Central Command (CENTCOM), the military unit mandated to defend US interests in the Middle East (Colgan 2013a, 157).

Oil also had an indirect effect on America's 2003 invasion of Iraq. As we have seen in this chapter, it is because of oil that the Persian Gulf became vital to US national security interests. Without oil, the United States would be less likely to intervene in the Persian Gulf, just as it rarely engages in major interventions in Africa. Hence, the presence of oil in Iraq and the wider Persian Gulf created the strategic conditions for the US presence in the region, and it certainly increased the likelihood of the 2003 invasion of Iraq (Alfonsi 2006; Gause 2009).

CONFLICT AND OTHER SOURCES OF ENERGY

While the literature focuses on oil, there is also some research on natural gas, coal, and nuclear energy. The politics of natural gas has increased in importance since 1973 (Barnes et al. 2006; Barnes and Jaffe 2006). Japan and Europe especially have increased their natural gas imports to diversify their energy portfolios. A key difference between natural gas and oil is that gas is mainly traded on regional pipelines rather than through maritime shipping, meaning there is no global market. While regions are interconnected, there is no single global price of gas, as there is for oil, despite the growing significance of the market for liquefied natural gas (LNG). States cannot easily respond to supply shocks by shifting their commercial relations and importing gas from other countries, as they can do with oil. This has important implications for international security. It makes producers, consumers, and transit countries vulnerable to supply-line disruptions, and it allows them to use gas as a "weapon."

Yet the existing geography of pipeline infrastructures also limits coercive capabilities in the international gas trade. On the one hand, it ensures that the effects of supply-line disruptions remain limited to specific regions and countries. For instance, gas disputes in Europe do not necessarily affect China, India, or the United States (Abdelal 2015). Moreover, some scholars see the interdependence between Russia and Belarus as leading to cooperation (Hancock 2006). On the other hand, the international gas pipelines create mutual dependencies that might strengthen international cooperation. If countries cannot get out of a commercial relationship, they have strong incentives to prevent the escalation of international disputes (Stulberg 2015). The effect of gas on international conflict thus remains unclear. Moreover, how this relationship will develop in the future depends on infrastructure investments such as pipelines and LNG port terminals.

Scholars have paid even less attention to coal than to natural gas. Coal remains a major source of energy, especially in developing countries like China and India. Until the 1960s, coal was primarily traded domestically. An international market for coal did not emerge until the 1973 oil crisis, which created strong incentives for oil-consuming states to replace oil with coal for electricity generation. Between 1980 and 2000, the use of coal in power generation in OECD countries increased by 61 percent, while the use of oil in that sector fell by 41 percent (Thurber and Morse 2015, 13). Coal power plants are on average more capital intensive than oil or gas power plants, but the major advantage of coal is that it is more widely available than either oil or gas. Europe and the United States have large reserves of coal, as do China and India. Furthermore, a well-functioning global market for coal has emerged that allows countries to respond flexibly to short-term bottlenecks or disruptions in supply. The coercive potential associated with coal is thus very limited, and international conflicts over coal or access to coal remain unlikely (Thurber and Morse 2015).

Finally, we analyze civilian nuclear energy and how it affects international conflict. We do not address nuclear weapons, which is an issue too large to be covered in this chapter. Nuclear power is a capital-intensive source of energy that requires large initial investments and advanced technological capacities. It reduces dependency on fossil fuel imports and mitigates exposure to international market volatilities. Nuclear power plants proliferated starting in the postwar years, a trend that culminated in the 1970s in the wake of the global oil crisis. Since then, however, the construction of new nuclear power plants has declined significantly in advanced industrial states, in part because accidents at nuclear plants have demonstrated the risks associated with this source of energy (e.g., the 1979 Three Mile Island accident, the 1986 Chernobyl disaster, and the 2011 Fukushima accident). Demand for nuclear energy thus comes primarily from high-growth countries such as Brazil, Russia, India, and China (BRIC), which currently account for more than 68 percent of new nuclear plants under construction (Gourley and Stulberg 2013, 32). Scholars debate whether nuclear energy programs facilitate the proliferation of nuclear weapons (Fuhrmann 2012; Miller 2017).

We end our discussion with some considerations of how energy has shaped the conflict between Russia and Ukraine in recent years (van de Graaf and Colgan 2017). It was not a conflict over energy resources per se, but energy played an important contextual role. Disputes over gas prices increased tensions between Russia and Ukraine in the years prior to the so-called Maidan revolution that triggered Russia's annexation of Crimea. For instance, Russia suspended all gas exports to Ukraine for three weeks in winter 2009, leading to an energy crisis in many central European countries. Russia's behavior can also be seen in terms of the petro-aggression mechanism. Though Putin is not a revolutionary leader, he does seem to have aggressive preferences, and income from oil and gas exports has allowed him to finance the annexation of Crimea and Russia's military intervention in Syria.

The case of the Russian-Ukrainian conflict also shows the limits of energy, in this case natural gas, as a coercive tool in international disputes. Gas is transported through pipelines. Russia cannot simply cut off Ukraine and Europe from gas deliveries and instead sell its gas to China. Yet Europe, which relies on Russian gas deliveries, refrained from imposing sanctions on key Russian energy interests. According to Stulberg (2015, 113), the parties in the Russian-Ukrainian conflict "avoided uncontrolled energy brinkmanship that marred earlier stand-offs" and "deepened mutual energy ties as the crisis unfolded."

A FUTURE RESEARCH AGENDA

Oil and energy not only shape the strategies of states, they can act as a causal factor in international wars by interacting with other variables. The history of international conflict since World War I illustrates how eight distinct causal mechanisms link oil to war. Natural gas, coal, and nuclear energy also affect international conflict and security.

Our analysis suggests that energy will remain a major theme in international security in the future. Six broad groups of questions emerge from our discussion. First, to what extent will oil scarcity and the quest for energy security continue to shape the grand strategies of great powers (see Jewell and Brutschin in this volume)? Energy security is a major concern for Chinese and European strategists. The relationship between energy and great power grand strategy will thus remain an important issue for international security analysts.

Second, to what extent will energy politics shape the Middle East and its relationship with external powers in the twenty-first century? Oil turned the Middle East into one of the most contested strategic regions of the world after the 1973 oil crisis. The Persian Gulf remains crucial for global oil markets, but recent geopolitical changes and unconventional energy sources, which may make the United States self-sufficient in energy, have altered perceptions of the region's geopolitical significance (O'Sullivan 2017). How these changes will affect global oil markets and the fragile political environment in the Persian Gulf is a major question for the future.

Third, to what extent will energy shape international rivalries among the great powers? Today, the United States and China compete over control of strategic maritime oil supply routes and sea lines of communication in the South China Sea. In Europe, disputes over natural gas and strategic pipelines shape the dynamics of the Russian-Ukrainian conflict and the wider relations between Russia and the European Union. A deeper understanding of the ways in which oil and other energy sources shape conflict between the great powers will be crucial to address these geopolitical challenges.

Fourth, to what extent will petro-aggression and related mechanisms continue, and how will great powers respond? In the past, oil allowed revolutionary leaders in petro-states to pursue an aggressive foreign policy and to provide funding for terrorists and insurgent groups. One possibility is that consumer economies, motivated in part by ethical considerations, will begin to boycott so-called blood oil (Wenar 2016).

Fifth, how will future demand for energy, especially oil, affect international conflict? If prices declined over the long run, they would lower the value of territory that contains oil and gas resources, thus weakening incentives for territorial conquest. This might be good news in the light of maritime resource disputes in the South China Sea, an area that is rich in oil and gas resources (Nemeth et al. 2014). Yet decreasing oil prices might also undermine governance institutions in petro-states dependent on income from oil and lead to domestic unrest and civil war that could affect neighboring countries or trigger external military interventions.

Sixth, how will the growth of renewables affect international conflict? Historically, energy transitions have had major political consequences (Fouquet 2008). A burgeoning literature investigates the geopolitics of renewables and how such energy sources might disrupt politics (Aklin and Urpelainen 2018; Scholten 2018).

In light of these questions, we propose a research agenda centered on international order and the role that energy plays within it. That agenda should focus on energy in the context of the biggest issues in international relations: war and peace, environmental sustainability, and economic prosperity. It should address a variety of countries and regions, ranging from Russia to Venezuela and from Europe to the Middle East. Yet two issues seem especially important: the US role in the Middle East and energy in the US-Chinese relationship.

On the first issue, there is now an active debate about whether the United States should maintain its security commitments and military presence in the Persian Gulf (Glaser and Kelanic 2016; Rovner and Talmadge 2014; O'Sullivan 2014). The region continues to be the cornerstone of the global oil market, but changes in the international security and energy landscape suggest that the United States could reduce its military footprint in the region. For instance, the Iraqi state and its military are weak, and Saudi Arabia shows no interest in expansion. Iran is hostile, but not necessarily expansionist. It is relatively unlikely to threaten the Persian Gulf or attack Saudi Arabia's oil production (Shifrinson and Priebe 2011; Talmadge 2008). Moreover, research suggests that oil markets adapt quickly to most supply shocks (Gholz and Press 2010, 2013), and governments have created large oil reserves that mitigate their vulnerability to such shocks. That leads some to suggest that a large US military presence in the Persian Gulf is no longer necessary (Glaser and Kelanic 2016). The debate over the US role in the Middle East is far from over, however. A recent study, for instance, shows that Western "oil-for-security" deals with petro-states like Saudi Arabia and Qatar tend to reduce militarized interstate disputes, compared to other states in the region (Colgan 2017). Hence, US disengagement from the Persian Gulf might increase the risk of conflict and instability, which threaten global oil markets.

On the second issue, some scholars see an oil-driven security dilemma between China and the United States (Glaser 2013). China depends on oil imports through the South China Sea and the Strait of Malacca. The US Navy, however, controls this area and might try to blockade China's oil imports during a conflict. China thus has an incentive to enhance its strategic position in this region to protect and defend vital sea lines of communication (Downs 2004; Gholz et al. 2017; Lind and Press 2018). That position would also allow China to blockade Taiwan and to disrupt the maritime transportation routes of US allies such as Japan and South Korea (Biddle and Oelrich 2016). China's naval expansion program, its maritime disputes, and its island building and militarization activities should be seen in this light. The United States views China's behavior as threatening, and it is currently responding by deepening its own security ties in the

Asia-Pacific region. As both states need to control the same area, tensions will continue to escalate, potentially leading to great power conflict (Glaser 2013).

In sum, the connections between energy and security form an important and vibrant field of inquiry. A better understanding of how oil and energy affect international security remains crucial to make sense of major problems and fault lines in international politics and the behavior of great powers.

REFERENCES

Abdelal, Rawi. 2015. "The Multinational Firm and Geopolitics: Europe, Russian Energy, and Power." *Business and Politics* 17, no. 3: 553–576.

Aklin, Michaël, and Johannes Urpelainen. 2018. *Renewables: The Politics of a Global Energy Transition*. Cambridge: Massachusetts Institute of Technology Press.

Alfonsi, Christian. 2006. *Circle in the Sand: Why We Went Back to Iraq*. New York: Doubleday.

Barnes, Joe, Mark H. Hayes, Amy Myers Jaffe, and David G. Victor. 2006. "Introduction and Context." In *Natural Gas and Geopolitics: From 1970–2040*, edited by Joe Barnes, Mark H. Hayes, Amy M. Jaffe, and David G. Victor, 3–24. Cambridge, MA: Cambridge University Press.

Barnes, Joe, and Amy Myers Jaffe. 2006. "The Persian Gulf and the Geopolitics of Oil." *Survival* 48, no. 1: 143–162.

Basedau, Matthias, and Jann Lay. 2009. "Resource Curse or Rentier Peace? The Ambiguous Effects of Oil Wealth and Oil Dependence on Violent Conflict." *Journal of Peace Research* 46, no. 6: 757–776.

Bellin, Eva. 2004. "The Robustness of Authoritarianism in the Middle East." *Comparative Politics* 36, no. 2: 139–157.

Biddle, Stephen, and Ivan Oelrich. 2016. "Future Warfare in the Western Pacific: Chinese Antiaccess/Area Denial, U.S. AirSea Battle, and Command of the Commons in East Asia." *International Security* 41, no. 1: 7–48.

Blair, Clay. 2001. *Silent Victory: The U.S. Submarine War against Japan*. Annapolis, MD: Naval Institute Press.

Bronson, Rachel. 2006. *Thicker Than Oil: America's Uneasy Partnership with Saudi Arabia*. New York: Oxford University Press.

Byman, Daniel. 2016. "Understanding the Islamic State—A Review Essay." *International Security* 40, no. 4: 127–165.

Colgan, Jeff D. 2010. "Oil and Revolutionary Governments: Fuel for International Conflict." *International Organization* 64, no. 4: 661–694.

Colgan, Jeff D. 2013a. "Fueling the Fire: Pathways from Oil to War." *International Security* 38, no. 2: 147–180.

Colgan, Jeff D. 2013b. *Petro-Aggression: When Oil Causes War*. Cambridge, UK: Cambridge University Press.

Colgan, Jeff D. 2014. "The Emperor Has No Clothes: The Limits of OPEC in the Global Oil Market." *International Organization* 68, no. 3: 599–632.

Colgan, Jeff D. 2015. "Oil, Domestic Conflict, and Opportunities for Democratization." *Journal of Peace Research* 52, no. 1: 3–16.

Colgan, Jeff D. 2017. "Oil-for-Security Deals in the Middle East." Working Paper. Providence, RI: Brown University.

Collier, Paul, and Anke Hoeffler. 2004. "Greed and Grievance in Civil War." *Oxford Economic Papers* 56, no. 4: 563–595.

Cramer, Jane K., and A. Trevor Thrall, eds. 2012. *Why Did the United States Invade Iraq?* New York: Routledge.

Crane, Keith, Andreas Goldthau, Michael Toman, Thomas Light, Stuart E. Johnson, Alireza Nader, et al. 2009. *Imported Oil and U.S. National Security*. Santa Monica, CA: RAND Corporation.

Deutch, J. M., J. R Schlesinger, and D. G Victor. 2006. *National Security Consequences of US Oil Dependency: Report of an Independent Task Force*. Washington, DC: Council on Foreign Relations Press.

Downs, Erica S. 2004. "The Chinese Energy Security Debate." *China Quarterly*, no. 177: 21–41.

Duffield, John. 2007. *Over a Barrel: The Costs of U.S. Foreign Oil Dependence*. Stanford, CA: Stanford University Press.

Fouquet, Roger. 2008. *Heat, Power and Light: Revolutions in Energy Services*. Cheltenham, UK: Edward Elgar.

Fuhrmann, Matthew. 2012. *Atomic Assistance: How "Atoms for Peace" Programs Cause Nuclear Insecurity*. Ithaca, NY: Cornell University Press.

Gause, F. Gregory, III. 2009. *The International Relations of the Persian Gulf*. Cambridge, MA: Cambridge University Press.

Gholz, Eugene, and Daryl G. Press. 2010. "Protecting 'The Prize': Oil and the U.S. National Interest." *Security Studies* 19, no. 3: 453–485.

Gholz, Eugene, and Daryl G. Press. 2013. "Enduring Resilience: How Oil Markets Handle Disruptions." *Security Studies* 22, no. 1: 139–147.

Gholz, Eugene, Umul Awan, and Ehud Ronn. 2017. "Financial and Energy Security Analysis of China's Loan-for-Oil Deals." *Energy Research & Social Science* 24: 42–50.

Giraldo, Jeanne K., and Harold A. Trinkunas. 2007. *Terrorism Financing and State Responses: A Comparative Perspective*. Stanford, CA: Stanford University Press.

Glaser, Charles L. 2013. "How Oil Influences U.S. National Security." *International Security* 38, no. 2: 112–146.

Glaser, Charles L., and Rosemary Ann Kelanic. 2016. *Crude Strategy: Rethinking the U.S. Military Commitment to Defend Persian Gulf Oil*. Washington, DC: Georgetown University Press.

Gleditsch, Kristian Skrede, Idean Salehyan, and Kenneth Schultz. 2008. "Fighting at Home, Fighting Abroad: How Civil Wars Lead to International Disputes." *Journal of Conflict Resolution* 52, no. 4: 479–506.

Gourley, Bernard, and Adam N. Stulberg. 2013. "Correlates of Nuclear Energy: Back to the Future or Back to Basics?" In *The Nuclear Renaissance and International Security*, edited by Adam N. Stulberg and Matthew Fuhrmann, 19–36. Stanford, CA: Stanford University Press.

Graaff, Naná de. 2012. "Oil Elite Networks in a Transforming Global Oil Market." *International Journal of Comparative Sociology* 53, no. 4: 275–297.

Hancock, Kathleen. 2006. "The Semi-Sovereign State: Belarus and the Russian Neo-Empire." *Foreign Policy Analysis* 6, 117–136.

Hancock, Kathleen J., and Vlado Vivoda. 2014. "International Political Economy: A Field Born of the OPEC Crisis Returns to its Energy Roots." *Energy Research & Social Science* 1: 206–216.

Hayward, J. 1995. "Hitler's Quest for Oil: The Impact of Economic Considerations on Military Strategy, 1941–42." *Journal of Strategic Studies* 18, no. 4: 94–135.

Hendrix, Cullen S. 2017. "Oil Prices and Interstate Conflict." *Conflict Management and Peace Science* 34, no. 6: 575–596.

Hughes, Llewelyn, and Austin Long. 2015. "Is There an Oil Weapon? Security Implications of Changes in the Structure of the International Oil Market." *International Security* 39, no. 3: 152–189.

Kelanic, Rosemary A. 2016. "The Petroleum Paradox: Oil, Coercive Vulnerability, and Great Power Behavior." *Security Studies* 25, no. 2: 181–213.

Kim, Inwook, and Jackson Woods. 2016. "Gas on the Fire: Great Power Alliances and Petrostate Aggression." *International Studies Perspectives* 17, no. 3: 231–249.

Klare, Michael T. 2004. *Blood and Oil: The Dangers and Consequences of America's Growing Dependency on Imported Petroleum*. New York: Metropolitan Books.

Koubi, Vally, Gabriele Spilker, Tobias Böhmelt, and Thomas Bernauer. 2014. "Do Natural Resources Matter for Interstate and Intrastate Armed Conflict?" *Journal of Peace Research* 51, no. 2: 227–243.

Kuperman, Alan J. 2013. "A Model Humanitarian Intervention? Reassessing NATO's Libya Campaign." *International Security* 38, no. 1: 105–136.

Le Billon, Philippe. 2012. *Wars of Plunder: Conflicts, Profits and the Politics of Resources*. New York: Columbia University Press.

Lee, Chia-yi. 2018. "Oil and Terrorism Uncovering the Mechanisms." *Journal of Conflict Resolution* 62, no. 5: 903–928.

Lehmann, Timothy C. 2009. "Keeping Friends Close and Enemies Closer: Classical Realist Statecraft and Economic Exchange in U.S. Interwar Strategy." *Security Studies* 18, no. 1: 115–147.

Lind, Jennifer, and Daryl G. Press. 2018. "Markets or Mercantilism? How China Secures Its Energy Supplies." *International Security* 42 no. 4: 170–204.

Lujala, Paivi. 2010. "The Spoils of Nature: Armed Civil Conflict and Rebel Access to Natural Resources." *Journal of Peace Research* 47, no. 1: 15–28.

Marcel, Valerie. 2006. *Oil Titans: National Oil Companies in the Middle East*. London and Baltimore, MD: Brookings Institution Press and Chatham House.

Markowitz, Lawrence P. 2013. State Erosion: *Unlootable Resources and Unruly Elites in Central Asia*. Ithaca, NY: Cornell University Press.

Meierding, Emily. 2016. "Dismantling the Oil Wars Myth." *Security Studies* 25, no. 2: 258–288.

Miller, Nicholas L. 2017. "Why Nuclear Energy Programs Rarely Lead to Proliferation." *International Security* 42, no. 2: 40–77.

Moran, Daniel, and James Avery Russell. 2009. *Energy Security and Global Politics: The Militarization of Resource Management*. New York: Routledge.

Nemeth, Stephen C., Sara McLaughlin Mitchell, Elizabeth A. Nyman, and Paul R. Hensel. 2014. "Ruling the Sea: Managing Maritime Conflicts through UNCLOS and Exclusive Economic Zones." *International Interactions* 40, no. 5: 711–736.

Nevers, Renée de. 2015. "Sovereignty at Sea: States and Security in the Maritime Domain." *Security Studies* 24, no. 4: 597–630.

O'Sullivan, Meghan L. 2013. "The Entanglement of Energy, Grand Strategy, and International Security." In *The Handbook of Global Energy Policy*, edited by Andreas Goldthau, 30–47. Oxford: Wiley-Blackwell.

O'Sullivan, Meghan L. 2014. *North American Energy Remakes the Geopolitical Landscape: Understanding and Advancing the Phenomenon*. Cambridge, MA: Belfer Center, Harvard University.

O'Sullivan, Meghan L. 2017. *Windfall: How the New Energy Abundance Upends Global Politics and Strengthens America's Power*. New York: Simon & Schuster.

Paine, Jack. 2016. "Rethinking the Conflict 'Resource Curse': How Oil Wealth Prevents Center-Seeking Civil Wars." *International Organization* 70, no. 4: 727–761.

Paine, Sarah C. M. 2017. *The Japanese Empire: Grand Strategy from the Meiji Restoration to the Pacific War*. Cambridge, UK: Cambridge University Press.

Painter, David S. 1986. *Oil and the American Century: The Political Economy of U.S. Foreign Oil Policy, 1941–1954*. Baltimore, MD: Johns Hopkins University Press.

Ross, Michael L. 2013. *The Oil Curse: How Petroleum Wealth Shapes the Development of Nations*. Princeton, NJ: Princeton University Press.

Ross, Michael L. 2015. "What Have We Learned about the Resource Curse?" *Annual Review of Political Science* 18: 239–259.

Ross, Michael L., and Erik Voeten. 2016. "Oil and International Cooperation." *International Studies Quarterly* 60, no. 1: 85–97.

Rovner, Joshua, and Caitlin Talmadge. 2014. "Hegemony, Force Posture, and the Provision of Public Goods: The Once and Future Role of Outside Powers in Securing Persian Gulf Oil." *Security Studies* 23, no. 3: 548–581.

Salehyan, Idean. 2009. *Rebels without Borders: Transnational Insurgencies in World Politics*. Ithaca, NY: Cornell University Press.

Scholten, Daniel, ed. 2018. *The Geopolitics of Renewables*. Switzerland, Cham: Springer.

Schultz, Kenneth A. 2010. "The Enforcement Problem in Coercive Bargaining: Interstate Conflict over Rebel Support in Civil Wars." *International Organization* 64, no. 2: 281–312.

Shaffer, Brendan. 2009. *Energy Politics*. Philadelphia: University of Pennsylvania Press.

Shifrinson, J. R. I., and M. Priebe. 2011. "A Crude Threat: The Limits of an Iranian Missile Campaign against Saudi Arabian Oil." *International Security* 36, no. 1: 167–201.

Smith, B. 2004. "Oil Wealth and Regime Survival in the Developing World, 1960–1999." *American Journal of Political Science* 48, no. 2: 232–246.

St. John, Ronald Bruce. 1987. *Qaddafi's World Design: Libyan Foreign Policy, 1969–1987*. London: Saqi Books.

Stern, Roger J. 2016. "Oil Scarcity Ideology in US Foreign Policy, 1908–97." *Security Studies* 25, no. 2: 214–257.

Stulberg, Adam N. 2015. "Out of Gas? Russia, Ukraine, Europe, and the Changing Geopolitics of Natural Gas." *Problems of Post-Communism* 62, no. 2: 112–130.

Talmadge, Caitlin. 2008. "Closing Time: Assessing the Iranian Threat to the Strait of Hormuz." *International Security* 33, no. 1: 82–117.

Thurber, Mark C., and Richard K. Morse. 2015. "The Asia-Centric Coal Era." In *The Global Coal Market: Supplying the Major Fuel for Emerging Economies*, edited by Mark C. Thurber and Richard K. Morse, 3–34. Cambridge, UK: Cambridge University Press.

Tooze, Adam. 2007. *Wages of Destruction: The Making and Breaking of the Nazi Economy*. New York: Penguin Books.

Van de Graaf, Thijs, and Jeff D. Colgan. 2017. "Russian Gas Games or Well-Oiled Conflict? Energy Security and the 2014 Ukraine Crisis." *Energy Research and Social Science* 24: 59–64.

Venn, Fiona M. 1986. *Oil Diplomacy in the Twentieth Century*. London: Palgrave Macmillan.

Victor, David G. 2007. "What Resource Wars?" *The National Interest*, no. 92: 48–55.

Vitalis, Robert. 2006. *America's Kingdom: Mythmaking on the Saudi Oil Frontier*. Stanford, CA: Stanford University Press.

Wenar, Leif. 2016. *Blood Oil: Tyrants, Violence, and the Rules That Run the World*. Oxford: Oxford University Press.

Winegard, Timothy C. 2016. *The First Oil War*. Toronto: Toronto University Press.

Yergin, Daniel. 1991. *The Prize: The Epic Quest for Oil, Money & Power*. New York: Simon & Schuster.

Yetiv, Steven A. 2004. *Crude Awakenings: Global Oil Security and American Foreign Policy*. Ithaca, NY: Cornell University Press.

Yetiv, Steven A. 2011. *The Petroleum Triangle: Oil, Globalization, and Terror*. Ithaca, NY: Cornell University Press.

CHAPTER 14

....

ENERGY AS AN
INSTRUMENT IN
GLOBAL POLITICS

....

LIOR HERMAN

On August 2, 1990, the Iraqi army invaded Kuwait and in a swift victory consolidated control over the country within days. The invasion was the culmination of long-standing disputes between the two countries, Iraq claiming that Kuwait constituted part of its Basra province, as had been the case under Ottoman rule. Oil-related issues fueled these disputes; Iraq argued that Kuwait's overproduction of oil, beyond its OPEC commitments, had reduced oil prices, causing economic losses. Iraq further accused Kuwait of drilling across the border into Iraq's Rumaila oil field. The invasion of Kuwait and the threat of a potential Iraqi invasion of oil-rich Saudi Arabia resulted in the First Gulf War between Iraq and an international coalition headed by the United States.

Following the invasion of Kuwait, the United Nations (UN) Security Council imposed comprehensive economic sanctions on Iraq, primarily involving an embargo on the Iraqi oil trade, the country's main source of income. Despite the devastating consequences of the sanctions, they proved ineffective in changing the policies of the Iraqi president, Saddam Hussein. In a related and striking event, Jordan refused to join the international coalition against Iraq. This silent support of Iraq is noteworthy considering the wide coalition membership (thirty-five countries), which included even nations with strong anti-American sentiments. At the time, Jordan was the most pro–United States Arab state and enjoyed significant aid from several countries threatened by Iraq, as well as incoming remittances from Jordanian workers employed in those countries. Nevertheless, at the outset of the war Jordan was heavily dependent on Iraqi oil, with approximately 80 percent of its oil imports originating from that country. Iraq rewarded Jordan's support and provision of transportation routes and trade with preferential prices for oil purchases.

Oil played a prominent role in both triggering the First Gulf War and influencing its course, in addition to constituting an important foreign policy instrument, both as a carrot and a stick (respectively, positive and negative instruments to advance a given foreign policy objective, either encouraging and rewarding or coercing and punishing). Multilateral energy sanctions were the key policy instrument of choice in the conflict, despite their cost and ineffectiveness. Simultaneously, Iraq's energy carrots—preferential oil prices—were instrumental in garnering Jordan's support in the face of considerable international pressure to join the coalition against Iraq. Indeed, Iraq's energy inducements, in contrast to the failure of the financial aid provided by Gulf countries, suggest that energy foreign policy instruments possess certain attributes that distinguish them from other foreign policy tools of coercion and inducement.

Energy is intertwined with global politics because the energy system critically interacts and interrelates with virtually all other human technological systems. There is perhaps no other area that affects our security, economic, and social well-being, and the environment, as much as energy. Available, affordable, and reliable energy is a necessary condition for economic and human progress. Energy shapes the development trajectories of states, making it an important goal and means of national strategies and politics.

National agendas place energy at the top because supply and demand needs create interdependencies (for in-depth analysis of energy interdependencies, see Wilson in this volume). These needs stem from the uneven distribution of energy resources across the world, endowing some countries with more resources than others. Under these conditions, and in a world without a global authority, countries seek to meet their energy needs using a range of strategies, among them aggression and coercion, trade and cooperation, and unilateralism and self-reliance. Conflicts over energy resources and their transportation routes; cross-border energy trade; joint energy infrastructure; development of regional and international cooperation; and governance for trade, finance, investment, and standards are all part of global energy politics.

Energy interdependence pushes energy-poor countries to trade with energy-rich countries, with many of the latter relying on energy revenues. Some energy-rich countries are themselves also significant energy importers (e.g., China), while in certain cases export revenues are less crucial (e.g., Australia). Nevertheless, even the least dependent countries are affected by price and market conditions that have ramifications for the relative costs of energy, in addition to related finance, investment, transportation, and infrastructure decisions. Transit nations, which provide a water or land bridge for energy trade between nonadjacent countries, similarly benefit from trade revenues. Indeed, some academics, politicians, and commentators argue that the transition to renewable energy will facilitate energy self-reliance and independence (Johansson 2013; Harrington 2017). However, renewable energy is not a panacea for global energy politics challenges and is not likely to become so in the foreseeable future. Considerable reliance on fossil energy resources will continue, and at the same time, the potential to harness renewable energies varies between countries, given disparities in access to water (hydroelectric energy), solar radiation (solar energy), and wind conditions (wind energy). Thus, energy is a distinct element of global politics, a significant goal and means that countries pursue in the global arena and that involves a multitude of other state and nonstate actors.

Within the framework of this volume, this chapter focuses on analyzing how scholars conceptualize the link between energy and global politics, particularly how state and nonstate actors employ energy means to advance their foreign policy goals. While this chapter emphasizes the use of energy as a means and a target in global politics, other chapters engage with closely related subjects, such as energy interdependence (Wilson), energy regionalism (Hancock, Palestini, and Szulecki), energy security (Jewel and Brutschin), and international conflict (Colgan and Stockbruegger).

This chapter begins with a broad discussion of how scholarly literature perceives energy and global politics. It then discusses energy carrots and sticks, state goals, and the range of actors involved in using energy as carrots and sticks. Subsequently, it examines issues of design and effectiveness, followed by an analysis of how resource differences, supply chains, and market structure influence the foreign policy toolbox. The final section suggests a future research agenda.

GLOBAL ENERGY POLITICS

Surprisingly, the extensive extant literature relating directly and indirectly to energy and global politics has yielded little theorization of the field. Much of the literature is descriptive and prescriptive and focuses too much on oil and gas, neglecting other fossil and non-fossil resources and electricity. Indeed, one may argue that there is no need for specific theorization of particular commodities or resources in global politics. Yet energy is exceptional in terms of its strategic relationships with politics, security, and economics; possesses unique sociotechnical features; and affects nations' fortunes. In recent years scholars have increasingly recognized this lacuna (Hancock and Vivoda 2014; Keohane 2009; Shaffer 2009; Sovacool 2014; Van de Graaf et al. 2016).

Nevertheless, international relations paradigms, particularly the basic assumptions underlying realism and liberalism, have oriented much of the scholarly debate concerning how scholars understand the link between energy and global politics. A key question influencing the debate is whether energy predominantly follows an economic or a security rationale. This implicit division between realism and liberalism has also been framed as an "energy diplomacy vs. energy governance" debate (respectively).[1]

While realist assumptions are somewhat simplistic and often fail to accurately portray the importance of nonstate actors and the degree to which cooperation occurs, they nevertheless constitute the most dominant perception and conceptualization of global energy politics. Realism, sometimes also termed *statism* or *mercantilism*, is a well-entrenched worldview according to which global politics is characterized by anarchy due to the absence of an authority above states. States are the primary and most important actors, and while their domestic politics may differ, they tend to behave similarly in world politics. In such a situation of anarchy, all states are concerned for their security and even survival; therefore, they attempt to increase their power. Given the uncertainty and distrust prevailing in the international system, states are reluctant to cooperate with each other. When they do so, such cooperation is temporary and does not involve relinquishing sovereignty. Cooperation is viewed with suspicion, and states judge gains as relative and zero-sum (Donnelly 2000).

The realist approach to global energy politics is sometimes referred to as "energy diplomacy" (Goldthau 2010; Herranz-Surrallés 2016). Scholars working explicitly and implicitly within the realist school of energy politics regard energy as a strategic asset, crucial for state power and security (Andersen, Goldthau, and Sitter 2016; O'Sullivan 2017). They conceptualize energy in both defensive and offensive terms.[2] The defensive view, which is mostly applied to energy-importing countries, regards access to energy as a national priority and thus a vulnerability (Kelanic 2016). Dependence on energy imports exposes the state to the threat of shortages and price hikes; it therefore undermines national security. Import vulnerability affects three key state structures. First, the military is highly dependent on energy, particularly in effective day-to-day operations, fighting over long periods of time, and fulfilling long-range missions (Kreft 2006). Second, affordable and available energy is vital for any state's production structure; a lack thereof or price increase can significantly affect productivity, competitiveness, and employment. Third, affordable energy is required to maintain social peace, since high energy prices, particularly for electricity and transport, are a source of social unrest (Kelanic 2016). The offensive view, which scholars often employ with regard to energy-exporting or energy-affluent countries, considers other countries' energy vulnerabilities an opportunity to increase state power and security. This perception resonates with Hirschman's famous theory of foreign trade as an instrument of national power policy. Because foreign trade generates dependence relations, exporting countries can coerce their importing partners by interrupting trade or reward importers with trade advantages that make it difficult for them not to comply (Hirschman 1945). The 1973 oil shock reinforced the realist view of global energy politics. The Organization of the Petroleum Exporting Countries (OPEC) members' decision to impose an oil boycott, in an effort to influence Western attitudes toward the Arab-Israeli conflict, resulted in a global energy crisis, exposing the vulnerabilities of energy-importing countries (Engdahl 2004; Van de Graaf 2013a). In the aftermath of the oil shock, the US government created the Department of Energy, and for the first time scholars devoted serious attention to the strategic and security roles of energy and their use in foreign policy (Nance and Boettcher 2017).

O'Sullivan (2013) employs this logic to theorize about the relationship between energy and foreign policy, using a grand strategy argument. She discusses the interplay between energy and security from several angles. First, when energy constitutes an objective of a state's grand strategy, the government can meet this goal through a range of political, economic, military, and diplomatic means, including deliberate use of force, punitive actions, or conflicts that are indirect byproducts of the competition for energy resources. Second, energy can function as a key instrument in achieving national security strategies and other security objectives, a political weapon, and a tool for cementing alliances (O'Sullivan 2013). Recent changes in the US energy market have led scholars to believe that unconventional oil and gas[3] will mark a new chapter in global energy politics. Some argue that the United States can now pursue energy diplomacy in ways that were not possible before and that undermine the ability of competing powers (e.g., Russia) to successfully apply energy diplomacy against allies of the United States (Blackwill and O'Sullivan 2014; Blackwill and Harris 2016; Miller 2017). Nevertheless, many have noted that the effectiveness of such policies is rather dubious. Countries, including the United States, have experienced limited success in employing such tactics, in particular because global market realities are beyond any state's control and because energy is one of many national objectives and means (Boersma and Johnson 2018; Goldthau 2010).

Energy mercantilism drives states to adopt strategies for reducing energy dependence through self-sufficiency and diversification of resources and suppliers (or clients, in the case of exporters). The transition to renewable energy is often portrayed as a means to realize such strategies (Sivaram and Saha 2018). Energy mercantilism discerns little room for international interactions based on market relations. Indeed, states maintain national control over energy resources, related infrastructure, and ownership of energy firms, and at the same time attempt to gain influence in the energy sectors of other countries, as many argue with regard to Russia and China (Karasac 2002).

In particular, some scholars argue that oil scarcity is driving new and inevitable resource wars (Klare 2002, 2014). They attribute resource conflicts to the growing demands of mercantilist countries like China (Kaplan 2011); peak oil production fears (Friedrichs 2010); and the fact that large oil and gas resources are located in areas under the control of authoritarian, fragile, revisionist, and extreme regimes that are more prone to conflicts (e.g., in Central Asia, Africa, and the Middle East) (Colgan 2010; Klare 2002). Scholars have recently emphasized the race to obtain the rare materials necessary for certain renewable energies as a potential source of new conflicts (Criekemans 2018).

The liberal approach moves away from realism's state-centric worldview. It depicts a complex world wherein markets, consumers, firms, international institutions, and nongovernmental organizations (NGOs) are significant players, in addition to states. Domestic politics matter and influence international relations, either by affecting governments' foreign policies or due to the involvement of nongovernmental players. Conflict, according to liberalism, is not inevitable, and international cooperation is both feasible and desirable. In addition, it is driven by actors striving to maximize absolute gains (Baylis, Smith, and Owens 2017).

Scholars analyzing global energy politics through the lens of liberalism do not downplay the importance of energy for states and nonstate actors. These scholars, who sometimes frame their approach as "energy governance" (Chaban and Knodt 2015; Herranz-Surrallés 2016), reject the notion that energy has unique characteristics, which makes it exceptional from a strategic point of view. Thus, emphasizing energy dependence, they highlight interdependence and the mutual gains actors can obtain from energy trade and cooperation. Whereas energy realism harnesses economics for political and security objectives, energy liberalism concerns the separation of these spheres. Markets, not politics, are appropriate arenas for energy relations. Contrary to mercantilist notions, private ownership and liberalization of domestic energy markets can yield greater energy security than that attained through state intervention (Goldthau and Witte 2009). Moreover, energy resource scarcity is not regarded as a determinist state of affairs; markets and profit-maximizing actors continuously seek new resource reserves and technologies to avoid the dismal predictions of peak oil/gas (Dannreuther and Ostrowski 2013).

Those scholars who apply an energy liberalism perspective see greater opportunities for international cooperation. States cooperate with one another, and with nonstate actors, in international organizations, regional forums, and other platforms. These international governance structures yield long-term benefits, reduce uncertainties, and provide common solutions by developing common norms, rules, standards, arbitration mechanisms, and forums for dialogue and problem-solving. Scholars emphasize that international institutions, such as the World Trade Organization, the Organisation for Economic Co-operation and Development export credit arrangement, and the International Energy Agency (IEA), can reduce mercantilist and realist tendencies (Evans and Downs 2006; Selivanova 2010), albeit noting that regional cooperation has been more successful (Selivanova 2010). In that regard, the European Union is an exceptional case in terms of its extensive energy governance (Andersen, Goldthau, and Sitter, 2016). Finally, some explain global energy politics in light of the interplay between domestic and international politics. Hence, differences between regimes elucidate variations in state behavior, as exemplified by the greater propensity for conflict and coercive behavior among rentier and authoritarian energy-rich countries in comparison to democratic states. This issue, and additional market explanations, are discussed further later in the chapter (Ross 2015).

ENERGY CARROTS AND STICKS

As noted in the preceding discussion, actors use a variety of instruments to advance their foreign policy goals. We can categorize and analyze energy foreign policy instruments as carrots and sticks (Newnham 2011; Shaffer 2013). While this fails to capture the full breadth of foreign policy tools (e.g., energy diplomatic negotiations), it is useful in creating a taxonomy that includes the majority of instruments that states employ. The following section on actors widens the discussion, also including nonstate actors.

Energy sticks are energy-related measures that deprive the targeted actor of something (resources, recognition, membership status, etc.) it previously possessed, in the expectation of compliance with a specific demand (or demands) (Wallensteen and Staibano 2005). Scholars typically refer to two different kinds of sticks (or sanctions): economic or noneconomic. Noneconomic energy sticks include measures such as the obstruction and blockade of maritime routes, such as Egypt's closure of the Straits of Tiran and the Suez Canal in 1957, which restricted the access of oil tankers to Israel and Europe (Painter 2012), or the United Kingdom's 1965 oil maritime blockade of Southern Rhodesia (Mobley 2002), supported by the UN Security Council. These examples illustrate that energy plays an instrumental role as a tool (Fischhendler, Herman, and Maoz 2017; Hufbauer et al. 2007; Van de Graaf 2013a), a target (Singer 2008), or an enabling factor providing resource rents that motivates aggressive policies (Colgan 2013).

Most energy sticks are economic in nature (Hufbauer et al. 2007), focused on energy aspects of the target country's economic relations with the sender country or other states. The wide range of economic energy sanctions includes (among others) export and import restrictions, freezing of financial assets and revenue, and withdrawal of preferential pricing and energy and economic aid. Among the abundant examples are Russian gas supply cutoffs to the Ukraine in 2009 and oil and gas disruptions to Belarus, as well as retraction of energy subsidies during several disputes in the last decade and half (Jirušek and Kuchyňková 2018).

In opposition, energy carrots are energy-related measures that offer or deliver valuables to the targeted actor in anticipation of behavioral change or as a reward for certain behavior (Wallensteen 2005). Carrots are often referred to as positive sanctions; a sender country extends them to a target state in exchange for the latter's compliance and cooperation (Davis 2002; Solingen 2012). They typically add something (e.g., a resource, membership), as opposed to sticks, which deprive the target country of something. Carrots are widely utilized in foreign policy and include a range of gestures and differential favorable policies, among them debt relief, foreign aid, concessions, and technology transfer, using a variety of tools such as supply continuity and preferential pricing. Indeed, supply continuity, amid changing domestic market and political circumstances that exert pressure for supply disruption, is intended to strengthen relations with the target country (Shaffer, 2013). Similarly, the supply of energy below current or potential market prices is a preferential subsidy extended to secure long-term relations between the sender and target states (Bruce 2005; Goldthau 2008). Few scholars have explored energy carrots, and thus this body of literature remains underdeveloped.

The categorization of carrots and sticks in foreign policy does not assume that energy foreign policy measures intrinsically possess a coercive or rewarding value. Rather, the contrary is true: the practice of energy foreign policy measures as carrots and sticks depends on senders' objectives, how target countries interpret the signals, and the context in which these measures are embedded, as in the preceding examples of preferential energy prices. Russia has used its subsidized supply of gas and oil to neighboring nations such as Moldova, Ukraine, and Belarus both to induce and coerce, depending on the circumstances (Newnham 2011). Hence, not only can similar energy tools be employed as both carrots and sticks, but these tools are likewise interrelated: the deprivation or removal of a carrot is a stick, while the removal of an existing stick constitutes an act of inducement.

Goals

Countries employ energy carrots and sticks for many different purposes. These can be grouped into several categories: changing the target state's political behavior; influencing or changing its political regime; undermining or strengthening the sender's military capacity and economic well-being; affecting territorial, armed, and other disputes and conflicts; and serving various energy goals.

While few publications discuss energy carrots, numerous articles and books analyze specific cases of energy sanctions (e.g., Kropatcheva 2011; Licklider 1998; Newnham 2011, 2015; Van de Graaf 2013a). This focus on case studies results in several caveats. First, most of the literature tends to be descriptive, largely failing to explain the selection of specific goals and methods. Explanations concentrate rather on targets' responses and interactions (e.g., Licklider, 1988; Veebel and Markus 2015). Second, and no less significantly, whereas many case studies provide rich and detailed analysis, they concentrate on a particular event, a specific sender country, or a certain target state (Newnham 2011). Thus, future research can benefit from longitudinal and quantitative accounts explaining how the goals and measures of energy sticks (and carrots) evolve over time, across countries, regions, and political regimes. Indeed, several studies providing quantitative analysis of economic sanctions over an extended period also discuss energy sanctions. Yet these studies do not specifically code energy sanctions or address energy carrots; therefore they contribute little to theory-building (Hufbauer et al. 2007; Morgan, Bapat, and Kobayashi 2014).

Statistical methods face significant challenges for two main reasons. First, despite the large number of sanctions cases, most states do not officially declare them, resulting in a limited number of available cases for study. Second, scholars cannot easily code success and failure. For example, energy sanctions are often imposed as part of a wider sanction regime, which also includes nonenergy sanctions. In these cases it is difficult to isolate the "energy" effect of the sanction and distinguish it as success or failure. Energy sanctions are also multidimensional and change across time, raising a further obstacle in terms of coding a changing measure. An exception is Fischhendler, Herman, and Maoz's study (2017), which expands on the data set presented by Hufbauer et al. (2007), specifically addressing energy sanctions. This study distinguishes among divergent goals of energy sanctions, determining that sender states use sticks mainly to alter and influence the political behavior of target states (38 percent of cases) and promote regime change (30 percent). The study also discerns differences between key sender countries and the purposes for which they use energy sticks. Thus, for example, while the US government employs energy sticks to advance a variety of goals, Russia has a narrower set of goals, focusing mainly on influencing regional territorial disputes. (See Balmaceda and Heinrich this volume for more information on Russia's energy politics.) Cases of multilateral sanctions by international institutions (e.g., the UN) are more limited; these are implemented on extreme occasions, such as attempts to alter political regimes (Fischhendler, Herman, and Maoz 2017). Nevertheless, although the data set encompasses energy sanctions from 1938 to 2017, its coverage of countries and cases is limited.

Design and Effectiveness

Scholars disagree on the effectiveness of energy sanctions and rewards. Some argue that energy sanctions can be effective, as in the case of those imposed by the United States and Britain against Iran following the latter's 1951 nationalization of the Anglo-Iranian

Oil Company and its subsequent repeal in 1954 (Hufbauer et al. 2007). However, others are more skeptical, pointing to numerous cases in which sanctions have failed and to the existence of an expectations-capabilities gap between ambitious goals and the capacity to affect or change the target state's policy (e.g., Baldwin and Pape 1998; Hufbauer et al. 2007; Hughes and Long 2015; Pape 1997; Van de Graaf and Colgan 2017). One explanation for the continued use of carrots and sticks, despite their disputed efficacy, is that policy makers in sender countries are concerned by audience costs; thus, they use carrots and sticks to avoid domestic accusations of ineptitude and indifference (Martin 2011).

A key issue concerning effectiveness and the costs of using sticks is whether they are comprehensive or targeted (also known as "smart"). Comprehensive sanctions are universal measures that do not differentiate between those affected by them, as opposed to targeted sanctions, which are more selective with regard to subjects and means (Drezner 2011; Gharibnavaz and Waschik 2018). Comprehensive energy sticks include supply cutoffs and boycotts. Examples of targeted measures are the freezing of assets and revenues and restricting the movement of individuals and energy technology flow, such as in the sanctions imposed on Russia following its invasion of Crimea. The general literature on carrots has not yet addressed questions of comprehensiveness and smartness satisfactorily. Nevertheless, a recent contribution finds that carrots can be both smart and targeted; furthermore, targeted energy carrots encompass measures such as tariff reductions, debt relief, and preferential pricing to specific population segments and market actors (Herman and Fischhendler n.d.).

The use of energy carrots and sticks incurs a cost for both sender and target countries, in addition to other parties, such as transit nations, energy companies, and transport providers. Energy sanctions imposed by exporters entail loss of income, while importers' use of energy sticks threaten supply. These costs increase in the absence of alternative energy trade partners. States that employ energy sticks must likewise consider the potential loss of infrastructure investments, which in certain energy markets are particularly large, for example, in the natural gas trade (Shaffer 2013). Costs likewise extend to enforcement, such as payments and rewards to third parties vital in effectively implementing sanction regimes (Goldthau and Witte 2009; Kelanic 2012). Energy carrot costs generally involve a loss of income (e.g., for preferential pricing and aid), competitiveness (e.g., transfer of technology), and domestic supply (e.g., continuous supply to a target country despite domestic shortage in the sender state, as in the case of electricity grid interconnections) (Fischhendler, Herman, and Anderman 2016). A recent case in point is China's continuous losses over its loan-for-oil deals, which scholars explain as a foreign aid medium to gain political influence in recipient countries (Gholz, Awan, and Ronn 2017).

The target country's political regime type constitutes a variable that affects the successful use of carrots and sticks. Targeted sanctions are likely to be more successful in autocratic regimes, which rely on small groups. However, reliance on popular support increases the susceptibility of democracies to comprehensive sanctions (Blanchard and Ripsman 1999; Brooks 2002). While some argue that the effect of carrots is neutral to regime type, others claim that carrots are more effective when given to democracies or as part of an international regime (Drezner 1999).

Carrots are used to encourage coalitions in a target country that supports the sender nation's policy aims. Yet targeted carrots can also construct preferences and interests, creating new support and coalitions that did not previously exist (Abdelal and Kirshner 1999). Similarly, carrots are more effective when domestic coalitions or leadership in the target state have an interest in international markets or are acutely dependent on energy (Licht 2010). In this sense, carrots and sticks operate differently. Carrots can develop pro-sender constituencies, while sticks create backlash, particularly when comprehensive, and tend to have an adverse effect on domestic opposition in the target country, strengthening its regime internally (Newnham 2000). Effectiveness is also a matter of longevity. Evidence indicates that whereas sticks endure over the long term, carrots are ephemeral in terms of changing a target country's behavior (Cortright 1997; Crumm 1995; Nincic 2010).

Actors

In accordance with the realist orientation apparent in much of the literature, scholars of international relations attribute significance to states as the key and relevant actors in global energy politics. This conviction, however, misses the increasing importance of many nonstate actors and has been criticized by the emerging scholarship on the international political economy of energy (Hancock and Vivoda 2014; Van de Graaf 2013b). Thus, government-owned companies, multilateral banks, private energy firms, investors and financiers, civil society groups, and organizations all play a role in shaping and influencing global energy politics. This section initially expands on the role of three categories of states, subsequently discussing several nonstate actors.

Exporting, Importing, and Transit States

In 1973, believing that oil could help the countries that produce it to achieve their political aims, several Arab states imposed an oil embargo on the United States and the Netherlands. Their aim was to alter Western states' behavior toward Israel. Contrary to common belief, this was not an OPEC embargo—not all Arab OPEC countries participated in it (e.g., Iraq and Oman)—and similarly, not all OPEC members were Arab states. Its consequences made the 1973 oil shock exceptional. Previous attempts by Arab oil-producing nations to impose embargos in 1956 and 1967 had proven unsuccessful. Whereas in past attempts prices had mildly increased and then immediately dropped, the 1973 embargo resulted in a price hike of more than 400 percent, continuing long after the end of the crisis and causing inflation, recession, and decline in economic growth, together with rising unemployment all around the world, particularly in Europe, the United States, and Japan. Concurrently, sender countries enjoyed rising incomes, their economic and social circumstances improved, and their political prestige increased (Colgan 2014).

In retrospect, we cannot attribute the consequences of the oil shock solely to a mere 5 percent production decrease that effectively lasted for only a few months. Other factors were at play, among them the reduced production capacity of the United States, the timing of the crisis (which coincided with the beginning of the winter), and the shortage of oil tankers. Nevertheless, the oil embargo and its apparent causes cemented an enduring perception of oil as a weapon—a coercive foreign policy tool—in the hands of oil-exporting countries (Hughes and Long 2015; Hughes and Gholz 2016; Licklider 1988, 1998; Van de Graaf 2013a). Exporters' petro-sticks and carrots are thus considered key foreign policy tools. In relations with its neighbors, Russia accords petro-carrots through energy subsidies to countries such as Armenia, Belarus, and Ukraine (under Kuchma's presidency), while coercing others—Ukraine (under Yushchenko's presidency), Georgia, and Moldova—by increasing prices and disrupting supply (Newnham 2011, 2015).

Energy interdependence is a double-edged sword. Importers can also utilize energy trade to influence exporting countries. While energy importers' use of energy sticks is not a new phenomenon (Bohi and Russell 1978; Van de Graaf 2013a), there is growing recognition of the monopsony power among energy-consuming states (Hughes and Gholz 2016), although its effectiveness is contested. The IEA was created in response to the 1973 oil shock in order to increase the bargaining power of importing countries. In so doing, importers attempted (and largely failed over time) to soften the potential edge of the oil weapon, instituting an importers' regime to deter coercion by exporters through coordination, creation of stockpiles, and information sharing (Hughes and Lipscy 2013; Keohane 1984). During the Cold War, the United States used its consumer power to restrain and limit its own imports from the Soviet Union (Bohi and Russell 1978), later imposing unilateral sanctions against countries such as Iran and Libya and also attempting to deter third states from investing in these nations' energy sectors (Nincic 2010). A more recent example, which has attracted considerable scholarly and policy interest, occurred in 2012, when the United States and European Union imposed sanctions on Iran, including an embargo on purchasing Iranian oil and other measures against Iran's energy sector (Gharibnavaz and Waschik 2018; Van de Graaf 2013a). Nevertheless, the rise of new, large energy consumers in the developing world, for example India and China, may erode the ability of the United States, European Union, and their allies to use their monopsony powers against exporters (Hughes and Gholz 2016; Overland and Kubayeva 2018).

Transit countries constitute an important link between energy exporters and importers, particularly in the natural gas trade. They enable the flow of oil and gas between nonadjacent states via pipelines, critical maritime routes (e.g., the Suez Canal and Straits of Malacca), or liquefied natural gas (LNG) liquidation and regasification terminals, as well as providing storage facilities in their territories. The literature on transit countries and their usage of energy as a foreign policy instrument is rather limited and descriptive, and engages with typologies (e.g., Bilgin 2009; Lee 2017; Pirani, Stern, and Yafimava 2009; Stern 2006; Yafimava 2010). The ability of transit countries to use transit monopoly power varies widely. Some act as hubs or pivots, connecting exporters and importers of oil and gas, whereas others import gas themselves, limiting their ability to use energy as a foreign policy tool (Bilgin 2010). Similarly, a nation that functions simultaneously as an energy exporter and transit country enjoys limited ability to use energy in influencing foreign policy (Liesen 1999). The use of transit capacity, particularly the pipeline weapon, has a particular coercive appeal for the transit country. By restricting the flow of energy through its pipelines, a state can exert pressure on the exporting and importing countries, inflicting long-term damage on the exporting country's reputation (and that of the transit country) (Gnedina and Emerson 2009; Guillet 2007). The use of carrots and sticks always involves externalities toward other actors, but in the case of transit countries' sanctions against exporters, the collateral damage also directly affects importers. This is perhaps why transit nations attempt to hide or deny using sanctions against exporters. Denial, such as in several Ukrainian-Russian disputes, may create the impression that the transit country is not involved while concurrently generating an unintentional conflict between the exporting and importing states (Bouwmeester and Oosterhaven 2017; Lee 2017; Westphal 2009). However, this also illustrates that exporters can sanction importers, using transit countries as scapegoats (Yafimava 2010).

Nonstate Actors: National and Private Energy Firms and Civil Society

There is growing scholarly interest in the role of energy firms, both nationally owned and private. In this regard, the literature devoted to the Seven Sisters is exceptional and reflects the significant influence they wielded in the oil sector. The Seven Sisters were seven oil multinationals that dominated the international oil industry, particularly Middle Eastern oil, from the 1940s until the mid-1970s.[4] At the time, these companies controlled some 85 percent of the world's known oil reserves, exerting considerable political influence, particularly in the developing world. The Seven Sisters were able to affect foreign and domestic policies due to their control of the market, vertical integration of the supply chain, and cartel organization. However, the power of these multinationals considerably declined following the nationalization of oil industries by Middle Eastern nations, the rise of OPEC, and other market changes, for example the increased use of natural gas and the emergence of state-owned oil and gas companies (Blair 1976; Marcel 2006; Painter 2012; Pratt 2012; Sampson 1975; Yergin 1996).

Energy market transformations in recent years, such as low oil prices, growth of the unconventional oil and gas industries, and greater capital constraints on firms' ability to borrow, have further altered the relations between private firms, particularly multinational/international oil companies (IOCs), and governments (Waterworth and Bradshaw 2018). Nowadays many of the firms in OECD countries have been privatized. Presently, four of the original Seven Sisters produce less than 10 percent of the world's oil and gas and hold 3 percent of the reserves, while according to estimates, some 90 percent of the global oil and gas reserves are located in countries wherein national oil companies (NOCs) operate (World Energy Council 2016). Under these conditions, national influence on IOCs has declined (Hughes 2014a).

At the same time, government-owned energy companies, such as NOCs, national gas companies, and utilities, either wholly or partially owned by governments, have assumed a crucial role in energy markets, especially in developing countries. Western sanctions imposed by the European Union, United States, and several other countries on Russia following its 2014 annexation of Crimea specifically targeted Russian government-owned companies like Gazprom, Gazprom Neft, and Rosneft (Overland and Kubayeva 2018). A recent study suggests that although they did not *cause* a shift eastward, the 2014 sanctions *accelerated* Russian energy companies' move toward the Chinese market. This eastward shift partially compensated the multinationals for the market loss resulting from the sanctions (Abramova and Garanina 2017). While government-owned companies report to their governments, scholars note that this relationship is not unidimensional and that firms may also direct governments' actions (Goldthau 2010). Indeed, some NOCs are important economic actors in the international arena, such as China's NOCs, which have increasingly expanded overseas in recent years: searching for oil, buying shares in production fields and companies, and building energy infrastructure and transportation and processing facilities (Hughes and Kreyling 2010; Gholz, Awan, and Ronn 2017; Taylor 2006; Xu 2007). The evidence so far remains inconclusive. For example, according to recent research regarding Russian energy companies, they have been instrumentalized by the Russian government to deliver various foreign policy goals, including defense mechanisms to counter potential energy sanctions against Russia (Jirušek and Kuchyňková 2018). More nuanced results were detected in Israeli-Palestinian energy relations, wherein market and political tensions shape how the Israeli electricity utility company acts as a foreign policy tool and at the same time pushes the government to employ various carrots and sticks to advance corporate interests (Herman and Fischhendler n.d.).

Little is known about how civil society influences global energy politics (Cauchon, this volume). A plausible reason for the lack of scientific knowledge is that security and economic interests dominate the energy and foreign policy realms, leaving little scope or interest for civil society actors. However, such an assumption disregards the fact that civil society has been active in other areas of foreign policy involving nonenergy issues, such as trade and investment boycotts, and foreign aid. In a rare contribution on civil society and global energy politics, Sparks (2017) examines the anti-apartheid oil boycott. He argues that the Shipping Research Bureau (SRB), a Dutch civil society organization, was highly instrumental in enforcing international sanctions against South Africa. Staffed by no more than two to four members throughout the organization's existence, the SRB created a global network of informants and ship-spotters, including port agents, sailors, dock workers, "deep throats" in shipping companies, journalists, and other anti-apartheid minded citizens involved in maritime affairs (Sparks 2017). Initiatives such as TankerTrackers.com on Twitter are recent examples demonstrating the potential power of civil society to monitor and provide transparency and evidence, which can enhance or undermine the use of energy foreign policy tools.[5] Using the powers of the Internet and satellite footage, drawing on informants around the world (similarly to the SRB), and followed by thousands, TankerTrackers.com exposes international energy traffic; uncovers attacks on infrastructure (e.g., in Iran and Libya during December 2017); provides information; and exposes violations of energy sanctions, such as Chinese oil shipments to North Korea (e.g., February 14 and 15, 2018).

MARKETS AND RESOURCE TYPES

The energy foreign policy literature has evolved in tandem with the changes underway in the structure of global supply. Hence, emphasizing the oil weapon and realist politics was more common when oil markets were concentrated. As oil markets liberalized and the use of natural gas increased, scholarly attention shifted accordingly. Another shift in the literature is now underway as unconventional oil and gas, LNG, renewable energy, and cross-border electricity trade are becoming more important and changing the nature of energy markets. While scholars' views regarding the use of different types of energies in global politics have indeed changed, the conceptual foundations of scholarship have largely remained intact, leading to conceptual contradiction. Thus, scholars continue to perceive energy as a commodity that in principle differs from other goods and services due to its strategic essence, yet they acknowledge that the increased integration of most energy markets reduces the potential to manipulate energy for political ends (Hughes and Gholz 2016).

Energy markets are influenced by technological changes affecting the structure of both demand and supply, for instance, higher demand for natural gas due to LNG technologies or increased supply of oil and natural gas due to hydraulic fracturing. Other key factors influencing energy markets are price fluctuations, resource discoveries, organization of supply chains, and environmental concerns (Yergin 1996). Paradoxically, the weakening of the oil weapon can be partially interpreted as an endogenous effect of using sanctions; following the 1973 oil shock and the nationalization of Middle East energy markets, governments implemented diversification and efficiency measures (Moran 2009), which eventually weakened exporters' future ability to use oil sanctions.[6]

Oil

The transformation of oil into a globally traded commodity significantly reduced the potential to employ oil sanctions, carrots, and other means. In recent years the multiplication of suppliers and the introduction of shale oil furthered this trend (Goldthau and Witte 2009). Resource diversification and substitution in the production of electricity have reduced relative demand for oil, although oil remains a key resource for transportation. Despite the slow infiltration of new technologies, considering the required switching costs for private consumers, combined with the necessary infrastructure changes and expected detrimental effects on performance, it is unlikely that oil will be replaced in the transportation and distribution sectors within the next five to ten years (Hughes and Gholz 2016).

Natural Gas

Natural gas markets are also evolving; while natural gas remains largely confined to regional trade through pipelines, the trade in LNG is increasing. As LNG prices decline and demand for it rises in countries such as Japan, China, and South Korea, the possibility of using natural gas as a coercive or rewarding foreign policy tool is likely to decline. This is furthered by the construction of national and regional LNG hubs, development of LNG spot markets, and the European shift from point-to-point pipelines to gas networks (Stulberg 2017). These developments erode pipeline exporters' capacity to wield monopoly powers and force consumers to enter into long-term contracts. In general, greater liquidity in LNG markets reconstructs them in ways that are likely to resemble the oil market. Prices are likely to move from regional to global, making it easier to substitute one supplier for another and thus limiting the power of natural gas as a foreign policy tool.

Unconventional Gas and Oil

Hydraulic fracturing of shale gas and tight oil have altered the production of energy, particularly in the United States, contributing to the Obama administration's removal of the crude oil export ban. The growing supply of oil and gas may support reduced resource dependence in the United States. Indeed, some argue that the United States will consequently enjoy greater freedom in using energy as a foreign policy tool; it will be able to sanction exporters more effectively and provide energy as a carrot to support European allies on the one hand while reducing the petro-power of countries like Russia, Iran, and Venezuela on the other (Kim and Blank 2015; Medlock III, Jaffe, and Hartley 2011). However, as some scholars note, these projections overestimate the impact of the hydraulic fracturing ("fracking") revolution on oil markets, geopolitics, and climate change; in fact, the impact is likely to be modest and will not endow the United States with a powerful foreign policy tool (Boersma and Johnson 2018; Colgan and Van de Graaf 2017). A similar conclusion applies regarding the potential role of fracking and renewables in making states energy independent, noting that energy autarky is neither feasible nor desirable for enhancing security (Nance and Boettcher 2017). Hughes finds that oil abundance in the United States may contribute to the perception that oil independence will provide greater security and afford the United States more room to maneuver in foreign policy. However, this potential effect will be conditioned by whether policy makers view oil independence as important and their willingness to intervene in the market (i.e., unilateralist legislators) (Hughes 2014b).

Renewable Energy

How will the shift toward renewable energies affect the potential use of energy as a reward or a punitive foreign policy stick? This question has received little attention so far and is likely to become increasingly relevant as the role of renewables in production and consumption grows. It is also connected to the question of whether the shift to renewables will increase energy cooperation and international trade in energy or, alternatively, drive countries toward energy independence.

Prima facie, it seems that renewables lessen the importance of energy as a foreign policy tool, for several reasons. First, freed of the requirements of fuel trade, renewable energy is less susceptible to energy sanctions, reducing the vulnerability of target countries and decreasing senders' capacity. Every nation has at least some access to renewable energy, blurring the distinction between net-exporters and net-importers and reducing interstate dependence. Second, the shift to renewables is also a shift from monopolistic and oligopolistic fossil markets—characterized by large and often international energy companies and government-owned companies—to more competitive markets with multiple suppliers who are smaller in size, take on new roles, and apply new business models. In this constellation, it is more difficult to manipulate market power for foreign policy ends (Valdés Lucas, Escribano, and San Martín González 2016; Scholten 2018). Third, according to expectations, electricity—fueled largely or even exclusively by renewable energy—will become more important, and regional cross-border grid interconnections will attain greater importance. The growing significance of electricity supply may similarly increase its importance for foreign policy (Fischhendler, Herman, and Anderman 2016; Scholten 2018). This point also illustrates that research on renewable energy and foreign policy should distinguish among different types of renewable energies. For example, hydropower, the main renewable energy used today, creates vulnerabilities in cases where rivers used to make power cut across borders. Nevertheless, by 2040 renewable energy is expected to account for no more than 18 percent of the global energy mix and 29 percent of electricity production (EIA 2016). While the transformation is uneven and is occurring in some countries at a faster pace, it seems unlikely that renewables will considerably affect the use of energy in foreign policy within the next decade (Scholten and Bosman 2016; Scholten 2018). It is also improbable that renewables (via electricity) will replace oil in the transportation sector in the coming decade.

Electricity

Scholars of energy and geopolitics largely ignore the use of electricity in foreign policy or simply assume that electricity interconnectivity, as in the case of the European Union, is a cooperative foreign policy tool (Puka and Szulecki 2014). Recent contributions highlight the connection among grid interconnections, interdependence, and security (Moore 2017). They likewise examine the ways in which electricity is extensively played out over time as both a carrot and stick in bilateral and regional relations concerning sovereignty, political, and security issues (Fischhendler, Herman, and Anderman 2016; Herman and Fischhendler n.d.).

Supply Chains

Scholars have begun to focus on the link between the ability to exploit energy for foreign policy ends and the structure of supply chains. Thus, rather than investigating the transport segment of particular resources (e.g., the difference between oil and gas transport) (Victor, Jaffe, and Hayes 2006), it is necessary to examine the ability to coerce (or reward) across the chain of supply, as in the case of oil: from upstream production to midstream transport and downstream refinement. Hughes and Long discern that the potential to coerce varies along the oil supply chain and that over time, declining market concentration in the supply chain leads to lower coercive potential (Hughes and Long 2015). A further study examines the production, transmission, and distribution segments in electricity relations between Israel and the Palestinians, noting that control of the distribution segment is critical because in its absence, the sanctioning country cannot exercise targeted sanctions and could be deterred from imposing comprehensive sanctions (Herman and Fischhendler n.d.). Balmaceda (2018) connects the physical characteristics of fossil resources and their supply chains, applying a systematic approach to examine oil, natural gas, and coal and their impact on both international relations and the exercise of power. By comparing the physical characteristics of these fossil fuels, she endeavors to understand how transportability, size, and location of markets; the required processing activities; and obstructability all affect relations between actors and the possibility of employing energy as a mean, and as a constitutive, power (Balmaceda 2018).

A FUTURE RESEARCH AGENDA

This section flags three main directions for future research, namely (a) theory development and methodological challenges; (b) the role of actors, particularly nonstate actors; and (c) renewable energy and electricity politics.

The theoretical underdevelopment of global energy politics is perhaps a reminder of a wider problem: the undertheorization of energy relations in social sciences. There is scope to move from largely empirically driven research to theory development in global energy politics. This new research agenda should attempt to explain systematically the complex interactions among energy, security, political, and other societal factors across domestic and international levels. In particular, it should combine international relations, political science, and international political economy literatures with technological and technical knowledge, creating an integrated theoretical framework. Such a direction can expose distinct energy qualities and help us to move away from existing, oversimplified conceptualizations of global energy politics in the realist or liberal traditions of international relations.

A theoretical strand addressing the social constructions and ideologies that inform and shape both structure and agents is of particular importance. Global energy politics should not be viewed as given but as socially constructed (Wendt 1992), suggesting that the relationship between energy and security is a matter of perception. Hence, future research should analyze the agents involved in constructing threatening or peaceful perceptions of energy, their strategies, and means, and the ways in which external events act as defining moments, altering collective understandings and shared perceptions. An example is Fischhendler and Nathan's (2014) discursive analysis based on securitization theory, concerning the manipulation of energy security in the struggle between various actors over the exportation of Israel's natural gas. Another example examines the link between ideology and resource nationalism (Stevens 2008).

Methodologically, it is vital to expand the empirical spectrum of research concerning global energy politics to new regions and different countries, beyond the current emphasis on the United States, European-Russian relations, and the Middle East. For the most part, the literature currently engages with several countries, mostly large exporters and importers, and their relations with one another or with smaller states (e.g., Eastern European countries). This challenge also relates in a more specific way to the study of foreign policy instruments, such as carrots and sticks. Despite several problems previously identified, econometric research can significantly improve theory development on the design, use, and effectiveness of energy tools. Qualitative methodologies, such as archival work, can also help to expose new cases in which energy instruments were used, even if this was not officially declared. Such research will shed light on the domestic processes underlying the use of the energy instrument in global politics.

Future research should also further explore the roles that transit nations, and several nonstate actors, play. Greater theoretical attention should be devoted to examining the economic and political conditions that influence transit nations' behavior. Future research should likewise distinguish between different types of transit nations and transit capacities, for example, transit through pipelines, electricity grids, maritime routes, and regional LNG hubs. These transit capacities include trade-offs and affect issues such as the energy volume in transit, need for storage capacity, possible transit distance, geographical bottlenecks, and resource or electricity reverse flow.

The evolution of energy markets necessitates further research on private and government-owned energy companies and the considerations and actions guiding the actions of these companies as markets change. In particular, studies should focus on resource diversification, ownership, and production structures in primary and secondary markets. A notable recent study along these lines, concerning the oil industry, observed variations in the responses of state firms in the United States, Japan, and France. The OECD governments today are more limited in their ability to manipulate markets than they previously were. Firms' characteristics influence how governments respond to their demands; in turn, the firms affect how governments choose to regulate oil markets. Context and history also play a role in this regard (Hughes 2014a). Future research should furthermore explore the interplays between private and government-owned companies; in many cases these either compete or cooperate with one another. Firms' access to capital and their relations with financiers and lending institutions may also affect the ways in which markets and politics intertwine, particularly with regard to investment decisions in countries that are subject to higher political risks and contestations.

Scholars have paid little attention to the role of energy sovereign wealth funds (SWFs) in global politics. These are state-owned investment funds that derive their revenues from resource exports, usually oil and gas, or other government surpluses (Badian and Harrington 2008, 2009). There are more than seventy SWFs around the world, of which energy SWFs are usually the largest, including those in Norway, Saudi Arabia, Qatar, and the United Arab Emirates. They invest abroad to prevent domestic currency appreciations against the "Dutch disease" phenomenon.[7] Thus, through their investment portfolio, SWFs can reward, induce, and coerce (by divestment) foreign countries. Further research is required to examine how profit maximization considerations and autonomy in investment decisions coincide with governments' foreign policy considerations. Indeed, one study indicates that following Norway's threat to divest its investments from Israel's national electricity utility, the latter revoked its decision to cut the electricity connection with Gaza (Herman and Fischhendler n.d.). There is also evidence that Russia's and Qatar's energy SWFs have been utilized for foreign policy aims (Truman 2010). One research avenue deriving from these examples concerns whether governments' use of SWFs in attaining foreign policy objectives depends on political regime type.

The research gap concerning civil society's role in global energy politics offers scope for the study of how society participates in providing energy carrots, serving as a provider of energy-related finance, technology, and know-how. Civil society may also intervene by furnishing off-grid electricity solutions, as various NGOs in developing countries and conflict areas have done. Such interventions may increase or decrease political tensions. Future research should address the ways and forms through which civil society initiatives organize and mobilize domestically and transnationally; interactions among civil society groups, states, and firms; the extent to which civil society constitutes an audience and the audiences with whom NGOs communicate; and the tools that civil society groups employ to influence global energy politics.

Finally, future research should explore the effects of renewables on global politics and the extent to which they differ from fossil energies. In the absence of clear case studies, scholars have so far principally discussed the potential impact of renewables. Yet as renewable energies become an increasingly salient feature of the energy mix, there is scope for empirical research. Moreover, research can benefit from unbundling the phrase "renewable energy" into specific energies, with a view to understanding the significance of the differences between renewable energies for global energy politics.

For example, solar and wind energies may not necessitate international cooperation, while hydroelectric energy often involves shared international water resources and large infrastructures. Renewables also increase the demand for international electricity trade, calling for future research that goes beyond an examination of the technical and economic aspects of grid interconnectivity to explore how geopolitical considerations influence states' decisions and how interdependence affects producers and consumers.

ACKNOWLEDGMENTS

I am grateful to the editors and two anonymous referees for their excellent feedback and helpful suggestions.

NOTES

1. Several recent contributions have addressed this issue from a number of angles and provide extensive discussions, including those concerning constructivism, Marxism, and other critical theories. See Belyi (2016), Dannreuther and Ostrowski (2013), Van de Graaf et al. (2016), Herranz-Surrallés (2016), and Goldthau (2010).
2. This distinction is not the same as offensive realism and defensive realism, which explain states' behavior under conditions of anarchy as seeking sufficient (defensive) or maximum (offensive) power to ensure their security and survival by maintaining (defensive) or rejecting (offensive) the balance of power in the system.
3. For a detailed discussion of conventional and unconventional fossil fuels, see Tutuncu in this volume.
4. The Seven Sisters were Anglo-Iranian Oil (now BP), Gulf Oil (later Chevron), Dutch Royal Shell, Standard Oil Company of California (SoCal, now Chevron), Standard Oil Company of New Jersey (Esso, later Exxon, now part of ExxonMobile), Standard Oil Company of New York (later Mobile, now part of ExxonMobile), and Texaco (later merged into Chevron).
5. https://twitter.com/TankerTrackers.
6. Nevertheless, certain investments in non-OPEC countries, driven by price signals rather than geopolitics, preceded 1973, for example, in the North Sea and the Gulf of Mexico.
7. The Dutch disease describes a situation where discovery of tradable natural resources in an economy (or an increase in resource prices) leads to real exchange rate appreciation, and as a result reduce the competitiveness of other tradable sectors, increase wages and may lead to labor relocation from other sectors to the resource sector.

REFERENCES

Abdelal, Rawi, and Jonathan Kirshner. 1999. "Strategy, Economic Relations, and the Definition of National Interests." *Security Studies* 9, nos. 1–2: 119–156. doi:10.1080/09636419908429397.
Abramova, Anna, and Olga Garanina. 2017. "The Role of Sanctions in the Internationalization of Russian Multinationals Toward China: The Case of Energy and ICT Sectors." In *The Challenge of Bric Multinationals*, edited by Alain Verbeke, Jorge Carneiro, and Maria Alejandra Gonzalez-Perez, 451–479. Bingley, UK: Emerald.

Andersen, Svein S., Andreas Goldthau, and Nick Sitter, eds. 2016. *Energy Union: Europe's New Liberal Mercantilism?* London: Palgrave.

Badian, Laura, and Gregory Harrington. 2008. "The Politics of Sovereign Wealth." *International Economy* 22, no. 1: 52.

Badian, Laura, and Gregory Harrington. 2009. "The Evolving Politics of Sovereign Wealth Funds." *Revue d'économie financière* (English ed.) 9, no. 1: 143–156.

Baldwin, David A., and Robert A. Pape. 1998. "Evaluating Economic Sanctions." *International Security* 23, no. 2: 189–198.

Balmaceda, Margarita M. 2018. "Differentiation, Materiality, and Power: Towards a Political Economy of Fossil Fuels." *Energy Research & Social Science* 39: 130–140. doi:10.1016/j.erss.2017.10.052.

Baylis, John, Steve Smith, and Patricia Owens. 2017. *The Globalization of World Politics: An Introduction to International Relations.* Oxford: Oxford University Press.

Belyi, Andrei V. 2016. *Transnational Gas Markets and Euro-Russian Energy Relations.* Houndmills, UK: Palgrave.

Bilgin, Mert. 2009. "Geopolitics of European Natural Gas Demand: Supplies from Russia, Caspian and the Middle East." *Energy Policy* 37, no. 11: 4482–4492. doi:10.1016/j.enpol.2009.05.070.

Bilgin, Mert. 2010. "Turkey's Energy Strategy: What Difference Does It Make to Become an Energy Transit Corridor, Hub or Center?" UNISCI Discussion Papers 23.

Blackwill, Robert D., and Jennifer M. Harris. 2016. *War by Other Means: Geoeconomics and Statecraft.* Cambridge, MA: Harvard University Press.

Blackwill, Robert D., and Meghan L. O'Sullivan. 2014. "America's Energy Edge: The Geopolitical Consequences of the Shale Revolution." *Foreign Affairs* 93: 102.

Blair, John M. 1976. *The Control of Oil.* New York: Pantheon.

Blanchard, Jean-Marc F., and Norrin M. Ripsman. 1999. "Asking the Right Question: When Do Economic Sanctions Work Best?" *Security Studies* 9, nos. 1–2: 219–253. doi:10.1080/09636419908429400.

Boersma, Tim, and Corey Johnson. 2018. *US Energy Diplomacy.* New York: Center on Global Energy Policy, Columbia University.

Bohi, Douglas R., and Milton Russell. 1978. *Limiting Oil Imports: An Economic History and Analysis.* New York: Routledge.

Bouwmeester, Maaike C., and J. Oosterhaven. 2017. "Economic Impacts of Natural Gas Flow Disruptions Between Russia and the EU." *Energy Policy* 106: 288–297. doi:10.1016/j.enpol.2017.03.030.

Brooks, Risa A. 2002. "Sanctions and Regime Type: What Works, and When?" *Security Studies* 11, no. 4: 1–50. doi:10.1080/714005349.

Bruce, Chloë. 2005. *Fraternal Friction or Fraternal Fiction? The Gas Factor in Russian-Belarusian Relations.* Oxford: Oxford Institute for Energy Studies.

Chaban, Natalia, and Michèle Knodt. 2015. "Energy Diplomacy in the Context of Multistakeholder Diplomacy: The EU and BICS." *Cooperation and Conflict* 50, no. 4: 457–474. doi:10.1177/0010836715573541.

Colgan, Jeff D. 2010. "Oil and Revolutionary Governments: Fuel for International Conflict." *International Organization* 64, no. 04: 661–694. doi:10.1017/S002081831000024X.

Colgan, Jeff D. 2013. *Petro-Aggression: When Oil Causes War.* Cambridge, UK: Cambridge University Press.

Colgan, Jeff D. 2014. "The Emperor Has No Clothes: The Limits of OPEC in the Global Oil Market." *International Organization* 68, no. 3: 599–632. doi:10.1017/S0020818313000489.

Colgan, Jeff D., and Thijs Van de Graaf. 2017. "A Crude Reversal: The Political Economy of the United States Crude Oil Export Policy." *Energy Research & Social Science* 24: 30–35. doi:10.1016/j.erss.2016.12.012.

Cortright, David, ed. 1997. *The Price of Peace: Incentives and International Conflict Prevention, Carnegie Commission on Preventing Deadly Conflict*. Lanham, MD: Rowman & Littlefield Publishers.

Criekemans, David. 2018. "Geopolitics of the Renewable Energy Game and Its Potential Impact upon Global Power Relations." In *The Geopolitics of Renewables*, edited by Daniel Scholten, 37–73. Cham, Switzerland: Springer.

Crumm, Eileen M. 1995. "The Value of Economic Incentives in International Politics." *Journal of Peace Research* 32, no. 3: 313–330.

Dannreuther, Roland, and Wojciech Ostrowski. 2013. *Global Resources: Conflict and Cooperation*. Houndmills, UK: Palgrave.

Davis, Patricia Annette. 2002. *The Art of Economic Persuasion: Positive Incentives and German Economic Diplomacy*. Ann Arbor: University of Michigan Press.

Donnelly, Jack. 2000. *Realism and International Relations*. Cambridge, UK: Cambridge University Press.

Drezner, Daniel W. 1999. *The Sanctions Paradox: Economic Statecraft and International Relations*. Cambridge, UK: Cambridge University Press.

Drezner, Daniel W. 2011. "Sanctions Sometimes Smart: Targeted Sanctions in Theory and Practice." *International Studies Review* 13, no. 1: 96–108. doi:10.1111/j.1468-2486.2010.01001.x.

EIA. 2016. *International Energy Outlook 2016 with Projections to 2040*. Washington: US Department of Energy, Energy Information Administration.

Engdahl, William. 2004. *A Century of War: Anglo-American Oil Politics and the New World Order*. London; Ann Arbor, MI: Pluto Press.

Evans, Peter C., and Erica S. Downs. 2006. *Untangling China's Quest for Oil Through State-Backed Financial Deals*. Washington, DC: Brookings Institution.

Fischhendler, Itay, Lior Herman, and Jaya Anderman. 2016. "The Geopolitics of Cross-border Electricity Grids: The Israeli-Arab Case." *Energy Policy* 98: 533–543.

Fischhendler, Itay, Lior Herman, and Nir Maoz. 2017. "The Political Economy of Energy Sanctions: Insights from a Global Outlook 1938–2017." *Energy Research & Social Science* 34: 62–71. doi:10.1016/j.erss.2017.05.008.

Fischhendler, Itay, and Daniel Nathan. 2014. "In the Name of Energy Security: The Struggle over the Exportation of Israeli Natural Gas." *Energy Policy* 70, no. 0: 152–162. doi:10.1016/j.enpol.2014.03.020.

Friedrichs, Jörg. 2010. "Global Energy Crunch: How Different Parts of the World Would React to a Peak Oil Scenario." *Energy Policy* 38, no. 8: 4562–4569. doi:10.1016/j.enpol.2010.04.011.

Gharibnavaz, Mohammad Reza, and Robert Waschik. 2018. "A Computable General Equilibrium Model of International Sanctions in Iran." *World Economy* 41, no. 1: 287–307. doi:10.1111/twec.12528.

Gholz, Eugene, Umul Awan, and Ehud Ronn. 2017. "Financial and Energy Security Analysis of China's Loan-for-Oil Deals." *Energy Research & Social Science* 24: 42–50. doi:10.1016/j.erss.2016.12.021.

Gnedina, Elena, and Michael Emerson. 2009. *The Case for a Gas Transit Consortium in Ukraine: A Cost-Benefit Analysis*. Brussels: CEPS.

Goldthau, Andreas. 2008. "Rhetoric Versus Reality: Russian Threats to European Energy Supply." *Energy Policy* 36, no. 2: 686–692. doi:10.1016/j.enpol.2007.10.012.

Goldthau, Andreas. 2010. "Energy Diplomacy in Trade and Investment of Oil and Gas." In *Global Energy Governance: New Rules of the Game*, edited by Andreas Goldthau and Jan Martin Witte, 25–47. Washington, DC: Brookings Institution.

Goldthau, Andreas, and Jan Martin Witte. 2009. "Back to the Future or Forward to the Past? Strengthening Markets and Rules for Effective Global Energy Governance." *International Affairs* 85, no. 2: 373–390. doi:10.1111/j.1468-2346.2009.00798.x.

Guillet, Jérôme. 2007. "Gazprom as a Predictable Partner: Another Reading of the Russian-Ukrainian and Russian-Belarusian Energy Crises." *Russie Nei Visions* 18, no. 1: 4–24.

Hancock, Kathleen J., and Vlado Vivoda. 2014. "International Political Economy: A Field Born of the OPEC Crisis Returns to its Energy Roots." *Energy Research & Social Science* 1: –216. doi:10.1016/j.erss.2014.03.017.

Harrington, Rebecca. 2017. "There's Only One Way for the US to Reach Energy Independence." *Business Insider*, July 15. https://www.businessinsider.com/how-can-america-be-energy-independent-adopt-renewables-2017-7.

Herman, Lior, and Itay Fischhendler. 2019. "Energy as a Rewarding and Punitive Foreign Policy Instrument: The Case of Israeli–Palestinian Relations." *Studies in Conflict & Terrorism*, doi:10.1080/1057610X.2019.1567997.

Herranz-Surrallés, Anna. 2016. "An Emerging EU energy Diplomacy? Discursive Shifts, Enduring Practices." *Journal of European Public Policy* 23, no. 9: 1386–1405. doi:10.1080/135 01763.2015.1083044.

Hirschman, Albert O. 1945. *National Power and the Structure of Foreign Trade.* Berkeley: University of California Press.

Hufbauer, Gary Clyde, Jeffrey J. Schott, Kimberly Ann Elliott, and Barbara Oegg. 2007. *Economic Sanctions Reconsidered.* 3rd ed. London: Institute for International Economics.

Hughes, Llewelyn. 2014a. *Globalizing Oil.* Cambridge, UK: Cambridge University Press.

Hughes, Llewelyn. 2014b. "The Limits of Energy Independence: Assessing the Implications of Oil Abundance for U.S. Foreign Policy." *Energy Research & Social Science* 3, no. 1: 55–64. doi:10.1016/j.erss.2014.07.001.

Hughes, Llewelyn, and Eugene Gholz. 2016. "Energy, Coercive Diplomacy, and Sanctions." In *The Palgrave Handbook of the International Political Economy of Energy*, edited by Thijs van de Graaf, Benjamin K. Sovacool, Arunabha Ghosh, Florian Kern, and Michael T. Klare, 487–504. London: Palgrave.

Hughes, Llewelyn, and Sean J. Kreyling. 2010. "Understanding Resource Nationalism in the 21st Century." *Journal of Energy Security* (July), http://www.ensec.org/index.php?option= com_content&view=article&id=253:resource-nationalism-in-the-21st-century&catid=108: energysecuritycontent&Itemid=365.

Hughes, Llewelyn, and Phillip Y. Lipscy. 2013. "The Politics of Energy." *Annual Review of Political Science* 16: 449–469.

Hughes, Llewelyn, and Austin Long. 2015. "Is There an Oil Weapon? Security Implications of Changes in the Structure of the International Oil Market." *International Security* 39, no. 3: 152–189. doi:10.1162/ISEC_a_00188.

Jirušek, Martin, and Petra Kuchyňková. 2018. "The Conduct of Gazprom in Central and Eastern Europe: A Tool of the Kremlin, or Just an Adaptable Player?" *East European Politics and Societies* 0, no. 0: 0888325417745128. doi:10.1177/0888325417745128.

Johansson, Bengt. 2013. "Security Aspects of Future Renewable Energy Systems—A Short Overview." *Energy* 61: 598–605. doi:10.1016/j.energy.2013.09.023.

Kaplan, Robert D. 2011. "The South China Sea Is the Future of Conflict." *Foreign Policy*, no. 188: 76.

Karasac, Hasene. 2002. "Actors of the New 'Great Game': Caspian Oil Politics." *Journal of Southern Europe and the Balkans* 41, no. 1: 15–27.

Kelanic, Rosemary A. 2016. "The Petroleum Paradox: Oil, Coercive Vulnerability, and Great Power Behavior." *Security Studies* 25, no. 2: 181–213. doi:10.1080/09636412.2016.1171966.

Kelanic, Rosemary Ann. 2012. "Black Gold and Blackmail: The Politics of International Oil Coercion." PhD diss., University of Chicago.

Keohane, Robert O. 2009. "The Old IPE and the New." *Review of International Political Economy* 16, no. 1: 34–46. doi:10.1080/09692290802524059.

Keohane, Robert Owen. 1984. *After Hegemony: Cooperation and Discord in the World Political Economy*. Princeton, NJ: Princeton University Press.

Kim, Younkyoo, and Stephen Blank. 2015. "US Shale Revolution and Russia: Shifting Geopolitics of Energy in Europe and Asia." *Asia Europe Journal* 13, no. 1: 95–112. doi:10.1007/s10308-014-0400-z.

Klare, Michael T. 2002. *Resource Wars: The New Landscape of Global Conflict*. New York: Henry Holt and Company.

Klare, Michael T. 2014. "From Scarcity to Abundance: The Changing Dynamics of Energy Conflict." *Pennsylvania State Journal of Law & International Affairs* 3: 10.

Kreft, Heinrich. 2006. "China's Quest for Energy." *Policy Review* 139 (October/November): 61–70.

Kropatcheva, Elena. 2011. "Playing Both Ends Against the Middle: Russia's Geopolitical Energy Games with the EU and Ukraine." *Geopolitics* 16, no. 3: 553–573. doi:10.1080/146500 45.2011.520863.

Lee, Yusin. 2017. "Interdependence, Issue Importance, and the 2009 Russia-Ukraine Gas Conflict." *Energy Policy* 102: 199–209. doi:10.1016/j.enpol.2016.11.038.

Licht, Amanda Abigail. 2010. "Private Incentives, Public Outcomes: The Role of Target Political Incentives in the Success of Foreign Policy." PhD diss., University of Iowa.

Licklider, Roy. 1988. "The Power of Oil: The Arab Oil Weapon and the Netherlands, the United Kingdom, Canada, Japan, and the United States." *International Studies Quarterly* 32, no. 2: 205–226.

Licklider, Roy. 1998. *Political Power and the Arab Oil Weapon: The Experience of Five Industrial Nations*. Berkeley: University of California Press.

Liesen, Rainer. 1999. "Transit Under the 1994 Energy Charter Treaty." *Journal of Energy & Natural Resources Law* 17, no. 1: 56–73. doi:10.1080/02646811.1999.11433156.

Marcel, Valerie. 2006. *Oil Titans: National Oil Companies in the Middle East*. London: Chatham House.

Martin, Lisa L. 2011. "Credibility, Costs, and Institutions: Cooperation on Economic Sanctions." *World Politics* 45, no. 3: 406–432. doi:10.2307/2950724.

Medlock, Kenneth B., III, Amy Myers Jaffe, and Peter R. Hartley. 2011. *Shale Gas and US National Security*. Houston, TX: Rice University.

Miller, Eric A. 2017. *To Balance or Not to Balance: Alignment Theory and the Commonwealth of Independent States*. London: Routledge.

Mobley, Richard. 2002. "The Beira Patrol." *Naval War College Review* 55, no. 1: 63–84.

Moore, Sharlissa. 2017. "Evaluating the Energy Security of Electricity Interdependence: Perspectives from Morocco." *Energy Research & Social Science* 24: 21–29. doi:10.1016/j.erss.2016.12.008.

Moran, Theodore H. 2009. "Managing an Oligopoly of Would-Be Sovereigns: The Dynamics of Joint Control and Self-Control in the International Oil Industry Past, Present, and Future." *International Organization* 41, no. 4: 575–607. doi:10.1017/S0020818300027612.

Morgan, Clifton T., Navin Bapat, and Yoshiharu Kobayashi. 2014. "Threat and Imposition of Economic Sanctions 1945–2005: Updating the TIES Dataset." *Conflict Management and Peace Science* 31, no. 5: 541–558. doi:10.1177/0738894213520379.

Nance, Mark T., and William A. Boettcher. 2017. "Conflict, Cooperation, and Change in the Politics of Energy Interdependence: An Introduction." *Energy Research & Social Science* 24: 1–5. doi:10.1016/j.erss.2016.12.020.

Newnham, Randall E. 2000. "More Flies with Honey: Positive Economic Linkage in German Ostpolitik from Bismarck to Kohl." *International Studies Quarterly* 44, no. 1: 73–96. doi:10.1111/0020-8833.00149.

Newnham, Randall E. 2011. "Oil, Carrots, and Sticks: Russia's Energy Resources as a Foreign Policy Tool." *Journal of Eurasian Studies* 2, no. 2: 134–143. doi:10.1016/j.euras.2011.03.004.

Newnham, Randall E. 2015. "Georgia on My Mind? Russian Sanctions and the End of the 'Rose Revolution.'" *Journal of Eurasian Studies* 6, no. 2: 161–170. doi:10.1016/j.euras.2015.03.008.

Nincic, Miroslav. 2010. "Getting What You Want: Positive Inducements in International Relations." *International Security* 35, no. 1: 138–183. doi:10.1162/ISEC_a_00006.

O'Sullivan, Meghan L. 2013. "The Entanglement of Energy, Grand Strategy, and International Security." In *The Handbook of Global Energy Policy*, edited by Andreas Goldthau, 30–47. Chichester, UK: John Wiley & Sons.

O'Sullivan, Meghan L. 2017. *Windfall: How the New Energy Abundance Upends Global Politics and Strengthens America's Power*. New York: Simon and Schuster.

Overland, Indra, and Gulaikhan Kubayeva. 2018. "Did China Bankroll Russia's Annexation of Crimea? The Role of Sino-Russian Energy Relations." In *Russia's Turn to the East: Domestic Policymaking and Regional Cooperation*, edited by Helge Blakkisrud and Elana Wilson Rowe, 95–118. Cham, Switzerland: Springer International Publishing.

Painter, David S. 2012. "Oil and the American Century." *Journal of American History* 99, no. 1: 24–39.

Pape, Robert A. 1997. "Why Economic Sanctions Do Not Work." *International Security* 22, no. 2: 90–136.

Pirani, Simon, Jonathan Stern, and Katja Yafimava. 2009. *The Russo-Ukrainian Gas Dispute of January 2009: A Comprehensive Assessment*. Oxford: Oxford Institute for Energy Studies.

Pratt, Joseph A. 2012. "Exxon and the Control of Oil." *Journal of American History* 99, no. 1: 145–154. doi:10.1093/jahist/jas149.

Puka, Lidia, and Kacper Szulecki. 2014. "The Politics and Economics of Cross-Border Electricity Infrastructure: A Framework for Analysis." *Energy Research and Social Science* 4: 124–134.

Ross, Michael L. 2015. "What Have We Learned about the Resource Curse?" *Annual Review of Political Science* 18, no. 1: 239–259. doi:10.1146/annurev-polisci-052213-040359.

Sampson, Anthony. 1975. *The Seven Sisters: The Great Oil Companies and the World They Shaped*. New York: Viking Press.

Scholten, Daniel, ed. 2018. *The Geopolitics of Renewables*. Cham, Switzerland: Springer.

Scholten, Daniel, and Rick Bosman. 2016. "The Geopolitics of Renewables: Exploring the Political Implications of Renewable Energy Systems." *Technological Forecasting and Social Change* 103: 273–283. doi:10.1016/j.techfore.2015.10.014.

Selivanova, Yulia. 2010. "Managing the Patchwork of Agreements in Trade and Investment." In *Global Energy Governance: New Rules of the Game*, edited by Andreas Goldthau and Jan Martin Witte, 49–72. Washington, DC: Brookings Institution.

Shaffer, Brenda. 2009. *Energy Politics*. Philadelphia: University of Pennsylvania Press.

Shaffer, Brenda. 2013. "Natural Gas Supply Stability and Foreign Policy." *Energy Policy* 56, no. 0: 114–125. doi:10.1016/j.enpol.2012.11.035.

Singer, Clifford E. 2008. *Energy and International War: From Babylon to Baghdad and Beyond.* Hackensack, NJ: World Scientific.

Sivaram, Varun, and Sagatom Saha. 2018. "The Geopolitical Implications of a Clean Energy Future from the Perspective of the United States." In *The Geopolitics of Renewables*, edited by Daniel Scholten, 125–162. Cham, Switzerland: Springer.

Solingen, Etel, ed. 2012. *Sanctions, Statecraft, and Nuclear Proliferation.* Cambridge, UK: Cambridge University Press.

Sovacool, Benjamin. 2014. "What Are We Doing Here? Analyzing Fifteen Years of Energy Scholarship and Proposing a Social Science Research Agenda." *Energy Research and Social Science* 1: 1–29. doi:10.1016/j.erss.2014.02.003.

Sparks, Stephen. 2017. "Crude Politics: The ANC, the Shipping Research Bureau and the Anti-Apartheid Oil Boycott." *South African Historical Journal* 69, no. 2: 251–264. doi:10.1080/025 82473.2017.1310285.

Stern, Jonathan. 2006. "Natural Gas Security Problems in Europe: The Russian–Ukrainian Crisis of 2006." *Asia-Pacific Review* 13, no.1: 32–59. doi:10.1080/13439000600697522.

Stevens, Paul. 2008. "National Oil Companies and International Oil Companies in the Middle East: Under the Shadow of Government and the Resource Nationalism Cycle." *Journal of World Energy Law & Business* 1, no. 1: 5–30. doi:10.1093/jwelb/jwn004.

Stulberg, Adam N. 2017. "Natural Gas and the Russia-Ukraine Crisis: Strategic Restraint and the Emerging Europe-Eurasia Gas Network." *Energy Research & Social Science* 24: 71–85. doi:10.1016/j.erss.2016.12.017.

Taylor, Ian. 2006. "China's Oil Diplomacy in Africa." *International Affairs* 82, no. 5: 937–959. doi:10.1111/j.1468-2346.2006.00579.x.

Truman, Edwin M. 2010. *Sovereign Wealth Funds: Threat or Salvation?* Washington, DC: Peterson Institute.

Valdés Lucas, Javier Noel, Gonzalo Escribano, and Enrique San Martín González. 2016. "Energy Security and Renewable Energy Deployment in the EU: Liaisons Dangereuses or Virtuous Circle?" *Renewable and Sustainable Energy Reviews* 62: 1032–1046. doi:10.1016/j. rser.2016.04.069.

Van de Graaf, Thijs. 2013a. "The 'Oil Weapon' Reversed? Sanctions Against Iran and U.S.-EU Structural Power." *Middle East Policy* 20, no. 3: 145–163. doi:10.1111/mepo.12040.

Van de Graaf, Thijs. 2013b. *The Politics and Institutions of Global Energy Governance.* Houndmills, UK: Palgrave.

Van de Graaf, Thijs, and Jeff D. Colgan. 2017. "Russian Gas Games or Well-Oiled Conflict? Energy Security and the 2014 Ukraine Crisis." *Energy Research & Social Science* 24: 59–64. doi:10.1016/j.erss.2016.12.018.

Van de Graaf, Thijs, Benjamin K. Sovacool, Arunabha Ghosh, Florian Kern, and Michael T. Klare. 2016. *The Palgrave Handbook of the International Political Economy of Energy.* Houndmills, UK: Palgrave.

Veebel, Viljar, and Raul. Markus. 2015. "Lessons from the EU-Russia Sanctions 2014–2015." *Baltic Journal of Law & Politics* 8, no. 1: 165–194.

Victor, David G., Amy M. Jaffe, and Mark H. Hayes, eds. 2006. *Natural Gas and Geopolitics: From 1970 to 2040.* Cambridge, UK: Cambridge University Press.

Wallensteen, Peter. 2005. "Positive Sanctions: On the Potential of Rewards and Target Differentiation." In *International Sanctions: Between Words and Wars in the Global System*, edited by Peter Wallensteen and Carina Staibano, 229–241. London: Routledge.

Wallensteen, Peter, and Carina Staibano, eds. 2005. *International Sanctions: Between Words and Wars in the Global System*. London: Routledge.

Waterworth, Alec, and Michael J. Bradshaw. 2018. "Unconventional Trade-offs? National Oil Companies, Foreign Investment and Oil and Gas Development in Argentina and Brazil." *Energy Policy* 122: 7–16. doi:10.1016/j.enpol.2018.07.011.

Wendt, Alexander. 1992. "Anarchy Is What States Make of It: The Social Construction of Power Politics." *International Organization* 46, no. 02: 391–425.

Westphal, Kirsten. 2009. *Russian Gas, Ukrainian Pipelines, and European Supply Security: Lessons of the 2009 Controversies*. Berlin: SWP.

World Energy Council. 2016. *World Energy Resources 2016*. London: World Energy Council.

Xu, Xiaojie. 2007. *Chinese NOC's Overseas Strategies: Background, Comparison and Remarks*. Houston, TX: James A. Baker II Institute for Public Policy, Rice University.

Yafimava, Katja. 2010. *The June 2010 Russian-Belarusian Gas Transit Dispute: A Surprise That Was to Be Expected*. Oxford: Oxford Institute for Energy Studies.

Yergin, Daniel. 1996. *The Prize: The Epic Quest for Oil, Money and Power*. New York: Simon & Schuster.

CHAPTER 15

....

THE POLITICS OF OIL
MARKETS

....

WOJTEK WOLFE

As new international crises flare up, are reminded of the reality that geopolitics has the power to alter the status quo despite the longevity of the economic principles undergirding the structure and function of global oil markets. This chapter focuses on how variables such as politics, conflict, and geography affect oil production, trade, and consumption. Oil markets are based on economic principles, but they do not live in a political vacuum; when geopolitical tensions impact supply and demand capabilities, markets have to adjust to new and dynamic geopolitical realities. History shows that resource conflict occurs on the supply side (Klare 2001) and among the more politically and economically vulnerable states connected to energy trade (Le Billon 2004). Accordingly, if geopolitical tensions increase along sea lanes and oil transportation routes, then we will continue to see more price volatility that will challenge the stability of globally integrated oil markets.

Over the past decade, we have witnessed the three most impactful changes to the oil market: the US shale oil revolution, attempts by the Organization of the Petroleum Exporting Countries (OPEC) and Saudi Arabia to counter the growth of the United States as a top oil producer, and the People's Republic of China's (PRC's) growing economic issues as it continues to be the world's second largest oil consumer. Although oil production and consumption variables are typically economic in nature, this chapter attempts to provide an interdisciplinary approach by introducing politics into a traditionally economic-oriented dialogue about why these three changes carry significant explanatory weight toward our understanding of the politics of oil markets.

Oil markets are an integral part of the global economy and often play a considerable role in international relations (Keohane 2009; Van de Graaf et al. 2016). Given the political nature of international relations, there is a need for political analysis to provide us with a deeper understanding of oil politics within the changing global political landscape. This need will grow as the top energy producers and consumers continue to attempt to influence oil- and energy-related markets in their efforts to gain a relative advantage.

As state actions affecting oil production, trade, and transportation become more common, the resulting price volatility will test oil market and commodity exchange stability. While oil production sources are transitioning, markets are becoming more susceptible to outside influence. As the United States expands its shale oil operations and becomes a dominant energy producer, OPEC's market share and political influence will continue to diminish. On the consumer side, China has continued to hedge its global oil market imports by exploiting its financial advantage throughout the energy value chain. According to classical economics, markets seek to maintain relative levels of equilibrium, but geopolitical factors can push markets out of equilibrium, requiring politically informed explanations and solutions.

International and domestic sources of political influence over global trade are increasing, and the research field is ripe with opportunities for value added political analysis. Despite the high cost of entry for social science researchers seeking to be heard in policy journals dominated by economists (Sovacool 2014), international political economy of energy (IPEE) has successfully grown into a developed and influential area of study (Hughes and Lipscy 2013). IPEE scholars have continued to ask important and necessary questions about energy issues varying from market volatility to China's economic impact on those markets (Keohane 2009). The fundamental purpose driving IPEE literature is the call to put politics back into energy policy analysis, alongside the market-based perspectives dominating the literature (Hancock and Vivoda 2014).

This chapter focuses specifically on oil markets, as oil and oil products still account for 90 percent of global energy consumption and fuel nearly all of the world's commercial transportation sectors (O'Sullivan 2017b). This is due to the fact that oil benefits from product adaptability, purchasing contract flexibility, and global commodity exchange accessibility. Natural gas and renewables have earned their rightful positions within the energy market matrix and continue to increase in market share, market integration, and reliability. However, oil maintains greater accessibility since it is not affected by the same regional hub limitations that affect natural gas, and oil's flexible contractual options are only starting to become more available in natural gas markets. While natural gas is a rapidly growing component of energy markets, oil still maintains an overwhelming global market share.

OIL MARKET PHASES

The history of oil market investments can be split into four phases. The first phase existed before oil became the primary global energy commodity (Bressand 2013, 25–26). The second phase began when OPEC successfully gained majority influence over global oil prices but ended decades later when OPEC no longer held that influence. The third phase has been consistent with classic economics as the driving force behind global energy market functions, with supply and demand curves maintaining influence over energy prices and limiting state influence over the energy pricing process. Most states have lacked the capabilities needed to overpower the supply and demand variables that have been the main backbone of the current oil pricing regime (Markus 2016). However, a small number of states are becoming more effective in taking advantage of their relative strengths in order to influence market options, and this change indicates that the oil market may be entering into transition from the third to the fourth phase, which exhibits more frequent and effective attempts by states to influence energy resources, especially by energy producers and net oil importers (Bressand 2013).

The US shale oil revolution and Saudi Arabia's attempts to counter it are important examples of states attempting to exert political and economic power to change oil market dynamics. Consequently, energy markets are experiencing more changes in the supply and demand curves emanating out of the larger energy-producing and -consuming states, such as Saudi Arabia, the United States, and China. These states could have the potential to push existing oil market structures beyond their functional capacities, an outcome that would have tremendous impact on our understanding of the political economy of oil. These concerns are especially true among emerging Asian economies, which continue to account for the largest oil import increases in recent history (Aalto 2014).

OIL MARKETS

Oil markets maintain a dualism in their simplicity of explanation and their complexity of prediction. They can appear to be deceptively simple when they follow cyclical changes based on market supply, demand, and equilibrium models, especially since the supply and demand equation is the basis for energy market pricing models, market forecasting, and price discovery (Lin Lawell 2008). However, macro level events can have a substantial impact on oil market segments and introduce increased complexity to pricing models (Karali and Ramirez 2014). As globalization promotes further integration, it can also increase exposure to politically unstable regions and introduce additional sources of exogenous volatility for supply and demand factors (Coleman 2012). Some of the sources of volatility are states, nongovernmental organizations, national oil companies, privately owned energy conglomerates, financial regimes, and other factors that possess the geoeconomic capability and will to disrupt oil markets throughout the upstream, midstream, and downstream sectors.

The energy industry combines multiple entities within industrial sectors that participate in the extraction, transportation, and refining of petroleum energy products. The upstream sector pursues the exploration and production of crude oil and natural gas energy at the source site. The midstream sector transports crude oil and natural gas using marine transport, rail, and pipelines, with the majority of international energy transportation moving over sea-lane trading routes. After arriving at an appropriate downstream storage facility, terminal, or natural gas site, the crude oil and gas will be refined and processed into products such as gasoline, diesel fuel, and chemical products used in consumer goods. (For a technical discussion of fossil fuels, see Tutuncu in this volume. For more on oil and gas infrastructure, see Coburn in this volume.)

OIL FUTURES MARKET, PRICE VOLATILITY, AND PRICE SPECULATION

In pursuing an interdisciplinary explanation of the politics of oil, it may be beneficial to discuss the structural aspects of commodity markets and their functions. Oil markets rely on market fundamentals to determine price, as is the case in all other commodity markets; production supply and buyer demand shape market fundamentals and determine price (Simkins and Simkins 2013). As demand increases, the supply side increases production, leading to increased market share and profit margins for the producer. Conversely, when demand decreases, the supply side will reduce production to balance out inventory and maintain stable market pricing. Demand decreases can be cyclical or part of a macroeconomic downturn. Higher oil prices contribute to higher profits and increased infrastructure investments on the supply side. Those investments are necessary for producers to maintain proper production capabilities and increase production capacity when needed to meet future demand increases. When oil markets experience long-term low energy prices, upstream producers will cut back their oil inventories and reduce future production investments to offset reduced profits.

The commodity exchange system is the basis for the majority of the world's oil trade (Hajiyev 2019). This background information describes the structure in which political variables function. If geopolitics impacts oil prices, then that impact can be seen through the price formation process as it evolves on the commodity exchange. Commodity trading typically involves futures contract trading on a commodities exchange, which provides a transparent, efficient, and regulated market to buy and sell products that would otherwise be impractical to trade physically. Since most traders do not hold a commodity futures contract until its maturity date, the futures exchange bypasses the difficulties that a commodities trader on the physical market would encounter if it had to prepare, for example, for the delivery of ten thousand pounds of soybeans upon contract maturity. Nevertheless, oil futures contracts are standardized to show specific trade size, location, and contract expiration.

The governing body overseeing futures and swaps markets in the United States is the US Commodity Futures Trading Commission (CFTC). The CFTC regulates and maintains fair and transparent exchange rules, enforcing clear counterparty rules and reducing counterparty risk.[1] The regulatory oversight reduces the likelihood that the entity on the other side of the trade will fail to deliver the underlying commodity as promised. The Chicago Mercantile Exchange (CME)[2] and the New York Mercantile Exchange

(NYMEX)[3] are the two main commodity exchanges in the United States. Both exchanges are under the CME Group and handle approximately three billion contracts per year, with an annual value of $1 quadrillion in the oil futures market, where sellers and buyers contend with each other to find a price equilibrium as prices fluctuate throughout the trading day.[4] Futures markets serve an economic purpose by providing for the risk transfer and price discovery of the underlying commodity.

The commodity exchange also helps to alleviate the problem of private information being misused to impact market price. The operating assumption for market participants comes from the efficient market hypothesis: that the commodity price contains all available and relevant information (Lean, McAleer, and Wong 2010). Real-time commodity prices are listed on various oil benchmarks such as the WTI, Brent, and Dubai/Oman markets and indicate the expected value of the contract's underlying commodity. These benchmarks account for the majority of the different regional crude oil markets, with the Brent benchmark accounting for two-thirds of the total oil traded around the world (Kurt 2014). Commodity futures and options prices do not forecast long-term future prices, but they provide an agreed-upon basis for price discovery. A commodity exchange also provides an allocative effect that helps market participants determine other pricing functions such as costs of oil refining and product delivery in the midstream and downstream segments (Williams 2001).

The oil futures market is considered to be more liquid than the physical market because it contains significantly more trade volume. The high number of participant transactions contributes to stronger pricing trends, even though the majority of the participants will not be taking physical possession of the underlying commodity. In spite of this, strictly enforced regulations guarantee that all futures contracts are based on the verified amount of the underlying commodity. Although it is unlikely, it is possible for all oil futures traders to take physical possession of their contract's underlying commodity upon contract maturity. Since traders are exchanging contracts backed by existing physical assets with tangible value, the market will remain solvent even if everyone chooses to physically collect on the underlying commodity.

When price divergence occurs between futures prices and physical market prices, traders take advantage of the divergence, thereby diminishing its impact on energy markets. Research shows that ultimately, oil futures prices and physical market prices are jointly determined and driven by the same supply and demand fundamentals (Kilian and Lee 2014). Oil futures traders buy and sell contracts and crude options derivatives to hedge their positions against unexpected price changes that would cause the value of their underlying commodity positions to decrease in value. However, even the practice of hedging against future risk now incorporates index-fund investments, suggesting the existence of strong equity market correlations (Hamilton and Wu 2014). While more research is needed to determine the specific linkages between oil prices and overall economic health (Kilian 2014), index fund correlations are a valid sign of economic linkages between energy markets and broader economic indicators. This evidence shows that the more oil prices are integrated into other investment markets, the more protected oil will be against sudden volatility and price manipulation.

Many oil futures traders place speculative trades on future market prices, with a bias that the market will move prices higher (long position) or lower (short position) relative to the trader's futures contract and options position, without ever planning on taking physical possession of the underlying commodity. Some evidence suggests that speculative demand raised oil prices between $5 and $14 for a short period of time in mid-2008. However, that evidence depended on inventory specification, and it did not show price correlations for the 2003–2008 run-up in oil prices (Kilian and Lee 2014). Researchers examining hedge funds engaged in oil commodity trading found that hedge funds exhibited poor market predictability during periods of market stress, concluding that speculative traders have limited ability in predicting price outcomes when speculating against market fundamentals (Büyükşahin and Robe 2014).[5]

The main shortcoming behind casting causal blame on speculative trading is that if speculative traders purchased futures contracts too far outside of current market fundamentals, and/or the market moved against their expectations, they would not be able to recoup their investment when trying to close their position. In the event of a margin call, the speculators will need to close their positions at a loss or pay the margin maintenance to stay in their losing position and risk further losses (Weiner 2002). Ultimately, even a large group of speculative oil futures traders that is capitalized adequately enough to influence intraday trades would still have to maintain a predictive accuracy of price formation and price timing to continue trading over longer time frames; otherwise they also risk losing their investment capital. The lack of evidence does not imply that market manipulation does not occur. However, in the case of oil futures contracts, successful large-scale market manipulation is inherently cost prohibitive.

When markets experience significant price shifts, speculators become relatively more visible to observers, but the evidence suggests that speculators do not cause meaningful price changes that overcome supply, demand, and inventory fundamentals (Knittel and Pindyck 2016). On the contrary, speculation that goes too far beyond current market pricing eliminates traders from the market. Recent findings indicate that oil price is endogenous to economic fundamentals, and speculative attempts to manipulate markets fail because of the sheer volume and cost of trading (Kilian 2014).

Geopolitical Events

While research does not identify oil speculation as a long-term causal variable in major oil markets, it does suggest that geopolitical events constitute exogenous forces that can impact energy demand and supply sides, causing increased price volatility. This effect was observed in the 2011 Libyan crisis and the 2012 Iranian nuclear issue (Kilian and Lee 2014). In those cases, geopolitical events raised oil prices by $3 to $12 per barrel in the Libyan crisis and up to $9 per barrel in the Iranian case because of the sanctions directed at Iran and its nuclear program. These types of oil shocks occur when sudden and unexpected price volatility reflects significant supply-side or demand-side changes. Demand-side shocks occur when global or regional economies experience drastic shifts, as was the case in the 2008 global financial crisis arising out of a credit market collapse, leading to the subsequent oil price collapse. Geopolitical events typically affect the supply side and can be especially pronounced when caused by regional conflicts such as those seen during the Arab Spring and the subsequent US and NATO Libya invasion (Auton and Slobodien 2016). The US and NATO actions in Libya resulted in the death of Muammar al-Gaddafi, the subsequent failure of the Libyan state, and the destruction of domestic oil production facilities. It is important to note that while the Arab Spring and the collapse of Libya caused increased short-term market volatility, energy markets remained stable over the long-term time frame (Darbouche and Fattouh 2011). Nonetheless, such geopolitical events provide potential opportunities for political scientists to examine geopolitics' exogenous role in supply and demand models and hypothesize about short-term market stability problems when facing geopolitical crises.

THE US SHALE OIL REVOLUTION AND OPEC's RESPONSE

The US shale oil revolution and its consequences is one of the most significant examples of how domestic and international politics can impact global oil markets. Over the past decade, global oil markets have experienced dramatic changes on the demand and supply sides. The United States is leaving the era of energy scarcity and entering into a period of energy abundance (Dale and Fattouh 2018; O'Sullivan 2017b).[6] According to the International Energy Agency (IEA), the United States was expected to become the "undisputed global leader for oil & gas" (Birol 2018). In 2018, the United States surpassed both Saudi Arabia and Russia to become the top global oil producer (Greenley 2019). Fatih Birol described the United States as having enormous shale oil production potential and identified its potential to become a silent revolution in the oil market. The executive director of the IEA estimated that US shale oil production will supply 60 percent of global demand by 2022 ("IEA Director Fatih Birol on Tariffs and US Oil Dominance" 2018). Production estimates indicate future output at eight million barrels per day (MBP/d), with a long-term production capacity outlook.

The US shale oil industry experienced a 500 percent, rapid growth increase in production in only six years when US shale oil production went from 1 MBP/d in 2011 to 5.5 MBP/d in 2017. During that time, the US shale oil industry faced declining demand in China and, more important, a Saudi Arabia–led OPEC attempt to protect its global market share. In 2014 the traders and investors expected to see Saudi oil production cuts; however, since Saudi Arabia and its OPEC allies could no longer control the origin of the resource, they sought to control the supply side. OPEC members wagered that by flooding the supply side inventory, they could drop oil prices low enough to force North

American shale oil producers into bankruptcy, allowing them to regain their lost market share. Even though the oil markets were seeing a concurrent demand slowdown out of East Asia, the Saudi decision to maintain production levels in the face of increased US oil production was responsible for a massive oil price drop in 2014 (Bataa and Park 2017). Both sides took extensive losses from OPEC's attempt to regain market share. Over one hundred North American shale oil producers filed for bankruptcy (Gore 2017), while Saudi Arabia and its oil-producing allies lost large amounts of expected income and were forced to cancel infrastructure investments necessary to maintain future production capacity. By 2017 Saudi Arabia had lost $220 billion in foreign currency reserves, and the country changed from a surplus economy to a deficit economy. As a result, Saudi Arabia was preparing to sell a 5 percent stake in its national oil company, Saudi Aramco, through an initial public offering (IPO). The sale was intended to recoup the state's oil losses, implement alternative sources of state revenue, and promote the crown prince's 2030 economic restructuring, which would bring Saudi Arabia into a new economic future (Markarian and Stockhausen 2018). The IPO was expected to bring in a $2 trillion valuation for the Saudi nationally owned company (NOC), but it was eventually canceled (*Reuters* 2018a).

The failed oil pricing scheme reflected Saudi Arabia's long-suspected internal turmoil (Wilson and Graham 1994) and its regional competition with Iran (Rezaei 2019). While reductions in global oil demand may have contributed to increased instability among oil producers (Rowland and Mjelde 2016), Saudi Arabia failed to account for the inherent flexibility of shale oil production costs (Behar and Ritz 2017), which proved critical to North American shale oil producers' survival. Shale oil producers cut costs by canceling future wells and instead focused on completed and proven wells. After drilling the wells, shale oil overhead costs fell because of relatively lower maintenance costs. By focusing on already proven wells and avoiding the higher expense of drilling new exploratory wells, many producers were able to cut operating costs. The already proven "sweet spot" wells strategy generated enough profits that producers were able to stay solvent and survive OPEC's attempt to regain market share. The US shale oil market continued to recover as oil prices increased from their 2014 lows to a high of $70 per barrel spot price in 2018 (EIA 2018).

Given the capital investment constraints affecting oil producers in 2014, many important lessons have been learned about how shale oil producers can come out of a price slump and then move to the top of the market. Those lessons have paid off as "capital efficiency has increased so much since the price collapse that one dollar of expenditure today will yield two and a half times the oil that it would have at the end of 2014" (O'Sullivan 2017b). The 2014 crude oil slump put many oil producers out of business, but it forced the remaining companies to improve their operating efficiencies, lower their service costs, and adopt new technologies to improve their shale oil extraction results (Kuuskraa 2018). The combination of increased efficiency, enhanced oil well productivity, and lower oilfield service costs reduced average break-even costs from $71 per barrel at the beginning of the slump to $44 per barrel in 2017. These break-even costs are expected to continue to decrease as technological advances in extraction methods within the shale oil production sector increase in efficiency. The overall North American recovery strategy proved successful, and the United States reached 7.9 MBP/d shale oil output in 2018 (*Reuters* 2018b).

Shale oil constitutes 50 percent of US total crude oil production, but its geological composition dictates unconventional extraction methods that translate into varying production cycles. The rapid increase of shale-oil-specific technologies is improving the industry as a whole, and we can expect future technologies to continue to progress by increasing efficiency levels and quality of extraction while lowering break-even costs (Kuuskraa). As technological advances adapt to regional and local needs, it is realistic to expect future exploration and extraction projects in currently inaccessible and cost-prohibitive regions such as China, where the clay-rich areas pose their own geological challenges to extraction (Wu et al. 2017).

OPEC's 2014 decision to maintain production levels forced US producers to reduce their oil rig counts by 80 percent before prices began to recover (Perry 2015), but OPEC's decision continues to be a contributing factor to other unintended consequences for oil markets and financing. Most notably, North American shale oil producers came out from under bankruptcy with more cost-efficient business models, more effective extraction technologies, and significantly lower break-even costs. In the end, Saudi Arabia was unable to maintain solidarity in its push for lower price formation, and the OPEC oil cartel proved unprepared to maintain the push for the length of time that would have been necessary to take US shale oil production entirely offline. More important, the broader energy producer landscape is changing. The Saudi Arabia that once led OPEC continues to be the major player in the field, but OPEC no longer maintains the degree of oil price influence it was previously accustomed to, and important questions have been raised about its perceived status as a commodity cartel (Colgan 2014; O'Sullivan 2017b; Van de Graaf 2017).

Another important lesson for US shale oil producers comes out of energy financing's role in the shale oil recovery. Since US shale oil producers are relatively small companies, they seek financing on a much smaller scale than traditional oil companies. We can find capital expenditure (CAPEX) data by looking at a company's investments in maintaining current and future oil production projects. Many of the producers and their financial backers discovered that small changes in financing can have a substantial impact on production (Diwan 2018). Unlike the much larger national and international oil companies that are engaged in the world's most capital-intensive business sector (Bressand 2013), many of the actors involved in US shale oil extraction are small operations that are staying financially solvent by relying on longer term contracts and rig count flexibility.

Given the significant availability of capital, if oil prices stay in the $60 range or increase, then US producers will have an easy time increasing their production investments, which were lacking during the market share battle with OPEC and the market slowdown in Asia. OPEC's secretary general Mohammad Barkindo recently explained that the 2015–2016 oil market rout created the unintended consequence of a $1 trillion shortfall in infrastructure investments that are necessary for future oil production projects. According to the head of Saudi Aramco, the oil industry needs $20 trillion to be invested in the industry over the next twenty-five years (Rosenbaum 2018).

As technological latecomers to the energy industry, US shale oil producers have had opportunities to adopt new technologies at a rapid pace, unhindered by a history of institutional practices. This is partly due to the fact that the US shale oil industry consists of many small, privately owned companies that have the opportunity to upgrade their capabilities as needed without concern for the industry as a whole. If US shale oil producers functioned like a cartel, they would have to acquiesce to a level of operational independence for the greater good of the institution. However, the fact that shale plays differ greatly within North America forces producers to operate in ways that are beneficial to each geological and logistical situation. Given the increase in capital expenditures for 2018 (Slater 2018), US shale producers will be able to adapt to new technologies more quickly and efficiently than their OPEC counterparts.

Saudi Arabia holds the swing producer title within the OPEC conglomerate, but after OPEC's failure to put a price floor into the market in 2014, this resulted in an oil price crash. US producers weathered the storm and emerged with a stronger upstream sector and increased global market share. This outcome poses the question of whether or not the United States could become a swing producer and exert enough influence to change global energy market fundamentals within a short period of time. If the United States develops the technical and geological potential to rapidly adjust production levels to meet market demands, then it will gain strategic geopolitical influence over the global oil trade. If that comes to fruition, then it will have significant political and market impact, but its current technological capabilities are not there yet. Saudi Arabia continues to carry the swing producer title within OPEC, but its menu of policy options is diminishing.

Despite earlier estimates that the United States did not have the production capacity potential necessary to become a net oil exporter, more recent estimates show that the Bakken basin alone still has eight billion barrels of technically recoverable oil (Smith 2018). International Energy Agency and the US Energy Information Agency assessments support long-term projections that the United States will be able to produce up to twelve million barrels per day in the 2020s. Technological developments in shale oil production have led to the biggest intensification of oil production in US history. However, it is important to point out that although the US shale oil industry is experiencing a growing energy oil boom, its business structure is unlike that of other major oil producers. The US shale energy industry is not a unitary actor and does not function like a nationally owned energy company, with interconnected corporate governance structures designed to operate in a uniform and rapid manner.

US shale oil producers consist of numerous companies pursuing different shale plays. EOG Resources, Pioneer Natural Resources, ExxonMobil, Chesapeake Energy, and Whiting Petroleum are some of the biggest shale players in the United States, but there are many smaller family-owned shale oil producers operating in North America. Consequently, operational structures and individual budgets are based on regional geological challenges and midstream considerations that would conflict with the loosely organized cartel structure that is familiar to OPEC members. When maintaining solvency during low oil price cycles and raising funds to invest in future development infrastructure, US shale oil producers would have found it challenging to pursue collective directives to guide their production activities. Research simulations indicate that US shale production would not be able to meet the one million barrels per day capacity increase needed within a ninety-day period that may be required of an oil production swing state (Newell and Prest 2017). The same simulations show that if oil prices increased by 50 percent, a one- to two-million-barrels-per-day capacity increase would take one to two years to fulfill, based on 2017 technology and infrastructure.

The scholars and analysts cited in this literature agree that oil markets are seeing significant structural changes to the supply side where geopolitical tension typically occurs within markets (Klare 2001). There is also little doubt that those tensions will continue to increase and dictate foreign policy changes among the top energy producers and consumers. As pointed out elsewhere in this Handbook (see Colgan and Stockbruegger in this volume), the topic of energy and international conflict is ripe for more research, especially research that includes perspectives from both the foreign policy world and the energy market world. Interdisciplinary perspectives from foreign policy scholars and energy market practitioners are needed to better inform their audiences about the structural and geopolitical factors that will dictate future foreign policy and energy market options. Numerous researchers express the view that maintaining a productive interdisciplinary approach is time intensive, but the results inform both fields more accurately and provide a more effective and impactful policy approach (O'Sullivan 2017a). As changes to the supply side continue to evolve and the US shale oil revolution grows, political scholars will find it worthwhile to stay abreast of the technological and economic variables in energy markets.

On the US shale governance topic, that specific industry faces numerous obstacles to being considered a cartel or a swing producer. The nature of the US shale oil industry creates a collective action problem that will continue to stand in the way of the creation of a North American commodity cartel. Moreover, the shale oil production process prevents it from functioning as a swing producer that could cut or increase production capacity to meet anticipated needs (O'Sullivan 2017b). Finally, the industry's financial backers are too numerous to hold to collectively coordinated political guidance on production output. The cartel issues notwithstanding, the American shale oil boom raises interesting questions about the oil market's current transition, how it would react to the volatility of US–OPEC energy production competition, and how it will absorb increasing US–China economic and security tensions.

China's Oil Market Impact

With much of the oil market integrated into the global economy, unexpected oil supply and price shocks continue to be the key concern for globalized markets and many industries beyond oil. China, which is now the world's top oil importer, will continue to shape global energy market trends well into the future (Birol 2018), thereby increasing the oil market's risk exposure to China's economic fluctuations. As the world's largest oil importer, China's economic health is the main determinant of its oil consumption and its resulting reliance on global oil markets.[7] Therefore, it's no surprise that its fiscal practices and economic health are receiving more close attention from OPEC, the IEA, and the United States. All states with significant trade linkages are carefully watching for leading indicators of oil import slowdowns by the PRC (Tan 2017).

Observers have been keeping a close watch on China's use of its strategic petroleum reserve facilities (SPR), which can be used for stockpiling oil as a hedge against rising prices. China's SPR increased in use in 2016 and 2017 with indications of physical facility expansion (Meng, Meng, and Woo, Ryan 2017). While SPR reliance has limited long-term value, it can have varying levels of short-term impact on oil producers when profit margins are thin. China's role in the global oil market will continue to remain on OPEC member states' radar, and significantly expanded SPR facilities can indicate increased oil price stability concerns.

Looking beyond its oil consumption, China continues to have a significant impact on global energy markets because of its massive expansion of credit as a domestic and international economic growth tool, a practice that is now gaining closer international attention since the beginning of its economic slowdown in 2015 (Magnier 2016). If China's economic growth is based on credit in lieu of true profit, then the country and its credit-backed ventures are at risk of suffering a cascading collapse that would create a price shock for the energy markets.

In 2015 China's economic downturn placed heavy pressure on already low commodity prices (Wiseman 2015), and that economic shift had a negative impact on China's energy investments abroad. When China decreased its foreign direct commodity investments abroad, the host energy production economies experienced the negative effects of decreased investment dollars and increased unemployment. Although such outcomes are to be expected in market downturns, these effects are increased in countries that were already weak due to their levels of domestic political instability, poor human rights records, and high poverty records. The practice of creating new trade linkages with politically or economically vulnerable states was part of China's going-out energy security strategy that began in the early 1990s and gained significant momentum after the 2008 global financial crisis (Wolfe and Tessman 2012).

The 2008 global financial crisis had relatively less impact on China than the United States and the European Union (EU), but it spurred a massive wave of credit capitalization or the use of loans as investment capital. Consequently, credit capitalization also grew within China's energy sector to allow China's NOCs to expand their global ventures into politically and economically high-risk investments. This approach shielded the NOCs from Western oil company competition, while it also provided them with opportunities to mature their international energy trade experience. China's NOCs pursued these activities by focusing on bilateral equity oil contracts, which encompass only a small minority portion of the global oil trade (Wolfe and Tessman 2012).

These energy deals were financed by the China Development Bank (CDB) through the use of loans and new lines of credit. When China began encouraging its going-out policy by funding and underwriting investment risks through the CDB, the energy deals went beyond OPEC countries and other already established oil producers. China's energy-seeking strategy included questionable investments in less internationally competitive states (Gholz, Awan, and Ronn 2017; Moreira 2013). Many of those states contained significant economic and political liabilities, which increased the risk of default on the new loans and lines of credit. Consequently, over the last decade China's NOCs, the CDB, and the China Export and Import Bank (CHEXIM) have absorbed energy production and processing infrastructure losses in significant overseas investment ventures. The most notable losses occurred in Libya, when China lost billions of US dollars in investments after civil unrest led to the destruction of energy infrastructure facilities ("Heavy Losses for Chinese Companies Operating in Libya" 2011). Prior to those losses, analysts observed that these deals proved to be helpful to China's NOCs and the banks underwriting the investments because the investments helped them gain market experience and expand their future global acquisitions potential. The early going-out experience resulted in numerous energy and commodity projects in Central Asia, Russia, Pakistan, and Myanmar (Downs 2011).

The going-out strategy continues but on a much larger scale as China emerges as a peer among other top global lenders offering general project financing and energy project financing (Gallagher et al. 2016). China's power plant technology exports are double the size of US global market share (Kong and Gallagher 2017). China first began its going-out policy nearly three decades ago, relying extensively on its policy banks, the CDB and the CHEXIM, to globalize its ability to finance energy infrastructure projects. Throughout this time, China has been providing energy infrastructure services through its NOCs. The fruit of their labor over the past decade has put them at the forefront of the industry. In 2016 China created the Asian Infrastructure Investment Bank (AIIB), which now lists eighty-four member states. China was also party to establishing the New Development Bank (NDB) in partnership with other BRICS (Brazil, Russia, India, China, and South Africa) states. As credit-based investment increased, China's nonfinancial sector credit-to-GDP ratio increased, from 135 percent of gross domestic product (GDP) before the 2008 global financial crisis to 235 percent of GDP in 2016 ("Global Financial Stability Report" 2018). The consequence of this meant that the concurrent rise of sovereign and corporate debt has promoted credit as an alternative asset class with its own inherent financial risks.

China's Credit Markets

China's credit market issues could contribute to a negative cascading effect that net oil import economies have on energy markets during economic downturns. Economic downturns are a normal part of the broader fiscal cycle, but structural credit weaknesses intensify those downturns, causing greater fiscal damage than would have otherwise occurred. The boundaries between financial institutions and financial markets are increasingly porous, creating increased systemic risk as alternative forms of financing saturate the energy industry. This is relevant to the politics of oil markets because of China's significant influence on global oil demand and the resulting economic stability of energy-producing countries. Energy markets have benefited from China's multiple decades of double-digit economic growth. However, as China's debt-to-GDP ratio is expected to rise to over 320 percent by 2022 (Hamlin and Zhao 2018), China's trading partners will face negative consequences in the event of a significant and lengthy economic downturn, which will be intensified through China's expansion into energy financing.

Analysts have long warned investors about the potential of a hard landing for China's economy (Brown 2012), and the International Monetary Fund (IMF) issued repeated warnings about the inherent risks behind China's attempts to stabilize its economy through credit allocation, specifically in the energy sector ("Global Financial Stability Report" 2018). In response to growing concerns, the Central Commission of Comprehensive Reforms has endorsed new regulations on capital requirements for credit financing (Tang 2018), and China's credit problems are now under President Xi Jinping's direct regulatory focus as the China Banking Regulatory Commission has vowed to deal with the problem through increased oversight (Jiaxin 2018). However, China's record-breaking use of credit to undergird its economy continues, while its fundamental financial stabilizers have been weakening since 2012 (Wright and Rosen 2018). In 2019 there was little progress toward limiting China's expanding debt problem (Yu and Jiefei 2019), and the issue is now affecting a widening cross-section of businesses (Leng 2018).

China's debt problem is compounded as banks and nonbanking organizations still issue loans to unprofitable firms, thereby increasing the size of China's shadow banking industry (Trivedi 2017). Shadow banking occurs when nonbanking institutions facilitate credit risk transfers, leverage, and financial transformations using short-term loans or other cash-like liabilities to fund long-term assets. These institutions engage in core banking functions similar to those that played a role in the 2008 global financial crisis (Kodres 2013). Shadow banking is a common practice by entities that are not banking institutions but function as banks without the institutional oversight of banking regulations. If markets move unexpectedly, causing the long-term assets to lose value, then the institutions will lose their investments and could cease to function. This type of bankruptcy commonly occurs in failed nonbank ventures, including insurance firms, microloan organizations, and payday lending businesses. However, if shadow banks have direct linkages to regulated banking institutions, shadow bank failures will then expose the banking sector to wider systemic risk. Using a broad measure, the Financial Stability Board estimates that among the EU and twenty-one jurisdictions accounting for 80 percent of the global GDP, nonbank financing contributes $160 trillion to the global GDP ("Global Shadow Banking Monitoring Report 2017" 2018). China has integrated credit-based growth and shadow banking into its economic model, which could lead to price shocks and significant volatility in oil markets.

China's debt problem and its oil trading issues are beginning to gain more traction with political researchers, but the literature presented in this section shows that there is ample room for future theoretical contributions from the political perspective. Since the majority of the sources cited in this chapter come from economics, they focus on price, market fundamentals, finance, and econometrics. The main criticism of economics-based literature is the lack of consideration for political variables, but its strength is evident in its ability to identify and describe the economic structures underpinning the oil market events. Future research should focus on developing more political models that can bring political analysis to create a more interdisciplinary approach to oil market analysis.

A FUTURE RESEARCH AGENDA

In capitalizing on IPEE's relative advantage, research topics should focus on examining how political variables explain outcomes within the different sectors of the oil market's supply and demand value chain and how those political variables impact market reliability and stability. Oil markets are intended to absorb changes in energy supply and demand values, but market data do not interpret political activity. The researcher's challenge is to operationalize political variables to function as lead indicators of energy market changes that cannot be explained by cyclical market patterns.

The topic of market volatility would benefit from IPEE research examining political sources of market instability. The existence of market volatility itself is not a detriment to market function, but if research helped practitioners and policy makers better understand how politics plays a role in decreasing risk perception in energy markets, that would aid in reducing volatility duration and frequency, which is currently measured through the volatility index. The volatility index or VIX was created by the Chicago Board Options Exchange to measure market volatility and infer future volatility levels. The VIX is commonly referred to as the "fear index." It derives its values from S&P 500 Index options and is entirely financial in nature. Successfully developing an energy and politics volatility index inclusive of qualitative variables that impact energy market movements would be highly beneficial for both scholars and practitioners. The current market assumption, which underlies the construction of the popular VIX, is that market buy and sale prices across commodities and investment products are inclusive of the political variables in effect at the time. However, the political variables assumed in the price are left unidentified, and there is no causal explanation. A blended approach of price data and political variables within a parsimonious index would have tremendous value in measuring political effects on energy market volatility.

Much of the VIX literature is heavily quantitative in nature, but the broader reviews will provide helpful insights into the predictive potential of the tool (Bekaert and Hoerova 2014). It may also be helpful to conceptualize how to use the VIX as part of a broader systemic risk assessment that includes factors such as trade linkages when determining the risks of future economic and/or political shocks (Blancher et al. 2013). Such an approach opens the door to more politically oriented variables that are not explicitly captured by econometric models.

Another research area that could benefit from more attention is the political economy of sovereign wealth funds, which is an especially important issue in high energy production and consumption states (Hancock and Vivoda 2014). As the China discussion in this chapter notes, the economic health of countries with relatively large influence on oil markets is a crucial explanatory variable for researchers and practitioners seeking to better ascertain future oil trends. Three of the top five global sovereign wealth funds invest in oil, and their combined value is estimated at $3.3 trillion ("Sovereign Wealth Fund Rankings" 2018). China has the world's second most valued sovereign wealth fund, and although it officially does not invest in oil, it was in talks to become a principal investor in Saudi Arabia's Aramco public offering, which could have given China a significant political advantage within the organization. Given sovereign wealth funds' substantial fiscal power and the reality that these funds are intended to represent state interests, it would be prudent for IPEE scholars to examine the role of sovereign wealth funds not only for their impact on oil markets but also more specifically for their impact on oil producers, refiners, and transportation logistics.

Turning once again to China, there are many future research topics to consider that deal with China's increased impact on oil markets, energy financing, and emerging market economies, all of which affect global oil demand and market stability. Emerging markets can account for oil demand shocks on upstream, midstream, and downstream industry segments. Because energy production is one of the most capital-intensive global industries, it has the potential to produce far-reaching economic consequences for energy-producing economies. Credit risk is a pervasive issue for China, with increasing financial contagion concerns. When oil trade is combined with extensive credit risk exposure, it adds complexity and risk to the oil market equilibrium and exposes emerging market economies to financial spillover effects (Mwase et al. 2016). Crude oil commodity linkages among emerging economies are especially susceptible to industrial shock contagion (Kolerus, N'Diaye, and Saborowiski 2016). In identifying future risk variables for energy market watchers, the significant question to ask is whether sovereign debt or corporate debt contains greater risk of default. If state debt is the primary concern, then how can a globalized oil industry limit its exposure to historically inevitable market shocks? Researchers seeking to explain these oil market dynamics may benefit from examining the wide-ranging diversity of market participants, the extensive use of derivatives as trading instruments, and the rapidly changing technological developments that affect extraction and refining operations.

Finally, IPEE researchers may benefit from examining the evolving foreign policy outcomes of the United States becoming a major global energy producer and how that role is changing existing oil market structures to accommodate the technical aspects of shale oil production. The non-conglomerate nature of the shale oil industry prevents the existence of an OPEC-like cartel over shale oil and its financial backers. As the industry continues to thrive and expand, can it develop into an influential political actor despite its non-conglomerate nature? This industry is experiencing its share of growing pains, but given its economic and political potential for the United States, how will it change oil market structures, and will it challenge the global nature of oil markets?

Notes

1. See U.S. Commodity Futures Trading Commission (2019).
2. See CME Group (2019a).
3. See CME Group (2019b).
4. All currency references are in US dollars.
5. These findings do not include regional or national markets that may be prone to speculative swings due to low trading volume, limited trade execution transparency, or poor trade regulation enforcement.
6. This section is inclusive of additional energy products such as shale oil, also known as tight oil. The purpose of this section is to discuss US energy production as a significant change to the supply side status quo and as an emerging geopolitical variable.
7. China's economic stability plays a direct role in its internal political stability and the longevity of the current government. It is assumed that a political downturn in China would be detrimental to the country's economy and to the energy producers that are dependent on China's economic growth.

References

Aalto, Pami. 2014. "Energy Market Integration and Regional Institutions in East Asia." *Energy Policy* 74: 91–100. doi:10.1016/j.enpol.2014.08.021.

Auton, Graeme P., and Jacob R. Slobodien. 2016. "The Contagious of Regional Conflict." *Journal of International Affairs* 69, no. 2: 3–18.

Bataa, Erdenebat, and Cheolbeom Park. 2017. "Is the Recent Low Oil Price Attributable to the Shale Revolution?" *Energy Economics* 67 (September): 72–82. doi:10.1016/j.eneco.2017.08.011.

Behar, Alberto, and Robert A. Ritz. 2017. "OPEC vs US Shale: Analyzing the Shift to a Market-Share Strategy." *Energy Economics* 63 (March): 185–198. doi:10.1016/j.eneco.2016.12.021.

Bekaert, Geert, and Marie Hoerova. 2014. "The VIX, the Variance Premium and Stock Market Volatility." *Journal of Econometrics* 183, no. 2: 181–192. doi:10.1016/j.jeconom.2014.05.008.

Birol, Fatih. 2018. "World Energy Outlook 2017." Presented at the IEA's World Energy Outlook 2017, Center for Strategic & International Studies, January 16. https://www.csis.org/events/ieas-world-energy-outlook-2017.

Blancher, Nicolas R., NBlancher@imf.org, Srobona Mitra, SMitra@imf.org, Hanan Morsy, HMorsy@imf.org, Akira Otani, et al. 2013. "Systemic Risk Monitoring ('SysMo') Toolkit—A User Guide." *IMF Working Papers* 13, no. 168: i. doi:10.5089/9781484383438.001.

Bressand, Albert. 2013. "The Role of Markets and Investment in Global Energy." In *The Handbook of Global Energy Policy*, 1st ed., 15–29. Handbooks of Global Policy Series. New York: John Wiley & Sons.

Brown, Mark. 2012. "China Hard Landing Scenario Shows Uneven Global Impact – Fitch Ratings." *Fitch Wire*. Fitch Ratings. https://www.fitchratings.com/gws/en/fitchwire/fitch-wirearticle/China-Hard-Landing?pr_id=776242.

Büyükşahin, Bahattin, and Michel A. Robe. 2014. "Speculators, Commodities and Cross-Market Linkages." *Journal of International Money and Finance* 42 (April): 38–70. doi:10.1016/j. jimonfin.2013.08.004.

Chen, Sally, and Joong Shik Kang. 2018. "Credit Booms—Is China Different?" Working Paper no. 18/2. International Monetary Fund. https://www.imf.org/en/Publications/WP/Issues/2018/01/05/Credit-Booms-Is-China-Different-45537.

CME Group. 2019a. "Futures & Options Trading for Risk Management." http://www.cme-group.com.

CME Group. 2019b. "NYMEX." https://www.cmegroup.com/company/nymex.html.

Coleman, Les. 2012. "Explaining Crude Oil Prices Using Fundamental Measures." *Energy Policy* 40 (January): 318–324. doi:10.1016/j.enpol.2011.10.012.

Colgan, Jeff D. 2014. "The Emperor Has No Clothes: The Limits of OPEC in the Global Oil Market." *International Organization* 68, no. 03: 599–632. doi:10.1017/S0020818313000489.

Dale, Spencer, and Bassam Fattouh. 2018. "Peak Oil Demand and Long-Run Oil Prices." The Oxford Institute for Energy Studies. https://www.oxfordenergy.org/publications/peak-oil-demand-long-run-oil-prices/.

Darbouche, Hakim, and Bassam Fattouh. 2011. *The Implications of the Arab Uprisings for Oil and Gas Markets.* Oxford: Oxford Institute for Energy Studies.

Diwan, Roger. 2018. "The Short-Term Outlook for U.S. Tight Oil Production—Financial Appetite for Investors? New Business Model for Producers?" Presented at The Short-Term Outlook for U.S. Tight Oil Production, Washington, DC, February 27. https://www.csis.org/events/short-term-outlook-us-tight-oil-production.

Downs, Erica S. 2011. "China Development Bank's Oil Loans: Pursuing Policy and Profit." https://www.brookings.edu/articles/china-development-banks-oil-loans-pursuing-policy-and-profit/.

EIA. 2018. "Cushing, OK WTI Spot Price FOB (Dollars per Barrel)." March 18. https://www.eia.gov/dnav/pet/hist/LeafHandler.ashx?n=PET&s=RWTC&f=D.

Gallagher, Kevin P., Rohini Kamal, Yongzhong Wang, and Yanning Chen. 2016. "Fueling Growth and Financing Risk: The Benefits and Risks of China's Development Finance in the Global Energy Sector." GEGI Working Paper no. 2. 05/2016. Boston University Global Economic Governance Initiative. https://open.bu.edu/handle/2144/23650.

Gholz, Eugene, Umul Awan, and Ehud Ronn. 2017. "Financial and Energy Security Analysis of China's Loan-for-Oil Deals." *Energy Research & Social Science* 24 (February): 42–50. doi:10.1016/j.erss.2016.12.021.

"Global Financial Stability Report." 2018. International Monetary Fund. http://www.imf.org/en/Publications/GFSR/Issues/2018/04/02/Global-Financial-Stability-Report-April-2018.

"Global Shadow Banking Monitoring Report 2017." 2018. Financial Stability Board. http://www.fsb.org/2018/03/global-shadow-banking-monitoring-report-2017/.

Gore, Gareth. 2017. "Back from the Dead: US Shale Is Booming Again." IFRe, March 10. http://www.ifre.com/back-from-the-dead-us-shale-is-booming-again/21282139.article.

Greenley, Heather L. 2019. "The World Oil Market and U.S. Policy: Background and Select Issues for Congress." R45493. Congressional Research Service, Library of Congress. https://crsreports.congress.gov.

Hajiyev, Nazim. 2019. *World Market Price of Oil: Impacting Factors and Forecasting.* S.l.: Springer.

Hamilton, James D., and Jing Cynthia Wu. 2014. "Risk Premia in Crude Oil Futures Prices." *Journal of International Money and Finance* 42 (April): 9–37. doi:10.1016/j.jimonfin.2013.08.003.

Hamlin, Kevin, and Yinan Zhao. 2018. "The Biggest Threats to China's Economy in 2018." *Bloomberg*, January 1. https://www.bloomberg.com/news/articles/2018-01-01/china-warms-up-for-2018-critical-battles-with-cooling-economy.

Hancock, Kathleen J., and Vlado Vivoda. 2014. "International Political Economy: A Field Born of the OPEC Crisis Returns to Its Energy Roots." *Energy Research & Social Science* 1: 206–216. doi:10.1016/j.erss.2014.03.017.

"Heavy Losses for Chinese Companies Operating in Libya." 2011. AsiaNews.It, February 26. http://www.asianews.it/news-en/Heavy-losses-for-Chinese-companies-operating-in-Libya-20887.html.

Hughes, Llewelyn, and Phillip Y. Lipscy. 2013. "The Politics of Energy." *Annual Review of Political Science* 16, no. 1: 449–469. doi:10.1146/annurev-polisci-072211-143240.

"IEA Director Fatih Birol on Tariffs and US Oil Dominance." 2018. CNBC, March 6. https://www.cnbc.com/video/2018/03/06/iea-director-fatih-birol-on-tariffs-and-us-oil-dominance.html.

Jiaxin. 2018. "Economic Watch: China Steps up Banking Oversight to Prevent Risks—Xinhua/English.News.Cn." Xinhuanet, January 22. http://www.xinhuanet.com/english/2018-01/22/c_136915449.htm.

Karali, Berna, and Octavio A. Ramirez. 2014. "Macro Determinants of Volatility and Volatility Spillover in Energy Markets." *Energy Economics* 46 (November): 413–421. doi:10.1016/j.eneco.2014.06.004.

Keohane, Robert O. 2009. "The Old IPE and the New." *Review of International Political Economy* 16, no. 1: 34–46. doi:10.1080/09692290802524059.

Kilian, Lutz. 2014. "Oil Price Shocks: Causes and Consequences." *Annual Review of Resource Economics* 6, no. 1: 133–154.

Kilian, Lutz, and Thomas K. Lee. 2014. "Quantifying the Speculative Component in the Real Price of Oil: The Role of Global Oil Inventories." *Journal of International Money and Finance* 42 (April): 71–87. doi:10.1016/j.jimonfin.2013.08.005.

Klare, Michael. 2001. *Resource Wars: The New Landscape of Global Conflict.* New York: Metropolitan Books.

Knittel, Christopher R., and Robert S. Pindyck. 2016. "The Simple Economics of Commodity Price Speculation." *American Economic Journal: Macroeconomics* 8, no. 2: 85–110. doi:10.1257/mac.20140033.

Kodres, Laura E. 2013. "What Is Shadow Banking?" *IMF Finance & Development* 50, no. 2. http://www.imf.org/external/pubs/ft/fandd/2013/06/basics.htm.

Kolerus, Christina, Papa N'Diaye, and Christian Saborowiski. 2016. "China's Footprint in Global Commodity Markets." Spillover Notes. International Monetary Fund. doi:10.5089/9781475541069.062.

Kong, Bo, and Kevin P. Gallagher. 2017. "Globalizing Chinese Energy Finance: The Role of Policy Banks." *Journal of Contemporary China* 26, no. 108: 834–851. doi:10.1080/10670564.2017.1337307.

Kurt, Daniel. 2014. "Understanding Benchmark Oils: Brent Blend, WTI and Dubai." Investopedia, October 23. https://www.investopedia.com/articles/investing/102314/understanding-benchmark-oils-brent-blend-wti-and-dubai.asp.

Kuuskraa, Vello. 2018. "Evolution of U.S. Tight Oil Development and Its Applicability to Other Global Plays." Presented at The Short-Term Outlook for U.S. Tight Oil Production, February 27. https://www.csis.org/events/short-term-outlook-us-tight-oil-production.

Le Billon, Philippe. 2004. "The Geopolitical Economy of 'Resource Wars.'" *Geopolitics* 9, no. 1: 1–28. doi:10.1080/14650040412331307812.

Lean, Hooi Hooi, Michael McAleer, and Wing-Keung Wong. 2010. "Market Efficiency of Oil Spot and Futures: A Mean-Variance and Stochastic Dominance Approach." *Energy Economics* 32, no. 5: 979–986. doi:10.1016/j.eneco.2010.05.001.

Leng, Sidney. 2018. "Why China's Private Firms Are Falling into a Shadowy Debt Black Hole." *South China Morning Post*, July 18. https://www.scmp.com/news/china/economy/article/2155706/caught-chinas-cash-crunch-why-private-companies-are-collapsing.

Lin Lawell, C.-Y. Cynthia. 2008. "Estimating Supply and Demand in the World Oil Market." Working Paper no. 225893. University of California, Davis, Department of Agricultural and Resource Economics. https://econpapers.repec.org/paper/agsucdavw/225893.htm.

Magnier, Mark. 2016. "China's Economic Growth in 2015 Is Slowest in 25 Years." *Wall Street Journal*, January 19, World section. http://www.wsj.com/articles/china-economic-growth-slows-to-6-9-on-year-in-2015-1453169398.

Markarian, Garen, and Tobias Stockhausen. 2018. "Quo Vadis: Politics, Uncertainty and Saudi Aramco." *The Journal of World Energy Law & Business* 11, no. 6: 487–505. doi:10.1093/jwelb/jwy027.

Markus, Ustina. 2016. "The International Oil and Gas Pricing Regimes." In *The Palgrave Handbook of the International Political Economy of Energy*, edited by Thijs Van de Graaf, Benjamin K. Sovacool, Arunabha Ghosh, Florian Kern, and Michael T. Klare, 225–246. London: Palgrave Macmillan UK. doi:10.1057/978-1-137-55631-8_9.

Meng, Meng, and Ryan Woo. 2017. "UPDATE 2-China Accelerates Stockpiling of State Oil Reserves Over." *Reuters*, December 29. https://www.reuters.com/article/china-crude-reserves/update-2-china-accelerates-stockpiling-of-state-oil-reserves-over-2016-17-idUSL4N1OT2HF.

Moreira, Susana. 2013. "Learning from Failure: China's Overseas Oil Investments." *Journal of Current Chinese Affairs* 42, no. 1: 131–165.

Mwase, Nkunde, Papa M. N'Diaye, Hiroko Oura, Frantisek Ricka, Katsiaryna Svirydzenka, and Yuanyan S Zhang. 2016. "Spillovers from China; Financial Channels." IMF Spillover Notes 16/05. International Monetary Fund. https://EconPapers.repec.org/RePEc:imf:imfson:16/05.

Newell, Richard G., and Brian Prest. 2017. "Is the US the New Swing Producer? The Price Responsiveness of Tight Oil." SSRN Scholarly Paper ID 3093968. Rochester, NY: Social Science Research Network. https://papers.ssrn.com/abstract=3093968.

O'Sullivan, Meghan. 2017a. "Columbia | SIPA Center on Global Energy Policy | Windfall: How the New Energy Abundance Upends Global Politics and Strengthens America's Power." Columbia University, September 11. https://energypolicy.columbia.edu/events-calendar/windfall-how-new-energy-abundance-upends-global-politics-and-strengthens-americas-power.

O'Sullivan, Meghan. 2017b. *Windfall*. Simon & Schuster. https://www.simonandschuster.com/books/Windfall/Meghan-L-OSullivan/9781501107948.

Perry, Mark. 2015. "Saudis' Drive to Kill US Shale Has Backfired." AEI, May 26. http://www.aei.org/publication/saudis-drive-to-kill-us-shale-has-backfired/.

Reuters. 2018a. "Exclusive: Aramco IPO Halted, Oil Giant Disbands Advisers—Sources," *Reuters*, August 23. https://www.reuters.com/article/us-saudi-aramco-ipo-exclusive-idUSKCN1L71TZ.

Reuters. 2018b. "U.S. Shale Oil Output to Hit Record High 7.9 Million Barrels Per Day in December: EIA." November 13. https://www.reuters.com/article/us-usa-oil-productivity-idUSKCN1NI2JV.

Rezaei, Farhad. 2019. "Iran and Saudi Arabia: The Struggle for Regional Hegemony and Islamic Primacy." In *Iran's Foreign Policy After the Nuclear Agreement*, by Farhad Rezaei, 163–187. Cham: Springer International Publishing. doi:10.1007/978-3-319-76789-5_7.

Rosenbaum, Eric. 2018. "OPEC's Barkindo: 'Sowing Seeds for Future Global Energy Crisis.'" CNBC, March 6. https://www.cnbc.com/2018/03/06/opecs-barkindo-sowing-seeds-for-future-global-energy-crisis.html.

Rowland, Christopher S., and James W. Mjelde. 2016. "Politics and Petroleum: Unintended Implications of Global Oil Demand Reduction Policies." *Energy Research & Social Science* 11 (January): 209–224. doi:10.1016/j.erss.2015.10.003.

Simkins, Betty J., and Russell E. Simkins, eds. 2013. *Energy Finance and Economics: Analysis and Valuation, Risk Management, and the Future of Energy*. The Robert W. Kolb Series in Finance. Hoboken, NJ: Wiley.

Slater, Neal. 2018. "Confidence and Control: The Outlook for the Oil and Gas Industry in 2018." DNV GL. https://www.dnvgl.com/news/research-forecasts-oil-and-gas-capex-and-r-d-spending-boosts-in-2018-but-industry-still-promises-to-keep-a-cap-on-costs-110318.

Smith, James L. 2018. "Estimating the Future Supply of Shale Oil: A Bakken Case Study." *Energy Economics* 69 (January): 395–403. doi:10.1016/j.eneco.2017.11.026.

Sovacool, Benjamin K. 2014. "What Are We Doing Here? Analyzing Fifteen Years of Energy Scholarship and Proposing a Social Science Research Agenda." *Energy Research & Social Science* 1 (March): 1–29. doi:10.1016/j.erss.2014.02.003.

"Sovereign Wealth Fund Rankings." 2018. Sovereign Wealth Fund Institute. https://www.swfinstitute.org/sovereign-wealth-fund-rankings/.

Tan, Huileng. 2017. "China Is Downside Risk for Oil Prices as OPEC Meets: Analyst." CNBC, May 24. https://www.cnbc.com/2017/05/24/up.html.

Tang, Frank. 2018. "China's Leaders Sign off on New Rules to Crack down on 'Shadow Banking.'" *South China Morning Post*, March 30. http://www.scmp.com/news/china/economy/article/2139695/chinas-leaders-sign-new-rules-crack-down-shadow-banking.

Trivedi, Anjani. 2017. "China's $20 Trillion Shadow Banking Business Won't Be Easily Tamed." *Wall Street Journal*, October 17, Markets section. https://www.wsj.com/articles/chinas-greatest-challenge-1508137030.

U.S. Commodity Futures Trading Commission. 2019. Home page. https://www.cftc.gov/.

Van de Graaf, Thijs. 2017. "Is OPEC Dead? Oil Exporters, the Paris Agreement and the Transition to a Post-Carbon World." *Energy Research & Social Science* 23 (January): 182–188. doi:10.1016/j.erss.2016.10.005.

Van de Graaf, Thijs, Benjamin K. Sovacool, Arunabha Ghosh, Florian Kern, and Michael T. Klare, eds. 2016. *The Palgrave Handbook of the International Political Economy of Energy*. London: Palgrave Macmillan UK. doi:10.1057/978-1-137-55631-8.

Weiner, Robert J. 2002. "Sheep in Wolves' Clothing? Speculators and Price Volatility in Petroleum Futures." *Quarterly Review of Economics and Finance* 42, no. 2: 391–400. doi:10.1016/S1062-9769(02)00135-7.

Williams, Jeffrey C. 2001. "Chapter 13 Commodity Futures and Options." In *Handbook of Agricultural Economics* 1: 745–816. Elsevier. doi:10.1016/S1574-0072(01)10021-6.

Wilson, Peter W., and Douglas F. Graham. 1994. *Saudi Arabia: The Coming Storm*. London and New York: Routledge.

Wiseman, Paul. 2015. "China's Economic Slowdown Is Biggest Business Story of 2015." NBC News, December 27. https://www.nbcnews.com/storyline/2015-year-in-review/china-s-economic-slowdown-biggest-business-story-2015-n484131.

Wolfe, Wojtek M., and Brock F. Tessman. 2012. "China's Global Equity Oil Investments: Economic and Geopolitical Influences." *Journal of Strategic Studies* 35, no. 2: 175–196. doi:10.1080/01402390.2011.635467.

Wright, Logan, and Daniel Rosen. 2018. "Credit and Credibility: Risks to China's Economic Resilience." Center for Strategic & International Studies. https://www.csis.org/analysis/credit-and-credibility-risks-chinas-economic-resilience.

Wu, Jin, Feng Liang, Wen Lin, Hongyan Wang, Wenhua Bai, Chao Ma, Shasha Sun, et al. 2017. "Characteristics of Shale Gas Reservoirs in Wufeng Formation and Longmaxi Formation in Well WX2, Northeast Chongqing." *Petroleum Research* 2, no. 4: 324–335. doi:10.1016/j.ptlrs.2017.05.002.

Yu, Zhang, and Liu Jiefei. 2019. "China Sees Setback in Efforts to Keep Debt in Check." *Caixin*, Finance section. https://www.caixinglobal.com/2019-05-29/china-sees-setback-in-efforts-to-keep-debt-in-check-101421350.html.

CHAPTER 16

....

THE POLITICS
OF ENERGY AND
CLIMATE CHANGE

....

LLEWELYN HUGHES

CARBON dioxide (CO_2) is a byproduct produced during the burning of fossil fuels such as oil, coal, and natural gas. It constitutes the largest share of greenhouse gases (GHG) in the atmosphere attributable to human behavior, although gases such as methane also matter (Blanco et al. 2014, 354). Human activities producing GHG emissions are already estimated to be responsible for 1 degree Celsius of global warming above preindustrial levels (IPCC 2018), and the risk of catastrophic future changes in the climate is sufficiently worrisome that signatories to the 1992 United Nations Framework Convention on Climate Change (UNFCCC) agreed that the "lack of full scientific certainty should not be used as a reason for postponing . . . measures" (United Nations 1992).

The emission of GHGs is linked to the provision of heating, lighting, transport, and other energy products and services that are fundamental to human societies (Unruh 2000). Solving the climate change problem requires rapidly transforming the technological, institutional, and social systems that underpin the energy infrastructure providing these services. In terms of policy levers, mitigating climate change implies targeting population growth, gross domestic product (GDP) per capita, the energy intensity of GDP, and the GHG intensity of energy use (Rosa and Dietz 2012). Policy overwhelmingly focuses on the latter two factors, given ethical concerns with limiting populations or economic growth.

Social science has a crucial role to play in helping to decarbonize global energy systems by identifying which policies are feasible and effective in reducing the energy needed and transforming the types of energy used (Barbier and Pearce 1990). Social science can also inform policy makers and others about political and institutional strategies conducive to implementing more ambitious policies, by deepening our understanding of the responses of individuals and organizations toward different climate-policy mixes in the energy sector and showing how domestic and international institutions structure the bargaining power of these actors.

In the first section of this chapter I review major avenues of research in the political science subfield that consider the politics of energy and climate change. I emphasize work that presents general findings, although there are a large number of important studies that focus on single states or economic sectors, and some of these are included. I also concentrate on more recent results, referring readers to reviews that summarize earlier findings on aspects of the politics of climate change and the politics of energy (Bernauer 2013; Hancock and Vivoda 2014; Goldthau and Keating 2018; Hughes and Lipscy 2013).

Political science has only recently begun to engage more deeply with energy policy in the context of climate change as a discipline, and there are many important areas of research that require attention as a result. The role of supply-side policies in restricting the use of fossil fuels, for example, is a new and urgent focus of research (Green and Denniss 2018). Understanding the politics of climate adaptation is also critical as the effects of climate change become apparent.

In the second section of the chapter I highlight three issues with the potential to promote more rapid decarbonization of energy systems, but which have not been a sustained focus of research to date. The first is the politics of low-carbon economic development. The vast bulk of future energy demand is projected to lie in lower-income states, with India and China particularly important due to their large populations. Yet there is much still to be learned about the relationship between politics and climate-related energy politics in many of these states. Despite the myriad successes in deploying renewable energy sources such as solar photovoltaic (PV) and wind power in the electricity sector, demand for fossil fuels continues to grow. The world needs to rapidly increase the rate at which we slow and reverse the growth in energy-related GHG emissions. Thus, a second area of potential research lies in identifying how governments can help innovate and deploy new technologies more quickly in order to decarbonize energy systems. Third, our collective failure to date to reduce GHG emissions at a rate required to avoid potentially catastrophic levels of climate change increases the possibility that we will need to rapidly develop and deploy negative emissions and geoengineering technologies at scale. An important research question is how politics might affect technology choices and levels of investment in negative emissions and geoengineering technologies in the energy sector.

The chapter begins with a brief overview of the relationship between energy use and climate change. The main section summarizes the state of knowledge on the relationship between politics and energy and climate change, discussing political actors involved in shaping climate-related energy policy, beginning with individuals, then addressing business and civil society. The chapter then discusses the role of government, understood either as a political actor or as a set of institutions that shapes interactions between other actors. In the last section I discuss the politics of climate-related energy policy in lower-income states, technological innovation and deployment, and the politics of negative emissions and geoengineering.

ENERGY AND CLIMATE CHANGE

The Intergovernmental Panel on Climate Change (IPCC) has found that growing concentrations of GHGs in the atmosphere, along with other anthropogenic drivers of climate change, are *"extremely likely* to have been the dominant cause of the observed warming since the mid-20th century" (IPCC 2014, 2–4).[1] Much of this is attributable to the increase in CO_2, with atmospheric concentrations higher than they have been in at least 800,000 years. Changes in the climate will continue hundreds of years into the future, even if humans were immediately to stop emitting GHGs, with the added risk of negative feedback loops caused by human-induced warming (Wagner and Weitzman 2016). Projected changes include sea level rise and more intense rainfall, drought, and heat waves, with projected impacts on natural and human systems growing in severity as the temperature increases (IPCC 2018). Demand continues to increase for fuels that emit GHGs—primarily CO_2 but including methane and other gases—as a byproduct of providing energy services (See Figure 16.1).

The continued increase in GHG emissions is occurring despite the rapid rise in the deployment of renewable energy sources such as solar PVs and wind power, and despite improvements in efficiency of energy use (See Figure 16.2). Renewable energy, for example, has increased its share of total global energy consumption. However, total demand continues to increase (REN21 2018), and this has been met mostly by natural gas and crude oil. Even the demand for coal increased by 1 percent in 2017, driven largely by consumption increases in India and China (BP 2018, 2). (For detailed discussions of the politics of energy in India and China, see Powell and Nahm, respectively, in this volume.)

Some analysts and practitioners argue that nuclear energy and carbon capture and sequestration are important for reducing GHG emissions. However, the high costs and technical and perceived safety challenges of these two technologies mean they continue to face challenges in being deployed at scale. As such, they are not addressed in this chapter. (For background on nuclear energy, see Fitzwater, and for carbon capture, see Tutuncu's chapter on fossil fuels, both in this volume.)

While the growth of low-carbon energy sources is impressive, far more needs to be done to scale-up their deployment in order to ensure energy produced by these sources rapidly replaces the use of coal, oil, and natural gas in meeting global energy demand. This process is inherently political, due to its enormous distributional implications. Failure to stabilize GHG emissions to date by replacing fossil fuels with low-carbon energy sources means future reductions will need to occur even more rapidly in order to reduce the probability of catastrophic climate change, absent the widespread deployment of negative emissions technologies (NETs) at scale.

In the next section I examine the evidence regarding the actors and institutions involved in the politics of climate-related energy policy, beginning with individuals and then moving on to discuss the business sector.

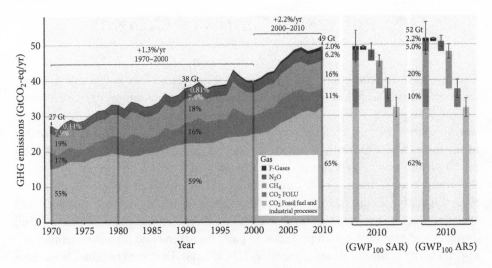

FIGURE 16.1 Total annual anthropogenic GHG emissions by gases 1970–2010 Total annual anthropogenic greenhouse gas (GHG) emissions (gigatonne of CO_2-equivalent per year, $GtCO_2$-eq/yr) for the period 1970 to 2010 by gases: CO_2 from fossil fuel combustion and industrial processes; CO_2 from Forestry and Other Land Use (FOLU); methane (CH_4); nitrous oxide (N_2O); fluorinated gases covered under the Kyoto Protocol (F-gases). Right hand shows 2010 emissions, using alternatively CO_2- equivalent emission weightings based on IPCC Second Assessment Report (SAR) and AR5 values. Unless otherwise stated, CO_2-equivalent emissions in this report include the basket of Kyoto gases (CO_2, CH_4, N_2O as well as F-gases) calculated based on 100-year Global Warming Potential (GWP_{100}) values from the SAR (see Glossary in IPCC 2014). Using the most recent GWP_{100} values from the AR5 (right-hand bars) would result in higher total annual GHG emissions (52 $GtCO_2$-eq/yr) from an increased contribution of methane, but does not change the long-term trend significantly.

Source: Image and caption from *IPCC, 2014: Climate Change 2014: Synthesis Report. Contribution of Working Groups I, II and III to the Fifth Assessment Report of the Intergovernmental Panel on Climate Change* [Core Writing Team, R.K. Pachauri and L.A. Meyer (eds.)]. IPCC, Geneva, Switzerland, pp. 46. https://www.ipcc.ch/site/assets/uploads/2018/02/SYR_AR5_FINAL_full.pdf

Actors and Institutions

The ubiquity of energy use means citizens, acting individually or collectively through civil society organizations, join business and government in having an interest in climate-related energy policies. In this section I discuss how these different political actors form their preferences regarding energy policies, beginning with citizens and then discussing business and governments.

Citizens and the Politics of Framing

A foundational issue in the politics of climate-related energy policies is understanding how citizens form preferences regarding climate-related energy policies and what

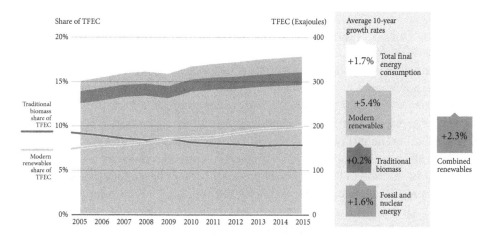

FIGURE 16.2 Growth of renewables in total final energy consumption, 2005–2015.

Source: REN21, 2018, *Global Status Report 2018*, 31, Paris, REN21 Secretariat.

their influence is over climate-related energy policies.[2] Most simply, as consumers of energy services, individuals' demand for access to less carbon intensive sources of energy reduces the rate of GHG emissions growth, given the large share of total energy use the residential sector represents (Stern 2014).[3] In democratic states, citizens also vote, and voting choices collectively affect policies enacted by governments. In the case of Germany, for example, the participation in government of the Green Party, which incorporated decarbonization in its party platform, contributed to the introduction of financial incentives that directly induced the rapid deployment of renewable energy (Laird and Stefes 2009). Citizens can also choose to act collectively in seeking to change the consumption and production of energy, as elaborated in the following discussion.

In general terms, cross-national surveys typically show that large pluralities of populations across high-income states are concerned about climate change (Shwom et al. 2015). Yet the effect of this generalized concern about attitudes toward energy policies is less certain. One reason may be that individuals believe decarbonizing energy systems will force them to incur higher costs, a reasonable concern given that policy costs can be passed on to final consumers. In the United States, for example, consumers' levels of expressed support for climate policies fall when they are asked to consider a trade-off between electricity costs and the environmental benefits from shifting to the greater use of wind, solar, and hydropower (Ansolabehere and Konisky 2014). Similarly, low consumer subscription rates to "green power" schemes in Australia favoring renewable energy generation have been linked to their perceived financial costs (Hobman and Frederiks 2014). These results suggest that individuals are sensitive to costs when considering whether to support energy policies designed to mitigate the effects of climate change. That said, there is some evidence that individuals' willingness to pay (WTP) for climate change measures is not a simple function of the expected policy costs. Economic downturns and worsening individual economic circumstances appear not to affect individuals' willingness to prioritize climate change (Mildenberger and Leiserowitz 2017).

The provision of energy reports that compare electricity usage to neighbors has also been found to affect household usage, suggesting that social norms affect energy behavior (Allcott 2011).

Given sensitivity to policy costs, an important issue is how individual views about climate-related energy policies will be affected by rapidly falling renewable energy prices, as experienced in the solar PV and battery storage sectors, and particularly whether such price changes increase individuals' willingness to support climate change mitigation using energy policy. One possibility is that falling renewable energy costs will have little effect on support for more stringent climate-related energy policies among the public. In addition to the problem of costs, individuals have imperfect information about the range of possible long-term climate outcomes, and this uncertainty influences their WTP for policies that would reduce energy sector emissions (Ingham, Ma, and Ulph 2007; Kotchen, Boyle, and Leiserowitz 2013).

Crucially, in the face of imperfect information, individuals' willingness to bear the costs of decarbonizing energy systems to reduce the risks of future climate change is also susceptible to organized efforts at issue framing. Framing has been used effectively by groups opposed to more stringent climate-related energy policies, for example, by emphasizing scientific uncertainty or focusing attention on the negative effects policies may have on consumer welfare (Cann and Raymond 2018). Business, in particular, has played an active role in sponsoring information campaigns designed to undermine support for more stringent climate action (Dunlap and McCright 2011; Farrell 2016; Supran and Oreskes 2017). Decarbonization has also been linked to values such as ideological commitments to negative liberty, in which regulating carbon emissions is framed as an unacceptable level of state intervention, with voluntarism identified as the appropriate response to climate change (Bohr 2016; Jacques and Knox 2016).

Alternative frames have been used by proponents of more active climate-related energy policies. Decarbonization has been associated with national security co-benefits, for example, in the form of reduced energy import dependence, in order to mobilize individuals (Pralle and Boscarino 2011; Vezirgiannidou 2013). Policies reducing transport-related emissions have also been framed in terms of national security and environmental justice (Alló and Loureiro 2014). Frames such as "ecological citizenship"—in which individuals are defined as part of a collective identity with a given ecological burden—can also affect individual support for policy change (Wolf, Brown, and Conway 2009). Some conservative groups have also sought to frame clean energy policies based on national economic advantage and religious stewardship of the environment (Hess and Brown 2017).

A key question, given multiple conflicting efforts to frame energy-related climate policies in politically polarized environments such as the United States (Dunlap and McCright 2008), is how exposure to these multiple frames affects individuals' views (Bolsen and Druckman 2018). Here, there is some evidence that the benefits of framing policies in terms of environmental or national security co-benefits dissipate when confronted with counterframing (Aklin and Urpelainen 2013). But there is a real need to understand the effects of counterframes more deeply, including across other jurisdictions in both high- and lower-income states.

In addition to how framing affects citizens' preferences about climate-related energy policies, a second question is how individuals prioritize climate-related energy policy relative to other issues. Consistent with findings that economic factors affect individual preferences, a perception of higher costs increases the salience of energy policies among the public (Lowry and Joslyn 2014). Direct experience of weather events—such as flooding—also appears to increase individuals' willingness to reduce energy consumption (Spence et al 2011). Other events, such as international climate negotiations, have also been found to increase the salience of energy and climate change issues (Bakaki and Bernauer 2017).

The longevity of increases in issue salience related to external shocks is questionable, however. Experiencing extreme weather, for example, has only a small effect on concerns about climate change compared to socioeconomic factors such as educational level or ideological predisposition (Marquart-Pyatt et al. 2014). The effects of exposure to weather shocks are also small and transient for individuals' support for adaptation policies (Ray et al. 2017). It is nevertheless worth considering whether external shocks, such as heat waves, droughts, and other types of extreme weather, or factors such as international climate negotiations, present windows of opportunity for policy makers by increasing the importance of individuals' support for more stringent climate-related energy policies. In the financial sector, for example, low issue salience has been identified with "insider politics" dominated by technocratic policymaking and the influence of organized interest groups, while greater public salience is argued to increase political attention to individual preferences (Culpepper 2010). Thus, one political strategy may lie in taking advantage of external shocks that increase issue salience to promote policies promoting sustainable energy transitions.

Households have been characterized as "price-takers" that exert little collective influence (Smith, Stirling, and Berkhout 2005); however, evidence shows that citizens can choose to act collectively. Grassroots movements that mobilize individuals seeking to change patterns of energy supply and demand, for example, have been studied across multiple jurisdictions. Under the Obama administration, so-called blue-green alliances of labor and environmental activists sought to promote decarbonization policies in the name of environment and industry policy. This was reflected in state ballot initiatives, such as Michigan's Proposition 3 in 2012, which proposed to increase the renewable portfolio standard (RPS) for electricity from 10 percent to 25 percent (Hess 2014).

Citizens can also organize collectively in the process of energy transition. Citizen participation in planning processes has been found to be important to the successful development of wind power projects in England, Wales, Denmark, France, and Germany (Enevoldsen and Sovacool 2016; Hager 2016; Langer, Decker, and Menrad 2017; Loring 2007). Citizens are also directly owning facilities involved in energy production. Community ownership in the Netherlands, developing technologies such as biomass and solar PV, has been observed (Van Der Schoor and Scholtens 2015). Policies that enable business models that directly involve citizens in the production of energy to flourish thus present one strategy for promoting decarbonization in the energy sector, although the scale of energy demand—and the important political role of business in the energy sector described in the following discussion—means additional policies are needed.

Analyses of citizen engagement with renewable energy production extend to the energy democracy movement, which frames decarbonization as an opportunity for individuals to bring about change directly through the use of distributed renewable energy technologies. In doing so, energy democracy ties shifting control over stages of the energy supply chain to local communities through community ownership to a broader political and social project focused on democratization (Burke and Stephens 2018). (For more on citizen action and energy more generally, see Cauchon in this volume.) The distributional effects of energy choices are also linked to normative concerns about how policies can be made more just (Jenkins et al. 2016). (For more on energy justice, see Fuller in this volume.)

Business and Climate-Related Energy Policy

Calls to democratize energy supply in response to climate change can be understood as a reaction to the perceived political influence of firms that own and operate large, centrally managed fossil fuel infrastructure that dominates the global provision of energy services. There are valid reasons to expect businesses to influence climate-related energy policies. Fossil fuels industries have high capital costs and assets that are durable and not readily redeployable. Relation-specific asset theory suggests industries with these characteristics will tend to lobby collectively and will be politically influential. Indeed, the theory of "regulatory capture" employed the oil refining industry as its paradigmatic case (Stigler 1971).

The pervasive influence of large energy firms through political access and the strategic use of information has substantially slowed the deployment of low-carbon energy sources (Geels 2014). This influence has led to claims that the existing energy infrastructure suffers from carbon lock-in, through a combination of technological and institutional forces (Unruh 2000). Historical evidence from previous energy transitions shows that incumbent industries have indeed slowed the emergence of products that have challenged their dominance (Fouquet 2016).

Yet a sole focus on the political influence of incumbents makes it difficult to explain recent changes in the energy sector centered on the extraordinary rise in renewable energy capacity. Many electricity companies are threatened by the rapid rise in renewable energies, such as wind and solar PV, and electricity utilities are often well-resourced and with substantial market power, which are characteristics that might lead us to expect them to be politically influential.

One explanation for the rise of renewable energy is that large shocks, such as the oil shocks of the 1970s and the more recent 2011 tsunami and nuclear disaster in Japan, enable shifts in the trajectories of energy systems (Aklin and Urpelainen 2018). (Lipscy and Incerti in this volume provide a more detailed discussion of the role of exogenous shocks in energy politics in Japan.) Another possibility is that competitive threats from emerging niche technologies are initially ignored by incumbents, which only mobilize politically once the markets for new low-carbon technologies have matured (Stokes and Breetz 2018).

Evidence also shows there is substantial diversity between firms operating within emissions-intensive energy industries regarding climate change policy. During negotiations in the 1990s to create an international agreement with binding emissions ceilings, for example, US oil majors chose to challenge the scientific consensus on climate change, while BP and Shell attempted to shape the final agreement (Levy and Kolk 2002). This situation raises the possibility that intra-industry heterogeneity creates a collective action problem that might dilute the influence of large firms over energy-related climate policy. Exploring the sources and implications of heterogeneity in business interests remains a fruitful area for research.

One plausible reason for intra-industry heterogeneity lies in differences in the implications of policies for the value of the assets held by companies. Among the international oil and gas majors, for example, Shell has a portfolio that is weighted toward natural gas, proposed as a transition fuel useful for supplanting coal in power markets. Extrapolating from the implications of policies for the value of assets, we might expect Shell to favor regulatory and other policies that favor natural gas over coal. Differences in the portfolio of assets extend to the national oil companies (NOCs) that dominate ownership of global reserves of crude oil and are increasingly international in scope (Nasiritousi 2017). In 2017 the Danish NOC DONG (Danish Oil and Natural Gas) was renamed Ørsted and committed to fully divesting from oil and natural gas operations, and in 2018 the Norwegian NOC Statoil changed its company name to Equinor, reflecting its commitment to increasing revenues from renewable energy. Companies in the oil and gas sector are also diversifying into renewable energy sources, as they did in the 1980s (Zhong and Bazilian 2018).

Business opposition to climate-related energy policies may also be diminishing (Sæverud and Skjærseth 2007). One reason for this shift is that business preferences about climate-related energy policies are not a pure function of their assets, but is also influenced by the broader policy and social environment. The choice of cap-and-trade, rather than carbon taxes, as the preferred policy instrument for reducing GHG emissions in the energy sector, for example, followed a switch in strategy by some firms from opposition to favor shaping the distributional effects of climate policies (Meckling 2011). This more complex interpretation of business interests and strategies suggests the existence of "tipping points," in which the benefits of engagement in shaping policy are judged to outweigh continued opposition, although care needs to be taken to ensure presumed cooperation is not driven by an attempt to reduce compliance costs by reducing the stringency of climate-related energy policies (Meckling 2015; Vormedal 2011).

Shareholder pressure may also hasten the shift. The divestment movement is characterized as a transnational advocacy network that aims to "shame, pressure, facilitate, and encourage investors … to relinquish their holdings of fossil fuel stocks" and is argued to be influential (Ayling and Gunningham 2017). Exxon, for example, was forced by shareholders in 2017 to report on the impact of climate change on its business, thus introducing the possibility that management will be forced to address the issue of stranded assets as a result of climate change. Summarizing the options available to companies, Meckling (2015) proposes that companies can choose to hedge by shaping policies in favor of least cost designs, supporting, or opposing climate-related energy policy proposals.

While the oil industry has been a key focus of research into the role of business in shaping climate-related energy policies, the electricity sector is increasingly important due to the rise of renewable energy in power generation and the potential for electrification as a strategy for decarbonizing the transport sector. Here, again, industry preferences are heterogeneous. Electricity companies consume different mixes of fuels in the power plants they operate, participate in different segments of the power market, and are different sizes. In the European Union (EU), the positions that large power generators adopted toward emissions trading reflected the mix of fuels they use to generate power. Companies that had high levels of nuclear and hydropower generation had substantially different interests than those with fossil-fuel-heavy generation portfolios (Markussen and Svendsen 2005). The mix of fuels electricity utilities used to generate power also affected their preferences about climate-related energy legislation. Companies with more renewables and natural gas tended to support more stringent climate legislation likely to increase the value of their assets, while companies weighted toward coal adopted the opposition position (Kim, Urpelainen, and Yang 2016).

Public policies promoting renewable energy generation thus have distinct political and environmental benefits. Some power utilities already identify renewable energy as an opportunity (Richter 2013). Over a decade ago, Spanish power utilities, for example, saw wind power as complementary to existing capabilities and supported policies enabling greater penetration of wind power (Stenzel and Frenzel 2008). German utilities owning and operating transmission grids, on the other hand, were not supportive of regulatory reform to power grids enabling greater penetration of wind power. Instead, Germany's success in renewable energy may be attributable to the influence of smaller power-generating companies that stood to gain from selling renewable power into the wholesale power market (Wassermann, Reeg, and Nienhaus 2015). Large utilities also failed to understand the competitive threat that renewables could represent (Kungl 2015). Regardless, the key link here, as with the oil and gas sectors, is the distributive implications of the policy for company assets and how these effects influence the policy preferences of the companies about climate-related energy policies (Cheon and Urpelainen 2013). By extension, offering financial compensation to carbon-intensive power generators may be a good strategy for weakening business opposition to more stringent climate policies (Jotzo and Mazouz 2015).

Diversity in the interests of the business sector extends to the renewable energy industry itself. Here, there appears to be a negative side to the relationship between company investments and the positions they adopt toward climate-related energy policies. Renewable energy–related trade disputes are increasing in frequency, for example, and evidence shows solar PV companies adopt different positions toward the imposition of tariffs on solar-related imports due to differences in their positions within global supply chains (GSCs) (Lewis 2014; Meckling and Hughes 2017). A key factor here may be the rise of GSCs in producing renewable energy products, as has occurred in other manufacturing sectors. GSCs are characterized by the geographic dispersion of production and the segmentation of production into multiple, distinct stages. The politics of trade in renewable energy is thus likely to be increasingly affected by intra-industry heterogeneity, as has occurred in other sectors.

Far from being unified, there appears to be tremendous heterogeneity in the interests of business in climate-related energy policies, which remains to be explored. Differences in policy preferences appear to be shaped not only by the diversity of assets held by companies operating in different sectors, but also by differences in the distributive effects of various policy instruments on the value of those assets, as well as other factors. Identifying the sources of these differences is a first step in understanding how policy can be designed to increase support for, and weaken opposition to, more stringent climate-related energy policies.

Political Institutions

The structure of political institutions affects the bargaining power of companies and other actors with interests in climate-related energy policymaking (Karapin 2016; Purdon 2015). A general finding is that rates of policy adoption decline as political institutions increase the number of actors with veto power. Change is also more likely to be incremental, as it will be likely to lead veto players to invest political resources in opposing a given policy (Madden 2014. Thus, the greater number of veto points evident in legislative procedures in the United States is found to have slowed the pursuit of more ambitious decarbonization policies, including in the energy sector, compared to the European Union (Skjærseth, Bang, and Schreurs 2013).

Electoral institutions also matter in shaping the political success of green parties. Electoral systems using proportional representation, in particular, are more conducive to green participation in government, and by extension, more ambitious climate-related energy policies (Hughes and Urpelainen 2015; Richardson and Rootes 2006). Mainstream parties are also given an incentive to incorporate elements of green party policies into their own political programs, rather than simply ignore the issue (Dumas. Rising, and Urpelainen 2016). The result can be a loss in votes for the green party but may lead to more ambitions climate-related energy policies than might otherwise have been adopted (Meguid 2005). Electoral systems can also make it easier, or more difficult, for policy makers to impose higher energy costs on consumers (Lipscy 2018).

The degree to which authority is devolved to subnational levels of government also matters for climate-related energy policies (Lyon and Yin 2010). Decentralized ownership models, for example, may be effective in part because they shift the institutional structure in which decision-making occurs, decreasing the influence of large, entrenched veto players in the fossil fuel sector (Burke and Stephens 2018). As noted in Allison and Parinandi in this volume, local- and state-level politicians in the United

States have been at the forefront in implementing climate-related energy policies such as RPSs, which require electricity retailers to supply a given amount of power from renewable energy sources (Yi and Feiock 2012). The implementation of more ambitious RPSs in the United States has also been associated with Democratic control of state legislatures, in part because of the increased influence of environmental groups at the state level (Berry, Laird, and Stefes 2015). Subnational levels of government, such as cities, are also increasingly involved in transnational politics, which is potentially significant given that urban areas dominate GHG emissions globally (Lee 2013). Local governments have also played a key role in the development of industrial capabilities in China's wind and solar PV sectors (Nahm 2017 and Nahm in this volume). Potential drawbacks include increased regulatory complexity and leakage of more carbon-intensive activities to locations with less stringent policies, undermining overall effectiveness (Lutsey and Sperling 2008).

Macro-institutions can also shape the balance of negotiating power between social actors. Thus China's more corporatist approach to state-business relations is proposed to produce manufacturing-centered policies, in contrast to Brazil's focus on public-private partnerships that provided sectoral success in promoting wind power development but were less successful in solar PV (Hochstetler and Kostka 2015). Here, the state is identified both as a set of rules and as an actor with interests in shaping climate-related energy policy.

There is thus tremendous heterogeneity in the preferences of business about energy-related climate policies, which remains open for scholarly investigation. A key area of fruitful research identifies how actors can use different institutional arrangements strategically to overcome resistance to the implementation of more stringent policies (Meckling and Nahm 2018). Governing parties, for example, have actively designed climate-related policy instruments to ensure successful passage into legislation. One policy instrument, the feed-in tariff, which provides a guaranteed return on investment for investors in renewable energy sources, has proven effective at spurring renewable energy deployment. It is also useful politically, however, because rural constituents are able to benefit from renewable energy investments, which can be electorally beneficial (Bayer and Urpelainen 2016).

Transnationalism and the Politics of Energy and Climate Change

The Paris Agreement on climate change, negotiated under the UNFCCC, institutionalized a new approach to international cooperation by introducing common obligations for developed and developing states and committing governments to an iterative pledge-and-review process.

The ubiquity of energy use in climate change–related emissions means national determined contributions (NDCs) made by governments under the Paris Agreement, although stated as commitments to alter GHG emissions levels relative to baseline, have enormous implications for states' energy policies. The specific policy instruments applied to achieve national commitments are left in the hands of national governments, meaning domestic factors are key in determining the level of states' commitments under the Paris Agreement.[4] The agreement thus gave primacy to national politics as the price for a more inclusionary agreement (Bodansky 2016).

The primacy of the UNFCCC-centered regime is also challenged by the proliferation of agreements between nongovernmental and subnational actors institutionalizing rules and practices promoting more stringent climate policies (Bulkeley et al. 2014). Transnational nongovernmental organizations (NGOs) are also increasing in diversity and number, leading to coordination challenges (Hadden 2015). In the energy sector, a consistent theme of studies on transnational cooperation is the existence of multiple, overlapping institutions (Goldthau and Witte 2010; Zelli and van Asselt 2013). Functionalist explanations for fragmentation point to the need for flexible and diverse forms of cooperation capable of incorporating different actors involved in energy policy and the various challenges presented by energy use in the context of economic development, security, and environmental challenges (Cherp, Jewell, and Goldthau 2011). Critics suggest that fragmentation in the international institutions promoting energy cooperation impedes cooperation, leaving governance gaps (Dubash and Florini 2011).

Multiple organizations promote cooperation in climate-related energy policy, including the International Energy Agency (Colgan, Keohane, and Van de Graaf 2012; Van de Graaf 2012), the G8 and G20 (Van de Graaf and Westphal 2011), the World Trade Organization (Lewis 2014), climate finance (Pickering, Jotzo, and Wood 2015), and the Sustainable Energy for All initiative (Rogelj et al. 2013). A key site of new and formal cooperation over climate-related energy policy is the International Renewable Energy Agency (IRENA), created in 2009 with the goal of promoting renewable energy primarily in lower-income states, with a focus on capacity building and technological support. However, the creation of new, multilateral bodies focused on promoting international cooperation is increasingly rare (Urpelainen and Van de Graaf 2015).

Given the urgency of responding to climate change and the infrequency with which multilateral organizations are created, one expectation is that alternative forms of cooperation will emerge into the climate regime, incorporating different groups of actors and focusing on different aspects of the climate mitigation problem. A particular focus is cooperation between private actors in environmental governance, including in climate-related energy policy (Falkner 2003), and between private actors and governments in the form of public-private partnerships (Bäckstrand 2008). International cooperation also occurs through private forms of authority, as firms, NGOs, and other actors create standards that codify appropriate behavior (Green 2013). Technology-oriented international agreements focused on knowledge sharing; research, development, and deployment; technology transfer; and standards agreements constitute an additional form of private governance within the realm of climate-related energy policy (De Coninck et al. 2008). Greenhouse gas emissions trading systems have also diffused globally as a form of transnational carbon management (Paterson et al. 2014.

Aside from documenting the emergence and effectiveness of new regimes affecting climate-related energy policy choices, a crucial issue is improving understanding of the interactions and gaps that exist in this multiple, layered, and non-hierarchical regime (Falkner 2014). Interactions between energy and other environmental issues also suggest it is important to map the effects of forms of cooperation across a wider range of environmental issues (Green and Hale 2017). The enormous demand that energy systems commonly place on water resources suggest this as a particularly important area of research (Siddiqi and Anadon 2011). Finally, in all cases, the projected marginal demand growth in lower-income states favors a focus on the interaction of cooperation in development and climate-related energy policy.

FUTURE RESEARCH AGENDA: DEVELOPMENT, INNOVATION, NEGATIVE EMISSIONS, AND GEOENGINEERING

This discussion suggests that while there remain important political impediments to decarbonizing energy systems, the direction of change of climate-related energy policies is positive. The reality of a global carbon budget means, however, that the rate of change is crucial. Here, data are of greater concern. While renewable energy is growing rapidly, fossil fuels continue to dominate. More worrisome, the global consumption of fossil fuels is growing more rapidly than renewable energy is, when measured by the volume of energy used (Tollefson 2018).

In this section I introduce three areas of research that are understudied and are important for addressing these problems. The first focuses on the politics of climate-related energy policy in lower-income states, which dominate projected growth in energy demand in the coming decades. The second addresses the politics of energy-related innovation, which is a key factor affecting the more rapid deployment of better performing low-carbon technologies in the energy sector. Third, and finally, I address the politics of negative emissions and geoengineering. Integrated models suggest negative emissions will be required at scale if politics fails to deliver adequate emissions reductions.

Energy, Climate Change, and Development

This discussion has focused largely on findings on the politics of climate-related energy policy drawn from data in the high-income states. This group of states is overrepresented in the scholarly literature (Aklin and Urpelainen 2018; Nordhaus 1995). Yet a focus on developed economies alone is woefully inadequate in understanding the politics of climate-related energy policy (Hendrix 2017). China accounts for approximately half of global coal consumption and is the largest importer of crude oil. While total energy demand growth in China is projected to slow, it will continue to be crucial to global energy demand (International Energy Agency 2017). India has over three hundred million people lacking access to electricity, representing 14 percent of the global total (Byravan et al. 2017). There is thus a real need to integrate issues such as poverty into analyses of energy politics, in addition to the more traditional focuses on energy security of supply and environmental sustainability (Bazilian, Nakhooda, and Van de Graaf 2014). And it is as crucial to increase our understanding of how energy choices are affected by political variables in these states as it is for states in Southeast Asia, Africa, and elsewhere. The feasibility of decarbonization is likely to differ across sectors in India and elsewhere due to political factors, as it does in the high-income states, yet systematic knowledge about the factors affecting climate-related energy choices remains limited (Busby and Shidore 2017). (For an analysis of energy politics in emerging markets and lower-income states, see Huda and Ali [Asia-Pacific region], Powell [India], and Delina [sub-Saharan Africa], all in this volume.)

There are also reasons to expect the politics of climate-related energy policies to differ across states based on their economies and histories (Harrison and Kostka 2014. Returning to the role of individuals, one plausible hypothesis is that individuals in states with lower levels of income per capita weigh non-economic factors, such as responding to climate change, less than policies promoting economic growth, a finding referred to as the Environmental Kuznets Curve. By extension, levels of policy effort in lower-income states may be expected to be less than in high-income states, quite aside from the ethical responsibility of high-income states to shoulder a greater burden of climate mitigation costs. Emissions-intensive industries should also fall in importance through development as the services sector increases in size. There is also the most government ownership of energy firms in lower-income states. Although not tested, we can again posit that this change in industrial structure could have distinct political effects by weakening the relative influence of emissions-intensive industries in the design and implementation of climate-related energy policies.

Despite its plausibility, empirical evidence in support of the Environmental Kuznets Curve is mixed. While some relationship may exist for local particulates, this may not be generalizable to other forms of pollution, including CO_2 and other GHGs. Evidence from China suggests that a distinct political logic may exist in which local governments that are more fiscally stable are in a position to enforce transparency around pollution, while those that are more fiscally constrained cannot (van der Kamp, Lorentzen, and Mattingly 2017). Understanding how individuals in India, China, and elsewhere weigh climate-related energy policy choices is thus an important area for research.

A second plausible difference between higher-income and other states is the political implications of energy infrastructure investments. Carbon lock-in means governments in higher-income states must transform existing infrastructure toward less carbon-intensive technologies. Governments of lower-income states, in contrast, can focus in part on meeting rising demand for energy services by supporting investment in new energy-related infrastructure. Given these distinctions, we can plausibly expect companies that have existing infrastructure invested in carbon-intensive technologies to oppose policies that undermine the value of those assets more intensely than companies that have yet to invest in building infrastructure in meeting new demand.

A clear trend in terms of this investment is toward increasing electrification, with electricity continuing to increase as a share of energy consumption. An important question is whether electrification in lower-income states will follow the path of the high-income states by relying on carbon-intensive fossil fuels provided through centralized electricity grids, or whether it will leapfrog carbon-intensive technologies (Stram 2016). Here, there is some room for optimism. South Asia, for example, has seen growth in grid-scale and decentralized renewable energy—in the form of solar PVs—utilized to improve energy access (Palit 2013). Renewable energy auctions have also been employed across a large number of lower-income states as a way of promoting lower carbon development (Rio 2017).

The politics surrounding these choices remain poorly understood. What is certain, however, is that the range of choices and possibilities is too complex to be understood as a simple trade-off between economic growth and environmental concerns. One solution for expanding energy access while limiting carbon emissions growth, for example, is to deploy distributed power generation systems that are substantially powered by solar PVs, although rural energy demand remains low on a household basis (Ulsrud et al. 2011). Here, studies suggest rural communities are willing to pay a higher price for electricity if reliability can be increased at peak times (Graber et al. 2018). There are clearly also important distributional issues at stake. Different rates of improved energy access, for example, could increase levels of inequality between those households that are able to afford access to energy and those that are not, with implications for long-term decarbonization pathways that remain unclear (Van Gevelt 2016). In sum, understanding the politics of climate-related energy politics is crucial to the decarbonization agenda, and there remain numerous opportunities for research.

Energy Innovation and Climate Change

Integrated assessment models (IAMs) suggest that meeting climate targets without relying on NETs, such as bioenergy with carbon capture and storage (BECCS), requires rapid and broad change, such as the widespread electrification of energy use and rapid deployment of best-available technologies (van Vuuren et al. 2018). Spurring innovation that improves the performance and lowers the costs of low-carbon technologies is an important policy option available to policy makers in promoting more rapid decarbonization. Governments increasingly understand that pursuing green growth strategies in the energy sector is important (REN21 2017). An important question that follows is what political variables affect rates of innovation and deployment of new low-carbon technologies.

Carbon taxes, which increase the cost of carbon-intensive fuels, are commonly proposed as an effective and efficient policy response to climate change. Taxes can also induce firms to innovate in order to reduce consumption of the taxed fuel relative to alternatives (Calel and Dechezlepretre 2016; Popp 2002). While carbon pricing may be feasible and durable politically (Rabe 2018), governments also commonly employ other policies (REN21 2018). One reason may be that policy instruments such as direct subsidies have attractive political features. Subsidies, for example, are likely to be supported by the beneficiaries, while costs remain generalized. This positive political characteristic is an explanation for the success of the feed-in-tariff, which provides a fixed rate of return for investors in renewable energy while commonly distributing costs among households. Such political benefits, in addition to economic efficiency, effectiveness, or other factors, can justify the use of non-price-based policies (Hepburn 2006).

Non-price-based policy instruments have other attractive features. Political leaders commonly appeal to the job and growth benefits of investing in low-carbon technologies. Research and development, and deployment policies that promote the early adoption of new innovations, for example, may provide increased export opportunities (Beise and Rennings 2005; Iyer 2016). The creation of lead markets for low-carbon innovations may also cause a "California Effect," providing an incentive for governments in other jurisdictions to follow suit (Vogel 1997). There is evidence that such an effect exists in automobile emissions standards (Perkins and Neumayer 2012).

More broadly, the transnational effects of green industrial policies supporting sustainable energy transitions remain an important area of research (Meckling and Hughes 2018). There is a question, for example, about whether national competitive advantages created through policies promoting low-carbon innovation are durable. Danish wind power companies were early leaders in promoting wind power technology; however, their competitive position is threatened (Iyer 2016). Chinese producers dominate the production of solar PV modules, despite early German leadership (Hughes and Meckling 2017). As renewable energy industries become increasingly transnational, competition is emerging as an important feature of the politics surrounding climate-related energy policies, with the potential to weaken domestic coalitions supporting low carbon transitions. Innovation systems themselves are increasingly globalized, with patterns of integration affected by government policies as well as technological characteristics (Nahm 2017). Differences in innovation systems can also create complementarities between companies headquartered in different states. Thus, rather than being in direct competition, the German and Chinese solar PV industries co-evolved through the exploitation of comparative advantages (Quitzow 2015). Better understanding of this interaction among politics, innovation, and the characteristics of technologies can lay the foundations for more transformative and politically robust climate-related energy policies (Schmidt and Sewerin 2017).

Negative Emissions and Geoengineering Technologies

Current trends in energy consumption show the global response to climate change is inadequate. Reflecting this, climate models increasingly depend on NETs, such as BECCS, in developing scenarios that keep mean global temperature increases within a 2 degree Celsius limit (Fridahl and Lehtveer 2018; Rogelj et al. 2018). Lomax et al. (2015) argue that one implication of this is that researchers should increase attention to the policy and technology options that are available to remove GHGs from the atmosphere at the scale required to limit warming to accepts levels.

If we accept that political constraints exist to the deployment of new technologies, then it is important to integrate political factors into analyses of different negative emissions options, such as BECCS, direct air capture, CO_2 sequestration, monitoring, utilization, and others (Fuss et al. 2014). There is a wide range of NETs, and many remain niche, or unproven, making them difficult to study. Governments have also been found to prioritize BECCS lower than other emissions technologies (Haikola, Hansson, and Fridahl 2018). Social science has a crucial role to play in investigating public understanding and acceptance of NETs, the barriers to deployment and scaling up, and their potential social and political implications (Buck 2016). A number of political and social barriers to the development and deployment of BECCS at scale have already been identified, including competition from alternative technologies, the need for an effective carbon price to make it cost competitive, the potential for conflicts over land use, and potential opposition from social groups (Bellamy and Healey 2018).

Preliminary analyses point to substantial variation in the extent to which political factors are likely to limit deployment (McLaren 2012). In the case of the deployment of biofuels as part of BECCS, for example, distributional and other issues have been identified that are worthy of attention (Buck 2016; Rhodes and Keith 2008). An examination of key carbon capture and storage (CCS) demonstration projects globally suggests that public opinion has had an important effect on progress in some cases, and that there are also differences in the methods used to incorporate the various community, public, and private organizations with interests in the projects (Markusson, Ishii, and Stevens 2011). Honegger and Reiner (2018) find that political factors can represent important impediments to scaling up NETs, even if adequate financial incentives are put in place.

Regardless, engagement across interdisciplinary boundaries represents a crucial task for understanding the possibilities for NETs (Tavoni and Socolow 2013). The International Conference on Negative CO2 Emissions, held in 2018, began the process of laying the groundwork for consideration of the technical, political, and social issues involved in effectively using NETs, and it is important for public policy scholars and political scientists to contribute to this work (Chalmers University of Technology 2018).

Finally, depending on our success in responding to the challenge of rapidly decarbonizing energy production and use globally, the politics of geoengineering will increase in importance. Here, preliminary evidence suggests that there is little support for deployment of climate engineering technologies among publics, who fear the potential for large environmental costs. This raises the question of how geoengineering might be deployed if faced with widespread public opposition.

There remains a broad research agenda in understanding attitudes toward geoengineering across both high- and lower-income states, as well as how businesses and governments understand the development and deployment of different geoengineering technologies and what this means for their likely adoption (Wibeck et al. 2017). Game theoretic work also strongly suggests that intergovernmental coordination will be crucial. Countries that suffer from climate change may resort to the unilateral deployment of geoengineering technologies such as solar radiation management (SRM). If the unilateral use of SRM adversely affects countries bearing less significant climate change costs, however, this could lead to retaliation through economic means or through the deployment of technologies designed to negate the effects of the initial deployment of SRM (Heyen, Horton, and Moreno-Cruz 2019). Given such challenges, five principles have been proposed as the basis for governing its study, centered on the regulation of geoengineering as a public good, the importance of public participation in decision-making, the transparent disclosure of research, the independent assessment of geoengineering, and the need to build governance structures prior to any deployment (Rayner et. al. 2013).

Acknowledgments

The author thanks Michaël Aklin, Jonas Meckling, Jonas Nahm, Leah Stokes, Johannes Urpelainen, and two anonymous reviewers and the editors for helpful comments and suggestions.

Notes

1. Emphasis in original. "Extremely likely" expresses a confidence level of 95 to 100 percent (IPCC 2014, 2).
2. There is a large literature on public opinion about climate change–related policies. I focus here on findings on public opinion specific to the energy sector.
3. Increasing the efficiency of energy consumption, on the other hand, can lead to an increase in demand ("the rebound effect"), as a result of a decrease in the effective price for energy services (Greening et al. 2000; Vivanco et al. 2016).
4. This section is limited to reviewing key themes in forms of international cooperation specifically designed to facilitate climate-related energy policy coordination. For a review of developments under the Paris Agreement within the UNFCCC, see Viñuales et al. (2017). [FIXED]

References

Aklin, Michaël, Patrick Bayer, S. P. Harish, and Johannes Urpelainen. 2018. *Escaping the Energy Poverty Trap: When and How Governments Power the Lives of the Poor.* Cambridge, MA: MIT Press.

Aklin, Michaël, and Johannes Urpelainen. 2013. "Debating Clean Energy: Frames, Counter Frames, and Audiences." *Global Environmental Change* 23, no. 5: 1225–1232.

Aklin, Michaël, and Johannes Urpelainen. 2018. *Renewables: The Politics of a Global Energy Transition.* Cambridge, MA: MIT Press.

Allcott, Hunt. 2011. "Social Norms and Energy Conservation." *Journal of Public Economics* 95, nos. 9–10: 1082–1095.

Alló, Maria, and Maria L. Loureiro. 2014. "The Role of Social Norms on Preferences towards Climate Change Policies: A Meta-analysis." *Energy Policy* 73: 563–574.

Ansolabehere, Stephen, and David M. Konisky. 2014. *Cheap and Clean: How Americans Think about Energy in the Age of Global Warming.* Cambridge, MA: MIT Press.

Ayling, Julie, and Neil Gunningham. 2017. "Non-state Governance and Climate Policy: The Fossil Fuel Divestment Movement." *Climate Policy* 17, no. 2: 131–149.

Bäckstrand, Karin. 2008. "Accountability of Networked Climate Governance: The Rise of Transnational Climate Partnerships." *Global Environmental Politics* 8, no. 3: 74–102.

Bakaki, Zorzeta, and Thomas Bernauer. 2017. "Do Global Climate Summits Influence Public Awareness and Policy Preferences Concerning Climate Change?" *Environmental Politics* 26, no. 1: 1–26.

Barbier, Edward B., and David W. Pearce. 1990. "Thinking Economically about Climate Change." *Energy Policy* 18, no. 1: 11–18.

Bayer, Patrick, and Johannes Urpelainen. 2016. "It Is All about Political Incentives: Democracy and the Renewable Feed-in Tariff." *The Journal of Politics* 78, no. 2: 603–619.

Bazilian, Morgan, Smita Nakhooda, and Thijs Van de Graaf. 2014. "Energy Governance and Poverty." *Energy Research & Social Science* 1: 217–225.

Beise, Marian, and Klaus Rennings. 2005. "Lead Markets and Regulation: A Framework for Analyzing the International Diffusion of Environmental Innovations." *Ecological Economics* 52, no. 1: 5–17.

Bellamy, Rob, and Peter Healey. 2018. "'Slippery Slope' or 'Uphill Struggle'? Broadening Out Expert Scenarios of Climate Engineering Research and Development." *Environmental Science & Policy* 83: 1–10.

Bernauer, Thomas. 2013. "Climate Change Politics." *Annual Review of Political Science* 16: 421–448.

Berry, Michael J., Frank N. Laird, and Christoph H. Stefes. 2015. "Driving Energy: The Enactment and Ambitiousness of State Renewable Energy Policy." *Journal of Public Policy* 35, no. 2: 297–328.

Blanco Gabriel, Reyer Gerlagh, Sangwon Suh, John Barrett, Heleen C. de Coninck, Cristobal Felix Diaz Morejon, Ritu Mathur, et al. 2014. "2014: Drivers, Trends and Mitigation." In *Climate Change 2014: Mitigation of Climate Change. Contribution of Working Group III to the Fifth Assessment Report of the Intergovernmental Panel on Climate Change,* [edited by Ottmar Edenhofer, Ramón Pichs-Madruga, Youba Sokona, Ellie Farahani, Susanne Kadner, Kristin Seyboth, Anna Adler, et al.],. Cambridge, UK, and New York: Cambridge University Press.

Bodansky, Daniel. 2016. "The Paris Climate Change Agreement: A New Hope?" *American Journal of International Law* 110, no. 2: 288–319.

Bohr, Jeremiah. 2016. "The 'Climatism' Cartel: Why Climate Change Deniers Oppose Market-Based Mitigation Policy." *Environmental Politics* 25, no. 5: 812–830.

Bolsen, Toby, and James N. Druckman. 2018. "Do Partisanship and Politicization Undermine the Impact of a Scientific Consensus Message about Climate Change?" *Group Processes & Intergroup Relations* 21, no. 3: 389–402.

BP. 2018. BP Statistical Review of World Energy. Available at: https://www.bp.com/en/global/corporate/energy-economics/statistical-review-of-world-energy.html.

Buck, Holly Jean. 2016. "Rapid Scale-up of Negative Emissions Technologies: Social Barriers and Social Implications." *Climatic Change* 139, no. 2: 155–167.

Bulkeley, Harriet, Liliana B. Andonova, Michele M. Betsill, Daniel Compagnon, Thomas Hale, Matthew J. Hoffmann, Peter Newell, et al. 2014. *Transnational Climate Change Governance.* New York: Cambridge University Press.

Burke, Matthew J., and Jennie C. Stephens. 2018. "Political Power and Renewable Energy Futures: A Critical Review." *Energy Research & Social Science* 35: 78–93.

Busby, Joshua W., and Sarang Shidore. 2017. "When Decarbonization Meets Development: The Sectoral Feasibility of Greenhouse Gas Mitigation in India." *Energy Research & Social Science* 23: 60–73.

Byravan, Sujatha, Mohd Sahil Ali, Murali Ramakrishnan Ananthakumar, Nihit Goyal, Amit Kanudia, Pooja Vijay Ramamurthi, Shweta Srinivasan, et al. 2017. "Quality of Life for All: A Sustainable Development Framework for India's Climate Policy Reduces Greenhouse Gas Emissions." *Energy for Sustainable Development* 39: 48–58.

Calel, Raphael, and Antoine Dechezlepretre. 2016. "Environmental Policy and Directed Technological Change: Evidence from the European Carbon Market." *Review of Economics and Statistics* 98, no. 1: 173–191.

Cann, Heather W., and Leigh Raymond. 2018. "Does Climate Denialism Still Matter? The Prevalence of Alternative Frames in Opposition to Climate Policy." *Environmental Politics* 27, no. 3: 433–454.

Chalmers University of Technology. 2018. "Final Program." Presented at 2018 International Conference on Negative CO_2 Emissions, University of Gothenberg, Sweden.

Cheon, Andrew, and Johannes Urpelainen. 2013. "How Do Competing Interest Groups Influence Environmental Policy? The Case of Renewable Electricity in Industrialized Democracies, 1989–2007." *Political Studies* 61, no. 4: 874–897.

Cherp, Aleh, Jessica Jewell, and Andreas Goldthau. 2011. "Governing Global Energy: Systems, Transitions, Complexity." *Global Policy* 2, no. 1: 75–88.

Colgan, Jeff D., Robert O. Keohane, and Thijs Van de Graaf. 2012. "Punctuated Equilibrium in the Energy Regime Complex." *The Review of International Organizations* 7, no. 2: 117–143.

Culpepper, Pepper D. 2010. *Quiet Politics and Business Power: Corporate Control in Europe and Japan*. New York. Cambridge University Press.

De Coninck, Heleen, Carolyn Fischer, Richard G. Newell, and Takahiro Ueno. 2008. "International Technology-Oriented Agreements to Address Climate Change." *Energy Policy* 36, no. 1: 335–356.

del Río, Pablo. 2017. "Designing Auctions for Renewable Electricity Support: Best Practices from around the World." *Energy for Sustainable Development* 41: 1–13.

Dubash, Navroz K., and Ann Florini. 2011. "Mapping Global Energy Governance." *Global Policy* 2: 6–18.

Dumas, Marion, James Rising, and Johannes Urpelainen. 2016. "Political Competition and Renewable Energy Transitions over Long Time Horizons: A Dynamic Approach." *Ecological Economics* 124: 175–184.

Dunlap, Riley E., and Aaron M. McCright. 2008. "A Widening Gap: Republican and Democratic Views on Climate Change." *Environment: Science and Policy for Sustainable Development* 50, no. 5: 26–35.

Dunlap, Riley E., and Aaron M. McCright. 2011. "Organized Climate Change Denial." *The Oxford Handbook of Climate Change and Society* 1: 144–160.

Enevoldsen, Peter, and Benjamin K. Sovacool. 2016. "Examining the Social Acceptance of Wind Energy: Practical Guidelines for Onshore Wind Project Development in France." *Renewable and Sustainable Energy Reviews* 53: 178–184.

Falkner, Robert. 2003. "Private Environmental Governance and International Relations: Exploring the Links." *Global Environmental Politics* 3, no. 2: 72–87.

Falkner, Robert. 2014. "Global Environmental Politics and Energy: Mapping the Research Agenda." *Energy Research & Social Science* 1: 188–197.

Farrell, Justin. 2016. "Corporate Funding and Ideological Polarization about Climate Change." *Proceedings of the National Academy of Sciences* 113, no. 1: 92–97.

Fouquet, Roger. 2016. "Historical Energy Transitions: Speed, Prices and System Transformation." *Energy Research & Social Science* 22: 7–12.

Fridahl, Mathias, and Mariliis Lehtveer. 2018. "Bioenergy with Carbon Capture and Storage (BECCS): Global Potential, Investment Preferences, and Deployment Barriers." *Energy Research & Social Science* 42: 155–165.

Fuss, Sabine, Josep G. Canadell, Glen P. Peters, Massimo Tavoni, Robbie M. Andrew, Philippe Ciais, Robert B. Jackson, et al. 2014. "Betting on Negative Emissions." *Nature Climate Change* 4, no. 10: 850.

Geels, Frank W. 2014. "Regime Resistance against Low-Carbon Transitions: Introducing Politics and Power into the Multi-level Perspective." *Theory, Culture & Society* 31, no. 5: 21–40.

Goldthau, Andreas, and Michael F. Keating, eds. 2018. *Handbook of the International Political Economy of Energy and Natural Resources.* Edward Elgar Publishing.

Goldthau, Andreas, and Jan Martin Witte, eds. 2010. *Global Energy Governance: The New Rules of the Game.* Washington DC. Brookings Institution Press.

Graber, Sachiko, Tara Narayanan, Jose Alfaro, and Debajit Palit. 2018. "Solar Microgrids in Rural India: Consumers' Willingness to Pay for Attributes of Electricity." *Energy for Sustainable Development* 42: 32–43.

Green, Fergus, and Richard Denniss. 2018. "Cutting with Both Arms of the Scissors: The Economic and Political Case for Restrictive Supply-side Climate Policies." *Climatic Change* 150, nos. 1–2: 73–87.

Green, Jessica F. 2013. "Order Out of Chaos: Public and Private Rules for Managing Carbon." *Global Environmental Politics* 13, no. 2: 1–25.

Green, Jessica F., and Thomas N. Hale. 2017. "Reversing the Marginalization of Global Environmental Politics in International Relations: An Opportunity for the Discipline." *PS: Political Science & Politics* 50, no. 2: 473–479.

Greening, Lorna A., David L. Greene, and Carmen Difiglio. 2000. "Energy Efficiency and Consumption—the Rebound Effect—a Survey." *Energy Policy* 28, nos. 6–7: 389–401.

Hadden, Jennifer. 2015. *Networks in Contention: The Divisive Politics of Climate Change.* New York: Cambridge University Press.

Hager, Carol. 2016. "The Grassroots Origins of the German Energy Transition." In *Germany's Energy Transition,* by Carol Hager and Christoph Stefes, 1–26. New York: Palgrave Macmillan.

Haikola, Simon, Anders Hansson, and Mathias Fridahl. 2018. "Views of BECCS among Modelers and Policymakers." In *Bioenergy with Carbon Capture and Storage: From Global Potentials to Domestic Realities,* edited by Mathias Fridahl, 17–30. Stockholm: European Liberal Forum.

Hancock, Kathleen J., and Vlado Vivoda. 2014. "International Political Economy: A Field Born of the OPEC Crisis Returns to Its Energy Roots." *Energy Research & Social Science* 1: 206–216.

Harrison, Tom, and Genia Kostka. 2014. "Balancing Priorities, Aligning Interests: Developing Mitigation Capacity in China and India." *Comparative Political Studies* 47, no. 3: 450–480.

Hendrix, Cullen S. 2017. "The Streetlight Effect in Climate Change Research on Africa." *Global Environmental Change* 43: 137–147.

Hepburn, Cameron. 2006. "Regulation by Prices, Quantities, or Both: A Review of Instrument Choice." *Oxford Review of Economic Policy* 22, no. 2: 226–247.

Hess, David J. 2014. "Sustainability Transitions: A Political Coalition Perspective." *Research Policy* 43, no. 2: 278–283.

Hess, David J., and Kate Pride Brown. 2017. "Green Tea: Clean-Energy Conservatism as a Countermovement." *Environmental Sociology* 3, no. 1: 64–75.

Heyen, D., J. Horton, and J. Moreno-Cruz. 2019. "Strategic Implications of Counter-geoengineering: Clash or Cooperation?" *Journal of Environmental Economics and Management* 95: 153–177.

Hobman, Elizabeth V., and Elisha R. Frederiks. 2014. "Barriers to Green Electricity Subscription in Australia: Love the Environment, Love Renewable Energy…but Why Should I Pay More?" *Energy Research & Social Science* 3: 78–88.

Hochstetler, Kathryn, and Genia Kostka. 2015. "Wind and Solar Power in Brazil and China: Interests, State–Business Relations, and Policy Outcomes." *Global Environmental Politics* 15, no. 3: 74–94.

Honegger, Matthias, and David Reiner. 2018. "The Political Economy of Negative Emissions Technologies: Consequences for International Policy Design." *Climate Policy* 18, no. 3: 306–321.

Hughes, Llewelyn, and Phillip Y. Lipscy. 2013. "The Politics of Energy." *Annual Review of Political Science* 16: 449–469.

Hughes, Llewelyn, and Jonas Meckling. 2017. "The Politics of Renewable Energy Trade: The US-China Solar Dispute." *Energy Policy* 105: 256–262.

Hughes, Llewelyn, and Johannes Urpelainen. 2015. "Interests, Institutions, and Climate Policy: Explaining the Choice of Policy Instruments for the Energy Sector." *Environmental Science & Policy* 54: 52–63.

Ingham, Alan, Jie Ma, and Alistair Ulph. 2007. "Climate Change, Mitigation and Adaptation with Uncertainty and Learning." *Energy Policy* 35, no. 11: 5354–5369.

Intergovernmental Panel on Climate Change. 2018. "Global Warming of 1.5 °C: An IPCC Special Report on the Impacts of Global Warming of 1.5 °C above Pre-industrial Levels and Related Global Greenhouse Gas Emission Pathways, in the Context of Strengthening the Global Response to the Threat of Climate Change, Sustainable Development, and Efforts to Eradicate Poverty: Summary for Policymakers." Incheon, Republic of Korea: IPCC.

International Energy Agency. 2017. *World Energy Outlook 2017*. Paris. Organisation for Economic Co-operation and Development, OECD.

IPCC. 2014. *Climate Change 2014: Synthesis Report*. Contribution of Working Groups I, II and III to the Fifth Assessment Report of the Intergovernmental Panel on Climate Change. [Edited by R. K. Pachauri and L. A. Meyer]. Geneva: IPCC. https://www.ipcc.ch/site/assets/uploads/2018/02/SYR_AR5_FINAL_full.pdf.

Iyer, Gokul C., Leon E. Clarke, James A. Edmonds, and Nathan E. Hultman. 2016. "Do National-Level Policies to Promote Low-Carbon Technology Deployment Pay Off for the Investor Countries?" *Energy Policy* 98: 400–411.

Jacques, Peter J., and Claire Connolly Knox. 2016. "Hurricanes and Hegemony: A Qualitative Analysis of Micro-level Climate Change Denial Discourses." *Environmental Politics* 25, no. 5: 831–852.

Jenkins, Kirsten, Darren McCauley, Raphael Heffron, Hannes Stephan, and Robert Rehner. 2016. "Energy Justice: A Conceptual Review." *Energy Research & Social Science* 11: 174–182.

Jotzo, Frank, and Salim Mazouz. 2015. "Brown Coal Exit: A Market Mechanism for Regulated Closure of Highly Emissions Intensive Power Stations." *Economic Analysis and Policy* 48: 71–81.

Karapin, Roger. 2016. *Political Opportunities for Climate Policy: California, New York, and the Federal Government*. New York: Cambridge University Press.

Kim, Sung Eun, Johannes Urpelainen, and Joonseok Yang. 2016. "Electric Utilities and American Climate Policy: Lobbying by Expected Winners and Losers." *Journal of Public Policy* 36, no. 2: 251–275.

Kotchen, Matthew J., Kevin J. Boyle, and Anthony A. Leiserowitz. 2013. "Willingness-to-Pay and Policy-Instrument Choice for Climate-Change Policy in the United States." *Energy Policy* 55: 617–625.

Kungl, Gregor. 2015. "Stewards or Sticklers for Change? Incumbent Energy Providers and the Politics of the German Energy Transition." *Energy Research & Social Science* 8: 13–23.

Laird, Frank N., and Christoph Stefes. 2009. "The Diverging Paths of German and United States Policies for Renewable Energy: Sources of Difference." *Energy Policy* 37, no. 7: 2619–2629.

Langer, Katharina, Thomas Decker, and Klaus Menrad. 2017. "Public Participation in Wind Energy Projects Located in Germany: Which Form of Participation Is the Key to Acceptance?" *Renewable Energy* 112: 63–73.

Lee, Taedong. 2013. "Global Cities and Transnational Climate Change Networks." *Global Environmental Politics* 13, no. 1: 108–127.

Levy, David L., and Ans Kolk. 2002. "Strategic Responses to Global Climate Change: Conflicting Pressures on Multinationals in the Oil Industry." *Business and Politics* 4, no. 3: 275–300.

Lewis, Joanna I. 2014. "The Rise of Renewable Energy Protectionism: Emerging Trade Conflicts and Implications for Low Carbon Development." *Global Environmental Politics* 14, no. 4: 10–35.

Lipscy, Philip. 2018. "The Institutional Politics of Energy and Climate Change." Unpublished manuscript.

Lomax, Guy, Timothy M. Lenton, Adepeju Adeosun, and Mark Workman. 2015. "Investing in Negative Emissions." *Nature Climate Change* 5, no. 6: 498.

Loring, Joyce McLaren. 2007. "Wind Energy Planning in England, Wales and Denmark: Factors Influencing Project Success." *Energy Policy* 35, no. 4: 2648–2660.

Lowry, William R., and Mark Joslyn. 2014. "The Determinants of Salience of Energy Issues." *Review of Policy Research* 31, no. 3: 153–172.

Lutsey, Nicholas, and Daniel Sperling. 2008. "America's Bottom-up Climate Change Mitigation Policy." *Energy Policy* 36, no. 2: 673–685.

Lyon, Thomas P., and Haitao Yin. 2010. "Why Do States Adopt Renewable Portfolio Standards? An Empirical Investigation." *The Energy Journal* 31, no. 3: 133–157.

Madden, Nathan J. 2014. "Green Means Stop: Veto Players and Their Impact on Climate-Change Policy Outputs." *Environmental Politics* 23, no. 4: 570–589.

Markussen, Peter, and Gert Tinggaard Svendsen. 2005. "Industry Lobbying and the Political Economy of GHG Trade in the European Union." *Energy Policy* 33, no. 2: 245–255.

Markusson, Nils, Atsushi Ishii, and Jennie C. Stephens. 2011. "The Social and Political Complexities of Learning in Carbon Capture and Storage Demonstration Projects." *Global Environmental Change* 21, no. 2: 293–302.

Marquart-Pyatt, Sandra T., Aaron M. McCright, Thomas Dietz, and Riley E. Dunlap. 2014. "Politics Eclipses Climate Extremes for Climate Change Perceptions." *Global Environmental Change* 29: 246–257.

McLaren, Duncan. 2012. "Governance and Equity in the Development and Deployment of Negative Emissions Technologies." In *Lund Conference on Earth System Governance*, edited by Lund, 18–20. http://www.earthsystemgovernance.org/lund2012/LC2012-paper237.pdf.

Meckling, Jonas. 2011. "The Globalization of Carbon Trading: Transnational Business Coalitions in Climate Politics." *Global Environmental Politics* 11, no. 2: 26–50.

Meckling, Jonas. 2015. "Oppose, Support, or Hedge? Distributional Effects, Regulatory Pressure, and Business Strategy in Environmental Politics." *Global Environmental Politics* 15, no. 2: 19–37.

Meckling, Jonas, and Llewelyn Hughes. 2017. "Globalizing Solar: Global Supply Chains and Trade Preferences." *International Studies Quarterly* 61, no. 2: 225–235.

Meckling, Jonas, and Llewelyn Hughes. 2018. "Global Interdependence in Clean Energy Transitions." *Business and Politics* 20, no. 4: 467–491.

Meckling, Jonas, and Jonas Nahm. 2018. "The Power of Process: State Capacity and Climate Policy." *Governance* 31, no. 4: 741–757.

Meguid, Bonnie M. 2005. "Competition between Unequals: The Role of Mainstream Party Strategy in Niche Party Success." *American Political Science Review* 99, no. 3: 347–359.

Mildenberger, Matto, and Anthony Leiserowitz. 2017. "Public Opinion on Climate Change: Is There an Economy–Environment Tradeoff?" *Environmental Politics* 26, no. 5: 801–824.

Nahm, Jonas. 2017. "Renewable Futures and Industrial Legacies: Wind and Solar Sectors in China, Germany, and the United States." *Business and Politics* 19, no. 1: 68–106.

Nasiritousi, Naghmeh. 2017. "Fossil Fuel Emitters and Climate Change: Unpacking the Governance Activities of Large Oil and Gas Companies." *Environmental Politics* 26, no. 4: 621–647.

Nordhaus, William D. 1995. "The Ghosts of Climates Past and the Specters of Climate Change Future." *Energy Policy* 23, nos. 4–5: 269–282.

Pachauri, Rajendra K., Myles R. Allen, Vicente R. Barros, John Broome, Wolfgang Cramer, Renate Christ, John A. Church, et al. "Climate Change 2014: Synthesis Report." Contribution of Working Groups I, II and III to the fifth assessment report of the Intergovernmental Panel on Climate Change. IPCC.

Palit, Debajit. 2013. "Solar Energy Programs for Rural Electrification: Experiences and Lessons from South Asia." *Energy for Sustainable Development* 17, no. 3: 270–279.

Paterson, Matthew, Matthew Hoffmann, Michele Betsill, and Steven Bernstein. 2014 "The Micro Foundations of Policy Diffusion toward Complex Global Governance: An Analysis of the Transnational Carbon Emission Trading Network." *Comparative Political Studies* 47, no. 3: 420–449.

Perkins, Richard, and Eric Neumayer. 2012. "Does the 'California Effect' Operate across Borders? Trading- and Investing-up in Automobile Emission Standards." *Journal of European Public Policy* 19, no. 2: 217–237.

Pickering, Jonathan, Frank Jotzo, and Peter J. Wood. 2015. "Sharing the Global Climate Finance Effort Fairly with Limited Coordination." *Global Environmental Politics* 15, no. 4: 39–62.

Popp, David. 2002. "Induced Innovation and Energy Prices." *American Economic Review* 92, no. 1: 160–180.

Pralle, Sarah, and Jessica Boscarino. 2011. "Framing Trade-offs: The Politics of Nuclear Power and Wind Energy in the Age of Global Climate Change." *Review of Policy Research* 28, no. 4: 323–346.

Purdon, Mark. 2015. "Advancing Comparative Climate Change Politics: Theory and Method." *Global Environmental Politics* 15, no. 3: 1–26.

Quitzow, Rainer. 2015. "Dynamics of a Policy-Driven Market: The Co-evolution of Technological Innovation Systems for Solar Photovoltaics in China and Germany." *Environmental Innovation and Societal Transitions* 17: 126–148.

Rabe, Barry G. 2018. *Can We Price Carbon?* Cambridge, MA: MIT Press.

Ray, Aaron, Llewelyn Hughes, David M. Konisky, and Charles Kaylor. 2017. "Extreme Weather Exposure and Support for Climate Change Adaptation." *Global Environmental Change* 46: 104–113.

Rayner, Steve, Clare Heyward, Tim Kruger, Nick Pidgeon, Catherine Redgwell, and Julian Savulescu. 2013. "The Oxford Principles." *Climatic Change* 121, no. 3: 499–512.

REN21, R. 2017. *Global Status Report 2017*. Paris: REN21 Secretariat.

REN21, R. 2018. *Global Status Report 2018*. Paris: REN21 Secretariat.

Rhodes, James S., and David W. Keith. 2008. "Biomass with Capture: Negative Emissions within Social and Environmental Constraints, an Editorial Comment." *Climatic Change* 87, no. 3: 321–328.

Richardson, Dick, and Chris Rootes. 2006. "The Green Challenge: Philosophical, Programmatic and Electoral Considerations." In *The Green Challenge: The Development of Green Parties in Europe*, edited by Dick Richardson and Chris Rootes, 13–26. London: Routledge.

Richter, Mario. 2013. "Business Model Innovation for Sustainable Energy: German Utilities and Renewable Energy." *Energy Policy* 62: 1226–1237.

Rogelj, Joeri, David L. McCollum, and Keywan Riahi. 2013. "The UN's' Sustainable Energy for All Initiative Is Compatible with a Warming Limit of 2 C." *Nature Climate Change* 3, no. 6: 545.

Rogelj, Joeri, Alexander Popp, Katherine V. Calvin, Gunnar Luderer, Johannes Emmerling, David Gernaat, Shinichiro Fujimori, et al. 2018. "Scenarios towards Limiting Global Mean Temperature Increase below 1.5 C." *Nature Climate Change* 8, no. 4: 325.

Rosa, Eugene A., and Thomas Dietz. 2012. "Human Drivers of National Greenhouse-Gas Emissions." *Nature Climate Change* 2, no. 8: 581.

Sæverud, Ingvild Andreassen, and Jon Birger Skjærseth. 2007. "Oil Companies and Climate Change: Inconsistencies between Strategy Formulation and Implementation?" *Global Environmental Politics* 7, no. 3: 42–62.

Schmidt, Tobias S., and Sebastian Sewerin. 2017. "Technology as a Driver of Climate and Energy Politics." *Nature Energy* 2, no. 6: 17084.

Shwom, Rachael L., Aaron M. McCright, Steven R. Brechin, Riley E. Dunlap, Sandra T. Marquart-Pyatt, and Lawrence C. Hamilton. 2015. "Public Opinion on Climate Change." In *Climate Change and Society: Sociological Perspectives*, edited by Riley E. Dunlap and Robert J. Brulle, . Oxford University Press: 269–299.

Siddiqi, Afreen, and Laura Diaz Anadon. 2011. "The Water–Energy Nexus in Middle East and North Africa." *Energy Policy* 39, no. 8: 4529–4540.

Skjærseth, Jon Birger, Guri Bang, and Miranda A. Schreurs. 2013. "Explaining Growing Climate Policy Differences between the European Union and the United States." *Global Environmental Politics* 13, no. 4: 61–80.

Smith, A., A. Stirling, and F. Berkhout. 2005. "The Governance of Sustainable Socio-technical Transitions." *Research Policy* 34, no. 10: 1491–1510.

Spence, Alexa, Wouter Poortinga, Catherine Butler, and Nicholas Frank Pidgeon. 2011. "Perceptions of Climate Change and Willingness to Save Energy Related to Flood Experience." *Nature Climate Change* 1, no. 1: 46.

Stenzel, Till, and Alexander Frenzel. 2008. "Regulating Technological Change—The Strategic Reactions of Utility Companies towards Subsidy Policies in the German, Spanish and UK Electricity Markets." *Energy Policy* 36, no. 7: 2645–2657.

Stern, Paul C. 2014. "Individual and Household Interactions with Energy Systems: Toward Integrated Understanding." *Energy Research & Social Science* 1: 41–48.

Stigler, George J. 1971. "The Theory of Economic Regulation." *The Bell Journal of Economics and Management Science* 2, no. 1: 3–21.

Stokes, Leah C., and Hanna L. Breetz. 2018. "Politics in the US Energy Transition: Case Studies of Solar, Wind, Biofuels and Electric Vehicles Policy." *Energy Policy* 113: 76–86.

Stram, Bruce N. 2016. "Key Challenges to Expanding Renewable Energy." *Energy Policy* 96: 728–734.

Supran, Geoffrey, and Naomi Oreskes. 2017. "Assessing ExxonMobil's Climate Change Communications (1977–2014)." *Environmental Research Letters* 12, no. 8: 084019.

Tavoni, Massimo, and Robert Socolow. 2013. "Modeling Meets Science and Technology: An Introduction to a Special Issue on Negative Emissions." *Climatic Change* 118, no. 1: 1–14.

Tollefson, Jeff. 2018. "Can the World Kick Its Fossil-Fuel Addiction Fast Enough?" *Nature Climate Change* 556: 422–425.

Ulsrud, Kirsten, Tanja Winther, Debajit Palit, Harald Rohracher, and Jonas Sandgren. 2011. "The Solar Transitions Research on Solar Mini-grids in India: Learning from Local Cases of Innovative Socio-technical Systems." *Energy for Sustainable Development* 15, no. 3: 293–303.

United Nations. 1992. United Nations Framework Convention on Climate Change.

Unruh, Gregory C. 2000. "Understanding Carbon Lock-in." *Energy Policy* 28, no. 12: 817–830.

Urpelainen, Johannes, and Thijs Van de Graaf. 2015. "The International Renewable Energy Agency: A Success Story in Institutional Innovation?" *International Environmental Agreements: Politics, Law and Economics* 15, no. 2: 159–177.

Van de Graaf, Thijs. 2012. "Obsolete or Resurgent? The International Energy Agency in a Changing Global Landscape." *Energy Policy* 48: 233–241.

Van de Graaf, Thijs, and Kirsten Westphal. 2011. "The G8 and G20 as Global Steering Committees for Energy: Opportunities and Constraints." *Global Policy* 2: 19–30.

van der Kamp, Denise, Peter Lorentzen, and Daniel Mattingly. 2017. "Racing to the Bottom or to the Top? Decentralization, Revenue Pressures, and Governance Reform in China." *World Development* 95: 164–176.

Van Der Schoor, Tineke, and Bert Scholtens. 2015. "Power to the People: Local Community Initiatives and the Transition to Sustainable Energy." *Renewable and Sustainable Energy Reviews* 43: 666–675.

Van Gevelt, T., C. Canales Holzeis, B. Jones, and M. T. Safdar. 2016. "Insights from an Energy Poor Rwandan Village." *Energy for Sustainable Development* 32: 121–129.

van Vuuren, Detlef P., Elke Stehfest, David E. H. J. Gernaat, Maarten Berg, David L. Bijl, Harmen Sytze Boer, Vassilis Daioglou, et al. 2018. "Alternative Pathways to the 1.5 C Target Reduce the Need for Negative Emission Technologies." *Nature Climate Change* 8, no. 5: 391.

Vezirgiannidou, Sevasti-Eleni. 2013. "Climate and Energy Policy in the United States: The Battle of Ideas." *Environmental Politics* 22, no. 4: 593–609.

Viñuales, Jorge E., Joanna Depledge, David M. Reiner, and Emma Lees. 2017. "Climate Policy after the 2015 Paris Conference." Special issue, *Climate Policy* 17, no. 1.

Vivanco, David Font, René Kemp, and Ester van der Voet. 2016. "How to Deal with the Rebound Effect? A Policy-Oriented Approach." *Energy Policy* 94: 114–125.

Vogel, David. 1997. "Trading Up and Governing Across: Transnational Governance and Environmental Protection." *Journal of European Public Policy* 4, no. 4: 556–571.

Vormedal, Irja. 2011 "From Foe to Friend? Business, the Tipping Point and US Climate Politics." *Business and Politics* 13, no. 3: 1–29.

Wagner, Gernot, and Martin L. Weitzman. 2016. *Climate Shock: The Economic Consequences of a Hotter Planet*. Princeton, NJ: Princeton University Press.

Wassermann, Sandra, Matthias Reeg, and Kristina Nienhaus. 2015. "Current Challenges of Germany's Energy Transition Project and Competing Strategies of Challengers and Incumbents: The Case of Direct Marketing of Electricity from Renewable Energy Sources." *Energy Policy* 76: 66–75.

Wibeck, Victoria, Anders Hansson, Jonas Anshelm, Shinichiro Asayama, Lisa Dilling, Pamela M. Feetham, Rachel Hauser, et al. 2017. "Making Sense of Climate Engineering: A Focus Group Study of Lay Publics in Four Countries." *Climatic Change* 145, nos. 1–2: 1–14.

Wolf, Johanna, Katrina Brown, and Declan Conway. 2009. "Ecological Citizenship and Climate Change: Perceptions and Practice." *Environmental Politics* 18, no. 4: 503–521.

Yi, Hongtao, and Richard C. Feiock. 2012. "Policy Tool Interactions and the Adoption of State Renewable Portfolio Standards." *Review of Policy Research* 29, no. 2: 193–206.

Zelli, Fariborz, and Harro van Asselt. 2013. "Introduction: The Institutional Fragmentation of Global Environmental Governance; Causes, Consequences, and Responses." *Global Environmental Politics* 13, no. 3: 1–13.

Zhong, Minjia, and Morgan D. Bazilian. 2018. "Contours of the Energy Transition: Investment by International Oil and Gas Companies in Renewable Energy." *The Electricity Journal* 31, no. 1: 82–91.

PART III

MAJOR ENERGY PLAYERS AND REGIONS

CHAPTER 17

....

THE ENERGY POLITICS
OF THE UNITED STATES

....

JULIANN EMMONS ALLISON AND
SRINIVAS PARINANDI

On April 10, 2010, the BP *Deepwater Horizon* exploded in the Gulf of Mexico. More than four million barrels of oil flowed out of the Maconda well over eighty-seven days, making it the largest oil spill in US history; globally, it was the second worst spill. The explosion and fire killed eleven crew members and injured an additional seventeen; the oil spill destroyed four square miles of seafloor and more than thirteen hundred miles of coastline, killing tens of thousands of birds and sea animals and causing the region's tourism and fishing industries to collapse (Ebinger 2016; Jarvis 2010). The disaster cost BP over $144.89 billion, including cleanup, government response, property and natural resource damage, economic losses associated with the spill, litigation and settlement costs, and restoration expenses (Lee, Garza-Gomez, and Lee 2018; Smith, Smith, and Ashcroft 2011). The magnitude of the tragedy undermined public faith in offshore drilling for oil and gas; national and regional surveys alike have demonstrated that much of the public negatively viewed BP and the federal government immediately following the spill and for some time afterward (*ABC News/Washington Post* 2010; Bishop 2014; Lilley and Firestone 2013; Mukherjee and Rahman 2016; Rosentiel 2010; Safford, Ulrich, and Hamilton 2012).

The BP *Deepwater Horizon* oil spill highlights persistent weaknesses inherent in US energy politics, despite the country's statutory commitment to secure access to affordable energy resources without unwarranted environmental damage (Energy Policy Act of 2005; Hultman 2010). The fact that many major sources of energy—coal, crude oil, natural gas, biomass, and nuclear—are dangerous to extract and produce contributes to the energy regulation challenge. Offshore drilling for oil and gas, for example, especially in deepwater, depends on a complex drilling system that entails rigs, moorings, pipelines, shoreside processing, and supply lines covering thousands of miles (see Coburn in this volume), with numerous weak points prone to accidents, the worst being explosions and spills. There have been forty-four major oil spills in US waters since 1969 and three major spills in the Gulf of Mexico (National Oceanic and Atmospheric Administration n.d.). While hurricane damage to oil and gas infrastructure is the leading cause of spills, other causal factors of these accidents are equipment failure, weather, human error, and collisions (Meyers et al. 2018). Corporate safety management and regulatory oversight should diminish these accident risks. Yet analyses of the BP *Deepwater Horizon* explosion and spill by government agencies (Bureau of Safety and Environmental Enforcement 2011; Graham and Reilly 2011; US Chemical Safety and Hazard Investigation Board 2014), energy and environmental researchers (Birkland and Young 2011; Ebinger 2016; Osofsky 2011), and the media (Hoffman 2010) point to the following causes: equipment failure complicated by human error as a result of inadequate government and corporate regulation; poor discharge of responsibility by employees of BP, Transocean Offshore Drilling Inc., and Haliburton; and lack of any emergency planning by involved companies or the US Coast Guard. Ebinger (2016, 1) argues that evidence provided via legal and regulatory proceedings make it "clear that there was gross negligence on the part of BP and its partners who placed short-term profits against technically sound drilling practices" (see also Neill and Morris 2012).

Effectively regulating entities such as BP is complicated by the US decentralized political structure, which makes decisive action at the national level difficult. Even though the United States is one of the world's largest producers and consumers of energy as well as a key innovator in energy technology (Nanda, Younge, and Fleming 2014; see also Tutuncu in this volume), the country's national energy policy is piecemeal, with individual states taking the lead in devising their own energy and climate policies and engaged activists among the public taking the lead in pushing issues of environmental protection to the fore. Politics explains why actors other than the national government have crafted much of contemporary US energy policy. The structure of Congress, combined with the heterogeneity (in terms of ideology, constituent pressure, and economic interest) of districts represented there, makes changing the status quo difficult; hence, national energy policy still bears the imprint of the 1950s–1970s, the period during which it was created (Volden and Wiseman 2014). Individual states are less heterogeneous, making unified action at that level relatively easier. Activists understand disparities between national and state audiences and have demonstrated an ability to bring appropriate awareness to issues concerning them.

This chapter examines the politics of US energy policy, with an emphasis on three themes: the distribution of authority to regulate energy between national (or federal) and subnational governments, the relationship between energy and environmental policy and regulation, and the role of climate action in energy politics. It begins with an overview of contemporary energy production and consumption in the United States. The chapter then proceeds with a history of national energy politics that includes the role of federalism and the development of environmental policies associated with the nation's transition to renewable energy and unconventional sources of energy. This section suggests that, politically, US national energy policy was a tenuous prospect until the post–World War II rise to power made continuation of modern economic growth a national priority; the 1970s oil crisis then demonstrated that economic growth could be wiped out by disruptions in energy supply. The success of postwar economic growth and the commitment to fuel it, regardless of ecological impacts, catalyzed opposition from environmentalists and, later, climate activists. This overview is followed by a critical review of the literatures on federalism and energy politics and policy, the increasing integration of energy and environmental policies, and the effects of climate action on energy policy. The chapter concludes with a discussion of a research agenda to guide scholarship going forward.

ENERGY PRODUCTION AND CONSUMPTION IN THE UNITED STATES

Although the geographic distribution of energy production and consumption within its borders is highly uneven, the United States is overall one of the world's largest producers and consumers of energy (Nanda, Younge, and Fleming 2014; see also Tutuncu in this volume). Figure 17.1 summarizes US electricity generation in 2018 by source, including fossil fuels (coal, petroleum from crude oil and natural gas, and natural gas); nuclear; and renewables, consisting of wind, biomass, solar, geothermal, and hydropower. Fossil fuels make up roughly 64 percent of the current mix of energy resources used for electricity generation; nuclear energy contributes about 20 percent of the mix; and renewables, which have received significant attention for their extraordinary growth—67 percent in

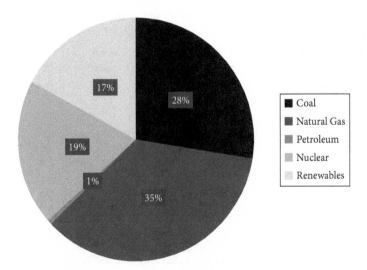

FIGURE 17.1 US electricity production by source, 2018* * Numbers do not add up to 100 because other sources not included make up the difference in electricity production.

Source: Data from US Energy Information Administration (2018d).

the 2010–2016 decade (Center for Climate and Energy Solutions 2016)—make up the remaining 16 percent. As of 2017, the top five producing states overall, including all sources of energy, were Texas, with 17,573 trillion British thermal units (BTUs); Pennsylvania, with 8,168 trillion BTUs; Wyoming, with 7,788 trillion BTUs; West Virginia, with 4,418 trillion BTUs; and Oklahoma, with 4,160 trillion BTUs. The top five consuming states as of 2017 were Texas, at 13,365 trillion BTUs; California, at 7,881 trillion BTUs; Louisiana, at 4,481.8 trillion BTUs; Florida, at 4,208.5 trillion BTUs; and Illinois, at 3,871.5 trillion BTUs (US Energy Information Administration 2017).

Most US efforts to foster green energy growth are directed at increasing the renewables' share of electricity generation. In this endeavor, some states, by virtue of natural resource endowments, regulatory policymaking choices, or both, have more developed renewables sectors than others. Yet electricity generation in many states continues to feed primarily on fossil fuel resources. Table 17.1, which lists the top five states by energy source used for electricity generation, provides important insights that guide the remainder of this chapter. First, the explicit emphasis on states rather than the nation underscores the decentralized nature of energy policy in the United States. Second, the diversity of sources and states in the table illustrates the strong local dimension of energy politics in the United States due to the tendency of dominant resource sectors to seek to codify, enhance, and build their advantage through governmental action in their "home" states. And third, as demonstrated by Texas, fossil fuels and renewables can be important sources of revenue and energy within the same state. As Table 17.1 indicates, Texas is the nation's top consumer of natural gas and wind for electricity generation; that state is also the nation's top producer of natural gas and wind power. Thus, conventional (fossil fuels) and emerging (renewables) energy resources are not necessarily in opposition.

Electricity generation is instructive but does not reflect patterns of energy resource production and consumption in other areas, most notably transportation. Twenty-eight percent of all of the energy used in the United States in 2019 was consumed by transportation (US Energy Information Agency 2019d). Figure 17.2 provides a breakdown of total US energy use as of 2018 by source across the nation's electricity, transportation, and

Table 17.1 Top States Based on Energy Source Used for Electricity

Coal	Natural Gas	Nuclear	Biomass	Hydropower	Solar Photovoltaic	Wind
Texas	Texas	Illinois	California	Washington	California	Texas
Indiana	Florida	Pennsylvania	Georgia	California	North Carolina	Oklahoma
West Virginia	Pennsylvania	South Carolina	Florida	Oregon	Arizona	Iowa
Missouri	California	New York	Virginia	New York	Texas	Kansas
Kentucky	Louisiana	Alabama	Alabama	Alabama	Nevada	California

Note: Rankings denote year-to-year changes between 2018 and 2019 (US Energy Information Administration 2019a). Hydropower in this context refers to electricity obtained through conventional hydroelectric generation.

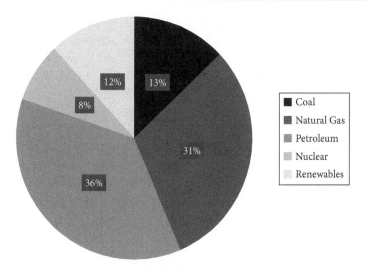

FIGURE 17.2 Total US energy use by source, 2018.

Source: Data from U.S. Energy Information Administration (2018d).

industrial sectors. The chart reveals that due to its use for transportation, petroleum is the largest energy resource used in the United States. According to the US Energy Information Administration (2018d), 92 percent of the transportation sector is fueled by petroleum. Petroleum is also used widely as a feedstock for industrial processes. Energy resources other than petroleum are used primarily for electricity generation and as industrial feedstocks (US Energy Information Administration 2018b). The resilience of fossil fuels despite the growth of renewables suggests oil and gas resources will continue to play some role in US energy politics even as the nation embraces a decarbonizing future.

In the context of transitioning to lower-carbon energy sources in the United States, hydraulic fracturing, or "fracking," is arguably the most controversial fossil fuel issue in the United States, where it is currently the primary method of shale oil and gas extraction (Powell 2017; see also Tutuncu in this volume). Fracturing is a complicated and expensive process that involves injecting fluid—water and sand or other proppants suspended by thickening agents—at high pressure into subsurface formations to fracture, or create cracks in, (chiefly shale) rock formations to release oil, natural gas, and brine. Combined with horizontal drilling, which provides greater access to oil and gas reservoirs, fracturing is an effective extraction process whenever market prices for these energy resources are high enough to warrant the associated economic, environmental, and social costs. The rapid rise in oil prices from less than $30/barrel in 2000 to over $90 at the start of the 2008[1] recession provided the ideal conditions for the US shale boom.

Initially scholars as well as energy and environmental policy makers were enthusiastic about the viability of shale gas. The US oil and gas industries arguably "staged a remarkable recovery" as a consequence of fracturing and were positioned to increase self-sufficiency, reverse the nation's trade deficit, and revive industries (Dunn and McClelland 2013, 1411). Others heralded fracturing because the carbon dioxide emissions—a key greenhouse gas (GHG)—associated with the combustion of natural gas are lower than comparable emissions from gasoline or coal (Burnham et al. 2011; Hayhoe et al. 2002). Some of that eagerness later waned when evidence that natural gas, which consists mostly of methane, is a more potent GHG than carbon dioxide threatened to derail commitments to climate change mitigation strategies at all levels of government. Howarth, Santoro, and Ingraffea's (2011) critical review of natural gas as a "transition fuel" finds that fracturing is less likely to ensure transition from coal to natural gas than it is to increase overall dependence on fossil fuels. Though other scholars are more optimistic about the potential for natural gas to reduce carbon dioxide emissions and some forms of air pollution (Jackson et al. 2014; see Hughes in this volume), fracturing remains strongly tied to the process's role in land degradation, water contamination, and air pollution (Jackson et al. 2014).

THE POLITICS OF NATIONAL ENERGY POLICY IN THE UNITED STATES IN RETROSPECT

The US federal structure, as well as the behavior of individuals and groups within it, has impacted the content and nature of energy politics and policy in the nation. For much of the nation's history there was no comprehensive national energy policy. The dominance of individual states, combined with the weakness of executive institutions through the mid-twentieth century, yielded decentralized energy policy that was localized in character (Gailmard and Patty 2013; Kollman and Chibber 2004; Tulis 2017). Prior to the mid-twentieth century, energy policy was local or regional in scope and designed to facilitate the development and transport of dominant energy sources to commercial, industrial, and residential customers demanding power (Gormley 1983). For instance, New York advanced its own hydroelectric interests while Ohio developed a significant coal industry (Rueb 2017; Siegel and Cheung 2016); there was little effort to synchronize New York's interests with Ohio's in the form of national policy (Chubb 1983; Commoner 1979;). Until the 1960s, public engagement with energy policy was similarly limited to "smoke nuisances" and other local issues related to increased reliance on fossil fuels in dense urban areas (Melosi 1980; Morgan 1973; Stradling 2002). While individual victims of air pollution sued perpetrators throughout the first century of US history, the first municipal antismoke ordinances were not passed until the 1880s (in Chicago, Illinois, and Cincinnati, Ohio, both of which were then among the nation's top ten most populous cities); legislation governing counties and states followed in 1913 (Albany County, New York) and 1952 (Oregon), respectively (Stradling and Thorsheim 1999; and Stern 1982).

Three developments converged in the mid-twentieth century to generate the political conditions necessary to develop greater regulation of the electricity and natural gas systems and the oil industry. First, US involvement in two world wars, along with the construction of a post–World War II American-led alliance system, gave the United States the opportunity to act globally in the pursuit of its energy and, later, environmental goals (DeSombre 2000; Yergin 1990). Second, the development of the "modern presidency" during the Roosevelt administration, the modern bureaucracy, and the modern party system strengthened national executive power and facilitated presidential and congressional coordination in articulating a national energy policy (Aldrich 2011; Chick 2007; Neustadt 1980). A president with ample staff at his or her disposal can deal with Congress from a position of equality rather than subservience and can direct a national bureaucracy to create a centralized energy policy (Neustadt 1980). These institutional innovations, including frequent use of executive orders (Lisowski 2002; Olson 1984; Shanley 1983), also spurred the development of air and water quality policy in response to activists opposed to "unchecked pollution" associated with fossil fuel extraction and combustion (Childs 2011; DeSombre 2000; Dunlap and Mertig 2014; Scheraga 1994). And third, industrialization and the rise of a predominantly urban population necessitated greater coordination with respect to the procurement, generation, and distribution of energy (Cherp and Jewell 2011; Hughes and Lipscy 2013), including preparing for and responding to environmental externalities and emergencies associated with energy generation and use (Hays 1987).

In the aftermath of World War II and for much of the nearly three-decade Western economic boom that followed it, the US government's principal energy goal consisted of finding and securing petroleum deposits for itself and its allies (Crafts and Toniolo 2012; Hughes and Lipscy 2013). Continued close US involvement with Aramco and the Saudi Arabian government (Bronson 2008) and cordial relationships with Iran during the Pahlavi regime (Castiglioni 2015) and with Venezuela prior to Hugo Chavez's rule (Miller 2016; see Rosales and Sánchez in this volume) were predicated on the desire not only to secure oil deposits in these countries but also to prevent the Soviet Union and its allies from accessing these deposits. From the 1940s to the 1970s, the US goal of securing unfettered access to oil had bipartisan support due to the centrality of oil to the transportation sector and manufacturing processes (OPEC Secretariat 2015); electoral fears of Democrats regarding accusations of being weak concerning national security (Daalder and Lindsay 2005); and the possibility that the salience of the civil rights movement deflected attention from energy issues (Ellis 2013). Research on how presidents balance managerial roles with desires for legislative success suggests that with rare exceptions—for example, President Barack Obama regarding the Clean Power Plan—presidents did not use their visibility to move away from an energy policy designed to ensure access to fossil fuels (Beckmann 2010). Studies of bureaucratic freedom to maintain policy stability (see Gailmard and Patty 2013) indicate that regulators have little autonomy and act according to the dictates of their executive and legislative bosses.

The event that upended American foreign policy concerning oil was the 1973 oil embargo by the Organization of the Petroleum Exporting Countries (OPEC), which increased the price of oil dramatically. President Richard Nixon responded by creating the Federal Energy Office, an organization that coordinated the US response to the embargo; it was succeeded by the Federal Energy Administration (FEA) in 1974

(Anders 1980). The FEA's charge included maintaining quotas and price controls on oil and associated derivatives and gathering data on energy sources and energy production and consumption patterns to reduce dependence on foreign petroleum. Greater federal regulation of energy in response to the oil crisis included congressional involvement. The passage of the Energy Reorganization Act in 1974 fostered the development of the Nuclear Regulatory Commission, along with increased investment in energy research. In addition, the passage of the Energy Policy and Conservation Act of 1975 established the Strategic Petroleum Reserve (up to 727 billion gallons), the Energy Conservation Program for Consumer Products, and Corporate Average Fuel Economy (CAFE) standards, which are levied on new vehicles according to class of vehicle (Knittel 2011). Finally, the passage of the Department of Energy Organization Act in 1977 subsumed the FEA within the Department of Energy (DOE), which administers energy regulation and research efforts under the supervision of the president and Congress. The same act retained the Federal Power Commission (FPC), which had licensed power plants and electricity transmission since 1920 and natural gas facilities and pipelines since 1935, in the new Federal Energy Regulatory Commission (FERC). FERC regulates public utility transmission and sales for resale in interstate commerce, leaving decisions about supplying energy to users up to individual states.

The extension of federal regulation of energy production and usage coincided with the rise of popular protest against "the relentless degradation" of the US natural environments (Rothman 2017). Reliance on fossil fuels contributed to New York City's killer smog events during the 1950s and 1960s and a well blowout off California's coast in 1969 that spilled over 400,000 gallons of oil, in addition to many of the more than 100,000 deaths due to air pollution each year through 1990 (Zhang et al. 2018). President Richard Nixon responded to these crises by establishing the Environmental Protection Agency (EPA) in 1970. The EPA is responsible for environmental assessment—completing environmental impact statements (EIS) in the context of specific projects and/or strategic environmental assessments (SEA) in the case of state policies, plans, and programs—research, and education, as well as the administration of national statutes in consultation with state and tribal governments. While the DOE and FERC seek "to keep energy prices low and supplies ample" (Freeman 2017, 341), the EPA and environmental regulatory agencies focus on reducing and mitigating the adverse consequences of securing stable supplies of affordable energy. Despite claims that environmental agencies fail to consider the effects of regulation on energy markets and costs and electrical system reliability, and that energy regulators do not consider the impacts of their regulatory choices on public health and the natural environment, "environmental law increasingly has become a driver of energy policy, and energy regulation has begun to seriously address environmental concerns" (Freeman 2017, 340).

The federal government's movement in the 1970s toward increased regulation of energy resources in response to the oil crisis represented a new status quo. Prior to the crisis, political debate concerned whether the federal government should regulate energy procurement, production, and consumption at all, except for securing petroleum and maintaining the safety of workers. Debate following the crisis shifted to how vigorous federal regulation must be to ensure energy security and sustainability, including environmental and socioeconomic concerns (Kuhlman and Farrington 2010; McCollum, Krey, and Riahi 2011). Politics concerning the federal government's role with regard to increasing domestic oil and gas production or adopting carbon emissions limits has occurred in the context of this post–oil crisis perspective on regulation.

The flurry of energy, and environmental, regulatory activity that characterized the 1970s was followed by a lull until passage of the 1992 Energy Policy Act, which stimulated competition in electricity generation, paving the way for the current period of deregulation (Watkiss and Smith 1993; see Hoika and MacArthur in this volume). Lower energy costs, which may be attributable to deregulation (Milstein and Tishler 2011; Pollitt 2012; Razeghi, Shaffer, and Samuelsen 2017), buttressed conservative opposition to incentivizing energy efficiency and/or less polluting fuel sources, despite growing concern about climate change evidenced by the 1992 Earth Summit in Rio de Janeiro. A decade later, "rising energy prices...shaped by competing concerns about energy security, environmental quality, and economic growth" (VandeHei and Blum 2005, 1) prompted passage of the 2005 Energy Policy Act. Although this legislation required the addition of renewable fuels to gasoline sold in the United States, it increased reliance on fossil fuels by incentivizing oil and gas extraction on public lands and fossil fuel production. President George W. Bush claimed the act would prove to be "a vital step toward a more secure and more prosperous nation that is less dependent on foreign sources of energy" (VandeHei and Blum 2005). Opponents argued that it "continues to subsidize the well-established oil and gas industries that really don't need subsidizing" (Roberts 2005, 1).

The years since the 2005 Energy Policy Act was enacted have witnessed an extraordinary rise in political polarization between American liberals and conservatives—elites as well as the mass public—worsened by an "echo chamber" in terms of media consumption (Flaxman, Goel, and Rao 2016; McCarty, Poole, and Rosenthal 2006; Shor and McCarty 2011). Ideological echo chambers have mapped onto energy and environmental issues (Jasny, Waggle, and Fisher 2015). The politics of energy policy in the United States is now divided along party lines. Democrats have advocated regulatory activity to reduce reliance on oil and gas and transition to renewable energy sources, while Republicans have emphasized energy security through increased domestic fossil fuel production and private sector investment in alternative and renewable energy (Brown and Hess 2016; Gromet, Kunreuther, and Larrick 2013; Lyon and Yin 2010). This discord is central to the politics of climate change attributable to increased levels of atmospheric carbon dioxide released during fossil fuel use (Cook et al. 2013). The United States is one of the world's largest emitters of carbon (World Bank 2019) and stands to experience more severe weather events, diminished agricultural productivity, and reduced quality of life (Goudie 2019). Liberals favor stronger federal regulation to reduce carbon dioxide and other GHG emissions to mitigate the effects of a changing climate. Conservatives generally begrudge policies intended to curb GHG emissions, insofar as they might impinge on the economic and political benefits that have long accrued to the fossil fuel industries. This conservative-liberal divide has influenced current national-level debates about energy, which we examine in greater detail in the next section.

NATIONAL POLICY DEBATES ON ENERGY, THE ENVIRONMENT, AND THE CLIMATE

The overwhelming majority of research on climate change indicates that average global temperatures are rising as a consequence of increased GHG emissions and that the sharp upward trend since the Industrial Revolution is due to human activity, especially that resulting from fossil fuel combustion, deforestation, and changes in land use (Cook et al. 2013). Impacts of our changing climate are evident in the United States, as they are worldwide, and include human health threats; altered agricultural production and food insecurity; disrupted water supplies; and more pressing concerns regarding transportation systems, energy supplies, and ecologies (US Climate Change Research Program 2018). These threats challenge the federal government to act. Specifically, those on the ideological Left have advocated using federal regulation to increase the costs of generating carbon emissions, while those on the ideological Right have exhibited three distinct responses (Dryzek, Norgaard, and Schlosberg 2011; McCright 2008). A small number of conservatives agree with progressives that climate change is anthropogenic and represents a serious public policy challenge. Prior to 2018's extended and devastating wildfire season, their support for climate adaptation policies emphasized tax credits to spur growth in renewables (Hochschild and Hochschild 2018; Siegel 2018). Many others understand that climate change is occurring but do not believe humans are responsible for it or that regulation can undo what they regard to be a natural process (Friedman 2019). The final group of those on the Right are skeptical that climate change is occurring and generally support conventional energy usage without restriction (Bohr 2016).

These distinct ideological responses to contemporary climate science have so far undermined the legislative consensus necessary to develop effective, national policy to reduce carbon dioxide and other GHG emissions. Specifically, economists and other policy analysts consider imposing a carbon tax directly on consumers to be the most effective way to reduce carbon production, because consumers themselves would face direct financial repercussions for the amount of carbon that they emit (Avi-Yonah and Uhlmann 2009; Goulder and Schein 2013; Harrison 2010; International Panel on Climate Change 2019). Yet even left-leaning politicians at the US federal level have largely refrained from advocating a direct carbon tax on consumers for political reasons; politicians fear that making consumers pay directly for the carbon will engender voter anger and hamper their electoral prospects (Harrison 2010; Rabe 2011). Evidence from nations that have enacted carbon taxes suggests that their concerns are well-founded; hence, "carbon pricing has, so far, played only a supporting role in efforts to mitigate global warming" (Plumer and Popavich 2019).

Advocates of increased carbon regulation have similarly been unable to create a nationwide cap and trade system, although such schemes have been effective for California and, at the regional level, in the Northeast and in western North America (Betsill et al. 2006 Union of Concerned Scientists 2018). These systems include increasingly strict "caps" on GHG emissions and a market in which companies can "trade" emissions allowances. In practice, major polluters buy and sell allowances to produce carbon dioxide emissions; emissions reductions occur over time as the maximum number of tradable allowances is reduced pursuant to policy goals (Elkins and Baker 2001). Scholars consider a cap and trade system to be less effective than a carbon tax (Avi-Yonah and Uhlmann 2009; Goulder and Schein 2013; Stavins 2008). They argue that cap and trade provides an indirect incentive to reduce GHG-producing activities, compared with the direct incentive posed by a carbon tax. Of course, cap and trade participants *could* pass the costs of carbon emissions on to consumers in the form of higher prices but are unlikely to risk losing customers (Schmalensee and Stavins 2015). Though the effects of cap and trade on individuals are low compared to a carbon tax, opposition in Congress from representatives of states whose economies rely on resource extraction and from presidents whose electoral fortunes are dependent on votes from those states has doomed efforts to adopt nationwide emissions trading programs (Stavins 2011).

In the absence of successful legislative efforts to craft a national energy policy that would facilitate climate change adaptation, the executive and judicial branches have emerged as the key federal battlegrounds with respect to energy and climate policy. During the Barack Obama administration, the Environmental Protection Agency (EPA) used the Supreme Court's ruling in *Massachusetts v. EPA* (2007) to regulate carbon dioxide under the Clean Air Act to devise the Clean Power Plan (CPP) (Bulman-Pozen 2017). The plan established the first ever US limits on carbon emissions from power plants but granted states the opportunity to design local and regional policies to achieve emissions targets by shifting electricity production away from coal toward natural gas and renewables and/or increasing energy efficiency. The CPP aimed to reduce emissions from electricity generation by 32 percent below 2005 levels by 2030. The Obama administration also signed the Paris Agreement, which strengthened the 1992 United Nations Framework Convention on Climate Change (UNFCCC) by committing signatories to work individually and collectively to limit global temperature increase to no more than 2°C.

The problem with executive actions, including those derived from judicial decisions, is that they are entirely reversible. The Supreme Court has no way of enforcing its decisions without cooperation from the president or congressional action that forces presidential compliance with the Court (Rabe 2011). Decisions made by one presidential administration without congressional approval can also be overturned by the next presidential administration (Chiou and Rothenberg 2017). Both the Obama administration's CPP and its commitment to the Paris Agreement were abandoned by the Donald Trump administration that followed, despite the anticipated high environmental and economic costs associated with doing so (Linn, Burtraw, and McCormack 2016; Nong and Siriwardana 2018). This "quashing" (Dunlap, McCright, and Yarosh 2016) of optimism concerning climate action at the federal level supports scholars' and policy makers' continuing expectation that national and international agreements to reduce GHG will aggregate and emulate successful approaches that emerge at lower levels of governance (Cooper 2018; Meckling 2015; Stokes and Warshaw 2017). "It is not participation that matters, but compliance," according to Cooper (2018, 440). By 2019, nearly two dozen states, representing more than 40 percent of the nation's carbon emissions, had enacted policies capable of ensuring compliance with the aims of the Paris Agreement (Cooper 2018). If fully implemented, these policies, in combination with efforts by cities, businesses, and other organizations invested in climate action, "could come within striking distance of the US Paris Agreement commitment, resulting in emissions that are 17–24 percent below 2005 levels in 2025" (Climate Action Tracker 2019).

State and Regional Energy Politics and Policy in the Twenty-first Century

Absent sufficient, effective national initiatives, the locus of US energy policy had shifted to states by 2001 (see Bryner 2012; Mintrom 2009; Rabe 2011). As dissenting justice Louis D. Brandeis noted in *New State Ice Co. v. Liebmann* (1932), the well-developed US system of federalism allows for individual states to act independently of the national government and adopt policies supported by their respective electorates. The result, when combined with federal inaction on renewable energy development and climate change, is that states—independently and regionally—have responded to pressing energy and environmental challenges by enacting policies designed to reduce carbon dioxide production by spurring growth in renewable—or sustainable, in the case of nuclear (Plumer 2019)—energy (Boehmke and Skinner 2012; Byrne et al. 2007; Bryner 2012; Callander 2011b; Engel 2006; Karch 2007; Rabe 2011; Sovacool 2008). Lutsey and Sperling (2008) argue that the scale and procedural success of these initiatives provide evidence of greater US commitment to climate action than is usually recognized (see Hughes in this volume). By 2019, twenty-four states and Puerto Rico had joined the US Climate Alliance in support of the Paris Agreement. (Climate Action Tracker 2019; Green 2019).

State-level energy policy motivated by climate politics includes legislation to improve efficiency, accelerate the introduction of zero-emission vehicles, finance climate resilience projects, and increase reliance on renewable energy. The most widespread "green energy" policy among these is the renewable portfolio standard (RPS). An RPS typically requires electric utility companies operating in a state to procure or generate a specified percentage of the electricity sold to consumers from renewable sources (Barbose 2018; Rabe 2004). It is more feasible politically than a carbon tax because electric utility companies are the targets of regulation; in addition, these standards promote the emergence of more electric utility options for consumers. Iowa adopted a prototypical RPS in 1983. Since that time, half of the states have established renewable energy targets. Twenty-nine states, Washington D.C., and three territories—most of which are clustered on the coasts and in the Great Lakes region—have adopted RPS programs; eight states and one territory have set renewable energy goals (National Conference of State Legislatures 2019). By 2018 these initiatives applied to more than 55 percent of retail electricity sales in the United States (Barbose 2018). Many states, including California and New York, have successfully mandated large renewable energy generation requirements for electric utilities to meet. In 2018 California's legislature accelerated its RPS program to require 60 percent of retail electricity sales to be renewable by 2030 and production of all of the state's electricity to be carbon-free by 2045. As of 2017, all retail electricity sellers were meeting or exceeding the interim 27 percent target; moreover, 36 percent of the electrical power provided by California's three largest investor-owned utilities (IOUs) was renewable, and that percentage was 50 percent among the state's community choice, or municipal, aggregators (California Public Utilities Commission 2019). The National Conference of State Legislatures (NCSL 2019) reports that half the growth in US renewable energy generation since 2000 is due to policies like California's (see also Allison et al. 2016).

Not all states have constructed their RPS programs intending to reduce fossil fuel consumption, though. West Virginia's Alternative and Renewable Energy Portfolio Standard (AREPS) required 25 percent of the energy supplied by large investor-owned utilities to be alternative or renewable energy by 2025; however, the policy included advanced coal technology, coalbed methane, natural gas, fuel from coal gasification or liquefaction, synthetic gas, integrated gasification combined-cycle technologies, waste coal, and tire-derived fuel among the "alternative or renewable" options. AREPS was repealed in 2015, affirming West Virginia's desire to rely on a "coal-powered economy" (Small 2015; Parinandi 2020). Similarly, Ohio's RPS—passed by a Democratic governor and a majority Republican legislature in 2008—established a 12.5 percent renewable energy goal by 2026 but was "frozen" for two years beginning in 2014 due to opposition by coal companies, utilities, think tanks, nonprofit foundations, and political action committees (Beirne 2015; Weiner and Hasemyer 2017). Currently, 5 percent of Ohio's energy is produced from renewables, and commitment to the state's RPS remains a dubious prospect (Small 2015; US Energy Information Administration 2019c).

Research on state and other subnational energy politics and policies considers the factors that might cause variation in states' RPS programs. One obvious possibility is that the importance of fossil fuel extraction to a state's economy affects its adoption of RPS programs and willingness to permit fossil fuel sources to be used for RPS requirements. Coal mining has played a significant role in West Virginia's economy since the mid-nineteenth century. Today, West Virginia is the nation's second largest producer of coal, after Wyoming, and 90 percent of the state's electricity comes from coal (US Energy Information Administration 2018a). Yet research suggests that while state affluence and regional economic competition are important, the relationship between the economic importance of fossil fuel and support for RPS programs is not so simple (Chandler 2009; Dincer, Payne, and Simkins 2014; Fredriksson and Millimet 2002a; Matisoff, 2008; Matisoff and Edwards 2014). Rather, research conducted in the 2010s supports Rabe's (2006) claim that state RPS programs are mostly "home grown." Carley and Miller's (2012) cogent review suggests that while state RPS programs vary in stringency—measured in terms of requisite share of the electrical load and rate of change in renewable generation over time—there are commonalities. Early work indicates that politics, especially "partisanship and political culture" (Fowler and Breen 2013), best accounts for states' RPS adoptions and variations among their specific requirements (Huang et al. 2007; Lyon and Yin 2010; Matisoff 2008; Matisoff and Edwards 2014; Yi and Feiok 2012). Dincer, Payne, and Simkins (2014) underscore the greater import of citizens' demands and lobbyists' influence rather than regional political-economic competition, even though RPS programs in the Northeast, Midwest, and West tend to be more stringent than those in the South.

Other research suggests that the geographic pattern of successful state commitments to renewable energy targets and RPS programs explains the variation among states. Voters in some regions may be more willing to sustain the costs of these policies. RPS programs typically impose short-term costs on utility companies, which must upgrade their infrastructure to comply with new, more stringent fuel requirements and emissions standards. Many states allow utility companies to pass some of the costs of upgrading infrastructure on to consumers, meaning rates may rise in the short term. While the costs of compliance and electricity rates vary across states and can be volatile (Borenstein and Bushnell 2015), a recent survey (Stokes and Warshaw 2017) suggests that consumers' support for RPS programs depends on "how a policy is designed and presented" (Stauffer 2017). Stokes and Warshaw's (2017) strongest finding is that consumers are least likely to support their state's RPS if they believe residential energy costs will rise. This result is consistent with related research on public responses to policies and regulatory changes that might increase energy costs (Aklin and Urpelainen 2013; Bang, Hovi, and Sprinz 2012; Besley and Coate 2003; Bushnell et al. 2017). Specifically, energy costs are more salient to voters' choices regarding public utilities commissioners than they are in gubernatorial or legislative elections (Besley and Coate 2003), possibly because whereas commissioners are evaluated on capacity to establish rates equitably and ensure uninterrupted electricity and gas power services, elected officials, including governors and state legislators, are judged more broadly (Aklin and Urpelainen 2013; Bang, Hovi, and Sprinz 2012). Besley and Coate (2003) argue that electricity prices are lower in states where voters select commissioners and expect them to prioritize low cost over environmental protection.

The diversity of states' RPS programs notwithstanding, there have been attempts to synchronize climate change policies at the regional level (Byrne et al. 2007; Lutsey and Sperling 2008). These include the Regional Greenhouse Gas Initiative (RGGI), a cap and trade program that currently commits nine northeastern states to reduce carbon dioxide emissions from power generators; the Western Climate Initiatives (WCI), which includes compatible cap and trade programs for GHG emissions covering California and the Canadian provinces of Ontario and Quebec; and the Pacific Coast Collaborative (PCC) among the northwestern states, provinces, and cities (British Columbia, Washington, Oregon, California, British Columbia, and the cities of Vancouver, Seattle, Portland, San Francisco, Oakland, and Los Angeles), which together constitute the world's fifth largest economy and have committed to increasing resilience to climate change by transforming power grids and transportation systems. The RGGI is the most advanced of these initiatives (Murray and Maniloff 2015; see also Mildenberger and

Stokes in this volume). While states have enforcement authority internally, participation is voluntary (Engel 2006, and states can withdraw freely, as New Jersey did in 2011 pursuant to then governor Chris Christie's executive order (Engel 2006; Ranson and Stavins 2016). The RGGI is also not an effective substitute for national involvement in designing and implementing a cap and trade system; while the compact reduced electricity-related emissions in the Northeast and mid-Atlantic regions, many observers argue that a national solution is necessary to achieve significant reductions in carbon dioxide and other GHG emissions (Bryner 2012; Engel 2006; Sovacool 2008; Weatherholtz 2017; Wallach 2019).

Contrary to scholars' and policy makers' claims that subnational policies could fulfill national climate action responsibilities (Cooper 2018; Meckling 2015; Stokes and Warshaw 2017), research suggests that states—alone or in regional collaboration—are unlikely to serve as federal energy policy leaders. Ensuring adequate supplies of affordable, if not always increasingly "green," energy remains central to sustaining national security and global economies, whatever their impact on climate change and the natural environment more generally. Moreover, the only well-supported case of state leadership is California, with respect to auto emissions standards (Allison et al. 2016; Fredriksson and Millimet 2002b). The "California effect" (Vogel 1997) refers to the 1970 Clean Air Act Amendment, which includes an exemption for California to enact lower emissions standards than those required nationwide (Bryner and Hankins 2018). Once adopted, section 177 of the Clean Air Act permitted other states to sign on, and fourteen states had done so as of 2018 (Jervey 2018). The Trump administration's opposition to stringent fuel economy and tailpipe emissions standards represents the first threat to California's air quality authority in nearly fifty years (Mernit 2018). As this chapter goes to press, the Trump administration has announced it will repeal the waiver. Still, revoking California's Clean Air Act waiver would be burdensome for the EPA, which would have to prove in court that the state's "compelling and extraordinary circumstances" with respect to air pollution no longer exist.

RPS programs and regional initiatives, such as the RGGI, illuminate an emerging debate in the literature on US federalism concerning states' strategic adoption of energy or environmental policies to influence federal legislation or rulemaking. Research on this issue suggests that states seeking to protect fossil fuel industries are more likely to preempt federal action than catalyze it (Byrne et al. 2007; Peterson and Rose 2006; Willie 2011). Ohio is one of three states (the others are Michigan and West Virginia) that adopted RPS programs within a year of Obama's election as president. Ohio relied heavily on increasingly costly coal imports, making the state long ripe for a transition to alternatives, including wind and solar (Union of Concerned Scientists 2018). By 2011, conservative political advocacy groups, including Americans for Prosperity and the American Legislative Exchange Council (ALEC), had begun to champion natural gas— an economical source of energy due to developments in hydraulic fracturing and horizontal drilling (see chapters by Coburn, Mildenberger and Stokes, and Tutuncu in this volume)—in opposition to renewables (Fisk 2016; Wiener and Hasemyer 2017). Natural gas production in Ohio was 28 percent higher in 2018 than it was in 2012 (US Energy

Information Administration 2019c). While there is no direct evidence that Ohio's, or any other state's, RPS or fracturing regulations impacted the CPP promulgated by the Obama administration, that plan did support greater reliance on natural gas as part of a larger decarbonization strategy that also supports the growth of renewable energy sources (Bushnell et al. 2017; Davis, Bollinger, and Dijkema 2016; Peters and Hertel 2017).

Local Energy Politics in the United States

The persistence of state and regional energy politics underscores Rabe's (2011) claim that climate change, the central context for energy, and environmental, policymaking, is "far more complex than originally anticipated" and requires an "intergovernmental lens to understand the factors that foster and deter policy formation at multiple governmental levels as well as the interactive dynamics across them" (495). That lens increasingly must incorporate local energy politics. Metropolitan areas are major sources of GHG emissions, and those who live there suffer most from the pollution, extreme weather, and harm to natural environments associated with climate change (Kammen and Sunter 2016; International Panel on Climate Change 2018). Despite the logic of collective action (Olson 2009), which would obviate municipal action in favor of free riding on the efforts of state and federal governments, many cities—individually and collectively—have developed GHG emissions reporting programs, committed to regional RPS programs, and created their own climate action plans in addition to participating in state-level plans.

Much of this undertaking occurs under the auspices of Local Governments for Sustainability, a global network of local and regional governments committed to urban sustainability, or the US Mayors' Climate Protection Agreement (MCPA), signed by over one thousand US mayors pledged to reduce their carbon dioxide emissions to below 1990 levels (United States Conference of Mayors 2019). Though these commitments are not binding, they accurately reflect US cities' authority over climate and energy policy, including electrical power production and transportation (Krause 2011). By 2019, six—Aspen, Colorado; Burlington, Vermont; Georgetown, Texas; Greensburg, Kansas; Kodiak Island, Alaska; and Rockport, Missouri—of the ninety-nine cities committed to 100 percent renewable energy had achieved the goal of reducing emissions below 1990 levels (Kaldjian and Barua 2019). These cities are small, with populations ranging from 977 (Greensburg) to 49,562 (Georgetown); middle class (incomes range from $38,571 in Greensburg to $64,594 in Aspen); and sustained by industries that do not rely on fossil fuels.

Academic scholarship is circumspect regarding subnational energy initiatives. Krause's review (2011) of intergovernmental relations and climate action suggests that municipal "best practices" (see Betsill and Bulkeley 2006; Bulkeley 2013) emphasize local co-benefits of renewable energy and related climate policies; elevate local leaders; and focus on less costly "low hanging fruit," which might include incentives for car- and/or ride-sharing or energy conservation. While energy conservation represents a long-standing strategy for modifying and reducing energy demand, neither popular nor scholarly research to date suggests car-sharing (e.g., Zipcar, auto rental, or Lyft) or ride-sharing (e.g., Uber Pool, cabs, and employer van pools) necessarily reduces energy demands or GHG emissions (see Bliss 2018; Jung and Koo 2018). The few studies that seek to explain cities' motivations to advance these strategies do not support the municipal vulnerability narrative (Krause 2011; Zahran, Brody, et al. 2008). Rather, cities with high levels of human capital in demographic terms—for example, income, education, left partisanship, and environmental action—are more likely to participate in climate action networks and enact energy and transportation policies to reduce GHG emissions (Krause 2011; Zahran, Brody, et al. 2008; Zahran, Grover, et al. 2008). In contrast to the literature on states, cities that are more dependent on manufacturing and other industries associated with high levels of GHG emissions are less likely to encourage transitions to renewables or other, cleaner fuel sources (Krause 2011; Zahran, Grover, et al. 2008). Also contrary to research on state energy initiatives, clean—that is, efficient and/or low carbon—energy commitments do diffuse among cities (Krause 2011), more so in states with RPS programs (Yin and Powers 2010).

State politics and local politics also differ in their relationships to national energy policy. Historically, cities followed states, which adopted positions on water and the natural environment (e.g., Crowder et al. 2006), public hazards (e.g., Schneider 1992), and energy and climate change (e.g., Bulkeley 2013; Bulkeley and Betsill 2013, Byrne et al. 2007), reflecting an amalgam of municipal concerns and positions on these issues (Bulkeley 2013; Bulkeley and Betsill 2013; Wright, Weber-Burdin, and Rossi 2013). That calculus is different today, due to the obvious and imminent threat of climate change for communities (Bulkeley 2013; Bulkeley and Betsill 2013). Bulkeley and Betsill (2013) argue that local governments have become "fundamental" to restructuring intergovernmental relations around "carbon control." Cities do continue to support state initiatives in some cases; San Francisco, New York, and Miami have rallied behind state clean energy initiatives. San Francisco is notably one of ten California municipalities that recently committed to 100 percent renewable energy, following the state's enactment of legislation mandating that all of the state's electricity come from clean power sources, by 2045—one of only two states (the other is Hawaii) to do so (Daly 2018). Because transportation is the greatest source of GHG emissions in California, local support for the state's decision to continue strengthening auto emissions standards annually, with the support of major automakers (Ford, Volkswagen, BMW, and Honda as of summer 2019), is significant (Chavez 2019; State of California 2019).

Cities increasingly also oppose state positions with respect to the policy direction taken by the federal government. Municipal opposition to the "localized costs" of "fracking" is a case in point (Fisk 2016). The 2005 Energy Policy Act effectively divorced the federal government from regulation of fracturing by exempting "underground injection" from meeting the requirements of the Safe Drinking Water Act (Energy Policy Act 2005, 102). This maneuver altered the balance of regulatory power over nonconventional sources of energy in favor of state and local governments and created a disconnect between fossil fuel advocates championing potential state "venues" of operation and environmentalists seeking greater federal regulation (Davis 2014; Davis and Hoffer, 2012). As a result, environmentalists have allied with residents in communities opposed to the noise, migrant gas workers, water pollution, and earthquakes associated with nearby fracturing operations. In Youngstown, Ohio, a drastic increase in seismic activity is linked to wastewater disposal from fracturing, and the combined wastewater-earthquake crisis has allowed for the formation of common cause between residents and environmental groups (Fischetti 2012).

This situation has created dilemmas for state and local governments seeking to increase economic growth and local investment provided by gas companies, while also hoping to assuage increasingly hostile constituents upset over the social and environmental costs related to fracturing. Research (Goho 2012; Warner and Shapiro 2013) suggests that energy and environmental regulators at the state level tend to endorse jobs and develop rules ensuring a fair and predictable environment for gas companies. Local responses have ranged from cooperating with gas companies to ensure environmental protection without jeopardizing job growth, to regulating where fracturing can occur without undue harm to residents and natural environments, to outright confrontation—moratoria and bans (Fisk 2016). Although a city's response choice depends on its experiences with oil and gas extraction, Fisk's (2016) examination of municipal defiance in Colorado, Ohio, and Texas—three of the US shale gas flashpoints—suggests that better-resourced, more autonomous cities are more likely to strengthen "environmental" regulation at the expense of expanding energy production (Davis 2012, 2014; Davis and Fisk 2014a, 2014b). Still, "states win" due to preemption clauses in state oil and gas statutes, according to Davis (2017), except when state constitutional provisions elevate environmental concerns over other issues, as in New York and Pennsylvania (Davis 2014, 2017; Rabe 2014).

AN AGENDA FOR FUTURE RESEARCH

The research discussed in this chapter explains the development of energy policy in the United States in terms of a complex, intergovernmental distribution of regulatory authority; the increasing integration of energy and environmental policies; and the politics of state local action to reduce air and water pollution and respond to climate change challenges. This history and review of research suggests fruitful avenues for future research on federalism and energy politics in a changing climate and an "energy democracy" that integrates "radical" federalism with the decarbonization of energy.

Federalism and Energy Politics in a Changing Climate

Current research and politics (see Pew Research Center 2017) support the prioritization of transitioning to renewable energy sources to improve water and air quality but remain ideologically divided over how to do so. Those on the political Right champion the lower carbon footprint of natural gas and believe market forces are sufficient to limit pollution. The political Left expects that increasing the production and use of even the cleanest fossil fuel (natural gas) will delay the transition to renewables and trusts government regulation, rather than markets, to reduce pollution associated with fossil fuel combustion. The Left's opposition to expanded reliance on fossil fuels is so strong that a majority, including Green New Deal champions, would support nuclear power as well as renewable sources (Meyers et al. 2018; Roberts 2019).[2] So would most conservatives (Roberts 2019). Zero emissions nuclear power is a climate action star, but it is more expensive to produce than solar or natural gas; hence, as of 2018, while ninety-nine commercial nuclear reactors remained in operation, fourteen were scheduled for shutdown by 2025 (Abdulla 2018), and no US state is moving forward with building new nuclear power plants (Fitzwater, Tidwell, and Schneider 2015).

This situation raises a number of questions to motivate future research. What are the likely economic, social, and environmental implications of relaxing regulations on coal production? How would any changes in the balance among the nation's use of fossil fuels, renewables, and even nuclear power impact future energy politics? While zero-sum framing of fossil fuels and renewables can make political compromise on a future energy strategy difficult, Kumar, Fujii, and Managi (2015) are among those who demonstrate that fossil fuels and renewables are often complementary sources in key industries, such as food and pulp. Scholars might interrogate the bases for either (fossil fuels) or (renewables) thinking and explore the ways in which new technologies enable the use of renewable energy sources and processes to mitigate carbon production. The use of geothermal energy to support carbon sequestration is one such possibility (Rahmouni et al 2014; Randolph and Saar 2011).

Thinking more politically than technically, how might the US withdrawal from its international commitments to lower GHG impact, or be impacted by, its (local, state, and) federal energy and environmental policies? Could broad-based support for nuclear energy, despite associated safety risks, reverse its ongoing decline (Abdulla 2018)? Can the political polarization around energy policy and environmental regulation be reduced in this or some other way to at least the point of bipartisan support for climate action reached in 2008 (Jaffe 2017)? If not, is there a path toward leveraging the efforts of state and local governments to rely more on renewable sources of energy and regulate environmental quality more stringently (Guy et al. 2014)? Can the California effect provide not only lessons (Allison et al. 2016) but also leadership (see Bulkeley and Schroeder 2012; Engel 2006; Fredriksson and Millimet 2002a, 2002b)?

Answers to these questions bear heavily on global efforts to implement market-based polices, such as carbon taxes or cap and trade systems to reduce carbon dioxide emissions (see Hughes in this volume). Whether the US federal government takes decisive action, as some analysts argue will be necessary (see Weatherholtz 2017), or "follows" states and/or local governments (Engel 2006; Sovacool 2008) may depend on what voters believe it will "cost" them directly. Stigler (1971) argues that organized special interests—for example, the fossil fuel sector—pay closer attention to regulatory issues than the public does and are better able to influence policy makers; Parinandi and Hitt's

(2018) critique shows that elected officials side with ordinary voters instead if they expect electoral "punishment" for endorsing organized interests and higher costs. Another fruitful direction for future researchers would be to examine how to sustain voters' attention on the virtues of renewable energy as a means of incentivizing politicians to respond to voters rather than organized interests.

Energy Democracy

Considering the significant role of subnational governments and politics in the development and implementation of energy policy and related environmental regulations, a wide-open area for future research is energy democracy. Energy democracy is a social movement for renewable energy transitions that embodies resistance to fossil-fuel extraction, the fossil fuel industry, and the governments and politicians that endorse dependence on hydrocarbons for energy and advocates for democratically restructured energy regimes. It refers to both "the *normative goal* of decarbonization and energy transformation, and existing *examples* of decentralized and mostly bottom-up civic energy initiatives" (Szulecki 2018, 23). Given public support for renewable energy and the activity of (state and) local governments on the energy and environment front, energy democracy offers a means for reconceptualizing and advancing energy politics in the United States (see Burke and Stephens 2017). Meng (2018) argues that contemporary conflicts around fracturing embody the essence of energy democracy. Specifically, achieving energy justice in this context requires attending to the expected benefits—local as well as national—and the personal and environmental costs of unconventional fossil fuels *and* engaging all relevant stakeholders.

Most research concerning such radical democratic politics around energy issues focuses on disenfranchised communities outside of the United States; however, studies of local resistance associated with the siting of polluting industries offer many relevant examples of homegrown, bottom-up politics (Pellow and Brulle 2005; see also Szulecki 2018). Furthermore, in addition to Meng (2014, 2018), Canfield, Klima, and Dawson's (2015) study of deliberative democracy and energy policy in Pittsburgh, Pennsylvania, which explores the role of knowledge in shaping public perceptions and opinions on climate change and adaptive energy policies, represents the kind of detailed research required to understand the ideological foundations for contemporary energy politics on a warming planet. An energy democracy framework might prove particularly useful for studying local renewable energy transitions, such as those under way in California. San Diego County's Regional Comprehensive Plan, for example, is supported by the Fourteenth Amendment (US Const. amend. XIV) and President Clinton's Executive Order on Environmental Justice (Clinton 1994), as well as California legislation, including SB 115 (1999), the first state-level statute on EJ, and SB 375 (2006), which requires a bottom-up approach to regional planning to achieve the state's targets for reducing GHG emissions.

A more provocative venue for studying the potential for energy democracy would be communities that have historically depended on coal production. The idea of reviving the US coal industry is popular in the nation's coal-mining regions, despite the social injustices associated with coal mining and combustion—for example, environmental degradation and health risks, including respiratory disease and cancer (Morrice and Colagiuriits 2013)—and poor chances of long-term success (Carley, Evans, and Konisky 2018). The decline of the US coal industry invites research on what members of these communities understand about available energy resources, climate change, and the mining industry's capacity to influence their social and economic prospects. How do these communities seek to balance attachment to place with the desire for better health and social welfare prospects? What means are available for them to mobilize and empower themselves to manage the local impacts of ongoing decarbonization? How might they guide the transition from coal to cleaner energy sources and also improve their economic situations, mental and physical health outcomes, and social welfare (Linn and McCormack 2019)?

Notes

1. InflationData.com, with data provided by Plains All American pipeline (https://inflationdata.com/articles/inflation-adjusted-prices/historical-crude-oil-prices-table/).
2. Some scholars and policy makers argue that nuclear energy is a renewable energy source, though most contend nuclear energy cannot be considered renewable. Nuclear reactors do not produce air pollution or carbon dioxide while operating; however, the processes for mining and refining uranium ore and making reactor fuel all require large amounts of energy. In addition, nuclear power plants are constructed out of metal and concrete, which require additional energy to manufacture. "If fossil fuels are used for mining and refining uranium ore, or if fossil fuels are used when constructing the nuclear power plant, then the emissions from burning those fuels could be associated with the electricity that nuclear power plants generate" (US Energy Information Administration 2019b).

References

ABC News/Washington Post. 2010. "Spill Response Rated Worse Than Katrina; Most Favor Pursuit of Criminal Charges." June 7. http://abcnews.go.com/images/PollingUnit/1110a1%20Oil%20Spill.

Abdulla, Ahmed. 2018. "The Demise of U.S. Nuclear in 4 Charts." *The Conversation,* August 1. https://theconversation.com/the-demise-of-us-nuclear-power-in-4-charts-98817.

Aklin, Michaël, and Johannes Urpelainen. 2013. "Political Competition, Path Dependence, and the Strategy of Sustainable Energy Transitions." *American Journal of Political Science* 57, no. 3: 643–658.

Aldrich, John. 2011. *Why Parties? A Second Look.* Chicago: University of Chicago Press.

Allison, Juliann, Daniel Press, Cara Horowitz, Adam Millard-Ball, and Stephanie Pincetl. 2016. "Paths to Carbon Neutrality: Lessons from California." *Collabra: Psychology* 2, no. 1: 21. doi:10.1525/collabra.66

Anders, Roger. 1980. "The Federal Energy Administration." United States Department of Energy Brief.

Avi-Yonah, Reuven S., and David M. Uhlmann. 2009. "Combating Global Climate Change: Why a Carbon Tax Is a Better Response to Global Warming Than Cap and Trade." *Stanford Environmental Law Journal* 28: 3.

Bang, Guri, Jon Hovi, and Detlef F. Sprinz. 2012. "US Presidents and the Failure to Ratify Multilateral Environmental Agreements." *Climate Policy* 12, no. 6: 755–763.

Barbose, Galen. 2018. "U.S. Renewables Portfolio Standards: 2018." Annual Status Report, November 28. Lawrence Berkeley National Laboratory.

Beckmann, Matthew. 2010. *Pushing the Agenda: Presidential Leadership in U.S. Lawmaking, 1953–2004.* New York: Cambridge University Press.

Beirne, Samuel. 2015. "West Virginia Sticks with Coal Despite Trends in Favor of Cleaner Energy." Available at https://www.eesi.org/articles/view/west-virginia-sticks-with-coal-despite-trends-in-favor-of-cleaner-energy.

Besley, Timothy, and Stephen Coate. 2003. "Elected Versus Appointed Regulators: Theory and Evidence." *Journal of the European Economic Association* 1, no. 5: 1176–1206.

Betsill, Michelle M., and Harriet Bulkeley. 2006. "Cities and the Multilevel Governance of Global Climate Change." *Global Governance* 12: 141.

Birkland, Thomas A., and Sarah E. DeYoung. 2011. "Emergency Response, Doctrinal Confusion, and Federalism in the Deepwater Horizon Oil Spill." *Publius: The Journal of Federalism* 41, no. 3: 471–493.

Bishop, Bradford. H. 2014. "Focusing Events and Public Opinion: Evidence from the Deepwater Horizon Disaster." *Political Behavior* 36, no. 1: 1–22.

Bliss, Laura. 2018. "Uber and Lyft Could Do a Lot More for the Planet." *Citylab*, April 30.

Boehmke, Frederick, and Paul Skinner. 2012. "State Policy Innovativeness Revisited." *State Politics and Policy Quarterly* 12, no. 3: 303–329.

Bohr, Jeremiah. 2016. "The 'Climatism' Cartel: Why Climate Change Deniers Oppose Market-Based Mitigation Policy." *Environmental Politics* 25, no. 5: 812–830.

Borenstein, Severin, and James Bushnell. 2015. "The US Electricity Industry after 20 Years of Restructuring." *Annal Review of Economics* 7, no. 1: 437–463.

Bronson, Rachel. 2008. *Thicker Than Oil: America's Uneasy Partnership with Saudi Arabia.* New York: Oxford University Press.

Brown, Kate, and David Hess. 2016. "Pathways to Policy: Partisanship and Bipartisanship in Renewable Energy Legislation." *Environmental Politics* 25, no. 6: 971–990.

Bryner, Gary. 2012. *Integrating Climate, Energy, and Air Pollution Policies.* Cambridge, MA: MIT Press.

Bryner, Nicholas, and Meredith Hankins. 2018. "Why California Gets to Write Its Own Auto Emissions Standards: 5 Questions Answered." *The Conversation*, April 6. https://theconversation.com/why-california-gets-to-write-its-own-auto-emissions-standards-5-questions-answered-94379.

Bulkeley, Harriet. 2013. *Cities and Climate Change.* New York, NY: Routledge.

Bulkeley, Harriet, and Michelle M. Betsill. 2013. "Revisiting the Urban Politics of Climate Change." *Environmental Politics* 22, no. 1: 136–154.

Bulkeley, Harriet, and Heike Schroeder. 2012. "Beyond State/Non-State Divides: Global Cities and the Governing of Climate Change." *European Journal of International Relations* 18, no. 4: 743–766.

Bulman-Pozen, Jessica. 2017. "Federalism All the Way up: State Standing and the New Process Federalism." *California Law Review* 105: 1739.

Bureau of Safety and Environmental Enforcement. 2011. "Deepwater Horizon Joint Investigative Team Report." Volumes I and II. Available at https://www.bsee.gov/newsroom/library/deepwater-horizon-reading-room/joint-investigation-team-report.

Burke, Matthew J., and Jennie C. Stephens. 2017. "Energy Democracy: Goals and Policy Instruments for Sociotechnical Transitions." *Energy Research & Social Science* 33: 35–48.

Burnham, Andrew, Jeongwoo Han, Corrie E. Clark, Michael Wang, Jennifer Dunn, and Ignasi Palou-Rivera. 2011. "Life-Cycle Greenhouse Gas Emissions of Shale Gas, Natural Gas, Coal, and Petroleum." *Environmental Science & Technology* 46, no. 2: 619–627.

Bushnell, James B., Stephen P. Holland, Jonathan E. Hughes, and Christopher R. Knittel. 2017. "Strategic Policy Choice in State-Level Regulation: The EPA's Clean Power Plan." *American Economic Journal: Economic Policy* 9, no. 2: 57–90.

Byrne, John, Kristen Hughes, Wilson Rickerson, and Lado Kurdgelashvili. 2007. "American Policy Conflict in the Greenhouse: Divergent Trends in Federal, Regional, State, and Local Green Energy and Climate Change Policy." *Energy Policy* 35, no. 9: 4555–4573.

Callander, Steven. 2011. "Searching for Good Policies." *American Political Science Review* 105 (November): 643–662.

California Public Utilities Commission. 2019. "Renewables Portfolio Standard Program." Available at https://www.cpuc.ca.gov/renewables/.

Canfield, Casey, Kelly Klima, and Tim Dawson. 2015. "Using Deliberative Democracy to Identify Energy Policy Priorities in the United States." *Energy Research & Social Science* 8: 184–189.

Carley, Sanya, Tom Evans, and David Konisky. 2018. "Adaptation, Culture, and the Energy Transition in American Coal Country." *Energy Research and Social Science* 37: 133–139.

Carley, Sanya, and Chris J. Miller. 2012. "Regulatory Stringency and Policy Drivers: A Reassessment of Renewable Portfolio Standards." *Policy Studies Journal* 40, no. 4: 730–756.

Castiglioni, Claudia. 2015. "No Longer a Client, Not Yet a Partner: the U.S.-Iranian Alliance in The Johnson Years." *Cold War History* 15, no. 4: 491–509.

Center for Climate and Energy Solutions. 2016. "Nuclear Energy." https://www.c2es.org/content/nuclear-energy/.

Chandler, Jess. 2009. "Trendy Solutions: Why Do States Adopt Sustainable Energy Portfolio Standards?" *Energy Policy* 37: 3274–3281.

Chavez, Chris. 2019. "Local Government and Clean Air." Coalition for Clean Air blog, February 13. https://www.ccair.org/local-government-clean-air/.

Cherp, Aleh, and Jessica Jewell. 2011. "The Three Perspectives on Energy Security: Intellectual History, Disciplinary History, and the Potential for Integration." *Current Opinion in Environmental Sustainability* 3, no. 4: 202–212.

Chick, Martin. 2007. *Electricity and Energy Policy in Britain, France and the United States since 1945*. Northampton, MA: Edward Elgar Publishing.

Childs, William R. 2011. "Energy Policy and the Long Transition in America." *Origins: National Event in Historical Perspective* 5, no. 2. http://origins.osu.edu/article/energy-policy-and-long-transition-america.

Chiou, Fang-Yi, and Lawrence S. Rothenberg. 2017. *The Enigma of Presidential Power: Parties, Policies and Strategic Uses of Unilateral Action*. New York, NY: Cambridge University Press.

Chubb, John. 1983. *Interest Groups and the Bureaucracy: The Politics of Energy*. Stanford, CA: Stanford University Press.

Climate Action Tracker. 2019. "USA Country Summary." https://climateactiontracker.org/countries/usa/.

Clinton, William J. 1994. "Federal Actions to Address Environmental Justice in Minority Populations and Low-Income Populations." Executive Order (E.O.) 12898.

Commoner, Barry. 1979. *The Politics of Energy*. New York: Random House.

Cook, John, Dana Nuccitelli, Sara A. Green, Mark Richardson, Bärbel Winkler, Rob Painting, Robert Way, et al. 2013. "Quantifying the Consensus on Anthropogenic Global Warming in the Scientific Literature." *Environmental Research Letters* 8, no. 2: 024024.

Cooper, Mark. 2018. "Governing the Global Climate Commons: The Political Economy of State and Local Action, after the US Flip-Flop on the Paris Agreement." *Energy Policy* 118: 440–454.

Crafts, Nicholas, and Gianni Toniolo. 2012. "'Les trente glorieuses': From the Marshall Plan to the oil crisis." In *The Oxford Handbook of Postwar European History*, edited by Dan Stone, 356–378.

Crowder, Larry B., Gail Osherenko, Oran Young, Satie Airamé, Elliot A. Norse, Nancy Baron, John C. Day, et al. 2006. "Resolving Mismatches in US Ocean Governance." *Science* 313: 617–618.

Daalder, Ivo, and James Lindsay. 2005. "Why the Democrats Have a Hard Time Gaining Trust in Diplomacy and Security." *Brookings*, May 1. https://www.brookings.edu/articles/why-the-democrats-have-a-hard-time-gaining-trust-in-diplomacy-and-security/.

Daley, Jason. 2018. "What to Know About California's Commitment to 100 Percent Clean Energy by 2045." *Smithsonian Magazine Smart News*, September 12. https://www.smithsonianmag.com/smart-news/california-commits-100-percent-clean-energy-2045-180970262/.

Davis, Charles, and Jonathan M. Fisk. 2014a. "Analyzing Public Support for Fracking in the U.S." *Review of Policy Research* 31: 1–16.

Davis, Charles, and Jonathan Fisk. 2014b. "Energy Abundance or Environmental Worries? Analyzing Public Support for Fracking in the United States." *Review of Policy Research* 31, no. 1: 1–16.

Davis, Charles, and Katherine Hoffer. 2012. "Federalizing Energy? Agenda Change and the Politics of Fracking." *Policy Science* 45: 221–241.

Davis, Charles E. 2012. "The Politics of 'Fracking': Regulating Natural Gas Drilling Practices in Colorado and Texas." *Review of Policy Research* 29: 177–191.

Davis, Charles E. 2014. "Substate Federalism and Fracking Policies: Does State Regulatory Authority Trump Local Land Use Autonomy?" *Environmental Science & Technology* 48, no. 15: 8397–8403.

Davis, Charles E. 2017. "Shaping State Fracking Policies in the United States: An Analysis of Who, What, and How." *State and Local Government Review* 49, no. 2: 140–150.

Davis, Chris, Andrew Bollinger, and Gerard P. J. Dijkema. 2016. "The State of the States: Data-Driven Analysis of the US Clean Power Plan." *Renewable and Sustainable Energy Reviews* 60: 631–652.

DeSombre, Elizabeth. 2000. *Domestic Sources of International Environmental Policy: Industry, Environmentalists, and US Power*. Cambridge, MA: MIT Press.

Dincer, Oguzhan, James E. Payne, and Kristi Simkins. 2014. "Are State Renewable Portfolio Standards Contagious?" *American Journal of Economics and Sociology* 73, no. 2: 325–340.

Dryzek, John S., and Richard B. Norgaard. 2011. "Climate Change and Society: Approaches and Responses." In *The Oxford Handbook of Climate Change and Society* 3–17.

Dunlap, Riley E., and Angela G. Mertig. 2014. "The Evolution of the US Environmental Movement from 1970 to 1990: An Overview." In *American Environmentalism*, 13–22. Taylor & Francis.

Dunlap, Riley E., and Aaron M. McCright, and Jerrod H. Yarosh. 2016. "The Political Divide on Climate Change: Partisan Polarization Widens in the US." *Environment: Science and Policy for Sustainable Development* 58, no. 5: 4–23.

Dunn, David Hastings, and Mark J. L. McClelland. 2013. "Shale Gas and the Revival of American Power: Debunking Decline?" *International Affairs* 89, no. 6: 1411–1428.

Ebinger, Charles K. 2016. "Six Years from the BP Horizon Oil Spill: What We've Learned and What We shouldn't Misunderstand." Brookings *PlanetPolicy* (blog), April 20. https://www. brookings.edu/blog/planetpolicy/2016/04/20/6-years-from-the-bp-deepwater-horizon-oil-spill-what-weve-learned-and-what-we-shouldnt-misunderstand/.

Elkins, Paul, and Terry Baker. 2001. "Carbon Taxes and Carbon Emissions Trading." *Journal of Economic Surveys* 15, no. 3: 325–376.

Ellis, Sylvia. 2013. *Freedom's Pragmatist: Lyndon Johnson and Civil Rights*. Gainesville: University Press of Florida.

Engel, Kirsten. 2006. "State and Local Climate Change Initiatives: What Is Motivating State and Local Governments to Address a Global Problem and What Does This Say about Federalism and Environmental Law." *Urban Law* 38: 1015.

Fischetti, Mark. 2012. "Ohio Earthquake Likely Caused by Fracking Wastewater." *Scientific News*, January 4. http://esciencenews.com/sources/scientific.american/2012/01/04/ohio. earthquake.likely.caused.fracking.wastewater.

Fisk, Jonathan M., 2016. "Fractured Relationships: Exploring Municipal Defiance in Colorado, Texas, and Ohio." *State and Local Government Review* 48, no 2: 75–86.

Fitzwater, Savanna, Abraham Tidwell, and Jen Schneider. 2015. "The Nuclear Pipeline: Integrating Nuclear Power and Climate Change." *Engineering Identities, Epistemologies and Values: Engineering Education and Practice in Context* 2: 271–286.

Flaxman, Seth, Sharad Goel, and Justin Rao. 2016. "Filter Bubbles, Echo Chambers, and Online News Consumption." *Public Opinion Quarterly* 80, no. 1: 298–320.

Fowler, Luke, and Joseph Breen. 2013. "The Impact of Political Factors on States' Adoption of Renewable Portfolio Standards." *The Electricity Journal* 26, no. 2: 79–94.

Fredriksson, Per G., and Daniel L. Millimet. 2002a. "Strategic Interaction and the Determination of Environmental Policy across US States." *Journal of Urban Economics* 51, no. 1: 101–122.

Fredriksson, Per G., and Daniel J. Millimet. 2002b. "Is There a 'California Effect' in US Environmental Policymaking?" *Regional Science and Urban Economics* 32, no. 6: 737–764.

Freeman, Jody. 2017. "The Uncomfortable Convergence of Energy and Environmental Law." *Harvard Environmental Law Review* 41: 339.

Friedman, Lisa. 2019. "In a Switch, Some Republicans Start Citing Climate Change as Driving Their Policies." *New York Times*, April 30. https://www.nytimes.com/2019/04/30/climate/ republicans-climate-change-policies.html.

Gailmard, Sean, and John Patty. 2013. *Learning While Governing: Expertise and Accountability in the Executive Branch*. Chicago: University of Chicago Press.

Goho, Shaun A. 2012. "Municipalities and Hydraulic Fracturing: Trends in State Pre-emption." *Planning & Environmental Law* 64: 3–9.

Gormley, William. 1983. *The Politics of Public Utility Regulation*. Pittsburgh: University of Pittsburgh Press.

Goudie, Andrew. 2019. *Human Impact on the Natural Environment*. 8th ed. Hoboken, NJ: Wiley and Sons.

Goulder, Lawrence H., and Andrew R. Schein. 2013. "Carbon Taxes versus Cap and Trade: A Critical Review." *Climate Change Economics* 4, no. 3: 1350010.

Graham, Bob, and William Reilly. 2011. "The National Commission on the BP Deepwater Horizon Spill and Offshore Drilling." In *Deep Water: The Gulf Oil Disaster and the Future of Offshore Drilling: Report to the President* NYC and Washington, DC. https://unfoundation.org/.

Green, Chandler. 2019. "7 Ways U.S. States are Leading Climate Action." New York, NY: United Nations Foundation. https://unfoundation.org/blog/post/7-ways-u-s-states-are-leading-climate-action/.

Gromet, Dena, Howard Kunreuther, and Richard Larrick. 2013. "Political Ideology Affects Energy-Efficiency Attitudes and Choices." *Proceedings of the National Academy of Sciences of the United States of America* 110, no. 23: 9314–9319.

Guy, Sophie, Yoshihisa Kashima, Iain Walker, and Saffron O'Neill. 2014. "Investigating the Effects of Knowledge and Ideology on Climate Change Beliefs." *European Journal of Social Psychology* 44, no. 5: 421–429.

Harrison, Kathryn. 2010. "The Comparative Politics of Carbon Taxation." *Annual Review of Law and Social Science* 6: 507–529.

Hayhoe, Katherine, Haroon S. Kheshgi, Atul K. Jain, and Donald J. Wuebbles. 2002. "Substitution of Natural Gas for Coal: Climatic Effects of Utility Sector Emissions." *Climatic Change* 54, nos. 1–2: 107–139.

Hays, Warren. 1987. *Beauty, Health, and Permanence: Environmental Politics in the United States, 1955–1985*. New York, NY: Cambridge University Press.

Hochschild, Arlie, and David Hochschild. 2018. "More Republicans Than You Think Support Action on Climate Change." *New York Times*, December 29. https://www.nytimes.com/2018/12/29/opinion/sunday/republicans-climate-change-polls.html.

Hoffman, Carl. 2010. "Special Report: Why the BP Oil Rig Blowout Happened." *Popular Mechanics*, September 2. https://www.popularmechanics.com/science/energy/a6065/how-the-bp-oil-rig-blowout-happened/.

Hongtao, Yi, and Richard C. Feiock, 2012. "Policy Tool Interactions and the Adoption of State Renewable Portfolio Standards." *Review of Policy Research, Policy Studies Organization* 29, no. 2: 193–206.

Howarth, Robert W., Renee Santoro, and Anthony Ingraffea. 2011. "Methane and the Greenhouse-Gas Footprint of Natural Gas from Shale Formations." *Climatic Change* 106, no. 4: 679.

Huang, Ming-Yuan, R. Janaki, R. Alvalapati, Douglas Carter, and Matthew Langholtz. 2007. "Is the choice of renewable portfolio standards random?" *Energy Policy* 35, no. 11: 5571–5575.

Hughes, Llewelyn, and Phillip Lipscy. 2013. "The Politics of Energy." *Annual Review of Political Science* 16: 449–469.

Hultman, Nathan. 2010. "Beyond Petroleum: The Broader Effects of the Deepwater Horizon Oil Spill." Brookings, August 24. https://www.brookings.edu/opinions/beyond-petroleum-the-broader-effects-of-the-deepwater-horizon-oil-spill/.

International Panel on Climate Change. 2018. "Summary for Urban Policy Makers: What the IPCC Special Report on Global Warming of 1.5 Degrees Celsius Means for Cities." https://www.ipcc.ch/site/assets/uploads/sites/2/2018/12/SPM-for-cities.pdf.

International Panel on Climate Change. 2019. "Special Report: Global Warming of 1.5 Degrees C." https://www.ipcc.ch/sr15/.

Jackson, Robert B., Avner Vengosh, William Carey, Richard J. Davies, Thomas H. Darrah, Francis O'Sullivan, and Gabrielle Pétron. 2014. "The Environmental Costs and Benefits of Fracking." *Annual Review of Environment and Resources* 39: 327–362.

Jaffe, Cale. 2017. "Melting the Polarization Around Climate Change Politics." *Georgetown International Environmental Law Review* 30: 455.

Jarvis, Alice-Azania. 2010. "BP Oil Spill: Disaster by the Numbers." *Independent*, September 14. https://www.independent.co.uk/environment/bp-oil-spill-disaster-by-numbers-2078396.html.

Jasny, Lorien, Joseph Waggle, and Dana Fisher. 2015. "An Empirical Examination of Echo Chambers in US Climate Policy Networks." *Nature Climate Change* 5, no. 8: 782–786.

Jervey, Ben. 2018. "Trump Administration to Halt Clean Air Standards, Revoke California's Right to Regulate." DeSmog blog, July 24. https://www.desmogblog.com/2018/07/24/trump-administration-halt-clean-car-standards-revoke-california-s-right-regulate.

Jung, Jiyeon, and Yoomo Koo. 2018. "Analyzing the Effects of Car Sharing Services on the Reduction of Greenhouse Gas (GHG) Emissions." *Sustainability* 10: 539.

Kaldjian, Emily, and Priya Barua. 2019. "The US Underwent a Quiet Clean Energy Revolution Last Year." World Resources Institute, January 23. https://www.wri.org/blog/2019/01/us-underwent-quiet-clean-energy-revolution-last-year

Kammen, Daniel M., and Deborah A. Suntor. 2016. "City-Integrated Renewable Energy for Urban Sustainability." Featured Research. Goldman School of Public Policy, UC Berkeley. https://gspp.berkeley.edu/research/featured/city-integrated-renewable-energy-for-urban-sustainability.

Karch, Andrew. 2007. *Democratic Laboratories: Policy Diffusion among the American States.* Ann Arbor: University of Michigan Press.

Knittel, Christopher. 2011. "Automobiles on Steroids: Product Attribute Trade-Offs and Technological Progress in the Automobile Sector." *American Economic Review* 101, no. 7: 3368–3399.

Kollman, Kenneth, and Pradeep Chhibber. 2004. *The Formation of National Party Systems: Federalism and Party Competition in Canada, Great Britain, India, and the United States.* Princeton, NJ: Princeton University Press.

Krause, Rachel. 2011. "Policy Innovation, Intergovernmental Relations, and the Adoption of Climate Protection Initiatives by US Cities." *Journal of Urban Affairs* 33, no. 1: 45–60.

Kuhlman, Tom, and John Farrington. 2010. "What Is Sustainability?" *Sustainability* 2, no. 11: 3436–3448.

Kumar, Surender, Hidemichi Fujii, and Shunsuke Managi. 2015. "Substitute or Complement? Assessing Renewable and Nonrenewable Energy in OECD Countries." *Applied Economics* 47, no. 14: 1438–1459.

Lee, Yong Gyo, Xavier Garza-Gomez, and Rose M. Lee. 2018. "Ultimate Costs of the Disaster: Seven Years After the *Deepwater Horizon* Oil Spill." *Journal of Corporate Accounting & Finance* 29, no. 1. doi:10.1002/jcaf.22306.

Lilley, Jonathan, and Jeremy Firestone. 2013. "The Effect of the 2010 Gulf Oil Spill on Public Attitudes toward Offshore Oil Drilling and Wind Development." *Energy Policy* 62: 90–98.

Linn, Joshua, Dallas Burtraw, and Kristen McCormack. 2016. "An Economic Assessment of the Supreme Court's Stay of the Clean Power Plan and Implications for the Future." Resources for the Future Discussion Paper, 16–21.

Linn, Joshua, and Kristen McCormack. 2019. "The Roles of Energy Markets and Environmental Regulation in Reducing Coal-Fired Plant Profits and Electricity Sector Emissions." *Rand Journal of Economics*, 50, no. 4: 1–35.

Lisowski, Michael. 2002. "Playing the Two-Level Game: US President Bush's Decision to Repudiate the Kyoto Protocol." *Environmental Politics* 11, no. 4: 101–119.

Lutsey, Nicholas, and Daniel Sperling. 2008. "America's Bottom-up Climate Change Mitigation Policy." *Energy Policy* 36, no. 2: 673–685.

Lyon, Thomas, and Haitao Yin. 2010. "Why Do States Adopt Renewable Portfolio Standards? An Empirical Investigation." *The Energy Journal* 31, no. 3: 133–157.

Massachusetts v. EPA, 549 U.S. 497 (2007).

Matisoff, D.C. 2008. "The Adoption of State Climate Change Policies and Renewable Portfolio Standards: Regional Diffusion or Internal Determinants?" *Review of Policy Research* 25, no. 6: 527–546.

Matisoff, Daniel C., and Jason Edwards. 2014. "Kindred Spirits or Intergovernmental Competition? The Innovation and Diffusion of Energy Policies in the American States (1990–2008)." *Journal of Environmental Politics* 23, no. 5: 795–817.

McCarty, Nolan, Keith Poole, and Howard Rosenthal. 2006. *Polarized America: The Dance of Ideology and Unequal Riches*. Cambridge, MA: MIT Press.

McCollum, David L., Volder Krey, and Keywan Riahi. 2011. "An Integrated Approach to Energy Sustainability." *Nature Climate Change* 1, no. 9: 428.

McCright, Aaron M. 2008. "The Social Bases of Climate Change Knowledge, Concern, and Policy Support in the US General Public." *Hofstra Law Review* 37: 1017.

Meckling, Jonas, Nina Kelsey, Eric Biber, and John Zysman. 2015. "Winning Coalitions for Climate Policy." *Science* 349, no. 6253: 1170–1171.

Melina, Remy. 2010. "Why Is Offshore Drilling So Dangerous?" *LiveScience*, May 28. https://www.livescience.com/32614-why-is-offshore-drilling-so-dangerous-.html.

Melosi, Martin V. 1980. *Pollution and Reform in American Cities: 1870–1930*. Austin, TX: University of Texas Press.

Meng, Qingmin. 2014. "Modeling and Prediction of Natural Gas Fracking Pad Landscapes in the Marcellus Shale Region, USA." *Landscape and Urban Planning* 121: 109–116.

Meng, Qingmin. 2018. "Fracking Equity: A Spatial Justice Analysis Prototype." *Land Use Policy* 70: 10–15.

Meyers, Joe, Benjamin Roberts, Brandon Lee, and Shannon Hill. 2018. "Outer Continental Shelf Oil Spill Causal Factors Report." US Department of the Interior, Bureau of Ocean Energy, Alaska OCS Region.

Miller, Storm Aragon. 2016. *Precarious Paths to Freedom: The United States, Venezuela, and The Latin American Cold War*. Albuquerque: University of New Mexico Press.

Milstein, Irena, and Asher Tishler. 2011. "Intermittently Renewable Energy, Optimal Capacity Mix and Prices in a Deregulated Electricity Market." *Energy Policy* 39, no. 7: 3922–3927.

Mintrom, Michael, and Phillipa Norman. 2009. "Policy Entrepreneurship and Policy Change." *Policy Studies Journal* 37, no. 7: 649–667.

Mernit, Judith Lewis. 2018. "Can the EPA Roll Back California's Clean Air Standards?" *The American Prospect*, August 10. https://prospect.org/article/can-epa-roll-back-californias-clean-air-standards.

Morgan, H. Wayne, 1973. "America's First Environmental Challenge, 1865–1920." *Essays on the Gilded Age*: 87–108.

Morrice, Emily, and Ruth Colagiuri. 2013. "Coal Mining, Social Injustice and Health: A Universal Conflict of Power and Priorities." *Health & Place* 19: 74–79.

Mukherjee, Deep, and Mohammad Arshad Rahman. 2016. "To Drill or Not to Drill? An Econometric Analysis of US Public Opinion." *Energy Policy* 91: 341–351.

Murray, Brian, and Peter Maniloff. 2015. "Why Have Greenhouse Emissions in RGGI States Declined? An Econometric Attribution to Economic, Energy Market, and Policy Factors." *Energy Economics* 51: 581–589.

Nanda, Ramana, Ken Younge, and Lee Fleming. 2014. "Innovation and Entrepreneurship in Renewable Energy." In *The Changing Frontier: Rethinking Science and Innovation Policy*, 199–232. Cambridge, MA: National Bureau of Economic Research.

National Conference of State Legislatures. 2019. "State Renewable Portfolio Standards and Goals." Available at https://www.ncsl.org/research/energy/renewable-portfolio-standards.aspx.

National Oceanic and Atmospheric Administration, Office of Response and Restoration. n.d. "Largest Oil Spills Affecting U.S. Waters Since 1969." https://response.restoration.noaa.gov/oil-and-chemical-spills/oil-spills/largest-oil-spills-affecting-us-waters-1969.html.

Neill, Katharine A., and John C. Morris. 2012. "A Tangled Web of Principals and Agents: Examining the Deepwater Horizon Oil Spill through a Principal–Agent Lens." *Politics & Policy* 40, no. 4: 629–656.

Neustadt, Richard. 1980. *Presidential Power and the Modern Presidents*. Hoboken, NJ: Wiley.

New State Ice Co. v. Liebmann, 285 U.S. 262 (1932).

Nong, Duy, and Mahinda Siriwardana. 2018. "Effects on the US Economy of Its Proposed Withdrawal from the Paris Agreement: A Quantitative Assessment." *Energy* 159: 621–629.

Olson, Erik D. 1984. "The Quiet Shift of Power: Office of Management & Budget Supervision of Environmental Protection Agency Rulemaking under Executive Order 12,291." *Virginia Journal o of Natural Resources Law* 4, no. 1: 1–80b.

Olson, Mancur. 2009. *The Logic of Collective Action* Vol. 124. Cambridge, MA: Harvard University Press.

OPEC Secretariat. 2015. "Oil Demand and Transportation: An Overview." *OPEC Energy Review* 39, no. 4: 349–375.

Osofsky, Howard J., Joy D. Osofsky, and Tonya C. Hansel. 2011. "Deepwater Horizon Oil Spill: Mental Health Effects on Residents in Heavily Affected Areas." *Disaster Medicine and Public Health Preparedness* 5, no. 4: 80–286.

Parinandi, Srinivas. 2018. "Invention and Borrowing among State Legislatures." Working Paper.

Parinandi, Srinivas, and Matthew Hitt. 2018. "How Politics Influences the Energy Pricing Decisions of Elected Public Utilities Commissioners." *Energy Policy* 118: 77–87.

Parinandi, Srinivas. 2020. "Policy Inventing and Borrowing among State Legislatures." American Journal of Political Science. https://doi/abs/10.1111/ajps.12513

Pellow, David N., and Robert J. Brulle. 2005. *Power, Justice, and the Environment: A Critical Appraisal of the Environmental Justice Movement*. Cambridge, MA: MIT Press.

Peters, Jeffrey C., and Thomas W. Hertel. 2017. "Achieving the Clean Power Plan 2030 CO2 Target with the New Normal in Natural Gas Prices." *The Energy Journal* 38, no. 5. doi:10.5547/01956574.38.5.jpet

Peterson, Thomas D., and Adam Z. Rose. 2006. "Reducing Conflicts between Climate Policy and Energy Policy in the US: The Important Role of the States." *Energy Policy* 34, no. 5: 619–631.

Pew Research Center. 2017. "Public Divides Over Environmental Regulation and Energy Policy." https://www.pewresearch.org/science/2017/05/16/public-divides-over-environmental-regulation-and-energy-policy/.

Plumer, Brad. 2019. "Blue States Roll out Aggressive Strategies. Red States Keep to the Sidelines." *New York Times*, June 21. https://www.nytimes.com/2019/06/21/climate/states-climate-change.html.

Plumer, Brad, and Nadja Popavich. 2019. "These Countries Have Prices on Carbon: Are They Working?" *New York Times*, April 2. https://www.nytimes.com/interactive/2019/04/02/climate/pricing-carbon-emissions.html.

Pollitt, Michael G. 2012. "The Role of Policy in Energy Transitions: Lessons from the Energy Liberalisation Era." *Energy Policy* 50: 128–137.

Powell, Tarika. 2017. "Is Your Natural Gas Actually Fracked?" Sightline Institute, October 30. https://www.sightline.org/2017/10/30/is-your-natural-gas-actually-fracked/.

Rabe, Barry. 2004. *Statehouse and Greenhouse: The Emerging Politics of American Climate Change Policy.* Washington, DC: Brookings.

Rabe, Barry. 2011. "Contested Federalism and American Climate Policy." *The Journal of Federalism* 41, no. 3: 494–521.

Rabe, Barry. 2006. "Race to the Top: The Expanding Role of US State Renewable Portfolio Standards." *Sustainable Development Law and Policy* 7: 10.

Rabe, Barry. 2014. "Shale Play Politics: The Intergovernmental Odyssey of American Shale Governance." *Environmental Science & Technology* 48, no. 15: 8369–8375.

Rahmouni, Soumia, Noureddine Settou, Nasreddine Chennouf, Belkhir Negrou, and Mustapha Houari. 2014. "A Technical, Economic, and Environmental Analysis of Combining Geothermal Energy with Carbon Sequestration for Hydrogen Production." *Energy Procedia* 50: 263–269.

Randolph, Jimmy, and Martin Saar. 2011. "Combining Geothermal Energy Capture with Geologic Carbon Dioxide Sequestration." *Geophysical Research Letters* 38, no. 10: 1–7.

Ranson, Matthew, and Robert Stavins. 2016. "Linkage of Greenhouse Gas Emissions Trading Systems: Learning from Experience." *Climate Policy* 16, no. 3: 284–300.

Razeghi, G., B. Shaffer, and S. Samuelsen. 2017. "Impact of Electricity Deregulation in the State of California." *Energy Policy* 103: 105–115.

Roberts, David. 2019. "Americans Love Clean Energy: Do They Care If It Includes Nuclear?" *Vox*, April 23. https://www.vox.com/energy-and-environment/2019/4/23/18507297/nuclear-energy-renewables-voters-poll.

Roberts, Joel. 2005. "Bush Signs Sweeping Energy Bill." *CBS News*, August 8. https://www.cbsnews.com/news/bush-signs-sweeping-energy-bill/2/.

Rosentiel, Tom. 2010. "Oil Spill Seen as Ecological Disaster." Pew Research Center, May 11. https://www.pewresearch.org/2010/05/11/oil-spill-seen-as-ecological-disaster/.

Rothman, Lily. 2017. Here's Why the Environmental Protection Agency Was Created." *Time*, March 22. http://time.com/4696104/environmental-protection-agency-1970-history/.

Rueb, Emily. 2017. "How New York City Gets Its Electricity." *New York Times*, February 10. https://www.nytimes.com/interactive/2017/02/10/nyregion/how-new-york-city-gets-its-electricity-power-grid.html.

Safford, Thomas G., Jessica D. Ulrich, and Lawrence C. Hamilton. 2012. "Public Perceptions of the Response to the Deepwater Horizon Oil Spill: Personal Experiences, Information Sources, and Social Context." *Journal of Environmental Management* 113: 31–39.

Shanley, Robert. 1983. "Presidential Executive Orders and Environmental Policy." *Presidential Studies Quarterly* 13: 405–16.

Scheraga, Joel D. 1994. "Energy and the Environment Something New under the Sun?" *Energy Policy* 22, no. 10: 798–803.

Schmalensee, Richard, and Robert Stavins. 2015. "Lessons Learned from Three Decades of Experience with Cap-and-Trade." National Bureau of Economic Research Working Paper Series (21742). https://www.nber.org/papers/w21742.pdf.

Schneider, Saundra K. 1992." Governmental Response to Disasters: The Conflict between Bureaucratic Procedures and Emergent Norms." *Public Administration Review*: 52, no. 2: 135–145.

Shor, Boris, and Nolan McCarty. 2011. "The Ideological Mapping of American Legislatures." *American Political Science Review* 105, no. 3: 530–551.

Siegel, Josh. 2018. "Republicans Learn to Love Wind and Solar Jobs after Once Mocking Them." *Washington Post*, October 23. https://www.washingtonexaminer.com/policy/energy/republicans-learn-to-love-wind-and-solar-jobs-after-once-mocking-them.

Siegel, Robert, and Jessica Cheung. 2016. "In Ohio Coal Country, Job Prospects Lie with Neither Coal Nor Trump's Promises." *National Public Radio All Things Considered*, December 13. https://www.npr.org/2016/12/13/504829671/in-ohio-coal-country-job-prospects-lie-with-neither-coal-nor-trumps-promises.

Small, Laura. 2015. "West Virginia Sticks with Coal Despite Trends in Favor of Cleaner Energy." Environmental and Energy Study Institute. https://www.eesi.org/articles/view/west-virginia-sticks-with-coal-despite-trends-in-favor-of-cleaner-energy.

Smith, Lawrence C., Murphy Smith, and Paul Ashcroft. 2011. "Analysis of Environmental and Economic Damages from British Petroleum's Deepwater Horizon Oil Spill." *Albany Law Review* 74, no. 1: 563–585.

Sovacool, Benjamin K. 2008. "The Best of Both Worlds: Environmental Federalism and the Need for Federal Action on Renewable Energy and Climate Change." *Stanford Environmental Law Journal* 27: 397.

State of California. 2019. "California and Major Automakers Reach Groundbreaking Framework Agreement on Clean Emissions Standards." Office of Governor Gavin Newsome, July 25. https://www.gov.ca.gov/2019/07/25/california-and-major-automakers-reach-groundbreaking-framework-agreement-on-clean-emission-standards/.

Stauffer, Nancy W. 2017. "State-Level Renewable Energy Standards: Strengthening Critical Public Support." *MIT Energy Initiative News*, June 30. http://energy.mit.edu/news/state-level-renewable-energy-policies/.

Stavins, Robert N. 2008. "A Meaningful US Cap-and-Trade System to Address Climate Change." *Harvard Environmental Law Review* 32: 293.

Stavins, Robert. 2011. "The Problem of the Commons: Still Unsettled after 100 Years." *American Economic Review* 101, no. 1: 81–108.

Stern, Arthur C. 1982. "History of Air Pollution Legislation in the United States." *Journal of the Air Pollution Control Association* 32, no. 1: 44–61.

Stigler, George. 1971. "The Theory of Economic Regulation." *Bell Journal of Economics and Management* 2, no. 1: 3–21.

Stokes, Leah, and Christopher Warshaw. 2017. "Renewable Energy Policy Design and Framing Influence Public Support in the United States." *Nature Energy* 2, no. 17107: 1–6.

Stradling, David. 2002. *Smokestacks and Progressives: Environmentalists, Engineers, and Air Quality in America, 1881–1951*. Baltimore, MD: John Hopkins Univeristy Press.

Stradling, David, and Peter Thorsheim. 1999. "The Smoke of Great Cities: British and American Efforts to Control Air Pollution, 1860–1914." *Environmental History* 4, no. 1: 6–31.

Szulecki, Kacsper. 2018. "Conceptualizing Energy Democracy." *Environmental Politics* 27, no. 1: 21–41.

Tulis, Jeffrey. 2017. *The Rhetorical Presidency*. Princeton, NJ: Princeton University Press.

Union of Concerned Scientists. 2018. "Existing Cap-and-Trade Programs to Cut Global Warming Emissions." https://www.ucsusa.org/global-warming/solutions/reduce-emissions/regional-cap-and-trade.html.

United States Census. 2019. "Quarterly Residential Vacancies and Homeownership, Second Quarter 2019." Release Number: CB19-98. https://www.census.gov/housing/hvs/files/currenthvspress.pdf.

United States Conference of Mayors. 2019. "Mayors Climate Protection Agreement." https://www.usmayors.org/mayors-climate-protection-center/.

US Chemical Safety and Hazard Investigation Board. 2014. "Investigation Report: Explosion and Fire at the Macondo Well." https://www.csb.gov/assets/1/7/overview_-_final.pdf.

US Climate Change Research Program. 2018. "Fourth National Climate Assessment, Volume II: Impacts, Risks and Adaptation in the United States." https://www.globalchange.gov/nca4.

US Const. amend. XIV, § 1.

US Energy Information Administration. 2017. "State Profiles and Energy Estimates—Rankings." https://www.eia.gov/state/rankings/.

US Energy Information Administration. 2018a. "In 2018, the United States Consumed More Energy Than Ever Before." https://www.eia.gov/todayinenergy/detail.php?id=39092#.

US Energy Information Administration. 2018b. "Use of Energy Explained." https://www.eia.gov/energyexplained/use-of-energy/.

US Energy Information Administration. 2018c. "Use of Energy Explained: Energy Use for Transportation." https://www.eia.gov/energyexplained/use-of-energy/transportation.php.

US Energy Information Administration. 2018d. "What Is U.S. Electricity Generation by Energy Source?" https://www.eia.gov/tools/faqs/faq.php?id=427&t=3.

US Energy Information Administration. 2019a. *Electric Power Monthly* series. https://www.eia.gov/electricity/monthly/.

US Energy Information Administration. 2019b. "Nuclear Explained: Nuclear Energy and the Environment." https://www.eia.gov/energyexplained/nuclear/nuclear-power-and-the-environment.php.

US Energy Information Administration. 2019c. "State Profile and Energy Estimates: Ohio." https://www.eia.gov/state/?sid=OH.

US Energy Information Administration. 2019d. "Use of Energy Explained." https://www.eia.gov/energyexplained/use-of-energy/transportation.php.

VandeHei, Jim, and Justin Blum. 2005. "Bush Signs Energy Bill, Cheers Steps Toward Self-Sufficiency." *Washington Post*, August 9. http://www.washingtonpost.com/wp-dyn/content/article/2005/08/08/AR2005080800124.html.

Vogel, David. 1997. "Trading Up and Governing Across: Transnational Governance and Environmental Protection." *Journal of European Public Policy* 4, no. 4: 556–571.

Volden, Craig, and Alan Wiseman. 2014. *Legislative Effectiveness in the United States Congress.* New York, NY: Cambridge University Press.

Wallach, Phillip. 2019. "Where Does U.S. Climate Policy Stand in 2019?" Brooking Center on Regulation and Markets, March 22. https://www.brookings.edu/2019/03/22/where-does-u-s-climate-policy-stand-in-2019/.

Warner, Barbara, and Jennifer Shapiro. 2013, "Fractured, fragmented federalism: A study in fracking regulatory policy." *Publius: The Journal of Federalism* 43, no. 3: 474–496.

Watkiss, Jeffrey D., and Douglas W. Smith. 1993. "The Energy Policy Act of 1992—A Watershed for Competition in the Wholesale Power Market." *Yale Journal on Regulation* 10: 447.

Weatherholtz, Tiffany. 2017. "Separating Controversy and Climate Change: How the United States Could Lead Climate Change and Energy Reform with the Growth of Renewable Energy Sources Globally." *Emory International Law Review* 32: 581.

Weiner, Brad, and David Hasemyer. 2017. "How Fossil Fuel Allies Are Tearing Apart Ohio's Embrace of Clean Energy." *Inside Climate News*, October 20. https://insideclimatenews.org/news/29102017/renewable-energy-ohio-rps-law-fossil-fuel-political-donations-coal.

Willie, Matt. 2011. "Hydraulic Fracturing and Spotty Regulation: Why the Federal Government Should Let States Control Unconventional Onshore Drilling." *BYU Law Review*: 1743.

World Bank. 2019. "CO2 Emissions (Metric Tons per Capita)." https://data.worldbank.org/indicator/en.atm.co2e.pc

Wright, James D., Eleanor Weber-Burdin, and Peter H. Rossi. 2013. *Natural Hazards and Public Choice: The State and Local Politics of Hazard Mitigation*. New York, NY: Elsevier.

Yergin, Daniel. 1990. *The Prize: The Epic Quest for Oil, Money, and Power*. New York: Simon and Schuster.

Yin, Haitao, and Nicholas Powers. 2010. "Do State Renewable Portfolio Standards Promote In-State Renewable Generation?" *Energy Policy* 38, no. 2: 1140–1149.

Zahran, Sammy, Samuel D. Brody, Arnold Vedlitz, Himanshu Grover, and Caitlyn Miller. 2008. "Vulnerability and Capacity: Explaining Local Commitment to Climate-Change Policy." *Environment and Planning C: Government and Policy* 26: 544–562.

Zahran, Sammy, Himanshu Grover, Samuel D. Brody, and Arnold Vedlitz. 2008. "Risk, Stress and Capacity: Explaining Metropolitan Commitment to Climate Protection." *Urban Affairs Review* 43: 447–474.

Zhang, Yuqiang, Jason West, Rohit Mathur, Jia Xing, Christian Hogrefe, Shawn J. Roselle, Jesse O. Bash, et al. 2018. "Long-Term Trends in the Ambient PM 2.5-and O 3-Related Mortality Burdens in the United States under Emission Reductions from 1990 to 2010." *Atmospheric Chemistry and Physics* 18, no. 20: 15003–15016.

CHAPTER 18

THE ENERGY POLITICS OF NORTH AMERICA

MATTO MILDENBERGER AND LEAH C. STOKES

WHEN energy infrastructure companies began work on the Keystone XL Pipeline in 2010, the plan seemed straightforward, like any other pipeline built over the preceding years. This one would cross the border, bringing Albertan oil from Canada to refineries in Texas and elsewhere in the United States. But by 2011 environmental groups in the United States had the pipeline in their sights. Given scientific research, they believed that increasing Albertan oil sand production would mean game over for the planet; there simply was not enough of a carbon budget available if the world aimed to avert disastrous climate change (McGlade and Ekins 2015; Swart and Weaver 2012). After years of effort, US activists successfully stalled approval under the Barack Obama administration, frustrating Canadian decision makers and oil companies. Shortly after the Donald Trump administration took office, the Keystone XL began moving forward again. The Canadian government was pleased by this development (Tasker 2017). However, a strong movement of environmentalists and indigenous communities across both countries continued to contest and resist the pipeline's completion through protest and litigation (Elbein 2017; Hodges and Stocking 2016; Romo 2018). The Keystone Pipeline was first proposed in 2008 and still has not been completed.

The Keystone XL Pipeline is just one example of energy politics unfolding across the North American continent. More recently, the United States, Canada, and Mexico renegotiated the North American Free Trade Agreement (NAFTA). The new United States-Mexico-Canada Agreement (USMCA) eliminated long-contentious investor-state dispute settlement (ISDS) rules, which allowed companies in one country to sue a different North American government for legal changes that jeopardized their corporate investments (Gertz 2018; Tankersley 2018). For example, after President Obama denied TransCanada's permit, the energy company filed for arbitration through ISDS (Kent et al. 2018). Energy companies touted the ISDS rules as protection for their foreign investments and against government abuse of power (Kent et al. 2018). Under the USMCA, oil and gas companies maintained ISDS rights for their Mexican investments, despite the elimination of most ISDS provisions in the broader agreement. In another major shift, the new agreement eliminated the contentious "proportionality" clause that had guaranteed the United States proportional access to Canadian energy production.

Debates over energy resources sit at the core of both policymaking and electoral battles across North America (Clarkson and Mildenberger 2011; Rippy 1972; Oreskes and Conway 2010; Stokes 2015, 2016). Yet in contrast to Europe, strong international institutions to manage continental energy and environmental policy have not developed in North America. While oil, natural gas, and electricity are traded across the region, energy policies remain the purview of national and subnational governments in Canada, Mexico, and the United States. Regional energy policy is thus shaped by two opposing tendencies: integration and independence. Growing economic interdependence among the three states has generated pressure from economic stakeholders to integrate energy policy at the regional level, particularly in favor of US energy interests. However, the decentralized nature of energy institutions and policies means that North American national and subnational governments have different electricity markets, energy mixes, regulations, and commitments to the energy transition. In this chapter we map the trajectory of North American energy policymaking, with a focus on the role of politics. We describe how continental energy politics are shaped by four key factors: the federalist nature of North American countries, the absence of effective continental energy institutions, regional economic interdependence, and the relative power asymmetries between the United States and its neighbors.

First, federalist institutions in all three countries dramatically affect energy politics across the region (Clarkson 2008; Selin and VanDeveer 2009). In the United States and Canada, subnational governments enjoy unusually broad latitude in energy policymaking. Canadian provinces and American and Mexican states often work against the energy policies of their federal counterparts, both in support of and in opposition to the energy transition. Subsequently, North American energy politics is shaped by shifting coalitions of subnational actors, often working across national borders. As a result of this decentralization, energy and climate policymaking priorities across federal and subnational levels in North America are rarely synchronized.

Second, integrated regional energy institutions have not developed in North America. The states have not been willing to delegate energy planning authority to continental institutions. As a result, regional-scale energy planning has consisted of trilateral policy harmonization efforts, which have tended toward voluntary and informal institutions (Selin and VanDeveer 2005). For example, in the early 2000s the North American Energy Working Group supported US efforts to guarantee access to Canadian and Mexican energy resources; however, this trilateral energy initiative lacked regulatory teeth. At most, these institutions and negotiations have shaped each country's understanding of its national energy interests.

Third, all three North American economies remain interdependent. Consequently, the presence of a large, integrated energy market dominated by the United States gives that state substantial power over Mexican and Canadian energy policies. Over the course of the twentieth century, Canadian and Mexican energy resources came to be seen in Washington as part of US energy self-interests. The United States pressured Canada (successfully) and Mexico (unsuccessfully) to guarantee access to their energy resources. Under this proportionality clause, since eliminated as part of the 2018 USMCA agreement, the Canadian government could not restrict energy exports to the United States without proportionally reducing domestic production and consumption. In turn, energy markets in Canada and Mexico developed in the shadow of these US needs. Correspondingly, Canada and Mexico often saw themselves as rule-followers with respect to US regulatory decisions in the energy and climate space. The US market's size largely explains why the United States is the leader and Canada and Mexico are the followers (Studer 2013). Both countries depend more economically on the United States than it does on them. Consequently, Canada and Mexico take pains to avoid regulations that might limit their access to US markets or weaken investment and capital flows from the United States into their markets. For instance, federal Canadian policy makers have repeatedly invoked the importance of aligning domestic climate policies with the United States out of competitiveness concerns. Similarly, Canada likely took cues from the United States when it chose to withdraw from the Kyoto Protocol (Studer 2013).

Fourth, regional trends in energy policymaking often involve independent Canadian and Mexican engagement with US policymaking agendas, rather than coordinated regional planning. Scholars have described this as a form of "double bilateralism," with the United States managing independent and differentiated yet simultaneous policy conversations with Canada and Mexico (Clarkson 2008). Generally, US-Canadian bilateralism operated under a different set of rules and institutions than the US-Mexican relationship, even in the context of NAFTA. For instance, Canadian oil is deeply integrated into US markets, and Canada formally guaranteed the United States access to its oil as part of the Canada-US Free Trade Agreement (CUFTA) in the 1980s. However, Mexico refused similar provisions as part of NAFTA. While both Canada and Mexico moved to decrease their reliance on the US market in the 1980s, the political context was much more favorable for Mexico to hold its ground (Lock and Kryzda 1993).

Taken together, these features of North American energy regionalism distinguish it in both form and dynamics from energy politics in Europe and Asia. The North American energy system is an example of regional energy management in which a single dominant state pulls neighbors into a regional but fragmented institutional framework (Clarkson and Mildenberger 2011). Scholars have described continental environmental governance as "less than meets the eye" (Clarkson, 2008, 128). This conclusion applies equally to continental energy governance.

We begin this chapter with background information on energy resources in North America. Given that there is another chapter in this volume focused on US energy politics (Allison and Parinandi in this volume), we focus here on Canada's and Mexico's energy relationships with the United States. Next we consider the regional politics of oil, natural gas, and electricity production. Third, we trace the trajectory of energy and climate policymaking in North America, outlining how shifting coalitions of subnational actors have been the major forces in shaping regional energy policies. Fourth, we describe a series of stunted attempts to develop trilateral North American energy institutions. Finally, we offer a research agenda for the study of North American energy politics moving forward. Throughout, we highlight the complex empirical reality of North American energy policymaking. Given the sparseness of scholarship on continental energy politics, we hope this survey can help precipitate coordinated efforts to place American, Canadian, and Mexican energy politics in their regional context. (For analysis of regionalism literature, see Hancock, Palestini, and Szulecki in this volume.)

NORTH AMERICAN ENERGY: FACTS AND FIGURES

To understand North American energy politics, we must contrast the size and nature of Canadian and Mexican markets against their dominant economic neighbor. We highlight the relative importance of these regional energy flows to all three North American economies. Figure 18.1 illustrates the scale and size of these trade flows, charting select US energy exports and imports with Canada and Mexico in 2017.

These regional trade and energy market relationships are, in turn, shaped by a diversity of institutional contexts. All North American countries have federal systems of government, though energy policymaking authority varies across each federalist system. At the extreme, Canadian provinces enjoy almost exclusive autonomy over Canadian energy policymaking, with energy issues delegated to these provinces under the Canadian constitution (Harrison 1996). Federal efforts to plan and harmonize Canadian energy

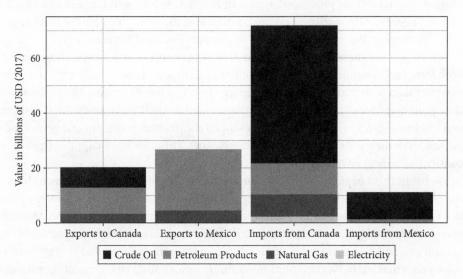

FIGURE 18.1 US Import and Export Flows of Select Energy Products.

Note: Crude Oil includes US Census End Use Code 11100 only. Petroleum Products includes both Fuel Oil (11110) and Petroleum Products, other (11120). Natural Gas includes both Natural Gas Liquids (11130) and Gas-Natural (11200). Electricity includes Electric Energy (11400) only.

Source: Data from US Census Bureau (2018).

policy require negotiation and coordination of provincial efforts, and as we discuss later in this chapter, have generated substantial conflicts (Richards, Noble, and Belcher 2012; Pollard 1986). For instance, while the Canadian federal government has exclusive authority to negotiate international agreements—including international climate agreements—its capacity to implement these agreements is constrained by provinces' willingness to comply with Ottawa's priorities (Cameron and Simeon 2002; Lachapelle, Borick, and Rabe 2012).

The US federal government maintains relatively more control over energy planning than the central government in Canada does. That said, US states still enjoy substantial energy autonomy relative to other states and governments around the world. As a result, US energy policymaking involves a blend of federal and state legislative and regulatory efforts (Byrne et al. 2007). For example, the Obama administration's proposed Clean Power Plan sought to use regulatory authority under the federal Clean Air Act to set standards for the carbon intensity of state-level energy production. In practice, however, the proposal required individual states to submit plans to the federal government on how they would implement the new federal standard. This effort is representative of many energy policies in the United States that offer substantial subnational flexibility to states. Thus US energy policy tends to be the joint product of state and federal efforts (Lutsey and Sperling 2008).

In contrast to the United States and Canada, Mexican energy policymaking remains largely centralized (Páez 2010). Major state-owned entities still play dominant roles in both electricity and resource extraction markets. While subnational Mexican states have engaged in some forms of energy regulation and management, Mexican energy policy remains far more shaped by its federal government than either the United States or Canada.

Canada

Canada has a long history as an energy-rich state. Oil production from the Albertan tar sands makes the country the fourth largest oil producer globally (US Energy Information Administration 2018). This oil production primarily flows to the United States: more than 75 percent of Canada's domestic production or more than three million barrels of crude oil per day (Government of Canada 2018a). These exports flow through a growing network of proposed and operational pipelines that transport Canadian oil to refineries and other facilities on the US Gulf Coast. Canada exports provide 41 percent of US crude oil imports (Government of Canada 2018a). Canada also exports substantial natural gas, again via pipelines, to the United States (Government of Canada 2018b). Despite the development of US shale gas, Canada continues to be a net exporter of natural gas. In the United States, both domestic supplies of natural gas from hydraulic fracturing and imports of natural gas from Canada are important sources of energy for the country.

In terms of its electricity production, Canada's mix is mostly non-fossil fuels, dominated by a very large hydropower sector (59 percent), and a tiny but growing wind and solar market (5 percent) (National Energy Board 2017). As with oil and natural gas trading across the Canadian-US border, the electricity sector is similarly integrated. Canada exports about 10 percent of its electricity production to the United States, particularly hydropower produced in the Canadian provinces of Manitoba and Quebec. In total, Canadian power exports supply about 1.4 percent of US electricity demand (US Energy Information Administration 2015). Its trade occurs across thirty transmission linkages between the two countries, amounting to just under 60 TWh of power flows in 2014 (US Energy Information Administration 2015).

Mexico

Like Canada, Mexico has historically exported crude oil to the United States. However, both declining oil production and a diversification of Mexican export markets have reduced this flow in recent years to under 600,000 barrels per day, around one-fifth of the Canadian supply (US Energy Information Administration 2017). By contrast, Mexico is a substantial net importer of petroleum products and natural gas from the United States. Mexican imports of natural gas have grown in recent years, to supply the Mexican electricity sector. Currently, a pipeline network is under construction to facilitate this regional flow (US Energy Information Administration 2017). It is likely that Mexico will continue to import cheap natural gas from the United States, given the latter's boom in hydraulic fracturing.

Mexican electricity production and transmission continues to be managed by the state-owned Comisión Federal de Electricidad (CFE). Since 1992 there have been limited opportunities for private providers to contract production to the CFE, including some companies backed by US investors. The Mexican electricity markets remain highly fossil-fuel dependent, with almost 75 percent of the mix coming from coal, gas, and oil. Mexico has only limited hydropower (19 percent) capacity. The Mexican grid has interconnections to the United States and Belize, but imports and exports are on a substantially smaller scale than between the United States and Canada. Over the past decade, Mexico has been either a small net importer or an exporter to the United States, though only in a locally bounded way that does not factor significantly into US electricity demand (US Energy Information Administration 2013).

NORTH AMERICAN ENERGY SYSTEMS RESOURCES AND POLICIES

Next we survey the current state of North American energy politics. We begin with a discussion of oil and gas resources. In this domain, opposing forces of regional integration and disintegration have characterized North American fossil fuel markets

(Bird and Heintzelman 2018; Craik, Studer, and VanNijnatten 2013). While Mexican energy resources were developed with an eye to maintaining independence from US control, Canadian resources became institutionally bound to US demand throughout the latter half of the twentieth century. Second, we consider North American electricity markets. Overall, the United States benefits enormously in terms of energy supply from the cross-border trade in energy (oil and electricity), particularly from Canada. In 2015, $140 billion of energy trade occurred between the United States and its neighbors, with $100 billion of that value from imports. Third, we evaluate linkages between national and subnational North American governments in energy and climate policy planning. We find substantial policy fragmentation across the continent, but also point to important cross-national and cross-jurisdictional linkages. Finally, we survey efforts to develop truly regional energy institutions. In contrast to other parts of the world, regional institutions to manage energy are not present in North America, and attempts to develop such institutions have repeatedly stalled.

Oil and Gas Resources

When Mexico proclaimed its independence in 1917, it prohibited foreign development of national resources, including oil. Some US interests still maintained oil operations in Mexico for a few decades, but President Lázaro Cárdenas eventually implemented a full nationalization of the oil sector in 1937. In the face of declining oil production and a desire for more foreign capital investment, reforms to open up Mexican oil and gas markets began more than half a century later, in the 2000s. However, these reforms proved deeply controversial with the Mexican public (*Economist* 2013; Wilkinson 2014). Overall, while Mexico still spent much of the second half of the twentieth century as an important source of US oil imports, the relationship was one of two countries that happened to share a common geography rather than an integrated market. Mexican oil and gas policies have never followed a North American governance logic.

By contrast, Canadian oil production was incrementally integrated into a shared US-Canadian market over the twentieth century.[1] After the discovery of Albertan oil, US officials lobbied Canadians to develop an integrated supply chain south to US markets, rather than moving Canadian oil east to Quebec and Ontario. This orientation became formalized in Canada's 1961 National Oil Policy. By 1970 an official US task force report conceptualized Canadian-American oil production as an integrated whole because of "the existence of an integrated transport system and the likelihood the two countries would consult closely during a crisis" (Schultz Report, 1970, para. 252b). When Prime Minister Pierre Trudeau proposed that Canada reorient its energy production and consumption toward domestic needs as part of his 1980 National Energy Policy (NEP), US actors joined with subnational Albertan political officials to oppose the reform. Regional economic interests felt the NEP was an unconstitutional imposition on their resource management autonomy. Albertan preferences for regional cross-border energy planning won out, and the NEP faltered. In this way, subnational Canadian actors helped channel energy planning according to a regional rather than national logic. Since the NEP's contentious debates, Canadian federal governments have been particularly sensitive about antagonizing provinces on energy issues.

Despite the NEP's failure, the United States continued to worry that Canada might revisit an NEP-like policy in the future, pivoting away from its commitment to US energy exports. This fear, echoed by domestic Canadian constituencies looking to guarantee access to US markets, animated negotiations for CUFTA in 1987. Under the agreement's "proportionality clause," Canada gave up the right to restrict oil exports to the United States if it did not simultaneously reduce domestic consumption by the same amount. CUFTA thus eroded the Canadian federal government's ability to shape Canadian oil production patterns and institutionalized a continental logic into patterns of Canadian fossil fuel development. Some US political actors have subsequently rejected the notion that Canadian oil is foreign altogether (Taber 2010).

However, when CUFTA was expanded into NAFTA, Mexico strongly objected to the inclusion of any similar proportionality clause that might hamper its resource autonomy. In contrast to CUFTA, NAFTA explicitly acknowledged Mexico's autonomous control over its oil resources. Powerful economic interest groups with a stake in the economic status quo were able to block Mexican energy liberalization during this period (Rodriguez-Padilla and Vargas 1996). Instead, reforms to Mexican energy markets only materialized two decades later, in 2014, partly the result of declining oil output and a perceived need for foreign investment in the national energy sector (Alpizar-Castro and Rodriguez-Monroy 2016). However, energy liberalization proponents have criticized these reforms as being incomplete (Ibarra-Yunez 2015).

Debates over fossil fuel production in North America have more recently shifted away from negotiating market access toward the physical integration of energy supply chains. Over the past decade, natural and oil pipelines have risen to the top of the North American political agenda. Oil and gas pipelines form the physical backbone of integrated North American energy markets. As Canadian oil production from the Albertan tar sands increased in the 1990s and 2000s, proposed infrastructure projects to transport and deliver this energy across the continent generated high-profile, contentious politics. One of the most prominent conflicts was over the Keystone XL Pipeline. The Keystone XL line proposed to expand capacity under an existing pipeline network, providing an easier route to transport Albertan oil to Gulf Coast markets. However, the pipeline proposal became a major point of conflict between the industry and environmentalists and North American indigenous peoples over the project's climate impacts. It was delayed by the Obama administration, but the Trump administration tried to facilitate the project's construction in early 2017; legal and technical barriers remain at the time of this chapter's writing.

Similar conflicts over pipelines exist within Canada and the United States. For example, efforts to develop infrastructure to carry Albertan oil to the Pacific Ocean via an expansion of the Kinder Morgan Trans Mountain pipeline have pitted the governments of British Columbia and Alberta against one another. The Canadian federal government has intervened, backing Alberta's continuing oil production by agreeing to purchase the half-built pipeline outright. In May 2018 a left-leaning Albertan government took the extraordinary step of passing legislation to give it power to restrict oil and gas flows to British Columbia in an effort to strong-arm its provincial peer into approving the pipeline expansion. In the United States, indigenous and environmentalist protests against the Dakota Access Pipeline (DAPL) from North Dakota to Illinois became a focal point of climate and energy debates in recent years.

Compared with these high-profile oil pipelines, the construction of new natural gas infrastructure in North America has generated less resistance, particularly pipelines south from the United States to Mexico. Mexico increasingly imports cheap natural gas from the United States (Fang 2014; Parfomak, Campbell, and Pirog 2017). This natural gas supports Mexico's growing electricity production. However, liquefied natural gas (LNG) facilities have proven contentious (Boudet and Ortolano 2010). As part of LNG terminal planning, differential regulations across North America have created something of a continental logic. While LNG terminals are operational in Maryland, Georgia, and some parts of the Gulf Coast, they have been more difficult to build in other parts of the United States, such as on the West Coast. As a result, some US companies have opened terminals just over the border in Mexico to import gas from overseas while avoiding more contentious regulatory environments. Similarly, efforts to site LNG terminals in Maine stalled for over fifteen years in the face of opposition from groups concerned with environmental risks. By contrast, an LNG terminal across the border in Saint John, New Brunswick, was conceived as a gateway to US natural gas imports. In these ways, the ability of fossil fuel corporations to move their goods across national borders remains central to their business and profitability.

Electricity Markets

Like the physical infrastructure for the oil and gas industry in North America, electricity infrastructure and markets are also integrated across the continent, in this case through regional transmission networks that cross national boundaries; for instance, the United States and Canada share thirty-seven major electricity interconnections. This Integration of regional electricity grids predates NAFTA. Important regional transmission organizations (RTOs) that cross the US-Canadian border include the Midwest Independent System Operator (MISO) (US Energy Information Administration 2012). Overall, Canada has had net exports to the United States since 1990, with significant growth in exports over the past decade (Vine 2017). Almost two-thirds of Canadian exports come from Quebec and Ontario to the Northeast United States, with an additional fifth of the supply coming from British Columbia to the Pacific Northwest (Vine 2017). There are also plans for additional transmission interconnections between Canada and the United States, particularly in provinces from Ontario eastward. Under the Canadian constitution, provinces have lead authority to develop their electricity resources, and there is potential for greater connections between some provinces and US states. The Federal Energy Regulatory Agency (FERC) also plays a role in overseeing US-Canadian electricity ties.

If the United States and Canada increased their electricity interconnections, these efforts might be particularly beneficial for North American action on climate change. Canadian hydropower, which dominates that country's electricity grid, has inherent storage and therefore the ability to balance intermittent renewables (Vine 2017). Indeed, Canada is the world's second largest hydropower producer (Rowlands 2017). Ontario has led in decarbonizing its electricity grid, with its 2003 goal to phase out coal from its grid achieved in 2014 (Rowlands 2017; Stokes 2013; Vine 2017). Given that the Canadian federal government proposed a policy in 2018 that would accelerate the phase-out timeline for coal to 2030, Canadian electricity supplies will continue to decarbonize. Research has shown that greater connections between the two countries could also help balance intermittent resources and reduce emissions overall (Amor et al. 2011). Further, these international electricity connections require less transmission capacity than bringing wind resources from the Midwest (Ek and Fergusson 2014).

While there are links through the electricity grid, there has been less effort to link sub-national renewable energy policies across the continent. Instead, there is likely learning across jurisdictions about what works and does not work. For example, a policy entrepreneur from California was instrumental in getting Ontario to adopt a feed-in tariff (FIT) policy in the mid-2000s (Stokes 2013). Later, when this policy struggled under poor design, other North American jurisdictions took note, steering away from this option toward other policies, such as renewable portfolio standards (Stokes and Breetz 2018).

Not all of this cross-border action and learning is pro-renewables, however. The United States has challenged Ontario's FIT on trade grounds (Stokes 2013). Many anti-wind groups have linked up via the Internet, creating networks that cross borders to develop strategies to block wind development, particularly in Ontario and the US Northeast (Stokes 2016). Electricity interests in the United States have also attempted to shape domestic energy policy in an effort to block certain types of electricity trade. For instance, Rowlands (2009) describes how US-Canadian trade in electricity shapes incentives to jointly support renewable energy capacity. Many of these debates have centered on the classification of large-scale hydropower. For example, while Quebec has lobbied US states to include such hydropower within its renewable portfolio standards, some states have resisted this inclusion. These debates echo earlier controversies about hydropower exports to the United States, including a successful effort by US environmental groups to pressure New York to cancel a $17 billion contract with Hydro-Quebec in 1992 on environmental grounds (Rowlands 2009). In these ways, North American electricity policy remains fragmented despite the presence of cross-border grid interconnections.

INTERDEPENDENT AND INCONGRUENT
CLIMATE POLICIES

North American environmental policymaking has long been shaped by cross-border interactions, both between Canada and the United States (Dorsey 1998; Le Prestre and

Stoett 2006; Rabe and Zimmerman 1995) and in a more limited way between the United States and Mexico (Mumme 2003). In some environmental disputes, economic interdependence has led to regulatory interdependence (Harrison and Hoberg 1991). In the case of Canada and the United States, networks of mid-level bureaucrats and scientists have a history of working together to manage technical features of shared environmental challenges (VanNijnatten 2004). (For more on the politics of energy and climate change, see Hughes in this Handbook.)

That said, the federal governments of Canada, Mexico, and the United States have rarely been on the same page in terms of their international climate commitments. Canada and Mexico ratified the Kyoto Protocol, while the United States withdrew from the process under President George W. Bush. When Canada later withdrew, then prime minister Stephen Harper cited economic ties with the United States to justify slowing down on addressing the climate crisis. Given economic integration, Harper argued that Canadian federal climate policy needed to be de facto harmonized with US efforts. However, after the Obama administration began to take a more aggressive set of climate stances in 2008, Harper's Conservatives maintained their resistance to global climate policies. While the election of Justin Trudeau's Liberals briefly aligned Canadian and US leadership on the climate file, the Trump administration brought any plans for continental climate policy cooperation to a swift end, including the administration's stated intention to withdraw entirely from the Paris Protocol. Thus, regional integration is used more as an excuse than as a binding constraint on either country's climate actions.

In Mexico, domestic considerations have structured climate policy debates, including domestic scientific and bureaucratic pressures (Pulver 2009). Mexico hosted the 2010 United Nations Framework Convention on Climate Change (UNFCCC) Conference of Parties talks in Cancun and was widely perceived as playing a promising leadership role. Its national climate commitments have remained delinked from political developments in Canada and the United States. Mexico has committed to the development of a national-level carbon market and has signaled a strong commitment to harmonizing this system with North American jurisdictions that are pursuing parallel cap and trade systems, including Quebec and California (McCarthy 2018). System development is ongoing as of late 2018.

But while national actions receive greater attention internationally, subnational climate action in North America has consistently been ahead of federal leadership across all three countries (Harrison 2013). These subnational actors have a long history of linking up climate action across national borders through regional cooperation (Rabe 2004, 2007, 2010; Selin and VanDeveer 2005, 2011). Three significant groups of subnational actors have worked to control carbon across the continent, from the US East Coast to the Midwest and the West. While some of these links have been very slow to develop from plans on paper to actual cooperation, there are some success stories.

The first effort began on the East Coast. Beginning in the mid-2000s, a series of regional carbon pollution trading schemes was proposed across the United States, which also drew interest from Canadian provinces (Betsill 2009; Bernstein et al. 2010). In the

US Northeast, this regional cooperation grew from a preexisting institution: an annual meeting that has long brought New England governors and eastern Canadian premiers together (Selin and VanDeveer 2009). These subnational jurisdictions developed a shared 2001 Climate Change Action Plan to coordinate climate mitigation policies and carbon pollution reduction targets. The plan was revised in 2017. Importantly, the American governors in this area developed a Regional Greenhouse Gas Inventory (RGGI) program covering carbon pollution from regional power plants, setting up emissions trading for this pollution in 2009. The Atlantic Canadian provinces, alongside Quebec and Ontario, all undertook preliminary conversations with their regional US state counterparts about joining in the program (Selin and VanDeveer 2005), but no Canadian jurisdiction ever moved beyond observer status for the program. Likewise, the Midwestern Greenhouse Gas Reduction Accord was signed in 2007 with the Canadian province of Manitoba as a signing partner and Ontario as an official observer; however, the effort to develop a regional trading scheme in the Midwest region failed.

In 2007 California began coordinating the Western Climate Initiative. Four Canadian provinces had signed onto this initiative by 2008: British Columbia, Ontario, Quebec, and Manitoba. Observers included the Canadian province of Saskatchewan and six Mexican states: Baja California, Chihuahua, Coahuila, Nuevo Leon, Sonora, and Tamaulipas. These links mirrored other bilateral conversations across the US-Mexican border. For instance, Arizona and the Mexican state of Sonora signed a 2005 bilateral agreement to coordinate carbon pollution reductions in the region, though this was a purely symbolic effort that did not generate reform momentum in either jurisdiction. Like earlier initiatives in the Northeast and Midwest, these efforts struggled to move past symbolic discussions toward concrete policy action. By 2011 only California remained committed to establishing a regional emissions trading scheme among the western US states. Instead, the first jurisdiction to join the state's trading market was Quebec in 2014, followed by an announced commitment by Ontario in 2015, although the agreement with Ontario was not signed until 2017. In Ontario, the carbon market remains controversial. In that province, the opposition Progressive Conservatives ran their 2018 election campaign on a promise to eliminate Ontario's carbon price and withdrew from the market after their election win. At the 2016 Climate Summit of the Americas, Quebec, Ontario, and Mexico agreed to expand the market. Mexico has not yet joined the Western Climate Initiative in practice, but there are still ongoing plans to integrate the national market with California and Quebec's linked system (McCarthy 2018). Before linking— and then delinking—their carbon pricing strategies, Ontario and California also signed an agreement to coordinate fuel efficiency standards for cars in 2007.

In summary, North American subnational governments have coordinated policies across international borders to pursue reforms at odds with their domestic peers' and federal governments' priorities. These subnational, cross-border relationships continue to support the emerging architecture of North American climate policymaking (Rabe 2007). Some scholars suggest that because federal governments are laggards in climate action, it is increasingly important to turn to transboundary governance on the subnational level (Bird and Heintzelman 2018; VanNijnatten and Olvera 2018). However, these plans have struggled to move into practice, with only California and Quebec currently operating linked carbon markets across international borders. Given growing skepticism that linked carbon markets are preferable, particularly if there is over-allocation due to political capture, this may not necessarily be a bad thing (Green 2017). However, if provinces and states quit regional initiatives and instead do little to nothing to address climate change, this is equally if not more problematic. Thus, the norms that regional cooperation creates for action may be important, even if linking carbon markets waters down the stringency of the policies.

Continental Energy and Environmental Initiatives

North America as a region is less than the sum of its parts (Clarkson 2008). This is acutely true for its energy and environmental politics, in which only a few truly regional-level institutions have emerged. By and large, these institutions have not had a significant impact on continental policymaking. The most prominent institution for regional cooperation in North American has been NAFTA. Scholars have analyzed the impact of NAFTA on environmental policymaking in North America and find little evidence that the agreement has boosted environmental outcomes (Audley 1997; Deere and Esty 2002; Gallagher 2004; Markell and Knox 2003). The first major trilateral environment institution grew out of NAFTA. After President Bill Clinton took office in 1993, he brought Mexico, Canada, and the United States together to negotiate labor and environmental side agreements to the treaty. NAFTA's environment provisions were enacted despite substantial opposition from the Mexican Ernesto Zedillo administration, which was uncomfortable formalizing links between trade and environmental policy (Deere and Esty 2002). The environmental side agreement established the North American Council for Environmental Cooperation (CEC), funded jointly by all three countries. Prior to NAFTA, trilateral environmental cooperation had been rare (Clarkson 2008, 118).

But while the CEC was established in 1994, its principals—the environmental ministers in all three countries—have never funded it broadly or provided it with serious regulatory or enforcement power. Consequently, its interventions in North American energy and environment debates have remained limited to writing reports—few of which have had a material impact on energy or environmental trade patterns. While the CEC included an innovative mechanism for citizens and nongovernmental organizations (NGOs) to bring environmental claims against polluting actors, an opaque claim review process that relied on private sector actors' voluntary disclosures ensured this process remained ineffectual. Some speculative conversations that the CEC could provide effective institutional context to establish a "tri-national emissions trading scheme" within continental electricity markets never gained traction because the idea had no political support from member governments (Betsill 2009). More generally, there is not a lot of evidence that environmental provisions within NAFTA have reshaped continental policymaking (Audley 1997; Gallagher 2004).

A decade after the CEC was established, the George W. Bush administration oversaw a more specific effort to support integrated North American energy planning. Following the publication of an energy taskforce report spearheaded by Vice President Dick Cheney, the US government facilitated the establishment of the North American Energy Working Group (NAEWG) in 2001. The NAEWG was a response to the Cheney report's arguments that US strategic interests were served by fostering access to Canadian and Mexican resources. The NAEWG meet twice annually and largely comprised mid-level actors (Clarkson and Mildenberger, 2011). Tasked with reorienting energy planning across all countries to conceptualize energy management at the continental level, the group prepared a series of technical and regulatory reports to exchange information and facilitate policy harmonization.

Later, NAEWG provided support for the 2005 Security and Prosperity Partnership of North America (SPP), which incorporated a push for integrated continental energy planning within its broader security policy ambitions. SPP conversations helped play a role in driving Mexican commitment to gradual liberalization of its oil sector, including to the United States as a regional ally (Clarkson and Mildenberger 2011). This liberalization included both the partial reforms of 2008 as well as the more dramatic liberalization reforms pursued by the Mexican government in 2014. However, the SPP's broader impact on North American energy policymaking remained limited, and it was phased out in favor of an annual North American Leaders summit in 2009. SPP dialogue may also have undermined other forms of continental environmental cooperation by splitting discussions of environmental issues from economic debate (VanNijnatten 2007). Further, North American summits declined in importance over the 2010s and have not been held since the election of Donald Trump to the US presidency.

Most recently, the renegotiation of NAFTA will have a bearing on regional energy reforms, but the long-term impacts of the new trade agreement still remain unclear. The Trump administration's interest in dropping NAFTA's existing investor-state settlement provisions, which industry believed was critical to protecting energy-related investments from such threats as nationalization, initially complicated negotiations. More generally, had NAFTA negotiations collapsed, some analysts believed this could have disrupted continental oil and gas markets (Denning 2018). Conversely, the new USMCA is viewed as a boon to the energy industry. For example, in a major win for fossil fuel producers, in the final treaty investor-state settlement provisions were maintained for Mexican energy investments.

A FUTURE RESEARCH AGENDA

This chapter has reviewed existing academic literature on energy politics and policy in North America. Where would future research prove most productive? We recommend research focus on several key areas: how to scale up energy and climate cooperation to regional levels, how corporate and business power shapes continental energy politics, and how the Trump presidency and the renegotiated USMCA will reshape energy policymaking priorities. As this chapter has shown, trade and access to fossil fuels, most notably the export of oil to the United States from Canada and Mexico, have long structured North American energy cooperation. Yet we are at the beginning of a major global transition away from fossil fuels toward low-carbon sources due to the climate crisis. North American cooperation will eventually need to shift from a focus on access to and trade in fossil fuels toward other energy sources. In the future, research could also take up a wider array of methods than those that have been used to date. While most work has involved case studies and process tracing, future research could also rely on econometric tools of quantitative causal inference now used widely in political science.

Around the world, governments are grappling with how to scale up cooperation on energy and climate policies across international borders. The 2015 Paris agreement allows countries to propose their own post-2020 carbon pollution targets; it does not specify a minimum ambition for these targets, nor does it spell out how the international community can enforce these commitments. In doing so, it delegates to each country the responsibility to propose self-determined climate commitments—even though every country will be impacted unless all countries act jointly. The Paris agreement's success will depend on simultaneous and decentralized decarbonization and energy transition efforts by all countries.

The fate of the energy transition in North America is no different. The region's energy policy will remain a function of distributive energy and climate politics at national and subnational levels. Despite substantial attention to some of the positive anomalies— cities or states and provinces that have taken early action to push clean energy—many other jurisdictions across the continent have actively resisted such efforts. Future research will need to grapple with the limits of this approach, particularly as some policies fail. How does this variation in reform enactment interact with the strong federal and weak regional institutions that structure North American energy politics? The nascent emergence of some cross-border emissions trading linkages, critically between California and Quebec, suggests a possible route for regionalism during the energy transition. Future scholars may wish to think of low-carbon energy sources as shared resources that can cross borders to benefit global decarbonization. The alternative is a system in which Canada retains very inexpensive hydropower resources but does not use them optimally, as shown for example in Quebec's lack of energy efficiency efforts (Langlois-Bertrand et al. 2015). Additional research is needed on trade in electricity and renewable energy technologies across the region.

However, these efforts must simultaneously grapple with the reality of entrenched carbon-intensive economic interests in all three North American countries. Climate and energy policy opponents, particularly in the oil and gas communities, still enjoy a privileged position within energy policy debates (Mildenberger 2019). We still know too little about the strategies that these actors take to shape political debates and the conditions under which the social and economic needs of North American publics for a safe climate can override the economic needs of these private companies. In this way, shifting coalitions of energy and climate reformers have brought North American governments together to promote and oppose decarbonization over the past two decades. These coalitions supporting climate action have largely proved more unstable than those supporting the fossil fuel status quo. To gain traction on these issues, scholars may need to bring in a wider array of data, from public opinion to vulnerability assessments to campaign contributions and lobbying data.

Further, the federal governments' energy priorities in Canada, Mexico, and the United States have rarely been synchronized. To date, analyses of these cross-national linkages may be overly optimistic. Some analysts tout federalist systems as an opportunity for policy experimentation. They point to the ability of subnational units to pursue climate and energy reforms even in the absence of national policymaking efforts. Yet over a decade of efforts to develop meaningful cross-border subnational climate policies in North America has not cohered into serious policy gains. The ability to drive the North American energy transition "from below" remains an open question. In part, this will require more attention to issues of distributional compensation in the face of necessary climate and energy reforms. Energy and climate policies will need to restructure some of the economic institutions that quite literally fuel the contemporary North American economy. Carbon will have to be kept in the ground, at the expense of companies seeking to profit from its extraction and the workers whose jobs depend on these efforts. Some existing infrastructure may need to be mothballed, leading to stranded assets. Scholars will need to make sense of how to manage these transitions in equitable fashion. One place to begin this effort may be to study the politics of post-coal communities across the continent. These areas may be experiencing some of the dislocation and political upheaval that oil-dependent communities may face in the coming decades as the climate crisis deepens and more extreme policy action becomes necessary to protect public welfare. Political science scholars have a role to play in outlining what the social and political repercussions are of the energy transition and how the needs and interests of these dislocated communities can be met by public policy.

There are also conceptual questions about whether "North America" is a relevant analytical category to make sense of developments in the energy space. Trilateral efforts to negotiate energy policy have never developed, despite the efforts of some North American proponents (Pastor 2001). Despite the existence of an integrated economic zone under NAFTA, US energy relations still tend to develop separately along bilateral Canadian and Mexican tracks. More broadly, studies of North American regionalism have only rarely included comparative analysis of both US-Canadian and US-Mexican relations (but see Clarkson 2008; Clarkson and Mildenberger 2011). To what degree does the region as a whole bound the politics of energy, rather than acting as an arbitrary geographic delimiter? For instance, is Mexican energy and climate policy best understood through a North American lens? Or should it be conceived within the context of an emerging economy that happens to have a shared geography with the United States?

Finally, what will the lasting consequences of the Trump administration be for North American climate and energy policymaking? While Canada and Mexico should be mostly viewed as sources of security, economic, and energy strength for the United States (Clarkson and Mildenberger 2011), the Trump administration has instead framed North American trade and US-Mexican migration as major threats. The consequences of this disruptive shift in the US executive branch's orientation toward its North American neighbor remain to be seen. The administration has begun efforts to abandon the Clean Power Plan and promote oil, coal, and gas resources; however, is not clear that these efforts are shifting secular changes in the US energy mix. Federal opposition to the Paris agreement, if anything, seems to have precipitated a new wave of state and local declarations of commitment to climate reforms, which may seed a new wave of coordinated, subnational reforms. And what will be the long-term consequences of a renegotiated NAFTA agreement on North American energy flows? Some of the features of NAFTA that most privileged the United States—for instance the proportionality clause that guaranteed Canadian energy exports to the United States—were removed in the new USMCA. Will the United States still use its economic advantage to maintain informal control over patterns of North American energy production and investment? And how will new entrants into continental energy production reshape continental-level policy conflict? In this regard, scholars may need to look beyond the North American continent to understand resource flows, particularly given China's massive investment of more than $20 billion from 2009 to 2013 in the Canadian oil sands (Jacobs 2017). To what extent is China emerging as an alternative market for Canadian crude oil, and how will that affect climate commitments globally?

Clearly there are many open questions on energy politics and policy in North America. Unlike in Europe, regional energy policymaking in North America has remained fragmented, echoing in the policy domain divergences across the continent in public energy and climate beliefs (Mildenberger et al. 2016; Lachapelle, Borick, and Rabe 2012). Diverse national and subnational governments continue to push competing policy and institutional reforms to facilitate or block the energy transition. Ultimately, energy policymaking in all three countries is conditioned by the North American context without being fully constrained by a continental logic. How the shared geography of Canada, Mexico, and the United States constructs and constrains twenty-first-century energy conflict deserves further study.

NOTE

1. The following policy histories of Canadian and Mexican oil and gas relationships with the United States are drawn from the histories offered in Clarkson and Mildenberger (2011), which remains one of the few systematic surveys of the politics of North American energy relationships.

REFERENCES

Alpizar-Castro, Israel, and Carlos Rodríguez-Monroy. 2016. "Review of Mexico's Energy Reform in 2013: Background, Analysis of the Reform and Reactions." *Renewable and Sustainable Energy Reviews* 58: 725–736.

Amor, Mourad Ben, Pierre-Olivier Pineau, Caroline Gaudreault, and Réjean Samson. 2011. "Electricity Trade and GHG Emissions: Assessment of Quebec's Hydropower in the Northeastern American Market (2006–2008)." *Energy Policy* 39: 1711–1721.

Audley, John. 1997. *Green Politics and Global Trade: NAFTA and the Future of Environmental Politics.* Washington, DC: Georgetown University Press.

Bernstein, Steven, Michele Betsill, Matthew Hoffmann, and Matthew Paterson. 2010. "A Tale of Two Copenhagens: Carbon Markets and Climate Governance." *Millennium: Journal of International Studies* 39, no. 1: 161–173.

Betsill, Michele M. 2009. "NAFTA as a Forum for CO2 Permit Trading?" In *Changing Climates in North American Politics: Institutions, Policymaking, and Multilevel Governance*, edited by Henrik Selin and Stacy VanDeveer, 161–180. Cambridge, MA: MIT Press.

Bird, Stephen, and Martin D. Heintzelman. 2018. "Canada/US Transboundary Energy Governance." In *Transboundary Environmental Governance across the World's Longest Border*, edited by Stephen Brooks and Andrea Olive, 175–199. East Lansing, MI: Michigan State University Press.

Boudet, Hilary Schaffer, and Leonard Ortolano. 2010. "A Tale of Two Sitings: Contentious Politics in Liquefied Natural Gas Facility Siting in California." *Journal of Planning Education and Research* 30, no. 1: 5–21.

Byrne, John, Kristen Hughes, Wilson Rickerson, and Lado Kurdgelashvili. 2007. "American Policy Conflict in the Greenhouse: Divergent Trends in Federal, Regional, State, and Local Green Energy and Climate Change Policy." *Energy Policy* 35, no. 9: 4555–4573.

Cameron, David, and Richard Simeon. 2002. "Intergovernmental Relations in Canada: The Emergence of Collaborative Federalism." *Publius: The Journal of Federalism* 32, no. 2: 49–71.

Clarkson, Stephen. 2008. *Does North America Exist? Governing the Continent after NAFTA and 9/11.* Toronto and Washington, DC: University of Toronto Press and Woodrow Wilson Center Press.

Clarkson, Stephen, and Matto Mildenberger. 2011. *Dependent America? How Canada and Mexico Construct US Power.* Toronto and Washington, DC: University of Toronto Press and Woodrow Wilson Center Press.

Craik, Neil, Isabel Studer, and Debora L. VanNijnatten, eds. 2013. *Climate Change Policy in North America: Designing Integration in a Regional System.* Toronto: University of Toronto Press.

Deere, Carolyn, and Daniel Esty, eds. 2002. *Greening the Americas: NAFTA's Lessons for Hemispheric Trade.* Cambridge, MA: MIT Press.

Denning, Liam. 2018. "How a Nafta Breakdown Could Blow Back Into Shale Patch." Bloomberg. https://www.bloomberg.com/news/articles/2018-01-16/trump-would-jeopardize-energy-dreams-with-nafta-exit.

Dorsey, Kurkpatrick. 1998. *The Dawn of Conservation Diplomacy: U.S.-Canadian Wildlife Protection Treaties in the Progressive Era.* Seattle, WA: University of Washington Press.

Economist, The. 2013. "Giving It Both Barrels." August 16. https://www.economist.com/the-americas/2013/08/16/giving-it-both-barrels

Ek, Carl, and Ian Fergusson. 2014. *Canada-U.S. Relations.* Washington, DC: Congressional Research Service.

Elbein, Saul. 2017. "The Keystone XL Pipeline Fight Is Not Over Yet." *Rolling Stone.* 21 November. https://www.rollingstone.com/politics/politics-news/the-keystone-xl-pipeline-fight-is-not-over-yet-119346/

Fang, Yongjie. 2014. "Reflections on Stability Technology for Reducing Risk of System Collapse Due to Cascading Outages." *Journal of Modern Power Systems and Clean Energy* 2, no. 3: 264–271.

Gallagher, Kevin. 2004. *Free Trade and the Environment: Mexico, NAFTA, and Beyond.* Stanford, CA: Stanford University Press.

Gertz, Geoffrey. 2018. "5 Things to Know about USMCA, the New NAFTA." Brookings. https://www.brookings.edu/blog/up-front/2018/10/02/5-things-to-know-about-usmca-the-new-nafta/.

Government of Canada. 2018a. "Crude Oil Facts." Natural Resources Canada. http://www.nrcan.gc.ca/energy/facts/crude-oil/20064.

Government of Canada. 2018b. "Natural Gas Facts." Natural Resources Canada. http://www.nrcan.gc.ca/energy/facts/natural-gas/20067.

Green, Jessica F. 2017. "Don't Link Carbon Markets." *Nature* 543, no. 7646: 484–486.

Harrison, Kathryn. 1996. *Passing the Buck: Federalism and Canadian Environmental Policy.* Vancouver, BC: University of British Columbia Press.

Harrison, Kathryn. 2013. "Federalism and Climate Policy Innovation: A Critical Reassessment." *Canadian Public Policy* 39, Supplement 2: S95–S108.

Harrison, Kathryn, and George Hoberg. 1991. "Setting the Environmental Agenda in Canada and the United States: The Cases of Dioxin and Radon." *Canadian Journal of Political Science* 24, no. 1: 3–27.

Hodges, Heather E., and Galen Stocking. 2016. "A Pipeline of Tweets: Environmental Movements' Use of Twitter in Response to the Keystone XL Pipeline." *Environmental Politics* 25, no. 2: 223–247.

Ibarra-Yunez, Alejandro. 2015. "Energy Reform in Mexico: Imperfect Unbundling in the Electricity Sector." *Utilities Policy* 35: 19–27.

Jacobs, Justin. 2017. "Canada Looks to Beijing for New Oil Sands Investment." *Petroleum Economist.* https://www.petroleum-economist.com/articles/upstream/exploration-production/2017/canada-looks-to-beijing-for-new-oil-sands-investment

Kent, Rachael D., Naboth van den Broek, Rachel Jacobson, Danielle Morris, and Nathaniel B. Custer. 2018. "Infrastructure Series: NAFTA Renegotiation; Energy Infrastructure and Investor-State Disputes." https://www.wilmerhale.com/en/insights/client-alerts/2018-05-03-infrastructure-series-nafta-renegotiation-energy-infrastructure-and-investor-state-disputes.

Lachapelle, Erick, Christopher P. Borick, and Barry Rabe. 2012. "Public Attitudes toward Climate Science and Climate Policy in Federal Systems: Canada and the United States Compared." *Review of Policy Research* 29, no. 3: 334–357.

Langlois-Bertrand, Simon, Mohamed Benhaddadi, Maya Jegen, and Pierre Olivier Pineau. 2015. "Political-Institutional Barriers to Energy Efficiency." *Energy Strategy Reviews* 8: 30–38.

Le Prestre, Philippe, and Peter Stoett. 2006. "From Neglect to Concern: The Study of Canadian-American Ecopolitics." In *Bilateral Ecopolitics: Continuity and Change in Canadian-American Environmental Relations*, edited by Philippe Le Prestre and Peter Stoett, 1–17. London, UK: Routledge.

Lock, Reinier, and Bill F Kryzda. 1993. "Mexico-United States Energy Relations and NAFTA." *United States—Mexico Law Journal* 1: 235–256.

Lutsey, Nicholas, and Daniel Sperling. 2008. "America's Bottom-up Climate Change Mitigation Policy." *Energy Policy* 36, no. 2: 673–685. doi:10.1016/j.enpol.2007.10.018.

Markell, David, and John Knox. 2003. *Greening NAFTA: The North American Commission for Environmental Cooperation.* Stanford, CA: Stanford University Press.

McCarthy, Shawn. 2018. "Ontario, Quebec Sign Climate Policy Deal with Mexico." *The Globe and Mail*, May 17. https://www.theglobeandmail.com/report-on-business/international-business/latin-american-business/ontario-quebec-sign-climate-policy-deal-with-mexico/article31637425/.

McGlade, Christophe, and Paul Ekins. 2015. "The Geographical Distribution of Fossil Fuels Unused When Limiting Global Warming to 2°C." *Nature* 517, no. 7533: 187–190.

Mildenberger, M. 2019. *The Logic of Double Representation in Climate Politics*. Forthcoming. Cambridge, MA: MIT Press.

Mildenberger, M., P. Howe, E. Lachapelle, L. Stokes, J. Marlon, and T. Gravelle. 2016. "The Distribution of Climate Change Public Opinion in Canada." *PLoS ONE* 11, no. 8.

Mumme, Stephen P. 2003. "Environmental Politics and Policy in U.S.-Mexican Border Studies: Developments, Achievements, and Trends." *Social Science Journal* 40, no. 4: 593–606.

National Energy Board. 2017. "Canada's Energy Future 2016: Province and Territory Outlooks." https://www.neb-one.gc.ca/nrg/ntgrtd/ftr/2016pt/prvnc-trrtrl-cmprsn-eng.html.

Oreskes, Naomi, and Erik Conway. 2010. "Defeating the Merchants of Doubt." *Nature* 465 (June): 686–687.

Páez, Armando. 2010. "Energy-Urban Transition: The Mexican Case." *Energy Policy* 38, no. 11: 7226–7234. doi:10.1016/j.enpol.2010.07.053.

Parfomak, Paul W., Richard J. Campbell, and Robert Pirog. 2017. "Cross-Border Energy Trade in North America: Present and Potential." https://digital.library.unt.edu/ark:/67531/metadc958654/.

Pastor, Robert. 2001. *Toward a North American Community: Lessons From the Old World for the New*. Washington, DC: Peterson Institute Press.

Pollard, Bruce G. 1986. "Canadian Energy Policy in 1985: Toward a Renewed Federalism?" *Publius: The Journal of Federalism* 16, no. 3: 163–174. doi:10.2307/3330018.

Pulver, Simone. 2009. "Climate Change Politics in Mexico." In *Changing Climates in North American Politics*, edited by Henrik Selin and Stacy VanDeveer, 25–46. Cambridge, MA: MIT Press.

Rabe, Barry G. 2004. *Statehouse and Greenhouse: The Emerging Politics of American Climate Change Policy*. Washington, DC: Brookings Institution Press.

Rabe, Barry G. 2007. "Beyond Kyoto: Climate Change Policy in Multilevel Governance Systems." *Governance: An International Journal of Policy, Administration and Institutions* 20, no. 3: 423–444.

Rabe, Barry G. 2010. "Introduction: The Challenges of U.S. Climate Governance." In *Greenhouse Governance: Addressing Climate Change in America*, edited by Barry Rabe, 3–23. Washington, DC: Brookings Institution Press.

Rabe, Barry G., and Janet B. Zimmerman. 1995. "Beyond Environmental Regulatory Fragmentation: Signs of Integration in the Case of the Great Lakes Basin." *Governance* 8, no. 1: 58–77. doi:10.1111/j.1468-0491.1995.tb00197.x.

Richards, Garrett, Bram Noble, and Ken Belcher. 2012. "Barriers to Renewable Energy Development: A Case Study of Large-Scale Wind Energy in Saskatchewan, Canada." *Energy Policy* 42 (March): 691–698. doi:10.1016/j.enpol.2011.12.049.

Rippy, Merrill. 1972. *Oil and the Mexican Revolution*. Leiden, Netherlands: Brill.

Rodriguez-Padilla, Victor, and Rosio Vargas. 1996. "Energy Reform in Mexico. A New Development Model or Modernization of Statism?" *Energy Policy* 24, no. 3: 265–274.

Romo, Vanessa. 2018. "Native American Tribes File Lawsuit Seeking to Invalidate Keystone XL Pipeline Permit." NPR. https://www.npr.org/2018/09/10/646523140/native-american-tribes-file-lawsuit-seeking-to-invalidate-keystone-xl-pipeline-p.

Rowlands, Ian. 2009. "Renewable Electricity Politics Across Borders." In *Changing Climates in North American Politics: Institutions, Policymaking, and Multilevel Governance*, edited by Henrik Selin and Stacy VanDeveer: MIT Press.

Rowlands, Ian H. 2017. "U.S.-Canadian Subnational Electricity Relations." In *Towards Continental Environmental Policy? North American Transnational Networks and Governance*, edited by Owen Temby and Peter Stoett, 334–356. Albany: State University of New York Press.

Schultz Report. 1970. United States, Cabinet Task Force on Oil and Import Control. *The Oil Import Question: A Report on the Relationship of Oil Imports to National Security. ('Schultz Report)* Washington, DC: 1970.

Selin, Henrik, and S. D. VanDeveer. 2005. "Canadian-US Environmental Cooperation: Climate Change Networks and Regional Action." *American Review of Canadian Studies* 35, no. 2: 353–378.

Selin, Henrik, and Stacy D. VanDeveer. 2009. "Changing Climates and Institution Building across the Continent." In *Changing Climates in North American Politics: Institutions, Policymaking, and Multilevel Governance*, 3–22. Cambridge, MA: MIT Press.

Selin, Henrik, and Stacy D. VanDeveer. 2011. "Climate Change Regionalism in North America." *Review of Policy Research* 28, no 3: 295–304.

Stokes, Leah C. 2013. "The Politics of Renewable Energy Policies: The Case of Feed-in Tariffs in Ontario, Canada." *Energy Policy* 56 (January): 490–500.

Stokes, Leah C. 2019. *Short Circuiting Policy: Organized Interests in the American States and the Erosion of Clean Energy Laws*. Unpublished manuscript.

Stokes, Leah C. 2016. "Electoral Backlash against Climate Policy: A Natural Experiment on Retrospective Voting and Local Resistance to Public Policy." *American Journal of Political Science* 60, no. 4: 958–974.

Stokes, Leah C., and Hanna L. Breetz. 2018. "Politics in the U.S. Energy Transition: Case Studies of Solar, Wind, Biofuels and Electric Vehicles Policy." *Energy Policy* 113: 76–86.

Studer, Isabel. 2013. "Supply and Demand for a North American Climate Regime." In *Climate Change Policy in North America: Designing Integration in a Regional System*, edited by Neil Craik, Isabel Studer, and Debora VanNijnatten, 35–67. Toronto: University of Toronto Press.

Swart, Neil C., and Andrew J. Weaver. 2012. "The Alberta Oil Sands and Climate." *Nature Climate Change* 2, no. 3: 134–136.

Taber, Jane. 2010. "U.S. Senator Sold on the Oil Sands." *The Globe and Mail*, September 17. https://www.theglobeandmail.com/news/politics/ottawa-notebook/us-senator-sold-on-the-oil-sands/article4190089/.

Tankersley, Jim. 2018. "Trump Just Ripped Up Nafta: Here's What's in the New Deal." *New York Times*, October 1. https://www.nytimes.com/2018/10/01/business/trump-nafta-usmca-differences.html?action=click&module=TopStories&pgtype=Homepage.

Tasker, John Paul. 2017. "Trudeau Welcomes Trump's Keystone XL Decision." CBC. https://www.cbc.ca/news/politics/trudeau-cabinet-keystone-xl-1.3949754.

US Census Bureau. 2018. "US International Trade Data." https://www.census.gov/foreign-trade/data/index.html

US Energy Information Administration. 2012. "Canada Week: Integrated Electric Grid Improves Reliability for United States, Canada." Today in Energy. https://www.eia.gov/todayinenergy/detail.php?id=8930.

US Energy Information Administration. 2013. "Mexico Week: U.S.-Mexico Electricity Trade Is Small, with Tight Regional Focus." Today in Energy. https://www.eia.gov/todayinenergy/detail.php?id=11311.

US Energy Information Administration. 2015. "U.S.-Canada Electricity Trade Increases." Today in Energy. https://www.eia.gov/todayinenergy/detail.php?id=21992.

US Energy Information Administration. 2017. "U.S. Energy Trade with Mexico: U.S. Export Value More Than Twice Import Value in 2016." Today in Energy. https://www.eia.gov/todayinenergy/detail.php?id=29892.

US Energy Information Administration. 2018. "International." https://www.eia.gov/beta/international/index.php?view=production.

VanNijnatten, D. 2007. "The Security and Prosperity Agreement as an 'Indicator Species' for the Emerging North American Environmental Regime." *Politics & Policy* 35, no. 4: 664–682.

VannijNatten, Debora L. 2004. "Canadian-American Environmental Relations: Interoperability and Politics." *American Review of Canadian Studies* 34, no. 4: 649–664.

VannijNatten, Debora L., and Marcela Lopez-Vallejo Olvera. 2018. "Canada–United States Relations and a Low-Carbon Economy for North America?" In *Transboundary Environmental Governance across the World's Longest Border*, edited by Stephen Brooks and Andrea Olive, 201–226. East Lansing, MI: Michigan State University Press.

Vine, Doug. 2017. "Interconnected: Canadian and U.S. Electricity." Center for Climate and Energy Solutions. https://www.c2es.org/site/assets/uploads/2017/05/canada-interconnected.pdf

Wilkinson, Tracy. 2014. "Debate Rages over Mexico's Plan to Open Energy Markets." *LA Times*, July 30. http://www.latimes.com/world/mexico-americas/la-fg-mexico-energy-20140730-story.html.

....

CHAPTER 19

THE ENERGY POLITICS
OF THE EUROPEAN
UNION

....

KIRSTEN WESTPHAL

THE European Union (EU) is the world's most significant regional integration organization. In 2015 Jean-Claude Juncker, EU Commission president, announced the creation
of the Energy Union: "For too long, energy has been exempt from the fundamental free-
doms of our Union. Current events show the stakes—as many Europeans fear they may
not have the energy needed to heat their homes. This is about Europe acting together, for
the long term. I want the energy that underpins our economy to be resilient, reliable,
secure and growingly renewable and sustainable" (European Commission 2015a). The
Energy Union was one of the ten priorities of the Juncker Commission (2014-2019),
shaping energy relations among the twenty-eight EU member states. As with so many
EU issues, complex politics underlie myriad energy issues.

The EU's approach to energy policy was shaped by several rounds of enlargement
between 1973 and 2013; during that period, the EU expanded from six to twenty-eight
member states. Brexit (the name given to the decision by voters in the United Kingdom
in a 2016 referendum to leave the EU) is the first time a state has left the EU on 31 January
2020. This will have a profound impact on the rest of the union and by extension on the
energy politics in the region.

Overall, the EU relies most heavily on oil and natural gas, as is true of most countries.
The EU collectively uses more nuclear power than many countries, primarily because of
France, which derives 73 percent of its electricity from nuclear power plants (see
Figures 19.1 and 19.2).

The EU's energy consumption by fuel, CO_2 emissions, and level of imports varies
significantly by state (see Figures 19.2 and 19.3). Overall, the EU is highly dependent
on imported oil (87.1 percent) and natural gas (70.4 percent) (see Figure 19.4).
However, some countries (Denmark and the Netherlands) still produce enough natural gas—although the volume is shrinking—for exports. Other member states have

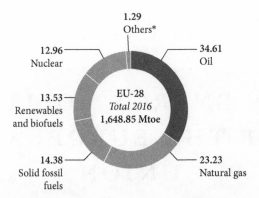

FIGURE 19.1A EU28: Gross inland consumption by fuel (data in percent, 2016).
*Non-RES waste, peat, oil shale and sands, manufactured gases.

Source: Data from EU Commission, DG Energy, Unit A4. Energy Datasheets: EU28 Countries, July 2019.
© 2019 Stiftung Wissenschaft und Politik (SWP).

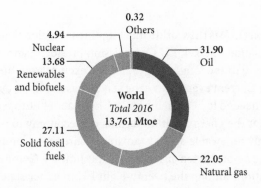

FIGURE 19.1B World: Gross inland consumption by fuel (data in percent, 2016).

Note: Solid fuels includes hard coal, lignite, and peat, as well as derived fuels. Petroleum and (petroleum) subproducts comprises crude oil, NGL, feedstock, and additives, as well as other hydrocarbons. RES (renewables) is equal to the sum of hydro, geothermal, solar PV, solar thermal, tide, wind, municipal waste, primary solid biofuels, biogases, bio, gasoline, biodiesel, other biofuels, nonspecific biofuels, and charcoal energy. Industrial waste not included. *Source*: Data from European Union, "EU Energy in Figures." Statistical pocketbook, Luxembourg Office of the European Union. © 2019 Stiftung Wissenschaft und Politik (SWP).

been largely dependent on imports from Russia (e.g., Latvia, Estonia, Finland, and Slovakia) (Noël 2008).

As the figures illustrate, in addition to the variation in resource endowments, countries have different energy consumption and production patterns. Figure 19.3 displays significant differences among big member states with regard to national greenhouse gas emission balances, power mix, and greenhouse gas emissions stemming from the power mix.

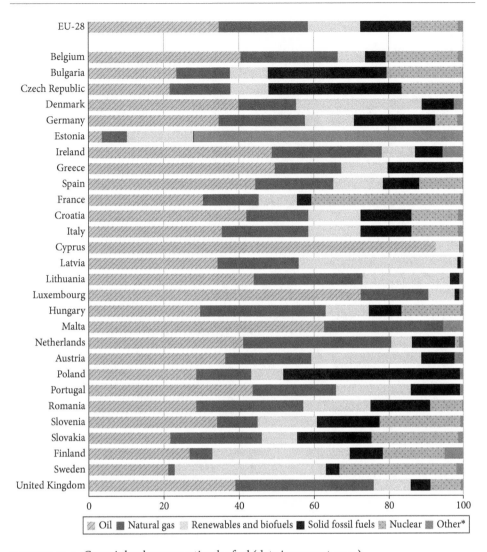

FIGURE 19.2 Gross inland consumption by fuel (data in percent, 2017).

*Non-RES waste, peat, oil shale and sands, manufactured gases.

Source: Data from EU Commission, DG Energy, Unit A4. Energy Datasheets: EU28 Countries, October 2019.

© 2019 Stiftung Wissenschaft und Politik (SWP).

This chapter focuses on energy policies, with some discussion of climate policy. It first provides a historical overview of the early years of integration. It then moves on to the complex legal framework and institutions created after 2009 as a result of the Lisbon Treaty. The third part shows how scholars approach EU energy politics. In a nutshell, intergovernmentalism and supranationalism are the major theories applied to analyze EU policies. *Intergovernmentalism* refers to situations in which national sovereignty is not undermined. Governments decide about "the extent and nature of the cooperation" (Nugent 2017, 436). This means that they are in control of the outcomes, and cooperation

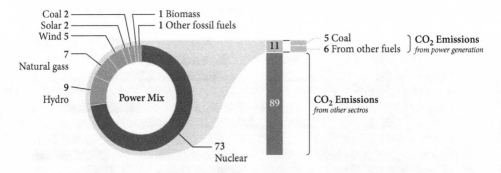

FIGURE 19.3A France's power mix compared to its CO_2 emissions (data in percent).

Source: Data from Tajani (2018).

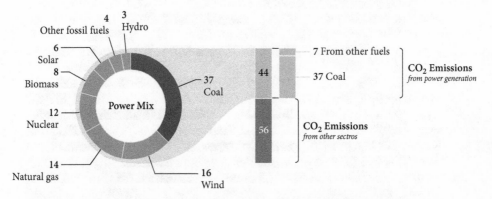

FIGURE 19.3B Germany's power mix compared to its CO_2 emissions (data in percent).

Source: Data from Tajani (2018).

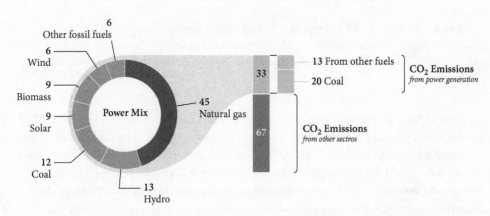

FIGURE 19.3C Italy's power mix compared to its CO_2 emissions (data in percent).

Source: Data from Tajani (2018).

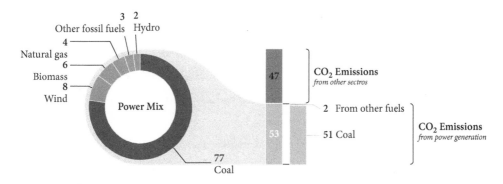

FIGURE 19.3D Poland's power mix compared to its CO_2 emissions (data in percent).

Source: Data from Tajani (2018).

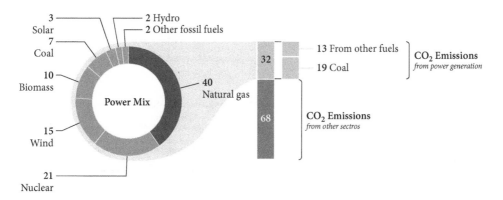

FIGURE 19.3E The United Kingdom's power mix compared to its CO_2 emissions (data in percent).

Source: Data from Tajani (2018).

is based on common interest (Nugent 2017, 436). *Supranationalism* in turn refers to a situation in which states are cooperating in such a way that no state is in full command of the outcomes and developments (Nugent 2017, 436). States can find themselves in situations in which they have to subordinate their preferences and political will to a common policy. Integration translates into a certain loss of sovereignty (Nugent 2017, 436).

The development of energy policies can roughly be grouped into three strands: internal market, environment and climate, and security of supply; each strand has developed incrementally. As enshrined in Article 194 of the Lisbon Treaty, member states have a major say in energy policies. This implies a prevalence of national approaches to energy policy, a consequence highlighted by analysts focusing on intergovernmentalism. These analysts find that intergovernmental bargains often result in compromises based on the least common denominator; for example, in the case of energy, agreeing on targets rather than on concrete energy pathways. On the other hand, scholars guided by

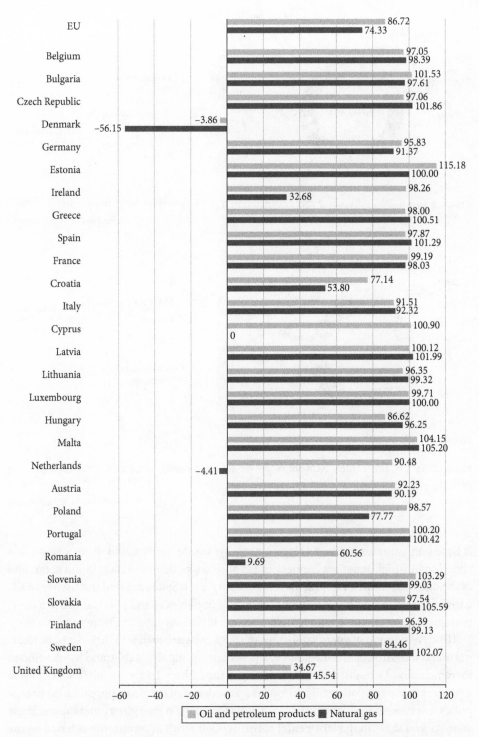

FIGURE 19.4 Import dependency by fuel (percentage of imports in total energy consumption, 2017).

Note: Negative rate indicates a net exporter. Values over 100 percent indicate stock buildup.
Source: Data from EU Commission, DG Energy, Unit A4. Energy Datasheets: EU28 Countries, December 2019.
© 2019 Stiftung Wissenschaft und Politik (SWP).

neofunctionalism/supranationalism emphasize the functional logics arising from the creation of an internal market for electricity and gas, which successively results in a harmonization of energy policies and functional spillovers. The fourth part outlines the creation of the Energy Union between 2014 and 2019, followed by the fifth section, which covers foreign energy policy. Finally, the chapter highlights emerging topics of research. Although the EU has been the primary example of energy regionalism (see Hancock, Palestini, and Szulecki in this volume), it faces the major challenge of remaining an integrated and united energy region in an environment increasingly shaped by geopolitics and great power rivalries. Last but not least, the energy transition as part of the Green Deal and a stronger geopolitical role will reshape energy politics in the EU under the new von der Leyen Commission which took office in November 2019.

The extant literature on EU energy politics is abundant, multifaceted, and manifold. This chapter aims to offer a sample of research avenues into the subject that have been largely informed by integration theory, the theoretical concepts of intergovernmentalism and neofunctionalism/supranationalism, as well as multilevel governance concepts and principal-agent theory.

The Early Years of European Integration and Energy Politics

Energy has been part of the EU project from the very beginning. The EU's predecessor, the European Community (EC), was founded in 1951 by six European countries (Belgium, France, Federal Republic of Germany, Italy, Luxemburg and the Netherlands). The EC started the integration process by establishing cross-jurisdictional control over two strategic sectors for military use: coal and steel (Kanellakis, Martinopoulos, and Zachariadis 2013, 1020). The European Community on Coal and Steel (ECCS) was seen as a cornerstone for establishing stability and peace in Europe. As Robert Schuman put it, establishing a centralized authority over the strategic assets makes war "materially impossible" (Schuman 1950 in Nies 2019c, 132). In 1957 the members founded the European Atomic Energy Community (Euratom) to ensure the safety and control of radioactive materials and the peaceful use of nuclear energy. Both treaties covered special sectors and specific projects rather than broad economic relations. This changed with the 1957 Treaty of the European Economic Community (EEC), which established a common market for goods. The EEC laid the path for the energy policies of today, which are defined by a common market and market regulation (Fischer 2014). These steps initiated the early phase of energy politics (see Figure 19.5, later in the chapter).

The next phase of West European integration was marked by a national energy primacy and a strategic asset approach (see Figure 19.5). The states were owning and providing common goods such as energy infrastructure (Nies 2019c). The Single European Act (1987) was designed to create a single market and to harmonize the regulation of

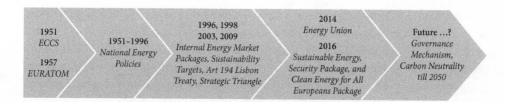

FIGURE 19.5 Timeline of institutional setup and guiding principles.
Source: Based on Nies (2019c). Translation and adaptation 2019 Stiftung Wissenschaft und Politik (SWP).

competition (Tosun, Biesenbender, and Schulze 2015, 4). In the process, it laid the foundation for a "flood of policies" (Buonanno and Nugent 2013, 8) and thus opened the door to creating EU energy policies. Energy policy only developed through common market competitiveness, environmental policies, and later energy security, starting in the late 1980s and the 1990s (Kanellakis, Martinopoulos, and Zachariadis 2013; Fischer 2011; Schubert, Pollak, and Kreutler 2016). In fact, electricity and gas market policies, which are now at the core of EU's energy policies, were relative latecomers into the EU's policy portfolio and went hand in hand with creating a common and liberalized European market.

As Nies (2019c) argues, the phase of the 1990s marks a fundamental change of "what energy is all about" (135): from a strategic asset approach (ECCS) and early strategic innovation (Euratom) to energy policy. The Maastricht Treaty (1993) was the first agreement to embed formal energy activities at the European level, yet without explicitly mentioning energy policy. Since then, the EU's policy involvement in the form of legal regulation has become considerable (Buchan 2010) in the areas of competition and market regulation. Thus, the legislative competences were borrowed from the chapter on the internal market and environmental protection (e.g., Eberlein 2012; Pollak and Slominski 2011), when the Commission kicked off the development of an internal market for electricity (1996) and gas (1998) (forming the first package). Later, the commission initiated the second (2003) and third (2007) energy market packages. In substance, the internal market packages aimed at creating a competitive, functioning, and integrated internal energy market.

Institutionalist approaches highlight that liberalization in the EU energy markets is inspired by the Anglo-Saxon and US models to liberalize markets (McGowan 2008, 91; Talus 2014). In particular, the Third Energy Market Package of 2007, with its provisions for unbundling, certification of transmission system operators, and third-party access to the natural monopolies of gas pipelines and electricity grids, significantly accelerated the implementation of a competitive and functioning internal energy market. To understand the development of the EU's policy portfolio, including when and how energy was added, one must draw on both economic integration theory and federal/institutional theory (Buonanno and Nugent 2013). Haas and Schmitter (1964, 705) famously looked into economic integration and differential patterns of political integration: "Does the economic integration of a group of nations automatically trigger political unity?" To an extent neofunctionalism and economic integration theory look at similar phenomena, as both suggest "spillover effects" from one economic sector into another, and ever closer economic ties also spill over into the political sphere (Buonanno and Nugent 2013, 29–30). Federalism has long had a place in the political debates and disputes about the fate and future of Europe. In analytical terms, the concept helps to grasp the gradual and "constant expansion of the EU's policy portfolio and of the powers of the EU-level institutions" (Buonanno and Nugent 2013, 34). It also helps to distinguish vertical and horizontal dynamics, that is, between the EU and its member states (vertical) and the "relationship and obligations between member states as co- equals, usually with minimal involvement (if any) from the central government" (horizontal) (Buonanno and Nugent 2013, 34). Horizontal federalism somewhat resembles intergovernmentalism. These processes have led to varying paces, degrees of EU involvement, and use of legal regulation in different policy areas. As a consequence of liberalization and creation of an internal energy market, institutions of all kinds (Nies 2019c, 136) and at all levels mushroomed in this third phase (see the section "Legal Framework and Institutional Setup Post-2009" and Figure 19.5, both later in this chapter).

Environmental policy was the second pathway to developing energy policy. Legislative power with regard to the environmental aspect of energy policy is shared between the EU and the member states. The environment became an area of EU competence with the Treaty of Amsterdam (1997). The chapter on environment provided the legal reference for the Directive on Renewable Energy (2001 and 2003) and for the introduction of the emission trading scheme in 2005 (Fischer 2011, 44). The EU's emissions trading system (ETS), which covers around 45 percent of the EU's greenhouse gas emissions, is the key policy tool for cutting emissions. The ETS covers emissions from large-scale facilities in the power and industry sectors as well as the aviation sector. The EU's climate policy and the crucial role of the Kyoto Protocol have been studied extensively (Skjærseth and Wettestad 2008, 2009, 2010).

In the EU, climate policy is part of environmental policy and has moved to the forefront since 2007. Climate policy also provides a good example of agenda setting by member states. In 2007, the then German Presidency of the Council of the EU pushed for an ambitious climate target to reduce the EU's emissions by 20 percent by 2020. The European Commission submitted the program "An Energy Policy for Europe," which was the most substantial action program in this policy area up until then. These steps in 2007 marked the beginning of a new era of EU energy policy, because the EU embarked on a common, integrated energy and climate policy framework. The Union and the member states started to develop policies for 2020 and then 2030, when 2050 emerged as a reference point to limit global warming to 2 degrees Celsius compared to preindustrial levels. The dominating theoretical approaches for analyzing this policy strand have been intergovernmentalism and governance (Fischer 2014; Fischer and Geden 2014; Skjærseth and Wettestad 2008, 2009, 2010; see also Delbeke and Vis 2019).

Energy security (see Jewell and Brutschin in this volume) is the latecomer on the EU's energy agenda (Fischer 2011); Tosun, Biesenbender, and Schulze (2015, 4) take a different view though, referring to ECCS and Euratom. In 2000, the Commission kicked off the debate with the Green Paper "Toward a European Strategy of the Security of Energy Supply" (European Commission 2000). Supply security was explicitly *not* "to maximize…autonomy in energy or to minimize…dependence, but to reduce the risks connected to the latter" (European Commission 2000, 9). In accordance with this goal, diversification in energy carriers, geographical origin, and transport routes was defined as a central goal. Only when the heads of state and government met informally in March 2005 at Hampton Court did energy security become an equally important objective together with sustainability and competitiveness (Fischer 2011). The new view reflected the United Kingdom's position, as it then had agenda-setting power. Energy security has remained on the political agenda since then. After the 2004 round of enlargement, in which the EU added ten new members, mostly former Communist states, the new members brought in a very different historical experience than the old member states as well as distinct contractual energy relations with Russia. Since the new members faced a high level of natural gas import dependency of up to 100 percent (Noël 2008), the major focal point for energy security became natural gas supply security (Landry 2018; Godzimirski and Nowak 2018). As Youngs (2009) emphasizes, energy security remains largely an intergovernmental affair, leaving national governments as the most powerful energy actors. The European Energy Security Strategy reflected these concerns by utilizing the key terms *diversity, affordability*, and *reliability* (European Commission 2014).

These three strands—competitiveness, climate friendliness, and energy security—form the "strategic triangle" that has guided energy policy since the early 2000s. One way to look at it is as a trilemma, since solutions to one objective could be linked to trade-offs for another objective; for example, the use of domestic lignite for supply security reasons reinforces the detrimental effects of climate change. The alternative is to think about the three strands as overlapping circles (Nies 2019c, 134–135) and to highlight the deep linkages and cross-fertilization, as sustainability can be seen from an economic perspective as taking external costs into account. What has also become evident is that energy policy is a crosscutting issue (Tosun, Biesenbender, and Schulze 2015; Knodt, Piefer, and Müller 2015, Ringel and Knodt 2018), integrating energy and climate explicitly since 2007 and stretching into trade, competition, technical and industrial policy, research and innovation, and foreign and security policies. These different starting points are the reason the respective policy processes involve different EU institutions and regulatory bodies.

LEGAL FRAMEWORK AND INSTITUTIONAL SETUP POST-2009

As previously described, energy policy was historically carried out through secondary legislation without regulating energy under primary law. Not until 2009 was energy included in the treaties as primary law, in the Lisbon Treaty (officially known as the Treaty on the Functioning of the European Union, signed in 2007 and entered into force in 2009). Energy policy evolved into a policy area with its own title (Ringel and Knodt 2018). The Lisbon Treaty marked a real shift of competences (see Figure 19.6). Since then, energy policy has become a shared competence between the Union and the member states. The Lisbon Treaty aimed at clarifying the division of competences between the Union and the member states in Article 194. Regarding the objectives of a single market as well as the preservation and improvement of the environment, the article (Art. 194[1] TFEU) lays out the following aims: (a) ensure the functioning of the energy market, (b) ensure security of energy supply in the Union, (c) promote energy efficiency and energy saving and the development of new and renewable forms of energy, and (d) promote the interconnection of energy networks. Moreover, the principle "in a spirit of solidarity" became part of the primary law of the EU (Art. 122[1] TFEU) in the Lisbon Treaty. Since then, it has been a major principle for the security of supply provisions and crisis mechanisms. In September 2019 the European Court applied this principle to a single infrastructure decision. This may have far-reaching consequences in the future because the potential impact on European energy security might have to be analyzed for every single infrastructure project.

At the same time, member states retain their sovereign right to decide about their energy mix in Article 194(2): "Such measures shall not affect a Member State's right to determine the conditions for exploiting its energy resources, its choice between different energy sources and the general structure of its energy supply." Not surprisingly, and against the backdrop of Article 194(2) of the TFEU, energy policy is (still) dominated by national policies and the prerogatives of the member states.

The EU still has insufficient competences based on primary law. As a result of the principle of subsidiarity, the EU lacks the competence to legislate "on unional, energetic matters" (ESYS 2019, 11). In competition policies, the EU has exclusive competence; with regard to the single energy market, legislative power is shared between the EU and the member states. In EU terminology, there are four categories of "competence" related to the power of the EU institutions relative to the member states: exclusive competence; shared competence; competence to support, coordinate, or supplement; and competence to provide arrangements within EU member states to coordinate policy.

Much of the EU literature in general, as well as on energy, focuses on the EU as a unique regional organization and its institutional setting (see Figure 19.6). Scholars have extensively described and analyzed the institutional setting (Schubert, Pollak, and Kreutler 2016; Fischer 2011; Nies 2019c). The Commission is the supranational body and the "guardian of the treaties"; acts independently from the member states (Schubert, Pollak, and Kreutler 2016, 128); and consists of several directorates general, among them the Directorate General for Energy. The Commission is the body that initiates EU law proposals and is responsible for ensuring their subsequent application. As Schubert, Pollak, and Kreutler (2016) outline, the Commission has a hybrid function as a legislative, but also as the executive, institution. All directives and regulations as well as green

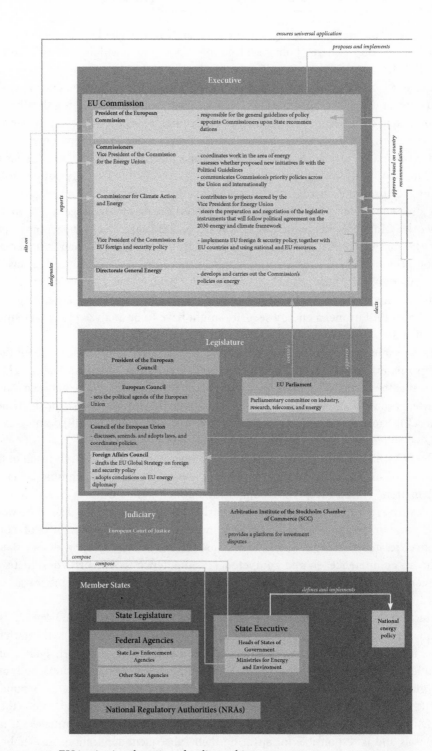

FIGURE 19.6 EU institutional setup and policymaking structures.

Source: Author's compilation, based on https://europeanconstitution.eu/wp-content/uploads/2018/03/European-Union-Current-Organisation-2.jpg.

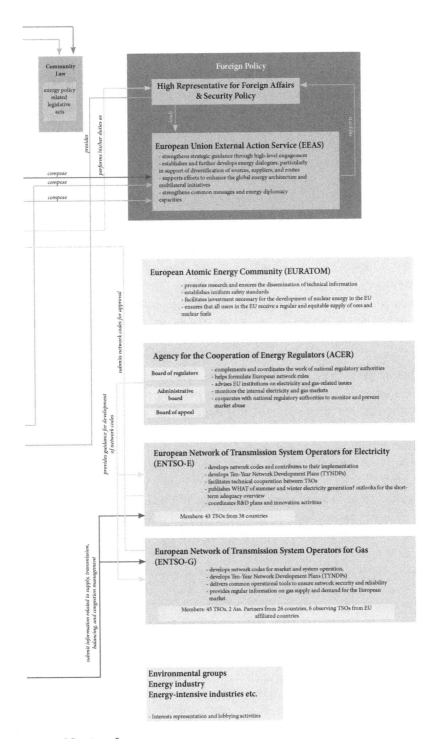

Foreign Policy

High Representative for Foreign Affairs & Security Policy

leads

European Union External Action Service (EEAS)
- strengthens strategic guidance through high-level engagement
- establishes and further develops energy dialogues, particularly in support of diversification of sources, suppliers, and routes
- supports efforts to enhance the global energy architecture and multilateral initiatives
- strengthens common messages and energy diplomacy capacities

supports

Community Law

energy policy related legislative acts

presides

performs his/her duties as

compose
compose
compose

European Atomic Energy Community (EURATOM)
- promotes research and ensures the dissemination of technical information
- establishes uniform safety standards
- facilitates investment necessary for the development of nuclear energy in the EU
- ensures that all users in the EU receive a regular and equitable supply of ores and nuclear fuels

Agency for the Cooperation of Energy Regulators (ACER)

Board of regulators

Administrative board

Board of appeal

- complements and coordinates the work of national regulatory authorities
- helps formulate European network rules
- advises EU institutions on electricity and gas-related issues
- monitors the internal electricity and gas markets
- cooperates with national regulatory authorities to monitor and prevent market abuse

submits network codes for approval

provides guidance for development of network codes

European Network of Transmission System Operators for Electricity (ENTSO-E)
- develops network codes and contributes to their implementation
- develops Ten-Year Network Development Plans (TYNDPs)
- facilitates technical cooperation between TSOs
- publishes WHAT of summer and winter electricity generation? outlooks for the short-term adequacy overview
- coordinates R&D plans and innovation activities

Members: 43 TSOs from 38 countries

European Network of Transmission System Operators for Gas (ENTSO-G)
- develops network codes for market and system operation,
- develops Ten-Year Network Development Plans (TYNDPs)
- delivers common operational tools to ensure network security and reliability
- provides regular information on gas supply and demand for the European market

Members: 45 TSOs, 2 Ass. Partners from 26 countries, 6 observing TSOs from EU affiliated countries

submit information related to supply, transmission, balancing, and congestion management

Environmental groups
Energy industry
Energy-intensive industries etc.

- Interests representation and lobbying activities

FIGURE 19.6 *(Continued).*

and white papers, and so on, are initially formulated by the Commission. Yet the body has little influence on the final draft of secondary legislation. This legislative process is carried out by the Parliament and the Council.

The European Council is composed of the heads of states and governments. The member states are the "owners of the treaties" and set the overall political directions. Even though votes with a qualified majority are possible in principle, in practice the majority of decisions are made unanimously. As a consequence, decisions often reflect the lowest common denominator among the member states. The ministers for energy meet within the Council on transport, telecommunications, and energy.

The role of the Parliament has increased significantly as the major co-legislative institution (Fischer 2011) together with the Council, due to the Lisbon Treaty. Majorities in the Parliament are often formed in line with personal convictions or origin rather than along party lines (Fischer 2011, 57). The Parliamentary Committee on Industry, Research & Energy (ITRE) is central for most of the legislation connected to energy. While the Parliament functions as a driver for Europeanization, the Council shelters national preferences and prerogatives. Trilogue negotiations between representatives of the Council, the European Parliament, and the Commission have become a dominant process for achieving compromises on legal and regulatory acts (Laloux 2017).

Last but not least, the Court of Justice is the judicial branch in the EU's institutional setting. It interprets EU law, has claimed authority over national law, is important for the interpretation of the treaties, and thus enforces EU law in cooperation with the Commission (Talus 2013; Tosun, Biesenbender, and Schulze 2015, 9).

The distribution of power is influenced by joint decision-making in the community, pooling of competences, or even supranational decisions (Schimmelfennig, Leuffen, and Rittberger 2015). Tosun, Biesenbender, and Schulze (2015) focus on the specific role each institution plays in agenda setting. As highlighted by Nies (2019c), the third phase of energy politics in the EU has caused a significant increase in agencies, institutions, and interest groups as energy markets have liberalized, natural monopolies have unbundled, and infrastructure has become a regulated business under the internal energy market packages. Moreover, with energy transformation taking place in liberalized markets, the expansion of renewables, small-scale prosumers, and start-ups has resulted in a cascading evolution of new companies, actors, and structures at the union, national, regional, and local levels. In sum, the interplay of public and private regulatory bodies (Maggetti 2014) varies in the three different strands of energy policy previously described and depending on their different degrees of Europeanization. Especially in terms of infrastructure and market regulation, the European Networks of Transmission System Operators for Electricity (ENTSOE) and for Gas (ENTSOG), as well as the Agency for the Cooperation of Energy Regulators (ACER), have a decisive impact on the formation of the internal market (see Borchardt and Leoz Martin-Casallo 2019; Staschus 2019; Pototschnig 2019).

THEORETICAL CONCEPTS EXPLAINING
EU ENERGY POLITICS

Methods widely used are literature analysis of primary and secondary sources as well as content review (e.g., Ringel and Knodt 2018). A plethora of secondary literature on the EU exists. Primary sources, such as official EU documents, are easily accessible, and the decision-making process is remarkably transparent (see appendix). Documents include not only treaties, directives, regulations, and green and white papers, but also proposals, communications, parliamentary hearings, policy reports, stakeholder position papers, and more. Most studies have followed qualitative methods.

Since 2009, with the Lisbon Treaty and Third Energy Market Package in force, energy policy scholars have started to analyze EU energy policy in much more detail. These approaches (Nies 2019a) correspond with the increasingly complex and cascading institutions and processes at the EU, national, regional, and local levels.

As with many scholarly debates about the EU, liberal intergovernmentalism and supranationalism have been used as major theoretical approaches to gain further insights into EU energy (and climate) policymaking, procedural aspects, and forms of governance. Besides intergovernmental and supranational policy modes, the variety of policy modes includes experimentalist forms of decision-making and governance (Buchan 2010; Von Homeyer 2010). The Commission and the Directorates (Sabel and Zeitlin 2008) act as policy entrepreneurs (Eberlein 2012; Oberthür and Pallemaerts 2010; Wettestad 2005). Other authors use principal-agent models (Laloux 2017) to explain the interactions between the Commission and member states.

Intergovernmentalist scholars analyzing EU policy classify member states as core actors and focus on national interests. Fundamental and strategic decisions are made by intergovernmental institutions and EU member states (Puetter 2014, 96; Tosun and Solorio 2011, 7). These scholars focus on rationalist bargaining approaches, transaction costs (Szulecki et al. 2016), and mechanisms of coordination (Thaler 2016). Diverging national energy mixes as well as differing energy and climate agendas are viewed as major root causes for intergovernmental policymaking in the domain of energy. As scholars outline (Andoura, Hancher, and van der Woude 2010; Andoura 2013; Thaler 2016), energy, the security of energy supplies in particular, became a field that increasingly required coordination among the Union and the member states. The greater need for coordination seems to be a functional consequence, as coordinated action is needed to build a competitive and integrated internal market, to implement infrastructure projects of common interest (to interconnect energy networks), and to face security of supply challenges. Bargaining and cooperation mechanisms can be widely observed in the area of integrated energy and climate policy: the 20-20-20 targets for 2020 were set in 2007 and became legislation in 2009. The member states agreed on an effort-sharing decision in 2009, which set binding national emission reduction or limitation targets for 2020 to meet the target of 20 percent reduction in greenhouse gas emissions. Renewable energy and energy efficiency targets were included as well, with a 20 percent target of EU renewable energy for the EU as a whole (Held et al. 2014; Maxian Rusche 2015) and a 20 percent improvement in energy efficiency (Zygierewicz 2016). The bargaining and cooperation mechanisms become apparent in the member states' national action plans, which are designed to implement their specific national targets. These targets vary to reflect the countries' different starting points for renewable energy production and ability to further increase it. In this context, Central and Eastern European member states were substantially compensated and exempted from ambitious targets under the existing framework. This variation became even more evident with the 2030 framework for energy and climate of 2014, which emphasizes the roles of both national strategies and intergovernmental bargains (Fischer 2014, 1). It was also negotiated to establish a reliable and predictable framework till 2030 (Fischer and Geden 2014), and indeed, there is evidence for the stabilizing effect of common energy policies; while some member states, such as Spain and Italy, had made retroactive cuts into their support schemes in the past, the EU as a whole has stuck to its targets. The 2030 framework relies more on compromises with a high level of ambiguity, the opportunity to change the goals through consensual intergovernmental decisions, and "extensive financial transfers and exemptions for the blocking states" (Fischer 2014, 3). Ambitions were raised in 2018: greenhouse gas emission should be cut by at least 40 percent till 2030, and the original target of at least 27 percent for energy efficiency and renewables were increased as well, to 32.5 percent and 32 percent, respectively. Essentially, the integrated energy and climate policy is characterized by deep-cutting cleavages "healed by ambiguous formula compromises" (Fischer 2014; Fischer and Geden 2014).

In the EU, the vertical relationship between Brussels and the respective capitals and horizontal relationships between member states continue to matter equally and to attract research interest. Therefore, scholars also investigate the vertical relations between member states and Brussels (e.g., Ceglarz and Ancygier 2015; Łada et al. 2015); Germany is a particular case in point, with its integrated approach toward energy and climate policies and its "Energiewende" (Duffield and Westphal 2011; Fischer and Geden 2014; Westphal 2019). Further analyses highlight the horizontal relationships among member states (Gephart, Tesnière, and Kleßmann 2015; Gawlikowska-Fyk et al. 2017). Within this strand of literature the role of agenda-setting previously mentioned is important. Given the British influence in this policy field, with the United Kingdom as a net payer and advocate for decarbonization (Gaventa 2017) as well as for market-based policies, Brexit may have a strong impact (Fischer and Geden 2016).

In contrast to the intergovernmentalists, scholars who analyze the EU through the lens of supranationalist approaches such as neo-institutionalism or functionalism emphasize the positive spillover effects of integration (Szulecki et al. 2016). The creation of the internal market for gas (Boersma 2015a, 2015b) and electricity (Gene-Creux 2019; Nies 2019b), driven by the Commission, is the example par excellence. DG Competition has played a significant role in supervising the functioning of markets and abuse of scompetition law (Art.101ff TFEU) by breaking the opposition of member states and incumbents through antitrust proceedings and infringement procedures (Thaler 2016). Functionalist thinking assumes that common trade provisions spill over to regulation, policies, and infrastructure, but this assertion has been revealed to have fundamental flaws (Kustova 2017, 97). Scholars have assessed that legal and regulatory acts have been implemented at different speeds and with varying rigor. Goldthau and Sitter (2014, 2015a) and Andersen, Goldthau, and Sitter (2017) have pioneered research about EU's regulatory power in shaping a competitive buyers' market and making regulation the Commission's major tool inside the EU and beyond.

As Schimmelfennig, Leuffen, and Rittberger (2015, 779) note, the integration development in the EU in general is characterized by deepening, widening, and differentiation. Differing speeds and depth of integration, as well as emerging administrative-regulatory spaces, challenge the management of heterogeneity (Andersen and Sitter 2015) inside the EU. Contraction as a consequence of Brexit may be added to this list in the future. Differentiation has to be understood as an enduring feature of EU integration, with vertical differentiation between policy areas that have developed variably (Schimmelfennig, Leuffen, and Rittberger 2015), such as the internal market, climate policies, and energy security policy as the latecomer. Horizontal differentiation relates to diverging levels of implementation across member states and thus has a territorial and spatial dimension as well. As Sattich (2016) highlights, the EU encompasses members with "diverse political-economic configurations, various historical-technological and economic legacies" (789–790), which form a mosaic of energy mixes, technical systems, ownership structures, and regulatory responsibilities. Neither the hardware of physical infrastructure, production chains, and corporate structures nor the software of regulatory norms, network codes, and tariffs that guide technical operation and cross-border trade are uniformly developed in the EU. Beyond the energy mix, national approaches are influenced by the (changing) nature of economic and corporate structures (Yao, Shi, and Andrews-Speed 2018; Kustova 2018), which codetermine how a given member state deals with energy. Moreover, the technical infrastructure as well as cross-border production chains (Balmaceda 2018; Mabey and Gaventa 2016) and industrial clusters are the hardware of energy spaces. The "software" forms a second layer above the physical structures, consisting of regulatory norms, network codes, and tariffs that guide technical operation, and a third virtual layer of (cross-border) trade and commercial mechanisms. These processes can also be viewed as a stepping stone toward integration (Egenhofer and De Jong 2014). Cowles, Caporaso, and Risse (2001) focus on the compatibility between EU and domestic policies, which is increasing not only through the convergence of institutions and policy but also through dynamic processes of national adaptations driven by corresponding perceptions and interests and best practice sharing. Literature informed by neo-institutionalism points out that the idea that "form follows function" is evident in phenomena of regionalization and cross-border cooperation inside the EU. The EU's internal market reforms imply a spatial (re)organization through new physical interconnections as well as commercial and trade transactions. These phenomena are also palpable in energy politics; within the EU, regionalism is deepening (Gephart, Tesnière, and Kleßmann 2015; Maras 2015), for example in the Pentalateral Energy Forum and the Pentalateral Gas Platform (Benelux,

France, and Germany), as well as the Baltic Energy Market Interconnection Plan (BEMIP) and the Northern Seas High Level Forum, among others.

Within the concept of differentiated integration, some scholars consider the interaction between interdependence and politicization a major explanatory factor. Interdependence is evaluated as the key driver of integration (Schimmelfennig, Leuffen, and Rittberger 2015, 771), conceding that externalities and transnational exchanges vary with respect to costs and benefits. Politicization is defined as an "increase in polarization of opinions, interests or values and the extent to which they are publicly advanced towards the process of policy formation in the EU" (Schimmelfennig, Leuffen, and Rittberger 2015, 771). This definition entails the functional and discursive link to interdependence, namely, when an interdependent relation is increasingly framed in terms of vulnerability. The unintended electricity flows from Germany into neighboring countries, the "loop flows"—resulting from high wind electricity generation in Germany's north and distant load centers in the south without a direct grid interconnection through Germany—can serve as an empirical case study here. These electricity flows result in differentiation rather than in the deepening integration (Gawlikowska-Fyk et al. 2017) of Poland and Germany, yet have been dealt with through the Pentalateral Forum with Germany's western neighbors. To summarize, differentiation and politicization have increasingly shaped the political environment in the 2010s.

Finally, theoretical concepts of governance have been used to analyze the different modes of governance in broad terms of hierarchy, networks, and markets, in which different types of state, supranational, and nonstate actors cooperate (Ringel and Knodt 2018, 210; Maggetti 2014). Presumably, this strand of literature will evolve in the future, given the new governance mechanism introduced with the Energy Union.

A Step Forward: The EU's Energy Union

The idea to create an Energy Union was politically launched by then Polish prime minister Donald Tusk in response to the Russian military intervention in Ukraine and the annexation of Crimea in 2014, which severely destabilized fundamentals of the post–Cold War security order in Europe. Tusk drew on an idea of Jacques Delors and the then president of the European Parliament, Jerzy Buzek, from 2010. The two politicians had devised this concept to more effectively integrate the Central and Eastern European member states into a common energy security realm (Ringel and Knodt 2018). The wish to diversify away from Russia was the major impetus behind the proposal. Even though the security crisis has not resulted in an energy crisis, the EU's energy security came under ever closer scrutiny. According to the European Energy Security Strategy (European Commission 2014), "[t]he European Union's prosperity and security hinges on a stable and abundant supply of energy."

After his election in 2014 as president of the European Commission, Jean-Claude Juncker took up the idea of the Energy Union and defined ten priorities for the term through 2019, the Energy Union being one of them. In February 2015 Juncker launched the concept with the document "Energy Union Package: A Framework Strategy for a Resilient Energy Union with a Forward Looking Climate Policy" (European Commission 2015b). It differed substantially from Tusk's initial concept (Szulecki et al. 2016). The concept of the Energy Union (Andoura and Vinois 2015) was made more concrete, and the Energy Union's five dimensions were fleshed out by integrating the energy objectives of all EU-28 member states. Energy security, solidarity, and trust are ranked most important, followed by fully integrating an internal energy market; improving energy efficiency; decarbonizing the economy (not least by using more renewable energy); and supporting research, innovation, and competitiveness.

Constructing the Energy Union as something more than the sum of its parts (Helm 2015) proved to be not an easy task. The positions of the member states ranged from sole focus on energy security on the one hand, to a strong emphasis on energy efficiency and climate change on the other (Kreutler 2014; Zachmann 2015; De Jong, Pellerin-Carlin and Vinois 2015). In the course of developing the Energy Union, the Commission has increasingly attempted to fill in a more political role, to pool more political competences in Brussels, and to move the Union's clout beyond regulation and market reviews (Szulecki and Westphal 2018). As a consequence, growing tensions between the EU member states and the Commission over the distribution of powers in this area of policy are visible. The reasons for resistance to pooling more political competences are manifold: some member states categorically reject the shift of competences, some support pooling in specific policy areas, while others generally support a stronger Union approach in energy matters (Zachmann 2015; Leal Arcas and Ríos 2015) but not the current (external) policy approach. The persistent cleavages—for example, in energy transition and decarbonization-related issues—are highlighted by Ringel and Knodt (2018). They distinguish between North and Western European member states, which advocate a fast and more thorough energy transition and decarbonization, and the Visegrad states (Poland, Czech Republic, Slovakia, and Hungary) plus Bulgaria and Romania, which oppose a higher level of greenhouse gas emission reductions and prioritize security of supply issues (Ringel and Knodt 2018). Among scholars, the tension between the established market-based approach and the emergence of energy security and a more state-interventionist approach has also received attention, in particular in a volume edited by Szulecki (2018) (see also Slominski 2016; Lang and Westphal 2017).

Finally, the Commission itself aimed for functional and supranational effects, because an internal market for electricity and gas and an energy transition were seen as the basis for growth and socioeconomic cohesion after a decade of constant crises in the EU and in the face of existential threats (Juncker 2016), a vision that was also put forward by Andoura and Vinois (2015). Yet the Energy Union is also an attempt to merge the three different historical strands of energy policies under one roof.

Without doubt, the creation of the Energy Union marks a shift to link energy policies to hard security matters (Andersen, Goldthau, and Sitter 2017; Šefčovič 2018). The caesura is evident in natural gas stress tests launched in 2014 to test the Union's resilience to gas supply shortages. The stress tests clearly showed that cross-border cooperation and interconnections are improving the overall EU energy security level, making a strong argument for cooperation. To reflect the primary objective of energy/gas security (Landry 2018), the Commission came up with the Sustainable Energy Security Package in February 2016, which launched significant reforms of the gas security of supply directive, a heating and cooling strategy, a liquefied natural gas and storage strategy, and a proposal for intergovernmental agreements to respond to the initial concept of the Energy Union. The new regulation on gas security of supply measures has introduced the solidarity principle into secondary law for the first time (Fischer 2017).

The real paradigm shift and structural change in policymaking were initiated with the 2016 winter package Clean and Secure Energy for All Europeans, which aims to provide affordable, clean, stable, and secure electricity supplies to all end consumers. Its adoption was completed in early 2019. The paradigm shift from supply security to end consumer consumption marks an important step, as it allows the energy transition to move forward and implies cross-sectoral approaches beyond the energy-source-structured silos, which is a precondition for coupling sectors and increased electrification (Pellerin-Carlin et al. 2017). As enshrined in Article 194(2), the member states retain the sovereign right to decide on their energy mix, but the new package can be seen as a move to bridge the lacking competences of the Commission by pursuing decarbonization and the Europeanization of energy and climate policy (Ringel and Knodt 2018). The package consists of several directives and regulations that codify the politically agreed energy and climate targets of the EU and propose regulatory and nonregulatory measures (Ringel and Knodt 2018). The package consists of, for example, revised EU directives on the promotion of renewable energy and on energy efficiency, as well as texts on electricity markets and market design. Yet the centerpiece with regard to energy politics is the new governance mechanism (Ringel and Knodt 2018).

Most work on the new governance scheme focuses on procedural aspects (Fischer 2017; Buchan and Keay 2016) and on its coherence (Strambo and Nilsson 2018). The governance mechanism introduced with the Clean and Secure Energy for All Europeans Package is aimed at making "soft governance harder" (Ringel and Knodt 2018, 215). It demands that member states draft an integrated National Energy and Climate Plan (NECP) with a ten-year perspective and a low emissions strategy with a fifty-year perspective. Member states have to do their planning according to standardized templates and reporting. This is complemented by midterm updates. The task at the European level is twofold: the Commission has to assess progress and detect inconsistencies in this iterative process (Ringel and Knodt 2018). In addition, it has to provide feedback and take corrective action, in case of insufficient ambition. Member states "shall take utmost account of any recommendation from the Commission" (Ringel and Knodt 2018, 215). Ringel and Knodt note (2018, 210) that the related National Energy Efficiency Action Plans and the National Renewable Energy Action Plans are precursor governance models, but this new governance mechanism may still clearly tip the balance of power between the Commission and the member states. In a nutshell, the core components of the regulation are the integrated NECPs, the comprehensive monitoring process, and the "gap-filling mechanism," through which the Commission recommends the adoption of more ambitious strategies and measures (ESYS 2019, 12). However, at this early stage it is very difficult to predict to what extent this governance mechanism will ensure that the European targets are met without country-level binding contributions (ESYS 2019, 12) and without sharp tools in the Commission's hands. It may be argued that the intergovernmental mechanisms of reporting and monitoring are becoming similar to the UN approach of nationally determined contributions under the Paris Agreement.

EXTERNAL ENERGY POLITICS: MUCH TO DO STILL

All five topics of the Energy Union have an external dimension, but historically, external energy policies have evolved around energy security and import dependency. According to Far and Youngs (2015), the external dimension has only gradually been developed and somewhat represents the "undefined link."

External energy policy has been guided by liberal economic considerations of energy as a commodity and a service (Westphal 2006; Goldthau and Sitter 2014, 2015a), with public good characteristics (Andersen, Goldthau, and Sitter 2017) rather than strategic considerations, as is the case in Russia. (See Balmaceda and Heinrich on Eurasia in this Handbook.) By nature of the EU's institutions, policy tools, and available resources, the Commission has been bound to be a liberal actor (Goldthau and Sitter 2014, 2015a) sui generis. The EU is a multilateral undertaking, built around common rules and law. This has determined its approach to international affairs in general. The EU has therefore been one of the pillars of the liberal global order dominated by the West. In parallel, sustainability as a normative leitmotif has influenced the EU's external policies.

The EU Commission is limited to its regulatory power, while the EU's External Action Service with the High Representative has a certain role to play in energy diplomacy and external energy relations (see Figure 19.6, earlier in the chapter). Overall, external energy relations are still very much shaped by the member states. At the same time, they have received high political attention at the EU level. In July 2015, the Foreign Affairs Council adopted conclusions and the EU Energy Diplomacy Action Plan (Council of the European Union 2015) to ensure that "a strong, united EU engages constructively with its partners and speaks with one voice on energy and climate," according to Action Point 15 of the Energy Union Communication (European Commission 2015a). The Council and the Commission have laid down four priorities in this respect (Schubert, Pollak, and Kreutler 2016): to strengthen internal coordination of external energy policies, to strengthen EU cooperation with third countries, to deepen energy partnerships, and to support developing countries.

The EU's relations with international organizations and energy partnerships (Dreyer and Stang 2014; Knodt, Piefer, and Müller 2015; Leal-Arcas, Alemany Ríos, and Grasso 2015) have received far less attention in academic literature than its relations with Russia or the Eastern "neighborhood." Yet the EU is involved in a number of initiatives beyond the Energy Community, for example, with the Mediterranean countries, such as the Union for the Mediterranean, the MEDTSO, which is a common setting for transmission system operators. Another example is the MEDREG, which is a setting for regulators (Nies 2019c).

A major focus in the literature has centered on EU's bilateral relations with third countries, and in particular on Russia and natural gas relations (Belyi 2003; Aalto 2007; Westphal 2007; Noël 2008; Schmidt-Felzmann 2008; Kardas 2014; Dickel et al. 2014; Romanova 2016; Casier 2016; Dannreuther 2016; Fischer 2016; Sharples 2016; Hadfield 2016; Judge, Maltby, and Sharples 2016; Khrushcheva and Maltby 2016; Eyl-Mazzega 2018; Siddi 2018). The Russian-Ukrainian gas crises in 2006 and 2009 presented a focal point for EU gas security and transit issues, which have subsequently gained wide attention from scholars (e.g., Yafimava 2011; Belyi 2012).

The fact that supply security and diversification have predominantly shaped the EU's policy agenda is dealt with in the literature as well. Heinrich and Szulecki (2018) analyze the discursive process of framing energy through the security lens and relating it to significant risks. These processes offer ways to deal with energy supplies with other kinds of means (Buzan and Waever 2003; Strizel 2007) and to treat them as a matter of hard politics. Energy deliveries from Russia were framed as a security threat or risk for independence and national sovereignty, which did contribute to the politicization of external energy relations with Russia. Views inside the EU differ on whether or not (increased) Russian gas supplies and new pipeline projects undermine the Union's approaches and "jeopardize major national values and objectives" (Yergin 1988, 111). Whether energy deliveries can be used as a political tool in times of political conflict and security crises became an acute source of political and scientific debate; an early study by Larsson (2006) suggests that the risks of partial/short-term cuts increase in times of geopolitical crises. Nord Stream and even more so Nord Stream 2, two gas pipeline projects connecting Russia and Germany through the Baltic Sea, have been perceived as driving a wedge into the EU/Energy Union. Scholars debate whether the Third Energy Market Package can be used as leverage to obstruct construction and operation (Riley 2016) or not (Talus 2017). Others emphasize the Commission's function as guardian of the treaties as well as the commercial character of the project (Goldthau 2016; Fischer 2016) or analyze it through the lens of gas supply security (Heinrich 2018). There is an increasing literature arguing that the pipeline is a geopolitical project (Gawlikowska-Fyk et al. 2018), while Lang and Westphal (2017) emphasize the ambiguity of the project.

A specific strand of the literature on EU's foreign energy policy highlights the EU regulatory power in foreign energy relations. Goldthau and Sitter (2015b) argue that the EU's major tool is regulation and describe it as "soft power with a hard edge." The EU's regulatory toolbox is seen as a response to Russia's approach to energy policies and even more so to the strong market position of the Russian gas behemoth, Gazprom, in the EU market (Balmaceda and Heinrich, this Handbook). Since 2006, the European Energy Community has been the major tool to govern energy relations with the "Eastern Neighborhood," and this organization builds on exporting the EU's Energy Acquis Communautaire, for example, the internal energy market packages, to the Southern and Eastern "neighborhood," including to Ukraine. In doing so, the EU has disregarded multilateral processes, such as the European and International Energy Charter Process, in favor of the Energy Community and bilateral relations (Buschle and Talus 2015; Buschle 2016, 2019). Certain scholars have explored the EU's ability to export its energy rules (the Acquis Communautaire) to the "neighborhood" (Kustova 2017; Prange-Gstöhl 2009); others have been more skeptical (Belyi 2012; Kaim, Maull, and Westphal 2015; Pastukhova and Westphal 2016, 2018) and even have emphasized the danger of creating regulatory fault lines and barriers (Øverland et al. 2016; Scholl and Westphal 2017). Energy regionalism and the drive to project the single market beyond EU borders also imply struggles for regional domination and over spheres of influence (Schubert, Pollak, and Kreutler 2016, 209).

Yet in the face of a more mercantilist, realist, and multipolar world, the EU's attempt to project the single market beyond its borders (Goldthau and Sitter 2014, 2015a, 2015b) is of geoeconomic and even of geopolitical importance. External energy relations are becoming a matter of both soft and hard security, given the security challenge on the European continent. Externally, the Energy Union repositions the EU in the global energy landscape, which is marked geoeconomically by twin phenomena of coopera- tion and competition, interdependence, and multipolarity (Grevi 2009). The geopoliti- cal context of security conflicts in Europe, weakening power and dwindling cohesion of the West, and the liberal order under stress creates a less benign environment. International energy politics increasingly augments rivalries (Equinor 2019) in a more heterogeneous and diversified energy world in which competing over efficient energy (transformation) pathways, resources, and technologies and paying less attention to global public goods has begun to prevail. Against the backdrop of rising uncertainties and the liberal economic order in crisis, Andersen, Goldthau, and Sitter (2017) explore the idea of whether the EU is pursuing a new form of liberal mercantilism.

WHAT WILL COME NEXT? A FUTURE RESEARCH AGENDA

The EU is at a critical juncture regarding both its internal energy politics and its external relations and global position. As Kustova (2017, 99) rightly argues, scholarship should move beyond the mainstream and not nest in "orthodox-ism" approaches to analyze the EU's market model and energy power. The EU Commission's term in office ended on October 31, 2019. The newly elected president of the EU Commission, Ursula von der Leyen, has already outlined that she perceives climate change as a major challenge, that she strives for a "Green Deal," and that carbon neutrality by 2050 is one of her top priori- ties. This is in line with the "Clean Planet for All" strategy adopted ahead of COP 24. The von der Leyen Commission will be "a geopolitical Commission committed to sustain- able policies ... [and shall be] the guardian of multilateralism" (von der Leyen 2019).

What institutional framework and overarching theme will succeed the Energy Union? How will the Green Deal be translated into different dossiers and policies? How will the state versus market dichotomy play out in climate and energy politics? Future research should focus on three key areas: the EU's governance mechanism for achieving its own and international climate and energy targets, its role in a multipolar world with the liberal order in crisis, and energy transition and its impact on geoeconomics/geopolitics. Internally, the EU faces challenges of internal and social cohesion. Externally, the Energy Union has to flesh out and to readjust its external energy policies but also act to preserve key elements of the liberal international market order.

A first topic to investigate is the multilevel governance process to achieve the energy and climate targets. How will the interaction between horizontal and vertical as well as the internal and external differentiation evolve? Member states' priorities continue to diverge and display fundamental cleavages and conflict lines. This implies an intensified politicization or securitization (Judge, Maltby, and Szulecki 2018) of energy, resulting in politics increasingly driving policies. It is evident that conflicting interests and cleavages may lead to more differentiation and internal fragmentation, while risk exposure and mutualization of risks may well increase through technically driven processes. Will Brussels be able to deal with the governance deficits and weaknesses and overcome them within a Green Deal? Moreover, energy has always been a cross-cutting issue with other policy fields. The major challenge is how to deal with decarbonization of the economy, climate, and environment (see Andoura and Offenberg 2019), as well as digitization and sector coupling. How can the institutional structure of the EU be reconfigured to address these multifaceted challenges that transcend policy areas and jurisdictions? Further research needs to be done on the different dimensions of the challenges. The EU also provides an outstanding example for an administrative-regulatory space. Furthermore, a better understanding of the definition of roles and responsibilities of institutions and actors on the different supra-, national, regional, and local levels is needed.

Second, related to the literature on the EU's power and global role, how does the Energy Union reposition itself in the global energy landscape? The EU's relative market power is shrinking. It still represents a market of 450 million consumers and 460 bcm annual gas consumption but has to face China's rise (see Nahm in this volume) as well US energy dominance and extensive use of statecraft (Pascual 2015; O'Sullivan 2018). The EU's strategic toolbox is limited vis-à-vis a world characterized by the twin tracks of multipolarity and interdependence (Grevi 2009). As Schunz (2016) argues, a multipolar world leads to a highly differentiated global system, in which cooperation and competition coexist and issue-specific governance arrangements are negotiated. Whether the EU can exert leadership (Schunz 2016) and emerge as a unified pole in the multipolar world depends on the EU's ability to act collectively, strategically, and decisively (Smith 2013). The EU's regionalism, understood as a regional integration process of supranational delegation and pooling of authority (Börzel and Risse 2016) as well as a process of organizing social and political power over space (Bridge et al. 2013, 336), is affected by the multiple crises the EU has faced since the Eurozone crisis of 2009. The production of geographical difference (Bridge et al. 2013, 336) and heterogeneity

(Smith 2013) does enforce external differentiation, with its co-phenomena of competitive energy regionalism and regulatory fault lines (Scholl and Westphal 2017; Øverland et al. 2016). The potential for competitive regionalism to emerge between blocs, namely the EU, the EU/Energy Community, and the Eurasian Economic Union and the Shanghai Cooperation Organization, is evident.

The third topic is linked to the avenue laid out in conjunction with research about environmental and climate as well as market policies. Emerging new topics will be related to the energy transformation (Andoura and Offenberg 2019; Schülke 2019; Piebalgs 2018; Pistelli 2018; Sartori and Colantoli 2018; Szulecki and Kusznir 2018). The transformation of the energy systems will have multiple effects on many levels; for instance, energy geographies around Europe are quickly changing, driven by technical, socioeconomic, and political processes. As Bridge et al. (2013) argue, energy transition is also a geographical process, affecting the reconfiguration of current transactional patterns and scales of economic and social activity. The incumbent energy systems and the pathways of energy transformation will contribute to challenges of differentiation, heterogeneity, cohesion, and politicization. As previously described, energy presents a cross-cutting issue, but the focus of energy policies will most likely shift toward industrial and technology policy, as technically driven processes of conversion or storage of energy into end energy and services will increasingly matter (Goldthau, Keim, and Westphal 2018). This will in turn have implications for EU's energy security (Buschle and Westphal 2019). As a consequence, fewer fossil fuels will be imported from third countries, which in turn will have an effect on the EU's foreign energy policy. Energy transformation will most likely play out differently across the Union, and the differentiation will result in diverging techno-regulatory spaces. An interesting issue will be the question of how the energy transformation will affect the EU's foreign and energy toolbox. All countries will experience gains and losses (Øverland et al. 2019) and this changes the energy and foreign policy equation. So far, the extant literature has mainly focused on the traditional topics of oil and gas supply security.

Much work remains to be done on the politics of energy in the European Union. These three gaps—energy and cohesion, the EU's global role in the energy landscape, and the energy transition—are a good starting point.

ACKNOWLEDGMENTS

I would like to kindly thank anonymous reviewers for their useful comments and suggestions. My thanks also go to Maria Pastukhova, Julian Lasinger, and Victor Passfall for their support.

REFERENCES

Aalto, Pami, ed. 2007. *The EU-Russian Energy Dialogue. Europe's Future Energy Supply.* Aldershot/Burlington, UK: Ashgate.

Andersen, Svein S., Andreas Goldthau, and Nick Sitter, eds. 2017. *Energy Union. Europe's New Liberal Mercantilism?* London: Palgrave Macmillan.

Andersen, Svein S., and Nick Sitter. 2015. "Managing Heterogeneity in the EU: Using Gas Market Liberalisation to Explore the Changing Mechanisms of Intergovernmental Governance." *Journal of European Integration* 37, no. 3: 319–334.

Andoura, Sami. 2013. *Energy Solidarity in Europe: From Independence to Interdependence.* Paris: Notre Europe. https://institutdelors.eu/wp-content/uploads/2018/01/energysolidarity-andoura-ne-ijd-july13.pdf.

Andoura, Sami, Leigh Hancher, and Marc van der Woude. 2010. *Towards a European Energy Community: A Policy Proposal.* Paris: Notre Europe. http://www.europarl.europa.eu/meetdocs/2009_2014/documents/envi/dv/201/201006/20100602_envi_study_energy_policy_en.pdf.

Andoura, Sami, and Philipp Offenberg. 2019. "A Climate and Energy Union for the Future of Europe: What Comes after the 'Clean Planet for All' EU Strategy." In *The European Energy Transition: Actors, Factors, Sectors*, edited by Susanne Nies, 265–274. Deventer, Netherlands: Claeys & Casteels Law Publishers.

Andoura, Sami, and Jean-Arnold Vinois. 2015. *From the European Energy Community to the Energy Union—A New Policy Proposal.* Paris: Jacques Delors Institute. http://www.institutdelors.eu/wp-content/uploads/2018/01/energyunion-andouravinois-jdi-jan15.pdf.

Balmaceda, Margarita M. 2018. "Differentiation, Materiality, and Power: Towards a Political economy of Fossil Fuels." *Energy Research & Social Science* 39: 130–140.

Belyi, Andrei. 2003. "New Dimensions of Energy Security of the Enlarging EU and Their Impact on Relations with Russia." *Journal of European Integration* 25, no. 4: 351–369.

Belyi, Andrei. 2012. "The EU's Missed Role in International Transit Governance." *Journal of European Integration* 34, no. 3: 261–276.

Boersma, Tim. 2015a. *Energy Security and Natural Gas Markets in Europe: Lessons from the EU and the United States.* London, New York: Routledge.

Boersma, Tim. 2015b. "The Challenge of Completing the EU Internal Market for Natural Gas." *European Policy Analysis* 27. https://www.brookings.edu/wp-content/uploads/2016/07/2015_27_epa_-eng.pdf.

Borchardt, Klaus-Dieter, and Maria E. Leoz Martin-Casallo. 2019. "Regionalisation and Regional Cooperation in the European Electricity Markets." In *The European Energy Transition: Actors, Factors, Sectors*, edited by Susanne Nies, 153–173. Deventer, Netherlands: Claeys & Casteels Law Publishers.

Börzel, Tanja A., and Thomas Risse. 2016. "Three Cheers for Comparative Regionalism." In *The Oxford Handbook of Comparative Regionalism*, edited by Tanja A. Börzel and Thomas Risse, 621–648. Oxford: Oxford University Press.

Bridge, Gavin, Stefan Bouzarovski, Michael Bradshaw, and Nick Eyre. 2013. "Geographies of Energy Transition: Space, Place and the Low-Carbon Economy." *Energy Policy* 53: 331–340.

Buchan, David. 2010. "Energy Policy. Sharp Challenges and Rising Ambitions." In *Policy-making in the European Union*, edited by Helen Wallace, Mark A. Pollack, and Alasdair R. Young, 357–379. Oxford: Oxford University Press.

Buchan, David, and Malcolm Keay. 2016. *EU Energy Policy—4th Time Lucky?* Oxford: The Oxford Institute for Energy Studies. https://www.oxfordenergy.org/wpcms/wp-content/uploads/2016/12/EU-energy-policy-4th-time-lucky.pdf.

Buonanno, Laurie, and Neill Nugent. 2013. *Policies and Policy Processes of the European Union.* Basingstoke, UK: Palgrave Macmillan.

Buschle, Dirk. 2016. "The Enforcement of European Energy Law Outside the European Union—Does the Energy Community Live up to the Expectations?" *European Energy Journal* 6, no. 1: 26–44.

Buschle, Dirk. 2019. "The Energy Community—Ready for the Clean Energy Transition." In *The European Energy Transition: Actors, Factors, Sectors*, edited by Susanne Nies, 243–264. Deventer, Netherlands: Claeys & Casteels Law Publishers.

Buschle, Dirk, and Kim Talus. 2015. *The Energy Community: A New Energy Governance System*. Cambridge, UK: Intersentia.

Buschle, Dirk, and Kirsten Westphal. 2019. "A Challenge to Governance in the EU: Decarbonization and Energy Security." *European Energy Journal* 8, no. 3: 53–64.

Buzan, Barry, and Ole Waever. 2003. *Regions and Powers*. Cambridge, UK: Cambridge University Press.

Casier, Tom. 2016. "Great Game or Great Confusion: The Geopolitical Understanding of EU-Russia Energy Relations." *Geopolitics* 21, no. 4: 763–778.

Ceglarz, Andrzej, and Andrzej Ancygier. 2015. "The Polish Renewable Energy and Climate Policies under the Impact of the EU." In *The Transformative Power of Europe: The Case of Poland*, edited by Sus Karolewski, 137–168. Baden-Baden, Germany: Nomos.

Council of the European Union. 2015. *Council Information Note on External Energy Relations*. (13174/15, November 6). Brussels: Council of the European Union. http://data.consilium. europa.eu/doc/document/ST-13174-2015-INIT/en/pdf.

Cowles, Maria G., James A. Caporaso, and Thomas Risse. 2001. *Transforming Europe: Europeanization and Domestic Change*. Ithaca, NY: Cornell University Press.

Dannreuther, Roland. 2016. "EU-Russia Energy Relations in Context." *Geopolitics* 21, no. 4: 913–921.

De Jong, Jacques, Thomas Pellerin-Carlin, and Jean-Arnold Vinois. 2015. "Governing the Differences in the European Energy Union." Paris: Jacques Delors Institute. https://www .clingendaelenergy.com/files.cfm?event=files.download&ui=D70081B5-5254-00CF- FD0387C522867185.

Delbeke, Jon, and Peter Vis. 2019. "EU Climate Policy as a Driver of Change." In *The European Energy Transition: Actors, Factors, Sectors*, edited by Susanne Nies, 33–49. Deventer, Netherlands: Claeys & Casteels Law Publishers.

Dickel, Ralf, Elham Hassanzadeh, James Henderson, Anouk Honoré, Laura El-Katiri, Simon Pirani, et al. 2014. "Reducing European Dependence on Russian Gas: distinguishing natural gas security from geopolitics." OIES Paper NG 92. Oxford: OIES.

Dreyer, Iana, and Gerald Stang. 2014. *Energy Moves and Power Shifts: EU Foreign Policy and Global Energy Security*. Paris: EU Institute for Security Studies. https://www.iss.europa .eu/content/energy-moves-and-power-shifts-eu-foreign-policy-and-global-energy- security.

Duffield, John S., and Kirsten Westphal. 2011. "Germany and EU Energy Policy: Conflicted Champion of Integration?" In *Towards a Common European Union Energy Policy: Problem, Progress and Prospects*, edited by Vicky Birchfield and John S. Duffield, 169–186. New York: Palgrave Macmillan.

Eberlein, Burkard. 2012. "Inching Towards a Common Energy Policy: Entrepreneurship, Incrementalism, and Windows of Opportunity." In *Constructing a Policy-Making State? Policy Dynamics in the EU*, edited by Jeremy Richardson, 147–169. Oxford: Oxford University Press.

Egenhofer, Christian, and Jacques J. De Jong. 2014. *Thinking the Unthinkable: Promoting Regional Approaches to EU Energy Policies for a More United and Effective Europe*. Rome: Istituto Affari Internazionali. https://www.clingendaelenergy.com/files.cfm?event=files .download&ui=B83D7BE0-5254-00CF-FD03F122B6DF5885.

Equinor. 2019. *Energy Perspectives 201:9 Long-term Macro and Market Outlook*. Stavanger, Norway: Equinor.

ESYS. 2019. "Governance for the European Energy Union." Munich: National Academy of Science and Engineering; Halle: German National Academy of Sciences Leopoldina; Mainz: Union of the German Academies of Sciences and Humanities. https://www.akademienunion.de/fileadmin/redaktion/user_upload/Publikationen/Stellungnahmen/ESYS_Position_Paper_Energy_Union.pdf.

European Commission. 2000. "Green Paper—Towards a European Strategy for the Security of Energy Supply." https://eur-lex.europa.eu/legal-content/EN/TXT/?uri=celex:52000DC0769.

European Commission. 2014. "Communication from the Commission to the European Parliament and the Council." https://www.eesc.europa.eu/resources/docs/european-energy-security-strategy.pdf.

European Commission. 2015a. "COM(2015) 80 Final—A Framework Strategy for a Resilient Energy Union with a Forward-Looking Climate Change Policy." http://eur-lex.europa.eu/resource.html?uri=cellar:1bd46c90-bdd4-11e4-bbe1-01aa75ed71a1.0001.03/DOC_1&format=PDF.

European Commission. 2015b. "Energy Union: Secure, Sustainable, Competitive and Affordable Energy for Every European." https://europa.eu/rapid/press-release_IP-15-4497_en.htm.

Eyl-Mazzega, Marc-Antoine. 2018. "EU-Russia: A Relationship in Need of Rethinking." *World Energy Quarterly* 10, no. 38: 76–79.

Far, Shahrazad, and Richard Youngs. 2015. *Energy Union and EU Global Strategy: The Undefined Link*. Stockholm: Swedish Institute for European Policy Studies. http://www.sieps.se/en/publications/2015/energy-union-and-eu-global-strategy-the-undefined-link-20155/sieps_2015_5.

Fischer, Severin. 2011. *Auf dem Weg zur gemeinsamen Energiepolitik: Strategien Instrumente und Politikgestaltung in der Europäischen Union*. Baden-Baden, Germany: Nomos.

Fischer, Severin. 2014. "The EU's New Energy and Climate Policy Framework for 2030. Implications for the German Energy Transition." SWP Comment 2014/C 55. https://www.swp-berlin.org/fileadmin/contents/products/comments/2014C55_fis.pdf.

Fischer, Severin. 2016. "Nord Stream 2: Trust in Europe." *CSS Policy Perspectives* 4, no. 4. https://css.ethz.ch/content/dam/ethz/special-interest/gess/cis/center-for-securities-studies/pdfs/PP4-4.pdf.

Fischer, Severin. 2017. "Energy Union. Delivery Still Pending." *CSS Policy Perspectives* 5 (1). https://ethz.ch/content/dam/ethz/special-interest/gess/cis/center-for-securities-studies/pdfs/PP5-1.pdf.

Fischer, Severin, and Oliver Geden. 2014. "Moving Targets: Negotiations on the EU's Energy and Climate Policy Objectives for the Post-2020 Period and Implications for the German Energy Transition." SWP Research Paper 2014/RP 03. https://www.swp-berlin.org/fileadmin/contents/products/research_papers/2014_RP03_fis_gdn.pdf.

Fischer, Severin, and Oliver Geden. 2016. "BREXIT: Implications for the EU's Climate and Energy Policy." CSS Analysis in Security Policy No. 197. https://ethz.ch/content/dam/ethz/special-interest/gess/cis/center-for-securities-studies/pdfs/CSSAnalyse197-EN.pdf.

Gaventa, Jonathan. 2017. "Brexit and the EU Energy Union: Keeping Europe's Energy and Climate Transition on Track." E3G working Paper. https://www.e3g.org/docs/E3G_Brexit_and_the_EU_Energy_Union_030417.pdf.

Gawlikowska-Fyk, Aleksandra, Kai-Olaf Lang, Karsten Neuhoff, Ellen Scholl, and Kirsten Westphal. 2017. "Germany and Poland in the Energy Union: Moving from Controversies to Shared Interests?" *European Energy Journal* 2, no. 2: 49–59.

Gawlikowska-Fyk, Aleksandra, Marcin Terlikowski, Bartosz Wiśniewski, and Szymon Zaręba. 2018. *Nord Stream 2: Inconvenient Questions*. Warsaw: Polish Institute of International Affairs. https://www.europeangashub.com/wp-content/uploads/2018/07/PISM-Policy-Paper-no-5-165.pdf.

Gene-Creux, Christophe. 2019. "The European Electricity Market Integration Process." In *The European Energy Transition: Actors, Factors, Sectors*, edited by Susanne Nies, 289–301. Deventer, Netherlands: Claeys & Casteels Law Publishers.

Gephart, Malte, Lucie Tesnière, and Corinna Kleßmann. 2015. *Driving Regional Cooperation Forward in the 2030 Renewable Energy Framework*. Brussels: Heinrich-Boell-Stiftung. https://eu.boell.org/sites/default/files/hbfecofys_regional_cooperation.pdf.

Godzimirski, Jakub M., and Zuzanna Nowak. 2018. "EU Gas Supply Security: The Power of the Importer." In *Energy Security in Europe: Divergent Perceptions and Policy Challenges*, edited by Kacper Szulecki, 221–249. Basingstoke, UK: Palgrave Macmillan.

Goldthau, Andreas. 2016. "Assessing Nord Stream 2: Regulation, Geopolitics and Energy Security in the EU, Central Eastern Europe and the UK." European Centre for Energy and Resource Security [EUCERS].

Goldthau, Andreas, Martin Keim, and Kirsten Westphal. 2018. "The Geopolitics of Energy Transformation. Governing the Shift: Transformation Dividends, Systemic Risks and New Uncertainties." Berlin: SWP Comment 42.

Goldthau, Andreas, and Nick Sitter. 2014. "A Liberal Actor in a Realist World? The Commission and the External Dimension of the Single Market for Energy." *Journal of European Public Policy* 21, no. 10: 1452–1472.

Goldthau, Andreas, and Nick Sitter. 2015a. *A Liberal Actor in a Realist World: The European Union Regulatory State and the Global Political Economy of Energy*. New York: Oxford University Press.

Goldthau, Andreas, and Nick Sitter. 2015b. "Soft power with a hard edge: EU policy tools and energy security", *Review of International Political Economy* 22, no. 5: 941–965.

Grevi, Giovanni. 2009. *The Interpolar World: A New Scenario*. Paris: European Union Institute for Security Studies. https://www.iss.europa.eu/sites/default/files/EUISSFiles/op79.pdf.

Haas, Ernst B., and Philippe C. Schmitter. 1964. "Economics and Differential Patterns of Political Integration: Projections about Unity in Latin America." *International Organization* 18, no. 4: 705–737.

Hadfield, Amelia. 2016. "EU-Russia Strategic Energy Culture: Progressive Convergence or Regressive Dilemma?" *Geopolitics* 21, no. 4: 779–798.

Heinrich, Andreas. 2018. "Securitisation in the Gas Sector: Energy Security Debates Concerning the Example of the Nord Stream Pipeline." In *Energy Security in Europe: Divergent Perceptions and Policy Challenges*, edited by Kacper Szulecki, 61–91. Basingstoke, UK: Palgrave Macmillan.

Heinrich, Andreas, and Kacper Szulecki. 2018. "Energy Securitisation: Applying the Copenhagen School's Framework to Energy." In *Energy Security in Europe: Divergent Perceptions and Policy Challenges*, edited by Kacper Szulecki, 33–59. Basingstoke, UK: Palgrave Macmillan.

Held, Anne, Mario Ragwitz, Gustav Resch, Lukas Liebmann, and Fabio Genoese. 2014. "Implementing the EU 2030 Climate and Energy Framework: A Closer Look at Renewables and Opportunities for an Energy Union." Brussels: Centre for European Policy Studies. http://www.idaea.csic.es/sites/default/files/Implementing-the-EU2030-Climate-and-Energy-Framework-a-closer-look-at-renewables-and-opportunities-for-an-Energy-Union.pdf.

Helm, Dieter. 2015. "The EU Energy Union: More Than the Sum of Its Parts?" Center for European Reform. https://cer.eu/sites/default/files/publications/attachments/pdf/2015/pb_helm_energy_9nov15-12259.pdf.

Judge, Andrew, Tomas Maltby, and Jack D. Sharples. 2016. "Challenging Reductionism in Analyses of EU-Russia Energy Relations." *Geopolitics* 21, no. 4: 751–762.

Judge, Andrew, Tomas Maltby, and Kacper Szulecki. 2018. "Energy Securitisation: Avenues for Future Research." In *Energy Security in Europe: Divergent Perceptions and Policy Challenges*, edited by Kacper Szulecki, 149–173. Basingstoke, UK: Palgrave Macmillan.

Juncker, Jean-Claude. 2016. "State of the Union Address 2016: Towards a better Europe—A Europe That Protects, Empowers and Defends." Strasbourg. https://europa.eu/rapid/press-release_SPEECH-16-3043_en.htm.

Kaim, Markus, Hanns W. Maull, and Kirsten Westphal. 2015. "The Pan-European Order at the Crossroads: Three Principles for a New Beginning." SWP Comments 2015/C 18. March. Berlin: SWP.

Kanellakis, Marinos, Georgios Martinopoulos, and Theodoros Zachariadis. 2013. "European Energy Policy—A Review." *Energy Policy* 62: 1020–1030.

Kardas, Szymon. 2014. "The Tug of War: Russia's Response to Changes on the European Gas Market." OSW Studies. Warsaw: OSW. https://www.osw.waw.pl/sites/default/files/tug-o-_war_net.pdf.

Khrushcheva, Olga, and Tomas Maltby. 2016. "The Future of EU-Russia Energy Relations in the Context of Decarbonisation." *Geopolitics* 21, no. 4: 799–830.

Knodt, Michele, Nadine Piefer, and Franziska Müller, eds. 2015. *Challenges of European External Energy Governance with Emerging Powers*. Farnham, UK: Ashgate.

Kreutler, Maren. 2014. *Interest Group Coalitions in the European Union: An Analysis of (in) Formal Initiatives to Influence European Energy Policy*. Baden-Baden, Germany: Nomos.

Kustova, Irina. 2017. "Towards a Comprehensive Research Agenda on EU Energy Integration: Policy Making, Energy Security, and EU Energy Actorness." *Journal of European Integration* 39, no. 1: 95–101.

Kustova, Irina. 2018. "Unpacking the Nexus Between Market Liberalisation and Desecuritisation in Energy." In *Energy Security in Europe: Divergent Perceptions and Policy Challenges*, edited by Kacper Szulecki, 203–220. Basingstoke, UK: Palgrave Macmillan.

Łada, Agnieszka, Magdalena Skłodowska, Melchior Szczepanik, and Łukasz Wenerski. 2015. *The Energy Union: Views from France, Germany, Poland and the United Kingdom*. Warsaw: Instytut Spraw Publicznych. https://www.ifri.org/en/publications/publications-ifri/ouvrages-ifri/energy-union-views-france-germany-poland-and-united.

Laloux, Thomas. 2017. "Designing a Collective Agent for Trilogues in the European Parliament." In *The Principal Agent Model and the European Union*, edited by Tom Delreux and Johan Adriaensen, 83–103. New York: Springer Publishing.

Landry, Paulina. 2018. "Positive and Negative Security: A Consequentialist Approach to EU Gas Supply." In *Energy Security in Europe: Divergent Perceptions and Policy Challenges*, edited by Kacper Szulecki, 275–310. Basingstoke, UK: Palgrave Macmillan.

Lang, Kai-Olaf, and Kirsten Westphal. 2017. "Nord Stream 2—A Political and Economic Contextualisation." SWP Research Paper 2017/RP 03. March. Berlin: SWP.

Larsson, Robert L. 2006. "Russian Energy Policy: Security Dimensions and Russia's Reliability as an Energy Supplier." Stockholm: Swedish Defense Research Agency, FOI. https://ntrl.ntis.gov/NTRL/dashboard/searchResults/titleDetail/PB2007106453.xhtml#.

Leal-Arcas, Rafael, and Juan Alemany Ríos. 2015. "The Creation of a European Energy Union." *European Energy Journal* 5, no. 3: 24–60.

Leal-Arcas, Rafael, Juan Alemany Ríos, and Costantino Grasso. 2015. "The European Union and Its Energy Security Challenges." *Journal of World Energy Law and Business* 21, no. 8: 1–46.

Mabey, Nick, and Jonathan Gaventa. 2016. "A Perspective on Infrastructure and Energy Security in the Transition." Energy Union Choices. https://www.e3g.org/docs/Energy_Union_Choices.pdf.

Maggetti, Martino. 2014. "The Politics of Network Governance in Europe: The Case of Energy Regulation." *West European Politics* 37, no. 3: 497–514.

Maras, Isabelle. 2015. "Going Beyond the Symbolic to Realize Potential: France Germany Poland." In *Opening up the Franco-German Dialogue: How Trialogues Can Enhance European Integration*, edited by Claire Demesmay and Hans Stark, 15–17. Berlin: Deutsche Gesellschaft für Auswärtige Politik. https://dgap.org/en/article/getFullPDF/26834.

Maxian Rusche, Tim. 2015. *EU Renewable Electricity Law and Policy: From National Targets to a Common Market*. Cambridge, UK: Cambridge University Press.

McGowan, Francis. 2008. "Can the European Union's Market Liberalism Ensure Energy Security in a Time of 'Economic Nationalism'?" *Journal of Contemporary European Research* 4, no. 2: 90–106.

Nies, Susanne, ed. 2019a. *The European Energy Transition: Actors, Factors, Sectors*. Deventer, Netherlands: Claeys & Casteels Law Publishers.

Nies, Susanne. 2019b. "Security of Supply: A New Focus on Electricity." In *The European Energy Transition: Actors, Factors, Sectors*, edited by Susanne Nies, 51–73. Deventer, Netherlands: Claeys & Casteels Law Publishers.

Nies, Susanne. 2019c. "An Introductory Overview on Institutional Change." In *The European Energy Transition: Actors, Factors, Sectors*, edited by Susanne Nies, 131–173. Deventer, Netherlands: Claeys & Casteels Law Publishers.

Noël, Pierre. 2008. *Beyond Dependence: How to Deal with Russian Gas*. London: European Council on Foreign Relations. https://www.ecfr.eu/page/-/ECFR-09-BEYOND_DEPENDENCE-HOW_TO_DEAL_WITH_RUSSIAN_GAS.pdf.

Nugent, Neill. 2017. *The Government and Politics of the European Union*. Basingstoke, UK: Palgrave Macmillan.

Oberthür, Sebastian, and Marc Pallemaerts. 2010. "The EU's Internal and External Climate Policies: An Historical Overview." In *The New Climate Policies of the European Union: Internal Legislation and Climate Diplomacy*, edited by Sebastian Oberthür and Marc Pallemaerts, 27–63. Brussels: VUB Press.

O'Sullivan, Meghan. 2018. *Windfall: How the New Energy Abundance Upends Global Politics and Strengthens America's Power*. New York: Simon & Schuster.

Øverland, Indra, Morgan Bazilian, Roman Vakulchuk, Talgat Ilimbek Uulu, and Kirsten Westphal. 2019. "The GeGaLo index: Geopolitical Gains and Losses after Energy Transition" *Energy Strategy Reviews* 26 (November). https://www.sciencedirect.com/science/article/pii/S2211467X19300999?utm_campaign=STMJ_75273_AUTH_SERV_PPUB&utm_medium=email&utm_dgroup=Email1Publishing&utm_acid=30622914&SIS_ID=0&dgcid=STMJ_75273_AUTH_SERV_PPUB&CMX_ID=&utm_in=DM593500&utm_source=AC_30#!.

Øverland, Indra, Ellen Scholl, Kirsten Westphal, and Katja Yafimava. 2016. "Energy Security and the OSCE: The Case for Energy Risk Mitigation and Connectivity." SWP Comments 2016/C 26. May. Berlin: SWP.

Pascual, Carlos. 2015. *The New Geopolitics of Energy*. New York: SIPA, Center on Global Energy Policy. https://energypolicy.columbia.edu/sites/default/files/The%20New%20 Geopolitics%20of%20Energy_September%202015.pdf.

Pastukhova, Maria, and Kirsten Westphal. 2016. "A Common Energy Market in the Eurasian Economic Union. Implications for the European Union and Energy Relations with Russia." SWP Comments 2016/C 9. February. Berlin: SWP.

Pastukhova, Maria, and Kirsten Westphal. 2018. "Eurasian Economic Union Integrates Energy Markets—EU Stands Aside." SWP Comments 2018/C 5. January. Berlin: SWP.

Pellerin-Carlin, Thomas, Jean-Arnold Vinois, Eulalia Rubio, and Sofia Fernandes. 2017. *Making the Energy Transition a European Success: Tackling the Democratic, Innovation, Financing and Social Challenges of the Energy Union*. Paris: Jacques Delors Institute. http://www. institutdelors.eu/wp-content/uploads/2018/01/makingtheenergytransitionaeuropeansuccess-study-pellerincarlinfernandesrubio-june2017-bd.pdf.

Piebalgs, Andris. 2018. "Rethink Gas for the Future EU." *World Energy Quarterly* 10, no. 38: 20–23.

Pistelli, Lapo. 2018. "A Challenging Transition." *World Energy Quarterly* 10, no. 38: 32–35.

Pollak, Johannes, and Peter Slominski. 2011. "Liberalizing the EU's Energy Market. Hard and Soft Power Combined." In *The EU's Decision Traps: Comparing Policies*, edited by Gerda Falkner, 1–17. Oxford: Oxford Scholarship Online.

Pototschnig, Alberto. 2019. "The ACER Experience." In *The European Energy Transition: Actors, Factors, Sectors*, edited by Susanne Nies, 175–209. Deventer, Netherlands: Claeys & Casteels Law Publishers.

Prange-Gstöhl, Heiko. 2009. "Enlarging the EU's Internal Energy Market: Why Would Third Countries Accept EU Rule Export?" *Energy Policy* 37, no. 12: 5296–5303.

Puetter, Uwe. 2014. *The European Council and the Council*. Oxford: Oxford University Press.

Riley, Alan. 2016. "Nord Stream 2: A Legal and Policy Analysis." CEPS Special Report 151. Brussels: CEPS.

Ringel, Marc, and Michèle Knodt. 2018. "The Governance of the European Energy Union: Efficiency, Effectiveness and Acceptance of the Winter Package 2016." *Energy Policy* 112: 209–220.

Robert Schuman, Declaration of 9 May 1950, https://www.robert-schuman.eu/en/declaration-of-9-may-1950

Romanova, Tatiana. 2016. "Is Russian Energy Policy Towards the EU Only about Geopolitics? The Case of the Third Liberalisation Package." *Geopolitics* 21, no. 4: 857–879.

Sabel, Charles F., and Jonathan Zeitlin. 2008. "Learning from Difference: The New Architecture of Experimentalist Governance in the EU." *European Law Journal* 14, no. 3: 271–327.

Sartori, Nicolò, and Lorenzo Colantoni. 2018. "Transition Matters." *World Energy Quarterly* 10, no. 38: 61–63.

Sattich, Thomas. 2016. "Energy Imports, Geoeconomics, and Regional Coordination: The Case of Germany and Poland in the Baltic Energy System-Close Neighbours, Close(r) Cooperation?" *International Journal of Energy Economics and Policy* 6, no. 4: 789–800.

Schimmelfennig, Frank, Dirk Leuffen, and Berthold Rittberger. 2015. "The European Union as a System of Differentiated Integration: Interdependence, Politicization and Differentiation." *Journal of European Public Policy* 22, no. 6: 764–782.

Schmidt-Felzmann, Anke. 2008. "All for One? EU Member States and the Union's Common Policy Towards the Russian Federation." *Journal of Contemporary European Studies* 16, no. 2: 169–187.

Scholl, Ellen, and Kirsten Westphal. 2017. "European Energy Security Reimagined: Mapping the Risks, Challenges and Opportunities of Changing Energy Geographies." SWP Research Paper 2017/RP 04. March. Berlin: SWP.

Schubert, Samuel R., Johannes Pollak, and Maren Kreutler. 2016. *Energy Policy of the European Union*. London: Palgrave.

Schülke, Christian. 2019. "What Future for Gas and Gas Infrastructure in the European Energy Transition?" In *The European Energy Transition: Actors, Factors, Sectors*, edited by Susanne Nies, 313–325. Deventer, Netherlands: Claeys & Casteels Law Publishers.

Schunz, Simon. 2016. "The Prospects for Transatlantic Leadership in an Evolving Multipolar World." *European Foreign Affairs Review* 21, no. 3: 431–448.

Šefčovič, Maroš. 2018. "Energy Union: An Increasingly Resilient Energy System." *World Energy Quarterly* 10, no. 38: 10–12.

Sharples, Jack D. 2016. "The Shifting Geopolitics of Russia's Natural Gas Exports and Their Impact on EU-Russia Gas Relations." *Geopolitics* 21, no. 4: 880–912.

Siddi, Marco. 2018. "Identities and Vulnerabilities: the Ukraine Crisis and the Securitisation of the EU-Russia Gas Trade." In *Energy Security in Europe: Divergent Perceptions and Policy Challenges*, edited by Kacper Szulecki, 251–273. Basingstoke, UK: Palgrave Macmillan.

Skjærseth, Jon B., and Jørgen Wettestad. 2008. "Implementing EU Emissions Trading: Success or Failure?" *International Environmental Agreements* 8: 275–290.

Skjærseth, Jon B., and Jørgen Wettestad. 2009. "The Origin, Evolution and Consequences of the EU Emissions Trading System." *Global Environmental Politics* 9, no. 2: 101–122.

Skjærseth, Jon B., and Jørgen Wettestad. 2010. "Fixing the EU Emissions Trading System? Understanding the Post-2012 Changes." *Global Environmental Politics* 10, no. 4: 101–123.

Slominski, Peter. 2016. "Energy and Climate Policy: Does the Competitiveness Narrative Prevail in Times of Crisis?" *Journal of European Integration* 38, no. 3: 343–357.

Smith, Karen E. 2013. "Can the European Union Be a Pole in a Multipolar World?" *The International Spectator* 48, no. 2: 114–126.

Staschus, Konstantin. 2019. "The ENTSO-E Experience." In *The European Energy Transition: Actors, Factors, Sectors*, edited by Susanne Nies, 211–230. Deventer, Netherlands: Claeys & Casteels Law Publishers.

Strambo, Claudia, and Måns Nilsson. 2018. "The Energy Union: A Coherent Policy Package?" In *Handbook of the International Political Economy of Energy and Natural Resources*, edited by Andreas Goldthau, Michael F. Keating, and Caroline Kuzemko, 107–122. Cheltenham, UK: Edward Elgar Publishing.

Strizel, Holger. 2007. "Towards a Theory of Securitization: Copenhagen and Beyond." *European Journal of International Relations* 13, no. 3: 357–383.

Szulecki, Kacper, Severin Fischer, Anne Therese Gullberg, and Oliver Sartor. 2016. "Shaping the 'Energy Union': Between National Positions and Governance Innovation in EU Energy and Climate Policy." *Climate Policy* 16, no. 5: 548–567.

Szulecki, Kacper, and Julia Kusznir. 2018. "Energy Security and Energy Transition: Securitization in the Electricity Sector." In *Energy Security in Europe: Divergent Perceptions and Policy Challenges*, edited by Kacper Szulecki, 117–148. Basingstoke, UK: Palgrave Macmillan.

Szulecki, Kacper, and Kirsten Westphal. 2018. "Taking Security Seriously in EU Energy Governance: Crimean Shock and the Energy Union." In *Energy Security in Europe: Divergent Perceptions and Policy Challenges*, edited by Kacper Szulecki, 177–202. Basingstoke, UK: Palgrave Macmillan.

Tajani, Antonio. 2018. "The European Union's Sustainable Revolution." *World Energy Quarterly* 10, no. 38: 6–9.

Talus, Kim. 2013. *EU Energy Law and Policy: A Critical Account*. Oxford: Oxford University Press.

Talus, Kim. 2014. "United States Natural Gas Markets, Contracts and Risks: What Lessons for the European Union and Asia-Pacific Natural Gas Markets?" *Energy Policy* 74: 28–34.

Talus, Kim. 2017. "Application of EU Energy and Certain National Laws of Baltic Sea Countries to the Nord Stream 2 Pipeline Project." *Journal of Energy Law and Business* 10: 30–42.

Thaler, Philipp. 2016. "The European Commission and the European Council: Coordinated Agenda Setting in European Energy Policy." *Journal of European Integration* 38, no. 5: 571–585.

Tosun, Jale., Sophie Biesenbender, and Kai Schulze. 2015. *Energy Policy Making in the EU*. Munich: Springer.

Tosun, Jale, and Israel Solorio. 2011. "Exploring the Energy-Environment Relationship in the EU: Perspectives and Challenges for Theorizing and Empirical Analysis." *European Integration online Papers* 15, no. 1: 1–15.

Von der Leyen, Ursula. 2019. Quoted in: "The von der Leyen Commission: For a Union That Strives for More." European Commission Press Release, September 10. https://ec.europa.eu/commission/presscorner/detail/en/IP_19_5542.

Von Homeyer, Ingmar. 2010. "Emerging Experimentalism in EU Environmental Governance." In *Experimentalist Governance in the European Union: Towards a New Architecture*, edited by Charles F. Sabel and Jonathan Zeitlin, 121–150. Oxford: Oxford University Press.

Westphal, Kirsten. 2006. "Energy Policy between Multilateral Governance and Geopolitics: Whither Europe?" *Internationale Politik und Gesellschaft* 4: 44–63.

Westphal, Kirsten. 2007. "Germany and the EU-Russia Energy Dialogue." In *The EU-Russian Energy Dialogue. Europe's Future Energy Supply*, edited by Pami Aalto, 93–118. Aldershot/Burlington, UK: Ashgate.

Westphal, Kirsten. 2019. "Germany's Energiewende: Climate Change in Focus—Competitiveness and Energy Security Sidelined?" In *New Political Economy of Energy in Europe: Power to Project, Power to Adapt*, edited by Jakub M. Godzimirski, 165–194. Basingstoke UK: Palgrave Macmillan.

Wettestad, Jorgen. 2005. "The Making of the 2003 EU Emissions Trading Directive: Ultra-quick Process Due to Entrepreneurial Proficiency?" *Global Environmental Politics* 5, no. 1: 1–23.

Yafimava, Katja. 2011. *The Transit Dimension of EU Energy Security*. Oxford: OIES/OUP.

Yao, Lixia, Xunpeng Shi, and Philip Andrews-Speed. 2018. "Conceptualization of Energy Security in Resource-Poor Economies: The Role of the Nature of Economy." *Energy Policy* 114: 394–402.

Yergin, Daniel. 1988. "Energy Security in the 1990s." *Foreign Affairs* 67, no. 1: 110–132.

Youngs, Richard. 2009. *Energy Security: Europe's New Foreign Policy Challenge*. New York: Routledge.

Zachmann, Georg. 2015. "The European Energy Union: Slogan or an Important Step Towards Integration?" Bonn: Friedrich-Ebert-Stiftung. https://library.fes.de/pdf-files/wiso/11495.pdf.

Zygierewicz, Anna. 2016. "Implementation of the Energy Efficiency Directive (201227EU): Energy Efficiency Obligation Schemes; European Implementation Assessment." Brussels: European Parliamentary Research Service. http://www.europarl.europa.eu/RegData/etudes/STUD/2016/579327/EPRS_STU(2016)579327_EN.pdf.

PRIMARY SOURCES

The European Community on Coal and Steel (ECCS) (1951): https://eur-lex.europa.eu/
LexUriServ/LexUriServ.do?uri=CELEX:11951K:EN:PDF

European Atomic Energy Community (Euratom) (1957; consolidated version 2010): https://
europa.eu/european-union/sites/europaeu/files/docs/body/consolidated_version_
of_the_treaty_establishing_the_european_atomic_energy_community_en.pdf

European Economic Community (ECC) (1957): https://europa.eu/european-union/sites/
europaeu/files/docs/body/treaties_establishing_the_european_communities_single_
european_act_en.pdf

The Single European Act (1986): https://europa.eu/european-union/sites/europaeu/files/
docs/body/treaties_establishing_the_european_communities_single_european_act_
en.pdf

Maastrict Treaty (signed 1992): https://europa.eu/european-union/sites/europaeu/files/docs/
body/treaty_on_european_union_en.pdf

Treaty of Amsterdam (signed 1997): https://eur-lex.europa.eu/legal-content/EN/
TXT/?uri=CELEX%3A11997D%2FTXT

First Energy Market Package (1996 and 1998): https://eur-lex.europa.eu/legal-content/EN/
TXT/?uri=CELEX%3A31996L0092

https://eur-lex.europa.eu/legal-content/EN/TXT/?uri=uriserv:OJ.L_.1998.204.01.0001.01.
ENG&toc=OJ:L:1998:204:TOC

European Strategy of the Security of Energy Supply (2000): https://eur-lex.europa.eu/legal-
content/EN/TXT/?uri=celex:52000DC0769

Second Energy Market Package (2003): https://eur-lex.europa.eu/legal-content/EN/
TXT/?uri=CELEX%3A32003L0054

https://eur-lex.europa.eu/legal-content/EN/ALL/?uri=CELEX%3A32003R1228

https://eur-lex.europa.eu/legal-content/EN/TXT/?uri=celex:32003L0055

Directive on Renewable Energy (2001 and 2003)

https://eur-lex.europa.eu/legal-content/EN/TXT/?uri=celex%3A32001L0077

https://eur-lex.europa.eu/LexUriServ/LexUriServ.do?uri=OJ:L:2003:123:0042:0046:EN:PDF

Third Energy Market Package (2007): http://eur-lex.europa.eu/LexUriServ/LexUriServ.do?ur
i=OJ:L:2009:211:0055:0093:EN:PDF

http://eur-lex.europa.eu/LexUriServ/LexUriServ.do?uri=OJ:L:2009:211:0094:0136:en:PDF

http://eur-lex.europa.eu/LexUriServ/LexUriServ.do?uri=OJ:L:2009:211:0015:0035:EN:PDF

http://eur-lex.europa.eu/LexUriServ/LexUriServ.do?uri=OJ:L:2009:211:0036:0054:en:PDF

http://eur-lex.europa.eu/LexUriServ/LexUriServ.do?uri=OJ:L:2009:211:0001:0014:EN:PDF

An Energy Policy for Europe (EU Commission program) (2007): https://eur-lex.europa.eu/
legal-content/EN/TXT/?uri=LEGISSUM%3Al27067

Lisbon Treaty (signed 2007); http://www.europarl.europa.eu/ftu/pdf/en/FTU_1.1.5.pdf

European Energy Security Strategy (2014): https://www.eesc.europa.eu/resources/docs/
european-energy-security-strategy.pdf

Energy Union Package: A Framework Strategy for a Resilient Energy Union with a Forward
Looking Climate Policy (2015): https://europa.eu/rapid/press-release_IP-15-4497_en.htm

The Energy Union Communication (COM/2015/080 final): http://eur-lex.europa.eu/resource.
html?uri=cellar:1bd46c90-bdd4-11e4-bbe1-01aa75ed71a1.0001.03/DOC_1&format=PDF

EU Energy Diplomacy Action Plan (2015): http://data.consilium.europa.eu/doc/document/
ST-13174-2015-INIT/en/pdf

Sustainable Energy Security Package (February 2016): https://europa.eu/rapid/press-release_IP-16-307_en.htm

Clean and Secure Energy for all Europeans (November 2016): https://ec.europa.eu/energy/en/topics/energy-strategy-and-energy-union/clean-energy-all-europeans

New governance scheme under the Clean Energy for All Europeans Package: https://ec.europa.eu/energy/en/topics/energy-strategy-and-energy-union/governance-energy-union

Appendix of Relevant Internet Sources and Further Reading

EUR-Lex, Access to European Law: https://eur-lex.europa.eu/summary/chapter/energy.html?root_default=SUM_1_CODED=18

European Commission: Energy Topics (Overview): https://ec.europa.eu/energy/en/topics

European Commission: Energy market analysis: https://ec.europa.eu/energy/en/data-analysis/market-analysis

European Commission: Energy Union indicators: https://ec.europa.eu/energy/en/data-analysis/energy-union-indicators

European Commission: Renewable energy—Moving toward a low carbon economy: https://ec.europa.eu/energy/en/topics/renewable-energy

European Commission: Energy Efficiency—Saving energy, saving money: https://ec.europa.eu/energy/en/topics/energy-efficiency

European Commission: Imports and secure supplies—Diverse, affordable, and reliable energy: https://ec.europa.eu/energy/en/topics/imports-and-secure-supplies

European Council: Energy: http://www.consilium.europa.eu/en/topics/energy/

European Council: Tackling climate change in the EU: http://www.consilium.europa.eu/en/policies/climate-change/

European Parliament: Energy policy—general principles: http://www.europarl.europa.eu/atyourservice/en/displayFtu.html?ftuId=FTU_2.4.7.html

European Parliament: Renewable energy: http://www.europarl.europa.eu/atyourservice/en/displayFtu.html?ftuId=FTU_2.4.9.html

European Parliament: Energy efficiency: http://www.europarl.europa.eu/atyourservice/en/displayFtu.html?ftuId=FTU_2.4.8.html

European Parliament: Nuclear energy: http://www.europarl.europa.eu/atyourservice/en/displayFtu.html?ftuId=FTU_2.4.10.html

European External Action Service: Climate, Environment & Energy: https://eeas.europa.eu/topics/climate-environment-energy/42455/climate-environment-energy_en

European External Action Service: Energy Diplomacy: https://eeas.europa.eu/topics/energy-diplomacy/406/eu-energy-diplomacy_en

....

CHAPTER 20

THE ENERGY POLITICS
OF RUSSIA AND EURASIA

....

MARGARITA BALMACEDA AND ANDREAS HEINRICH

As one of the world's largest fossil fuel exporters, Russia is a key player in the global energy arena. It also plays a unique role in Eurasia, understood here as a region defined not only by physical features such as infrastructures that survived the dissolution of the Soviet Union in 1991 but also by economic and political legacies (Gleason 2010, 26).[1] As the biggest producer, exporter, consumer, and therefore polluter, as well as an important transit country, Russia is also the main player in former Soviet Union (FSU) energy policies (see Table 20.1). This role has been modified—but not erased—by the breakup of its unified energy structures; however, infrastructures and trade relationships still bind the former Soviet republics together—cooperatively as well as via conflict. These infrastructural dependencies left Russia in a dominant position vis-à-vis the other post-Soviet states because it continues to control most of the pipeline infrastructure and thereby also the energy exports of the other FSU producers. This unique role enabled Russia, at least throughout the early 2000s, to de facto dictate the main terms of energy (especially gas) governance. (For analysis of regionalism literature, see Hancock, Palestini, and Szulecki in this volume.)

The overarching narrative of energy relations in the region is a story of how these ties have been progressively eroding, but also of how the tension between economic and political imperatives—a tension in both Russia and the other states—has affected these relationships. Thus, policies in the region are often understood as the result of the interaction of inherited infrastructures, economic and ecological imperatives, and political considerations. In the case of rising producers such as Azerbaijan, Kazakhstan, Turkmenistan, and Uzbekistan, this tension manifested itself in their attempts to establish independent export routes and shake loose from Russian marketing arrangements (as local ruling elites came to enjoy increased revenues from direct exports). In the case of consumer states, such as Ukraine, this strain expressed itself first and foremost as rent-seeking, which limited the country's ability to set a truly independent and proactive energy policy (Balmaceda 2008). As for Russia, this tension showed itself in the interdependence between various "uses" of

Table 20.1 Production, Import, and Export of Crude Oil, Natural Gas and Coal in Eurasia, 2007–2015

		Crude Oil (Thousand Metric Tons)			Natural Gas (Terajoules)			Coal[a] (Thousand Metric Tons of Coal Equivalent)		
		Production	Import	Export	Production	Import	Export	Production	Import	Export
Armenia	2007	N/A	N/A	N/A	N/A	77,436	980	N/A	5	0
	2008	N/A	N/A	N/A	N/A	84,975	1,206	N/A	5	0
	2009	N/A	N/A	N/A	N/A	65,601	1,192	N/A	1	0
	2010	N/A	N/A	N/A	N/A	63,761	0	N/A	5	0
	2011	N/A	N/A	N/A	N/A	80,469	4,143	0	3	0
	2012	N/A	N/A	N/A	N/A	95,532	2,710	0	2	0
	2013	N/A	N/A	N/A	N/A	91,953	2,079	0	1	0
	2014	N/A	N/A	N/A	N/A	91,295	707	0	1	1
	2015	N/A	N/A	N/A	N/A	89,224	4,938	1	1	1
Azerbaijan	2007	41,342	0	34,780	421,780	0	71,003	N/A	N/A	N/A
	2008	42,190	0	36,858	636,110	0	204,826	N/A	N/A	N/A
	2009	48,354	1	44,332	635,663	0	228,449	N/A	N/A	N/A
	2010	48,581	0	44,508	651,236	0	241,672	N/A	N/A	N/A
	2011	43,445	N/A	37,268	638,553	0	266,272	N/A	6	N/A
	2012	41,015	N/A	34,728	673,082	N/A	258,460	N/A	5	N/A
	2013	40,726	N/A	34,260	698,627	N/A	285,450	N/A	5	N/A
	2014	39,443	N/A	32,903	735,031	N/A	316,112	N/A	2	N/A
	2015	39,035	N/A	32,843	751,362	N/A	318,152	N/A	1	N/A

		Crude Oil (Thousand Metric Tons)			Natural Gas (Terajoules)			Coal[a] (Thousand Metric Tons of Coal Equivalent)		
		Production	Import	Export	Production	Import	Export	Production	Import	Export
Belarus	2007	1,760	20,036	851	7,763	796,579	N/A	81z5	133	148
	2008	1,740	21,461	1,453	7,840	813,418	N/A	768	111	234
	2009	1,720	21,509	1,716	7,918	680,404	N/A	719	115	330
	2010	1,700	14,739	0	8,226	833,077	N/A	764	112	259
	2011	1,682	20,436	1,676	8,574	772,363	N/A	980	181	115
	2012	1,660	21,669	1,645	8,420	782,173	N/A	930	458	132
	2013	1,645	21,261	1,619	8,806	782,482	N/A	812	584	55
	2014	1,645	22,508	1,617	8,574	774,448	N/A	513	747	39
	2015	1,645	22,919	1,615	8,690	725,707	N/A	350	641	65
Georgia	2007	64	14	58	623	66,492	N/A	16	131	4
	2008	52	37	35	483	57,166	N/A	48	221	3
	2009	53	5	60	420	45,928	N/A	141	96	3
	2010	50	5	58	271	42,416	N/A	227	144	13
	2011	49	3	49	202	70,135	N/A	202	199	9
	2012	44	0	37	202	76,462	N/A	241	197	4
	2013	48	0	57	183	64,371	N/A	231	229	4
	2014	43	10	51	399	84,913	N/A	175	241	1
	2015	40	133	153	442	97,253	3,889	177	218	2

(continued)

Table 20.1 Production, Import, and Export of Crude Oil, Natural Gas and Coal in Eurasia, 2007–2015 (Continued)

		Crude Oil (Thousand Metric Tons)			Natural Gas (Terajoules)			Coal[a] (Thousand Metric Tons of Coal Equivalent)		
		Production	Import	Export	Production	Import	Export	Production	Import	Export
Kazakhstan	2007	55,265	7,050	46,36	1,153,500	249,025	303,341	61,790	1,048	16,897
	2008	58,646	3,187	48,979	1,283,362	241,873	243,438	69,780	865	20,962
	2009	64,354	6,029	57,030	1,402,492	84,069	258,345	63,260	780	18,124
	2010	68,084	5,978	52,800	1,459,620	137,089	243,105	69,353	875	19,670
	2011	67,765	4,526	57,621	1,542,539	176,296	237,129	72,708	771	19,221
	2012	66,475	5,919	57,943	1,572,507	169,698	418,484	75,376	921	20,417
	2013	69,483	7,494	58,078	1,654,686	201,109	398,355	74,913	845	21,181
	2014	67,908	969	53,879	1,694,994	162,714	409,593	71,343	1,054	19,300
	2015	79,457	74	63,581	1,551,868	227,408	495,794	67,300	843	19,493
Kyrgyzstan	2007	69	58	0	581	29,308	N/A	162	385	0
	2008	71	126	53	663	28,135	N/A	203	346	15
	2009	77	11	6	588	25,009	N/A	248	302	0
	2010	83	15	3	872	17,585	N/A	235	339	0
	2011	77	14	2	1,038	11,905	N/A	430	655	19
	2012	79	6	0	1,132	15,452	N/A	603	897	8
	2013	84	0	1	1,288	11,433	N/A	738	907	97
	2014	82	60	0	1,249	9,248	N/A	941	920	152
	2015	107	224	0	1,154	9,522	N/A	1,011	972	149

		Crude Oil (Thousand Metric Tons)			Natural Gas (Terajoules)			Coal[a] (Thousand Metric Tons of Coal Equivalent)		
		Production	Import	Export	Production	Import	Export	Production	Import	Export
Moldova	2007	8	N/A	N/A	4	44,199	0	N/A	114	N/A
	2008	15	N/A	N/A	5	41,541	0	N/A	131	N/A
	2009	17	N/A	N/A	8	38,158	0	N/A	87	N/A
	2010	11	N/A	N/A	3	40,218	0	N/A	118	N/A
	2011	13	0	N/A	2	39,011	N/A	N/A	131	N/A
	2012	11	0	N/A	4	37,091	N/A	N/A	150	N/A
	2013	1	1	N/A	4	34,921	N/A	N/A	217	N/A
	2014	8	0	N/A	3	35,655	N/A	N/A	120	N/A
	2015	7	0	N/A	3	34,146	N/A	N/A	135	N/A
Russia	2007	468,174	2,693	258,579	24,283,317	278,603	7,210,955	232,777	20,763	91,681
	2008	469,470	2,456	243,098	24,878,778	297,467	7,342,290	238,819	26,898	89,189
	2009	476,709	1,784	248,899	22,073,061	310,620	6,328,479	219,472	20,738	95,984
	2010	484,687	0	243,260	25,128,116	162,745	7,172,216	257,184	21,853	119,822
	2011	491,937	N/A	244,490	25,720,226	304,846	7,690,500	234,639	27,505	113,164
	2012	497,425	N/A	236,716	25,157,696	307,331	7,388,394	263,451	26,093	118,693
	2013	497,483	N/A	233,686	25,786,288	313,371	8,099,677	263,248	25,039	127,480
	2014	503,092	756	222,846	24,717,453	328,549	7,247,337	271,061	22,723	140,360
	2015	510,230	2,862	244,521	24,391,734	336,386	7,674,559	286,103	20,429	139,806

(continued)

Table 20.1 Production, Import, and Export of Crude Oil, Natural Gas and Coal in Eurasia, 2007–2015 (Continued)

		Crude Oil (Thousand Metric Tons)			Natural Gas (Terajoules)			Coal[a] (Thousand Metric Tons of Coal Equivalent)		
		Production	Import	Export	Production	Import	Export	Production	Import	Export
Tajikistan	2007	12	N/A	2	551	24,596	N/A	109	6	0
	2008	14	N/A	2	1,349	19,494	N/A	120	7	1
	2009	26	N/A	4	1,444	15,450	N/A	122	9	0
	2010	27	N/A	4	1,558	12,245	N/A	121	12	0
	2011	28	N/A	0	703	6,840	N/A	142	10	14
	2012	30	N/A	0	422	5,054	N/A	249	15	1
	2013	27	N/A	4	144	N/A	N/A	323	7	N/A
	2014	25	N/A	N/A	122	N/A	N/A	549	8	1
	2015	25	N/A	N/A	156	N/A	N/A	653	8	N/A
Turkmenistan	2007	9,000	N/A	1,900	2,609,794	N/A	1,799,728	N/A	N/A	N/A
	2008	10,178	N/A	2,400	2,671,175	N/A	1,856,562	N/A	N/A	N/A
	2009	9,250	N/A	2,000	1,445,465	N/A	744,226	N/A	N/A	N/A
	2010	8,700	N/A	1,800	1,716,372	N/A	909,668	N/A	N/A	N/A
	2011	10,465	N/A	2,300	2,508,631	N/A	1,620,432	N/A	N/A	N/A
	2012	10,903	N/A	3,100	2,616,235	N/A	1,700,139	N/A	N/A	N/A
	2013	11,651	N/A	3,600	2,972,013	N/A	2,031,476	N/A	N/A	N/A
	2014	11,800	N/A	3,200	3,033,014	N/A	2,078,710	N/A	N/A	N/A
	2015	12,050	N/A	3,450	3,171,309	N/A	2,178,093	N/A	N/A	N/A

		Crude Oil (Thousand Metric Tons)			Natural Gas (Terajoules)			Coal[a] (Thousand Metric Tons of Coal Equivalent)		
		Production	Import	Export	Production	Import	Export	Production	Import	Export
Ukraine	2007	3,310	9,808	4	738,239	1,954,395	156	48,018	13,347	3,566
	2008	3,184	6,568	9	750,124	2,010,286	192	48,073	12,277	4,779
	2009	2,904	7,182	8	751,685	1,426,247	178	44,751	7,097	5,430
	2010	2,582	7,765	0	717,826	1,375,095	214	44,307	10,866	6,315
	2011	2,438	5,679	0	722,386	1,683,533	0	56,096	11,236	7,686
	2012	2,290	1,522	0	716,824	1,237,329	0	57,628	14,180	7,419
	2013	2,172	729	0	745,543	1,051,134	0	58,440	12,984	8,950
	2014	2,042	179	41	700,102	731,493	N/A	46,225	14,820	6,926
	2015	1,877	227	8	689,341	618,333	N/A	24,914	14,199	616
Uzbekistan	2007	3,363	N/A	N/A	2,463,465	49,882	555,498	1,365	77	13
	2008	3,259	N/A	N/A	2,554,536	39,906	566,835	1,316	100	12
	2009	3,187	N/A	N/A	2,503,446	31,925	574,393	1,432	77	14
	2010	2,891	N/A	N/A	2,271,497	25,540	544,162	1,302	46	13
	2011	3,550	N/A	N/A	2,388,523	N/A	454,668	1,930	50	20
	2012	3,165	N/A	N/A	2,383,597	N/A	386,468	1,935	65	20
	2013	2,997	N/A	N/A	2,259,321	N/A	511,502	2,072	10	20
	2014	2,821	N/A	N/A	2,339,267	N/A	556,968	2,253	N/A	21
	2015	2,736	N/A	N/A	2,356,531	N/A	609,389	2,028	N/A	19

[a] Coal includes hard coal, brown coal, oil shale, and peat.
Sources: UN (2013, 2016, 2017).

energy policy: for economic development, safeguarding of political stability, and rewarding of loyal elites, but also for external political pressure.

Despite all the energy changes in the region since 1991, these tensions among inherited infrastructures, economic imperatives, and politics remain the central explanatory narrative in the literature. Given Russia's role as most important player in the region, this chapter puts it at the center of this narrative, discussing other key states in the region as they have an impact on Eurasia's broader energy relationships, particularly with the West. Domestic politics often also have international effects and repercussions. Therefore we discuss the relationship between energy and international as well as national politics in the Eurasian states.

Current Research

The literature on the politics of energy in Russia and Eurasia is far from even in quality nor focus. First, the focus differs significantly based on whether the scholars are from Russia/Eurasia or Europe and the United States. Much of the Russian literature focuses on policy and technical rather than theoretical issues, concentrating on issues such as the development of energy prices (Sitnikova 2009), the situation of specific companies (Balabin 2015), forecasts of future production (Makarov et al. 2014), the impact of the fuel and energy sector on regional development (Belousova 2015), the challenges of developing mature oil and gas fields (Khusainov and Afanasiev 2012), and issues of refinery capacity (Kryukov, Silkin, and Shmat 2012). In many cases these issues are approached more from a practical policy-oriented perspective (Kryukov, Tokarev, and Shmat 2016). More theoretical work exists concerning issues such as the development of natural monopolies (Bozo and Shmat 2011; Ulanov 2011) and the relationship between companies and the state (Pusenkova 2010; Yakovlev 2006), but it has become increasingly less visible as the Russian government has increased pressure on the sector and narrowed the space for open discussion.

Western scholars mostly cover the availability of resources (asking "can Russia produce enough?") (Sagers 2007; Söderbergh, Jakobsson, and Aleklett 2010; Solanko and Sutela 2009) and energy security (energy demand and supply management, forecasts, conflicts with transit countries, overreliance on one supplier) (Kaveshnikov 2010; Kazantsev 2012; Stulberg 2017; Yafimava 2011; Youngs 2009). As a result, they have mainly focused on large exporters and transit countries and on the most important fuels for Western energy markets and security issues in the West: oil and natural gas. Countries that are neither exporters nor transit countries (or transit countries that have not caused conflicts), as well as possessing less-developed energy technologies (such as some renewables) or traditionally less prominent fuels in Western politics of energy (such as coal) have received less attention (Hughes and Lipcsy 2013). Consequently, most Western analyses of energy politics in the region have focused on Russia, Kazakhstan, and Azerbaijan (and to a lesser degree Ukraine) and on oil and gas.

It is also interesting to note the ups and downs of academic interest in specific subregions. For example, after the Soviet Union broke up, the Caspian Sea region (and in particular Kazakhstan and Azerbaijan) was considered a "last frontier" for energy production and an alternative to Russian energy resources. This led to an increased interest in the region and related issues, such as ownership and potential transit route conflicts (Shaffer 2010).

In this chapter we organize the literature into three categories: an overview of the major energy players in the region, an assessment of concrete literature on related issues (such as governance, resource curse, justice, energy security and conflict, and environment/renewable energy), and a discussion of how the tension between economic and political imperatives has manifested itself in each of these areas and debates about them.

Markets, Trade, and Ownership: Main Players

Any discussion of trade in the region needs to start with a consideration of the main players. In the Russian gas sector, these are Gazprom, the majority-state-owned natural gas giant, as well a number of "independent" gas producers, whose role has increased significantly in recent years as a result of good connections to President Vladimir Putin's inner circle (such as Novatek), and oil companies producing natural gas as a by-product of oil production, such as Lukoil and Rosneft (Lunden et al. 2013). Other key actors are in the electricity sector, which relies primarily on natural gas. After the privatization of the state monopoly Unified Energy System of Russia (RAO UES), the electricity sector was divided among multiple providers, with Gazprom (owning over 20 percent of Russia's generation capacity) sharing the market with both national and foreign companies (Wengle 2015). In the oil sector, the main players have been Rosneft and Lukoil, as well as Yukos, which was disbanded in 2004.[2] In addition, oil pipeline monopolist Transneft has played a key role (see Table 20.2).

Table 20.2 Key Players in the Russian Energy Sector

	Primary Energy Type production	Secondary Energy Type Production	Ownership
Gazprom	Natural gas	Oil (through GazpromNeft); electricity (through ownership of generation capacity)	Majority state owned
Novatek	Natural gas	N/A	Independent
LUKoil	Oil	Natural gas (associated gas produced as by-product of oil production)	Private
Rosneft	Oil	Natural gas (associated gas produced as by-product of oil production)	Majority state owned
Rosatom	Nuclear energy	N/A	State owned

To understand the role of these actors, it is important to keep in mind the different institutional trajectories of the natural gas and oil sectors. Whereas the state retained control over a monopolized gas sector after 1991, the oil sector was (partially) privatized in the "loans-for-shares" program of the mid-1990s (in which the cash-strapped state put oil and other strategic industries up as collateral for large loans) into eleven vertically integrated companies. (See Appendix: Chronology of Main Energy Events for Russia and Eurasia, 1992–2018). In 2003–2004, after the virtual destruction of Yukos, the state was able to regain its key role in the sector. As a result, although oil exports generate significantly more revenue than gas exports, the latter have been more politically prominent both in Russian politics and in the scholarly literature (Stern 2009, 54–55). Since 2010 the strict division between the oil and gas sectors has been somewhat erased with the increased political weight of Rosneft and rising gas production by oil companies.

Company-State Relationships

The key role of players such as Gazprom, Russia's natural gas giant and largest company overall, and the growing roles of the state and state-supported actors in the oil sector since the turnaround signified by the dismantlement of Yukos in 2004, have been a major focus of the literature on company-state relationships. Different approaches to this issue also represent different visions of Russian domestic politics. Some authors have explained the attack on Yukos and increased state involvement in the oil sector from a new institutionalism perspective, noting the institutional incoherence between Russia's liberal governance structure at the time and the reality of frail market institutions and a weak rule of law, both of which led to short-term-focused strategies (such as asset stripping and lack of investment) by the newly privatized companies (Locatelli and Rossiaud 2011). With market incentives not sufficient to move oil companies to more long-term-focused strategies (Tompson 2010), a more direct state intervention in the area, such as the takeover of Yukos in 2004, was seen as largely unavoidable. Other authors, on the contrary, have interpreted Putin's assault on Yukos as mainly driven by political agendas (Fortescue 2006; Sakwa 2009, 2013) and the desire to destroy its owner, Mikhail Khodorkovsky, as a potential competitor for Putin's power.

The dynamics have been different in the natural gas industry, largely due to Gazprom's survival as a unified organization and virtual sector monopolist through the first two post-Soviet decades. Scholars have analyzed a system wherein Gazprom could accrue "points" with the Russian state through services provided domestically (providing subsidized gas as well as social services) or internationally (helping manage the relationship with Russia's neighboring states through price manipulations), "points" that could later be converted into advantages in other areas, such as monopoly rights on (pipeline) gas exports, access to credits, privileges in privatization contracts, and preferential access to especially strategic gas fields (Balmaceda 2006). However, since around 2013 Gazprom's export monopoly has been challenged by the rise of so-called independent (i.e., non-Gazprom) producers allowed to export liquefied natural gas (LNG), whose owners are widely believed to be close private associates of President Putin (Henderson 2014).

While the conventional narrative would argue that the changes in the Russian oil (and gas) sector after 2001 (with a change in Gazprom's leadership), including but not limited to Yukos's takeover, represented an increased level of *state* control over the sector or an instance of resource nationalism (Domjan and Stone 2010), others have presented a different reading of the situation. While state ownership in both sectors formally increased, this situation did not necessarily result in increased state (if one understands "state" as an entity with separate interests from the private interests of individual leaders) *control* of the sector. Three sets of issues have been key here. First is the coexistence of state, corporate, and personal, within-the-corporation interests in majority state-owned corporations such as Gazprom (Balmaceda 2013, ch. 3) and the ability of top managers to misuse their positions for personal power. Despite attempts by foreign shareholders in Gazprom to improve its governance structure, structural problems have persisted (Milov and Nemtsov 2008); this situation is part of broader principal-agent problems between the leadership of companies such as Rosneft and the state (Locatelli and Rossiaud 2011).

A second constraint on the state's ability to control the sector relates to competition among different factions (also within company leadership) with different agendas (Heinrich 2008), as reflected, for example, in often contradictory taxation regimes, which have limited the state's ability to steer the sector's long-term development.

Third, there is an increased concern that what is being presented as "state interests" may actually concern the private interests and "business capture" by close-to-the-Kremlin elites (Vahtra, Liuhto, and Lorentz 2007; Milov and Nemtsov 2008) and that the "statization" of the energy industry may be a veil covering what in actuality has been a process of private takeover of formally state property (Balmaceda 2013, ch. 3). For example, the rise of Rosneft may be interpreted not only in terms of an increase in state property, but also in terms of its control by close allies of Putin, such as Igor Sechin, with important private economic interests.

Russia's system of oil export duties, a unique feature of Russian oil sector governance not seen in other states, is telling for the competition between different factions and agendas in terms of state policies toward oil companies. In addition to their role in revenue collection, export taxes were also intended to fulfill several domestic goals, often in competition: to retain an instrument of leverage vis-à-vis companies and appropriate some of their rents by targeting companies' gross revenues rather than profits (Gaddy and Ickes 2009; Mitrova 2016, 26) and steering the balance of refined oil products exports to both ensure sufficient domestic supplies of gasoline in situations where their deficit threatened to spark social tensions (Gustafson 2012, 377), and to pursue broader objectives concerning modernization of the highly outdated refinery system. Between 2001 and 2011 this system not only created a confrontation between oil companies and the Ministry of Finance's desire to maximize export revenue but actually backfired: taxing revenues instead of profits—at an extremely high rate (Alexeev and Conrad 2009)—acted as a disincentive on new investments, and while the preferential treatment of some oil products over others actually subsidized production at outdated refineries, needed investments in the modernization of the mid- and upstream sectors were neglected.

Changes since 2011 have sought to reduce some of these imbalances, allowing oil companies to keep more of their revenue for investment (Fattouh and Henderson 2012). The taxation of Russian oil (and gas) exports to the FSU has also been subject to a variety of complex and changing regulations involving country-of-origin or country-of-destination application of taxes (Shiells 2005) and has been a key issue in Russian-led integration efforts (see "Eurasian Economic Union" later in this chapter).

While this chapter focuses on Russia as the key actor in the region, it is worth noting the situation in other energy-rich, post-Soviet states such as Kazakhstan and Uzbekistan. Much of the literature has paid attention to direct and indirect control of the energy sector by rulers' families and close associates (Radnitz 2012). In energy-rich countries of the region, well-connected elites have been able to transform the post-Soviet energy exports boom into personal gain.

Globalization and Energy Trade

Although control by the state or actors close to the political leadership has increased, it has simultaneously coincided with an increasingly globalized role of Russian energy companies. Russian oil companies in particular were able to internationalize their production and refining activities. One such example is LUKoil, which expanded its refining capacities to various European Union (EU) locations in the 2000s not only to be geographically closer to sale markets, but also to have access to more efficient refining facilities within an increasingly competitive and globalized oil refining market (Balmaceda and Westphal forthcoming; Grätz 2013; Heinrich 2005). Some authors (see Heinrich 2003) have emphasized the unique nature of the globalization strategies of Russian companies such as Gazprom: acting according to one set of standards at home and in the FSU and to another, globalizing set farther abroad.

Research on the impact of globalization of energy relationships in the region has focused on three key themes: (1) the impact of globalization on company strategies, (2) the effects of global energy price fluctuations on the ability of the Russian government to use export revenues for domestic goals, and (3) how global trends such as the demand for standards of corporate behavior and decarbonization imperatives (Lachapelle, MacNeil, and Paterson 2017; Stern 2017) are affecting energy players in the area.

A key factor has been how the use of new production technologies elsewhere has affected Eurasian energy politics. Thus the "unconventionals revolution" (increased hydrocarbon production through hydraulic fracturing, opening up of shale gas and oil resources, and use of tar sands; for more on unconventionals, see Tutuncu in this volume) has impacted Russia's energy role (Kropatcheva 2014). The growing unconventional natural gas production in the United States drove down prices for natural gas in that country, leading many domestic coal users to replace coal with natural gas, creating a surplus of low-priced coal, much of which found a market in Europe. This lower-price surplus coal (whose import prices in Europe fell more than 50 percent from March 2008 to May 2014; IEA 2014, 223) drove a temporary increase in coal use in the EU, including by many of Russia's traditional natural gas customers. In addition, this increased pressure on the Russian oil and gas industry to modernize its production and sectoral organization (Ćwiek-Karpowicz 2012; Gustafson 2012). Although in a more limited manner, there has also been a discussion of the impact of the unconventionals boom on the Central Asian energy producers' ability to continue to generate significant export revenues to continue as stable rentier states (Auping et al. 2016).

Returning to the central theme of the tension between political and economic imperatives, the possible impact of unconventional exploration on energy consumer states in the region has been contested. Some authors argue that increased supplies from the United States could diametrically change these states' dependency on energy supplies from Russia (O'Sullivan 2017). More cautious voices, however, have noted the governance-related and regulatory hurdles to new production in countries such as Ukraine (Georgiev 2016), and they argue that potential supplies from the United States in and of themselves do not solve the issue of the cost of imports (Goldthau and Boersma 2014).

One particular issue of energy trade and globalization is the rise (mid-1990s) and fall (starting around 2006) of cooperation between Russian and foreign companies, with the examples of failed cooperation around the Sakhalin I and II natural gas projects (Bradshaw 2010), as well the short-lived merger between TNK (Tyumen Oil Company) and BP oil companies (Ekin and King 2009), serving as prime examples. Most authors see regulatory mismatches as the reason, making institutional collaboration with foreign companies unable to survive the heavy shadow of politics and nationalization on Russia's energy policies (Henderson and Ferguson 2014; Locatelli 2006). Again, the tension between economic and political imperatives has been central in this question.

Energy and Governance

It was these tensions between Russian and foreign companies that inspired the creation of new energy governance initiatives in the 1990s, such as the Energy Charter Treaty (ECT) that was signed in December 1994 and entered into legal force in April 1998, to assure safe conditions for cross-border investment in energy resource development (originally by Western companies in Eastern Europe and Russia). The ECT also calls for equal access to energy transit infrastructure; that is, third parties' access cannot be blocked, and only transit fees can be charged (Axelrod 1996). These transit provisions should be supplemented (and extended) by a "transit protocol" within the ECT.

At a time of economic depression and political instability for the Eurasian countries, the international parties brought these reform ideas forward; the Eurasian countries remained largely passive recipients. Nevertheless, the ECT started with strong support from both the EU and Russia. However, Russia's attitude toward the ECT soon cooled; it was concerned that the ECT might be detrimental to the country's position as energy exporter by strengthening competition. In 2011 negotiations on the ECT's key transit protocol were suspended by Russia and others (Belyi 2013; Konoplyanik 2010); in 2014, Russia ceased its direct involvement in all ECT activities.

Kyoto and Paris Agreements

International treaties concerning environmental issues and carbon emissions have been an important part of international energy governance affecting the post-Soviet space. As one of the most energy- and carbon-intensive countries in the world, a significant emitter of greenhouse gases (GHG),[3] and fossil fuels exporter, Russia plays a crucial role in achieving a comprehensive solution to climate change.

The Kyoto Protocol, signed in December 1997, is an international climate agreement to fight global warming/climate change by reducing GHG emissions. Signatories agreed to a broad outline of emission targets and established an emission trading regime; countries that reduced carbon emissions under their base-year level (1990) would be able to sell "emission rights" to ones that emitted more than their allocations. The emission targets adopted for transition countries, such as Russia and Ukraine, far exceed their likely level of emissions, enabling them to sell their surplus (e.g., Korppoo, Karas, and Grubb 2006; Victor, Nakićenović, and Victor 2001). Russian climate politics was dominated by the sale of surplus emission rights; this revenue flow has rivaled its earnings from natural gas exports (Henry and Sundstrom McIntosh 2007). Russia's support for the Kyoto climate regime was also fueled by a desire to appear as a responsible global player, provided that positive distributional implications and domestic support from economic interest groups and top government bureaucracies persist (Andonova and Alexieva 2012).

However, the relatively easy terms they received under the Kyoto Protocol did not encourage Eurasian countries to engage forcefully in actual measures to curb carbon emissions, as their primary concern was advancing unconstrained economic growth (Andonova and Alexieva 2012; Falkner 2016). Under the 2015 Paris Climate Change Agreement, successor to the Kyoto Protocol, Russia made new pledges to limit GHG emissions, but its nationally determined contribution targets are still weak (Nosko 2017; Rogelj et al. 2017). Ukraine has so far not developed any legislative or policy frameworks to implement its emission targets (Soloviy 2017).

In most FSU states, technically outdated energy sectors cause huge energy wastage and carbon emissions. This situation is regarded by countries importing Eurasian energy as an increasing threat to energy security and as a major barrier to global climate change policy (Garbuzova and Madlener 2012; Henry and Sundstrom McIntosh 2014). Changing trade patterns due to restrictions on fossil fuel imports by Western consumers are considered a danger by the Russian government. So far, however, Russia has largely ignored the renewable energy business, which would also offer a chance to free the country of its dependence on fossil fuel exports (i.e., the resource curse). Instead, Russia plans to increase its coal production and launch new coal-fired plants until 2030 (Nosko 2017).

Eurasian Economic Union

Russia-led governance initiatives have also affected energy relationships in the region, as Russia has sought to use its energy resources as a stimulus for economic (and political) integration in Eurasia (e.g., Nygren 2008). Evolving from a series of unsuccessful regional integration attempts (cf. Dragneva and Wolczuk 2013; Dutkiewicz and Sakwa 2015), the Eurasian Economic Union (EAEU) came into force in January 2015 and, as of mid-2018, included Armenia, Belarus, Kazakhstan, Kyrgyzstan, and Russia. The EAEU, in an attempt to emulate the EU, seeks to establish a customs union (especially the elimination of nontariff barriers), a single market for goods and services (e.g., for energy), and mutual trade and investment flows, along with policy coordination among member states (Di Gregorio and Di Gregorio 2017; Vinokurov 2017). However, the EAEU was made possible by bilateral deals initiated by Russia rather than any particular enthusiasm for integration by the other member states (Dragneva and Wolczuk 2017). Already since 2014, for instance, Russia has made its discounts for oil and gas deliveries to Belarus conditional on the country's participation in the EAEU; Belarus has expressed dissatisfaction with the lack of a common energy market, which would allow it to purchase Russian oil at the lower domestic price, its key motivation to join the EAEU (Balkunets 2016; Kardaś and Kłysiński 2017).

Indeed, the EAEU's success in creating a single energy market has been limited at best. While it succeeded in harmonizing external customs tariffs and abolishing internal customs borders, it has made little progress on reducing nontariff barriers (Tarr 2016; Vinokurov 2017) or in establishing a supranational decision-making process, as Russia has refused to be constrained by the EAEU (Dragneva and Wolczuk 2017). Roberts (2017) explains this with the authoritarian member states' concerns over regime stability, which create antagonism and result in their inability to coordinate policy.

Energy and the Resource Curse

In addition to issues on the international level, domestic governance issues have been key in the region in terms of whether energy resource revenues can be managed soundly (Busse and Gröning 2013; Collier and Hoeffler 2009; Mehlum, Moene, and Torvik 2006; Robinson, Torvik, and Verdier 2006; Ross 2018). The term "resource curse" refers to the paradox that resource-rich countries (due to a lack of proper governance) have in general been unsuccessful in translating that wealth into economic development, social prosperity, and political stability (for an overview of the phenomenon in Eurasia see Gel'man and Marganiya 2010; Heinrich and Pleines 2012; Najman, Pomfret, and Raballand 2008).

In many cases, domestic institutions and practices in the FSU could not prevent the effects of the resource curse, especially worsening terms of trade, a price/revenue volatility, and the "Dutch disease"[4] (Ahrend 2005; Algieri 2011; Dülger et al. 2013). In a related development, the expansion of state ownership has often crowded out other investors (Heinrich 2008; Jones Luong and Weinthal 2001, 2010; Kalyuzhnova and Nygaard 2008; Vivoda 2009).

In addition, corruption, loose fiscal policies, and subsidies have been highly problematic. While such policies have been successful in the short term in terms of promoting social quiescence and increasing regime stability (Kendall-Taylor 2012), their long-term effects are more nefarious; large and untargeted energy subsidies to households and enterprises have led to overconsumption and waste (e.g., Azerbaijan, Russia, Turkmenistan). The scale and ease of natural resource rent extraction has led governments to postpone reform while simultaneously subsidizing uncompetitive manufacturing sectors (Auty 1997, 2003; Petri and Taube 2003). Energy-related corruption and rent-seeking by powerful interest groups in fossil fuel–producing countries further undermine their socioeconomic development by wasteful spending and crowding out innovation (Pleines 2012; Suslov 2014).

While the establishment of sovereign wealth funds (state-owned entities for the management of balance-of-payment surpluses, e.g., from commodity exports) in Azerbaijan, Kazakhstan, Russia, and Turkmenistan has helped mitigate some of the worse effects of the resource curse, there exist significant interregional income and wage disparities caused by the uneven distribution of natural resource rents. Resource-rich regions are significantly richer than other regions (Alexeev and Chernyavskiy 2015), yet hydrocarbons represent one of the leading determinants of an increased gap between the rich and poor in the producing regions (Buccellato and Mickiewicz 2009).

Energy and Justice

There has been relatively little written on the issue of energy justice (see Fuller in this volume) in Russia and Eurasia. A steady stream of research exists on energy justice issues in the Arctic, but this literature deals with Russia only indirectly (McCauley et al. 2016). The topic has been discussed in an indirect manner, first and foremost through the issue of whether the inhabitants (and in particular indigenous populations) of the main oil and gas production regions in Russia have received any positive results from energy production in their native areas, including environmental sustainability (Ogneva-Himmelberger and Agyeman 2009) and access to more reliable energy supplies (Nalimov and Rudenko 2015) as part of benefit-sharing agreements (Sirina 2010; Tysiachniouk and Petrov 2018). A comparative study on the Nenets and the Komi-Izhemtsi groups' ability to reach benefit-sharing agreements with LUKoil, for example, showed the importance of a group's domestic legal status (with officially recognized groups such as the Nenets finding an easier path to compensation for land and environmental damage) as well as partnerships with global environmentalist groups. The Komi-Izhemtsi, for example, recognized by international but not by Russian law, have been able to use international organizations and transnational networks to pressure LUKoil into a benefits-sharing agreement (on legal issues see Novikova 2016; Tysiachniouk et al. 2017).

A second way in which the issue of energy justice has been treated indirectly is through the issue of corporate social responsibility (CSR) (for an in-depth discussion of CSR, see Steinberg in this volume). This literature examines how Russian energy companies have adapted increasingly globalized models of CSR, both building upon and yet differing clearly from the "company as main provider" expectations of the Soviet period (Henry et al. 2016; Tysiachniouk et al. 2018). Other research sheds light on the issue of how Russian oil and gas companies seek to adapt to local landscapes and tap into energy and identity using cultural programs (Rogers 2015) and other means to increase their legitimacy and participate successfully in various "regional bargains" with the state (Pika 1999; Wengle 2015). Little has been written on the issue of gender energy justice— as well as on gender and energy in general—in Russia; in the case of the Central Asian states, the issue has been analyzed indirectly through the issue of women's access to energy (Calderon, Michelle, and Georgieva 2015) as well as the engagement of women for the support of renewable energy initiatives (Hoeck et al. 2007; see also Standal, Winther, and Danielsen in this volume).

Energy Security and Conflict

Despite its frequent usage, the term "energy security" is not clearly defined (see Jewell and Brutschin in this volume); it has thus "become an umbrella term for many different policy goals" (Winzer 2012, 36). Most of the literature uses a narrow concept of energy security as energy supply continuity, taking the position of energy-importing countries, which focus on possible supply disruptions and their geopolitical implications. However, the concept means different things for different stakeholders given their role as producers, consumers, and and/or transit countries (Chester 2010). The Russian understanding of energy security emphasizes the importance of security of demand, as opposed to the Western emphasis on security of supply. Demand security represents "the other side of the coin and, together with supply security, it forms global energy security" (Bahgat 2013; Romanova 2013, 255). Linking the issue of energy security and energy justice, the question of "security for whom?" (Cherp and Jewell 2014) becomes key as it understands energy security as "low vulnerability of vital energy systems."

As the FSU's largest energy producer, regional energy politics cannot be understood without bringing Russia into the picture (for more on energy regionalism, see Hancock, Palestini, and Szulecki in this volume). This situation requires a geopolitical perspective for the analysis, which has been adopted by a significant portion of the literature. The oldest strand of this discussion has emphasized Russia's use of its energy resources, in particular oil and gas, as foreign policy instruments ("weapons") vis-à-vis energy-poor former Soviet states (i.e., Ukraine, Belarus, Moldova, Armenia, Georgia, Tajikistan, and Kyrgyzstan). Given Russia's significant energy resources, in sharp contrast to the FSU energy consumers' high dependence on energy imports, and the fact that Russia's own strategic documents in the 2000s called for the use of energy resources as part of its foreign policy toolbox (Ministry of Energy of the Russian Federation 2003), such views are not surprising. In much of the literature, the image of weak neighboring states and a missing common EU energy policy was juxtaposed with a neorealist picture of a strong Russian state with centralized control of the energy sector, able to use "energy power" as a political weapon vis-à-vis its energy-dependent post-Soviet neighbors. The main focus of this approach has been on Russia's state power, export volumes, and the degree of energy dependence of these consumer states (Goldman 2009; Grigas 2017; Lucas 2014; Orban 2008).

While these views have been based on the assumption of the energy-dependent states as basically powerless vis-à-vis Russia's external energy power, other research has analyzed the domestic governance situation of key energy dependent states. It demonstrates the role of domestic governance issues (in particular the benefits accruable by corrupt groups from energy trade dynamics) in maintaining a high level of energy dependency on Russia as well as a highly nontransparent energy trade modus operandi in the region (Balmaceda 2008, 2013), which has facilitated the abuse of market power by Russian actors. Above and beyond corruption, participation in the value-added chains of Russian exporters (such as through the provision of transit, storage, and refining services) has created both the threat of dependency and the possibility of accruing significant profits from such participation (Balmaceda forthcoming). In Belarus, for instance, the import of Russian crude oil at lower-than-market prices and its subsequent refining and export at international prices created a revenue windfall that, trickling down to the population as a whole, made the survival of authoritarian president Aleksandr Lukashenka possible despite the lack of modernization of the economy as a whole (Balmaceda 2014).

Others have emphasized the importance of contractual (Pirani 2009) and commercial considerations (Stern, Pirani, and Yafimava 2009) in these relationships, elements not always trumping a desired use of energy supplies as political weapons, but at the very least contextualizing as well as constraining it (Orttung and Øverland 2011). While the literature on a Russian "energy weapon" has been mainly focused on post-Soviet energy importers, this approach has also been applied to EU-Russia energy relations; as argued by Casier (2011, 493), such relations have largely been analyzed in terms of "power, security and zero-sum geopolitical competition." However, this view has been countered by authors emphasizing the mutual nature of this dependency; while the EU as a whole derived around 30 percent of its natural gas, oil, and coal imports from Russia, Russian producers were also dependent on the EU market as their most profitable one (Casier 2011; Godzimirski and Nowak 2018; Westphal 2014). More recent literature has also questioned the security narrative in the area by highlighting how the connection between energy and security issues is not an objective "given" but can be variously framed as a result of securitization (Heinrich and Szulecki 2018; Szulecki 2018) and as de-securitization processes (Khrushcheva 2011; Szulecki and Kusznir 2018).

Another aspect of the impact of energy on security issues concerns how Russian-led integration processes—often in competition with EU-led processes such as the Eastern Partnership and (the prospect of) association agreements—have affected energy relationships in the region, in particular with consumer states (Pastukhova and Westphal 2016; see also the section "Eurasian Economic Union" in this chapter). After a long period as energy rule-setter and "absolute leader" in the gas sector, institutional changes in Russia's role in the region (Mitrova 2009, 21) seemed self-evident; since

2011, authors have discussed the competition between Moscow and Brussels in the post-Soviet energy sphere (Delcour and Wolczuk 2013; Pardo Sierra 2011), as well as the means used by the EU and the degree of success in transposing energy-sector rules to countries such as Ukraine (Wolczuk 2016).

Endogenous security events can also affect energy relations and their regulation, as the 2014 Russian annexation of Crimea demonstrates (Szulecki and Westphal 2018). While some authors have argued that energy issues such as gas pricing played an important contextual role (Van de Graaf and Colgan 2017), others have noted the desire to control Ukraine's Black Sea energy potential and facilities as an important reason for the annexation (Biersack and O'Lear 2014; Blockmans 2015).

Several authors have emphasized the fact that—given the mutual interdependence between Russia and the EU—political conflicts such as that between Russia and Ukraine should not spread into the economic and energy relationship between those parties (Westphal 2014). Although Russian actions in Ukraine led to EU and US economic sanctions against Russia, most authors have argued that the sanctions have been ineffectual. The Russian energy industry was most directly impacted through bans on technology exports used for Arctic offshore and deepwater exploration (Henderson 2015); the effects on oil production will not be so visible in the short term, but there will be long-term effects on the sector's ability to modernize, especially in areas of high-cost production such as the offshore Arctic (Aalto 2016; Larchenko and Kolesnikov 2017). However, the possibilities for indirect cooperation between Russian and Western companies in other areas have remained.

Much of the interdependence literature has focused on the limited effectiveness of sanctions (Ashford 2016; Dreger et al. 2016). Much of the economic pain that at first glance may have been ascribed to sanctions has actually been the result of the sharp decline in world oil prices which, starting in June 2014, has largely coincided with the EU and US sanctions.

Energy and the Environment

Most energy sources create environmental problems within their life cycle, that is, during production, transport, consumption, and disposal. The literature often focuses only on the problems caused by the consumption of energy, for example, GHG emissions. However, the production and transport of energy also cause serious liabilities and contribute to climate change. This situation applies especially to Eurasia, where Soviet legacies have resulted in highly energy-intensive spatial patterns of energy production (i.e., remote production sites and long distances to consumer markets), worn-out and outdated production and transport infrastructures, and a lack of awareness resulting in neglect and waste (see, e.g., Hill and Gaddy 2003; Khotin 2007). This environmental degradation also results in a deterioration of public health and increasing healthcare costs in production regions (e.g., Marples 1999; Netalieva, Wesseler, and Heijman 2005; Thomas 2015).

Two environmental problems related to energy production in Eurasia are especially alarming: (1) the flaring of associated petroleum gas and (2) risky nuclear energy production. The global flaring and venting of associated petroleum gas (hereafter "associated gas") in the oil industry results in the emission of air pollutants and GHGs and the waste of large amounts of resources. Russia is by far the world's largest gas-flaring country, with Kazakhstan and Uzbekistan following among the top-twenty polluters (Soltanieh et al. 2016). Since 2007 the reduction of flaring has been high on Russia's political agenda. A decree requiring each company to utilize a minimum of 95 percent of the associated gas by 2012 was adopted in 2009. Russia has sought to promote large-scale emission reductions through fines and incentives. However, maintaining the status quo to ensure (political) stability is often prioritized by the authorities at the expense of investments and structural reform (Evans and Roshchanka 2014; Loe and Ladehaug 2012). Regulatory issues have also affected the situation, as many oil companies are not allowed to market the associated gas they produce due to a lack of legislative clarity regulating the access to the Russian pipeline system and uncertainty concerning transportation tariffs. In addition, Russia has the largest oil and gas pipeline network in Eurasia and a huge potential to reduce its energy consumption for the pumping of these resources, as methane emissions from Russian natural gas pipelines are approximately 0.6 percent of the gas delivered (Lechtenböhmer et al. 2007).

Another environmental risk of global proportions is the nuclear energy production in the FSU, due to existing Soviet legacies. The most severe nuclear accident in the Soviet Union was the disaster at the Ukrainian Chernobyl' nuclear power plant in 1986 (e.g., Josephson 2005). Far from being isolated occurrences, problems with equipment, operating procedures, and the safety regime at Chernobyl' were endemic in the Soviet nuclear industry (Marples 2004). Solid containment structures to reduce the spread of radiation in the event of a worst-case scenario were missing at Chernobyl' and an entire class of Soviet-designed reactors. Ukraine and Armenia are still operating these dangerous reactors, even though they signed international agreements to close them (Scott et al. 1995; Thomas 1999). Meredith (2014) looks at how political decision makers weighed the enormous short-term costs of closing those reactors against the long-term benefits of compliance and how the political instability that dominated post-communist transitions impacted their choices. Meanwhile, Russia has become a major exporter of nuclear power equipment thanks to diplomatic and financial state support (Aalto et al. 2017; Sim 2017).

The use of renewable energy sources is often recommended to avoid environmental problems caused by fossil fuels. Not only rich in natural gas, oil, coal, and uranium, Eurasia also holds a considerable renewable energy resource base. Renewable energy sources are either boundlessly available or easily regenerative; they comprise solar, wind, hydropower, tidal wave, and geothermal energy; agrofuels (also called biofuels); and biomass. (See Bahr, Boeing, and Szarka in this volume for a detailed discussion of renewable energy.)

One particular type of renewable energy—hydropower—has a long tradition in the FSU. However, renewables were not used to preserve the environment and to mitigate climate change, but rather to complement the Soviet energy mix and to substitute for fossil fuels, for example in locations remote from major energy grids and where demand is too small to warrant large-capacity conventional units (Garnish 1976; Reznikov 1989). The development of large-scale dams and related water-diversion projects, in particular, caused severe environmental damage in the past (Turnbull 1991; Ziegler 1990). New large-scale hydroelectric projects, such as the Trans-Siberian hydropower plant project in the Russian Altai region, have adverse effects on the environment that are still largely ignored by the planners and investors, as are their high (social) costs and limited potential (Glazyrina et al. 2012; Kraudzun 2014).

The slow pace of transition to sustainable energy systems after the dissolution of the Soviet Union has been the result of several factors. While the starting points were very low, policy initiatives were for the most part ineffectual and/or misdirected and often failed to address the fundamental causes of climate change. The political and regulatory frameworks still support and promote fossil fuels, and governments even subsidize traditional energy forms. The Russian government, for instance, might be ready to adapt to climate change but not to mitigate it and tackle its root causes (Laruelle 2014; Karatayev et al. 2016; Smeets 2017).

Nevertheless, there are renewable energy projects in Eurasia (e.g., Doukas et al. 2012; Karatayev and Clarke 2014, 2016; Martinot 1999; Øverland and Kjærnet 2009), as Table 20.3 shows, such as tidal wave energy at the Caspian Sea (Amirinia, Kamranzad, and Mafi 2017; Rusu and Onea 2013) and solar energy (Abbasov 2016; Boute 2016; Nurlankyzy et al. 2016).

The wind power capacity installed in Eurasia represents less than 1 percent of the world share (Prokopenko 2013). However, Ukraine has obtained a leading position in wind energy development, as it is among the few countries that have made attempts to establish domestic serial production of licensed wind turbines (Konechenkov and Shmidt 2013). Overall, it seems that the surviving Soviet-style state planning of energy infrastructure still favors large-scale projects, such as big hydropower stations, instead of using existing wind energy potentials (Kraudzun 2014).

However, new renewable energy projects in Eurasia have also caused problems with land use for or carbon emission during the production of agrofuels (Plank 2016) or with the use of hydropower. Looking beyond Russia, hydroelectric plants have caused conflicts in Central Asia, as their use can create water scarcities in an arid climate where agriculture requires irrigation. While Uzbekistan, Turkmenistan, and Kazakhstan are rich in fossil fuels, they face significant water scarcity. The upstream riparian Tajikistan and Kyrgyzstan, on the other hand, control most of the water resources; they account for around 80 percent of the entire region's runoff. Tajikistan and Kyrgyzstan increase water discharge in the winter months to meet increased electricity consumption and reduce it in the summer in order to replenish the water reservoirs. But this leads to a shortage of irrigation and drinking water in the summer in Kazakhstan and Uzbekistan (Karimov et al. 2013; Uulu and Smagulov 2011).

A water quota system and energy exchange regime were established during the Soviet era. Kazakhstan and Uzbekistan delivered gas, coal, and petroleum products to

Table 20.3 Electricity Supply in Eurasia by Source (in Gigawatt Hours), 2007–2015

		Production							Imports	Exports
		Total	Thermal/Combustible Fuels	Hydro	Nuclear	Wind	Solar	Others		
Armenia	2007	5,898	1,489	1,856	2,553	N/A			419	451
	2008	6,114	1,854	1,797	2,461	2			338	360
	2009	5,672	1,154	2,020	2,494	4			295	325
	2010	6,491	1,438	2,556	2,490	7			246	1,061
	2011	7,433	2,390	2,489	2,548	6	N/A	N/A	205	1,533
	2012	8,036	3,399	2,311	2,322	4	N/A	N/A	98	1,696
	2013	7,710	3,173	2,173	2,360	4	N/A	N/A	148	1,313
	2014	7,750	3,289	1,992	2,465	4	N/A	N/A	206	1,314
	2015	7,799	2,801	2,206	2,766	3	1	N/A	174	1,424
Azerbaijan	2007	21,847	19,483	2,364	N/A	N/A			548	786
	2008	21,643	19,411	2,232	N/A	N/A			216	812
	2009	18,868	16,558	2,308	N/A	2			110	380
	2010	18,710	15,263	3,446	N/A	1			100	462
	2011	20,294	17,618	2,676	N/A	0	N/A	N/A	128	805
	2012	22,988	21,167	1,821	N/A	0	N/A	N/A	141	680
	2013	23,354	21,863	1,489	N/A	1	1	N/A	127	495
	2014	24,728	23,423	1,300	N/A	2	3	N/A	124	489
	2015	24,688	23,041	1,637	N/A	5	5	N/A	108	265

| | | Production | | | | | | | Imports | Exports |
		Total	Thermal/Combustible Fuels	Hydro	Nuclear	Wind	Solar	Others		
Belarus	2007	31,829	31,793	35	N/A	1			9,406	5,062
	2008	35,048	35,008	39	N/A	1			7,085	5,245
	2009	30,376	30,331	44	N/A	1			8,404	3,933
	2010	34,895	34,849	45	N/A	1			7,767	5,067
	2011	32,200	32,157	42	N/A	1	N/A	N/A	9,289	3,704
	2012	30,799	30,723	70	N/A	6	N/A	N/A	10,398	2,797
	2013	31,507	31,361	138	N/A	8	N/A	N/A	9,382	3,012
	2014	34,735	34,602	121	N/A	11	1	N/A	7,806	4,488
	2015	34,077	33,941	107	N/A	26	3	N/A	6,104	3,482
Georgia	2007	8,580	1,764	6,816	N/A	N/A			433	625
	2008	8,440	1,244	7,196	N/A	N/A			649	680
	2009	8,165	1,010	7,155	N/A	N/A			255	749
	2010	9,992	644	9,348	N/A	N/A			222	1,524
	2011	10,104	2,212	7,892	N/A	N/A	N/A	N/A	471	931
	2012	9,698	2,477	7,221	N/A	N/A	N/A	N/A	615	528
	2013	10,059	1,788	8,271	N/A	N/A	N/A	N/A	484	450
	2014	10,370	2,036	8,334	N/A	N/A	N/A	N/A	794	545
	2015	10,833	2,379	8,454	N/A	N/A	N/A	N/A	699	660
Kazakhstan	2007	76,621	68,450	8,171	N/A	N/A			3,269	3,616
	2008	80,326	72,866	7,460	N/A	N/A			2,788	2,483

(continued)

Table 20.3 Electricity Supply in Eurasia by Source (in Gigawatt Hours), 2007–2015   (Continued)

	Production							Imports	Exports
	Total	Thermal/Combustible Fuels	Hydro	Nuclear	Wind	Solar	Others		
2009	78,710	71,831	6,879	N/A	N/A	N/A	N/A	1,710	2,378
2010	82,646	74,624	8,022	N/A	N/A	N/A	N/A	2,914	1,757
2011	86,586	78,703	7,883	N/A	N/A	N/A	N/A	3,406	1,809
2012	92,817	85,177	7,637	N/A	3	N/A	N/A	4,252	2,933
2013	103,086	95,349	7,731	N/A	5	1	N/A	2,147	2,996
2014	105,068	96,791	8,263	N/A	13	1	N/A	1,749	2,917
2015	106,422	97,020	9,269	N/A	132	1	N/A	1,618	1,614
Kyrgyzstan									
2007	16,237	2,289	13,948	N/A	N/A			0	2,379
2008	11,877	1,137	10,740	N/A	N/A			10	545
2009	11,100	1,190	9,910	N/A	N/A			0	320
2010	12,063	1,733	10,330	N/A	N/A			0	680
2011	15,158	1,019	14,139	N/A	N/A	N/A	N/A	174	2,848
2012	15,168	989	14,179	N/A	N/A	N/A	N/A	177	1,840
2013	14,011	914	13,097	N/A	N/A	N/A	N/A	N/A	377
2014	14,572	1,274	13,298	N/A	N/A	N/A	N/A	286	72
2015	13,030	1,930	11,100	N/A	N/A	N/A	N/A	729	184
Moldova									
2007	1,100	1,067	33	N/A	N/A			2,931	0
2008	1,096	1,014	82	N/A	N/A			2,958	0
2009	1,032	977	55	N/A	N/A			2,941	0

	Year	Production							Imports	Exports
		Total	Thermal/Combustible Fuels	Hydro	Nuclear	Wind	Solar	Others		
	2010	1,064	985	79	N/A	N/A	N/A	N/A	3,033	0
	2011	1,016	940	76	N/A	0	N/A	N/A	3,145	N/A
	2012	932	898	34	N/A	0	N/A	N/A	846	N/A
	2013	905	859	45	N/A	1	N/A	N/A	1,456	N/A
	2014	963	902	59	N/A	1	1	N/A	731	N/A
	2015	939	886	50	N/A	2	1	N/A	18	N/A
Russia	2007	1,015,333	675,820	178,982	160,039	492			5,670	18,468
	2008	1,040,379	710,113	166,711	163,085	470			3,105	20,738
	2009	991,980	651,810	176,118	163,584	468			3,066	17,923
	2010	1,038,030	698,709	168,397	170,415	509			1,644	19,091
	2011	1,054,765	713,689	167,608	172,941	5	N/A	522	1,558	24,111
	2012	1,070,734	725,399	167,319	177,534	5	N/A	477	2,661	19,143
	2013	1,059,092	703,481	182,654	172,508	5	N/A	444	4,706	18,382
	2014	1,064,207	705,598	177,141	180,757	96	160	455	6,623	14,671
	2015	1,067,544	701,220	169,914	195,470	148	335	457	6,586	18,244
Tajikistan	2007	17,494	380	17,114	N/A	N/A			4,361	4,259
	2008	16,147	347	15,800	N/A	N/A			5,297	4,421
	2009	16,117	317	15,800	N/A	N/A			4,304	4,247
	2010	16,410	565	15,845	N/A	N/A			339	180

(continued)

Table 20.3 Electricity Supply in Eurasia by Source (in Gigawatt Hours), 2007–2015 (Continued)

	Total	Production Thermal/Combustible Fuels	Hydro	Nuclear	Wind	Solar	Others	Imports	Exports
2011	16,234	38	16,196	N/A	N/A	N/A	N/A	172	197
2012	16,998	74	16,924	N/A	N/A	N/A	N/A	114	775
2013	17,115	44	17,071	N/A	N/A	N/A	N/A	117	1,061
2014	16,472	160	16,312	N/A	N/A	N/A	N/A	13	1,366
2015	17,162	262	16,900	N/A	N/A	N/A	N/A	63	1,400
Turkmenistan									
2007	14,880	14,877	3	N/A	N/A	N/A		N/A	1,950
2008	15,040	15,037	3	N/A	N/A			N/A	1,530
2009	15,980	15,977	3	N/A	N/A			N/A	2,100
2010	16,660	16,657	3	N/A	N/A			N/A	2,410
2011	17,220	17,220	0	N/A	N/A	N/A	N/A	N/A	2,550
2012	17,750	17,750	0	N/A	N/A	N/A	N/A	N/A	2,720
2013	18,870	18,870	N/A	N/A	N/A	N/A	N/A	N/A	2,850
2014	20,400	20,400	N/A	N/A	N/A	N/A	N/A	N/A	3,210
2015	22,534	22,534	N/A	N/A	N/A	N/A	N/A	N/A	3,201
Ukraine									
2007	196,251	93,405	10,259	92,542	45			3,383	12,554
2008	192,586	91,188	11,512	89,841	45			2,101	8,831
2009	173,619	78,716	11,936	82,924	43			25	4,294
2010	188,584	86,229	13,152	89,152	51			23	4,078
2011	194,947	93,634	10,946	90,248	89	30	N/A	35	6,327

	Production							Imports	Exports
	Total	Thermal/Combustible Fuels	Hydro	Nuclear	Wind	Solar	Others		
2012	198,878	97,126	10,994	90,137	288	333	N/A	93	11,560
2013	194,377	95,487	14,472	83,209	639	570	N/A	39	9,929
2014	182,815	83,549	9,318	88,389	1,130	429	N/A	89	8,523
2015	163,682	67,523	6,971	87,627	1,084	477	N/A	2,241	3,591
Uzbekistan									
2007	48,950	42,550	6,400	N/A	N/A			11,360	11,442
2008	49,400	38,040	11,360	N/A	N/A			11,464	11,547
2009	49,950	40,620	9,330	N/A	N/A			11,592	11,676
2010	51,710	40,870	10,640	N/A	N/A			12,000	12,087
2011	52,400	42,160	10,240	N/A	N/A	N/A	N/A	12,500	12,411
2012	52,500	41,290	11,210	N/A	N/A	N/A	N/A	12,524	12,435
2013	54,200	42,640	11,560	N/A	N/A	N/A	N/A	12,930	12,838
2014	55,400	43,570	11,830	N/A	N/A	N/A	N/A	13,216	13,122
2015	57,280	45,450	11,830	N/A	N/A	N/A	N/A	11,336	12,384

Sources: UN (2013, 2016, 2017).

Kyrgyzstan and Tajikistan, while the latter, in turn, discharged water during the growing season and supplied electricity. But since independence, this energy exchange has broken down, Soviet-era governance structures have eroded, and unilateral action has become the norm (Granit et al. 2012; Kushkumbayev and Kushkumbayeva 2013; Uulu and Smagulov 2011). In addition, Kyrgyzstan and Tajikistan wish to further develop their hydropower potential (Kraudzun 2014; Wegerich, Olsson, and Froebrich 2007).

Toward a New Research Agenda

Specialized energy-related journals, such as *Energy Policy*, *Resources Policy*, and *Energy*, focus to a large degree on technical aspects of energy, neglecting to place these issues within a broader social and political context. The same applies to Russian publications on energy issues. Overall, many of these studies are empirical, missing a theoretical focus. Western scholars often have a bias toward focusing on the interests of energy consumer countries only (e.g., regarding energy security). These studies often follow fashions of interest (e.g., in the aftermath of a crisis), trying to provide policy advice and "easy answers" from a geopolitical perspective.

The topic of energy politics per se, in particular as related to energy sources other than oil, is still widely neglected or covered only in passing by journals from the fields of political science, international relations, (international) political economy, sociology, and anthropology. In particular, the nontechnical aspects of issues such as climate change agreements (such as the Kyoto Protocol) in the region are largely missing. This is especially regrettable, as global governance initiatives will eventually push fossil fuel producers toward a low carbon transition—maybe not directly and out of conviction, but indirectly through a change in behavior among energy consumer countries.

The Eurasian fossil fuel exporters are some of the most energy- and carbon-intensive countries in the world, are significant emitters of GHGs, and have a weak track record on climate change mitigation. This situation is regarded by countries importing energy from the FSU as an increasing threat to security of supply and as a major barrier to global climate change policy (Garbuzova and Madlener 2012). United Nations climate agreements such as the Paris Agreement have the potential to shift global energy consumption from a mix dominated by fossil fuels to one driven by low-carbon technologies. Energy producers will be increasingly more vulnerable to this shift than energy consumers (Romanova 2013, 255), as low-carbon scenarios are associated with lower energy trade and higher diversity of energy options, especially in the transport sector (Anceschi and Symons 2012; Jewell, Cherp, and Riahi 2014). In addition, the EU has been institutionalizing energy efficiency in EU external energy relations, in particular toward Russia (Boute 2013; Paltsev 2016). Thus energy producers will have to adjust their economies to reflect lower export earnings from fossil fuels.

These trends are likely to become increasingly important in the coming decades. They also represent key social, political, and environmental issues that scholars of energy politics in Eurasia should make an effort to address in order to remain relevant even in the midst of changing global energy conditions. These trends also force us to rethink our understandings of energy security and to increasingly ask "security for whom?" (Jewell and Brutschin in this volume), not only in terms of producer and consumer states, but in terms of all users of "vital energy systems." This approach opens the road for detailed exploration of vulnerabilities as a combination of exposure to risks and resilience and of the links between vital energy systems and critical social functions.

As new types of energy (i.e., renewable energy sources) slowly but surely make inroads in the region, some of the following questions may offer especially interesting insights: Up to what extent can one assume that new types of energy will bring in new actors able and willing to reshape sectors highly affected by corruption and renterism, or does one simply see the same oligarchic elites expanding into new sectors (Plank 2016)? Similarly, recent research extending the resource curse from fossil fuels and mineral resources to agricultural produce and renewable energy sources (i.e., hydropower) (Hancock and Sovacool 2018; Markowitz 2017; Williams and Le Billon 2017) appears especially promising. This new line of research would also include Central Asian countries poor in fossil fuels, so far neglected in the resource curse literature.

Overall, analyses of Eurasian energy policy should try to enhance a deeper understanding of the inner workings of decision-making processes in the field and to identify veto players and underlying paradigms (e.g., energy security concepts of energy producers). In this regard, researchers can also have an agenda-setting function and can raise awareness of the problems of the future instead of staying on traditional, well-trampled research paths.

Notes

1. Here the term "Eurasia" describes most of the area of the FSU, comprising twelve countries: Armenia, Azerbaijan, Belarus, Georgia, Kazakhstan, Kyrgyzstan, Moldova, Russia (the Russian Federation), Tajikistan, Turkmenistan, Ukraine, and Uzbekistan. The Baltic States (Estonia, Latvia, and Lithuania), even though they also formerly belonged to the Soviet Union, are not covered because their development has been strongly influenced by their accession to the European Union (EU).
2. After an overzealous—and, according to many, politically motivated—scrutiny of the company in 2003–2004 for tax evasion, Yukos's filing for bankruptcy to cover the government's tax claims facilitated the sale of its assets to largely state-owned Rosneft.
3. Greenhouse gases (GHGs) caused by burning fossil fuels include carbon dioxide, methane, and oxides of nitrogen, as well as other air pollutants such as sulfur oxide.
4. The term "Dutch disease" broadly refers to the harmful consequences of large, but perhaps temporary, increases in a country's income based on exchange rates and eventually on trade balances, domestic production, and the availability and costs of credit.

REFERENCES

Aalto, Pami. 2016. "Modernisation of the Russian Energy Sector: Constraints on Utilising Arctic Offshore Oil Resources." *Europe-Asia Studies* 68, no. 1: 38–63.

Aalto, Pami, Heino Nyyssönen, Matti Kojo, and Pallavi Pal. 2017. "Russian Nuclear Energy Diplomacy in Finland and Hungary." *Eurasian Geography and Economics* 58, no. 4: 386–417.

Abbasov, Elnur. 2016. "Sustainable Solution for Increasing the Share of Solar Photovoltaic Usages on Residential Houses in Azerbaijan." *Environmental Research, Engineering and Management* 71, no. 4: 11–18.

Ahrend, Rüdiger. 2005. "Can Russia Break the 'Resource Curse'?" *Eurasian Geography and Economics* 46, no. 8: 584–609.

Alexeev, Michael, and Andrey Chernyavskiy. 2015. "Taxation of Natural Resources and Economic Growth in Russia's Regions." *Economic Systems* 39, no. 2: 317–338.

Alexeev, Michael, and Robert Conrad. 2009. "The Russian Oil Tax Regime: A Comparative Perspective." *Eurasian Geography and Economics* 50, no. 1: 93–114.

Algieri, Bernardina. 2011. "The Dutch Disease: Evidences from Russia." *Economic Change and Reconstruction* 44, no. 3: 243–277.

Amirinia, Gholamreza, Bahareh Kamranzad, and Somayeh Mafi. 2017. "Wind and Wave Energy Potential in Southern Caspian Sea Using Uncertainty Analysis." *Energy* 120: 332–345.

Anceschi, Luca, and Jonathan Symons, eds. 2012. *Energy Security in the Era of Climate Change: The Asia-Pacific Experience.* Basingstoke, UK: Palgrave Macmillan.

Andonova, Liliana B., and Assia Alexieva. 2012. "Continuity and Change in Russia's Climate Negotiations Position and Strategy." *Climate Policy* 12, no. 5: 614–629.

Ashford, Emma. 2016. "Not-So-Smart Sanctions: The Failure of Western Restrictions against Russia." *Foreign Affairs* 95: 114–123.

Auping, Willem L., Sijbren de Jong, Erik Pruyt, and Jan H. Kwakkel. 2016. "The Geopolitical Impact of the Shale Revolution: Exploring Consequences on Energy Prices and Rentier States." *Energy Policy* 98: 390–399.

Auty, Richard M. 1997. "Does Kazakhstan Oil Wealth Help or Hinder the Transition?" Development Discussion Paper no. 615. Cambridge, MA: Harvard Institute for International Development, Harvard University.

Auty, Richard M. 2003. "Natural Resources and 'Gradual' Reform in Uzbekistan and Turkmenistan." *Natural Resources Forum* 27: 255–266.

Axelrod, Regina S. 1996. "The European Energy Charter Treaty: Reality or Illusion?" *Energy Policy* 24, no. 6: 497–505.

Bahgat, Gawdat. 2013. "Oil Producer's Perspectives on Energy Security." In *International Handbook of Energy Security*, edited by Hugh Dyer and Maria J. Trombetta, 258–272. Cheltenham, UK: Edward Elgar.

Balabin, A. A. 2015. "Zachem 'Gazpromu' rynochnaya kapitalizatsiya?" *EKO: Vserossiiskii ekonomicheskii zhurnal* 3: 98–116.

Balkunets, D. V. 2016. "Russian–Belarusian Energy Cooperation." *Problems of Economic Transition* 58, no. 6: 512–525.

Balmaceda, Margarita M. 2006. "Russian Energy Companies in the New Eastern Europe: The Cases of Ukraine and Belarus." In *Russian Business Power: The Role of Russian Business in Foreign and Security Policy*, edited by Andreas Wenger, Jeronim Perovic, and Robert W. Orttung, 67–87. London: RoutledgeCurzon.

Balmaceda, Margarita M. 2008. *Energy Dependency, Politics and Corruption in the Former Soviet Union: Russia's Power, Oligarchs' Profits and Ukraine's Missing Energy Policy, 1995–2006.* London: Routledge.

Balmaceda, Margarita M. 2013. *The Politics of Energy Dependence: Ukraine, Belarus and Lithuania between Domestic Oligarchs and Russian Pressure.* Toronto: University of Toronto Press.

Balmaceda, Margarita M. 2014. *Living the High Life in Minsk: Russian Energy Rents, Domestic Populism and Belarus' Impending Crisis.* Budapest: Central European University Press.

Balmaceda, Margarita M. Forthcoming. *Russian Energy Chains: the Remaking of Technopolitics from Siberia to Ukraine to the European Union.* New York: Columbia University Press.

Balmaceda, Margarita M., and Kirsten Westphal. "Cross-Regional Production Chains, Regional Fault Lines and Competitive Regional Processes in Eurasia," article in preparation for "Energy Regionalism" special issue, *Review of Policy Research.*

Belousova, S. V. 2015. "Resursnye regiony: Ekonomicheskie bozmozhnosti i finansovaya spravedlivost." *EKO: Vserossiiskii ekonomicheskii zhurnal* 6: 40–48.

Belyi, Andrei V. 2013. "Energy Security Governance in Light of the Energy Charter Process." In *International Handbook of Energy Security*, edited by Hugh Dyer and Maria J. Trombetta, 273–294. Cheltenham, UK: Edward Elgar.

Biersack, John, and Shannon O'Lear. 2014. "The Geopolitics of Russia's Annexation of Crimea: Narratives, Identity, Silences, and Energy." *Eurasian Geography and Economics* 55, no. 3: 247–269.

Blockmans, Steven. 2015. "Crimea and the Quest for Energy and Military Hegemony in the Black Sea Region: Governance Gap in a Contested Geostrategic Zone." *Southeast European and Black Sea Studies* 15, no. 2: 179–189.

Boute, Anatole. 2013. "Energy Efficiency as a New Paradigm of the European External Energy Policy: The Case of the EU–Russian Energy Dialogue." *Europe-Asia Studies* 65, no. 6: 1021–1054.

Boute, Anatole. 2016. "Off-grid Renewable Energy in Remote Arctic Areas: An Analysis of the Russian Far East." *Renewable and Sustainable Energy Reviews* 59: 1029–1037.

Bozo, N. V., and V. V. Shmat. 2011. "Neftegazovaya 'monopol'ka' v Rossii." *EKO: Vserossiiskii ekonomicheskii zhurnal* 10: 78–101 and 11: 74–93.

Bradshaw, Michael. 2010. "A New Energy Age in Pacific Russia: Lessons from the Sakhalin Oil and Gas Projects." *Eurasian Geography and Economics* 51, no. 3: 330–359.

Buccellato, Tullio, and Tomasz Mickiewicz. 2009. "Oil and Gas: A Blessing for the Few. Hydrocarbons and Inequality within Regions in Russia." *Europe-Asia Studies* 61, no. 3: 385–407.

Busse, Matthias, and Steffen Gröning. 2013. "The Resource Curse Revisited: Governance and Natural Resources." *Public Choice* 154, nos. 1–2: 1–20.

Calderon, Rebosio, P. Michelle, and Sophia V. Georgieva. 2015. *Toward Gender-informed Energy Subsidy Reforms.* Washington, DC: World Bank.

Casier, Tom. 2011. "Russia's Energy Leverage over the EU: Myth or Reality?" *Perspectives on European Politics and Society* 12, no. 4: 493–508.

Cherp, Aleh, and Jessica Jewell. 2014. "The Concept of Energy Security: Beyond the Four As." *Energy Policy* 75: 415–421.

Chester, Lynne. 2010. "Conceptualising Energy Security and Making Explicit Its Polysemic Nature." *Energy Policy* 38, no. 2: 887–895.

Collier, Paul, and Anke Hoeffler. 2009. "Testing the Neo-con Agenda: Democracy in Resource-rich Societies." *European Economic Review* 53, no. 3: 293–308.

Ćwiek-Karpowicz, Jarosław. 2012. "Russia's Gas Sector: In Need of Liberalization in the Context of the Shale Gas Revolution and Energy Relations with the European Union." *Journal of East-West Business* 18, no. 1: 54–65.

Delcour, Laure, and Kataryna Wolczuk. 2013. "Eurasian Economic Integration: Implications for the EU Eastern Policy." In *Eurasian Economic Integration: Law, Policy and Politics*, edited by Rilka Dragneva and Kataryna Wolczuk, 179–203. Cheltenham, UK: Edward Elgar.

Di Gregorio, A., and Angela Di Gregorio, eds. 2017. *The Eurasian Economic Union and the European Union: Moving toward a Greater Understanding.* The Hague: Eleven International Publishing.

Domjan, Paul, and Matt Stone. 2010. "A Comparative Study of Resource Nationalism in Russia and Kazakhstan 2004–2008." *Europe-Asia Studies* 62, no. 1: 35–62.

Doukas, Haris, Vangelis Marinakis, Charikleia Karakosta, and John Psarras. 2012. "Promoting Renewables in the Energy Sector of Tajikistan." *Renewable Energy* 39: 411–418.

Dragneva, Rilka, and Kataryna Wolczuk, eds. 2013. *Eurasian Economic Integration: Law, Policies and Politics.* Cheltenham, UK: Edward Elgar.

Dragneva, Rilka, and Kataryna Wolczuk. 2017. *The Eurasian Economic Union: Deals, Rules and the Exercise of Power.* London: Chatham House.

Dreger, Christian, Konstantin A. Kholodilin, Dirk Ulbricht, and Jarko Fidrmuc. 2016. "Between the Hammer and the Anvil: The Impact of Economic Sanctions and Oil Prices on Russia's Ruble." *Journal of Comparative Economics* 44, no. 2: 295–308.

Dülger, Fikret, Kenan Lopcu, Almıla Burgaç, and Esra Balli. 2013. "Is Russia Suffering from Dutch Disease? Cointegration with Structural Break." *Resources Policy* 38, no. 4: 605–612.

Dutkiewicz, Piotr, and Richard Sakwa, eds. 2015. *Eurasian Integration: The View from Within.* London: Routledge.

Ekin, A. Cemal, and Thomas R. King. 2009. "A Struggling International Partnership: TNK-BP Joint Venture." *International Journal of Strategic Business Alliances* 1, no. 1: 89–106.

Evans, Meredydd, and Volha Roshchanka. 2014. "Russian Policy on Methane Emissions in the Oil and Gas Sector: A Case Study in Opportunities and Challenges in Reducing Short-lived Forcers." *Atmospheric Environment* 92: 199–206.

Falkner, Robert. 2016. "The Paris Agreement and the New Logic of International Climate Politics." *International Affairs* 92, no. 5: 1107–1125.

Fattouh, Bassam, and James Henderson. 2012. "The Impact of Russia's Refinery Upgrade Plans on Global Fuel Oil Markets." Working Paper WPM no. 48. Oxford: Oxford Institute for Energy Studies.

Fortescue, Stephen. 2006. "Business-State Negotiations and the Reform of the Tax Procedures in Post-Yukos Russia." *Law in Context* 24, no. 3: 36–59.

Gaddy, Clifford, and Barry W Ickes. 2009. "Russia's Declining Oil Production: Managing Price Risk and Rent Addiction" *Eurasian Geography and Economics* 50, no. 1: 1–13.

Garbuzova, Maria, and Reinhard Madlener. 2012. "Towards an Efficient and Low Carbon Economy Post-2012: Opportunities and Barriers for Foreign Companies in the Russian Energy Market." *Mitigation and Adaptation Strategies for Global Change* 17, no. 4: 387–413.

Garnish, J. D. 1976. "Geothermal Energy as an 'Alternative' Source." *Energy Policy* 4, no. 2: 130–143.

Gel'man, Vladimir, and Otar Marganiya, eds. 2010. *Resource Curse and Post-Soviet Eurasia: Oil, Gas, and Modernization*. Lanham, MD: Lexington Books.

Georgiev, Atanas. 2016. "Shale and Eastern Europe; Bulgaria, Romania, and Ukraine." In *The Global Impact of Unconventional Shale Gas Development: Economics, Policy, and Interdependence*, edited by Yongsheng Wang and William E. Hefley, 75–96. Cham, Switzerland: Springer.

Glazyrina, I. P., I. E. Mikheev, E. G. Egidarev, and E. A. Simonov. 2012. "Ekonomicheskii demping v planakh razvitiya Sibiri i Dal'nego Vostoka." *EKO: Vserossiiskii ekonomicheskii zhurnal* 10: 35–51.

Gleason, Abbott. 2010. "Eurasia: What Is It? Is It?" *Journal of Eurasian Studies* 1, no. 1: 26–32.

Godzimirski, Jakub M., and Zuzanna Nowak. 2018. "EU Gas Supply Security: The Power of the Importer." In *Energy Security in Europe: Divergent Perceptions and Policy Challenges*, edited by Kacper Szulecki, 221–249. Cham, Switzerland: Palgrave Macmillan.

Goldman, Marshall. 2009. *Petrostate*. Oxford: Oxford University Press.

Goldthau, Andreas, and Tim Boersma. 2014. "The 2014 Ukraine-Russia Crisis: Implications for Energy Markets and Scholarship." *Energy Research & Social Science* 3: 13–15.

Granit, Jakob, Anders Jägerskog, Andreas Lindström, Gunilla Björklund, Andrew Bullock, Rebecca Löfgren, et al. 2012. "Regional Options for Addressing the Water, Energy and Food Nexus in Central Asia and the Aral Sea Basin." *International Journal of Water Resources Development* 28, no. 3: 419–432.

Grätz, Jonas. 2013. *Russland als globaler Wirtschaftsakteur: Handlungsressourcen und Strategien der Öl- und Gaskonzerne*. Munich: Oldenbourg Verlag.

Grigas, Agnia. 2017. *The New Geopolitics of Natural Gas*. Cambridge, MA: Harvard University Press.

Gustafson, Thane. 2012. *Wheel of Fortune: The Battle for Oil and Power in Russia*. Cambridge, MA: Belknap Press of Harvard University Press.

Hancock, Kathleen J., and Benjamin K. Sovacool. 2018. "International Political Economy and Renewable Energy: Hydroelectric Power and the Resource Curse." *International Studies Review* 20, no. 4: 615–632. doi:10.1093/isr/vix058.

Heinrich, Andreas. 2003. "Internationalisation of Russia's Gazprom." *Journal for East European Management Studies* 8, no. 1: 46–66.

Heinrich, Andreas. 2005. "Why Corporate Governance in the Russian Oil and Gas Industry Is Improving." *Corporate Governance: The International Journal of Business in Society* 5, no. 4: 3–9.

Heinrich, Andreas. 2008. "Under the Kremlin's Thumb: Does Increased State Control in the Russian Gas Sector Endanger European Energy Security?" *Europe-Asia Studies* 60, no. 9: 1539–1574.

Heinrich, Andreas, and Heiko Pleines, eds. 2012. *Challenges of the Caspian Resource Boom: Domestic Elites and Policy-making*. Basingstoke, UK: Palgrave Macmillan.

Heinrich, Andreas, and Kacper Szulecki. 2018. "Energy Securitization: Applying the Copenhagen School's Framework to Energy." In *Energy Security in Europe: Divergent Perceptions and Policy Challenges*, edited by Kacper Szulecki, 33–59. Cham, Switzerland: Palgrave Macmillan.

Henderson, James, ed. 2014. *The Russian Gas Matrix: How Markets Are Driving Change*. Oxford: Oxford University Press.

Henderson, James. 2015. "Key Determinants for the Future of Russian Oil Production and Exports." Working Paper WPM no. 58. Oxford: Oxford Institute for Energy Studies.

Henderson, James, and Alastair Ferguson. 2014. "The Turbulent History of Foreign Involvement in the Russian Oil and Gas Industry." In *International Partnership in Russia: Conclusions from the Oil and Gas Industry*, edited by James Henderson and Alastair Ferguson, 1–60. London: Palgrave Macmillan.

Henry, Laura, S. Nysten-Haarala, S. Tulaeva, and M. Tysiachniouk. 2016. "Corporate Social Responsibility and the Oil Industry in the Russian Arctic: Global Norms and Neo-paternalism." *Europe-Asia Studies* 68, no. 8: 1340–1368.

Henry, Laura A., and Lisa Sundstrom McIntosh. 2007. "Russia and the Kyoto Protocol: Seeking an Alignment of Interests and Image." *Global Environmental Politics* 7, no. 4: 47–69.

Henry, Laura A., and Lisa Sundstrom McIntosh. 2014. "Climate Change Policies in the Post-Socialist World." *Current History* 113, no. 765: 278–283.

Hill, Fiona, and Clifford Gaddy. 2003. *The Siberian Curse: How Communist Planners Left Russia Out in the Cold*. Washington, DC: Brookings Institution Press.

Hoeck, Tobias, Roman Droux, Thomas Breu, Hans Hurni, and Daniel Maselli. 2007. "Rural Energy Consumption and Land Degradation in a Post-Soviet Setting: An Example from the West Pamir Mountains in Tajikistan." *Energy for Sustainable Development* 11, no. 1: 48–57.

Hughes, Llewelyn, and Phillip Y. Lipscy. 2013. "The Politics of Energy." *Annual Review of Political Science* 16: 449–469.

International Energy Agency (IEA). 2014. "Energy Policies of IEA Countries: European Union." 2014 Review. Paris: IEA/OECD.

Jewell, Jessica, Aleh Cherp, and Keywan Riahi. 2014. "Energy Security under De-carbonization Scenarios: An Assessment Framework and Evaluation under Different Technology and Policy Choices." *Energy Policy* 65: 743–760.

Jones Luong, Pauline, and Erika Weinthal. 2001. "Prelude to the Resource Curse: Explaining Oil and Gas Development Strategies in the Soviet Successor States and Beyond." *Comparative Political Studies* 34, no. 4: 367–399.

Jones Luong, Pauline, and Erika Weinthal. 2010. *Oil Is Not a Curse: Ownership Structure and Institutions in Soviet Successor States*. Cambridge, UK: Cambridge University Press.

Josephson, Paul R. 2005. *Red Atom: Russia's Nuclear Power Program from Stalin to Today*. Pittsburgh, PA: Pittsburgh University Press.

Kalyuzhnova, Yelena, and Christian Nygaard. 2008. "State Governance Evolution in Resource-rich Transition Economies: An Application to Russia and Kazakhstan." *Energy Policy* 36, no. 6: 1829–1842.

Karatayev, Marat, and Michèle L. Clarke. 2014. "Current Energy Resources in Kazakhstan and the Future Potential of Renewables: A Review." *Energy Procedia* 59: 97–104.

Karatayev, Marat, and Michèle L. Clarke. 2016. "A Review of Current Energy Systems and Green Energy Potential in Kazakhstan." *Renewable and Sustainable Energy Reviews* 55: 491–504.

Karatayev, Marat, Stephen Hall, Yelena Kalyuzhnova, and Michèle L. Clarke. 2016. "Renewable Energy Technology Uptake in Kazakhstan: Policy Drivers and Barriers in a Transitional Economy." *Renewable and Sustainable Energy Reviews* 66: 120–136.

Kardaś, Szymon, and Kamil Kłysiński. 2017. "The Story That Never Ends: A New Stage in the Energy Dispute between Russia and Belarus." OSW Commentary no. 242. Warsaw: Ośrodek Studiów Wschodnich. https://www.osw.waw.pl/sites/default/files/commentary_242.pdf.

Karimov, Khasan S., Khakim M. Akhmedov, Muhammad Abid, and Georgiy N. Petrov. 2013. "Effective Management of Combined Renewable Energy Resources in Tajikistan." *Science of the Total Environment* 461/462: 835–838.

Kaveshnikov, Nikolay. 2010. "The Issue of Energy Security in Relations between Russia and the European Union." *European Security* 19, no. 4: 585–605.

Kazantsev, Andrey. 2012. "Policy Networks in European–Russian Gas Relations: Function and Dysfunction from a Perspective of EU Energy Security." *Communist and Post-Communist Studies* 45, nos. 3–4: 305–313.

Kendall-Taylor, Andrea. 2012. "Purchasing Power: Oil, Elections and Regime Durability in Azerbaijan and Kazakhstan." *Europe-Asia Studies* 64, no. 4: 737–760.

Khotin, Leonid. 2007. "A Siberian Curse?" *Problems of Economic Transition* 49, no. 9: 35–50.

Khrushcheva, Olga. 2011. "The Creation of an Energy Security Society as a Way to Decrease Securitization Levels between the European Union and Russia in Energy Trade." *Journal of Contemporary European Research* 7, no. 2: 216–230.

Khusainov, V. M., and S. V. Afanasiev. 2012. "Kak izvlekat' zapasy nefti na pozdnikh stadiyakh razrabotki?" *EKO: Vserossiiskii ekonomicheskii zhurnal* 1: 41–47.

Konechenkov, Andriy, and Galina Shmidt. 2013. "Ukraine: 'Licensed' Way to Develop Wind Industry." In *Wind Power for the World. International Reviews and Developments*, edited by Preben Maegaard, Anna Krenz and Wolfgang Palz, 510–534. Singapore: Pan Stanford Publishing.

Konoplyanik, Andrei A. 2010. "Why Is Russia Opting Out of the Energy Charter?" *International Affairs* 56, no. 2: 84–96.

Korppoo, Anna, Jacqueline Karas, and Michael Grubb, eds. 2006. *Russia and the Kyoto Protocol: Opportunities and Challenges*. London: Chatham House.

Kraudzun, Tobias. 2014. "Bottom-up and Top-down Dynamics of the Energy Transformation in the Eastern Pamirs of Tajikistan's Gorno Badakhshan Region." *Central Asian Survey* 33, no. 4: 550–565.

Kropatcheva, Elena. 2014. "He Who Has the Pipeline Calls the Tune? Russia's Energy Power against the Background of the Shale 'Revolutions'." *Energy Policy*, 66: 1–10.

Kryukov, V. A., V. Yu. Silkin, and V. V. Shmat. 2012. "Na krayu propasti, ili kak my zabludilis' v poiskakh legkikh putei." *EKO: Vserossiiskii ekonomicheskii zhurnal* 8: 71–96.

Kryukov, V. A., A. N. Tokarev, and V. V. Shmat. 2016. "How Can We Preserve Our Oil and Gas 'Hearth'?" *Problems of Economic Transition* 58, no. 2: 73–95.

Kushkumbayev, S., and A. Kushkumbayeva. 2013. "Water and Energy Issues in the Context of International and Political Disputes in Central Asia." *Chinese Journal of International Law* 12, no. 2: 211–218.

Lachapelle, Erick, Robert MacNeil, and Matthew Paterson. 2017. "The Political Economy of Decarbonisation: From Green Energy 'Race' to Green 'Division of Labour'." *New Political Economy* 22, no. 3: 311–327.

Larchenko, Lyubov V., and Roman A. Kolesnikov. 2017. "The Development of the Russian Oil and Gas Industry in Terms of Sanctions and Falling Oil Prices." *International Journal of Energy Economics and Policy* 7, no. 2: 352–359.

Laruelle, Marlène. 2014. *Russia's Arctic Strategies and the Future of the Far North*. Armonk, NY: M. E. Sharpe.

Lechtenböhmer, Stefan, Carmen Dienst, Manfred Fischedick, Thomas Hanke, Roger Fernandez, Don Robinson, et al. 2007. "Tapping the Leakages: Methane Losses, Mitigation Options and Policy Issues for Russian Long-Distance Gas Transmission Pipelines." *International Journal of Greenhouse Gas Control* 1: 387–395.

Locatelli, Catherine. 2006. "The Russian Oil Industry between Public and Private Governance: Obstacles to International Oil Companies' Investment Strategies." *Energy Policy* 34, no. 9: 1075–1085.

Locatelli, Catherine, and Sylvain Rossiaud. 2011. "A Neoinstitutionalist Interpretation of the Changes in the Russian Oil Model." *Energy Policy* 39, no. 9: 5588–5597.

Loe, Julia S., and Olga Ladehaug. 2012. "Reducing Gas Flaring in Russia: Gloomy Outlook in Times of Economic Insecurity." *Energy Policy* 50: 507–517.

Lucas, Edward. 2014. *The New Cold War*. New York: St. Martin's Press.

Lunden, Lars, Daniel Fjaertoft, Indra Øverland, and Alesia Prachakova. 2013. "Gazprom vs. Other Russian Gas Producers: The Evolution of the Russian Gas Sector." *Energy Policy* 61: 663–670.

Makarov, A., A. Galkina, E. Grushevenko, D. Grushevenko, V. Kulagin, T. Mitrova, and S. Sorokin. 2014. "Perspektivy mirovoi energetiki do 2040 g." *Mirovaia ekonomika i mezhdunarodnye otnosheniia* 1: 3–20.

Markowitz, Lawrence P. 2017. "The Resource Curse Reconsidered: Cash Crops and Local Violence in Kyrgyzstan." *Terrorism and Political Violence* 29, no. 2: 342–358.

Marples, David R. 1999. "Environmental and Health Problems in the Sakha Republic." *Post-Soviet Geography and Economics* 40, no. 1: 62–77.

Marples, David R. 2004. "Chernobyl: A Reassessment." *Eurasian Geography and Economics* 45, no. 8: 588–607.

Martinot, Eric. 1999. "Renewable Energy in Russia: Markets, Development and Technology Transfer." *Renewable and Sustainable Energy Reviews* 3, no. 1: 49–75.

McCauley, Darren, Raphel Heffron, Maria Pavlenko, Robert Rehner, and Ryan Holmes. 2016. "Energy Justice in the Arctic: Implications for Energy Infrastructural Development in the Arctic." *Energy Research & Social Science* 16: 141–146.

Mehlum, Halvor, Karl Moene, and Ragnar Torvik. 2006. "Institutions and the Resource Curse." *Economic Journal* 116, no. 508: 1–20.

Meredith, Spencer B. 2014. *Nuclear Energy Safety and International Cooperation: Closing the World's Most Dangerous Reactors*. London: Routledge.

Milov, Vladimir, and Boris Nemtsov. 2008. *Putin and Gazprom: An Independent Expert Report*. Moscow: Novaya Gazeta.

Ministry of Energy of the Russian Federation. 2003. *Energeticheskaya Strategia Rossii v Period do 2020*. Moscow: Ministry of Energy.

Mitrova, Tatiana. 2009. "Natural Gas in Transition: Systemic Reform Issues." In *Russian and CIS Gas Markets and Their Impact on Europe*, edited by Simon Pirani, 13–53. Oxford: Oxford University Press for the Oxford Energy Institute.

Mitrova, Tatiana. 2016. *Shifting Political Economy of Russian Oil and Gas*. Washington, DC: CSIS.

Najman, Boris, Richard Pomfret, and Gaël Raballand, eds. 2008. *The Economics and Politics of Oil in the Caspian Basin: The Redistribution of Oil Revenues in Azerbaijan and Central Asia*. New York: Routledge.

Nalimov, Pavel, and Dmitry Rudenko. 2015. "Socio-economic Problems of the Yamal-Nenets Autonomous Okrug Development." *Procedia Economics and Finance* 24: 543–549.

Netalieva, Indira, Justus Wesseler, and Wim Heijman. 2005. "Health Costs Caused by Oil Extraction Air Emissions and the Benefits from Abatement: The Case of Kazakhstan." *Energy Policy* 33, no. 9: 1169–1177.

Nosko, P. A. 2017. "Parizhskoe soglashenie po klimatu kak opredelyayoshchii faktor budushchego mirovoy ekonomiki i posledstbiya dlya Possii." *Financy: Teoriya i praktika* 21, no. 1: 145–150.

Novikova, Natalya I. 2016. "Who Is Responsible for the Russian Arctic? Co-operation between Indigenous Peoples and Industrial Companies in the Context of Legal Pluralism." *Energy Research & Social Science* 16: 98–110.

Nurlankyzy, Sabina, Yi Xiong, Mengliang Luo, and Ke Wang. 2016. "Investigation on Solar Energy Industry Development Model in Kazakhstan." *Open Journal of Business and Management* 4, no. 3: 393–400.

Nygren, Bertil. 2008. "Putin's Use of Natural Gas to Reintegrate the CIS Region." *Problems of Post-Communism* 55, no. 4: 3–15.

Ogneva-Himmelberger, Yelena, and Julian Agyeman, eds. 2009. *Environmental Justice and Sustainability in the Former Soviet Union.* Cambridge, MA: The MIT Press.

Orban, Anita. 2008. *Power, Energy, and the New Russian Imperialism.* Westport, CT: Praeger.

Orttung, Robert W., and Indra Øverland. 2011. "A Limited Toolbox: Explaining the Constraints on Russia's Foreign Energy Policy." *Journal of Eurasian Studies* 2, no. 1: 74–85.

O'Sullivan, Meghan. 2017. *Windfall: How the New Energy Abundance Upends Global Politics and Strengthens America's Power.* New York: Simon & Schuster.

Øverland, Indra, and Heidi Kjærnet. 2009. *Russian Renewable Energy: The Potential for International Cooperation.* Farnham, UK: Ashgate.

Paltsev, Sergey. 2016. "The Complicated Geopolitics of Renewable Energy." *Bulletin of the Atomic Scientists* 72, no. 6: 390–395.

Pardo Sierra, Oscar B. 2011. "No Man's Land? A Comparative Analysis of the EU and Russia's Influence in the Southern Caucasus." *Communist and Post-Communist Studies* 44, no. 3: 233–243.

Pastukhova, Maria, and Kirsten Westphal. 2016. *A Common Energy Market in the Eurasian Economic Union: Implications for the European Union and Energy Relations with Russia.* SWP Comments 9/2016. Berlin: SWP.

Petri, Martin, and Günther Taube. 2003. "Fiscal Policy Beyond the Budget: Quasi-fiscal Activities in the Energy Sectors of the Former Soviet Union." *Emerging Markets Finance and Trade* 39, no. 1: 24–42.

Pika, A. 1999. *Neotraditionalism in the Russian North: Indigenous Peoples and the Legacy of Perestroika.* Seattle: University of Washington Press.

Pirani, Simon, ed. 2009. *Russian and CIS Gas Markets and Their Impact on Europe.* Oxford: Oxford University Press for the Oxford Institute for Energy Studies.

Plank, Christina. 2016. "The Agrofuels Project in Ukraine: How Oligarchs and the EU Foster Agrarian Injustice." In *Fairness and Justice in Natural Resource Politics,* edited by Melanie Pichler, Cornelia Staritz, Karin Küblböck, Christina Plank, Werner Raza, and Fernando Ruiz Peyré, 218–236. London: Routledge.

Pleines, Heiko. 2012. "The Role of Corruption in the Governance of the Oil and Gas Industry." In *Challenges of the Caspian Resource Boom: Domestic Elites and Policy-making,* edited by Andreas Heinrich and Heiko Pleines, 205–216. Basingstoke, UK: Palgrave Macmillan.

Prokopenko, Alina. 2013. "Wind Power Sector Development in the Russian Federation and Other Countries of the Commonwealth of the Independent States (CIS)." In *Wind Power for the World: International Reviews and Developments,* edited by Preben Maegaard, Anna Krenz, and Wolfgang Palz, 510–534. Singapore: Pan Stanford Publishing.

Pusenkova, N. N. 2010. "Gosudarstvo v neftyanoi otrasli." *EKO: Vserossiiskii ekonomicheskii zhurnal* 9: 50–68.

Radnitz, Scott. 2012. "Oil in the Family: Managing Presidential Succession in Azerbaijan." *Democratization* 19, no. 1: 60–77.

Reznikov, A. P. 1989. "Utilizing the Solar Energy Resources of the Eastern and High-latitude Regions of the USSR." *Soviet Geography* 30, no. 7: 576–585.

Roberts, Sean P. 2017. "The Eurasian Economic Union: The Geopolitics of Authoritarian Cooperation." *Eurasian Geography and Economics* 58, no. 4: 418–441.

Robinson, James, Ragnar Torvik, and Thierry Verdier. 2006. "Political Foundations of the Resource Curse." *Journal of Development Economics* 79, no. 2: 446–468.

Rogelj, Joeri, Oliver Fricko, Malte Meinshausen, Volker Krey, Johanna J. J. Zilliacus, and Keywan Riahi. 2017. "Understanding the Origin of Paris Agreement Emission Uncertainties." *Nature Communications* 8: 15748. doi:10.1038/ncomms15748.

Rogers, Douglas. 2015. *The Depths of Russia: Oil, Power, and Culture after Socialism*. Ithaca, NY: Cornell University Press.

Romanova, Tatiana. 2013. "Energy Demand: Security of Suppliers?" In *International Handbook of Energy Security*, edited by Hugh Dyer and Maria J. Trombetta, 239–257. Cheltenham, UK: Edward Elgar.

Ross, Michael. 2018. "The Politics of the Resource Curse: A Review." In *Oxford Handbook of the Politics of Development*, edited by Carol Lancaster and Nicolas van de Walle, 200–223. Oxford: Oxford University Press.

Rusu, Eugen, and Florin Onea. 2013. "Evaluation of the Wind and Wave Energy Along the Caspian Sea." *Energy* 50: 1–14.

Sagers, Matthew J. 2007. "Developments in Russian Gas Production Since 1998: Russia's Evolving Gas Supply Strategy." *Eurasian Geography and Economics* 48, no. 6: 651–698.

Sakwa, Richard. 2009. *The Quality of Freedom: Putin, Khodorkovsky and the Yukos Affair*. Oxford: Oxford University Press.

Sakwa, Richard. 2013. *Putin and the Oligarch: The Khodorkovsky–Yukos Affair*. London: I. B. Tauris & Co.

Scott, Michael J., Jeffery E. Dagle, Krista L. Gaustad, Marylynn Placet, Joseph M. Roop, Lawrence A. Schienbein, et al. 1995. "Dark after Chernobyl? Closing Former Soviet Power Reactors." *Energy Policy* 23, no. 8: 703–717.

Shaffer, Brenda. 2010. "Caspian Energy Phase II: Beyond 2005." *Energy Policy* 38, no. 11: 7209–7215.

Shiells, Clinton R. 2005. "VAT Design and Energy Trade: The Case of Russia and Ukraine." *IMF Staff Papers* 52, no. 1: 103–119.

Sim, Li-Chen. 2017. "Economic Diversification in Russia: Nuclear to the Rescue?" In *Economic Diversification Policies in Natural Resource Rich Economies*, edited by Sami Mahroum and Yasser Al-Saleh, 175–202. London: Routledge.

Sirina, Anna A. 2010. "Oil and Gas Development in Russia and Northern Indigenous Peoples." In *Russia and the North*, edited by Elana Wilson Rowe, 187–202. Ottawa: University of Ottawa Press.

Sitnikova, O. V. 2009. "Sotsial'no-orientirovannaya tarifnaya politika v energetike regiona." *EKO: Vserossiiskii ekonomicheskii zhurnal* 2: 172–176.

Smeets, Niels. 2017. "Similar Goals, Divergent Motives: The Enabling and Constraining Factors of Russia's Capacity-based Renewable Energy Support Scheme." *Energy Policy* 101: 138–149.

Söderbergh, Bengt, Kristofer Jakobsson, and Kjell Aleklett. 2010. "European Energy Security: An Analysis of Future Russian Natural Gas Production and Exports." *Energy Policy* 38, no. 12: 7827–7843.

Solanko, Laura, and Pekka Sutela. 2009. "Too Much or Too Little Russian Gas to Europe?" *Eurasian Geography and Economics* 50, no. 1: 58–74.

Soloviy, V. I. 2017. "Climate Finance in the Context of the Paris Agreement: Opportunities and Cautions for the Ukraine." *Naukovii visnik NLTU Ukraini: Seriya ekonomichna* 27, no. 2: 38–41.

Soltanieh, Mohammad, Anigineh Zohrabian, Mohammad J. Gholipour, and Eugenia Kalnay. 2016. "A Review of Global Gas Flaring and Venting and Impact on the Environment: Case Study of Iran." *International Journal of Greenhouse Gas Control* 49: 488–509.

Stern, Jonathan. 2009. "The Russian Gas Balance to 2050: Difficult Times Ahead." In *Russian and CIS Gas Markets and Their Impact on Europe*, edited by Simon Pirani, 54–92. Oxford: Oxford University Press for the Oxford Institute for Energy Studies.

Stern, Jonathan. 2017. "The Future of Gas in Decarbonising European Energy Markets." OIES Paper NG no. 116. Oxford: Oxford Institute for Energy Studies.

Stern, Jonathan, Simon Pirani, and Katja Yafimava. 2009. "The Russo-Ukrainian Gas Dispute of January 2009: A Comprehensive Assessment." OIES Paper NG no. 27. Oxford: Oxford Institute for Energy Studies.

Stulberg, Adam N. 2017. "Natural Gas and the Russia-Ukraine Crisis: Strategic Restraint and the Emerging Europe-Eurasia Gas Network." *Energy Research & Social Science* 24: 71–85.

Suslov, N. I. 2014. "Rent Is Our Everything." *Problems of Economic Transition* 56, no. 10: 78–89.

Szulecki, Kacper, ed. 2018. *Energy Security in Europe: Divergent Perceptions and Policy Challenges*. Cham, Switzerland: Palgrave Macmillan.

Szulecki, Kacper, and Julia Kusznir. 2018. "Energy Security and Energy Transition: Securitization in the Electricity Sector." In *Energy Security in Europe: Divergent Perceptions and Policy Challenges*, edited by Kacper Szulecki, 117–148. Cham, Switzerland: Palgrave Macmillan.

Szulecki, Kacper, and Kirsten Westphal. 2018. "Taking Security Seriously in EU Energy Governance: Crimean Shock and the Energy Union." In *Energy Security in Europe: Divergent Perceptions and Policy Challenges*, edited by Kacper Szulecki, 177–202. Cham, Switzerland: Palgrave Macmillan.

Tarr, David G. 2016. "The Eurasian Economic Union of Russia, Belarus, Kazakhstan, Armenia, and the Kyrgyz Republic: Can It Succeed Where Its Predecessor Failed?" *Eastern European Economics* 54, no. 1: 1–22.

Thomas, Marzhan. 2015. "Social, Environmental and Economic Sustainability of Kazakhstan: A Long-term Perspective." *Central Asian Survey* 34, no. 4: 456–483.

Thomas, Steve. 1999. "Economic and Safety Pressures on Nuclear Power: A Comparison of Russia and Ukraine since the Break-up of the Soviet Union." *Energy Policy* 27, no. 13: 745–767.

Tompson, William. 2010. "Back to the Future? Thoughts on the Political Economy of Expanding State Ownership in Russia." In *Institutions, Ideas and Leadership in Russian Politics*, edited by Julie M. Newton and William J. Tompson, 67–87. New York: Palgrave Macmillan.

Turnbull, M. 1991. *Soviet Environmental Policies: The Most Critical Investment*. Brookfield, VT: Dartmouth.

Tysiachniouk, Maria, Laura A. Henry, Machiel Lamers, and Jan P. M Van Tatenhove. 2017. "Oil Extraction and Benefit Sharing in an Illiberal Context: The Nenets and Komi-Izhemtsi Indigenous Peoples in the Russian Arctic." *Society & Natural Resources* 31, no. 5: 556–579.

Tysiachniouk, Maria, Laura A. Henry, Machiel Lamers, and Jan P. M Van Tatenhove. 2018. "Rethinking Equity and Governance in Benefit Sharing Agreements." *Energy Research & Social Science* 37: 140–152.

Tysiachniouk, Maria, and Andrey Petrov. 2018. "Benefit Sharing in the Arctic Energy Sector: Perspectives on Corporate Policies and Practices in Northern Russia and Alaska." *Energy Research & Social Science* 39: 29–34.

Ulanov, V.L. 2011. "O putyakh reformirovaniya estestvennykh monopolii." *EKO: Vserossiiskii ekonomicheskii zhurnal* 6: 139–146.

United Nations (UN). 2013. *2010 Energy Statistics Yearbook*. New York: United Nations, https://unstats.un.org/unsd/energy/yearbook/2010eyb.pdf.

United Nations (UN). 2016. *2014 Energy Statistics Yearbook*. New York: United Nations, https://unstats.un.org/unsd/energy/yearbook/2014.htm.

United Nations (UN). 2017. *2015 Energy Statistics Yearbook*. New York: United Nations, https://unstats.un.org/unsd/energy/yearbook/2015.htm.

Uulu, Bakhtiar B., and Kadyrzhan Smagulov. 2011. "Central Asia's Hydropower Problems: Regional States' Policy and Development Prospects." *Central Asia and the Caucasus* 12, no. 1: 81–87.

Vahtra, Peeter, Kari Liuhto, and Harri Lorentz. 2007. "Privatization of Re-nationalisation in Russia." *Journal of East-European Management Studies* 12, no. 4: 273–296.

Van de Graaf, Thijs, and Jeff D. Colgan. 2017. "Russian Gas Games or Well-oiled Conflict? Energy Security and the 2014 Ukraine Crisis." *Energy Research & Social Sciences* 24: 59–64.

Victor, David G., Nebojša Nakićenović, and Nadejda Victor. 2001. "The Kyoto Protocol Emission Allocations: Windfall Surpluses for Russia and Ukraine." *Climatic Change* 49, no. 3: 263–277.

Vinokurov, Evgeny. 2017. "Eurasian Economic Union: Current State and Preliminary Results." *Russian Journal of Economics* 3, no. 1: 54–70.

Vivoda, Vlado. 2009. "Resource Nationalism, Bargaining and International Oil Companies: Challenges and Change in the New Millennium." *New Political Economy* 14, no. 4: 517–534.

Wegerich, Kai, Oliver Olsson, and Jochen Froebrich. 2007. "Reliving the Past in a Changed Environment: Hydropower Ambitions, Opportunities and Constraints in Tajikistan." *Energy Policy* 35, no. 7: 3815–3825.

Wengle, Suzanne. 2015. *Post-Soviet Power: State-led Development and Russia's Marketization*. New York: Cambridge University Press.

Westphal, Kirsten. 2014. *Russian Energy Supplies to Europe: The Crimea Crisis, Mutual Dependency, Lasting Collateral Damage and Strategic Alternatives for the European Union*. Berlin: SWP (SWP Comments 16/2014).

Williams, Aled, and Philippe Le Billon. 2017. *Corruption, Natural Resources and Development: From Resource Curse to Political Ecology*. Cheltenham, UK: Edward Elgar.

Winzer, Christian. 2012. "Conceptualizing Energy Security." *Energy Policy* 46: 36–48.

Wolczuk, Kataryna. 2016. "Managing the Flows of Gas and Rules: Ukraine between the EU and Russia." *Eurasian Geography and Economics* 57, no. 1: 113–137.

Yafimava, Katja. 2011. *The Transit Dimension of EU Energy Security: Russian Gas Transit across Ukraine, Belarus, and Moldova*. Oxford: Oxford University Press.

Yakovlev, Andrei. 2006. "The Evolution of Business-State Interaction in Russia: From State Capture to Business Capture?" *Europe-Asia Studies* 58, no. 7: 1033–1056.

Youngs, Richard. 2009. *Energy Security: Europe's New Foreign Policy Challenge*. London: Routledge.

Ziegler, Charles. 1990. *Environmental Policy in the USSR*. Amherst: University of Massachusetts Press.

APPENDIX: CHRONOLOGY OF MAIN ENERGY EVENTS FOR RUSSIA AND EURASIA, 1992–2018

1992	A presidential decree calls for the breakup of the Soviet oil monopoly.
1993	Remnants of the Soviet Ministry of Gas Industry are transformed into a state-controlled, vertically integrated company, Gazprom.
1995	As a result of the "loans for shares" program, oil companies Sidanko, Yukos, and Sibneft become the property of private banks.
1996	The restructuring of the oil sector is completed, with the former oil monopolist divided among eleven vertically integrated, partially privatized companies.
2003	The merger of TNK, Sideanko, and Onako with BP's Russian assets creates the largest foreign investment in Russia.
2004	Yukos is disbanded.
2005	State ownership of Gazprom reaches over 50 percent.
2006	The first Ukrainian-Russian gas crisis (a three-day suspension of gas supplies) occurs in January.
2009	In January a 14-day suspension of gas supplies by Russia to Ukraine stops all Russian supplies to Bulgaria, Romania, Macedonia, Serbia, Bosnia-Herzegovina, and Croatia.
2010	The construction of the Nord Stream gas pipeline, connecting Russia and Germany directly under the Baltic Sea, is started.
2011	Privatization of the electricity generator RAO EES is completed; the sector is divided among multiple providers.
2013	Russia's LNG exports are liberalized.
2013	Rosneft's takeover of TNK-BP is completed, making Rosneft the world's largest-output oil producer.
2014	Gazprom signs a 30-year, $400 billion contract to supply gas to China.
2014	Sanctions on Russian oil gas sectors are imposed as a result of Russian intervention in Ukraine.
2018	The United States announces new sanctions on Russian energy companies, further tightening their access to financing and technology.

CHAPTER 21

....

THE ENERGY POLITICS
OF CHINA

....

JONAS NAHM

CHINA's energy sector is a study in contradictions. Each new Five-Year Plan issued by the central government in Beijing exceeds the previous one in its ambitions to transition to cleaner sources of energy. In 2016 China accounted for 81 percent of the world's manufacturing capacity of silicon solar cells. It also installed 42 percent of the world's wind turbines, virtually all of them manufactured domestically (Ball et al. 2017; GWEC 2017). Yet in spite of China's progress toward meeting its target of installing 315 gigawatts (GW) of wind and solar power by 2020, rapid economic growth and lax enforcement of energy and environmental regulations have triggered an air pollution crisis of unprecedented magnitude. Along with transport and industrial emissions, relentless investment in new coal power generation has spread an environmental problem once confined to centers of industrialization in Northeast China to coastal and interior provinces, where pollution levels in cities at times exceed conventional measurement scales (Davidson, Kahrl, and Karplus 2017; Guan et al. 2009).

The coexistence of ambitious clean energy policies and continued investment in fossil fuels in China is both confounding and important. It is confounding because China's authoritarian context in principle offers the central leadership strong policy levers to follow through on its commitments. And it is important because China is the world's largest emitter of greenhouse gases, making the future trajectory of its domestic energy sector central to any effort to limit anthropogenic climate change. This chapter reviews the literature in Chinese politics to provide an overview of key patterns that have shaped politics and policymaking in China's energy sector. Much of the literature explains contradictions inherent in China's energy sector through the lens of fragmented authoritarianism. Paying close attention to the role of institutions and incentives, this perspective regards Chinese politics as the result of bargaining among the many functional and regional administrative entities with distinct bureaucratic goals and organizational interests tasked with policy formulation, implementation, and enforcement (Lieberthal and Oksenberg 1988; Lieberthal 1992; Mertha 2005). Policy makers respond to divergent institutional incentives, causing the Chinese state to pursue policies and implementation strategies with contradictory goals.

The empirical focus of this chapter is the politics of shifting to cleaner sources of energy. Not only is China's clean energy transition of critical importance to a global politics of energy and climate change, but it also provides a particularly lucid window into the role of institutional incentives in structuring policymaking in China against opposition from vested interests. Space limitations preclude a full survey of all aspects of China's energy sector governance here, yet the empirics and theoretical approaches covered here apply to broader patterns of energy policymaking in China. While overseas direct investment in oil and hydropower, China's domestic nuclear energy program, and attempts to curb industrial energy consumption receive only brief treatment in this chapter, the same concepts and theoretical approaches apply.

The chapter proceeds as follows. The first section reviews China's overall energy and fuel mix. This is followed by a review of theoretical approaches to energy politics in China, and then a discussion of the role of institutions and incentives in three key energy subsectors: renewables, coal, and oil and gas. The final section concludes and spells out implications for future research.

Energy Demand, Supply, and Fuel Mix

China's progress toward a low carbon energy economy has not been without obstacles. Since the beginning of economic reforms in 1978, China's domestic economy has expanded more than twentyfold. Gross domestic product (GDP) increased from US$395 billion in 1980 to US$9.2 trillion in 2015; between 2000 and 2015 alone, economic activity more than tripled. Improvements in energy intensity over this period have not been able to offset the rise in energy demand caused by rapid economic growth (Figure 21.1). An export-oriented manufacturing economy; the attraction of energy-intensive industries such as steel, aluminum, and cement manufacturing; and rising living standards, among other factors, caused energy consumption to soar by a factor of six between 1980 and 2015 (IEA 2017a).

China's economy continues to be more energy intensive than Organisation for Economic Co-operation and Development (OECD) economies. As a result of lower per capita GDP—in 2017, per capita GDP was only 23 percent of the average for OECD states—per capita energy consumption continues to trail advanced industrialized economies. With a population of more than 1.4 billion, China has nevertheless become the largest energy consumer in the world and is now also the largest emitter of greenhouse gases (IEA 2017a; World Bank 2017). In 2015, industry accounted for half of domestic energy demand, with iron and steel, cement (nonmetallic minerals), and petrochemical industries making up two-thirds of industrial energy consumption (Figure 21.2). Residential energy use and transportation constituted 16.4 and 15.7 percent of total final consumption, respectively (IEA 2017a).

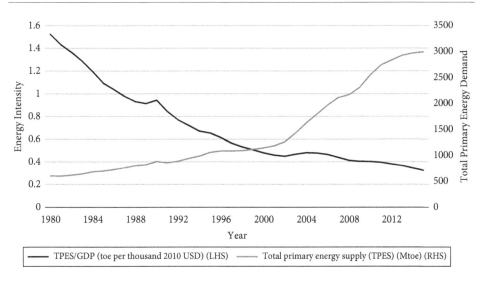

FIGURE 21.1 Energy demand and energy intensity (1980–2015).

Source: Based on data from IEA (2017a).

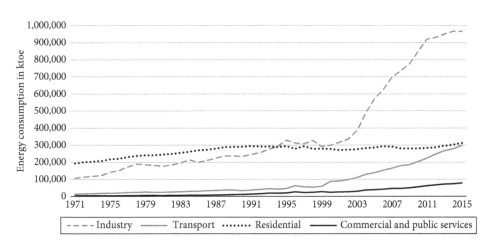

FIGURE 21.2 Energy consumption by sector in China (1971–2015).

Source: Based on data from IEA (2017a).

Only a fraction of China's energy demand comes from low carbon sources (Figure 21.3). Although increasing private car ownership is expected to increase oil demand, the nation continues to rely on coal for most of its energy needs (*Economist* 2016). In 2015 coal accounted for two-thirds of energy supply, followed by oil at 18 percent. China's power sector relied on coal for 70 percent of electricity generation in 2015, down from 80 percent in 2005. Coal-powered power plants generated 4,109 terawatt hours (TWh) in 2015, compared to 1,471 TWh in the United States (IEA 2017a). Carbon

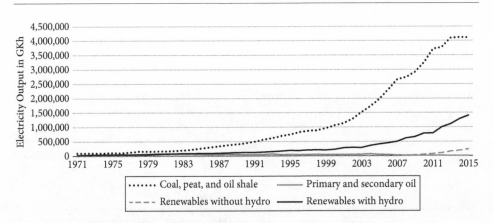

FIGURE 21.3 Electricity generation by fuel source.

Source: Based on data from IEA (2017a).

emissions and air pollution from China's heavy reliance on coal are two reasons China's central government has attempted to diversify domestic energy sources; a growing reliance on imports is a second motivation to encourage investment in renewable sources of energy. China has relied on imported oil since 1993. It is now the world's largest importer of crude oil, outstripping the United States as a result of increased demand in China and increased domestic production in the United States. In 2015, 62 percent of crude oil consumed domestically came from foreign sources (Andrews-Speed 2012; Hornby 2017; IEA 2017b; Sheppard and Meyer 2015).

ENERGY POLITICS IN CHINA: ACTORS AND INCENTIVES

Literature on China's energy sector has identified institutions as a central factor in the discrepancy between state ambitions to transition to a low carbon economy and a domestic energy sector that continues to be dominated by fossil fuels. Although formally a unitary, authoritarian state under the rule of the Chinese Communist Party (CCP), China is not monolithic. Its system of policymaking institutions continues to resemble what Lieberthal termed "fragmented authoritarianism": policies issued by the central government in Beijing are shaped by a plethora of bureaucratic goals and organizational interests of functional and regional administrative entities charged with policy implementation (Kostka and Nahm 2017; Lieberthal and Oksenberg 1988; Lieberthal 1992; Mertha 2005).

Institutional fragmentation is of course not the only explanatory framework applied to Chinese politics. Scholars have argued that the key to understanding China's policymaking practices is not a set of institutional incentives but its under-institutionalization

(Ang 2016). Perry and Heilmann contend that policymaking in China, including in the energy sector, is an adaptive system of experimentation that defies conventional paradigms in political science. Perry and Heilmann do not deny the importance of China's decentralized governance institutions, but focus on governance practices rooted in the CCP's revolutionary origins that allow for bottom-up policy input by combining ongoing local experimentation with the threat of central government interference (Heilmann and Perry 2011; Heilmann 2018).

Others have critiqued the institutional approach by pointing to the role of ties, networks, and competing factions among CCP officials (Cai and Treisman 2006). Personal ties and networks among executives of China's national oil companies (NOCs), for instance, led to the establishment of a "petroleum clique" with significant influence over government policymaking. In an attempt to reassert its power against competing factions, the Xi administration removed a number of oil industry executives tied to the "petroleum clique" after corruption probes (Liao 2015; Zhiyue 2016). Scholarship on leadership, networks, and factions is frequently concerned with the politics of institutional change, while research focused on experimentation and institutional fragmentation is often primarily interested in the incentives for officials' behavior within the existing macro-institutional context.

Nonetheless, research in the institutional tradition has far outweighed alternative approaches, not least because of methodological difficulties. While policies, institutions, and incentives are relatively well documented, including in myriad yearbooks published at all levels of government, access to study elite politics in China has been notoriously difficult to achieve (Heimer and Thøgersen 2006). The fragmented nature of policymaking institutions carries particular weight in China's energy sector, where governance of various subsectors is distributed across competing bureaucracies at the central government level as well as subnational governments with distinct regional interests, economic opportunities, and resource endowments. For instance, offices of central government agencies at provincial and municipal levels of government formally report vertically to Beijing and horizontally to the provincial and municipal leadership at the same administrative levels that often pursue conflicting mandates. In this context, policy outcomes are determined by bargaining along both vertical and horizontal administrative hierarchies, referred to as *tiao-kuai* (Mertha 2005; Remick 2002).

For an economy with ambitious goals for a transition to cleaner sources of energy, the lack of a central agency tasked with comprehensive energy sector governance is striking. Horizontally, policymaking responsibility is distributed across competing administrative agencies at the central government level in Beijing. Historically, each energy sector—coal, electricity, petroleum, and petrochemicals—was governed by a distinct ministry within the central government in Beijing (Lieberthal and Oksenberg 1988). Despite repeated attempts at creating a single administrative agency in charge of energy governance, functional divisions remain in place. Under the overall direction of the State Council, energy policymaking is divided among eight central government ministries in addition to the National Development and

Reform Commission (NDRC), China's primary government agency in charge of economic policymaking. Additional agencies are charged with supervision of state-owned enterprises—including the NOCs Sinopec and the China National Petroleum Corporation (CNPC), which succeeded the former Ministries for Petroleum and Petrochemicals—regulatory tasks, and coordination between energy sector governance and economy-wide policy areas such as climate change (Andrews-Speed 2012; Chen 2010).

Since 2012, as part of a broader program to centralize energy sector governance under the Xi administration (IEA 2017b; Kostka and Nahm 2017), a number of previously independent agencies were brought under the umbrella of the NDRC, and previously independent climate and environmental tasks were unified in the Ministry of Ecology and Environment (Figure 21.4). Similar reforms may lead to a central energy ministry in the future. As of yet, conflicting interests continue to coexist within the various branches of central government as well as the state-owned oil and coal companies that were created under previous reforms (Grünberg 2017). It is not surprising that the NOCs, agencies tasked with developing policy to reduce reliance on fossil fuels, and the grid companies asked to integrate a rapidly changing energy mix are advocating for distinct visions of energy sector reform.

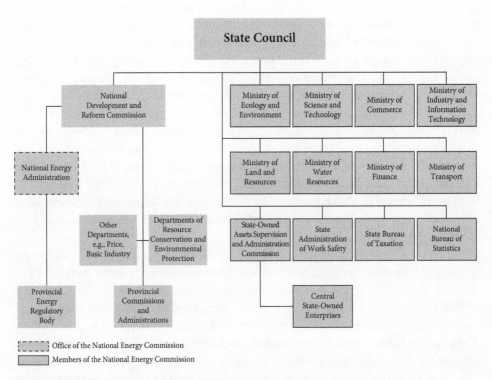

FIGURE 21.4 China's national administrative structure for energy.

Source: Adapted from IEA (2017b). © OECD/IEA 2017 World Energy Outlook, IEA Publishing, License: http://www.iea.org/t&c; as modified by Jonas Nahm.

In addition to fragmentation of government institutions at the central level in Beijing, policymaking in China is subject to vertical fragmentation of responsibility across levels of government. China's administrative hierarchy is divided into five levels of government: central, provincial, prefecture, county, and township. Among scholars of Chinese politics, it is common to refer to subnational governments as "local" governments (Oi 1995; Weingast, Jin, and Qian 2005). Local governments in China possess substantial policymaking autonomy, particularly on economic matters, but are also tasked with implementing and enforcing policies and directives coming from central government agencies in Beijing.

Beginning in the 1980s, fiscal and administrative decentralization was a means to introduce incentives for growth-oriented behavior among subnational government officials as China was transitioning away from the planned economy. By rewarding them for economic growth at the margin, local officials were given incentives to experiment with good economic policy, while reducing the temptation to interfere with a budding private sector in the absence of formal property rights (Montinola, Qian, and Weingast 1995; Weingast, Jin, and Qian 2005). Multiple reforms have since partially reversed decentralization, yet much of the day-to-day business of governing remains the domain of local officials, who continue to have incentives to prioritize economic growth above all else (Heberer and Schubert 2012; Wong 2013; Xu 2011). Using both qualitative analysis (Davidson, Kahrl, and Karplus 2017; Kostka and Hobbs 2012; Mertha 2008; Nahm 2017a) and large-n quantitative methods (van der Kamp, Lorentzen, and Mattingly 2017), scholars have documented officials' resistance to implementing key central policy mandates when they have threatened local economic interests in areas of energy and environmental governance.

Such challenges have been compounded by incentives for local officials that primarily reward short-term economic growth. The combination of local policymaking autonomy with central government control over officials' careers has created tournament-like performance competition among local officials. In this context, studies have confirmed prevalent views about the benefits of decentralized governance as more accountable, efficient, and better informed about local conditions (Birney 2014; Xu 2011; Zhou 2007). However, others have warned that local officials currently receive long lists of binding targets and priority tasks, not all of which are compatible, and not all of which can be accounted for in a comprehensive index for promotion. Faced with conflicting mandates and competing incentives, officials at provincial or municipal levels of government have tended to prioritize short-term economic rewards over environmental protection, investments in sustainability, or the pursuit of long-term upgrading targets (Bo 1996; Guo 2007; Li and Zhou 2005; Lü and Landry 2014; Minzner 2009; Nahm 2017a; O'Brien and Li 1999). Hence, institutional fragmentation along vertical lines and horizontal dependence on local governments have generally led subnational offices of central agencies to adopt the growth-oriented policy preferences of local officials. Perverse incentives have further encouraged collusion among local officials, lax implementation of central government mandates, and poor monitoring (Economy 2010; Van Rooij 2003; Van Rooij et al. 2017).

POLICIES AND IMPLEMENTATION

Five-Year Plans have been central to policymaking in China since the early 1950s. Starting with the period of administrative and fiscal decentralization of the 1980s and 1990s and China's transition away from a planned economy, Five-Year Plans no longer issued directives, but began to lay out broad policy directions envisioned by the central government and the CCP. Five-Year Plans set the top policymaking priorities' targets for government performance, but protected the autonomy and flexibility of government agencies at the central and local levels charged with implementation (Heilmann and Melton 2013). Five-Year Plans issued by the central government are followed by a string of ministry and industry-specific plans, first at the center and then at subnational levels of government. These specific plans defined policy programs to meet central government targets and set implementation schedules. For example, the 13th Five-Year Plan, covering the period 2016–2020, was accompanied by eighteen central-level plans for the energy sector, ranging from the "Medium-and Long-Term Plan for Renewable Energy" to the "13th Five Year Work Plan for Controlling Greenhouse Gas Emissions." Agencies responsible for implementation included the State Council and the National Energy Administration (NEA), but depending on the target sector, also extended responsibility to the Ministry of Finance and the Ministry of Industry and Information Technology (Koleski 2017).

As the main policy documents outlining China's overarching policy trajectory, Five-Year Plans contain the key targets related to China's clean energy transition (Yuan and Zuo 2011). In the 13th Five-Year Plan, covering 2016–2020, ten out of twenty-five core targets were related to energy and the environment, and all ten were on the list of thirteen binding targets that officials have to achieve by 2020. The plan announced the establishment of a national cap-and-trade system for carbon emissions, updated targets for the share of energy generated from renewable sources (from 9.5 percent under the 12th Five-Year Plan to 15 percent), and declared the need for a further reduction of carbon intensity by 18 percent and energy intensity by 15 percent. The plan also set the first cap on overall energy consumption for the nation (Koleski 2017).

The affirmative language included in China's Five-Year Plans can give the impression of a monolithic state capable of directing a centralized policy program to meet government targets. However, as previously discussed, China scholars have refuted the characterization of the Chinese state as monolithic, pointing instead to bureaucratic bargaining, unintended consequences, and perverse incentives of subnational officials in the process of policy implementation. The remainder of this section reviews approaches to the study of Chinese energy politics in the context of energy policy implementation, focusing in particular on renewable energy, coal, and oil and gas as the largest energy subsectors in China.

Clean Energy in the Electric Power Sector

A key element of China's clean energy transition has been the focus on non-carbon sources of energy in the electric power sector. (For an introduction to various types of renewable energy, see Bahr, Boeing, and Szarka in this volume.) This emphasis has included, since the 1990s, an active effort by the central government to promote the development of domestic nuclear power plants. The central government has set a target of 58 GW of installed capacity and 30 GW under construction by 2020, making China the largest market for nuclear power plants in the world (Zeng et al. 2016). Although scholars of Chinese politics have paid relatively little attention to the development of China's nuclear energy industry, it is clear that China's nuclear energy sector has benefited from substantial R&D support, credit financing from China's state-owned development banks, and international technology transfers, which have often been a contractual requirement for foreign vendors (Metzler and Steinfeld 2013; Steinfeld 2015). In contrast to advanced industrialized economies, China only briefly halted its domestic nuclear program after the Fukushima incident, and surveys indicate a positive public attitude toward nuclear power in China (He et al. 2013; Yuan et al. 2017).

Despite these favorable conditions, China has repeatedly missed its nuclear development targets. Xu (2010), in one of the few book-length analyses of nuclear power in China, warns that the nuclear energy sector is a classic case of fragmented authoritarianism. In the past, the lack of a central agency in charge of nuclear power, poor coordination capacity among firms and administrative agencies in charge of nuclear power development, and competing commercial interests, not least from the fossil fuel industry, have frequently hindered the efficient implementation of central government guidelines. Whether recent administrative reforms and leadership changes under the Xi administration have removed such obstacles to nuclear power development remains to be seen. A recent review of nuclear energy development suggests that a slowing economy and electricity demand, electricity sector reforms that remove some of the commercial advantages of centralized base-load power generation, and technological innovation in other sectors have cast uncertainty over the future trajectory of China's nuclear power sector (Hibbs 2018).

As such, the nuclear power sector shares key characteristics with the wind and solar industries, which have received more extensive scholarly attention. Both wind and solar sectors were targeted by central and subsequently local government agencies with demand-side policies to accelerate domestic deployment and through supply-side incentives to encourage the development of domestic wind and solar manufacturing industries. However, divergent interests of central government agencies, state-owned companies, and subnational actors have resulted in implementation gaps between state goals and outcomes.

Wind Energy

China is the world's largest wind energy market; it is on track to meet its stated target of 250 GW installed capacity by 2020 (GWEC 2017). Yet the successful deployment of large-scale wind generation capacity obscures the complex bargaining among government agencies and state-owned enterprises that occurred during policy implementation.

In 2006, coinciding with the beginning of the 11th Five-Year Plan, China's first Renewable Energy Law established a comprehensive national framework for wind power installation. It included a wind power feed-in tariff, which in 2009 replaced a previous concession program that had tendered 2.6 GW of wind power development permits since 2003. The concession system was effective in rapidly expanding renewable energy capacity on the grid, yet fragmentation within central government institutions allowed state-owned energy companies to exploit the implementation process and prevent access for nonstate actors (Han et al. 2009; Hochstetler and Kostka 2015; Lema and Ruby 2007; Nahm and Steinfeld 2014a). The new law established mandatory access to the grid, set a designated price for wind power, and established a cost-sharing arrangement among provinces, through which the cost of subsidies for renewable energy was distributed to alleviate the financial burden on provinces with high wind power potential (Lewis 2013; Zhang, Andrews-Speed, and Zhao 2013). Incentives for renewable energy deployment were coupled with policies to support the growth of a domestic turbine manufacturing industry (Lewis 2014b).

Subsequent implementation of wind energy policy was shaped in particular by divergent interests of central and local actors. Global wind turbine manufacturers and component suppliers set up manufacturing facilities in China and transferred know-how and technology to local partners through licensing agreements, joint ventures, and joint development agreements (Lewis 2013). Incentives for local officials to target short-term economic gains yielded generous land deals, tax breaks, and preferential bank loans for turbine manufacturers in local development zones. Turbine manufacturers responded by focusing on the rapid scale-up of production regardless of the domestic market environment, pushed by continued support from provincial and municipal governments. While manufacturing investment led to rapid cost declines as a result of economies of scale and the development of strong technological capabilities focused on manufacturing innovation among some manufacturers, it also yielded overcapacity and large numbers of domestic manufacturers lacking technical skills. By 2011 some eighty turbine manufacturers were operating in China, many propped up by local governments. Only a fraction was competitive by international standards (Gosens and Lu 2014; Kirkegaard 2017; Nahm 2017b; Nahm and Steinfeld 2014a).

As China's wind power capacity expanded rapidly over the course of the 11th and 12th Five-Year Plans, China's fragmented energy governance institutions continued to give rise to new problems, including a high proportion of turbines lacking grid connection, frequent breakdowns among the domestic turbine fleet, and poor coordination in grid planning. Rather than mandating a percentage of energy generated from wind, capacity targets included in central government plans offered local officials the ability to meet goals without actually ensuring a grid connection. At least in the short term, this practice reduced competition for local coal power plants, which were an important source of revenue for municipal and provincial administrations (Williams and Kahrl 2008). Although the Chinese central government retained planning approval authority for wind parks with more than 50 MW capacity, local officials—to shore up investment, tax revenue, and local jobs—resorted to the common practice of splitting up larger parks to retain approval authority. In approving individual installations just below 50 MW capacity, local governments had few incentives to consider overall grid capacity or the long-term development needs of the domestic power market. The central government's authority to approve the construction of transmission lines further contributed to a mismatch between local investments in generation capacity and overall grid design (Zhang, Andrews-Speed, and Zhao 2013; Zhang et al. 2016).

Despite the central government's requiring turbine manufacturers to improve their technological capabilities, noneconomic considerations continued to hinder local implementation, undermining views that China has developed a highly adaptive policy-making system that rapidly incorporates corrections and feedback from local experimentation (Heilmann 2018; Lewis 2013). Local protectionism prevented cross-provincial electricity transfers in China's six regional grids. Such protectionism contributed to China's high levels of wind energy curtailment, essentially a practice of preventing wind power generators feeding all the available wind power into the grid. Curtailment and the associated waste of available wind energy was particularly prevalent in China's northern provinces, where concentrated wind resources far outpaced low local electricity demand. While the central government called for improved coordination, separate arms of the state continued to conduct grid planning and capacity planning. Interprovincial transfers were administratively determined, providing officials with the opportunity to limit energy imports in favor of local power generators. Power exchange prices negotiated by provincial administrators further reflected political and economic preferences of local officials, contributing to average national curtailment rates for wind power of 17 percent in 2016. Northern provinces reached seasonal wind power curtailment rates of up to 60 percent (Davidson, Kahrl, and Karplus 2017; Dupuy 2017; Hurlbut et al. 2017; Yin et al. 2017).

A set of electricity sector reforms announced in 2015 by the State Council to forge the creation of regional power markets and establish priority dispatch for renewable sources of power had not been implemented by 2017. Central and local governments and state-owned enterprises, including grid operator State Grid, have sought to use the reform process to advance their interests and influence the national policy in their favor (Davidson, Kahrl, and Karplus 2017; Xu 2016; Zhang, Andrews-Speed, and Li 2018). Flattening demand for power due to a slowing economy is likely to exacerbate such distributional fights in a restructured domestic power industry (IEA 2017b). Hence, the politics of power sector reform in China remains an important field of study, not just for its implications for the future of wind power in China, but also for China's broader ability to meet its ambitious climate goals.

Solar Energy

China's energy governance institutions gave rise to a set of solar sector policies that were at least initially driven by local government initiative. Until the central government established a mechanism to support a domestic solar photovoltaic (PV) market in 2009, preferential policies were available from local governments and primarily targeted solar PV manufacturing. High-technology zones (HTZs) became convenient vehicles for local governments to rapidly increase economic growth and tax revenues within their jurisdiction by shifting to support mass production rather than long-term investments in innovation, as originally intended (Breznitz and Murphree 2011; Sutherland 2005). For solar firms setting up production facilities, local governments offered tax breaks, land deals, and access to financing, channeling bank loans and other forms of funding to local firms. Such loans from local branches of state-owned development banks were frequently guaranteed by municipal government entities. The China Development Bank alone, one of three state-owned policy banks charged with raising funds for infrastructure and development projects, extended US$29 billion in credit to the fifteen largest renewable energy manufacturers (Bakewell and White 2011). Local government backing was critical in securing such loans, but local government guarantees also allowed firms to obtain waivers on loan conditions usually attached to large investments in high-risk industries (Nahm 2017b; Trina Solar 2010, 2013; Yingli Solar 2013).

Although a set of so-called indigenous innovation (*zizhu chuangxin*) policies issued by the central government in 2007 emphasized the importance of homegrown technological innovation without the assistance of foreign partners, solar firms used bank loans and government research and development (R&D) subsidies to expand manufacturing capacity. Continuing to rely on production equipment and components sourced abroad, firms' R&D departments prioritized cost reductions and the improvement of manufacturing processes (Nahm and Steinfeld 2014b). Credit lines to expand manufacturing capacity continued to be available to solar firms even in the years after the global financial crisis, when the collapse particularly of European markets led to overcapacity in global solar markets. Between 2009 and 2011, the capacity utilization of existing solar PV manufacturing plants fell from just over 60 percent to just under 50 percent, yet local governments continued to lend to "their" local solar PV manufacturers (Nahm 2017a; Zhao, Wan, and Yang 2015). Although scholars have attempted to trace financial practices in the solar industry to determine the flow of funds from state-owned banks to the solar sector, access to data remains notoriously difficult. Researchers largely rely on deal announcements and financial filings that do not fully reveal how the firms are able to obtain financing, how much, and on what terms, adding uncertainty to our knowledge of government support of the sector.

Demand-side subsidies were not introduced for the solar sector until 2009 (Lew 2000; Ru et al. 2012; Wang 2010). As a consequence, China's solar PV firms have historically exported the vast majority of their production. The collapse of European export markets in the wake of the global financial crisis exacerbated overcapacity created as a result of indiscriminate lending by local governments. The combination of fiscal constraints and the heavy reliance on GDP growth in cadre performance evaluations created incentives to protect the local industrial base against market competition. The focus on GDP in cadre performance evaluations provided further incentives for officials to bail out loss-making local businesses, often using debt financing to do so (Huang 2002, 2003; Segal and Thun 2001). Manufacturers were joined by local governments in insisting on demand-side policies to create a domestic alternative to export production (Hochstetler and Kostka 2015). Starting in 2009, demand-side subsidies offered by the central government created a domestic market for solar PV technologies, with additional subsidy programs available to support both residential customers and developers of utility-scale solar PV installations (Fischer 2012, 2014).

Rapid cost reductions, central government policies, and local government support led China to become the world's largest solar market in 2012. By 2015 China had overtaken the United States in installed solar PV capacity. In spite of growing domestic markets, ongoing overcapacity led to a number of high-profile bankruptcies. In an attempt to regain control over solar sector governance due to concerns about debt exposure and local protectionism, the central government began to restrict local government support to domestic manufacturers. Suntech, once China's largest solar manufacturer, defaulted on its loans in 2013, after the central government blocked additional bailouts from the city of Wuxi (Gruss and ten Brink 2016). Even as the overall export share of China's solar PV industry declined over time, the sheer size of manufacturing capacity and rapid cost declines caused friction with global trading partners. Both the European Union and the United States accused China of unfair trade practices and enacted a series of measures to slow Chinese imports (Lewis 2014b; Meckling and Hughes 2017).

Coal

China is the world's largest consumer and producer of coal and continues to rely on coal for the majority of its energy needs. Although China has made impressive advances in improving the efficiency of its coal power fleet, reducing reliance on coal remains central to improving urban air pollution and meeting greenhouse gas reduction goals (Steinfeld, Lester, and Cunningham 2009). Central government efforts to reduce coal consumption—a consumption cap was introduced in the 13th Five-Year Plan—have been met with resistance from local state-owned enterprises and subnational governments, for whom proceeds from mining and coal power generation remain important sources of revenue.

The central role of subnational governments in China's coal sector has its origins in the 1980s, when administrative decentralization and the encouragement of small nonstate mines were a means to increase domestic coal supply and end energy shortages. The coal sector reforms rapidly increased both private ownership and output of mines. What had once been a sector dominated by central government ownership became an industry of local governments and nonstate firms. By 1998 the Ministry of Coal estimated that ninety-five central state-owned mines, two thousand local state-owned mines, and more than fifty thousand mines with various forms of nonstate ownership were in operation. Nonstate mines were mostly private, but could still include indirect ties to the state, for instance when state-owned enterprises were among the investors (Thomson 2003; Wright 2012). By 2006, 52 percent of coal was produced by nonstate or locally owned mines. Nearly 40 percent of production came from local nonstate mines

(Cunningham 2015). Between the early 1983 reforms and 2006, domestic output increased by a factor of six, to 3.4 billion tons annually (National Bureau of Statistics of China 2017; Peng 2009).

As mines without direct ties to the central government became the dominant source of domestic coal, they became important streams of fiscal revenue for subnational governments. In areas with abundant coal resources, up to 80 percent of local government funds came from direct or taxable revenue from the local mining industry. The economic reliance on coal mining created incentives for local governments to approve new mining operations, often ignoring production safety standards issued by the Ministry of Coal and environmental regulations coming from the Ministry of Environmental Protection and its predecessors (Wang 2008). Low-cost production methods of non-state mines undercut the production costs of state-owned ones and led to periods of overcapacity (Thomson 2003). The 11th Five-Year Plan included the target of closing 50 percent of small mines by 2010 (National Development and Reform Commission 2006). Yet local governments frequently resisted shutdown directives and ignored the operations of unlicensed coal mines. Hence, the 13th Five-Year Plan on the Production Safety of Coal Mines, covering the period from 2016 to 2020, still included targets for reducing the number of safety incidents in the coal industry and the closure of small mines (China State Administration of Work Safety and State Administration of Coal Mine Safety 2016).

By the early 2000s, increasingly liberalized domestic markets had largely aligned with rising international prices, creating further incentives for local governments to approve new mines. After decades of expansion, China's coal consumption began to plateau by 2010, peaking in 2013. As local government approvals increased the domestic coal supply, a slowing economy, a changing energy mix, and government efforts to reduce air pollution resulted in falling coal consumption from 2014 onward, leading to oversupply and falling domestic prices (Lin 2017). Spot prices for coal fell by half between 2011 and 2015 (Cunningham 2015). Due to the spread between thermal generation cost and benchmark prices, coal power plants offered short-term profit opportunities; in combination with a benchmark electricity price that was not indexed to fuel cost, the falling price of coal created incentives for subnational governments to invest heavily in additional coal power plants. Although the government has published conflicting numbers, official statistics show that in 2013 up to 47 percent of generation capacity was owned by local administrations and affiliated entities. An administratively determined dispatch order allowed officials to prioritize local thermal plants, just as the central government ratcheted up green energy targets (Davidson, Kahrl, and Karplus 2017). At the same time, the NEA, the NDRC, and the Ministry of Environmental Protection delegated environmental impact assessments for new thermal plants to provincial agencies, further supporting a rapid surge in the number of thermal projects under construction (Ministry of Environmental Protection 2015).

Investment in additional thermal capacity at the hands of subnational governments exacerbated existing problems with overcapacity in the power sector and further complicated central government efforts to solve China's unusually high wind power curtailment rates. In a renewed effort to exert control over investments in generation capacity, the NEA in 2016 released four policy notices on controlling coal-fired power generation projects and shutting down inefficient thermal plants (National Development and Reform Commission and National Energy Administration 2016a, 2016b, 2016c; National Energy Administration 2016). The notices banned the approval of new coal power plants in provinces with overcapacity, and the NEA became directly involved in enforcing these statutes. In September 2016 it canceled fifteen approved coal power projects in nine provinces. A further one hundred newly approved coal plants were suspended by the NEA in 2017, defying subnational governments' plans (Gao 2017; Zhang 2016). To ensure compliance, the NEA announced a series of policy measures to deter shirking by subnational governments, including sanctions on ownership groups that failed to adhere to cancellation orders, a halt on business permits, a ban on grid connection for projects without approval, and new rules to limit access to financial capital (Zhang 2016). Decades after local governments were first given sweeping authority over the coal industry, the central government appeared determined to exert control of the sector to meet green energy targets and industrial policy goals (Blondeel and Van de Graaf 2018). Planned power sector reforms, discussed previously, further seek to improve grid access for non-carbon sources of electricity at the expense of coal power operators.

Oil and Gas

China is the world's largest oil importer and the world's seventh largest producer of oil (IEA 2017b). After four decades of institutional reform and experimentation, China's oil and gas sectors remain dominated by three large state-owned national oil and gas companies, each responsible for resource extraction, refining, the construction and operation of pipelines, overseas investment, and the nation's strategic petroleum reserves. Compared to renewable energy sectors and its domestic coal industry, governance institutions in China's oil and gas sectors are far more centralized. The small number of state-owned enterprises with quasi-ministerial rank at the central government level have prevented much of the vertical fragmentation between central and local governments that has shaped policymaking in other sectors of China's energy economy. Nonetheless, horizontal fragmentation and bureaucratic bargaining between oil and gas companies and central government ministries have allowed oil and gas firms to advance their own interests by exerting influence over the national policy agenda (Andrews-Speed and Dannreuther 2011).

China's National Offshore Oil Corporation (CNOOC) was created in 1982 under the umbrella of the Ministry of Petroleum Industry (MPI) and tasked with offshore exploration and production. In 1983 the State Council established Sinopec to house the refining and petrochemical assets that had previously belonged to the MPI. By 1988 the MPI itself was restructured into the CNPC, which was tasked with onshore oil and gas exploration as well as the administrative and regulatory functions previously conducted by the MPI (Kong 2009). The organization of China's domestic oil and gas sectors into three state-owned enterprises with distinct functional responsibilities along the supply chain became financially unsustainable over the course of the 1990s, prompting another set of reforms. A series of price reforms, in particular partial liberalization of crude oil prices, led to increasing profitability of upstream exploration and production activities conducted by the CNPC. The downstream market for oil products remained heavily regulated, leading to increasing losses for the company charged with refining and distribution, Sinopec (Cunningham 2015).

The central government responded by returning to administratively determined prices in 1994, while restructuring the three NOCs in 1998 to ensure that each held both upstream and downstream assets. After a short period during which provincial and local companies forayed into oil and gas sectors alongside foreign importers, the central government reestablished the monopoly of the three centrally owned oil and gas firms (Andrews-Speed 2000; Fesharaki and Tang 1995). While the central government initially attempted to create five or more domestic oil companies that would operate in competition with one another, Sinopec and the CNPC were able to prevent such restructuring. Through a simple asset swap, the two were able to maintain their duopoly over the domestic market (Andrews-Speed and Dannreuther 2011; Cunningham 2015).

In the years immediately following the creation of vertically integrated NOCs in 1998, regulatory responsibility was formally given to the newly created State Petroleum and Chemical Industry Bureau (SPCIB), which ranked below the oil and gas companies in the administrative hierarchy of the central government, preventing it from exerting regulatory power. After a series of administrative reforms, the Energy Bureau, predecessor to the NEA, was charged with oil and gas sector regulation, yet shared its responsibility for energy sector regulation with twenty-eight other commissions and ministries under the State Council. Although the NEA was eventually elevated to vice-ministerial rank in 2008, it continued to lack formal authority to enforce coordination among ministries, NOCs, and regulatory commissions (Andrews-Speed and Dannreuther 2011; Kong 2009). Formally, China's NOCs remained under the control of the State Assets Supervision and Administration Commission (SASAC), which in turn reported to the State Council. As such, the three NOCs required administrative approval from SASAC on issues ranging from mergers and acquisitions to the liquidation of substantial assets. As with other critical state-owned enterprises administered at the central government level, the CCP also had significant influence on China's NOCs, particularly over appointment and removal of management personnel. Although administrative rankings for executives of state-owned enterprises were formally abolished, in practice the leadership of NOCs was often considered as holding de facto ministerial or vice-ministerial ranking, since the procedure for appointment was identical to that of comparable positions within the government (Kong 2009).

The influence of SASAC and the CCP on the strategic direction of China's NOCs has led some scholars to question the applicability of the fragmented authoritarianism framework to China's relatively concentrated oil and gas sectors. From this perspective, bureaucratic authoritarianism better captures the substantial capacity of the Chinese state to chart the development of its oil and gas industry (Taylor 2014). Yet institutional fragmentation within the central government and the lack of a centralized energy bureaucracy nevertheless provided China's NOCs with considerable power to evade regulation, exert political influence, and engage in bureaucratic bargaining to advance their own interests. Domestically, China's NOCs successfully prevented the entry of competitors, both domestic and foreign, into a market that had been carefully divided among the existing players. The CNPC only consolidated its control over the domestic gas market, controlling more than half of crude oil production and three-quarters of natural gas supply (Cunningham 2015). In addition to such resistance to energy sector reform, the CNPC and Sinopec, China's main domestic players, also directly exploited their positions vis-à-vis a fragmented central government bureaucracy to avoid environmental regulations. For instance, in 2011 China's NOCs successfully delayed the implementation of vehicle emissions standards (Zhang, He, and Huo 2012).

Internationally, both the oil and gas companies and the central government have sought to secure resources beyond China's borders, with limited coordination between them. NOCs invested in more than fifty countries to secure resources to meet China's growing energy demand. They have frequently exploited the lack of coordination within the central government, setting precedent through investments on the ground while at times leaving China's foreign policy bureaucracy struggling to align with their overseas investment strategy (Andrews-Speed and Dannreuther 2011). Even in China's authoritarian context, research has shown that the state only rarely acts as a veto player to shape NOCs' outward investment strategy in a state-led fashion, holding little control over an internationalization strategy largely shaped by NOCs themselves (Meckling et al. 2015).

A FUTURE RESEARCH AGENDA

Energy politics in China displays two prominent characteristics that have defined policymaking since the beginning of the reform era. First, the governance of China's energy sector reflects broader cycles of centralization and decentralization that have long shaped Chinese politics (Baum 1996; He 1996). As the discussion of individual subsectors illustrates, periods of administrative decentralization are almost always followed by attempts by the central government to recentralize policymaking. Such patterns of "letting go" and "tightening up" (*fang/shou*) were visible in the solar sector when the center intervened to slow indiscriminate lending, leading to a series of high-profile bankruptcies and industry consolidation. In the coal sector, the center halted investment in new power generation and exerted renewed control over approval of mining projects, after overcapacity and safety problems had become too costly to tolerate (Kostka and Nahm 2017).

A second key feature and great strength of energy policymaking in China is the substantial room for experimentation and institutional flexibility afforded by China's system of fragmented authoritarianism (Heilmann and Perry 2011; Heilmann, Shih, and

Hofem 2013). It is easy to focus on the inefficiencies produced by governance institutions that contain multiple command lines, overlapping responsibilities, and conflicting incentives for bureaucrats. Yet it is equally important to acknowledge that in the face of the substantial challenges involved in managing a clean energy transition, the central government in Beijing was able to resort to local experimentation in search of policy solutions. This practice has created new hurdles in energy sector governance that have been well-documented in existing scholarship, including overcapacity in wind, solar, and coal (Lewis 2014a, 2014b); local protectionism in domestic electricity markets (Davidson, Kahrl, and Karplus 2017); and weak incentives to enforce environmental regulations in the energy sector (Wong and Karplus 2017). But experimentation, institutional flexibility, and bureaucratic bargaining are also responsible for unprecedented investments in the deployment of renewable energy; the rapid cost declines in global wind and solar technologies as a result of China's manufacturing capabilities (Lewis 2013; Nahm and Steinfeld 2014b); one of the most efficient coal power fleets in the world (Hart, Bassett, and Johnson 2017); and not least, the ability to provide energy reliably throughout a period of unparalleled increases in energy demand.

Against this background, three structural changes affecting China's energy sector are opening promising avenues for future research. First, under Xi Jinping's leadership China has seen a renewed effort to recentralize policymaking in Beijing. Xi has asserted much greater control over policymaking than his immediate predecessors did, including in economic, environmental, and energy policymaking. Much attention has been paid to Xi's elevation to "core leader" (*hexin lingdao*), his anticorruption campaign, and the constitutional amendment to remove term limits (Brødsgaard 2015; Pei 2018). Changes in Beijing have altered the balance of power between the center and subnational governments in ways that remain to be explored. The establishment of new institutions to increase monitoring of subnational officials—including environmental protection bureaus with direct command lines to Beijing (Van Rooij et al. 2017)—and renewed central government efforts to enforce subnational compliance (Donaldson 2016) have coincided with the announcement of widespread energy sector reforms to reduce local protectionism and remove discretion from local officials (Gao 2017; Zhang 2016). New scholarship should examine whether current efforts of the central government to exert control fall within the cyclical patterns of decentralization and centralization that have long structured Chinese politics or are the beginning of a break with past policymaking practices. The central discussion of climate change, environmental protection, and the urgent need to reduce air pollution during the 19th Party Congress in the fall of 2017 suggests that Beijing will continue to set ambitious targets (Xi 2017). As such goals are not yet backed by a centralized energy ministry, future research should investigate attempts to centralize energy sector governance.

Second, China has aggressively ramped up its international engagement on energy issues. As mentioned previously, China's oil and gas companies have long invested in projects around the world to secure sufficient supply during periods of rapidly rising domestic demand. China has stepped up such investments as part of its "One Belt One Road" initiative, under which China has attempted to strengthen its foreign policy footprint through infrastructure investments. What began as a resurrection of the economic ties of the silk road rapidly expanded to investments in resource extraction, energy pipelines, ports, and power generation facilities along an economic belt that may eventually include sixty countries (Ferdinand 2016). At the same time, China has actively forayed into transnational climate governance and declared its willingness to become an active agent in support of global progress toward limiting anthropogenic climate change (Hale and Roger 2017). While these developments undoubtedly shape international relations in the region and beyond, they likely will also affect domestic energy sector politics in ways that remain to be studied. How will China's international engagement affect the interests and power balance in its domestic energy sector?

Third, China's economy is undergoing structural change, with important consequences for domestic energy politics. China's recent economic slowdown, a shift away from manufacturing, rising living standards, increased demand for environmental protection, and a leveling off of energy demand are changing the politics of a sector that has for the past twenty years been primarily characterized by rapid expansion. As China's domestic priorities shift from increasing energy supply to increasing the quality of energy supply, which actors and institutions are likely to lose, and who will benefit? It is conceivable that this period of structural change and consolidation will lead to reduced tolerance for the energy governance inefficiencies of the past, which were tolerated by the central government in the service of increasing energy supply and encouraging experimentation. As of 2018, it also remains to be studied whether flattening energy demand in China will add further incentives for producers of renewable energy technology to export. Such broader structural changes could potentially add further strain to China's trade relationship with the United States, which has already been affected by accusations of unfair trade practices and a series of tariffs against Chinese imports (Lewis 2014b).

The broader consequences of the centralization of power under Xi, the increased international links of China's domestic energy sector, and structural changes affecting the Chinese economy remain unclear. Understanding whether contemporary changes will strengthen incentives for subnational actors to protect local policymaking autonomy, tip the scales toward centralization, or merely empower some subnational actors over others is a key challenge facing future research on energy politics in China.

References

Andrews-Speed, Philip. 2000. "Reform of China's Energy Sector: Slow Progress to an Uncertain Goal." In *The Chinese Economy under Transition*, edited by Sarah Cook, Shujie Yao, and Juzhong Zhuang, 111–130. London: Palgrave Macmillan.

Andrews-Speed, Philip. 2012. *The Governance of Energy in China: Transition to a Low-Carbon Economy*. Houndsmill, UK: Palgrave Macmillan.

Andrews-Speed, Philip, and Roland Dannreuther. 2011. *China, Oil and Global Politics*. New York: Routledge.

Ang, Yuen Yuen. 2016. *How China Escaped the Poverty Trap*. Ithaca, NY: Cornell University Press.

Bakewell, Sally, and Todd White. 2011. "Chinese Renewable Companies Slow to Tap $47 Billion Credit." Bloomberg Business. http://www.bloomberg.com/news/articles/2011-11-16/chinese-renewable-companies-slow-to-tap-47-billion-credit-line.

Ball, Jeffrey, Dan Reicher, Xiaojing Sun, and Caitlin Pollock. 2017. *The New Solar System: China's Evolving Solar Industry and Its Implications for Competitive Solar Power in the United States and the World*. Stanford, CA: Stanford University, Steyer-Taylor Center for Energy Policy and Finance.

Baum, Richard. 1996. *Burying Mao: Chinese Politics in the Age of Deng Xiaoping*. Princeton, NJ: Princeton University Press.

Birney, Mayling. 2014. "Decentralization and Veiled Corruption under China's 'Rule of Mandates.'" *World Development* 53: 55–67.

Blondeel, Mathieu, and Thijs Van de Graaf. 2018. "Toward a Global Coal Mining Moratorium? A Comparative Analysis of Coal Mining Policies in the USA, China, India and Australia." *Climatic Change* 150, no. 2: 89–101. doi:10.1007/s10584-017-2135-5.

Bo, Zhiyue. 1996. "Economic Performance and Political Mobility: Chinese Provincial Leaders." *Journal of Contemporary China* 5, no. 12: 135–154.

Breznitz, Dan, and Michael Murphree. 2011. *Run of the Red Queen: Government, Innovation, Globalization and Economic Growth in China*. New Haven CT: Yale University Press.

Brødsgaard, Kjeld Erik. 2015. "Assessing the Fourth Plenum of the Chinese Communist Party: personnel management and corruption." *Asia Policy* 20, no. 1: 30–37.

Cai, Hongbin, and Daniel Treisman. 2006. "Did Government Decentralization Cause China's Economic Miracle?" *World Politics* 58, no. 4: 505–535.

Chen, Ling. 2010. "Playing the Market Reform Card: The Changing Patterns of Political Struggle in China's Electric Power Sector." *The China Journal*, no. 64: 69–95.

China State Administration of Work Safety, and State Administration of Coal Mine Safety. 2016. "13th Five-Year Plan (2016–2020) on the Production Safety of Coal Mines" [非煤矿山安全生产 "十三五"规划].

Cunningham, Edward A. 2015. "The State and the Firm: China's Energy Governance in Context." Global Economic Governance Initiative Working Paper Series. Boston: Boston University.

Davidson, Michael R., Fredrich Kahrl, and Valerie J. Karplus. 2017. "Towards a Political Economy Framework for Wind Power: Does China Break the Mould?" In *The Political Economy of Clean Energy Transitions*, edited by Douglas Arent, Channing Arndt, Mackay Miller, Finn Tarp, and Owen Zinaman, 250–270. Oxford: Oxford University Press.

Donaldson, John A. 2016. "China's Administrative Hierarchy: The Balance of Power and Winners and Losers within China's Levels of Government." In *Assessing the Balance of Power in Central–Local Relations in China*, edited by John A. Donaldson, 105–137. New York: Routledge.

Dupuy, Max. 2017. "China's Power Sector Reform: Progress for Clean Energy." Regulatory Assistance Project. http://www.raponline.org/blog/chinas-power-sector-reform-progress-clean-energy/.

Economist, The. 2016. "Where India's and China's Energy Consumption Is Heading." November 24.https://www.economist.com/special-report/2016/11/24/where-indias-and-chinas-energy-consumption-is-heading

Economy, Elizabeth. 2010. *The River Runs Black: The Environmental Challenge to China's Future*. Ithaca, NY: Cornell University Press.

Ferdinand, Peter. 2016. "Westward Ho—the China Dream and 'One Belt, One Road': Chinese Foreign Policy under Xi Jinping." *International Affairs* 92, no. 4: 941–957.

Fesharaki, Fereidun, and Frank C Tang. 1995. "China-Evolving Oil Trade Patterns and Prospects to 2000." Natural Resources Forum 19, no. 1: 47–58.

Fischer, Doris. 2012. "Challenges of Low Carbon Technology Diffusion: Insights from Shifts in China's Photovoltaic Industry Development." *Innovation and Development* 2, no. 1: 131–146.

Fischer, Doris. 2014. "Green Industrial Policies in China—The Example of Solar Energy." In *Green Industrial Policies in Developing Economies*, edited by Anna Pegels, 69–103. London: Routledge.

Gao, Yu. 2017. "The National Energy Administration Halts Coal Power Projects in 11 Provinces with a Total Investment of 430 Billion Yuan" [国家能源局再次叫停11省煤电项目 投资总额约4300亿元]. Caixin. http://companies.caixin.com/2017-01-17/101044635.html?ulurcmd=0_comdf_art_0_841f5a6e-9fb1-4c3d-9682-99c28320e4ed&source3EntityID=101043363.

Gosens, Jorrit, and Yonglong Lu. 2014. "Prospects for Global Market Expansion of China's Wind Turbine Manufacturing Industry." *Energy Policy* 67: 301–318. doi:10.1016/j.enpol.2013.12.055.

Grünberg, Nis. 2017. "Revisiting Fragmented Authoritarianism in China's Central Energy Administration." In *Chinese Politics as Fragmented Authoritarianism*, edited by Kjeld Erik Brødsgaard, 15–37. New York: Routledge.

Gruss, Laura, and Tobias ten Brink. 2016. "The Development of the Chinese Photovoltaic Industry: An Advancing Role for the Central State?" *Journal of Contemporary China* 25, no. 99: 453–466. doi:10.1080/10670564.2015.1104914.

Guan, Dabo, Glen P. Peters, Christopher L. Weber, and Klaus Hubacek. 2009. "Journey to World Top Emitter: An Analysis of the Driving Forces of China's Recent CO2 Emissions Surge." *Geophysical Research Letters* 36, no. 4: L04709. doi:10.1029/2008GL036540.

Guo, Gang. 2007. "Retrospective Economic Accountability under Authoritarianism: Evidence from China." *Political Research Quarterly* 60, no. 3: 378–390.

GWEC. 2017. *Global Wind Report Annual Market Update 2016*. Brussels: Global Wind Energy Council.

Hale, Thomas, and Charles Roger. 2017. "Domestic Politics and Chinese Participation in Transnational Climate Governance." In *Global Governance and China: The Dragon's Learning Curve*, edited by Scott Kennedy, 250–271. New York: Routledge.

Han, Jingyi, Arthur P. J. Mol, Yonglong Lu, and Lei Zhang. 2009. "Onshore Wind Power Development in China: Challenges Behind a Successful Story." *Energy Policy* 37, no. 8: 2941–2951. doi:10.1016/j.enpol.2009.03.021.

Hart, Melanie, Luke Bassett, and Blaine Johnson. 2017. *Research Note on U.S. and Chinese Coal-Fired Power Data*. Washington, DC: Center for American Progress.

He, Baogang. 1996. "Dilemmas of Pluralist Development and Democratization in China." *Democratization* 3, no. 3: 287–305.

He, Guizhen, Arthur P. J. Mol, Lei Zhang, and Yonglong Lu. 2013. "Public Participation and Trust in Nuclear Power Development in China." *Renewable and Sustainable Energy Reviews* 23: 1–11. doi:10.1016/j.rser.2013.02.028.

Heberer, Thomas, and Gunter Schubert. 2012. "County and Township Cadres as a Strategic Group: A New Approach to Political Agency in China's local state." *Journal of Chinese Political Science* 17, no. 3: 221–249.

Heilmann, Sebastian. 2018. *Red Swan: How Unorthodox Policy-Making Facilitated China's Rise.* Hong Kong: Chinese University Press.

Heilmann, Sebastian, and Oliver Melton. 2013. "The Reinvention of Development Planning in China, 1993–2012." *Modern China* 39, no. 6: 580–628.

Heilmann, Sebastian, and Elizabeth J. Perry. 2011. "Embracing Uncertainty: Guerrilla Policy Style and Adaptive Governance in China " In *Mao's Invisible Hand*, edited by Sebastian Heilmann and Elizabeth J. Perry, 1–29. Cambridge, MA: Harvard University Press.

Heilmann, Sebastian, Lea Shih, and Andreas Hofem. 2013. "National Planning and Local Technology Zones: Experimental Governance in China's Torch Programme." *The China Quarterly* 216: 896–919. doi:10.1017/S0305741013001057.

Heimer, Maria, and Stig Thøgersen. 2006. *Doing Fieldwork in China.* Honolulu: University of Hawaii Press.

Hibbs, Mark. 2018. *The Future of Nuclear Power in China.* Washington, DC: Carnegie Endowment for International Peace.

Hochstetler, Kathryn, and Genia Kostka. 2015. "Wind and Solar Power in Brazil and China: Interests, State–Business Relations, and Policy Outcomes." *Global Environmental Politics* 15, no. 3: 74–94.

Hornby, Lucy. 2017. "China's Emergence as Top US Oil Buyer Highlights Economic Ties." *Financial Times*, April 5. https://www.ft.com/content/8a144f2e-19c8-11e7-a53d-dfo9f373be87

Huang, Yasheng. 2002. "Between Two Coordination Failures: Automotive Industrial Policy in China with a Comparison to Korea." *Review of International Political Economy* 9, no. 3: 538–573.

Huang, Yasheng. 2003. *Selling China—Foreign Direct Investment During the Reform Era.* Cambridge, UK: Cambridge University Press.

Hurlbut, David, Ella Zhou, Lori Bird, and Qin Wang. 2017. *Transmission Challenges and Best Practices for Cost-Effective Renewable Energy Delivery across State and Provincial Boundaries.* Golden, CO: National Renewable Energy Laboratory.

IEA. 2017a. *World Energy Balances.* Paris: International Energy Agency.

IEA. 2017b. *World Energy Outlook 2017.* Paris: International Energy Agency.

Kirkegaard, Julia Kirch. 2017. "Tackling Chinese Upgrading Through Experimentalism and Pragmatism: The Case of China's Wind Turbine Industry." *Journal of Current Chinese Affairs* 46, no. 2: 7–39.

Koleski, Katherine. 2017. *The 13th Five-Year Plan.* Washington, DC: U.S.-China Economic and Security Review Commission.

Kong, Bo. 2009. *China's International Petroleum Policy.* Santa Barbara, CA: Praeger Security International.

Kostka, Genia, and William Hobbs. 2012. "Local Energy Efficiency Policy Implementation in China: Bridging the Gap between National Priorities and Local Interests." *The China Quarterly* 211: 765–785. doi:10.1017/S0305741012000860.

Kostka, Genia, and Jonas Nahm. 2017. "Central–Local Relations: Recentralization and Environmental Governance in China." *The China Quarterly* 231: 567–582.

Lema, Adrian, and Kristian Ruby. 2007. "Between Fragmented Authoritarianism and Policy Coordination: Creating a Chinese Market for Wind Energy." *Energy Policy* 35, no. 7: 3879–3890. doi:10.1016/j.enpol.2007.01.025.

Lew, Debra J. 2000. "Alternatives to Coal and Candles: Wind Power in China." *Energy Policy* 28, no. 4: 271–286. doi:10.1016/S0301-4215(99)00077-4.

Lewis, Joanna I. 2013. *Green Innovation in China: China's Wind Power Industry and the Global Transition to a Low Carbon Economy*. New York: Columbia University Press.

Lewis, Joanna I. 2014a. "Industrial Policy, Politics and Competition: Assessing the Post-crisis Wind Power Industry." *Business and Politics* 16, no. 4: 511–547.

Lewis, Joanna I. 2014b. "The Rise of Renewable Energy Protectionism: Emerging Trade Conflicts and Implications for Low Carbon Development." *Global Environmental Politics*. doi:10.1162/GLEP_a_00255.

Li, Hongbin, and Li-An Zhou. 2005. "Political Turnover and Economic Performance: The Incentive Role of Personnel Control in China." *Journal of Public Economics* 89, nos. 9–10: 1743–1762.

Liao, Janet Xuanli. 2015. "The Chinese Government and the National Oil Companies (NOCs): Who Is the Principal?" *Asia Pacific Business Review* 21, no. 1: 44–59. doi:10.1080/13602381.2014.939893.

Lieberthal, Kenneth. 1992. "Introduction: The 'Fragmented Authoritarianism' Model and Its Limitations." In *Bureaucracy, Politics, and Decision Making in Post-Mao China*, edited by Kenneth Lieberthal and David M. Lampton, 1–32. Berkeley: University of California Press.

Lieberthal, Kenneth, and Michel Oksenberg. 1988. *Policy Making in China: Leaders, Structures, and Processes*. Princeton, NJ: Princeton University Press.

Lin, Alvin. 2017. "Understanding China's New Mandatory 58% Coal Cap Target." NRDC. https://www.nrdc.org/experts/alvin-lin/understanding-chinas-new-mandatory-58-coal-cap-target.

Lü, Xiaobo, and Pierre F Landry. 2014. "Show Me the Money: Interjurisdiction Political Competition and Fiscal Extraction in China." *American Political Science Review* 108, no. 3: 706–722.

Meckling, Jonas, and Llewelyn Hughes. 2017. "Globalizing Solar: Global Supply Chains and Trade Preferences." *International Studies Quarterly* 61, no. 2: 225–235.

Meckling, Jonas, Nina Kelsey, Eric Biber, and John Zysman. 2015. "Winning Coalitions for Climate Policy." *Science* 349, no. 6253: 1170–1171. doi:10.1126/science.aab1336.

Mertha, Andrew C. 2005. "China's 'Soft' Centralization: Shifting Tiao/Kuai Authority Relations." *The China Quarterly* 184: 791–810.

Mertha, Andrew C. 2008. *China's Water Warriors: Citizen Action and Policy Change*. Ithaca, NY: Cornell University Press.

Metzler, Florian, and Edward Steinfeld. 2013. "Sustaining Global Competitiveness in the Provision of Complex Products and Systems: The Case of Civilian Nuclear Power Technology." In *Production in the Innovation Economy*, edited by Richard M. Lock and Rachel L. Wellhausen, 175–210. Cambridge, MA: MIT Press.

Ministry of Environmental Protection. 2015. "Notice on Publishing the Catalog for the List of Construction Projects That Require Environmental Impact Assessment Approval from the Ministry of Environmental Protection" [环境保护部审批环境影响评价文件的建设项目目录]. Beijing.

Minzner, Carl F. 2009. "Riots and Cover-ups: Counterproductive Control of Local Agents in China." *University of Pennsylvania Journal of International Law* 31: 53.

Montinola, Gabriella, Yingyi Qian, and Barry R. Weingast. 1995. "Federalism, Chinese Style: The Political Basis for Economic Success." *World Politics* 48, no. 1: 50–81.

Nahm, Jonas. 2017a. "Exploiting the Implementation Gap: Policy Divergence and Industrial Upgrading in China's Wind and Solar Sectors." *The China Quarterly* 231: 705–727.

Nahm, Jonas. 2017b. "Renewable Futures and Industrial Legacies: Wind and Solar Sectors in China, Germany, and the United States." *Business and Politics* 19, no. 1: 68–106.

Nahm, Jonas, and Edward Steinfeld. 2014a. "The Role of Innovative Manufacturing in High-Tech Product Development: Evidence from China's Renewable Energy Sector." In *Production in the Innovation Economy*, edited by Richard M. Locke and Rachel L. Wellhausen, 139–174. Cambridge, MA: MIT Press.

Nahm, Jonas, and Edward S. Steinfeld. 2014b. "Scale-up Nation: China's Specialization in Innovative Manufacturing." *World Development* 54: 288–300. doi:10.1016/j.worlddev.2013.09.003.

National Bureau of Statistics of China. 2017. "Statistical Communiqué of the People's Republic of China on the 2016 National Economic and Social Development." http://www.stats.gov.cn/english/PressRelease/201702/t20170228_1467503.html.

National Development and Reform Commission. 2006. "Eleventh Five-Year Plan (2006–2010)" [煤炭工业发展的十一五计划].

National Development and Reform Commission and National Energy Administration. 2016a. "Notice on Establishing the Early-Warning Mechanism on the Risks in Planning and Construction of Coal-Fired Power Plants" [关于建立煤电规划建设风险预警机制暨发布2019年煤电规划建设风险预警的通知]. Beijing.

National Development and Reform Commission and National Energy Administration. 2016b. "Notice on Further Eliminating Outdated Coal-Fired Electricity Generation Capacity" [关于进一步做好煤电行业淘汰落后产能工作的通知]. Beijing.

National Development and Reform Commission and National Energy Administration. 2016c. "Notice on Promoting the Orderly Development of Coal Power in China" [关于促进我国煤电有序发展的通知]. Beijing.

National Energy Administration. 2016. "Working Plan for Supervision on the Planning and Construction of Coal-Fired Power Plants" [关于开展煤电项目规划建设情况专项监管工作]. Beijing.

O'Brien, Kevin J., and Lianjiang Li. 1999. "Selective Policy Implementation in Rural China." *Comparative Politics* 31, no. 2: 167–186.

Oi, Jean C. 1995. "The Role of the Local State in China's Transitional Economy." *The China Quarterly* 144: 1132–1149. doi:10.1017/S0305741000004768.

Pei, Minxin. 2018. "China in 2017: Back to Strongman Rule." *Asian Survey* 58, no. 1: 21–32.

Peng, Wuyuan. 2009. "The Evolution of China's Coal Institutions." Program on Energy and Sustainable Development. Stanford, CA. https://pesd.fsi.stanford.edu/publications/evolution_of_chinas_coal_institutions_the

Remick, Elizabeth J. 2002. "The Significance of Variation in Local States: The Case of Twentieth Century China." *Comparative Politics* 34, no. 4: 399–418.

Ru, Peng, Qiang Zhi, Fang Zhang, Xiaotian Zhong, Jianqiang Li, and Jun Su. 2012. "Behind the Development of Technology: The Transition of Innovation Modes in China's Wind Turbine Manufacturing Industry." *Energy Policy* 43: 58–69. doi:10.1016/j.enpol.2011.12.025.

Segal, Adam, and Eric Thun. 2001. "Thinking Globally, Acting Locally: Local Governments, Industrial Sectors, and Development in China." *Politics and Society* 29, no. 4: 557–588.

Sheppard, David, and Gregory Meyer. 2015. "China Oil Imports Surpass Those of US." *Financial Times*, May 10. https://www.ft.com/content/342b3a2e-f5a7-11e4-bc6d-00144feab7de

Steinfeld, Edward. 2015. "Teams of Rivals: China, the U.S., and the Race to Develop Technologies for a Sustainable Energy Future." Watson Institute for International Studies

Research Paper No. 2015–26. Providence, RI. https://papers.ssrn.com/sol3/papers.cfm?abstract_id=2606000

Steinfeld, Edward S., Richard K. Lester, and Edward A. Cunningham. 2009. "Greener Plants, Grayer Skies? A Report from the Front Lines of China's Energy Sector." *Energy Policy* 37, no. 5: 1809–1824.

Sutherland, Dylan. 2005. "China's Science Parks: Production Bases or a Tool for Institutional Reform?" *Asia Pacific Business Review* 11, no. 1: 83–104. doi:10.1080/1360238052000298399.

Taylor, Monique. 2014. *The Chinese State, Oil and Energy Security*. Basingstoke, UK: Palgrave Macmillan.

Thomson, Elspeth. 2003. *The Chinese Coal Industry: An Economic History*. London: RoutledgeCurzon.

Trina Solar. 2010. "Annual Report 2009—Form 20-F".

Trina Solar. 2013. "Annual Report 2012—Form 20-F."

van der Kamp, Denise, Peter Lorentzen, and Daniel Mattingly. 2017. "Racing to the Bottom or to the Top? Decentralization, Revenue Pressures, and Governance Reform in China." *World Development* 95: 164–176.

Van Rooij, Benjamin. 2003. "Organization and Procedure in Environmental Law Enforcement: Sichuan in Comparative Perspective." *China Information* 17, no. 2: 36–64.

Van Rooij, Benjamin, Qiaoqiao Zhu, Li Na, and Wang Qiliang. 2017. "Centralizing Trends and Pollution Law Enforcement in China." *The China Quarterly* 231: 583–606.

Wang, Puqing. 2008. Policy Analysis of the Development Problem of Small-scale Coal Mines [小煤矿发展问题及政策分]. Beijing, Institute of Sociology, Chinese Academy of Social Sciences.

Wang, Qiang. 2010. "Effective Policies for Renewable Energy—The Example of China's Wind Power: Lessons for China's Photovoltaic Power." *Renewable and Sustainable Energy Reviews* 14, no. 2: 702–712. doi:10.1016/j.rser.2009.08.013.

Weingast, Barry, Hehui Jin, and Yingyi Qian. 2005. "Regional Decentralization and Fiscal Incentives: Federalism, Chinese Style." *Journal of Public Economics* 89: 1719–1742.

Williams, James H., and Fredrich Kahrl. 2008. "Electricity Reform and Sustainable Development in China." *Environmental Research Letters* 3, no. 4: 044009.

Wong, Christine. 2013. "Reforming China's Public Finances for Long-term Growth." In *China: A New Model for Growth and Development*, edited by Ross Garnaut, Cai Fang, and Ligang Song, 199–219. Canberra: Australian National University Press.

Wong, Christine, and Valerie J Karplus. 2017. "China's War on Air Pollution: Can Existing Governance Structures Support New Ambitions?" *The China Quarterly* 231: 662–684.

World Bank. 2017. *World Development Indicators: Energy Dependency, Efficiency and Carbon Dioxide Emissions*. Washington, DC: World Bank.

Wright, Tim. 2012. *The Political Economy of the Chinese Coal Industry: Black Gold and Blood-Stained Coal*. London: Routledge.

Xi, Jinping. 2017. "Full Text of Xi Jinping's Report at 19th CPC National Congress." *China Daily*, November 4. http://www.chinadaily.com.cn/china/19thcpcnationalcongress/2017-11/04/content_34115212.htm.

Xu, Chenggang. 2011. "The Fundamental Institutions of China's Reforms and Development." *Journal of Economic Literature* 49, no. 4: 1076–1151.

Xu, Chong-Yi. 2010. *Politics of Nuclear Energy in China*. London: Palgrave Macmillan.

Xu, Yi-Chong. 2016. *Sinews of Power: The Politics of the State Grid Corporation of China*. Oxford: Oxford University Press.

Yin, Shangying, Sufang Zhang, Philip Andrews-Speed, and William Li. 2017. "Economic and Environmental Effects of Peak Regulation Using Coal-Fired Power for the Priority Dispatch of Wind Power in China." *Journal of Cleaner Production* 162: 361–370. doi:10.1016/j.jclepro.2017.06.046.

Yingli Solar. 2013. "Milestones." http://www.yinglisolar.com/en/about/milestones/.

Yuan, Xueliang, and Jian Zuo. 2011. "Transition to Low Carbon Energy Policies in China—from the Five-Year Plan Perspective." *Energy Policy* 39, no. 6: 3855–3859. doi:10.1016/j.enpol.2011.04.017.

Yuan, Xueliang, Jian Zuo, Rujian Ma, and Yutao Wang. 2017. "How Would Social Acceptance Affect Nuclear Power Development? A Study from China." *Journal of Cleaner Production* 163: 179–186.

Zeng, Ming, Shicheng Wang, Jinhui Duan, Jinghui Sun, Pengyuan Zhong, and Yingjie Zhang. 2016. "Review of Nuclear Power Development in China: Environment Analysis, Historical Stages, Development Status, Problems and Countermeasures." *Renewable and Sustainable Energy Reviews* 59: 1369–1383.

Zhang, Hui. 2016. "The National Energy Administration Cancels 15 Coal-Fired Power Projects" [国家能源局取消15个煤电项目]. Jiemian. http://www.jiemian.com/article/869400.html.

Zhang, Qiang, Kebin He, and Hong Huo. 2012. "Cleaning China's Air." *Nature* 484: 161. doi:10.1038/484161a.

Zhang, Sufang, Philip Andrews-Speed, and Sitao Li. 2018. "To What Extent Will China's Ongoing Electricity Market Reforms Assist the Integration of Renewable Energy?" *Energy Policy* 114: 165–172.

Zhang, Sufang, Philip Andrews-Speed, and Xiaoli Zhao. 2013. "Political and Institutional Analysis of the Successes and Failures of China's Wind Power Policy." *Energy Policy* 56: 331–340. doi:10.1016/j.enpol.2012.12.071.

Zhang, Yuning, Ningning Tang, Yuguang Niu, and Xiaoze Du. 2016. "Wind Energy Rejection in China: Current Status, Reasons and Perspectives." *Renewable and Sustainable Energy Reviews* 66: 322–344. doi:10.1016/j.rser.2016.08.008.

Zhao, Xin-gang, Guan Wan, and Yahui Yang. 2015. "The Turning Point of Solar Photovoltaic Industry in China: Will It Come?" *Renewable and Sustainable Energy Reviews* 41, no. 0: 178–188. doi:10.1016/j.rser.2014.08.045.

Zhiyue, Bo. 2016. *China's Political Dynamics Under Xi Jinping*. Singapore: World Scientific.

Zhou, Li An. 2007. "Governing China's Local Officials: An Analysis of Promotion Tournament Model [J]." *Economic Research Journal* 7: 36–50.

CHAPTER 22

....

THE ENERGY POLITICS
OF INDIA

....

LYDIA POWELL

THE "grid failure" on July 31, 2012, in Northern India is listed as the world's worst electricity blackout in the last fifty years in terms of the number of people affected (Duddu 2015). More than seven hundred million people, about 60 percent of India's population, were reportedly affected (Pidd 2012). The inquiry committee established to investigate causes of the failure reclassified it as a rather mild incident of grid disturbance and concluded that the northern grid had drawn excess power from the eastern and western grids, which led to the disturbance (Ministry of Power 2012). Most of the material presented in the inquiry committee report focused on technical details such as which transmission line started drawing excess power first and explained scientifically how this irregularity disturbed the grid.

The report did not answer political questions about why excess power was drawn despite regulatory constraints and who permitted the use of excess power. The failure of the monsoon (electricity demand increased to pump ground water for irrigation) was listed among the reasons for unanticipated demand for electricity, but the overall framing was a technical fault that could be addressed primarily through technical and managerial interventions. Because the inquiry commission demanded only proximate causes rather than underlying causes—notably, socioeconomic stratification that has trapped millions in monsoon-dependent subsistence farming, the growing regionalization of the political process, and the emergence of new hegemonic social groups, including farmers (Das 2001)—significant actors in the politics of energy were not discussed.

The blackout and the subsequent analysis capture the essence of India's key energy problem—chronic energy scarcity and low per person energy consumption (energy poverty)—and the false conclusion that these are strictly technical or managerial problems. This approach is reflected in most of India's five-year plans, which have decided the course of India's energy investments and interventions for the past six decades (Bagchi 1991). The Indian intellectual and technical elite who authored the five-year plans assumed that meticulous scientific projections for economic growth and technical planning and investment for energy supply would spontaneously produce social outcomes such as equitable access to energy and energy security. Scholarly analyses of the five-year plans have challenged the view of the Planning Commission, but mostly on technicalities such as the assumptions behind projections or the inclusion or exclusion of certain parameters (Chikkatur and Chakravarty 2008; Pachuri and Srivastava 1988; Sengupta 1992; Shenoy 2017).

Scholars explain the poor outcomes on energy policy that show evolutionary rather than revolutionary progress as the consequence of resource scarcity, bureaucratic incompetence, and technical inefficiency (Ganapathy 1984; Kannan and Pillai 2001; Khanna and Zilberman 1999). The extant literature does not adequately address structural or foundational factors that relate to contextual aspects, such as history, geography, and the nation's deeply ingrained economic and social stratification. Such socio-historical ignorance partially explains failures in India's energy policy.

INDIA'S ENERGY PROFILE

Despite impressive growth in energy demand in the last few decades, most Indians continue to experience energy poverty. India's per-person energy consumption of about 630 kilogram oil equivalent (Kgoe) in 2016 was a tenth of North America's, a sixth of Western Europe's, and about a fourth of China's (World Bank 2016). The average household electricity consumption of about 100 kWh per month (Central Electricity Authority 2017) is not adequate for a decent quality of life. Kerosene lamps are still common in rural households because electricity supply is unreliable; air conditioners and heaters are uncommon even in extremely hot summer and cold winter seasons.

Overall, electricity generation has grown at over 8 percent a year on average in the last six decades, but at least a tenth of households are yet to be connected to the grid (Central Electricity Authority 2018a). Electricity supply to rural households that are connected to the grid averages less than four hours per day (Bharat 2017). The plight of rural Indians belies the nation's overall high level of energy consumption, which is comparable to that of the largest energy-consuming nations given the size of its population. In 2016 India, with over 6 percent of global primary energy consumption, was the third largest energy consumer after China and the United States, whose share in global energy consumption was 21 and 15 percent, respectively (International Energy Agency 2017).

Coal accounted for over 44 percent of India's primary energy supply in 2016, estimated at about 890 million tons of oil equivalent (mtoe), and generated about three-quarters of all electricity supplied (see Figure 22.1). Indian coal consumption was 11 percent of the global coal consumption in 2016, making India the world's second largest coal consumer after China (British Petroleum 2018). India was the third largest oil consumer in 2016, accounting for 4.6 percent of the global total (International Energy Agency 2017). Unprocessed biomass (informally collected firewood and dried animal dung), which is the primary cooking fuel in over half of Indian households (NSSO 2016),

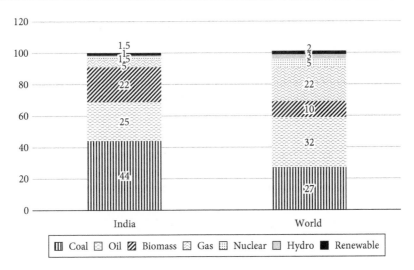

FIGURE 22.1 Primary energy basket: India and the world (2016).

Source: Data from World Energy Outlook 2017, IEA.

contributed almost as much energy as oil in terms of energy content; however, useful energy derived from burning biomass was as low as 30 percent of the energy content in fossil fuels.

Natural gas accounted for about 5 percent of the total primary energy supply in India in 2016, while nuclear energy, hydropower and renewable energy accounted for the remaining 4 percent. The large share of coal and the disproportionately large share of unprocessed biomass in India's energy basket represent two significant deviations from the average global energy basket (see Figure 22.1). Imported oil, which accounted for over 80 percent of oil consumption in 2016, is a source of economic risk because it constitutes the largest component of India's trade deficit. In addition, it is a source of geopolitical risk because more than 60 percent of India's crude oil supply is sourced from countries in the Persian Gulf and transported along contested sea lanes.

In the context of providing energy access (providing electricity and cooking fuels to poor households that cannot access these through markets) and energy security (lower dependence on imported energy), this chapter explores ideological conflicts and the notion of scarcity, which are sources of continuity in Indian energy politics, as well as the interactions between businesses and the state, which generate narratives of market failure and state failure, a source of discontinuity in energy politics. The persistent gap between policy goals of energy access and energy security is the result of energy politics dominated by strategic and commercial concerns rather than the result of bureaucratic inefficiency and implementation failures. Equitable access to energy and energy security persist in policy statements and political discourses because these narratives offer social and political legitimacy to the government. Technocratic and managerial analyses of policy and its outcomes marginalize political and social issues, offer scientific legitimacy for policies, and also generate excuses for policy failures.

POLITICS OF ENERGY ACCESS

India has a large number of households without access to modern energy sources such as electricity, as shown in Figure 22.2 (Bhide and Monroy 2011; Chancel and Piketty 2017; Jewitt and Raman 2017). As such, increasing energy access to poor households, primarily in rural India, remains among the most consistent wealth redistribution policies prioritized by all governments since independence in 1947 (Cisler, Bush, and Tauber 1966; Hanson 1966; Planning Commission 1969–1990, 1990–2002, 2002–2017).

The Planning Commission's first five-year plan emphasized electricity access; household cooking fuels were discussed only in terms of negative externalities, such as pollution (Planning Commission 1951; Murty 1987; Kudaisya 2009). Seventy years later, policies and political declarations continue to focus on improving energy access for poor households. The most recent energy policy document puts "increasing access to affordable energy as the first of its four primary policy goals (Niti Aayog 2017). In 2016 the *pradhan mantri ujjwala yojana* (the prime minister's plan for lighting up lives) was launched by the federal government to provide access to bottled liquid petroleum gas (LPG) as fuel for cooking to fifty million poor households in rural areas. The *sahaj bijli har ghar yojana* or *saubhagya* (electricity for all households) plan promoted in 2017 aimed to provide electricity connections to over forty million poor families in rural and urban areas by December 2018 (Ministry of Power 2019).

Though the government has presented these efforts as innovative and path-breaking, they differ only marginally from a number of earlier programs launched by Indian governments at the federal and regional levels over the last six decades (Banerjee et al. 2015; Modi 2005; Pachuri et al. 2004; Patnaik and Tripathi 2017; Reddy 1999; Samanta and

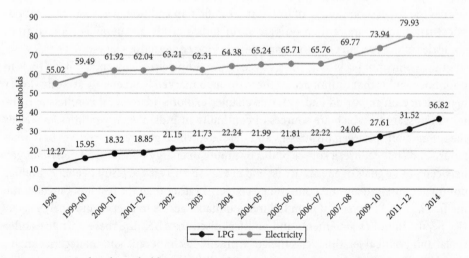

FIGURE 22.2 Indian household access to modern energy sources 1998–2014.

Source: Data from National Sample Survey Organization (NSSO) surveys; various rounds.

Sundaram 1983; Sengupta 1989; Sreekumar and Dixit 2011). Compared to Brazil, South Africa, and China, India's energy access programs have shown poorer outcomes, even over longer time frames (Coelho and Goldemberg 2013; Powell et al. 2012).

The literature critiquing India's electricity access policies focuses on technical and financial inadequacies (Deloitte 2013; Kamalapur and Udaykumar 2012; Sengupta 1989). Subsidies for capital equipment, such as rural transformers and electric poles, along with discounts on energy charges that are embedded in these plans, are debated extensively in terms of their economic rationale and macroeconomic impact (Badiani, Jessoe, and Plant 2012; Jain 2006; Mundle and Rao 1991; Rejikumar 2005). Leakages of subsidy benefits due to poor targeting are also discussed (Dubash 2008; Mayer 2015; Wolak 2008). The media describe the political attractiveness of energy access policies despite their inadequacies as populism, but these issues have not been strongly analyzed and critiqued in scholarly literature on energy (Dhume 2018; Marlow, Pradhan, and Chaudhary 2019; Tripathi 2018). Instead, it is the literature on the politics of redistribution in India that helps explain poor outcomes of energy access policies.

The first prime minister of India ensured that institutional support for socialist-based redistributive policies was clear and explicit (Mahalanobis 1964; Nehru 1946). The Planning Commission was directed to "prevent the operative economic system from concentrating wealth and means of production," which justified the strong redistributive principle embedded in energy access policies (Planning Commission 1951). As institutional support for redistribution of energy (and other public goods, such as education and healthcare) was unambiguous, poor outcomes of India's distributional policies have been explained as administrative problems rooted in the history and nature of the bureaucracy.

Administrative habits and procedures that evolved to preserve law and order under the colonial ruler were seen to be inadequate for a newly independent state that wished to induce rapid development through planning (Patnaik 1986). Even recent literature has labeled the Indian bureaucracy as a "commander" of public services rather than a "partner" to society and the private sector (Kumar 2015). The possibility of changing the bureaucratic culture is regarded as limited because it is the "steel frame" of an administration incapable of adapting to the forces of change (Satish 2004). Reform of colonial bureaucracies "to improve rules or just to better enforce ones on the books" is said to be impossible, as they are "beholden to their past" (Acemoglu, Johnson, and Robinson 2001).

India's ideology of a mixed economic growth model, which attempted to balance the role of the market with that of state planning for redistribution, was also blamed for policy failures (Ahluwalia 2002; Das 2015; Lal 1998; Nayyar 2006). Redistributive policies (including but not limited to electricity access) embedded in bureaucratic planning received greater criticism (Joseph 2007; Kurian 1968). as India shifted from being a "reluctant pro-capitalist state with a socialist ideology" to an "enthusiastic pro-capitalist state with a neo-liberal ideology" (Bajpai and Sachs 1998; Hone 1968; Kelkar 1999; Kohli 2007; Kurian 1968; Swamy 2005).

More incisive commentaries on the failure of redistributive policies argue that failure is part of the design, rather than the consequence of inadequacies in policy design or shortcomings in implementation (Desai and Bhagwati 1975; Myrdal 1968; Steeten 1995). The separation between bold radicalism in principle and extreme conservation in practice is described as accepted and well-established practice in Indian policymaking (Myrdal 1968). The central tendency of India's redistributive policy is described as "first round socialism," as socialist plans eventually wind up being aborted or subverted in execution in the second round (Desai and Bhagwati 1975; Kohli 2010). The need to placate the elite and the state's class character compromise redistributive energy policies that are derived from socialistic ideology (Kohli 2007; Patnaik 2015).

In this context, the observation that India is one of the world's least controlled or planned economies, yet also beholden to its socialist history (Galbraith 1958), serves as a useful framework to understand the politics of energy access in India. Under this thesis, the evolutionary progress in increasing energy access is a case of market failure to provide equitable access and also state failure to correct market failure. The subsequent sections explore these ideas in the context of the politics of providing access to electricity and LPG.

Accessto Electricity: Redistribution Confronts Market Reform

India's Planning Commission offered broad policy direction for electricity access in line with the Indian Constitution, which assigns the regional government responsibility for implementing plans (Rao 2017; Ruet 2005) State electricity boards (SEBs) that were set up under the 1948 Electricity Act and successive amendments provide household access to electricity. Federal financial assistance for electricity access programs was channeled through the rural electrification corporation (REC), set up in 1969 (Samanta and Sundaram 1983).

The creation of the SEBs and the REC shifted responsibility for electricity access from the private to the public sector. SEBs provided the last mile electricity connections to households and the last mile connection to the flow of revenue back into the electricity system (Bhattacharya and Patel 2011). Because of this key role, the SEBs came under attack for most of the inefficiency in the Indian power sector, including failure to increase energy access (Kannan and Pillai 2001; Salgo 1998).

When India partially opened its economy to market forces in the 1990s, international development funding agencies, such as the World Bank, targeted technical and managerial inefficiency of SEBs as the cause of low electricity access. Neoliberal narratives derived from the language of development funding agencies were reflected in the academic literature (Chattopadhyay 2001; Das and Parikh 2000; Dubash and Chella Rajan 2001). According to the World Bank, the "root cause [of inefficiency] was the pervasive politicization of most decisions affecting SEB operations and lack of commercial outlook in its functioning" (Salgo 1998). The bank accused regional governments of treating SEBs as their extensions and using them to further political objectives. Notably, the policy to increase electricity access at the cost of economic and technical efficiency was attacked by the World Bank.

Inspired by development funding agencies, a major theme explored in the academic literature in the late 1990s and early 2000s was exposing the power sector to market forces and private sector investment (Dubash and Chella Rajan 2001; Dubash and Singh 2005; Kale 2004; Morris 1996; Rao 2001; Ranganathan 2004; Sagar 2006; Sharma 2002; Smith 1993). The World Bank model of unbundling electricity generation, transmission, and distribution segments; privatizing (or corporatizing) each segment; and setting up regulatory bodies received particular attention. Academics argued that introducing private capital was necessary not only to increase efficiency to produce and supply energy but also to reduce corruption (Thomas 2005; Upadhyay 2000; Wood and Kodwani 1997).

Some analysts criticized the World Bank approach as an effort to subordinate interests of the state and society to those of capital (D'Sa, K. V., and Reddy 1999; Ghosh 1997; Godbole 1997; Purkayastha 2001; Reddy 2001). However, the more "bottom-up" approach did not take root, for reasons the academic literature has not explored. The nature of dominant fuels, such as coal and oil, which require upfront capital investment and centralized control for extraction, processing, and distribution, might explain the continued dominance of the top-down, capital-led approach, but this is yet to be established by scholarly literature. Scholars critical of the neoliberal approach used the collapse of some of the power generation projects undertaken by independent power producers that were introduced under the reform model and the financial liabilities this imposed on the state to make their case (Godbole 1999; Srinivasan 1995).

If viewed in a broader political and socioeconomic context, SEBs do not qualify as inefficient enterprises but rather as administrations whose nature is to pursue objectives that are heterogeneous and so incompatible with the sole criteria of economics (Ruet 2005). In the light of development externalities created by electricity networks at the macro level, such as food security, briefly discussed later in this chapter, SEBs not only achieved a reasonable level of village electrification (driven by electrification of groundwater pumping for irrigation) but also facilitated agricultural development through the green revolution (Samanta and Sundaram 1983).

Historic records provide evidence for this observation. When water resources were divided between India and Pakistan during independence, India got a smaller share of irrigated land relative to the size of its population. This concern was reflected in the first five-year plan, which recommended that the area under irrigation be doubled by the 1960s through the provision of "cheap electricity" that would enable the pumping of water from wells and tanks to irrigate arable land for food production (Planning Commission 1951). Over three decades (1951–1979) were dedicated to policies that increased electricity generation and distribution for the primary purpose of pumping groundwater (Dasgupta 1977).

Planning Commission documents demonstrate that increased spending on rural electrification, driven by the strategic concern of food security between 1960 and 1980, contributed more to village electrification than other policies for electrification

(Figure 22.3). Village electrification did not spontaneously translate into household electrification, as electricity was primarily for pumping groundwater rather than for lighting poor households, as shown in Figure 22.3. In the early 2000s, for example, 86 percent of Indian villages were considered "electrified," yet less than 30 percent of households had electricity connections, and electricity was not used to generate economic activity in these "electrified" villages (Planning Commission 2002). The government responded by redefining village electrification to improve outcomes. The original definition stated that "a village is deemed electrified if electricity is used in the inhabited locality within the revenue boundary of the village for any purpose whatsoever." In 2004 the definition was revised: "a village would be declared as electrified, if (1) basic infrastructure such as distribution transformer and distribution lines are provided in the inhabited locality as well as the Dalit basti (hamlet) where it exists, (2) electricity is provided to public places like schools, panchayat (village level) office, health centers, dispensaries, community centers etc., and (3) the number of households electrified is at least 10 percent of the total number of households in the village."

The redefinition demonstrates the influence of social and structural factors on energy policy. Concentration of power and agency in upper caste and relatively affluent households pushed the government to install electrical infrastructure in areas occupied by

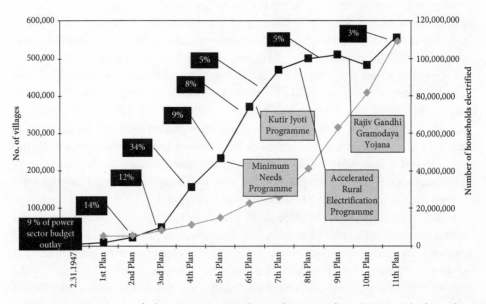

FIGURE 22.3 Progress of electricity access plans, plan periods 1 (1951–1956) through 11 (2007–2012).

Note: The figures in black boxes show the share (in percent) of budgetary outlay for power sector spent on rural electrification; the gray boxes give a selection of plans for rural electrification. The solid black line represents village electrification (left axis) and the grey line represents household electrification (right axis). The steeper slope for village electrification shows faster rates for village electrification than for household electrification.

Source: Data from first to eleventh plan documents.

upper caste households. Government policy reflected in the revised definition showed explicit emphasis on installing infrastructure in the areas with "*dalit*" (lower castes and invariably also poor) households so that access to electricity would be more evenly distributed among upper and lower caste (or affluent and poor) households (DDUGJY 2014).

The revised definition neither guarantees electrification of all households nor assures the supply of electricity (Sreevatsan 2018). Connecting a mere 10 percent of the households to the electric grid is sufficient to claim that a village is "electrified" even if no electricity is actually supplied to the village. This low benchmark accommodates the political interests of the state (Raghavan 2018). Under this generous definition, the government was able to claim, in April 2018, that India had achieved 100 percent electrification of its villages, even though about thirty million households (about 12 percent) were yet to be connected to the grid, and 20–30 percent of the households connected to the gird did not receive continuous electricity supply (Mohammad and Srivas 2018; Powell 2012).

The definition of village electrification has interesting implications for populist narratives (Powell 2014). It allows the federal government to appropriate the political gains of the rhetoric of "electrifying villages," almost immediately while passing on the long-term material cost of supplying electricity to "electrified villages" to SEBs controlled by the regional governments (Powell 2014). The federal government expects SEBs, which are under pressure to improve their commercial viability, to shoulder this "social" burden (Ministry of Power 2017a). The financial provision for this service is indefinitely deferred by the federal government, which adds to the financial distress of SEBs owned by regional governments.

The *ujwal discom assurance yojana* (UDAY), a federal financial restructuring plan for SEBs implemented in 2015, lists only financial goals and not social goals (Ministry of Power 2017a, 2017b). Without immediate support from the federal government for meeting redistributive goals, meeting commercial goals often means curtailing electricity access to poor households. Scholars and policy makers have not adequately addressed this contradiction between federal policy pronouncements and household level outcomes mediated by SEBs. Poor rural households shoulder the opportunity cost of poor quality (unreliable) electricity supply as uninterrupted supply is diverted to urban and commercial consumers (Tongia 2017). This cost is essentially a subsidy from the poor to the rich, and it is true not only of electricity but also of basic public goods, such as water, sanitation, education, and healthcare.

Access to Modern Cooking Fuels: Political Externalities Take Precedence

The transition from biomass to modern cooking fuels such as LPG in Indian households not only had a much later start but also followed a much slower pace than that of household electrification (see Figure 22.2, which shows the share of households with access to electricity and LPG based on household level surveys) (Commerce Annual 1977; NCAER 1959). In 1977, only 2.5 percent of the households had LPG connections, reaching 11 percent of the households only in the 1990s (Planning Commission 1969–1990; Central Statistical Institute 1970; Planning Commission 1982). According to household level surveys in 2015–2016, 40 percent of households in India had access to LPG, but most of these were urban households. The government's claim that over 80 percent of households had access to LPG in 2018 is based on figures from LPG dealer registrations, which must be treated with some caution, as they are less reliable than household level surveys (NSSO 2017; PPAC 2018).

The discourse around household cooking fuels offers clues about the state's and ruling elite's priorities (Mathur and Mathur 2005). From the start of independence, the government treated rural household cooking fuel needs as collateral damage in the larger project of nation-building. Consequently, rural cooking fuels were seen primarily as sources of inefficiency and pollution not relevant for development. In the 1960s and 1970s, the use of dried animal dung as cooking fuel (Fuel Policy Committee 1974) was seen as wasteful because animal dung was thought to be more valuable as manure to strengthen food production (Maulik 1986). Wood used as household fuel was blamed for rapid deforestation (Maulik 1986) by both the government planners and energy scholars, who recommended that "social forests" be developed by allocating fifty acres of land per village for cultivation of fuel wood (1960) so as to limit externalities such as deforestation.

None of the recommendations proposed by experts within and outside the government acknowledged the need for modern cooking fuels to substitute for wood in rural households to produce positive externalities such as better quality of life, especially for women, until the issue emerged as part of the global development agenda in the 1990s. Current climate change literature reflects a similar sentiment, in which pollution caused by rural cookstoves that burn biomass in India and elsewhere is highlighted without acknowledging the political, economic, social, and geographic marginalization that has left rural households without any choice of cooking fuels (Morelli, Cashman, and Rodgen 2017). In these narratives, the rural poor become the perpetrators of pollution and climate change rather than victims of political and social marginalization. (See Standal et al. in this volume for a focus on how gender intersects with energy politics.)

The distribution of material wealth, power, and agency within the household is another factor influencing energy choices of households (Palit and Govindan 2017). Women are the primary users of cooking fuels but have little or no influence on or agency in the choice of household cooking fuel (Batiwala 1983). In this context, the political rhetoric of inclusion that underpins the distribution of subsidized LPG bottles to economically and socially marginalized segments of the population (women and lower castes) gains significance.

The federal government portrays the *ujjwala yojana* (plan for brightness) program to distribute subsidized LPG bottles to poor women in rural areas as giving "respect and dignity" to women because it will "free women from the drudgery of collecting fuel" (Ministry of Petroleum & Natural Gas 2017). News outlets also present it as "socially transformative" because lower and marginalized castes in India will benefit (Press Trust of India 2018a). Popular narratives in energy platforms portray these polices as evidence of "politics working for women." Whether this is instead a case of "women working for politics" (Sasser 2018) is yet to be explored in academic literature. Clearly there is political value in subsidizing access to LPG because of the ability to galvanize support for parties that dispense these plans (Varshney 2013). Women voters match or exceed the number of male voters in many Indian regions, and the rhetoric of inclusion can influence electoral outcomes (Kapoor and Ravi 2014; Vishnoi 2017).

The long history of subsidized electricity for farmers illustrates the value of free or subsidized energy as a weapon in elections. Scholars have found that local government-owned utilities increase unbilled electricity for agriculture in the year prior to elections. The likelihood of a politician retaining his seat is positively correlated to the quantity of unbilled electricity in the constituency (Min and Golden 2014). Distributing subsidized LPG bottles to poor women is said to have produced a similar effect in regional elections in the largest regional province in India (Sehgal 2017). The short-term goal of winning elections partly explains the impotence of many of India's energy access plans in the longer term. The failure of plans for energy access (inconsistent or no delivery of electricity or LPG bottles on account of ambiguities in institutional accountability and underfunding of programs) enables the relaunch of plans many times over around multiple electoral cycles.

The rhetoric of redistribution and social justice that describes the subsidized LPG (or electricity) plans offers social legitimacy for the ruling alliance in India that has always been, at its core, an alliance of state and capital. Imperfect design of these programs offers comfort to pro-market, neoliberal stakeholders that the effort is likely to fail or have low impact eventually and consequently not drain public resources to the extent anticipated (Powell 2014). The sweeping claims of social transformation through energy access plans also oversimplifies complex social and political issues in India. The claim that technologies (such as LPG and electricity) can mediate deep-rooted social cleavages such as caste, class, and gender, which have resisted even the most committed and determined interventions is questionable, and this deserves deeper academic attention. The visual and rhetorical narratives of inclusion through energy access are compelling, but this does not constitute evidence of social transformation in the longer term.

POLITICS OF ENERGY INDEPENDENCE

Self-reliance or energy independence, interpreted as reduced dependence on imported energy sources, was part of India's energy strategy even before the oil crises of the 1970s. India's anti-imperial stand, signaled by the absence of foreign companies in almost every large industrial segment; its commitment to nonalignment, embedded in its nuclear policy; and its geopolitical preference for noninterference all favored self-reliance in energy. India's third five-year plan (1961–66), for example, projected nuclear energy as an option for power generation and a means for improving India's "self-reliance" in the context of energy (Planning Commission 1961).

As an independent country, India focused on developing a state-owned domestic energy industry consistent with the industrial policy resolutions of 1948 and 1956, which captured the government's aspiration to reserve core industries like petroleum with all future development for public sector undertakings (Bhatia 1983). In 1955 the government created the oil and natural gas directorate, which evolved into the Oil and Natural Gas Corporation (ONGC), India's largest upstream oil company today (ONGC 2018). The Indian government also established oil refineries such as the Indian Oil Corporation (IOC), which gained market share from international oil companies that dominated the sector in the early years after independence (Chakrabarti 2002).

India's entry into the oil industry was achieved at a time when international oil companies wielded global power over the supply and price of oil in India. International oil companies controlled refining capacity in India and set prices for oil products such as petrol (gasoline) and diesel (Chaudhury 1977). The state managed to counter the power of international oil companies using multiple levers, such as the sourcing of cheap Soviet petroleum products, limiting the allotment of foreign exchange required to import crude oil by international oil companies, purchasing crude oil from new independent oil companies such as Philips Petroleum, and establishing state-owned refineries using Soviet and other socialist-country technology to process the crude from independent oil producers that internationally owned refineries refused to process (Chaudhury 1977). The Indian state also resisted strong pressure from the World Bank and the International Monetary Fund (IMF) not to set up public sector refineries (Chaudhury 1977). Despite these early achievements in reducing dependence, India's dependence on foreign oil continued to increase in the 1970s and 1980s.

The importance of motorized transportation in economic activity and trade favored an increase in the use of oil (Visvanath 1997). From 1965 to 1969 coal consumption growth stagnated while oil consumption increased by over 50 percent (Maulik 1986). The increase alarmed Indian planners, especially because the years leading up to the oil crisis in the Persian Gulf were financially the most difficult for India. The growing cost of imported oil added to the costs of a brief war with Pakistan, rehabilitating refugees from Bangladesh, managing successive droughts, importing food and fertilizer, and aid to Bangladesh (Power 1975). When the oil crisis broke out in the Persian Gulf, India was importing two-thirds of its oil requirements. India's oil import bill increased from $447 million in 1973 to over $1.35 billion in 1975 (Planning Commission 1974). The failure of seasonal rain in 1973, along with the broader impacts of the oil crisis, produced unprecedented inflation of 27 percent (Planning Commission 1974). Consequent demonstrations contributed partly to the declaration of "emergency" and the suspension of democratic rights (Thomas 1982).

India subsequently nationalized refining companies owned by international oil companies, citing the companies' refusal to accept price controls proposed by the government (Kelkar 1980). Nationalization was achieved without much resistance: India accounted for only 2.9 percent of the Persian Gulf production that was nationalized during the crisis (Chaudhury 1977; Patra 2004).

To attain self-reliance, India invested heavily in securing hydrocarbon assets and relationships with hydrocarbon-rich countries (Government of India 2000; Planning Commission 2006). However, asset ownership did not prove to be a hedge against market forces that dominate global energy (particularly oil) in the 2000s (Collins et al. 2011; Constantin 2005) But the narrative of self-reliance served commercial and political interests. Self-reliance expressed in terms of "national security" and "energy security" offered commercial entities an excellent allegory for using state power to protect commercial interests—whether of state-owned or private companies (Ghose 1968). Diplomatic support to acquire hydrocarbon assets overseas helped companies reduce negotiation cost and increased the chance of success (Rajamohan and Powell 2015).

Domestic oil companies surely understood that their equity oil supplies were no more secure from political or logistical disruptions than long-term contract supplies or market purchases. In fact, domestic oil companies may have seen commercial merit in investing overseas, as it would safeguard investments and profits from predatory rent- or tax-seeking governments at home (Rajamohan and Powell 2015). Given the low probability of large oil discoveries and declining production from oil fields in India, it also made commercial sense for Indian companies to throw their weight behind any policy that encouraged investments abroad (Bhattacharya and Batra 2009). Making oil supply a matter of security also increased the influence of the traditional security community (such as the Ministry of Defense) on energy policy (Khurana 2007). This then led to unfamiliar terms such as "sea lanes of security" being added to the energy policy literature (Chellaney 2010).

India attempted to limit the economy's exposure to crude oil prices by relying on domestic resources such as coal, hydropower, and nuclear energy (Chakrabarti 1990; Planning Commission 1980). However, this strategy has not succeeded to the extent expected in India's plan documents. In 2017 coal accounted for over 58 percent of installed power generation capacity and over 76 percent of actual generation (Ministry of Power 2017a). Coal's dominance has led to an increase in imported coal.

In the last decade, imported coal grew three times faster than coking coal (with which India is not richly endowed), increasing from 8.7 million tons (MT) in 2003–2004 to over 212 MT in 2014–2015 (Ministry of Statistics and Program Implementation 2018). This growth occurred despite the fact that India has the world's third largest proved coal reserves, estimated at over 131 billion tons (BT), and is the world's third largest coal producer in volume (Coal Controllers Office 2015). The growing emphasis on the quality of thermal coal (Indian thermal coal is known to be of poor quality both in terms of energy content and chemical composition) was used as a reason for opening the option of coal imports (Reuters 2018; Russel 2016).

A directive by the Ministry of Environment, Forests and Climate Change stipulated that the ash content in coal transported over five hundred kilometers should be less than 34 percent from the beginning of January 2015 (Ministry of Environment, Forests and Climate Change 2014); this led to increased imports of low ash non-coking coal (Bam, Powell, and Sati 2017). Other factors contributing to the growth of coal imports include the rapid investment in coal-based power generation by the private sector and the unavailability of cheap domestically produced coal due to rigid supply controls through the publicly owned monopoly Coal India Limited (CIL) and control of coal transport by state-owned Indian Railways (Tandon 2010).

The option of blending imported low ash coal with domestic coal allowed private power generators to meet not only shortfalls in domestic coal but also restrictions on the transport of high ash coal. Private producers of power used the narrative of scarcity of domestic coal (Gupta, Joshi and Harihar 2010) to import coal with implicit state support in the form of favorable regulations and reduced duties. As a result, private power producers, who accounted for just over 9 percent of power generation capacity in gigawatts (GW) and 9 percent power generation in gigawatt hours (GWh) in 2003, increased their share of generation capacity to over 45 percent and of power generation to 36 percent by 2018 (Central Electricity Authority 2018b).

Private sector growth in power generation is a significant political and economic achievement, given the complex political economy of India's power sector, and this could not have been achieved without a compromise in the state policy of self-reliance that opened a way for coal imports. The Indian power sector puts private generators at a disadvantage compared to public sector generators in accessing relatively cheap domestic coal and in obtaining long-term power purchase agreements from SEBs. In 2016–2017, energy imports accounted for over 37 percent of India's primary energy basket or 48 percent of its commercial energy basket (Ministry of Statistics and Program Implementation 2018; see Figure 22.4). The high and volatile cost of energy imports is the single largest destabilizing factor in India's trade deficit.

Some argue that private commercial interests used the narrative of the state's failure to supply sufficient coal to begin importing coal (Mahajan 2013; Roy Chowdhury 2016; Singh 2017). But it may also be argued that market forces, both global and domestic, favored the import of energy fuels, and the state tacitly approved of imports because

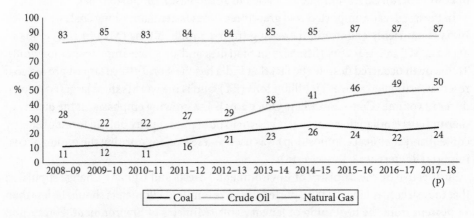

FIGURE 22.4 Share of imports (oil, natural gas, and thermal coal).

Source: Data from Ministry of Coal, Ministry of Commerce & Industry, Ministry of Petroleum & Natural Gas, Response to Questions in the Parliament, various dates. Gross crude oil imports are presented in the figure (excluding export of refined products).

they would facilitate integration of the Indian coal market with the global market and make the case for deregulating the coal industry (CCI 2013; Loh & Singh 2018; Russel 2018). These arguments may be also applied to natural gas, nuclear energy, and solar energy in future research. In the early 2000s, new gas discoveries led India to believe it could be self-sufficient in meeting natural gas demand, but today more than 50 percent of gas is imported (Niti Aayog 2017). Nuclear energy, which is held up as the means to "self-reliance" in all of India's policy documents, depends on imported nuclear technology and fuel (DAE 2019; Niti Aayog 2017). India's growing solar industry is almost entirely dependent on imported equipment (Niti Aayog 2017; Press Trust of India 2018b).

Returning to the case of coal, the notion of scarcity of coal on account of state failure to produce coal was used to generate a discourse that provided the desired rationalization and needed description to shape interactions between the government and commercial interests to simulate investment and financial support for importing coal, albeit at the cost of the state goal of self-reliance (Bhattacharjee 2017; CAG 2012; Mukherjee 2018). The notion of scarcity increased the value of domestic natural resources (coal and natural gas), which the state rations out to public and private commercial interests in exchange for political and financial support (Crabtree 2018; Mahalingam and Sharma 2017; Prasad 2007). Incentives, such as tax breaks and duty exemptions, favored commercial interests that sought greater international trade in energy fuels (Dillon et al. 2016; Gowda and Sharalaya 2016; Khatri and Ojha 2016).

Overall, when commercial investors have felt strong enough to take over a domain such as electricity generation or oil and gas exploration that had been reserved for the public sector, the private sector has tended to demand liberalization and openness to trade (Azad, Bose, and Dasgupta 2017; Breman 2014; Dela Rama and Rowley 2017; Mazumdar 2008). However, if the domain is in a nascent stage with large uncertainties over technology and cost, the private sector has tended to demand strong support from the state, as shown by the case of decarbonizing the energy sector, briefly discussed previously.

POLITICS OF DECARBONIZATION

The global emphasis on decarbonizing the energy sector to reduce local and global emissions of carbon has shifted policy from the quantity of energy to the quality of energy (Balachandra and Reddy 2002). Decentralized renewable energy, which had historically been treated as a form of "low-quality" energy suitable for the rural poor in India, emerged as a form of "high-quality" energy that would socially transform and environmentally sustain the country (Luthra et al. 2015).

The budget for 2015–2016 announced by the current government revised the target (non-binding) for renewable energy capacity to 175 GW by 2022, including 100 GW of solar (from about 17 GW), 60 GW of wind (from about 32 GW), 10 GW of biomass, and

5 GW of small hydropower (Ministry of Finance 2015; Ministry of Environment, Forests and Climate Change 2015). The government also increased the target for solar water pumps to over 100,000 from less than a thousand. To reach this target for renewable energy capacity, India would have to develop, in just seven years, renewable energy capacity that exceeds the coal-based generation capacity India developed over the last sixty years.

For its part, the government has justified investment in low carbon energy and reconciled policies for decarbonization with policies for poverty alleviation through the concept of "co-benefits," articulated in its national action plan on climate change (NAPCC) (Ministry of Environment, Forests and Climate Change 2008). The premise of the "co-benefits" concept is that unintended development outcomes would offset the cost of investment in low carbon energy sources. For example, the increase in the cost of energy on account of renewables may exclude the poor from energy access, but the decentralized nature of these energies may also increase access to energy for remote rural communities (Planning Commission 2012). Consequently, low carbon technologies, such as wind and solar, would be "neutral" (rather than negative) on the primary policy goal of inclusion (not excluding the poor from access to energy and other services).

In general, energy literature that is optimistic about technology anticipates decentralized renewable energy mediated by emerging automation and information technologies to enable the poor in India to "leap-frog" to a low carbon energy system that will also meet their developmental needs in an equitable and efficient manner (Bhattacharya 2010; Confederation of Indian Industry 2008; Dubey, Chatpalliwar, and Krishnaswamy 2014; Shukla et al. 2015). This is supplemented by an abundance of speculative literature on how this sustainable future is likely to unfold in India (Aswathanarayana 2008; Chella Rajan and Byravan 2011; Mathur et al. 2014; Sharma, Tiwari, and Sood 2012; Singh 2016; TERI 2015).

But there is inadequate literature on the present implications of using low carbon renewable energy. For example there is no systematic evidence generated about changes in savings, spending, business creation, time spent working or studying, or other broader indicators of socioeconomic development on account of low carbon energy sources such as off-grid solar electricity systems introduced in rural households (Aklin et al. 2017). Whether this assessment is due to limited services provided by off-grid solar energy (mainly lighting) or on account of the technological complexity and transaction costs imposed on poor households in mediating in intermittency of solar energy is yet to be established.

International literature that supports aggressive decarbonization targets for India argues that renewable energy will reduce the health cost of local pollution from fossil fuels (Public Health Foundation of India & Centre for Environmental Health 2017). These studies show the social cost (health cost) of fossil fuel use to be much higher than the economic cost of renewable energy. A notable counterview is that the social cost of coal and gas may be overestimated to the extent that electricity will actually replace much worse forms of energy in large parts of India where households use kerosene and wood stoves (Ghosh, Sharma, and Subramanian 2017). The underlying assumption in this argument is that the poor may value energy today more than good health tomorrow. The discount rates of the poor are generally much higher than those of the rich, which means that they would assign lower value to future gains (such as longer life) in today's decisions (such as obtaining access to energy).

Technocratic analysis (Gaba, Cormier, and Rogers 2011; Sathaye et al. 2011) and simulated projections for future low carbon outcomes (Kathuria, Ray, and Bandyopadhyay 2015) treat the trade-offs between development and decarbonization (Machingura and Lally 2017) as unimportant or insignificant compared to the larger goal of limiting global average temperature increases to less than 1.5°C to 2°C. Achieving the instrumental goal of limiting average temperature increases in the future at the cost of intrinsic values such as poverty alleviation today (Solow 1996) is seen as unavoidable. This approach justifies socialization of the cost of energy transitions.

The entrenched role of the state in the Indian energy sector may facilitate the deflection and diffusion of the cost of decarbonization onto the whole society, including the poor. The socialization of the cost of decarbonization would essentially benefit commercial interests, as all costs, including the cost of writing off stranded fossil fuel assets, can be passed on to either rate payers (of electricity) or taxpayers without consent or consultation. In implementing policies for decarbonization, federal and regional governments have so far used mainly contracts and auctions rather than bilateral markets. Decisions on investment in low carbon energy sources are made through centralized mechanisms in which consumers do not necessarily participate (Niti Aayog 2017; SECI 2018; Sree Ram 2018). The costs determined centrally are passed through to consumers administratively rather than through responsive and consultative price mechanisms (Ghosh, Sharma, and Subramanian 2017; Globaldata Energy 2018,).

For private investors, state intervention to correct market failure in providing environmental goods such as clean air not only creates new markets but also reduces financial risks as the state guarantees revenue far into the future. As the state can effectively diffuse cost externalities of decarbonization onto the society, the private sector, which had until very recently portrayed the role of the state in the energy sector as a key liability, is now treating it as a source of strength. Demand from the private sector for subsidies, incentives, targets, and mandates from the government for low carbon energy has become more strident. The use of subsidies and other incentives will enable the state to generate new markets for low carbon energy for the private sector at public risk. As explained previously, the relationship between the state and capital is a key source of power in India (Mukherji 2009) that strongly influences outcomes of energy policy goals such as decarbonization. Ambitious targets for decarbonization also produce benefits for the state in the international arena. High aspirations (even if non-binding) enhance state prestige in multilateral bargaining environments such as the conference of parties for combating climate change. Future literature may explore whether the newfound multilateralism in India's recent progressive stand in climate change action is predicated upon its capacity for domestic intervention (Ruggie 1982).

Achievement of the policy goal of decarbonization lies in the future, but as long as the social and political contexts from which policies emerge are the same, the path to decarbonization is unlikely to differ significantly from the policy path to energy access or that of energy security. The evidence must of course be generated by future literature.

An Agenda for Future Research

The issues presented here highlight major opportunities for research on the politics of energy issues in India. As the discussion demonstrates, few scholars have used political science theories, frameworks, and methods to shed light on energy in India, particularly in the current era. In addition, a wide range of issues is coming to the fore as part of decarbonization discussions and actions. Future research would be most productive in three key areas: (1) the political economy of energy access programs in India, (2) the nature of the relationship between the state and capital in the energy sector, and (3) the politics of decarbonization and the redistribution of the costs of decarbonization.

Energy supply and access has long been a political rather than a technical problem in India (Kristoferson 1973; Nayyar 1998; Venkataraman 1987). The technocratic analyses that dominate the literature tend to frame India's energy problems as managerial problems of inefficacy or as problems arising from scarce domestic resources rather than as political or social problems (Castle 1978; Kumar and Shekhar 2015; Makhijani 1977). This framing has served commercial and state interests but compromised achievement of key policy goals. The rhetoric of inclusive access has offered social legitimacy for the ruling alliance, while the rhetoric of energy security and scarcity has served commercial interests.

Energy literature, influenced strongly by reports from commercial consultancies and nongovernmental agencies that often depend on funding from international agencies, demonstrates contempt for social disciplines, possibly because in India social sciences do not have the same scientific legitimacy as technocratic analysis. Consequently, societal responses to interventions by the state or industry are undertheorized (Patnaik 1986). Literature that problematizes economic and environmental inefficiency effectively endorses rather than critiques prevailing national and international technocratic narratives. Analyses that question the foundations of state policy are generally avoided or postponed to the future, when policy choices and its implications will effectively be history.

In this context, the first promising area for future research is exploration of the political and social reasons for success of electrification for irrigation and food production in India. Why did the policy for village electrification achieve some success that has not been replicated in other national energy policy goals? Are strategic goals, such as food security, a necessary precondition for achieving other social goals such as energy access? A related issue for study may include investigating the role of regional provinces in southern and western India that have managed to achieve higher rates of electrification than provinces in the northern and eastern regions under the same federal policy environment. Regional disparities in household electrification highlight the importance of regional governments in meeting energy goals. Regional provinces with high rates of household electrification are also better economic performers. Apart from economic growth and industrialization, other factors that may be investigated as drivers of electrification are single-party majority governments at the federal and regional levels; the relationship between the federal and regional political leadership; and more important, the influence of rural interest groups such as large farmers. The narrative of the poor subsidizing the rich in the context of energy access contests the narrative of populism, and this deserves more scholarly attention.

Second, as decarbonization using renewable energy is taking off in India, it opens up a wide range of issues for research. There is a top-down portrayal of decentralized (off-grid) renewable energy systems (particularly solar) as the means for rural India to escape energy poverty and "leap-frog" into a sustainable and affluent low carbon world. There are relatively few studies on whether this view is shared by the rural poor (bottom-up view). In addition, development outcomes (increase in time spent on education, improved health outcomes, and employment generation) expected from existing decentralized solar energy programs in rural India are yet to be clearly established by rigorous academic studies.

Finally, apart from anecdotal evidence, there is little empirical work on whether capital and other forms of subsidies for low carbon energy sources are displacing investment in basic public goods such as clean drinking water, housing, basic healthcare, and education. In this context a question for research is whether the poor value modern energy today, even if it is from fossil fuels (such as grid-based electricity and LPG), more than better health tomorrow. Work on this question will contribute to answering the broader question of the cost of decarbonizing the energy system and how these costs will be distributed in a country that has just about completed the seven-decade-old project of connecting households to the electricity grid.

REFERENCES

Acemoglu, Daron, Simon Johnson, and James A. Robinson. 2001. "The Colonial Origins of Comparative Development: A Empirical Investigation." *American Economic Review* 91, no. 5: 1369–1401.

Ahluwalia, Motek Singh. 2002. "Economic Reforms in India since 1991: Has Gradualism Worked?" *The Journal of Economic Perspectives* 16, no. 3: 67–88.

Aklin, Michael, Patrick Bayer, Harish S. P., and Johannes Urpelainen. 2017. "Does Basic Energy Access Generate Socio Economic Benefits?: A Field Experiment with Off-grid Solar Power in India." *Science Advances* 3: 1–8.

Aswathanarayana, U. 2008. "A Low Carbon Technology Driven Strategy for India's Energy Security." *Current Science* 44, no. 4: 440–441.

Azad, Rohit, Prasenjit Bose, and Dasgupta Zico. 2017. "Riskless Capitalism in India." *Economic & Political Weekly* 52, no. 31: 85–98.

Badiani, Reena, Katrina Jessoe, and Suzanne Plant. 2012. "Development & Environment: The Implications of Agricultural Electricity Subsidies in India." *The Journal of Environment & Development* 21, no. 2: 244–262.

Bagchi, Amiya Kumar. 1991. "From a Fractured Compromise to a Democratic Consensus: Planning & Political Economy in Post-Colonial India." *Economic & Political Weekly* 26: 611–628.

Bajpai, Nirupam, and Jeffrey D. Sachs. 1998. "Strengthening India's Strategy for Economic Growth." *Economic and Political Weekly* 33, nos. 29/30: 1935–1942.

Balachandra, P., and Sudhakara Reddy. 2002. "A Sustainable Energy Security Strategy India Revisited." *Economic & Political Weekly* 37, no. 52: 5264–5273.

Bam, Swagat, Lydia Powell, and Akhilesh Sati. 2017. *Coal Beneficiation in India: Status and Way Forward.* New Delhi: Observer Research Foundation.

Banerjee, Ghosh Sudeshna, Dougles Barnes, Bipul Singh, Kristy Mayer, and Hussain Samad. 2015. *Power for All: Electricity Access Challenges in India.* World Bank Studies. Washington, DC: World Bank.

Batiwala, Srilath. 1983. "Women and Cooking Energy." *Economic & Political Weekly* 18, nos. 52/53: 2227–2230.

Bharat, Jairaj. 2017. "Issues to Watch as India Reaches Ambitious Energy Access Target." World Resources Institute. February 21. http://www.wri.org/blog/2017/02/5-issues-watch-india-reaches-ambitious-energy-access-target.

Bhatia, R. 1983. *Planning for Petroleum & Fertilizer Industries: Programming Model for India.* New Delhi: Oxford University Press.

Bhattacharjee. 2017. *India's Coal Story: From Damodar to Zambezi.* New Delhi: Sage.

Bhattacharya, B. B., and Amita Batra. 2009. "Fuel Pricing Policy Reform in India: Implications and Way Forward." *Economic & Political Weekly* 44, no. 29: 77–86.

Bhattacharya, Subhes C. 2010. "Shaping a Sustainable Energy Future for India: Management Challenges." *Energy Policy* 38, no. 8: 4173–4185.

Bhattacharya, Sugata, and R. Urjit Patel. 2011. "Does the Exuberance in the Indian Electricity Sector Have Legs?" Working Paper no. 45, Brookings Institute.

Bhide, Anjali, and Carlos Rodriquez Monroy. 2011. "Energy Poverty: A Special Focus on Energy Poverty in India and Renewable Energy Technologies." *Renewable Energy & Sustainable Energy Reviews* 15, no. 2: 1057–1066.

Breman, Jan. 2014. "The Gujarat Model of Growth, Development & Governance." *Economic & Political Weekly* 49, no. 39: 27–29.

British Petroleum. 2018. "BP Statistical Review of World Energy." British Petroleum.

CAG. 2012. "Report of the Comptroller & Auditor General of India on Allocation of Coal Blocks and Argumentation of Coal Production." New Delhi: Ministry of Coal, Government of India.

Castle, Emery N. 1978. "Property Rights and the Political Economy of Resource Scarcity." *American Journal of Agricultural Economics* 60: 1–9.

CCI. 2013. "Case Number 59 of 2013." Competition Commission of India. https://www.cci.gov.in/sites/default/files/592013_2.pdf.

Central Electricity Authority. 2017. *Growth of the Electricity Sector in India 1947–2017.* New Delhi: Government of India.

Central Electricity Authority. 2018a. *Growth of the Electricity Sector 1947–2018.* New Delhi: Government of India.

Central Electricity Authority. 2018b. "Annual Report," October 4. http://www.cea.nic.in/reports/annual/annualreports/annual_report-2018.pdf.

Central Statistical Institute. 1970. *Statistical Abstracts*. New Delhi: Government of India.

Chakrabarti, Prabhas Kumar. 2002. *Investment Decisions in the Indian Public Sector*. New Delhi: Northern Book Centre.

Chakrabarti, Prabhas Kumar. 1990. *Coal Industry in West Bengal*. New Delhi: Northern Book Centre.

Chancel, Lucas, and Thomas Piketty. 2017. "Indian Income Inequality 1922–2015: From British Raj to Billionaire Raj." WID Working Paper. World Inequality Lab. https://wid.world/document/chancelpiketty2017widworld/.

Chattopadhyay, P. 2001. "Electricity Reforms." *Economic & Political Weekly* 36, no. 31: 2902–2983.

Chaudhury, Saumitra. 1977. "Nationalization of Oil Companies in India." *Economic & Political Weekly* 12, no. 10: 437–444.

Chella Rajan, Sudhir, and Sujatha Byravan. 2011. "Development Benefit from Low Carbon Pathways." *Economic & Political Weekly* 46, no. 34: 20–26.

Chellaney, Brahma. 2010. "Indian Ocean Maritime Security; Energy, Environment and Climate Challenges." *Journal of the Indian Ocean Region* 6, no. 2: 155–168.

Chikkatur, Ananth, and Shaoibol Chakravarty. 2008. "Need for Integrated Energy Modelling Institutions in India." *Economic & Political Weekly* 43, no. 21: 64–69.

Cisler, W. L., A. E. Bush, and H. Tauber. 1966. "Review of the Report of Energy Survey of India Committee." *Institute of Electrical and Electronics Engineers (IEEE) Transactions on Power Apparatus and Systems* PAS-85, no. 8: 864–879.

Coal Controllers Office. 2015. "Provisional Coal Statistics." Government of India.

Coelho, Suani T., and Jose Goldemberg. 2013. "Energy Access: Lessons Learnt in Brazil and Perspectives for Replication in Other Countries." *Energy Policy* 61: 1018–1096.

Collins, Gabe, Andrew S. Erikson, Yufan Hao, Mikkal E. Herberg, Hughes Llewelyn, Weihua Liu, and Jane Nakano. 2011. "Asia's Energy & Resource Nationalism: Implications for the United States, China and the Asia Pacific Region." NBR Special Report, The National Bureau of Asian Research.

Commerce Annual. 1977. "Energy in Indian Economy: A Statistical Profile." *Commerce Annual*, 203–216.

Confederation of Indian Industry. 2008. "Building a Low Carbon Indian Economy." CII.

Constantin, Christian. 2005. "China's Conception of Energy Security: Sources and International Impacts." Working Paper. University of British Columbia.

Crabtree, James. 2018. *Billionaire Raj: A Journey through India's Gilded Age*. HarperCollins.

DAE. 2019. "Meeting Demand Projections." Department of Atomic Energy. http://www.dae.nic.in/?q=node/129.

Das, Anjana, and Jyoti Parikh. 2000. "Making Maharashtra Electricity Board Commercially Viable." *Economic & Political Weekly* 35, no. 14: 1201–1208.

Das, Raju. 2001. "The Political Economy of India: Review Essay." *New Political Economy* 6, no. 1: 103–117.

Das, Raju K. 2015. "Critical Observations on Neo-Liberalism and Indian Economic Policy." *Journal of Cotemporary Asia* 45, no. 4: 715–726.

Dasgupta, Biplab. 1977. "India's Green Revolution." *Economic & Political Weekly* 12, no. 618: 241–260.

Ministry of Power. 2014. "Definition of Electrified Village." Government of India. http://www.ddugjy.gov.in/page/definition_electrified_village.

Dela Rama, Marie, and Chris Rowley. 2017. *The Changing Face of Corruption in the Asia Pacific: Current Perspectives and Future Challenges*. Amsterdam: Elsevier.

Deloitte. 2013. "Securing Tomorrow's Energy Today: Energy Access for the Poor, Policy & Regulations." https://www2.deloitte.com/content/dam/Deloitte/in/Documents/energy-resources/in-enr-long-term-energy-security-noexp.pdf.

Desai, Padma, and Jagdish Bhagwati. 1975. "Socialism and Indian Economic Policy." *World Development* 3, no. 4: 213–221.

Dhume, Sadanand. 2018. "Modi Abandons Reform for Populist Nostrums." *Wall Street Journal*, August 23, https://www.wsj.com/articles/modi-abandons-reform-for-populist-nostrums-1535063402.

Dillon, A., P. Krishnan, M. Patnam, and C. Perroni. 2016. "Electoral Accountability and the Natural Resource Curse: Theory and Evidence from India." CEPR Discussion Paper no. 11377. https://www.kcl.ac.uk/sspp/research/economics/People/DhillonNRMP-30-Jan2017.pdf.

D'Sa, Antonette, Narasimha Murthy K. V., and Amulya K. N. Reddy. 1999. "India's Power Sector Liberalization: An Overview." *Economic & Political Weekly* 34, no. 23: 1423–1434.

Dubash, Navroz K. 2008. "The Electricity-Groundwater Conundrum: Case for a Political Solution to a Political Problem." *Economic & Political Weekly* 42, no. 52: 45–55.

Dubash, Navroz K., and Sudhir Chella Rajan. 2001. *Politics of Power Sector Reform in India.* New Delhi: World Resources Institute.

Dubash, Navroz K., and Daljit Singh. 2005. "Of Rocks and Hard Places: A Critical Overview of Recent Global Experience with Electricity Restructuring." *Economic & Political Weekly* 40, no. 50: 5249–5259.

Dubey, Sunita, Siddharth Chatpalliwar, and Srinivas Krishnaswamy. 2014. *Electricity for All in India: Why Coal Will Not Always Be King.* New Delhi: Vasudha Foundation.

Duddu, Praveen. 2015. "The 10 Worst Blackouts of the Last 50 Years." January 13. https://www.power-technology.com/features/featurethe-10-worst-blackouts-in-the-last-50-years-4486990/.

Fuel Policy Committee. 1974. "Report of the Fuel Policy Committee." New Delhi: Government of India.

Gaba, Kwawu Mensan, Charles Joseph Cormier, and John Allen Rogers. 2011. *Energy Intensive Sections of the Indian Economy: Path to Low Carbon Development.* Washington: World Bank ESMAP.

Galbraith, John Kenneth. 1958. "Rival Economic Theories on India." *Foreign Affairs* 36: 587–596.

Ganapathy, R. S. 1984. "Energy Planning in India: A Review." Working Paper 04-01_00580. Ahmedabad: Indian Institute of Management.

Ghose, Aurobindo. 1968. "Interaction of Private and Public Sector: Case of Petroleum & Coal." *Economic & Political Weekly* 3: 229–232.

Ghosh, Arun. 1997. "Break-up and Privatization of SEB in Andhra Pradesh: An Upcoming Scam." *Economic & Political Weekly* 32, no. 29: 1782–1785.

Ghosh, Rangeet, Navneeraj Sharma, and Arvind Subramanian. 2017. "Renewables May Be the Future but Are They the Present: Coal, Energy and Development in India." Sixteenth Darbari Seth Memorial Lecture. New Delhi: TERI.

Globaldata Energy. 2018. Solar PV Module, Update 2018 - Global Market Size, Competitive Landscape and Key Country Analysis to 2022, December 2018. London.

Godbole, Madhav. 1999. "Enron Revisited." *Economic & Political Weekly* 34, no. 12: 661–663.

Godbole, Madhav. 1997. "Future of State Electricity Boards: Tunnel Vision." *Economic & Political Weekly* 32, no. 35: 2222–2224.

Government of India. 2000. "Hydrocarbon Vision 2025." New Delhi.

Gowda, M. V. R., and N. Sharalaya. 2016. "Crony Capitalism and India's Political System." In *Crony Capitalism in India: Establishing Robust Counteractive Institutional Frameworks*, edited by N. Khatri and A. K. Ojha, 131–158. Palgrave Studies in Indian Management. London: Palgrave Macmillan.

Gupta, Rajan, Sunjoy Joshi, and Shankar Harihar. 2010. "Energy, Development & Climate Change." *Seminar* 606: 30–34.

Hanson, A. H. 1966. *The Process of Planning: A Study of the Indian Five Year Plans 1950–1964*. London: Oxford University Press for the Royal Institute of International Affairs.

Hone, Angus. 1968. "Tangled Wires of State Electricity Boards." *Economic & Political Weekly* 3, no. 29: 1151–1154.

International Energy Agency. 2017. *World Energy Outlook*. Paris: International Energy Agency.

Jain, Varinder. 2006. "Political Economy of Electricity Subsidies: Evidence from Punjab." *Economic & Political Weekly* 41, no. 38: 4072–4080.

Jewitt, Sarah, and Sujatha Raman. 2017. "Energy Poverty, Institutional Reform and Challenges for Sustainable Development: The Case of India." *Progress in Development Studies* 17, no. 2: 173–185.

Joseph, Sarah. 2007. "Neo-liberal Reforms and Democracy in India." *Economic & Political Weekly* 42, no. 31: 3213–3218.

K. L., X. 1960. "Domestic Fuels in India." *Economic & Political Weekly Annual* (January): 131–132.

Kale, Sunila S. 2004. "Current Reforms: The Politics of Policy Change in India's Electricity Sector." *Pacific Affairs* 77, no. 3: 467–491.

Kamalapur, G. D., and R. Y. Udaykumar. 2012. "Rural Energy in the Changing Paradigm of Power Sector Reform in India." *International Journal of Electrical and Computer Engineering* 2, no. 2: 147–154.

Kannan, K. P., and Vijaymohanan N. Pillai. 2001. "Plight of the Power Sector in India: Physical Performance of SEBs." *Economic & Political Weekly* 36, no. 2: 130–139.

Kapoor, Mudit, and Shamika Ravi. 2014. "Women Voters in Indian Democracy: A Silent Revolution." *Economic & Political Weekly* 49, no. 12: 63–67.

Kathuria, Rajat, Saon Ray, and Kuntala Bandyopadhyay. 2015. "Low Carbon Pathways for Growth in India: Assessment of Climate Models." Indian Council for Research on International Economic Relations (ICRIER).

Kelkar, Vijay. 1999. "India's Emerging Economic Challenges." *Economic and Political Weekly* 34, no. 33: 2326–2329.

Kelkar, Vijay Laxman. 1980. "India and World Economy: Search for Self-reliance." *Economic & Political Weekly* 15, no. 5-6-7: 245–258.

Khanna, Madhu, and David Zilberman. 1999. "Barriers to Energy Efficiency in Electricity Generation in India." *The Energy Journal* 20, no. 1: 25–41.

Khatri, N., and Abhoy K. Ojha, eds. 2016. *Crony Capitalism in India Establishing Robust Counteractive Institutional Frameworks*. London: Palgrave Macmillan.

Khurana, Gurpreet S. 2007. "The Maritime Dimension of India's Energy Security." *Strategic Analysis* 31, no. 4: 583–601.

Kohli, Atul. 2007. "State and Redistributive Development in India." UN Research Institute for Social Development.

Kohli, Atul. 2010. *Democracy and Development in India: From Socialism to Pro-Business*. New Delhi: Oxford University Press.

Kristoferson, Lars. 1973. "Energy in Society." *Ambio* 2: 178–185.

Kudaisya, Medha. 2009. "A Mighty Adventure: Institutionalizing the Idea of Planning in Post-Colonial India 1947–60." *Modern Asian Studies* 43: 939–978.

Kumar, Cheruku Jeevan. 2015. "Civil Service Reforms in India: Policy and Perspectives." *International Journal of Political Science* 1, no. 1: 15–26.

Kumar, Deepak, and Sulochana Shekhar, 2015. "Rural Energy Supply Models for Smart Villages." *School of Earth Sciences, Central University of Karnataka, Gulbarmartga-585367, Karnataka, India* 1, no. 5: 1–8. https://www.researchgate.net/profile/Dr_Kumar59/publication/277250356_RURAL_ENERGY_SUPPLY_MODELS_FOR_SMART_VILLAGES/links/55654cb408ae94e957205984.pdf.

Kurian, C. T. 1968. "Planning in India: A Theoretical Critique." *Economic & Political Weekly* 3, no. 9: 389–396.

Lal, Deepak. 1998. *Unfinished Business: India in the World Economy 1820–1992.* New York: Oxford University Press.

Loh, Tim, and Rajesh Kumar Sing, 2018. "Hurting for Buyers, U.S. Coal Miners Are Learning toLoveIndia."Bloomberg,July12,2018.https://www.bloomberg.com/news/articles/2018-07-11/u-s-coal-miners-hurting-for-buyers-are-learning-to-love-india.

Luthra, Sunil, Sanjay Kumar, Dixit Garg, and Abid Heleem. 2015. "Barriers to Renewable Energy/Sustainable Energy Technology Adoption; Indian Perspective." *Renewable Energy Sustainable Energy Reviews* 41: 726–776.

Machingura, Fortunate, and Steven Lally. 2017. "Sustainable Development Goals and Their Trade-Offs." Case Study Report. London: Overseas Development Institute.

Mayer, Kristy; Banerjee, Sudeshna Ghosh; Trimble, Chris. 2015. Elite Capture: Residential Tariff Subsidies in India. World Bank Study;. Washington, DC: World Bank. © World Bank. https://openknowledge.worldbank.org/handle/10986/20538 License: CC BY 3.0 IGO.

Mahajan, Anish S. 2013. "Import Lobby and Imported Coal—A Tale of Two Fridays." *Business Today*, June 24. https://www.businesstoday.in/current/perspective/import-coal-power-tariff/story/196085.html.

Mahalanobis, P. C. 1964. "Statistical Tools and Techniques in Perspective Planning in India." *Sankhya: The Indian Journal of Statistics* 26 (Series B, 1960-2002): 29–44.

Mahalingam, Sudha, and Sharma Deepak. 2017. "Political Economy of Independent Regulation in India's Natural Gas Industry." *Economic & Political Weekly* 52, no. 20: 44–50.

Makhijani, Arjun. 1977. "Energy Policy for Rural India." *Economic and Political Weekly* 12, no. 33/34: 1451–1464.

Marlow, Iain, Bibhudatta Pradhan, and Archana Chaudhary. 2019. "Modi Flicks Populist Switch as Tight India Election Draws Closer," *Bloomberg*, February 2. https://www.bloomberg.com/news/articles/2019-02-01/modi-flicks-populist-switch-as-tight-india-election-draws-closer.

Mathur, Jaskiran Kaur, and Dhiraj Mathur. 2005. "Dark Homes and Smoky Hearths: Rural Electrification and Women." *Economic & Political Weekly* 40, no. 7: 638–643.

Mathur, Ritu, Leena Srivastava, Atul Kumar, Aayush Awasthy, and Llika Mohan. 2014. "Pathways to deep De-carbonization: India." Research Report, Sustainable Development Solutions Network.

Maulik, T. K. 1986. "Energy and Development Options: The Case of India." Working Paper no. 622. Ahmedabad: Indian Institute of Management.

Mazumdar, Surajit. 2008. "Crony Capitalism & India: Before and After Liberalization." Working Paper, March 2008/04. Institute for Studies on Indian Development.

Min, Brian, and Miriam Golden. 2014. "Electoral Cycles in Electricity Losses in India." *Energy Policy* 65 (February): 619–625.

Ministry of Environment, Forests and Climate Change. 2008. "National Action Plan on Climate Change." Government of India.

Ministry of Environment, Forests and Climate Change. 2014. *The Gazette of India*. General Statutory Rules (G.S.R) 02 E (January 14).

Ministry of Environment, Forests and Climate Change. 2015. "Intended Nationally Determined Contribution." Submission to the Paris Agreement. New Delhi: Government of India.

Ministry of Finance. 2015. "Key Features of the Budget 2015–16." Government of India.

Ministry of Petroleum & Natural Gas. 2017. "PM Ujjwala Yojana." http://www.pmujjwalayojana.com/about.html.

Ministry of Power. 2012. "Report of the Enquiry Committee of the Grid Disturbance." Government of India.

Ministry of Power. 2017a. "Electricity Sector at a Glance." December 31. https://powermin.nic.in/en/content/power-sector-glance-all-india.

Ministry of Power. 2017b. "UDAY." https://www.uday.gov.in/home.php.

Ministry of Power. 2019. "Guidelines Pradhan Mantri Sahaj Bijlu Har Ghar Yojana." https://powermin.nic.in/en/content/guidelines-pradhan-mantri-sahaj-bijli-har-ghar-yojana.

Ministry of Statistics and Program Implementation. 2018. "Energy Statistics 2018." Government of India.

Modi, Vijay. 2005. "Improving Electricity Services in Rural India: An Initial Assessment of Recent Initiatives and Some Recommendations." Centre for Global Sustainable Development Working Paper. The Earth Institute, Columbia University.

Mohammad, Noor, and Anju Srivas. 2018. "Modi Announces 100% Electrification—But That Doesn't Mean Everyone Has Power." *The Wire*, April 29. https://thewire.in/government/narendra-modi-government-rural-electrification-power.

Morelli, Ben, Sarah Cashman, and Molly Rodgen. 2017. "Lifecycle Assessment of Cook-stoves and Fuels in India, China, Kenya and Ghana." US Environment Protection Agency (USEPA).

Morris, Sabastian. 1996. "Political Economy of Electric Power in India." *Economic & Political Weekly* 31, no. 21: 1274–1285.

Mukherjee, Prashant. 2018. "Fuel Shortage Crippling India's Thermal Power Projects." *Economic Times Prime*, October 29. https://prime.economictimes.indiatimes.com/news/66406734/energy/fuel-shortage-is-crippling-indias-thermal-power-plants-coal-india-and-costly-imports-can-save-the-day-but-not-for-long.

Mukherji, Rahul. 2009. "The State, Economic Growth and Development in India." *The India Review* 8, no. 1: 81–106.

Mundle, S., and M. G. Rao. 1991. "Volume and Composition of Subsidies in India 1987–88." *Economic & Political Weekly* 26, no. 18: 1157–1172.

Murty, M. N. 1987. "Prices for Public Electricity Supply in India: Efficiency, Distributional Equity & Optima; Structure." *Economic & Political Weekly* 22, no. 41: 1762–1769.

Myrdal, Gunnar. 1968. *Asian Drama: An Inquiry into the Poverty of Nations*. Vol. I. London: Alan Lane/The Penguin Press.

Nayyar, Deepak. 1998. "Economic Development and Political Democracy: Interaction of Economics & Politics in Independent India." *Economic & Political Weekly* 33, no. 49: 3121–3131.

Nayyar, Deepak. 2006. "Economic Growth in Independent India: Lumbering Elephant or Running Tiger." *Economic & Political Weekly* 41, no. 15: 1451–1458.

NCAER. 1959. *Domestic Fuels in India*. National Council on Applied Economic Research. Bombay: Asia Publishing House.

Nehru, Jawaharlal. 1946. *The Discovery of India*. New Delhi: Penguin Books.

Niti Aayog. 2017. "Draft National Energy Policy." Version as on 27.06.2017. New Delhi: Government of India.

NSSO. 2016. "Swachhta Status Report." National Sample Survey Organization, Ministry of Statistics and Programme Implementation, Government of India.

NSSO. 2017. "Millennium Development Goals - Final Country Report of India." National Sample Survey Organization. Ministry of Statistics and Programme Implementation, Government of India.

ONGC. 2018. Home page. http://www.ongcindia.com/wps/wcm/connect/ongcindia/Home/Company/History/.

Pachuri, R. K., and Leena Srivastava. 1988. "Indian Energy Policy: A Modelling Approach." *The Energy Journal* 9, no. 4: 35–48.

Pachuri, Sonali, Adrian Mueller, Andreas Kemmler, and Daniel Spreng. 2004. "On Measuring Energy Poverty in Indian Households." *World Development* 32, no. 12: 2083–2104.

Palit, Debajit, and Mini Govindan. 2017. "A Glaring Omission in India's Energy Policy: Gender Justice." October 13. https://medium.com/energy-access-india/a-glaring-omission-in-indias-energy-policy-gender-justice-afc63375eb20.

Patnaik, Prabhat. 2015. "The Nehru-Mahalanobis Strategy." *Social Scientist* 43: 3–10.

Patnaik, Sasmita, and Saurabh Tripathi. 2017. *Access to Clean Cooking Energy in India: State of the Sector*. New Delhi: Centre for Energy, Environment and Water.

Patnaik, Utsa. 1986. "The Agrarian Question and Development of Capitalism in India." *Economic & Political Weekly* 21: 781–793.

Patra, C. D. 2004. *Oil Industry in India*. New Delhi: Mittal Publishers.

Pidd, Helen. 2012. "India Blackouts Leave 700 Million without Power." *The Guardian*, July 31. https://www.theguardian.com/world/2012/jul/31/india-blackout-electricity-power-cuts.

Planning Commission. 1951. *First Five Year Plan*. New Delhi: Government of India.

Planning Commission, 1961. *Third Five Year Plan*, New Delhi: Government of India

Planning Commission. 1969–1990. *Five Year Plans*. New Delhi: Government of India.

Planning Commission. 1974. *Fifth Five Year Plan*. New Delhi: Government of India.

Planning Commission. 1980. *Sixth Five Year Plan*. New Delhi: Government of India.

Planning Commission. 1982. *Report of the Fuelwood Study Committee*. New Delhi: Government of India.

Planning Commission. 1990–2002. *Five Year Plans*. New Delhi: Government of India.

Planning Commission. 2002. *Tenth Five Year Plan*. New Delhi: Government of India.

Planning Commission. 2002–2017. *Five Year Plans*. New Delhi: Government of India.

Planning Commission. 2006. *Integrated Energy Policy*. Vol. XXVI: 9 and 57. New Delhi: Government of India.

Planning Commission. 2012. *Twelfth Five Year Plan*. New Delhi: Government of India.

Powell, Lydia. 2012. "Energy Access in India: Has Policy Performed?" Presentation at the ORF-Asia Centre Conference on Shaping the Future: Energy Security in India organized by the Asia Centre, Paris & the Observer Research Foundation, New Delhi, October 11–12.

Powell, Lydia. 2014. "Energy Access in BRICS Countries" Presentation at the Observer Research Foundation (ORF), Conference on BRICS organized by the Economic Policy Forum and ORF, February 28.

Powell, Lydia, Akhilesh Sati, Alexis Scholtz, Zhongyi Yin, and Igor Makarov. 2012. "Energy Access in BRICS Countries." Economic Policy Forum and Observer Research Foundation.

Power, Paul F. 1975. "The Energy Crisis and Indian Development." *Asian Survey* 15: 328–345.

Power-Technology. 2018. "Time for Rethink as Yet Another Auction Fails in India." November 13. https://www.power-technology.com/comment/clean-energy-time-rethink-yet-another-auction-fails-india/

PPAC. 2018. "LPG Profile." Petroleum Planning and Analysis Cell, Ministry of Petroleum and Natural Gas, Government of India.

Prasad, Neerabh K. 2007. "Regulation of Natural Gas in India." *Economic & Political Weekly* 43, no. 39: 21–24.

Press Trust of India. 2018a. "Ujjwala Yojna Has Led to Social Transformation: PM Modi." *Times of India*, May 28,. https://www.indiatoday.in/pti-feed/story/ujjwala-yojna-has-led-to-social-transformation-pm-1243479-2018-05-28.

Press Trust of India. 2018b. "India's Import Dependence for Solar Equipment over 90 Percent." *Economic Times*, July 19. https://economictimes.indiatimes.com/industry/energy/power/indias-import-dependence-for-solar-equipment-over-90-per-cent-in-last-3-fiscal-government/articleshow/65055838.cms.

Public Health Foundation of India & Centre for Environmental Health. 2017. "Air Pollution and Health in India: Review of Current Evidence and Opportunities for the Future." New Delhi: https://www.ceh.org.in/wp-content/uploads/2017/10/Air-Pollution-and-Health-in-India.pdf.

Purkayastha, Prabir. 2001. "Power Sector Policies and New Electricity Bill: From Crisis to Disaster." *Economic & Political Weekly* 36, no. 25: 2251–2262.

Raghavan, Sharad T. C. A. 2018. "Power Ministry Feels No Need to Change Electrification Definition." *The Hindu*, April 30. https://www.thehindu.com/news/national/power-ministry-feels-no-need-to-change-electrification-definition/article23732316.ece.

Rajamohan, C., and Lydia Powell. 2015. "Energy Rivalry Between India and China: Less Than Meets the Eye." In *The New Politics of Strategic Resources Energy and Food: Security Challenges in the 21st Century*, edited by David Steven, Emily O'Brian, and Bruce Jones, 144–167. Washington: Brookings Institution.

Ranganathan, V. 2004. "Electricity Act 2003: Moving to a Competitive Environment." *Economic & Political Weekly* 39, no. 20: 2001–2005.

Rao, M. Govinda. 2017. "Public Finances in India in the Context of India's Development." Working Paper no. 219. NIPFP, National Institute of Public Finance & Policy NIPFP.

Rao, S. L. 2001. "Electricity Bill 2001: What It Reflects of Power Policy." *Economic & Political Weekly* 36, no. 38: 3608–3613.

Reddy, Amulya. 1999. "Goals, Strategies and Policies for Rural Energy." *Economic & Political Weekly* 34, no. 49: 3435–3445.

Reddy, Amulya K. N. 2001. "Indian Power Sector Reforms for Sustainable Development: The Public Benefit Imperative." *Energy for Sustainable Development* 5, no. 2: 74–81.

Rejikumar, R. 2005. "National Electricity Policy: A Critical Review." *Economic & Political Weekly* 40, no. 20: 2028–2032.

Reuters. 2018. "India's Coal Imports Surge in July Despite Advancing Prices." *The Hindu Business Line*, July 26. https://www.thehindubusinessline.com/markets/commodities/india-coal-imports-surge-in-july-despite-advancing-prices/article24518311.ece.

Roy Chowdhury, Indronil. 2016. "Here's How India's Green Energy Plan Is Making the Global Coal Lobby Jittery." *Financial Express*, September 7. https://www.financialexpress.com/economy/heres-how-indias-green-energy-plan-is-making-global-coal-lobby-jittery/369506/.

Ruet, Joel. 2005. *Privatizing Power Cuts: Ownership and Reform of State Electricity Boards in India*. Edited by P. D. Kausik. New Delhi: Academic Foundation.

Ruggie, Gerard John. 1982. "International Regimes, Transnational Change & Embedded Liberalism in the Post War Economic Order." *International Organization* 36, no. 2: 379–415.

Russel, Clyde. 2016. "India's Changing Coal Imports Show Quality over Quantity." *Reuters*, June 21. https://www.reuters.com/article/us-column-russell-coal-india-idUSKCN0Z70GI.

Russel, Clyde. 2018. "Why India Hasn't Cut Back on Coal Imports Despite Rising Prices." *The Hindu Business Line*, August 20. https://www.thehindubusinessline.com/markets/commodities/why-india-hasnt-cut-back-on-coal-imports-despite-rising-prices/article24735514.ece.

Sagar, Jagdish. 2006. "Electricity Reforms." *Economic & Political Weekly* 41, no. 1: 80.

Salgo, H. 1998. "Power Sector Reform and the Privatization of Distribution in India." International Working Document, World Bank.

Samanta, B. B, and A. K. Sundaram. 1983. "Socio-economic Impact of Rural Electrification in India." Discussion Paper D 730. Resources for the Future. ,Washington, DC.

Sasser, Jade S. 2018. *On Infertile Ground: Population Control and Women's Rights in the Era of Climate Change.* New York: New York University Press.

Sathaye, Jayant A., Stephane de la Rue du Can, Maithili Iyer, Michael A. McNeil, Klaas Jan Kramer, Joyashree Roy, Moumita Roy, et al. 2011. "Strategies for Low Carbon Growth in India: Industry and Non-Industry Sectors." LBNL-4557E. Berkeley Lab.

Satish, T. 2004. "Civil Service Reforms." Centre for Good Governance, November. http://cgg.gov.in/core/uploads//2017/07/CivilServicesReform.pdf.

SECI. 2018. "RfS for Selection of Solar Power Developers for Setting up of 2000MW (250MW x 8) ISTS Connected Solar Power Projects under Global Competitive Bidding." Solar Energy Corporation of India.

Sehgal, Rashme. 2017. "UP Election Results 2017: Centre's Pro-women Plans Worked in BJP's Favor." *First Post*, March 11. https://www.firstpost.com/politics/up-election-results-2017-centres-pro-women-plans-worked-in-bjps-favour-3329612.html.

Sengupta, D. P. 1989. "Rural Electrification in India: The Achievements and the Shortcomings." Institute of Electrical and Electronics Engineers.

Sengupta, Ramprasad. 1992. "Energy Planning for India: A Critique of the Existing Methodology." *Indian Economic Review* 27: 425–437.

Sharma, Manoj Kumar. 2002. "Power Sector Reforms and Issues." Presented at National Power Systems Conference, NPSC.

Sharma, Naveen Kumar, Prashant Kumar Tiwari, and Yograj Sood. 2012. "Solar Energy in India: Strategies, Policies, Perspectives and Future Potential." *Renewable Energy & Sustainable Energy Review*, no. 16: 933–941.

Shenoy, Bhamy V. 2017. "Need to Redo the Draft National Energy Policy." *Economic & Political Weekly* 52, no. 30: 18–21.

Shukla, P. R., Minal Pathak, Darshini Mahadevia, and Amit Garg. 2015. "Pathways to Deep Decarbonizing in India." Sustainable Development Solutions Network (SDSN) and Institute for Sustainable Development and International Relations (IDDRI).

Singh, Kartikeya. 2016. "Business Innovation and Diffusion of Off-grid Solar Technology in India." *Energy for Sustainable Development*, 30: 1–13.

Singh, Rajesh Kumar. 2017. "Chemical Industries, Aluminum Smelters Mulling Coal Imports as Power Takes Priority." Livemint, December 14. https://www.livemint.com/Industry/qcNxY-QuphRwbunXsRBeF3I/Chemical-industries-aluminum-smelters-mulling-coal-imports.html.

Smith, Thomas B. 1993. "Indian Electric Power Crisis: Why Do the Lights Go Out?" *Asian Survey* 33, no. 4: 376–392.

Solow, M. Robert. 1996. "Intergenerational Equity Yes but What about Inequality Today."
    http://hdr.undp.org/en/content/inter-generational-equity-yes-what-about-inequity-today.

Sree Ram, R. 2018. "India's Renewable Energy Sector Awaits a Reboot." Livemint, December 26.
    https://www.livemint.com/Money/gczJsMignHqSXYg3F7iexI/India-renewable-energy-
    sector-awaits-a-reboot.html.

Sreekumar, N., and Shantanu Dixit. 2011. "Challenges in Rural Electrification." *Economic &
    Political Weekly* 46, no. 43: 27–33.

Sreevatsan, Ajay. 2018. "How Every Village Got Electricity and Why That Is Still Not Enough."
    Livemint, May 1. https://www.livemint.com/Politics/oKTPIug2MPuP4KpRVU8kuL/How-
    every-village-got-electricity-and-why-that-is-still-not.html.

Srinivasan, Kannan. 1995. "Indian Law and the Enron Agreement." *Economic & Political
    Weekly* 30, no. 20: 1153–1154.

Steeten, Paul Patrick. 1995. *Thinking about Development*, edited by Alessandro Pio. Cambridge:
    Cambridge University Press.

Swamy, Subramanian. 2005. "Political Structure and Economic Reforms: A comparative
    Appraisal of India and China." *Economic & Political Weekly* 40, no. 10: 934–940.

Tandon, Gulshan Lal. 2010. "Reflections on the Indian Coal Sector." Kumaramanglam
    Memorial Lecture.

TERI. 2015. *Energy Security Outlook: Defining a Secure and Sustainable Future for India*. New
    Delhi: The Energy Resources Institute.

Thomas, Raju G. C. 1982. "Energy Politics in Indian Security." *Pacific Affairs* 55, no. 1 (Spring
    1982): 32–53.

Thomas, Stephen. 2005. "British Experience of Electricity Liberalization: A Model for India?"
    Economic & Political Weekly 40, no. 50: 5260–5268.

Tongia, Rahul. 2017. "Delhi's Household Electricity Subsidies: Highly Generous but
    Inefficient?" IMPACT Series no.042017. Brookings Institution.

Tripathi, Bhasker. 2018. "UP Discoms Are Bleeding, Politics Is to Blame: New Study."
    IndiaSpend, April 2. https://www.indiaspend.com/up-discoms-are-bleeding-politics-is-to-
    blame-new-study-98750/.

Upadhyay, Anil K. 2000. "Power Sector Reforms: Indian Experience and Global Trends."
    Economic & Political Weekly 35, no. 12: 1023–1028.

Varshney, Ashutosh. 2013. *Battles Half Won: India's Improbable Democracy*. New Delhi:
    Penguin India.

Venkataraman, A. 1987. "Policy Making in India: Energy Sector." *The Indian Journal of Political
    Science* 48, no. 3 (July-Sept): 354–369.

Vishnoi, Anubhuti. 2017. "UP Elections 2017: Women Voters Exceed Men by a Wider Margin
    Than in 2012." *Economic Times*, March 7. https://economictimes.indiatimes.com/news/
    politics-and-nation/up-elections-2017-women-voters-exceed-men-by-wider-margin-
    than-2012-polls/articleshow/57544701.cms.

Visvanath, Dr. S. N. 1997. *A Hundred Years of Oil*. Oil India Limited. New Delhi: Vikas
    Publishing House.

Wolak, Frank. 2008. "Reforming the Indian Electricity Supply Industry." In *Sustaining India's
    Growth Miracle*. New York: Columbia University Press, 115–155.

Wood, Douglas, and Devendra Kodwani. 1997. "Privatization Policy & Power Sector Reforms:
    Lessons from British Experience for India." *Economic & Political Weekly* 32, no. 37:
    2350–2358.

World Bank. 2016. "World Bank Open Data." https://data.worldbank.org/.

CHAPTER 23

···

THE ENERGY POLITICS
OF JAPAN

···

TREVOR INCERTI AND PHILLIP Y. LIPSCY

On March 11, 2011, a powerful magnitude 9.0 earthquake shook Japan. The ensuing tsunami flooded the Fukushima Daiichi Nuclear Plant, triggering a series of catastrophic
events that led to core meltdowns and the displacement of over 110,000 people
(Samuels 2013). The disaster forced Japan to shut down all of its nuclear reactors and
fundamentally reexamine the basic premises of its energy policy. The ruling Democratic
Party of Japan (DPJ) came under intense criticism for its handling of the disaster, clear-
ing the way for the conservative Liberal Democratic Party (LDP) to reassume power
under Prime Minister Abe Shinzo in December 2012. The Abe government thus
assumed power at a pivotal moment for Japanese energy policy. Would Japan abandon
or resuscitate nuclear power? Would Japanese policy makers prioritize fossil fuels or
decarbonization to compensate for the loss of nuclear energy? Would Japan assume
leadership or step back from international climate change cooperation? Would the government break the power of regional monopolies or return to business as usual?

Japan is an important case in understanding the comparative politics and international relations of energy. With limited natural resources, energy security has loomed
large for Japan throughout its modern history. The US oil embargo of 1941—instituted in
response to the Japanese occupation of French Indochina—demonstrated the country's
vulnerability to supply disruptions, contributing to "energy angst" (Calder 1993) and an
"energy-cum-national security mindset" (Samuels 1981). The government responded to
the 1970s oil shocks with a variety of measures to encourage energy conservation
(Ikenberry 1986; Morse 1981; Murakami 1982). Japan emerged as an energy efficiency
leader and diversified away from fossil fuels, primarily through investments in nuclear
energy. Japan's regulatory policies for energy efficiency, such as the "top runner" program, exemplify successful collaboration between the public and private sectors.

However, the Japanese model has run into serious problems in recent years. Japanese
energy efficiency gains and conservation efforts stagnated in the 1990s following political changes and economic stagnation. Japan then shocked the international community

by abandoning the second commitment period of the Kyoto Protocol in 2010. The Fukushima nuclear disaster exposed fundamental flaws in Japan's nuclear regulatory structure and called into question basic premises of long-term energy policymaking (Asahi Shimbun Tokubetsu Hodobu 2012; Funabashi 2016; Independent Investigation Commission on the Fukushima Nuclear Accident 2014; Kurokawa et al. 2012; Kushida 2012; Lipscy, Kushida, and Incerti 2013). What accounts for the struggles of Japanese energy policy? What lessons can be learned to illuminate the politics of energy in other countries?

Understanding Japanese energy policy and politics requires consideration of factors common to many countries as well as some specific to Japan. Among the former are energy security concerns, the rise of environmentalist movements, and the domestic and international politics of climate change. Factors relatively specific to Japan include the politics of "reciprocal consent," the impact of institutional changes—such as the 1994 electoral reform—and a complicated relationship with nuclear energy reflecting memories of Hiroshima and Nagasaki.

HISTORICAL AND POLITICAL CONTEXT

The acquisition and production of energy has occupied a prominent role in modern Japanese politics (Akao 1983; Bobrow and Kudrle 1987; Calder 1993; Fukai 1988; Morse 1981; Samuels 1987; Vivoda 2014). From the Meiji Restoration to the 1940s, resource scarcity served as an important motive for colonialism and war. After World War II, Japan grew heavily reliant on oil imports, until the 1970s oil shocks necessitated major policy shifts. Leveraging its successful energy conservation and source diversification efforts, Japan assumed an important role in early global climate change negotiations. However, the Japanese government has struggled to maintain and extend its prior achievements in recent decades.

Coal reserves powered Japan's industrial development after the Meiji Restoration (Samuels 1987, 68). By the mid-1930s Japan had become the third largest producer of coal in the world (Lockwood 1970, 92). However, domestic coal quickly became insufficient to fuel rapid economic growth; by 1938, Japan was importing 6.5 million tons of coal, primarily from Karafuto and Northern China/inner Mongolia. In 1943 coal accounted for two-thirds of Japanese energy consumption. However, coal imports declined sharply as Allied forces severed shipping lanes during World War II (US SBS 1946 9–19).

Electricity use became widespread during the late Meiji era. Electric power was extended to every region of Japan by the end of the nineteenth century (Samuels 1987, 136). Initially, electricity was provided by small steam (coal) plants, but Japan gradually shifted toward large hydroelectric plants and thermal generation (Hein 1990, 73). During World War I, lightly regulated utilities "experienced turbulent, uncontrolled, and fratricidal expansion," and five major utilities accounted for one-quarter of total power generated (Samuels 1987, 138). In the 1930s global economic turbulence associated with the Great Depression and militarization led to calls for state control of electric utilities in order to ensure a supply of cheap, plentiful, and stable energy. These demands culminated in the creation in 1938 of the Japan Electric Power Generation and Transmission Company (Nippatsu), a public-private partnership supervised by both government and private leaders. Japanese electricity was organized around Nippatsu and nine regional distribution companies. Strong public-private coordination and large, monopolistic utilities were therefore already a feature of the Japanese electricity market prior to 1945. During the postwar US occupation, the Supreme Commander of the Allied Powers (SCAP) dissolved much of the centralized mechanisms of control established during the war effort and attempted to privatize the electric power industry. In reality, important prewar institutional legacies remained as Nippatsu was absorbed by the previous nine regional distribution companies, which were reorganized into nine private regional monopolies (Samuels 1987, 160–161).

Resource conservation and top-down management of natural resources began early in Japan. The first major policy aimed at energy efficiency (*nensho shido*, or technical guidance for fuel burning) was promulgated during the interwar years to increase the efficient use of coal. Several prefectural governments formalized private sector certification for the fuel economy of boilers in the 1910s, which evolved into a national policy by the 1930s (Kobori 2007). Centralized management of energy efficiency in coal resources continued into the postwar years with the institutionalization of heat management (Ogawa, Noda, and Yamashita 2010). However, these policies were focused on coal and faded in importance as Japan's economy moved toward reliance on other forms of energy. Major national efficiency initiatives were not seen again until after the oil price shocks of the 1970s.

After the 1930s, Japan became increasingly dependent on foreign oil, first as an energy source for the Imperial Navy and subsequently as the principal energy source for postwar growth (Lockwood 1970, 107). Japan's oil reserves are limited, making the country reliant on oil imports; by 1934, domestic crude accounted for only one-tenth of the refined products market (Samuels 1987, 171–178). The US oil embargo in 1941 effectively threatened to shut down Japan's navy, leading Japanese decision makers to conclude that gambling on a risky war was a rational choice (Sagan 1988).

Following World War II, Japan reverted to relying primarily on coal and hydropower. However, with abundant, cheap Middle East oil, Japanese petroleum consumption skyrocketed, growing 11 percent annually from 1963 to 1973 (see Figure 23.1). The oil share of Japan's primary energy supply increased from under 40 percent to nearly 80 percent (see Figure 23.2). Japan's dependence on Middle East oil moderated after the oil shocks of 1973 and 1979. Diversification into nuclear, natural gas, and coal led to a reduction of oil from around 80 percent to 50 percent of primary energy supply. This diversification has not reduced Japan's dependence on energy imports—even nuclear energy in Japan requires imported uranium—but it has reduced the country's vulnerability to Middle East supply disruptions.

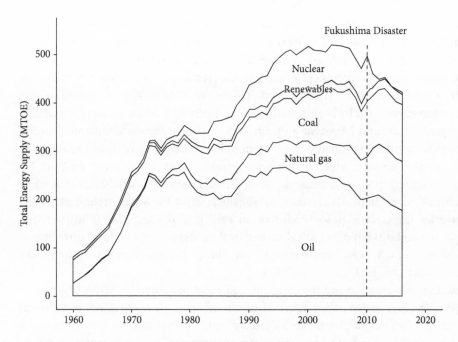

FIGURE 23.1 Japan's energy mix (MTOE), 1960–2016.

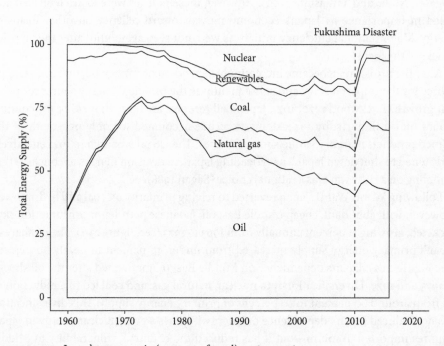

FIGURE 23.2 Japan's energy mix (percent of total), 1960–2016.

Note: Annual data.

Source: *Data from* IEA (2017).

Japan remains heavily dependent on foreign energy sources (see Figure 23.3). The 2011 Fukushima disaster exacerbated Japan's energy security challenge by forcing a temporary shutdown of nuclear power generation. Japan's energy self-sufficiency ratio—domestic primary energy production as a percentage of total energy consumption—fell to a historical low of 6 percent after the Fukushima disaster (IEA 2017). Japanese policy makers responded to the crisis by increasing reliance on imported fossil fuels (particularly natural gas), reducing overall energy consumption, and encouraging renewable energy production, though renewables still remain a small share of the overall energy mix.

Contemporary Political Context

Before moving to a detailed discussion of energy politics, we provide a basic overview of contemporary Japanese politics. Those familiar with Japanese politics may prefer to skip this section. Japan is a multiparty bicameral democracy. The country ranks high in all widely used quantitative measures of democratic development and stands out in Asia for the stability of its democratic institutions; since World War II, Japanese democracy has continued uninterrupted (Boix, Miller, and Rosato 2013; Marshall, Gurr, and Jaggers 2010). Three basic features are useful to highlight in understanding the political context of Japanese energy policy.

First, Japan's postwar experience is defined by the predominance of a single moderate conservative political party—the LDP—since 1955. LDP rule has only been interrupted on two occasions: once in 1993 by an eight-party coalition government, and again in

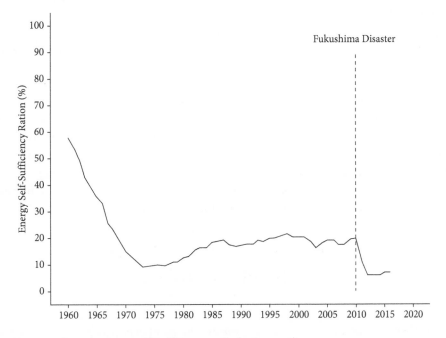

FIGURE 23.3 Japan's energy self-sufficiency ratio (1960–2016).

Note: Annual data.

Source: Data from IEA (2017).

2009 in a landslide victory by the opposition center-left DPJ (Kushida and Lipscy 2013; Lipscy and Scheiner 2012). The DPJ was in power during the Fukushima nuclear disaster and was sharply criticized for its crisis response. The LDP regained power in 2012 under Prime Minister Abe Shinzo. This history of success by a single party means that Japanese policymaking has been heavily influenced by the LDP, working in close coordination with bureaucratic ministries—particularly the Ministry of International Trade and Industry (MITI), now reorganized as the Ministry of Economy, Trade and Industry (METI)—and private industry, in contrast to the partisan and policy rotation found in many other democracies (Curtis 1988; Johnson 1982; Okimoto 1990; Ramseyer and Rosenbluth 1993; Samuels 1987).

Second, important shifts altered the context of politics in Japan starting in the 1990s. The end of the Cold War unsettled the long-standing ideological cleavage between the LDP and opposition Socialist Party, and Japan's economy began to struggle after the bursting of twin asset price bubbles in real estate and equities in 1991 (Hoshi and Kashyap 2004). With the rise of new opposition parties, the LDP saw its dominance weaken, and it has ruled since then in coalition with smaller parties, particularly Komei (Ehrhardt et al. 2014). Japan's powerful bureaucracy, once glorified for orchestrating the country's economic miracle and successful response to the oil shocks, fell from grace amid economic stagnation and embarrassing corruption scandals (Carlson and Reed 2018; Pharr 2000).

Third, Japan's political system underwent fundamental transformations in the 1990s that also affected the context of energy policymaking. The 1993–1994 non-LDP coalition government enacted electoral reform. Under the electoral system in place from 1947 to 1994, voters had cast a single non-transferable vote (SNTV) for an individual candidate. Multiple seats were awarded in each electoral district (multimember districts, or MMD), and seats were won by the top several candidates in each district. These seats were often contested by multiple LDP candidates, requiring the cultivation of personal support networks and pork-barrel spending rather than reliance on party label. In January 1994 new rules were implemented, which replaced Japan's former multimember districts with three hundred single-member districts (SMDs) and two hundred proportional representation (PR) seats. This electoral reform reduced incentives to cultivate regionally targeted pork-barrel projects and instead increased incentives to appeal broadly to Japanese voters (Catalinac 2016; Rosenbluth and Thies 2010). In addition, administrative reforms initiated by Prime Minister Hashimoto Ryūtarō in 1996 shifted power away from bureaucrats and backbenchers, centralizing greater power in the cabinet office of the prime minister (Estevez-Abe 2006; Mulgan 2017; Takenaka 2006).

ELECTRICITY, NUCLEAR ENERGY, AND FUKUSHIMA

Richard Samuels famously characterized the development of energy policy in Japan as a process of constant conflict, bargaining, and compromise between the state and private firms. Through what Samuels (1987) calls "reciprocal consent," private industry accepts significant state jurisdiction over market structure but also receives access to public goods, extensive inclusion in policymaking processes, and considerable autonomy to self-regulate. Neither the state nor the private sector dominates the policy process; instead they remain in a state of constant negotiation and accommodation (Dauvergne 1993; Samuels 1987).

However, close ties between the state and private firms in the energy sector have been increasingly questioned in recent years, and criticism intensified after the 2011 Fukushima disaster. Japan's power sector has been heavily dominated by ten regional monopolies. Historically, these regional utilities enjoyed limited competition in power generation, which allowed them to charge higher electricity prices than counterparts abroad (Hosoe 2006; Moe 2012). As the sole providers of nuclear energy, regional utilities have a strong stake in maintaining nuclear power in Japan's energy mix and tend to resist policies to strengthen competition or renewable energy. They also maintain close ties with the LDP, making substantial campaign contributions to LDP politicians that far outweigh those of other players in the energy sector (Duffield and Woodall 2011; Vivoda 2012). Close public-private ties, including *amakudari* (literally descent from heaven: the movement of retired officials from the bureaucracy to private firms), have been criticized for fostering lax regulations and energy policy stasis (Moe 2012).

The Development of Nuclear Power in Japan

Japan pursued nuclear power generation beginning in the 1950s, only a decade after becoming the only country to suffer nuclear attacks at Hiroshima and Nagasaki. This turn toward nuclear energy was initiated by Japanese public and private leaders, such as Nakasone Yasuhiro and Shoriki Matsutaro (Arima 2008; Kelly 2014; Low 1994), and supported by the United States through its "Atoms for Peace" program. In 1955 Japan jumpstarted its nuclear energy program with passage of the Atomic Energy Basic Law, which established the Atomic Energy Commission, comprising the Nuclear Safety Commission, tasked with ensuring safe production of nuclear energy, and the Atomic Energy Research Institute for state-funded research in nuclear technology. Japan succeeded in generating electricity using nuclear power for the first time in 1963. Nuclear power grew sharply in the aftermath of the 1970s oil shocks (see Figure 23.4).

Supporters saw nuclear energy as a path to energy self-sufficiency for Japan. However, Japanese nuclear power generation ultimately relies on imported uranium and hence is not a completely domestic energy source. MITI therefore committed to investing in "breeder" reactor technology beginning in the 1950s, aimed at providing a source of domestic plutonium (Cochran et al. 2010; Pickett 2002). The project, of which 80 percent was funded by the government, culminated in the Monju fast breeder project in 1994 (Dauvergne 1993). Monju operated for only approximately a year before shutting down over safety concerns. Thus, nuclear power never truly fulfilled its self-sufficiency promise in Japan (Pickett 2002). By 2005, METI's long-term plan for nuclear power had moved its target for fast breeder commercialization to 2050, compared to the original

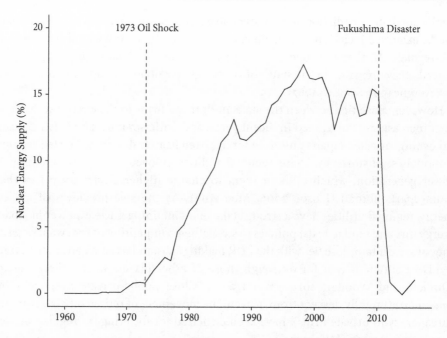

FIGURE 23.4 Japanese nuclear energy supply as a percentage of total energy, 1960–2016.

Source: Data from IEA (2017).

goal of commercialization in the 1980s (Cochran et al. 2010; Walker 2000). Nevertheless, it continued to emphasize the construction of new nuclear power plants.

The Politics of Nuclear Energy Prior to Fukushima

Japan is often described as having a "nuclear allergy" stemming from its experience of being the first victim of nuclear warfare at Hiroshima and Nagasaki (Hook 1984; Hymans 2011). In 1954 a third of Japanese citizens signed petitions against nuclear weapons and nuclear power (Aldrich 2013). Institutionally, Japan's Atomic Energy Basic Law limits atomic energy development to peaceful purposes; a 1967 Diet resolution pledges Japan not to possess, manufacture, or allow the introduction of nuclear weapons onto Japanese soil; and Japan has ratified both the Treaty on the Non-Proliferation of Nuclear Weapons in 1976 and the Comprehensive Nuclear Test Ban Treaty in 1997. Japan has also been able to rely on the US nuclear umbrella for its defense. Although Japan could develop nuclear weapons quickly based on its existing capabilities, these factors have served as important constraints (Hughes 2007; Hymans 2011; Solingen 2010).

Despite its "allergy" toward nuclear weapons, Japan successfully developed an extensive nuclear power program, with a total capacity exceeded only by the United States and France. Cohen, McCubbins, and Rosenbluth (1995) argue that there were few political access points for civil society groups to intervene to stop or delay broader nuclear power development, and that environmental groups were outside of the LDP electoral coalition and so could not influence LDP policy. However, the adoption of nuclear energy was not without opposition. Local groups sometimes thwarted the construction of nuclear plants, and fishing cooperatives were particularly successful at blocking or delaying plant construction in some areas (Lesbirel 1998). Japan also has a long history of environmental civil society activism and local antinuclear movements, which have often successfully resisted construction of nuclear plants (Hasegawa 2004; Hirabayashi 2013; LeBlanc 2010).

Utilities have sidestepped such local opposition by siting nuclear plants in rural areas where civil society opposition was weak (Aldrich 2007). The Japanese government then targeted these communities with informational campaigns and incentives designed to shift public opinion in a pronuclear direction. These incentives were both economic—subsidies, loans, job training programs, and infrastructure projects—and political, such as televised ceremonies for cooperative local politicians (Aldrich 2007, 2013).

By the late 1980s, Japan began to face serious political obstacles to the further expansion of nuclear power. The 1986 Chernobyl disaster caused a shift in public opinion, with a majority of Japanese citizens opposed to nuclear power for the first time, and large antinuclear demonstrations increased throughout the 1980s (Dauvergne 1993; Pickett 2002). The LDP, METI, and utilities, however, maintained their support for nuclear power and responded to growing popular anxiety by launching a public relations campaign promoting nuclear safety and offering increased compensation to communities willing to host nuclear plants. As grassroots opposition increased, more prefectures and municipalities opposed the construction of new nuclear plants and waste facilities, slowing the potential for nuclear expansion. Growing opposition from prefectural governors was particularly problematic, as they possessed effective veto power over plant construction (Hymans 2011; Pickett 2002). Although the government maintained ambitious nuclear power goals as part of its energy security strategy, shifts in public opinion and local opposition decreased the rate of nuclear expansion by the late 1980s.

Post-Fukushima Nuclear Energy Politics and Policy

On March 11, 2011, a tsunami triggered by the magnitude 9.0 great Tohoku earthquake inundated the Fukushima Daiichi nuclear plant, causing a nuclear meltdown. (For more on Fukushima as one of three major nuclear disasters, see Fitzwater in this volume.) Following the disaster, the DPJ government shut down all of Japan's nuclear reactors for safety reevaluations. While the scale of the disaster was significant—more than twenty thousand people were killed in the tsunami—the tsunami was not without precedent. The 1896 Meiji-Sanriku earthquake generated a tsunami of comparable heights in the same geographic region (Samuels 2013). While the tsunami affected several nuclear plants in Japan simultaneously, only one—Fukushima Daiichi—suffered core meltdowns.

Fukushima Daiichi housed six reactors, three of which were in active operation at the time of the earthquake. While all three operating reactors successfully shut down in response to the earthquake, the quake destroyed the power lines connecting Fukushima Daiichi to the external power grid. The plant therefore needed to rely on its emergency backup systems to provide power to the reactor cooling pumps. The ensuing tsunami, however, exceeded the plant's ten-meter seawall and flooded the backup power systems, rendering them useless. Without primary or secondary power to operate the cooling pumps, the plant's fuel rods could not be cooled, ultimately leading to meltdowns in all three operating reactors. Fukushima Daiichi was therefore deficient in three key attributes: plant elevation, sea wall elevation, and location and status of backup generators. Higher elevations for any of these three variables, or watertight protection of backup power systems, likely would have prevented the disaster (Lipscy, Kushida, and Incerti 2013).

In the aftermath of the disaster, critics pointed out inadequacies in Japan's nuclear regulatory regime, many of which stem from close ties between government officials and private utilities under the politics of reciprocal consent. The regulatory body charged with ensuring nuclear safety—the Nuclear and Industrial Safety Agency (NISA)—had been housed within METI, which was also responsible for promoting nuclear power. In addition, many retired METI bureaucrats routinely assumed positions in regional utilities such as Tokyo Electric Power Company, intensifying potential conflicts of interest. Regulatory capture has been widely cited as a contributing factor to the Fukushima nuclear accident, including by the government's Independent Investigation Commission (Ferguson and Jansson 2013; Kingston 2013; Kurokawa et al. 2012; Vivoda and Graetz 2015). This has raised important questions about the viability of Japan's traditional approach toward power regulation.

Future Prospects for Nuclear Energy in Japan

Despite the Fukushima disaster, Japanese nuclear policy reform has been stalemated by the competing interests of entrenched actors within Japan's energy policy establishment (Arase 2012; Hymans 2015; Vivoda and Graetz 2015). In addition, the LDP, which regained power in 2012, has adopted a conspicuously pronuclear policy stance. The party proposed that Japan generate roughly 20–22 percent of its energy supply from nuclear power by 2030. While this target represents a reduction from the pre-Fukushima goal of 50 percent, it would still require the restart of virtually all of Japan's shuttered plants, an unlikely prospect due to public and local opposition. The LDP has struggled to restart plants in cases where scientific experts concluded they would be unsafe (Scalise 2015). In contrast to the LDP's pronuclear stance, opinion polls generally show large majorities of the Japanese public prefer a reduction or elimination of nuclear power (see Figure 23.5). Major opposition parties have proposed a phaseout of nuclear energy over the coming decades, and many local courts and politicians—including some LDP members—are unenthusiastic about nuclear restarts in their own backyards.

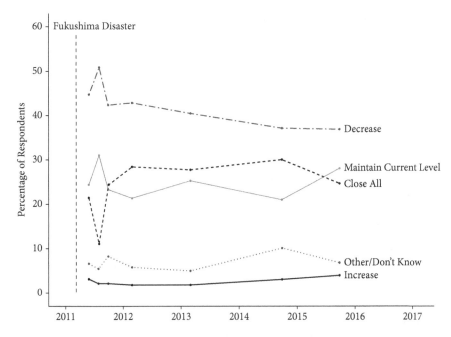

FIGURE 23.5 Public opinion on nuclear power in Japan: What do you think should be done with the current number of nuclear plants in Japan?

Note: Dashed vertical line at March 11, 2011.

Source: NHK Research. Adapted from Incerti and Lipscy (2018, 607–634).

One important reform after Fukushima was the replacement of NISA by the new Nuclear Regulatory Authority (NRA) (Koppenborg 2019). The NRA was housed within the Ministry of Environment (MOE) rather than METI, which separated nuclear regulation from nuclear promotion. The NRA both creates new nuclear regulations and determines whether plants can resume operations. It has scrutinized restarts more closely than its predecessor did. For example, as of mid-2019, the NRA had declined to grant permission to reopen for Hokkaido Electric Power Company's Tomari plant, requiring construction of a 1.4-kilometer long seawall and an investigation to determine if a fault line running underneath the plant is active. In contrast, NISA had granted permission for the same plant to reopen only five months after the Tohoku earthquake (World Nuclear Association 2018; Asahi Shimbun 2017). KEPCO's Ōi plant was also given permission to restart by NISA in 2012, but the NRA later determined that seismic upgrades were necessary. Additional reactors have been granted preliminary approval by the NRA, but only after safety upgrades not originally required by NISA.

Restarts have also been hampered by local political opposition (Aldrich and Fraser 2017). Antinuclear voters have only exerted limited influence at the national level due to the lackluster performance of opposition parties, but they have greater influence over the policy positions and actions of local representatives. Local government approval has generally been accepted as an informal precondition for the restart of nuclear plants. This means pronuclear policy implementation is often checked by local courts and governments (Aldrich and Platte 2014; Samuels 2013; Vivoda 2012). The strength of local opposition makes it unlikely Japan will return to pre-Fukushima nuclear levels anytime soon, if ever. Local governments have often shaped energy and climate change policy in Japan. For example, Tokyo and Kyoto introduced local climate change programs that exceeded national goals (Schreurs 2008). However, opposition to nuclear restarts has sharply elevated local government influence over national energy policy.

A number of plants under NRA review or approved for restart encountered opposition from local governments. The governor of Fukushima called for the decommissioning of the four remaining reactors at Fukushima Daini (Samuels 2013). The mayor of Tōkai as well as a majority of Ibaraki mayors publicly opposed the restart of JAPCO's Tōkai 2 (Japan Times 2017b; Mainichi Shimbun 2017; World Nuclear Association 2018). The restart of Chubu Electric's Hamaoka 4 was opposed by all municipalities within a thirty-kilometer radius of the plant, and the governor of Shizuoka prefecture stated that the restart should be put to a popular referendum (Mainichi Shimbun 2016). Finally, while the NRA ruled in October 2017 that TEPCO's Kashiwazaki Kariwa plant could restart, the governor of Niigata prefecture campaigned against the restart, stating that a restart would be conditional on the prefecture's independent review (Japan Times 2017c).

Local courts have also played an important role in delaying restarts. For example, in May 2014 the Fukui District Court ruled that it would not permit the restart of KEPCO's Ōi reactors following the filing of a local lawsuit, citing "structural deficiencies" in earthquake safety measures (Japan Times 2014). Restart was not permitted (for two of four reactors) until March 2018, after the lower court decision was overturned by the Osaka High Court in 2017 (World Nuclear Association 2018). The Takahama plant received NRA approval to restart but was blocked by the Fukui and Otsu District Courts. Once again, two reactors restarted only after lower court decisions were overturned by the Osaka High Court in 2017 (World Nuclear Association 2018). Restart of Shikoku Electric's Ikata 3 reactor was also hampered by court decisions. A Hiroshima District Court allowed the restart of the plant in March 2017, but after only four months in operation, the Hiroshima High Court overturned the decision and ordered a suspension, citing risks from nearby volcanoes (Japan Times 2017a). One year later, the High Court accepted an appeal by Shikoku Electric and permitted the reactor to restart.

These examples demonstrate that local governments and courts have the ability to block or delay the implementation of nuclear restarts. Thus far, this has primarily been a story of delay rather than outright blockage. Opposition to nuclear power appears to diminish as decisions move further up from the local level in the court system. Local court decisions have blocked restarts and closed plants, but prefectural high courts and the Supreme Court have often overturned these decisions. Nevertheless, success in blocking or slowing restarts shows that local antinuclear opinion cannot be ignored by the LDP. As long as the LDP continues its approach of securing local support for hosting nuclear plants (Aldrich 2007), it will face challenges in implementing its pronuclear ambitions.

More stringent safety regulations and local political opposition have kept the number of operating Japanese nuclear reactors to a mere nine (as of December 2018), compared to the fifty in operation prior to the accident. As of December 2018, utilities had applied to restart twenty-seven reactors and chose to decommission nineteen. Given regulatory, political, and technical constraints, the LDP's goal to achieve 20–22 percent nuclear power by 2030 appears unlikely to come to fruition.

Deregulation

The post-Fukushima reduction in domestic power generation has strengthened the hand of advocates for deregulation in the Japanese government. Deregulation can increase competition in the retail power sector, reduce energy prices, and increase supply by encouraging new entrants. However, deregulation threatens the profitability of Japan's vertically integrated regional monopolies, which have traditionally controlled electricity generation, retail, and transmission. With generation decoupled from transmission, a regional monopoly will no longer be able to discriminate against electricity produced by rival generators, and with generation decoupled from retail, a producer with market power should no longer be able to discriminate against other retailers. General industry groups, however, support deregulation due to its potential to lower electricity prices. Keidanren, Japan's most powerful business federation, is split over energy deregulation, as it contains members from both general industry and the energy sector (Vogel 2006). Electricity market deregulation began in 1995 with an amendment to the Electricity Utility Industry Law that allowed for independent producers of electric power and is planned to come to full fruition in 2020, when electricity producers will no longer be permitted to own transmission infrastructure or to sell electricity to consumers (Incerti and Lipscy 2018).

The Abe government, which took power in 2012, has undercut regional monopolies through deregulation, but it has simultaneously offered supportive measures. For example, the MOE—a strong advocate of transformational approaches to climate change mitigation and renewable energy adoption—took on a more active role in energy policymaking under the DPJ government. The LDP, however, returned METI to its traditional lead role (Kameyama 2016). The Abe government also dramatically scaled back Japan's feed-in-tariff (FIT) scheme. The FIT was enacted under Prime Minister Kan Naoto of the DPJ as a condition for stepping down in the aftermath of the Fukushima disaster. The scheme encouraged the adoption of renewable energy, particularly solar, by forcing utilities to buy into the grid electricity generated by renewables at an above-market rate. Utility companies such as Tokyo Electric lobbied heavily against the FIT, which they saw as a competitive and economic threat. The LDP's scale back of the FIT caused the cancellation of around twenty-eight million kilowatts of solar installations, equivalent to about 10 percent of Japanese household electricity consumption (Incerti and Lipscy 2018).

THE POLITICS OF ENERGY EFFICIENCY AND CONSERVATION POLICY IN JAPAN

Environmental movements in Japan gained momentum beginning in the late 1960s, pushing for stricter regulation of industrial pollutants (Broadbent 1998; Imura and Schreurs 2005; Reed 1981). Criticism of severe environmental degradation and health hazards that developed with postwar economic development—including the infamous Minamata disease, a neurological disease caused by mercury poisoning—compelled the government to strengthen regulations on environmental pollution. After the 1970s oil shocks, Japan emerged as a global leader in energy efficiency and conservation, and Japan's energy-efficient technologies became among the most advanced in the world (Barrett 2005; Barrett and Therivel 1991; Lipscy and Schipper 2013). In 1990 Japan became an early adopter of the official "Action Program to Arrest Global Warming," seeking to freeze CO_2 emissions at 1990 levels through conservation, technological development, and promotion of lifestyle changes (Fukasaku 1995). How did Japan emerge as a leader in energy conservation and efficiency after the oil shocks?

Throughout most of the postwar period, Japan did not possess an overarching, single energy policy framework. Instead, energy policy was determined through a mix of laws, such as the Act on Rationalizing Energy Use of 1979, and administrative measures designed to encourage energy efficiency and security. This lack of a cohesive framework partially changed with the passage of the Basic Act on Energy Policy in 2002, which establishes energy security, environmental sustainability, and reliance on market mechanisms as three broad goals of energy policy and tasks METI with drafting new energy plans every three years (Duffield and Woodall 2011).

Japanese energy efficiency policy reflects a pattern of close collaboration between government bureaucrats and private industry, a relationship also seen in the utilities sector. Even while industrial policy has diminished in most sectors along with economic development, METI has retained an outsized role in energy policymaking (Hughes 2012). One notable regulatory policy innovation that reflects close public-private cooperation is the Top Runner program, introduced under the 1998 Law Concerning the Rational Use of Energy. Top Runner automates energy efficiency improvements through the setting of regulations based on the current product with the highest energy efficiency level on the market (Agency for Natural Resources and Energy 2010). Standards are adjusted upward based on this highest-performance product. Top Runner has advantages over conventional regulatory approaches, such as minimum and average energy performance standards. By basing standards on currently available products, the regulations are inherently realistic and feasible. In addition, the standards are quite stringent, as they require producers to meet best practices and pursue continual improvements in energy efficiency. Policy makers also note that the program reduces the scope for protracted policy formulation and industrial lobbying, as the standards are based mechanically on the most energy-efficient products available (Lipscy and Schipper 2013).

Transportation has also been an important policy arena for Japanese energy efficiency. Japan was one of the first countries to implement automobile fuel economy standards, and the standards remain relatively stringent. While automakers in the United States lobbied against increased emissions regulations throughout the 1970s (Levy and Rothenburg 2002), Japanese auto firms largely embraced more stringent fuel economy standards introduced by the Ministry of Land, Infrastructure, and Transport (MLIT) in 1979, which gave their fuel-efficient cars a competitive advantage.

Japan has imposed some of the highest costs of vehicle ownership in the industrialized world, which has contributed to an outsized share of passenger transportation being accounted for by energy-efficient rail. Rail represents over 30 percent of passenger travel in Japan, as opposed to roughly 10 percent in Western Europe and less than 1 percent in the United States, and bus ridership is similarly higher than in peer countries (Kiang and Schipper 1996; Lipscy 2012; Lipscy and Schipper 2013).

After the 1970s oil shocks, Japanese policy makers were able to implement a series of policies that sharply raised the price for energy-inefficient consumption, particularly for transportation and electricity. Lipscy (2012) argues that this was possible because of "efficiency clientelism," a series of policies that imposed high prices on diffuse, energy-inefficient consumption and redistributed the revenues or rents to concentrated interest groups that supported the ruling LDP. These policies—such as gasoline taxes, regulations that allowed high electricity prices, various automobile taxes, and subsidies for lightweight automobiles—were incentive compatible with Japanese political arrangements in the late twentieth century, such as one-party dominance under the LDP; an electoral system that favored particularistic interest groups at the expense of diffuse consumers; and a strong, autonomous bureaucracy that prioritized energy security objectives. In addition, revenues often funded semipublic corporations that provided lucrative employment opportunities for retired bureaucrats.

For example, a unique feature of Japanese transport policies has been extensive subsidies for *keijidōsha*, or lightweight automobiles. Low *kei* taxes encourage Japanese consumers to purchase *kei* vehicles, which are subject to idiosyncratic regulations and only sold by Japanese automakers. Vehicles older than thirteen years receive a higher weight tax than new vehicles, encouraging consumers to drive newer, more efficient vehicles. Tax breaks, therefore, not only encourage the adoption of energy-efficient vehicles by consumers, but also encourage consumers to buy Japanese cars and to buy them frequently, and incentivize Japanese automakers to remain leaders in efficient and alternative fuel technologies. *Kei* cars are also disproportionately utilized in rural areas, and the associated policies have effectively served as subsidies for rural voters (Lipscy 2012).

Stagnation of Japanese Energy Conservation Policy

As outlined previously, the political context of Japan's energy policy transformed in fundamental ways during and after the 1990s: the LDP fell from power for the first time in 1993, the 1990s saw major scandals that delegitimized the elite bureaucracy and led to administrative reforms that shifted power toward the cabinet office, and electoral reform made it less feasible for politicians to return to office by securing narrow support from organized interest groups. As a consequence of these changes, some basic underpinnings of Japanese energy conservation policy have unraveled. Most important, politicians now face strong electoral incentives to deliver lower energy prices to diffuse voters and to dismantle traditional policies that favored organized interest groups. However, lower energy prices cut against energy conservation and climate change mitigation goals (Lipscy 2018).

Since the mid-1990s, Japanese policy makers have struggled to sustain improvements in energy conservation achieved in the two prior decades. Despite intensifying international pressure to mitigate greenhouse gases, Japan has implemented very little in the way of new policy measures to combat climate change, and Japanese energy prices, once among the highest in the world, have been overtaken by numerous European countries. The transformation was highlighted in 2010 when Japan withdrew from the second commitment period of the Kyoto Protocol, cementing its status as a laggard on climate change, particularly compared to the European Union (Schreurs and Tiberghien 2007).

These struggles were compounded by the 2011 Fukushima disaster. However, the Japanese response to the disaster was also a remarkable demonstration of the country's latent ability to achieve greater energy savings. As nuclear plants shut down in the aftermath of the disaster, the government required businesses in the Tokyo Metropolitan Area to decrease energy consumption by 15 percent in an effort to avoid rolling blackouts. Office workers were encouraged to don "Super Cool Biz" attire by MOE, thermostats were set above 28 degrees Celsius in offices, shops and subway stations turned off air conditioning, and automakers shifted production to weekends to avoid using power during peak periods. This campaign—known as *setsuden* ("energy saving")—successfully averted serious blackouts (Yagita et al. 2012). The Japanese government also accelerated energy-saving measures such as the use of LED lightbulbs and energy-efficient air conditioners (Agency for Natural Resources and Energy 2018).

Climate Change and Renewable Energy

Relative to Japan's population and economy, greenhouse gas (GHG) emissions have been modest. GHG emissions on a per capita and per GDP basis are well below those of the United States (see Figures 23.6 and 23.7). However, Japan has made little progress on energy efficiency or GHG mitigation since the 1990s. Japan's GHG emissions levels have remained relatively static over the past twenty-five years, a period during which other advanced industrialized countries have generally made modest progress. As a result, while Japanese emissions by these measures were below OECD Europe in 1990, this has now reversed.

Japan lags behind many of its peers in renewable energy production. Japan has taken advantage of its capacity for hydroelectric power, but further growth is constrained by geography. Excluding hydroelectric power, Japan lags behind its international peers in

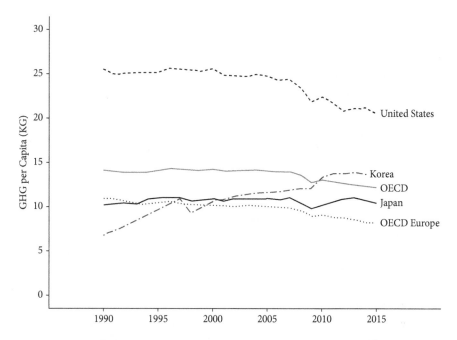

FIGURE 23.6 Greenhouse gas emissions per capita, 1990–2016.

Source: Data from IEA (2017).

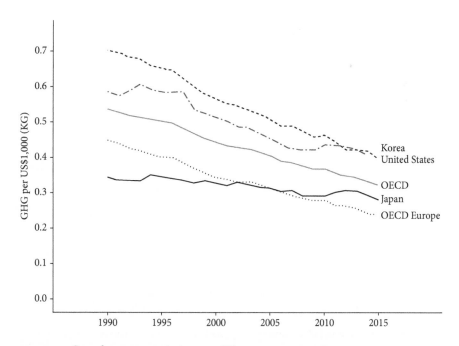

FIGURE 23.7 Greenhouse gas emissions per US$1,000, 1990–2016.

Source: Data from IEA (2017).

terms of its percentage of energy supply derived from renewables. Unlike European states, which have sharply increased renewable energy production in recent years, Japan's renewable share has increased only modestly and remains below levels in the United States (see Figure 23.8).

Many observers expected Japan to shift toward renewable energy following the Fukushima nuclear disaster, since the country lost approximately 20 percent of its energy supply. However, Japan's commitment to increased renewable energy production has been uneven. While the DPJ government implemented a FIT intended to support renewable energy in 2011 (Huenteler, Schmidt, and Kanie 2012; Kingston 2011), the LDP government under Abe Shinzo reemphasized nuclear and coal-fired power plants and weakened the FIT, curtailing the expansion of solar power. Japan has also avoided outright or implemented minimalist energy pricing schemes to address climate change (Carl and Fedor 2016).

The anemic development of Japanese renewables, on the one hand, and the resurgence of fossil fuels, particularly coal, on the other, is an important puzzle for ongoing research. Decarbonization will become increasingly crucial if the country is to make progress toward reducing its GHG emissions and energy imports. Historically, resistance from vested interests in the energy sector, particularly large utility companies, has been a major impediment (Moe 2012). However, after the Fukushima disaster, Japan's utilities were delegitimized and lost considerable political clout. Nonetheless, policy change has been slow (Aldrich, Lipscy, and McCarthy 2019). An emerging literature is

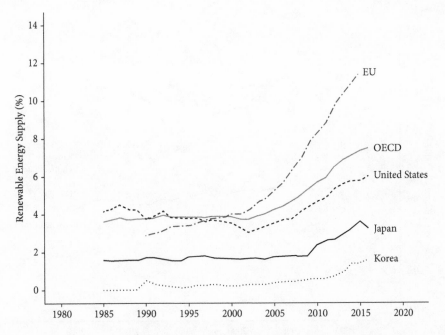

FIGURE 23.8 Cross-national renewable energy share, excluding hydropower, 1990–2017.

Note: Renewables includes geothermal, solar, tide, wind, and biofuels and waste. Hydro power is excluded.

Source of data: IEA (2017). Adapted from Incerti and (2018, 607–634).

examining the political impediments to renewable energy in Japan (Cherp et al. 2017; Incerti and Lipscy 2018; Moe and Midford 2014; Ohira 2017; Raupach-Sumiya et al. 2015; Ueda and Yamaka 2017), as well as specific energy sources such as wind (Maruyama, Nishikido, and Iida 2007; Motosu and Maruyama 2016) and geothermal energy (Hymans and Uchikoshi 2018). However, much work remains to be done on this critical issue.

A Future Research Agenda

As this chapter demonstrates, energy policy has occupied an important place in modern Japanese political economy. Japan is a useful case for scholars and students interested in the politics of energy. The country offers fascinating variation over time: from energy self-sufficiency in the early twentieth century to near total dependence on foreign energy, from victim of nuclear bombs to adopter of nuclear energy, and from global energy efficiency leader to climate change laggard. We conclude by offering several suggestions for future research.

There is scope for more interdisciplinary research on the politics of energy in Japan. Understanding the politics of energy necessarily requires expertise from multiple fields, but the technical literature on Japanese energy policy is still largely separate from the literature on energy politics. The Japanese-language literature has often focused on technical and administrative aspects rather than the political economy of energy (Takahashi 2017). Closer collaboration among experts in Japanese politics, energy policy, nuclear engineering, and climate science will be important to move the field forward.

Scholars should continue to seek productive ways to merge studies of Japanese energy politics with broader theoretical and empirical literatures. Significant insights have been gained by analyzing Japanese energy politics through lenses such as the politics of civil society (Aldrich 2007), embedded symbolism (Tiberghien and Schreurs 2007), veto players (Hymans 2011), and electoral politics (Lipscy 2018). Similarly, scholars have analyzed energy in conjunction with other aspects of Japanese politics, such as industrial policy (Hughes 2012; Samuels 1987), transportation policy (Lipscy and Schipper 2013), and municipal mergers (Chang 2010).

Another fruitful area for future research is placing Japanese energy policy more firmly within a cross-national and international relations context. Language and cultural barriers often make the intricacies of Japanese politics impenetrable for outside scholars. However, there is more room for work that marries deep-area expertise of Japanese energy politics with comparative qualitative or quantitative examination of multiple countries. Work in this vein has examined environmental politics (Schreurs 2002), the politics of oil markets (Hughes 2014), and energy conservation policies (Lipscy 2018). One of the most important lessons of the Fukushima disaster was a failure of international learning (Blandford and Sagan 2016); if Japanese nuclear plants had adopted watertight backup power generators implemented in France and the United States after incidents in those countries, the disaster likely would have been avoided (Lipscy, Kushida, and Incerti 2013). Hence, the politics of international learning, influence, and information exchange deserves greater attention.

There is also greater scope for the application of rigorous causal identification strategies to salient questions of Japanese energy policy. There has recently been a surge in innovative survey studies that examine the energy policy preferences and behavior of Japanese citizens (Hassard et al. 2013; Horiuchi, Smith, and Yamamoto 2018; Ito, Ida, and Tanaka 2018; Iwasaki, Sawada, and Aldrich 2017; Murakami et al. 2015; Nakamura 2017, 2018; Werfel 2017). This work nicely complements existing data on popular and elite preferences in Japan (Taniguchi 2017). Some work has also leveraged the exogeneity of natural disasters and institutional changes to draw inferences about the politics surrounding energy issues in Japan (Aldrich 2016; Lipscy 2018; Lipscy, Kushida, and Incerti 2013). However, there is still considerable scope for rigorous methodological studies that speak to major themes in the qualitative literature on Japanese energy policy, such as the politics of deregulation, regulatory capture, civil society activism, and energy security.

Finally, the politics of decarbonization in Japan is an area ripe for study. While Japan's institutional changes since the 1990s make it difficult for Japanese leaders to use price incentives as a means of energy conservation, the politics of decarbonization is characterized by a different logic and may offer a more plausible way forward for Japan. Llewelyn Hughes describes Japanese power market and renewable energy policies as "radical incrementalism," combining substantial shifts in policy with path dependencies stemming from institutional constraints (Hughes 2018). One impediment to major changes after Fukushima has been Prime Minister Abe's prioritization of economic growth over decarbonization (Incerti and Lipscy 2018). This will not necessarily continue indefinitely. A salient question for scholars to examine is what type of political arrangements and bargains are emerging that could support radical decarbonization in Japan in the long run.

Acknowledgments

We thank Juliann Allison, Kathleen Hancock, and two anonymous reviewers for their excellent feedback.

References

Agency for Natural Resources and Energy. 2010. *Top Runner Kijun: Sekai Saiko No Sho Energy Kiki No Soshutsu Ni Mukete.* Tokyo: METI.

Agency for Natural Resources and Energy. 2018. *Energy Hakusho (White Paper).* Tokyo: Ministry of Economy, Trade, and Industry (Japan).

Akao, Nobutoshi. 1983. *Japan's Economic Security: Resources as a Factor in Foreign Policy.* Aldershot, Hampshire, UK: Royal Institute of International Affairs.

Aldrich, Daniel, Phillip Y. Lipscy, and Mary M. McCarthy. 2019. "Japan's Opportunity to Lead." *Nature Climate Change* 9, no. 7: 492. doi:10.1038/s41558-019-0510-0.

Aldrich, Daniel, and James Platte. August 15, 2014. "After the Fukushima Meltdown, Japan's Nuclear Restart Is stalled." *Washington Post.* https://www.washingtonpost.com/news/monkey-cage/wp/2014/08/15/after-the-fukushima-meltdown-japans-nuclear-restart-is-stalled/

Aldrich, Daniel P. 2007. *Site Fights: Divisive Facilities and Civil Society in Japan and the West.* Ithaca, NY: Cornell University Press.

Aldrich, Daniel P. 2013. "Rethinking Civil Society–State Relations in Japan after the Fukushima Accident." *Polity* 45, no. 2: 249–264. doi:10.1057/pol.2013.2.

Aldrich, Daniel P. 2016. "It's Who You Know: Factors Driving Recovery from Japan's 11 March 2011 Disaster." *Public Administration* 94, no. 2: 399–413. doi:10.1111/padm.12191.

Aldrich, Daniel P., and Timothy Fraser. 2017. "All Politics Is Local: Judicial and Electoral Institutions' Role in Japan's Nuclear Restarts." *Pacific Affairs* 90, no. 3: 433–457.

Arase, David M. 2012. "The Impact of 3/11 on Japan." *East Asia* 29, no. 4: 313–336. doi:10.1007/s12140-012-9182-3.

Arima, Tetsuo. 2008. *Genpatsu, Shoriki, CIA: Kimitsu Bunsho de Yomu Showa Uramenshi* [Nuclear power, Shoriki, and the CIA: The backstory of the Showa Era as revealed by secret documents]. Tokyo: Shincho Shinsho.

Asahi Shimbun. 2017. "Screenings for Restart of Tomari Nuke Plant likely to Be Prolonged." *The Asahi Shimbun,* December 11.

Asahi Shimbun Tokubetsu Hodobu. 2012. *Promethus no Wana: Akasarenakatta Fukushima Genpatsu no Shinjitsu* [The Prometheus trap: The hidden truth of the Fukushima nuclear accident]. Tokyo: Gakken Publishing.

Barrett, Brendan. 2005. *Ecological Modernization and Japan.* London: Routledge.

Barrett, Brendan F. D., and Riki Therivel. 1991. *Environmental Policy and Impact Assessment in Japan.* London: Routledge.

Blandford, Edward D., and Scott Douglas Sagan. 2016. *Learning from a Disaster: Improving Nuclear Safety and Security after Fukushima.* Stanford, CA: Stanford University Press.

Bobrow, Davis, and Robert Kudrle. 1987. "How Middle Powers Can Manage Resource Weakness: Japan and Energy." *World Politics* 39, no. 4: 536–565.

Boix, Carles, Michael Miller, and Sebastian Rosato. 2013. "A Complete Data Set of Political Regimes, 1800–2007." *Comparative Political Studies* 46, no. 12: 1523–1554. doi:10.1177/0010414012463905.

Broadbent, Jeffrey. 1998. *Environmental Politics in Japan: Networks of Power and Protest.* Cambridge, UK: Cambridge University Press.

Calder, Kent E. 1993. "Japan's Energy Angst and the Caspian Great Game." *NBR Analysis* 12, no. 1: 1–46.

Carl, Jeremy, and David Fedor. 2016. "Tracking Global Carbon Revenues: A Survey of Carbon Taxes versus Cap-and-Trade in the Real World." *Energy Policy* 96: 50–77. doi:10.1016/j.enpol.2016.05.023.

Carlson, Matthew M., and Steven R. Reed. 2018. *Political Corruption and Scandals in Japan.* Ithaca, NY: Cornell University Press.

Catalinac, Amy. 2016. "From Pork to Policy: The Rise of Programmatic Campaigning in Japanese Elections." *Journal of Politics* 78, no. 1: 1–18.

Chang, Jung Ouk. 2010. "Genpatsu ritchi chiiki no gappei to chiiki keizai: chihou zaisei no henka nitsuite: Ehime-ken Ikata-chō wo chūshin ni [Municipal mergers and economies of nuclear power plant host communities: On changing regional municipal revenue: Focusing on Ikata, Ehime Prefecture]." *Matsuyama Daigaku Ronshu* 22, no. 3: 1–26.

Cherp, Aleh, Vadim Vinichenko, Jessica Jewell, Masahiro Suzuki, and Miklós Antal. 2017. "Comparing Electricity Transitions: A Historical Analysis of Nuclear, Wind and Solar Power in Germany and Japan." *Energy Policy* 101: 612–628. doi:10.1016/j.enpol.2016.10.044.

Cochran, Thomas B., Harold A. Feiveson, Walt Patterson, Gennadi Pshakin, M. V. Ramana, Mycle Schneider, Tatsujiro Suzuki, et al. 2010. *Fast Breeder Reactor Programs: History and Status*. Princeton, NJ: International Panel on Fissile Materials (IPFM).

Cohen, Linda, Mathew McCubbins, and Frances Rosenbluth. 1995. "The Politics of Nuclear Power in Japan and the United States." In *Structure and Policy in Japan and the United States*, edited by Peter Cowhey and Mathew McCubbins, 177–202. Cambridge: Cambridge University Press.

Curtis, Gerald L. 1988. *The Japanese Way of Politics*. New York: Columbia University Press.

Dauvergne, Peter. 1993. "Nuclear Power Development in Japan: 'Outside Forces' and the Politics of Reciprocal Consent." *Asian Survey* 33, no. 6: 576–591. doi:10.2307/2645007.

Duffield, John S., and Brian Woodall. 2011. "Japan's New Basic Energy Plan." *Energy Policy* 39, no. 6: 3741–3749.

Ehrhardt, George, Axel Klein, Levi McLaughlin, and Steven R. Reed. 2014. *Kōmeitō: Politics and Religion in Japan*. Berkeley: Institute of East Asian Studies, University of California, Berkeley.

Estevez-Abe, Margarita. 2006. "Japan's Shift Toward a Westminster System: A Structural Analysis of the 2005 Lower House Election and Its Aftermath." *Asian Survey* 46, no. 4: 632–651. doi:10.1525/as.2006.46.4.632.

Ferguson, Charles D., and Mark Jansson. 2013. "Regulating Japanese Nuclear Power in the Wake of the Fukushima Daiichi Accident." Washington, DC: Federation of American Scientists Issues Briefs. https://fas.org/wp-content/uploads/2013/05/Regulating_Japanese_Nuclear_13May131.pdf

Fukai, Shigeko N. 1988. "Japan's Energy Policy." *Current History*, April 1988, 169.

Fukasaku, Yukiko. 1995. "Energy and Environment Policy Integration: The Case of Energy Conservation Policies and Technologies in Japan." *Energy Policy* 23, no. 12: 1063–1076.

Funabashi, Yoichi. 2016. *Count Down: Meltdown*. Tokyo: Bungei Shunju.

Hasegawa, Koichi. 2004. *Constructing Civil Society in Japan: Voices of Environmental Movements*. Melbourne, Australia: Trans Pacific Press.

Hassard, Harry A., Joshua K. Y. Swee, Moustafa Ghanem, and Hironobu Unesaki. 2013. "Assessing the Impact of the Fukushima Nuclear Disaster on Policy Dynamics and the Public Sphere." *Procedia Environmental Sciences* 17: 566–575. doi:10.1016/j.proenv.2013.02.072.

Hein, Laura. 1990. *Fueling Growth: The Energy Revolution and Economic Policy in Postwar Japan*. Cambridge, MA: Harvard University Press.

Hirabayashi, Yuko. 2013. "Genpatsu okotowari chiten to han-genpatsu undo [Locations rejecting nuclear plants and the anti-nuclear movement]." *Ohara Shakai Mondai Kenkyujo Zasshi*, no. 661: 36–51.

Hook, Glenn D. 1984. "The Nuclearization of Language: Nuclear Allergy as Political Metaphor." *Journal of Peace Research* 21, no. 3: 259–275. doi:10.1177/002234338402100305.

Horiuchi, Yusaku, Daniel M. Smith, and Teppei Yamamoto. 2018. "Measuring Voters' Multidimensional Policy Preferences with Conjoint Analysis: Application to Japan's 2014 Election." *Political Analysis* 26, no. 2: 190–209. doi:10.1017/pan.2018.2.

Hoshi, Takeo, and Anil K. Kashyap. 2004. "Japan's Financial Crisis and Economic Stagnation." *Journal of Economic Perspectives* 18, no. 1: 3–26. doi:10.1257/089533004773563412.

Hosoe, Nobuhiro. 2006. "The Deregulation of Japan's Electricity Industry." *Japan and the World Economy* 18, no. 2: 230–246.

Huenteler, Joern, Tobias S. Schmidt, and Norichika Kanie. 2012. "Japan's Post-Fukushima Challenge—Implications from the German Experience on Renewable Energy Policy." *Energy Policy* 45: 6–11. doi:10.1016/j.enpol.2012.02.041.

Hughes, Llewelyn. 2007. "Why Japan Will Not Go Nuclear (Yet): International and Domestic Constraints on the Nuclearization of Japan." *International Security* 31, no. 4: 67–96.

Hughes, Llewelyn. 2012. "Climate Converts: Institutional Redeployment and Public Investment in Energy and Environment in Japan." *Journal of East Asian Studies* 12, no. 1: 89–117.

Hughes, Llewelyn. 2014. *Globalizing Oil: Firms and Oil Market Governance in France, Japan, and the United States*. Cambridge, UK: Cambridge University Press.

Hughes, Llewelyn. 2018. "Japan's Radical Incrementalism in Power Market Regulation and Renewable Energy." In *Japan's Energy Conundrum: A Discussion of Japan's Energy Circumstances and U.S.-Japan Energy Relations*, edited by Phyllis Yoshida, 59–67. Washington, DC: Sasakawa Peace Foundation.

Hymans, Jacques E. C. 2011. "Veto Players, Nuclear Energy, and Nonproliferation: Domestic Institutional Barriers to a Japanese Bomb." *International Security* 36, no. 2: 154–189. doi:10.1162/ISEC_a_00059.

Hymans, Jacques E. C. 2015. "After Fukushima: Veto Players and Japanese Nuclear Policy." In *Japan: The Precarious Future*, edited by Frank Baldwin and Anne Allison, 110–138. New York: New York University Press.

Hymans, Jacques E. C., and Fumiya Uchikoshi. 2018. "Social Determinants of Geothermal Energy Project Siting in Japan." In *American Political Science Association 2018 Annual Meeting*.

Ikenberry, G. John. 1986. "The Irony of State Strength: Comparative Responses to the Oil Shocks in the 1970s." *International Organization* 40, no. 1: 105–137.

Imura, Hidefumi, and Miranda Alice Schreurs. 2005. *Environmental Policy in Japan*. Cheltenham, UK: Edward Elgar Publishing.

Incerti, Trevor, and Phillip Y. Lipscy. 2018. "The Politics of Energy and Climate Change in Japan under Abe: Abenergynomics." *Asian Survey* 58, no. 4: 607–634.

Independent Investigation Commission on the Fukushima Nuclear Accident. 2014. *The Fukushima Daiichi Nuclear Power Station Disaster: Investigating the Myth and Reality*. New York: Routledge.

International Energy Agency (IEA). 2017. *World Energy Statistics and Balances*.

Ito, Koichiro, Takanori Ida, and Makoto Tanaka. 2018. "Moral Suasion and Economic Incentives: Field Experimental Evidence from Energy Demand." *American Economic Journal: Economic Policy* 10, no. 1: 240–267.

Iwasaki, Keiko, Yasuyuki Sawada, and Daniel P. Aldrich. 2017. "Social Capital as a Shield against Anxiety among Displaced Residents from Fukushima." *Natural Hazards* 89, no. 1: 405–421. doi:10.1007/s11069-017-2971-7.

Japan Times. 2014. "Reflect on Fukui Nuclear Ruling." The Japan Times, May 23.

Japan Times. 2017a. "Hiroshima High Court Orders Suspension of Ikata Nuclear Reactor in Ehime Prefecture, Revoking District Court Ruling." The Japan Times, December 13.

Japan Times. 2017b. *Ibaraki Gov. Hashimoto Denied Seventh Term after Losing to Ruling Coalition-backed Rookie*. The Japan Times, August 28.

Japan Times. 2017c. "'Several Years' Needed to Restart Kashiwazaki-Kariwa Plant: Niigata Governor." *The Japan Times*, January 5.

Johnson, Chalmers A. 1982. *MITI and the Japanese Miracle: The Growth of Industrial Policy, 1925–1975*. Stanford, CA: Stanford University Press.

Kameyama, Yasuko. 2016. *Climate Change Policy in Japan: From the 1980s to 2015*. Abingdon, UK: Routledge.

Kelly, Dominic. 2014. "US Hegemony and the Origins of Japanese Nuclear Power: The Politics of Consent." *New Political Economy* 19, no. 6: 819–846. doi:10.1080/13563467.2013.849673.

Kiang, Nancy, and Lee Schipper. 1996. "Energy Trends in the Japanese Transportation Sector." *Transport Policy* 3, no. 1: 21–35.

Kingston, Jeff. 2011. "Ousting Kan Naoto: The Politics of Nuclear Crisis and Renewable Energy in Japan." *The Asia-Pacific Journal* 9, no. 39: 1–16.

Kingston, Jeff. 2013. "Japan's Nuclear Village." In *Critical Issues in Contemporary Japan*, edited by Jeff Kingston, 107–119. New York: Routledge.

Kobori, Satoru. 2007. "Japanese Energy-saving Policy during the Interwar Era." *Rekishi to Keizai* 49, no. 3: 48–64.

Koppenborg, Florentine. 2019. "Legal Fallout from the Fukushima Nuclear Accident: Reforming Nuclear Safety Administration in Japan." In *Fukushima and the Law*, edited by Julius F. Weizdörfer and Kristian C. Lauta. Cambridge, UK: Cambridge University Press.

Kurokawa, Kiyoshi, K. Ishibashi, K. Oshima, H. Sakiyama, M. Sakurai, K. Tanaka, and Y. Yokoyama. 2012. "The National Diet of Japan Fukushima Nuclear Accident Independent Investigation Commission." Japan: The National Diet of Japan.

Kushida, Kenji E. 2012. *Japan's Fukushima Nuclear Disaster: Narrative, Analysis, Recommendations*. Stanford, CA: Shorenstein APARC Working Paper Series. https://papers.ssrn.com/sol3/papers.cfm?abstract_id=2118876.

Kushida, Kenji E., and Phillip Y. Lipscy. 2013. *Japan under the DPJ: The Politics of Transition and Governance*. Stanford, CA: Brookings Institution/Shorenstein APARC.

LeBlanc, Robin. 2010. *The Art of the Gut: Manhood, Power, and Ethics in Japanese Politics*. Berkeley: University of California Press.

Lesbirel, S. Hayden. 1998. *Nimby Politics in Japan: Energy Siting and the Management of Environmental Conflict*. Ithaca, NY: Cornell University Press.

Levy, David L., and Sandra Rothenberg. 2002. "Heterogeneity and change in environmental strategy: technological and political responses to climate change in the global automobile industry." *Organizations, policy and the natural environment: institutional and strategic perspectives*, 173–193. Stanford, CA: Stanford University Press.

Lipscy, Phillip Y. 2012. "A Casualty of Political Transformation? The Politics of Japanese Energy Efficiency in the Transportation Sector." *Journal of East Asian Studies* 12, no. 3: 409–439.

Lipscy, Phillip Y. 2018. *The Institutional Politics of Energy and Climate Change*. Stanford, CA: Stanford University Press.

Lipscy, Phillip Y., Kenji E. Kushida, and Trevor Incerti. 2013. "The Fukushima Disaster and Japan's Nuclear Plant Vulnerability in Comparative Perspective." *Environmental Science & Technology* 47, no. 12: 6082–6088. doi:10.1021/es4004813.

Lipscy, Phillip Y., and Ethan Scheiner. 2012. "Japan under the DPJ: The Paradox of Political Change without Policy Change." *Journal of East Asian Studies* 12, no. 3: 311–322.

Lipscy, Phillip Y., and Lee Schipper. 2013. "Energy Efficiency in the Japanese Transport Sector." *Energy Policy* 56: 248–258.

Lockwood, William Wirt. 1970. *Economic Development of Japan*. Princeton: Princeton University Press.

Low, Morris F. 1994. "Japan: The Political Economy of Japanese Science: Nakasone, Physicists, and the State." In *Scientists and the State: Domestic Structures and the International Context*, edited by Etel Solingen, 116. Ann Arbor: University of Michigan Press.

Mainichi Shimbun. 2016. "Shizuoka, Hamaoka genpatsu zenmen teishi gonen, saikadō sansei nashi, 30 kiro jichitai, Mainichi Shimbun Ankēto" [No municipalities within 30km Hamaoka nuclear plant want restart: Survey]. May 14. https://mainichi.jp/articles/20160514/k00/00m/040/125000c.

Mainichi Shimbun. 2017. "Ibaraki Tōkai Daini genpatsu, hinan keikaku nankō, 'musekinen' enchō shinsei wo hyōmei, jimoto jyūmin wa hanpastu" [Concerns raised after utility announces plan for nuclear reactor lifespan extension]. November 11. https://mainichi.jp/articles/20171122/ddm/041/040/099000c.

Marshall, Monty G., Ted Robert Gurr, and Keith Jaggers. 2010. *Polity IV Project: Political Regime Characteristics and Transitions, 1800–2009*. Veinna, VA: Center for Systemic Peace.

Maruyama, Yasushi, Makoto Nishikido, and Tetsunari Iida. 2007. "The Rise of Community Wind Power in Japan: Enhanced Acceptance through Social Innovation." *Energy Policy* 35, no. 5: 2761–2769. doi:10.1016/j.enpol.2006.12.010.

Moe, Espen. 2012. "Vested Interests, Energy Efficiency and Renewables in Japan." *Energy Policy* 40: 260–273. doi:10.1016/j.enpol.2011.09.070.

Moe, Espen, and Paul Midford. 2014. *The Political Economy of Renewable Energy and Energy Security: Common Challenges and National Responses in Japan, China and Northern Europe*. London: Palgrave Macmillan UK.

Morse, Ronald A. 1981. *The Politics of Japan's Energy Strategy: Resources-Diplomacy-Security*. Berkeley: Institute of East Asian Studies, University of California.

Motosu, Memi, and Yasushi Maruyama. 2016. "Local Acceptance by People with Unvoiced Opinions Living Close to a Wind Farm: A Case Study from Japan." *Energy Policy* 91: 362–370. doi:10.1016/j.enpol.2016.01.018.

Mulgan, Aurelia George. 2017. *The Abe Administration and the Rise of the Prime Ministerial Executive*. Abingdon, UK: Routledge.

Murakami, Kayo, Takanori Ida, Makoto Tanaka, and Lee Friedman. 2015. "Consumers' Willingness to Pay for Renewable and Nuclear Energy: A Comparative Analysis between the US and Japan." *Energy Economics* 50: 178–189. doi:10.1016/j.eneco.2015.05.002.

Murakami, Teruyasu. 1982. "The Remarkable Adaptation of Japan's Economy." In *Global Insecurity: A Strategy for Energy and Economic Renewal*, edited by Daniel Yergin and Martin Hillenbrand, 138–167. Boston: Houghton Mifflin.

Nakamura, Hidenori. 2017. "Political and Environmental Attitude toward Participatory Energy and Environmental Governance: A survey in Post-Fukushima Japan." *Journal of Environmental Management* 201: 190–198. doi:10.1016/j.jenvman.2017.06.053.

Nakamura, Hidenori. 2018. "Willingness to Know and Talk: Citizen Attitude toward Energy and Environmental Policy Deliberation in Post-Fukushima Japan." *Energy Policy* 115: 12–22. doi:10.1016/j.enpol.2017.12.055.

Ogawa, Junko, Fuyuhiko Noda, and Yukari Yamashita. 2010. "Japan's Energy Management Policy Experiences and Their Implications for Developing Countries." *IEEJ Energy Journal* (August): 1–42.

Ohira, Yoshio. 2017. "Renewable-Energy Policies and Economic Revitalization in Fukushima: Issues and Prospects." In *Rebuilding Fukushima*, edited by Mitsuo Yamakawa and Daisaku Yamamoto, 136–151. New York: Routledge.

Okimoto, Daniel I. 1990. *Between MITI and the Market: Japanese Industrial Policy for High Technology*. Stanford, CA: Stanford University Press.

Pharr, Susan J. 2000. "Official's Misconduct and Public Distrust: Japan and the Trilateral Democracies." In *Disaffected Democracies: What's Troubling the Trilateral Countries?*, edited by Susan J. Pharr and Robert D. Putnam, 173–201. Princeton, NJ: Princeton University Press.

Pickett, Susan E. 2002. "Japan's Nuclear Energy Policy: From Firm Commitment to Difficult Dilemma Addressing Growing Stocks of Plutonium, Program Delays, Domestic Opposition and International Pressure." *Energy Policy* 30, no. 15: 1337–1355.

Ramseyer, Mark, and Frances McCall Rosenbluth. 1993. *Japan's Political Marketplace.* Cambridge, MA: Harvard University Press.

Raupach-Sumiya, Jörg, Hironao Matsubara, Andreas Prahl, Astrid Aretz, and Steven Salecki. 2015. "Regional Economic Effects of Renewable Energies—Comparing Germany and Japan." *Energy, Sustainability and Society* 5, no. 1: 10. doi:10.1186/s13705-015-0036-x.

Reed, Steven R. 1981. "Environmental Politics: Some Reflections Based on the Japanese Case." *Comparative Politics* 13, no. 3: 253–270.

Rosenbluth, Frances McCall, and Michael F. Thies. 2010. *Japan Transformed: Political Change and Economic Restructuring.* Princeton, NJ: Princeton University Press.

Sagan, Scott D. 1988. "The Origins of the Pacific War." *The Journal of Interdisciplinary History* 18, no. 4: 893–922. doi:10.2307/204828.

Samuels, Richard J. 1981. "The Politics of Alternative Energy Research and Development in Japan." In *The Politics of Japan's Energy Strategy: Resources-Diplomacy-Security*, edited by Ronald A. Morse, 134–166. Berkeley: Institute of East Asian Studies, University of California.

Samuels, Richard J. 1987. *The Business of the Japanese State: Energy Markets in Comparative and Historical Perspective.* Ithaca, NY: Cornell University Press.

Samuels, Richard J. 2013. *3.11: Disaster and Change in Japan.* Ithaca, NY: Cornell University Press.

Scalise, Paul. 2015. "In Search of Certainty: How Political Authority and Scientific Authority Interact in Japan's Nuclear Restart Process." In *Policy Legitimacy, Science, and Political Authority: Knowledge and Action in Liberal Democracies*, edited by Michael Heazel and John Kane, 141–164. New York: Routledge.

Schreurs, Miranda A. 2002. *Environmental Politics in Japan, Germany, and the United States.* Cambridge, UK: Cambridge University Press.

Schreurs, Miranda A. 2008. "From the Bottom Up: Local and Subnational Climate Change Politics." *The Journal of Environment & Development* 17, no. 4: 343–355. doi:10.1177/1070496508326432.

Schreurs, Miranda A., and Yves Tiberghien. 2007. "Multi-Level Reinforcement: Explaining European Union Leadership in Climate Change Mitigation." *Global Environmental Politics* 7, no. 4: 19–46.

Solingen, Etel. 2010. "The Perils of Prediction: Japan's Once and Future Nuclear Status." In *Forecasting Nuclear Proliferation in the 21st Century*, Volume 2, *A Comparative Perspective*, edited by William C. Potter and Gaukhar Mukhatzhanova, 131–157. Stanford, CA: Stanford University Press.

Takahashi, Hiroshi. 2017. *Energy Seisakuron* [Theory of energy policy]. Tokyo: Iwanami Shoten.

Takenaka, Harukata. 2006. *Shusho Shihai: Nihon Seiji no Henbo.* Tokyo: Chuko Shinsho.

Taniguchi, Masaki. 2017. The UTokyo-Asahi Survey (UTAS). University of Tokyo and Asahi Shimbun.

Tiberghien, Yves, and Miranda A. Schreurs. 2007. "High Noon in Japan: Embedded Symbolism and Post-2001 Kyoto Protocol Politics." *Global Environmental Politics* 7, no. 4: 70–91.

Ueda, Kazuhiro, and Kimio Yamaka. 2017. *Saisei Kanou Energy Seisaku no Kokusai Hikaku* [International comparison of renewable energy]. Kyoto: Kyoto University Press.

United States Strategic Bombing Survey. 1946. *Summary Report (Pacific War)*. Washington, D.C.: United States Government Printing Office.

Vivoda, Vlado. 2014. *Energy Security in Japan: Challenges after Fukushima*. Farnham, UK: Ashgate Publishing Limited.

Vivoda, Vlado. 2012. "Japan's Energy Security Predicament Post-Fukushima." *Energy Policy* 46: 135–143. doi:10.1016/j.enpol.2012.03.044.

Vivoda, Vlado, and Geordan Graetz. 2015. "Nuclear Policy and Regulation in Japan after Fukushima: Navigating the Crisis." *Journal of Contemporary Asia* 45, no. 3: 490–509.

Vogel, Steven K. 2006. *Japan Remodeled*. Ithaca, NY: Cornell University Press.

Walker, William. 2000. "Entrapment in Large Technology Systems: Institutional Commitment and Power Relations." *Research Policy* 29, nos. 7–8: 833–846.

Werfel, Seth H. 2017. "Household Behaviour Crowds Out Support for Climate Change Policy When Sufficient Progress Is Perceived." *Nature Climate Change* 7: 512. doi:10.1038/nclimate3316. https://www.nature.com/articles/nclimate3316#supplementary-information.

World Nuclear Association. 2018. *Nuclear Power in Japan*. London, UK: World Nuclear Association.https://www.world-nuclear.org/information-library/country-profiles/countries-g-n/japan-nuclear-power.aspx.

Yagita, Yoshie, Yumiko Iwafune, Miyuki Ogiwara, and Goshi Fujimoto. 2012. "Household Electricity Saving Behavior after the Great East Japan Earthquake." *Journal of Japan Society of Energy and Resources* 33, no. 4: 7–16.

CHAPTER 24

....

THE ENERGY POLITICS
OF THE ASIA-PACIFIC
REGION

....

MIRZA SADAQAT HUDA AND SALEEM H. ALI

ENERGY encapsulates the entire milieu of politics in Asia. From multilateral trade and cooperation through organizations such as the Association of Southeast Asian Nations (ASEAN), to bilateral competition for resources between India and China, to grassroots environmental movements in countries as diverse as Mongolia and Vietnam, to the importance of electricity in domestic electoral manifestos, energy is a pervasive presence in the politics of the region. In the near future, the politics of energy in Asia will continue to be shaped by technological developments, including regional integration projects such as the Belt and Road Initiative (BRI), which will facilitate cooperation on energy on an unprecedented scale. (For analysis of regionalism literature, see Hancock, Palestini, and Szulecki in this volume.)

Energy politics in Asia are underpinned by the region's rapid economic development, skewed distribution of economic and political power, territorial disputes, separatist and insurgency movements, political and cultural heterogeneity, historical trauma, and low levels of economic and security integration (Ascher and Mirovitskaya 2013; Beeson 2014; Christensen 1999; Vivoda 2017). In the last few decades strong regional growth driven by export-oriented strategies has largely contributed to a reduction in extreme poverty, from 29.7 percent in 2000 to 10.3 percent in 2010 (ESCAP 2018). Despite such progress, some four hundred million people in the region still live in extreme poverty, and income, gender, and ethnic inequality has created significant social and political turbulence (Ofreneo 2013). Real and perceived inequalities and marginalization have fueled insurgencies in Northeast India, Northwest Pakistan, and the Southern regions of Thailand and the Philippines. The activities of these insurgent groups have significant cross-border and regional implications, most recently resulting in military conflict between India and Pakistan in February 2019. Regional cohesion in the Asia-Pacific region is further undermined by rapid militarization and the territorial conflicts in Kashmir and the South China Sea (Saunders 2017).

National energy policies in Asia are influenced to a great extent by such regional realities as well as the foreign policy overtures of extra-regional actors. A number of scholars have given priority to the economic aspects of energy issues in formulating national or regional policies (Lesbirel and Sun 2017; Zafar et al. 2019). Others, however, have convincingly argued that energy policies are shaped by broader political issues, rather than only by the commercial aspects of energy security (Ebinger 2011; Eder 2014; Pant 2015; Tow 2007; Van de Graaf and Sovacool 2014). These political determinants of energy have been the subject of a growing body of literature that can broadly be classified under the field of energy geopolitics, defined by Bradshaw (2009) as the influence of geographical factors, such as the distribution of centers of supply and demand, on state and non-state actions to ensure adequate, affordable, and reliable supplies of energy.

Despite its importance, energy in Asia is significantly underresearched. In an analysis of 4,444 articles on energy in three major energy journals (*The Energy Journal*, *Energy Policy*, and *Electricity Journal*), Sovacool discovered that only 2.7 percent addressed political, geopolitical, political economy, and international relations issues. In addition, only 17 percent focused on Asia (Sovacool 2014), of which a majority were on China, Japan, and India, owing to the geopolitical importance of these countries (Vivoda 2017). Consequently, there is enormous potential for a future research agenda in this field.

In this chapter we critically analyze the literature and identify existing gaps. Our analysis is divided into three parts. First, we provide a geopolitical and socioeconomic overview of Asia and classify the contemporary geographic definitions of the region and its subregions. Second, we undertake an examination of the prevalent features, strengths, weaknesses, and contestations within the body of the literature. Last, while recognizing that our findings are limited by constraints of time and space, we identify a number of issues that can form the future research agenda.

DEFINING THE ASIA-PACIFIC REGION

The most commonly accepted boundaries place Asia to the east of the Suez Canal, the Ural River, and the Ural Mountains, and south of the Caucasus Mountains and the Caspian and Black Seas (The National Geographic 2018). This massive continent constitutes 32.7 percent of the total area of the planet. Various interpretations of the composition of subregions exist. The United Nations Department of Economic and Social Affairs categorizes fifty Asian countries into five subregions: Eastern Asia, Central Asia, Southern Asia, Southeastern Asia, and Western Asia (UN 2018). The World Energy Outlook and the BP Statistical Review of World Energy categorize Asia into three broad subregions: Eurasia, the Middle East, and the Asia Pacific (BP 2017; IEA 2017b). Overall, while in geographic terms the continent of Asia constitutes all three subregions, within the literature on energy politics, the term "Asia" has often been used to describe the countries of the Asia-Pacific region (Caballero-Anthony, Chang, and Putra 2012; Dulal et al. 2013; Oecallaghan and Spagnoletti 2013; Vivoda 2017). For this reason, we focus on the geographic area of the Asia-Pacific region, thereby complementing the analyses of Eurasia (Balmaceda and Heinrich), Japan (Lipscy and Incerti), and China (Namh) in this volume.

Even within the narrower category of the Asia-Pacific region, energy scholars differ over what countries are included. Most scholars define the term to include countries of East Asia, South Asia, Southeast Asia, and Oceania collectively, as illustrated in Figure 24.1. An exception is Janardhanan (2017), who includes the Central Asian countries of Uzbekistan and Kazakhstan. The vast majority of studies have not provided an exclusive geographic definition of the Asia-Pacific region, and the use of the term has been largely contextual (Jo 2015; Samuelson 2014; Weeks 2011).

Within the existing literature on energy politics, some scholars have included the entire Asia-Pacific region within the scope of their analysis, despite the complexities of undertaking research on such a vast and diverse landscape (Intriligator 2015; Sovacool 2013; Vivoda 2010, 2017). A majority of energy studies on the Asia-Pacific region focus on one of the four subregions of Asia, namely South Asia, East Asia, Southeast Asia, and Oceania. Such variance in geographic focuses generates diverse research findings. Geopolitics is a major focus of studies on South Asia, which reflects the region's status as one of the most conflict-prone areas of the world. Studies often highlight political challenges as the greatest impediment to energy cooperation (Huda and McDonald 2016; Singh 2013). Studies on East Asia and Southeast Asia mostly evaluate the political economy of energy cooperation, and while challenges such as resource nationalism are prominently mentioned, studies from this region generally consider the economic and social aspects of energy, in addition to the political issues (Aalto 2014; Chang 2013; Chen 2014; Dent 2013; Hashim 2015; Motomura 2014). Within studies on Oceania, the focus is more on renewables, stakeholder engagement, and legislative issues, rather than nationalism or international conflict (Eusterfeldhaus and Barton 2011; Ko, Jeong, and Kim 2015; Martin and Rice 2015).

Regardless of subregional diversity in literature, there is overall consensus on the importance of energy for Asia's future, as described in the following section.

THE EVOLVING IMPORTANCE OF ENERGY IN ASIA

Three broad issues have enhanced the relevance of energy research in Asia. First is the spectacular economic growth of the region, which has spurred the demand for energy resources. The Asia-Pacific region continues to be the main growth engine of the world and is projected to grow by 5.6 percent in 2017 and 5.5 percent in 2018 (IMF 2017). The region currently accounts for 42 percent of the world's energy consumption and is the

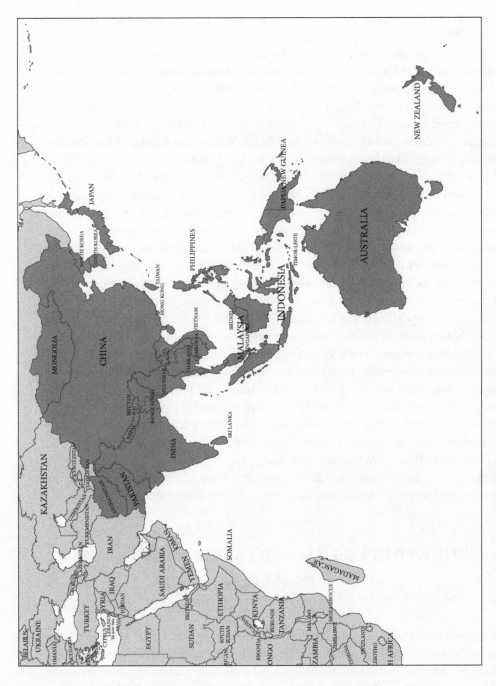

FIGURE 24.1 Commonly accepted composition of the Asia-Pacific region.

Source: Map created with online software from mapchart.net. Licensed under CC BY-SA 4.0 https://creativecommons.org/licenses/by-sa/4.0/

largest consumer of oil, coal, hydroelectricity, and renewables (BP 2017). It is estimated that by 2040 Asia's primary energy consumption will increase to 8,794 Mtoe, accounting for 60 percent of global energy consumption growth (IEE Japan 2014).

Second, due to the dependence on fossil fuels of states in the region, it currently accounts for more than 48 percent of the world's emissions, and this is likely to increase by 3.6 percent per year (BP 2017). Emissions take a tremendous toll on health in the region; ambient air pollution in Southeast Asia is expected to result in 300,000 premature deaths in 2040, a 70 percent increase from current levels (IEA 2017a). Despite the health impacts, Asian countries have justified the use of fossil fuels, particularly coal, as a cost-effective means of providing access to electricity, thereby reducing poverty. Even with coal, the region has 421 million people without access to electricity and is home to the largest number of poor people in the world (ESCAP 2017; Guanghua and Sebastian 2011). In terms of energy in the region, the trade-off between development imperatives and environmental obligations is set to intensify in the near future.

Third, the paradoxical presence of intense civil and international conflict, along with significant cooperation, makes the Asia-Pacific region an interesting subject for energy scholars. In 2018 there were seven international conflicts and more than ten domestic conflicts of varied intensity in the region (CFR 2018; IRIN 2018), which invariably impact energy cooperation. The perpetual conflict between India and Pakistan is one of the factors that led to the shelving of the Iran-Pakistan-India pipeline. Yet cooperation on energy can reduce existing conflicts, as exemplified by the thawing of relations between Algeria and Morocco as a result of their participation in the Maghreb-Europe Pipeline project (Ali 2010).

However, the Asia-Pacific region also has a plethora of bilateral, multilateral, and regional organizations, which have had varied levels of success; more than fifteen multilateral energy and connectivity projects are being planned in the region (GICA 2018). The newly opened Asian Infrastructure Investment Bank (AIIB) is also set to boost the financing of regional energy projects and complement the efforts of the Asian Development Bank and World Bank. In the near future, the politics of energy in Asia will be underpinned as much by the Kashmir conflict and the South China Sea dispute as by the Turkmenistan-Afghanistan-Pakistan-India (TAPI) Pipeline and BRI.

Academics have attempted to address some of these critical queries on energy in Asia using a variety of methodologies, conceptual frameworks, and energy sources. Taking into account the wide range of studies, we identify five common themes: analytical frames, securitization, cooperation, environmental issues, and energy justice. Each of these themes is developed in a separate subsection here.

Analytical Frames

Regardless of geographic focus, studies on international energy affairs are relatively under conceptualized and do not seem to fully benefit from the wider bodies of literature on international relations (IR) theories. In an extensive review of the extant literature, Stoddard (2013) finds that many accounts of energy politics exhibit forms of implicit theorization, employing concepts drawn loosely from the fields of political realism or neoliberalism. Stoddard argues that while realism and geopolitical issues are often deliberated, they rarely systematically relate to the wider body of scholarship on political realism (Stoddard 2013). Some noted exceptions are provided by Hancock and Vivoda (2014) and Kuzemko et al. (2012), who use an international political economy framework to analyze global energy politics.

Consistent with most energy literature, studies on Asia have generally not developed or worked with international relations frameworks (Aalto 2014; Dulal et al. 2013; Kohli 2012; Singh 2013). Although geopolitical issues and the interplay between security concerns and development objectives receive frequent mention, these issues are generally not exclusively linked to the literature on realism, liberalism, international political economy, and other variants of IR theory. Only a handful of studies have formed explicit theoretical frameworks. Ali (2010) uses "contested regionalism" and "rational regionalism" to frame the political issues on oil and gas pipelines in Asia. Pande (2013) analyzes energy cooperation through the theoretical lens of absolute and relative gains. Cao, Andrew, and Chuyu (2016) use a political economy framework to examine renewable energy politics in China. While these studies make important contributions in terms of policy, their use of conceptual frameworks is mostly ad hoc, and they do not undertake a systematic, in-depth analysis of IR theories.

One of the reasons for the theoretical shortcomings of energy studies in Asia is that almost all mainstream IR theories are dominated by Western-centric schools of thought. In a critique of the universal applicability of mainstream IR theories, Sondhi (2006) has stated that the sovereign state that lies at the heart of such concepts is at odds with the weak nature of governance in many Asian countries and the fact that internal security concerns in these countries far outweigh issues such as the international balance of power. The challenge for future researchers therefore is not only to apply existing theoretical frameworks to energy issues but also to develop concepts steeped in the existing political realities of the region.

Securitization

In Asia, while official energy policies often focus on regional cooperation and sustainability (MOF 2009; PD 2014; NITI Ayog 2017), in terms of implementation, governments have prioritized national security, domestic political compulsions, and energy independence over other goals (Ebinger 2011; Weeks 2011). Vlado (2017) has argued that intense competition for scarce resources, existing political conflicts, and regional mistrust have resulted in the "securitization" of energy discourse in Asia, a process through which conflicts over availability and pricing of energy are perceived as threats to national security. This link between national security and energy issues in Asia has been further conceptualized by some analysts as the "the security dilemma" of Asian energy dynamics, which implies that increases in the security of one state decrease the security of others (Herz 1950; Vivoda 2017, 275), a zero-sum game, to use IR terminology. Marketos (2008), Sun et al. (2011), and Wilson (2014) provide important insights in regard to great power politics and regional rivalries that influence energy issues. Several analysts have argued that the emphasis on energy's importance to defense and national security and great power politics can further aggravate existing tensions among regional countries, such as China, Japan, Australia, and Indonesia (Singh 2013; Sovacool 2011; Vivoda 2017; Wilson 2017). In recent years analysts have paid particular attention to bilateral energy competition between China and Japan (Evron 2017; Minoura 2011) and China and India (Janardhanan 2015; Zhao 2012).

Drawing from our broad analysis, here we discuss in more detail three topics of increasing importance to the securitization of energy in Asia: oil and gas pipelines, maritime energy trade, and cybersecurity of energy systems. We have chosen these three topics because oil and gas pipelines, maritime trade, and the computer systems used to control them are important nodes of contemporary integration projects, notably the BRI, which is set to revolutionize energy cooperation in the near future. A literature review of these three topics is therefore of particular importance for creating the future research agenda for this field.

Oil and Gas Pipelines

Within contemporary literature, transnational oil and gas pipelines have garnered increasing academic attention. Due to the presence of several insurgent groups, such as the Baloch Liberation Army (BLA), and ongoing territorial conflicts in South and Southeast Asia, the small body of literature on Asian pipelines has been dominated by studies that have focused on security issues and energy geopolitics (Iqbal and Afridi 2017; Kandiyoti 2008; Nathan, Kulkarni, and Ahuja 2013). The vast majority of analysts of Asian pipelines use the security and defense paradigm, largely overlooking the cooperative potential of energy infrastructure. Only a handful of studies have examined the peace-building potential of pipelines in the region (Huda and Ali 2017; Sovacool 2010a).

In addition, the issue of transnational governance has been addressed by only a few studies, such as Dadwal (2011), who examines the viability of governing South Asia's pipelines through regional frameworks such as the Energy Charter Treaty. However, the most concerning gap within this body of literature is the lack of studies that address pipeline projects from the interests of nonstate actors. There is almost a complete absence of studies that examine issues such as resettlement, land rights, and social safeguards as they relate to the development of pipeline infrastructure. In this context, the human rights violations committed by the Burmese junta during the construction of the Yadana pipeline serve as a cautionary tale about how large energy projects, if not perceived from a microeconomic perspective, can have significant adverse impacts on communities (Khanna 2011). The inclination of analysts to focus on geopolitical perspectives rather than human security issues is also apparent in the literature on pipeline projects in other parts of the world. Studies of pipelines in Europe (Szul 2011), Africa (Watkins 2011), and the Middle East (Vogler 2017) focus almost exclusively on the interactions within and between states and multinational energy companies. Only a handful of studies on pipelines have examined the interests of a wider group of stakeholders such as community members and nongovernmental organizations (NGOs) (Le Billon and Savage 2016). Therefore, the existing literature on Asia's pipelines has not yet fully addressed some key issues related to peace and conflict, governance, and human rights.

Maritime Energy Trade

A growing body of literature has explored the link between energy markets and maritime security in Asia. Within this context, a small number of studies have explored the impact of piracy and "maritime terrorism" on the security of oil tankers and liquefied natural gas (LNG) carriers. For instance, Chaturvedi and Samdarshi (2011) argue that the exploitation of container shipping by fundamentalist and terrorist groups is a significant threat to maritime energy trade. Kosai and Unesaki's (2016) study derives a composite maritime security index to evaluate the vulnerability of seventeen main energy shipping routes, in which the Far East Asia–Europe route is found to be most vulnerable. Several analysts have argued that energy security will be impacted by the disruptions to shipping lanes instigated by China's expansionist naval strategy and Beijing's ongoing territorial disputes with Southeast Asian countries (Malik 2014; Phillips 2013; Wirth 2012). Within this group of literature, an increasing number of studies are addressing the rivalry between India and China in regard to vital energy shipping lanes in the Indian Ocean and the South China Sea (Weimar 2013). Some studies have also highlighted Beijing's concerns regarding the "Malacca dilemma": the possibility that the United States will block energy supplies to China that pass through the Malacca Strait (Noël 2014; Ramadhani 2015; Zhang 2011).

As with the literature on pipelines, studies on maritime issues have almost exclusively focused on geopolitical and security aspects of energy. The environmental issues related to energy trade through shipping lanes in Asia, such as carbon emissions, have not been subject to sufficient academic scrutiny, although this issue in the context of maritime trade in general has been explored by some academics (Fitzgerald, Howitt, and Smith 2011; Lee, Lam, and Lee 2016). Qiu, Wong, and Lam (2018) argue that significant reductions in CO_2 can be obtained through sharing of vessels by companies and countries involved in maritime trade. Future researchers may consider the viability of such sharing arrangements for maritime energy trade.

The literature on the geopolitics of maritime energy trade also does not adequately reflect contemporary political developments in this area. US president Donald Trump's administration's trade embargo against China, the evolving denuclearization efforts in the Korean Peninsula, the revival of the Quadrilateral Security Dialogue (Malik 2016), and China's development of the rail gun and arming of artificial islands in the South China Sea (Saunders 2017) are issues that will impact the security of seaborne energy supplies in the near future but have not yet attracted sufficient academic interest.

Cybersecurity of Energy Systems

While political scientists have evaluated the "hardware" of energy infrastructure, issues regarding the security of computer networks that control smart energy grids, pipelines, and hydroelectric dams have not garnered enough attention. Studies in this field are mostly technical in nature (Xu et al. 2019), and while some studies exist on the political issues, the geographic focus is predominantly on Europe (Pearson 2011) or North America (Baggett and Simpkins 2018). A stark research gap exists on the politics of cybersecurity as it relates to Asia's energy projects, particularly the proposed and already under-construction transnational pipelines and smart electricity grids.

Regional Cooperation

In contrast to the securitization of energy in Asia, a considerable amount of literature exists on regional energy cooperation. This body of literature includes academic studies (Paik 2012; Tan 2018; Zhao 2011) as well as reports by institutions such as the World Bank (ESMAP 2010) and the Asian Development Bank (ADB 2013; Wijayatunga and Fernando 2013). Studies in this genre have highlighted the economic, environmental, and political benefits of energy cooperation (Aalto 2014; Paik 2012; Singh 2013). While such studies have established the rationale for regional energy cooperation, they have failed to explain the incremental progress of such collaboration in the region. Where explanations have been provided, they have mostly been of a generic nature, such as the presence of political challenges, nationalistic sentiments, and lack of trust (Andrews-Speed and Adnan 2013; Gippner 2010; Nathan, Kulkarni, and Ahuja 2013; Zhao and Zhang 2016). Findings from these studies are also limited by an overreliance on secondary data. Only a handful of studies have used primary data collection methodologies to analyze the constituents of the often-quoted but poorly understood political impediments to energy cooperation (Huda and McDonald 2016; Sovacool 2010b). Sovacool (2010b) uses more than one hundred interviews and extensive fieldwork in multiple countries to evaluate the political economy of the Trans-ASEAN Gas Pipeline (TAGP) Network. Huda and McDonald (2016) use interviews with forty-five policy makers in four countries of South Asia to understand political challenges to regional energy cooperation.

Scholars of energy cooperation have made a number of recommendations about how practitioners could enhance the prospects for cooperation. Broadly, these recommendations have included the use of international frameworks, creating regional energy governance mechanisms, and greater engagement across the energy sectors (Andrews-Speed and Adnan 2013; Dadwal 2011; WB 2012). However, given the prevailing international environment of intense energy competition, it is highly unlikely political leaders will implement these recommended policies. In addition, the extant literature has mostly perceived the benefits of energy cooperation from a statist perspective. Apart from a few exceptions, such as Uddin and Taplin (2015) and Ebinger (2011), most existing studies have only briefly explored the potential benefits of regional energy cooperation for human development and poverty alleviation. Given that more than four hundred million people in the region still do not have access to electricity, energy access should be incorporated more broadly within regional cooperation agendas.

Environmental Issues

Scholars diverge in their analysis of the environmental impacts of energy use in Asia. Some have conceptualized environmental issues within the context of a nexus among food, water, and energy security (Fan 2016; Makoto, Masuhara, and Burnett 2017; Rasul and Sharma 2016; White et al. 2018). These studies have successfully placed energy and environmental issues within broader goals of climate change mitigation and sustainable economic development. However, with the exception of a few studies (e.g., Pittock et al. 2015), literature in this genre does not delve sufficiently into the political and bureaucratic impediments, such as lack of coordination between various government ministries and endemic corruption, that impinge on the development and implementation of policies based on the nexus concept.

The environmental issues related to the use of renewable energy in Asia have been the subject of a number of studies (Anbumozhi and Kalirajan 2016; Chang, Zheng, and Yanfei 2016; Dent 2013; Liu, Zhang, and Bae 2018; Ng and Tao 2016). These studies have explored issues such as the financing and trade liberalization of renewable energy technologies, the impact of such technologies on economic growth and the environment, and the various obstacles to their adoption and development. A small number of studies have also focused exclusively on the political aspects of renewable energy in Asia (Cao, Andrew, and Chuyu 2016; Hughes and Meckling 2017). Much of this literature has focused on East Asia; the growing renewable capabilities of South Asia and opportunities for collaboration in this aspect between India and Pakistan are subjects that have not been sufficiently explored in the literature.

In addition to renewables, some studies have also examined the impact of the use of fossil fuels on the environment (Froggatt 2013; Lesbirel and Sun 2017). Of particular importance to energy policies are studies that have measured the environmental impact of the use and extraction of fossil fuels on health (Colagiuri and Morrice 2015), water resources (Ali et al. 2017; Wright, Belmer, and Davies 2017), and societal harmony (Li et al. 2017; McDuie-Ra and Kikon 2016). These studies mostly have a national focus; few studies examine the political repercussions of the environmental impact of fossil fuel consumption on a transboundary level (Koplitz et al. 2017; Simpson 2014).

Within studies on energy and environment in Asia, hydroelectric projects, particularly large-scale multilateral dams, have come under increasing academic attention (Chang 2013; Huda 2016; Tan-Mullins, Urban, and Mang 2017). This body of literature mostly focuses on the national security aspects of hydroelectric dams, such as the potential for "water wars" and regional conflicts arising out of unilateral diversions of shared rivers, particularly between India and China (Chellaney 2013). Within these studies, the environmental issues related to the production of hydroelectricity are perceived purely as catalysts for geopolitical conflict, and social impacts of hydrological changes such as resettlement and loss of livelihoods are not comprehensively explored. As Alley, Hile, and Chandana (2014) argue, regional hydroelectric dams in Asia will fail to bring about sustainable development unless innovative research can account for the social, political, and environmental costs associated with such projects.

Among studies on climate change and energy in Asia, the majority focus on the technical aspects of mitigation (Calvin 2012; Fulton et al. 2017; Koljonen and Lehtila 2012; Reed, Mendelsohn, and Abidoye 2017). Studies that exclusively focus on the political milieu around complex policy choices between energy security and climate change mitigation are limited (Anceschi and Symons 2012; Simpson and Smits 2018). Overall, sufficient space exists for research that can create cohesive links among the existing discourses on politics, energy, and the environment in Asia.

Energy Justice

The extant literature explores a number of issues related to energy justice, although the level of academic attention has varied among topics and countries. (For an extensive discussion of the energy justice literature, see Fuller in this volume.) A growing body of literature has explored energy justice issues related to mining-induced displacement and resettlement in Asia (O'Callaghan and Graetz 2017; Van der Ploeg and Vanclay 2017; Owen and Kemp 2016). These studies have made important contributions to the development of concepts and policies related to greater corporate social responsibility and social safeguards in the mining industry. In terms of geographic scope, while some studies exist on mining-induced resettlement in India (Ekka 2006; Mishra and Mishra 2017; Sharma 2010), research on China is relatively rare (Yang, Zhao, and Ho 2017). In addition, only a handful of scholars have examined the human rights issues in the context of mining in Mongolia (McIntyre et al. 2016), Vietnam (Vo 2013), and Pakistan (Makki, Ali, and Van Vuuren 2015).

As mentioned in the previous section, scholars who focus on the national security aspects of hydroelectric dams broadly ignore the issue of human rights. Energy justice scholars, however, put considerable emphasis on links between hydroelectric projects in Asia and resettlement. A substantial amount of literature exists on the social impact of large dams in India (Bidoglio, Berger, and Finkbeiner 2018; Chowdhury 2018; Kipgen 2017; Nayak 2013). Literature on China is not inconsiderable (Faure 2015; Lee 2013) but is incommensurate with the number of dams in the country, which is by far the highest in Asia: There is a considerable dearth of studies that measure the socioeconomic impacts of proposed multilateral hydroelectric projects among Bangladesh, Bhutan, India, and Nepal in the Ganges-Brahmaputra-Meghna Basin.

Some studies have delved into the rights of workers employed in energy-related industries. Lahiri-Dutt (2012) undertakes an important study on the gradual decline in women's participation in Indian collieries. Other studies have broadly covered the labor rights of workers employed in the extraction, processing, and transfer of energy resources, with gender issues, health, and compensation for accidents getting particular attention (Chen et al. 2013; Liu 2011; Rodriguez-Fernandez et al. 2016). The scope of studies within this field is quite broad and includes domestic issues, such as tribal rights and coal mining in India (McDuie-Ra and Kikon 2016), and transnational issues, such as the use of slave labor in the construction of the Yadana pipeline between Myanmar and Thailand (Simpson 2014). The subject of labor rights in energy-related industries offers ample scope for prospective researchers, with child labor in coal mines in South Asia being a topic that is yet to receive substantial academic focus, despite contemporary media attention on the issue (Chandran 2016).

FUTURE RESEARCH AGENDA

The preceding analysis highlighted several research gaps within existing literature. These gaps have broadly informed the eleven elements of the future research agenda described here: conceptual frameworks, a broader geographic focus, comparative analyses, unraveling political challenges, regional integration projects and energy, Arctic resources, deep sea oil and gas exploration, cybersecurity of energy systems, politics of energy subsidies, social and environmental impacts of transnational energy projects, and the politics of environment and energy.

Conceptual Frameworks

One of the defining features of literature on energy politics in Asia is the dearth of studies that use IR theories to frame the research. While future researchers should take into account the importance of using theoretical frameworks, a more important contribution can be made toward concepts themselves. The lack of IR theories that have originated in Asia means that concepts such as realism, liberalism, and even constructivism cannot completely account for the plethora of social, historical, political, and economic factors that determine the energy politics of the region. Future researchers should therefore not only use existing concepts to frame energy politics in Asia, but also highlight where such concepts fall short in accounting for regional realities. Research on this area can contribute to existing theories by giving them more Asia-centric ontological axioms, or even create the grounding for non-Western IR theories. Foundations for such IR theories can be found within Asian perceptions of world affairs such as the ASEAN Way, the distinct political cultures in Java, Indonesia (Sebastian and Lanti 2009), or the texts of the Indian philosopher Kauṭilya (Behara 2009).

A Broader Geographic Focus

The majority of extant literature on energy in Asia focuses on China, Japan, and India. While this exclusivity has been driven to some extent by the disproportionate influence of these countries on regional and even global energy politics, important issues related to smaller countries and subregions of Asia have not been analyzed sufficiently. This includes coal mining and sustainable development in Mongolia, transnational hydroelectric projects in South and Southeast Asia, and the development of nuclear energy in Bangladesh. Undertaking analysis in these countries and regions will play an important role in the development of the field.

Comparative Analysis

In our review of literature on regional energy cooperation, we have argued that most of the policy recommendations within these studies are ambiguous and far removed from the reality of energy competition in Asia. In a region dominated by zero-sum perspectives and entrenched mistrust, calls for "greater confidence building measures" (Pande 2013, 107) as a way of enhancing energy cooperation have little policy relevance. To meet this gap, future scholars may consider undertaking comparative analyses of energy cooperation through detailed process-tracing of particular energy projects. For instance, studies that compare the planning processes of the Baku-Tbilisi-Ceyhan (BTC) Pipeline in Eurasia with those of Asian pipelines currently under construction, such as the TAPI, may have significant policy and academic value. Similarly, comparative analyses should be undertaken between existing hydroelectric dams in the Mekong Basin and proposed multilateral dams in the Ganges-Brahmaputra-Meghna Basin.

Unravelling Political Challenges

A common explanation for the incremental progress of transnational energy projects in Asia is political challenges. Despite their apparent importance, only a few studies, such as Sovacool (2010a), have systematically analyzed the political challenges to energy cooperation, apart from vague interpretations of energy geopolitics. To some extent, this research gap is due to a dearth of studies that use primary data. To understand the political challenges to energy in Asia, the future research agenda should combine research methodologies such as household surveys and key informant interviews. Such diversity in research methodologies will facilitate an understanding of political challenges at the domestic, national, and regional levels.

Regional Integration Projects and Energy

A number of regional integration projects, including the BRI, are currently being conceptualized or implemented in Asia. Given the importance of these projects to the region broadly and to specific states, notably China, there is a growing need for research into the impact of such initiatives on the region's energy politics. The future research agenda should therefore examine the impact on energy trade of projects such as the Bangladesh-Bhutan-India-Nepal (BBIN) Group, the International North-South Transport Corridor (INSTC), the South Asia Subregional Economic Cooperation

(SASEC), and the Bangladesh-China-India-Myanmar Economic Corridor (BCIM) (Baruah 2018; Huda and Ali 2018; Passi 2017). In this context, researchers may evaluate the impact of Asia's integration projects on energy governance and trade as well as resource-based cooperation and competition.

Arctic Resources

The US Geological Survey estimates that the Arctic holds 30 percent of the world's natural gas reserves and 13 percent of its oil (Gautier et al. 2009). Scientists have pointed out that the melting of ice induced by climate change will make such resources more accessible. While Russia and the United States have been seen as traditional rivals in this area, more recently, China and Japan have expressed interests in claiming their share of the energy resources of the Arctic. Of great relevance is China's Polar Silk Road Initiative, which aims to develop the oil and gas resources of the region (Hawksley 2018). Both China and Japan are cooperating with Russia to develop energy infrastructures in the Arctic, which may have important ramifications for energy geopolitics in the future (Hayashi 2018). In addition, Asian countries have participated in important forums such as the Arctic Circle Assembly, which brings together international actors on a number of issues, including resource extraction in the Arctic region (AC 2019). The overtures of Asian countries to access the resources of the Arctic are therefore set to become an important area for future research.

Deep Sea Oil and Gas Exploration

The exploration of oil and gas in the contested waters of the South China Sea can significantly impact regional geopolitics in the near future. Currently, the South China Sea dispute includes overlapping territorial and maritime claims among several sovereign states, namely Brunei, China, Taiwan, Malaysia, Indonesia, the Philippines, and Vietnam. There are approximately 11 billion barrels (bbl) of oil reserves and 190 trillion cubic feet (Tcf) of natural gas reserves in the South China Sea (EIA 2013). Future researchers should consider how China's approach to extracting oil and gas in the contested areas of the South China Sea can impact energy politics of the region. Research in this area should consider not only the actions of countries involved in the dispute but also responses by the United States, international energy companies, and the ASEAN.

Cybersecurity of Energy Systems

The recent international scrutiny of Chinese telecom giant Huawei (Cellan-Jones 2018) has brought into focus the increasing role of cybersecurity in geopolitics. While the controversy surrounding Huawei is contemporary, it raises broader questions regarding the use of Chinese technology for energy systems. Given that a disproportionate number of energy projects in Asia are being conceptualized and implemented by Chinese companies, and the general unease that some countries have expressed about giving access to sensitive networks to overseas companies, the geopolitics of cybersecurity, particularly as it relates to energy systems, is set to become an important area of research. While it may be tempting to use a realist prism to frame the cybersecurity issues of smart grids and pipelines, researchers should also consider exploring the political determinants that can foster greater cooperation in Asia on cybersecurity of energy systems.

Politics of Energy Subsidies

Energy subsidies play an important role in the domestic politics of South and Southeast Asia (Chattopadhyay and Jha 2014). However, while there is increasing recognition that subsidies have put many governments under significant financial stress and delayed development of cleaner fuels and renewable technologies, energy subsidies in Asia have increased over time. One of the priorities of future energy researchers should be to understand the myriad political issues that perpetuate the use of energy subsidies in Asia. Research should evaluate the links between electoral politics and energy prices, political violence related to price hikes of fuels, and the international repercussions of domestic energy subsidies, such as trade wars over agricultural and other products.

Social and Environmental Impacts of Transnational Energy Projects

Considerable scope exists for academic inquiry into the social and environmental impacts of proposed and already under-construction transnational energy projects in Asia. Of particular contemporary relevance are the Central Asia-South Asia (CASA-1000) power project and the Turkmenistan-Uzbekistan-Tajikistan-Afghanistan-Pakistan (TUTAP) electricity project (Daisuke and Nakayama 2015). In this context, comparative studies can be undertaken with existing literature on regional hydropower development of the Mekong River in Southeast Asia (Edward et al. 2015; Green and Baird 2016). Research in this area can contribute to the wider bodies of literature on social and environmental safeguards related to energy infrastructure development, energy governance, and energy justice.

Politics of Environment and Energy

Finally, the future research agenda should include studies that focus exclusively on the political milieu of complex policy choices between energy security and environmental conservation in Asia. In addition to domestic and regional issues, scholarly work on this topic may also explore the political issues surrounding the participation of Asian countries in the United Nations Framework Convention on Climate Change (UNFCCC) and other international processes that aim to reduce the impact of energy consumption on the environment. The geopolitical aspects of renewable energy, particularly technological and trade issues between China and the United States, can also form part of the research agenda.

Energy politics in Asia is a subject that has seen growing academic attention, yet significant research gaps exist across a range of subtopics and themes. To develop this field in the future, researchers should address these gaps through the use of innovative methodologies, particularly the use of primary data collection and interdisciplinary frameworks. While "politics" in the context of this topic broadly refers to inter-state interactions, in cognizance of regional poverty alleviation, climate change, and energy access goals, academics may consider the economic, environmental, and societal aspects of energy within broader political frames. Economic and population growth, the dynamic nature of international relations, and technological advancements in resource extraction and renewable technologies, among other developments, will impact the future direction of research on energy politics in Asia. While regional rivalries and great power struggles around energy are unlikely to fade, future research in this field may contribute somewhat to a peaceful, energy secure, and prosperous region.

References

Aalto, P. 2014. "Energy Market Integration and Regional Institutions in East Asia." *Energy Policy* 74: 91–100.

ADB. 2013. "Energy outlook for Asia and the Pacific." Manila: The Asian Development. Bank. https://www.adb.org/sites/default/files/publication/30429/energy-outlook.pdf

Ali, S. 2010. "Energizing Peace: The Role of Pipelines in Regional Cooperation." Brookings Doha Center Analysis Paper Number 2. https://www.brookings.edu/research/energizing-peace-the-role-of-pipelines-in-regional-cooperation/

Ali, A., V. Strezov, P. Davies, and I. Wright. 2017. "Environmental Impact of Coal Mining and Coal Seam Gas Production on Surface Water Quality in the Sydney Basin, Australia." *Environmental Monitoring & Assessment* 189, no. 8: 1–16.

Alley, K. D., R. Hile, and M. Chandana. 2014. "Visualizing Hydropower across the Himalayas: Mapping in a Time of Regulatory Decline." *Himalaya* 34, no. 2: 52–66.

Anbumozhi, V., and K. Kalirajan. 2016. "Effect of Trade Liberalization on Low-Carbon Energy Technology Dissemination in Asia." *Asian Economic Papers* 15, no 3: 95–108.

Anceschi, L., and J. Symons, eds. 2012. *Energy Security in the Era of Climate Change: The Asia-Pacific Experience.* London: Palgrave Macmillan.

Andrews-Speed, P., and H. Adnan. 2013. "Institutional and Governance Dimensions of ASEAN Energy Market Integration." AEMI Working Paper. http://www.asean-aemi.org/wp-content/uploads/2013/09/AEMI-Working-Paper-Institutional-and-governance-dimensions-of-ASEAN-Energy-Market-Integration.pdf.

Arctic Circle. 2019. "About." http://www.arcticcircle.org/about/about/.

Ascher, W., and N. Mirovitskaya, eds. 2013. *Development Strategies, Identities, and Conflict in Asia.* New York: Palgrave Macmillan.

Baggett, R. K., and B. K. Simpkins. 2018. *Homeland Security and Critical Infrastructure Protection*. Santa Barbara CA: Praeger.

Baruah, D. 2018. "India's Answer to the Belt and Road: A Road Map for South Asia." Carnegie India Working Paper. https://carnegieendowment.org/files/WP_Darshana_Baruah_Belt_Road_FINAL.pdf.

Beeson, M. 2014. "Security in Asia." *Journal of Asian Security and International Affairs* 1, no. 1: 1–23.

Behara, N. C. 2009. "Re-imagining IR in India." In *Non-Western International Relations Theory: Perspectives on and Beyond Asia*, edited by A. Acharya and B. Buzan, 92–116. London: Routledge.

Bidoglio, G., M. Berger, and M. Finkbeiner. 2018. "An Environmental Assessment of Small Hydropower in India: The Real Costs of Dams' Construction under a Life Cycle Perspective." *International Journal of Life Cycle Assessment* 34, no. 3: 419–440.

BP. 2017. *BP Statistical Review of World Energy June 2017*. London: BP. https://www.bp.com/content/dam/bp-country/de_ch/PDF/bp-statistical-review-of-world-energy-2017-full-report.pdf.

Bradshaw, M. J. 2009. "The Geopolitics of Global Energy Security." *Geography Compass* 3, no. 5: 1920–1937.

Caballero-Anthony, M., Y. Chang, and N. A. Putra, eds. 2012. *Rethinking Energy Security in Asia: A Non-traditional View of Human Security*. Heidelberg, Germany: Springer.

Calvin, K. 2012. "The Role of Asia in Mitigating Climate Change: Results from the Asia Modeling Exercise." *Energy Economics* 34, no. 3: S251–S260.

Cao, X., K. Andrew, and L. Chuyu. 2016. "Why Invest in Wind Energy? Career Incentives and Chinese Renewable Energy Politics." *Energy Policy* 99: 120–131.

Cellan-Jones, R. 2018. "Tech Tent: Can We Trust the Telecoms Giants?" BBC News, December 7. https://www.bbc.com/news/technology-46488969.

CFR. 2018. "Global Conflict Tracker." The Council on Foreign Relations. https://www.cfr.org/interactives/global-conflict-tracker#!/global-conflict-tracker.

Chandran, R. 2016. "Children Working in India's Coal Mines Came as 'Complete Shock', FilmmakerSays." Reuters, July 6. https://www.reuters.com/article/us-india-mines-childlabour-idUSKCN0ZM1DZ.

Chang, F. K. 2013. "The Lower Mekong Initiative & U.S. Foreign Policy in Southeast Asia: Energy, Environment & Power." *Orbis* 57, no. 2: 282–299.

Chang, Y., F. Zheng, and L. Yanfei. 2016. "Renewable Energy Policies in Promoting Financing and Investment among the East Asia Summit Countries: Quantitative Assessment and Policy Implications." *Energy Policy* 95: 427–436.

Chattopadhyay, D., and S. Jha. 2014. "The Impact of Energy Subsidies on the Power Sector in Southeast Asia." *The Electricity Journal* 27, no. 4: 70–83.

Chaturvedi, A., and S. K. Samdarshi. 2011. "Energy, Economy and Development (EED) Triangle: Concerns for India." *Energy Policy* 39: 4651–4655.

Chellaney, B. 2013. *Water, Peace, and War: Confronting the Global Water Crisis*. New York: Rowman & Littlefield.

Chen, H., F. Qun, L. Ruyin, and Q. Hui. 2013. "Focusing on Coal Miners' Occupational Disease Issues: A Comparative Analysis between China and the United States." *Safety Science* 51, no. 1: 217–222.

Chen, S. 2014. "China's Energy Rise and Implications to Southeast Asia." *China: An International Journal* 12, no. 2: 46–65.

Chowdhury, A. R. 2018. "State Formation from Below: Social Movements of Dam Evictees and Legal Transformation of the Local State in India, 1960–76." *South Asia-Journal of South Asian Studies* 41, no. 1: 194–211.

Christensen, T. J. 1999. "China, the U.S.-Japan Alliance, and the Security Dilemma in East Asia." *International Security* 23, no. 4: 49–80.

Colagiuri, R., and E. Morrice. 2015. "Do Coal-Related Health Harms Constitute a Resource Curse? A Case Study from Australia's Hunter Valley." *The Extractive Industries and Society* 2, no. 2: 252–263.

Dadwal, S. R. 2011. "Can the South Asian Gas Pipeline Dilemma Be Resolved through a Legal Regime?" *Strategic Analysis* 35, no. 5: 757–769.

Daisuke, S., and M. Nakayama. 2015. "A Study on the Risk Management of the CASA-1000 Project." *Hydrological Research Letters* 9, no. 4: 90–96.

Dent, C. M. 2013. "Wind Energy Development in East Asia and Europe." *Asia Europe Journal* 11, no. 3: 211–230.

Dulal, H. B., K. U. Shah, C. Sapkota, G. Uma, and B. R. Kandel. 2013. "Renewable Energy Diffusion in Asia: Can It Happen without Government Support?" *Energy Policy* 59: 301–311.

Ebinger, C. K. 2011. *Energy and Security in South Asia: Cooperation or Conflict?* Washington, DC: Brookings Institution Press.

Eder, T. S. 2014. *China-Russia Relations in Central Asia: Energy Policy, Beijing's New Assertiveness and 21st Century Geopolitics.* Wiesbaden, Germany: Springer.

Edward, J. A., B. Guillaume, M. Besset, M. Goichot, P. Dussouillez, and V. L. Nguyen. 2015. "Linking Rapid Erosion of the Mekong River Delta to Human Activities." *Scientific Reports* 5, no. 14745: 1–14.

EIA. 2013. "South China Sea." United States Energy Information Administration. https://www.eia.gov/beta/international/regions-topics.php?RegionTopicID=SCS.

Ekka, A. 2006. "Mitigating Adverse Social Impacts of Coal Mining: Lessons from the Parej East Open Caste Project." *Social Change* 36, no 1: 153–174.

ESCAP. 2017. *Global Tracking Framework 2017—Progress toward Sustainable Energy.* United Nations Economic and Social Commission for Asia and the Pacific. Bangkok: The United Nations. https://www.unescap.org/sites/default/files/122017_GTF_Findings%20Overview.pdf.

ESCAP. 2018. *Handbook on Negotiating Sustainable Development Provisions in Preferential Trade Agreements.* United Nations Economic and Social Commission for Asia and the Pacific. Bangkok: The United Nations. https://www.unescap.org/resources/handbook-negotiating-sustainable-development-provisions-preferential-trade-agreements.

ESMAP. 2010. *Regional Power Sector Integration: Lessons from Global Case Studies and a Literature Review.* Energy Sector Management Assistance Program Washington, DC: The World Bank. http://documents.worldbank.org/curated/en/456981468154776209/Literature-review.

Eusterfeldhaus, M., and B. Barton. 2011. "Energy Efficiency: A Comparative Analysis of the New Zealand Legal Framework." *Journal of Energy and Natural Resources Law* 29, no. 4: 431–470.

Evron, Y. 2017. "China-Japan Interaction in the Middle East: A Battleground of Japan's Remilitarization." *Pacific Review* 30, no. 2: 188–204.

Fan, S. 2016. "A Nexus Approach to Food, Water, and Energy: Sustainably Meeting Asia's Future Food and Nutrition Requirements." *Pakistan Development Review* 55, no. 4: 297–311.

Faure, A. 2015. "Public International Law Debate Concerning Forced Evictions in China." Paper presented at Regional Conference on Social and Economic Human Rights, Rennes.

Fitzgerald, W., O. Howitt, and I. Smith. 2011. "Greenhouse Gas Emissions from the International Maritime Transport of New Zealand's Imports and Exports." *Energy Policy* 39, no. 3: 1521–1531.

Froggatt, A. 2013. "The Climate and Energy Security Implications of Coal Demand and Supply in Asia and Europe." *Asia Europe Journal* 11, no. 3: 285–303.

Fulton, L., A. Mejia, A. Magdala, K. Dematera, and O. Lah. 2017. "Climate Change Mitigation Pathways for Southeast Asia: CO_2 Emissions Reduction Policies for the Energy and Transport Sectors." *Sustainability* 9, no. 7: 1160.

Gautier, Donald L., et al. 2009. "Assessment of Undiscovered Oil and Gas in the Arctic." *Science* 324, no. 5931: 1175–1179.

GICA. 2018. "Connectivity Initiatives Around the World." Global Infrastructure Connectivity Alliance. https://www.gica.global/maps.

Gippner, O. 2010. *Energy Cooperation in South Asia: Prospects and Challenges.* Kathmandu, Nepal: South Asia Watch on Trade, Economics and Environment (SAWTEE).

Green, W. N., and I. G. Baird. 2016. "Capitalizing on Compensation: Hydropower Resettlement and the Commodification and Decommodification of Nature–Society Relations in Southern Laos." *Annals of the American Association of Geographers* 106, no. 4: 853–873.

Guanghua, W., and I. Sebastian. 2011. *Poverty in Asia and the Pacific: An Update.* Philippines: The Asian Development Bank. https://www.adb.org/publications/poverty-asia-and-pacific-update.

Hancock, K. J., and V. Vivoda. 2014. "International Political Economy: A Field Born of the OPEC Crisis Returns to Its Energy Roots." *Energy Research & Social Science* 1: 206–216.

Hashim, J. 2015. "Challenges of Energy and Water in Southeast Asia." *International Journal of Epidemiology* 44, no. 1: i7.

Hawksley, H. 2018. "China's Arctic Plan Spreads a Chill." *Nikkei Asian Review* (February 16). https://asia.nikkei.com/Politics/International-relations/China-s-Arctic-plan-spreads-a-chill.

Hayashi, S. 2018. "Japan Joins race to develop Arctic resources." *Nikkei Asian Review* (October 5). https://asia.nikkei.com/Politics/International-relations/Japan-joins-race-to-develop-Arctic-resources.

Helms, R., and S. E. Costanza. 2014. "Energy Inequality and Instrumental Violence: An Empirical Test of a Deductive Hypothesis." *SAGE Open* 4, no. 2: 1–16.

Herz, J. H. 1950. "Idealist Internationalism and the Security Dilemma." *World Politics* 2, no. 2: 157–180.

Huda, M. S. 2016. "Envisioning the Future of Cooperation on Common Rivers in South Asia: A Cooperative Security Approach by Bangladesh and India to the Tipaimukh Dam." *Water International* 42, no. 1: 54–72.

Huda, M. S., and S. Ali. 2017. "Energy Diplomacy in South Asia: Beyond the Security Paradigm in Accessing the TAPI Pipeline Project." *Energy Research & Social Science* 34: 202–213.

Huda, M. S., and S. Ali. 2018. "Environmental Peacebuilding in South Asia: Establishing Consensus on Hydroelectric Projects in the Ganges-Brahmaputra-Meghna (GBM) Basin." *Geoforum* 96: 160–171.

Huda, M. S., and M. McDonald. 2016. "Regional Cooperation on Energy in South Asia: Unraveling the Political Challenges in Implementing Transnational Pipelines and Electricity Grids." *Energy Policy* 98: 73–83.

Hughes, L., and J. Meckling. 2017. "The Politics of Renewable Energy Trade: The US-China Solar Dispute." *Energy Policy* 105: 256–262.

IEA. 2017a. *Southeast Asia Energy Outlook 2017*. Paris: International Energy Agency. https://www.iea.org/southeastasia/.

IEA. 2017b. *World Energy Outlook 2017*. Paris: International Energy Agency. https://www.iea.org/weo2017/.

IEE. Japan 2014. *Asia/World Energy Outlook*. Tokyo: The Institute of Energy Economics Japan. https://eneken.ieej.or.jp/data/7199.pdf.

IMF. 2017. *Regional Economic Outlook: Asia Pacific*. Washington, DC: International Monetary Fund. https://www.imf.org/en/Publications/REO/APAC/Issues/2017/10/09/areo1013.

Intriligator, M. D. 2015. "Energy Security in the Asia-Pacific Region." *Contemporary Economic Policy* 33, no. 1: 221–227.

Iqbal, M., and M. K. Afridi. 2017. "New Great Game in Central Asia: Conflicts, Interests and Strategies of Russia, China and United States." *Dialogue* 12, no. 3: 229–246.

IRIN. 2018. "Mapped—a World at War." Integrated Regional Information Networks. https://www.irinnews.org/content/about-us.

Janardhanan, N. 2015. "India-China Energy Geopolitics: Dominating Alternative Energy Market in Pacific Asia." *International Studies* 52, no. 1–4: 66–85.

Janardhanan, N. 2017. "Nuclear Power and Climate Change Mitigation: Search for Low-Carbon Energy Mix in Asia." In *Resurgence of Nuclear Power: Challenges and Opportunities for Asia*, edited by N. Janardhanan, G. Pant, and R. B. Grover, 71–88. Singapore: Springer.

Jo, C. H. 2015. "Renewable Energy in Asia-Pacific Region." *Energy* 81: 1–2.

Kandiyoti, R. 2008. *Pipelines: Flowing Oil and Crude Politics*. London: I. B. Tauris & Co Ltd.

Khanna, P. 2011. *How to Run the World*. New York: Random House.

Kipgen, N. 2017. "The Enclosures of Colonization: Indigeneity, Development, and the Case of Mapithel Dam in Northeast India." *Asian Ethnicity* 18, no. 4: 505–521.

Ko, D. H., S. T. Jeong, and Y. C. Kim. 2015. "Assessment of Wind Energy for Small-Scale Wind Power in Chuuk State, Micronesia." *Renewable and Sustainable Energy Reviews* 52: 613–622.

Kohli, P. P. 2012. "Achieving Energy Security in South Asia." *The Environmentalist* 32, no. 3: 360–362.

Koljonen, T., and A. Lehtila. 2012. "The Impact of Residential, Commercial, and Transport Energy Demand Uncertainties in Asia on Climate Change Mitigation." *Energy Economics* 34, no. 3: S410–S420.

Koplitz, S. N., D. J. Jacob, M. P. Sulprizio, L. Myllyvirta, and C. Reid. 2017. "Burden of Disease from Rising Coal-Fired Power Plant Emissions in Southeast Asia." *Environmental Science & Technology* 51, no. 3: 1467–1476.

Kosai, S., and H. Unesaki. 2016. "Conceptualizing Maritime Security for Energy Transportation Security." *Journal of Transportation Security* 9, nos. 3–4: 175.

Kuzemko, C., A. Belyi, A. Goldthau, and M. Keating, eds. 2012. *Dynamics of Energy Governance in Europe and Russia*. London: Palgrave Macmillan.

Lahiri-Dutt, K. 2012. "The Shifting Gender of Coal: Feminist Musings on Women's Work in Indian Collieries." *South Asia: Journal of South Asian Studies* 35, no. 2: 456–476.

Le Billon, P., and E. Savage,. 2016. "Binding Pipelines? Oil, Armed Conflicts, and Economic Rationales for Peace in the Two Sudans." *African Geographical Review* 35, no. 2: 134–150.

Lee, T., J. S. Lam, and P. Lee. 2016. "Asian Economic Integration and Maritime CO2 Emissions." *Transportation Research, Part D: Transport and Environment* 43: 226–237.

Lee, Y. B. 2013. "Global Capital, National Development and Transnational Environmental Activism: Conflict and the Three Gorges Dam." *Journal of Contemporary Asia* 43, no. 1: 102–126.

Lesbirel, S. H., and S. Sun. 2017. "Oil Import Diversification in the Asia-Pacific (1976–2014)." *Journal of the Asia Pacific Economy* 22, no. 4: 621–625.

Li, Q., N. Stoeckl, D. King, and E. Gyuris. 2017. "Exploring the Impacts of Coal Mining on Host Communities in Shanxi, China—Using Subjective Data." *Resources Policy* 53: 125–134.

Liu, Chaojie. 2011. "Failures of Enterprise-Level Unionization in China: Implications for Coalmine Safety and Beyond." *International Labour Review* 150, nos. 1–2:163–175. doi:10.1111/%28ISSN%291564-913X/issues.

Liu, X., S. Zhang, and J. Bae. 2018. "Renewable Energy, Trade, and Economic Growth in the Asia-Pacific Region." *Energy Sources, Part B: Economics, Planning, and Policy* 13, no. 2: 96–102.

Makki, M., S. Ali, and K. Van Vuuren. 2015. "Religious Identity and Coal Development in Pakistan: Ecology, Land Rights and the Politics of Exclusion." *The Extractive Industries and Society* 2: 276–286.

Makoto, T., N. Masuhara, and K. Burnett. 2017. "Water, Energy, and Food Security in the Asia Pacific Region." *Journal of Hydrology: Regional Studies* 11: 9–19.

Malik, M. 2014. *Maritime Security in the Indo-Pacific: Perspectives from China, India, and the United States*. Lanham, MD: Rowman & Littlefield Publishers.

Malik, M. 2016. "Balancing Act: The China-India-U.S. Triangle." *World Affairs* 179, no. 146: 46–57.

Marketos, N. T. 2008. *China's Energy Geopolitics: The Shanghai Cooperation Organization and Central Asia*. New York: Routledge.

Martin, N., and J. Rice. 2015. "Improving Australia's Renewable Energy Project Policy and Planning: A Multiple Stakeholder Analysis." *Energy Policy* 84: 128–141.

McDuie-Ra, D., and D. Kikon. 2016. "Tribal Communities and Coal in Northeast India: The Politics of Imposing and Resisting Mining Bans." *Energy Policy* 99: 261–269.

McIntyre, N., N. Bulovic, I. Cane, and P. McKenna. 2016. "A Multi-disciplinary Approach to Understanding the Impacts of Mines on Traditional Uses of Water in Northern Mongolia." *Science of the Total Environment* 557–558: 404–414.

Minoura, H. 2011. "Energy Security and Japan-China Relations: Competition or cooperation?" Master's diss., The George Washington University.

Mishra, S. K., and P. Mishra. 2017. "Do Adverse Ecological Consequences Cause Resistance against Land Acquisition? The Experience of Mining Regions in Odisha, India." *The Extractive Industries and Society* 4, no. 1: 140–150.

MOF. 2009. "Integrated Energy Plan 2009–2022." Ministry of Finance, Government of Pakistan. http://climateinfo.pk/frontend/web/attachments/data-type/MoF_EEG%20(2009)%20Integrated%20energy%20plan%202009-22.pdf.

Motomura, M. 2014. "Japan's Need for Russian Oil and Gas: A Shift in Energy Flows to the Far East." *Energy Policy* 74: 68–79.

Nathan, H. S. K., S. S. Kulkarni, and D. R. Ahuja. 2013. "Pipeline Politics—A Study of India's Proposed cross Border Gas Projects." *Energy Policy* 62: 145–156.

The National Geographic. 2018. "Asia: Physical Geography." https://www.nationalgeographic.org/encyclopedia/asia/.

Nayak, A. K. 2013. "Development, Displacement and Justice in India: Study of Hirakud Dam." *Social Change* 43, no. 3: 397–419.

Ng, T. H., and J. Y. Tao. 2016. "Bond Financing for Renewable Energy in Asia." *Energy Policy* 95: 509–517.

NITI Ayog. 2017. "Draft National Energy Policy." New Delhi: NITI Ayog. https://niti.gov.in/writereaddata/files/new_initiatives/NEP-ID_27.06.2017.pdf.

Noël, P. 2014. "Asia's Energy Supply and Maritime Security." *Survival* 56, no. 3: 201–216.

O'Callaghan, T., and G. Graetz, eds. 2017. *Mining in the Asia-Pacific: Risks, Challenges and Opportunities*. Cham: Springer.

O'Callaghan, T., and B. Spagnoletti. 2013. "Let there be light: a multi-actor approach to alleviating energy poverty in Asia". *Energy Policy* 63: 738–746.

Ofreneo, Rene E. 2013. *Asia and the Pacific: Advancing Decent Work amidst Deepening Inequalities*. Singapore: ITUC-Asia Pacific.

Owen, J. R., and D. Kemp. 2016. "Can Planning Safeguard against Mining and Resettlement Risks?" *Journal of Cleaner Production* 133: 1227–1234.

Paik, H. 2012. "Northeast Asian Energy Corridor Initiative for Regional Collaboration." *East Asian Economic Review* 16, no. 4: 395–410.

Pande, S. 2013. "Developing Energy Corridor from Central and West Asia to South Asia." In *Towards an Asian Century: Future of Economic Cooperation in SAARC Countries*. 101–118. Islamabad, Pakistan: Islamabad Policy Research Institute.

Pant, G., ed. 2015. *India's Emerging Energy Relations: Issues and Challenges*. New Delhi: Springer.

Passi, R. 2017. "Money Matters: Discussing the Economics of the INSTC." ORF Occasional Paper no 112. New Delhi: The Observer Research Foundation. https://www.orfonline.org/research/money-matters-discussing-the-economics-of-the-instc/.

PD. 2014. "Vision/Mission Statement and Major Functions." Power Division, Ministry of Power, Energy and Mineral Resources, Government of the Peoples Republic of the Bangladesh. https://powerdivision.portal.gov.bd/sites/default/files/files/powerdivision.portal.gov.bd/page/f6d0e100_e2d8_47e7_b7cd_e292ea6395d3/4.%20VSPSPSectorReform.pdf

Pearson, I. L. G. 2011. "Smart Grid Cybersecurity for Europe." *Energy Policy* 39, no. 9: 5211–5218.

Phillips, A. 2013. "A Dangerous Synergy: Energy Securitization, Great Power Rivalry and Strategic Stability in the Asian Century." *The Pacific Review* 26, no. 1: 17–38.

Pittock, J., S. Orr, L. Stevens, M. Aheeyar, and M. Smith. 2015. "Tackling Trade-offs in the Nexus of Water, Energy and Food." *Aquatic Procedia* 5: 58–68.

Qiu, X., E. Y. C. Wong, and J. S. L. Lam. 2018. "Evaluating Economic and Environmental Value of Liner Vessel Sharing along the Maritime Silk Road." *Maritime Policy and Management* 45, no. 3: 336–350.

Ramadhani, E. 2015. "China in the Indian Ocean Region: The Confined 'Far-Seas Operations.'" *India Quarterly* 71, no. 2: 146–159.

Rasul, G., and B. Sharma. 2016. "The Nexus Approach to Water–Energy–Food Security: An Option for Adaptation to Climate Change." *Climate Policy* 16, no. 6: 682–702.

Reed, B., R. Mendelsohn, and B. O. Abidoye. 2017. "The Economics of Crop Adaptation to Climate Change in Southeast Asia." *Climate Change Economics* 8, no. 3: 1–20.

Rodriguez-Fernandez, R., N. Ng, D. Susilo, J. Prawira, M. J. Bangs, and R. M. Amiya. 2016. "The Double Burden of Disease among Mining Workers in Papua, Indonesia: At the Crossroads between Old and New Health Paradigms." *BMC Public Health* 16, no. 1: 951.

Samuelson, R. D. 2014. "The Unexpected Challenges of Using Energy Intensity as a Policy Objective: Examining the Debate over the APEC Energy Intensity Goal." *Energy Policy* 64: 373–381.

Saunders, I. 2017. "The 'South China Sea Award', Artificial Islands and Territory." *Australian Year Book of International Law* 34: 31–39.

Sebastian, L. C., and I. G. Lanti. 2009. "Perceiving Indonesian Approaches to International Relations Theory." In *Non-Western International Relations Theory: Perspectives on and Beyond Asia*, edited by A. Acharya, and B. Buzan, 149–173. London: Routledge.

Sharma, R. N. 2010. "Changing Facets of Involuntary Displacement and Resettlement in India." *Social Change* 40, no. 4: 503.

Simpson, A. 2014. *Energy, Governance and Security in Thailand and Myanmar (Burma): A Critical Approach to Environmental Politics in the South*. Surrey, UK: Ashgate.

Simpson, A., and M. Smits. 2018. "Transitions to Energy and Climate Security in Southeast Asia? Civil Society Encounters with Illiberalism in Thailand and Myanmar." *Society & Natural Resources* 31, no. 5: 580–598.

Singh, B. K. 2013. "South Asia Energy Security: Challenges and Opportunities." *Energy Policy* 63: 458–468.

Sondhi, S. 2006. "South Asia in International Relations." *South Asia Politics* 4, no 11:

Sovacool, B. K. 2010a. "A Critical Stakeholder Analysis of the Trans-ASEAN Gas Pipeline (TAGP) Network." *Land Use Policy* 27, no. 3: 788–797.

Sovacool, B. K. 2010b. "Exploring the Conditions for Cooperative Energy Governance: A Comparative Study of Two Asian Pipelines." *Asian Studies Review* 34, no. 4: 489–511.

Sovacool, B.K. 2011. "An international comparison of four polycentric approaches to climate and energy governance." *Energy Policy* 39, no. 6: 3832–3844.

Sovacool, B. K. 2013. "A Qualitative Factor Analysis of Renewable Energy and Sustainable Energy for All (SE4ALL) in the Asia-Pacific." *Energy Policy* 59: 393–403.

Sovacool, B. K. 2014. "What Are We Doing Here? Analyzing Fifteen Years of Energy Scholarship and Proposing a Social Science Research Agenda." *Energy Research & Social Science* 1: 1–29.

Stoddard, E. 2013. "Reconsidering the Ontological Foundations of International Energy Affairs: Realist Geopolitics, Market Liberalism and a Politico-Economic Alternative." *European Security* 22 no. 4: 437–463.

Sun, X., J. Li, D. Wu, and S. Yi. 2011. "Energy Geopolitics and Chinese Strategic Decision of the Energy-Supply Security: A Multiple-Attribute Analysis." *Journal of Multi-Criteria Decision Analysis* 18, nos. 1/2: 151–160.

Szul, R. 2011. "Geopolitics of Natural Gas Supply in Europe—Poland Between the EU and Russia." *European Spatial Research and Policy* 18, no. 2: 47–67.

Tan, S. 2018. Regime Complex and Energy Cooperation in Southeast Asia. Master's diss., Nanyang Technological University.

Tan-Mullins, M., F. Urban, G. and Mang. 2017. "Evaluating the Behaviour of Chinese Stakeholders Engaged in Large Hydropower Projects in Asia and Africa." *China Quarterly* 230: 464–488.

Tow, W. 2007. "Strategic Dimensions of Energy Competition in Asia." In *Energy Security in Asia*, edited by M. Wesley, 161–173. New York: Routledge.

Uddin, N., and R. Taplin. 2015. "Regional Cooperation in Widening Energy Access and Also Mitigating Climate Change: Current Programs and Future Potential." *Global Environmental Change* 35: 497–504.

UN. 2018. "Standard Country or Area Codes for Statistical Use." United Nations. https://unstats.un.org/unsd/methodology/m49/.

Van de Graaf, T., and B. K. Sovacool. 2014. "Thinking Big: Politics, Progress, and Security in the Management of Asian and European Energy Megaprojects." *Energy Policy* 74: 16–27.

Van der Ploeg, L., and F. Vanclay. 2017. "A Human Rights Based Approach to Project Induced Displacement and Resettlement." *Impact Assessment and Project Appraisal* 35, no. 1: 34–52.

Vivoda, V. 2010. "Evaluating Energy Security in the Asia-Pacific Region: A Novel Methodological Approach." *Energy Policy* 38: 5258–5263.

Vivoda, V. 2017. "Energy Security Issues in Asia." In *Routledge Handbook of Energy in Asia*, edited by S. C. Bhattacharyya, 272–283. London: Taylor and Francis.

Vo, M. 2013. "Government-Managed Resettlement in Vietnam: Structure, Participation and Impoverishment Risks in the Case of the Thach Khe Iron Ore Mine." PhD diss., The University of Queensland.

Vogler, G. 2017. *Iraq and the Politics of Oil: An Insider's Perspective.* Lawrence: University Press of Kansas.

Watkins, E. 2011. "Trouble in Sudan's Pipeline." *Oil & Gas Journal* 109, no. 14: 44–45.

Weeks, D. 2011. "An East Asian Security Community: Japan, Australia and Resources as 'Security.'" *Australian Journal of International Affairs* 65, no. 1: 61–80.

Weimar, N. D. 2013. "Sino-Indian Power Preponderance in Maritime Asia: A (Re-)source of Conflict in the Indian Ocean and South China Sea." *Global Change, Peace & Security* 25, no. 1: 5–26.

White, D. J., K. Hubacek, K. Feng, L. Sun, and B. Meng. 2018. "The Water-Energy-Food Nexus in East Asia: A Tele-connected Value Chain Analysis Using Inter-regional Input-Output Analysis." *Applied Energy* 210: 550–567.

Wijayatunga, P., and P. N. Fernando. 2013. "An Overview of Energy Cooperation in South Asia." Manila: Asian Development Bank. https://www.adb.org/publications/overview-energy-cooperation-south-asia.

Wilson, J. D. 2014. "Northeast Asian Resource Security Strategies and International Resource Politics in Asia." *Asian Studies Review* 38, no. 1: 15–35.

Wilson, J. D. 2017. *International Resource Politics in the Asia-Pacific: The Political Economy of Conflict and Cooperation.* Cheltenham, UK: Edward Elgar.

Wirth, C. 2012. "Ocean Governance, Maritime Security and the Consequences of Modernity in Northeast Asia." *Pacific Review* 25, no. 2: 223–245.

World Bank. 2012. *Assessing the Investment Climate for Climate Investments: A Comparative Clean Energy Framework for South Asia in a Global Context.* Washington, DC: World Bank https://openknowledge.worldbank.org/handle/10986/26739.

Wright, I. A., N. Belmer, and P. J. Davies. 2017. "Coal Mine Water Pollution and Ecological Impairment of One of Australia's Most 'Protected' High Conservation-Value Rivers." *Water, Air and Soil Pollution* 228, no. 3: 1–18.

Xu, Y., H. Xia, F. Gao, W. Chen, Z. Liu, and P. Gu, eds. 2019. *Nuclear Power Plants: Innovative Technologies for Instrumentation and Control Systems.* Singapore: Springer.

Yang, X., H. Zhao, and P. Ho. 2017. "Mining-Induced Displacement and Resettlement in China: A Study Covering 27 Villages in 6 Provinces." *Resources Policy* 53: 408–418.

Zafar, M. W., M. Shahbaz, F. Hou, and A. Sinha. 2019. "From Nonrenewable to Renewable Energy and Its Impact on Economic Growth: The Role of Research & Development Expenditures in Asia-Pacific Economic Cooperation Countries." *Journal of Cleaner Production* 212: 1166–1178.

Zhang, Z. 2011. "Viewpoint: China's Energy Security, the Malacca Dilemma and Responses." *Energy Policy* 39: 7612–7615.

Zhao, H. 2011. "China-Myanmar Energy Cooperation and Its Regional Implications." *Journal of Current Southeast Asian Affairs* 30, no 4: 89–109.

Zhao, H. 2012. *China and India: The Quest for Energy Resources in the 21st Century*. New York: Routledge.

Zhao, S., and Z. Zhang. 2016. "The Political Economy of Energy Resources between China and ASEAN States: Opportunity and Challenge." *The Chinese Economy* 49, no. 6: 456–466.

CHAPTER 25

....

THE ENERGY POLITICS
OF BRAZIL

....

ELIZA MASSI AND JEWELLORD NEM SINGH

THE study of energy politics in Brazil is, essentially, about the role of the state and its various policy instruments and institutions–notably state-owned enterprises–in promoting economic development. This should not come as a surprise given the near consensus regarding the three main pillars of Brazilian economic development: the construction of state capacity and autonomy as part of political modernization (Lessa 1964; Sikkink 1991; Skidmore 1986), the prominence of state-backed finance and state-owned enterprises (SOEs) (Massi 2014; Trebat 1982), and the rise of technocratic expertise and of an extensive bureaucratic machinery to implement developmentalism[1] throughout most of the twentieth century (Daland 1981; Evans 1995; Sola 1982). Owing to its limited supply of fossil fuels, Brazil designed its energy policy to secure a stable supply, with the state playing a vital role in the promotion of industrialization as well as in the diversification of energy resources (Goldemberg and Moreira 2005, 217).

The literature on energy politics in Brazil is mostly technical studies about energy efficiency and how reforms and state regulations have been implemented since the 1990s. Studies often probe energy governance through the lens of the state and its capacity to drive investment in energy (Goldemberg et al. 2014; Leite 2014) Hence, many studies emphasize the balance between SOE reform and sectoral regulations as opposed to privatization and market competition (Amann, Baer, and Coes 2011; Oliveira et al. 2011), with reference to reforms in three main sectors: oil and gas, electricity, and ethanol/biofuels (Oliveira 2012; Massi and Nem Singh 2018). This chapter argues that existing research highlights the evolving role of the state in energy development. Future research, however, must critically examine how political economy and related disciplines can shed light on policy dynamics in energy.

A BRIEF OVERVIEW OF BRAZILIAN
ENERGY GOVERNANCE

Brazil gained its independence from Portugal in 1822. Given its vast territory, the country's elites were often divided by regional allegiances and periodic challenges to the centralization of political authority, thereby weakening the cohesion of the state. As the Great Depression and collapse of commodity prices brought an end to the liberal exports model (1880–1930), the 1930s Revolution and the coming to power of Getúlio Vargas (1930–1945) ushered in—and eventually consolidated—the modernization of the Brazilian state with a new growth model centered on industrialization. The Vargas government was arguably a dictatorship, which limited any political discussion as the logic of state capitalism became embedded in Brazilian political life. Backed by the military, the Varguista legacy involved an unprecedented process of state centralization, political incorporation of labor and industrial elites, and economic modernization.

Energy security was a major concern in realizing Brazil's industrialization drive. Securing energy resources became a key policy objective. To this end, Brazil established a series of SOEs as the principal means to carry out an import substitution industrialization (ISI) program. The ISI model also relied on a complex set of incentives and subsidies, varying from import controls to subsidized credit, tax exemptions, and direct state investment via SOEs. This growth model prioritized state ownership of basic industries as a means of capital accumulation, with SOEs expected to coordinate and finance sectoral expansion. State intervention and the ideology of economic nationalism is well-documented. While examining the logic of state action is an established tradition in Brazilian political economy, there are also those who highlight the importance of state-business relations and state-labor relations as co-constitutive of the logic of state capitalism in Brazil (Sikkink 1991; Stepan 1973, 1981). Worth noting is the fact that Brazil's economic miracle was achieved through an industrial development strategy pursued by the government since the 1930s and deepened during the military dictatorship (1964–1985). The development model, however, was sustained through imported oil and low-interest foreign loans. To minimize dependence on imported oil after the first oil shock, the government adopted a two-pronged policy of energy substitution. In the long term, it aimed to expand the use of ethanol from sugarcane for transportation; in the short term, it intended to provide the industry with electricity at reasonable prices through the expansion of hydropower (Esposito 2012, 198–199).

However, the decline of the statist model in the late 1970s coincided with a fiscal crisis in the 1980s, leading to the re-democratization of the country in 1985. Brazil today is governed by a civilian-led democracy with a multiparty system in place. The military initiated and led the political liberalization, which resulted in the institutionalization of a democratic constitution in 1988. The return of democracy also meant the proliferation of political parties. The constitutionally mandated emphasis on party politics meant that (1) fragmentation caused by the large number of political parties could only be overcome through coalitional politics built through a system of clientelism and patronage, and (2) tensions between the federal and state governments constantly arose due to different jurisdictions across a variety of policy fields (Hagopian 1996; Hunter 2010; Kingstone and Power 2017). Nevertheless, most scholars agree that despite liberal reforms, *developmentalism* remains the organizing logic of Brazilian economic development (Ban 2013; Döring, Santos, and Pocher 2017; Font 2003; Nem Singh and Massi 2016, Massi and Nem Singh 2018). In this context, the study of Brazilian energy politics after 1985 can be divided into two major fields of enquiry: (1) the persistence of state capitalism and (2) continuity in understanding energy security as the foundation of economic modernization.

First, energy policy has been predominantly understood in terms of how SOEs and domestic enterprises promote the energy needs of the country. Petrobras, the national oil company, is the most important energy player in Brazil. In analyzing Petrobras, scholars have focused on three areas: (1) its historical development and role in promoting industrialization (Biasetto 2016; Philip 1982; Priest 2007, 2016; Randall 1993; Smith 1976); (2) the impact of regulatory reforms, especially oil fiscal regimes in national oil companies' performance (Gudmestad, Zolotukin, and Jarlsby 2010; Ramírez-Cendrero and Paz 2017); and (3) institutional continuity in Brazil's oil and gas sector despite market liberalization, which coalesced around the intertwining logics of developmentalism and energy security (Nem Singh 2014; Massi and Nem Singh 2018; Oliveira 2012). The second key energy player is Eletrobras, the state's largest utilities company. Eletrobras is often discussed in the context of a complex regulatory environment, in which recurrent tensions arise between the federal and state governments over infrastructure investments in electricity supply and distribution (Leite 2014; Trebat 1982; Villela 1984). Overall, fewer scholars have explored the politics behind Eletrobras than behind Petrobras, in part because Petrobras is historically associated with the military's industrialization program and national security. Petrobras's impact on the economy is well-documented; special emphasis is given to the pivotal role of the company in establishing competitive sectors deemed relevant for industrialization, notably transport, petrochemicals, and shipbuilding (Oliveira 2012; Randall 1993). The introduction of privatization in many segments of the Brazilian economy from 1990s onward did not put an end to the state-capitalism model; on the contrary, energy policy remains under the purview of the state. At best, policy debates in Brazil have been limited to partial market competition, such as partial privatizing of energy distribution. The overall approach to market reforms has been to enable the entry of market players without compromising the national development agenda.

Second, political scientists have emphasized the role of the military in Brazilian politics, which also means that energy security was a major policy concern to successfully carry out an industrialization program (Evans 1979, 1981; Stepan 1973, 1981). The military understood industrialization and access to energy as a key component of national defense (Guimarães 2003; Fiori 2012; Massi 2014; Oliveira 1976). Security policy was at the core of the doctrine; as a result, no development plan could be designed without taking into consideration national security. For example, the creation of Petrobras in

1952—amid the absence of proven oil reserves—reflected the military's distrust of foreign ownership of the country's natural resources. As Leite (2014) puts it, energy security is a reflection of the Brazilian state's attempts at bringing together economic development and national security.

Nevertheless, the widespread adoption of privatization and liberalization has given rise to a new agenda. Early scholarship evaluated whether SOEs can become as productive as their private counterparts (Bridgman, Gomes, and Teixeira 2011; Randall 1993); succeeding studies focused instead on the politics of creating regulatory agencies to manage market competition (Ramírez-Cendrero and Paz 2013; Sant Ana, Jannuzzi, and Bajay 2009). As part of the reform agenda, the National Council of Energy Policy was created in 1997 to advise the president of the republic on energy policy. The Ministry for Mines and Energy (MME) gained powers and became the primary institution responsible for the formulation of energy policy. In response to demands for greater competition, two agencies were set up: the National Petroleum, Natural Gas and Biofuels Agency (ANP) and the National Electricity Agency (ANEEL). Overall, privatization was not implemented on purely ideological grounds; it was part of a strategy conceived to ensure the soundness of the country's fiscal accounts following the macroeconomic stability achieved with the Real Plan in 1994 (Modiano 2000; Pinheiro 1999). In significant ways, the end of the state monopoly and the introduction of market competition were constitutive of a critical juncture in Brazilian political economy. The debates in Brazil throughout the 1990s were essentially focused on how to improve the competitiveness and productivity of domestic firms vis-à-vis foreign players.

In this context, Luiz Inácio Lula da Silva and his Workers' Party (PT) government were a mix of continuity and change. Scholars explored the consolidation of a new growth strategy based on "new developmentalism" (Ban 2013; Döring et al. 2017; Milanez and Santos 2015) as well as the return of Petrobras, not only as a key energy player but also as a national champion in the context of its discovery of offshore oil reserves in 2007 (Nem Singh 2012, 2014; Nem Singh and Massi 2016, Massi and Nem Singh 2018). In the oil and gas sector, the PT government pushed to strengthen Petrobras and its dominant position. Lula da Silva sought to rebuild industrial policy through local content policies, subsidized loans, and investments in infrastructure. In electricity, the PT government carried out reforms emphasizing security of supply and implementing a hybrid system that promoted state-led centralization operating alongside market competition. In many ways, Lula da Silva and his successor, Dilma Rousseff (2011–2016) adopted energy policies that sought continuity in promoting economic development and national security. However, by 2014 the Brazilian political and intellectual landscape had become preoccupied with a corruption scandal known as *Lava Jato*, which involved Petrobras as a focal point of investigation. As the scandal deepened, the investigation moved on toward mapping out a complex web of corruption, bribery, and rent-seeking among elected politicians and construction firms (Massi and Nem Singh 2018; MPF 2018). In the following sections we focus on the politics of Brazil's three main energy sources: oil and other liquids, ethanol, and electricity.

OIL AND OTHER LIQUIDS

The scholarship that emerged in analyzing the oil sector—and Petrobras—has stressed (1) the historical role of Petrobras in linking energy security with industrialization, (2) the impact of market competition and economic liberalization in the industry, and (3) the politics of rent-seeking and corruption in the context of Brazil's discovery of pre-salt oil from 2008 onward (Alveal 1993; de Biasi, Pinto, and Cecchi 2012; Florêncio 2016; Maceda e Silva 1985; Mahdavi 2014; Massi and Nem Singh 2018; Oliveira 2012; Philip 1982; Ramírez-Cendrero and Paz 2017). Most research deploys either in-depth case study, paired comparisons, or statistical techniques applied to a set of oil-exporting countries. Brazil is also compared with Norway and the United Kingdom due to their geological characteristics: offshore as opposed to onshore reserves, which shaped their respective regulatory frameworks (Mendes, Matos, and Silvestre 2014). Studies about the development of the Brazilian oil industry are linked to debates about Petrobras and its economic performance.

Methodologically, most studies faced difficulties in data collection. Given the strategic importance of Petrobras, few authors have managed to conduct interviews with state bureaucrats and top management of the SOE. In general, research on oil and gas often relies on company reports and publicly available government documents. As an alternative source of primary data, the government has several publications on the public sector and on Petrobras's policies and commercial activities (Almeida, Oliveira, and Schneider 2014; De Negri 2011a, 2011b, 2011c; Ramos Xavier 2012).

Furthermore, scholars who study Petrobras often frame questions as a development issue. The literature on resource nationalism and the oil curse falls short in explicating the unique role of Petrobras in Brazilian oil politics. While scholars agree that national oil companies were created to maximize fiscal revenues in oil-exporting states (Mahdavi 2014; Victor 2013), none of these analyses applies to Brazil because Petrobras's mandate was to "provide a secure oil supply while saving scarce hard currencies and supporting the country's broader industrialization" (Oliveira 2012, 534). While oil exporting countries nationalized their energy sector to capture the oil largesse, Vargas viewed oil nationalization as a political decision to control the commanding heights of the economy. With the backing of nationalists, who campaigned for state control of the sector (*O Petróleo é Nosso*—The Oil Is Ours), Vargas passed legislation against the presence of international oil companies (IOCs) in Brazil. The campaign wanted to prevent "backdoor dealing" with IOCs and advocated restrictions on foreign capital in oil exploration (Evans 1979, 90–92; Randall 1993, 9–12). Unlike Mexico and Venezuela, Petrobras was created to achieve energy self-sufficiency amid the limited availability of reserves.

Petrobras's history in promoting development is well-documented (Oliveira 2012; Philip 1982; Randall 1993). The company began its operations by acquiring small refineries after the passage of the law on state monopoly. Given its limited profits, the company was shielded from rent-seeking, while its objective of reducing oil imports and supporting industrialization was clearly articulated. Petrobras also stood out from other national oil companies for its ability to develop a professional cadre, taking advantage of its relative discretion over management policies, such as hiring professionals and appointing foreign experts, to help develop the oil industry (Nem Singh 2014; Philip 1982). Although it began with the objective of finding oil, this eventually changed to supplying the country's energy needs as Brazil began to deepen its ISI model. As early as 1964, Petrobras already had moved away from onshore exploration to focus on the development of the domestic energy market. It invested in offshore engineering technology after the Link Report[2] categorically concluded that there was limited availability of onshore reserves. To develop the domestic market, Petrobras enjoyed market monopoly and had corporate autonomy; it also benefited from limited labor resistance. The military government also eased foreign exchange controls and gave the company access to state resources. This enabled the company to implement policies aimed at vertical and horizontal integration of the sector (Randall 1993, 32). Scholars agree that Petrobras's strength stems from its culture of innovation, its ability to make commercial decisions despite being an SOE, and investment in human capital formation (Dantas and Bell 2009, 2011). Petrobras's commercial decisions were also influenced by growing state pressures to address increasing energy demand. Indeed, by 1954 oil already accounted for one-fifth of Brazil's total imports, so price increases would have debilitating effects on economic growth. Over time, the company became highly diversified, with market power in upstream and downstream activities.

As macroeconomic instability and foreign borrowing negatively affected the IS model, research on market opening and privatization reforms gained momentum (Birdsall and Nellis 2003; Goldstein 1999; Shirley 1999). Fernando Henrique Cardoso (1995–2003) introduced reforms in the oil and gas sector; in 1995 the National Congress ratified constitutional amendment no. 5, which broke the monopoly of Petrobras across the hydrocarbon commodity chain. This was followed by the 1997 Petroleum Law (Law 9478), which established the concessions regime. Under this regime, oil exploration and production are undertaken at the risk of oil companies, which retain ownership of the oil produced. The Petroleum Law reflects the essence of the "Norwegian model," which promotes a clear delineation of functions for the national oil company as a regulator and as a market competitor. It likewise established an independent regulatory agency, ANP, to oversee contract bidding and overall sectoral regulation. ANP's oversight powers also served to curb Petrobras's market power and influence in the transition from monopoly to a competitive market (see Trojbicz 2017).

The liberalization phase, marked by increased participation of private oil companies was interrupted by a new critical juncture: Petrobras's discovery of offshore reserves in the pre-salt layer in 2007 (Massi and Nem Singh 2018; Tyler 2016). Two important factors explicate the change in policy and academic debates in Brazil. First, the international circumstances—namely high oil prices in the 2000s—made deep ocean exploration commercially viable and therefore attracted foreign private interest. Given Petrobras's technological expertise in offshore ultra-deep engineering, international companies perceived partnerships and joint ventures with Petrobras as a low-risk, high-reward investment. Table 25.1 shows that Petrobras retained its market power despite liberalization. Second, the perception of risk from the government's perspective has also changed as a result of the pre-salt discovery. When Lula da Silva came to power in 2003, oil policy remained unchanged. However, the discovery provided a justification for the PT government to introduce a new law aimed at increasing state participation in the sector. In 2010 the government enacted Law 12.350—the Pre-Salt Law—which restructured the market, favoring state control and Petrobras. The law established the production-sharing regime for the pre-salt and areas considered strategic. Accordingly, oil companies bear the risks of oil exploration even though oil and gas production belongs to the state. The law also named Petrobras the leader of all operations in the pre-salt area, granting the SOE a minimum 30 percent stake in every project. The discovery itself has transformed oil into one of the most important sectors of the economy, and it therefore became an emerging field for social sciences and economics. Some studies examine the potential for oil-based industrialization and reinforce the importance of state-led development (Massi and Nem Singh 2018; Nem Singh and Massi 2016; Oliveira 2012). Amid potential windfall, other scholars have explored critical questions about how to allocate oil rents productively, the merits of creating a national social fund, and whether compulsory investments in R&D projects aimed at technological development can work as a strategy for industrialization (Mancini and Paz 2018; Postali 2009; Postali and Nishijima 2013; Tyler 2016).

However, the fortunes of Brazil changed after 2012. The country experienced an economic recession, a collapse in oil prices, and in 2014 a corruption scandal—known as Car Wash (*Lava Jato*)—all of which were structural conditions conducive to a major crisis in governance and political legitimacy. The *Lava Jato* investigation, on its own, negatively affected public trust in state institutions. It showed how major political parties institutionalized corruption into an illicit financial scheme that enabled domestic private firms, especially construction companies, to overprice services while also financing political campaigns. This scandal, in turn, played a crucial role in the

Table 25.1 Oil and Natural Gas Production in Brazil by Operator, 2015

	Oil (in Barrels)		Natural Gas (in Cubic Millimeters)	
TOTAL	889,667,381		35,126,447	
Petrobras	822,051,381.5	92%	33,115,158.6	94%
Statoil Brasil	26,459,293.4	3%	36,773.1	0%
Shell Brasil	23,460,667.4	3%	265,679.3	1%
Chevron Frade	8,500,306.9	1%	92,041.3	0%
OGX	4,900,627.0	1%	15,407	0%
Others	4,295,104.8	0%	1,601,387.7	5%

Source: ANP, *ANP Annuário 2016*, p. 82 (adapted).

impeachment of Rousseff (2011–2016), which paved the way for the return of the conservative right in 2016. Emerging research today has only begun to discuss the implications of this political crisis for Brazil's model of state capitalism, the changing nature of corruption and rent-seeking, and the extent to which democratic politics—especially the system of coalitional presidentialism—can withstand future challenges (Hunter and Power 2019; Katz 2018).

Since the exposition of the *Lava Jato* scandal, critical discussions about its complex nature are often found in newspapers, academic blogs, and selected reports about Petrobras; however, a systematic account regarding how rent-seeking, corruption, and the oil industry are interlinked has yet to be published (see Massi and Nem Singh 2018). In this context, we outline some preliminary analysis here of how Petrobras responded to the changing economic and political environment. With already costly investments in offshore drilling, the discovery of pre-salt reserves created divergent interests between Petrobras and the state. While the former sought gradual and strategic investment to explore the new reserves, politicians, who had very limited understanding of the risks involved in the sector, aimed to extract oil and swiftly move toward its commercialization. Indeed, the 2010 Petroleum Law outlined specific clauses to ring-fence oil rents toward targeted expenditures (Nem Singh 2012). The rush to exploit the pre-salt and the large investments required to make it commercially viable created the conditions for the indebtedness of Petrobras.

Further aggravating the problems of Petrobras, in 2008, in an attempt to control inflation, the federal government froze the prices of diesel and gasoline, forcing the company to sell fuel below cost (Goldemberg 2018, 369; Pinto et al. 2016). In other words, Petrobras absorbed the costs of the government's pricing policy, as inflation became a major concern for the PT government. Almost simultaneously, the corruption investigation exposed a decade-long scheme defrauding Petrobras on contracts, adding fuel to growing discontent with the PT government. A separate political process involving Rousseff's economic management began in parallel to the judicial investigation. An impeachment process against Rousseff in Congress abruptly ended the PT government in 2016, bringing Michel Temer (2016–2019) to the government. Temer reintroduced market liberalization despite low levels of popular support. The Petrobras's then president, Pedro Parente, asked Temer to respect the company's autonomy by giving him the latitude to adjust prices according to international oil prices and to freely sell non-performing assets to reduce the company's debt burden. In an attempt to encourage private investment, Temer (2016–2019) amended the Pre-Salt Law, allowing foreign companies to become operators and removing the requirement that Petrobras take a 30 percent stake in future projects. It must be noted, however, that Petrobras still has preference because the law granted the company the "right of first refusal"; in other words, it can choose in which projects it wishes to participate. The ability of Petrobras to recover from its financial losses and the constant pressure from the government to develop the pre-salt shape the conditions upon which oil policy in Brazil will remain the same or change.

ETHANOL SECTOR

Although much attention in the Brazilian energy literature has been directed to Petrobras and the pre-salt oil region, biofuel—mainly ethanol produced from sugarcane—has played an important role in transforming Brazil's energy matrix due to its widespread use as an automotive fuel. According to Santos (2016a, 11), the sum of ethanol production plus the electricity generated from the burning of sugarcane bagasse and straw account for 16 percent of total energy. The sector is also the second largest electricity generator. Currently Brazil is the world's second largest consumer and producer of ethanol[3] (EIA 2017).

The literature on the ethanol sector is prolific. Studies vary, from the technical aspects of production, productivity, and supply chain structures (Martines-Filho, Burnquist, and Vian 2006; Santos 2016b); determinants of crisis (Santos, Garcia, and Shikida 2015; Santos et al. 2016); technological innovation (Berger 2010; Demetrius 1990; Santos and Wehrmann 2016); and geopolitics (Afionis et al. 2016; Schutte and Barros 2010); to social, environmental, and economic impacts of ethanol production (Drabik et al. 2015; Galli 2011; Regitano d'Arce et al. 2009; Ribeiro 2013; Santos and Ferreira Filho 2017).

To analyze the political economy of ethanol requires familiarity with the politics of sugar—a major commodity of Brazil since the colonial era. Unlike in oil and electricity, the scope of government intervention in sugar production was shaped by the relationship of the state with sugar producers (Leite 2009, 127–128). Accordingly, the trajectory of the sugarcane agroindustry in Brazil can be divided into three periods: 1889–1930, 1930–1990, and 1990–present (Ramos 2016, 47). The first period was mainly characterized by the sugar industry's efforts to modernize and recuperate market share. Authors, such as De Carli (1942) and Perruci (1978), discuss the structure of the industry, its development, and forms of state assistance. As in other sectors considered strategic, government support was fundamental to technological development and market expansion. State intervention, according to Ramos (2016, 48–49), was directly linked to all aspects of the industry, from technical changes, the search for new markets, pricing, financing, and research, to the creation of a captive market.

The development of the ethanol sector was tied to the economic fate of the sugar industry, particularly after the 1930 worldwide depression. As Vargas sought for industrialization and to shift away from primary commodities, sugar producers—and the regional agricultural elites more broadly—rallied for state protection (Ramos 2001, 2007). Policies adopted by developed countries provided the incentives for the creation of preferential markets and expansion of sugar production and consumption (Ramos 2001). The use of ethanol as an additive to gasoline was introduced in 1931. The world depression severely impacted the sugar market and the agricultural sector, which led Vargas to create the Sugar and Alcohol Institute (IAA) in 1933 to regulate and promote the sector, establishing, among other measures, production quotas and price controls (Ramos 1999, 2016). Crucially, ethanol production was encouraged, and its addition to gasoline became mandatory (Leite 2009; Ramos 2016). This policy, however, viewed ethanol production as a subsidiary activity and an effective means to reduce sugar surpluses (Ramos 2007).

In the mid-1970s the military government created the Proálcool Program (National Ethanol Program) to stimulate the production and use of ethanol as fuel, particularly after the first oil shock. Scholars agreed that this strategy was part of a larger effort to decrease Brazil's dependence on imported sources of energy (Berger 2010; Demetrius 1990; Leite 1990). Under the Geisel government's Second National Development Plan (PND II), technological development and research became a central objective, which included reorienting energy policy to address high oil prices and investment in strategic sectors such as agriculture (Baumgarten 2008; Dias 2012). To promote ethanol production, several measures, such as low-interest loans, production targets, and price parity between ethanol and sugar, were adopted (Geller 2003; Leite 2009; Milanez and Nykos 2012; Ramos 2016). This policy reflected the influence of the sugar and automobile sectors. Most authors agree that the program served a dual purpose: to reduce oil imports and to protect the sugar industry, because soaring oil prices were accompanied by a sharp drop in the international price of sugar (Bermann 2001; Ramos 2016; Scandiffio 2005). Sugar prices declined more than 70 percent from 1974 to 1975 (Tourinho, Ferreira and Pimentel 1987); as a result, by the mid-1970s idle capacity was as high as 50 percent in some mills (Castro Santos 1993). The Proálcool not only mitigated the effects of the oil crisis and helped the sugar industry, but also served the interests of the auto industry. By the 1970s the Brazilian auto industry was well-established, and the car had become the main mode of transport, so the program, and later the adoption of ethanol-powered cars, were vital for the maintenance of profits and further expansion of the industry (Lorenzi 2018, 60).

In 1979 the second oil shock and a further rise in oil prices prompted the government to expand the program, providing incentives, such as fixed prices and tax reductions and exemptions, for the adoption of vehicles running exclusively on ethanol (Michellon, Santos, and Rodrigues 2008). As a result, ethanol production rose from 0.6 billion litter in 1975 to almost 12 billion liters in 1985 (Milanez and Nykos 2012, 67). Given the incentives and subsidies provided by the government, ethanol-powered vehicles were readily adopted by the population, and by 1986, 96 percent of all new vehicles sold were ethanol-powered (Unica 2007).

Despite the apparent success of the Proálcool Program, the debt crisis of the 1980s crippled the industry. Not only did incentives and subsidies virtually disappear, but ethanol as a substitute for fossil fuels remained unviable. Several studies emphasize the high production costs of biofuels compared with oil and its derivatives (Ferreira and Motta 1986; Pelin 1985; Tourinho, Ferreira, and Pimentel 1987). For example, enhancing the competitiveness of biomass-based fuels would require a transition period combined with a systematic policy aimed at reducing production costs (Pelin 1985). Others, in turn, argue that the government failed to create the right incentives for producers to invest and build distilleries at cost-effective rates; in other words, there was limited innovation and competitiveness due to protectionism (Ramos 2016, 63). The supply crisis of 1989–1990 further reflected the weakness of the industry, as ethanol production could not accompany the rapid increase in demand (Berger 2010; Ramos 2009, 2016). This was further aggravated by the removal of direct state intervention in the sugarcane agroindustry, extinction of the IAA, deregulation of the sector, and removal of subsidies and tax advantages. The liberalization of the sector was completed in 1999 when all price controls in the sugarcane agroindustry were abolished (Ramos 2016; Távora 2011). Unable to compete with fossil fuels, ethanol cars nearly disappeared from the market, and ethanol production remained stagnant until 2004.

In 2003 the industry experienced a rebirth with the introduction of flex-fuel vehicles: cars with engines that can run on either ethanol or gasoline. The sector experienced a wave of new investments; production rose from 12.6 billion liters in 2002 to 28.2 billion liters in 2010 (Milanez and Nykos 2012, 67). Sugarcane bagasse and straw, in turn, became widely used as an input for electricity generation in ethanol distilleries. As discussed in the electricity section of this paper, as reforms promoted the de-verticalization of the power sector, competition increased in the generation and commercialization segments.

Expansion of the production capacity of the ethanol sector was also boosted by the prospect of higher international demand. For instance, studies by the Centre for Strategic Studies of the University of Campinas (UNICAMP) and Organisation for Economic Co-operation and Development (OECD) estimated that given the proper public policies, world demand for ethanol could reach 150 billion liters by the second half of the 2010s (CGEE 2009; OECD 2010; Ramos 2016, 66). Put simply, there were expectations of ethanol becoming a *commodity* (Santos, Garcia, and Shikida 2015; Santos et al. 2016). In 2007 the presidents of Brazil and the United States—the two biggest producers of ethanol—launched an effort to promote ethanol and transform it into a global commodity. However, domestic policy failures and changing international perceptions of biofuels, especially related to the food security-energy nexus, defeated the prospects of the initiative (Afionis and Stringer 2014; Afionis et al. 2016). In an analysis of Brazil's failure to promote ethanol leadership internationally ("ethanol diplomacy"), Fröhlich (2018) suggests that the Brazilian government's priority in exploiting the pre-salt oil discoveries overshadowed efforts to promote ethanol as a global commodity. For others, while Brazil has the material and scientific resources to exercise leadership, its efforts lacked vision and direction (Afionis et al. 2016, 145).

Finally, recent studies have focused on the determinants of the most recent crisis in the sector, between 2009 and 2014. Multiple factors contributed to the recent crisis. Among the most cited in the literature are high credit costs due to the 2008 economic crisis (Mendonça, Pitta, and Xavier 2012; Santos, Garcia, and Shikida 2015; Santos et al. 2016); high production costs (Nachiluk and Oliveira 2013; Santos, Garcia, and Shikida 2015; Santos et al. 2016); low productivity, high capacity, and debt levels prompted by the period of optimism discussed previously (Santos, Garcia, and Shikida 2015; Santos et al. 2016); and controls imposed by the government on gasoline prices (Lorenzi 2018; Pereira 2015; Santos, Garcia, and Shikida 2015; Santos et al. 2016). Price control over gasoline is considered by many scholars to be the factor that has most negatively affected the performance of the ethanol industry in recent years since, as previously discussed, domestic gasoline prices were kept artificially low despite high international oil prices (Lorenzi 2018; Pereira 2015; Santos, Garcia, and Shikida 2015; Santos et al. 2016). Rousseff's pricing policy plunged Petrobras into debt and reduced the competitiveness of ethanol (Costa and Burnquist 2016). The end of the fuel price controls and higher oil prices has boosted ethanol production in recent years. Yet the competitiveness of the sector is not guaranteed, as the industry is affected by both internal and external factors and, since the liberalization, it lacks a long-term policy.

THE ELECTRICITY SECTOR

The main debate in the electricity sector revolves around (1) the tensions arising from federal- and state-level governments and (2) the recurring role of state intervention and supply crisis. As shown in Figure 25.1, renewable sources account for over 80 percent of the installed capacity (Brazil 2018, 14–17). Hydropower is the main source of electricity, accounting for over 65 percent of generating capacity.

The literature on electricity is often technical, written mostly by engineers and economists, or focused on public policy and regulation (Ferreira 2000; Kligermann 2009;

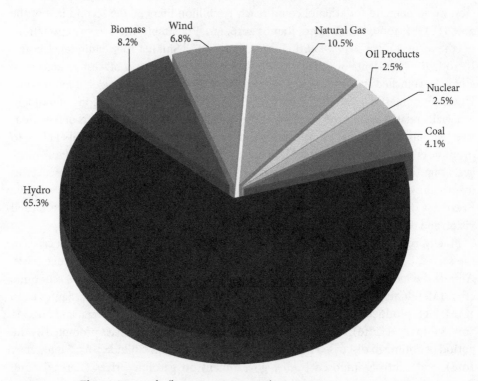

FIGURE 25.1 Electricity supply (by source type, 2018).

Source: Original chart based on data from National Energy Balance (2018).

Magalhães and Parente, 2009; Oliveira 2011; Santana 1993). Prior to the liberalization of the 1990s, discussions were mostly concerned with technical aspects of the integrated system or embedded into the overall development literature, as electricity was seen as an input to industrialization. Similar to the oil industry, the electricity sector has been characterized by state control, in which SOEs—Eletrobras and its subsidiaries—operated, planned, coordinated, and financed the development of the sector. This structure prevailed from the mid- to the late part of the twentieth century. In the 1990s liberal reforms yielded privatization, changes in regulations, and the establishment of the regulatory agency ANEEL.

The focus of earlier studies on electricity was on the importance of state control, born out of concerns over the dominant role of foreign companies as well as the persistent gap between generation capacity and increasing demand (Villela 1984). Starting in the late nineteenth century, the Brazilian electricity sector was primarily driven by private companies. Foreign capital investments in distribution and generation penetrated major cities as urbanization rapidly transformed the country. By the 1930s the sector had a capital structure that was predominantly foreign, decentralized, and geographically concentrated in large urban areas (Esposito 2012, 194–196; Pinto and Almeida 2007).

Vargas's industrialization plans identified electricity as a strategic and essential input to industrialization, which meant the dominance of foreign companies in power generation was incompatible with economic nationalism. In other words, foreign capital participation in electricity generation (as well as in other sectors) was extremely politicized (Oliveira 2009). In practice, state control began through the intensification of sectoral regulation. Until the 1930s, there was no comprehensive legislation, and the operation of the electricity sector was governed by concession contracts between private companies and federal, state, or municipal governments. A key provision in concession contracts was the "gold clause," which allowed tariffs to be automatically readjusted when the exchange rate was devalued (Pinto and Almeida 2007). After the 1930 Revolution, the regulation and control of the sector became part of the functions of the federal government. The Water Code, promulgated in 1934 (Decree 24643), became the basic legal instrument for the regulation of the sector, establishing the exclusive competence of the federal government to regulate the use of water resources (Corrêa 2005; Espósito Neto 2015). The gold clause was eliminated, and tariffs were established based on the historical cost of capital, with a fixed rate of return (Corrêa 2005; Pinto and Almeida 2007). State control over the sector was augmented by the Constitution of 1934, which incorporated many of the provisions of the Water Code and adopted the same principles of economic nationalism and federal rights over natural resources (Corrêa 2005; Federal Constitution of 1934, art. 5, ch. 1).

Most literature that analyzed developments in the 1940s and 1950s highlighted the persistence of tension between private sector and state regulation in the context of rapid urbanization and industrialization. There were intermittent supply crises as demand for power escalated and investments in the sector failed to catch up, leading to growing state intervention at the federal and state levels (Leite, 1997). To address investment problems in the sector, in 1954 Congress approved the creation of a tax on electricity consumption

(Imposto Único sobre Energia Elétrica–IUEE), which was channeled into the Federal Electrification Fund. However, it was only when the Kubitschek government's (1956–1961) national development plan (the Target Plan) was implemented that power generation issues were prioritized, receiving massive amounts of investment (Orenstein and Sochaczewski 1990). Baer and McDonald (1997, 16) argue that the period was also marked by a growing division of labor in the sector, where SOEs, both at the federal and state levels, were responsible for investments in electricity generation, while distribution remained in the hands of the private sector. There was, however, no proper policy of sectoral expansion or planning (Mercedes, Rico, and Pozzo 2015).

Despite the growing presence of the national state, coordination among electricity companies was poor or nonexistent. Scholars point to the establishment of Eletrobras in 1962 as the critical juncture that resolved the problems of coordination, lack of centralization, and investment (Ferreira 2000, 184; Oliveira 2009). The expansion of the sector was influenced by the continental dimensions of the country and the large hydroelectric potential (and dependence), which provided for significant economies of scale (Ferreira 2000, 184). The significant costs of building large plants and extensive transmission lines led to a model in which cooperation rather than competition was viewed as the most efficient option (Oliveira 2009). Therefore, centralization yielded not only the most efficient model in technical and economic terms, but it was also a politically acceptable arrangement given the predominance of state capitalism.

Through Eletrobras, the federal and state governments gradually took control of electricity generation, transmission, and distribution (Ferreira 2000; Walvis and Gonçalves 2014). Esposito (2012), however, argues that this period was characterized by a hybrid system that combined aspects of centralization and decentralization. While at the federal level Eletrobras and its subsidiaries controlled most of the generation and transmission network, the distribution of electricity—an activity once controlled by foreign private companies—was gradually transferred to the states. To a great extent, this decentralization of distribution reflected the nature of shared power in the Brazilian federal system (Oliveira 2009). In addition, wealthy states challenged and resisted centralization by establishing their own vertically integrated SOEs, which resulted in constant disputes between the state-level SOEs and Eletrobras (Ferreira 2000; Walvis and Gonçalves 2014, 27).

Notwithstanding the problems of partial centralization, Eletrobras was responsible for coordinating, financing, and planning sectoral expansion at the national level. It did so through its ability to manage significant financial resources. In significant ways, Eletrobras set targets and operated as a de facto "development bank" for the sector, financing projects it considered strategic (Walvis and Gonçalves 2014: 24). The company also directed the two main steering committees established to coordinate the sector: the Interconnected Operation Coordination Group (GCOI), created in 1973 to manage the interconnected grids; and the System Planning Coordination Group (GCPS), established in 1982 to plan generation and transmission expansion (Esposito 2012; Oliveira 2009; Walvis and Gonçalves, 2014). Scholars tend to consider the centralization and coordination achieved with the creation of Eletrobras successful (Ferreira 2000; Esposito 2012;

Oliveira 1976; Villela 1984). There was substantial expansion of transmission and generation capacity; for instance, the installed generation capacity increased from 4.8 GW in 1960 to 11.5 GW in 1970, 33.5 GW in 1980, and 53.1 GW in 1990 (Esposito 2012, 228). However, despite its apparent success, a number of factors undermined the financial structure of the sector and led to the exhaustion of the model and reform and privatization in the 1990s.

As mentioned previously, power generation was essential to industrialization. Electricity tariffs, then, became an instrument of industrial policy and of inflationary control (Esposito 2012, 199; Oliveira 2009; Walvis and Gonçalves 2014). Tariffs were also used to advance social policy. In an attempt to reduce regional economic disparities, the government introduced a single tariff regime throughout the country in 1974. Consequently, low-cost, efficient, and profitable companies were forced to transfer resources to high-cost, less efficient ones (Baer and McDonald 1997; Oliveira 2009). There was no incentive to control costs, which in turn resulted in a sharp deterioration of the financial health of electricity companies. Faced with a dearth of financial resources and a need to further invest, SOEs sought foreign loans, worsening the indebtedness of the sector. With the deterioration of the international economic environment in the early 1980s and rising international interest rates, external indebtedness became unsustainable. To exacerbate the financial difficulties of the sector, the 1988 Constitution redefined the spheres of responsibilities between the federal government, the states, and municipalities and promoted fiscal decentralization (Stepan 2000). In many ways, this was the prelude to the liberalization of the electricity sector and privatizations.

Similar to the oil industry, sectoral reforms commenced in 1993 and focused on market opening. Scholars have examined the multiple policies put in place to address the energy crisis, such as the abolition of the single tariff and leeway for electricity companies to charge tariffs based on their costs with an appropriate rate of return, increasing access for private firms to the federal transmission network, and establishment of an independent regulatory agency (Ferreira 2000; Oliveira 2009; Walvis and Gonçalves 2014). In 1995 Congress approved the Concessions Law (Law 8987), establishing the rules by which the state could grant concessions and initiating the privatization of the sector. The objectives of the reform were (a) de-verticalization, (b) privatization and introduction of competition, and (c) creation of an independent regulator (Mercedes et al. 2015; Santana 2015).

From 1995 onward, Cardoso expanded the scope of the privatization program by breaking up monopoly rights of state companies and giving state governors the freedom to launch their own privatization programs (Pinheiro 1999). Goldemberg and Prado (2003), however, argue that there were divergent views within the government on how to tackle the problems of the sector. On the one hand, there were those who believed that liberal reforms would lead to a rapid change in the role of the state since it would lead to the rise of markets and participation of multinational corporations. On the other, many technical experts of the electricity industry sought reforms within the existing organizations and structure of the sector (Goldemberg and Prado 2003). However, given that Cardoso was preoccupied with achieving fiscal balance and macroeconomic stability, sectoral liberalization and privatization became a credible option for the state. As with other sectors, the debate in the literature then focused on policy proposals to break from Brazil's developmentist past, as opposed to gradual reforms of the existing economic model.

As privatization plans rolled out, most studies have focused on the shortcomings and consequences of liberalization (Mello 1996; Pires, 2000; Sauer 2002; Santos et al. 2008; Mercedes et al. 2015). Scholars were critical of the government strategy, given that privatization was carried out in the absence of a regulatory framework and its main objective was to maximize revenues rather than develop a proper regulatory framework and long-term planning for the sector (Oliveira 2009; Santana 2015; Walvis and Gonçalves 2014). The privatization program, however, halted after the transfer to the private sector of about 60 percent of the distribution segment. The currency crises in Asia and Russia forced the government to devalue the currency, making privatization unattractive to investors (Tankha 2008). As a result, transmission remained in the hands of the state, which also retained control of about 80 percent of the generation capacity (Santana 2015).

The literature from 2000 onward focused on the limitations of the reforms carried out in the 1990s, particularly in the context of another supply crisis (Almeida and Pinto 2004; Mercedes et al. 2015; Oliveira 2009; Prado et al. 2016). Some scholars pointed to the complexity of the sector and flawed regulatory framework, which explain the low rates of private investment (Almeida and Pinto 2004; Oliveira 2009). Others stressed the negative effect of dismantling the planning structures and the weakening of Eletrobras (Goldemberg and Prado 2003; Santana 2015; Tankha 2008). As part of the reforms, Eletrobras's planning body was disbanded; its functions were then transferred to the Ministry of Mines and Energy, which did not have "the institutional set up to absorb such complex function" (Tankha 2008, 158). The crisis triggered further reforms, with emphasis on energy security and greater generation capacity (Prado et al. 2016), providing incentives for expanding capacity, notably of gas-based thermal plants (Almeida and Pinto 2004).

In 2003 Lula da Silva took power with the intention of introducing a new regulatory framework that prioritizes the security of supply, universalization of access, and low tariffs. The new framework—Laws 10847 and 10848 and Decree 5163—brought several changes, among them the removal of Eletrobras from the privatization program, the creation of the Energy Research Company (EPE) to centralize sectoral planning and coordination activities, and a commitment to principles of market competition (Tankha 2008).

However, under the current system, thermal plants are used to compensate for the reduced generation capacity of hydro-plants, particularly during periods of drought, at the expense of high emissions and financial costs (Prado et al. 2016). Yet any efforts to expand hydropower are deeply controversial given that unexplored resources are located in the Amazon region. While there are strong economic arguments in favor of dam building, the socio-ecological imprints of megaprojects are often intertwined with identity politics and contentious social mobilization. Scholars have focused on the direct and indirect impacts of exploration in the Amazon region, in terms of deforestation, and threats to biodiversity, local food security, culture, and traditional communities (Fearside 2002, 2004, 2005; Finer and Jenkins 2012; Prado et al. 2016; Reis and Bloemer 2001; Soito and Freitas 2011; Stickler et al. 2013). Yet without further investments in alternative sources, Brazil will continue to wrestle with the high economic and environmental costs of using thermal plants to meet its energy needs.

FUTURE RESEARCH AGENDA

The politics of energy governance in Brazil is an exciting field for political science, business, economics, and law. As the chapter elucidates, there is no consensus among scholars on what constitutes energy governance. Instead, researchers have focused on explaining distinctive energy sources and their relationship with Brazil's industrialization. We argue that energy security should be understood as part of a wider developmental strategy. However, there is still much needed research on Brazilian energy politics. There are at least three key areas for future research. First, we need a better understanding of the policy dynamics that underpin Brazil's changing model of governance and its impact on the country's energy matrix. Scholars agree that state capitalism is likely to stay, albeit modified and responsive to external factors, but how this is likely to impact energy policy and Brazil's continuing efforts to meet its energy needs remains a matter of investigation. Although we know that reforms separating ownership and management of SOEs have been partially successful in attaining greater efficiency, the penetration of market-oriented thinking within the Brazilian state can change policy direction, and in some cases, create contradictions within institutions. Researchers might be interested in looking at how policy continuity and change occur in the energy sector and beyond.

Second, the recent crisis and changing winds in Brazilian politics present an excellent opportunity to study political and economic development in an emerging market. While the election of Jair Bolsonaro indicates a move toward further liberalization, the extent to which he will succeed in implementing difficult reforms in strategic and politically sensitive sectors remains to be seen. Market reforms in Brazil are intrinsically political, subject to veto players constantly playing tug-of-war to draw the state inside and outside of the market (Kingstone 1999; Schneider 2016). The strategic position of energy—both renewable and nonrenewable—will mean that new policies or reformulations of old ones (for example, rules of domestic content) are bound to be path dependent. According to the Ministry of Mines and Energy, the oil, natural gas, and biofuels segments already have guaranteed investments of about R$800 billion (approximately US$194 billion at current exchange rates) until the end of the next decade (Rittner 2018). In a few years, Brazil is expected to become a net oil exporter; IEA estimates forecast that by 2022, net oil exports will pass one million barrels/day. These data point to continuing evidence for scholars to focus their research on energy policy as a vital component of industrial development.

Finally, we must introduce more "politics" into the analysis of energy policy in Brazil. For instance, Petrobras's technological development efforts and market dominant position are likely to be shaped by its ever-persistent relationship with the government. In Evans's (1995) words, "embedded autonomy" was the purview of Brazil's relative industrial success. Tracking the nature of relationships within state institutions (see Nem Singh and Chen 2018) is likely to be an important research field given that privatization of state assets and actual retreat of governments in strategically controlled industries are likely to face resistance from societal forces. Accordingly, Brazil's recurring electricity supply crisis is equally political because there are currently no viable alternatives to hydropower. With megaprojects conceived as highly politicized due to their complex environmental and social implications, environmental activism comes into contact with the national state over how to best promote sustainable development (Hochstetler and Keck 2007). Beyond hydropower, social scientists are equipped with the analytical tools to explore energy from a wider frame of reference, bringing into the discussion concepts such as energy justice, poverty, and the environment (McCauley 2018; Sovacool and Dworkin 2014).

In summary, energy policy in Brazil has been, and remains, a pragmatic approach to the energy needs of the country. Brazil is likely to keep its commitment to diversify its portfolio of energy resources, particularly in light of technological advances in renewable energy. Future researchers can therefore focus on how the Brazilian state is increasingly using market mechanisms amid a crisis context to design regulatory governance frameworks. While SOEs remain important, the economic crisis that hit Brazil is likely to reduce state participation in the further development of the sector. Hence, policies aimed at increasing private capital participation, including foreign players, might become an important source of sectoral development. How precisely the Brazilian state will facilitate this process will be a matter of empirical investigation.

Author Note

The views expressed in this chapter are those of the authors and do not reflect the official policy or position of the Brazilian government or any of its agencies.

Notes

1. The term *developmentalist* refers to the centralized and interventionist state that took shape after the 1930 revolution and lasted up to the mid-1980s (Massi 2014; Guimarães 2003).
2. Petrobras commissioned Walter Link from Jersey Standard to set up its exploration department and to assess the potential for oil exploration in every region of Brazil. In the Link Report, he stated that if Petrobras really wanted to find more oil, it should look offshore and overseas (Nem Singh 2012, 140).
3. In Brazil, ethanol is produced as anhydrous and as hydrated ethanol; the former is blended with gasoline, while the latter is used in flex-fuel cars.

References

Afionis, Stavros, and Lindsay C. Stringer. 2014. "The Environment as a Strategic Priority in the European Union–Brazil Partnership: Is the EU Behaving as a Normative Power or Soft Imperialist?" *International Environmental Agreements: Politics, Law and Economics* 14, no. 1: 47–64.

Afionis, Stravos, Lindsay C. Stringer, Nicola Favretto, Julia Tomeir, and Marcos S. Buckeridge. 2016. "Unpacking Brazil's Leadership in the Global Biofuels Arena: Brazilian Ethanol Diplomacy in Africa." *Global Environment Politics* 16, no. 3: 127–150.

Almeida, Edmar Luiz Fagundes, and Helder Queiroz Pinto Jr. 2004. "Reform in Brazilian Electricity Industry: The Search for a New Model." Energy Economics Group. Institute of Economics. Federal University of Rio de Janeiro. http://www.ie.ufrj.br/datacenterie/pdfs/seminarios/pesquisa/reform_in_brazilian_electricity_industry_the_search_for_a_ne.pdf.

Almeida, Mansueto, Renato Lima de Oliveira, and são Ross Schneider. 2014. "Política Industrial e Empresas Estatais no Brasil: BNDES e Petrobras." 2013 Texto para Discussão. Brasilia: IPEA.

Alveal, Edelmeria del Carmen. 1993. *Os Desbravadores: A Petrobras e a Construção do Brasil Industrial*. Rio de Janeiro: Relume/Dumara.

Amann, Edmund, Werner Baer, and Donald Coes, eds. 2011. *Energy, Biofuels and Development: Comparing Brazil and the United States*. London: Routledge.

Baer, Werner, and Curt McDonald. 1997. "Um Retorno ao Passado? A Privatização de Empresas de Serviços Públicos no Brasil: O Caso do Setor de Energia Elétrica." *Planejamento e Políticas Públicas* 16: 5–38.

Ban, Cornel. 2013. "Brazil's Liberal Neo-developmentalism: New Paradigm or Edited Orthodoxy?" *Review of International Political Economy* 20, no. 2: 298–331.

Baumgarten, Maíra. (2008). *Conhecimento e Sustentabilidade: Políticas de Ciência, Tecnologia e Inovação no Brasil Contemporâneo*. Porto Alegre: UFRGS.

Berger, Elena M. 2010. "Dynamics of Innovation of Biofuel Ethanol: Three Decades of Experience in the U.S. and Brazil." PhD thesis, Georgia Institute of Technology.

Bermann, Célio. 2001. *Energia no Brasil: Para quê? Para Quem? Crise e Alternativas para um País Sustentávesão*. Sao Paulo: FASE e Editora Livraria da Física.

Biasetto, Bruno. 2016. "The Poisoned Chalice: Oil and Macroeconomics in Brazil (1967–2003)." PhD diss., Georgetown University.

Birdsall, Nancy, and John Nellis. 2003. "Winners and Losers: Assessing the Distributional Impact of Privatization." *World Development* 31, no. 10: 1617–1633.

Brazil. Ministry of Mines and Energy. 2018. "National Energy Balance." http://epe.gov.br/pt/publicacoes-dados-abertos/publicacoes/balanco-nergetico-nacional-2018.

Bridgman, Benjamin, Victor Gomes, and Arilton Teixeira. 2011. "Threatening to Increase Productivity: Evidence from Brazil's Oil Industry." *World Development* 39, no. 8: 1372–1385.

Castro Santos, Maria Helena. 1993. *Política e Políticas de uma Energia Alternativa: O Caso do Proáalcool*. Rio de Janeiro: Notrya.

CGEE (Centro de Gestão e Estudos Estratégicos). 2009. *Bioetanol Combustível: Uma Oportunidade para o Brasil*. Brasília: CGEE.

Corrêa, Maria Letícia. 2005. "Contribuição para uma História da Regulamentação do Setor de Energia Elétrica no Brasil: O Código de Águas de 1934 e o Conselho Nacional de Águas e Energia Elétrica." *Política & Sociedade* 6: 255–291.

Costa, Cinthia Cabral, and Heloisa Lee Burnquist. 2016. "Impactos do Controle do Preço da Gasolina sobre o Etanol Biocombustível no Brasil." *Estudos Econômicos* 46, no. 4: 1003–1028.

Daland, Robert. 1981. *Exploring Brazilian Bureaucracy: Performance and Pathology*. Washington, DC: University Press of America.

Dantas, Eva, and Martin Bell. 2009. "Latecomer Firms and the Emergence and Development of Knowledge Networks: The Case of Petrobras in Brazil." *Resources Policy* 38, no. 5: 829–844.

Dantas, Eva, and Martin Bell. 2011. "The Co-Evolution of Firm-Centered Knowledge Networks and Capabilities in Late Industrializing Countries: The Case of Petrobras in the Offshore Oil Innovation System in Brazil." *World Development* 39, no. 9: 1570–1591.

De Biasi Cordeiro, Guilherme, Helder Queiroz Pinto, and José Cesário Cecchi. 2012. "Evaluating the Natural Gas Legal Framework in Brazil: Regulatory Reform Developments and Incompleteness." *The Journal of World Energy Law and Business* 5, no. 2: 114–124.

Dé Carli, Gileno. 1942. *Aspectos da Economia Açucareira*. Rio de Janeiro: Irmãos Pongetti.

De Negri, João Alberto, ed. 2011a. *Poder de Compra da Petrobras: Impactos Econômicos nos seus Fornecedores*. Vol. 1. Brasilia: IPEA and Petrobras.

De Negri, João Alberto, ed. 2011b. *Poder de Compra da Petrobras: Impactos Econômicos nos seus Fornecedores*. Vol. 2. Brasilia: IPEA and Petrobras.

De Negri, João Alberto, ed. 2011c. *Poder de Compra da Petrobras: Impactos Econômicos nos seus Fornecedores*. Vol. 3. Brasilia: IPEA and Petrobras.

Demetrius, Joseph F. 1990. *Brazil's National Alcohol Program: Technology and Development in an Authoritarian Regime*. New York: Praeger.

Dias, Rafael de Brito. 2012. *Sessenta Anos de Política Científica e Tecnológica*. Campinas: Editora UNICAMP.

Döring, Heike, Rodrigo Salles Pereira dos Santos, and Eva Pocher. 2017. "New Developmentalism in Brazil? The Need for Sectoral Analysis." *Review of International Political Economy* 24, no. 2: 332–362.

Drabik, Dusan, Harry de Gorter, David R. Just, and Govinda R. Timilsina. 2015. "The Economics of Brazil's Ethanol-Sugar Markets, Mandates, and Tax Exemptions." *American Journal of Agricultural Economics* 97, no. 5: 1433–1450.

EIA. U.S. Energy Information Administration. 2017. "Country Analysis Brief: Brazil." https://www.eia.gov/beta/international/analysis_includes/countries_long/Brazil/brazil.pdf.

Empresa de Pesquisa Energética (EPE). 2018. *Brazilian Energy Balance*. Rio de Janeiro. EPE.

Esposito, Alexandre Siciliano. 2012. "O Setor Elétrico Brasileiro e o BNDES: Reflexões sobre o Financiamento aos Investimentos e Perspectivas." BNDES. https://web.bndes.gov.br/bib/jspui/bitstream/1408/920/1/O%20setor%20el%C3%A9trico%20brasileiro%20e%20o%20BNDES_reflex%C3%B5es_P-final.pdf.

Espósito Neto, Tomaz. 2015. "Uma Análise Histórico-jurídica do Código de Águas (1934) e o Início da Presença do Estado no Setor Elétrico Brasileiro no Primeiro Governo Vargas." *História em Reflexão* 9, no. 17: 1–16.

Evans, Peter. 1979. *Dependent Development: The Alliance of Multinational, State, and Local Capital in Brazil*. Princeton, NJ: Princeton University Press.

Evans, Peter. 1981. "Collectivized Capitalism: Integrated Petrochemical Complexes and Capital Accumulation in Brazil." In *Authoritarian Capitalism: Brazil's Contemporary Political and Economic Development*, edited by Thomas Bruneau and Philippe Faucher, 85–125. Boulder, CO: Westview Press.

Evans, Peter. 1995. *Embedded Autonomy: States and Industrial Transformation*. Princeton, NJ: Princeton University Press.

Fearside, Phillip M. 2002. "Avança Brazil: Environmental and Social Consequences of Brazil's Planned Infrastructure in Amazonia." *Environmental Management* 30, no. 6: 735–747.

Fearside, Phillip M. 2004. "Greenhouse Gas Emissions from Hydroelectric Dams: Controversies Provide a Springboard for Rethinking a Supposedly 'Clean' Energy Source." *Climatic Change* 66, nos. 1–2: 1–8.

Fearside, Phillip M. 2005. "Do Hydroelectric Dams Mitigate Global Warming? The Case of Brazil's Curuá-Uma Dam." *Mitigation and Adaptation Strategies for Global Change* 10, no. 4: 675–691.

Ferreira, Carlos Kawall Leal. 2000. "Privatização do Setor Elétrico no Brasil." In *A Privatização no Brasil: O caso dos Serviços de Utilidade Pública*, edited by Armando Castelar Pinheiro and Kiichiro Fukasaku, 179–220. Rio de Janeiro: BNDES.

Ferreira, Léo da Rocha, and Ronaldo Serôa da Motta. 1986. "Reavaliação Econômica e Novos Ajustamentos do Proáalcool." *Revista Brasileira de Economia* 41, no. 1: 117–133.

Finer, Matt, and Clinton N. Jenkins. 2012. "Proliferation of Hydroelectric Dams in the Andean Amazon and Implications for Andes-Amazon Connectivity." *PLoS One* (April 18). doi:10.1371/journal.pone.0035126.

Fiori, José Luis. 2012. "Para Reler o 'Velho Desenvolvimentismo.'" https://www.cartamaior.com.br/?/Coluna/Para-reler-o-velho-desenvolvimentismo-/20888.

Florêncio, Pedro. 2016. "The Brazilian 2010 Oil Regulatory Framework and Its Crowding-out Investment Effects." *Energy Policy* 98: 378–389.

Font, Maurício. 2003. *Transforming Brazil: A Reform Era in Perspective*. Lanham, MD, & Oxford: Rowman and Littlefield Publishers.

Fröhlich, Thomas M. 2018. "Why Did Brazil's Ethanol Diplomacy Fail?" FGV Energia. https://fgvenergia.fgv.br/sites/fgvenergia.fgv.br/files/coluna_opiniao_novembro_-_ethanol_-_thomas_m.pdf

Galli, Ester. 2011. "Frame Analysis in Environmental Conflicts: The Case of Ethanol Production in Brazil." PhD thesis, Stockholm: Royal Institute of Technology (KTH).

Geller, Howard. 2003. *Energy Revolution*. Washington, DC: Island Press.

Goldemberg, José, and José Roberto Moreira. 2005. "Política Energética no Brasil." *Estudo Avançados* 19, no. 55: 215–228. http://www.scielo.br/pdf/%0D/ea/v19n55/14.pdf.

Goldemberg, José. 2018. "Energy in Brazil: Past and Future." In *The Oxford Handbook of the Brazilian Economy*, edited by Edmund Amann, Carlos Azzoni, and Werner Baer, 358–376. Oxford: Oxford University Press.

Goldemberg, José, and Luiz Tadeu Siqueira Prado. 2003. "Reforma e Crise do Setor Elétrico no Período FHC." *Tempo Social* 15, no. 2: 219–235.

Goldemberg, José, Roberto Schaeffer, Alexandre Szklo, and Rodrigo Lucchesi. 2014. "Oil and Gas Prospects in South America: Can the Petroleum Industry Pave the Way for Renewables in Brazil?" *Energy Policy* 64: 58–70.

Goldstein, Andrea. 1999. "Brazilian Privatization in International Perspective: The Rocky Path from State Capitalism to Regulatory Capitalism." *Industrial and Corporate Change* 8, no. 4: 673–711.

Gudmestad, Ove, Anatoli Zolotukin, and Erik Jarlsby. 2010. *Development of Petroleum Resources with Emphasis on Offshore Fields*. Southampton/Boston: WIT Press.

Guimarães, Alexandre Queiroz. 2003. "Institutions, State Capacity and Economic Development: The Political Economy of Import Substitution Industrialization in Brazil." PhD thesis, University of Sheffield.

Hagopian, Frances. 1996. *Traditional Politics and Regime Change in Brazil*. Cambridge, UK: Cambridge University Press.

Hochstetler, Kathryn, and Margaret Keck. 2007. *Greening Brazil. Environmental Activism in State and Society*. Durham, NC: Duke University Press.

Hunter, Wendy. 2010. *The Transformation of the Workers' Party in Brazil, 1989–2009*. Cambridge, UK: Cambridge University Press.

Hunter, Wendy, and Timothy Power. 2019. "Bolosonaro and Brazil's Illiberal Backlash." *Journal of Democracy* 30, no. 1: 68–82.

Katz, Andrea S. 2018. "Making Brazil Work? Brazilian Coalitional Presidentialism at 30 and its Post-*Lava Jato* Prospects." *Revista de Investigações Constitucionais* 5, no. 3: 77–102.

Kingstone, Peter. 1999. *Crafting Coalitions for Reform: Business Preferences, Political Institutions, and Neoliberal Reform in Brazil*. University Park: Pennsylvania State University Press.

Kingstone, Peter, and Timothy Power. 2017. *Democratic Brazil Divided*. Pittsburgh: Pittsburgh University Press.

Kligermann, Alberto S. 2009. "Um Sistema de Apoio à Decisão Bicritério para o Planejamento da Operação Energética." PhD thesis, Fluminense Federal University.

Leite, Antonio Dias. 1997. *A Energia do Brasil*. Rio de Janeiro: Editora Nova Fronteira.

Leite, Antonio Dias. 2009. *Energy in Brazil*. London: Earthscan.

Leite, Antonio Dias. 2014. *A Energia do Brasil. 3a Edição. Revista e Atualizada*. Rio de Janeiro: Lexikon.

Leite, Rogério Cézar de Cerqueira. 1990. *Pro-Álcool—A Única Alternativa para o Futuro*. Campinas: Editora Unicamp.

Lessa, Carlos. 1964. "Fifteen Years of Economic Policy in Brazil." *Economic Bulletin for Latin America* 2 (December):.

Lorenzi, Bruno Rossi. 2018. "Etanol de Segunda Geração no Brasil: Política e Translações." PhD thesis, Federal University of São Carlos.

Maceda e Silva, Antonio Carlos. 1985. *Petrobras: A Consolidação do Monopólio Estatal e Empresa Privada*. Campinas: Instituto de Economia-Campinas.

Magalhães, Gerusa, and Virginia Parente. 2009. "Do Mercado Atacadista à Câmara de Comercialização de Energia Elétrica: A Evolução de um Novo Paradigma Regulatório no Brasil." *Revista Brasileira de Energia* 15, no. 2: 55–79.

Mahdavi, Paasha. 2014. "Why Do Leaders Nationalize the Oil Industry? The Politics of Resource Expropriation." *Energy Policy* 75: 228–243.

Mancini, Lorenzo, and María José Paz. 2018. "Oil Sector and Technological Development: Effects of the Mandatory Research and Development (R&D) Investment Clause on Oil Companies in Brazil." *Resources Policy* 58: 131–143.

Martines-Filho, João, Heloisa L. Burnquist, and Carlos E. F. Vian. 2006. "Bioenergy and the Rise of Sugarcane-Based Ethanol in Brazil." *Choice* 21, no. 2: 91–96.

Massi, Eliza. 2014. "The Political Economy of Development Finance: The BNDES and Brazilian Industrialization." PhD thesis, SOAS, University of London.

McCauley, Darren. 2018. *Energy Justice: Re-balancing the Trilemma of Security, Poverty and Climate Change*. London: Palgrave Macmillan.

Mello, Maria Figueira. 1996. "Os Impasses da Privatização do Setor Elétrico." Discussion Paper no. 365. PUC-RIO. www.econ.puc-rio.br/biblioteca.php/trabalhos/download/1235.

Mendes, Pietro, Jeremy Hall, Stelvia Matos, and Bruno Silvestre. 2014. "Reforming Brazil's Offshore Oil and Gas Safety Regulatory Framework: Lessons from Norway, the United Kingdom, and the United States." *Energy Policy* 74: 443–453.

Mendonça, Maria Luisa, Fábio T. Pitta, and Carlos V. Xavier. 2012. "A Agroindústria Canavieira e a Crise Econômica Mundial: Rede Social de Justiça e Direitos Humanos." https://www.social.org.br/relatorioagrocombustiveis2012.pdf.

Mercedes, Sonia Seger Pereira, Julieta A. P. Rico, and Liliana de Ysasa Pozzo. 2015. "Uma Revisão Histórica do Planejamento do Setor Elétrico Brasileiro." *Revista USP* 104: 13–36.

Michellon, Ednaldo, Ana Aracelly L. Santos, and Juliano R. A. Rodrigues. 2008. "Breve Descrição do Proálcool e Perspectivas Futuras para o Etanol Produzido no Brasil." Sociedade Brasileira de Economia, Adminstração e Sociologia Rural. http://www.sober.org.br/palestra/9/574.pdf.

Milanez, Artur Yabe, and Deigo Nykos. 2012. "O Futuro do Setor Sucroenergético e o Papel do BNDES." https://www.bndes.gov.br/SiteBNDES/bndes/bndes_pt/Galerias/Convivencia/ Publicacoes/Consulta_Expressa/Tipo/BNDES_Setorial/201210_11.html.

Milanez, Bruno, and Rodrigo Salles Pereira dos Santos. 2015. "Topsy-Turvy Neo-Developmentalism: An Analysis of the Current Brazilian Model of Development." *Revista de Estudios Sociales* 53: 12–28.

Modiano, Eduardo. 2000. "Um Balanço das Privatizações nos Anos 90." https://www.bndes. gov.br/SiteBNDES/bndes/bndes_pt/Galerias/Convivencia/Publicacoes/Consulta_ Expressa/Tipo/Livro/200002_1.html.

MPF. Federal Prosecutor's Office. 2018. "Operação Lava Jato." http://www.mpf.mp.br/grandes-casos/lava-jato, http://www.mpf.mp.br/para-o-cidadao/caso-lava-jato.

Nachiluk, Katia, and Marli D. M. Oliveira. 2013. "Cana-de-acucar: Custos nos Diferentes Sistemas de Producao nas Regiões do Estado de São Paulo." *Informações Econômicas* 43, no. 4: 45–81.

National Agency of Petroleum, Natural Gas and Biofuels (ANP). *ANP Annuário 2016*, Rio de Janeiro: ANP, 2016.

Nem Singh, Jewellord. 2012. "States, Markets and Labour Unions: The Political Economy of Oil and Copper in Brazil and Chile." PhD thesis, University of Sheffield.

Nem Singh, Jewellord. 2014. "Towards Post-neoliberal Resource Politics? The International Political Economy (IPE) of Oil and Copper in Brazil and Chile." *New Political Economy* 19, no. 3: 329–358.

Nem Singh, Jewellord, and Geoffrey Chen. 2018. "State-owned Enterprises and the Political Economy of State-State Relations in the Developing World." *Third World Quarterly* 39, no. 6: 1077–1097.

Nem Singh, Jewellord, and Eliza Massi. 2016. "Resource Nationalism and Brazil's Post-neoliberal Strategy." In *The Political Economy of Natural Resources and Development: From Neoliberalism to Resource Nationalism*, edited by Paul A. Haslam and Pablo Heidrich, 158–186. Abingdon: Routledge.

Nem Singh, Jewellord, and Eliza Massi. 2018. "Industrial Policy and State-making: Brazil's Attempt at Oil-based Industrialization." *Third World Quarterly* 39, no. 6: 1133–1150.

OECD (Organization for Economic Co-operation and Development). 2010. *OECD-FAO Agricultural Outlook 2010–2019*. Paris: OECD/FAO.

Oliveira, Adilson. 2009. "Political Economy of the Brazilian Power Industry Reform." In *The Political Economy of Power Sector Reform*, edited by David G. Victor, 31–75. Cambridge, UK: Cambridge University Press.

Oliveira, Adilson. 2011. "Setor Elétrico: Desafios e Oportunidades." CEPAL-IPEA Discussion Paper. http://repositorio.ipea.gov.br/bitstream/11058/1376/1/TD_1551.pdf.

Oliveira, Adilson. 2012. "Brazil's Petrobras: Strategy and Performance." In *Oil and Governance: State-Owned Enterprises and the World Energy Supply*, edited by David Victor, David Hults, and Mark Thurber, 515–556. Cambridge, UK: Cambridge University Press.

Oliveira, Adilson, Eduardo Pontual Ribeiro Rosemarie Bröker Bone, and Luciano Losekann. 2011. "Energy Restrictions to Growth: The Past, Present and Future of Energy Supply in Brazil." In *Energy, Bio Fuels and Development: Comparing Brazil and the United States*, edited by Edmund Amann, Warner Baer ad Donald Coes, 51–64. London: Routledge.

Oliveira, Eliézer Rizzo. 1976. *As Forças Armadas: Política e Ideologia no Brasil (1964–1969)*. Petropolis, RJ: Editora Vozes Ltda.

Orenstein, Luiz, and Antonio Claudio Sochaczewski. 1990. "Democracia com Desenvolvimento: 1956–1961." In *A Ordem do Progresso: Cem Anos de Política Econômica Republicana*, edited by Marcelo de Paiva Abreu, 171–195. Rio de Janeiro: Editora Campos.

Pelin, Eli Roberto. 1985. *Avaliação Econômica do Álcool Hidratado Carburante no Curto e Médio Prazos*. São Paulo: IPEA.

Pereira, Wellington da Silva. 2015. "A Participação do Estado no Fomento ao Etanol como uma Oportunidade Estratégica de Desenvolvimento Econômico: As Políticas Federais de Estímulo ao Etanol no Brasil e nos EUA." PhD thesis, Parana Federal University.

Perucci, Gadiel. 1978. *A Republica das Usinas*. Rio de Janeiro: Paz e Terra.

Philip, George. 1982. *Oil and Politics in Latin America: Nationalist Movements and State Companies*. Cambridge, UK: Cambridge University Press.

Pinheiro, Armando Castelar. 1999. "Privatização no Brasil: Por Quê? Até Onde? Até Quando?" In *A Economia Brasileira nos Anos 90*, edited by Fabio Giambiagi and Maurício Mesquita Moreira, 147–182. Rio de Janeiro: BNDES.

Pinto, Eduardo Costa, José Paulo Guedes Pinto, Grasiela Baruco, Alexis Saludijan, Paulo Balanco, Carlos Schonerwald, et al. 2016. "A Economia Política dos Governos Dilma: Acumulação, Bloco no Poder e Crise." IE-UFRJ Texto Para Discussao no. 004, Rio de Janeiro.

Pinto, Helder Queiroz, Jr., and Edmar Fagundes de Almeida. 2007. *Economia da Energia: Fundamentos Econômicos, Evolução Histórica e Organização Industrial*. Rio de Janeiro: Elsevier.

Pires, José Caludio Linhares. 2000. "Desafios da Reestruturação do Setor Elétrico Brasileiro." Discussion Paper no. 76. BNDES. https://www.bndes.gov.br/SiteBNDES/export/sites/default/bndes_pt/Galerias/Arquivos/conhecimento/td/Td-76.pdf.

Postali, Fernando. 2009. "Petroleum Royalties and Regional Development in Brazil: The Economic Growth of Recipient Towns." *Resources Policy* 34, no. 4: 205–213.

Postali, Fernando, and Marislei Nishijima. 2013. "Oil Windfalls in Brazil and their Long-term Social Impacts." *Resources Policy* 38, no. 1: 94–101.

Prado, Fernando Alemeida, Jr., Simone Athayde, Joann Mossa, Stephanie Bohlman, Flavia Leite, and Anthony Oliver-Smith. 2016. "How Much Is Enough? An Integrated Examination of Energy Security, Economic Growth and Climate Change Related to Hydropower Expansion in Brazil." *Renewable and Sustainable Energy Reviews* 53: 1132–1136.

Priest, Tyler. 2007. *The Offshore Imperative: Shell Oil's Search for Petroleum in Post War America*. College Station, TX: A&M Press.

Priest, Tyler. 2016. "Petrobras in the History of Offshore Oil." In *New Order and Progress: Development and Democracy in Brazil*, edited by Ben Ross Schneider, 53–77. Oxford: Oxford University Press.

Ramírez-Cendrero, Juan, and Maria Paz. 2013. "How Important Are National Companies for Oil and Gas Sector Performance? Lessons from the Bolivian and Brazilian Case Studies." *Energy Policy* 61: 706–716.

Ramírez-Cendrero, Juan, and Maria Paz. 2017. "Oil Fiscal Regimes and National Oil Companies: A Comparison between Pemex and Petrobras." *Energy Policy* 101: 473–483.

Ramos, Pedro. 1999. *Agroindústria Canavieira e Propriedade Fundiária no Brasil*. São Paulo: Hucitec.

Ramos, Pedro. 2001. "O Mercado Mundial de Açúcar no Período 1930–1960." *Revista de Política Agrícola* 4: 26–33.

Ramos, Pedro. 2007. "Os Mercados Mundiais de Açúcar e a Evolução da Agroindústria Canavieira do Brasil entre 1930 e 1980: Do Açúcar ao Álcool para o Mercado Interno." *Economia Aplicada* 11, no. 4: 559–585.

Ramos, Pedro. 2009. "A Agroindústria no Sistema de Biocombustíveis." In *Agroindústria: Uma Análise no Contexto Socioeconômico e Jurídico Brasileiro*, edited by Darcy W. Zibetti and Lucas A. Barroso, 239–259. São Paulo: LEUD.

Ramos, Pedro. 2016. "Trajetória e Situação Atual da Agroindústria Canavieira do Brasil e do Mercado de Álcool Carburante." In *Quarenta Anos de Etanol em Larga Escala no Brasil: Desafios, Crises e Perspectivas*, edited by Gesmar Rosa dos Santos, 257–282. Brasília: IPEA.

Ramos Xavier, Carlos Eduardo, Jr. 2012. "Políticas de Conteúdo Local no Setor Petrolífero: O Caso Brasileiro e a Experiência Internacional." 1775 Texto para Discussão, Brasilia: IPEA.

Randall, Laura. 1993. *The Political Economy of Brazilian Oil*. Westport, CT: Praeger.

Regitano d'Arce, Marisa Aparecida, Thais Maria Ferreira de Souza Vieria, and Thiago Libório Romanelli. 2009. *Agroenergy and Sustainability*. São Paulo: Editora da Universidade de São Paulo.

Reis, Maria José, and Neusa Maria Sens Bloemer. 2001. *Hidroelétricas e Populações Locais*. Florianopolis: Editora Cidade Futura.

Ribeiro, Barbara Esteves. 2013. "Beyond Commonplace Biofuels: Social Aspects of Ethanol." *Energy Policy* 57: 355–362.

Rittner, Daniel. 2018. "Petróleo e Gás Vão Movimentar R$1,2 Tri Até 2030." Valor Economico. https://www.valor.com.br/brasil/5398535/petroleo-e-gas-vao-movimentar-r-12-tri-ate-2030.

Sant Ana, Paulo Henrique de Melo, Gilberto de Martino Jannuzzi, and Sérgio Bajay. 2009. "Developing Competition while Building up the Infrastructure of the Brazilian Gas Industry." *Energy Policy* 37: 308–317.

Santana, Carlos Henrique Vieira. 2015. "Políticas de Infraestrutura Energética e Capacidades Estatais nos BRICS." Discussion Paper 2045. Institute of Applied Economic Research (IPEA). http://www.ipea.gov.br/portal/index.php?option=com_content&view=article&id=24684

Santana, Eduardo Alves. 1993. "Questões Fundamentais para o Estudo da Economia de Escala do Setor Elétrico Brasileiro." *Textos de Economia* 4, no. 1: 53–62.

Santos, Antônio Galvão, Eduardo Kaplan Barbosa, José Francisco Sanches da Silva, and Ronaldo da Silva de Abreu. 2008. "Por que as Tarifas Foram para os Céus? Propostas para o Setor Elétrico Brasileiro." *Revista do BNDES* 14, no. 29: 435–474.

Santos, Gesmar Rosa, ed. 2016a. *Quarenta Anos de Etanol em Larga Escala no Brasil: Desafios, Crises e Perspectivas*. Brasília: IPEA.

Santos, Gesmar Rosa dos. 2016b. "A Produtividade na Agroindústria Canavieira: Uma Olhada a Partir da Etapa Agrícola." In *Quarenta Anos de Etanol em Larga Escala no Brasil: Desafios, Crises e Perspectivas*, edited by Gesmar Rosa dos Santos, 165–186. Brasília: IPEA.

Santos, Germar Rosa, Eduardo Afonso Garcia, and Pery Francisco Assis Shikida. 2015. "A Crise na Produção do Etanol e as Interfaces com as Políticas Públicas." *Radar* 39: 27–38.

Santos, Gesmar Rosa, Eduardo Afonso Garcia, Pery Francisco Assis Shikida, and Darcy Jacob Rissardi Jr. 2016. "A Agroindústria Canavieira e a Produção de Etanol no Brasil: Características, Potenciais e Perfil da Crise Atual." In *Quarenta Anos de Etanol em Larga Escala no Brasil: Desafios, Crises e Perspectivas*, edited by Gesmar Rosa dos Santos, 17–46. Brasília: IPEA.

Santos, Gesmar Rosa dos, and Magda Eva S. de Faria Wehrmann. 2016. "Desafios e Caminhos da Pesquisa e Inovação no Setor Sucroenergético no Brasil." In *Quarenta Anos de Etanol em Larga Escala no Brasil: Desafios, Crises e Perspectivas*, edited by Gesmar Rosa dos Santos, 257–282. Brasília: IPEA.

Santos, Jeronimo Alves, and Joaquim Bento de Souza Ferreira Filho. 2017. "Substituição de Combustíveis Fósseis por Etanol e Biodiesel no Brasil e seus Impactos Econômicos: Uma Avaliação do Plano Nacional de Energia 2030." *Pesquisa e Planejamento Econômico* 47, no. 3: 185–216.

Sauer, Ildo. 2002. "Um Novo Modelo para o Setor Elétrico Brasileiro." University of São Paulo. https://professorildosauer.files.wordpress.com/2010/01/umnovomodeloparaosetoreletri-codez2002.pdf.

Scandiffio, Mirna I. G. 2005. "Análise Prospectiva do Álcool Combustível no Brasil—Cenário 2004–2014." PhD thesis, University of Campinas.

Schneider, Ben Ross. 2016. *New Order and Progress: Development and Democracy in Brazil.* Oxford: Oxford University Press.

Schutte, Giorgio Romano, and Pedro Silva Barros. 2010. "A Geopolítica do Etanol." *Boletim de Economia e Política Internacional* 1: 33–43.

Shirley, Mary. 1999. "Bureaucrats in Business: The Roles of Privatization versus Corporatization in State-owned Enterprise Reform." *World Development* 27, no. 1: 115–136.

Sikkink, Kathryn. 1991. *Ideas and Institutions: Developmentalism in Brazil and Argentina.* Ithaca, NY: Cornell University Press.

Skidmore, Thomas. 1986. *Politics in Brazil: 1930–1964.* New York: Oxford University Press.

Smith, Peter Seaborn. 1976. *Oil and Politics in Modern Brazil.* Toronto: Macmillan of Canada.

Soito, João Leonardo da Silva, and Marcos Aurélio Vasconcelos Freitas. 2011. "Amazon and the Expansion of Hydropower in Brazil: Vulnerability, Impacts and Possibilities for Adaptation to Global Climate Change." *Renewable and Sustainable Energy Reviews* 15, no. 6: 3165–3177.

Sola, Lourdes. 1982. "The Political and Ideological Constraints to Economic Management in Brazil, 1945–1963." PhD thesis, Oxford University.

Sovacool, Benjamin, and Michael Dworkin. 2014. *Global Energy Justice: Problems, Principles, Practices.* Cambridge, UK: Cambridge University Press.

Stepan, Alfred. 1973. *Authoritarian Brazil: Origins, Policies and Future.* New Haven, CT: Yale University Press.

Stepan, Alfred. 1981. *The Military in Politics: Changing Patterns in Brazil.* Princeton, NJ: Princeton University Press.

Stepan, Alfred. 2000. "Brazil's Decentralized Federalism: Bringing Government Closer to the Citizens?" *Deadalus* 129, no. 2: 145–169.

Stickler, Claudia M., Michael T. Coe, Marcos H. Costa, Daniel C. Nepstad, David G. McGrath, Livia C. P. Dias, Hermann O. Rodrigues, et al. 2013. "Dependence of Hydropower Energy Generation on Forests in the Amazon Basin at Local and Regional Scales." *Proceedings of the National Academy of Sciences of the United States of America* 110, no. 23: 9601–9606.

Tankha, Sunil. 2008. "From Market to Plan: Lessons from Brazilian Power Reforms on Reducing Risks in the Provision of Public Services." *Policy and Society* 27: 151–162.

Tavora, Fernando Lagares. 2011. "História e Economia dos Biocombustíveis no Brasil." Discussion Paper 89. National Senate Consulting and Studies Centre.

Tourinho, Otávio A. F., Léo R. Ferreira, and Ruderico F. Pimentel. 1987. "Agricultura e Produção de Energia: Um Modelo de Programação Linear para Avaliação do Proálcool." *Pesquisa e Planejamento Econômico* 17, no. 1: 19–63.

Trebat, Thomas. 1982. *Brazil's State-owned Enterprises: A Case Study of the State as Entrepreneur.* Cambridge, UK: Cambridge University Press.

Trojbicz, Beni. 2017. "Ideas and Economy in the Policy Reforms of the Brazilian Oil Sector: 1995 to 2010." *Brazilian Journal of Public Administration* 51, no. 5: 767–787.

Tyler, Priest. 2016. "Petrobras in the History of Offshore Oil." In *New Order and Progress: Development and Democracy in Brazil*, edited by Ben Ross Schneider, 53–77. Oxford: Oxford University Press.

UNICA (União da Indústria de Cana-de-Açucar). 2007. "Produção e Uso do Etanol Combustível no Brasil." http://arquivos.ambiente.sp.gov.br/etanolverde/producao_etanol_unica.pdf.

Victor, David G. 2013. "National Oil Companies and the Future of the Oil Industry." *Annual Review of Resource Economics* 5: 445–462.

Villela, Annibal Villanova. 1984. *Empresas do Governo como Instrumento de Política Econômica: Os Sistemas Siderbrás, Eletrobrás, Petrobrás e Telebrás*. Rio de Janeiro: IPEA.

Walvis, Alida, and Edson Daniel Lopes Gonçalves. 2014. "Avaliação das Reformas Recentes no Setor Elétrico Brasileiro e sua Relação com o Desenvolvimento do Mercado Livre de Energia." FGV CERI. https://ceri.fgv.br/publicacoes/avaliacao-das-reformas-recentes-no-setor-eletrico-brasileiro-e-sua-relacao-com-o, https://bibliotecadigital.fgv.br/dspace/bitstream/10438/18588/avaliacao_das_reformas_recentes_no_setor_eletrico_brasileiro.pdf.

CHAPTER 26

THE ENERGY POLITICS
OF VENEZUELA

ANTULIO ROSALES AND MIRIAM SÁNCHEZ

THE discovery of an oil well in 1921 in the Maracaibo Basin created an indissoluble link between oil and Venezuela's economic and political evolution. The response from various social strata to the discovery of the largest oil reserves in the country was an augury of the change in social dynamics that the oil industry would bring to Venezuela. Political and economic elites and transnational oil interests celebrated the country's initial pumping of 100,000 barrels of oil per day (bpd), indicating the enormous reserves remaining below the nation's surface (Tinker 2015). Then Juan Vicente Gomez, a caudillo who ruled the country with an iron fist, granted concessions that permitted more than one hundred foreign oil companies to enter Venezuela. The rural population that lived near the wells saw their lives completely transformed. The oil discoveries provided many Venezuelans with one of the highest standards of living in Latin America, while a significant part of the population continued to live in poverty. For instance, while a handful of powerful families monopolized land, thousands of Venezuelans had to be relocated due to the first extraction works. This conflict of interests between those who viewed the discovery as a potential source of wealth and those who suffered the negative consequences of the economic model persisted throughout most of the twentieth century (Johnson 2018).

Venezuela has historically been a significant oil producer globally, and it is crucial to analyze how different governments have used this fact to improve their positions or even challenge power structures in the international system. With 302 billion barrels of untapped reserves, the country has the world's largest oil reservoir (Petróleos de Venezuela 2017). Most of these are unconventional heavy and extra-heavy crudes located in the Orinoco River belt. Nevertheless, Venezuela's presence in the global oil market is also changing rapidly. From 1929 until the late 1960s, Venezuela was the world's largest oil exporter (Salazar-Carrillo and West 2004). Today it exports less than one million bpd, and the national oil company (NOC), Petróleos de Venezuela (PDVSA), is nearing bankruptcy.

Oil is central to understanding Venezuelan economic development and has also shaped political attitudes and social values that prevail in large sectors of the population. Even before the nationalization of the industry, the population recognized the centrality of oil to Venezuela's development. Political disagreements have focused on appropriation, control, and distribution of the rents but have not challenged the rentier model. Alternatives to rentierism, focused on the need for economic diversification, have failed, and Venezuela remains dependent on oil (Monaldi 2018). The significance of the Venezuelan experience lies in its potential to provide insights for the political development of other oil-dependent states (Coronil 1997; Di John 2009; Karl 1997; McBeth 1983; Tugwell 1975).

The objective of this chapter is to explain how oil wealth has shaped state-society relations in Venezuela and positioned the nation as a major producer in regional and global markets. The rents, or payments in excess of production costs, associated with oil extraction in Venezuela have remodeled the nation's power relations, rent distribution logics, state-business relations, and collective identities, making it impossible to abandon the oil-development model. Venezuela's economy remains dependent on the oil industry not only for exports but also for government revenue. Political science scholarship on the politics of oil in Venezuela has been concerned with two overall debates: (1) the social uses of oil wealth and (2) the state's relationship with the oil industry.

The first debate, on the state's use of oil wealth for the improvement of society as a whole, focuses on how oil wealth and dependence on rents have molded sociocultural features of Venezuelan society (Coronil 1997; Karl 1997; Urbaneja 2013). Regardless of transformations in the appropriation and distribution of oil rents throughout Venezuelan history, the desire for control over them remains constant, and decisions on how the money is spent depend on politics rather than economic principles. During oil booms, different forms of rent distribution have contributed to social improvements, yet today's deep crisis questions the validity of these policies, especially in the past two decades. Criticisms directed toward Venezuela's current situation often refer to resource curse arguments, as if the failure of resource-rich countries to benefit adequately from natural resource endowment is a universal truth. The curse thesis rightly questions links between extraction and development; however, it is essential to avoid the determinism prevalent in much of this literature. Rather, categorizing the curses of extraction into external, internal, and intrinsic sheds light on the parallelisms and divergences between the different developmental extractive cases and makes it possible to identify the trends that are unique to Venezuela.

The second debate regarding Venezuela's oil politics concerns the state's relations with the oil industry. The evolution of alliances, tensions, control, and ruptures between the state and international oil companies (IOCs) or its own NOC in charge of extracting, transporting, refining, and trading oil has been at the center of Venezuela's role as a global oil producer (Boué 2002, 1993; Dunning 2010; Manzano and Monaldi 2010; Mommer 2002, 2010, 1999; Philip 1999; Rosales 2018). From 1943 until 1975, Venezuela specialized in regulating oil concessionaires and extracting rents from them via royalties and taxes. Despite formally exerting full control over the company as sole stakeholder, the state struggled with PDVSA, which behaved autonomously, like "a state within the state" (Rodríguez Araque 1997; Mommer 2003). These struggles have been at the core of Venezuela's contemporary political shifts and the ultimate control over PDVSA by the government and explain the fate of today's crisis in the sector. The problems explored here are internal and relate to the state's weakening institutional framework and descent into authoritarianism. They also reflect elites' lack of incentive to solve problems inherent to the extraction model and break away from rent dependence.

These discussions illuminate the reasons behind the paradoxical mismatch between the country's capacity as a major oil producer and its currently indebted and inefficient industry. Although Venezuela is a crucial case of rentier society, one standard model of rentier society does not exist. Thus it is essential to question the rentier state paradigm, which automatically links natural resources extraction to authoritarian regimes, explained by the state capacity to appropriate an essential part of the rent income, and the distribution of it creates political legitimation. Analysis of Venezuela's rentier society provides insights into the challenging question of why political and economic decisions to decrease oil dependence and transform the country's development model have not worked. For instance, the Bolivarian Revolution that followed the accession of Hugo Chávez in 1999 encouraged rent-seeking, instead of productive, activity by avoiding both domestic taxation and the systems of accountability associated with it (Rapier 2017).[1] Yet these approaches have conceptual and methodological defects that complicate a proper understanding of rentier societies. For instance, a central argument shared by opponents of the resource curse thesis is that resource-dependent countries lack sound institutions, accountability, and efficiency. These deficiencies cannot be accepted uncritically; rather, it is necessary to recognize regional and national differences, including how the distribution of the oil rent generates social inequalities, privileges, and exclusion, and shapes class structures.

The Blessing of the Oil Curse and the Magic of Rentier Capitalism

Venezuela holds the world's largest oil reserves and is one of the most troubled economies on the globe. Distorted government policies, soaring levels of corruption, authoritarianism, and a reckless political agenda have fueled the crisis. Why have some oil-rich countries ended up performing worse than resource-poor countries? Scholars in economics, political science, development, and international studies regularly discuss this question as a part of their research agendas (see, for example, Auty 1993; Karl 1997; Ross 2015).

The historical relationship between the state and the oil industry is crucial in the development of the Venezuelan political economy. In 1997 two of the most cited books on the politics of oil in Venezuela were published: Fernando Coronil's *Magical State* and

Terry L. Karl's *Paradox of Plenty*. Each explores the nature of the state in Venezuela and its intrinsic relation to oil as a source of wealth. At the core of these studies is the task of comprehending the emergence of Venezuela's modern state as concomitant with the discovery of oil and the establishment of the oil industry. These studies cement the notion of Venezuela as a prototypical petro-state (Foster 2007; Hidalgo 2007; Lander 2014) because it depends on oil extraction as the primary source of revenue. In this sense, Venezuela is a revealing case of the impact of oil booms on oil-exporting countries whose institutions have been molded by oil-led development. According to these ideas, petro-states are unable to handle oil booms without running into almost unpayable debt and undermining their democratic institutions.

Venezuela represents the typical "rentier state," whose economy, social structures, and political institutions are dependent on the inflow of considerable rent income from abroad (above 40 percent of government income). Rentier states are entities that easily succumb to the natural resource curse derived from oil wealth flowing into immature institutional apparatuses. The rentierism establishes the features of a dysfunctional state bureaucracy and state-society relations built upon the dispute over those rents (Ross 2015). For almost one hundred years, rent income from oil has molded the economy, politics, and society in Venezuela. Between the 1920s and 1970s, oil revenues allowed Venezuela to achieve one of the world's fastest-growing economic rates (Peters 2017). With the relative success of oil-based development during this stage, the idea of a resource curse would have seemed impossible to economic planners and the population.

The resource curse paradigm suggests a negative correlation between the abundance of natural resources and the economic development of countries. The commodity-based development model leads to reduced financial results in the long term because it prevents structural change, economic diversification, and industrialization (Peters 2017). Auty (1993) explains the differences in economic growth rates between countries with lack of resources and high growth rates (Japan, Korea, Singapore, etc.) and states with resource abundance but low growth rates (Angola, Nigeria, Sudan, etc.). According to Sachs and Warner's (1995) empirical studies, there is a strong correlation between resources and poor economic performance. Oil booms are accompanied by economic growth and positive outcomes in social development, but a fall in prices inflicts damage on exporting countries, widening budget deficits, and has been connected to a lack of good governance. Shaxson (2007) established that resource extraction strengthens patronage politics, and the revenue obtained by extractive industries is the primary source of national income. Thus rent-seeking activities are deepened, enhancing the relationship between economic actors and government and damaging the links between citizens and government.

Besides the volatility in oil prices, the poor economic performance of resource-rich nations is explained by the "Dutch disease": when a country strikes hydrocarbons, the unexpected flow of revenues leads to a sharp appreciation in the domestic currency, which makes non-oil sectors less competitive in the national economy (Beblawi 1987; Frankel 2010; Karl 1997). The Dutch disease became endemic in Venezuela after 1934, when the government kept the currency overvalued and used the exchange policy as a mechanism to transfer underground rents to other sectors of the economy, most notably agriculture. The inherent volatility in commodity prices harms more poor people, as they are least able to hedge the risks. Additionally, the resource revenues are concentrated in a few hands and are more prone to mismanagement.

In this context, governments have little need to raise incomes through taxes, and the motivation to develop non-oil sources of wealth is almost nonexistent. The channeling of these rents to private hands translated into processes whereby economic and social actors claimed portions of this rent to the state (Urbaneja 2013). That fact links to the most pervasive *political* implications of the resource curse, such as the rise of corruption and cronyism, as windfall rents do not depend on the productive tax base of the economy, allowing political elites to become "autonomous" from their populations, undermining accountability and democracy (Haslam 2016). In Coronil's terms (1997), the state becomes a "magical" entity capable of pulling tricks on its audience, the body politic of the nation, through its ownership over oil and its rents.

The resource curse has been tested, and many scholars have critically reconsidered the different dimensions, questioning the approach that establishes the negative correlation between natural resources and poor economic performance and development. These critiques distinguish among the several cases that demonstrate features of the resource curse by highlighting the variety of experiences possible and underlining the role of context and politics (Peters 2017). Gonzalez-Vicente (2011) proposes a framework that divides the curse associated with extraction into external, internal, and intrinsic forms. The external curse indicates those evident aspects of the relationships between resource-producing countries and importers, which shows the linkages of economic disadvantages with the world economy. For instance, the external curse can be illustrated by unfavorable terms of trade for resources, the Dutch disease, commodity prices' instability, and the dependence on core economies. The internal curses include patronage politics in resource-rich countries, structures that do not allow the development of democratic regimes, corruption, disputes over the use of natural resources, economic inequality, and low national expenditure in boosting productive competences. Finally, intrinsic curses include those that are unavoidable in resource extraction, basically referring to depletion of resources and environmental degradation.

Critical scholars refer instead to a system of "rent capitalism" that connects the struggles between landed property and capital to an international capitalist system in which the landlord state seeks to maximize ground rent (Hellinger 2017; Chodor 2016; Purcell 2017). In this context, the phenomenon of the resource curse is tied to the postcolonial nature of petro-states, highlighting their "dependent" condition in a global system of capital accumulation (Chodor 2016; Purcell 2017; Rodriguez Araque 2012). As Coronil rebrands it, the "colonial disease" also replicates "relations of colonial dependence between these formally independent nations and metropolitan centers" (Coronil 2008). Venezuela's identity as a landlord state has therefore permeated not only its struggles over ground rent with extractive companies, but also its relationships with foreign powers, wherein resource nationalism emerges as a prominent feature. Hence the idea of breaking away from a dependent form of capitalism is connected to the capacity of the landlord state to enact its control over underground wealth (Chodor 2016).

Guided in part by ideas of dependent capitalism and revolutionary politics, control over the oil industry has been a central component of progressive political discourse and action in Venezuela throughout the twentieth and, most notably, during the first decades of the twenty-first centuries. While the tensions of an autonomous sector and the desire for control have been present since the creation of PDVSA, they have never been as crucial as in the last two decades. During the Bolivarian Revolution, the use of oil wealth and the control over the oil industry converged into one goal, which ironically risked the sustainability of the rentier state.

The Bolivarian government failed to make structural economic changes to diversify the economy; thus, the problems linked with the resource curse have become more visible lately. Although huge public spending cut poverty from 49 to 37 percent by 2005, the project proved to be expensive and ineffective over the long term. In turn, poverty has risen in the past few years to around 90 percent of households, with increasing malnutrition rates and a wave of migration that has reached four million (UCAB 2018; UNHCR 2019). The Maduro government (2013–) has recognized its incapacity to transcend the rentier model and, due to the collapse in prices from 2014 onward, has claimed a desire to diversify away from oil. Nevertheless, Nicolás Maduro's policies have further entrenched rentierism by promoting gold mining, which has deepened the intrinsic and internal features of the resource curse (Rosales 2019).

Despite all the resources invested in social programs, the government did not improve the necessary infrastructure, and much of the oil rents were used without transparency (Aznarez 2018). Instead of reforming institutions, the Venezuelan government just created parallel structures such as "Missions."[2] These structures produced high expenditures on bureaucracy and the duplication of responsibilities, while securing political loyalty and control.

RESOURCE NATIONALISM AND CHANGES IN THE LEGAL FRAMEWORK

The period 2003–2013 was a heady time in Latin America, with economies across the region growing faster than during any previous decade. However, during the commodities boom, several experts expressed concern that the region's dependence on its resource-led growth could deepen economic reliance on foreign consumers of commodities such as China (Gallagher 2016). Venezuela's currently perilous financial situation is an outcome of both external and internal factors.

The governance of global resource industries is constantly changing. During oil booms, many resource-rich countries adopt nationalist policies in an attempt to lead economic activity in the energy sector toward established national goals. Resource nationalism takes several forms across different commodities-based economies. It reflects a state's response to the cyclical recovery in commodities' international prices or is the result of the negotiations between countries and firms. It has economic and political drivers, and it is essential to ponder the role of institutions in the process of resource nationalist policies. For instance, in rentier states, governments generally execute direct ownership over resources to get full control of the distribution of wealth and to consolidate power (Wilson 2015). In developmental resource nationalism, the government uses interventionist policies to influence resource production for different developmental goals. In neoliberal regimes, states use market mechanisms to promote output expansion.

Understanding resource nationalism's dynamic requires analysis of the cycles of opening and expropriation in the oil sector. These cycles represent incentives faced by political leaders under different scenarios of international oil prices, stages of the investment cycle, production, and reserve tendencies. The expropriation scenarios tend to occur when prices rise abruptly—that is, when the economic benefits for the government increase. It is also likely in an environment of increasing reserves and production (Wilson 2015). In some cases, the macroeconomic basis becomes vague gradually, even though the growing cash flow from commodity exports alleviates problems due to government willingness to relax important fiscal and budgetary rules.

During the 1990s the Venezuelan government changed the hydrocarbon legislation to attract foreign investors by pursuing "Oil Opening". It tried to incorporate new technology and skills from foreign corporations into the oil business and to increase PDVSA's access to new markets. PDVSA devised a plan to open untapped fields of unconventional heavy crudes in the Orinoco River belt for investment (Philip 1999). As has been argued elsewhere (Rosales 2018), the ideas of the landlord state as traditionally espoused by the Venezuelan government, focused on maximizing rents, clashed with PDVSA's global oil producer concerns: to maximize output. Overall, these operational agreements allowed private firms to participate in thirty-two oilfields, including the assets in the Orinoco River belt. Regulating the oil industry and learning about oil was a simultaneous process that gradually increased confidence vis-á-vis foreign companies but also provoked transformations within the modern state.

The opening was successful at increasing investment and output (Hults 2012b; Manzano and Monaldi 2010). In sum, the oil opening produced thirty-two operating agreements, eight explorations at risk and profit-sharing contracts, four strategic associations, and one association agreement for the production of Orimulsion. In terms of output, the Oil Service Association (OSA) contracts generated up to 600,000 bpd by the end of the 1990s. The other association agreements produced 200,000 bpd then and totaled 650,000 by the mid-2000s. Increasing production was not smooth, as Venezuela was constrained by Organization of the Petroleum Exporting Countries (OPEC) quotas.

By the end of the 1990s the corporate logic of the company was established as the center of the country's oil policy, and Venezuela increased output by about 800,000 bpd, which meant a shift from the logics of a rentier state to that of a global oil producer. In the words of Urbaneja, with the oil opening, "there was a productive philosophy regarding oil—rather than a rentier one—which pointed to the expansion of the industry and production even at the expense of rent per barrel" (Urbaneja 2013, 352). Indeed, the Venezuelan government allowed PDVSA to increase output, sacrificing rent intake, in a process analyzed by Dunning (2010) as the result of a competitive political system in which a relatively weak incumbent had little incentive to increase rent appropriation.

While plans for internationalization and oil opening were carried out, the government led by Carlos Andrés Pérez failed at executing a neoliberal plan in 1989, which provoked massive protests and unprecedented repression. Rather than renovating the traditional party and institutional structures, the neoliberal experiment weakened them. Increasing inequality and poverty rates were seen as a result of a growing disconnect between the political elite and the general population (Buxton 2003).

Throughout the 2003–2013 commodity boom, the Venezuelan government used the profits for social development, primarily to reduce poverty and inequality (Urbaneja 2013). However, it fell short in using those revenues for upgrading technology and innovation in the oil sector, and the drop in prices highlighted structural and macroeconomic problems. Failure to implement long-term development policies and fiscal and budget policies dependent on energy commodities are the leading causes of the current critical economic situation.

The state is fundamental in challenging the problems associated with extractivism and trying to achieve viable models of resource-led development. Even though it is difficult to replicate others' experiences, successful cases should be taken into consideration. Canada, Norway, and Australia, for example, were able to move from extraction into processing. Even less-developed countries governed by the Left, such as Ecuador and Bolivia, managed to invest underground rents for productive purposes, allowing them to avoid deep crises after the price bust. The key has been state intervention that guarantees a shift from one stage to the next. It is essential to protect nascent industries and to ensure further technological upgrading.

THE RETURN OF STATE CONTROL AND COLLAPSE OF THE OIL INDUSTRY

When Chávez took power, the government introduced significant changes in the oil industry's legal framework (Manzano and Monaldi 2010). His oil policy highlighted maintaining the national character of PDVSA and increasing the state's intake of rents via royalties. These plans were carried out in tandem with fierce anti-imperialist rhetoric and a revolutionary agenda critical of the traditional party structures, evolving into the socialism of the twenty-first century.

In 2001 the executive decreed a new law of hydrocarbons via special powers given by the parliament. The Organic Law on Hydrocarbons, governing the contractual arrangements under which foreign oil companies operate, was renegotiated as part of Chávez's plans to retain higher oil revenues and to boost the role of the state in the management of the national oil industry (Petróleos de Venezuela 2006). The law also secured government ownership of existing refineries and their potential expansion or improvement. Nevertheless, the law also included private sector participation through joint ventures, mandating that an NOC own at least 50 percent of assets (Petróleos de Venezuela 2006).

Within this legal reorganization, the percentage of royalties that foreign firms would pay to the government was established (33.33 percent royalty), while reducing corporate tax to 50 percent. PDVSA would lead all new oil exploration and production projects, while foreign oil companies could only hold a minority stake. The state controlled the oil rent and assumed a fundamental role in its distribution (social missions, subsidies, currency overvaluation, labor policies, and the creation of jobs). The law sought to erode the oil opening, as it did not contemplate operating contracts and profit-sharing agreements (Rosales 2018). The government argued that these tax and royalty conditions were not difficult for the ongoing projects to meet, as their extraction costs had already shrunk due to improved technologies and enhanced learning in these oil fields.[3]

Yet while this process of partial nationalization worked thanks to the continued investments coming from foreign corporations, PDVSA was used as a bankroll agency to funnel spending, and it did not reinvest in the oil fields or technology upgrading (Rapier 2017; Rosales 2018). The deterioration of the oil industry is the root cause of the Venezuelan economic collapse that began in 2013. The deepening troubles at PDVSA threaten to continue destabilizing the nation, which faces recession, soaring inflation, high crime rates, and shortages of food and medicine. The Venezuelan oil industry complex is in a state of severe deterioration; a lack of investment connected with cash flow difficulties and chronic problems in infrastructure have affected operations and led to a massive outflow of workers who cannot rely on their meager wages. With oil facilities around the country extremely deteriorated, the government was incapable of taking advantage of higher prices to increase production and ramp up refinery operations (Monaldi 2018).

There are two related causes for the decline of Venezuela's oil production despite the sustained increase in the country's proved reserves: (1) lack of adequate technical expertise and (2) socialist politics associated with the Chávez government (Rapier 2017). First, the lack of expertise required to develop the country's heavy oil resulted from the massive firing of PDVSA's employees in 2003 and the decrease in international capital. Once Chávez arrived in power, his first targets included the technocrats at PDVSA, who challenged his view of the industry and the country. Second, Chávez aimed to fully control PDVSA and maximize its revenue to fund his socialist agenda. The main issue was that PDVSA's key managers at that time wanted to raise production, which required reinvesting more in the company instead of handing over revenues to the government. By the end of 2002, labor groups were calling for a national strike, trying to pressure a collapse of the Chávez government. Oil workers, especially PDVSA managers, backed up this effort, setting the stage for the future crisis. In the end, the government shut down the strike and fired more than half of the company's employees, effectively purging the company of dissenting voices and ensuring loyalty (Philip and Panizza 2013; Luong and Sierra 2015; Manzano and Monaldi 2010). The loss of PDVSA's human capital was the most damaging of Chávez's moves against the company.

Since then, PDVSA has become the regime's political and economic strong right arm and has included many social programs as part of its finances. The use of oil rents for the achievement of the government's political project has become synonymous with a new oil nationalization. In 2006, after a systematic increase in oil prices, the government decided to force a complete migration of all operating contracts signed under the oil opening to fit the legal framework of the 2001 hydrocarbons law (Petróleos de Venezuela 2006).

Moreover, Chávez took billions of dollars of PDVSA's revenue to finance social programs. First, his government enacted a policy of capital and exchange controls that overvalued the legal tender and centralized the distribution of foreign currency (Dachevsky and Kornblihtt 2017; Palma 2013; Saboin García 2017). Second, it established ad hoc dollar-denominated funds from "surplus" oil rents (above the level of the national budget) for the discretionary use of the presidency (Balza Guanipa 2017; Rosales 2016). This model allowed the government to enact social policies that lowered poverty rates for a few years and secured a remarkable electoral performance for Chávez and his party (Corrales and Penfold 2011; Urbaneja 2013). This strategy worked in the short term, but it was harmful in the long term because PDVSA invested little in the industry.

From 2004 until 2012, capital markets were happy to lend money to Venezuela because of its large oil reserves and climbing oil prices. Then in 2013, while oil prices were still high, capital markets stopped lending to Venezuela due to the country's increasing fiscal deficit (Bo and Gallagher 2016). The economic recession worsened in 2014 when oil prices collapsed. Over 95 percent of Venezuela's foreign currency income comes from crude oil exports. External debt amounts to around US$185 billion, including bondholders, commercial creditors, and China (Petróleos de Venezuela 2017).

Imports declined by about 80 percent between 2013 and 2018, which contributed to the collapse of national production and per capita income. One source of this decline was a combination of mismanagement, unpaid suppliers' bills, and underinvestment; domestic oil production declined steadily. In 1998, the year before Chávez was elected, Venezuelan oil production was 3.7 million barrels per day (mbpd), but since 2007 there has been a continuing decline in output. By mid-2019, crude accounted for 96 percent of export revenues, and the national oil output was below one million bpd (OPEC 2019). The production decline was particularly steep in camps operated solely by PDVSA. Thus production relied more heavily on joint ventures conducted with foreign companies (Hernández and Monaldi 2016; Petróleos de Venezuela 2017).

The second explanation for the decline of oil production in Venezuela is related to the incapacity of Chávez's and Maduro's administrations to understand the level of capital expenditure required to continue developing the country's oil industry. Maduro faced a dramatic drop in oil prices from 2014 onward and the gradual collapse of the Bolivarian Revolution's socialist rentierism, characterized by price controls, high social spending, and generalized subsidies (Rosales 2016; Vera 2008). One of the most dramatic consequences of this crisis has been the declining capacity of Venezuela's NOC to keep up production. The country's oil industry entered an unprecedented crisis in 2014, with a production decline of over 50 percent over five years, more than two million bpd (OPEC 2018; Monaldi 2018).

During the oil boom, the Venezuelan government used billions of dollars to fund the country's social programs, but it failed to reinvest in this capital-intensive industry. The Venezuelan refineries have fallen into severe disrepair, leading to a sharp cutback in operations. As production has declined, the company's crude exports have also dropped dramatically. For instance, shipments to the United States (PDVSA's top foreign market) plunged to 475,165 bpd in 2019, the lowest level since 2003. This situation was further complicated after April 2019 by an oil embargo imposed by the United States, which does not recognize the government of Maduro as legitimate.

Despite the government's nationalist rhetoric, investment in the oil sector has always been necessary, making external financing necessary. The government chose to sacrifice the technical expertise of the company for the expediency of having a compliant company, eventually leading to the collapse of the rentier model. Despite attempts to break away from dependence on foreign capital, the Bolivarian Revolution has deepened it. In a desperate effort to cope with the crisis, the Maduro government opted for a fire sale of assets, both abroad and in the country, this time receiving less-enthusiastic interest from China and instead increasing the stake of Russian state capital in Venezuela's oil industry, thus deepening the external features of the oil curse (Kahn 2017; Monaldi 2018).

FOREIGN RELATIONS IN THE CONTEXT OF A RENTIER STATE

Venezuela's relationships to the global economy through oil are not remote from the interests and connections of foreign political and economic actors. During most of the twentieth century, the United States arose as the leading international actor in Venezuela, mainly as an oil consumer and as a source of investment and cooperation (Rosales 2016). When Chávez reached the presidency in 1999, he tried to diversify export markets, especially replacing US demand with Chinese demand (Serbin and Serbin Pont 2017). Despite the diplomatic altercations between Venezuela and the United States, the economic relationship always revolved around the oil trade and investment. In this sense, a functional relationship was essential to both because a disturbance would extinguish a crucial source of cash for Venezuela and compromise the viability of the CITGO Petroleum Corporation retailers in the United States, as happened in 2019 with the freezing of PDVSA assets by Donald Trump's administration. Avoiding overdependence on the United States may have been a constructive act, but while Chávez's antagonism to the United States encouraged an "anti-imperialist" discourse, it did little to achieve specific developmental goals (Gonzalez-Vicente 2011).

Venezuelan foreign policy has long been focused on the aspiration to make the country a regionally relevant actor, but also an international player, through the creation of a regional and international support network of alliances and partnerships, using oil as the main tool. Venezuela tried to establish close links with extra-regional powers such as Russia, China, and Iran (Ellner 2012). In Latin America and the Caribbean, Venezuela built a network of South-South cooperation through oil arrangements and ideological convergences. When favorable international circumstances contributed to a rise in oil prices, the government used these resources to promote national interests, especially among its Andean neighbors, and in Central America and the Caribbean. In 2005 Chávez created Petrocaribe, an agreement that negotiated low-interest oil sales with Caribbean and Central American countries. The payment system allowed nations to buy oil at only a portion of the market value, with the remainder paid through a twenty-five-year financing arrangement at 1 percent interest. They could also pay their debts through goods and services to Venezuela. For instance, in 2012 Venezuela sent Cuba around ninety thousand bpd, in exchange for the services of thirty thousand doctors. Even when these credits were a substantial economic burden, Chávez and Maduro safeguarded Petrocaribe, which bought Caracas political support in the United Nations and in the Organization of American States (Schipani 2015).

During the Bolivarian Revolution, dependence on oil rents deepened, and the country's linkage with foreign powers became more acute. *Chavismo* built important alliances with emerging powers, especially China and Russia, while attempting to break away from US dominance. These new relationships were also rooted in the traditional position of a peripheral provider of natural resources in exchange for capital and technology in the form of oil-backed loans and investments in the oil industry (Rosales 2016; Sanderson and Forsythe 2012; Sebastián Paz 2011). As a consequence of rising commodity prices, resource-endowed countries no longer needed to depend on their relations with a small group of Western investors, so the conditions of these countries in the global economy improved. However, in Venezuela a new dependence on China has been encouraged by elites that seek ultimately to preserve political control instead of following a developmental path. China's foreign policy approach, based on nonintervention in internal affairs, has permitted it to support isolated regimes, allowing them to tolerate internal and external pressures.

As the country's relationship with the United States worsened, then president Chávez tried to rely on China as an oil consumer, investor, and provider of cooperation funds. Simultaneously, China wanted access to a stable source of resources, to enter the domestic market, and to provide its enterprises with a new space to do business in Latin America. The offers made by China to access resources were received positively because they revitalized important infrastructure projects all over the continent. In Venezuela, the China Development Bank designed servicing mechanisms such as oil for loans, keeping the payment risk to a minimum level. According to this logic, during a period of high oil prices, Venezuela can quickly increase production and pay the credit back (Bo and Gallagher 2016). China is a critical source of financing for countries with relatively limited access to international capital markets, such as Venezuela, Ecuador, Brazil, and Argentina. However, this could raise the risk of debt distress in some borrower countries, and more debtors are rethinking the implications of the loans offered by Chinese policy banks for infrastructure projects because they could be trapped in a debt cycle.

China's loan details have not been published, and critical voices are no longer limited to Western spectators; disapproval is also emerging in recipient countries. In some cases the Chinese commodities-backed loan arrangements in the developing world have saddled many of the debtor nations with unsustainable sovereign loan burdens and left promises of development unfulfilled. China's debt deals have strengthened some of the strongest accusations, mainly about how its investment and lending programs lead to a debt trap for vulnerable countries around the world, fueling corruption and autocratic behavior. Kaplan (2018) argues that higher government budgets are related to Chinese bilateral lending as a segment of a country's total external financing. Chinese policy banks do not unveil the conditions of lending, making it difficult to assess a country's debt's value to China (Hurley, Morris, and Portelance, 2018). At the national level, Chinese support has empowered the Venezuelan authoritarian ruling elites. While China does not try to promote a particular political system, it has indirectly reinforced negative consequences for political and economic national development.

Rendon and Baumunk (2018) have highlighted the negative impact of Chinese involvement in Venezuela by arguing that China's focus on the Venezuelan energy sector is neither transparent nor commercially oriented, but can be viewed as a strategy to gain influence over Venezuelan political configurations. Through loans and investments, Venezuela's dependence on Chinese, and more recently Russian, financing has increased, taking advantage of the precarious economic situation to sign one-sided financial agreements that perpetuate the economic distortions affecting the country.

A FUTURE RESEARCH AGENDA

The pursuit of rent appropriation and maximization in Venezuela's oil politics has at times conflicted with the expectations of oil-producing companies, both national and foreign. Research suggests that this unsurprising situation is the result of the struggle between the landlord state and forces of capital (Hellinger 2017; Mommer 2010). Once the nationalization of the industry took place, this struggle occurred within the state, prompting tectonic tensions with implications for the country's political economy but also for the global oil market. After almost two decades of socialist experimentation, it is clear that for rent maximization to be sustainable, a functioning oil industry is required. Thus, Venezuela's capacity to overcome its current economic collapse depends to a large degree on its ability to put the oil industry back on its feet.

This chapter and the research agenda proposed in this section recognize that this challenge is not new. Resolving it will require establishing a balance between autonomy and control over the oil industry, between the state's right to exercise sovereignty over its resources and the inherent interdependence of the globalized oil industry. During much of Chávez's era, the government applied a hybrid governance model that welcomed foreign investment on the one hand and exercised state control and increased state participation in the industry on the other. This model of high royalties and majority stakes for the state worked when oil prices were high. But PDVSA under *chavismo* demonstrated that if the NOC is responding to political objectives that distract it from its task, such a hybrid form of governance can deepen the country's dependence on foreign partners—paradoxically, the same dependence left-leaning nationalists sought to break away from. Thus one area for future research is extending and deepening analysis of conflicts over rent appropriation and distribution. What is the range of state-society relationships that might enable society to benefit more equitably from oil extraction?

The apparent paradox previously described leads to the second point of discussion for the future. What should be the role of the NOC in the economy? Historically, the Venezuelan state has shifted between two extremes regarding its NOC. The state allowed PDVSA to act autonomously, which encouraged a world-class oil company but distanced that company from its main shareholder and the rest of society. The other extreme proved disastrous. As a politically controlled bankroll agency, PDVSA came to its knees; it was hugely indebted and became unable to extract oil, threatening the existence of the rentier state itself. As Hults (2012a) explains, some states clearly define the lines between policymaking, the regulator, and the operator of the oil policy (the "Norwegian model"). Due to the complexity and technical nature of the industry, companies tend to develop knowledge and capacities that distance them from the bureaucracy of regulators and policy makers. This can lead to a form of "capture" in which the operator's interests can obscure those of the regulator or, in the Venezuelan case, the emergence of a "state within the state." For the separation of functions to succeed in balancing the interests of production, rent intake, and generating developmental linkages, high institutional capacity is required, and a competitive political context is necessary. A competitive and open political context lowers the incentives of incumbents to reap the benefits of increasing rent appropriation while allowing long-term policymaking to take hold (Dunning 2010; Thurber, Hults, and Heller 2011).

In Venezuela, the tendency toward autonomy in the industry has been present since its inception, as has the state's desire for control. Despite some periods of stable growth and industrialization, a developmental form of "embedded autonomy," as Evans (1995) argues, in which state and industry harbor innovation with autonomy and strong social ties, has been elusive. In the coming years, rebuilding state capacity as regulator and technical skills in the industry will require working hand in hand with the consolidation of a competitive political system. A final area of future research includes engagement in the politics of oil policy necessary to achieve this goal. Absent such attention, the oil sector's increased dependence on foreign capital, especially Chinese and Russian interests, and the strengthening of the current authoritarian political elite in power are likely to impede the development of both Venezuela's oil industry and its sociopolitical structure.

NOTES

1. The Bolivarian Revolution is the political process brought about by Hugo Chávez after his election in 1998. This process sought to transform the Venezuelan political system into a

participatory democracy, doing away with forty years of representative, liberal democracy. Later on, it embraced socialism of the 21st century.

2. One of the first missions was Barrio Adentro, under which in return for subsidized oil, sixteen thousand Cuban doctors and dentists were sent by the Cuban government throughout the country, but especially where medical services were deficient. The government could provide social services that poor people previously lacked. At the same time, this created a clientelistic program in return for political loyalty.

3. The new law revoked the 1943 hydrocarbons law, the 1971 reversion law, and the 1975 nationalization law together with three other minor laws.

References

Auty, Richard. 1993. *Sustaining Development in Mineral Economies: The Resource Curse Thesis.* London: Routledge.

Aznarez, Juan. 2018. "La oposicion venezolana tropieza con el mito." *El Pais*, July 31.

Balza Guanipa, Ronald. 2017. "El FONDEN, 'Fondos Chinos' y Sector Externo En Venezuela: 2005 a 2014." In *Fragmentos de Venezuela: 20 Escritos Sobre Economía*, edited by Ronald Balza Guanipa and Humberto García Larralde. Caracas: Universidad Catolica Andres Bello.

Beblawi, Hazem. 1987. "The Rentier State in the Arab World." *Arab Studies Quarterly* 9: 383–398.

Bo Kong and Kevin Gallagher. 2016. "The Globalization of Chinese Energy Companies: The Role of the State Finance." Boston University: Global Economic Governance Initiative.

Boué, Juan Carlos. 1993. *Venezuela: The Political Economy of Oil*. Oxford University Press for the Oxford Institute for Energy Studies.

Boué, Juan Carlos. 2002. "El Programa de Internacionalización de Pdvsa: ¿Triunfo Estratégico o Desastre Fiscal?" *Revista Venezolana de Economía y Ciencias Sociales* 8, no. 2: 237–282.

Buxton, Julia. 2003. "Economic Policy and the Rise of Hugo Chávez." In *Venezuelan Politics in the Chávez Era: Class, Polarization, and Conflict*, edited by Steve Ellner and Daniel Hellinger, 13–130. Boulder: Lynne Rienner Publishers.

Chodor, Tom. 2016. "A Different Kind of Magic? Oil, Development and the Bolivarian Revolution in Venezuela." In *Energy, Capitalism and World Order*, edited by Tim Di Muzio and Jesse Salah Ovadia, 94–110. London: Palgrave Macmillan.

Coronil, Fernando. 1997. *The Magical State: Nature, Money, and Modernity in Venezuela.* Chicago: University of Chicago Press.

Coronil, Fernando. 2008. "It's the Oil Stupid!!!" *ReVista: Harvard Review of Latin America.* Fall 2008: 19–35.

Corrales, Javier, and Michael Penfold. 2011. *Dragon in the Tropics: Hugo Chavez and the Political Economy of Revolution in Venezuela*. Washington DC: Brookings Institution Press.

Dachevsky, Fernando, and Juan Kornblihtt. 2017. "The Reproduction and Crisis of Capitalism in Venezuela under Chavismo." *Latin American Perspectives* 44, no. 1: 78–93. doi:10.1177/0094582X16673633.

Di John, Jonathan. 2009. *From Windfall to Curse? Oil and Industrialization in Venezuela, 1920 to the Present*. Pennsylvania: Penn State Press.

Dunning, Thad. 2010. "Endogenous Oil Rents." *Comparative Political Studies* 43, no. 3: 379–410.

Ellner, Steve. 2012. "The Distinguishing Features of Latin America's New Left in Power: The Chavez, Morales, and Correa Governments." *Latin American Perspectives* 39, no. 1: 96–114.

Evans, Peter. 1995. *Embedded Autonomy: States and Industrial Transformation*. Princeton, NJ: Princeton University Press.

Foster, D. 2007. "Political State and the Venezuela Petro-State," Hamilton Edu, https://www. hamilton.edu/documents/levitt-center/foster_article_2008.pdf, 38.

Frankel, Jeffrey A. 2010. "The Natural Resource Curse: A Survey." National Bureau of Economic Research. http://www.nber.org/papers/w15836.

Gallagher, Kevin. 2016. *The China Triangle: Latin America's China Boom and the Fate of the Washington Consensus*. New York: Oxford University Press.

Gonzalez-Vicente, Ruben. 2011. "China's Engagement in South America and Africa's Extractive Sectors: New Perspectives for Resource Curse Theories." *The Pacific Review* 24, no. 1: 65–87.

Haslam, Paul Alexander. 2016. "Overcoming the Resource Curse: Reform and the Rentier State in Chile and Argentina, 1973–2000." *Development and Change* 47, no. 5: 1146–1170. doi:10.1111/dech.12259.

Hellinger, Daniel. 2017. "Oil and the Chávez Legacy." *Latin American Perspectives* 44, no. 1: 54–77. doi:10.1177/0094582X16651236.

Hernández, Igor, and Francisco Monaldi. 2016. "Weathering Collapse: An Assessment of the Financial and Operational Situation of the Venezuelan Oil Industry." Working Paper. Center for International Development at Harvard University, November 2016. https:// growthlab.cid.harvard.edu/files/growthlab/files/venezuela_oil_cidwp_327.pdf.

Hidalgo, Manuel. 2007. "A Petro-State: Oil, Politics, and Democracy in Venezuela." Real Instituto Elcano, Working Paper 47, 19. https://www.files.ethz.ch/isn/46855/WP%2049,%20 2007.pdf.

Hults, David R. 2012a. "Hybrid Governance: State Management of National Oil Companies." In *Oil and Governance: State-Owned Enterprises and the World Energy Supply*, edited by David Victor, David Hults, and Mike Thurber, 62–120. Cambridge: Cambridge University Press.

Hults, David R. 2012b. "Petróleos de Venezuela, SA (PDVSA): From Independence to Subservience." In *Oil and Governance: State-Owned Enterprises and the World Energy Supply*, edited by David Victor, David Hults, and Mike Thurber, 418–477. Cambridge: Cambridge University Press.

Hurley, J., S. Morris, and G. Portelance. 2018. "Examining the Debt Implications of the Belt and Road Initiative from a Policy Perspective." Center for Global Development. CGD Policy Paper 121. March. https://www.cgdev.org/sites/default/files/examining-debt-implications-belt-and-road-initiative-policy-perspective.pdf.

Johnson, Keith. 2018. "How Venezuela Struck It Poor." *Foreign Policy*, July 16.

Kahn, Robert. 2017. "Venezuela after the Fall: Financing, Debt Relief and Geopolitics." CIGI Paper Series. Waterloo, Canada: Centre for International Governance Innovation. https:// www.cigionline.org/publications/venezuela-after-fall-financing-zdebt-relief-and-geopolitics.

Kaplan, Stephen. 2018. "The Rise of Patient Capital: The Political Economy of Chinese Global Finance." George Washington University, Institute for International Economic Policy. https://papers.ssrn.com/sol3/papers.cfm?abstract_id=3108215.

Karl, Terry Lynn. 1997. *The Paradox of Plenty: Oil Booms and Petro-States*. Vol. 26. Berkeley: University of California Press.

Lander, Edgardo. 2014. "Venezuela: Terminal Crisis of the Rentier Petro-state." TNI. https:// www.tni.org/en/publication/venezuela-terminal-crisis-of-the-rentier-petro-state.

Luong, Pauline Jones, and Jazmín Sierra. 2015. "The Domestic Political Conditions for International Economic Expansion." *Comparative Political Studies* 48, no. 14: 2010–2043. doi:10.1177/0010414015592647.

Manzano, Osmel, and Francisco Monaldi. 2010. "12 The Political Economy of Oil Contract Renegotiation in Venezuela." In *The Natural Resources Trap: Private Investment without Public Commitment*, 409.

McBeth, Brian Stuart. 1983. *Juan Vicente Gómez and the Oil Companies in Venezuela, 1908–1935*. Vol. 43. Cambridge: Cambridge University Press.

Mommer, Bernard. 1999. "Venezuela, Política y Petróleos."*Cuadernos Del CENDES*, no. 42: 63–107.

Mommer, Bernard. 2002. *Global Oil and the Nation State*. New York: Oxford University Press, USA.

Mommer, Bernard. 2003. "Subversive Oil." In *Venezuelan Politics in the Chávez Era: Class, Polarization, and Conflict*, edited by Steve Ellner and Daniel Hellinger, 131–146. Boulder: Lynne Rienner Publishers.

Mommer, Bernard. 2010. *La Cuestión Petrolera*. 3rd ed. Plena Soberanía Petrolera. Caracas: Fondo Editorial Darío Ramírez PDVSA.

Monaldi, Francisco. 2018. "The Collapse of the Venezuelan Oil Industry and Its Global Consequences." Working Paper. http://www.atlanticcouncil.org/images/AC_VENEZUELAOIL_Interactive.pdf.

OPEC. 2018. "OPEC Monthly Oil Market Report." Vienna: OPEC. https://www.opec.org/opec_web/static_files_project/media/downloads/publications/MOMR%20December%202018.pdf.

OPEC. 2019. "OPEC Monthly Oil Market Report May 2019." Vienna: OPEC. https://momr.opec.org/pdf-download/index.php.

Palma, Pedro A. 2013. "Tsunamis Cambiarios." In *Las Circunstancias Mundiales y Venezuela: Cambios Imaginarios y Reales*, edited by Luis Mata Mollejas, 23–29. Caracas: Academia Nacional de Ciencias Económicas Coloquio "Alberto Adriani."

Peters, Stefan. 2017. "Beyond Curse and Blessing: Rentier Society in Venezuela." In *Contested Extractivism, Society and the State, Development, Justice and Citizenship*, edited by B. Engels and K. Dietz, 45–68. London: Palgrave Macmillan.

Petroleos de Venezuela. 2006. "Ley Orgánica de Hidrocarburos." http://www.pdvsa.com/images/pdf/marcolegal/LEY_ORGANICA_DE_HIDROCARBUROS.pdf.

Petróleos de Venezuela. 2017. "Informe Anual de Gestión 2016." Business report. Caracas: PDVSA.

Philip, George. 1999. "When Oil Prices Were Low: Petroleos de Venezuela (PdVSA) and Economic Policy-Making in Venezuela since 1989." *Bulletin of Latin American Research* 18, no. 3: 361–376.

Philip, George, and Francisco Panizza. 2013. *The Triumph of Politics*. New York: John Wiley & Sons.

Purcell, Thomas F. 2017. "The Political Economy of Rentier Capitalism and the Limits to Agrarian Transformation in Venezuela." *Journal of Agrarian Change* 17, no. 2: 296–312. doi:10.1111/joac.12204.

Rapier, Robet, "How Venezuela Ruined Its Oil Industry." *Forbes*, May 7, 2017.

Rendon, Moises, and Sarah Baumunk. 2018. "When Investment Hurts: Chinese Influence in Venezuela." CSIS, April 3. https://www.csis.org/analysis/when-investment-hurts-chinese-influence-venezuela.

Rodríguez Araque, Alí. 1997. *El Proceso de Privatización Petrolera En Venezuela*. Los Teques: Fondo editorial ALEM.

Rodríguez Araque, Alí. 2012. *Antes de Que Se Me Olvide: Conversación con Rosa Miriam Elizalde*. La Habana: Editora Política.

Rosales, Antulio. 2016. "Deepening Extractivism and Rentierism: China's Role in Venezuela's Bolivarian Developmental Model." *Canadian Journal of Development Studies/Revue Canadienne d'études Du Développement* (August): 1–18. doi:10.1080/02255189.2016.1208605.

Rosales, Antulio. 2018. "Pursuing Foreign Investment for Nationalist Goals: Venezuela's Hybrid Resource Nationalism." *Business and Politics* 20, no. 3. doi:10.1017/bap.2018.6.

Rosales, Antulio. 2019. "Statization and De-nationalization Dynamics in Venezuela's ASM-large-scale Mining Interface." *Resources Policy* 63. doi:10.1016/j.resourpol.2019.101422.

Ross, Michael. 2015. "What Have We Learned about the Resource Curse?" *Annual Review of Political Science* 18, no. 1: 239–259, doi:10.1146/annurev-polisci-052213-040359.

Saboin García, José Luis. 2017. "Determinantes Del Tipo de Cambio Paralelo En Venezuela: Un Enfoque Empírico." In *Fragmentos de Veneuzela: 20 Escritos Sobre Economía*, edited by Ronald Balza Guanipa and Humberto García Larralde, 379–400. Caracas: Universidad Catolica Andres Bello.

Sachs, Jeffrey, and Andrew Warner. 1995. *Natural Resource Abundance and Economic Growth.* NBER Working Paper No.5398. Cambridge, MA: NBER.

Salazar-Carrillo, Jorge, and Bernadette West. 2004. *Oil and Development in Venezuela During the 20th Century.* Westport, CT: Greenwood Publishing Group.

Sanderson, Henry, and Michael Forsythe. 2012. *China's Superbank: Debt, Oil and Influence-How China Development Bank Is Rewriting the Rules of Finance.* New York: John Wiley & Sons.

Schipani, Andres. 2015. "Petrocaribe: A Legacy That Is Both a Blessing and a Curse." *Financial Times*, April 17.

Sebastián Paz, Gonzalo. 2011. "China and Venezuela: Oil, Technology, and Socialism." In *China Engages Latin America: Tracing the Trajectory*, edited by Adrian H. Hearn and José Luis León-Marnríquez, 221–234. Boulder, CO: Lynne Rienner Publishers.

Serbin, Andres, and Andrei Serbin Pont. 2017. "The Foreign Policy of the Bolivarian Republic of Venezuela: The Role and Legacy of Hugo Chávez." *Latin American Policy* 8, no. 2: 232–248

Shaxson, Nicholas. 2007. "Oil, Corruption and the Resource Curse." *International Affairs* 83: 1123–1140. doi:10.1111/j.1468-2346.2007.00677.x

Thurber, Mark C., David R. Hults, and Patrick R. P. Heller. 2011. "Exporting the 'Norwegian Model': The Effect of Administrative Design on Oil Sector Performance." *Energy Policy* 39, no. 9: 5366–5378.

Tinker Salas, Miguel. 2015. *Venezuela: What Everyone Needs to Know.* Oxford: Oxford University Press.

Tugwell, Franklin. 1975. *The Politics of Oil in Venezuela.* Stanford, CA: Stanford University Press.

UCAB. 2018. "Encuesta Nacional Sobre Condiciones de Vida Venezuela 2017." Caracas: Universidad Católica Andrés Bello. https://www.ucab.edu.ve/investigacion/centros-e-institutos-de-investigacion/encovi-2017/.

UNHCR. 2019. "Refugees and Migrants from Venezuela Top 4 Million: UNHCR and IOM." June 7. https://www.unhcr.org/news/press/2019/6/5cfa2a4a4/refugees-migrants-venezuela-top-4-million-unhcr-iom.html.

Urbaneja, Diego. 2013. *La Renta y El Reclamo: Ensayo Sobre Petróleo y Economía Política en Venezuela.* Caracas: Alfa.

Vera, Leonardo V. 2008. "Políticas Sociales y Productivas en un Estado Patrimonialista Petrolero: Venezuela 1999–2007." *Nueva Sociedad* 215: 111–129.

Wilson, Jeffrey. 2015. "Understanding Resource Nationalism: Economic Dynamics and Political Institutions." *Contemporary Politics* 21, no. 4: 399–416.

CHAPTER 27

....

THE ENERGY POLITICS
OF LATIN AMERICA

....

SYLVIA GAYLORD

THIS chapter focuses on overall trends in energy politics in Latin America, with more detail on the larger countries: Argentina, Bolivia, Brazil, Chile, and Colombia. Two major states are not covered in detail here because they have Handbook chapters dedicated to them: Brazil (see chapter by Nem Singh and Massi in this volume) and Venezuela (see chapter by Rosales in this volume). In addition, Mexico is covered in the chapter on North America by Mildenberger and Stokes in this volume. More so than in developed countries, debates regarding energy governance in Latin America are closely tied to the region's most fundamental policy questions and dilemmas: the roles of the market and the state in the economy and the relationship between natural resources and inclusive and sustainable development. The first debate, over the proper roles for the state and the market, has been ongoing since the 1930s, when states in Latin America took a leading role in energy infrastructure development. It resurfaced during the privatization wave of the 1990s and then again as globalization offered new opportunities and limits on state action (Cárdenas, Ocampo, and Thorp 2000; Evans 1979; Mares 2010; Williamson 2009). The second question dates even further back, to the patterns of resource-dependent development locked in during Latin America's colonial period and the perpetual quest thereafter to harness natural resources to overcome poverty and deep, structural inequality (Kingstone 2018; Leamer et al. 1999; Sachs and Warner 2001; Thorpe 1998). (For analysis of regionalism literature, see Hancock, Palestini, and Szulecki in this volume.)

The domestic political context and global economic conditions in which these debates play out is also relevant. Latin America is enjoying the longest democratic period in its history, with unprecedented regime stability and improved socioeconomic indicators; in the first decade of the twenty-first century, extreme poverty in the region fell from 27 to 14 percent, moderate poverty from 41 to 28 percent and the middle classes expanded by 50 percent (Ferreira et al. 2013). The first decade and a half of the century also brought to power presidents from the center Left in a number of countries, among them the energy-rich Argentina, Bolivia, Brazil, Ecuador, and Venezuela (Blanco and Grier 2013; Castañeda 2012; Petras 1999; Seligson 2007; Weyland, Madrid, and

Hunter 2010). Global market trends in the first decade of the century ushered in a period of record high prices for agricultural and mineral commodities, as well as oil and gas, and along with new technologies, the discovery of significant new reserves of hydrocarbons, including unconventional plays (Fryklund 2012; Gruss 2014; Ocampo 2007). The debates regarding national priorities in the exploitation of energy reflect these trends, with governments advocating a new role for national oil companies (NOCs) in Argentina, Bolivia, Brazil, and Venezuela and reasserting the role of the state in energy markets through nationalization and increased control over reserves and production (Tissot 2012).

A more nationalist political environment, combined with the resource and commodity booms, has refocused energy policy on the role of the state in allocating resources and reaping the benefits of hydrocarbon extraction and on the effects of resource extraction on socioeconomic outcomes. The highly globalized environment and the effects of external shocks have reignited opposition to neoliberalism and unregulated markets. At the same time, critics of increasing state intervention point to the state's inability to create regulatory and institutional conditions for competitive markets to exist, beginning a new round of debates on market versus government failure. Finally, there is increasing concern over the effects of international market pricing and unfettered development of natural resources on social welfare; specifically, governments intervene significantly in energy pricing but fail to deliver a sense of shared opportunities and costs.

The first section of this chapter addresses the evolving debate on state-market relations in energy: state ownership, regulatory performance, and energy subsidies. The second section addresses political trends emerging from below, in particular the growing frequency of social protest related to energy projects. This trend is not unique to Latin America, or to energy—extractive activities and large infrastructure projects have also spurred protest and activism in other parts of the world (Özkaynak et al. 2015). The last four decades of democracy have consolidated an active and increasingly effective civil society that has taken up a range of causes, from sexual identity to the environment (Escobar and Álvarez [1992] 2018). There has also been an expansion of social movements and government policies promoting the rights of indigenous peoples to self-determination and a growing awareness of the social and environmental impacts of large extractive and infrastructure projects on the lives of local communities (Van Cott 2010). The increase in opposition to energy projects also responds to the emergence of new technologies in energy extraction and production that have spread activity to areas previously unaffected and often well populated. Fracking technology has opened up new areas to exploration and extraction, while nonconventional renewables, such as wind and solar, have large land requirements. Market integration projects, such as natural gas pipelines, traverse vast distances and touch many lives. As a result of the integration of these new energy technologies, the expansion of markets, and the continuous growth in demand, many more people are coming into contact and conflict with energy projects. The chapter ends with brief remarks on future lines of research.

STATE AND MARKET

During the second half of the twentieth century Latin American countries, with some exceptions, followed a model of state-led development. This model included vertically integrated electric utilities and NOCs, with varying degrees of participation by the private sector; Brazil and Mexico had constitutionally mandated monopolies over oil and electricity, while Argentina, Bolivia, and Colombia combined state control of oil, at times exclusive, with reliance on private participation (Echeverry et al. 2009; Vargas Suárez 2009). The model of state-led development experienced a crisis in the 1980s and underwent significant reforms in the 1990s that rolled back state participation and opened up the economy to private ownership and operation. Since then the region has been in a permanent state of reform, oscillating between moving further in the direction of the market and reasserting the state as an agent of development.

Debates regarding the role of the state in the energy sector in Latin America in the twenty-first century are strongly shaped by the unpopularity of neoliberalism on the one hand (Checchi and Carrera 2009; Chong and López-de-Silanes 2004; Harris 2003; Kingstone 2018) and the imperative of embracing globalization on the other (Keeling 2004; Schroeder 2007). Using survey data from Latinobarómetro, a survey conducted every year on a representative population sample in seventeen Latin American countries, Checchi, Florio, and Carrera (2009) report opposition to privatization increasing from an already significant nearly 45 percent of the population in 1998 to more than 70 percent after 2005. They find that discontent with privatization is driven mostly by a concern with distributive fairness—it is highest among people from the lower income strata—and with the privatization of public utilities. Regarding electricity, the authors report that price increases implemented immediately before privatization, presumably to make the companies more attractive and more profitable to investors, were the source of negative perceptions. McKenzie and Mookherjee (2002) explore public discontent with the outcomes of privatization of public utilities in four countries (Argentina, Bolivia, Mexico, and Nicaragua) and find that while price increases on average cannot explain public disenchantment, the adverse impact on employment can, as the number of employees laid off was very high and those laid off from state-owned utilities suffered long-term economic consequences.

Opposition to market—and foreign—control over energy resources also stemmed from the sense that precious patrimony was being usurped by foreign interests through the privatization of the NOCs. Argentina and Bolivia, for example, underwent the deepest pro-market reforms in the 1990s, having fully privatized their flagship oil companies, YPFB and YPF, respectively, and both countries renationalized their NOCs twenty years later. Created in 1922, YPF of Argentina was the first national oil company in the world outside of the Soviet Union and remains the most important player in the country's hydrocarbon sector. It was restructured and sold in the early 1990s in one of the largest public offerings at the time; the privatization was considered a best practice in privatization in part because of the government's successful efforts at diffusing and dis-articulating opposition from pressure groups, such as the oil workers' union (Grosse and Yáñez 1998). In the case of Bolivia, the government began to reduce its role in its flagship oil and gas enterprise, YPFB, in 1985 and in 1996 split the company into six functional units; ownership was transferred to private operators in exchange for investment (capitalization) but without payment for existing assets (Kaup 2010).

The privatization of YPFB was successful in increasing investment and in turn in increasing production, but the predicted trickle-down effects were not visible, and opposition mounted. There was also a perception that foreign firms (including Petrobrás of Brazil) were reaping excessive profits and effectively defining policy for the sector (Gjelten 2012; Zissis 2006). In 2005 the Bolivian government held a referendum in which Bolivians voted to nationalize the country's hydrocarbons, recapitalize YPFB, and increase taxes and royalties on foreign energy firms. A new division of ownership and control did not come into existence until a year later, when President Evo Morales came to power. The nationalization consisted mainly of taking back control of the underground resources, which according to Bolivia's constitution belong to the state, and renegotiating contracts with customers and suppliers and increasing the state's take from the business (Kaup 2010). In 2012 Bolivia also nationalized the main hydroelectric plant and the power grid operator, which controls 74 percent of the electricity lines in the country (Azcui 2012).

In the case of Argentina, the decision to renationalize a controlling share of YPF from the Spanish company Repsol in 2012 came from above, from a government seeking to regain control over the country's flagship energy company with an eye to the newly discovered shale deposits of Vaca Muerta. The nationalization received wide support from all parties in Congress and was hailed as a victory for sovereignty and a necessary move toward fixing the country's falling energy production and reaching energy self-sufficiency (Mares 2014). Other countries, such as Brazil, Chile, and Uruguay, opted for a more moderate, reformist approach as a reaction to neoliberal policies (Kingstone 2018). Rather than privatizing outright, Brazil opted to transform the NOC Petrobrás into a market-traded company, with majority ownership remaining in the hands of the state, and to end the monopoly it had held over all hydrocarbon activities since 1953, allowing private companies to participate alongside the government.

The balance between Petrobrás and private companies, however, evolved after the end of the monopoly in response to global trends and domestic political conditions. The government of Brazil sought to prioritize the national interest by keeping production and the benefits thereof in national hands while at the same time creating conditions attractive to foreign investors. Until 2010 a concession model was used in which companies bid for exploration rights and in the event of a commercial discovery had exclusive property rights over production after payment of taxes and the applicable government take. With oil prices reaching historical highs and vast reserves discovered deep in the ocean off the coast of Rio de Janeiro, the government changed the rules, giving Petrobrás exclusive rights to operate the extraction of new deposits. These "pre-salt" deposits—due to their location deep in the ocean floor beneath geologic layers of rock and salt—extend five hundred miles along Brazil's Atlantic coast and could move Brazil from being self-sufficient in oil to being a net exporter. The government also enacted an ambitious local content policy (Guimarães 2012) and moved to dilute private ownership by exchanging oil reserves for equity (Monaldi 2014).

While there have been almost no new privatizations in Latin America since the end of the 1990s, public opinion of privatization and neoliberalism, as the cases discussed illustrate, remains relevant to energy politics. The discussion has come to encompass the larger phenomenon of globalization and its effects on the exploitation of energy resources and the fortunes of developing countries more generally. Broad sectors of society in Latin America are critical and fearful of globalization and understand it to be a driver of profound structural change that, like privatization and neoliberalism before it, brings uneven benefits and threatens more disadvantaged sectors of society (Keeling 2004). The trend, however, is not to return to the model of state-led energy development favored before the 1990s; governments are seeking greater control and better terms but continue to rely strongly on the investment acumen and the technological and operational know-how of private firms, especially with respect to developing unconventional deposits and unconventional renewables, such as solar and wind. Two years after the expropriation of YPF, the government of Argentina created new and attractive conditions for Chevron to develop the shale gas deposits in Vaca Muerta. Bolivia too has signed new deals with private oil and gas companies after a period of wariness following the renegotiation of contracts.

Regulatory Performance

Another dimension of the state-market debate in the energy politics of Latin America pertains to the quality of state management of energy resources, enterprises, and services (Levy and Spiller 1996). Economists blame privatization's poor reputation on opaque processes and inadequate and insufficient deregulation, which failed to create conditions that would attract capital and reduce the cost of investment in public services (Chong and López-de-Silanes 2004; Villalonga 2000). Yet a significant literature points to the difficulties of creating adequate regulatory systems in countries with underdeveloped institutions of governance and where cost recovery conflicts with addressing the needs of the poor. This literature on regulatory performance can be organized around two themes: fostering competition and resolving conflicts of interest.

One of the challenges of introducing private participation in the financing and delivery of energy services is that many are natural monopolies, meaning that competition is unlikely to develop on its own. As a result, states must rely on regulatory systems that simultaneously create attractive conditions for investment and police the revenues and costs of energy firms (Kirkpatrick, Parker, and Zhang 2006). Zhang, Parker, and Kirkpatrick (2008) test the effect of privatization, deregulation, and competition on per capita electricity output, capacity utilization, and investor confidence and find that privatization and regulation on their own do not lead to improved performance.

Their main finding is that competition is a strong determinant of improved performance, and that in the presence of weak competition, improvements from private participation are dependent on an effective regulatory regime. A case in point is Chile, which pioneered market-oriented electricity reforms in the region. In Chile, private investors entered the electricity market by purchasing existing state-owned assets. Market rules, however, allowed some early players to become dominant, and in a few years one company came to own nearly 60 percent of the generation market in Chile's Central System, as well as transmission and distribution, and controlled most of the country's water rights. Two companies alone were responsible for nearly half of all investment in new electricity-generating capacity between 1984 and 2004. On the whole, the Chilean reform introduced market-driven incentives that greatly improved the performance of the system, while at the same time allowing high levels of market concentration. Consumer prices declined, but not as much as wholesale prices, which fell nearly 40 percent in the first decade, with distribution companies capturing the difference. It took Chile nearly twenty years to overhaul its regulatory system to address the cost and uncertainty caused by vertical integration and other limitations to competition created by the initial legislation, because existing players in the system became vested in maintaining it, and the regulatory agencies and courts were either unable or unwilling to intervene (Díaz and Soto 1999; Pollitt 2004; Serra and Fischer 2007). Learning from its neighbor's experience, Argentina adopted market rules that forbid majority cross ownership across generation, transmission, and distribution; they also forbid any generator owning more than ten percent of installed capacity (CEE N.d.). At the time of reform, Argentina was suffering power shortages and blackouts, and with market reforms the number of generating companies increased from twenty-five to forty-three. Open access to the grid and cost-based dispatch led to the gradual elimination of older, less-efficient facilities as well as a significant decline in prices and profit margins.

A second challenge identified in the literature is the conflicts of interest that arise from the multiple roles assigned to institutions in the energy field. The advice imparted by the World Bank, the International Energy Agency (IEA), and other institutions engaged in international development has been to unbundle electricity markets. In electricity this has meant separating the different components of the service (generation, transmission, and distribution) and creating separate bodies to deal with daily operation and long-term planning (Zhang, Parker, and Kirkpatrick 2005). In the case of hydrocarbons, the model promoted is that of Norway, where petroleum resources are administered by three separate bodies: a NOC, a government ministry, and a regulatory body. In this model, the NOC manages commercial functions, the ministry determines policy, and the regulatory agency provides oversight (Al-Kasim 2006; Collins 2003). The advice widely promoted by international agencies such as the World Bank was to adopt mechanisms of accountability to the government and the public, create autonomy of management from political authorities and budgetary independence, protect personnel from arbitrary removal, and assure the transparency of decision-making processes (Shah 2007).

Most nations in Latin America followed this advice. Seventy percent of the countries in the region now have a separate entity to regulate electricity markets (Andres et al. 2007), and many of the major producers of hydrocarbons also have dedicated regulatory agencies. Some, such as the ANP (Agência Nacional do Petróleo) in Brazil, predate the deregulation of the 1990s, and others, such as the ANH (Agencia Nacional de Hidrocarburos) in Colombia and PetroPeru in Peru, were purposefully created to address the incorporation of private companies. Though Espinasa (2012) reports the generally positive results attributed to implementing these regulatory frameworks in Brazil, Colombia, and Peru, overall performance has been uneven because much escapes the regulatory capabilities of any agency. Regulatory agencies in lower income nations often must navigate a delicate balance between what is public and what is private in a context of high expectations for the state in the management of the nation's patrimony and the provision of basic services. NOCs, like public utilities, are often the sole providers of distribution services, which gives them extraordinary market power that regulators are not always able to curb. In energy as well as in other sectors, state-owned enterprises generally maintain close ties to the national treasury despite nominal budgetary independence, which defines a set of incentives and behaviors unlike those faced by private actors. NOCs are not only the most important players in the hydrocarbon sectors of their respective countries because of their size, but they are also influential because their goals and strategies are part of the government's agenda. In the case of Mexico and Brazil, the NOC needs formal government approval of investment projects, and the appointment of the directory is highly correlated with the electoral cycle, meaning that new management gets appointed by incoming governments in an effort to ensure convergence between company plans and government agendas (Musacchio and Lazzarini 2014).

In Argentina, regulating the hydrocarbon sector includes the additional challenge of a federal system that gives significant power to the governments of the ten provinces where hydrocarbons are located. Simultaneously with the shift from national to private ownership of YPF, there was a process underway to decentralize governance of underground resources. In the first decade of the twenty-first century, and later with the discovery of unconventional resources, provincial governments created their own oil and gas companies (sub-NOCs) and required private companies to enter into exploration and development partnerships with them in order to be licensed to operate in their jurisdictions. The renationalization of YPF in 2012 and the subsequent deal with Chevron reversed this trend and reasserted the national government's authority on energy deals over that of the provincial governments (Vásquez 2016). Argentina does not have a separate regulatory agency for hydrocarbons; government policy is channeled via YPF and the national and provincial executives.

While there is agreement in the literature that the success of market liberalization and privatization in the energy sector has been partial and that unsatisfactory regulatory performance is to a great extent to blame, some argue against rigid ideological commitments to liberalization and to the wholesale importation of institutional models. Millan (2005) argues that the inadequate separation of state roles that predated liberalization (in which the state was at once policy maker, regulator, entrepreneur, and client) was insufficiently addressed by reducing the scope of the state and the importance of policymaking while leaving regulation to independent agencies and entrepreneurship to private companies. This arrangement did not reduce conflicts of interest or clarify the limits between policymaking and regulation, but effectively reduced the ability of the state to perform any role (Perotti 2004). Gabriele (2004) points at the risks inherent in energy market liberalization, such as the creation of private monopolies and insufficient attention to long-term energy supply, as well as the loss of technical and managerial capability by the state. He recommends a flexible, nonideological approach that allows developing countries to combine private and public attributes in accordance with their needs. Thurber, Hults, and Heller (2011) also doubt the wisdom of exporting the Norwegian model to countries with low political competition and low institutional capacity; they suggest consolidating rather than separating functions in countries where both weaknesses are present. Other suggestions include focusing on developing technical and institutional capacity and consolidating functions first, only moving on to unbundling once there is evidence of a pluralistic political environment.

In recommending pragmatism over boilerplate solutions, these authors identify with a broader body of institutionalist research that focuses on the greater challenges and constraints of developing countries and is skeptical of notions of convergence toward a universal best practice (Dixit 2004; Rodrik 2007). Two contrasting experiences illustrate this point. First, Argentina is an example of regulatory functions not surviving the economic and political disruptions that are frequent in the developing world. A major crisis in 2001 included a massive devaluation of the local currency, which in turn caused the government to intervene in the pricing of services, effectively freezing electricity tariffs at nominal prices for nearly fifteen years. Long-term planning took a back seat to short-term needs, and regulatory functions were reduced to overseeing the provision of daily service. The initial policy, carried out as an emergency measure, became entrenched and costly for politicians to eliminate (Bril-Mascarenhas and Post 2015; Valverde Camiña 2012). Even as the sector recovers capacity with new investments in renewables, regulatory functions continue to be concentrated in the executive cabinet and tied to the government's agenda, which has complicated plans to return energy tariffs to market levels (Ganem n.d.).

Second, Mexico deregulated much later than other countries in the region and has benefited from their experiences and succeeded in implementing a combination of the sector's best practices. It was also helpful that unlike other Latin American nations, Mexico implemented reforms in the absence of an electricity crisis. Auctions have attracted investment in natural gas and nonconventional renewables at competitive prices. The institutional design has evolved as expected, with separate entities assuming responsibilities for operation and oversight. Mexico is also ahead of other countries in introducing brokering into the electricity system, which indicates a shared expectation among actors that the system will produce reliable market signals (Bracho 2018).

Energy Subsidies

At the core of energy policy and politics in a developing region like Latin America lies the challenge of attracting sufficient investment to assure supply while maintaining reasonable consumer prices. As mentioned previously, consumers have become wary of market-based reform based on the perception that there is a disconnect between economic efficiency and the public good, understood as an improved and sustained quality of life, in particular for those less favored by development (Kingstone 2018). Historically, the price of energy in Latin America was an economic variable used for macro-economic management. The market-oriented reforms of the 1990s sought to change this arrangement, returning prices (of energy, transportation, telecommunications, and other public services) to the realm of the market and aligning the allocation of resources with market conditions. A core belief behind the utility reforms was that low tariffs were a key cause of poor performance (Bates 1997). Agencies such as the World Bank and US Agency for International Development (USAID) recommended setting consumer prices for electricity to levels that promoted the efficient allocation of resources, allowed for the complete pass-through of production costs, and were consistent with the utilities' expected rate of return (Besant-Jones 1993; Corduckes 1994; Menke and Fazzari 1994). The transformation produced by these reforms was uneven; in some areas, such as telecommunications, market prices have prevailed (though often with a significant additional tax burden), while in transportation and energy, the state continues to intervene in markets with a variety of goals and instruments (Estache, Goicoechea, and Trujillo 2006).

By the first decade of the twenty-first century, the pendulum was starting to swing away from neoliberal precepts toward greater state intervention. The region experienced the arrival to power of governments with unfavorable views of private companies owning public services and of the arm's-length regulation that was promoted in the 1990s (Cleary 2006; Estache, Goicoechea, and Trujillo 2006). The commodity boom was bringing fiscal surpluses to the region and financing investment in social programs and income redistribution while at the same time increasing the price of fuel; these combined events created pressure to provide energy subsidies even in countries that are energy rich, such as Bolivia. For the region as a whole, energy subsidies account for nearly 5 percent of GDP (Coady et al. 2015), well above the world average of 1 percent of global GDP (Commander 2012). Electricity subsidies are more common in low-income countries, particularly in Central America and the Caribbean, where small scale and dependence on fuel imports result in high electricity prices, while subsidies to oil and gas consumption are more common in energy-rich countries (Di Bella et al. 2015). The instruments of subsidization also vary. Peru and Colombia use a stabilization fund to adjust domestic prices, while Costa Rica and Uruguay pay for adjustments through foregone taxes. Energy subsidies in Bolivia are created by selling in the domestic market at prices lower than export parity. By 2012 energy subsidies in Bolivia amounted to nearly 10 percent of GDP. Motivations for the adoption of energy subsidies also vary, but the most common across Latin America are transferring income to the poor and giving preferential treatment to groups with lobbying power (Commander 2012).

Subsidies in Latin America, as in the rest of the world, are under scrutiny. In addition to the traditional critiques of inefficiency, energy subsidies are increasingly opposed by environmental groups, such as Greenpeace, on the grounds that they encourage the overconsumption of fossil fuels and are a major obstacle to decarbonization policies (Hancevic et al. 2016; Sovacool 2017). In Latin America the main reason for energy subsidies becoming a major policy issue has been their fiscal cost and the growing recognition that the bulk of what is spent on energy subsidies is captured by social groups that were not the intended beneficiaries. Despite aiming at alleviating negative welfare effects, energy subsidies are generally regressive, providing more benefits for the upper income segments of the population. For South and Central America combined, for the period 2003–2008 the top quintile of the population received 42 percent of the resources spent on subsidies for gasoline, kerosene, and LPG, while the bottom quintile received 5 percent (Arze del Granado, Coady, and Gillingham 2012, 2247). In Bolivia, for the period 2005–2016 the highest income decile received a subsidy to natural gas and oil five times greater than that received by the lowest decile (Laserna 2018, 20). This ratio extends approximately to all fuel consumption in developing countries, with the richest 20 percent of the population capturing six times more subsidies than the poorest 20 percent (Arze del Granado, Coady, and Gillingham 2012, 2238). Sometimes price adjustment mechanisms work perversely against the interests of consumers, in particular those in the lower income categories. Mexico uses a gasoline excise tax to compensate for price fluctuations, such that when the international price is higher than the domestic price set by the government, the tax becomes negative, effectively subsidizing consumers, while in the reverse situation it generates revenue for the government. This tax has generated revenue for the government in twenty-eight of the thirty-six years it has been in existence (Aguilera 2017).

Energy subsidies are also motivated by concerns over adequate investment in production and by the interests of producers themselves. Often, price control mechanisms that are initially introduced as a reaction to an external shock remain on the books during market slumps, with subsidies switching from consumers to producers. In Argentina the government established price controls for crude during the height of the market but decided to keep these controls after prices declined, guaranteeing producers prices for oil and natural gas well above international prices. The government justified this policy as necessary to attract investment in exploration by giving price incentives to gas produced from new wells using unconventional technologies (Mares 2013).

The recommendations emerging from the literature on reforming energy policy and reducing subsidies recognize that while subsidies are expensive and inefficient, removing them could have a significantly adverse effect on poorer segments of the population that rely on lower energy prices to meet household consumption needs, and they promote the use of targeted efforts to compensate the poor for the cost of energy without encouraging excessive consumption of fossil fuels (Feng et al. 2018; Commander 2012). The recommendation is to replace blanket subsidies with direct cash transfer programs to the poor—as is done in the Dominican Republic, Ecuador, El Salvador, and Nicaragua (Di Bella et al. 2015)—and with other in-kind measures, such as subsidized public transportation and electrification of poor and rural areas. Finally, as in the case of regulation, there is a recognition that solutions are best if designed for the specific conditions found in each country and market, rather than employing an idealized notion of the market and of convergence on a single model of best practice (Commander 2012; Feng et al. 2018; Williams and Ghanadan 2006).

Social Conflict

One of the longer lasting political debates in Latin America refers to the relationship between natural resources and sustainable and equitable development. During the twentieth century the relationship between centuries of extraction and persistent underdevelopment produced theories such as structuralism and dependent development. The focus of these theories was the structure of the national and world economies and the roles that states and social actors, in particular the elites, played in reinforcing the conditions that led to underdevelopment (Cardoso and Faletto 1979; Prebisch 1950). In the twenty-first century the relationship between resource extraction and development has been captured by the term "Commodities Consensus" (Svampa 2015). According to Svampa, the Commodities Consensus is the new paradigm of development driven by the world's insatiable appetite for natural resources. It is characterized by its enormous scale and by the absorption of areas previously not considered productive. This new phase of extractivism, as well as the conflict and dilemmas it generates, includes not only mining, but also the expansion of the energy frontier through the use of new technologies to tap unconventional deposits, the installation of mega-energy projects, and the expansion of large-scale agriculture.

The Commodities Consensus includes corporate and financial interests, but also states, and the shared optimism of progressively minded governments across the region that the commodity boom will pave the way out of poverty. Yet the literature reflects anything but consensus; it is focused primarily on the conflicts and transformations that define a new geography, politics, and language of extractivism. The first point to note is the significant increase in resource- and land-related conflicts in the region. According to the Observatory of Mining Conflicts in Latin America (Observatorio de Conflictos Mineros en América Latina), there are 246 ongoing conflicts in the region distributed across twenty-one countries (OCMAL 2018). Activities related to the extraction, processing, and transportation of hydrocarbons have attracted significant opposition as well. In Colombia, public acts seeking to obstruct activity related to hydrocarbons increased from 38 in 2010 to 343 in 2015 (Sáenz 2016), and five referenda, or popular consultations, were carried out in 2017, all resulting in an overwhelming vote against oil and mining activity (Bristow 2017). In some respects, Colombia is a unique case given the legacy of armed guerrilla conflict in the relationship between oil companies and local communities. For decades the companies' main concern was security, which has led to a defensive and mistrustful stance relative to the surrounding communities (Cuéllar 2016).

The protests in Colombia nonetheless reflect concerns expressed throughout the region over environmental degradation, unmet expectations of employment and overall economic development, and the violation of the right to consultation.

Extractive energy activities are not the only sources of conflict. Hydroelectric dam projects, and megadams in particular, have been the focus of protest and opposition. Examples include the Agua Zarca Dam in Honduras, which lost its funding after banks pulled out following violent conflict, including the assassination of a community leader, Berta Cáceres (Raftopoulos 2017); HydroAysén in southern Chile, which underwent an eight-year legal battle that culminated with the suspension of the project; the projects in the Tapajós basin in Brazil, which are stalled; and the Oxec and Oxec II projects suspended by Guatemala's Supreme Court for failing to consult the 29,000 residents in the project's affected area. With 412 dams projected to be built in the Amazon region as of 2015 (including 77 in Peru, 55 in Ecuador, 14 in Bolivia, 6 in Venezuela, and 2 in Guyana) and the success of many opposition movements, the trend of protest and conflict can be expected to continue (Vidal 2017).

The literature addressing these conflicts can be organized into three themes: geography, identity, and collective action. According to Bebbington (2009), the latest commodity boom in Latin America has created new "development geographies," defined in part by the scale and pace of projects; the scope of regional infrastructure initiatives, such as the Initiative for the Integration of the Regional Infrastructure of South America (IIRSA); and the new landscape of open-pit mines and heap-leaching operations. Another physical feature observed by Bebbington that shapes these conflicts is the diminished use of skilled labor and the increased use of water, energy, and land, which leads to fewer protests regarding working conditions led by organized labor and more protests from local residents competing with projects for natural resources. These localized protests, though numerous, are highly dispersed and constitute a fragmented geography of protest against resource-extracting projects, which severely limits the possibility of creating a non-extractivist development model (López and Vértiz 2015). Barton, Román, and Fløysand (2012) present these contrasting visions of development as different understandings of space and place, with megaprojects representing the international commodification of *spaces* and local communities advocating the organic development of *places* (see also Haarstad 2012).

The issue of land has been the focus of research on resource-related conflicts, not only because mineral extraction and infrastructure projects have advanced into new, more populated areas, but also because the right to the land is the primary objective of rural and indigenous groups in Latin America (Jackson and Warren 2005). This factor has caused renewable energy projects to also generate conflict. Mexico in particular has faced numerous conflicts related to wind farm projects in the Tehuantepec Isthmus (Ávila-Calero 2017), where the best wind resources are located, and the Yucatán Peninsula (Zárate Toledo and Fraga 2016). While renewable energy technologies do not pose environmental hazards comparable to a potential oil spill, as many communities in Colombia have experienced over the years (Cuéllar 2016; Sáenz 2016), the issues that generate conflict are very similar, and land tenure figures prominently among these. In addition to disputes over the use of water, rural communities see little long-term benefit to welcoming these projects because they provide few economic gains after the initial phase of construction to offset the disruption they cause to agricultural life (Flemmer and Schilling-Vacaflor 2016; Riethof 2017). In addition, in many rural and indigenous communities in Mexico land is owned through communal arrangements that are difficult to reconcile with the contractual needs of energy projects (Jackson and Warren 2005; Payan and Correa-Cabrera 2014).

The issue of land is also closely related to that of identity. Jackson and Warren (2005) observe that indigenous movements in Latin America have advocated for a notion of territory that is intrinsic to the formation of social and cultural values that are at the core of an indigenous identity and the quest for self-determination. In protesting megaprojects, indigenous peoples are defending a relationship with the natural world that is "better expressed in the language of kinship than in the language of property" (Blaser, 2013, 14). In Bolivia the conflict over the development of natural gas resources involves identities that are spatially rooted: the indigenous people of the highlands, who embrace traditional roots and resist certain aspects of globalization, and the mestizo class in the lowlands, who favor full engagement with the extractive model and the global economy (Schroeder 2007). The language of protest has changed as well in this new era, sidelining questions of poverty and exclusion in favor of demands for dignity and self-determination (Svampa 2015). Perhaps the most important development has been conceptualizing opposition to megaprojects and extractive development as a human right. The framework of human rights has provided a symbolic and legal basis to socio-environmental conflicts and allowed an alternative narrative and a powerful critique to develop from the immediate issues felt by communities neighboring project sites (Gearty 2010; Riethof 2017). Communities opposed to energy projects have increasingly called upon the UN Declaration of the Rights of Indigenous Peoples (UNDRIP) and the International Labor Organization's Convention 169, The Indigenous and Tribal People's Convention, to bolster their claims. The Convention was passed in 1989 and ratified by twenty-two countries, eighteen of which are in Latin America. It recognizes "the aspirations of [Indigenous] peoples to exercise control over their own institutions, ways of life, and economic development and to maintain and develop their identities, languages and religions, within the framework of the States in which they live" (Art. 44). The Convention also creates an obligation for governments and corporations to consult indigenous peoples regarding activities that may impact their communities and territories. UNDRIP also gives indigenous peoples substantive and procedural rights to the land, which includes the legal recognition of land and its use (Raftopoulos 2017).

Appealing to a human rights agenda has allowed rural and marginalized communities access to transnational movements and amplified the visibility of their cause. The Mapuche community of Chile forged links with national and international environmental and human rights organizations and activists, such as the Defenders of the Chilean Forest, a well-established organization, alongside newer, more politicized groups, such as the Institute of Political Ecology and The Observatory of Indigenous People's Rights, led by José Aylwin, that provided legal services to Mapuche activists.

These organizations in turn provided links to international groups, such as the American Anthropological Association's Committee for Human Rights, California's South and Meso American Indian Rights, and Human Rights Watch, that allowed an otherwise remote and marginalized community to launch a series of campaigns of protest and awareness and forge better relations with the state agencies involved in environmental permitting and energy projects. As a result of their activism, Chilean society has also become more aware of the linkage between environmental issues and social justice. Joining forces with international actors across the environmental-human rights spectrum has given the Mapuche a measure of agency that would not otherwise have been possible given the power imbalances among rural, indigenous communities and political elites (Carruthers and Rodriguez 2009, 752). The power of international linkages was perhaps most evident in the campaign against HydroAysén's five megadam hydroelectric projects. The coalition that led this effort included Chilean and international nongovernmental organizations (NGOs), including the Pumalín Foundation, Conservación Patagónica, the Council for the Defense of Patagonia, and Deep Ecology, and was able to launch a well-funded media campaign that included full-page ads and TV spots (Tompkins Conservation 2018). It finally succeeded in persuading the Chilean government to cancel the projects in the Aysén region and approve instead 700 MW of solar and wind energy (Chivers 2016). There is some evidence that at the regional level governments are retreating from megadam construction, starting with a statement from the Brazilian government that the country's hydropower policy may need to be reconsidered in the face of public opposition (Watts 2018). Many countries in the region have also been pursuing non-hydro renewables as a form of complementing large hydro, tripling installed capacity in the region between 2006 and 2015 (IRENA 2016).

Much of the literature on socio-environmental conflict, however, focuses on the limitations of protest movements. One issue noted often in the literature is the (apparent) contradiction between the Left's embrace of the extractive and large infrastructure development model and the dispossession it visits on social groups that it purports to represent and that have contributed to its electoral success (Farthing and Riofrancos 2017; Raftopoulos 2017; Riethof 2017; Svampa 2015). The constitutions of Bolivia and Ecuador were modified by the leftist governments of Evo Morales and Rafael Correa to recognize the rights of all indigenous nations and of nature itself, yet the very same governments that promoted these changes have shown little sympathy toward those opposing resource extraction (Farthing and Riofrancos 2017), resorting to authoritarian methods of policymaking combined with occasional use of force and efforts to delegitimize those who question extraction (Bebbington and Bebbington 2012). As Gudynas (2010) points out, however, more than a contradiction, this phenomenon is evidence of the endurance of ideas of development based on the achievement of modernity based on material progress and the appropriation of nature. This legacy also affects the legal systems that often frustrate social movements against extractivism and megaprojects because these systems are designed to perpetuate human domination of nature and have a difficult time recognizing other types of relationships (Cullinan 2010). An example of this phenomenon is the absence of legislation to define and regulate the meaning of The Indigenous and Tribal People's Convention within the respective national legal frameworks and to give legal specificity to the right of consultation and the mandate to respect and protect alternative notions of development. In other cases, such as the fight against megadams in Brazil (Flemmer and Schilling-Vacaflor 2016), apparently successful domestic and international legal campaigns eventually were blocked by a government not willing to recognize and enforce legal decisions (Riethof 2017). A final observation on the limited progress made by social movements in achieving an alternative model of resource and energy use is the absence of clear and agreed-upon objectives and viable political strategies among protesters (Jackson and Warren 2005). Communities living alongside major infrastructure projects find it difficult to obtain information about a project and its consequences and lack the tools to formulate alternatives that have clear benefits for the community and can also appeal to potential allies outside the community. Often, language barriers and lack of knowledge of legal procedures leave communities with few avenues of action other than physically impeding the progress of a project (DPLF 2011). The actions that garner international notoriety and support and are able to deploy sophisticated, multifront legal and political strategies, such as the campaigns against megadams in Chile and Brazil, are few, and the cases of success are even fewer.

AN AGENDA FOR FUTURE RESEARCH

There is considerable scholarship on the role of states and markets in energy politics in Latin America that has focused on the ideological frontier between the two and the relative position of governments (and societies) in relation to that divide. The literature covered in this chapter documents the recurring concern with neoliberalism and the difficulty in developing alternative modes of energy exploitation and use. The literature on reform, however, points to an important topic that would benefit from further exploration: state capacity. The research cited on regulatory frameworks (Dixit 2004; Gabriele 2004; Millán 2005; Rodrik 2007; Thurber, Hults, and Heller 2011), as well as that on the removal of energy subsidies (Commander 2012; Feng et al. 2018; Williams and Ghanadan 2006), emphasizes the importance of tailoring policy solutions to each country's circumstances and discourages the wholesale adoption of best-model solutions. Among the institutional attributes that affect the quality of policy is state capacity. While it is a subject that has received substantial attention in the political science literature on the Latin American state (Geddes 1994; Evans, Rueschemeyer, and Skocpol 1985; O'Donnell 1993; Tommasi 2011), fruitful research could be conducted that is specific to energy policy and to contemporary commodity booms. The research by Dargent, Feldmann, and Luna (2017) on the uneven improvement in state capacity in Peru following the most recent commodity boom is one example. This work builds on other scholarship on commodities and state building, such as Saylor's (2014) and Soifer's (2016; 2008), which trace variation in state capacity to elite behavior and the commodity booms of the nineteenth century. The work by Dargent and his colleagues is innovative in that it focuses on the effects of the commodity boom not only on actors that benefit from, and demand, state capacity, as elites did in the past, but also on actors that oppose state strengthening, such as peasants, informal miners, and illegal agents. The issue of uneven state capacity is another fruitful line of research. This unevenness can be observed across subnational units (Luna and Soifer 2017) and across functional units of the state (Hochstetler 2011). Hochstetler, for example, documents the growth in state capacity in Brazil with reference to environmental licensing for energy projects and the relative power that licensing agencies have over the course of energy policy. This line of research also intersects with the issue of social conflict and, on the one hand, the ability of the state to preempt opposition, as Hochstetler points out in the case of Brazil, and on the other hand, the ability of groups that mobilize against infrastructure and other projects to limit the reach of the state and in so doing undermine the construction of state capacity.

Second, more research should focus on societal preferences regarding new technologies, such as fracking and renewable energy. Research on public attitudes toward environmental questions in Latin America has been dominated by the study of opposition and protest movements, and little is known about the effectiveness of organizations that promote (and succeed in) the adoption of particular activities and behaviors. Organizations such as the National Assembly of Environmental Casualties (Asamblea Nacional de Afectados Ambientales), which congregates over ninety environmental NGOs in Mexico; the Brazilian Network of Environmental Justice (Rede Brasileira de Justiça Ambiental), which includes over eighty social movements, labor unions, NGOs, and indigenous peoples' organizations; and Patagonia without Dams (Patagonia sin Represas) in Chile, which congregates coalitions of citizens, community groups, and international NGOs, are most visible for exposing the plight of those adversely affected by resource extraction and large infrastructure and for their strategies of resistance. Little is known about the effectiveness of these movements in representing alternative policy solutions and promoting change. The case of the abandonment of the Aysén Hydro projects in Chile in favor of solar and wind projects could be a starting point for a more comprehensive look at grassroots movements in the energy space. Recent research by Madariaga and Allain (2018) documents how environmental coalitions in Chile have been influential in advancing an agenda for renewable energy. An interesting angle explored in this research is the construction of contingent coalitions that congregate actors with a variety of agendas, such as labor, feminist groups, and environmentalists, as an effective way of mobilizing human resources and pushing forward policy agendas. These coalitions are formed with specific policy goals in mind and disband once that goal has been reached, thus avoiding some of the collective action problems identified by Jackson and Warren (2005) among indigenous movements.

Our understanding of societal influences on energy policy would also benefit from more research on corporate interests and how they combine with societal preferences to form coalitions for and against different energy policy options. Surveys such as Latinobarómetro, an annual public opinion survey, find that a large majority of the population of Latin America, 71 percent, believes fighting climate change should be a priority regardless of the potential impacts on economic growth (Latinobarómetro 2017). Research on the renewable energy discourse networks, however, finds that "economic incentives" and "exploiting an abundant resource" prevail as motives to adopt green energy over issues of ecology or sustainability in middle-income countries such as South Africa, Thailand, and Mexico (Rennkamp et al. 2017). According to this network analysis, environmental NGOs have not been in the vanguard of the adoption of renewable technologies. In South Africa, for example, the industrial sector has been a leading voice in support of renewable energy, enticed by policies such as local content requirements for renewable energy projects. Another phenomenon worth investigating is that of corporations adopting a green energy policy for their own consumption and later diversifying into the renewable energy business. The United States has the example of Facebook, Google, and Apple committing to 100 percent renewable energy targets, which has given an important push to the renewable energy agenda. The next step, becoming providers of renewable energy using cloud and commercial know-how, is now considered just a matter of time (Mackinnon 2018; Reid 2018). In Latin America the phenomenon of corporate consumers becoming active participants in the energy market seems to be somewhat circumscribed to Mexico, which can be explained by the type of regulatory framework adopted and the opportunities it provides for large consumers and corporate self-producers to profitably diversify into the renewable energy business (Bracho 2018). Other markets in Latin America, such as that of Central America, which is fossil-energy poor and rich in renewable sources such as solar, and where the state infrastructure capacity is weak (with the exception of Costa Rica), could benefit from the leadership of corporate actors, such as large industrial and commercial consumers of electricity, in the construction of renewable energy. More research is needed on the types of conditions and incentives that need to be present for the business sector to participate in coalitions that support renewable energy.

In the second decade of the twenty-first century, energy politics in Latin America is playing out in a setting broadly defined by two trends: new political actors and agendas enabled by the consolidation of democracy, and the emergence of new economic opportunities in resource extraction and renewable energy. The confluence of these factors, along with unique historical and institutional legacies, defines the paths available for societies to navigate their participation in the region's collective energy future. Further research on individual country experiences and comparative case studies would help us better understand the conditions under which particular energy strategies are formulated and deployed.

References

Aguilera, Rodrigo. 2017. "The Absurd Logic behind Mexico's Gasoline Price Hike." *Huffington Post*, January 16. https://www.huffingtonpost.com/rodrigo-aguilera/the-absurd-logic-behind-m_b_14197100.html (updated January 17, 2018).

Al-Kasim, Farouk. 2006. "Managing Petroleum Resources: The 'Norwegian Model' in a Broad Perspective." Oxford: Oxford Institute for Energy Studies.

Andres, Luis, José Luis Guasch, Makhtar Diop, and Sebastián Lopez Azumendi. 2007. "Assessing the Governance of Electricity Regulatory Agencies in the Latin American and Caribbean Region: A Benchmarking Analysis." Washington, DC: World Bank.

Arze del Granado, Francisco, David Coady, and Robert Gillingham. 2012. "The Unequal Benefits of Fuel Subsidies: A Review of Evidence for Developing Countries." *World Development* 40, no. 11: 2234–2248.

Ávila-Calero, Sofia. 2017. "Contesting Energy Transitions: Wind Power and Conflicts in the Isthmus of Tehuantepec." *Journal of Political Ecology* 24, no. 1: 922–1012.

Azcui, Mabel. 2012. "Evo Morales nacionaliza la filial de Red Eléctrica en Bolivia." *El País*, May 1. http://economia.elpais.com/economia/2012/05/01/actualidad/1335887717_799794.html/.

Barton, Jonathan, Álvaro Román, and Arnt Fløysand. 2012. "Resource Extraction and Local Justice in Chile: Conflicts Over the Commodification of Spaces and the Sustainable Development of Places." In *New Political Spaces in Latin American Natural Resource Governance*, edited by Håvard Haarstad, 107–128. Basingstoke, UK: Palgrave Macmillan.

Bates, Robin. 1997. "Bulk Electricity Pricing in Restructured Markets: Lessons for Developing Countries from Eight Case Studies." IEN Occasional Paper no. 10. Washington, DC: The World Bank Industry and Energy Department.

BBC. 2017. "Amazon Culture Clash over Brasil's Dams." *BBC News*, January 10. http://www.bbc.com/news/world-latin-america-38391377.

Bebbington, Anthony. 2009. "Latin America: Contesting Extraction, Producing Geographies." *Singapore Journal of Tropical Geography* 30, no. 1: 7–12.

Bebbington, Denise Humphreys, and Anthony Bebbington. 2012. "Post-What? Extractive Industries, Narratives of Development and Socio-Environmental Disputes Across the (Ostensibly Changing Andean Region)." In *New Political Spaces in Latin American Natural Resource Governance*, edited by Håvard Haarstad, 17–37. Basingstoke, UK: Palgrave Macmillan.

Besant-Jones, John, ed. 1993. "Power Supply in Developing Countries: Will Reform Work?" Proceedings of a Roundtable. Occasional Paper no. 1. Washington, DC: World Bank, Industry and Energy Department and Electricité de France.

Blanco, Luisa, and Robin Grier. 2013. "Explaining the Rise of Left in Latin America." *Latin American Research Review* 48, no. 1: 68–90.

Blaser, Mario. 2013. "Notes Towards a Political Ontology of 'Environmental Conflicts'." In *Contested Ecologies: Dialogues in the South on Nature and Knowledge*, edited by Lesley Green, 13–27. Cape Town, South Africa: HSRC Press.

Bracho, Riccardo. 2018. Interview with Senior Project Leader, International Programs NREL. Golden, CO, February 1.

Bril-Mascarenhas, Tomás, and Alison Post. 2015. "Policy Traps: Consumer Subsidies in Post-Crisis Argentina." *Studies in Comparative International Development* 50, no. 1: 98–120.

Bristow, Matthew. 2017. "Colombia Has Oil, but Voters Want to Keep it Underground." *Bloomberg Businessweek*, September 7. https://www.bloomberg.com/news/articles/2017-09-07/colombia-needs-oil-colombians-say-no.

Cárdenas, Enrique, José Antonio Ocampo, and Rosemary Thorp, eds. 2000. *An Economic History of Twentieth-Century Latin America*. Vol. 3. New York: Palgrave.

Cardoso, Fernando and Enzo Faletto. 1979. *Dependency and Development in Latin America*. Berkeley, CA: University of California Press.

Carruthers, David, and Patricia Rodriguez. 2009. "Mapuche Protest, Environmental Conflict and Social Movement Linkage in Chile." *Third World Quarterly* 30, no. 4: 743–760.

Castañeda, Jorge. 2012. *Utopia Unarmed: The Latin American Left after the Cold War*. New York: Random House.

Center for Energy Economics (CEE). N.d. "Results of Electricity Sector Restructuring in Argentina." Center for Energy Economics, Bureau of Economic Geology, Jackson School of Geosciences, The University of Texas at Austin.

Checchi, Daniele, Massimo Florio, and Jorge Carrera. 2009. "Privatisation Discontent and Utility Reform in Latin America." *The Journal of Development Studies* 45, no. 3: 333–350.

Chivers, Danny. 2016. *Renewable Energy: Cleaner, Fairer Ways to Power the Planet*. ON: .

Chong, Alberto, and Florencio López-De-Silanes. 2004. "Privatization in Latin America: What Does the Evidence Say? [with Comments]." *Economía* 4, no. 2: 37–111.

Cleary, Matthew. 2006. "A 'Left Turn' in Latin America? Explaining the Left's Resurgence." *Journal of Democracy* 17, no. 4: 35–49.

Coady, David, Ian Parry, Louis Sears, and Baoping Shang. 2015. "How Large Are Global Energy Subsidies?" IMF Working Paper no. 105. Washington, DC: International Monetary Fund.

Collins, Tom, 2003. "NOC Reform: Restructuring, Commercialization and Privatization." World Bank National Oil Companies Workshop, Current Roles and Future. Washington, DC: World Bank

Commander, Simon. 2012. "A Guide to the Political Economy of Reforming Energy Subsidies." Policy Paper no. 52. Bonn, Germany: Altura Partners, EBRD, IE Business School and IZA.

Cordukes, Peter, ed. 1994. "Submission and Evaluation of Proposals for Private Power Generation in Developing Countries." Occasional Paper no. 2. Washington, DC: World Bank Industry and Energy Department and USAID.

Cuéllar, Alfonso. 2016. "Oil and Peace in Colombia: Industry Challenges in the Post-War Period." Washington, DC: Wilson Center Latin America Program.

Cullinan, Cormac. 2010. "Earth's Jurisprudence: From Colonization to Participation." In *State of the World*, edited by Erik Assadourian, 143–148. Washington, DC: Worldwatch Institute.

Dargent, Eduardo, Andreas Feldmann, and Juan Pablo Luna. 2017. "Greater State Capacity, Lesser Stateness: Lessons from the Peruvian Commodity Boom." *Politics & Society* 45, no. 1: 3–34.

Di Bella, Gabriel, Lawrence Norton, Joseph Ntamatungiro, Sumiko Ogawa, Issouf Samaké, and Marika Santoro. 2015. "Energy Subsidies in Latin America and the Caribbean: Stocktaking and Policy Challenges." IMF Working Paper no. 15/30, Washington, DC.

Díaz, Carlos, and Raimundo Soto. 1999. "Open-Access Issues in the Chilean Telecommunications and Electricity Sectors." Paper presented at the Inter-American Development Bank Conference Second Generation Issues in the Reforms of Public Services, Washington, DC, October.

Dixit, Avinash. 2004. *Lawlessness and Economics: Alternative Modes of Governance*. Princeton, NJ: Princeton University Press.

Due Process of Law Foundation (DPLF). 2011. "The Rights of Indigenous Peoples to Prior Consultation." Washington, DC: Due Process of Law Foundation, Oxfam.

Echeverry, Juan Carlos, Jaime Navas, Verónica Navas, and María Paula Gómez. 2009. "Oil in Colombia: History, Regulation and Macroeconomic Impact." Documentos Cede 005428. Bogota, Colombia: Universidad de los Andes-Cede.

Escobar, Arturo, and Sonia Álvarez, eds. (1992) 2018. *The Making of Social Movements in Latin America: Identity, Strategy, and Democracy*. New York: Taylor & Francis.

Espinasa, Ramón, 2012. "Los dos mundos petroleros de América Latina." *Debates Iesa* 17, no. 2: 26–27.

Estache, Antonio, Ana Goicoechea, and Lourdes Trujillo. 2006. "Utilities Reforms and Corruption in Developing Countries." Policy Research Working Paper no. 4081. Washington, DC: World Bank.

Evans, Peter. 1979. *Dependent Development: The Alliance of Multinational, State, and Local Capital in Brazil*. Princeton, NJ: Princeton University Press.

Evans, Peter, David Rueschemeyer, and Theda Skocpol, eds. 1985. *Bringing the State Back In*. Cambridge, UK: Cambridge University Press.

Farthing Linda, and Thea Riofrancos. 2017. "The State of the Left in Latin America: Ecuador and Bolivia after the Pink Tide." NACLA, July 19. https://nacla.org/news/2017/07/20/state-left-latin-america-ecuador-and-bolivia-after-pink-tide.

Feng, Kuishuang, Klaus Hubacek, Yu Liu, Estefanía Marchán, and Adrien Vogt-Schilb. 2018. "Managing the Distributional Effects of Energy Taxes and Subsidy Removal in Latin America and the Caribbean." Working Paper no. 947. Washington, DC: Inter-American Development Bank.

Ferreira, Francisco, Julian Messina, Jamele Rigolini, Luis Felipe López-Calva, Maria Ana Lugo, and Renos Vakis. 2013. "Economic Mobility and the Rise of the Latin American Middle Class." Latin America and Caribbean Studies. Washington, DC: World Bank.

Flemmer, Riccarda, and Almut Schilling-Vacaflor. 2016. "Unfulfilled Promises of the Consultation Approach: The Limits to Effective Indigenous Participation in Bolivia's and Peru's Extractive Industries." *Third World Quarterly* 37, no. 1: 172–188.

Fryklund, Bob. 2012. "South America: Will Resource Plays Lead the Next Wave?" *Houston Geological Society Bulletin* 54, no. 8: 29–31.

Gabriele, Alberto. 2004. "Policy Alternatives in Reforming Energy Utilities in Developing Countries." *Energy Policy* 32: 1319–1337.

Ganem, Carlos. N.d. "Taking Stock of the Macri Energy Reform Agenda: Tariffs and Subsidy Reduction." La Jolla, CA: Institute of the Americas Energy and Sustainability Program.

Gearty, Conor. 2010. "Do Human Rights Help or Hihumannder Environmental Protection?" *Journal of Human Rights and the Environment* 1: 7–22.

Geddes, Barbara. 1994. *Politician's Dilemma: Building State Capacity in Latin America*. Berkeley: University of California Press.

Gjelten, Tom. 2012. "The Dash for Gas: The Golden Age of an Energy Game-Changer." *World Affairs* 174 (January/February). http://go.galegroup.com/ps/i.do?id=GALE.

Grosse, Robert, and Juan Yáñez. 1998. "Carrying Out a Successful Privatization: The YPF Case." *Academy of Management Executive* 12, no. 2: 51–63.

Gruss, Bertrand. 2014. "After the Boom—Commodity Prices and Economic Growth in Latin America and the Caribbean." Working Papers no. 14/154. Washington, DC: International Monetary Fund.

Guimarães, Eduardo. 2012. "Política de conteúdo local na cadeia de petróleo e gás: uma visão sobre a evolução do instrumento e a percepção das empresas investidoras e produtoras de bens." Rio de Janeiro: Confederação Nacional da Indústria.

Gudynas, Eduardo. 2010. "The New Extractivism of the 21st Century: Ten Urgent Theses about Extractivism in Relation to Current South American Progressivism." Americas Program Report. Washington, DC: Center for International Policy.

Haarstad, Håvard. 2012. "Extraction, Regional Integration, and the Enduring Problem of Local Political Spaces." In *New Political Spaces in Latin American Natural Resource Governance*, edited by Håvard Haarstad. Studies of the Americas, 83–105. New York: Palgrave Macmillan.

Hancevic, Pedro, Walter Cont and Fernando Navajas. 2016. "Energy populism and household welfare." *Energy Economics*, 56: 464–474.

Harris, Richard L. 2003. "Popular Resistance to Globalization and Neoliberalism in Latin America." *Journal of Developing Societies* 19, nos. 2–3: 365–426.

Hochstetler, Kathryn. 2011. "The Politics of Environmental Licensing: Energy Projects of the Past and Future in Brazil." *Studies in Comparative International Development* 46, no. 4: 349–371.

International Renewable Energy Agency (IRENA). 2016a. "Latin America's Renewable Energy Market Analysis." November 17. http://www.irena.org/newsroom/articles/2016/Nov/Latin-Americas-Renewable-Energy-Market-Analysis.

International Renewable Energy Agency (IRENA). 2016b. "How Corporates Are Taking the Lead in Renewable Energy: IRENA Newsroom." November 15. https://irenanewsroom.org/2016/11/15/how-corporates-are-taking-the-lead-in-renewable-energy/.

Jackson, Jean, and Kay Warren. 2005. "Indigenous Movements in Latin America, 1992–2004: Controversies, Ironies, New Directions." *Annual Review of Anthropology* 34: 549–573.

Kaup, Brent. 2010. "A Neoliberal Nationalization? The Constraints on Natural-Gas-Led Development in Bolivia." *Latin American Perspectives* 37, no. 3: 123–138.

Keeling, David. 2004. "Latin American Development and the Globalization Imperative: New Directions, Familiar Crises." *Journal of Latin American Geography* 3, no. 1: 1–21.

Kingstone, Peter. 2018. *The Political Economy of Latin America: Reflections on Neoliberalism and Development after the Commodity Boom*. New York: Routledge.

Kirkpatrick, Colin, David Parker, and Yin-Fang Zhang. 2006. "Foreign Direct Investment in Infrastructure in Developing Countries: Does Regulation Make a Difference?" *Transnational Corporations* 15, no. 1: 143–171.

Laserna, Roberto. 2018. "Energy Dividends in Bolivia: Are There Any Alternatives to Price Subsidies?" Policy Paper no. 130. Washington, DC: Center for Global Development.

Latinobarómetro. 2017. *Informe*. Buenos Aires, Argentina: Corporación Latinobarómetro.

Leamer, Edward, Hugo Maul, Sergio Rodriguez, and Peter Schott. 1999. Does natural resource abundance increase Latin American income inequality? *Journal of Development Economics* 59: 3–42.

Levy, Brian, and Pablo Spiller. 1996. *Regulations, Institutions, and Commitment*. Cambridge, UK: Cambridge University Press.

López, Emiliano, and Francisco Vértiz. 2015. "Extractivism, Transnational Capital, and Subaltern Struggles in Latin America." *Latin American Perspectives* 42, no. 5: 152–168.

Luna, Juan Pablo, and Hillel Soifer. 2017. "Capturing Sub-National Variation in State Capacity: A Survey-Based Approach." *American Behavioral Scientist* 61, no. 8: 887–907.

Mackinnon, Lawrence. 2018. "The Next Phase of the Energy Transformation: Platform Thinking." *Renewable Energy World*, March 19. https://www.renewableenergyworld.com/articles/print/volume-21/issue-2/features/all-renewables/the-next-phase-of-the-energy-transformation-platform-thinking.html.

Madariaga, Aldo, and Mathilde Allain. 2018. "Contingent Coalitions in Environmental Policymaking: How Civil Society Organizations Influenced the Chilean Renewable Energy Boom." *Policy Studies Journal*, November 20. https://onlinelibrary.wiley.com/doi/epdf/10.1111/psj.12298.

Mares, David. 2010. "The Changing Pattern of Exclusion in Latin America and the Caribbean." Working Paper. James Baker III Institute for Public Policy, Rice University.

Mares, David. 2013. "Political Economy of Shale Gas in Argentina." Working Paper. James Baker III Institute for Public Policy, Rice University.

Mares, David. 2014. "Argentine Shale Developments-On Track?" *International Shale Gas & Oil Journal* 3: 27–30.

McKenzie, David, and Dilip Mookherjee. 2002. "Distributive Impact of Privatization in Latin America: An Overview of Evidence from Four Countries." Paper commissioned by the InterAmerican Development Bank and the Universidad de las Américas-Puebla. Mimeo.

Menke, Christopher, and Gregory Fazzari. 1994. "Improving Electric Power Utility Efficiency: Issues and Recommendations." Technical Paper no. 243. Washington, DC: World Bank.

Millán, Jaime. 2005. "Power Sector Reform in Latin America: Accomplishments, Failure and Challenges." *Economic and Political Weekly* 40, no. 50: 5291–5301.

Monaldi, Francisco. 2014. "Is Resource Nationalism Fading in Latin America? The Case of the Oil Industry." Issue Brief (September). Baker Institute for Public Policy, Rice University.

Musacchio, Aldo, and Sergio Lazzarini. 2014. *Reinventing State Capitalism: Leviathan in Business, Brazil and Beyond.* Cambridge, MA: Harvard University Press.

Observatorio de Conflictos Mineros de América Latina (OCMAL). 2018. "Conflictos Mineros en América Latina." https://mapa.conflictosmineros.net/ocmal_db-v2/.

Ocampo, José Antonio. 2007. "The Macroeconomics of the Latin American Economic Boom." *CEPAL Review* 93 (December): 7–28.

O'Donnell, Guillermo. 1993. "On the State, Democratization and Some Conceptual Problems: A Latin American View with Some Glances at Post Communist Countries." *World Development* 21, no. 8: 1355–1369.

Özkaynak, Begüm, Beatriz Rodríguez-Labajos, and Cem Iskender Aydin. 2015. "Towards Environmental Justice Success in Mining Resistances: An Empirical Investigation." EJOLT Report 14 (April).

Payan, Tony, and Guadalupe Correa-Cabrera. 2014. "Land Ownership and Use Under Mexico's Energy Reform." Issue Brief 10.29.14. The Baker Institute for Public Policy, Rice University.

Perotti, Enrico. 2004. "State Ownership: A Residual Role?" Policy Research Working Paper Series, no. 3407. Washington, DC: World Bank.

Petras, James. 1999. *The Left Strikes Back Class Conflict in Latin America in the Age of Neoliberalism.* New York: Westview Press.

Pollitt, Michael. 2004. "Electricity Reform in Chile." Working Paper. Center for Energy and Environmental Policy Research, University of Cambridge.

Pollitt, Michael. 2008. "Electricity Reform in Argentina: Lessons for Developing Countries." *Energy Economics* 30: 1536–1567.

Prebisch, Raúl. 1950. "The Economic Development of Latin America and Its Principal Problems, United Nations Department of Economic Affairs, Economic Commission for Latin America (ECLA), New York, NY.

Raftopoulos, Malayna. 2017. "Contemporary Debates on Social-Environmental Conflicts, Extractivism and Human Rights in Latin America." *The International Journal of Human Rights* 21, no. 4: 387–404.

Reid, Gerard. 2018. "Coming Soon: The Amazon of Rnergy." Energypost.eu, March 16. https://energypost.eu/coming-soon-the-amazon-of-energy.

Rennkamp, Britta, Sebastian Haunss, Kridtiyaporn Wongsa, Araceli Ortega, and Erika Casamadrid. 2017. "Competing Coalitions: The Politics of Renewable Energy and Fossil

Fuels in Mexico, South Africa and Thailand." *Energy Research & Social Science* 34 (December): 214–223.

Riethof, Marieke. 2017. "The International Human Rights Discourse as a Strategic Focus in Socio-environmental Conflicts: The Case of Hydro-electric Dams in Brazil." *The International Journal of Human Rights* 21, no. 4: 482–499.

Rodrik, Dani. 2007. *One Economics, Many Recipes: Globalization, Institutions, and Economic Growth*. Princeton, NJ: Princeton University Press.

Sachs, Jeffrey, and Andrew Warner. 2001. "The Curse of Natural Resources." *European Economic Review* 45, nos. 4–6: 827–838.

Sáenz, Jorge. 2016. "Conflictos en el sector de hidrocarburos han costado $217.000 millones." *El Espectador*, July 24. https://www.elespectador.com/noticias/economia/conflictos-sector-de-hidrocarburos-han-costado-217000-m-articulo-645090.

Saylor, Ryan. 2014. *State Building in Boom Times: Commodities and Coalitions in Latin America and Africa*. New York: Oxford University Press.

Schroeder, Kathleen. 2007. "Economic Globalization and Bolivia's Regional Divide." *Journal of Latin American Geography* 6, no. 2: 99–120.

Seligson, Mitchell. 2007. "The Rise of Populism and the Left in Latin America." *Journal of Democracy* 18, no. 3: 81–95.

Serra, Pablo, and Ronald Fischer. 2007. "Efectos de la Privatización de Servicios Públicos en Chile." Serie de estudios económicos y sociales. Washington, DC: Inter-American Development Bank.

Shah, Anwar, ed. 2007. "Performance Accountability and Combating Corruption." Public Sector and Governance Accountability Series. Washington, DC: The World Bank.

Soifer, Hillel. 2008. "State Infrastructural Power: Approaches to Conceptualization and Measurement." *Studies in Comparative International Development* 43, nos. 3–4: 231–251.

Soifer, Hillel. 2016. *State Building in Latin America*. Cambridge, UK: Cambridge University Press.

Sovacool, Benjamin. 2017. "Reviewing, Reforming, and Rethinking Global Energy Subsidies: Towards a Political Economy Research Agenda." *Ecological Economics* 135: 150–163.

Svampa, Maristella. 2015. "Commodities Consensus: Neoextractivism and Enclosure of the Commons in Latin America." *South Atlantic Quarterly* 114, no. 1: 65–82.

Thorpe, Rosemary. 1998. *Progress, Poverty and Exclusion: An Economic History of Latin America in the 20th Century*. Washington, DC: Inter-American Development Bank.

Thurber, Mark, David Hults, and Patrick Heller. 2011. "Exporting the 'Norwegian Model': The Effect of Administrative Design on Oil Sector Performance." *Energy Policy* 39: 5366–5378.

Tissot, Roger. 2012. *Latin America's Energy Future*. Washington, DC: Inter American Development Bank

Tommasi, Mariano. 2011. "Latin America: How State Capacity Determines Policy Success." *Governance* 24, no. 2: 199–203.

Tompkins Conservation. 2018. "Patagonia sin Represas." http://www.tompkinsconservation. org/patagonia_sin_represas.htm.

Valverde Camiña, Verónica. 2012. "Hacia un Estado Regulador en América Latina: El fortalecimiento institucional a través de la práctica informal de los organismos reguladores del sector energético de Argentina and Brasil." Paper presented at XII World Congress of Political Science, Madrid, Spain.

Van Cott, Donna Lee. 2010. "Indigenous Peoples' Politics in Latin America." *Annual Review of Political Science* 13: 385–405.

Vargas Suárez, Rosío. 2009. "La nacionalización de los hidrocarburos bolivianos en la presidencia de Evo Morales Ayma." *Latinoamérica* 49: 11–34.

Vásquez, Patricia. 2016. "Argentina's Oil and Gas Sector: Coordinated Federalism and The Rule of Law." Washington, DC: Wilson Center Latin America Program. https://www.wilsoncenter.org/sites/default/files/argentinasoilgas.vasquez.pdf.

Vidal, John. 2017. "Why Is Latin America So Obsessed with Mega Dams?" *The Guardian*, May 23. https://www.theguardian.com/global-development-professionals-network/2017/may/23/why-latin-america-obsessed-mega-dams.

Villalonga, B. 2000. "Privatization and Efficiency: Differentiating ownership effects from political, organizational, and dynamic effects." *Journal of Economic Behaviour & Organization* 42, 43–74.

Watts, Jonathan. 2018. "Brazil Raises Hopes of a Retreat from New Mega-dam Construction." *The Guardian*, January 4. https://www.theguardian.com/environment/2018/jan/04/brazil-raises-hopes-of-a-retreat-from-new-mega-dam-construction.

Weyland, Kurt, Raúl Madrid, and Wendy Hunter. 2010. *Leftist Governments in Latin America: Successes and Shortcomings*. New York: Cambridge University Press.

Williams, J., and R. Ghanadan. 2006. "Electricity Reform in Developing and Transition Countries: A Reappraisal." *Energy* 31: 815–844.

Williamson, John. 2009. "A Short History of the Washington Consensus Preface." *Law and Business Review of the Americas* 15, no. 1: 7–26.

Zárate Toledo, Ezequiel, and Julia Fraga. 2016. "La política eólica mexicana: Controversias sociales y ambientales debido a su implantación territorial; Estudios de caso en Oaxaca y Yucatán. *Travaux et Recherches dans les Amériques du Centre* 69: 65–95.

Zhang, Yin-Fang, David Parker, and Colin Kirkpatrick. 2005. "Competition, Regulation and Privatisation of Electricity Generation in Developing Countries: Does the Sequencing of Reforms Matter?" *The Quarterly Review of Economics and Finance* 45, nos. 2–3: 358–379.

Zhang, Yin-Fang, David Parker, and Colin Kirkpatrick. 2008. "Electricity Sector Reform in Developing Countries: An Econometric Assessment of the Effects of Privatization, Competition and Regulation." *Journal of Regulatory Economics* 33: 159–178.

Zissis, Carin. 2006. "Bolivia's Nationalization of Oil and Gas." New York: Council on Foreign Relations. http://www.cfr.org/economics/bolivias-nationalization-oil-gas/p10682.

CHAPTER 28

THE ENERGY POLITICS OF THE MIDDLE EAST AND NORTH AFRICA (MENA)

ECKART WOERTZ

OIL and gas play a paramount role in economic development, the domestic social contract, and the international relations of the Middle East and North Africa (MENA). Oil revenues dominate state income in about half of the states of the region, buying political acquiescence with services, public sector jobs, and welfare payments (Beblawi and Luciani 1987). The social contract of local rentier states is no taxation and no representation. Even semi-rentier states with limited resource endowments such as Egypt, Syria, and Jordan relied on modest oil exports until the end of the 2000s in the case of the former two and have benefitted from migrant remittances and strategic transfer payments from oil-rich Gulf countries.

In addition to domestic politics, oil has impacted the international relations of the region. Oil became a strategic commodity when the British navy switched from coal to oil on the eve of World War I. The MENA was not yet important as a producer, but there were beginnings of oil production in Iran, and later advances on royalty payments by the US company CASOC underwrote early Saudi state building in the 1930s. By 1944 US diplomats regarded the oil of the Arabian Peninsula as the "greatest single prize in all history" (Yergin 1991, 393). After World War II, the European energy mix shifted from coal to oil, and MENA production increased steeply. Oil became a primary reason for external power involvement in the region, whose international relations have been affected by compromised sovereignty in a "penetrated system" of overlapping national, international, and local interests (Brown 1984).

The exporter countries of the MENA, in turn, sought to maximize their benefits via the Organization of the Petroleum Exporting Countries (OPEC) and the nationalization of oil companies (Marcel 2006). In some Gulf countries, exploitation of associated natural gas started in the 1970s, fueling residential energy consumption and ambitious diversification efforts in refining, petrochemicals, and heavy industries (Luciani 2012b). In other countries such economic diversification remained limited (e.g., Libya, Kuwait) or failed (e.g., the import substituting industrialization drives in Iraq and Algeria). Newly built cities in the Gulf followed the US model. They were based on suburbanization along car-centered traffic lanes and were energy intensive. Propagated by Western city planners, the city designs supported the housing of a depoliticized, docile, and consumer-oriented populace during the Cold War era (Menoret 2014).

Skyrocketing domestic demand now threatens to diminish export capacities. With lower oil prices, many states have had to tighten their fiscal belts and cut energy, water, and food subsidies. The social contract is under threat. Economic diversification and job creation in the private sector for the burgeoning youth population are urgent priorities. Rulers are developing other energy sources, such as renewables and nuclear, to safeguard crude for export, support domestic energy consumption, and satisfy the social contract (Griffiths 2017; Kamrava 2012; Krane 2019).

Most greenhouse gas (GHG) emissions happen in an urban context. Many cities in the MENA region belong to the largest GHG emitters on a per capita basis. Yet climate policies play a subdued role in politics and policy formulation. The focus continues to be on export revenues from and domestic subsidized pricing of hydrocarbons (Verdeil 2016, 2014; Verdeil et al. 2015). Central governments are reluctant to share control over these issues, while cities have no real autonomy and do not figure prominently in national energy debates. The main driving forces for renewable energy transitions are not climate policies, but the improved economics of solar panels and their possible contribution to diversifying domestic energy supplies.

With the possible exception of wind (in some locations) and photovoltaic (PV) solar energy, whose price has recently declined dramatically, the new energy sources will not be as cheap as the conventional hydrocarbons, and none is as suitable for export. These energy sources might be able to free up hydrocarbons for export that have been hitherto consumed domestically, but in their own right they will not generate the kind of rent that exports of low-cost oil provided in the past. Energy transitions will likely involve sociopolitical transformation processes.

Against this backdrop, this chapter first discusses the idea of the Middle East and how it has been shaped by the impact of oil. The geographical scope and definition of the MENA can mean different things to different people and have changed over time. Second, the chapter provides a statistical overview of energy mixes, export revenues, and resource endowments and identifies countries of importance in the region. Third, historical production profiles and production policies are analyzed to illustrate the crucial role of energy exports in the region's rentier states. Fourth, the chapter shows how rents relate to the social contract and economic diversification efforts and how they have developed over time. Fifth, energy transitions toward renewables, nuclear, and in some isolated cases also coal are discussed. Finally, possible areas of future research are outlined. (For analysis of regionalism literature, see Hancock, Palestini, and Szulecki in this volume.)

How Oil Shaped the Idea of the
Middle East (and North Africa)

The term "Middle East" was rarely used before World War II. Its combining with North Africa to form "MENA" is even more recent. As a vague notion of a troublesome region somewhere between Europe and India, it has a longer history of precursor terms (Bonine, Amanat, and Gasper 2012; Khalil 2014). Currently the World Bank and the International Monetary Fund (IMF) use MENA as a category. They include Iran and all Arab League states, except the Comoros, including Somalia, Djibouti, and Mauritania and excluding Turkey and Israel. Considerable ambiguities remain. MENA definitions sometimes include Israel, Turkey, or Mauritania and sometimes not. More recently the US second Bush administration even included Afghanistan and Pakistan in its "Greater Middle East Initiative."

If we cannot exactly tell *where* the Middle East is, we can clearly state *what* it is: a geopolitical concept that emerged in the nineteenth century and came to full fruition in the twentieth. We cannot define it by language, religion, or ethnicity, as it hosts a variety of these, and we cannot define it by geography, either: it includes mountains, deserts, and green coastal areas and spans two continents, actually three if we include Turkey, parts of which are located in Europe.

Carl Brown has described the geopolitics of the MENA as a "penetrated system" of compromised sovereignty and overlapping international, national, and local interests (Brown 1984). Countries in the region have been too weak to ward off foreign influence and control local pockets of autonomy, but strong enough to play one external power against the other (e.g., Gamal Abdel Nasser and Anwar Sadat in Egypt). The motives of external power intervention have changed, but the rules of the game have stayed the same. If it was about the Bosporus Strait and the Suez Canal in the nineteenth century, it is about oil today. Fred Halliday criticized Brown for structural essentialism and pleaded for an approach rooted in historical sociology. Yet from a different angle he also highlighted the crucial role of oil in state formation and international power competition (Halliday 2005).

The importance of oil in the global economy has grown considerably since 1945. After World War II, Europe's economy was still largely coal based. The little oil it consumed was mostly imported from the United States. By the 1970s its energy mix was dominated by oil, most of it imported from the MENA, whose production took off in the postwar decades. From the 1970s onward the MENA developed into an important producer, if not exporter, of natural gas as well (Yergin 1991).

Except for oil and gas reserves, the MENA is energy poor, which has hampered its economic development historically. It lacks meaningful reserves of coal and other minerals that were crucial for industrialization, such as iron ore. It also lacks the "white coal" of hydropower, as there are only a few rivers. Another of its geographic eccentricities is the interspersed settlement patterns of urban and nomadic lifestyles (McNeill 2013).

As a result, there were ample draft animals available, and the economic incentive to use water and wind power for industry, grinding, water lifting, and drainage was limited. The MENA did not develop the "advanced organic economy" in medieval and early modern times that Europe did (Ashtor 1976).

Thus, when industrialization began, the MENA was at a disadvantage. The MENA remained an energy importer for a long time. Coal was used in desalination plants in Jeddah and on trains in Iraq. During the nineteenth century and until World War II, coal was still the dominant fuel in the MENA and was imported from faraway places such as Great Britain and South Africa (Barak 2015; Woertz 2014).

The oil age thoroughly transformed MENA societies and economic development models. In no other world region has oil income so thoroughly influenced economic, social, and political structures. For this reason, rentier state theory emerged from Middle East area studies. The MENA region is heterogeneous, but the direct and indirect importance of oil revenues is such that resource endowments are instrumental in the developmental classification of different countries, ranging from resource rich/labor poor (the Gulf countries and Libya) to resource rich/labor abundant (Algeria, Iran, Iraq), to resource poor/labor abundant (Morocco, Tunisia, Egypt, Jordan, Palestine, Lebanon). The mineral production in Syria, Yemen, and Sudan has been affected by conflict and maturing oil fields, so their status more and more resembles that of resource poor/labor abundant countries as well. Israel and Turkey are the only Organisation for Economic Co-operation and Development (OECD) countries in the region and are outliers with a diversified economic structure (Cammett et al. 2015; Henry and Springborg 2010).

SHORT STATISTICAL OVERVIEW AND COUNTRIES OF IMPORTANCE

The Middle East is a formidable force in the global energy world because of its shares in global oil and gas production and reserves (see Figure 28.1). Before the unconventional hydrocarbon revolution in the United States, it was a widespread expectation that more Middle East reserves would need to be developed urgently to satisfy growing global demand. (For more on the energy politics of the United States, see Allison and Parinandi, this volume). Now the International Energy Agency expects 80 percent of the net increase in oil supply until 2025 to come from the United States; only after that will reliance on OPEC countries again be crucial, as US production is expected to plateau and then decline toward 2040 amid slowing growth in demand (IEA 2017).

The Middle East is not only a major oil and gas producer; it also has become one of its own best customers. Energy demand has skyrocketed since the 1970s, fueled by population and economic growth, subsidies, and the establishment of energy-intensive heavy industries. The Middle East consumes almost 30 percent of its own oil production and

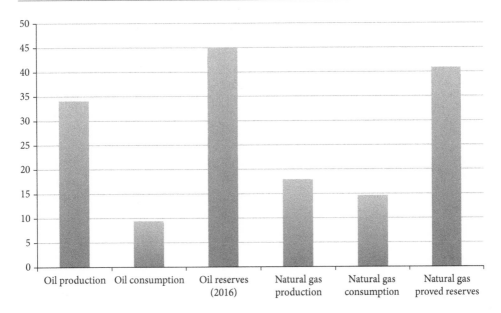

FIGURE 28.1 Oil and natural gas: Middle East global shares by percent, 2017.

Source: Data from BP (2018).

more than 80 percent of its natural gas production. Apart from Qatar, no country in the region currently has a meaningful natural gas export capacity. Israel might develop into a medium-sized exporter of regional importance once it ramps up production in its newly developed Mediterranean gas fields (Darbouche, El-Katiri, and Fattouh 2012). The potential in Iran is higher, as it is the world's second largest holder of natural gas reserves after Russia, but it has been unable to develop them as planned due to sanctions and domestic inefficiencies. It was a gas net importer for much of the 2000s. The United Arab Emirates (UAE), Kuwait, and Egypt also have become net importers of natural gas. Saudi Arabia burns large amounts of diesel, fuel oil, and crude in power stations, as its natural gas production is outstripped by domestic demand. Demand growth threatens to reduce the ability to export oil if left unchecked. The search for additional natural gas production and alternative energies, such as nuclear, renewables, and even coal has become an urgent priority in order to safeguard oil export capacity, whose foreign exchange generation is crucial for the budgetary needs of the social contract.

Among the oil exporters, the Gulf countries stand out in terms of production and reserves, Saudi Arabia in particular, followed by Iran, Iraq, the UAE, and Kuwait (see Table 28.1). Iraq has large undeveloped reserves. Its production more than doubled between 2007 and 2017, and it holds potential for further production increases. Saudi Arabia commands a majority of OPEC spare capacity, which it can use to calm markets in case of supply shortfalls elsewhere. Saudi Arabia's role as a "swing producer" is of great geopolitical importance. The country has been anxious to maintain its ability to fulfill this role with capacity expansions in the 2000s, but the costly provision of such a public good to global markets is not without domestic critics. Saudi Arabia's importance has

Table 28.1 MENA Oil and Natural Gas: Production, Consumption, and Reserves, 2017

	Oil Production, 2017 ('000 bpd)	Oil Consumption, 2017 ('000 bpd)	Oil Reserves, 2016 (in billion barrels)	Natural Gas Production, 2017 (in billion cm)	Natural Gas Consumption, 2017 (in billion cm)	Natural Gas Proved Reserves, 2017 (in trillion cm)
Iran	4,982	1,816	157.2	223.9	214.4	33.2
Iraq	4,520	791	148.8	10.4	12.0	3.5
Kuwait	3,025	449	101.5	17.4	22.2	1.7
Oman	971	189	5.4	32.3	23.3	0.7
Qatar	1,916	354	25.2	175.7	47.4	24.9
Saudi Arabia	11,951	3,918	266.2	111.4	111.4	8.0
Syria	25	n/a	2.5	3.1	n/a	0.3
UAE	3,935	1,007	97.8	60.4	72.2	5.9
Yemen	52	n/a	3.0	0.7	n/a	0.3
Other Middle East	220	520	0.1	9.5	23.7	n/a
Total Middle East	31,597	9,290	807.7	659.9	536.5	79.1
Egypt	660	816	3.4	49.0	56.0	1.8
Libya	865	n/a	48.4	11.5	n/a	1.4
Algeria	1,540	411	12.0	91.2	38.9	4.3

Note: Oil figures include natural gas liquids (NGL) besides crude oil.
Source: Data from BP (2018).

diminished somewhat in recent years with the supply surge in the United States, which now provides a sort of buffer, as high-cost tight oil producers enter and exit the market depending on oil price levels. Syria and Yemen used to command significant oil production, but maturing oil fields and conflict have caused production to plummet. Egypt also has become an oil net importer since the late 2000s.

Iran and Qatar are by far the largest producers and reserve holders of natural gas in the region. In North Africa, Algeria is a major player in this area. Like Saudi Arabia, it also has significant resources of unconventional natural gas. However, the scarcity of water resources, which are required for its production, is a major challenge. Gas flaring is still substantial in Iraq and Iran and constitutes an untapped production potential (IEA 2018).

Table 28.2 MENA Energy Mixes: Share in Primary Energy Consumption (%), 2017

	Oil	Natural Gas	Coal	Nuclear Energy	Hydroelectric	Other Renewables
Iran	31	67	0	0.6	1.4	0.1
Iraq	78	21	0	0	1.0	0
Israel	45	33	20	0	0	1.6
Kuwait	51	49	0	0	0	0
Oman	32	68	0	0	0	0
Qatar	25	75	0	0	0	0.1
Saudi Arabia	64	36	0	0	0	0
UAE	41	57	1	0	0	0.1
Other Middle East	54	43	1	0	0.7	1.3
Total Middle East	47	51	1	0.2	0.5	0.2
Algeria	37	63	0	0	0	0.2
Egypt	43	53	0	0	3.3	0.7
Morocco	67	5	23	0	1.4	4.0
Total World	34	23	28	4.4	6.8	3.6
OECD	39	26	16	7.9	5.6	5.4
Non-OECD	31	22	36	1.9	7.6	2.3

Source: Data from BP (2018).

The domestic energy mixes of MENA countries are dominated by oil and natural gas, with shares in primary energy consumption of 47 percent and 51 percent, respectively. The share of natural gas is particularly high in Iran, Oman, Qatar, and Algeria, while Iraq, Saudi Arabia, and Morocco rely heavily on oil, also for power generation (see Table 28.2). Coal does not play a role in the MENA, apart from Morocco, Israel, and Turkey. In contrast to global trends, however, its role might increase due to expansion plans in Egypt, Turkey, the UAE, and Oman. Nuclear energy is only used by Iran so far. The first of four newly built nuclear plants in the UAE was completed in 2018 and is expected to come online in the near future. Hydroelectricity makes a modest contribution in Egypt and Iran.

The metric of primary energy consumption understates the importance of renewables in final energy consumption, as they do not have the kind of conversion losses that are associated with hydrocarbon and nuclear power plants. Still, the share of other renewables such as solar and wind is insignificant in most countries and far below the world average. Morocco is a marked exception and in line with global trends. In addition to Morocco, renewables other than hydropower play some role in Tunisia, Israel, Turkey, Yemen, and Egypt. The renewable share in Gulf countries is remarkably low;

however, all of them have ambitious plans to expand, especially the UAE and Saudi Arabia. Costs for PV cells have come down dramatically in recent years. Solar power is now in many cases the cheapest newly installed capacity in the Gulf, with costs as low as 2.42 US cents per kWh (Abdul Kader 2017). The main challenge for expansion of renewables is no longer cost but rather intermittency, which would need to be tackled via storage solutions and flexible smart grids.

Per capita energy consumption in the MENA is high to extraordinarily high. In Gulf countries, it is above the already substantial levels of North America, especially in Qatar. Energy efficiency per gross domestic product (GDP) dollar is also low in international comparison (United Nations 2018). Governments have started to try to curb consumption by cutting back subsidies for electricity, fuel, and water, whose provision relies extensively on energy-intensive desalination (IMF 2017). Desalination accounted for 5 percent of total energy consumption in the Middle East in 2016. Led by the UAE, Saudi Arabia, and other Gulf countries, the region accounts for 90 percent of global thermal energy use for desalination (IEA 2018).

OIL EXPORT REVENUES AND PRODUCTION POLICIES

Oil remains paramount for the budgetary needs and social contracts of many MENA countries, not only in the Gulf. Oil prices, production levels, and domestic consumption needs influence the amount of oil revenues that ends up in state coffers. A look at historical production profiles illustrates some of the risks that this oil reliance entails for MENA states and what choices they face as a result (see Figure 28.2).

After the oil boom of the 1970s, oil prices came under pressure in the 1980s as a result of new production in the North Sea and the Gulf of Mexico and some demand destruction. Saudi Arabia sought to stabilize prices by cutting back production from over 10 mbpd (million barrels per day) in 1980 to 3.6 mbpd in 1985. But finally it had to throw in the towel: at the end of 1985 it started to reopen the spigots to regain market share. Oil prices collapsed and remained low for most of the rest of the 1980s and the 1990s. Oil production of the Middle East has increased since the mid-1980s, mainly driven by the Gulf countries. Only Kuwait had to overcome a production collapse in the wake of the Iraqi occupation in 1990/1991.

Given the importance of oil revenues for state building and socioeconomic development, production policies of state-owned oil companies in the region go beyond commercial considerations and have longer time horizons than a private company with the sole goal of profit maximization would have (Luciani 2013; Marcel 2006).

Production levels in Iran, Iraq, and Libya have been volatile as a result of violent conflict and sanctions. Domestic unrest after the fall of the shah in Iran in 1979 and the onset of the Iran-Iraq War (1980–1988) caused plummeting production in both countries. The

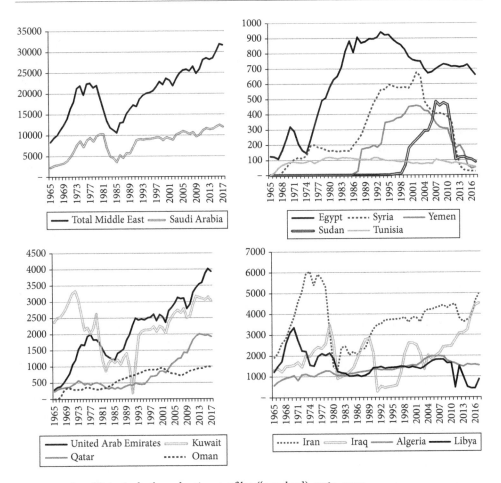

FIGURE 28.2 Historical oil production profiles ('000 bpd), 1965–2017.

Source: Data from BP (2018).

multilateral UN embargo (1990–2003) against Iraq massively affected the country's production. The same is true of the tightening of US, EU, and UN sanctions against Iran that caused oil exports to fall in 2012. Like the Libyan civil war, since 2011 it can be clearly seen as a production bump in Figure 28.2. Remarkably, the civil war in Algeria in the 1990s did not affect oil and gas production levels in the country (Aissaoui 2001). The regime managed to maintain security of installations. Insurgents attempted to sabotage pipelines, but they could be repaired quickly, and the insurgents never managed to target compressor stations.

A final category comprises countries whose production volumes have been in steep, possibly terminal decline, causing severe economic distress. Production growth was an economic lifeline for Egypt from the mid-1970s to 1990, in Yemen and Syria from the mid-1980s to 2000, and in Sudan in the 2000s. In Egypt production peaked in 1993 and has trended lower since then. In Syria and Yemen the decline was more abrupt, caused by maturing oil fields and domestic production challenges. In both countries, oil production peaked in 2002 and had about halved a decade later when domestic conflict ravaged the industry and pushed production levels down even further, to almost zero. In Sudan conflict in the wake of the separation of South Sudan in 2011 and the inability of both governments to agree on transit fees for the pipelines from South Sudanese fields to Port Sudan were a factor. Combined production levels in 2017 were less than half those in 2010, when Sudan was still united.

Between 2011 and 2015 the unconventional oil revolution in the United States added more than three mbpd to global oil supplies, making up for political supply disruptions of similar magnitude elsewhere (Libya, Iran, Nigeria, Yemen, Syria, Sudan). Together with sluggish demand in OECD countries in the wake of the global financial crisis, this caused prices to fall from over $100 in the first half of 2014 to below $30 at the beginning of 2016. In contrast to the first half of the 1980s, Saudi Arabia did not try to stabilize prices. It rather sought to maintain market share right from the beginning and push high-cost producers out of the market. Oil projects in the deep seas and the Arctic were most affected, but the US tight oil producers proved remarkably resilient, managed to cut costs, and benefited from technological innovations. In 2016 Saudi Arabia recognized that its initial strategy was not working. It changed tack and cut production in coordination with OPEC and non-OPEC producer Russia (Fattouh and Economou 2018). Others have interpreted this about-face as a logical next step rather than an acknowledgment of past failure. Using game theory, they have argued that OPEC policy aims at securing a market share that is conducive to profit maximization rather than a certain price level. Once the former was achieved, production cuts became a policy option again (Lasry, Halff, and Rostand 2017).

There has been a recovery since then, but prices of around $60–80 per barrel of Brent remain below budget break-even prices for many oil producers (IMF 2018a). This metric has gained increased popularity in many analyses, but it needs to be used with caution. Estimates vary from one author to another and between different years. Any impact depends again on a variety of factors. Flexible exchange rates, access to international capital markets, and overseas assets all cushion the impact (Clayton and Levi 2015). Iran and Russia were helped by flexible exchange rates; their revenues in dollars declined, but not necessarily in their devaluing local currencies. The Gulf countries, on the other hand, faced the question of whether they would be able to maintain their dollar currency pegs, but their unfettered access to international financial markets and substantial overseas assets put them in a better position to cope than sanctions-ridden Iran.

Hence, one should refrain from making assumptions about a mechanical transmission of oil markets below budget break-even prices into concrete policies. However, most Middle East producers have had to repatriate assets or issue debt since 2015 to cover their ongoing expenditure, in particular Bahrain, Oman, and Saudi Arabia. They increasingly have to reckon with an environment in which unconventional oil adds to supply, while demand might be affected by electric mobility and environmental legislation in the longer run (Fattouh, Poudineh, and West 2018). Light oil imports in the

United States have plummeted, affecting countries such as Libya, Algeria, and Nigeria. However, US refiners have continued to import large quantities of heavy crude from the Gulf, as they need these crude varieties for their feedstock mixes. If a possible peak in oil supplies was a prominent topic of discussion in the 2000s (Campbell and Laherrère 1998; Simmons 2005), some experts now worry about the opposite: a peak in oil demand that would affect prices negatively and would motivate oil producers to turn to a high-volume/low-price strategy, producing as much as they can before their oil resources end up being stranded assets (Dale and Fattouh 2018). Predictions of a possible peak date vary widely depending on assumptions. Electric cars might lead to demand destruction in the gasoline and diesel markets, but petrochemicals are slated for continued expansion, and kerosene, diesel, and fuel oil would still be needed for airplanes, trucks, and ships because of their high energy density. Fuel cell technology has attracted less attention than battery driven cars in recent years, but it offers advantages in terms of range, energy density, and refueling speed, and hydrogen could theoretically be produced with renewables as well. Middle East oil producers are clearly concerned about such energy transitions as they seek to diversify their economies, cut subsidies, rein in domestic energy consumption to maintain export capacity, and raise new revenues via taxes.

Economic Diversification and the Social Contract

External rents from natural resources such as oil and natural gas have played an important role in the political economy of the region's rentier states and their processes of state building (Beblawi and Luciani 1987; Vitalis 2007). Total natural resources rents as a percentage of GDP are high in the MENA; they average 16.9 percent, as opposed to 1.9 percent globally and 0.5 percent in OECD countries (World Bank 2018b). Even compared to sub-Saharan Africa (8.3 percent) and non-MENA oil producers such as Russia (11.5 percent), Nigeria (5.4 percent), and Norway (5.8 percent), the MENA ranks high. The rent dependency in Gulf countries is far above the already high MENA average. In Kuwait and Saudi Arabia it stood at 44.7 and 27.2 percent, respectively, in 2016. In the more diversified UAE it was at 15.3 percent. Most of these rents come from oil. Even in Qatar, the largest LNG exporter of the world, only 4.8 percent of its 21.1 percent GDP share of natural resources rents comes from natural gas (World Bank 2018a). The fiscal discretion of the country largely relies on rents from its oil production. In Morocco, Tunisia, and Jordan phosphate and potash mining contributes to their limited share of rents in the lower single digits of GDP (World Bank 2018b).

The relative share of rents in GDP and on a per capita basis has fluctuated over time, depending on prices, production levels, and population growth. The respective shares tend to be lower than during the heyday of the oil boom of the late 1970s and early 1980s, despite recovery over the 2000s (see Figures 28.3 and 28.4). In absolute terms

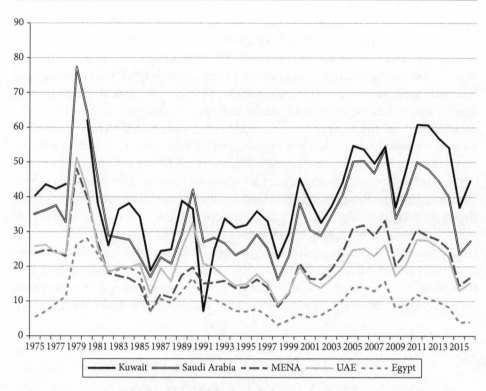

FIGURE 28.3 Natural resources rent (% of GDP).

Source: Data from World Bank (2018b).

rents are still substantial in the Gulf countries, with the exception of Bahrain (see Figure 28.5). But even in the former they have fallen. The economic reliance on rents is increasingly perceived as a liability. Governments are thus cutting spending and diversifying their economies.

The rentier state paradigm postulates that oil has affected not only the economies of oil-exporting countries, but also their societies. External rents have made rentier states relatively autonomous vis-à-vis their populations. Rather than relying on support from tax income, the governments support their populations via discretionary spending of oil rent and expect political acquiescence in return. The social contract is no taxation and no representation (Luciani 1987). Yet this structural approach risks overlooking the considerable role of human agency and vastly differing socioeconomic outcomes between different oil states. The theory tells us that oil states will likely end up being authoritarian but does not tell us how they do so (Hertog 2010b). In the late 1990s Herb argued, against the rentier state theory, that considerable moral economies of accountability exist, regardless of whether a state finances itself via rents, taxes, or debt issuance. He deemed a transition from dynastic monarchies to constitutional monarchies possible, especially in the case of Kuwait (Herb 1999). There was indeed a limited "liberalization from above" in the 2000s in the Gulf (Ehteshami and Wright 2008;

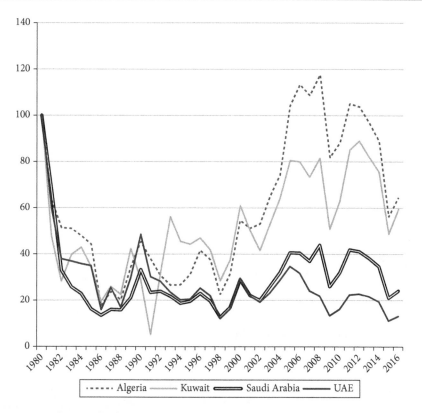

FIGURE 28.4 Change of inflation adjusted rents per capita, 1980–2016.
**PPP, constant 2011 US$, 1980 = 100.

Source: Data from World Bank (2018b) and IMF (2018b).

Teitelbaum 2009). Even in Saudi Arabia, there were municipal elections. Yet these steps have been limited and were possibly undertaken for the international gallery, and there has been a broad-based authoritarian backlash since the Arab Spring started in December 2010. States of the region seek economic modernization and might even allow for some cultural and social opening, but they painstakingly avoid any political liberalization.

Vastly differing economic, if not political, outcomes require a more nuanced view of rentier states. More recently, Herb has suggested differentiating between rent dependence and rent abundance of an economy and has come up with a three-tiered categorization of rentier states: extreme rentiers with very high rents per capita (Kuwait, Qatar, UAE, Brunei); middling rentiers (Saudi Arabia, Oman, Bahrain, Norway, Libya, Equatorial Guinea); and poor rentiers, who only have a high rent share because their economies do not produce much else (Iran, Iraq, Algeria, Yemen, Angola, Nigeria) (Herb 2014). In semi-rentier states of the region such as Egypt, Syria, and Jordan, the rent endowment per capita has been still smaller, too small to enjoy the same distributional discretion as the full rentier states. Yet besides some domestic rents, they have

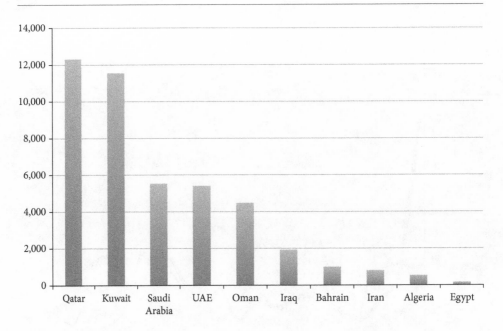

FIGURE 28.5 Resource rents per capita in US$, 2016.

Source: Data from World Bank (2018b) and IMF (2018b).

been integrated in the regional flows of oil rent via strategic transfer payments from Gulf countries, and their respective economies have benefited from migrant remittances (Pawelka 1993).

The decline in oil rents in the 1980s and 1990s created a legitimacy problem. Gulf rentier states typically tried to save on investments and stretched payments, while maintaining payroll and welfare payments as far as possible. Similar reactions can be observed since 2014.

Attempts at economic diversification have some history in the MENA. Oil producers have sought to expand their influence along the value chain via investments in refining, transporting, and distribution companies, such as BP (Kuwait), Tamoil (Libya), CEPSA (UAE), and Vela (Saudi Aramco). Gulf countries have built up petrochemical and heavy industries since the 1970s to capitalize on their competitive advantage of cheap energy feedstock (Luciani 2012a; Kvande 2012). Rather than exporting only crude oil, the strategic aim is to become providers of a variety of refined products and take better advantage of the heavy oil resources of the region (Krane 2019, 2015).

Bahrain and Dubai, a country and an emirate with limited hydrocarbons, have been at the forefront of diversification attempts, not only in heavy industries (e.g., Dubai Aluminum and Aluminum Bahrain), but also in sectors that are less energy related, such as trade, logistics, finance, and tourism (Hvidt 2009). In Saudi Arabia, the influential young crown prince Mohammed bin Salman seeks to undertake similar diversification steps in a more populous rentier economy with the much-publicized Saudi Vision 2030 (Kingdom of Saudi Arabia 2018). However, any success would only materialize in the middle and long run and has been cast into doubt by foreign policy adventures, the arrest of prominent representatives of the business community in Riyadh's Ritz Carlton in an ostensible anticorruption drive, and the political ramifications of the murder of Saudi journalist Jamal Khashoggi in the Saudi consulate in Istanbul.

Gulf countries have built competitive state-owned companies such as SABIC, Emirates, Dubai Ports World, and Aluminum Bahrain (ALBA). They have given them considerable leeway and have insulated them as "pockets of efficiency" from bloated bureaucratic structures of rent distribution (Hertog 2010a). As such they have seemingly defied economic orthodoxy and the resource curse theory (Luciani 2012b). This sets them apart from more negative diversification examples in the region (e.g., Libya, Iraq, Kuwait) and beyond (e.g., Venezuela, Nigeria) and calls for a more nuanced discussion of the economic impacts of resource rents (Luciani 2012b) than a plain reading of the resource curse literature might suggest (Ross 2012). The role of the private sector in the MENA, especially of larger business conglomerates, has grown. In addition to construction and trade, it has made forays into sectors that were formerly state dominated, such as education, media, and health. However, the private sector remains strongly dependent on subcontracting from the state, has only limited autonomy, and has faced renewed assertiveness of the public sector in recent years (Harris 2013; Hertog 2010b; Hertog, Luciani, and Valeri 2013).

An assessment of the socioeconomic implications of energy politics in the MENA is complicated by difficulty of access to and quality of data (Clark and Cavatorta 2018). Authoritarian regimes are disinclined to share information about their strategically important energy sectors. In the case of the oil exporters, capacities to collect data are underdeveloped compared to states that predominantly rely on tax income and need to maintain fiscal bureaucracies that reach into society. As a result, quantitative social science research on the MENA is relatively scarce and often focuses on a few countries where research conditions (e.g., survey collection) are better, such as Tunisia and Jordan (Pellicier and Wegener 2018). Comparative area studies (CAS) has emerged as an approach to bridging the gap between disciplinary specializations that seek to unearth nomothetic generalizations and the contextual expertise of area studies. This can include intraregional, cross-regional, and interregional comparisons (Ahram, Köllner, and Sil 2018).

ENERGY TRANSITIONS (RENEWABLES, NUCLEAR, COAL)

Growing domestic energy demand in the MENA countries increases the budgetary burden of energy subsidies and threatens to diminish oil export capacity. In some countries, such as Saudi Arabia, domestic demand for natural gas has outstripped domestic production. As a result environmentally more problematic diesel, fuel oil, and crude continue to be major factors in power generation. Since Gulf countries invested in the expansion of deep conversion refineries in the 2000s, unwanted fuel oil is not as readily available anymore, as local refineries manage to produce more value-added products for export, such as diesel (Luciani 2012a). However, global fuel oil demand will likely decline and shift to diesel-like products when the new reduced-sulfur marine fuel standards from the International Maritime Organization (IMO) take effect in January 2020 (Halff 2017). As maritime fuels account for about 7 percent of global oil demand, demand destruction for fuel oil will be substantial, and its market availability might not be affected as much despite the modernization of Gulf refineries.

All Gulf countries except Qatar are now suffering natural gas shortages or have started to import natural gas. Egypt has also turned from being a gas exporter to a gas importer. With the discovery of the giant Zohr gas field in 2015 off its Mediterranean coast, the country hopes to reverse that trend. Saudi Arabia and Algeria put their hopes in the development of unconventional sources of natural gas, which poses a challenge, as the water that is necessary for their production is scarce.

In addition to these shifts within the two dominant sources of the region's energy mix, MENA countries now eye alternative energies. Israel, Morocco, and Turkey are examples of countries with a substantial coal share in the energy mix (see Table 28.2). Currently the UAE and Oman are developing coal-fired power plants for the production of base load electricity, and Egypt and Turkey have significant expansion plans (Al-Sarihi 2018). Without carbon capture and storage (CCS), this will lead to increased emissions. CCS is in its infancy; only a few pilot plants exist globally, and the technology would significantly increase the costs of coal utilization (Supekar and Skerlos 2015). Unless CCS becomes economical and widespread, global coal demand will likely remain subdued and targeted by environmental regulations.

However, good conditions for other CCS applications exist in the Gulf region. In Abu Dhabi the world's first large-scale CCS project in the iron and steel industry started operating in 2016 (McAuley 2016; IEA 2017). Carbon dioxide can be used for injection into oil fields to maintain reservoir pressure, replacing the precious natural gas that is currently used. As such CCS would not be just a costly disposal process in the Gulf, but would carry economic benefits, as it would free up natural gas for other purposes (Ustadi, Mezher, and Abu-Zahra 2017). Oil reservoirs are also in close vicinity to power generation facilities, minimizing transport costs. Not surprisingly, Qatar, Saudi Arabia, and the UAE, alongside hydrocarbon producers Norway and Australia, pushed during the Cancun climate summit in 2010 to include CCS among the eligible technologies for funding under a United Nations clean development mechanism (CDM), which hitherto had focused on renewable energy, energy efficiency, and limiting the emissions from landfills (Luomi 2012).

Currently only Iran uses nuclear energy for civilian purposes in the MENA. The UAE will follow suit soon, and Turkey started construction of a reactor in 2018. Jordan and Egypt are less advanced but have committed plans and are developing the necessary legal and regulatory framework. Saudi Arabia has well-developed plans, but commitment is pending, and initial plans for sixteen reactors over a period of twenty to twenty-five years have been scaled back to only two. Israel, Algeria, and Morocco are only at the stage of developing plans. Israel already has a nuclear reactor for military and scientific purposes at Dimona, which was completed in the early 1960s (World Nuclear Association 2019).

Nuclear energy raises issues of costs, proliferation, security, and waste disposal (Kamrava 2012). Iran and the UAE represent two different approaches. On the one hand, Iran has sought to master the nuclear fuel cycle domestically and reduce its reliance on foreign providers of fuels and services for strategic reasons. The UAE, on the other hand, relies on foreign partners for construction, fuel provision, and waste disposal.

The enrichment and reprocessing of uranium on domestic soil for civilian purposes is legal under the Nuclear Non-Proliferation Treaty (NPT), but it has developed into a hot potato in regional negotiations. It was taken away from Iran via UN Security Council Resolution No. 1696 in 2006 to preclude any possible weaponization. The UAE voluntarily relinquished the right to enrich and reprocess uranium in its 123 nuclear cooperation agreement with the United States in 2009, but it remains a sticking point in the negotiations of a similar agreement between the United States and Saudi Arabia and Jordan; the latter two have domestic uranium reserves that they seek to develop (Woertz 2014).

Renewable energies are the most promising alternative energy source in the MENA and the world at large because of their limited environmental impact and improving economics, which are in stark contrast to habitual cost overruns of nuclear power projects. Between 2010 and 2017 the levelized cost of electricity (LCOE) for utility scale PV projects fell by 73 percent globally, for concentrated solar power (CSP) by 33 percent, and for onshore wind by 23 percent. Auctioning prices for PV projects in the Gulf broke record levels in 2017, with costs at and below $0.3 per kWh. The International Renewable Energy Agency (IRENA) in Abu Dhabi expects that "electricity from renewables will soon be consistently cheaper than from fossil fuels" (IRENA 2018). Main drivers have been technology improvements, competitive procurement, and a growing base of experienced, internationally active project developers. Further cost declines are expected from better economies of scale, learning rates, improved regulations, competitive market environment, and technological advances such as nanotechnology. Renewable energies are now competitive with conventional energy sources. Their main challenge is not cost anymore, but intermittency. Possible remedies in the form of storage solutions and integrated smart grids that can even out supply/demand mismatches have moved to the center of the debate.

MENA countries have announced ambitious renewable goals, which must be treated with caution (Brand 2016). The UAE was a pioneer of renewable energies in the Gulf region when it announced its Masdar initiative in 2006, which comprised a variety of multibillion renewable energy projects. The resulting reputational gain helped Abu Dhabi to attract IRENA in 2009, outbidding international competitors in Bonn and Copenhagen. However, in the same year Masdar's ambitions were downsized significantly in the wake of economic recession. Similarly, Saudi Arabia has walked back several ambitious renewable targets in recent years. The Public Investment Fund (PIF) for example spoke in 2018 of a stunning 200 gigawatts (GW) of solar power by 2030, but it was soon downgraded to a vague "long-term goal" (Mills 2018).

The Desertec Industrial Initiative was launched in 2009 with the ambitious vision of producing 15 percent of Europe's power needs by 2050 from CSP plants in North Africa. The transport of the electricity to Europe was planned via direct current cables, which have less transmission loss than alternating current. By 2014 the export-based part of the vision had collapsed. Most of the mainly German companies (e.g., Siemens, Bosch, E.ON, Bilfinger) withdrew from the consortium. In the wake of the global financial crisis and the Arab Spring, the project was deemed too risky. Even solar proponents had argued that electricity exports over such large distances are questionable and that solar production should focus primarily on domestic and regional markets. Expected incentives for local stakeholders were limited in the form of employment and knowledge transfer. To some the project appeared to be a gadget of European engineers. CSP can be combined with heat storage of energy via molten salts and/or conventional gas-fired plants. It thus offers solutions for intermittency, but due to more rapid cost declines of PV cells and advances in electricity storage via batteries, PV is seen as increasingly more attractive than CSP. Siemens actually closed down its CSP department.

Afterward the thrust of the initiative focused on an intergovernmental cooperation effort under the umbrella of the Mediterranean Solar Plan (MSP), championed by the Union for the Mediterranean (UfM) in Barcelona. The MSP hoped to deploy 20 GW of renewable energy capacity by 2020, which would have entailed a surge of transmission capacity and interconnections across borders. The MSP failed as well. Regulatory and infrastructure issues on the European side were major impediments. The Iberian Peninsula is an "energy island" within Europe. Its grid interconnection with France is limited to only 3 percent of daily capacity. As a result Spain is unable to export its renewable energy surpluses, which it generates on sunny and windy days. In the wake of the Great Recession (2007–2009), it cut subsidies to its domestic renewables producers. Additional competition via interconnections with southern Mediterranean countries was a nonstarter, especially as France objected to additional northern interconnections, fearing increased competition for its electricity producers (Carafa and Escribano 2017).

Hence renewable energy development in North Africa has focused on projects for domestic energy provision, such as the 160 MW/$3.9 billion Noor CSP plant in Ouarzazate, Morocco, which relied on World Bank financing (Carafa, Frisari, and Vidican 2016). Grid integration within and across borders remains an important challenge of renewable energy transitions. Electric storage solutions for intermittent renewables have moved to the center of attention, among them electric cars, as battery costs decreased by 40 percent between 2010 and 2016, and the IEA expects a further decrease of about two-thirds by 2040 (IEA 2017). While these changes portend declining demand for gasoline and diesel, they can also offer opportunities for the sun-rich MENA countries, especially those that do not own hydrocarbon resources and are not held back by considerations of stranded hydrocarbon assets (Woertz and Martinez 2018).

It remains to be seen how transitions toward renewable energies in the MENA will look in scope and detail, but two thing are certain: they will not constitute a comparable export commodity to hydrocarbons, and they will not provide the same amount of rents to MENA rulers. In 2015 then Saudi oil minister Ali Al-Naimi suggested that one day

Saudi Arabia could export electricity from renewables instead of oil (Clark 2015). This is unlikely to happen. Solar and wind power are distributed much more evenly across the globe than hydrocarbons, and transmission losses make electricity transportation over thousands of kilometers uneconomical with increasing distance. Saudi Arabia has a lot of sun and should make use of it, but its solar radiation hardly constitutes the same scarcity value as its oil does today. Technology trumps location in terms of strategic importance as the global energy mix transitions toward renewables. Energy systems as a whole will change: their infrastructures, markets, and regulations, not just the source powering them (Scholten 2018). The relative importance of commodities will decline and will partially shift to other raw materials such as rare earth minerals, cobalt, and lithium. Even if MENA countries managed to carve out their niche successfully, remunerations will accrue to the providers of labor and capital along the renewable value chains, not the owners of a particular resource. The wind and the sun are free and do not generate rent apart from the land needed to build renewable power systems. The more decentralized nature of renewable energy production and consumption will also empower new economic and possibly political actors, which could prompt either accommodation or suppression by authoritarian regimes and their public sectors.

FUTURE RESEARCH AGENDA

As energy issues continue to evolve in the MENA, political scientists can make important contributions in a number of areas. Six issues, elaborated in this section, are particularly promising: the role of environmental history, redefining the rentier state, varied diversification records and the role of state-owned enterprises and business communities, integration in global oil markets at a time of energy transitions and expansion of domestic refining, urban studies and the role of cities in the energy system, and the regulation of renewables and nuclear energy during the energy transition.

First, the MENA before the advent of oil deserves attention and can draw on the emerging field of environmental history in the region (Mikhail 2013). The essential question is how the MENA's environmental eccentricities have shaped its socioeconomic development since medieval times and how it was integrated into the British-led global coal economy of the nineteenth and early twentieth centuries.

Second, once oil appeared on the scene, it played a crucial role in state building and international relations of the MENA, especially in the Gulf. Here the rentier state paradigm could be refined, describing in more detail how this happened, how it was affected by human agency, and how regional flows of rent beyond oil-producing states affected the region's political economy.

Third, results of resource allocation of rentier states and their diversification record have differed widely across the region. Some have diversified considerably and have managed to build up "pockets of efficiency": well-run, mostly state-owned companies that have been insulated from bloated bureaucratic structures of rent distribution. More granularity is needed than a conventional reading of the resource curse literature suggests. In this context national oil companies in the MENA would merit further research as they position themselves amid domestic pressures and globalization strategies.

Fourth, the impact of the unconventional oil and gas revolution in the United States and possible future impact of increased electric mobility raise important questions about the region's interaction with OPEC and international oil markets. They also invite historical comparisons with the downturn in international oil markets in the mid-1980s. Due to the diversification efforts in refining of some MENA countries, much of the region's integration in global energy markets now happens in petroleum products' markets, not in the market for crude oil. This also affects logistical requirements, such as transportation and storage.

Fifth, cities play an increasingly important role in international politics and are the locus where much of the global resources is being consumed. Hence, they are indispensable agents in the localization processes of the Sustainable Development Goals (SDGs). Cities in the MENA do not have the same level of autonomy as cities in Europe and the Americas, yet MENA energy studies should go beyond the national and international dimensions, engage with urban studies and include issues of municipal energy management, including public transportation solutions, which a number of MENA cities have tried to expand to address problems of congestion and environmental pollution (e.g., Dubai, Riyadh, Istanbul, and the satellite cities of Cairo) (Lorraine 2017; Woertz 2018).

Finally, renewables will play an increasing role in the region's energy mixes, especially PV, as well as CSP and wind power. Nuclear expansion plans raise crucial issues about regulations and international agreements such as the NPT and 123 cooperation agreements of the United States. In addition to economic and technical aspects of energy transitions, one must not lose sight of social and political implications. What will rentier states do without rents, and what social and political changes will come with energy transitions?

References

Abdul Kader, Binsal, 2017. "Solar Energy Costs to See Record Lows in 2017." *Gulf News*, January 19. https://gulfnews.com/news/uae/environment/solar-energy-costs-to-see-record-lows-in-2017-1.1964780.

Ahram, Ariel I., Patrick Köllner, and Rudra Sil, eds. 2018. *Comparative Area Studies: Methodological Rationales and Cross-Regional Applications.* Oxford and New York: Oxford University Press.

Aissaoui, Ali. 2001. *Algeria: The Political Economy of Oil and Gas.* The Political Economy of Oil Exporting Countries. Oxford and New York: Oxford University Press for the Oxford Institute for Energy Studies.

Al-Sarihi, Aisha. 2018. "Why Oil- and Gas-Rich Gulf Arab States Are Turning to Coal." The Arab Gulf States Institute in Washington, August 21. https://agsiw.org/oil-gas-rich-gulf-arab-states-turning-coal/.

Ashtor, Eliyahu. 1976. *A Social and Economic History of the Near East in the Middle Ages.* Berkeley: University of California Press.

Barak, On. 2015. "Outsourcing: Energy and Empire in the Age of Coal (1820–1911)." *International Journal of Middle East Studies* 47, no. 3: 425–445. doi:10.1017/S0020743815000483.

Beblawi, Hazem, and Giacomo Luciani, eds. 1987. *The Rentier State: Nation, State, and Integration in the Arab World*. London and New York: Croom Helm.

Bonine, Michael E., Abbas Amanat, and Michael Ezekiel Gasper, eds. 2012. *Is There a Middle East? The Evolution of a Geopolitical Concept*. Stanford, CA: Stanford University Press.

BP. 2018. "Statistical Review of World Energy 2017." https://www.bp.com/en/global/corporate/energy-economics/statistical-review-of-world-energy.html.

Brand, Bernhard. 2016. "The Renewable Energy Targets of the MENA Countries: Objectives, Achievability, and Relevance for the Mediterranean Energy Collaboration." In *Regulation and Investments in Energy Markets*, edited by Alessandro Rubino, Maria Teresa Costa Campi, Veronica Lenzi, and Ilhan Ozturk, 89–100. New York: Academic Press.

Brown, L. Carl. 1984. *International Politics and the Middle East: Old Rules, Dangerous Game*. Princeton Studies on the Near East. Princeton, NJ: Princeton University Press.

Cammett, Melani, Ishac Diwan, Alan Richards, and John Waterbury. 2015. *A Political Economy of the Middle East*. 4th ed. Boulder, CO: Westview Press.

Campbell, Colin J., and Jean H. Laherrère. 1998. " The End of Cheap Oil." *Scientific American* 278, no. 3: 78–83.

Carafa, Luigi, and Gonzalo Escribano. 2017. "Renewable Energy in the MENA: Why Did the Desertec Approach Fail?" In *Handbook of Transitions to Energy and Climate Security*, edited by Robert E. Looney, 66–78. London and New York: Routledge.

Carafa, Luigi, Gianleo Frisari, and Georgeta Vidican. 2016. "Electricity Transition in the Middle East and North Africa: A De-risking Governance Approach." *Journal of Cleaner Production* 128: 34–47. doi:10.1016/j.jclepro.2015.07.012.

Clark, Janine A., and Francesco Cavatorta, eds. 2018. *Political Science Research in the Middle East and North Africa: Methodological and Ethical Challenges*. Oxford and New York: Oxford University Press.

Clark, Pilita. 2015. "Kingdom Built on Oil Foresees Fossil Fuel Phase-out This Century." *Financial Times*, May 21. https://www.ft.com/content/89260b8a-ffd4-11e4-bc30-00144feabdc0.

Clayton, Blake, and Michael A. Levi. 2015. "Fiscal Breakeven Oil Prices: Uses, Abuses, and Opportunities for Improvement." Discussion Paper, November 30. New York: Council on Foreign Relations. http://www.cfr.org/oil/fiscal-breakeven-oil-prices-uses-abuses-opportunities-improvement/p37275.

Dale, Spencer, and Bassam Fattouh. 2018. "Peak Oil Demand and Long-Run Oil Prices." Energy Insight no. 25. Oxford: The Oxford Institute for Energy Studies.

Darbouche, H., L. El-Katiri, and B. Fattouh. 2012. "East Mediterranean Gas: What Kind of a Game Changer?" Report NG71, December. Oxford: Oxford Institute for Energy Studies.

Ehteshami, Anoushiravan, and Steven M. Wright. 2008. *Reform in the Middle East Oil Monarchies*. Reading and Berkshire, UK: Ithaca Press.

Fattouh, Bassam, and Andreas Economou. 2018. "What to Make of Saudi Arabia's Recent Shift in its Output Policy?" Oxford Energy Comment, August. Oxford: The Oxford Institute for Energy Studies.

Fattouh, Bassam, Rahmatallah Poudineh, and Rob West. 2018. "The Rise of Renewables and Energy Transition: What Adaptation Strategy for Oil Companies and Oil-Exporting Countries?" OIES Paper, MEP 19, May. Oxford: The Oxford Institute for Energy Studies.

Griffiths, Steven. 2017. "A Review and Assessment of Energy Policy in the Middle East and North Africa Region." *Energy Policy* 102: 249–269. doi:10.1016/j.enpol.2016.12.023.

Halff, Antoine. 2017. "Slow Steaming to 2020: Innovation and Inertia in Marine Transport and Fuels." August 18. Columbia University Center on Global Energy Policy. https://energy-policy.columbia.edu/research/report/slow-steaming-2020-innovation-and-inertia-marine-transport-and-fuels.

Halliday, Fred. 2005. *The Middle East in International Relations: Power, Politics and Ideology*. The Contemporary Middle East. Cambridge, UK, and New York: Cambridge University Press.

Harris, Kevan. 2013. "The Rise of the Subcontractor State: Politics of Pseudo-Privatization in the Islamic Republic of Iran." *International Journal of Middle East Studies* 45, no. 1: 45–70. doi:10.1017/S0020743812001250.

Henry, Clement M., and Robert Springborg. 2010. *Globalization and the Politics of Development in the Middle East*. 2nd ed. The Contemporary Middle East. Cambridge, UK, and New York: Cambridge University Press.

Herb, Michael. 1999. *All in the Family: Absolutism, Revolution, and Democracy in the Middle Eastern Monarchies*. SUNY Series in Middle Eastern Studies. Albany: State University of New York Press.

Herb, Michael. 2014. *The Wages of Oil: Parliaments and Economic Development in Kuwait and the UAE*. Ithaca, NY: Cornell University Press.

Hertog, Steffen. 2010a. "Defying the Resource Curse: Explaining Successful State-Owned Enterprises in Rentier States." *World Politics* 62, no. 2: 261–301.

Hertog, Steffen. 2010b. *Princes, Brokers, and Bureaucrats: Oil and the State in Saudi Arabia*. Ithaca, NY, and London: Cornell University Press.

Hertog, Steffen, Giacomo Luciani, and Marc Valeri, eds. 2013. *Business Politics in the Middle East*. London and New York: Hurst and Oxford University Press.

Hvidt, Martin. 2009. "The Dubai Model: An Outline of Key Development-Process Elements in Dubai." *International Journal of Middle East Studies* 41, no. 3: 397–418. doi:10.1017/S0020743809091120.

International Energy Agency (IEA). 2017. "World Energy Outlook 2017." Paris:

International Energy Agency (IEA). 2018. "Outlook for Producer Economies: What Do Changing Energy Dynamics Mean for Major Oil and Gas Exporters?" World Energy Outlook Special Report. https://webstore.iea.org/weo-2018-special-report-outlook-for-producer-economies.

International Monetary Fund (IMF). 2017. "Gulf Cooperation Council: The Economic Outlook and Policy Challenges in the GCC Countries." GCC Surveillance Report. https://www.imf.org/en/Publications/Policy-Papers/Issues/2017/12/14/pp121417gcc-economic-outlook-and-policy-challenges.

International Monetary Fund (IMF). 2018a. "World Economic Outlook Database." April. https://www.imf.org/external/pubs/ft/weo/2018/01/weodata/index.aspx.

International Monetary Fund (IMF). 2018b. "Regional Economic Outlook: Middle East and Central Asia, Statistical Appendix." November. https://www.imf.org/~/media/Files/Publications/REO/MCD-CCA/2018/November/En/CCA/reo-statistical-appendix-cca.ashx.

International Renewable Energy Agency (IRENA). 2018. "Renewable Power Generation Costs in 2017." http://www.irena.org/publications/2018/Jan/Renewable-power-generation-costs-in-2017.

Kamrava, Mehran. 2012. *The Nuclear Question in the Middle East*. London: Hurst & Co.

Khalil, Osamah F. 2014. "The Crossroads of the World: U.S. and British Foreign Policy Doctrines and the Construct of the Middle East, 1902–2007*." *Diplomatic History* 38, no. 2: 299–344. doi:10.1093/dh/dht092.

Kingdom of Saudi Arabia. 2018. "Vision 2030." http://vision2030.gov.sa/en.

Krane, Jim. 2015. "A Refined Approach: Saudi Arabia Moves Beyond Crude." *Energy Policy* 82: 99–104. doi:10.1016/j.enpol.2015.03.008.

Krane, Jim. 2019. *Energy Kingdoms: Oil and Political Survival in the Persian Gulf.* New York: Columbia University Press.

Kvande, Halvor. 2012. "The GCC Aluminum Industry—The Development of Aluminum Production Capacity in the Middle East." In *Resources Blessed: Diversification and the Gulf Development Model*, edited by Giacomo Luciani, 213–232. Berlin and London: Gerlach Press.

Lasry, Jean-Michel, Antoine Halff, and Antoine Rostand. 2017. "OPEC Market Share Explained by Game Theory." *Kayrros: The Oil Games* 3.

Lorraine, Dominique, ed. 2017. *Métropoles en Méditerranée: Gouverner par les rentes.* Paris: Sciences Po Les Presses.

Luciani, Giacomo. 1987. "Allocation vs. Production States. A Theoretical Framework." In *The Rentier State: Nation, State, and Integration in the Arab World*, edited by Hazem Beblawi and Giacomo Luciani, 63–82. London and New York: Croom Helm.

Luciani, Giacomo. 2012a. "GCC Refining and Petrochemical Sectors in Global Perspective." In *Resources Blessed: Diversification and the Gulf Development Model*, edited by Giacomo Luciani, 183–212. Berlin and London: Gerlach Press.

Luciani, Giacomo, ed. 2012b. *Resources Blessed: Diversification and the Gulf Development Model.* Berlin and London: Gerlach Press.

Luciani, Giacomo. 2013. *Security of Oil Supplies: Issues and Remedies.* Vol. 4, *European Energy Studies.* Deventer and Leuven, Belgium: Claeys & Casteels.

Luomi, Mari. 2012. *The Gulf Monarchies and Climate Change: Abu Dhabi and Qatar in an Era of Natural Unsustainability.* Power and Politics in the Gulf. London: Hurst & Company.

Marcel, Valérie. 2006. *Oil Titans: National Oil Companies in the Middle East.* Washington, DC: Brookings Institution Press.

McAuley, Anthony. 2016. "Abu Dhabi Starts Up World's First Commercial Steel Carbon Capture Project." *The National*, November 5. https://www.thenational.ae/business/abu-dhabi-starts-up-world-s-first-commercial-steel-carbon-capture-project-1.213295.

McNeill, J. R. 2013. "The Eccentricity of the Middle East and North Africa's Environmental History." In *Water on Sand: Environmental Histories of the Middle East and North Africa*, edited by Alan Mikhail, 27–50. Oxford and New York: Oxford University Press.

Menoret, Pascal. 2014. *Joyriding in Riyadh: Oil, Urbanism, and Road Revolt.* Cambridge Middle East Studies. Cambridge, UK, and New York: Cambridge University Press.

Mikhail, Alan, ed. 2013. *Water on Sand: Environmental Histories of the Middle East and North Africa.* New York: Oxford University Press.

Mills, Robin. 2018. "Saudi Arabia Shelves SoftBank Solar Effort, Reflecting Challenges with Megaprojects." The Arab Gulf States Institute in Washington, October 9. https://agsiw.org/saudi-arabia-shelves-softbank-solar-effort-reflecting-challenges-with-megaprojects/.

Pawelka, Peter. 1993. *Der Vordere Orient und die internationale Politik.* Stuttgart, Germany: W. Kohlhammer.

Pellicier, Miquel, and Eva Wegener. 2018. "Quantitative Research in MENA Political Science." In *Political Science Research in the Middle East and North Africa: Methodological and Ethical Challenges*, edited by Janine A. Clark and Francesco Cavatorta, 187–196. Oxford and New York: Oxford University Press.

Ross, Michael Lewin. 2012. *The Oil Curse: How Petroleum Wealth Shapes the Development of Nations.* Princeton, NJ: Princeton University Press.

Scholten, Daniel, ed. 2018. *The Geopolitics of Renewables*. Vol. 61 of *Lecture Notes in Energy*. Cham, Switzerland: Springer.

Simmons, Matthew R. 2005. *Twilight in the Desert: The Coming Saudi Oil Shock and the World Economy*. Hoboken, NJ: John Wiley & Sons.

Supekar, Sarang D., and Steven J. Skerlos. 2015. "Reassessing the Efficiency Penalty from Carbon Capture in Coal-Fired Power Plants." *Environmental Science & Technology* 49, no. 20: 12576–12584. doi:10.1021/acs.est.5b03052.

Teitelbaum, Joshua. 2009. *Political Liberalization in the Persian Gulf*. New York: Columbia University Press.

United Nations. 2018. "2018 Energy Statistics Pocket Book." https://unstats.un.org/unsd/energy/pocket/default.htm.

Ustadi, Iman, Toufic Mezher, and Mohammad R. M. Abu-Zahra. 2017. "The Effect of the Carbon Capture and Storage (CCS) Technology Deployment on the Natural Gas Market in the United Arab Emirates." *Energy Procedia* 114: 6366–6376. doi:10.1016/j.egypro.2017.03.1773.

Verdeil, Éric. 2014. "The Contested Energy Future of Amman, Jordan: Between Promises of Alternative Energies and a Nuclear Venture." *Urban Studies* 51, no. 7: 1520–1536. doi:10.1177/0042098013500085.

Verdeil, Éric. 2016. "Beirut, Metropolis of Darkness and the Politics of Urban Electricity Grids." In *Geographies of the Electric City*, edited by A. Luque-Ayala and J. Silver. London: Routledge.

Verdeil, Éric, Elvan Arik, Hugo Bolzon, and Jimmy Markoum. 2015. "Governing the Transition to Natural Gas in Mediterranean Metropolis: The Case of Cairo, Istanbul and Sfax (Tunisia)." *Energy Policy* 78: 235–245. doi:10.1016/j.enpol.2014.11.003.

Vitalis, Robert. 2007. *America's Kingdom: Mythmaking on the Saudi Oil Frontier*. Stanford Studies in Middle Eastern and Islamic Societies and Cultures. Stanford, CA: Stanford University Press.

Woertz, Eckart. 2014. "Mining Strategies in the Middle East and North Africa." *Third World Quarterly* 35, no. 6: 939–957. doi:10.1080/01436597.2014.907706.

Woertz, Eckart, ed. 2018. *"Wise Cities" in the Mediterranean? Challenges of Urban Sustainability*. *Colección Mongrafías*. Barcelona: CIDOB.

Woertz, Eckart, and Irene Martinez. 2018. "Embeddedness of the MENA in Economic Globalization Processes." MENARA Working Paper no. 8, June. Rome: Istituto Affari Internazionali.http://www.iai.it/it/pubblicazioni/embeddedness-mena-economic-globalization-processes.

World Bank. 2018a. "Oil Rents (% of GDP)." https://data.worldbank.org/indicator/ny.gdp.petr.rt.zs?locations=kw.

World Bank. 2018b. "Total Natural Resources Rents (% of GDP)." https://data.worldbank.org/indicator/ny.gdp.totl.rt.zs.

World Nuclear Association. 2019. "Emerging Nuclear Energy Countries." March. http://www.world-nuclear.org/information-library/country-profiles/others/emerging-nuclear-energy-countries.aspx

Yergin, Daniel. 1991. *The Prize: The Epic Quest for Oil, Money, and Power*. New York: Simon & Schuster.

CHAPTER 29

THE ENERGY POLITICS OF SOUTH AFRICA

LUCY BAKER, JESSE BURTON, AND HILTON TROLLIP

This chapter has been written in the aftermath of nearly a decade of state capture and a national discourse on corruption that emerged at the end of 2016. While the extent of state capture is still coming to light (Joffe 2018), the country's electricity sector has been at its center. Within this context, we focus on key processes within the electricity sector and the state-owned utility Eskom that evolved under the presidency of Jacob Zuma from his inauguration in 2009 until he was forced out of office in February 2018. Zuma's presidency was riddled with allegations of corruption and graft that include but have gone far beyond the electricity sector. As we discuss here, the challenges associated with the design and implementation of national policies on energy have been intertwined with intensifying national political conflict and broader political battles within the ruling national party, the African National Congress (ANC), and the state. Since Zuma was ousted from power, a number of key sticking points in the electricity sector have been reversed by current (2019) president Cyril Ramaphosa. Yet while Zuma is facing charges that include corruption, racketeering, fraud, and tax evasion—charges that were dropped prior to his becoming president in 2009—many of Zuma's cronies remain in power (Momoniat 2018). The impact this will continue to have on national politics and the politics of electricity will require further political analysis over the coming years.

Eskom, the state-owned, vertically integrated monopoly utility, generates 85 percent of electricity from coal. Privately owned, utility-scale renewable energy makes a small contribution to electricity generation of approximately 5 percent, along with other independent power producers (IPPs), but is dependent on Eskom as the single buyer and transmission operator to purchase this electricity. Nuclear power accounts for 6 percent of electricity production, gas/diesel for 2 percent, and the remainder comes from imported hydro (Eskom 2017) (see Figure 29.1).

South Africa's energy sector is dominated by coal, which accounts for approximately 75 percent of primary energy. Of total national coal production of approximately 250 million metric tons per annum, 41 percent is converted into electricity and 15 percent

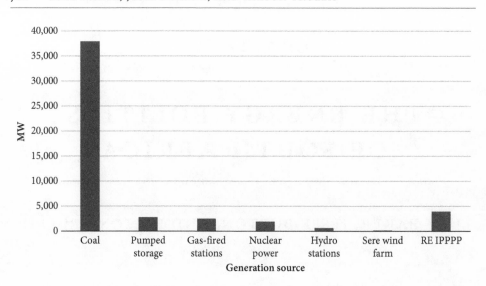

FIGURE 29.1 South Africa's installed capacity, 2018.

Sources: Data from Eskom (2019b) and IPP Office (2018).

into liquid fuels, and 8 percent is used directly by industry (Hartley et al, 2019); the remainder is exported, primarily to the Pacific market.

An electricity supply crisis that gripped the country over the period 2007–2015 has been succeeded by stagnant demand (Steyn, Burton, and Steenkamp 2017). This situation is partly a result of increasing electricity prices; the average standard tariff increased from R0.18 ($0.13)[1] in 2006/2007 to R0.82 ($0.59) in 2016/2017, an increase of 355 percent, while inflation increased by 74 percent over the same period and is projected to continue rising (Eskom 2019a). At the same time there has been a decline in economic growth, from around 4 percent between 2000 and 2010 to 2 percent between 2010 and 2015, and to 1 percent or lower since 2016 (IMF 2019). This has been accompanied by a parallel reduction in demand from the country's energy-intensive mineral-extraction industries, whose industrial sales shrank by 13 percent between 2013/2014 and 2017/2018 (Eskom 2018). While the commissioning of some units of the country's largest coal-fired power stations, Medupi and Kusile, currently still under construction, has somewhat alleviated the supply shortages, chronic underfunding for the maintenance of coal-storage and coal-fired infrastructure remains a risk. With 30 percent of Eskom's plant out of service due to planned and unplanned outages (Eskom 2018), this led to further load shedding in late 2018 and early 2019, despite a large capacity margin. Indeed, in 2018 available dispatch generation capacity stood at 32GW out of 47GW net maximum capacity (Eskom 2019b).

This chapter develops theoretical perspectives on the political economy of South Africa's electricity sector that have analyzed its embeddedness within the context of the country's "minerals-energy complex" (MEC) (Fine and Rustomjee 1996). We account for shifts that have taken place since 2009, focusing in particular on the introduction of a national planning process for electricity; the implementation of a procurement program for privately generated electricity from renewable energy; and a highly controversial nuclear procurement program, since scrapped under President Ramaphosa (Baker et al. 2015; DoE 2018; Eberhard, Kolker, and Leighland, 2014).

This chapter advances our combined long-standing and in-depth expertise and insights into South Africa's electricity sector and political economy (Baker and Burton 2018; Baker, Newell, and Phillips 2014; Baker et al. 2015). In addition to an academic literature review, our theoretical development is informed by an extensive content analysis of gray literature pertaining to energy and related sectors, including government documents, national policies, parliamentary transcriptions, and industry reports, as well as a systematic consultation of relevant media, including sources such as *Business Day*, *Engineering News*, and *ESI Africa*.

In this chapter we first explain the nature of South Africa's MEC as a descriptive and theoretical starting point for understanding the historical and contemporary development of the labor-intensive, energy-intensive, and carbon-intensive economy in which the electricity sector is embedded. We next examine the crises currently being experienced in the electricity sector and the way in which it has been involved in and affected by processes of state capture. This examination is followed by a discussion of the political and economic challenges to key processes in the electricity sector in recent years. Finally, we suggest a future research agenda that focuses on alternative framings for the technological and political nature of South Africa, including concepts of a political economy of electricity and the role of the state in energy transitions.

National Context: The Minerals-Energy Complex and Beyond

The political economy of South Africa's electricity sector has been characterized by the country's MEC (Fine and Rustomjee 1996), a concept coined at the end of apartheid that has continued to be used as the dominant framework for a critical analysis of South Africa's political economy, including its energy sector and industrial dynamics. The MEC has long provided a descriptive starting point for understanding the nature of South Africa's capital-intensive, energy-intensive, and carbon-intensive economy. It also provides a critical analytical framework for understanding key trends in the country's economic and political history as well as the structural causes of socioeconomic inequality and environmental injustice, such as the effects of continued coal development on local communities (Hallowes 2014; Peek and Taylor 2014).

The MEC refers to the country's unique and evolving system of accumulation, which historically was based on cheap coal for generating cheap electricity. Coupled with cheap labor, this combination provided input into export-oriented mining and minerals processing and beneficiation[2] (Fine and Rustomjee 1996). Historically, the MEC has been characterized by an evolving relationship and set of linkages between highly concentrated ownership structures of the state, state-owned enterprises, corporate capital, and a powerful financial system (Ashman and Fine 2013). Indeed, Marquard (2006, 71) described the South African economy as an associated "industrial policy complex," "consisting of a number of overlapping policy networks...and coordinated by what can be termed an 'industrial policy elite'...with close connections to the political elite." The inter-linkages have been characterized by a particular historical dynamic of "conflict and coordination" (Baker et al. 2015, 7).

The MEC has offered an analytical framework to address the socioeconomic and political legacy of apartheid and the nature of state and capital relations in contemporary South Africa (Padayachee 2010, 2). The MEC has been understood as an "architecture" (Freund 2010) that encompasses critical links and networks of power between the financial sector, government, the private sector, and state-owned enterprises, which are commercial corporations wholly or majority owned by the government, such as the Industrial Development Corporation (IDC) and Eskom. Various studies have applied an MEC framing to the electricity sector (Büscher 2009; Hallowes and Munnik 2007; McDonald 2009). More recent analyses have extended this framing to the country's new renewable energy industry and in so doing have drawn from the sociotechnical transitions literature to incorporate a perspective that is more aware of the nature of technological development, infrastructure, and innovation than the otherwise political and socioeconomic analyses (Baker 2015, 2016; Baker, Newell, and Phillips 2014).

A number of changes have been made to the MEC framework since its earlier use. First, twenty-five years after the transition to democracy, the assumed homogeneity of the MEC and the formal and informal institutions underpinning it have been subject to economic, political, and technical change, due to a combination of endogenous and exogenous factors. Such changes include shifts in the contribution of different sectors to gross domestic product (GDP), including the increased role of finance and tertiary sectors in the country's economy (Ashman and Fine 2013). For instance, South Africa's financial and business services now account for 24 percent of the county's GDP (Bhorat, Cassim, and Hirsch 2014) and form the country's single largest economic sector in terms of contribution to GDP, leading to what Ashman and Fine (2013, 146) describe as a "financialised MEC." At the same time, declining prices in international commodity markets have reduced the international competitiveness of many of South Africa's beneficiated exports. While elements of the relationship between the state and energy-intensive businesses have remained intact, emerging changes have arisen from parallel economic, technological, and ideological pressures.

A second change is the formation of a new black economic and political elite following socioeconomic redistribution policies introduced after the end of apartheid under black economic empowerment (BEE) policies and legislation,[3] and more recently the country's mining charter and minerals legislation. In the energy sector, this new elite has played an important role in diversifying ownership of the country's coal-mining houses, which were previously owned by a small number of large international conglomerates (such as Anglo American and BHP-Billiton). Eskom now purchases almost 40 percent of its coal from smaller, BEE-owned mines, at much higher delivered costs (Burton, Caetano and McCall et al. 2018).

Further shifts in the coal market have included changes in international demand for the country's coal (from Europe to India), depletion of the country's cheaper coal resources as a result of increased demand from China and India, and the end of long-term coal contracts between tied coal mines and Eskom. Consequently, the era of cheap coal in South Africa has come to an end (Burton and Winkler 2014; Spencer et al. 2017). This, in addition to international greenhouse gas emissions agreements, will in the long term require the structural phaseout of coal in South Africa.

A third change in the MEC is the increasing dispersal and fragmentation of previously entrenched relationships between and within different political, state, industrial, and financial institutions, which spells a fundamental reshaping of South Africa's political economy. As McDonald (2009) has argued, the relationship between "big state and big capital is changing." This change has been accompanied by growing factional battles within the ruling ANC, as well as political battles in other key parts of the polity. As a post-colonial liberation movement, the ANC accommodated organized labor, the Congress of South African Trade Unions (COSATU), and the South African Communist Party (SACP), with which it forms the Tripartite Alliance. This "broad church" (Gumede 2007, 305) has always brought with it ideological tensions. Not least, organized labor has fallen into internal disarray, with COSATU splitting apart and giving rise to a new union federation that is no longer aligned with the ANC, and there is growing competition and fragmentation between unions competing within sectors (Bezuidenhout and Tshoaedi 2017).

The means by which Zuma came to power and the dynamic of his presidency highlighted factional divisions within the party that were often more about networks of patronage than about questions of policy (Butler and Southall 2015). Moreover, while the ANC has demonstrated its willingness to put the party before the constitution and the public interest, it is clear that contemporary South Africa is no longer about the one-party state, but is experiencing an unraveling of long-standing political strongholds (Butler and Southall 2015).Understanding the dynamics of political factions and their interests and influence over policy decisions is a key area of further research.

AN ELECTRICITY SECTOR IN CRISIS AND THE ROLE OF STATE CAPTURE

At the heart of South Africa's MEC sits the state-owned monopoly utility Eskom, which has been integral to balancing the interests of the state and businesses for almost a century. South Africa's relative international isolation under apartheid meant that the country avoided the global trend of electricity sector liberalization pushed by the World Bank and other multilateral and bilateral donors as part of structural adjustment programs during the 1980s and 1990s (Gratwick and Eberhard 2008). Therefore, Eskom has essentially retained its monopoly over electricity generation, transmission, and the majority of distribution despite various failed attempts to liberalize it over the years. While there are long-standing tensions within government and related institutions and a spectrum of ideological differences between those advocating state ownership of the electricity sector at one end and those for liberalization and market reform at the other, factions within Eskom and related interests have long resisted the introduction of IPPs and the creation of an independent systems operator for transmission that would undermine Eskom's current monopoly control (Baker and Burton 2018). The long-running ideological battle over ownership has been overlaid with a crisis partly caused by techno-institutional shifts in the sector and partly by runaway costs of large coal-fired power plants still under construction, operating expenses, and coal supplies, which have in turn been exacerbated by corruption (Eberhard and Godinho 2017b; Steyn, Burton, and Steenkamp 2017). National debates over whether or not to keep Eskom as a vertically integrated monopoly or under state ownership have continued under the new era of governance heralded by President Ramaphosa (National Treasury 2019; Moneyweb 2019).

Facing a financial and management crisis, Eskom has been at the center of national scandals on state capture and failures of corporate and financial management, as discussed later in the chapter (Bhorat et al. 2017; Public Protector 2016). A huge program for the construction of new electricity generation capacity, initiated in 2005, is now several years delayed, more than 200 percent over budget, and subject to its own corruption allegations (Mntongana 2018). As a result, the state is now heavily exposed to Eskom's debt as a result of guarantees it has provided to the utility (National Treasury 2018), as are other institutions that also hold Eskom's debt, such as the Public Investment Corporation (which manages the pensions of government employees). The utility's sales base is in decline, and regulated tariffs are not rising in line with the applications Eskom has made to the country's energy regulator, NERSA, for rate increases. On the brink of bankruptcy, the largest recipient of state guarantees and bailouts and loans from development finance institutions, and with a capital budget larger than that of any other state-owned entity, Eskom is simply too big to fail. Eskom's financial failure would impose a fundamental threat to the South African economy. The utility's bonds are no longer considered creditworthy by investors (Laing 2018), it faces insolvency, it ran at a loss in financial year 2018/2019, and it has received various state bailouts in recent years. In the context of these crises, in the next section we discuss three key processes: the politics of electricity planning, renewable energy procurement from independent power producers, and nuclear procurement.

KEY PROCESSES IN THE ELECTRICITY SECTOR

Under Zuma, state capture evolved into massive corruption by a predatory elite. The term "state capture" was first used for South Africa by the country's former public protector.[4] who as part of a nationwide investigation was among the first to expose the systemic corruption within Eskom and other state-owned enterprises in a groundbreaking report published in November 2016 (Public Protector 2016).

In October 2017, based on the 2016 report, the parliament began an enquiry into the state capture of Eskom and other state-owned enterprises (Levy 2018). Beyond the public protector's report, the sheer extent and nature of state capture has been described in detail in a growing body of evidence, including by journalists and academics (Bhorat et al. 2017; Merten 2018; Pauw 2017;). Such evidence clearly illustrates ANC-sanctioned corruption across the economy and government. In brief, it has involved the ransacking and infiltration of public finances and government departments, including the intelligence networks; tax collection authorities (the South African Revenue Service); the National Prosecuting Authority; and state-owned enterprises, not least Eskom, but also transport (Transnet), aviation (South African Airways), and defense (Denel). Brian Molefe, the then chief executive officer of Eskom, was heavily implicated in multiple corruption scandals in different sectors and involving different levels of government. A judicial commission of inquiry into allegations of state capture, corruption, and fraud in the public sector has been looking into the contracts between Eskom's power stations and its coal suppliers, in particular the irregular sale of the Optimum coal mine by mining giant Glencore to a company co-owned by the infamous Gupta family[5] and former president Zuma's son. The sale implicated the minister of mineral resources and the head of the electricity generation division at Eskom, among others (Eberhard and Godinho 2017b). Formal corruption investigations have resulted in a strongly worded parliamentary report recommending criminal investigations (Parliament of South Africa 2018), and a Judicial Commission of Enquiry has been hearing evidence under oath since August 2018, much of it damning (Hoffman 2019; Swilling 2019; Turok 2018; Zondo Commission 2019). The extension of capture throughout the state and state-owned enterprises, which have been "repurposed" for the benefit of a narrow elite within the ANC, highlights that the politics of energy must be analyzed in light of the broader politics within South Africa. Yet thus far theoretical research remains limited.

The Politics of Electricity Planning

During apartheid there was no formal public process for electricity planning. Instead, planning was carried out by Eskom, which made all decisions about electricity new build. Only after the Electricity Regulation Act was introduced in 2006 were the necessary powers established for the country's Department of Energy (DoE) to conduct an open planning process for electricity. Under the act, responsibility was formally allocated to the energy minister to approve the construction of new electricity generation capacity. Subsequently, in 2011 South Africa's first public electricity plan, the Integrated Resource Plan (IRP), was finally put forward in the government gazette (DoE 2011). The plan's negotiation was heavily contested, leading to delays. However, the delay allowed for the effective participation of a broad range of new political actors. It is therefore considered something of a breakthrough in light of the public process that accompanied its development (Baker et al. 2015).

The IRP delivered both a new institutional process and the potential for a fundamental break with the long-standing coal-dependent electricity system. It set a renewable energy target of 17.8 GW, which if built would deliver 9 percent of electricity supply by 2030. It also included 9.6 GW of new nuclear capacity and new coal-fired power stations. The Zuma administration was unwilling, however, to update the 2011 IRP to reflect new technological and demand realities, since these would lead to the exclusion of new coal and nuclear.

Consequently, in violation of the requirement that the plan be updated periodically, revisions of the IRP stalled. For instance, an updated version was released in 2013 for public comment (DoE 2013) but was never formally adopted by the government. Reportedly, the main reason was that the draft advised against the new nuclear construction included in the 2010 plan, for two reasons. First, due to a decline in economic growth and reduced energy intensity in the economy, the 2013 draft projected a lower electricity demand up until 2030 and therefore a reduced requirement for constructing new capacity, stating that "the revised demand projections suggest that no new nuclear baseload capacity is required until after 2025 (and for lower demand not until at earliest 2035)" (DoE 2013, 8). Second, the draft questioned the high costs of nuclear technology.

A second IRP draft was released in late 2016 (DoE 2016) but was also contested. The renewable energy industry and civil society expressed concerns about how the document placed constraints on the uptake of renewable energy and assumed that the prices of renewable energy technologies were much higher than those achieved in the recent auctions submitted under the country's renewable energy independent power producers program (RE IPPPP) (CSIR 2017), as discussed later in the chapter.

By early 2018 the latest draft of the IRP had yet to be finalized, in part because of pressure from the former minister of energy, David Mahlobo, to ensure that all technologies were represented. As a result of such delays, the IRP was now almost a decade out of date and based on assumptions that no longer applied (McCall et al. 2019). With multiple delays and revisions, and contestation over the inclusion of new coal and nuclear, the IRP 2019 was finalized only at the end of October 2019. As Baker et al. (2015) have argued, despite the gains that the first IRP represented in terms of increased transparency in post-apartheid energy policymaking, the stalling of the 2013, 2016, and 2018 versions signaled a return to the highly secretive decision-making characteristic of energy policy under apartheid. Such uncertainty is one of various challenges facing the future of the country's renewable energy sector and the electricity sector more broadly.

While the IRP process has been contested, academic analysis of planning and the technology interest groups involved is relatively limited. Three scholarly frameworks have been used for this analysis. First, some have applied sociotechnical transitions and political economy frameworks to understand the political nature of an otherwise technical policy process and the strong lobbying power of the energy-intensive users and associated factions in its design (Baker 2016; Froestad et al. 2018). Second, others have applied the advocacy coalition framework (Martin 2016) and discourse network analysis (Rennkamp et al. 2017), both of which seek to understand the coalitions in support of or opposed to renewable energy. Finally Rennkamp and Bhuyan (2017) have analyzed opposing political coalitions relating to nuclear power, arguing that it is the strength of political interest groups, rather than the technical merits of nuclear power, that gave rise to the inclusion of a large technical fleet in the IRP, as discussed later in the chapter.

The Stalling of Renewable Energy Procurement

The second process under way in the electricity sector is the stalling of renewable energy procurement. The 2011 introduction of the renewable energy independent power producers' procurement program (RE IPPPP) facilitated the generation of electricity from renewable energy sources and by IPPs for the first time. It has since attracted over R200 billion in investment. The RE IPPPP's trajectory and that of the industry it has generated have been influenced by a number of developments at the international and national levels, including a dramatic decline in the cost of renewable energy technologies, as a result of which they have become competitive with new coal power plants globally and in South Africa (Bischof-Niemz and Creamer 2018); enormous electricity rate hikes in South Africa in recent years; and a decline in the country's economic growth and related energy demand. Yet despite the RE IPPPP's initial successes, which were celebrated internationally, political, economic, and technical challenges have led to delays that have generated significant uncertainty for renewable energy investors and stakeholders, thus threatening the future of renewables in South Africa.

Renewable energy from IPPs can be seen as a small but significant change to Eskom's monopoly control and as both a technological and institutional break with the centralized, state-owned electricity sector of the past. The political barriers facing the program highlight new aspects of the politics of South African energy and offer significant potential for further theoretical analysis.

Most significantly, in 2015 Eskom made clear its refusal to sign power purchase agreements (PPAs) for thirty-seven projects approved under the RE IPPPP, a stalemate that continued until the end of Zuma's presidency. A further procurement round, which was to have been announced in 2016, was also stalled. Eskom's resistance to RE IPPPP began to be felt in late 2015 when it announced it would not provide the budget quotes for a renewable energy project to connect to the grid. The utility subsequently announced in July 2016 that it would not sign any new PPAs with IPPs beyond those selected under round four of RE IPPPP and refused to sign a PPA for a concentrated solar power project approved under round three (Baker 2017).

Though the utility never provided a formal reason for refusing to sign the PPAs, it claimed first that it would suffer a loss by having to purchase energy from IPPs (SAREC 2017) and second that the country's energy supply had stabilized since the most recent round of load-shedding in 2014/2015; therefore, Eskom argued, additional capacity from renewable energy was no longer necessary and would make "the future outlook for Eskom operationally and financially unsustainable" (Eskom 2017). However, many argued that its refusal to sign the PPAs represented a clear attempt by the utility to challenge the procurement of further independent power generation (cf. Baker 2017).

Moreover, in refusing to sign the PPAs, Eskom was acting beyond its mandate, given that it is the DoE's role to make policy on energy under the 2006 Electricity Regulation Act, and procurement is the remit of the DoE. While Treasury and the DoE eventually condemned the move, over a year later the impasse endured, and despite a pledge by Zuma in February 2017 in his "state of the nation" address that the PPAs would be signed in April 2017, they were not signed until early 2018 (Yelland and Lilley 2018).

The approval of RE IPPPP projects faced further opposition from organized labor and coal interests. Not only did the Coal Transporters Forum (an advocacy group for coal trucking interests) mount a legal challenge against the procurement program (Saflii 2019), but a leading South African union, National Union of Metalworkers (NUMSA), also attempted to interdict the signing of PPAs in early 2018 (Legal Brief Environmental 2019). The unions claimed they were motivated by concerns for workers in the coal sector and fears that they will lose their jobs as coal plants are closed to make way for the RE IPPPP projects. The newly appointed minister for energy in the Ramaphosa regime finally ensured that the stalled PPAs were signed in April 2018, but opposition to the program from coal incumbents persists. Trade unions in particular assert that the privatization of electricity and the introduction of IPPs will act against the interests of the working class and "will result in electricity being expensive and unaffordable to the poor" (David Sipunzi, the general secretary of the National Union of Mineworkers, cited in Industriall 2019).

The role of RE IPPPP and the introduction of renewable energy in South Africa have been analyzed from various angles, and there has been burgeoning national and international interest in RE IPPPP's conception and implementation, resulting in numerous empirical and theoretical studies. Major contributions include the empirical explorations of the nature of the policymaking process (Eberhard and Kåberger 2016); more theoretical analyses of renewable energy as a sociotechnical "niche" that has posed a significant challenge to the country's coal-fired "regime" (Baker 2015, 2016; Baker and Burton 2018); an examination of the opportunities opened up by renewable electricity generation for alternative configurations of urban energy governance (Davies, Swilling and Wlokas 2018); studies of the potential of the new renewable industry to generate opportunities for local industrial development and job creation (Ettmayr and Lloyd 2017; Rennkamp and Boyd 2013); and studies that have considered the challenges of RE IPPPP's stated aims to generate opportunities for community empowerment and socioeconomic development in a country with gross socioeconomic inequality (Wlokas, Westoby, and Soal 2017), including how the program could draw lessons from the mining industry (Marais et al. 2018).

Nuclear Program Pushed by the Presidency

A deal that lies at the heart of state capture, the nuclear program was long considered a legacy project for Zuma. Prior to Zuma's departure, Eskom, backed by the presidency, seemed set to pursue its plans for a 9.6 GW, state-driven nuclear fleet despite clear evidence from independent analyses showing that building the fleet would lead to higher electricity costs and negative economic impacts for South Africa (ERC 2015).[6] The revised nuclear determination of December 2016 transferred nuclear procurement responsibilities from the DoE to Eskom and the South African Nuclear Energy Corporation. Subsequently, Zuma's unexpected cabinet shuffle in March 2017 removed Finance Minister Pravin Gordhan because of his alleged opposition to the nuclear program and installed a new energy minister believed to be in favor of it. Then, in a case brought by civil society organizations Earthlife Africa Johannesburg and The South African Faith Communities Environment Institute (SAFCEI) in late April 2017, the Western Cape High Court judged that the intergovernmental agreements on nuclear cooperation signed in 2014 between South Africa and five countries were unconstitutional and unlawful, particularly in the case of the agreement signed between Eskom and Russia's state-owned nuclear company Rosatom (Ensor 2017). Despite this ruling, the government subsequently announced that the nuclear procurement program would start afresh. Given the centralized nature of the technology, it would seem that nuclear power would serve to bolster the interests of a monopoly-controlled electricity system while marginalizing renewable energy (Baker and Burton 2018). In late January 2018, shortly after taking office, Ramaphosa announced at the World Economic Forum that South Africa does not have the financial capacity or need for additional nuclear power and would abandon plans to build nuclear plants.

Questions have been raised about what the entanglement between developments in the electricity sector and national politics means for the future of Eskom and its role in the political economy of South Africa. Since Ramaphosa took over from Zuma as head of the ANC and as president of the country, he has reversed actions on a number of key sticking points in the electricity sector to which Zuma had held steadfast, including an overhaul of the utility board and the extension by banks of a R20 billion short-term credit line. Yet with Eskom crisis ridden and struggling with high levels of debt, there are questions about over how long it will maintain its generation, transmission, and distribution monopoly, and what implications this might have for realizing decarbonization and accommodating rapid technological change in energy.

FUTURE RESEARCH AGENDA

As we have discussed, key shifts in South Africa's political economy have resulted in the reconfiguration of formerly well-established structures, institutions, and relationships within and between the state, the ruling party, and the private sector. The political and economic interests of various ANC factions, networks of patronage, and technology interests continue to have an outsize influence on the shape of electricity policy in South Africa. There is still rich potential for future theoretical development, however, in particular the way in which techno-economic debates have become caught up in broader political and ideological battles. With this in mind, we first propose how concepts of political economy can be incorporated into the wide-ranging literature on sociotechnical transitions. While a political economy approach provides critical tools with which to analyze networks and institutions of economic and political power, sociotechnical transition frameworks conceptualize technological change as unpredictable, long term, and involving complex interactions between different actors (Elzen, Geels, and Green 2004).

Of particular interest is that the term "transition" is central to these two diverse sets of literatures. First, for political economy, the term refers to South Africa's post-apartheid socioeconomic and political transition and the ongoing struggle to uphold principles of justice and democracy (Michie and Padayachee 1997). Such a struggle is ongoing not least in light of the state capture and corruption that have permeated state-owned enterprises and institutions, as discussed. For the sociotechnical transitions literature the term "transition" denotes low-carbon technological and societal shifts, which have had a significant impact on the way in which electricity is owned and governed. A number of other parallels can be identified between these two approaches: both place emphasis on linkages between developments, institutions, and actors at multiple levels; both talk about the need to revise and reconfigure structural changes and relationships (for instance in technology, infrastructure, political, and economic institutions) for any transition to take place (Rip and Kemp 1998); and both underline the importance of a historical understanding (e.g., Elzen, Geels, and Green 2004; Hughes 1983, 2; Milonakis and Fine 2009). A political economy of electricity is therefore necessarily context specific, understood via a localized exploration that includes political, economic, technological, and social complexities; institutional architecture; infrastructural and industrial development; comparative technological advantage; and geophysical factors. It further allows for the consideration of historical power relations, the role of vested interests and key networks, and complex relationships between political and economic institutions and state and nonstate actors involved in electricity governance.

Second, a key opportunity for further theoretical work lies in understanding better the role and interactions of different ANC and political factions, their influence over and role within the state, and the implications for national decisions in the energy sector. Such an approach adds value to the existing literature on South Africa's electricity sector, which has often underplayed the social, political, and economic complexities in favor of a more techno-economic and managerial approach, despite the growing acknowledgment of contextual difference and national and subnational factors (Eberhard and Godinho 2017a; Gratwick and Eberhard 2008). Such differences include how the electricity system is shaped by and interacts with differentiated patterns of domestic and industrial consumption, socioeconomic inequality and uneven access to services, processes of spatial development, and the strong influential role that vested interests can have in electricity policy and planning. With such factors in mind, South Africa's electricity sector can be considered a site of struggle over its governance, ownership, and regulation as well as over the allocation of access to electricity services (Gentle 2009; McDonald 2009).

Finally, the implications of South Africa's case raise the need for a greater and more explicit analysis of the role of the state and different aspects of state power over the electricity sector and how electricity is embedded within political and economic factions of capital. Indeed, the fact that the nuclear construction program was nearly carried out raises the need for further analysis of the political factions and interest groups in Eskom, the state, and the ANC as they pertain to the energy sector. While in recent years the literature on sociotechnical transitions has developed a more sophisticated analysis of politics and power (Geels 2014; Lockwood et al. 2017), it still has some way to go to develop a framework for analysis of the role of the state and different aspects of state power according to time and context. As Johnstone and Newell (2018) emphasize, there is a need to make the state "a focal point of analysis—as opposed to broader institutional account of decision-making" and to understand the nature of the state "in different contexts in more relational terms." With this in mind we therefore see significant theoretical value in merging more technically aware perspectives with recent country-specific analyses of South Africa's patronage politics and corruption and the evolving relationships between business and state (e.g. Beresford 2015; Butler and Southall 2015; Hyslop 2005; Lodge 2014). Such a merger would also enable these more politically focused analyses to consider how technologies, natural resources, and infrastructural systems can be found at the heart of national political economy.

NOTES

1. Based on exchange rate of R0.82 to$0.589 on July 22, 2019.
2. A process that creates a higher grade product.
3. Many, including ANC insiders, have criticized aspects of BEE policy for encouraging patronage and rent-seeking (Cargill, 2010); for an even more critical perspective, see Jeffery (2014).
4. The public protector is an independent institution established by the constitution, with a mandate to support and strengthen constitutional democracy. A supreme administrative oversight body, the public protector has the power to investigate, report on, and remedy improper conduct in all state affairs, and anyone may lodge a complaint with the protector for investigation (http://www.pprotect.org/).
5. An Indian family who became well-connected and influential within South Africa's political economy and were heavily implicated in the state capture investigation. Family members left South Africa when warrants were issued for their arrest.
6. In general new nuclear would require significant subsidies (due to its higher costs) compared to an alternative electricity pathway, and in particular the 9.6 GW fleet would exceed demand growth, leading to stranded assets, and reduce capital available to the rest of the economy, slowing growth (ERC 2015). All independent cost optimization modeling in South Africa has shown that new nuclear and new coal plants do not form part of a least-cost electricity pathway, even when ambitious decarbonization goals are included (Ireland and Burton 2018; Burton et al. 2018; McCall et al. 2019; CSIR 2017; Wright et al. 2018). There are already significant subsidies to electricity consumption and fossil fuels (Burton, Lott, and Rennkamp, 2018).

REFERENCES

Ashman, Sam, and Ben Fine. 2013. "Neo-liberalism, Varieties of Capitalism, and the Shifting Contours of South Africa's Financial System." *Transformation: Critical Perspectives on Southern Africa* 81/82: 144–178.

Baker, Lucy. 2015. "Renewable Energy in South Africa's Minerals-Energy Complex: A "Low Carbon" Transition?" *Review of African Political Economy* 42, no. 144: 245–261.

Baker, Lucy. 2016. "Sustainability Transitions and the Politics of Electricity Planning in South Africa." In *Handbook on Sustainability Transition and Sustainable Peace*, edited by H. G. Brauch, Ú. Oswald Spring, J. Grin, and J. Scheffran, 793–809. Cham, Switzerland: Springer International Publishing.

Baker, Lucy. 2017. "Post-apartheid Electricity Policy and the Emergence of South Africa's Renewable Energy Sector." In *The Political Economy of Clean Energy Transitions*, edited by Douglas Arent et al., 371–390.WIDER Studies in Development Economics. Oxford: Oxford University Press.

Baker, Lucy, and Jesse Burton. 2018. "The Politics of Procurement and the Low Carbon Transition in South Africa." In *Handbook on the IPE of Energy and Resources*, 91–106, edited by A. Goldthau, M. Keating, and C. Kuzemko, Cheltenham, UK: Edward Elgar.

Baker, Lucy, Jesse Burton, Catrina Godinho, and Hilton Trollip. 2015. "The Political Economy of Decarbonisation: Exploring the Dynamics of South Africa's Electricity Sector." Energy Research Centre, University of Cape Town.

Baker, Lucy, Peter Newell, and Jon Phillips. 2014. "The Political Economy of Energy Transitions: The Case of South Africa." *New Political Economy* 19, no. 6: 791–818.

Beresford, A., 2015. "Power, patronage, and gatekeeper politics in South Africa." *African Affairs* 114, no. 455: 226–248

Bezuidenhout, Andries, and Malehoko Tshoaedi. 2017. *Labour Beyond Cosatu: Mapping the Rupture in South Africa's Labour Landscape*. Johannesburg: Wits University Press.

Bhorat, Haroon, et al. 2017. "Betrayal of the Promise: How South Africa Is Being Stolen." https://pari.org.za/wp-content/uploads/2017/05/Betrayal-of-the-Promise-25052017.pdf.

Bhorat, Haroon, Aalia Cassim, and Alan Hirsch. 2014. "Policy Co-ordination and Growth Traps in a Middle-Income Country Setting." UNU-WIDER Working Paper 2014/155.

Bischof-Niemz, Tobias, and Terence Creamer. 2018. *South Africa's Energy Transition: A Roadmap to a Decarbonised, Low-cost and Job-rich Future*. Routledge: London, UK

Burton, Jesse, Tara Caetano, and Bryce McCall. 2018. "South Africa's Coal Transition: Understanding the Implications of a 2°C-Compatible Coal Phase Out Plan for South Africa." Energy Research Centre, University of Cape Town.

Burton, Jesse, Tawney Lott, and Britta Rennkamp. 2018. "Sustaining Carbon Lock in: Fossil Fuel Subsidies in South Africa." In *The Politics of Fossil Fuel Subsidies and Their Reform*, edited by Jakob Skovgaard and Harro van Asselt, 229–245. Cambridge, UK: Cambridge University Press.

Burton, Jesse, and Harald Winkler. 2014. "South Africa's Planned Coal Infrastructure Expansion: Drivers, Dynamics and Impacts on Greenhouse Gas Emissions." Energy Research Centre, University of Cape Town.

Büscher, Bram. 2009. "Connecting Political Economies of Energy in South Africa." *Energy Policy* 37, no. 10: 3951–3958.

Butler, Anthony, and Roger Southall. 2015. "Introduction: Understanding the ANC at Sub-national Level." *Transformation: Critical Perspectives on South Africa* 87: 1–12.

Cargill, Jenny. 2010. *Trick or Treat: Rethinking Black Economic Empowerment*. Jacana Media, Johnnesburg.

CSIR. 2017. "Formal Comments on the Integrated Resource Plan (IRP) Update Assumptions: Base Case and Observations 2016." Council for Scientific and Industrial Research.Pretoria

Davies, Megan, Mark Swilling, and Holle Wlokas. 2018. "Towards New Configurations of Urban energy Governance in South Africa's Renewable Energy Procurement Program." *Energy Research & Social Science* 36: 61–69.

Department of Energy (DoE). 2011. "Integrated Resource Plan for Electricity (IRP), 2010–2030." *Government Gazette* no. 34263 (May 6, 2011). Pretoria. http://www.energy.gov.za.

Department of Energy (DoE). 2013. "Integrated Resource Plan for Electricity (IRP), 2010–2030 Update." Pretoria. https://www.environment.gov.za/sites/default/files/docs/irp2010_2030.pdf.

Department of Energy (DoE). 2016. "Integrated Resource Plan: Assumptions, Base Case Results, and Observations, October 2016." http://www.energy.gov.za/IRP/irp-2016.html.

Department of Energy (DoE). 2018. "Draft Integrated Resource Plan 2018." Pretoria, August. https://www.ee.co.za/wp-content/uploads/2019/04/IRP-Update-2018-Draft-for-Comments.pdf.

Eberhard, A., and T. Kåbeger. 2016. "Renewable Energy Auctions in South Africa Outshine Feed-in Tariffs." *Energy Science and Engineering* 4, no. 3: 190–193.

Eberhard, Anton, and Catrina Godinho. 2017a. "A Review and Exploration of the Status, context and Political Economy of Power Sector Reforms in Sub-Saharan Africa, South Asia and Latin America." MIR Working Paper. https://assets.publishing.service.gov.uk/media/5a251ecee5274a75088c42a1/Eberhard_Godinho_2017.pdf.

Eberhard, Anton, and Catrina Godinho. 2017b. "Eskom Inquiry Reference Book." October. Graduate School of Business, State Capacity Research Project.

Eberhard, Anton, Joel Kolker, and James Leighland. 2014. "South Africa's Renewable Energy IPP Procurement Program: Success Factors and Lessons." World Bank Group, Washington, DC. https://openknowledge.worldbank.org/handle/10986/20039.

Elzen, Boelie, Frank Geels, and Ken Green. 2004. *System Innovation and the Transition to Sustainability: Theory Evidence and Policy*. Cheltenham, UK: Edward Elgar.

Energy Research Centre (ERC). 2015. "South Africa's Proposed Nuclear Build Plan: An Analysis of the Potential Socio-economic Risks." Technical Report, November. Energy Research Centre, University of Cape Town.

Ensor, Linda. 2017. "Lynne Brown Sticks to Her Guns on Eskom's IPP Deals." *Business Day*, https://www.businesslive.co.za/bd/national/2017-05-25-lynne-brown-sticks-to-her-guns-on-eskoms-ipp-deals/ May 25.

Eskom. 2017. "Integrated Report." March 31. http://www.eskom.co.za/OurCompany/Investors/IntegratedReports/Pages/Annual_Statements.aspx.

Eskom. 2018. "Integrated Report." March 31. http://www.eskom.co.za/OurCompany/Investors/IntegratedReports/Pages/Annual_Statements.aspx.

Eskom. 2019a. "Historical Average Prices and Increase." v20160707. http://www.eskom.co.za/CustomerCare/TariffsAndCharges/Pages/Tariff_History.aspx.

Eskom. 2019b. "Eskom Weekly System Status Report—2019 Week 24." (10/06/2019–16/06/2019). www.eskom.co.za/Whatweredoing/SupplyStatus/Pages/SupplyStatusT.aspx.

Ettmayr, Christopher and Hendrik Lloyd. 2017. "Local Content Requirements and the Impact on the South African Renewable Energy Sector: A Survey-Based Analysis". *South African Journal of Economic Management Sciences* 20, no. 1: 1–11.

Fine, Ben, and Zavareh Rustomjee. 1996. *The Political Economy of South Africa: From Minerals Energy Complex to Industrialisation*. London, UK: C. Hurst & Co Publishers.

Freund, Bill. 2010. "The Significance of the Minerals-Energy Complex in the Light of South African Economic Historiography." *Transformation: Critical Perspectives on Southern Africa* 71: 3–25.

Froestad, Jan, M. Nøkleberg, Clifford Shearing, and Hilton Trollip. 2018. "South Africa's Minerals-Energy-Complex: Flows, Regulation, Governance and Policing." In *Ending Africa's Energy Deficit and the Law. Achieving Sustainable Energy for All in Africa*, edited by Yinka Omorogbe and Ada Ordor, pp. 308–340. Oxford: Oxford University Press.

Geels, Frank. 2014. "Regime Resistance against Low-Carbon Energy Transitions: Introducing Politics and Power in the Multi-level Perspective." *Theory, Culture & Society* 31, no. 5: 21–40.

Gentle L. 2009. "Escom to Eskom: From Racial Keynesian Capitalism to Neo-liberalism (1910–1994)." In *Electric Capitalism: Recolonising Africa on the Grid*, edited by David McDonald, 50–72. Cape Town: HSRC Press.

Gratwick, Katherine, and Anton Eberhard. 2008. "Demise of the Standard Model for Power Sector Reform and the Emergence of Hybrid Power Markets." *Energy Policy* 36, no. 10: 3948–3960.

Gumede, William Merven. 2007. *Thabo Mbeki and the Battle for the Soul of the ANC*. London/ New York: Zed Books.

Hallowes, David. 2014. "Slow Poison: Air Pollution, Public Health and Failing Governance." Ground Work. http://www.groundwork.org.za/specialreports/Slow%20Poison(e).pdf.

Hallowes, David, and Viktor Munnik. 2007. "Peak Poison: The Elite Energy Crisis and Environmental Justice", Pietermaritzburg groundWork http://www.groundwork.org.za/reports/Peak%20Poison.pdf

Hartley, Faaiqa, Bruno Merven, Channing Arndt, and Gregory Ireland. 2019. "Quantifying the Macro- and Socio-Economic Benefits of a Transition to Renewable Energy in South Africa: Part 2: economic impacts". SA-TIED Working paper no 25. https://sa-tied.wider.unu.edu/sites/default/files/pdf/SATIED_WP25_January_2019_Hartley_Merven_Arndt_Ireland_1.pdf

Hoffman, P., 2019. "Why Is Nobody Going to jail?" *New Agenda: South African Journal of Social and Economic Policy*, no. 72: 28–29. https://journals.co.za/content/journal/10520/EJC-14fd4c0636.

Hughes, Thomas. 1983. *Networks of Power: Electrification in Western Society, 1880–1930*. Baltimore: JHU Press.

Hyslop, J. 2005. "Political Corruption: Before and after Apartheid", *Journal of Southern African Studies*, 31, no. 4: 773–789.

Industriall. 2019. "South African Unions Oppose Plans to Privatize Eskom." http://www.industriall-union.org/south-african-unions-oppose-plans-to-privatize-power-utility-eskom.

International Monetary Fund (IMF). 2019. "Report for Selected Countries and Subjects.". http://www.imf.org/~/media/Files/Publications/CR/2020/English/1ZAFEA2020002.ashx

IPP Office (2018) 'Independent Power Producers Procurement Programme (IPPPP) An Overview As at 31 March 2018' Department of Energy, National Treasury, Development Bank of South Africa [available at: https://www.ipp-projects.co.za/Publications]

Ireland, G., and J. Burton. 2018. "An Assessment of New Coal Plants in South Africa's electricity Future: The Cost, Emissions, and Supply Security Implications of the Coal IPP Program." Energy Research Centre, University of Cape Town. https://cer.org.za/wp-content/uploads/2018/05/ERC-Coal-IPP-Study-Report-Finalv2-290518.pdf

Jeffery, Anthea. 2014. *BEE: Helping or Hurting*. Cape Town: Tafelberg Press.

Joffe, Hilary "Futuregrowth's Report Is a Reminder of How Urgent Reform is at SoEs." *Business Day*, March 28. https://www.businesslive.co.za/bd/opinion/columnists/2018-03-28-hilary-joffe-futuregrowths-report-is-a-reminder-of-how-urgent-reform-is-at-soes/.

Johnstone, Philip, and Peter Newell. 2018. "Sustainability Transitions and the State". *Environmental Innovation and Societal Transitions* 27: 72–82.

Laing, Robert. 2018. "Fitch Pushes Eskom Deeper into Junk Territory." *Business Day*, February 1. https://www.businesslive.co.za/bd/companies/energy/2018-02-01-fitch-pushes-eskom-deeper-into-junk-territory/.

Legal Brief Environmental. 2019. "Court Action Delays IPP Contract Signing." November 14. https://legalbrief.co.za/diary/legalbrief-environmental/story/court-action-delays-ipp-contract-signing-3/print/.

Levy, M. 2018. "Notes from the House: Parliamentary Eskom Inquiry to Run Parallel to Zuma's State Capture Probe." *Daily Maverick*, January 23. https://www.dailymaverick.co.za/article/2018-01-23-notes-from-the-house-parliamentary-eskom-inquiry-to-run-parallel-to-zumas-state-capture-probe.

Lockwood, Matthew, et al. 2017. "Historical Institutionalism and the Politics of Sustainable Energy Transitions: A Research Agenda." *Environment and Planning C: Politics and Space* 35, no. 2: 312–333.

Lodge, Tom. 2014. "Neo-Patrimonial Politics in the ANC." *African Affairs* 113, no. 450: 1–23.

Marais, Lochner, Holle Wlokas, Jiska de Groot, Noleen Dube, and Andreas Scheba. 2018. "Renewable Energy and Local development: Seven Lessons from the Mining Industry." *Development Southern Africa* 35, no. 1: 24–38.

Marquard, Andrew. 2006. "The Origins and Development of South African Energy Policy." PhD thesis, University of Cape Town.

Martin, Brenda. 2016. "The politics of electricity planning in South Africa: A review of dominant advocacy coalitions seeking to influence the Integrated Resource Plan of 2010 (IRP2010), and its update in 2013." MPhil thesis. University of Cape Town.

McCall, B., J. Burton, A. Marquard, F. Hartley, F. Ahjum, G. Ireland, and B. Merven. 2019. 'Least-Cost Integrated Resource Planning and Cost-Optimal Climate Change Mitigation Policy: Alternatives for the South African Electricity System." Energy Research Centre, University of Cape Town.

McDonald, David. 2009. "Electric Capitalism: Conceptualizing Electricity and Capital Accumulation in (South) Africa." In *Electric Capitalism: Re-colonising Africa on the Power Grid*, edited by D. McDonald, 1–49. Cape Town: HSRC Press.

Merten, Marianne. 2018. "Analysis: Like the Nazis, the State Capture Culprits have left a Paper Trail for All to See." *Daily Maverick*, January 1, https://www.dailymaverick.co.za/article/2018-01-25-analysis-like-the-nazis-the-state-capture-culprits-have-left-a-paper-trail-for-all-to-see/#.Wrzte4jwbIU.

Michie, Jonathan, and Vishnu Padayachee, eds. 1997. *The Political Economy of South Africa's Transition*. London, UK: The Dryden Press.

Milonakis, Dimitri, and Ben Fine. 2009. *From Political Economy to Economics, Method, the Social and the Historical in the Evolution of Economic Theory*. London, UK: Routledge.

Mntongana, Lutho. 2018. "Eskom Considers Selling Assets as It Faces Battle to Shed Unsustainable Debt." *Business Day*, February 3. https://www.businesslive.co.za/bt/business-and-economy/2018-02-03-eskom-considers-selling-assets--as-it-faces-battle-to----shed-unsustainable-debt/.

Momoniat, Yunus. 2018. "Our Long Walk from Freedom." *Business Day*, March 19. https://www.businesslive.co.za/bd/opinion/2018-03-19-yunus-momoniat-our-long-walk-from-freedom-with-msholozi/.]

Moneyweb. 2019. "Eskom Union to Ramaphosa: No Job Cuts, No Split, Fire the Board." Moneyweb, June 20. www.moneyweb.co.za/news-fast-news/eskom-union-to-ramaphosa-no-job-cuts-no-split-fire-the-board/.

National Treasury. 2018. "Budget Review 2018: Government Debt and Contingent Liabilities." http://www.treasury.gov.za/documents/nationalper cent20budget/2018/review/Chapterper cent207.pdf.

National Treasury. 2019. "Budget Review 2019: Annexure W3—Fiscal Support for Electricity Market Reform." www.treasury.gov.za/documents/nationalper cent20budget/2019/review/Annexureper cent20W3.pdf.

Padayachee, Vishnu. 2010. "Re-introducing the Minerals-Energy Complex." *Transformation: Critical Perspectives on Southern Africa*, no. 71: 1–2.

Parliament of South Africa. 2018. "Report of The Portfolio Committee on Public Enterprises on the Inquiry into Governance, Procurement and the Financial Sustainability of Eskom, Dated 28 November 2018." http://pmg-assets.s3-website-eu-west-1.amazonaws.com/181128pcpubentreport.pdf

Pauw, Jacques. 2017. *The President's Keepers: Those Keeping Zuma in Power and Out of Prison*. Cape Town: Tafelberg.

Peek, Bobby, and Tristen Taylor. 2014. "Eskom Cannot Continue to Ignore Reality." *Business Day*, December 10. http://www.bdlive.co.za/opinion/2014/12/10/eskom-cannot-continue-to-ignore-reality.

Public Protector. 2016. "State of Capture." Report 6 of 2016/17. https://cdn.24.co.za/files/Cms/General/d/4666/3f63a8b78d2b495d88f10ed060997f76.pdf.

Rennkamp, Britta, et al. 2017. "Competing Coalitions: The Politics of Renewable Energy and Fossil Fuels in Mexico, South Africa and Thailand." *Energy Research & Social Science* 34: 214–223.

Rennkamp, Britta, and Anya Boyd. 2013. "Technological Capability and Transfer for Achieving South Africa's Development Goals." *Climate Policy* 15, no. 1: 12–29.

Rennkamp, Britta, and Radhika Bhuyan. 2017. "The Social Shaping of Nuclear Energy Technology in South Africa." In *The Political Economy of Clean Energy Transitions*, edited by D. Arent, C. Arndt, M. Miller, F. Tarp, and O. Zinaman, 271–291. Oxford: Oxford University Press.

Rip, Arie, and René Kemp. 1998. "Technological Change." In *Human Choice and Climate Change*, vol. 2, pp. 327–399, edited by S. Rayner and E. Malone, Columbus: Battelle Press.

South African Legal Information Institute (SAFLII). 2019. "Coal Transporters Forum v Eskom Holdings Limited and Others." (42887/2017) [2019] ZAGPPHC 76. March 26. http://www.saflii.org/za/cases/ZAGPPHC/2019/76.html.

South African Renewable Energy Council (SAREC). 2017. "Are Eskom's Concerns Relating to IPPs Valid?" May. http://sarec.org.za/wp-content/uploads/2017/05/Briefing-note_final-1.pdf

Spencer, Thomas, et al. 2017. "The 1.5°C Target and Coal Sector Transition: At the Limits of Societal Feasibility." *Climate Policy* 18, no. 3: 335–351.

Steyn, Grove, Jesse Burton, and Marco Steenkamp. 2017. "Eskom's Financial Crisis and the Viability of Coal-Fired Power in South Africa: Implications for Kusile and the Older Coal-Fired Power Stations." Meridian Economics, November.

Swilling, M. 2019. "Can Economic Policy Escape State Capture?" *New Agenda: South African Journal of Social and Economic Policy*, no. 72: 24–27. https://journals.co.za/content/journal/10520/EJC-14fd49b9a9.

Turok, B. 2018. "The ANC and the State Apparatus." *New Agenda: South African Journal of Social and Economic Policy*, no. 71: 5. https://journals.co.za/content/journal/10520/EJC-13714d0afd.

Wlokas, H., P. Westoby, and S. Soal. 2017. "Learning from the Literature on Community Development for the Implementation of Community Renewables in South Africa." *Journal of Energy in Southern Africa* 28, no. 1: 35–44.

Wright, J. G., J. Calitz, N. Ntuli, R. Fourie, M. Rampokanyo, and P. Kamera. 2018. "Formal Comments on the Draft Integrated Resource Plan 2018." CSIR. https://researchspace.csir.co.za/dspace/handle/10204/10493

Yelland, Chris, and Roger Lilley. 2018. "Cloak and Dagger Drama at the IPP Signing." April 16. https://www.ee.co.za/article/drama-at-the-signing-why-did-eskom-refuse-to-sign-the-ppas.html.

Zondo Commission. 2019. "Zondo Judicial Commission of Enquiry into State Capture." https://www.sastatecapture.org.za/.

CHAPTER 30

THE POLITICS OF ENERGY AND SUSTAINABLE DEVELOPMENT IN SUB-SAHARAN AFRICA

LAURENCE L. DELINA

THE United Nations General Assembly (2015), in its meeting on September 5, 2015, adopted the 2030 Agenda for Sustainable Development, a collection of seventeen Sustainable Development Goals (SDGs) with 169 targets that place "people, prosperity and planet" front and center in development. Energy—which came to be recognized as a key driver for social and economic development but was conspicuously absent in the Millennium Development Goals, the precursor to the SDGs—has been duly included in this global agenda as goal 7 (SDG7). It calls for universal energy access and increases in the deployment of renewable energy and energy efficiency technologies. But SDG7 does not operate in a vacuum. Delivering the targets of SDG7 by 2030 is a process rife with contentious and messy exercises, in which technical materiality interacts with power, discourse, and behavioral, social, and institutional forces. In short, it is difficult to divorce the politics of energy from the rhetoric of sustainable development for *all* (Chaurey et al. 2012; Meadowcroft 2009; Newell and Phillips 2016; Schillebeeckx et al. 2012; Sovacool 2013; Stirling 2014). How can we understand the surrounding politics in energy systems for sustainable development of people, prosperity, and planet? This chapter focuses on the world's most energy poor region, sub-Saharan Africa (SSA), to advance a research agenda that looks centrally at the politics of energy and sustainable development. (For analysis of regionalism literature, see Hancock, Palestini, and Szulecki in this volume.)

Scholars and practitioners—this chapter's intended audience—must consider energy and development in SSA more than other region, as this is where energy access is the lowest. SSA is home to 590 million people without access to electricity, more than half of the global total. While the region is economically, culturally, and politically diverse, as a whole it shares the problem of energy poverty. Roughly 57 percent of the SSA population still lacks access to reliable, sustainable, and affordable energy (see also Fuller in this Handbook). The International Energy Agency (IEA) (2017) reports that there has been encouraging progress in closing energy access gaps in the region, with twenty-six million people gaining access annually since 2012. This number has tripled since 2000, yet the number of those without access to electricity in SSA continues to be higher today than in 2000 (IEA 2017). The IEA projects that, with rapidly increasing population and urban migration, more than six hundred million people in the region will lack access to electricity by 2030 (cf. Keho 2016). Closing this energy access gap to meet the SDGs' 2030 deadline would require about $28 billion annual investment globally (IEA 2017). To date, however, SSA accounts for only 4 percent of total global energy investment (IEA 2017).

Beyond electrification, energy for cooking is still a key area for energy and development in SSA, where solid biomass, kerosene, and coal remain the cooking fuels of choice (see Hughes in this Handbook and Standal, Danielson, and Winther in this Handbook). Almost four-fifths of the SSA's population, or approximately 780 million people, still rely on these health- and environmentally risky cooking fuels (IEA 2017). For about sixty million people, kerosene is the primary cooking fuel, with over forty million of them living in Nigeria. The IEA (2017) is pessimistic about efforts to address this challenge, projecting that clean cooking initiatives could fail and an additional one hundred million people could be without clean cooking methods by 2030. Even with adequate access, people may still prefer biomass for cultural or culinary reasons (see Standal, Danielson, and Winther in this Handbook), thus adding complexity to an already messy relationship between energy and sustainable development.

Perhaps the most pressing rationale for studying energy and sustainable development concerns humanity's greatest challenge: climate change. About 60 percent of anthropogenic emissions are from energy systems, making them the principal focus of urgent action to address climate change (central to SDG13; see also Hughes in this Handbook). Fundamental to this goal is the transition to low-carbon energy systems, an animating force to achieve another international ambition—that of limiting warming to 1.5°C—enshrined in the Paris Agreement (see Hughes in this Handbook). More than 60 percent of African countries have, in their nationally determined contributions (NDCs) to the Paris Agreement, recognized energy access as a key enabler of their development (IEA 2017). Fifteen countries have specific targets for advancing electrification efforts in their NDCs. Nigeria, for instance, targets universal energy access by 2030; Sudan plans to provide 1.1 million solar home installations by 2030; and Ghana aims to provide 2 million households with solar lanterns (IEA 2017). Over 90 percent of these NDCs also indicate the need to prioritize renewables, with thirty-three NDCs including targets to increase the share of environmentally benign fuels in their energy mixes. The importance of energy efficiency is also recognized in 80 percent of these NDCs (IEA 2017). With 75 percent of installed power generation capacity being fossil based—and coal accounting for

35 percent—SSA stands as an important region in the energy transition challenge, especially given the region's renewable energy potential (see Hafner, Tagliapietra, and de Strasser 2018).

According to one analysis, 113 targets (about 65 percent of the SDG's total targets) require actions related to energy systems, at least 143 targets (or about 85 percent) have synergies with SDG7, and 65 targets represent trade-offs with SDG7 (Fuso Nerini et al. 2017). With energy systems affecting the delivery of a majority of the SDGs, energy is indeed at the core of sustainable development. But what of its politics? After all, energy *for* sustainable development involves processes involving actors and institutions with varying interests.

Drawing on the extant literature on energy and sustainable development in SSA, this chapter adds a fourth "p" to the "people, prosperity and planet" framework—politics—and progresses in two stages. First, the chapter reviews the linkages between the politics of energy and sustainable development using the framework of sustainable development for people, prosperity, and planet. A focus on "people" is concerned with the role energy systems play in "human well-being" and pertains to our individual and collective aspirations for greater welfare. A focus on "prosperity" is related to both physical and social energy infrastructure for achieving sustainable development for all. A focus on the "planet" is concerned with the sustainable management of energy resources. This analytical framework is consistent with other goal-level analysis done in contexts such as health and the SDGs (e.g., Waage et al. 2015). The chapter then proposes a research agenda arguing for conceptual, methodological, and empirical advances to better understand the politics of energy and sustainable development.

THE POLITICS OF ENERGY SYSTEMS FOR PEOPLE

Closing energy access gaps, increasing renewables, and adopting energy efficiency will assist in achieving a number of the SDGs, including ending poverty (SDG1), ending hunger and achieving food security (SDG2), ensuring healthy lives (SDG3), ensuring quality education (SDG4), achieving gender equality (SDG5), ensuring availability of water and sanitation (SDG6), improving household incomes (SDG8), making resilient livelihoods (SDG11), and providing entrepreneurship opportunities for women (SDG5). Scholars and practitioners are delving into the relationship between improving the human condition and access to environmentally benign and sustainable energy systems (e.g., Practical Action, 2014), suggesting, among other things, that when a typical household gains access to energy services, benefits accrue in terms of lighting (light bulbs), cooling (fans), and entertainment (television). If electricity access were bundled with energy efficient appliances in SSA, an IEA estimate suggests that an average household would see an annual cost reduction of 32 percent (about $150) (IEA 2017, 54). This amount represents substantial savings, given that nearly 75 percent of SSA households have an annual income of less than $1,500.

The literature is awash with studies on how people in SSA would benefit (and have benefited) from energy access. One particularly important strand analyzes the nexus between modern energy supply and the relatively low productivity of SSA agriculture.[1] However, these studies mostly focus on technical solutions such as electric water pumps in irrigation and mechanization, and on improving agricultural practices, such as in post-harvest processing. The African Development Bank (2015), for instance, suggests that women could benefit more from agriculture-based interventions, since 62 percent of economically active African women work in this sector; in Burkina Faso, Malawi, and Rwanda, up to 90 percent of women work in agriculture. Sovacool et al. (2014) have documented the importance of modern energy for efficiency gains in Malian agriculture. Kirubi et al. (2008) have studied how small-scale, often rural, community-based electric micro-grids have benefited small- and medium-sized Kenyan entrepreneurs. Other scholars report that positive effects may not always accrue. For example, Grimm et al. (2017) show that the adoption of simple but quality-verified solar photovoltaic kits—despite their positive effects on rural Rwandan household expenditures—is impeded by affordability. Jacobson (2007) also reveals that the Kenyan rural middle class—not essentially poor Kenyans—has captured the benefits of solar electrification, and that this intervention plays only a modest role in supporting productive energy use, with end users opting to prioritize appliance use, particularly television. Ahlborg (2018) shows how a small-scale, nongovernmental organization (NGO)-led, renewable energy project in Tanzania created social tensions that reconfigured political relations in a community.

Grimm et al. (2017), Jacobson (2007), and Ahlborg (2018) hint at one of the understudied aspects of energy and sustainable development in SSA: the underlying politics of energy interventions and their impacts on human well-being. Jacobson (2017) examines why the solar electrification program has contravened some of the normative ideals regarding energy and livelihoods (e.g., Food and Agricultural Organization of the United Nations 2011). All three articles ask why many people are trapped in perpetual poverty despite development interventions (Haider et al. 2018); in gist, why productive and economic energy use and energy access provision are difficult to link.

Electricity is not the only kind of power distributed across diverse societal subsystems and among many actors; scholars need to pay attention to the dynamics of institutional change in the context of political power distribution or maldistribution (Meadowcroft 2010; see also Carpenter and Greenberg, and Hoika and MacArthur, in this Handbook). The complex political interactions among several actors and institutions (i.e., public authorities, private businesses, civil society, and individuals) are captured in the features of modern society: diversity, complexity, and dynamics (Meadowcroft 2010) and pluralities and polarities (Delina and Janetos 2018; Leach et al. 2005; Stirling 2014). Scholars have begun exploring these features of modern life, including ways to govern sociotechnical, politically complex energy systems, using emergent concepts in the politics of energy, such as energy justice.

"Energy justice" has surfaced as a framework by which scholars and practitioners alike can analyze and navigate contemporary energy issues, including energy access and energy transitions. Energy justice, which revolves around the recognition of, consideration of, respect for, and utilization of plural voices in decision-making, resonates well with the politics of energy and sustainable development such as just institutions, strengthened rule of law, greater participation, transparency and accountability, access to information, and the reduction of corrupt practices (Delina and Sovacool 2018; Sovacool et al. 2016; for a full treatment of the politics of energy justice, see Fuller in this Handbook).

Scholars have already been documenting the politics of conventional forms of energy in SSA, for example in studies about oil and coal resources in Mozambique by Kirshner and Power (2015); petroleum investments and land acquisition in Tanzania (Pedersen and Kweka 2017); fuel subsidy (Joshua and Akinyemi 2017; cf. Schmidt, Matsuo, and Michaelowa 2017); and oil exploration and exploitation in Nigeria (Aworawo 2017). Hydropower, one of the region's fast-developing energy resources yet also contentious, has also been examined in terms of community participation in the siting and design of dams (Tilt, Braun, and He 2009) and concerns about their viability with changing river-flow conditions (cf. Chinzila 2017; Cole, Elliott, and Strobl 2014). Biofuels produced from lands originally planted with food crops are also an area in which the political impacts of energy systems on people have been duly studied, such as in the context of land grabs (Hunsberger et al. 2014). Scholars have also studied the resulting disparities in efforts aimed at increasing the affordability of energy. Monyei, Adewumi, and Jenkins (2018), for example, show that the policy to fill energy access gaps in South Africa has exacerbated poverty despite increasing generation capacity. Most of these studies, however, are largely focused on single-country studies and traditional and conventional energy systems (fossil fuel-based and large hydropower), often utilizing single-discipline conceptual frameworks.

Given the complexity of energy systems, scholars need to direct their research to energy and people in cross-country and even multiple energy resource comparisons, always in interdisciplinary efforts. Scholars have to acknowledge that the traditional, siloed approach to knowledge generation—that is, the isolation of energy-related knowledge in many different fuels and systems, disciplines and locations—no longer works effectively when studying the complexity of the politics of energy and sustainable development (cf. Sovacool 2014). In addition, research based on linear and deterministic assumptions about the impacts of energy on people are no longer valid (Brown et al. 2018)—such as the assumption that energy access provision leads to productive and economic use and impact. An extreme example is readily found in the voluminous research focused on technology design to deliver electricity at scale and mitigate carbon emissions at relatively low cost (see Sovacool 2014) without due consideration for other elements of energy provision, such as for cooking, information, communications, entertainment, transport, and motive power. As such, impact in this context is often quantitatively defined—for example, sales or provision of equipment, number of new connections or installations—hence missing opportunities to consider the implications of these interventions for people's quality of life and well-being.

A focus on people would thus bring front and center questions such as these: Who really benefits from interventions on energy access, on energy transition? What are these benefits and how they are chosen? What are the political dynamics that contribute to the delayed deployment of modern energy that benefits *all* people, not just the privileged few? What political capacities and institutions are necessary to close these gaps (e.g., Olaopa, Akinwale, and Ogundari 2017)? Responding to these questions requires essential considerations to view context-specific histories and ongoing political dynamics, not only at the national level but most important, at the local level—especially in the context of rural SSA, where rural elites possess "more" power than national governments (Mizuno 2016). Context-specific approaches suggest firmly that we do not restrict our comparisons to the level of the nation-states but also consider the "local." Studies geared at knowing what the people of SSA need, what their preferences and aspirations are (e.g., Winkler et al. 2017), and how they could take actions remain needed research areas (e.g., Ockwell and Byrne 2016), alongside studies on what formal and informal institutional arrangements exist (e.g., Olaopa, Akinwale and Ogundari 2017), who dominates these platforms (e.g., powerful rural elites [Mizuno 2016] and actors in the age of post-truth politics [Trotter and Maconachie 2018]), whose voices remain on the periphery, how to "speak truth to power," and so forth (Delina and Janetos 2018; Meadowcroft 2009; Stirling 2014).

The Politics of Energy Systems for Prosperity

Energy systems are key mechanisms in the social and physical infrastructure that led to the emergence of human civilization. For example, our modern democracy, according to Mitchell (2011), has developed from systems surrounding the exploration, mining, distribution, and use of conventional oil and coal. The ordering of our political infrastructure thus is closely linked to *what* energy resources we are tapping and *how* we distribute and use energy services. Sustainable development that puts a premium on our prosperity therefore will rest largely upon *how* we make decisions about our future energy systems, a clear nod to their institutional arrangements and decision-making processes.

Energy systems, both centralized and decentralized infrastructure, are necessary to achieve energy access and energy transition in the time contexts of the SDGs (2030) and the NDCs. The IEA (2017) has recognized that closing energy gaps in SSA would no longer simply require grid connection; small-scale, distributed systems also have roles (and the largest potential) to play in meeting this target (cf. Diaz-Maurin, Chiguvare, and Gope 2018), as well as in energy transition. This signals the need to rethink and remake not only technology infrastructures but also energy institutions (Bischof-Niemz and Creamer 2018; Olaopa, Akinwale, and Ogundari 2017). Beyond providing access and transitioning to more renewable energy, however, ensuring higher degrees of reliability—especially in SSA, where rolling blackouts are common—and affordability—so that everyone could have access to energy without incurring substantial cost—remain key challenges. In that regard, financing energy development is essential; however, the lack of institutional capacity in SSA limits implementation, resulting in lower take-up of projects related to energy access and transition (Adenle, Manning, and Arbiol 2017; Baker 2015; cf. Olaopa, Akinwale, and Ogundari 2017; Schwerhoff and Sy 2017; Trimble et al. 2016).

The ideals of reliable and affordable energy are not merely economic exercises; they are also political processes, involving, for example, what Meadowcroft (2010) calls "ideological steering": one technique among many to influence reform initiatives essential for achieving these ideals. The driver of political change in this approach is not necessarily hierarchical control, but rather the actors and institutions internalizing certain perspectives and independently orienting and reorienting their actions in consequence. In this context, "ideology" is not used in the classic sense of "political ideologies" (liberalism, socialism, etc.), but rather refers to the broader sets of social ideas that transcend political currents, including "concepts that concretize its orientation and articulate a more complete societal vision" (Meadowcroft 2010, 311). Following Meadowcroft (2010), imagining a prosperous future for all not only involves articulating desirable visions, it also comprises the design and fulfillment of concrete projects using blatant exercises of power (Jasanoff 2015). Connecting people's aspirations and preferences with their vision of prosperity—of which reliability and affordability of energy services are but two possible characteristics—requires scholars and practitioners to think beyond the multiple and complex dimensions of energy systems.

The shift in doing energy research and practice recognizes that the dominance of techno- and econo-centric approaches in policy and decision-making has been one of the greatest obstacles in achieving sustainable development (Baptista and Plananska 2017). The study of energy systems requires a turn in new ways that scholars and practitioners could respond to the multidimensionality and complexity of these systems, especially the politics. Trotter, Maconachie, and McManus (2018), for example, have identified that multilevel political factors are at play within African energy planning. These factors include external political pressure and commitments, national energy security and sovereignty, political institutions, political stability and instability, private political interests, and politicized land access. Beyond these conventional lenses of energy politics, a cosmopolitan understanding of the users of energy services and their needs, priorities, and aspirations and their means of attaining them is also required (cf. Delina and Janetos 2018). Miller et al. (2015), for example, found that the failed take-up of improved cookstoves is mainly due to durability issues in terms of handling large, heavy meals—a reason not strictly confined to the technology itself and its economics but primarily having to do with people's choices and local practices. This would mean that studies done about the cultural dimensions of energy systems (e.g., Ahlborg and Sjostedt 2015 in Tanzania; Jürisoo, Lambe, and Osborne 2018 in Kenya and Zambia; Ulsrud et al. 2015 in Kenya) have to be extended to include not only the understudied locations and cultures in SSA but also the ways and means by which people advance their imaginaries of energy prosperity.

"Urban energy" offers another rich site for highlighting some examples. In SSA, where rural-to-urban migration has resulted in increasing energy consumption in cities (Keho 2016), scholars have documented how spatial patterns in urban environments influence the way energy is used (e.g., Castán Broto 2017; Runsten, Fuso Nerini, and Tait 2018) and how infrastructure upgrades in the built environment could produce substantial gains in energy access (e.g., Smajgl, Ward, and Pluschke 2016; Viera and Ghisi 2016). There are also other dynamics at play. Chidebell-Emordi's (2015) work in Nigeria, for instance, reveals that urban dwellers shifted to appliances that consume more electricity, which led to poor payment collection. The United Nations Habitat (2016) shows that despite new access, some urban centers in Malawi, Mozambique, Rwanda, and Tanzania continue to have unreliable and expensive electricity issues. There also remain insecurities around land tenure in urban SSA, a perennial challenge that seems to be exacerbated by urban energy poverty (e.g., Runsten, Fuso Nerini, and Tait 2018; Singh et al. 2015). In many slums in urban SSA, the lack of proof of residence has often led into unauthorized and illegal means of accessing energy. This situation begs new research questions and development practices around institutional shifts that go beyond mere energy provision. A multifaceted approach would include, among other aspects, coherent policy linkages across land tenure, sustainable urban development, social inclusion, and institutional coordination (cf. Runsten, Fuso Nerini, and Tait 2018).

The specificity of urbanization in the SSA region—which occurred in the absence of industrialization (Fox 2012) but was due largely to colonial history, in which urban centers were used as coordinating points for extractive activities (Coquery-Vidrovitch 2005; Chikowero 2007; King 1990), and more recently is due to internal population growth, health care improvement, and circular migration (Fox 2012; Parnell and Pieterse 2014)—also offers a starting point that may echo similar conditions in other parts of the developing world. This focus on local level challenges brings to the fore the need to study the rise of urban centers as well as the middle class across SSA and ensuing inequalities. Of particular interest, among many features, would be the relationship between people's energy use in terms of transport preferences (which impacts SDG11) and people's "new" consumption behaviors and patterns (which relates to SDG12) (Melber 2016).

Scholars and practitioners thus need to acknowledge that energy systems are embedded in multiple aspects of modern life. Some illustrations of these complex realities, beyond what has been described here, have been documented in the following studies. Mavhunga (2013) demonstrates how charcoal is spatially embedded in the various aspects of Mozambican social life. Winther (2008) shows how Zanzibar's electrification intersected with various social relations, including the spiritual realm. Von Schnitzler (2016) reveals that electricity provision in post-apartheid South Africa intertwined with its apartheid history. Hiemstra-van der Horst and Hovorka's (2008) work in Botswana reveals that improved income levels do not necessarily lead to consumers using the most sophisticated possible energy source; instead, modern energy uptake complements fuelwood and does not abandon it. This study further illustrates how fuelwood maintains its dominance despite the rise of commercial fuel use in the country.

Future research and development interventions therefore need to pay attention to people's relationships with new technologies, including when and how uptake occurs (e.g., what drives the purchase of improved cookstoves and solar photovoltaic systems and their continued use; Jürisoo, Lambe and Osborne 2018; cf. Atteridge and Weitz 2017), as well as capacity development, not only in terms of new skills (which directly affect SDG4 and SDG9), particularly for women (to meet SDG4 and SDG5), but also for operating and managing existing or new institutional systems (related to SDG16 and SDG17) (Delina, 2018b), including at times of conflict and disaster (with direct relevance to SDG11). Understanding the political and institutional constraints on renewable energy deployment in SSA beyond countries such as South Africa, Kenya, and Ghana (e.g., Pueyo 2018) also remains necessary. More studies are needed to shed light on the important intersections of cultural, institutional, and political influences that drive the uptake—or refusal—of innovative renewable energy technologies. Such studies can inform the development of strategies to make energy access, renewable energy, and energy efficiency technologies more desirable, leading to improved odds of achieving sustainable development for prosperity.

THE POLITICS OF ENERGY SYSTEMS FOR THE PLANET

The foundation of human well-being and sustainable development for all is the natural environment, which provides the flows of valuable goods and ecosystem services. While energy systems depend on these stocks and flows, they also have profound impacts on the planet. One of these key impacts is the rising global anthropogenic emissions from energy systems, which drive rapid climate change. Even though the physics of climate change are already exacerbating extreme weather events, the politics of climate change remain a challenging terrain to navigate. For instance, it took governments more than twenty years to overcome the political hurdle of delivering an agreement to curtail future emissions, especially from fossil fuel–based energy systems—a long trip from Rio de Janeiro in 1992 to Paris in 2015. Regardless, the agreement that parties to the Climate Change Convention have forged is falling short of what the science indicates is necessary, according to analysis by Climate Action Tracker (2015). A special report from the Intergovernmental Panel on Climate Change (2018) even suggests we now direly need to accelerate progress in energy transition.

While scholars have analyzed the policy and politics of climate change, including works that wed the climate agenda to that of the SDGs (e.g., Creutzig et al. 2018; Delina 2018a; Hubacek et al. 2017; Rosenthal et al. 2018), more work needs to be done to link the politics of energy, specifically as it relates to sustainable development in SSA.

Understanding the underlying politics of climate change in SSA is key, given the uncertainties for achieving the ambitions of the Paris Agreement and the need for accelerating climate action. Specifically, scholars should shift their focus beyond understanding the implications of climate change for energy supply (e.g., Chinzila 2017) and the energy sector in general (e.g., Andrews and Nwapi 2018) to identifying the issues that arise from the tensions between neoliberal and developmental approaches to energy access and energy transition. In this regard, the politics of climate and energy has to capture these competing discourses, institutional change, and issues of power, all interacting in their expectedly polarized contexts (Delina and Janetos 2018; Simmet 2018).

For instance, Byrne, Mbeva, and Ockwell (2018), using the Kenyan solar photovoltaic (PV) sector as an illustration, argue that the neoliberal orientation of the Paris Agreement and the SDGs has created a potential for confrontation between neoliberalism in global agreements and developmentalism in national policy. Gore et al. (2018) also analyze the politics and resistance in the energy sector in Ghana, Tanzania, and Uganda, following the framework of contradictory ideologies. Simmet (2018) notes the contested imaginaries of Senegal's energy future, in which national vision continues to marginalize imaginaries from communities. Rafey and Sovacool (2011) show how competing discourses around coal development impacted the energy landscape in South Africa. Andrews and Nwapi (2018) have analyzed the emerging developmental state in the energy sector in Ghana, Mozambique, and Uganda, in contrast to the dominant neoliberal agenda that underpins development in other world regions. Further studies, however, remain necessary to better understand these political tensions arising from the confrontations among these discourses (i.e., liberalization, competition, unbundling, and resistance) as SSA countries (especially beyond well-studied countries such as Kenya, Ghana, Tanzania, and Uganda) chart and execute their climate-energy agendas (cf. Andreasson 2017).

The NDCs by SSA countries largely recognize the need for international support (also pertinent to SDG1 and SDG17) to increase their capacity to contribute to climate mitigation through energy access and transition. Scholars have produced studies focused on the history and dynamics of international cooperation, geopolitics, and diplomacy as they relate to the production of multiple future pathways for energy and development (e.g., Corkin 2012; Power et al. 2016), but other areas of interest remain open. These research areas include using the field of international political economy to investigate the roles and interventions of public and private finance (pertinent to SDG9), national and international institutions (related to SDG16 and SDG17), national and multinational development banks (relevant to SDG17), and rising powers (including Brazil, Russia, India, China, and South Africa). A postcolonial lens offers one possible way for scholars and practitioners to draw attention to the influences not only of national and international actors in energy and sustainable development (Andreasson 2017; Donou-Adonsou and Lim 2018), but also local actors, particularly powerful rural elites (Mizuno 2016). In this case, one way to view energy systems is to treat them as a type of neocolonial resource grab. Corkin (2012) has done this type of study in terms of Chinese state-owned enterprises and their relationship with and impact on Angola's construction sector. Shen and Power (2016) have explored the growing involvement of China in SSA's renewable energy deployment. Power et al.'s (2016) theorization in this area, using comparative analysis of Brazil-India-China relations with South Africa and Mozambique (see also Gu, Renwick and Xue 2018; Wilson 2015), has produced a framework that scholars can use.

Beyond climate change, the use of natural resources in energy systems also has profound impacts on ecosystem services, yet few studies have been undertaken to relate energy systems to, for example, water security (to meet SDG6), food security (to address SDG2), and health (to support SDG3). Schuenemaan, Msangi, and Zeller (2018) have shown how biomass energy can be sustainable in Malawi and hence should figure prominently in the SDGs; however, other authors have also shown that trade-offs are possible within this nexus (e.g., Damerau, Patt, and van Vliet 2016; Hess et al. 2016). With energy systems having direct impacts on both terrestrial and marine ecosystems and other natural resources (e.g., local pollution and competition for space, particularly land use), more scholarly work on these nexuses remains paramount.

Another potential area for research is the analysis of trade-offs when selecting energy policies to meet the energy needs of the growing SSA population, including not only the needs of urban dwellers (related to SDG11 and previously discussed), but also the need to protect critical ecosystems that support sustainable development in other areas. Of particular importance in the SSA context is the rising use of charcoal—the fuel of choice for many people in the region—and its impacts on emissions, forest cover, soil fertility, and biodiversity. Bailis, Ezzati, and Kammen (2005) have shown that charcoal-intensive future scenarios using practices of the time could increase emissions by 140 to 190 percent. With SSA undergoing changes in population profiles, it is time to update these scenarios while paying attention to ecosystem loss, deforestation, and degradation—which SDG15 aims to address, but which could contradict SDG7. Our current understanding of fuelwood and charcoal production for energy (e.g., Fuso Nerini, Ray, and Boulaid's [2017] Kenyan study) has to be complemented by scholarship that looks at the embedded politics of bioenergy (e.g., Branch and Martiniello's [2018] work in Uganda).

The key challenge in the politics of energy as it relates to sustainable development of the planet revolves around the need to decrease the natural resource intensity of energy systems. These actions include tapping opportunities to address climate change, biodiversity loss, and air and water pollution, while at same time ensuring economic growth (pertinent to SDG8). Energy is indeed necessary for mobilizing natural resources for ending poverty (SDG1), restoring water ecosystems (which directly impacts SDG6, SDG14, and SDG15), increasing water efficiency (related to meeting SDG6, SDG9, and SDG11), and sustainable irrigation management in food systems for increasing food production (SDG2). Protecting ecosystems (made clear in SDG15) is indeed intertwined with energy access and energy transitions, especially when livelihoods are heavily dependent on natural ecosystems (Daw et al. 2011). There are therefore profound trade-offs that SSA countries need to understand and account for in decision-making, yet very little research has been done on the politics of trade-offs arising from the interactions of energy interventions with the SDGs. Decision-making and leadership on energy systems have to account for these interdependencies, especially as actors and interests compete for dominance.

An Agenda for Future Research

Despite the considerable body of research now available on the politics of energy and sustainable development in SSA, gaps remain. The global SDG project in which no one is supposed to be left behind—that is, ensuring that sustainable development for all is *indeed* for people, prosperity, and planet—can be met through multiple pathways and trajectories. The plurality, polarity, messiness, and complexities of embedded politics in these pathways pose a challenge for policymaking at the same time that they offer a new, rich landscape for pushing the boundaries of scholarship and practice in this area. Navigating the tensions surrounding energy and sustainable development depends on how scholarship is produced and how practice is attuned to the complexities of the politics of energy systems. While most studies have largely focused on single countries, often utilizing single-discipline conceptual frameworks, future research should focus on three primary areas: studies of understudied states and actors in energy and sustainable development; analyses of the local, national, and global politics behind energy systems using multiple epistemic sources, traditions, and disciplines; and partnerships between scholars and practitioners, including among those based in African states and those in the global north in developing theories of energy politics. To achieve these ends, scholars and practitioners who want to extend the research on and practice of energy politics and sustainable development in SSA should focus on making their work inclusive, interdisciplinary, and influential. I now turn to this agenda.

Inclusiveness requires that scholars and practitioners value and emphasize the specificity of knowledge practices in locations where they do work and acknowledge the political dimension of energy systems. It begins with how scholars and practitioners treat energy technologies. Sovacool (2014) was right in pointing out that scholars tend to favor topics related to modern electricity while placing little emphasis on "mundane" technologies such as cookstoves, although the latter have the greatest impact on poor people's everyday lives, especially in SSA. Indigenous capacities for energy technology experimentation, learning, and reflection in the delivery of energy access need to be studied more deeply (Atteridge and Weitz 2017), including the robustness of measurement and verification frameworks (Tait 2017). How could the "local"—practices and people—be brought to the fore in the study and practice of energy and sustainable development? Doing so would most likely require new participatory mechanisms, including inclusive deliberations (Delina 2018b; Dryzek 2010) that nod at energy justice as a framework (see Delina and Sovacool 2018 for more details; cf. Jenkins et al. 2016). In this regard, scholars and practitioners could use their research and practice areas as platforms for raising the voices of traditionally marginalized actors in energy systems, including the poor, women, and indigenous peoples and their interests and aspirations. What methods and tools could be designed and used to ensure that the beneficiaries of interventions are regarded not only as technology receivers but also as observers of their changing worlds—and that their observations are made known to the world? Capacity development and/or strengthening (e.g., Colenbrander et al. 2015) and citizen science (Ottinger 2017) offer two promising opportunities. Beyond raising voices and bringing to the surface indigenous observations, however, what could be done to ensure that their imaginaries influence policy (Delina 2018c; Simmet 2018) and that they eventually become responsible owners of energy technologies and systems (Ikejemba et al. 2017)? In some parts of postcolonial SSA, where powerful rural elites control local political structures more than national governments (Mizuno 2016), what opportunities exist to formalize existing institutional rural arrangements in the energy and sustainable development milieu?

Also required is an *interdisciplinary* approach to the production of new knowledge (Newell 2001; Sovacool 2014) and in development practice. With multiple factors at play in the politics of energy and sustainable development, scholars need to study the politics through interdisciplinary lenses. Current gaps in the literature require addressing issues beyond the spatial (e.g., Bridge et al. 2013) or the historical (e.g., Baptista 2018) dimensions of energy systems. Sovacool (2014) lists some of these promising future areas of interdisciplinary research in the social studies of energy. In addition to consulting his exhaustive list, scholars and practitioners need to adopt a reflexive stance when doing their work. It is fitting to ask: How could scholars and practitioners design their research and interventions in ways that their work would recognize the multiple dynamics that power relations bring to the politics of energy systems in addition to its economics and technological complexities? In particular, how could new research embed climate change considerations in new energy development? How could scholars and practitioners increase the contributions of "lay expertise" and "indigenous knowledge" in their interdisciplinary work? Will inclusion result in a better understanding of why poor people are trapped in their circumstances despite development interventions (Haider et al. 2018) or is it the reverse? Enrolling SSA citizens and scientists in energy research and practice is the first step in this process, but a truly participatory work would ensure that "local" people truly benefit and that "helicopter" research is avoided (e.g., Nordling 2018; Rochmyaningsih 2018).

Doing interdisciplinary work in the politics of energy and sustainable development would require a suite of contextual and theoretical frameworks. Contemporary political economy, for instance, offers a frame by which scholars and practitioners can understand the histories and contemporary political pathways and contestations surrounding the dynamics and evolution of energy systems. Hancock and Vivoda (2014) have advanced a research agenda for scholarship in this area, suggesting bringing the politics back to policy. What they mean is that political variables and qualitative methods have to be increasingly included in policy analysis—in ways that are complementary to largely economics-led studies (e.g., Hamilton and Kelly 2017; Lucas et al. 2015; Ouedraogo 2017; Van der Zwaan et al. 2018)—using qualitative methods such as process-tracing (e.g., Byrne, Mbeva and Ockwell 2018; Gore et al. 2018). With current scholarship heavily tilted toward the political economy of conventional fuels, it is also about time to consider the political economy of "other fuels"—particularly renewables—and their contribution to policymaking; state formation; conflicts (along spatial, class, ethnic, and political lines; e.g., McEwan 2017); and interactions across national, international, public, and private institutions. Bringing to surface these contours of energy politics is a promising research agenda at the same time that it is also key for delivering effective development interventions. Research questions in this area linger: Who sets the national agenda for the future of energy systems? How is it done? How do future-setting processes affect and impact other processes of sustainable development? How is energy futuring attuned to the need for accelerating climate actions? What power relations are present in the nexus of state-capital-people, such as labor and indigenous peoples, and substate, interstate and suprastate relations? Responding to these questions requires the explanatory power of political science, alongside cognate disciplines of economics, geography, international relations, sociology, and anthropology, among others (cf. Sovacool 2014).

The *influence* of energy research and development interventions in achieving sustainable development for people, prosperity, and the planet manifests beyond the mere communication of research findings. Scholars and practitioners need to reflect how they can ensure that they are producing impact-focused and policy-relevant research and initiatives that promote the interface between the academic and nonacademic worlds. The methods offered by policy discourse, civic epistemology, and critical poverty analyses can make a difference when responding to these complex politics. To further the collaboration agenda in energy politics research, scholars also need to ask how they could increasingly engage not only their local and international colleagues in the academy but also their SSA partners, businesses, investors, civil society, communities and other local actors. Forging coalitions is necessary to extract influence, since coalition-building creates the political conditions for accelerating energy access provision and transitions (Roberts et al. 2018). With different actors attaching energy artifacts to a variety of utility and intentions (Newell and Phillips 2016; Power et al. 2016), scholars and practitioners need to reflect on the ways new research and practice could advance the way we understand how coalitions shape the trajectories of energy systems as they appear in discourses (e.g., Rafey and Sovacool 2011), how they are imagined (Delina 2018c; Jasanoff and Kim 2015; Simmet 2018), and/or how they are territorialized (Bridge et al. 2013). Also pertinent is to understand why SSA does not benefit from the wave of market-based approaches aimed at increasing investments in energy transitions (e.g., Pueyo 2018) and whether a regional approach is better suited to many institutionally challenged SSA countries (Adenle, Manning, and Arbiol 2017; Adeoye and Spataru 2018; Hancock 2015).

Energy systems that put people, prosperity, and planet first are the drivers of sustainable development, but politics are also embedded in these systems. In reviewing these linkages, this chapter notes SSA as a region full of potential for accelerating energy access provision and energy transition, at the same time that it also notes SSA's postcolonial histories and contemporary challenges as dynamic influencers of the politics of energy and sustainable development in the region. A better understanding of this politics remains crucial to make sense of SSA's major energy challenges.

Acknowledgments

This chapter is a product of "the future of energy systems in developing countries" project at Boston University. The author thanks Cynthia Barakatt, two anonymous reviewers, and this Handbook's editors for their helpful comments.

Note

1. The challenges to bringing about improved agricultural productivity in SSA remain huge and truly extend beyond mere interventions in energy supply. Most notably, there are factors related to poor-quality agricultural land; the limited use of irrigation; and unpredictable weather, including severe drought, flooding, and rising temperatures, that need to be accounted for.

References

Adenle, Ademola A., Dale T. Manning, and Joseph Arbiol. 2017. "Mitigating Climate Change in Africa: Barriers to Financing Low-Carbon Development." *World Development* 100: 123–132. doi:10.1016/j.worlddev.2017.07.033.

Adeoye, Omotola, and Catalina Spataru. 2018. "Sustainable Development of the West African Power Pool: Increasing Solar Energy Integration and Regional Electricity Trade." *Energy for Sustainable Development* 45: 124–134. doi:10.1016/j.esd.2018.05.007.

African Development Bank. 2015. *African Economic Outlook 2015*. Paris: OECD Publishing.

Ahlborg, Helene. 2018. "Changing Energy Geographies: The Political Effects of a Small-Scale Electrification Project." *Geoforum* 97:268–280. doi:10.1016/j.geoforum.2018.09.016.

Ahlborg, Helene, and Martin Sjöstedt. 2015. "Small-Scale Hydropower in Africa: Socio-Technical Design for Renewable Energy in Tanzanian Villages." *Energy Research & Social Science* 5: 20–33. doi:10.1016/j.erss.2014.12.017.

Andreasson, Stefan. 2017. "Fossil-Fuelled Development and the Legacy of Post-Development Theory in Twenty-first Century Africa." *Third World Quarterly* 38: 2634–2649. doi:10.1080/01436597.2017.1334544.

Andrews, Nathan, and Chilenye Nwapi. 2018. "Bringing the State Back in Again? The Emerging Developmental State in Africa's Energy Sector." *Energy Research & Social Science* 41: 48–58. doi:10.1016/j.erss.2018.04.004.

Atteridge, Aaron, and Nina Weitz. 2017. "A Political Economy Perspective on Technology Innovation in the Kenyan Clean Cookstove Sector." *Energy Policy* 110: 303–312. doi:10.1016/j.enpol.2017.08.029.

Aworawo, Friday. 2017. "The Impact of Oil Exploration and Exploitation in the Niger Delta, Nigeria." In *The Political Economy of Energy in Sub-Saharan Africa*, edited by Lucky E. Asuelime and Andrew Emmanuel Okem, 164–180. Abingdon, UK: Routledge.

Bailis, Robert, Majid Ezzati, and Daniel M. Kammen. 2005. "Mortality and Greenhouse Gas Impacts of Biomass and Petroleum Energy Futures in Africa." *Science* 308: 98–103. doi:10.1126/science.1106881.

Baker, Lucy. 2015. "The Evolving Role of Finance in South Africa's Renewable Energy Sector." *Geoforum* 64: 146–156. doi:10.1016/j.geoforum.2015.06.017.

Baptista, Idalina. 2018. "Space and Energy Transitions in Sub-Saharan Africa: Understated Historical Connections." *Energy Research & Social Science* 36: 30–35. doi:10.1016/j.erss.2017.09.029.

Baptista, Idalina, and Jana Plananska. 2017. "The Landscape of Energy Initiatives in Sub-Saharan Africa: Going for Systemic Change or Reinforcing the Status Quo?" *Energy Policy* 110: 1–8. doi:10.1016/j.enpol.2017.08.006.

Bischof-Niemz, Tobias, and Terence Creamer. 2018. *South Africa's Energy Transition: A Roadmap to a Decarbonised, Low-Cost and Job-Rich Future.* Abingdon, UK: Routledge.

Branch, Adam, and Giuliano Martiniello. 2018. "Charcoal Power: The Political Violence of Non-Fossil Fuel in Uganda." *Geoforum* 97: 242–252. doi:10.1016/j.geoforum.2018.09.012.

Bridge, Gavin, Stefann Bouzarovski, Michael Bradshaw, and Nick Eyre. 2013. "Geographies of Energy Transition: Space, Place and the Low-Carbon Economy." *Energy Policy* 53: 331–340. doi:10.1016/j.enpol.2012.10.066.

Brown, Ed, Ben Campbell, Long Seng To, Britta Turner, and Alistair Wray. 2018. "Low Carbon Energy and International Development: From Research Impact to Policymaking." *Contemporary Social Science* 13: 112–127. doi:10.1080/21582041.2017.1417627.

Byrne, Rob, Kennedy Mbeva, and David Ockwell. 2018. "A Political Economy of Niche-Building: Neoliberal-Developmental Encounters in Photovoltaic Electrification in Kenya." *Energy Research & Social Science* 44: 6–16. doi:10.1016/j.erss.2018.03.028.

Castán Broto, Vanessa. 2017. "Energy Landscapes and Urban Trajectories Towards Sustainability." *Energy Policy* 108: 755–764. doi:10.1016/j.enpol.2017.01.009.

Chaurey, Akaksha, P. R. Krithika, Debajit Palit, Smita Rakesh, and Benjamin K. Sovacool. 2012. "New Partnerships and Business Models for Facilitating Energy Access." *Energy Policy* 48: 687–697. doi:10.1016/j.enpol.2012.03.031.

Chidebell-Emordi, Chukwunonso. 2015. "The African Electricity Deficit: Computing the Minimum Energy Poverty Line Using Field Research in Urban Nigeria." *Energy Research & Social Science* 5: 9–19. doi:10.1016/j.erss.2014.12.011.

Chikowero, Moses. 2007. "Subalternating Currents: Electrification and Power Politics in Bulawayo, Colonial Zimbabwe, 1894–1939." *Journal of South African Studies* 33: 287–306. doi:10.1080/03057070701292590.

Chinzila, Chuma Banji. 2017. "Degradation and Climate Change: Implications for Sustainable Energy Supply in Zambia." In *The Political Economy of Energy in Sub-Saharan Africa*, edited by Lucky E. Asuelime and Andrew Emmanuel Okem, 119–136. Abingdon, UK: Routledge.

Climate Action Tracker. 2015. "2.7°C Is Not Enough—We Can Get Lower." https://climateactiontracker.org/documents/44/CAT_2015-12-08_2.7degCNotEnough_CATUpdate.pdf.

Cole, Matthew A., Robert J. R. Elliott, and Eric Strobl. 2014. "Climate Change, Hydro-Dependency, and the African Dam Boom." *World Development* 60: 84–98. doi:10.1016/j.worlddev.2014.03.016.

Colenbrander, Sarah, Jon Lovett, Mary Suzan Abbo, Consalva Msigwa, Bernard M'Passi-Mabiala, and Richard Opoku. 2015. "Renewable Energy Doctoral Programmes in Sub-Saharan Africa: A Preliminary Assessment of Capacity Deficits and Emerging Capacity-Building Strategies." *Energy Research & Social Science* 5: 70–77. doi:10.1016/j.erss.2014.12.010.

Corkin, Lucy. 2012. "Chinese Construction Companies in Angola: A Local Linkages Perspective." *Resources Policy* 37: 475–483. doi:10.1016/j.resourpol.2012.06.002.

Coquery-Vidrovitch, Catherine. 2005. *The History of African Cities South of the Sahara: From the Origins to Colonization.* Princeton. NJ: Markus Wiener Publishers.

Creutzig, Felix, Joyashree Roy, William F. Lamb, Inês M. L. Azevedo, Wändi Bruine de Bruin, Holger Dalkmann, Oreane Y. Edelenbosch, Frank W. Geels, Arnulf Grubler, Cameron Hepburn, Edgar G. Hertwich, Radhika Khosla, Linus Mattauch, Jan C. Minx, Anjali Ramakrishnan, Narasimha D. Rao, Julia K. Steinberger, Massimo Tavoni, Diana Ürge-Vorsatz, and Elke U. Weber. 2018. "Towards Demand-Side Solutions for Mitigating Climate Change." *Nature Climate Change* 8: 260–271. doi:10.1038/s41558-018-0121-1.

Damerau, Kerstin, Anthony G. Patt, and Oscar P. R. van Vliet. 2016. "Water Saving Potentials and Possible Trade-offs for Future Food and Energy Supply." *Global Environmental Change* 39: 15–25. doi:10.1016/j.gloenvcha.2016.03.014.

Daw, Tim, Katrina Brown, Sergio Rosendo, and Robert Pomeroy. 2011. "Applying the Ecosystem Services Concept to Poverty Alleviation: The Need to Disaggregate Human Well-Being." *Environmental Conservation* 38: 370–379. doi:10.1017/S0376892911000506.

Delina, Laurence L. 2018a. *Accelerating Sustainable Energy Transition(s) in Developing Countries: The Challenges of Climate Change and Sustainable Development.* Abingdon, UK: Routledge.

Delina, Laurence L. 2018b. "Energy Democracy in a Continuum: Remaking Public Engagement on Energy Transitions in Thailand." *Energy Research & Social Science* 42: 53–60. doi:10.1016/j.erss.2018.03.008.

Delina, Laurence L. 2018c. "Whose and What Futures? Navigating the Contested Coproduction of Thailand's Energy Sociotechnical Imaginaries." *Energy Research & Social Science* 35: 48–56. doi:10.1016/j.erss.2017.10.045.

Delina, Laurence L., and Anthony Janetos. 2018. "Cosmopolitan, Dynamic, and Contested Energy Futures: Navigating the Pluralities and Polarities in the Energy Systems of Tomorrow." *Energy Research & Social Science* 35: 1–10. doi:10.1016/j.erss.2017.11.031.

Delina, Laurence L., and Benjamin K. Sovacool. 2018. "Of Temporality and Plurality: An Epistemic and Governance Agenda for Accelerating Just Transitions for Energy Access and Sustainable Development." *Current Opinion in Environmental Sustainability* 34: 1–6. doi:10.1016/j.cosust.2018.05.016.

Diaz-Maurin, François, Zivayi Chiguvare, and Gideon Gope. 2018. "Scarcity in Abundance: The Challenges of Promoting Energy Access in the Southern African Region." *Energy Policy* 120: 110–120. doi:10.1016/j.enpol.2018.05.023.

Donou-Adonsou, Ficawoyi, and Sokchea Lim. 2018. "On the Importance of Chinese Investment in Africa." *Review of Development Finance* 8: 63–73. doi:10.1016/j.rdf.2018.05.003.

Dryzek, John. 2010. *Foundations and Frontiers of Deliberative Governance.* Oxford: Oxford University Press.

Food and Agricultural Organization of the United Nations. 2011. *Energy-Smart Food for People and Climate.* Rome: FAO.

Fox, Sean. 2012. "Urbanization as a Global Historical Process: Theory and Evidence from Sub-Saharan Africa." *Population and Development Review* 38: 285–310. doi:10.1111/j.1728-4457.2012.00493.x.

Fuso Nerini, Francesco, Antonio Andreoni, David Bauner, and Mark Howells. 2016. "Powering Production: The Case of the Sisal Fibre Production in the Tanga Region, Tanzania." *Energy Policy* 98: 544–556. doi:10.1016/j.enpol.2016.09.029.

Fuso Nerini, Francesco, Charlotte Ray, and Youssef Boulaid. 2017. "The Cost of Cooking a Meal: The Case of Nyeri County, Kenya." *Environmental Research Letters* 12: 065007. doi:10.1088/1748-9326/aa6fdo.

Fuso Nerini, Francesco, Julia Tomei, Long Seng To, Iwona Bisaga, Priti Parikh, Mairi Black, Aiduan Borrion, Catalina Spataru, Vanesa Castán Broto, Gabrial Anandarajah, Ben Milligan, and Yacob Mulugetta. 2017. "Mapping Synergies and Trade-offs between Energy and the Sustainable Development Goals." *Nature Energy* 3: 10–15. doi:10.1038/s41560-017-0036-5.

Gore, Christopher D., Jennifer N. Brass, Elizabeth Baldwin, and Lauren M. MacLean. 2018. "Political Autonomy and Resistance in Electricity Sector Liberalization in Africa." *World Development* 120: 193–209. doi:10.1016/j.worlddev.2018.03.003.

Grimm, Michael, Anicet Munyehirwe, Jörg Peters, and Maximilane Sievert. 2017. "A First Step Up the Energy Ladder? Low Cost Solar Kits and Household's Welfare in Rural Rwanda." *World Bank Economic Review* 31: 631–649. doi:10.1093/wber/lhw052.

Gu, Jing, Neil Renwick, and Lan Xue. 2018. "The BRICS and Africa's Search for Green Growth, Clean Energy and Sustainable Development." *Energy Policy* 120: 675–683. doi:10.1016/j.enpol.2018.05.028.

Hafner, Manfred, Simone Tagliapietra, and Lucia de Strasser. 2018. "Prospects for Renewable Energy in Africa." In *Energy in Africa: Challenges and Opportunities*, 47–75. Cham, Switzerland: Springer.

Haider, L. Jamila, Wiebren J. Boonstra, Garry J. Peterson, and Maja Schlüter. 2018. "Traps and Sustainable Development in Rural Areas: A Review." *World Development* 101: 311–321. doi:10.1016/j.worlddev.2017.05.038.

Hamilton, Thomas Gerald Adam, and Scott Kelly. 2017. "Low Carbon Energy Scenarios for Sub-Saharan Africa: An Input-Output Analysis on the Effects of Universal Energy Access and Economic Growth." *Energy Policy* 105: 303–319. doi:10.1016/j.enpol.2017.02.012.

Hancock, Kathleen J. 2015. "Energy Regionalism and Diffusion in Africa: How Political Actors Created the ECOWAS Center for Renewable Energy and Energy Efficiency." *Energy Research & Social Science* 5: 105–115. doi:10.1016/j.erss.2014.12.022.

Hancock, Kathleen J., and Vlado Vivoda. 2014. "A Field Born of the OPEC Crisis Returns to Its Energy Roots." *Energy Research & Social Science* 4: 23–35. doi:10.1016/j.erss.2014.03.017.

Hess, Tim M., J. Sumberg, T. Biggs, M. Georgescu, D. Haro-Monteagudo, G. Jewitt, M. Ozdogan, M. Marshall, P. Thenkabail, A. Daccache, F. Marin, and J. W. Knox. 2016. "A Sweet Deal? Sugarcane, Water and Agricultural Transformation in Sub-Saharan Africa." *Global Environmental Change* 39: 181–194. doi:10.1016/j.gloenvcha.2016.05.003.

Hiemstra-van der Horst, Greg, and Alice J. Hovorka. 2008. "Reassessing the 'Energy Ladder': Household Energy Use in Maun, Botswana." *Energy Policy* 36: 3333–3344. doi:10.1016/j.enpol.2008.05.006.

Hubacek, Klaus, Giovanni Baiocchi, Kuishuang Feng, and Anand Patwardhan. 2017. "Poverty Eradication in a Carbon Constrained World." *Nature Communications* 8: 912. doi:10.1038/s41467-017-00919-4.

Hunsberger, Carol, Simon Bolwig, Esteve Corbera, and Felix Creutzig. 2014. "Livelihood Impacts of Biofuel Crop Production: Implications for Governance." *Geoforum* 54: 248–260. doi:10.1016/j.geoforum.2013.09.022.

Ikejemba, Eugene C. X., Peter C. Schuur, Jos Van Hillegersberg, and Peter B. Mpuan. 2017. "Failures & Generic Recommendations towards the Sustainable Management of Renewable Energy Projects in Sub-Saharan Africa (Part 2 of 2)." *Renewable Energy* 113: 639–647. doi:10.1016/j.renene.2017.06.002.

Intergovernmental Panel on Climate Change. 2018. *Summary for Policymakers: Global Warming of 1.5C*. Seoul: IPCC.

International Energy Agency. 2017. *Energy Access Outlook 2017: From Poverty to Prosperity.* Paris: OECD/IEA.

Jacobson, Arne. 2007. "Connective Power: Solar Electrification and Social Change in Kenya." *World Development* 35: 144–162. doi:10.1016/j.worlddev.2006.10.001.

Jasanoff, Sheila. 2015. "Future Imperfect: Science, Technology, and the Imaginations of Modernity." In *Dreamscapes of Modernity: Sociotechnical Imaginaries and the Fabrication of Power*, edited by Sheila Jasanoff and Sang-Hyun Kim, 1–33. Chicago: Chicago University Press.

Jasanoff, Sheila, and Sang-Hyun Kim, eds. 2015. *Dreamscapes of Modernity: Sociotechnical Imaginaries and the Fabrication of Power.* Chicago: Chicago University Press.

Jenkins, Kirsten, Darren McCauley, Raphael Heffron, Hannes Stephan, and Robert Rehner. 2016. "Energy Justice: A Conceptual Review." *Energy Research & Social Science* 11: 174–182. doi:10.1016/j.erss.2015.10.004.

Joshua, Segun, and Opeyemi Akinyemi. 2017. "Exploring the Political Economy of Fuel Subsidy in Nigeria." In *The Political Economy of Energy in Sub-Saharan Africa*, edited by Lucky E. Asuelime and Andrew Emmanuel Okem, 152–163. Abingdon, UK: Routledge.

Jürisoo, Marie, Fiona Lambe, and Matthew Osborne. 2018. "Beyond Buying: The Application of Service Design Methodology to Understand Adoption of Clean Cookstoves in Kenya and Zambia." *Energy Research & Social Science* 39: 164–176. doi:10.1016/j.erss.2017.11.023.

Keho, Yaya. 2016. "What Drives Energy Consumption in Developing Countries? The Experience of Selected African Countries." *Energy Policy* 91: 233–246. doi:10.1016/j.enpol.2016.01.010.

King, Anthony D. 1990. *Urbanism, Colonialism, and the World-Economy: Cultural and Spatial Foundations of the World Urban System.* London: Routledge.

Kirshner, Joshua, and Marcus Power. 2015. "Mining and Extractive Urbanism: Postdevelopment in a Mozambican Boomtown." *Geoforum* 61: 67–78. doi:10.1016/j.geoforum.2015.02.019.

Kirubi, Charles, Arne Jacobson, Daniel M. Kammen, and Andrew Mills. 2008. "Community-Based Micro-Grids Can Contribute to Rural Development: Evidence from Kenya." *World Development* 37: 1208–1221. doi:10.1016/j.worlddev.2008.11.005.

Leach, Melissa, Ian Scoones, Brian Wynne, eds. 2005. *Science and Citizens: Globalization and the Challenge of Engagement.* London: Zed Books.

Lucas, Paul L., Jens Nielsen, Katherine Calvin, David L. McCollum, Giacomo Marangoni, Jessica Strefler, Bob C. C. van der Zwaan, and Detlef P. van Vuuren. 2015. "Future Energy System Challenges for Africa: Insights from Integrated Assessment Models." *Energy Policy* 86: 705–717. doi:10.1016/j.enpol.2015.08.017.

Mavhunga, Clapperton Chakanetsa. 2013. "Cidades Esfumaçadas: Energy and the Rural-Urban Connection in Mozambique." *Public Culture* 25: 261–271. doi:10.1215/08992363-2020593.

McEwan, Cheryl. 2017. "Spatial Processes and Politics of Renewable Energy Transition: Land, Zones and Frictions in South Africa." *Political Geography* 56: 1–12. doi:10.1016/j.polgeo.2016.10.001.

Meadowcroft, James. 2009. "What About the Politics? Sustainable Development, Transition Management, and Long Term Energy Transitions." *Policy Science* 42: 323–340. doi:10.1007/s11077-009-9097-z.

Meadowcroft, James. 2010. "Who Is in Charge Here? Governance for Sustainable Development in a Complex World." *Journal of Environmental Policy & Planning* 9: 3–4. doi:10.1080/15239080701631544.

Melber, Henning, ed. 2016. *The Rise of Africa's Middle Class: Myths, Realities and Critical Engagements.* London: Zed Books.

Miller, Clark A., Carlo Altamirano-Allende, Nathan Johnson, and Malena Agyemang. 2015. "The Social Value of Mid-Scale Energy in Africa: Redefining Value and Redesigning Energy to Reduce Poverty." *Energy Research & Social Science* 5: 67–69. doi:10.1016/j.erss.2014.12.013.

Mitchell, Timothy. 2011, *Carbon Democracy: Political Power in the Age of Oil*. London: Verso.

Mizuno, Nobohiro. 2016. "Political Structure as a Legacy of Indirect Colonial Rule: Bargaining between National Governments and Rural Elites in Africa." *Journal of Comparative Economics* 44: 1023–1039. doi:10.1016/j.jce.2016.03.002.

Monyei, Chukwuka Gideon, Aderemi O. Adewumi, and Kirsten Jenkins. 2018. "Energy (In) justice in Off-Grid Rural Electrification Policy: South Africa in Focus." *Energy Research & Social Science* 44: 152–171. doi:10.1016/j.erss.2018.05.002.

Newell, Peter, and Jon Phillips. 2016. "Neoliberal Energy Transitions in the South: Kenyan Experiences." *Geoforum* 74: 39–48. doi:10.1016/j.geoforum.2016.05.009.

Newell, William H. 2001. "A Theory of Interdisciplinary Studies." *Issues in Integrative Studies* 19: 1–25.

Nordling, Linda. 2018. "African Scientists Call for More Control of Their Continent's Genomic Data." *Nature*, April 18. doi:10.1038/d41586-018-04685-1.

Ockwell, David, and Rob Byrne. 2016. *Sustainable Energy for All: Innovation, Technology and Pro-poor Green Transformations*. Abingdon, UK: Routledge.

Olaopa, Olawale R., Yusuf O. Akinwale, and Ibikunle O. Ogundari. 2017. "Governance Institutions for Sustainable Energy Resources Management in Nigeria: Issues, Perspectives and Policy Agenda for action." In *The Political Economy of Energy in Sub-Saharan Africa*, edited by Lucky E. Asuelime and Andrew Emmanuel Okem, 82–101. Abingdon, UK: Routledge.

Ottinger, Gwen. 2017. "Making Sense of Citizen Science: Stories as a Hermeneutic Resource." *Energy Research & Social Science* 31: 41–49. doi:10.1016/j.erss.2017.06.014.

Ouedraogo, Nadia S. 2017. "Africa Energy Future: Alternative Scenarios and Their Implications for Sustainable Development Strategies." *Energy Policy* 106: 457–471. doi:10.1016/j.enpol.2017.03.021.

Parnell, Susan, and Edgar Pieterse, eds. 2014. *Africa's Urban Revolution*. London: Zed Books.

Pedersen, Rasmus Hundsbæk, and Opportuna Kweka. 2017. "The Political Economy of Petroleum Investments and Land Acquisition Standards in Africa: The Case of Tanzania." *Resources Policy* 52: 217–225. doi:10.1016/j.resourpol.2017.03.006.

Power, Marcus, Peter Newell, Lucy Baker, Harriet Bulkeley, Joshua Kirshner, and Adrian Smith. 2016. "The Political Economy of Energy Transitions in Mozambique and South Africa: The Role of the Rising Powers." *Energy Research & Social Science* 17: 10–19. doi:10.1016/j.erss.2016.03.007.

Practical Action. 2014. *Poor People's Energy Outlook*. London: Practical Action.

Pueyo, Ana. 2018. "What Constrains Renewable Energy Investment in Sub-Saharan Africa? A Comparison of Kenya and Ghana." *World Development* 109: 85–100. doi:10.1016/j.worlddev.2018.04.008.

Rafey, William, and Benjamin K. Sovacool. 2011. "Competing Discourses of Energy Development: The Implications of the Medupi Coal-Fired Power Plant in South Africa." *Global Environmental Change* 21: 1141–1151. doi:10.1016/j.gloenvcha.2011.05.005.

Roberts, Cameron, Frank W. Geels, Matthew Lockwood, Peter Newell, Hubert Schmitz, Bruno Turnheim, and Andy Jordan. 2018. "The Politics of Accelerating Low-Carbon Transitions: Towards a New Research Agenda." *Energy Research & Social Science* 44: 304–311. doi:10.1016/j.erss.2018.06.001.

Rochmyaningsih, Dyna. 2018. "Did a Study of Indonesian People Who Spend Most of Their Days under Water Violate Ethical Rules?" *Science*, July 26. doi:10.1126/science.aau8972.

Rosenthal, Joshua, Ashlinn Quinn, Andrew P. Grieshop, Ajay Pillarisetti, and Roger I. Glass. 2018. "Clean Cooking and the SDGs: Integrated Analytical Approaches to Guide Energy Interventions for Health and Environment Goals." *Energy for Sustainable Development* 42: 152–159. doi:10.1016/j.esd.2017.11.003.

Runsten, Simon, Francesco Fuso Nerini, and Louise Tait. 2018. "Energy Provision in South African Informal Urban Settlements: A Multi-Criteria Sustainability Analysis." *Energy Strategy Reviews* 19: 76–84. doi:10.1016/j.esr.2017.12.004.

Schillebeeckx, Simon J. D., Priti Parikh, Rahul Bansal, and Gerard George. 2012. "An Integrated Framework for Rural Electrification: Adopting a User-Centric Approach to Business Model Development." *Energy Policy* 48: 687–697. doi:10.1016/j.enpol.2012.05.078.

Schmidt, Tobias S., Tyeler Matsuo, and Axel Michaelowa. 2017. "Renewable Energy Policy as an Enabler of Fossil Fuel Subsidy Reform? Applying a Socio-Technical Perspective to the Cases of South Africa and Tunisia." *Global Environmental Change* 45: 99–110. doi:10.1016/j.gloenvcha.2017.05.004.

Schuenemaan, Franziska, Siwa Msangi, and Manfred Zeller. 2018. "Policies for a Sustainable Biomass Energy Sector in Malawi: Enhancing Energy and Food Security Simultaneously." *World Development* 103: 14–26. doi:10.1016/j.worlddev.2017.10.011.

Schwerhoff, Gregor, and Mouhamadou Sy. 2017. "Financing Renewable Energy in Africa— Key Challenge of the Sustainable Development Goals." *Renewable and Sustainable Energy Reviews* 75: 393–401. doi:10.1016/j.rser.2016.11.004.

Shen, Wei, and Marcus Power. 2016. "Africa and the Export of China's Clean Energy Revolution." *Third World Quarterly* 38: 678–697. doi:10.1080/01436597.2016.1199262.

Simmet, Hilton R. 2018. " 'Lighting a Dark Continent': Imaginaries of Energy Transition in Senegal." *Energy Research & Social Science* 40: 71–81. doi:10.1016/j.erss.2017.11.022.

Singh, Rozita, Xiao Wang, Juan Carlos Mendoza, and Emmanuel Kofi Ackom. 2015. "Electricity (In)accessibility to the Urban Poor in Developing Countries." *WIREs Energy and Environment* 4: 339–353. doi:10.1002/wene.148.

Smajgl, Alex, John Ward, and Lucie Pluschke. 2016. "The Water-Food-Energy Nexus: Realizing a New Paradigm." *Journal of Hydrology* 533: 533–540. doi:10.1016/j.jhydrol.2015.12.033.

Sovacool, Benjamin K. 2013. "Expanding Renewable Energy Access with Pro-poor Public Private Partnerships in the Developing World." *Energy Strategy Reviews* 1: 181–192. doi:10.1016/j.esr.2012.11.003.

Sovacool, Benjamin K. 2014. "What Are We Doing Here? Analyzing Fifteen Years of Energy Scholarship and Proposing a Social Science Research Agenda." *Energy Research & Social Science* 1: 1–29. doi:10.1016/j.erss.2014.02.003.

Sovacool, Benjamin K., Shannon Clarke, Katie Johnson, Meredith Crafton, Jay Eidsness, and David Zoppo. 2014. "The Energy-Enterprise-Gender Nexus: Lessons from the Multifunctional Platform (MFP) in Mali." *Renewable Energy* 50: 115–125. doi:10.1016/j.renene.2012.06.024.

Sovacool, Benjamin K., Raphael J. Heffron, Darren McCauley, and Andreas Goldthau. 2016. "Energy Decisions Reframed as Justice and Ethical Concerns." *Nature Energy* 1: 16024. doi:10.1038/nenergy.2016.24.

Stirling, Andy. 2014. "Transforming Power: Social Science and the Politics of Energy Choices." *Energy Research & Social Science* 1: 83–95. doi:10.1016/j.erss.2014.02.001.

Tait, Louise. 2017. "Towards a Multidimensional Framework for Measuring Household Energy Access: Application to South Africa." *Energy for Sustainable Development* 38: 1–9. doi:10.1016/j.esd.2017.01.007.

Tilt, Bryan, Yvonne Braun, and Daming He. 2009. "Social Impacts of Large Dam Projects: A Comparison of International Case Studies and Implications for Best Practice." *Journal of Environmental Management* 90: S249–S257. doi:10.1016/j.jenvman.2008.07.030.

Trimble, Chris, Masami Kojima, Ines Perez Arroyo, and Farah Mohammadzafeh. 2016. *Financial Viability of Electricity Sectors in Sub-Saharan Africa: Quasi-fiscal Deficits and Hidden Costs*. Washington, DC: The World Bank Group.

Trotter, Philipp A., and Roy Maconachie. 2018. "Populism, Post-Truth Politics and the Failure to Deceive the Public in Uganda's Energy Debate." *Energy Research & Social Science* 43: 61–76. doi:10.1016/j.erss.2018.05.020.

Trotter, Phillip A., Roy Maconachie, and Marcelle C. McManus. 2018. "Solar Energy's Potential to Mitigate Political Risks: The Case of an Optimized Africa-wide Network." *Energy Policy* 117: 108–126. doi:10.1016/j.enpol.2018.02.013.

Ulsrud, Kirsten, Tanja Winther, Debajit Palit, and Harald Rohracher. 2015. "Village-Level Solar Power in Africa: Accelerating Access to Electricity Services Through a Socio-Technical Design in Kenya." *Energy Research & Social Science* 5: 34–44. doi:10.1016/j.erss.2014.12.009.

United Nations General Assembly. 2015. "Transforming Our World: The 2030 Agenda for Sustainable Development." Resolution adopted by the General Assembly on September 25. A/RES/70/1.

United Nations Habitat. 2016. *World Cities Report 2016: Urbanization and Development—Emerging Futures*. Nairobi, Kenya: UN Habitat.

Van der Zwaan, Bob, Tom Kober, Francesco Dalla Longa, Anouk van der Laan, and Gert Jan Kramer. 2018. "An Integrated Assessment of Pathways for Low-Carbon Development in Africa." *Energy Policy* 117: 387–395. doi:10.1016/j.enpol.2018.03.017.

Viera, Abel Silva, and Enedir Ghisi. 2016. "Water-Energy Nexus in Low-Income Houses in Brazil: The Influence of Integrated On-site Water and Sewage Management Strategies on the Energy Consumption of Water and Sewerage Services." *Journal of Cleaner Production* 133: 145–162. doi:10.1016/j.jclepro.2016.05.104.

Von Schnitzler, Antina. 2016. *Democracy's Infrastructure: Techno-Politics & Protest after Apartheid*. Princeton, NJ: Princeton University Press.

Waage, Jeff, Christopher Yap, Sarah Bell, Caren Levy, Georgina Mace, Tom Pegram, Elaine Untelhalter, Niheer Dasandi, David Hudson, Richard Kock, Susanna Mayhew, Colin Marx, and Nigel Poole. 2015. "Governing the UN Sustainable Development Goals: Interactions, Infrastructures, and Institutions." *Lancet Global Health* 3: e251–e252. doi:10.1016/S2214-109X(15)70112-9.

Wilson, Jeffrey D. 2015. "Resource Powers? Minerals, Energy and the Rise of the BRICS." *Third World Quarterly* 36: 223–239. doi:10.1080/01436597.2015.1013318.

Winkler, Bastian, Stefanie Lemke, Jan Ritter, and Iris Lewandowski. 2017. "Integrated Assessment of Renewable Energy Potential: Approach and Application in Rural South Africa." *Environmental Innovation and Societal Transitions* 24: 17–31. doi:10.1016/j.eist.2016.10.002.

Winther, Tanja. 2008. *The Impact of Electricity: Development, Desires and Dilemmas*. Oxford: Berghahn Books.

PART IV

CONCLUSION

···

CHAPTER 31

ENERGY POLITICS

Research Contributions and Future Directions

···

KATHLEEN J. HANCOCK AND
JULIANN EMMONS ALLISON

THE most important finding of *The Oxford Handbook of Energy Politics* is that despite some earlier reports to the contrary (Hancock and Vivoda 2014; Hughes and Lipscy 2013), political science and international relations (IR) scholars have been actively researching and publishing about energy politics, both deepening long-standing research agendas (e.g., the resource curse, energy and conflict, and energy security) while adding new lines of research (e.g., climate change, renewable energy, comparative regionalism, and gender). Research currently covers oil, the traditional focus of energy politics, as well as renewable energy and nuclear energy, although to a lesser degree and with variation within those categories: less on wind and biofuels than on solar and wind, for example. Nevertheless, the extensive reference lists in all chapters provide ample evidence that energy politics is an active line of research.

Why has this significant research frequently gone unnoticed or even been expressly called out as deficient (Hancock and Vivoda 2014; Hughes and Lipscy 2013)? Several factors likely account for this mismatch between the body of literature revealed in this *Handbook* and perceptions of a lack of research. First, a review of the extensive reference lists shows that the vast majority of publications are not in the mainstream political science and international relations journals, which have typically been the targets for literature reviews. Second, and related to the first point, many *Handbook* authors identify a lack of theoretical focus and development as a shortcoming in the extant literature. Since the major mainstream journals highly value theoretical contributions, energy politics articles are published in other venues that may be less read and valued by scholars in top research universities or who do not themselves already focus on energy politics. Third, there has not been a systematic gathering of the literature across a wide range of political science perspectives, paradigms, and subdisciplines. While global energy politics and international political economy (IPE) of energy have recently received significant attention, this *Handbook* is the first to gather work across the subfields of political science, particularly in IR and comparative politics. Finally, scholars have not been using the term *energy politics* to identify their work, making it difficult to recognize a coherent body of work. Our goal is for the *Handbook* to recognize this significant body of research and in so doing further the larger research agenda, attracting new scholars and enabling current experts to recognize new lines of research. In addition, we expect engineers, policy makers, economists, and other social scientists will learn from the existing literature to better inform their own research and recommendations.

This chapter brings together strands of findings and future research agendas that emerge throughout the preceding thirty chapters, which include an introduction to the topic of energy politics, five technical chapters, ten chapters on political science and energy concepts, seven chapters on states that are major energy consumers and/or producers, and seven chapters on world regions. This chapter is divided into two parts: first we classify cross-cutting themes and critiques in the extant literature, and then we summarize major new lines of research recommended by several authors and identified by the editors by looking for larger gaps that emerge only after collectively reviewing individual chapters. It is important to note that this summary in no way substitutes for the detailed critical reviews and research agendas provided in the *Handbook's* substantive chapters.

CRITICAL REVIEWS OF THE EXTANT LITERATURE

Although we followed the lead of *Handbook* contributors regarding the substantive and theoretical foci of their chapters, this section discusses some of the major strands that cut across multiple chapters. These strands are characterized by the types of energy sources covered; methodological emphases and theory building; conventional issues of conflict and cooperation; more contemporary concerns with energy justice and gender; the intersections of energy, poverty, and economic development; energy policy and regulation; and the array of actors in energy politics.

Types of Energy Sources Covered

Mimicking global trends, the energy politics literature covers all types of energy resources and technologies, but the bulk of the research still focuses on fossil fuels. The international conflict chapter and markets chapter are exclusively about oil, given its global markets and the fact that it generally has no alternatives for transportation (ethanol in Brazil is an exception). Oil is the focus, although not the exclusive topic, of chapters on major producers (Russia and Eurasia, the United States, Venezuela) and consumers (China) and states for whom oil has important political power (Brazil).

Given many national trends away from coal, it is notable that coal plays a dominant role in the literature of many states, notably South Africa, India, and China. South Africa's energy sector is dominated by coal, accounting for 75 percent of installed capacity (Baker et al., this volume), while over 76 percent of India's generation is from coal (Powell). China has struggled to move away from coal, in part for political reasons (Nahm, this volume). For the United States, hydraulic fracturing and natural gas are the focus of many energy politics studies, although scholars continue to write about oil and are increasingly writing about the politics of renewable energy (Allison and Parinandi, this volume).

However, fossil fuels are not the key focus of all chapters. For some states and regions (or subregions), the literature instead focuses on renewable energy. There is a considerable body of research on renewable energy in Oceana, presumably because solar and wind are abundant (Huda and Ali, this volume). Hydropower is a key factor in North American energy politics, where Canada is the world's second largest hydropower producer (Mildenberger and Stokes, this volume). The literature on the EU's energy politics focuses on renewable energy going forward, although significant research also addresses the role of natural gas given many EU members' dependence on Russia. Little research has been done explicitly on the politics of wind or biofuels. As the world's largest wind energy market, China is the focus of some wind politics scholarship, with authors showing how policies were directly tied to creating the wind turbine industry and the jobs that come with it, and how this coupled well with local politicians' short-term economic growth goals (Nahm, this volume). Scholars of MENA, while mostly focusing on petroleum, note that some states are looking to renewables, particularly solar and, in light of increasing cost overruns, nuclear power (see Fitzwater, and Allison and Parinandi, this volume, on the limits of nuclear power as a renewable energy resource). Eckart Woertz, however, cautions that states have periodically made declarations without follow through. Few regionalism studies make renewables the primary focus of their analysis (Hancock et al., this volume)

Methods and Theory Building

With respect to methodology, scholars of energy politics have tended to focus on empirical research and have relied on qualitative methods, especially case studies, which has made it more difficult to generalize and then engage in systematic theory building beyond specific states or historical cases. In addition, of those authors who overtly discuss methods, the emphasis is often on secondary sources and/or the gray literature. For example, Mirza Sadaqat Huda and Saleem H. Ali note in their chapter that regional cooperation studies in Asia-Pacific rely too much on secondary sources. Lucy Baker, Jesse Burton, and Hilton Trollip; Eliza Massi and Jewellord Nem Singh; and Kirsten Westphal each note that their respective chapters on South Africa, Brazil, and the EU rely heavily on treaties, directives, regulations, hearings, and national government and parliamentary reports. Some authors note that scholars of their subject area (Brazil, EU, and CSR) often turn to reports written by firms. Lior Herman finds that the energy sanctions literature is mostly descriptive, usually without comparative analysis that would help scholars identify patterns of success and failure. Few literatures actively use interviews or combine qualitative and quantitative studies; energy security and energy justice are exceptions, albeit with room for improvement. Karina Standal, Tanja Winther, and Katrine Danielsen note in their chapter that quantitative studies on gender tend to look at a single indicator, such as how much time women use an energy source, rather than a bevy of indicators that would provide a fuller picture. Gender studies and energy justice studies have made good use of interviews; Sara Fuller notes interviews have been critical for documenting the "lived experience of energy poverty."

Most scholars actively publishing on energy politics lament the lack of strong theoretical focus and development in published research. Nevertheless, this criticism is not a uniform one. For several states and regions, the energy politics literature closely parallels broader theoretical frameworks and identified patterns within the state or region. In Latin America, the waves of privatization and nationalization are a key feature of energy politics as well as the economy in general (Gaylord, this volume). China scholars use the concept of fragmented authoritarianism, in which the central government issues orders that are then "shaped by a plethora of bureaucratic goals and organizational interests of functional and regional administrative entities charged with policy implementations" (Nahm, this volume). Scholars of the EU use the general concepts of supranationalism versus intergovernmentalism to explain energy outcomes (Westphal, this volume). Scholars of North America, the United States, and Brazil analyze energy from the federalism perspective, documenting the importance of subnational units (Mildenberger and Stokes; Allison and Parinandi; and Massi and Singh, this volume, respectively). For South Africa, most scholars use the concept of the mineral energy complex (MEC), not found in any of the other chapters, although it could feasibly apply to some other states if the concept were broadened. MEC refers to South Africa's evolving system of accumulations historically "based on cheap coal for generating cheap electricity" (Baker et al., this volume). It references "critical links and networks of power between the financial sector, government, the private sector, and SOEs (Baker et al., this volume). In analyzing electricity planning in South Africa, scholars have also used political economy frameworks, advocacy coalition networks, and discourse network analysis (Baker et al., this volume). A few scholars working on comparative regionalism have used the concepts from that genre, such as diffusion (Hancock et al., this volume).

Conflict and Cooperation

As in political science in general, a major theme cutting across all chapters is how energy politics intersects with conflict and cooperation at the national, regional, and global levels. Jeff D. Colgan and Jan B. Stockbruegger's entire chapter is dedicated to the extensive literature on the relationship between oil and domestic and international conflict. Security has long been the focus of Asia-Pacific energy politics. Energy's connection to national security hinders energy cooperation in the region (Huda and Ali, this volume). Japan's vulnerability from imported oil and coal was highlighted during World War II, when it was cut off by the Allies. In the war's aftermath, Japan turned to nuclear energy, a move supported by the United States (Incerti and Lipscy, this volume). In contrast, other chapters identify literatures on how energy creates opportunities for cooperation. For example, the Maghreb-Europe Pipeline project is credited with helping thaw the relationship between Algeria and Morocco. Recommendations for fostering energy cooperation, however, are often vague and unrealistic given nationalism and security challenges in the regions, such as Asia-Pacific (Huda and Ali, this volume). Cooperation in North America, however, is hindered by "different electricity markets, energy mixes, regulations and commitments to the energy transition (Mildenberger and Stokes, this volume).

Similarly, energy interdependence scholars divide into two groups that parallel cooperation and conflict debates: (1) energy governance, which follows the logic of liberalism, seeing opportunities for global governance and cooperation; and (2) the geopolitical perspective, which aligns with realism, seeing energy interdependence as leading to international conflict (resource wars) (Wilson, this volume). Kathleen J. Hancock, Stefano Palestini, and Kacper Szulecki find that energy interdependence within a geographic region can lead to conflict or cooperation. A related line of research considers how energy is used—as both sticks and carrots—in foreign policy to achieve mutual goals (Herman, this volume). For example, Russia is often cited as using regional oil and gas pipelines for foreign policy leverage—dubbed "pipeline politics"—with its neighbors (Balmaceda and Heinrich, this volume). During the Cold War, the United States developed a close relationship with Venezuela in part to prevent the Soviet Union and its allies from accessing deposits in Venezuela (Allison and Parinandi, this volume). Venezuela's foreign policy has long focused on making it a regional and international power, using oil as leverage and lubricant (Rosales and Sánchez, this volume). While much of this literature focuses on oil, renewable energy projects are not immune to creating conflict. In Latin America, hydroelectric dam projects have been the source of significant protests. In some cases the conflict is over the right to the land of indigenous and rural communities. In Mexico and Colombia, wind farms have been strongly opposed in part because they provide no long-term benefits to the local communities (Gaylord, this volume).

Energy Justice and Gender

Energy justice, like environmental and social justice, is a rapidly rising focus in energy politics scholarship. In addition to the chapter dedicated to this topic, several *Handbook* chapters discuss it. The concept broadly considers issues of distribution—"who gets what, where, and why"—as well as fair and equitable access to decision-making about energy. The concept has broadened over time to include energy poverty, fuel poverty, vulnerability, precarity, ethical consumption, and capabilities related to energy use and poverty. In the Asia-Pacific, energy justice has included the social impacts of big hydro-electric dams. Although not stated in terms of energy justice, scholarship on Latin America has a strong focus on distributive fairness, particularly whether private companies will undermine equitable access compared to the state, which has greater concerns beyond profit and in evaluating the usefulness of energy subsidies in alleviating poverty (Gaylord, this volume). In India, where most people continue to live with energy poverty, despite substantial growth in demand for energy, energy justice can be mere political rhetoric (Powell, this volume). Although oil and gas have been the focus of many energy justice studies, scholars have expanded research into renewable energy (Fuller, this volume).

Some gender analysis overlaps with energy justice; if access to energy is "a prerequisite for realizing economic and social rights" (Standal et al., this volume), then gender considerations must also be part of energy justice. While the *Handbook* dedicates a chapter to gender, this section highlights some of the other chapters that include related findings. It should first be noted that many chapters do not explicitly discuss gender, presumably because the literature does not cover the topic. Most research that does focus on gender examines women and energy in international development policy. This literature has been dominated by engineers and economists and has relied too much on gray literature from NGOs. Scholars find that engineers tended to ignore, or not expect, that women have preferences for their households that go beyond technological developments, such as aesthetics. There is a related literature on women in wealthier states: Italy, Norway, Serbia, Sweden, United Kingdom, and Ukraine (Standal et al., this volume). The Asia-Pacific chapter states that scholars observe significant gender inequality. They also link gender and labor rights such as the decline of women working in the coal mines and related infrastructure (Huda and Ali, this volume) The literature on India concludes that women are victims of social and geographic marginalization, leading to greater health risks from cooking stoves. Some perceived advances are more about using women for political purposes by using the right rhetoric (Powell, this volume).

Energy, Poverty, and Economic Development

Growth in energy access is often presented as a means out of poverty and into economic development. However, the *Handbook* chapters show how energy access, usually defined as being connected to a central electricity grid, does not always bring the benefits one might expect and can even create new political challenges. For example, the Kenyan rural middle class, rather than the essentially poor, captured the benefits of solar and then opted to use it for appliances, notably television, much to the disappointment of development experts. One of the greatest obstacles to sustainable development has been the dominance of technical and economic approaches over broader social and political approaches. For example, development experts and entrepreneurs have failed to understand cultural preferences for cookstoves, particularly that the modern stoves were not durable enough to handle the large, heavy meals preferred in many African rural societies (Delina, this volume). In India, the very definition of what constitutes energy access has become politicized; having at least 10 percent of total households in a village hooked up to electricity now counts as being "electrified" (Powell, this volume).

Related analyses consider the intersection between neoliberalism and energy more directly. The literature on Latin America places energy in the larger debate about the role of privatization and the costs and benefits of multinational corporations (Gaylord, this volume). Similarly, India has moved from a socialist state to one embracing neoliberalism as a path to economic development, the context that frames much of energy politics. In addition, independence and redistributive wealth are tied up in energy politics of India (Powell, this volume). In Brazil, the early focus was on energy for development. As such, energy was placed in the larger framework of import-substitution industrialization, with its subsidies, incentives, import controls, tax exemptions, and state-owned companies (Massi and Singh, this volume).

Policy, Regulations, and Subsidies

Much of the energy scholarship focuses on, or at least incorporates, policy recommendations. Although the *Handbook* does not have a single chapter dedicated to policy, given how extensive that literature is, many chapters, including the technical chapters, include policy. Policies and their relatives, regulations, can be dependent variables (outcomes to explain) as well as independent variables (explanations for observed outcomes).

Looking at policy as a dependent variable, explanations of varying US policies on renewable energy are explained in part by the importance of fossil fuel extraction in the individual states. In West Virginia, for example, 90 percent of electricity consumption comes from coal, which has played a key role in the state's economy since the mid-nineteenth century. However, the link is not so straightforward, with other factors playing key roles: partisanship, citizen demands, and lobbying influence (Allison and Parinandi, this volume). Some literature observes whether states have national energy policies but does not explore the why, how, and when of those policies. For example, until recently Japan lacked a national energy policy. Policy was instead "determined through a mix of laws, such as the Act on Rationalizing Energy Use of 1979, and administrative measures designed to encourage energy efficiency." Starting with the 2002 Basic Act Energy Policy, Japan has moved toward creating national plans (Incerti and Lipscy, this volume).

Looking at policy as an independent variable, Christina E. Hoicka and Julie MacArthur note in their chapter how policies have driven new technological developments and are reshaping cost curves for renewable energy. Feed-in-tariffs, mandates, targets, subsidies, and other incentives have all shaped energy profiles in individual states. Policy is part and parcel of energy security. Addressing issues of resilience, affordability, accessibility, and sustainability requires states to consider what policies will best tackle the perceived vulnerabilities (Jewell and Brutschin, this volume).

Regulations—generally, laws developed to implement policy—have been the subject of some scholarship. Some scholarship on Latin America has criticized poor regulatory practices, while others have pointed to the difficulty of "creating adequate regulatory systems in states with underdeveloped institutions of governance and where cost recovery conflicts with addressing the needs of the poor" (Gaylord, this volume). Scholars find that the United States has gone through waves of regulation and deregulation (Allison and Parinandi, this volume), and that the EU's regulatory power on energy (and other issues) is its major foreign policy tool (Westphal, this volume). One of the more interesting and innovative regulations is found in Japan, where the "Top Runner program automates energy efficiency improvements through the setting of regulations based on the current product with the highest energy efficiency level on the market" (Incerti and Lipscy, this volume). This regulatory strategy has pushed energy efficiency to higher levels.

Subsidies are a long-standing means for encouraging and discouraging certain types of energy production and consumption and related behavior. In developing states, subsidies are about ensuring supply while maintaining affordable rates for the population. Scholarship on subsidies is especially rich for the Latin American region. While Latin American states followed the World Bank and USAID's neoliberal advice in some markets, such as telecommunications, they continued to intervene in energy markets on behalf of consumers. Indeed, in Latin America subsidies account for nearly 5 percent of GPD, whereas 1 percent is the global average. Low-income states are more likely to subsidize electricity prices, whereas petroleum-rich states subsidize oil and gas consumption. Studies on subsidies in Latin America conclude that direct cash transfers would be more equitable than subsidies in alleviating poverty (Gaylord, this volume).

In China the government used subsidies for solar PV to create a local demand market in the face of falling demand from the EU during the 2008 global recession (Nahm, this volume). Despite a 2009 pledge to "phase out and rationalize over the medium-term inefficient fossil fuel subsidies" (Group of 20, 2009, as quoted in Wilson, this volume), member states have done little to reduce subsidies. Meanwhile, growing energy demand in MENA states is increasing the burden of energy subsidies (Woertz, this volume). In India, subsidies meant for the poor have been ineffective because of poor targeting. Subsidies for the oil and gas sector have in some cases, such as the United States under the 2005 Energy Policy Act, been enacted under the discourse of energy independence or energy security (Allison and Parinandi, this volume). Prioritizing energy efficiency, Japan subsidizes lightweight vehicles manufactured only by Japanese companies. These cars are disproportionately used in rural areas, thus particularly benefiting rural voters (Incerti and Lipscy, this volume).

Actors in Energy Politics

As is the case in many areas of IR and comparative politics research, the literatures reviewed collectively identify a number of state and nonstate actors, including international, regional, and nongovernmental organizations (IOs, ROs, and NGOs). Some of the other nonstate actors are newer to energy politics (renewable energy companies and agriculture); others are longtime "players" with well-developed research agendas surrounding them (oil and gas companies); and still others have been mostly ignored in earlier literatures (labor and bureaucracies).

International and Regional Organizations

Several *Handbook* chapters identify IOs, Ros, and other governance institutions and structures, mostly without strong effects on energy outcomes. The World Bank is mentioned most often. The World Bank appears in the Latin America, India, and South Africa chapters as advocating for neoliberal solutions, some of which were received with skepticism or even protests by the local populations (Gaylord; Powell; Baker et al., this volume, respectively). The World Bank finances critical energy infrastructure (Huda and Ali; Hancock et al., this volume) and, along with the International Monetary Fund, plays a role in CSR. In climate change research, scholars have documented the work of the International Energy Agency, G-8, G-20, Sustainable Energy for All (SE4A) initiative, and International Renewable Energy Agency (IRENA) (Hughes, this volume). Scholars note that the Organization of the Petroleum Exporting Countries , the oldest and best-known energy IO, is not as powerful as in the past. For example, in 2014 OPEC tried to flood the oil market to drop prices, which in turn would force out US producers. Both OPEC and the United States lost, with Saudi Arabia losing $220 billion in foreign currency reserves (Wolfe, this volume).

Regional organizations have mixed success, according to the *Handbook* authors. Some regions do not have institutions to manage energy policy (North America, Mildenberger and Stokes, this volume), while others have extensive treaties and regulations (Europe, Westphal, this volume). Those scholars focusing on energy governance argue there is an energy regime complex that cooperatively manages interdependent world markets. This regime is one of soft law in which governments favor organized dialogue to negotiate informal and voluntary reforms as opposed to more binding measures (Wilson, this volume).

State Actors

All the chapters on specific states and regions include extensive literatures on how their subject states have affected energy politics at the domestic, regional, and global levels. China's role in global energy politics is analyzed not only by China scholars but by those studying states and regions affected by China's energy demands and policies. For example, Venezuela under Chavez attempted to replace the United States with China as its major oil partner. China is also a critical source of financing for states with limited access to international financial markets, such as Argentina, Brazil, Ecuador, and Venezuela (Rosales and Sánchez, this volume). A few chapters summarize a literature on subgroups within the state. For example, the literature on Brazil (Massi and Singh, this volume) and India (Powell, this volume) includes extensive studies on the role of technocrats in creating energy policies. Subnational units are also highlighted in chapters focused on federal states in Latin America and North America (Gaylord; Mildenberger and Stokes;

Allison and Parinandi, this volume). Scholars of Japan find that local courts played a role in delaying restarts of nuclear plants (Incerti and Lipscy, this volume).

Some strands of literature recognize the interplay between state types and energy politics. First, in authoritarian states (e.g., Russia) and in technical democracies with low contestation (e.g., South Africa), energy and corruption often run hand in hand (Balmaceda and Heinrich; Baker et al., this volume). These factors also enable states to quickly change policy; Japan has been mostly governed by one party since World War II, which allowed the state to enforce strong energy efficiency policies (Incerti and Lipscy, this volume).

Some authors discuss how having a federal system rather than a centralized system affects energy politics. For Argentina, decentralizing governance of underground resources dovetailed with privatization of companies (Gaylord, this volume). The climate change chapter and US chapters demonstrate the importance of understanding subnational governments. At the subnational level, the entrenched multinational fossil fuel firms, which often act as veto players at the national level, have less influence, opening the door to policy shifts supporting renewable energy and climate change policy (Hughes; Allison and Parinandi, this volume). Matto Mildenberger and Leah C. Stokes find that federalism in all the North American countries (Canada, United States, and Mexico) has affected the ability of this continental region to integrate more fully. The Canadian provinces and American and Mexican states work against the federal policy makers. However, federalism does not tell the full story. For example, in Mexico, energy policy is largely centralized at the national level, whereas in the United States the national and subnational units share policymaking, and in Canada, the provinces have primary control (Mildenberger and Stokes, this volume). In Brazil, subnational governments gradually took control of electricity generation, transmission, and distribution (Massi and Singh, this volume). Subnational units have been ahead of federal governments on renewable energy policy in all three North American states (Mildenberger and Stokes, this volume). In the United States, states have passed legislation to "improve efficiency, accelerate the introduction of zero-emission vehicles, finance climate resilience projects, and increase reliance on renewable energy" (Allison and Parinandi, this volume).

Certain political institutions can shape climate change policy. For example, the greater number of veto points in the United States is seen as slowing policy change compared to European states. In addition, varying electoral institutions have enabled green parties, and their advocacy for climate change policies, to thrive in Europe but be shut out in the two-party system in the United States (Hughes, this volume).

Energy Companies

Before turning to nonstate actors we consider energy firms, which include privately owned and state-owned enterprises that may be partially privately owned. Energy companies include a variety of ownership models and cover the full range of energy services—including resource extraction, processing, refining, and delivery; and electricity production and delivery, including ownership of the electricity grid—and cover one or more renewable and/or nonrenewable energy sources. Within the energy politics field, one of the most important and often studied state actors is national oil companies (NOCs) or, more broadly, state-owned enterprises (SOEs). Some literature centers around the costs and benefits of nationalizing the energy sector, particularly oil companies (Gaylord; Massi and Singh; Powell; Rosales and Sánchez, this volume). Scholars also investigate hybrid forms of ownership, such as Petrobras in Brazil and Aramco in Saudi Arabia, which are market traded but majority owned by the state (Gaylord; and Woertz, respectively). NOCs play an important role in China's energy portfolio, including recently being tasked with lowering emissions (Nahm, this volume). Scholars find that some states, such as Russia and the OPEC members, engage in energy nationalism using SOEs to assert control over other states and the global markets (Wilson, this volume). Some SOEs are relatively efficient, such as SABIC, a Saudi petroleum manufacturing company (Woertz, this volume). Electricity SOEs are less commonly found in the literature, although Massi and Singh (this volume) discuss Brazil's Electrobras. State-owned Eskom is the focus of the energy politics chapter on South Africa (Baker et al., this volume).

Debates about neoliberalism intersect this literature. For example, Lydia Powell argues that the World Bank pushed India to liberalize its energy markets, unbundling electricity generation, transmission, and distribution segments and setting up regulatory bodies. In contrast, South Africa's apartheid regime was isolated and thus avoided the push to liberalize (Baker et al., this volume). These SOEs are often inefficient. China's NOCs are currently absorbing energy production and processing infrastructure losses in their overseas investments (Wolfe, this volume). Venezuela's PDVSA has been called a "state within a state" (Rosales and Sánchez, this volume).

Of course many energy companies are privately owned, and many states have a mix of private and publicly owned energy companies. In Japan, energy policy is the "process of constant conflict, bargaining, and compromise between the state and private firms." Regional utilities have played a key role in maintaining nuclear energy plants even after Fukushima (Incerti and Lipscy, this volume), and scholars have documented the importance of power utilities (notably for electricity and natural gas distribution) in climate change policy (Hughes, this volume).

Nonstate Actors

In addition to energy companies, the *Handbook* chapters identify a number of other nonstate actors, including mining companies, labor, and communities and individuals related to distributed energy. First, mining companies were found to push for regional power pools in Africa (Hancock et al., this volume). In this case, it was the demand for highly reliable electricity that led to the company pushing for new energy infrastructure.

Second, a few studies explore the role of labor in Asia Pacific, South Africa, and Venezuela. Significant literature exists on Asia-Pacific regarding slave labor moving between Myanmar and Thailand and health and compensation for injuries in the coal industry (Huda and Ali, this volume). In post-apartheid South Africa, the ruling African National Congress (ANC) "accommodated organized labor, the Congress of

South African Trade Unions (COSATU), and the South African Communist Party (SACP) with which it forms the Tripartite Alliance" (Baker et al., this volume). Labor groups in Venezuela, especially workers for PVSD, the NOC, called for a national strike aimed at bringing down the Chavez government. This led to the state firing more than half PVSD's employees, setting the stage for the national crisis (Rosales and Sánchez, this volume).

Third, a number of chapters highlight literatures on how individuals and communities affect energy politics. Community-owned enterprises developing biomass and solar PV projects become new proponents for renewable energy (Hughes, this volume). Individuals rely on "energy democracy" to bring about change through the use of distributed renewable energy technologies (Hughes; Allison and Parinandi; this volume). Japan originally put nuclear power plants in rural areas where civil society is weak. However, in the aftermath of Fukushima, local opposition increased enough to influence political leaders (Incerti and Lipscy, this volume). Others note that we know little about the relationship between civil society and energy-related sanctions (Herman, this volume).

Developing Sophistication

Energy politics scholars have shown increasing sophistication in their understanding of energy concepts. Much as political scientists had to learn more about economics to further develop the subfield of international political economy, so have social scientists become more educated on energy terminology and technology. While many *Handbook* authors have focused on the lack of theory building as a flaw in the scholarship, we should also acknowledge the conceptual advances scholars have made in the last ten years. Without these advances, a research agenda and its focus on theory and methods development would be much more distant goals. The following examples of conceptual development in the area of energy politics are illustrative, with many more examples found in each chapter.

First, energy politics scholars now routinely distinguish between oil and natural gas rather than conflating them or using *petroleum* and *oil* synonymously (petroleum includes oil and natural gas). Scholars understand that *natural gas, oil,* and *petroleum* cannot be used interchangeably and that doing so can obscure important processes, outcomes, and analysis (Balmaceda 2018). Second, scholars are unpacking the concept of a "resource rich" state. For example, while many consider MENA states to be energy rich, this is not uniformly the case. As a group, MENA states lack coal, iron ore, sufficient water for hydraulic fracturing, and rivers for hydroelectric dams. In addition, some are rich in oil but not natural gas (Woertz, this volume). Third, scholars are more carefully breaking down energy issues into supply chains: upstream, downstream and midstream; and production, transmission, and distribution. Who owns what determines the extent to which these segments can be exploited as tools of foreign policy (Herman, this volume) and explains various facets of energy security, including risks related to cyberattacks. Finally, scholars recognize heterogeneity among energy firms, within both the renewable energy sectors and fossil fuels sectors (Hughes, this volume). Making these distinctions allows scholars to better understand political variables such as interest group coalitions, For example, small, family-owned energy companies cannot wait as long for legislation, regulation, and negotiations as major oil and gas companies, which means they do not always lobby together.

A Combined Research Agenda

Each *Handbook* chapter concludes with a detailed research agenda proposed by the author(s). These agendas are often specific to the chapter's subject matter, but some recommendations suggest ideas that could be applied to other topics. This section summarizes some of the common recommendations as well as others that might also be taken up. The major categories are theory development; methods; policy, regulations, and subsidies; emerging and underdeveloped topics; and key state and nonstate actors.

Theory Development

Handbook authors demonstrate a wide variety of theoretical frameworks already used in energy politics, but widely recommend scholars further develop existing theories as well as new ones. First, nearly all authors recommend that scholars move beyond single-case studies and into methodologically sound comparative analysis between projects and states (Delina; Huda and Ali; Hancock et al.; Incerti and Lipscy, this volume). Scholars call for comparisons across issue areas, such as transportation policy, industrial policy, and municipal mergers, as well as between states and regions.

A second and also common recommendation is for interdisciplinary research and theory development. Engineers (especially electrical, mechanical, chemical, materials, and biological), economists, climate scientists, political scientists, and others must collaborate to ensure they are recognizing and overcoming the barriers and challenges associated with research in energy politics. This is true even for understanding politics, as Trevor Incerti and Phillip Y. Lipscy argue.

Third, scholars need a deeper understanding of decision-making, including energy veto players and underlying paradigms, in authoritarian states like Russia (Balmaceda and Heinrich, this volume). While this is discussed in the Russia chapter, scholars of other authoritarian regimes could benefit from this type of analysis as well.

Fourth, we need more research into the social and psychological barriers to greater adoption of technologies and behavior related to the energy transition (Hoicka and MacArthur). In other words, how do we change the norms of energy use? Research should both honor specific cultural and historical contexts, as many authors call for, while also paving the way for generalizations, leading to further theory development.

Fifth, some contributors call for theories on how to build state capacity to create policy solutions that fit individual states—underscored for Latin America (Gaylord), but relevant as well to other regions and states. We argue that capacity for governance is also uneven among substate units, an issue that needs further research to document inequalities and propose solutions.

Sixth, identity and gender are ripe areas for research on energy politics. Research should unpack state identities and how these matter for whether states pursue energy regionalism, for what gain, and the success or failure of regional identity formation (Hancock et al., this volume). An intersectional lens would improve scholarship on energy justice by identifying the ways in which categories of difference—gender, race, class, and so on—combine to advantage/disadvantage individuals and groups with respect to securing affordable and consistent access to (clean) energy (Fuller, this volume). Contributors who cover gender differences in energy access and power over energy policy suggest that gender should be adopted as both an analytical category (e.g., as in gender disaggregation of data) and an analytical tool (e.g., to identify power relations and access to resources associated with them) (Standal, et al., this volume).

Finally, contributors recommend discourse analysis for a deeper understanding of energy security, Indian politics, and development in Africa (Jewell and Brutschin; Powell; Delina respectively). The software for discourse analysis has become more sophisticated, making it relatively easy to analyze how language is used in energy politics and reveal how people are talking about an issue, potentially revealing barriers to the energy transition, for example.

Methods

The *Handbook* authors identify a number of specific ways to improve and expand on methods. While these address specific regions, states, or issues, most could be applied beyond the subject the authors address. First, a number of recommendations refer specifically to the global south, although they could be extended to include other regions. We need more local scholars, practitioners, and indigenous populations, both laypeople and scientists, working with Western scholars. Where possible, we need household surveys and structured interviews with elite actors and key informants (Huda and Ali, this volume). Scholars should create new participatory mechanisms, helping raise up voices often overlooked, including the poor, women, and indigenous peoples (Delina, this volume).

Second, scholars identify differing needs regarding qualitative and quantitative methods. On the one hand, we need qualitative measures of policy successes. Studies that use only quantitative measures, such as number of new connections to the electricity grid, miss how the interventions actually change the quality of life for the recipients. This limitation is especially critical for low and low-middle income states, where significant public funds received through multilateral and bilateral aid are supposed to be improving people's lives (Delina, this volume). Latin American studies would benefit from public opinion surveys to better understand views on renewable energy and related environmental issues (Gaylord, this volume). More process tracing is needed to understand how and why energy regions form (Hancock et al., this volume). On the other hand, Sara Fuller argues that we need new quantitative frameworks to capture the multidimensional nature of energy poverty; Lior Herman argues for more quantitative analysis on energy-related sanctions; and Matto Mildenberger and Leah C. Stokes call for scholars of North America to use more econometric tools.

Policy, Regulations, and Subsidies

While energy policy formation, explanations of policy, and analyses of policy effectiveness have been widely researched by energy politics scholars, *Handbook* authors conclude there is more to be done. First, scholars working at the intersection of basic research and policy need to more carefully think through the political realities of the states and regions for which they make recommendations. Calls for confidence-building measures are often simply too vague and perhaps unrealistic for regions marked by significant security conflicts such as the Asia-Pacific (Huda and Ali, this volume), and Laurence L. Delina (this volume) calls on scholars to do more research on energy in sub-Saharan Africa that is "impact-focused and policy-relevant."

Second, scholars need to keep analyzing the successes and failures of the wide variety of renewable energy subsidies, targets, feed-in-tariffs, and other incentives that have shaped the uptake of renewable energy, energy efficiency, and other low-carbon technologies. What is working, and under what circumstances? While carbon taxes are commonly proposed as effective, they may not be politically feasible. Subsidies are often politically more palatable. Policies that allow political leaders to appeal to job growth are especially attractive (Hughes, this volume). We need to continue to research the transnational effects of green industrial policies. Scholars should search for more policies that enable companies in different states to co-evolve industries, as the wind industries in China and Germany did (Hughes, this volume).

Finally, while there has been some important research on energy subsidies, much of that research has focused on the West, especially the United States. More could be done on other states and regions, including Asia, where subsidies have been increasing. This research should look at the connections "between electoral politics and energy prices, political violence related to price hikes of fuels, and the international repercussions of domestic energy subsidies, such as trade wars over agricultural and other products" (Huda and Ali, this volume). Are subsidies for renewable energy displacing investments in basic goods like clean drinking water, healthcare, and housing? Anecdotal evidence says yes, but we need more systematic investigation to know how extensive the problem might be (Powell, this volume). This question is not about analyzing the effectiveness of policies, as proposed in the second point above, but rather about unintended consequences, particularly in the less developed states.

Emerging and Underdeveloped Topics

The *Handbook* authors identify a number of emerging or underdeveloped topics that require more attention. First, several chapters cite literature analyzing how the transition to renewable energy—a change the *Handbook* authors take as a given—will affect energy politics. For example, Jessica Steinberg argues that CSR will be different for renewable energy projects. Many of the unique features of CSR as applied to energy refer only to fossil fuels projects. The transition may change how companies engage with communities.

Second, the politics around energy efficiency and transportation have received surprisingly little attention, given that both will be a key part of a low-carbon future. What are the political coalitions for energy efficiency, and why are some states more advanced in efficiency standards than others? What are international organizations, states, substate units, and individuals doing to reduce automobile use, and why are some states making more headway than others on electric vehicle fleets, for example?

Third, *Handbook* authors argue cybersecurity is a growing threat to energy security. We need more nontechnical studies, particularly beyond Europe, where much of the work is now done. Given China's state-owned companies as well as those privately owned but open to state manipulation, cybersecurity is set to be a major research area for a wide variety of issues (Huda and Ali, this volume).

Fourth, much more research needs to be done on energy regionalism (Hancock et al., this volume), in particular its drivers, institutional design, and effects. Of all the chapters, this one focuses most on a research agenda, arguing that very little has been done on the subject, and certainly there has been no coherent agenda.

Fifth, while some chapters show significant research on the history of energy politics and historical cases, some authors call for more research on the historical contexts of energy politics. First, on energy security, the authors recommend further analysis of historical energy disruptions, in particular to tease out the causes of these disruptions with an eye on whether these cases shed light on future potential disruptions (Jewell and Brutschin, this volume). Second, scholars need to better understand the historical development of MENA states. Woertz argues we need to know how the region's "environmental eccentricities shaped its socioeconomic development since medieval times and how it was integrated into the British-led global goal economy of the nineteenth and twentieth centuries." Third, despite extensive research on the rentier state, Woertz calls for more research on the processes through which states become rentier states, what role human agency plays, and how regional flows of rent affect the political economy of regions (Woertz, this volume), arguments that apply not only to MENA but also to Latin America, where there are rentier states. Finally, several authors argue that scholars must research and take seriously the rich and historical trajectories of individual states (Massi and Singh, Powell, Incerti and Lipscy, this volume).

Finally, there is little recent scholarship on the politics of nuclear energy, perhaps in part because of the move away from nuclear in many states, including the United States, Germany, and Japan. However, there are emerging technologies that may bring nuclear back onto the agenda (Fitzwater, this volume), some developing states are still looking at nuclear energy (Gaylord and Hancock 2013), France will retain its nuclear fleet for the foreseeable future, and some still hope to see a revival in the United States as a response to climate change. Among the developing states, Mirza Sadaqat Huda and Saleem H. Ali recommend research on nuclear politics in Bangladesh. Jonas Nahm finds that despite significant R&D support, state financing through credits, and technology transfers, as well as public opinion surveys that show support for nuclear, political scientists have not given China's development of nuclear energy much attention.

Key Actors: New and Underresearched

As in the critical analysis sections, contributors to the *Handbook* frequently discussed the role of state and nonstate actors as part of their proposed research agendas. While some of the actors that have long been part of energy politics—the United States is a notable case—will remain the focus of research, some relatively new actors—such as renewable energy companies—should receive considerable attention in future research.

State Actors

It is widely recognized that anyone studying energy issues at the global but also regional and local levels will have to understand China and the United States as the major countries shaping future global energy markets, through continually increasing oil and gas production in the United States and China's growing energy demands and contributions to renewable energy manufacturing as well as consumption. Political scientists should ask questions such as to what extent China is emerging as an alternative market for Canada's crude oil (Mildenberger and Stokes, this volume) and what that means for North America, US markets, and even geopolitics.

Some authors speculate that the energy transition will change the power of specific states, possibly in a positive way. For example, the shift from large-scale oil and gas projects to smaller, renewable energy projects and increased competition might lessen the power of states rich in renewables. The energy transition may then mean states have more difficulty manipulating market power for foreign policy (Herman, this volume). Scholarship should address this from an empirical and theoretical perspective.

The *Handbook* authors note that a number of states are underresearched and thus require more scholarly attention. In sub-Saharan Africa, scholars need to go beyond South Africa, Kenya, and Ghana (Delina, this volume). Authors of topics chapters tend to find that developing states are understudied. Topics that need much more research for developing states include social justice and climate change. These studies will be particularly important for analyzing how states that do not have "carbon lock-in" can leapfrog past the carbon-intensive energy system and straight into low-carbon systems (Hughes, this volume). Conversely, gender scholars need to study more of the global north, as currently much of the literature is embedded in international development studies (Standal et al., this volume).

Substate Actors

Beyond the unitary state, scholars of energy politics, first, can uniquely contribute to energy studies by analyzing the historical, current, and projected roles of actors within the state, most notably bureaucrats and public utility commissions and other regulators. The *Handbook* authors say little about bureaucrats, suggesting opportunities for research. There are a few exceptions that could be used for comparisons: Powell's arguments about the Indian bureaucracy as a "commander" of public services rather than a partner and Incerti and Lipscy's finding that the autonomous bureaucracy in Japan is in part responsible for Japan's success in pushing energy efficiency. What other roles have bureaucrats played, in what political climates are they successful, and on what types of energy issues are they effective?

Second, public utility commissions and similar regulators receive little attention in the scholarly literature, including in the *Handbook* chapters, yet are increasingly recognized as pushing states in various directions, whether toward or away from fossil fuels and energy efficiency. In the United States these are substate actors, but regulators in other states may be at the national level.

Third, cities are increasingly important actors and venues for policy (Hughes, this volume). Although cities in MENA do not have the same agency as in democracies, research on the MENA region should engage with urban studies and include municipal energy management (Woertz, this volume). City governance has been particularly important for renewable energy in South Africa, in part because of the potential for job growth (Baker et al., this volume). In the United States, the Mayors' Climate Protection Agreement (MCPA) has been signed by more than one thousand mayors pledging to reduce carbon dioxide emissions (Allison and Parinandi, this volume). Through comparative analysis, scholars should explore how and where cities make a difference in energy policy, increased use of renewable energy, and city job growth or decline in specific sectors, inter alia.

Fourth, sovereign wealth funds (SWF) have become players in energy politics and thus should be the subject of research (Herman; Wolfe, this volume). "Three of the top five global sovereign wealth funds invest in oil and their combined value is estimated at $3.3 trillion" (Wolfe, this volume). We need to better understand how they influence energy politics at the domestic and international levels.

Nonstate Actors

The *Handbook* authors point to a wide variety of nonstate actors that deserve much more research and could guide our understanding of the intricacies of energy politics and policy. First, scholars should look for racial and ethnic actors in energy. In South Africa, a new black economic and political elite has formed following Black Empowerment Enterprises (BEE) policies and legislation in the aftermath of apartheid. These new actors have diversified ownership of the coal mines, with small entities replacing international conglomerates like BHP-Billiton) (Baker et al., this volume) Will these new actors change how we understand energy politics in South Africa? Similarly, free prior and informed consent (FPIC) is a policy developed by the UN in which firms must get FPIC from indigenous communities before starting work there. How will this shape CSR activities related to energy?

Second, the role of labor and labor unions should be further explored. While Huda and Ali (this volume) report an extensive literature from scholars studying the Asia-Pacific, this research has focused only on coal mining. The literature should be expanded to other industries, looking for comparisons between industries and states. Huda and Ali also argue that child labor in energy projects has not been sufficiently analyzed.

Third, and related to the first two categories of nonstate actors considered, *Handbook* authors call for more research on social movements. For example, Latin America has vast social movement resources, such as the National Assembly of Environmental Casualties, with over ninety member groups (Mexico); the Brazilian Network of Environmental Justice, with over eighty labor unions; NGOs; indigenous people's groups; and Patagonia without Dams, with its coalition of individuals, community groups, and international NGOs (Chile). More research should be done on how effective these groups and similar social movements around the world are in achieving change, however defined.

Fourth, for many states and regions, further research should be done on the new and evolving role of renewable energy companies and others with a vested interest in renewable energy, such as agricultural sectors. In Brazil, the sugar industry played a key role in pushing for ethanol (Massi and Singh, this volume). In the United States, farmers now host wind turbines. How do these interests compare across states and regions in their influence?

Conclusion

Drawing from the extensive critical analyses and proposed research agendas, this chapter has identified key strands of the extant literature and where scholars should direct their research going forward. The individual chapters provide excellent narratives of energy politics within states and regions and around the world; we encourage scholars and practitioners to read in more depth these narratives, key findings, and recommendations.

Energy politics is an exciting line of research that has been underappreciated for the breadth and depth of research and findings. Even though we have much more work to do, one can no longer claim that political scientists have been ignoring energy.

References

Balmaceda, Margarita M. 2018. "Differentiation, Materiality, and Power: Towards a Political Economy of Fossil Fuels." *Energy Research & Social Science* 39: 130–140.

Gaylord, Sylvia, and Kathleen J. Hancock. 2013. "Developing World: National Energy Strategies." In *The International Handbook of Energy Security*, edited by Hugh Dyer and Maria Julia Trombetta, 206–235. Cheltenham, UK/Northampton, MA: Edward Elgar Publishing.

Hancock, Kathleen J., and Vlado Vivoda. 2014. "International Political Economy: A Field Born of the OPEC Crisis Returns to Its Energy Roots." *Energy Research and Social Science* 1, no. 1: 206–217.

Hughes, Llewelyn, and Phillip Y. Lipscy. 2013. "The Politics of Energy." *Annual Review of Political Science* 16: 449–469.

INDEX